British Archives

THIRD EDITION

To Tracy Tillotson

British Archives

THIRD EDITION

A Guide to Archive Resources in the United Kingdom

JANET FOSTER
& JULIA SHEPPARD

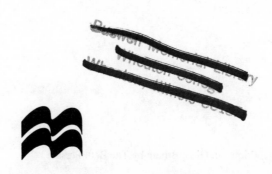

First published in Great Britain 1995 by
MACMILLAN PRESS LTD
Houndmills, Basingstoke, Hampshire RG21 6XS
and London.

Companies and representatives throughout the world.

ISBN 0-333-532-554

A catalogue record for this book is available from the British Library.

10   9   8   7   6   5   4   3   2   1
04   03   02   01   00   99   98   97   96   95

Published in the United States and Canada by
STOCKTON PRESS, 1995
345 Park Avenue South, 10th Floor, New York,
N.Y. 10010-1707

ISBN 1-56159-172-6

Printed in Great Britain by The Bath Press

Contents

Acknowledgements

As always this book would not have been possible without the help and contributions of the many archivists and custodians throughout the country who gave their time to supply us with information. In addition, we are very grateful to the Wellcome Institute for the History of Medicine and the Wellcome Trust for allowing us the use of their facilities and support services.

Many colleagues expressed appreciation of the second edition and gave us their encouragement in what, at times, was a daunting task. Those who have been particularly helpful include, as previously, Richard Storey, who supplied endless suggestions for new entries and helped with the Useful Publications section, as did John Davies and Helen Young. The staff at the National Register of Archives were again extremely obliging, especially Dr Rosemary Hayes and Alex Ritchie.

Staff in the Contemporary Medical Archives Centre have been very forbearing and we cannot thank them enough. Shirley Dixon, Lesley Hall, Isobel Hunter and Jennifer Smith have been staunch supporters throughout. Also Caroline Overy, who kindly checked bibliographical queries for the Useful Publications. It is, however, to Tracy Tillotson that we owe yet again the greatest debt of gratitude for her patience and persistence with the word-processing. Quite simply the book would not have been possible without her.

At Macmillan, we were fortunate to work with Grace Evans and Fiona Moffat, whilst Orlando Richards helped enthusiastically in telephoning recalcitrant and forgetful respondents. Again we benefited greatly from the meticulous and sensitive copy-editing of Caroline Richmond.

Our families and friends have endured our complaints and sustained us when the labour seemed endless. Henceforth they can look forward to supper on time!

Foreword

British Archives was first published in 1982, with a reprint in the same year and a paperback edition in 1984. Since the publication of the second edition in 1989 the book has been recognised as the principal reference work in its field – in fact the only book providing a general guide to archives in Britain. The editors, with the valued assistance of colleagues and friends, have constantly monitored the archival scene in the UK for changes and additions, with substantive work for this new edition having begun in January 1994.

Again the opportunity has been taken to expand the number and content of entries. A further 155 entirely new entries are included, although this is not reflected in the total (1109, from 1048 in the second edition) because a significant number of existing entries, principally institutions and local history libraries, indicated that they had transferred their archives to established archive repositories. It is to be hoped that this is an indication of a growing perception of the need for professional care of archives and a higher profile for archivists.

Respondents were also actively encouraged to improve their entries with additional information. Local authority record offices in particular were urged to do this, and most responded enthusiastically to this request. The content of each entry has also been expanded by the addition of fax numbers and details of conservation arrangements. Because of the resultant general increase of information, the layout has been changed to a double column format to keep the book to a manageable size and the binding has been strengthened.

It is worth noting that many local authority record offices have been moved within the administrative structures of their authorities, often becoming part of a general libraries, museums and archives section. This seems to be a reflection of the emphasis on 'heritage' which has developed in recent years and marks a significant departure from the traditional place of archives as part of the secretariat. Finally, it is appropriate to mention here the possible changes to archive provision which the proposed local government reorganisation may bring. Despite vigorous lobbying by the profession and its supporters, no guarantees have been given about the future of local authority archive services after reorganisation, and the experiences of 1974 show that any changes will by no means be uniform. Users of archives are therefore warned that information in the book about local authority record offices may be superseded by these events.

Janet Foster and Julia Sheppard

Introduction

Archives: What they are and how to use them

Strictly speaking, archives are the documents created in the normal course of the life of an institution or individual in order for them to function, and as such provide a historical record. Thus an archive is a cohesive body of original documents emanating from one source. However, the term is now used much more loosely to cover any primary source material in a variety of media whatever its origin (hence including documents, photographs, films and even printed material). Also it can be used to describe the physical place where records are held. Although the title of this book is *British Archives* we are taking the wider definition and including 'artificial' collections, so called because they have been consciously put together, usually around a subject area or a type of material, and have not accumulated naturally over the course of time.

In many cases archives will remain in the institution that has created them, and increasingly professional archivists are involved in their preservation. Many such bodies, however, have decided that they are neither able satisfactorily to house their older records nor adequately to make them available for historians to consult, hence there is also a steady transfer of such archives to established record repositories.

Researchers should bear in mind that consulting archives is not the same as looking up information in a book. Archives are unique: the reader cannot assume that they are freely available or easily accessible, or even that the originals can be consulted. They are never 'loaned', and copies are not necessarily obtainable. Finding aids – lists and indexes – vary greatly in style and detail in spite of recent moves to standardise listing; there is no single classification system, and in some places finding aids or guides may not exist. All this will depend greatly on the type of repository/library the reader visits, and the facilities and services of, for example, a large and well-staffed county record office cannot be expected everywhere. These larger or well-established repositories are actively involved in raising standards within repositories in general to meet the British Standard while the Royal Commission on Historical Manuscripts is in the process of implementing a policy of recognising repositories based upon its own published standard (see Useful Publications, p. lv). It will be obvious from consulting the entries in this guide that some of the archives are administered by librarians, clerks, secretaries, honorary archivists or other individuals whose chief priorities or duties may be elsewhere. Moreover the archives are frequently not stored readily to hand, or may be in use by others or being filmed or repaired. Increasingly, too, certain categories of records, especially in local authority record offices, may only be consulted on microfilm/fiche, and there may be heavy demand for use of the film/fiche reader.

For all these reasons it is therefore always advisable to make a prior appointment. Background reading and preparation are also essential if the reader is to grasp the significance of the archives and the types of documentation likely to be encountered. It must be remembered that records were not normally created with the needs of historical research in mind. It is easy to fall into the trap of assuming that records will directly answer a specific query; rather it is necessary to understand how and why they were created before embarking on any research into them. Archivists, being primarily custodians, are not necessarily authorities on all that their holdings contain, although they will do everything possible to direct the researcher towards the relevant material. If an enquiry is lengthy and a personal visit to the archive is impossible, the services of a professional researcher may be recommended. Some record offices maintain lists of approved professional researchers. See Useful Addresses for relevant organisations and the Society of Genealogists (p. lv).

Methodology

British Archives is not a commercial directory and no charge is made for an entry. Inevitably it cannot be comprehensive, since any organisation holding its own non-current records selected for preservation can claim to have an archive. Our approach has been to cover as many places as possible where archives, in the widest sense of the word, are held and are relatively accessible.

As with the second edition, restrictions on time and finance made it impossible to visit repositories. Therefore we have again relied on questionnaires, modified with explanatory notes, which we sent out accompanied by sample entries and a key subject word list. We are indebted to all those who so kindly took the time and trouble to complete and return the questionnaires.

Sources

We have drawn on a number of published reference works in order to locate archives, as well as monitoring professional archival publications and historical and other general works where primary sources were quoted. Approaches were also made to organisations which had advertised for archivists or whose existence was drawn to our attention by historians and colleagues. In addition a number of organisations requested to be included and the National Register of Archives computerised locations index was checked.

Exclusions

Again we have excluded businesses, which are the specific concern of the Business Archives Council (see p. il), although of course business archives will appear under the holdings of many of the repositories. There is also now an increasing number of published guide material to business records, noted in the list of Useful Publications (p. lv). In accordance with this policy a small number of anomalous entries in the second edition, e.g. *The Times* and the Savoy archives, have been deleted. Public utilities, however, despite privatisation, continue to be included either because their archives remain public records or because of their national importance.

Privately held collections of estate and family papers have not been extensively covered, although we have included several of the most well-known collections, especially if an archivist is employed. Further information about these collections is available from the Royal Commission on Historical Manuscripts (see p. liii) and in their forthcoming guide (see Useful Publications, p. lv).

No comprehensive coverage of the *c*2500 museums in Britain has been attempted, although most will have maintained some records of their administration and collections and management and some have accepted collections of archives and manuscripts. National museums and a limited number of other museums are included, however.

The many local history, archaeological, literary and philosophical societies have not been systematically listed, both because of the numbers involved and because information about them is normally available from local authority record offices. The latter may indeed hold these archives or have an agreement to administer them on behalf of the societies. Borough records have also not been systematically covered: the National Register of Archives (see p. liii) holds separate lists of these; local authority record offices should be able to advise on their whereabouts if they have not been deposited.

Information collection

On the whole we have relied on questionnaires, backed up with telephone calls to clarify queries or to confirm the current situation with those repositories which failed to respond. In January 1994 we started to send out questionnaires and key subject lists for new entries and in the summer of 1994 circulated those institutions with existing entries with their second edition entry, annotated where we considered more information could helpfully be forthcoming. We tried to encourage fuller responses where appropriate, and many organisations took the opportunity to revise their existing entry completely. For the first time information was requested about fax numbers and conservation arrangements.

Updating has been a continuous process up to proof stage (May 1995). In some cases it has not been possible to obtain final information prior to going to press. Office addresses, phone and fax numbers and staff are continually changing, and where revised information arrived too late for inclusion we apologise for any inconvenience caused.

The information sought was as follows:

Name of repository   In some cases related repositories under one parent body have been given the same entry number, with subsections 'A', 'B' etc (e.g., entry **194**, National Museum of Wales: **A** Library; **B** Welsh Folk Museum; **C** Welsh Industrial and Maritime Museum).

Parent organisation   This is included if applicable, although the historical background section may also yield the relevant information. It is appreciated that the colleges of the universities of Oxford and Cambridge do not strictly belong to a parent organisation; nevertheless we have included this category in their entries so that the reader may easily refer to all parts of the university.

Address   Post codes are comprehensively included in this edition. In a few cases the postal address is different from the address where the archives are stored.

Telephone   The new telephone codes introduced in April 1995 are given. British Telecom is liable to change codes yet again, so if a number is unobtainable for long periods it is worth checking that the code and/or number are still correct.

Fax   These numbers have been included where supplied.

Enquiries   Both title and name were requested but not always given. Qualifications have not been included. A contact address is given if necessary.

Open   This normally states opening arrangements, i.e., days and hours of opening and any regular annual closures apart from bank and other public holidays. Academic institutions are normally closed for longer periods over Easter and Christmas. Many smaller places are closed for lunch.

Access   This gives information about persons who may consult the records and whether there are any particular restrictions, e.g., closure periods. Where an appointment is necessary this is also indicated. A very few repositories charge for access: actual details of charges are liable to change and have not been included. Some local authority record offices operate the County Archives Research Network (CARN) system of issuing readers' tickets.

Historical background   Outline administrative history of the organisation is supplied, including details of predecessor bodies where appropriate and, if relevant, the development of the repository and/or collections. It is also noted if the repository is a Diocesan Record Office and/or recognised as a place of deposit for public records.

Acquisitions policy   The aims of the collecting policy and/or major subject areas may be given.

Archives of organisation   Outline details are provided, including dates if known. Where the formula 'usual local authority record holdings' has been used for local authority record offices, see the fuller description below (p. xiii).

Major collections   This category usually covers material acquired by the organisation as gifts or on deposit, and names significant collections, with covering dates where possible. This section has been omitted from the entries for certain national repositories whose collections by definition cover all types of archival material and subjects. Where the formula 'deposited local collections' has been used for local authority record offices, see the fuller description below (p. xiii).

Non-manuscript material   This lists any other materials, e.g., plans, drawings, photographs, maps, sound archives, films, and supporting printed material.

Finding aids   Unpublished catalogues, lists and indexes etc, available in the offices are mentioned here. In some cases it is stated whether lists are sent to the National Register of Archives (NRA) or the National Register of Archives (Scotland) (NRA(S)), and relevant list reference numbers may be given.

Facilities   Provisions for readers are given, usually specifying availability of reprographic facilities, e.g., photocopying, photography, microfilm/fiche reader/printer etc. Reading aids have not normally been included. Specific charges for services are not given.

Conservation   This notes where there are in-house facilities for paper conservation or whether work is contracted out, in some cases specifying if outside work is undertaken by the conservation staff.

Publications   Details are listed of guides or other relevant works about the repository or its holdings which have been published or may be consulted elsewhere.

If any section is not included in an entry, this indicates that no information of relevance was supplied. In some instances where it was impossible or inappropriate to have a full entry, the information was summarised in a brief statement or minimal entry.

It will be appreciated that the quality and detail of returns is not consistent. Although editorial persistence achieved a substantial measure of improvement in many cases, the guide is essentially based on information received and there is still considerable variation in the entries. Needless to say, the larger the repository the more general must be its return, and in those cases the value of information about published finding aids should be stressed. Where little information is supplied it may indicate that dealing with their archives is not a routine activity of the institution.

The appendices have been completely revised and cover only information acquired since publication of the second edition. As noted above, there has been a continual movement of archives into record offices; the Health Visitors' Association, for example, has placed its archives in the Wellcome Institute (entry **768**). These moves are noted in

Appendix I, as are other transfers of institutional archives of importance. Appendix II lists places which reported holding no archives, and Appendix III lists places which failed either to respond or to supply adequate information for a full entry. An asterisk * notes those places which indicated that they held archives.

Local authority record offices and libraries

Although proposed local government reorganisation may affect provision of archive services, at present it is possible to say that every county in England and Wales has at least one record office maintained by a local government authority. These began to be established formally by county councils in England from the 1930s and in Wales from the 1950s. Until local government reorganisation in 1974 there were no equivalent repositories in Scotland; therefore in Scotland, and to a certain extent in Wales, the responsibility for acquiring and housing archives fell to the respective national libraries.

Local authority record offices, that is county, city and some borough record offices, provide a comprehensive record service to the general public, collecting material, official and unofficial, which is of relevance to the history of the locality. Such record offices can be expected to produce a wide range of lists, indexes and catalogues which may also be available at the National Register of Archives. For these reasons the entries for local authority record offices were modified to save endless repetition of similar information. The formulae 'usual local authority record holdings' and 'deposited local collections' have often been used, with additional information when necessary on collections which the offices deemed were of wider significance.

'Usual local authority record holdings' can be described as follows:

Local government and related records: archives of the local authorities, which may range from charters of a medieval burgh to recent committee records of an urban district or county council. Quarter session records are also frequently held. Hence all aspects of local government – Poor Law, health, education etc – are likely to be covered.

'Deposited local collections' comprise the following main categories:

Ecclesiastical records: these may include parish records (all such records over 100 years old are now held at designated Diocesan Record Offices unless the parish itself provides special storage), as well as tithe, probate and non-conformist records, e.g., the non-current records of Methodists, Baptists and Quakers.

Estate and family archives, including manorial records: many of these archives are held, and include leases, deeds, maps and other documents relating to property as well as the personal correspondence and other papers of local families and individuals.

Solicitors' and estate agents' papers: including records of former clients' businesses or estates, auction and sale details.

Business and industrial records: records of local businesses, manufacturers and branches of national firms, as well as records from small family retail concerns. Such records may include accounts, correspondence, plans, photographs and publicity.

Voluntary organisations: records of charitable bodies, local societies, associations, clubs and branches of national bodies, mostly 19th–20th centuries.

Antiquarian collections: manuscripts, transcripts of documents etc assembled by an individual and usually relating to a specific area.

Public libraries' local history collections may contain a miscellany of items, primarily non-manuscript, consisting (apart from the books) of some or all of the following: census returns; Ordnance Survey and other maps; postcards and photographs; drawings; newspapers and cuttings; details of local functions; material assembled by local historians; ephemera, including programmes, theatre bills, advertising etc. Where manuscript material is held this might include rate books; local business records; papers of local residents and celebrities; written and oral memoirs; journals and correspondence.

* * *

Finally, users are reminded that this guide is a first step to discovering where to locate archives, since the entries do not comprise every place in the United Kingdom where archives and manuscripts are held. Developments in electronic information and increasing use of the Internet system to gain access to information about archives is likely to improve dramatically in the next few years. The third edition of *British Archives* will nevertheless, we hope, continue to give an overall view of the archives scattered throughout the country, and the editors trust that a fourth edition will be produced in due course. We would therefore welcome any additions or suggestions and invite comments to be sent to us c/o the Wellcome Institute for the History of Medicine, 183 Euston Road, London NW1 2BE.

How to Use this Book

The entries are arranged alphabetically by town and running heads of town names are given on each page. London is the area of postal districts only.

All listings and indexes refer to entry not page numbers unless specifically indicated otherwise.

The Alphabetical Listing (p. xvi) gives references to all sections of the book. The List of Entries by County (p. xxxii) refers to all main entries within each county. If you wish to trace a particular person or named collection, use the Index to Collections (p. 574); for subjects use the Guide to Key Subjects (p. 621). But remember there are limitations to both of these and the introductory remarks to them should be read.

Alphabetical Listing

List of Entries by County

National Trust for Scotland, 297
New College Library, 315C
Royal Botanic Garden Library, 298
Royal College of Nursing Archives, 299
Royal College of Physicians of Edinburgh, 300
Royal College of Surgeons of Scotland, 301
Royal Commission on the Ancient and
 Historical Monuments of Scotland, 295
Royal Highland and Agricultural Society of
 Scotland, 302
Royal Observatory, Edinburgh, 303
Royal Scots Regimental Museum, 304
Royal Scottish Academy, 305
Royal Society for the Relief of Indigent
 Gentlewomen of Scotland, 306
Royal Zoological Society of Scotland, 307
School of Scottish Studies, University of
 Edinburgh, 308
Scottish Catholic Archives, 309
Scottish Chamber of Agriculture, 833
Scottish Ethnological Archives, 310
Scottish Mining Museum Archives, 845
Scottish National Gallery of Modern Art,
 311
Scottish National Portrait Gallery, 312
Scottish Record Office, 313
Scottish United Services Museum, 314
University of Edinburgh Library, 315
West Lothian District Library, 60

Merseyside
Athenaeum, 464
Birkenhead Central Library, *see* Wirral
 Archives
British Psychological Society Archives, 465
King's (Liverpool) Regiment, 470
Knowsley Archives, 405
Liverpool Medical Institution, 466
Liverpool Record Office and Local History
 Library, 467
Liverpool School of Tropical Medicine, 468
Merseyside Record Office, 469
National Museums and Galleries on
 Merseyside, 470
Prescot Museum, 470
St Helens Local History and Archives Library,
 982
Science Fiction Foundation Collection, 471
Sefton Metropolitan Borough Libraries and
 Arts Service, 1023
Sydney Jones Library, *see* University of
 Liverpool
University of Liverpool, Archives Unit, 472
——, Sydney Jones Library, 473
Wirral Archives, 91

Mid Glamorgan
Cynon Valley Libraries Local Collection, 1
Merthyr Tydfil Central Library, 816

Treorchy Library, Rhondda Borough Council,
 1059

Norfolk
Ancient House Museum, 1052
Aylsham Town Council Archives, 35
East Anglian Film Archive, *see* University of
 East Anglia
Great Yarmouth Central Library, 362
History of Advertising Trust, 853
Holkham Hall, 1081
John Innes Centre, 854
King's Lynn Borough, 855
Lynn Museum, 427
Norfolk Museums Service, King's Lynn, *see*
 Lynn Museum
——, Thetford, *see* Ancient House Museum
Norfolk Record Office, 855
University of East Anglia, 856

North Yorkshire
Bar Convent, 1100
Borthwick Institute of Historical Research,
 1101
Castle Howard Archives, 1102
Company of Merchant Adventurers of York,
 1103
Film Music Resource Centre, 1104
Institute of the Blessed Virgin Mary, 1100
National Railway Museum Library, 1105
North Yorkshire County Library,
 Scarborough, 1000
——, Skipton, 1014
——, York, 1106
North Yorkshire County Record Office,
 Northallerton, 846
Scarborough Central Library, 1000
Skipton Branch Library, 1014
University College of Ripon and York St John,
 962
University of York, *see* Borthwick Institute of
 Historical Research; Film Music Resource
 Centre
York Central Library, 1106
York City Archives, 1107
York Health Archives, 1108
York Minster Archives, 1109
Yorkshire Film Archive, 962

Northamptonshire
British Steel, East Midlands Records Centre,
 1078
Castle Ashby, 201
Drayton House, 425
Northampton Museum, 847
Northamptonshire Record Office, 848
Northamptonshire Studies Collection, 849

Useful Addresses

Army Museums Ogilby Trust (see also entry 1082)
Secretary: Colonel P.S. Walton, 2 St Thomas Centre, Southgate Street, Winchester, Hants SO23 9EF. Tel. (01962) 841416; fax (01962) 811426.
The Army Museums Ogilby Trust (AMOT) aims to encourage regimental and corps museums of the army to achieve certain criteria of collections management. In support of that aim, the trust provides legal and corporate structural advice, encourages and grant-aids acquisitions, and represents military museums within the profession and elsewhere. The trust publishes work on certain aspects of regimental and corps antecedents and also maintains an archive related chiefly to the organisation, dress and equipment of regiments and corps and to associated paintings, drawings, prints and photographs. The archive is open to bona fide researchers, by appointment.

The Association of Genealogists and Record Agents
Joint Secretaries: 29 Badgers Close, Horsham, West Sussex RH12 5RU.
The association was founded in 1968 to promote high standards of professional conduct and expertise in genealogy, heraldry and record searching. It does not undertake research but publishes a booklet listing members and their interests.
The Scottish counterpart can be contacted at PO Box 174, Edinburgh EH3 5QZ.

Association of Independent Museums
Honorary Secretary: Andrew Patterson. Tel. (01744) 22766; fax (01744) 616966.
The association aims to assist all independent museums with advice and liaison with other bodies and to raise standards in the museums, many of which hold archives.

British Association for Local History
Secretary: 24 Lower Street, Harnham, Salisbury, Wilts SP21 8EY. Tel. (01722) 320115.
Established in 1982 to supersede the Standing Conference for Local History, it promotes knowledge and understanding of local history. A quarterly journal, *The Local Historian*, is published as well as a *Local History Newsletter*, and a full publications list is available on request. An insurance service for local societies is operated.

British Association of Picture Libraries and Agencies
Administrator: Ms S. Shuel, 13 Woodberry Crescent, London N10 1PJ. Tel. (0181) 444 7913.
This is a professional trade association which provides an information service for location of images. It publishes an annual *Directory*, listing its members, with a subject index, and an occasional *Journal*.

British Association of Sound Collections
Honorary Secretary: Alan Ward, National Sound Archive, 29 Exhibition Road, London SW7 2AS. Tel. (0171) 412 7407; fax (0171) 412 7441.
The association is the UK branch of the International Association of Sound Archives. It serves as a meeting ground for individuals and organisations involved in the making and preservation of sound recordings, in whatever form, and runs training courses on the

management of collections. It also organises special meetings on topics of related interest, e.g., new technology and copyright law.

British Records Association (BRA)
Honorary Secretary: 18 Padbury Court, London E2. Tel./fax (0171) 729 1415.
The association was founded in 1932 as a national organisation to co-ordinate and encourage the work of individuals, authorities, institutions and societies interested in the conservation and use of records. It also runs a Records Preservation Section which rescues and advises on the deposit of papers, deeds and documents of all kinds.

British Records Society
Honorary Secretary and Registrar: P.L. Dickinson, College of Arms, London EC4V 4BT. Tel. (0171) 236 9612.
A learned society founded in 1888, it is now concerned principally with publishing indexes to English probate records.

British Universities Film & Video Council
Information Officer: 55 Greek Street, London W1V 5LR. Tel. (0171) 734 3678; fax (0171) 287 3914.
The BUFVC was founded in 1948 by and for university teachers but now serves higher education as a whole. Its purpose is to encourage the use, production and study of audio-visual media for teaching and research and to provide a forum in this field. It maintains a reference library, which includes the Slade Film History Register on British cinema newsreels, an AV reference centre and a film and video library with viewing and editing facilities. BUFVC events organised anually include large-scale two-day conferences and one-day courses for researchers, lecturers and librarians. A publications list is available on request.

Business Archives Council (BAC)
Secretary General: Mrs Sharon Quinn-Robinson, The Clove Building, 4 Maquire Street, London SE1 2NQ. Tel. (0171) 407 6110; fax (0171) 234 0300.
The objects of the council are to promote the preservation of business records of historical importance, to supply advice and information on the administration and management of archives and modern records and to encourage interest in the history of business in Britain.

Business Archives Council (Scotland)
Honorary Secretary: Vicki Wilkinson, c/o The Royal Bank of Scotland Archives, 36 St Andrews Square, Edinburgh EH2 2YP. Tel. (0131) 523 5929; (Surveyor's Office) (0141) 330 6079.
The council does similar work to the BAC in London. It was established in 1960.

The Catholic Archives Society
Honorary Secretary: Innyngs House, Hatfield Park, Hatfield, Herts AL9 5PL.
The society was founded in 1979 to promote the care and preservation of the records of the dioceses, religious foundations, institutions and societies of the Roman Catholic Church in the UK and Eire. It arranges an annual conference and occasional seminars and publishes a yearly periodical, *Catholic Archives*, and a *Bulletin* to members.

Centre for Metropolitan History, *see* **Institute of Historical Research**

Ephemera Society
Membership Secretary: Valerie Harris, 146 Portobello Road, London W11 2DZ. Tel. (0181) 450 9998.
Founded in 1975, the society is concerned to promote the preservation and study of printed and MS ephemera of all types and subjects. It organises exhibitions, lectures and collectors' fairs and acts as an information forum for members through its publication *The Ephemerist.*

Federation of Family History Societies (FFHS)
Administrator: Benson Room, Birmingham and Midland Institute, Margaret Street, Birmingham B3 3BS.
The federation offers a forum for constituent societies as well as offering training and an international information service. Publications, aimed mainly at the genealogist, include many on different source materials. A list is available on request.

Friends of the National Libraries
Assistant Secretary: Mr R.G. Copnall, c/o The British Library, Great Russell Street, London WC1B 3DG. Tel. (0171) 412 7559.
The association was founded in 1931 with individuals and organisations as members. It aims to help acquire for the nation printed books, manuscripts and archives, in particular those which might otherwise leave the country. The Friends operate by making grants towards purchase, by eliciting and channelling benefactions and by organising appeals and publicity.

Greater London Archive Network (GLAN)
Chairman: David Mander, Hackney Archives Department, 43 De Beauvoir Road, London N1 5SQ. Tel. (0171) 241 2886; fax (0171) 241 6688.
This is an association of local authority archivists and librarians with archival responsibilities in Greater London to encourage co-operation and promote awareness of their holdings. It organises visits to various repositories and libraries and training meetings on various subjects which have attracted an increasing number of associate members. A regular newsletter, *Metropolitan Lines,* is published.

Historic Houses Archivists Group
Secretary: C. Shrimpton, Archivist to the Duke of Northumberland, Estates Office, Alnwick Castle, Alnwick, Northumberland NE66 1NQ. Tel. (01655) 51077.
The group was formed in 1986 to encourage the highest possible standards of care of the privately administered archives of historic estates.

The Historical Association
Association Secretary: Mrs M. Stiles, 59a Kennington Park Road, London SE11 4JH. Tel. (0171) 735 3901; fax (0171) 582 4989.
Founded in 1906, the association has a network of local branches which allows those with interests in history and the past, especially history education, to meet and exchange views. It also produces numerous publications.

Institute of Heraldic and Genealogical Studies (see also entry **189**)
Registrar: Mr Jeremy Palmer, 79-82 Northgate, Canterbury, Kent CT1 1BA. Tel. (01227) 768664; fax (01227) 765617.
The institute was founded in 1961 as an educational trust for study and research into the history and structure of the family. It provides training courses leading to professional qualifications in genealogy and publishes a journal, *Family History*.

Institute of Historical Research (see also entry **575**)
Academic Secretary: Senate House, Malet Street, London WC1E 7HU. Tel. (0171) 636 0272; fax (0171) 436 2183.
A postgraduate institute of the University of London, it provides extensive resources for bona fide historical students. It produces the *Victoria County History*, and in 1987 the Centre for Metropolitan History was established as a part of the institute. This provides a forum for the interchange of ideas on metropolitan history with particular emphasis on London, but in a countrywide context and in comparison with other metropolitan centres.

Institute of Paper Conservation
Secretary: Clare Hampson, Leigh Lodge, Leigh, Worcester WR6 5LB. Tel. (01886) 832323; fax (01886) 833688.
The institute is an international specialist organisation concerned with the conservation of paper and related materials. It aims to increase professional awareness by co-ordinating the exchange of information and facilitating contacts between its members through meetings, seminars and publications: a quarterly newsletter and an annual journal, *The Paper Conservator* (1976–).

International Council on Archives
Executive Secretary: 60 rue des Francs-Bourgeois, 75003 Paris, France.
The council was founded in 1948 with membership from over 140 countries and territories of national associations, archival institutions and individuals, with nine regional branches and various sections and specialised committees. An international congress is held every four years, and various publications are produced.

Library Association
Chief Executive: Mr R. Shimmon, 7 Ridgmount Street, London WC1E 7AE. Tel. (0171) 636 7543; fax (0171) 436 7281.
The professional association for all librarians, it produces numerous publications including indexes, abstracts and subject bibliographies.

List and Index Society
Secretary: c/o Department of Historical and Critical Studies, University of Central Lancashire, Preston, PR1 2HE (general enquiries).
Applications and publication orders to Assistant Secretary, c/o Public Record Office, Chancery Lane, London WC1A 2LR.
The society distributes copies of PRO lists and lists from other public archives to subscribing members. A typed catalogue of publications is available on request.

The London Archive Users Forum
Secretary: Isobel Watson, 29 Stepney Green, London E1 3JX. Fax (0171) 265 8236.
Founded in 1987, it provides a forum for the exchange of views between users and archivists concerning records in and of the London area, organises a range of meetings, and publishes a regular *Newsletter*.

Methodist Church Archives
Methodist Church Liaison Officer: Dr E. Dorothy Graham, 34 Spiceland Road, Northfield, Birmingham B31 1NJ. Tel. (0121) 475 4914.
The association deals with all queries relating to the location and deposit of Methodist archives.
See also Methodist Archives and Research Centre (entry **806B**).

Museums Association
42 Clerkenwell Road, London EC1R 0PA. Tel. (0171) 608 2933; fax (0171) 250 1929.
Founded in 1889 to promote professional standards in museums and art galleries by campaigning, training and publications, it is also concerned with archives and affiliated issues, e.g., copyright. It publishes a *Museums Yearbook* and *Museums Journal*; a list of other publications is available on request.

National Cataloguing Unit for the Archives of Contemporary Scientists (NCUACS)
Archivist: Peter Harper, University of Bath, Claverton Down, Bath BA2 7AY. Tel. (01225) 826826; fax (01225) 826381.
The successor body to the Contemporary Scientific Archives Centre (CSAC) of Oxford, the unit was set up in 1987. It is not an archive, but locates and catalogues papers of distinguished contemporary British scientists and engineers prior to placing them in appropriate repositories.

National Council on Archives
Secretary: Nicholas Kingsley, Birmingham City Archives, c/o Central Library, Chamberlain Square, Birmingham B3 3HQ. Tel. (0121) 235 4217; fax (0121) 233 4455.
The council was established in 1988 to bring together the major groupings of archivists, custodians and users. It provides a regular forum for the exchange of views and acts as a channel through which concerns in the archive field can be brought to the attention of the public and the government.

National Preservation Office
Mrs Valerie Ferris, The British Library, Great Russell Street, London WC1B 3DG. Tel. (0171) 412 7612; fax (0171) 412 7796.
The office was founded in 1984 to encourage high standards of preservation and security issues in libraries and repositories throughout the UK, by education and exchange of information.

The National Register of Archives (NRA)
Quality House, Quality Court, Chancery Lane, London WC2A 1HP. Tel. (0171) 242 1198; fax (0171) 831 3550.
Search room: Mon–Fri: 9.30-5.00.
The Royal Commission on Historical Manuscripts (see below) has maintained the NRA since its establishment in 1945 as a central collecting point for information about manuscript sources for British history outside the public records. More than 38,000

catalogues of manuscript collections are available for consultation in the public search room. Also available are the computerised business, personal names and subject indexes to the NRA. It is expected that these indexes will become available on the Internet by the end of 1995.

The National Register of Archives (Scotland) (NRA(S))
HM General Register House, Edinburgh EH1 3YY. Tel. (0131) 535 1314; fax (0131) 535 1360.
A counterpart to the National Register of Archives in London, it was established at the same time but as a branch of the Scottish Record Office. Copies of lists are sent to the NRA.

Postal History Society
Secretary: PO Box 77, Huntingdon, Cambs PE18 6TZ. Tel. (01480) 456254; fax. (01480) 456255.
This is a learned society concerned with the history of all aspects of postal and telegraphic communications. It publishes a quarterly journal, *Postal History*.

Press Association (PA) News Library and Picture Library
85 Fleet Street, London EC4P 4BE. Tel. (0171) 353 7440, ext. 3161 (News Library); ext. 3200 (Picture Library).
PA News is the national news agency of the UK and Republic of Ireland. The News Library dates back to 1928 and contains some 14 million cuttings from British national newspapers. It is updated daily. The Picture Library includes all work of PA photographers dating from the turn of the century, plus bought-in collections, and is a UK agent for several European agencies.

Records Management Society
Admin. Secretary: Mrs H. Farley, c/o Rooftop Secretarial Services, 6 Sheraton Drive, High Wycombe, Bucks HP13 6DE. Tel. (01494) 525040; fax (01494) 465488.
The society was started in 1983 to encourage the highest professional standards in records management. It is open to all working in the field and provides regular contact for members through its bi-monthly meetings and *Bulletin*.

The Royal Commission on Historical Manuscripts (HMC)
Secretary: Dr C.J. Kitching, Quality House, Quality Court, Chancery Lane, London WC2A 1HP. Tel. (0171) 242 1198; fax (0171) 831 3550.
Established in 1869 by Royal Warrant, its terms of reference were extended in 1959. The commission is concerned with all aspects of the location and preservation of records (other than public records) as well as maintaining manorial and tithe documents registers on behalf of the Master of the Rolls. It maintains the National Register of Archives (see above) and produces reports and publications.

Scots Ancestry Research Society
Secretary: Alison Munroe, 29b Albany Street, Edinburgh EH1 3QN. Tel./fax (0131) 556 4220.
The society was established in 1945. It is a non-profit making society for research into sources for tracing ancestry in Scotland.

Scottish Association of Genealogists and Record Agents, *see* Association of Genealogists and Record Agents

Scottish Genealogy Society
Library and Family History Centre, 15 Victoria Terrace, Edinburgh EH1 2JL. Tel. (0131) 220 3677.
Open: Tues: 10.30-5.30; Wed: 10.30-8.30; Sat: 10.00-5.00.
This is a learned society linked with other major Scottish family history societies. It has a library and publications programme covering all aspects of Scottish genealogy.

Scottish Records Association
c/o Scottish Record Office, HM Register House, Edinburgh EH1 3YY. Tel. (0131) 535 1314; fax (0131) 535 1360.
This has similar functions to the British Records Association in London but also produces *Datasheets* describing the holdings of various repositories.

Society of Archivists
Honorary Secretary: Information House, 20-24 Old Street, London EC1V 9AP. Tel. (0171) 253 5097/4488; fax (0171) 253 3942.
Originally founded in 1947 as the Society of Local Archivists and renamed in 1954, the society is the recognised professional body for archivists, archive conservators and record managers in the British Isles. It promotes the care and administration of archives and the education of archivists, and publishes in all these areas. The society maintains a voluntary register based on qualification, holds regular meetings and runs an in-service training scheme for archive conservators in Britain. Various publications are produced, including a *Journal*, a monthly *Newsletter* and a series of *Best Practice Guidelines*. A reference library is maintained at the Borthwick Institute, York (see entry **1101**).

Society of Genealogists (see also entry **745**)
14 Charterhouse Buildings, London EC1M 7BA. Tel. (0171) 251 8799.
The society provides information about regional genealogical societies and the work of individuals in this field. It maintains a reference library and an extensive document collection open to non-members on payment of a fee.

Standing Conference of National and University Libraries (SCONUL)
Secretary: Mr A.J.C. Bainton, 102 Euston Street, London NW1 2HA. Tel. (0171) 387 0317; fax (0171) 383 3197.
The association was established as a representative body concerned with the promotion of British academic libraries, the exchange of information and other collaborative efforts. It furthers the interest of its member institutions via meetings, newsletters etc with advisory panels, including a Manuscripts Panel.

Ulster Historical Foundation and Ulster Genealogical and Historical Guild
Balmoral Buildings, 12 College Square East, Belfast BT1 6DD. Tel. (01232) 332288; fax (01232) 239885.
The foundation is a genealogical research agency which provides a full research service for the historic province of Ulster and maintains a large collection of completed searches on Ulster families. The guild is an associated body which can be joined by family historians who wish to publicise their research interests. UHF has a wide range of publications and hosts annual genealogical conferences.

Useful Publications

Abraham, B. (ed.) and Aldridge, T.M. (consultant ed.): *Directory of Registers and Records* (London: Longman, 5/1993).

Allan, A.R.: *Para-Educational Forces: a Survey of Intra- and Supra-University Bodies and their Records* (Liverpool: Archives Unit, University of Liverpool, 1990).

Armstrong, J. and Jones, S.: *Business Documents: their Origins, Sources and Uses in Historical Research* (London: Mansell, 1987).

Atherton, L.: *'Never Complain, Never Explain': Records of the Foreign Office and State Paper Office, 1500–c1960* (London: Public Record Office Reader's Guide No. 7, 1994).

Baldock, R.W.: 'A Survey of Southern African Manuscripts in the United Kingdom', *Communications from the Basel Africa Bibliography*, Vol. 16 (1976), 3–27.

Ballantyne, J. (ed.): *Researcher's Guide to British Newsreels*, 3 vols (London: British Universities Film and Video Council, 1983–93).

——: *Researcher's Guide to British Film & Television Collections* (London: British Universities Film and Video Council, rev. 4/c1993).

Barbour, S.: *Museums Yearbook, including a Directory of Museums and Galleries of the British Isles* (London: Museums Association, annual).

Barrow, M.: *Women, 1870–1928: a Select Guide to Printed and Archival Sources in the United Kingdom* (London: Mansell, 1981).

Batts, J.S.: *British Manuscript Diaries of the Nineteenth Century: an Annotated Listing* (London: Centaur, 1976).

Bearman, D. and Edsall, J.T. (eds): *Archival Sources for the History of Biochemistry and Molecular Biology: a Reference Guide and Report* (Philadelphia: American Philosophical Society, 1980).

Bennett, J. and Tough, A. (comps) and Storey R. (ed.): *Trade Union and Related Records* (Coventry: University of Warwick, Occasional Publication No. 5, 6/1991).

Bridgeman, I. and Emsley, C.: *A Guide to the Archives of the Police Forces of England and Wales* (Leigh-on-Sea: Police History Society, 1989).

Bridson, G.D.R., Phillips, V.C. and Harvey, A.P.: *Natural History Manuscript Resources in the British Isles* (London: Mansell, 1980).

British Association of Picture Libraries: *BAPLA Directory* (1995).

British Film Institute: *National Film Archive Catalogue*, Vol. 1: *Non-Fiction Films*; Vol. 2: *Feature Films*; Vol. 3: *Newsreels* (London: British Film Institute, 1980–).

British Library: *Guide to Libraries and Information Units in Government Departments and other Organisations* (London: British Library Science Reference and Information Service, 1990–).

British Standards Institution: *Repair and Allied Processes for the Conservation of Documents*, BS4971 (London, 1988).

——: *Recommendations for the Storage and Exhibition of Archival Documents*, BS5454 (London, 1989).

Bryon, R.V. and Bryon, T.N. (eds): *Maritime Information: a Guide to Libraries and Sources of Information in the United Kingdom* (London: Maritime Information Association, 3/1993).

Burdett, A.L.P.: *Summary Guide to Archive and Manuscript Collections relevant to the Former British Colonial Territories in the United Kingdom* (London: Commonwealth Archivists Association, 1988).

Burnell, R.S.: *The Libraries Directory, 1988–90* (Cambridge: James Clarke, 1991).

Camp, A.J.: *Wills and their Whereabouts* (London: A.J. Camp, 4/1974).

Catholic Archives Society: *Directory of Catholic Archives in the United Kingdom and Eire* (Newcastle upon Tyne: Catholic Archives Society, 1984).

Chadwyck-Healey: *Index of Manuscripts in the British Library*, 10 vols (Cambridge: Chadwyck-Healey, 1984–6).

——: *National Inventory of Documentary Sources in the United Kingdom and Ireland* (Cambridge: Chadwyck-Healey, 1985–) [microfiches of lists of MSS and archives held by a variety of repositories nationally, with union index. Index on CD-Rom with User manual, 1994].

Clinker, C.R.: *Railway History Sources: a Handlist of the Principal Sources of Original Material with Notes and Guidance on its Use* (Bristol: Avon-Anglia, 1976).

Cockerell, H.A.L. and Green E.: *The British Insurance Business, 1547–1970: an Introduction and Guide to Historical Records in the United Kingdom* (London: Heinemann, 1976).

Cook, C. (ed.): *Sources in British Political History, 1900–1951* (London: Macmillan, 1975–):

Vol. 1: *A Guide to the Archives of Selected Organizations and Societies* (1975).

Vol. 2: *A Guide to the Papers of Selected Public Servants* (1975).

Vol. 3: *A Guide to the Private Papers of Members of Parliament, A–K* (1977).

Vol. 4: *A Guide to the Private Papers of Members of Parliament, L–Z* (1977).

Vol. 5 (with Weekes, J.): *A Guide to the Private Papers of Selected Writers, Intellectuals and Publicists* (1978).

Vol. 6: *First Consolidated Supplement* (1985).

Cook, C. and Waller, D.: *Sources in Contemporary British History*, Vol. 1: *Organisations and Societies* (London: Longman, 1994).

Cook, C., Leonard, J. and Leese, P.: *Sources in Contemporary British History*, Vol. 2: *Individuals* (London: Longman, 1994).

Cornish, G.P.: *Archival Collections of Non-Book Materials: a Listing and Brief Description of Major National Collections* (London: British Library Information Guide No. 3, 1986).

Cory, K.B.: *Tracing your Scottish Ancestry* (Edinburgh: Polygon, 1990).

Cox, A.: *Sources for the Study of Public Housing* (London: Guildhall Library and the London Archive Users' Forum, 1993).

Cox, J. and Padfield, T.: *Tracing your Ancestors in the Public Record Office*, ed. A. Bevan and A. Duncan (London: HMSO, 4/1990).

Cox, M. (ed.): *Exploring Scottish History: a Directory of Resource Centres in Scottish Local and National History in Scotland* (Edinburgh: Scottish Library Association, 1992).

Cox, R.: *History of Sport: a Guide to the Literature and Sources of Information* (Cheshire: British Society of Sport History in association with Sports History Publishing, 1994).

Coxe, H.O.: *Catalogue of the Manuscripts in the Oxford Colleges* (Oxford: Oxford University Press, 1852; repr. E.P. Publishing, 1972).

Davison, S. (ed.): *Northern Ireland and Canada: a Guide to Northern Ireland Sources for the study of Canadian history, c1705–1992* (Belfast: Queen's University/PRONI, 1994)

Donahue, C. (ed.): *The Records of the Medieval Ecclesiastical Courts*, part II: *England* (Berlin: Report of the Working Group on Church Court Records, Duncker and Humblot, 1994).

Eakins, R. (ed.): *Picture Sources UK* (London: Macdonald, 1985).

Ellis, J. (ed.): *Keeping Archives* (Port Melbourne: D.W. Thorpe in association with the Australian Society of Archivists, 2/1993).

Ellis, M.: *Using Manorial Records* (London: Public Record Office Reader's Guide No. 6, 1994).

Emmison, F.G. and Smith, W.J. (comps): *Material for Theses in Local Record Offices and Libraries* (London: Historical Association, 1982).

Evans, H. and Evans, M. (comps): *Picture Researcher's Handbook: an International Guide to Picture Sources and How to Use Them* (London: Chapman & Hall 5/1992).

Ferguson, J.P.S.: *Directory of Scottish Newspapers* (Edinburgh: National Library of Scotland, 1984).

Forbes, H. (comp.): *Local Authority Archive Services, 1992: a Survey Commissioned by the Royal Commission on Historical Manuscripts and National Council on Archives* (London: British Library R and D Report 6090, HMSO, 1993).

Foster, J.: *AIDS Archives in the UK* (London: London School of Hygiene and Tropical Medicine, 1990).

Fowler, S.: *Army Records for Family Historians* (London: HMSO, 1992).

Gibson, J.S.W.: *Unpublished Personal Name Indexes in Record Offices and Libraries* (Birmingham: FFHS, 2/1987).

——: *A Simplified Guide to Probate Jurisdictions: Where to Look for Wills* (Birmingham: FFHS, 2/1987).

——: *Local Newspapers 1750-1920: a Select Location List* (Birmingham: FFHS, 1987).

——: *Quarter Sessions Records for Family Historians: a Select List* (Birmingham: FFHS, 4/1995).

——: *Marriage, Census and other Indexes for Family Historians* (Birmingham: FFHS, 5/1994).

——: *Poll Books c1696–1872: a Directory to Holdings in Great Britain* (Birmingham: FFHS, 1994).

——: *Probate Jurisdictions: Where to Look for Wills* (Birmingham: FFHS, 4/1994).

Gibson, J.S.W. and Hampson, E.: *Census Returns, 1841–1891, in microform: a Directory to Local Holdings* (Birmingham: FFHS, 6/1994).

Gibson, J.S.W. and Medlycott, M.: *Local Census Listings, 1522–1930: Holdings in the British Isles* (Birmingham: FFHS, 1992).

Gibson, J.S.W. and Peskett, P.: *Record Offices: How to Find Them* (Birmingham: FFHS, 6/1993) [gives helpful maps of locations].

Gibson, J.S.W. and Rogers, C.: *Coroners' Records in England and Wales* (Birmingham: FFHS, 1988).

Gibson, J.S.W. and Walcot, M.: *Where to Find the International Genealogical Index* (Birmingham: FFHS, 1984).

Glanville, P.G.: *Councils, Committees and Boards: a Handbook of Advisory, Consultative, Executive and Similar Bodies in British Public Life.* (Beckenham: CBD Research, 8/1993).

Grenham, J.: *Tracing your Irish Ancestors: the Complete Guide* (Dublin: Gill and Macmillan, 1992).

Gunasingam, S. (ed.): *Directory of South Asian Library Resources in the UK and the Republic of Ireland* (London: South Asian Library Group, 1987).

Habgood, W. (ed.): *Chartered Accountants in England and Wales: a Guide to Historical Records* (Manchester: Manchester University Press, 1994).

Harper, P.: *Guide to the Manuscript Papers of British Scientists Catalogued by the Contemporary Scientific Archives Centre and the National Cataloguing Unit for the Archives of Contemporary Scientists, 1973–1993* (Bath: NCUACS, University of Bath, 1993).

Harrold, A.: *Academic Libraries in the United Kindgom and the Republic of Ireland* (London: Library Association, 2/1992).

Hartley, J.M.: *Guide to Documents and Manuscripts in the United Kingdom relating to Russia and the Soviet Union* (London: Mansell, 1987).

Harvey, J.H.: *Sources for the History of Houses* (London: British Records Association, Archives and the User No. 3, 1974).

Hawkings, D.T.: *Criminal Ancestors: a Guide to Historical Criminal Records in England and Wales* (Stroud: Sutton, 1993).

Hazlehurst, C. and Woodland, C.: *Guide to the Papers of British Cabinet Ministers, 1900-1951* (London: Royal Historical Society Guides and Handbooks Supplementary Series No. 1, 1974).

Helferty, S. and Refaussé, R.(eds): *Directory of Irish Archives* (Dublin: Blackrock, Irish Academic Press, 2/1993).

Henderson, G.P. and Henderson, S.P.A. (eds): *Directory of British Associations and Associations in Ireland* (Beckenham: CBD Research, 10/1990).

Hewitt, A.R.: *Guide to Resources for Commonwealth Studies in London, Oxford and Cambridge, with Bibliographical and other Information* (London: Athlone, 1957).

Higgs, E.: *Making Sense of the Census: the Manuscript Returns for England and Wales, 1801–1901* (London: HMSO, 1989).

Hindle, P.: *Maps for Local History* (London: Batsford, 1988).

History, Museums and Galleries, Sectional List 60 (London: HMSO, 1994) [includes information about officially published records, printed lists and indexes].

Holding, N.: *The Location of British Army Records: a National Directory of World War I Sources* (Birmingham: FFHS, 2/1987).

Honer, J. (ed.): *The Art Directory* (London: Macmillan, 1993) [a guide to the visual arts institutions and organisations in Britain, to be published annually].

Houston, P.: *Keepers of the Frame: the Film Archives* (London: British Film Institute, 1994).

Humphery-Smith, C. (ed.): *The Phillimore Atlas and Index of Parish Registers* (Chichester: Phillimore, 1984).

Index of English Literary Manuscripts (London: Mansell, 1980–):
    Vol. I: *1450–1625*, ed. P. Beal (1980).
    Vol. II: *1625–1700*, ed. P. Beal (1987–93).
    Vol. III: *1700–1800*, ed. M.M. Smith (1986–92).
    Vol. IV: *1800–1900*, eds B. Rosenbaum and P. White (1982–90).

Ingram, K.E.: *Sources for West Indian Studies: a Supplementary Listing, with Particular Reference to Manuscript Sources* (Zug: Inter Documentation, 1993).

Institute of Historical Research, University of London: *Historical Research for Higher Degrees in the UK*, comp. J.M. Horn, Part I: *Thesis Completed* [in the previous year]; Part II: *Theses in progress* [in the current year] (London: IHR, annually).

——: *History Theses, 1901–70*, comp. P.M. Jacobs (London, IHR, 1976).

——: *History Theses, 1971–80*, comp. J.M. Horn (London, IHR, 1984).

——: *History Theses, 1981–90*, comp. J.M. Horn (London, IHR, 1994).

International Council on Archives: *International Bibliography of Directories and Guides to Archival Repositories* (London: K.G. Saur, 1990).

Iredale, D.: *Discovering Local History* (Aylesbury: Shire, 2/1977; repr. Haverfordwest, 1985).

——: *Local History Research and Writing* (Chichester: Phillimore, 1980) [rev. edn of *Enjoying Archives* (Newton Abbott: David and Charles, 1973)].

Jones, C.A.: *Britain and the Dominions: a Guide to Business and Related Records in the United Kingdom concerning Australia, Canada, New Zealand and South Africa* (Boston: Hall, 1978).

Jones, P.: *Britain and Palestine, 1914–1948: Archival Sources for the History of the British Mandate* (Oxford: Oxford University Press for the British Academy, 1979).

Kamen, R.H.: *British and Irish Architectural History: a Bibliography and Guide to Sources of Information* (New York: Nichols, 1981).

Keen, R.: *Survey of Archives of Selected Missionary Societies* (London: Church Missionary Society, 1968) [TS available at HMC].

Keene, D. and Harding, V.: *A Survey of Documentary Sources for Property Holding in London before the Great Fire* (London: London Record Society, 1985).

Ker, N.R.: *Medieval Manuscripts in British Libraries*, Vols 1-4 (Oxford: Clarendon Press, 1969–92).

Kitching, C.J. (comp.): *Surveys of Historical Manuscripts in the United Kingdom : a Select Bibliography* (London: HMSO, 2/1994).

——: *The Central Records of the Church of England: a Report and Survey presented to the Pilgrim and Radcliffe Trustees* (London: Church Information Office, 1976).

——: *Archive Buildings in the United Kingdom, 1977–1992* (London: HMSO, 1993).

Knightbridge, A.: *Archive Legislation in the United Kingdom* (Society of Archivists Information Leaflet No. 3, 1986).

Kurucz, G.: *Guide to Documents and Manuscripts in Great Britain relating to the Kingdom of Hungary from the Earliest Times to 1800 (London: Mansell, 1992)*.

Lambert, D.: *Record of Documentary Sources for British Gardens, Gardening and Landscape Design: Report on the Pilot Study 1989–90* (York: Publication No.4, Centre for the Conservation of Historic Parks and Gardens, Institute of Advanced Architectural Studies, University of York, 1991).

Lance, D.: *An Archive Approach to Oral History* (London: Imperial War Museum, 1978).

Lannon, D. (ed.): *The Directory of Roman Catholic Archives* (Roman Catholic Archives Society, 1994).

Lenz, W.: *Archivalische Quellen zur deutschen Geschichte seit 1500 in Grossbritannien* [Archival sources for German history since 1500 in Great Britain] (Boppard am Rheim: Harald Boldt, 1975).

The Libraries Directory (Cambridge: James Clarke, 1991–) [biennial].

London Museum Service: *Museums in London* (London: Area Museums Service for South East England, 1988).

LRCC History Sub-Committee: *A Guide to History Libraries and Collections* (London: University of London, 5/1990).

Lumas, S.: *Making Use of the Census* (London: HMSO, 2/1993).

Macdonald, B.: *Broadcasting in the United Kingdom: a Guide to Information Sources* (London: Mansell, rev. 2/1994).

MacDougall, I. (comp. and ed.): *A Catalogue of some Labour Records in Scotland and some Scots Records outside Scotland* (Edinburgh: Scottish Labour History Society, 1978).

McKay, Peter H.: *A Guide to the Retention of Modern Records on Landed Estates* (Letchworth: Hall-McCartney for the Historic Houses Archivists Group, 1992).

MacLeod, R.M. and Friday, J.R.: *Archives of British Men of Science: Introduction and Index to the Publication in Microfiche of a Survey of Private and Institutional Holdings* (London: Mansell, 1972).

McNulty, A. and Troop, H. (comps): *Directory of British Oral History Collections* (Colchester: Oral History Society, 1981).

Mander-Jones, P.: *Manuscripts in the British Isles relating to Australia, New Zealand and the Pacific* (Canberra: Australian National University, 1972).

Marchant, L.: *A Guide to the Archives and Records of Protestant and Christian Missions from the British Isles to China, 1796–1914* (Nedlands: University of Western Australia Press, 1966).

Marsh, A. and Ryan, V.: *Historical Directory of Trade Unions*, 4 vols (Farnborough/ Aldershot: Gower, 1980-88) [includes the survival and location of records].

Martin, G. and McIntyre, S.: *A Bibliography of British and Irish Municipal History*. Vol. 1: *General Works* (Welwyn Garden City: Leicester University Press, 1972).

Mathias, P. and Pearsall, A.W.H. (eds): *Shipping: a Survey of Historical Records* (Newton Abbot: David & Charles, 1971).

Matthews, N.: *Materials for West African History in the Archives of the United Kingdom* (London: Athlone Press, 1973).

Matthews, N. and Wainwright, M.D. (eds): *A Guide to Manuscripts and Documents in the British Isles relating to the Far East* (Oxford: Oxford University Press, 1977).

——: *A Guide to Manuscripts and Documents in the British Isles relating to the Middle East and North Africa* (Oxford: Oxford University Press, 1980).

Matthews, W. (comp.): *British Diaries: an Annotated Bibliography of British Diaries Written between 1442 and 1942* (Gloucester, Mass.: Peter Smith, 1967).

Mayer, S.L. and Koenig, W.J.: *The Two World Wars: a Guide to Manuscript Collections in the United Kingdom* (London: Bowker, 1976).

Moody, D.: *Scottish Towns: Sources for Local Historians* (London: Batsford: 1986).

——: *Scottish Local History: an Introductory Guide* (Batsford: London, 1986).

Morgan, P. (comp.): *Oxford Libraries outside the Bodleian: a Guide* (Oxford: Bodleian Library, 2/1980).

——: *Select Index of Manuscript Collections in Oxford Libraries outside the Bodleian* (Oxford: Bodleian Library, 1991).

Morris, P.J.T. and Russell, C.A.: *Archives of the British Chemical Industry, 1750–1914: a Handlist* (Faringdon: British Sociey for the History of Science, 1988).

Morton, A. and Donaldson, G.: *British National Archives and the Local Historian: a Guide to Official Record Publications* (London: Historical Association, 1980).

Moulton, J.W.: *Genealogical Resources in English Repositories* (Columbus, Ohio: Hampton House, 1988).

Mullett, M.: *Sources for the History of Nonconformity, 1660–1830*, Archives and the User No.8 (London: British Records Association, 1991).

Munro, D.J. (comp.): *Microforms for Historians: a Finding-List of Research Collections in London Libraries* (London: Institute of Historical Research, University of London, 1990).

National Library of Ireland: *Manuscript Sources for the History of Irish Civilisation*, 11 vols (Boston: Hall, 1965); *First Supplement, 1965–1975*, 3 vols (Boston: Hall, 1979).

Orbell, J.: *A Guide to Tracing the History of a Business* (Aldershot: Gower, for the Business Archives Council, 1987).

Ottley, G.: *Railway History: a Guide to Sixty-One Collections in Libraries and Archives in Great Britain* (London: Library Association Subject Guide to Library Resources No. 1, 1973).

Pearson, J.D.: (comp.): *A Guide to Manuscripts and Documents in the British Isles relating to South and South-East Asia*, Vol. 1: *London*, Vol. 2: *British Isles* (London: Mansell, 1989, 1990).

——: *A Guide to Manuscripts and Documents in the British Isles relating to Africa*, Vol. 1: *London*; Vol. 2: *British Isles* (London: Mansell 1993, 1994).

Percival, J. (ed.): *A Guide to Archives and Manuscripts in the University of London*, Vol. 1 (London: University of London, LRCC, 1984).

Pinhorn, M.: *Historical, Archaeological and Kindred Societies: a List* (Newport: Pinhorns, 1985).

Post, J.B. and Foster, M.R.: *Copyright: a Handbook for Archivists* (London: Society of Archivists, 1992).

Pressnell, L.S. and Orbell, J.: *A Guide to the Historical Records of British Banking* (Aldershot: Gower, 1985).

Prochaska, A.: *Irish History from 1700: a Guide to Sources in the Public Record Office* (London: British Records Association, Archives and the User No. 6, 1986).

Publications of the Royal Commission on Historical Manuscripts, Sectional List 17 (London: HMSO, 1974).

The Public Records Acts (London: HMSO, 1958, 1967).

Raimo, J.W. (ed.): *A Guide to Manuscripts relating to America in Great Britain and Ireland* (London: Mansell, 1979).

Reynard, K.W. (ed.): *ASLIB Directory of Literary and Historical Collections in the UK* (London: ASLIB, 1993).

Reynard, K.W. and J.M.E. (eds): *The ASLIB Directory of Information Sources in the United Kingdom* (London: ASLIB, 8/1994).

Richard, S. (comp.): *Directory of British Official Publications* (London: Mansell, 2/1984).

——: *ASLIB Directory of Information Sources in the UK* (London: ASLIB, 8/1994).

Richardson, J.: *The Local Historian's Encyclopedia* (New Barnet: Historical Publications, 2/1986).

Richmond, L.M. and Stockford, B.: *Company Archives: a Survey of the Records of 1000 of the First Registered Companies in England and Wales* (Aldershot: Gower, 1986).

Richmond, L.M. and Turton, A. (eds): *The Brewing Industry: a Guide to Historical Records* (Manchester: Manchester University Press, 1990).

——: *Directory of Corporate Archives* (London: Business Archives Council, 3/1992).

——: *Record Sources for Local History* (London: Batsford, 1987).

Ringler, W.A.: *Bibliography and Index of English Verse in Manuscript, 1501–1558* (London: Mansell, 1992).

Ritchie, L.A. (ed.): *The Shipbuilding Industry: a Guide to Historical Records* (Manchester: Manchester University Press, 1992).

Roberts, S. et al.: *Research Libraries and Collections in the United Kingdom* (London: Clive Bingley, 1978).

Rogers, C.D.: *Tracing Missing Persons: an Introduction to Agencies, Methods and Sources in England and Wales* (Manchester: Manchester University Press, 1986).

Rowlands, J. (ed.): *Welsh Family History: a Guide to Research* (Llandysul: Association of Family History Societies of Wales, J.D. Lewis and Sons, Gomer Press, 1993).

Royal Commission on Historical Manuscripts: *Accessions to Repositories and Reports added to the National Register of Archives (1972–91 annually)* (HMSO, 1975–91) [annually; no longer published].

——: *A Guide to the Reports on Collections of Manuscripts of Private Families, Corporations and Institutions in Great Britain and Ireland*, 7 vols (HMSO, 1914–73).

——: *Guide to Sources for British History* (HMSO, 1982–):

——: *Papers of British Cabinet Ministers, 1782–1900* (1982).

——: *The Manuscript Papers of British Scientists, 1600–1942* (1982).

——: *Guide to the Location of Collections described in the Reports and Calendars Series, 1870–1980* (1982).

——: *Private Papers of British Diplomats, 1782–1900* (1985).

——: *Private Papers of British Colonial Governors, 1782–1900* (1986).

——: *Papers of British Churchmen, 1780–1940* (1987).

——: *Papers of British Politicians, 1782–1900* (1989).

——: *Records of British Business and Industry, 1760–1914: Textiles and Leather* (1990).

——: *Records of British Business and Industry, 1760–1914: Metal Processing and Engineering* (1994).

——: *Principal Collections of Family and Estate Papers in the United Kingdom, A–K* (1995).

——: *List of Accessions to Repositories (1956 onwards)* (HMSO, 1957–72) [annually].

——: *Record Repositories in Great Britain* (HMSO, 9/1991).

Seton, R. and Naish, E. (comps): *A Preliminary Guide to the Archives of British Missionary Societies* (London: School of Oriental and African Studies, 1992).

Shaw, G. and Tipper, A.: *British Directories: a Bibliography and Guide to Directories published in England and Wales (1850-1950) and Scotland (1773-1950)* (London: Leicester University Press, 1989).

Silverthorne, E.: *London Local Archives: a Directory of Local Authority Record Offices and Libraries* (Orpington: Guildhall Library and Greater London Archives Network, 3/1994).

Sinclair, C.: *Tracing your Scottish Ancestors: a Guide to Ancestry Research in the Scottish Record Office* (Edinburgh: Scottish Record Office, HMSO, 1990).

——: *Tracing Scottish Local History: a Guide to Local History Research in the Scottish Record Office* (Edinburgh: Scottish Record Office, HMSO, 1994).

Smallbone, L. (comp.) and Storey, R. (ed.): *Employers' and Trade Associations' History* (Warwick: University of Warwick, 1992).

Smith, C. (comp.): *Directory of Consultants and Researchers in Library and Information Science* (London: British Library, 1987).

Smith, D.M.: *Guide to Bishops' Registers of England and Wales: a Survey from the Middle Ages to the Abolition of Episcopacy in 1646* (London: Royal Historical Society, 1981).

Society of Archivists: *Directory of Suppliers of Materials, Equipment and Services for Archive and Book Conservation Storage and Display* (3/1994)

Society of Genealogists: *National Index of Parish Registers* (London, 1968–).

——: 'Original Parish Registers in Record Offices and Libraries'. *Local Population Studies*, supplements (1974, 1976, 1978, 1982).

A Standard for Record Repositories on Constitution and Finance, Staff, Acquisition, Access (London: HMSO, 1990).

Stephens, W.B.: *Sources for English Local History* (Cambridge: Cambridge University Press, 2/1981).

Stephens, W.B. and Unwin R.W.: *Materials for the Local and Regional Study of Schooling, 1700–1900* (London: British Records Association, Archives and the User No. 7, 1987).

Storey, R.A. and Madden, J.L.: *Primary Sources for Victorian Studies: a Guide to the Location and Use of Unpublished Materials* (London: Phillimore, 1977; updated, Leicester, 1987).

Stuart, D.: *Manorial Records: an Introduction to their Transcription and Translation* (Chichester: Phillimore, 1992).

Sturges, R.P.: *Economists' Papers, 1750-1950: a Guide to Archive and other Manuscript Sources for the History of British and Irish Economic Thought* (London: Macmillan, 1975).

Sutton, D. (ed.): *Location Register of Twentieth-Century English Literary Manuscripts and Letters: a Union List of Modern English, Irish, Scottish and Welsh Authors in the British Isles*, 2 vols (London: British Library, 1988).

Swann, B. and Turnbull, M.: *Records of Interest to Social Scientists, 1919 to 1939*, 3 vols (London: HMSO, 1971–78).

Tate, W.E.: *The Parish Chest: a Study of the Records of Parochial Administration in England* (Cambridge: Cambridge University Press, 3/1969).

Thompson, K.: *The Use of Archives in Education: a Bibliography* (Leicester: Society of Archivists. 1982).

Thurston, A.: *Guide to Archives and Manuscripts relating to Kenya and East Africa in the United Kingdom*, Vol. 1: *Official Records*; Vol. 2: *Non-Official Archives and Manuscripts* (London: Hans Zell, 1991).

——: *Sources for Colonial Studies in the Public Record Office*, Vol. I (London: Institute of Commonwealth Studies, University of London and Public Record Office, HMSO, 1995).

Turton, A. (ed.): *Managing Business Archives* (Oxford: Butterworth/Heinemann in association with the Business Archives Council, 1991).

Varley, G. (comp. & ed.): *Art and Design Documentation in the UK and Ireland: a Directory of Resources* (Bromsgrove: ARLIS, 1993).

Vaurie, A. (ed.): 'International Directory of Archives', *Archivum*, Vol. XXXIII (Munich and London: Saur, ICA, 1988).

Victoria County History (1900–; now published by Oxford University Press for the Institute of Historical Research) [*c*200 vols to all counties in England].

Walford's guide to Reference Material, 2 vols (London: Library Association, 6/1993-4).

Wall, J. (comp.): *Directory of British Photographic Collections* (London: Heinemann, 1977).

Walne, P. (ed.): *A Guide to Manuscript Sources for the History of Latin America and the Caribbean in the British Isles* (London: Oxford University Press, 1973).

——: *Dictionary of Archival Terminology: English and French with Equivalents in Dutch, German, Russian and Spanish* (Munich and London: Saur, ICA Handbook Series Vol. 7, 2/1988).

Ward, A.: *A Manual of Sound Archive Administration* (Gower: Aldershot, 1990).

Watson, A.G.: *Catalogue of Dated and Dateable Manuscripts, c435–1600, in Oxford Libraries*, 2 vols (Oxford: Clarendon Press, 1984).

Watt, I.: *A Directory of UK Map Collections* (London: Map Curators Group Publication No. 3, 2/1985).

Weerasinghe, L. and Silver, J. (comp. & ed.): *Directory of Recorded Sound Resources in the UK* (London: British Library, 1988).

West, J.: *Village Records* (London: Macmillan, 1962).

——: *Town Records* (Chichester: Phillimore, 1983).

Whittaker's Almanack (London, annually) [includes details of learned societies and associations, schools etc].

Williams, C.J. and Watts-Williams, S.J. (comps): *Cofrestri Plwyf Cymru/Parish Registers of Wales* (Aberystwyth: National Library of Wales, 1986).

Williams, J.A.: 'Sources for Recusant History (1559–1791) in English Official Archives', *Recusant History* (journal of the Catholic Records Society), Vol. 16, No. 4 (Oct 1983).

Williams, M.I. (ed.): *A Directory of Rare Book and Special Collections in the United Kingdom and the Republic of Ireland* (London: Library Association, 1985).

Williamson, B.: *Using Archives at National Trust Properties: a Practical Guide* (London: National Trust, 1985).

Wilson, B.G. (ed.) and Burdett A. (comp.): *Manuscripts and Government Records in the United Kingdom and Ireland relating to Canada* (Ottawa: National Archives of Canada, 1992).

Wise, T. and Wise. S.: *A Guide to Military Museums and other Places of Military Interest* (Knighton: Imperial Press, 8/1994).

Yeo, G. (comp.): *The British Overseas: a Guide to Records of their Births, Baptisms, Marriages, Deaths and Burials available in the United Kingdom* (London: Guildhall Library, 1984).

1 Cynon Valley Libraries Local Collection

Parent organisation: Cynon Valley Borough Council, Department of Leisure Services: Libraries Section

Address: Central Library, Green Street, Aberdare, Mid Glamorgan CF44 7AG

Telephone: (01685) 885318

Fax: (01685) 881181

Enquiries: The Assistant Reference Librarian, Miss Alice Percival

Open: Mon, Fri: 9.00–7.00 Tues, Wed: 9.00–6.00 Thurs: 9.00–5.00 Sat: 9.00–1.00

Access: Generally open to the public. Appointments advisable for microform sources.

Historical background: The Public Library Act was adopted in 1904. Cynon Valley Borough Council was formed from Aberdare and Llandwdano urban district councils (and Rhigos/Penderyn) in 1974. The local collection has been greatly expanded from the 1970s onwards.

Acquisitions policy: To collect any available material appertaining to the history of the Cynon Valley.

Archives of organisation: Council minutes, correspondence, etc, 1904–.

Non-manuscript material: Collections of local historians: W.W. Price Collection (1873–1967), mainly notes and pamphlets, c1920–1967; and Rev. Ivor Parry Collection (1908–75), mainly notes and articles from local newspapers, c1950–1970.
Extensive photographic collection, especially on Cynon Valley (c7000).
Aberdare Times, 1861–1902; *Aberdare Leader,* 1902–, and other local newspapers (on microfilm), 1833–.
Census returns, 1841–91 (on microfilm).
Maps and newspaper cuttings. Small collection of videos and films.
Sketches by Bacon sisters, 1827–8.

Finding aids: Newspaper indexes; document schedules; keys to maps; guide to photograph classification; list of videos and films.

Facilities: Photocopying. Photography by arrangement. Microfilm/fiche readers.

Conservation: Contracted out.

Publications: D.L. Davies: *A Guide to Local Genealogical Sources.*

2 Aberdeen Art Gallery and Museums
James McBey Reference Library

Parent organisation: City of Aberdeen

Address: Schoolhill, Aberdeen, Grampian AB9 1FQ

Telephone: (01224) 646333 ext. 230

Fax: (01224) 632133

Enquiries: The Librarian, Mrs C. Williams

Open: Mon–Fri: 10.00–12.00; 2.00–4.00

Access: Generally open to the public

Historical background: The original art gallery was built in 1885. The James McBey Print Room and Art Library, opened in 1961 as a memorial to James McBey (1883–1959), etcher and painter, was endowed by his widow.

Acquisitions policy: Accepts donations of local artists' papers.

Major collections: Sir George Reid RSA (1841–1913), letters and papers.
William Dyce, RSA (1806–64), papers.
Records of Messrs Berry and Mackay, marine opticians of Aberdeen, are held in the museum.

Non-manuscript material: Collection of James McBey's books and memorabilia.
Slide collection and videotapes.

Finding aids: Berry and Mackay: NRA 14565.

Facilities: Photocopying by arrangement. Microfiche reader.

3 Aberdeen Central Library

Parent organisation: City of Aberdeen, Arts and Recreation Division, Library Services

Address: Rosemount Viaduct, Aberdeen, Grampian AB9 1GU

Telephone: (01224) 634622

Fax: (01224) 641985

Enquiries: The Head of Library Services, Mr Alan R. Fulton

Open: Mon–Fri: 9.00–9.00 Sat: 9.00–5.00

Access: Generally open, except where depositors have stipulated otherwise.

Historical background: The Public Library Acts were adopted for Aberdeen in 1884, and the library service began in 1886 in the Mechanics' Institute building, Market Street. The present central library was opened in 1892, with extensions in 1905 and 1981–2. The library includes a well-stocked reference library and local studies department.

Acquisitions policy: Items relating to Aberdeen and the surrounding area are considered for acquisition by donation or purchase. Archive deposits by local societies are welcomed.

Major collections: Aberdeen Airport, aircraft movement log-books, 1972–.
Aberdeen Mechanics' Institute, reports, rules and regulations, library catalogues, handbills.
Papers relating to the Bruce family of Heatherwick Farm, Inverurie.
Journals and letter-books of George Sim (1835–1908), naturalist.

Non-manuscript material: Aberdeen city plan, 1661.
George Washington Wilson Photographic Collection.
Photographs of places, people and events in Aberdeen.
Local newspapers, 1747–.

Finding aids: TS lists and card catalogues.

Facilities: Photocopying. Microfilm/fiche readers/printers.

Conservation: Contracted out.

4 Aberdeen City Archives

Address: Town House, Aberdeen, Grampian AB9 1AQ

Telephone: (01224) 276276 ext. 2513/2521

Fax: (01224) 522491

Enquiries: The City Archivist, Miss J.A. Cripps

Open: Mon–Fri: 9.30–12.30; 2.00–4.30

Access: Generally open to the public, by appointment.

Archives of organisation: Royal Burgh of Aberdeen, 12th century–1975; Burgh of Old Aberdeen, 1603–1891; Burgh of Woodside 1868–91; Aberdeen Harbour Board, 1801–1935 (incomplete).

Major collections: Records of: Hall Russell Shipbuilders, 19th–20th centuries; Aberdeen Association for Prevention of Cruelty to Animals, 1872–1970; Aberdeen Congregational Churches, 1798–1971; Northern Cooperative Society, 1861–1993; Aberdeen Chamber of Commerce, 1856–1980.

Finding aids: Survey list, 1970. Detailed listing in progress.

Facilities: Photocopying. Photography by arrangement.

Publications: P.J. Anderson (ed.): *Charters Relating to Burgh of Aberdeen* (1890) [incorporates 40-page inventory of Burgh records].

5 Aberdeen University Library
Department of Special Collections and Archives

Parent organisation: University of Aberdeen

Address: King's College, Aberdeen, Grampian AB9 2UB

Telephone: (01224) 272599/8

Fax: (01224) 487048

Enquiries: The University Archivist and Head of Department, Mr C.A. McLaren

Open: Mon–Fri: 9.30–4.30; advance notice of visits is desirable.

Access: Approved readers. Written application preferred.

Historical background: For over 200 years there were two separate universities in Aberdeen, each with its own statutory rights and degree-granting privileges. The first, King's College, was founded in Old Aberdeen in 1495. The second, Marischal College, was founded in New Aberdeen by George Keith, 4th Earl Marischal of Scotland, in 1593. The two colleges remained rival institutions until 1860, when a royal ordinance united them under the title of the University of Aberdeen. The Manuscripts and Archives Section of the university library was established in its present form in 1969.
MSS and books formerly belonging to scholars of the north-east from the 16th century onwards now form part of the university library. Material has been transferred from the library of Christ's College. The archives of St Machar's Cathedral, which are stored in the cathedral charter room, are made available for study in the library reading room.

Acquisitions policy: The principal function of the section is the systematic accumulation and preservation of the university's archives. Non-archival material relating to the university is acquired as often as possible. Until 1976 the university acted as a repository for local historical material in the absence of a local authority record office in the region, under the terms of the agreement reached between the Scottish universities and the NRA(S). Since 1976 it has shared this activity with the Regional and District Record Offices.

Archives of organisation: Archives of King's College, Marischal College and the University of Aberdeen.

Major collections: Individual MSS and archival collections bought by the library, given to it, or deposited in it on loan (*c*4000– separate items and collections).
Collections of papyri, ostraca and non-European MSS.

Non-manuscript material: An oral history archive of the university is being built up.

Finding aids: All collections are catalogued briefly by title and entered in the university library on-line catalogue accessible via JANET. Standardised descriptive or summary lists, 1969–, are circulated via the NRA(S).

Facilities: Photocopying. Photography. Microfilm/fiche reader/printer.

Conservation: Presently contracted out. It is planned soon to extend the conservation service at Marischal Museum to cover paper conservation.

Publications: Guide to Sources of Information: Manuscripts and Archives (Aberdeen, 1979–).
M.R. James: *A Catalogue of the Medieval Manuscripts in the University Library Aberdeen* (Cambridge, 1932).
E.G. Turner: *Catalogue of Greek and Latin Papyri and Ostraca in the Possession of the University Library, Aberdeen,* Aberdeen University Studies, no.116 (Aberdeen, 1939).
L. Macfarlane: 'William Elphinstone's Library', *Aberdeen University Review,* xxxvii (1957–8), 253.
C. Roth: *The Aberdeen Codex of the Hebrew Bible,* Aberdeen University Studies, no.138 (Edinburgh, 1958).
N.R. Ker: *Medieval Manuscripts in British Libraries,* ii (Oxford, 1977), 2.
J. Carter and C. McLaren: *Crown and Gown:*

an Illustrated History of the University of Aberdeen, 1495–1995 (Aberdeen University Press, 1994).
Other descriptions can be found in Aberdeen University Library *Bulletin, Aberdeen University Review,* and *Northern Scotland, passim.*

6 Grampian Health Board Archives

Address: ARI Woolmanhill, Aberdeen, Grampian AB9 1EF

Telephone: (01224) 663456 ext. 55562

Fax: (01224) 840791

Enquiries: The Archivist, Miss F.R. Watson

Open: Mon–Fri: 9.00–5.00

Access: Generally open to the public, by appointment, subject to 30-, 75- and 100-year closure periods on certain records.

Historical background: Grampian Health Board was set up in 1974, the successor authority to the North Eastern Regional Hospital Board, itself established in 1947 under the National Health Service (Scotland) Act. The board is accountable to the Secretary of State for Scotland and to local people to improve health and ensure that appropriate services are available for the residents of Grampian. The archives department, formed in 1980, holds the records of hospitals, community services, NHS authorities and many other health-related predecessor authorities in the north-east of Scotland.

Acquisitions policy: To acquire by deposit or donation material relevant to health care and health-care institutions currently or formerly in existence in the Grampian area.

Archives of organisation: Archives of Grampian Health Board and North Eastern Regional Hospital Board and their constituents.

Major collections: Records of Aberdeen Royal Infirmary (f. 1739), including 18th-century case notes and estate papers of Kinnadie and Towie (Aberdeenshire); Royal Cornhill Hospital, Aberdeen (f. 1800); Royal Aberdeen Children's Hospital (f. 1877); district lunatic asylums in Aberdeen, Banff and Elgin.

Non-manuscript material: Photographs of hospitals in north-east Scotland, exteriors and interiors.

Finding aids: TS lists, copies of which

are held in Scottish Record Office (entry **313**). Index of north-east doctors, midwives, druggists, dentists, etc, mainly 18th and early 19th centuries, in preparation.

Facilities: Photocopying. Photography by arrangement.

7 Grampian Regional Archives

Parent organisation: Grampian Regional Council

Address: Old Aberdeen House, Dunbar Street, Aberdeen, Grampian AB9 1LU

Telephone: (01224) 481775

Enquiries: The Regional Archivist, Mrs Brenda R. Cluer

Open: Mon–Fri: 10.00–1.00; 2.00–4.00

Access: Generally open to the public.

Historical background: The regional council was established in 1975 at local government reorganisation and took over records from the previous local authorities, including county councils and burghs.

Major collections: Poor records, 1845–; valuation rolls, 1855–; school records, 1873–.

Acquisitions policy: To maintain local government archives.

Archives of organisation: County Councils of Aberdeen, Banff, Kincardine and Moray, joint authorities for fire, police and water services, development, planning and valuation in northeast Scotland, including Aberdeen City.

Finding aids: Lists.

Facilities: Photocopying. Photography.

Conservation: Contracted out.

Publications: Lists of sources.

8 North East of Scotland Library Service

Address: Meadows Industrial Estate, Meldrum Meg Way, Oldmeldrum, Aberdeen, Grampian AB51 0GN

Telephone: (01651) 872707 ext. 17

Fax: (01651) 872142

Enquiries: The Local History Librarian, Miss L. Donald
Enquiries for the Huntly and Strichen branch libraries should also be directed to the Oldmeldrum Headquarters

Open: Mon–Fri: 9.00–5.00

Access: Generally open to the public, although some prior notice is welcome and an appointments system is in operation for the microfilm reader.

Historical background: The service was formed in May 1975 on local government reorganisation to serve Banff and Buchan, Gordon, and Kincardine and Deeside districts.

Acquisitions policy: To strengthen existing primary and secondary collections of material on the local area by purchase and donation.

Major collections: Strichen Collection: Strichen estate records and plans; records of local societies and Auchmedden estate papers and a small collection of late 19th-century and early 20th-century photographs (originals at Oldmeldrum, microfilm at Strichen Branch Library).
George Macdonald Collection: MSS, letters, books and photographs relating to Macdonald (1824–1905), novelist (held at Huntly Library but queries to HQ).

Non-manuscript material: The local history collection includes maps and photographs of the area.
Council minutes, valuation rolls and voters' rolls for the area, mostly 1975–.
Community council newsletters and minutes of meetings, 1975–.

Finding aids: The collection is catalogued and classified. Maps index. Index to magazine articles, proceedings of local societies. Index to major reference sources. Anderson Memorial Library (Strichen collection): NRA 18764.

Facilities: Photocopying. Microfilm/fiche reader/printer.

9 Dyfed Archives Service
Cardiganshire Record Office

Parent organisation: Dyfed County Council

Address: Swyddfa'r Sir, Marine Terrace, Aberystwyth, Dyfed SY23 2DE

Telephone: (01970) 617581 ext. 2120

Enquiries: The Archivist

Open: Tues, Thurs: 9.00–4.45

Historical background: The office was established in 1974. Previously records for the area had been collected by the National Library of Wales (entry 10). The office acts as a Diocesan Record Office for St Davids but has no parish register. It is recognised as a place of deposit for public records.

Archives of organisation: Usual local authority record holdings.

Major collections: Deposited local collections.

Facilities: Photocopying. Microfilm readers.

10 National Library of Wales
Department of Manuscripts and Records

Address: Aberystwyth, Dyfed SY23 3BU

Telephone: (01970) 623816

Fax: (01970) 615701

Enquiries: The Keeper of Manuscripts and Records, Mr G. Jenkins

Open: Mon–Fri: 9.30–6.00 Sat: 9.30–5.00

Access: By reader's ticket; over 18 years of age.

Historical background: The library was established by Royal Charter in 1907 and is a copyright library. It is recognised as a place of deposit for public records.

Acquisitions policy: MS and archival material relating to Wales.

Archives of organisation: Complete organisational archive, 1907–.

Major collections: General Series of the National Library of Wales MSS.
Records of Great Sessions in Wales, 1542–1830.
Diocesan and capitular archives of the Church in Wales, including Llandaff Cathedral; many of the parish records.
Archives of the Welsh Calvinistic Methodist Church; substantial holdings for other nonconformist denominations.
Many large archives of Welsh estates, families, institutions, artists and writers.
Welsh Political Archive: papers of politicians.

Non-manuscript material: Department of Prints, Drawings and Maps includes MS maps.
Francis Frith Photographic Archive, 1860s–1960s (c35,000).
Audio-visual sub-department: film and sound

archives, television and radio tapes, including log of S4C programmes.

Finding aids: Calendars, schedules and lists (c600 vols, mostly TS); associated card indexes.

Facilities: Photographic department. Microfilm/fiche readers. Ultra-violet and infra-red equipment.

Conservation: In-house bindery, also paper, parchment and leather repair facilities.

Publications: *Annual Report* [includes list of accessions].
National Library of Wales Journal (1939–) [articles on the library's holdings].
Guide to the Department of Manuscripts and Records, the National Library of Wales (Aberystwyth, 1994).

11 National Monuments Record of Wales

Parent organisation: The Royal Commission on the Ancient and Historical Monuments of Wales

Address: Crown Building, Plas Crug, Aberystwyth, Dyfed SY23 1NJ

Telephone: (01970) 624381

Fax: (01970) 627701

Enquiries: The Head of Library and Archive, Mrs Hilary Malaws

Open: Mon–Fri: 9.30–4.00; restricted service 1.00–2.00

Access: Generally open to the public. No appointment is necessary but advance notice is always helpful.

Historical background: The Royal Commission was established in 1908 to make an inventory of the ancient and historical monuments of Wales and Monmouthshire. It is currently empowered by a Royal Warrant of 1992 to survey, record, publish and maintain a database of ancient and historical sites, structures and landscapes in Wales. It is responsible for the National Monuments Record (NMR) of Wales, for the supply of archaeological information to the Ordnance Survey for mapping purposes, for the coordination of archaeological aerial photography in Wales, and for the sponsorship of the regional Sites and Monuments Records.

Acquisitions policy: To collect, maintain and

make available a comprehensive record of the archaeological, architectural and historical monuments of Wales (including its territorial waters) from the earliest times to the present day. The NMR collects records created or held by the Royal Commission, other organisations such as Cadw and the Welsh Archaeological Trusts, and private sources. Generally these consist of modern records. Indexes and descriptions of records and archives held in other repositories and organisations are also acquired. A copy of the *Collecting Policy* is available on request.

Archives of organisation: Archive of Royal Commission fieldwork and research, including reports, notes, drawings, plans, photographs, 1908–.
National Buildings Record (NMR since 1964), Welsh section, photographs, drawings, surveys, documents, 1941–.

Major collections: Cadw: notices of 'listing' and associated photographs of buildings, notices of 'scheduling' of ancient monuments, field monument warden reports and photographs.
Ministry of Works: photographs of monuments in state care.
National Trust: North Wales Vernacular Buildings Survey, Welsh archaeological surveys of NT property.
Regional Archaeological Trusts: excavation records.
Ordnance Survey Archaeology Division: records, photographs and maps.
Property Services Agency: plans and drawings of government and public buildings.
Numerous private collections.

Non-manuscript material: Major national collection of photographs (c1 million) of ancient sites and historic buildings, including vertical and oblique air photographs, 1850s–.
Large-scale OS maps (c30,000), including incomplete set of original OS 25 inch second edition annotated plans. A few of these plans were never published at this scale.
Plans and drawings (originals or copies) from various sources, including architects (c25,000).

Finding aids: Card indexes currently in process of computerisation (mostly site-based); computerised accession register and embryonic catalogue.

Facilities: Photocopying. Photography. Microfiche reader. Also specialist library and

access to experts in archaeology, architectural history and industrial archaeology fields.

Conservation: Contracted out.

Publications: Annual Report (for Royal Commission including NMR). NMR leaflet.
Various thematic or area-based publications from the Royal Commission available.

12 University of Wales

Address: Hugh Owen Library, Penglais, Aberystwyth, Dyfed SY23 3DZ

Telephone: (01970) 622391

Fax: (01970) 622404

Enquiries: The Librarian, Mr W.W. Dieneman

Open: Term: Mon–Fri: 9.00–10.00 Sat: 9.00–1.00 Vacation: Mon–Fri: 9.00–5.30 Sat: subject to variation.
Closed for a week at Christmas and Easter, and on bank holidays during vacations.

Access: Visiting scholars and others engaged in serious research. They should supply a suitable testimonial and obtain the written permission of the librarian before they can use the library.

Historical background: The library has deposited in the National Library of Wales (entry 10) various materials from the Powell Collection and a collection of papers formed by E. R. G. Salisbury (1819–90), including some MS material on Welsh local history and a large accumulation of press cuttings on the history and topography of Wales and the Welsh border and on contemporary political events. These may be consulted there but may not be reproduced without the permission of the registrar and librarian of the university. In 1989 the College of Librarianship Wales amalgamated with the university and is now the Information and Library Studies Library. It is located on a separate campus at Llanbadarn Fawr, Aberystwyth, Dyfed SY23 3AS, tel. (01970) 622417, where a collection of films, sound recordings, photographs and architectural plans relating to libraries and librarianship is maintained.

Acquisitions policy: The library acquires papers of those associated with the university.

Archives of organisation: The registrar's office holds some internal records. The library has the

University of Wales MSS Collection: chiefly early library records, including stockbooks, accessions, donations, binding etc, and some MSS relating to the foundation of the university; also minute books of a number of student societies.

Major collections: George Powell Collection: George Powell of Nanteos near Aberystwyth, bequest includes *c*200 MSS, including music MSS, 17th–mid-19th century, and many autograph letters of writers, artists and musicians of the 19th century.
Thomas Webster MSS: letters to Thomas Webster (1773–1844), first professor of geology at University College London, 1818–44.
Richard Ellis (1865–1928) MSS: notebooks and correspondence *re* unfinished study of antiquarian Edward Lloyd.
David De Lloyd MSS: Professor of Music at the college, 1926–48, scores and notes on Welsh music and musical history and theory.
Thomas Francis Roberts MSS: Principal of the college, 1891–1919, correspondence relating to all university matters.
J.O.Francis Archive: TS and acting copies of his plays and broadcast talks.
Lily Newton Archives: *re* her work on river pollution in mid-Wales, mid-20th century.

Facilities: Photocopying. Photography. Microform readers.

Publications: J. Challinor (ed.): 'Some correspondence of Thomas Webster, geologist (1773–1844)', *Annals of Science*, xvii/3 (1961), 175–95; xviii/3 (1962), 147–75; xix/1 (1963), 59–79; xix/4 (1963), 285–97; xx/1 (1964), 59–80; xx/2 (1964), 143–64.
B.F. Roberts: *The Richard Ellis Papers: Handbook and Schedule* (Aberystwyth, 1983).

13 Wales Film and Television Archive/Archif Ffilm a Theledu Cymru

Parent organisation: Wales Film Council

Address: Unit 1, Aberystwyth Science Park, Llanbadarn Fawr, Aberystwyth, Dyfed SY23 3AH

Telephone: (01970) 626007

Fax: (01970) 626007

Enquiries: The Director, Iola Baines or The Outreach Officer, Gwenan Owen

Open: Mon–Fri: 9.00–5.30

Access: Bona fide researchers; sliding-scale of charges. An appointment is necessary.

Historical background: The Welsh Film Archive was established as a pilot project in 1989. The project was located at the National Library of Wales (entry 10) and much of the research was based on the small but valuable film collection already held by the library. It formulated policies for selection, preservation and access for a film archive for Wales. In 1992 the archive began a new and permanent phase with an increased funding level which has enabled it to move to new premises. The archive will continue to be responsible for the National Library of Wales's film collection and will work in collaboration with the library's own audiovisual department.

Acquisitions policy: To acquire film and video material (both amateur and professional) reflecting aspects of the social and cultural history of Wales and the Welsh people, 1896–. Paper records are acquired if relevant to the moving image collection.

Non-manuscript material: National Library of Wales Collection (*c*50% of holdings), including films of A.J. Sylvester and Sir Ifan ab Owen Edwards, Welsh Office films, amateur films, e.g. of National Eisteddfod, 1952–.
Welsh Film Board fictional and educational films, 1970s.

Finding aids: Printed catalogue in preparation. A bilingual computerised system is being developed which it is hoped will integrate all information about the collection and allow for subject, period, geographical and biographical searches.

14 Christ's Hospital

Address: 1 Station Road, Abingdon, Oxon OX14 3LQ

Telephone: (01235) 526487

Fax: (01235) 526481

Enquiries: The Clerk to the Governors

Open: By prior arrangement.

Christ's Hospital holds records of the Fraternity of the Holy Cross and the Guild of Our Lady, 1165–1547; records of Christ's Hospital, 1533–1918, and records (minutes and accounts)

of other charities, deriving from 17th–century benefactors, administered by the governors.

15 Radley College Archives

Address: Abingdon, Oxon OX14 2HR

Telephone: (01235) 525983/520294

Fax: (01235) 527495

Enquiries: The Archivist, Mr A.E. Money

Open: Term time only, by arrangement.

Access: Generally open to the public, by appointment.

Historical background: Radley College was founded as St Peter's College in 1847 by the high churchmen Rev. William Sewell of Exeter College, Oxford, and Rev. Robert Singleton, late headmaster of St Columba's College, Ireland. The college has had an archivist since 1945.

Acquisitions policy: Anything to do with the school is welcomed. Mainly written or photographic material, memoirs, diaries and letters.

Archives of organisation: Archives of the college, including minutes of Council meetings, 1860s-, and minutes of Radleian Society (f. 1887), 1911-.

Major collections: Diary of Rev. Robert Singleton, first warden (*d.*1881), 1847–8.
TS copies of the following papers:
Diary of Rev. William Wood, assistant master and later warden (*d.*1919), 1855–67.
Letters home of John A. Godley, later Lord Kilbracken (1847–1932), 1857–61.
Talbot letters: letters from the two sons of Hon. Gerald Talbot, Private Secretary to Lord Canning, Governor-General in India, 1856–7.

Non-manuscript material: Photographs of buildings, groups, individual boys and masters, 1850s-1860s. Some film material.

Facilities: Photocopying.

16 Airdrie Library, Archives and Local History Section

Parent organisation: Monklands District Council

Address: Wellwynd, Airdrie, Strathclyde ML6 0AG

Telephone: (01236) 763221

Enquiries: The Archivist, Mr C. Geddes

Open: Mon, Tues, Thurs, Fri: 9.30–7.30 Sat: 9.30–5.00

Access: Generally open to the public. Appointment necessary for microfilm readers.

Historical background: Airdrie Library was established in 1853 and local history material has been collected spasmodically since that date. In 1980 the Local Collection was set up to house the collections from the former burghs of Airdrie and Coatbridge, following local government reorganisation. An archivist was appointed in 1993.

Acquisitions policy: To provide a comprehensive collection of local material from the Monklands district.

Archives of organisation: Airdrie Burgh minutes, 1821–1974; Coatbridge Burgh minutes, 1885–1974.

Major collections: Airdrie Weavers Friendly Society minutes, 1781-.
Gartsherrie Estate minute books.
Drumpellier Estate papers, 1560–1961.
Archives of local firms, estates, unions, clubs and societies.

Non-manuscript material: Map collection, including 19th-century mining plans.
Complete run of local newspapers, parish registers and census returns on microfilm.
Photographs.
Oral history recordings.

Finding aids: Computerised listing in progress. Lists will be sent to NRA(S).

Facilities: Photocopying. Microfilm reader/printers.

Conservation: Contracted out.

17 The Britten–Pears Library

Parent organisation: The Britten-Pears Foundation

Address: The Red House, Aldeburgh, Suffolk IP15 5PZ

Telephone: (01728) 452615

Fax: (01728) 453076

Enquiries: The Librarian, Dr Paul Banks

Open: Mon–Fri: 10.00–5.00, by appointment only.

Access: Bona fide researchers at the discretion of the librarian and trustees.

Historical background: The Britten–Pears Library was set up in 1973 to house the working collection of printed and MS music, books and personal papers of Benjamin Britten (1913–76) and Peter Pears (1910–86). The main public-access area is the library built by Britten and Pears in the early 1960s; the rest of the collection is housed in converted farm buildings, and a purpose-built extension opened in 1993.

Acquisitions policy: To acquire, any major Britten MSS remaining at large. Book acquisition in the areas of 20th–century music, music printing and publishing, politics, art and literature. Also local history.

Major collections: Music and literary MSS, letters and diaries of Benjamin Britten and Peter Pears.
MSS of other composers, including Gustav Holst (1874–1934), Frank Bridge (1879–1941), Sir Michael Tippett and Armstrong Gibbs.
Archives of the English Opera Group/English Music Theatre.
A few literary MSS, including drafts for the libretti to Britten's operas.

Non-manuscript material: Annotated poetry and drama texts. Proof and other interim music material.

Finding aids: In-house lists.

Facilities: Photocopying. Microfilm/fiche readers.

Publications: J. Evans, P. Reed and P. Wilson (comps): *A Britten Source Book* (Aldeburgh, 1987).

18 Alderney Society Museum

Address: Alderney, Channel Islands GY9 3TG

Telephone: (01481) 823222

Enquiries: The Administrator, Mrs C. Grabham

Open: Easter–end of Oct: Mon–Fri: 10.00–12.00; 2.00–4.00 Sat, Sun: 10.00–12.00

Access: Generally open to the public, by appointment.

The society museum was established in 1966. It is maintained on a voluntary basis and holds local history collections relating to the history of Alderney, including materials on occupations, folk history and records of iron age archaeological excavations. Photocopying facilities are available.

19 Queen Alexandra's Royal Army Nursing Corps Museum (QARANC)

Address: Regimental Headquarters QARANC, Army Medical Services Training Group, Keogh Barracks, Ash Vale, Aldershot, Hants GU12 5RQ

Telephone: (01252) 24431 ext. 5294, or 340294

Fax: (01252) 24431 ext. 5224, or 340224

Enquiries: The Curator, Major (retd) Ethel McCombe

Open: Mon–Fri: 9.00–12.30; 2.00–4.00 Other times by arrangement.

Access: Generally open to the public, preferably by appointment. No charge but donations appreciated.

Historical background: The museum was established to give a pictorial history of army nursing from the Crimea to the modern day. In 1995 it moved from the Royal Pavilion, Aldershot (its location since 1966), to join the Royal Army Medical Corps Museum at the address shown above.

Acquisitions policy: To acquire, by purchase, gift, bequest, exchange or loan, items relevant to QARANC, QAMFNS, QAIMNS, TANS, Almeric Paget Massage Corps, VAD, PCANSR, ANS, Florence Nightingale and the nurses who accompanied her to the Crimea.

Major collections: Reports and papers of Dame Maud McCarthy (1858–1949), Matron-in-Chief, British Expeditionary Force, France, 1914–19.
Letters of Dame Katharine Jones, Matron-in-Chief, 1940–44.
Other MS collections relating to army nursing experience in war and peace.

Non-manuscript material: Photographic library.

Facilities: Photocopying.

Publications: J. Piggott: *History of QARANC* (Trowbridge, 2/1990).

20 Roman Catholic Records Office

Parent organisation: Ministry of Defence (Army)

Address: St Michael's House, Queen's Avenue, Aldershot, Hants GU11 2BY

Telephone: (01252) 21180 or 347061

Fax: (01252) 347180

Enquiries: The Senior Chaplain (RC) or The Notary

Open: Mon–Fri: 7.30–4.00

Access: Generally open to the public, by appointment only.

In 1952, a policy decision at the HQ of the Royal Army Chaplain's Department (RAChD) decreed that all sacramental records of marriages, baptisms, confirmations etc which had taken place in service RC churches worldwide for the tri-services should be housed centrally at Aldershot. Consequently, all chaplains sent the registers to St Michael's House, where they were collated by date into other registers, then card-indexed by surname. Some records date back to 1856. Since 1989, the records have been computerised as they come in, and it is hoped that in time the bulk of the 200,000 records will be on computer. The office is recognised as a place of deposit for public records. See also Royal Army Chaplain's Department Museum and Archives (entry 41).

21 Alnwick Castle
Duke of Northumberland's Estate Office

Address: Alnwick, Northumberland NE66 1NQ

Telephone: (01665) 510777

Fax: (01665) 510876

Enquiries: The Archivist, Colin Shrimpton

Open: Strictly by arrangement.

Access: Bona fide scholars, by appointment only.

The substantial archives and MS collections dating from 12th to 19th centuries are fully described in HMC Third Report, xii and App 45–125 (Alnwick Castle) (2); Fifth Report, xi (4); Sixth Report, xi and App 221–33 (Syon House) (5); and NRA 0836.

The archives comprise the following: estate and manorial records; legal papers; household records; official and professional correspondence; family papers and personal correspondence; miscellanea (including MS items, notes, catalogues, cuttings, photographs etc); borough records; business records; ecclesiastical records; forestry papers; Lord Lieutenancy, military and naval records; royal correspondence, late 14th century–.

22 Fusiliers of Northumberland Archives

Address: The Abbot's Tower, Alnwick Castle, Alnwick, Northumberland NE66 1NG

Telephone: (01665) 602152 or 510211

Fax: (01665) 603320

Enquiries: The Hon. Curator, Capt. (retd) P.H.D. Marr

Open: Mon: 10.30–4.30, or by arrangement.

Access: Generally open to the public. An appointment is necessary.

The regiment maintains its own archives, including records of service, 1688–, courts martial books, daily order books, regimental and battalion orders and letter-books, plus war diaries, World War I and World War II. Personal papers and diaries of former members are also accepted and there are large collections of these and of photograph albums. NRA 20951.

23 The Armitt Library

Parent organisation: The Armitt Trust

Address: Kelswick Road, Ambleside, Cumbria LA22 0BZ

Telephone: (015394) 33949

Enquiries: The Curator of Collections

Open: By arrangement.

Access: Bona fide researchers, by appointment.

Historical background: The Armitt Library is a

charitable institution founded in 1912 under the terms of the will of Mary Armitt (1851–1911), a scholar and local historian who collected books and artefacts which became the archives of the library. The Armitt Trust Library incorporated the Ambleside Book Club (f.1828), of which William Wordsworth (1770–1850) was a member, and the Ambleside Ruskin Society (f.1882) in association with John Ruskin (1819–1900). The library has acted as a repository for documents, especially of local history interest, from its origin. It may move to different premises within Ambleside in 1995.

Acquisitions policy: Collects material relevant to the literary and social history of the Lake District.

Archives of organisation: Minutes and other records relating to the administration of the trust and library, 1828–.

Major collections: Personal papers of the Armitt sisters, Mary, Annie and Sophia, authors and naturalists.
Documents relating to Harriet Martineau (1802–76), John Ruskin, William Wordsworth, W.G. Collingwood (1854–1932), Thomas Alcock Beck (1795–1846), Arthur Ransome (1884–1967), Hugh Walpole (1884–1941), Charlotte Mason, educationalist, and the Arnold family of Fox How.

Non-manuscript material: Topographical books on the Lake District. Prints and drawings of Lake District by William Green, early 19th century.
Beatrix Potter (1866–1943) watercolours (c400).
Works of art by Kurt Schwitters (1887–1948), Barbara Crystal Collingwood (1887–1961) and many others.
Herbert Bell photograph albums.
Ruskin books and memorabilia.

Finding aids: TS lists of collections.

Facilities: Photocopying.

24 Scottish Fisheries Museum

Parent organisation: Scottish Fisheries Museum Trust Ltd

Address: St Ayles, Harbourhead, Anstruther, Fife KY10 3AB

Telephone: (01333) 310628

Enquiries: The Curator, Robert Bracegirdle

Open: April-Oct: Mon–Sat: 10.00–5.30 Sun: 11.00–5.00 Nov-March: Mon–Sat: 10.00–4.30 Sun: 2.00–4.30

Access: Bona fide researchers, with proof of identity. An appointment is necessary.

The museum was opened in 1969 and virtually all its collections have been donated. These cover fisheries and cognate industries (e.g. boat building) in Scotland over the last 200 years and some local material relating to Anstruther. Apart from documents there are films, paintings and artefacts, drawings and plans (c5000), and photographs (c12,000). There are photocopying and photography facilities and catalogued indexes.

25 Arbroath Signal Tower Museum

Address: Ladyloan, Arbroath, Tayside DD11 1PU

Telephone: (01241) 875598

Enquiries: The Curator, Mrs Margaret H. King

Open: Mon–Sat: 10.00–5.00 July and Aug: Sun: 2.00–5.00

Access: Generally open to the public, on written application.

Historical background: The museum was opened in 1974 by Arbroath Town Council; since 1975 it has been part of Angus District Libraries and Museums.

Acquisitions policy: Any local material.

Major collections: Arbroath Burgess records, 1790–1849.
Arbroath Museum Society, 1843–1918.
Miscellaneous local private records, 18th–20th centuries.
Alex Shanks Dens Ironworks: engineers' catalogues of boilers, steam engines and lawnmowers, and papers, 1859–c1950.
William Sharpey (1802–80), physiologist: letterbook, diplomas and certificates, 1821–74.
Bell Rock Lighthouse visitor books.

Finding aids: Archive list. Sharpey: NRA 24032.

26 Cunninghame District Library Headquarters
Local Collection

Address: 39/41 Princes Street, Ardrossan, Strathclyde KA22 8BT

Telephone: (01294) 469137

Fax: (01294) 604236

Enquiries: The Library Services Manager, Mr Alasdair McNaughtan

Open: Mon–Fri: 9.00–5.00

Access: Generally open to the public, but preferably by appointment.

Historical background: The collection was developed after local government reorganisation in 1975. The Alexander Wood Memorial Library was donated to the new council by the old Burgh of Ardrossan and now forms an integral part of the library's local material.

Acquisitions policy: To acquire all possible material relating to the history of the area.

Major collections: Archives relating to the old county burghs prior to local government reorganisation.
Alexander Wood Memorial Library: collection of material with local connections through publisher, topic, author; includes MSS, maps and pamphlets.
Cunninghame of Auchenharvie papers.

Non-manuscript material: Small collection of maps and photographs.
Ardrossan and Saltcoats Herald, 1857–1966 (1857–1983, also 1986, on microfilm).
Microfilms of parish registers for North Ayrshire and census returns, 1841–91.

Finding aids: Lists. Catalogues.

Facilities: Photocopying. Microfilm/fiche readers/printer.

Publications: Local collection bibliography.
Ardrossan Shipyards, 1825–1983.
Burgh of Saltcoats: a Brief History.
W. Kenafick: *Ardrossan, The Key to the Clyde* (1993).

27 Clan Donald Centre Library

Parent organisation: Clan Donald Lands Trust

Address: Armadale, Ardvasar, Isle of Skye IV45 8RS

Telephone: (014714) 389 (Library) 227 (Trust Office)

Fax: (014714) 275

Enquiries: The Curator/Archivist, Ms Maggie Macdonald

Open: Easter–Oct: Mon–Sun: 9.30–5.30 Oct–Easter: Mon–Fri: 9.30–5.30, by appointment.

Access: Generally open to the public by day ticket to the centre or by annual membership season ticket. A charge is made.

Historical background: The Clan Donald Lands Trust was founded in 1971, when it purchased part of the Macdonald estate on the Isle of Skye. As well as developing a visitor centre with museum and historic gardens, the trust has built up a major collection of books and MSS relating to Clan Donald and the history of the Highlands and Islands. A study centre was opened in 1990.

Acquisitions policy: MSS, objects and other materials relating to the cultural heritage of the Lords of the Isles; the several clans within Clan Donald; the geographic areas from which those clans originated; the lives and careers of individual clansmen; the history of the trust's Skye estates.

Major collections: Macdonald Estate Papers, Skye and North Uist, mainly 18th and 19th century.
Macdonald of Glenalladale and Borrodale papers, 1759–1910.
Macdonald of Inchkenneth papers, 1825–60.
Papers of Hector Macdonald-Buchanan (*d* c1831) as factor to Mrs Anne Campbell or MacLeod of Strond, 1804–31.

Non-manuscript material: Reference library (7000 books), photographs, maps and plans, microfilms of censuses and parish records for Western Highlands and Islands; genealogical collections.

Finding aids: Detailed catalogue *Macdonald Estate Papers* (microfiche at NRA(S)); relevant indexes are in preparation. Catalogue, handlists and indexes of other MSS collections.

Facilities: Photocopying. Microfilm/fiche readers. Photography by arrangement.

Conservation: Contracted out.

28 Armagh County Museum

Address: The Mall East, Armagh, Co. Armagh
BT61 9BE

Telephone: (01861) 523070

Fax: (01861) 522631

Enquiries: The Curator, Mrs Catherine
McCullough

Open: Mon–Fri: 10.00–5.00 Sat: 10.00–1.00;
2.00–5.00

Access: Generally open to the public.

Historical background: Around 1839 the
Armagh Natural and Philosophical Society
started a museum, which moved to the present
address in 1857. Armagh County Council took
over the building and collections in 1931 and
opened Armagh County Museum in 1935. The
museum was rebuilt and enlarged in 1962 and
transferred to the Ulster Museum trustees as a
regional branch on local government reorganisation in 1973.

Acquisitions policy: To increase the collections
selectively, so as to illustrate the history of Co.
Armagh, and build up a supporting library and
archive for student reference.

Major collections: Armagh militia records,
1793–.
Charlemont estate papers, 19th century.
T.G.F. Paterson collection of MSS and TS on
genealogy and local history.
Correspondence of George Russell 'AE' (1867–
1935).
Sundry items of MSS, TS annotated published
pamphlets etc relating to Co. Armagh.

Non-manuscript material: Photographic
archive collection.
Books and pamphlets forming a reference collection to assist the study of museum collections
in the fields of history, local history, pre-
history, social history, art, genealogy etc.

Finding aids: Card index.

Facilities: Photocopying and photography may
be arranged subject to management discretion.

Publications: D.R.M. Weatherup: 'The
published writings of T.G.F. Paterson', *Sean-
chas Ardmacha*, vi/2 (1972).
——: 'Armagh County Museum: the Reference
Library', *Irish Booklore*, ii/1 (1972).

——: 'Armagh Public Library', *Irish Booklore*,
ii/2 (1976).

29 Armagh Observatory

Address: College Hill, Armagh, Co. Armagh
BT61 9DG

Telephone: (01861) 522928

Fax: (01861) 527174

Enquiries: The Librarian, John McFarland

Open: Mon–Fri: 9.00–5.00

Access: Normally research workers only; an
appointment is necessary.

Historical background: The Armagh Observatory was founded in 1790 by Richard Robinson
(1709–94), Archbishop of Armagh.

Acquisitions policy: To maintain the observatory archives.

Archives of organisation: Archives of the observatory, c1790–.

Major collections: Papers of members of staff,
including correspondence and MSS of E.J.
Opik; MSS by J.L.E. Dreyer (1852–1926),
director of the observatory.

Non-manuscript material: Photographic material: Palomar sky survey; SCR sky survey; ESO
sky survey; Boyden photographs (ADH telescope), South Africa.

Facilities: Photocopying. Microfiche reader.

Publications: P. Moore: *Armagh Observatory,
1790–1967* (Armagh, 1967).
J. Butler and M. Hoskin: 'The archives of
Armagh Observatory', *Journal for the History
of Astronomy*, 18 (1987), 295.
J.A. Bennett: *Church, State and Astronomy in
Ireland: 200 years of Armagh Observatory*
(Belfast, 1990).
Irish Astronomical Journal is produced from the
obervatory and includes annual reports.

30 Armagh Public Library (Robinson Library)

Address: The Library, Abbey Street, Armagh,
Co. Armagh BT61 7DY

Telephone: (01861) 523142

Fax: (01861) 524177

Enquiries: The Keeper, the Very Rev. H. Cassidy

Open: Mon–Fri: 9.00–1.00; 2.00–4.00

Access: Generally open to the public. An appointment is desirable.

Historical background: The library was founded in 1771 by Archbishop Robinson by Act of Parliament. He wanted a university for the northern part of the island of Ireland and decided the first requirement was a public library. Governors and guardians of the library are the Archbishop of Armagh (Chairman), the Dean and Chapter of the Cathedral and two lay members.

Acquisitions policy: Strengthening of the collection of Church of Ireland material, local history, and some theology.

Archives of organisation: Minute books, 1796–. Registers of borrowers and books borrowed, 1796–1828, 1828–1916.
Property rental books, 1840–90.

Major collections: Papers of Anthony Dopping, Bishop of Mereth (1682–97), and William Reeves, Bishop of Down (1882–96).
Correspondence of Lord John George Beresford, Archbishop of Armagh (1822–62).
Episcopal visitation records, 17th and 18th century.

Non-manuscript material: Large collection of 18th-century pamphlets.
Rokeby Collection of prints, including a 'Piranesi' set, 17th and 18th century.

Finding aids: Handwritten author catalogue, and card catalogue; computerised cataloguing in progress.

Facilities: Photocopying.

Conservation: Contracted out.

Publications: Catalogue of Manuscripts in the Public Library of Armagh (1928).

31 Armagh RC Diocesan Archives

Address: Ara Coeli, Armagh, Co. Armagh BT61 7QY

Telephone: (01861) 522045

Fax: (01861) 526182

Enquiries: The Diocesan Secretary

Open: By appointment only.

Access: Bona fide scholars; reference required.

The archives maintain the papers, including correspondence, of the Archbishops of Armagh, 1787–1927, and the diocesan baptismal records, in computerised form, to 1900. Photocopying is available.

32 Irish Studies Library

Parent organisation: Southern Education and Library Board

Address: Library Headquarters, 1 Markethill Road, Armagh, Co. Armagh BT60 1NR

Telephone: (01861) 525353 ext. 552

Fax: (01861) 526879

Enquiries: The Irish Studies Librarian, Mr Joe Canning

Open: Mon, Wed: 9.30–7.15 Tues, Thurs, Fri: 9.30–5.00

Access: Generally open to the public.

Historical background: The board was established in 1973 following the reorganisation of local government in Northern Ireland. The major part of the library's archives was inherited from Newry Public Library.

Acquisitions policy: To acquire material relating to the Board's area and material by local writers.

Archives of organisation: Annual reports and minutes of Library Committee, 1973–.

Major collections: Usual local history collection including Crosslé papers relating to history of Newry and district and of local families.

Finding aids: Lists.

Facilities: Photocopying. Microfilm/fiche reader/printers.

Conservation: Contracted out.

33 Arundel Castle
Duke of Norfolk's Library and Archives

Parent organisation: Arundel Castle Trustees Ltd

Address: Arundel, West Sussex BN18 9AB

Telephone: (01903) 882173

Enquiries: The Librarian, Dr J.M. Robinson

Open: Tues, Wed and some Sats, by written appointment.

Access: To all accredited scholars. A daily research fee is charged. Personal papers less than 100 years old are not normally available.

Historical background: The Duke of Norfolk's archives form one of the largest and most complete family collections in England and have a unique importance for the study of English Catholic history. Assistance is received from West Sussex Record Office (entry 211).

Archives of organisation: Records and papers of the Fitzalan-Howard family and their family estates in various counties, 13th century–.
Northern estate papers deposited at Sheffield Record Office (entry 1006), Carlton Towers and Herries (Everingham) papers deposited at the University of Hull (entry 403).

Major collections: Collection of illuminated MSS held in the library.

Non-manuscript material: Recusant collection: a large series of 17th-century printed pamphlets.

Facilities: Limited photocopying.

Publications: F.W. Steer (ed.): *Catalogue of the Earl Marshal's Papers at Arundel Castle* (1963–4).
——*Arundel Castle Archives* (Chichester, 1968–80) [4 vols].

34 Buckinghamshire Record Office

Parent organisation: Buckinghamshire County Council

Address: County Hall, Aylesbury, Bucks HP20 1UA

Telephone: (01296) 382587 (Enquiries) 382771 (Bookings)

Enquiries: The County Archivist, Mr Hugh Hanley. All postal enquiries should be accompanied by an SAE or international reply coupon from overseas.

Open: Tues–Thurs: 9.00–5.15 Fri: 9.00–4.45
Thurs (1st of each month) by appointment only. Closed for stock-taking for the 2nd full week of February each year.

Access: Generally open to the public. The office operates the CARN reader's ticket system.

Prior notice of a visit is advisable to reserve a seat. Reservations are held until 10.30 for the morning period, and 1.30 for the afternoon period.

Historical background: The office was established in 1938 with the appointment of its first archivist. It also acts as the Diocesan Record Office for Oxford (Archdeaconry of Buckingham) and is recognised as a place of deposit for public records. Buckinghamshire Archaeological Society (f.1848) has transferred its collections of deeds, maps and manorial and estate records to the office, whilst retaining its own archives, papers of local historians, transcripts of documents, monumental inscriptions and printed items. Contact Hon. Archivist, County Museum, Church Street, Aylesbury, Bucks HP20 2QP.

Archives of organisation: Usual local authority record holdings.

Major collections: Deposited local collections, of which the following contain papers of wider significance:
Hobart-Hampden MSS, including papers of Robert, 4th Baron Trevor and 1st Viscount Hampden, as diplomat at The Hague, 1736–46; Robert, Lord Hobart, as governor of Madras, 1794–8, and secretary of state for war and the colonies, 1801–4; Lord Vere Henry Hobart, as director-general of the Ottoman Bank, 1861–72, and governor and president of Madras, 1872–5; F.J. Robinson, Viscount Goderich and 1st Earl of Ripon, 1796–1835.
Fremantle MSS, including private and naval papers of Admiral Sir T.F. Fremantle (1765–1819), and Capt. S.G. Fremantle (1810–60); papers of Sir W.H. Fremantle relating to Ireland and as deputy ranger of Windsor Great Park, 1830–50, and Sir T.F. Fremantle (1798–1890), 1st Baron Cottesloe, as a Conservative minister, 1834, 1841–6, and deputy chairman/chairman of the Board of Customs, 1846–73.
Bulstrode MSS, including correspondence of Lord Webb Seymour (1777–1819); the 11th and 12th Dukes of Somerset, including official correspondence of the latter as First Lord of the Admiralty, 1859–66; papers of Sir John Ramsden (1831–1914), 5th Bart; miscellaneous papers, diary and note-books of Edward Horsmann (1807–76), MP.
Spencer Bernard MSS, including official correspondence of Scope Bernard (1758–1830) *re* Ireland and the Home Department; banking

papers of Morlands Bank (and predecessors), c1780–1832.

Howard–Vyse MSS, including official papers of FM Sir George Howard (1720–96) and Gen. Richard Vyse (1746–1825).

Hartwell MSS, including miscellaneous legal papers of Sir William Lee (1688–1754), as chief justice of King's Bench, and of Sir George Lee (1700–53), as Dean of Arches; correspondence of Dr John Lee (1783–1866).

Clayton MSS, including papers of Sir Robert Clayton (1629–1707), scrivener of London; official papers of George, Baron Jeffreys of Wem, as Lord Chancellor, 1685–8.

Carrington MSS, including letters of the 2nd Baron Carrington (1796–1868) to his family.

Grenville MSS, including correspondence of William Wyndham, Baron Grenville, (1759–1834), and Thomas Grenville (1755–1846).

Correspondence of Lydia Catherine, Dowager Duchess of Chandos, c1728–50.

Papers of William Henry Grenfell, Baron Desborough (1855–1945), including papers re British Olympics Association.

Literary papers of Thomas Wright (1859–1936), author and popular biographer and Theodora Roscoe (d 1962), author and poet.

Letters from George Church, convict transported to Tasmania, 1845–54.

Business records of E. Gomme Ltd, furniture manufacturers (G-Plan), and related firms, 1881–1980, including pattern books and catalogues; Hazell, Watson and Viney Ltd, printers, 1866–1993; and Wycombe Marsh Paper Mills, 1920–c1990.

Finding aids: Catalogues sent to NRA; draft guide with subject index; personal and place name indexes; consolidated personal and place name and subject indexes to annual *Lists of Accessions*, 1976–90.

Facilities: Photocopying. Photography and microfilming by arrangement. Microfilm readers.

Publications: *Annual Reports and Lists of Accessions* (1976–) [detailed].
Consolidated Indexes to Lists of Accessions, 1976–85, 1985–90.
House History: a Short Guide to Sources (1987).
Wartime Buckinghamshire 1939–45: a Brief Guide to Sources (1992).
The Buckinghamshire Sheriffs, 992–1992 (1992).
Archive Teaching Units: *Parliamentary Enclosure; Elections in Buckinghamshire, 1740–1832;*

Buckinghamshire in the French Revolutionary and Napoleonic Wars, 1792–1815.

35 Aylsham Town Council Archives

Address: Town Hall, Market Place, Aylsham, Norwich, Norfolk NR11 6EL

Telephone: (01263) 733354 (mornings only)

Enquiries: The Town Clerk, Mrs Maureen Reynolds or The Hon. Archivist, Ron Peabody, tel. (01263) 733230

Open: By appointment.

Access: Bona fide researchers.

Historical background: The collection was started by the second parish clerk, who was in office from 1897 to 1937, and has been continually augmented since then.

Acquisitions policy: Material relating to the history of Aylsham, mainly by donation or deposit, but a small purchase fund is available.

Archives of organisation: Minutes of the Parish Council; Poor Law records; material relating to the Aylsham Navigation Company and the Turnpike Trustees.

Major collections: Town Crier's books, 1899–1923. Papers relating to royal celebrations, 1887; 'Aylsham Derby' papers.

Non-manuscript material: Posters, photographs, slide collection, oral history collection, artefacts.

36 Ayrshire Sound Archive

Parent organisation: Ayrshire Federation of Historical Societies (AFHS)

Address: University of Paisley, Craigie Campus in Ayr, Beech Grove, Ayr, Strathclyde KA8 0SR

Telephone: (01292) 260321

Fax: (01292) 611705

Enquiries: The Craigie Campus Librarian, Ms A. Goodwin or The AFHS Secretary, Mr Robin Urquhart, Strathclyde Regional Archives, Ayr Sub-Office (entry 39)

Open: Craigie Campus Library: Term: Mon–Thurs: 9.00–8.00 Vacation: Mon–Fri: 9.00–12.30; 1.30–5.00

Access: Anyone may consult the recordings on request at Craigie Campus Library. Recordings may be borrowed only by those who join the library, and it is open to members of the public to do so at a modest annual charge.

Historical background: The AFHS is a voluntary organisation which has deposited its sound archive at Craigie Campus, Ayr, to allow public access. It is investigating the possibility of depositing further copies in other libraries. The sound archive has been built up by copying loaned recordings from schools, radio stations, historical societies and individuals.

Acquisitions policy: Records relevant to the locality and its inhabitants are accepted for copying at the discretion of AFHS.

Non-manuscript material: A wide range of recordings covering mining; textiles; rural life; schooling; World War 1; living and social conditions, 20th century (*c*200).

Finding aids: Catalogue.

Facilities: Listening facilities are available at Craigie Campus Library.

37 Burns' Cottage and Museum

Parent organisation: Trustees of Burns' Monument

Address: Alloway, Ayr, Strathclyde KA7 4PY

Telephone: (01292) 441215

Enquiries: The Curator, Mr John Manson

Open: By appointment.

Access: Generally open to the public by application in writing to the curator.

Historical background: The Trustees of Burns' Monument were formed in 1814 to build a monument in memory of Robert Burns (1759–96). This monument was built in 1823 and in 1881 the trustees acquired Burns' Cottage, the poet's birthplace. The trustees remain responsible for the upkeep of the two properties. Since 1881 the trustees have acquired a unique collection of Burns' MSS, an extensive library and authentic items which belonged to the poet.

Acquisitions policy: To add to existing collections.

Archives of organisation: Records of the Burns' monument and cottage, 1814–.

Major collections: Extensive collection of Robert Burns' MSS and correspondence, including the Graham of Fintry Collection and the Cunningham Collection.

Non-manuscript material: Memorabilia, pictures, statues, photographs, books.

Finding aids: Catalogue.

Facilities: Photography by arrangement.

Conservation: Contracted out.

38 Carnegie Library

Parent organisation: Kyle and Carrick District Libraries and Museums

Address: 12 Main Street, Ayr, Strathclyde KA8 8ED

Telephone: (01292) 286385

Fax: (01292) 611593

Enquiries: The Principal Officer, Libraries and Galleries

Open: Mon, Tues, Thurs, Fri: 9.00–7.30 Sat: 9.00–5.00

Access: Generally open to the public.

Historical background: The collection originally covered the whole of Ayrshire, but since local government reorganisation in 1974 has been restricted to Kyle and Carrick.

Acquisitions policy: To obtain, when possible, further material on Kyle and Carrick and Robert Burns.

Major collections: Kyle and Carrick Collection: minute books of various local societies, committees, etc.
Robert Burns (1759–96) Collection: the only original MS is the Visitors' Book for Burns' Cottage.
Other MS items are still being processed.

Non-manuscript material: Robert Burns Collection: *c*1200 books by and about Burns.
Kyle and Carrick Collection: photographs, slides, cassette recordings; newspapers, 1803–, some on microfilm/fiche.

Finding aids: Catalogue to Robert Burns Collection. Newspaper index being completed. Local collection being catalogued. NRA 18760.

Facilities: Photocopying. Microfilm reader/printer.

39 Strathclyde Regional Archives
Ayr Sub-Office

Parent organisation: Strathclyde Regional Council

Address: Regional Offices, Wellington Square, Ayr, Strathclyde KA7 1DR

Telephone: (01292) 612000 ext. 2138

Fax: (0141) 2268452

Enquiries: The Archivists, Mr R. Urquhart/ Miss A. Gardiner

Open: Wed: 10.00–1.00; 2.00–4.00

Access: Generally open to the public; appointment advisable but not necessary.

Historical background: Formed as sub-office of Strathclyde Regional Archives, Glasgow (entry 350) after local government reorganisation.

Archives of organisation: Usual local authority record holdings, principally the records of Ayr County Council and predecessor authorities, 1689–1975.

Major collections: Local estate papers and correspondence, including Kennedy of Kirkmichael, Cunninghame of Auchenharvie and the Woodburn family.
Solicitors' records.
Kirk session records for Church of England and secession churches within Ayr Presbytery, 17th–20th centuries.

Non-manuscript material: Portland Estate plans, c1760–1928.

Finding aids: Subject/name card index. Catalogues. Lists sent to NRA(S).

Facilities: Photocopying.

Conservation: In-house conservation unit at Strathclyde Regional Archives, Glasgow.

40 Badminton Muniments

Address: Badminton House, Badminton, Avon GL9 1DB

Telephone: (01454) 218202/3

Enquiries: The Archivist, Mrs M. Richards: family and household records and general enquiries.
County Archivist, Gloucestershire Record Office (GRO) (entry 357): estate records (Glos and Wilts).
National Library of Wales (NLW) (entry 10): Welsh estate records.

Open: Tues, Wed: 9.00–4.30
NB it is possible to make temporary deposits of material for research at GRO to overcome the difficulties of limited access.

Access: Badminton: His Grace's permission is needed for access, and requests should be addressed to the Duke. An appointment is necessary.

GRO: generally open to the public.
NLW: Duke's permission is needed for access and photocopying.

Historical background: Badminton has been the family seat since it was inherited in 1655 by the future 1st Duke of Beaufort. The present muniment room was built to a design prepared by James Gibbs for the 3rd Duke. The interior of the 'evidence room' was completed in 1758 to working drawings made by Stephen Wright, who advised the 4th Duchess that the shelving should be lined with wood to preserve the papers from damp. Successive Duchesses played an important part in preserving the papers now in the Badminton muniment room. An archivist was first appointed in 1940.

Acquisitions policy: To maintain the collections.

Archives of organisation: Correspondence and papers of the Earls and Marquess of Worcester, c1460–1698.
Political, financial and personal papers and correspondence of the Dukes and Duchesses of Beaufort, 1629–.
Household accounts and inventories, 1672–1941.

Major collections: Papers of the Berkeley, Coventry and Ormonde families, 17th and 18th centuries.
Family papers of the Culling Smith and Wellesley families.

Non-manuscript material: Architectural plans relating to Badminton House, 17th–19th centuries.
Maps (mainly at GRO).

Finding aids: HMC Report XII, appendix IX, 'The manuscripts of His Grace the Duke of Beaufort' (1891). Provisional catalogue of architectural plans. Glos and Wilts estate, family and household records fully catalogued and indexed. Copies of the catalogue (comp. 1989)

can be consulted at the NRA or GRO as well as at Badminton.

NLW: Catalogues of Welsh manorial records (6 vols), Badminton deeds and documents (2 vols), 1941–6; 'Preliminary Schedule' of more recent deposits, 1965 (NRA).

Facilities: Photocopying. Photography, if own equipment is provided. Duke of Beaufort's specific permission if family or household papers are involved.
NLW: Duke's permission needed for photocopying.

Conservation: Contracted out.

Publications: G. Cottesloe and D. Hunt: *The Duchess of Beaufort's Flowers* (1983).
A. Gomme: 'Badminton Revisited', *Architectural History*, 27 (1984) [architectural plans and drawings].
M. Brennan: 'Alexander Pope's "Epistle to Robert Earl of Oxford and Earl Mortimer": a new autograph manuscript', *The Library*, 6th series, 15/3 (Sept 1993).

41 Royal Army Chaplain's Department Museum and Archives

Parent organisation: Ministry of Defence (Army)

Address: Bagshot Park, Bagshot, Surrey GU19 5PL

Telephone: (01276) 471717 ext. 2845

Fax: (01276) 471717 ext. 2828

Enquiries: Maj. (retd) M.A. Easey

Open: Mon–Fri: 10.00–12.00; 2.00–4.00, by appointment.

Access: Military personnel and members of the public by arrangement only.

Historical background: The present department was formed, by Royal Warrant, in 1796. The museum, in its present form, dates from 1968, although there was a departmental collection of memorabilia before that. It is recognised as a place of deposit for public records. For the department's Roman Catholic records see Roman Catholic Records Office (entry 20).

Acquisitions policy: Actively acquires material from chaplains by loan or gift.

Archives of organisation: Church services regis-

ters and Precedent Books.
Records of Protestant marriages, baptisms and deaths. Registers of military cemeteries overseas.

Major collections: Letters of F.M. Montgomery. Personal papers and memorabilia, including POW material of various chaplains over the years.

Non-manuscript material: Many photographs, some drawings and prints. Medal collections and uniforms.

Finding aids: Partial card index.

Facilities: Photocopying. Photography.

42 Devonshire Collection

Parent organisation: The Trustees of the Chatsworth Settlement

Address: Chatsworth, Bakewell, Derbyshire DE45 1PP

Telephone: (01246) 582204

Enquiries: The Keeper of Collections, Mr P.J. Day or The Librarian and Archivist, Mr M.A. Pearman

Open: By written appointment.

Access: Accredited postgraduate students or scholars only; reading fees and search fees payable.

Historical background: There are now concentrated at Chatsworth the collections of art, books, estate archives and political and personal correspondence of the Cavendish family, Earls of Devonshire from 1618 to 1694, and Dukes of Devonshire from 1694 onwards. The family fortune and estates were founded in the mid-16th century by Sir William Cavendish and his wife Bess of Hardwick, who built the first Chatsworth. The house was rebuilt by the 1st Duke of Devonshire (1640–1707), a strong supporter of William of Orange, and the collections of art were founded by his son the 2nd Duke, a celebrated connoisseur. The 3rd and 4th Dukes served as Lords Lieutenant of Ireland, and the 4th Duke was briefly Prime Minister of England. The 6th Duke greatly extended the house and collections at Chatsworth, and the 8th Duke, as the Marquis of Hartington, was a prominent Liberal politician.

Acquisitions policy: To acquire works of art, books or archives that help to document the history of the family, their houses and collections.

Archives of organisation: MSS of the philosopher Thomas Hobbes (1588–1679), tutor to the Earls of Devonshire.
MSS of the scientist Henry Cavendish (1731–1810).
Political correspondence of the 3rd (1698–1755), 4th (1720–64) and 8th (1833–1908) Duke of Devonshire.
Correspondence of Sir Joseph Paxton (1803–65), gardener to the 6th Duke of Devonshire.
Building and household accounts for Chatsworth, Hardwick, Chiswick and Devonshire houses.
Estate archives for present and former family estates in England and Ireland.

Non-manuscript material: Old Master drawings and prints, 15th–17th centuries (*c*2000).
Designs for court masques by Inigo Jones (*c*400).
Rare printed books, 15th–19th centuries (*c*50,000).
Paintings (*c*1000).

Finding aids: Calendars of MSS and correspondence copied by NRA. Paintings, sculpture and drawings listed by Photographic Survey of the Courtauld Institute of Art.

Facilities: Photocopying. Photography.

Conservation: Contracted out.

Publications: International Exhibition Foundation: *Treasures from Chatsworth: the Devonshire Inheritance* (Washington, DC, 1978–9).

43 South Eastern Education and Library Board
Irish and Local Studies Section

Address: Library Headquarters, Windmill Hill, Ballynahinch, Co. Down BT24 8DH

Telephone: (01238) 562639 ext. 235/6/7

Fax: (01238) 565072

Enquiries: The Irish and Local Studies Librarian, Deirdre Armstrong

Open: Mon–Fri: 9.00–5.15
Closed 12 and 13 July.

Access: Generally open to the public; appointment preferable

Historical background: Originally the Down County Library Service, the SEELB came into being after local government reorganisation in 1973. The present service covers most of Co. Down, parts of south-western Antrim and the southern suburbs of Belfast.

Acquisitions policy: All material relevant to Ulster studies collected, particularly material on the SEELB area, including ephemera.

Archives of organisation: Minutes of the Down County Library Service and the SEELB, 1973–.

Major collections: Usual local history collection, with special emphasis on Co. Down and South Antrim.

Finding aids: Various indexes, lists, catalogues.

Facilities: Photocopying, Microfilm/fiche reader/printers.

Conservation: Contracted out.

Publications: Local history source lists for: The Ards, Castlereagh and Donaghadee (1980); The Mournes (1982); Camber (1984); and newspaper index series: *Co. Down Spectator*, 1904–64; *Downpatrick Recorder*, 1836–86; *Mourne Observer*, 1949–80; *Newtownards Chronicle*, 1873–1939; *Northern Herald*, 1833–6; *Northern Star*, 1792–97.

44 North Down Heritage Centre

Parent organisation: North Down Borough Council

Address: Town Hall, Bangor, Co. Down BT20 4BT

Telephone: (01247) 270371

Fax: (01247) 271370

Enquiries: The Manager, Mr I.A. Wilson

Open: Tues–Fri: 10.30–4.30

Access: Bona fide researchers, by appointment only.

Historical background: The council was formed in 1973, and inherited the records of Bangor Borough Council from 1927.

Acquisitions policy: Records relevant to the northern part of Co. Down, excluding material *re* textiles, folk life and agriculture.

Archives of organisation: Council records *re* public health, gas and the harbour, early 20th century.
Burial records of municipally owned cemeteries, 1895–.

Non-manuscript material: Extensive photographic archive.
Folio of maps by Thomas Raven, 17th century (64).
Cine film archive of the area, 1950s-60s.

Facilities: Photocopying. Photography.

Conservation: Contracted out.

45 University of Wales, Bangor
Department of Manuscripts

Address: The Library, University of Wales, Bangor, Gwynedd LL57 2DG

Telephone: (01248) 351151 ext. 2966

Fax: (01248) 370576

Enquiries: The Archivist and Keeper of Manuscripts, Mr Tomos Roberts

Open: Term: Mon, Tues, Thurs, Fri: 9.00–4.45
Wed: 9.00–8.50 Vacation: Mon–Fri: 9.00–4.45

Access: Generally open to the public; prior arrangement preferred.

Historical background: The library of the University of Wales, Bangor, previously University College of North Wales, has been an approved repository since 1927. It was therefore the first record office in North Wales (the Caernarvonshire Record Office opened in 1947, and the Flintshire Record Office in 1952). It is recognised as a place of deposit for public records.

Acquisitions policy: Deposits and donations are not solicited, but are gratefully accepted. Papers relating to all aspects of life in North Wales, past and present, are particularly welcome.

Archives of organisation: Records of UCNW, Bangor, 1883–, including student registers, 1884–1944.

Major collections: Holdings run to some 500,000 items, and include family and estate papers; mine and quarry papers; quarter sessions records (Borough of Beaumaris, acquired by purchase during World War II); literary MSS in Welsh and English; personal papers; deposits by solicitors etc.
Bangor (General) MSS; Baron Hill MSS; Beaumaris and Anglesey MSS; Bodorgan MSS; Bodrhyddan MSS; Carter Vincent MSS; Kinmel MSS; Lligwy MSS; Maesyneuadd MSS; Maenan MSS; Mostyn MSS; Nannau MSS; Penrhyn Castle MSS; Plas Coch MSS; Plas Newydd MSS; Porth yr Aur MSS.

Non-manuscript material: Printed ephemera, all topics.
OS maps, 2½ and 6 inch: Wales and borders.

Finding aids: Catalogues and indexes (Bangor MSS catalogue is continually in progress). Provisional Guide to Special Collections, 1962 (TS).

Facilities: Photocopying. Photography. Microfilm/fiche reader.

Conservation: In-house department.

46 Barnsley Archive Service

Address: Central Library, Shambles Street, Barnsley, South Yorks S70 2JF

Telephone: (01226) 773950

Enquiries: The Archivist

Open: Mon–Wed: 9.30–1.00; 2.00–6.00 Fri: 9.30–1.00; 2.00–5.00 Sat: 9.30–1.00

Access: Generally open to the public; advance notice preferred.

Historical background: The service was founded within the library in 1986. It inherited material relating to the Barnsley area, including records of Barnsley Borough and predecessor authorities which came into Barnsley in 1974.

Acquisitions policy: Material relating to the area covered by Barnsley Metropolitan District.

Archives of organisation: Borough minutes with rate books and papers from the early 19th century–; UDC and RDC minutes and papers.

Major collections: Deposited local collections, including records of Barnsley British Co-operative Society and West Riding Miners' Permanent Relief Fund Friendly Society.
Local Methodist and Congregational records.
Records of local societies and businesses, including Lancasters, estate agents, with valuation books, c1829–1963.
Papers of Lord Mason.

Non-manuscript material: Collection of illustrations, including: photographs from Barnsley Borough engineers, 1950s-60s (c1000), and the Biltcliff collection of postcards (c200).

Finding aids: Lists of some collections; other lists in progress.

Facilities: Photocopying. Photography. Microfilm/fiche reader/printer.

Publications: Information leaflet and family history handbook available on request.

47 National Union of Mineworkers

Address: 2 Huddersfield Road, Barnsley, South Yorks S70 2LS

Telephone: (01226) 284006

Fax: (01226) 285486

Enquiries: The President, Arthur Scargill

Open: Mon–Fri: 8.45–12.00; 1.15–5.00

Access: Bona fide researchers, by prior appointment.

Historical background: The union was established in 1944 by a number of regional coal-mining unions who had previously been affiliated to the Miners' Federation of Great Britain (set up in 1889). Few pre-1944 records survive due to loss and war damage. Areas frequently retain their own organisation and relief fund records.

Acquisitions policy: To maintain archives in conjunction with the regional organisations, which also retain their records.

Archives of organisation: MFGB: annual proceedings, 1889–1944; circulars and financial statements.
NUM: annual reports and minutes, 1944–; reports and minutes of area organisations, some correspondence and press cuttings.

Major collections: Papers of W.E. Jones (president, 1951–60) are at The Brynmor Jones Library, at the University of Hull (entry 403).

Non-manuscript material: Bound journals.

Publications: See C. Cook: *Sources in British Political History, 1900–1951*, vol. 1, pp. 195–7, vol. 5, pp. 75–7.

48 North Devon Record Office

Parent organisation: Devon Record Office

Address: North Devon Library and Record Office, Tuly Street, Barnstaple, Devon EX32 7EJ

Telephone: (01271) 388608/388607 (Local Studies Centre/microform bookings) 288611 (Beaford Photographic Archive)

Enquiries: The Senior Archivist, Mr T. Wormleighton or Beaford Photographic Archive Curator, Ms B. Harris

Open: Mon, Tues, Fri: 9.30–5.00 Thurs: 9.30–7.00 Wed, some Sats: 9.30–4.00

Access: Generally open to the public. Admission charge (season and exemption tickets available). Documents required between 12.00 and 2.00, and on the Saturdays on which the record office is open, should be ordered in advance.

Historical background: The office forms part of the North Devon Local Studies Centre, in cooperation with a branch local history library and the North Devon Athenaeum, a private free library. The centre opened in 1988, at which time records relating to north Devon were transferred from Devon Record Office, Exeter (entry 323).

Acquisitions policy: Records of the North Devon area.

Archives of organisation: Usual local authority record holdings, including parish records for Archdeaconry of Barnstaple; records of North Devon and Torridge District Councils and their predecessor authorities; North Devon area school, school board, Poor Law Union and hospital records.

Major collections: Deposited collections for North Devon area.
Archives of Chichester family of Arlington Court.

Non-manuscript material: Beaford Photographic Archive of historical and modern images of rural life.

Finding aids: Catalogues and indexes. Lists sent to NRA.

Facilities: Photocopying. Microfilm/fiche readers/printer.

Conservation: Provided by Devon Record Office, Exeter.

49 Cumbria Record Office, Barrow

Parent Organisation: Cumbria Archive Service

Address: 140 Duke Street, Barrow-in-Furness, Cumbria LA14 1XW

Telephone: (01229) 831269

Enquiries: The County Archivist, Mr Jim Grisenthwaite (service-wide enquiries) or the Area Archivist, Mr A.C.J. Jones (office enquiries)

Open: Mon–Fri: 9.00–5.00

Access: Generally open to the public. The office operates the CARN reader's ticket system.

Historical background: The present office was opened in 1979, but archives had been acquired in temporary premises since 1975. The office also hold records from the Furness Collection, originally collected from the early 20th century by the Central Library, Barrow. It acts as a Diocesan Record Office for Carlisle (south-western parishes) and is recognised as a place of deposit for public records. It is part of the Cumbria Archive Service, with offices also at Carlisle (entry **199**) and Kendal (entry **423**).

Acquisitions policy: Official and unofficial records for the former area of Lancashire North of the Sands and the County Borough of Barrow-in-Furness.

Archives of organisation: Usual local authority record holdings, including significant collections from Barrow Borough Council and from certain neighbouring authorities.

Major collections: Deposited local collections, including the following which have a wider significance:
Duke of Buccleuch's Furness estate records reflecting the iron-ore trade, c1854–1963.
Vickers Shipbuilding and Engineering Ltd, Barrow-in-Furness: gun mounting drawings, c1890–1950.
Ellen Rose Fieldhouse Collection: papers of a local enthusiast, covering local history and dialect, and relating chiefly to the parish of Kirby Ireleth.

Non-manuscript material: Soulby Collection of posters, handbills etc., mostly by J. Soulby, Ulverston printer, early 19th century.

Finding aids: Catalogues and indexes. Some collections are unlisted. Selected catalogues sent to NRA.

Facilities: Photocopying. Photography. Microfilming. Microfilm/fiche reader.

Publications: The Ellen Rose Fieldhouse Collection (Cumbria Archive Service, 1992).
Cumbrian Ancestors: Notes for Genealogical Searches (2/1993).

50 The Automobile Association

Address: AA Archives, Stenson Cooke Centre, Priestley Road, Basingstoke, Hants RG24 9NY

Telephone: (01256) 492392

Enquiries: The Archivist, Michael Passmore

Open: By arrangement only.

Access: Bona fide researchers only, strictly by appointment. Application should be made in writing to the archivist.

Historical background: The Automobile Association was founded in 1905. It is technically a club, although it now has several businesses related to it. The current records of the association are not under the archivist's control and the 'archives' are rather the historic holdings, some of which are the prewar records.

Acquisitions policy: To maintain the archival holdings which have been built up over the years and to add memorabilia.

Archives of organisation: Some minutes of committees, including Motor Legislation Committee, 1919–43.
Files *re* organisation of AGMs, motoring organisations, petrol rationing, AA vehicles and telephone boxes. Copies of all AA publications, including handbooks.

Major collections: Miscellaneous historical and associated material, including early correspondence.

Non-manuscript material: Photographs, badges, vehicles, press cuttings. Large collection of AA motoring memorabilia.

Finding aids: NRA 12322.

Publications: S. Cooke: *This Motoring* (1930).
D. Kier (ed.): *Golden Milestone* (1955).
H. Barty-King: *The AA: History of the first 75 years of the Automobile Association, 1905–1980* (1980).

51 American Museum in Britain

Address: The Library, Claverton Manor, Bath, Avon BA2 7BD

Telephone: (01225) 460503

Fax: (01225) 480726

Enquiries: The Curator, Miss Judith Elsdon

Open: Mon–Fri: 9.30–5.30

Access: Bona fide researchers only, by invitation, arising from telephone or postal enquiry. An appointment is necessary.

The museum was opened in 1961 and has acquired by donation material relevant to the American decorative arts from the 17th to the mid-19th centuries. The collection is very limited, but includes correspondence, wills, bills of sale and documents of slave hire and emancipation. Also US newspapers, 19th century; topographical postcards, 20th century; and fashion plates.

52 Bath Central Library

Parent organisation: County of Avon Community Resources Department

Address: 19 The Podium, Northgate Street, Bath, Avon BA1 5AN

Telephone: (01225) 428144

Enquiries: The Librarian-in-Charge

Open: Mon: 10.00–6.00 Tues–Thurs: 9.30–8.00 Fri: 9.30–6.00 Sat: 9.30–5.00

Access: Generally open to the public. Identification is required for some material. Advance notice may be necessary for material kept on a different site.

Historical background: The reference library was built in 1900 in conjunction with the Victoria Art Gallery to commemorate Queen Victoria's Jubilee. It received local collections previously held at the Guildhall and continued to build on these. In 1990 the reference and lending libraries were amalgamated to form the current central library in purpose-built accommodation.

Acquisitions policy: To expand and strengthen the existing collections, especially those relating to local history, by purchase and donation.

Major collections: Papers of the Walcot Estate,

17th–18th centuries, and Pulteney Estate, 18th–19th centuries.

James Thomas Irvine's papers relating to Bath, especially the Abbey restoration and Roman Bath excavations.

Napoleonic Collection relating to the French Revolution and Napoleonic newspapers (800 vols).

Some records of local societies, 19th and 20th centuries, including Bath Field Club correspondence.

Boodle Collection of scrapbooks relating to Bath and Somerset (39 vols).

Non-manuscript material: Extensive collections on the history of Bath, comprising pamphlets, maps, plans, prints, photographs and slides, including the following:

Buxton Collection of pamphlets of the Civil War period, most with Somerset interest.

Chapman Collection of books, maps and pamphlets.

Hunt Collection of scrapbooks containing original drawings, watercolours, maps and autograph letters relating to Bath and the surrounding area (6 vols).

Finding aids: Full card catalogues and (since 1986) some material included on computerised catalogue. Indexes to maps, plans and all illustrations. NRA 25737.

Facilities: Photocopying. Microfilm/fiche readers/printers. Photography by arrangement.

Conservation: In-house binding; other work contracted out.

53 Bath City Record Office

Parent organisation: Bath City Council

Address: Guildhall, Bath, Avon BA1 5AW

Telephone: (01225) 477000 ext. 2420/2421

Fax: (01225) 448646

Enquiries: The City Archivist, Mr C. A. Johnston

Open: Mon: 9.00–1.00; 2.00–8.00 Tues–Thurs: 9.00–1.00; 2.00–5.00 Fri: 9.00–1.00; 2.00–4.30

Historical background: The office was established by the Bath City Council in 1967 and is recognised as a place of deposit for public records. Records of Bath Municipal Charities and St John's Hospital, 17th–20th centuries, are housed at the hospital but made available at the City Record Office, which also has a catalogue of the records. Applications for access should be made to: The Clerk to the Trustees, Bath Municipal Charities and St John's Hospital, Thrings and Long, Midland Bridge Road, Bath; tel. (01225) 448494.

Archives of organisation: Usual local authority record holdings.

Major collections: Local deposited collections, including hospital records.
Records of Bath and West of England Society, 1777–.

Facilities: Photocopying. Microfilm/fiche readers.

54 Crafts Study Centre

Parent organisation: Holburne Museum

Address: Great Pulteney Street, Bath, Avon BA2 4DB

Telephone: (01225) 466669

Fax: (01225) 333121

Enquiries: The Curator, Barley Roscoe

Open: Mon–Fri 9.30–5.00

Access: Bona fide students and researchers, by appointment only (2–3 weeks' notice preferred).

Historical background: The Crafts Study Centre opened at the Holburne Museum in 1977 for the purpose of making a permanent collection of work by the finest British artist-craftspeople of the 20th century.

Acquisitions policy: To acquire, mainly by donation, photographs, books, documents and working notes pertaining to crafts and crafts-people.

Major collections: Papers of leading artist-craftsmen and women, including Bernard Leach, Michael Cardew, Katharine Pleydell-Bouverie, William Staite Murray, Ethel Mairet, Edward Johnston, Irene Wellington.
Records of the Red Rose Guild.

Finding aids: Leach catalogue in progress. Lists of other material in preparation.

Facilities: Photocopying. Photography.

Publications: J. Howes: *Edward Johnston: a Catalogue of the Crafts Study Centre Collection and Archive* (Bath, 1987).

55 Downside Abbey Archives

Parent organisation: English Benedictine Congregation

Address: Downside Abbey, Stratton-on-the-Fosse, Bath, Avon BA3 4RH

Telephone: (01761) 232295

Fax: (01761) 233575 or 232973

Enquiries: The Archivist, Dom Philip Jebb

Open: Open by prior arrangement only on most days, including weekends, except the first Sunday of Lent.

Access: Serious students, by appointment only. Application should be made in the first instance in writing to the archivist. Applicants need to indicate the nature of their research and to supply a reference. Personal papers of individuals (apart from strictly academic papers) are not normally available until 50 years after death.

Historical background: The Benedictine community of St Gregory the Great, now at Downside, has a history going back to 1605, when some English monks in Spanish and Italian monasteries came together to start a monastery in Douai, then part of the Spanish Netherlands. The community ran a school for English Catholics and sent priests (illegally) into England to support the recusants. In 1794, driven out of France by the Revolution, they came to England and settled in Downside in 1814. The community has run a school for English boys since the early 17th century, and been involved from the foundation in pastoral care of Catholics in England and Wales and engaged in historical and theological work. All these activities are reflected in the archives, although much material was lost during the French Revolution.

Acquisitions policy: English Benedictine history, but also histories of other religious communities which have ceased to exist and individuals in some way connected with the monastery or school. Also 19th and 20th century Catholic Australia, because the first two Archbishops of Sydney were monks of Downside.

Archives of organisation: Official papers and correspondence of the English Benedictine Congregation, 1617–, including minutes of General Chapters, constitutions and declarations, correspondence, records of Congregra-

tion officials and of individual houses (St Gregory's and others), bursar's, parish and other accounts, mainly mid-17th century–.
Records of Downside Weather Station and of St Gregory's Press.
Correspondence and official decisions of Presidents' General of the EBC, mainly 1790s-.
Records and financial accounts of pastoral work in England and Wales, 1640s-, and Australia, 1830–81.

Major collections: Annals and biographies, 1600–1850.
Collection of pamphlets, correspondence and diaries concerning the constitutional controversy, 1880–1900.
Personal papers of monks, mid-17th century–, including Cardinal Gasquet, Abbot Cuthbert Butler and Abbot Christopher Butler and of lay men and women (c100).
Papers of J. Harting, ornithologist and naturalist, 19th century.
World War I and II chaplains' correspondence.
Accounts of escapes from France, late 18th century, and voyages to Australia, 19th century.

Non-manuscript material: Postcards of European architectural and topographical interest, late 19th century– (c40,000).
Extensive collection of photographs and portraits, mainly of monks and nuns, other ecclesiastics, old boys of the school, 1850s-.
Architectural plans and drawings for Downside and churches elsewhere, including work by Pugin, Hanson, Cowper and Giles, Gilbert Scott, 19th and 20th centuries.
Copies of documents from continental archives in Spain, France and Italy relating to EBC history.

Finding aids: Card indexes and lists in progress. NRA 19936.

Facilities: Photocopying. Microfilm/fiche readers.

Publications: Dom Philip Jebb: 'Archives of the English Benedictine Congregation kept at St Gregory's, Downside', *Downside Review*, cxciii/312 (1975) [an updated version is in the *Bulletin* of the Catholics Archivist's Society, 14 (1994), 20–36].
Various articles by Dom Aidan Bellenger in *Catholic Archivist*.
Early editions of *Downside Review*, late 19th century, included a series of articles 'Among the Archives'.

56 Fashion Research Centre

Parent organisation: Bath City Council

Address: Bath Museums and Historic Buildings, 4 Circus, Bath, Avon BA1 2EW

Telephone: (01225) 461111 ext. 2752

Fax: (01225) 444793

Enquiries: The Assistant Keeper of Collections, Miss R. Tritton

Open: Mon–Thurs: 9.30–5.00 Fri: 9.30–4.30

Access: Generally open to the public.

Historical background: The centre was opened in 1974 as an extension to the Museum of Costume in Bath to make available study facilities in the history of dress. The aim is to provide a centre for reference and research from both documentary material and actual specimens of costume maintained in a study collection. The collections at both the museum and research centre deal mainly with fashionable dress in Europe for men, women and children from the late 16th century to the present day.

Acquisitions policy: To expand and strengthen existing primary and secondary collections in the history of costume and related subjects by donations and occasional purchases.

Major collections: Principally non-MS material.

Non-manuscript material: Fashion periodicals: titles of fashion magazines, 1802– (c100 titles).
Trade catalogues: catalogues from British firms, c1900– (c600).
Sunday Times Fashion Archive: fashion photographs, 1957–72 (c2000).
Worth/Paquin Archives: designs, photographs and press cuttings from house records of both firms, 1902–56.
Fashion plates, late 18th century-1920 (c2000).
Photographs: 19th- and 20th–century *cartes-de-visite* and photograph albums; fashion photographs; photographs of works of art from the medieval period to the 20th century (c10,000).
Paper dressmaking patterns, 1875–1980 (c500).
Miscellaneous designs and fashion illustrations.

Finding aids: Catalogues and indexes (e.g. to fashion designers represented in *Sunday Times* Fashion Archive or *Vogue* magazine, 1930–).

Facilities: Photocopying. Photography. Microfiche reader.

57 Provincial Archives of La Sainte Union Religious Congregation

Parent organisation: International Congregation of La Sainte Union, Rome

Address: La Sainte Union Convent, 29 Pulteney Road, Bath, Avon BA2 4EY

Telephone: (01225) 461984

Enquiries: The Archivist, Sr Elizabeth Ward, The Convent, Moorend Road, Charlton Kings, Cheltenham GL53 9AU, tel. (01242) 580472

Open: By advance appointment.

Access: All Sisters of the Congregation and to bona fide researchers. Restricted access to documents less than 50 years old.

Historical background: The Congregation of La Sainte Union was founded in Douai, France, in 1826, with special emphasis on work for the Christian Education of Youth. The Sisters were expelled by the French government at the end of the 19th century. The foundations of the Anglo-Hibernian province (UK and Ireland) were laid in 1858. The present provincial repository was formally established in Bath in 1980. It contains some valuable material on other LSU provinces founded from England, particularly the USA, Argentina and West Indies.

Acquisitions policy: Archives of the Congregation with special reference to foundation years, the life of the founder, the spread of the Congregation overseas, and, in particular, the establishment of new communities and schools in the UK and Ireland. Also material illustrating the lives and works of members of La Sainte Union.

Archives of organisation: Documents and reports received from general and provincial administration including six-year General Chapters, general and provincial councils, regional meetings, education conferences.
Records of spiritual formation and profession ceremonies.

Major collections: Letters and conferences of Fr Jean Baptise Debrabant, the founder, to the Sisters, 1828–76.
Collections of letters from Sisters who established the first houses of the Congregation in North and South America and later in the West Indies and Africa, early 20th century-.

Non-manuscript material: Photographs of the first LSU Mother House in Douai.
Biographies of the founder.
Histories of LSU schools and of the various pastoral and charitable works of the Congregation.
School journals.

Finding aids: Catalogues, lists and indexes.

Facilities: Photocopying.

58 Royal Photographic Society Collection

Address: The Octagon, Milsom Street, Bath, Avon BA1 1DN

Telephone: (01225) 462841 ext. 217/220

Fax: (01225) 448688

Enquiries: The Curator, Ms Pam Roberts

Open: Mon–Fri: 10.00–5.00

Access: Generally open to the public, by appointment. Non-members will be charged a research fee on a daily basis, depending on requirements.

Historical background: The Royal Photographic Society came into existence in 1853. The collection of photographs was not established until the 1920s, when J. Dudley Johnston was simultaneously president, secretary and curator. It was formed from the gifts of photographers of their own work and their personal collections. The material is mainly 19th century but extends into the 20th century, with the emphasis on pictorialism. However, it cannot be said to be representative of modern British photography.

Acquisitions policy: Material is acquired mainly by donation.

Archives of organisation: Archives of RPS, including early minute books, records of group meetings, 1853–; correspondence and catalogues, 1830s-.

Non-manuscript material: all forms of photographic images, including the work of: Julia Margaret Cameron (1815–79); Roger Fenton (1819–69), first secretary; D.O. Hill (1802–70) and Robert Adamson (1820–47); W.H. Fox Talbot (1800–77); also letters and documents; Horace Nicholls (1867–1941); Samuel Bourne (1834–1912); Francis Frith (1822–98); O.G.

Rejlander (1813–75); Linnaeus Tripe (1822–1902); H.P. Robinson (1830–1901); Frederick Evans (1852–1943); Alvin Langdon Coburn (1882–1966); Edward Steichen (1879–1973); Alfred Stieglitz (1864–1946); Clarence White (1871–1925); Alexander Keighley (1861–1947); Horsley Hinton (1863–1908); Nicéphore Niépce (1765–1833); J.D. Llewelyn (1810–82); Oxley Grabham (1865–1939); Frank M. Sutcliffe (1853–1941).
Kodak and other cameras and items of photographic equipment, including light meters and plates (6000).
Fox Talbot: *The Pencil of Nature*.
Du Mont Collection of books illustrated by photography.
Photographic periodicals and books, 1850s-.

Finding aids: Computerised catalogue for equipment. Card catalogue for books and photographs.

Facilities: Photocopying. Photography.

Conservation: Contracted out.

Publications: The Treasures of the RPS (Heinemann/RPS, 1980) [covers contents of photographic collection up to 1915].
Items about collection regularly appear in *The Photographic Journal*, published by the RPS, and *British Association of Picture Libraries and Agencies Journal*.
Various publications on individual photographers.

59 University of Bath Library

Address: Bath, Avon BA2 7AY

Telephone: (01225) 826835

Fax: (01225) 826229

Enquiries: The Librarian, Mr H.D. Nicholson

Open: Mon–Fri: 9.00–5.00

Access: Approved readers.

Historical background: The University of Bath received its charter in 1966, having developed from the Bristol College of Science and Technology. Since April 1987 the library has housed the National Cataloguing Unit for the Archives of Contemporary Scientists, the successor to the Oxford-based Contemporary Scientific Archives Centre.

Acquisitions policy: To maintain a collection in

support of the university's teaching and research interests.

Major collections: Pitman Collection: library and MS material of Sir Isaac Pitman (1813–97), the inventor of the Pitman Shorthand System, *re* the international development of the use of shorthand.
Watkins Collection of documents and photographs on the role of steam power in the British economy, 1850–1914.

Non-manuscript material: The library of the Initial Teaching Alphabet Foundation was received following the closing of that institution.

Facilities: Photocopying. Microfilm.

60 West Lothian District Library

Address: Wellpark, Marjoribanks Street, Bathgate, West Lothian EH48 1AN

Telephone: (01506) 652866/630300

Enquiries: The Local Collection Librarian, Mrs M.S. Cavanagh

Open: Mon–Thurs: 8.30–5.00 Fri: 8.30–4.00 Sat (1st of each month): 9.00–1.00

Access: Generally open to the public.

Historical background: The library service was started in 1924 and local material has probably been collected since that date.

Acquisitions policy: To improve existing collections relating to local history.

Major collections: Council minutes for Armadale Town, Bathgate Town, Linlithgow Town, Whitburn Town, and West Lothian County, 19th and 20th centuries.
District council minutes for Torphichen and Bathgate, East Calder, West Calder, Uphall and Whitburn, 19th and 20th centuries.

Non-manuscript material: Photographs (c4000), maps, videos.
Local newspapers, 1873–.
Parish records and census returns, 1811–91 (microfilm).

Finding aids: Catalogue of all holdings. Various lists and indexes.

Facilities: Photocopying. Microfilm/fiche reader/printer.

61 Bearsden and Milngavie District Libraries

Address: Library HQ, 166 Drymen Road, Bearsden, Glasgow G61 3RJ

Telephone: (0141) 9430121

Fax: (0141) 9430200

Enquiries: The Assistant Chief Librarian, Ms Elizabeth Brown

Open: Mon–Fri: 10.00–8.00 Sat: 10.00–5.00

Access: Generally open to the public. Appointment necessary if advice required.

Historical background: Bearsden and Milngavie joined together to form one district in 1975; the towns were previously part of Dumbarton County as New Kilpatrick parish.

Acquisitions policy: To develop holdings on the area of the present and historical geographical boundaries of New Kilpatrick parish.

Archives of organisation: Bearsden and Milngavie town and burgh minutes. Bearsden burgh records of formation, 1957/8.

Major collections: Local collections, including: Westerton Garden Suburb ledgers, 1912–66, and Co-operative Society minutes, 1915–25.
Bearsden Ladies Club records, 1947–83.
Federation of Bearsden Ratepayers Association records, 1959–76.
Douglas Park Golf Club records, 1897–1977.

Non-manuscript material: Local newspaper, 1901–.
Photographs and maps relating to district.

Finding aids: Computerised catalogue.

Facilities: Photocopying. Microfilm/fiche readers.

62 Beaulieu Archive

Parent organisation: Montagu Ventures Ltd

Address: John Montagu Building, Beaulieu, Brockenhurst, Hants SO42 7ZN

Telephone: (01590) 612345 exts 259/283

Fax: (01590) 612624

Enquiries: The Archivist, Miss Susan Tomkins

Open: Mon–Fri: 10.00–5.00

Access: Generally open to the public, by appointment.

Historical background: Originally family papers of the Lord Montagu of Beaulieu and papers of the Beaulieu Estate Steward, now expanded to include material relating to the Beaulieu leisure complex. See also National Motor Museum (entry **63**).

Acquisitions policy: Multi-media material relating to the Beaulieu Estate and Montagu family.

Archives of organisation: The Beaulieu Estate records, late 18th–19th century.
Poor House records, late 18th century-early 19th century.
Papers of Henry, 1st Lord Montagu of Beaulieu (1832–1905).
Records of Montagu Ventures Ltd.

Non-manuscript material: Oral history collection.

Finding aids: Catalogue. Some lists and indexes.

Facilities: Photocopying. Photography.

Conservation: Contracted out.

Publications: H.E.R. Widnell: *The Beaulieu Record* (1973).
F. Hockey: *Beaulieu: King John's Abbey* (1976).
A.J. Holland: *Buckler's Hard: a Shipbuilding Village* (1985).
C. Cunningham: *The Beaulieu River Goes to War* (1994).

63 National Motor Museum
BP Library of Motoring

Parent organisation: National Motor Museum Trust

Address: Trust Centre, Beaulieu, Brockenhurst, Hants SO42 7ZN

Telephone: (01590) 612345

Fax: (01590) 612655

Enquiries: The Reference Librarian, Annice Collett

Open: Mon–Sun: 10.00–12.30; 2.00–5.00

Access: Generally open to the public for reference; a reading room is provided.

The reference library was formed in 1961 and moved to its present position in 1972. Although there is some correspondence from the motor industry and sporting personalities, the bulk of the collection is printed material, including sales catalogues and owners handbooks. There is also a photographic library and sound archive. (See also Beaulieu Archives, entry **62**).

64 Bethlem Royal Hospital Archives and Museum

Parent Organisation: The Bethlem and Maudsley NHS Trust (for the hospital's own archives)
The Bethlem Art and History Collections Trust (for other historical and art collections)

Address: The Bethlem Royal Hospital, Monks Orchard Road, Beckenham, Kent BR3 3BX

Telephone: (0181) 776 4307/4227 (direct lines)

Fax: (0181) 777 1668

Enquiries: The Archivist and Curator, Patricia Allderidge

Open: Mon–Fri: 9.30–5.00

Access: Open to the public, by appointment. 100-year closure on medical and other records relating to individual patients; 30-year closure on other public records.

Historical background: The Bethlem Royal Hospital (the original 'Bedlam') was founded in 1247 as the Priory of St Mary of Bethlehem. It was a hospital for the insane by 1400. It has occupied sites in Bishopsgate (1247–1676); Moorfields (1676–1815); St George's Fields, Southwark (1815–1930); and the present location since 1930. It came under the control of the City of London in 1547, and was administered jointly with Bridewell Hospital from 1557 to 1948. It housed the first State Criminal Lunatic Asylum (replaced by Broadmoor Hospital) from 1816 to 1864. Under the National Health Service in 1948 Bethlem was united with the Maudsley Hospital, Denmark Hill. The Maudsley was opened in 1923 as a London County Council mental hospital and became the postgraduate Institute of Psychiatry in 1946. The joint hospital has been administered by a Board of Governors (1948–82), a Special Health Authority (1982–94), and an NHS trust (since 1994). The archives department was set up in 1967, and is recognised as a place of deposit for public records.

Acquisitions policy: Archives of Bethlem and Maudsley hospitals. Reference books and other material relating more generally to the history of psychiatry and to art and psychiatry are also collected.
Works by artists who have suffered mental disorders.

Archives of organisation: Bethlem Hospital: minutes of the Court of Governors of Bridewell and Bethlem, 1559–1948, and of the General Committee of Bridewell and Bethlem, 1737–1948 (on microfilm).
Patients admission registers, 1683–, casebooks, 1816–1948; various administrative and financial records, 18th century–; records of the State Criminal Lunatic Asylum 1816–64; title deeds (including some medieval), maps, plans and surveys relating to endowment estates; miscellaneous records, including photographs.
Maudsley Hospital: minute books and files transferred from LCC, 1923–48.
Records of the joint hospital, 1948–.

Non-manuscript material: Museum holdings include a collection of work by artists who have suffered from mental disorder, notably Richard Dadd, Louis Wain and Jonathan Martin.

Finding aids: NRA lists, 1958/9 (in process of revision). Indexes to Court and General Committee books, casebooks and admission registers.

Facilities: Photocopying. Microfilm reader.

Conservation: Full in-house service.

65 Raymond Mander and Joe Mitchenson Theatre Collection

Address: The Mansion, Beckenham Place Park, Beckenham, Kent BR3 2BP

Telephone: (0181) 658 7725

Fax: (0181) 663 0313

Enquiries: The Director, Mr Richard Mangan

Open: Mon–Fri: 10.30–4.30

Access: Bona fide researchers, by appointment only. An hourly charge is made.

Historical background: The collection was begun by Raymond Mander and Joe Mitchenson in the 1930s. Subsequently a charitable trust was formed with the two founders as directors.

Acquisitions policy: Anything and everything to do with the theatre and allied arts.

Non-manuscript material: Programmes, cuttings, photographs, posters, paintings,

designs, books, pottery relating mainly, but not exclusively, to London theatre. Also material on actors, actresses, playwrights, designers, composers, singers, dancers, music hall and variety.
Library (7000 books).

Finding aids: Indexes of pottery and designs. Book catalogue.

Facilities: Photocopying.

66 Bedford Central Library: Reference and Local Studies Library

Parent organisation: Bedfordshire County Council

Address: Harpur Street, Bedford MK40 1PG

Telephone: (01234) 350931

Fax: (0234) 342163

Enquiries: The Principal Librarian, Information Services (North East), Daniela Vuolo

Open: Mon–Fri: 9.30–7.00 Sat: 9.30–4.00

Access: Generally open to the public.

Historical background: The present collection is the result of the merger in 1985 of the Bedfordshire County Local Studies Collection, which started in 1925, with the Local Studies Collection of Bedford Central Library.

Acquisitions policy: To collect all published and pictorial material covering Bedfordshire, past and present.

Non-manuscript material: Usual local history collection, including John Bunyan Collection; newspapers, 1842–; photographs, 1880–; illustrations, 1700–; maps, 1765–; handbills and posters, 1800–; microfilms of parish registers, 1532–1812; census returns, 1841–91.

Finding aids: Catalogues and indexes. NRA 19222.

Facilities: Photocopying. Microfilm/fiche reader/printer.

67 Bedford Museum

Parent organisation: Bedford Borough Council

Address: Castle Lane, Bedford MK40 3XD

Telephone: (01234) 353323

Fax: (01234) 221606

Enquiries: The Curator, Mr H.J. Turner

Open: Tues–Sat: 11.00–5.00 Sun and bank holiday Mon: 2.00–5.00

Access: By appointment.

The museum maintains and collects archives relevant to its main collecting areas of recent local history, archaeology and natural history of the north Bedfordshire area (NRA 0560).

68 Bedford School Archive

Address: Burnaby Road, Bedford MK40 2TU

Telephone: (01234) 353436

Enquiries: The Archivist, R.G. Miller

Open: School hours, by arrangement.

Access: Generally open to the public via the archivist, by appointment.

Historical background: The school is a Tudor foundation with extensive archive material. The main body of pre-1800 material is held at the offices of the Harpur Trust, 101 Harpur Centre, Bedford. The school archive consists of post-1800 material collected in recent years and housed in three rooms in the school.

Acquisitions policy: To consolidate and extend the school's archive; material relating to Old Bedfordians is always accepted.

Archives of organisation: Administrative material concerning the school, its pupils and staff, finance, estates and architects, including G.F. Bodley (1827–1907) and Oswald Milne (1881–1968).

Major collections: Papers and memorabilia of old boys, including Sir Thomas Erskine May (1815–86) and Frederick Burnaby (1842–85); also extensive numbers of trench diaries, World War I.

Finding aids: Catalogued in part.

Facilities: Photocopying.

Publications: Sargeant and Hockliffe: *History of*

Bedford School.
Barlen, Stambach and Stileman: *Bedford School.*

69 Bedfordshire Record Office

Parent organisation: Bedfordshire County Council

Address: County Hall, Bedford MK42 9AP

Telephone: (01234) 228833/363222 ext. 2833

Fax: (01234) 228619 (main County Council fax)

Enquiries: The County Archivist, Mr C.J. Pickford

Open: Mon–Fri: 9.00–1.00; 2.00–5.00

Access: Open to the public without appointment. The conditions of access are stated in the Record Office Charter and Code of Conduct for searchroom users (available on request).

Historical background: Bedfordshire Record Office was established in 1913 under the auspices of the Records Committee formed by the County Council in 1898 and is the only officially designated archive repository in Bedfordshire. Bedfordshire was one of the pioneers of the local repository network and is the oldest county archives service. The Record Office moved to purpose-built premises in 1969, and in 1993 earned a Charter Mark award for excellence in public services. A full records management service for the authority was established in 1989. The office is recognised as a place of deposit for public records and designated as the Diocesan Record Office for St Albans (Archdeaconry of Bedford).

Acquisitions policy: The key aim is to secure archives illustrating all aspects of the life and history of the county and its people.

Archives of organisation: Usual local authority archive holdings, including Quarter Sessions records, 1651–; Poor Law Union records, 1834–; County Council archives, 1889–; and District and Parish Council records.

Major collections: Deposited local collections from businesses, landed estates, Anglican and non-conformist churches, public services, including hospitals, and papers of private individuals.

Non-manuscript material: Substantial collections of maps and plans, architectural drawings, and illustrations. There is a collection of local printed material on open access in the Record Office searchroom.

Finding aids: Most collections catalogued, with detailed subject index on cards. Holdings generally well indexed. Catalogues sent to the NRA.

Facilities: Photocopying (including large-scale and colour copying). Photography. Microfilming. Microfilm/fiche readers/printers. Laptop computers and tape-recorders permitted (subject to clearance with duty staff).

Conservation: In-house facilities with limited scope for outside work. Some contracting out.

Publications: Guide to the Bedfordshire Record Office (1957).
Guide Supplement (1966).
Guide to the Russell Estate Collections for Bedfordshire and Devon to 1910 (1966).
The Bedfordshire Parish Registers Series [80 vols, 1931–1992; indexed transcripts of all Bedfordshire parish registers up to 1812].
Newsletter [quarterly, 1986–].
National Inventory of Documentary Sources, (Chadwyck-Healey, microfiche 1984–).
Leaflets and short guides on a range of subjects.

70 Cranfield University

Address: Cranfield, Bedford MK43 0AL

Telephone: (01234) 750111 ext. 3722

Fax: (01234) 752391

Enquiries: The Librarian

Open: Mon–Fri: 8.30–9.00 Sat: 9.30–6.00

Access: Generally open to the public.

Historical background: Founded in 1946 as the College of Aeronautics, for the education of aeronautical engineers, the university became Cranfield Institute of Technology in 1970 with the power to award degrees. It now deals with many aspects of applied science, and changed its name to Cranfield University in 1993.

Acquisitions policy: To acquire books, periodicals and published material (e.g. reports) on those subjects taught at Cranfield. There is no formal acquisitions policy on historical material.

Major collections: Reports on aerodynamics, aeronautical engineering and related engineering subjects (c100,000).

Non-manuscript material: The institute has acquired the library of the Aeronautical Research Council.

Facilities: Photocopying. Microfiche readers/printer.

71 Belfast Central Library
Irish and Local Studies Department

Parent organisation: Belfast Education and Library Board

Address: Royal Avenue, Belfast BT1 1EA

Telephone: (01232) 243233

Enquiries: The Senior Librarian, Mr H. Russell

Open: Mon, Thurs: 9.30–8.00 Tues, Wed, Fri: 9.30–5.30 Sat: 9.30–1.00

Access: Generally open to the public.

Historical background: Since the 1920s the library has acquired the papers of local antiquarians and literary figures.

Acquisitions policy: To acquire material relating to the work of local historians and writers.

Major collections: Irish antiquarian and bibliographical studies: F.J. Bigger (1863–1926), 40,000 items; J.S. Crone (1858–1945), 10,000 items; A.S. Moore (1870–1961), 1000 items; A. Riddell (1874–1958), 5000 items.
Gaelic MSS: Bryson MacAdam Collection of Ulster Gaelic writings, 17th–18th centuries (44 MS vols).
MSS, TSS and/or correspondence of the following: Lynn Doyle (1873–1961); Alexander Irvine (1863–1941); Amanda McKittrick Ros, 1897–1939; Forrest Reid (1876–1947); Sam Thompson, 1956–65.

Non-manuscript material: Theatre and cinema posters and programmes, relating mainly to Belfast (c5000).
Photographs, political ephemera, postcards relating to Ireland.

Finding aids: Various lists and indexes.

Facilities: Photocopying. Limited photography. Microfilm/fiche reader/printer.

Publications: B. O'Buachalla: *Clar na Lamhscribhinni Gaeilge: 1 Leabharlainn Phoibli Bheal Feirste* (Baile Atha Cliath: An Chead Chlo, 1962).
Guide to Irish and Local Studies Department (1980).

72 Belfast Climate Office

Parent organisation: Meteorological Office

Address: Progressive House, 32 College Street, Belfast BT1 6BQ

Telephone: (01232) 328457

Fax: (01232) 328457

Enquiries: The Senior Meteorological Officer

Open: Mon–Thurs: 8.30–5.00 Fri: 8.30–4.30

Access: Generally open to the public, preferably by appointment. Meteorological records in the Public Record Office of Northern Ireland (entry **78**) may be consulted only on application to Belfast Climate Office.

Historical Background: The Meteorological Office originated as a department of the Board of Trade in 1855. Under Public Records Acts the office is authorised to select technical meteorological records for retention and maintain approved places of deposit at Belfast, Bracknell (entry **112**) and Edinburgh (entry **292**).

Acquisitions Policy: Responsible for original meteorological and climatological records from any source in Northern Ireland. Donations are welcomed.

Major collections: Comprehensive collection of weather observation registers and climatological returns for locations in Northern Ireland. Records older than ten years are deposited in the Public Record Office of Northern Ireland.

Finding aids: Full catalogue in the Public Record Office of Northern Ireland.

Facilities: Photocopying by arrangement.

73 Belfast Harbour Commissioners' Library

Address: Harbour Office, Corporation Square, Belfast BT1 3AL

Telephone: (01232) 234422

Fax: (01232) 242663

Enquiries: The Senior Administrative Officer, R. Yeates

Open: By arrangement only.

Access: Bona fide students, by appointment only.

Belfast Harbour Commissioners was set up by Act of Parliament in 1847. The library has acquired archival material from various bodies and its collections relate largely to Belfast and its port from 1600 onwards.

74 Belfast Library and Society for Promoting Knowledge
Linen Hall Library

Address: 17 Donegall Square North, Belfast BT1 5GD

Telephone: (01232) 321707

Fax: (01232) 438586

Enquiries: Mr John Gray

Open: Mon–Wed, Fri: 9.30–6.00 Thurs: 9.30–8.30 Sat: 9.30–4.00

Access: Members and approved readers, on application to the librarian.

Historical background: The library was founded in 1788 as the Belfast Reading Society, its stated aim being the 'collection of an extensive library, philosophical apparatus, and such productions of nature and art as tend to improve the mind and excite a spirit of general inquiry'. The library holdings cover the humanities and sciences, in particular the field of Irish history.

Acquisitions policy: To strengthen existing collections of Irish material.

Major collections: Blackwood Collection of local genealogies of Co. Down families.
Minute books of local societies, including Belfast Burns Society, early 20th century–; Natural History and Philosophical Society, early 19th century–; Belfast Anacreontic Society, late 18th century–.
Minutes of the Belfast Corporation, late 19th century–.

Facilities: Photocopying.

75 Campbell College

Address: Belmont Road, Belfast BT4 2ND

Telephone: (01232) 763076

Fax: (01232) 761894

Enquiries: The Archivist, Mr C.F. Gailey

Open: Term: Mon–Fri: 9.30–1.00

Access: Old Campbellians and others with suitable references, by appointment.

The college was opened in 1894 under the terms of the will of Henry James Campbell (1813–89) with the stated purpose of giving 'a superior liberal Protestant education' for boys. Although much of the early material was unfortunately destroyed, there remains a collection of Old Campbellians' historical reminiscences and photographs, which is being actively augmented. The register of the college is published in five volumes. A history of the school, *Neither Rogues nor Fools*, is available on application.

76 General Register Office, Northern Ireland

Address: Oxford House, 49–55 Chichester Street, Belfast BT1 4HL

Telephone: (01232) 252000

Fax: (01232) 252044/252120

Enquiries: The Deputy Registrar-General, Mr J.L. McKeag or The Assistants Registrar-General, Miss R. McGibbon and Mr S. Campbell

Open: Mon–Fri: 9.30–4.00

Access: Open to the public; fees vary.

Historical background: The Registrar General's Office was set up for the whole of Ireland and at the date of partition (1921) divided into General Register Office (Northern Ireland) and General Register Office (Republic of Ireland). Since 1973 the registrars of births, deaths and marriages have been local authority staff, paid for by the Department of Finance and Personnel, Northern Ireland.

Acquisitions policy: The Registrar General is required by statute to arrange for the registration of all births, marriages and deaths in Northern Ireland, and for the storage and safe keeping of all such records.

Major collections: Marriage records (Northern Ireland), 1844–.
Birth and death records (Northern Ireland), 1863–.

Non-manuscript material: Some pre-1921 birth and death indexes on microfilm. Post-1973 birth and death records on microfiche.

Computerised historic indexes: births, 1822–92, deaths and marriages, 1970– 1992.

Finding aids: Indexes to all records available.

Facilities: Index search facilities. Microfilm/ fiche readers.

Publications: Registrar General's annual reports, quarterly reports.

77 The Presbyterian Historical Society of Ireland

Parent organisation: The Presbyterian Church in Ireland

Address: Room 220, Church House, Fisherwick Place, Belfast BT1 6DW

Telephone: (01232) 322284

Enquiries: The Hon. Secretary, Rev. Dr W. D. Patton or The Assistant Secretary, Mr Robert H. Bonar

Open: Mon, Tues, Thurs, Fri: 10.00–12.30
Wed: 10.00–1.00; 2.00–4.00
Closed 12 and 13 July.

Access: Generally open to the public; an appointment is not normally necessary, but a telephone call is advisable. Presbytery records require the consent of the Clerks of Presbytery.

Historical background: The Presbyterian Historical Society was founded in 1907. Its constitution states 'the object of this Society shall be to collect and preserve the materials, and to promote the knowledge of the history, of the Churches of the Presbyterian order in Ireland.'

Acquisitions policy: The society's policy is to acquire, mostly by donation or deposit, material relevant to the history of the congregations in the Presbyterian Church in Ireland and their ministers.

Archives of organisation: Records of the General Synod of Ulster and the Seceders and, since 1840, of the General Assembly of the Presbyterian Church in Ireland.
Records relating to some presbyteries and congregations.
Files detailing records held by congregations; histories of congregations.

Major collections: Baptismal and marriage registers.
Writings by Presbyterian ministers.
Tenison Groves census records.

Fasti of the Irish Presbyterian Church, 1613– 1840, by Rev. James McConnell.

Non-manuscript material: Witness newspaper files; other publications of Presbyterian interest, e.g. *The Irish Presbyterian* and McComb's *Almanac.*
Some portraits and photographs and other artefacts of Presbyterian interest, e.g. communion vessels, hour glasses, offering ladles and communion tokens.
Collection of pamphlets on religious topics.

Finding aids: Indexes of ministers, congregations and church records. Computerised library list.

Facilities: Photocopying, photography by arrangement.

Publications: Annual Bulletin.
A History of Congregations in the Presbyterian Church in Ireland, 1610–1982.
J.M. Barkley: *Fasti of the General Assembly, 1840–1910* [in three parts].

78 Public Record Office of Northern Ireland

Address: 66 Balmoral Avenue, Belfast BT9 6NY

Telephone: (01232) 661621

Fax: (01232) 665718

Enquiries: The Director

Open: Mon–Fri: 9.15–4.45.
Documents are not produced after 4.15 (4.00 during July and August).
Closed first two weeks of December.

Access: Official records normally after 30 years. Private records open to public inspection except where the depositor has imposed restrictions.

Historical background: The Public Record Office of Northern Ireland was set up by the Public Records Act (Northern Ireland) 1923, to be responsible for the custody of official records of government departments, courts of law, statutory bodies etc. Provision was also made for the deposit of imperial records, i.e. those relating to Northern Ireland created by government at Westminster, and for the record office to accept records from private depositors.

Acquisitions policy: Official records are transferred to the Public Records Office of Northern Ireland under the terms of the 1923 Act. The office seeks to acquire a wide range of private records, in particular family, estate and business archives; ecclesiastical records; papers of clubs and societies; and emigrant letters.

Non-manuscript material: Very small collection of tapes and files.
Several large collections of photographic glass plate negatives.

Finding aids: Computerised and manual catalogues. Indexes. Deputy Keeper's reports, 1954–89.

Facilities: Photocopying. Photographic copies. Microfilm readers. Self-service microfilms for church records.

Conservation: Full in-house service.

Publications: A large number of publications, some published by HMSO, others by the Public Record Office; these include education facsimile packs, calendars, catalogues of selected papers, guides to various types of records. A publications list is available.

79 Queen's University Archives

Address: Main Library, Queen's University, Belfast BT7 1LS

Telephone: (01232) 245133 ext. 3604

Fax: (01232) 323340

Enquiries: The Librarian, Special Collections

Open: Term: Mon–Fri: 9.00–9.30 Vacation: Mon–Fri: 9.00–5.00 Summer vacation: Sat: 9.00–12.30

Access: Approved readers, by written application; appointment necessary. Certain categories of archives are not available to outside readers.

Historical background: Queen's College, Belfast, was founded in 1845, first opened in 1849, and formed a constituent college of Queen's University in Ireland from 1850. In 1882 Queen's University in Ireland was dissolved and Queen's College became part of the Royal University of Ireland. In 1908 Queen's College was elevated to university status as Queen's University of Belfast.

Acquisitions policy: To augment existing records with relevant material.

Archives of organisation: Minutes of Senate, Academic Council and other university committees. Calendars of Queen's College and University. Sets of examination papers.

Major collections: Personal and official papers of former senior officers.

Non-manuscript material: Plans and photographs of university property; photographs of former staff members.

Finding aids: Handlist.

Facilities: Photocopying.

80 The Royal Ulster Rifles Regimental Museum

Address: 5 Waring Street, Belfast BT1 2EW

Telephone: (01232) 247279

Enquiries: Maj. (retd) M. B. Murphy

Open: Mon–Fri: 10.00–12.30; 2.00–4.30

Access: Generally open to the public; an appointment is recommended.

The museum was first established at the regimental depot, Armagh, in 1932 and transferred to purpose-built premises in Belfast in 1962. Artefacts and papers connected with the Royal Ulster Rifles, the Royal Irish Rifles, the 83rd and the 86th Regimental and associated units are acquired. The holdings include personal papers, war diaries, record books, medal rolls, casualty lists, photograph albums and histories. A computerised listing is in progress and photocopying is available.

81 St Malachy's College

Address: 36 Antrim Road, Belfast BT15 2AE

Telephone: (01232) 748285

Enquiries: The Archivist, Dr Eamon Phoenix

Open: Term time, by appointment.

Access: Bona fide researchers.

Historical background: St Malachy's College was founded in 1833 as a Roman Catholic diocesan seminary. It is also the oldest Catholic grammar school in the north of Ireland. The archives were formally opened to researchers in 1987 and are housed in the associated library of Monsignor J. O'Laverty, PP (1828–1906), historian of the RC Diocese of Down and Connor, containing a unique collection of volumes on Irish history.

Acquisitions policy: Papers, photographs and

memorabilia relating to the college and its alumni are welcomed.

Archives of organisation: Archives of the college including lists of former students, *c*1856–1926, and account books, *c*1844–.

Major collections: Memoirs and diaries relating to the College and its alumni.
O'Laverty MSS: 16 Gaelic MSS.
Donellan MSS: two Gaelic MSS from the South Armagh/North Louth region, collected by Rev. L. Donnellan (*c*1900–1960), Co. Armagh.
Correspondence of Muiris ó Droiguneáin (Maurice Drinan), Gaelic scholar (1900–79), relating to Gaelic literature.

Non-manuscript material: Cuttings books of Laurence O'Neill, Lord Mayor of Dublin, *c*1918–24.
Photographs of students and college.

Finding aids: Catalogue.

Facilities: Photocopying.

Conservation: In-house.

Publications: C. O'Dochartaigh: 'Guide to O'Laverty Manuscripts', in *St Malachy's College Sesquiecentennial Record* (Belfast, 1983).

82 Ulster Museum

Address: Botanic Gardens, Belfast BT9 5AB

Telephone: (01232) 381251

Fax: (01232) 665510

Enquiries: The Librarian, Department of History

Open: Mon–Fri: 10.00–12.45; 2.00–5.00

Access: Bona fide enquirers, by appointment and by prior application in writing, by telephone or in person at the museum.

Historical background: The Ulster Museum has its roots in the Museum of the Belfast Natural History and Philosophical Society (f. 1831), and the Belfast Municipal Art Gallery and Museum (f. 1890), whose collections were amalgamated in 1910. In 1929 the Belfast Museum and Art Gallery was opened on the present site, and in 1962 it was transferred to a statutory board of trustees as the Ulster Museum.

Acquisitions policy: To build up comprehensive collections relating to the north of Ireland and, where appropriate, to Ireland as a whole, in the fields of antiquities, art, botany and zoology, geology, industrial archaeology, local history and numismatics.

Major collections: Antiquities Department: Aztec MS; four Tamil books.
Botany and Zoology Department: Templeton MSS: MSS of John Templeton (1766–1825), botanist, including his journal, 1806–25 (microfiche), Irish flora illustrated by himself, records of mosses and ferns and a list of Irish shells (*c*25 vols).
Hyndman MSS: numerous notes by George C. Hyndman (1796–1868), Belfast marine biologist and entomologist; also dredging papers, British Association Belfast Dredging Committee, 1844–57.
Thompson MSS: notes and correspondence of William Thompson (1805–52), Belfast naturalist and author of *Natural History of Ireland*.
Other small but important collections: notebooks of P.H. Grierson (1859–1952) on non-marine mollusca, and a checklist of Irish insects by Alexander Henry Haliday (1806–70).
Local History Department: Welch MSS: personal and excursion diaries, natural history notes, memoranda and lists of negatives of Robert J. Welch (1859–1936), photographer and amateur naturalist (*c*20 vols).
Barber MSS: MSS of Rev. Samuel Barber of Rathfriland, United Irishman.

Non-manuscript material: Local History Department: maps (*c*300); topographical drawings, paintings and prints (*c*1000); portraits (*c*250); posters, including playbills (*c*900); theatre programmes (*c*450); newspapers (*c*400); greetings cards (*c*2500).
Belfast and other locally printed books, pamphlets, chapbooks and broadsides (*c*500 items).
Welch Collection: glass plate negatives by R.J. Welch of Irish subjects (*c*600).
Hogg Collection: glass plate negatives (*c*550), lantern slides (*c*1500) and original prints by Alexander R. Hogg (1870–1939), of Irish (chiefly Belfast and Ulster) subjects, *c*1900–40.
Historical and Topographical Collection negatives (*c*3000); a few small and medium-sized collections, *c*1890–*c*1965 (*c*4000 items). Slides made in the field and from specimens.
Departments other than Local History keep their own specialised collections of negatives and slides.
Antiquities Department: Victorian sketch books of monuments and antiquities; watercolours of Indian temples and South African costume.

Art Department: topographical and portrait specimens (c2000).

Botany and Zoology Department: drawings and watercolours, including watercolours of shells and butterflies by Robert Templeton (1802–92) (c1000).

Geology Department: British Association for the Advancement of Science: Irish Collection photographs (c800 items).

Finding aids: Art and local history pictorial collections: computerised topographical index. Hogg Collection: classified card catalogue with subject index. Thompson MSS being catalogued.

Facilities: Photocopying. Photography. Microfiche reader.

Publications: A.W. Stelfox: 'John Templeton's Notes on Irish Land and Freshwater Mollusca', *The Irish Naturalist,* xxiii (1914), 29.
N. Fisher: 'George Crawford Hyndman's MSS', *Journal of Conchology,* xix (1931), 164.
E.E. Evans and B.S. Turner: *Ireland's Eye: the Photography of Robert John Welch* (Belfast, 1977).
A List of the Photographs in the R.J. Welch Collection in the Ulster Museum, 1: *Topography and History* (Belfast, 1979); 2: *Botany, Geology and Zoology* (Belfast, 1983).
R. Nash and H.C.G. Ross: *Dr Robert Templeton (1802–1892), Naturalist and Artist* (Belfast, 1980).
Concise Catalogue of the Drawings, Paintings and Sculptures in the Ulster Museum (Belfast, 1986).
W.A. Maquire *Caught in Time: the Photographs of Alexander Hogg of Belfast, 1870–1939* (Belfast, 1986).

83 Ruskin Galleries

Parent organisation: Education Trust

Address: Bembridge School, Isle of Wight PO35 5PH

Telephone: (01983) 872101

Fax: (01983) 872576

Enquiries: The Curator, J.S. Dearden

Open: By arrangement.

Access: Bona fide scholars, having already applied for permission to use material, by appointment.

Historical background: The collection was begun by J. Howard Whitehouse in the 1890s and brought to Bembridge with him in 1919, when he founded Bembridge School. It became part of the Education Trust property when the trust was established in 1921. The galleries at Bembridge were built by Whitehouse to house the collection in 1929. In 1932 he bought Brantwood at Coniston and opened it to the public as an international memorial to John Ruskin (1819–1900). Part of the collection was placed there but the bulk of the books and manuscripts remain at Bembridge. However, it is possible that these will be moved to Lancaster University.

Acquisitions policy: To acquire, by donation or purchase, material by or relating to Ruskin and his immediate circle.

Major collections: John Ruskin: correspondence with his parents and friends (c1000 items); letters to his cousin, 1864–95 (2500 items); diaries 1835–89 (26 vols); literary manuscripts and notebooks.

Non-manuscript material: Sketches and drawings by Ruskin (c1000) and by artists associated with him (c600). His collection of daguerreotypes; also large collection of photographs relating to him and of his works. Ruskin's Library (500 vols) and an extensive collection of books by and about him.

Finding aids: MS catalogue in the process of being computerised. See also NRA 11475.

Facilities: Photocopying.

84 Berwick upon Tweed Record Office

Parent organisation: Northumberland Archives Service

Address: Berwick upon Tweed Borough Council Offices, Wallace Green, Berwick upon Tweed, Northumberland TD15 1ED

Telephone: (01289) 330044 ext. 230

Fax: (01289) 330540

Enquiries: The Borough Archivist/Heritage Centre Officer

Open: Wed, Thurs: 9.30–1.00; 2.00–5.00

Access: Generally open to the public. Advance notice required for use of microfilm.

Historical background: A branch repository of the Northumberland Record Office (entry **838**) was opened in 1980 to provide access to the archives of the ancient borough of Berwick upon Tweed. Purpose-converted premises on the same site were opened in 1990 and the office now provides a comprehensive service for North Northumberland.

Archives of organisation: Usual local authority record holdings, including Berwick borough archives: Guild minute books, 1505–1837; borough accounts, 1603–1841; Freeman's records, 16th–20th centuries; Tweedmouth and Spittal manorial records, 1658–1926; borough court records, 17th–19th centuries; Quarter Sessions records, 1694–1951.

Major collections: Deposited local collections, including business records of Berwick Salmon Fisheries Company, 18th–20th centuries.
Family and estate records of Ford and Etal, Haggerston and Blake.
Non-conformist church records.

Facilities: Photocopying by arrangement. Microfilm/fiche readers.

Finding aids: Lists of collections.

85 Beverley Library
Local History Library

Parent organisation: Humberside County Council Leisure Services

Address: Champney Road, Beverley, North Humberside, HU17 9BQ

Telephone: (01482) 867108

Fax: (01482) 881861

Enquiries: The Team Leader, Reference and Information

Open: Mon, Wed: 9.30–5.00 Tues, Thurs, Fri: 9.30–7.00 Sat: 9.00–12.00; 1.00–4.00
Closed Tuesday after spring and August bank holidays.

Access: Generally open to the public; material available for consultation on request; an appointment is necessary for census microfilms and IGI fiche.

Historical background: Beverley Borough Library Local History Department was started in 1906, collecting standard material on all the Yorkshire Ridings, to which was added the former East Riding County Library Yorkshire collection. The library was taken over by Humberside Leisure Services in 1974.

Acquisitions policy: Purchase, donation and deposit of all types of material. All subject areas covered, more particularly in relation to Beverley, the East Riding of Yorkshire and Humberside, but also including other regions of Yorkshire.

Major collections: J.E. Champney Collection of Yorkshire material, donated in 1929.
A small collection of scrapbooks compiled by Gillyatt Sumner containing original MSS and copies of documents, chiefly on history of Beverley and immediate area, c1800–1850.
Small set of MS poll-books for Beverley parliamentary elections, c1800–1820.

Non-manuscript material: Census microfilms, East Riding, 1841–91 (includes some Hull reels, 1841–81, and complete 1891).
Newspaper microfilms.
Large collection of ephemera on Beverley parliamentary elections, c1790–1868; also some for East Riding county elections.
Substantial collection of Beverley playbills, 1817–21.

Facilities: Photocopying. Microfilm/fiche reader/printers.

86 Humberside County Archive Office

Parent organisation: Humberside County Council

Address: County Hall, Beverley, North Humberside HU17 9BA

Telephone: (01482) 885007

Fax: (01482) 885063

Enquiries: The County Archivist, Mr K.D. Holt

Open: Mon, Wed, Thurs: 9.00–4.45 Tues: 9.00–8.00 Fri: 9.00–4.00
Closed Tuesday after spring and August bank holidays.

Access: Generally open to the public, by appointment.

Historical background: The office was founded as the East Riding County Record Office in 1953. Following reorganisation in 1974 it became Humberside County Record Office, holding the same material with the exception of some private deposits placed in University of Hull Library (entry **403**) and one in the North Yorkshire Record Office (entry **846**). The office acts as the Diocesan Archive Office for York (parish records of the Archdeaconry of the East Riding) and is recognised as a place of deposit for manorial, tithe and public records.

Acquisitions policy: All records relating to the area of the present county. This headquarters office at Beverley covers North Humberside and Boothferry Borough Council area (formerly West Riding and Isle of Axholme in Lincolnshire). The Grimsby office (entry **364**) covers South Humberside east of the Trent.

Archives of organisation: Humberside County Council archives, 1974–, and those of all predecessor function authorities, including East Riding Quarter Sessions, 1706–.
Records of local authorities within the county area except the City of Hull, including Beverley Corporation, 12th–20th centuries; Hedon Corporation, 14th–20th centuries.
Urban and Rural District Council records, 1894–.
East Riding Register of Deeds, 1708–1976.

Major collections: Family and estate collections, including:
Beaumont family of Beverley and South Cave, 15th–19th centuries; Bethell family of Rise, 12th–20th centuries; Chichester-Constable family of Burton Constable, 12th–20th centuries; Grimston family of Kilnwick and Grimston Garth, 14th–20th centuries, including naval papers of Vice Admiral Henry Medley (*d* 1747); Harrison Broadley family of Hull and Welton, 16th–20th centuries; Hildyard family of Winestead, 14th–20th centuries; Howard Vyse family of Langton, 13th–19th centuries; Howden Manor estates (Bishopric of Durham), 15th–20th centuries; Kilnwick Percy estates, 16th–19th centuries; Londesborough settled estates, 16th–20th centuries; Osbaldeston and Mitford families of Hunmanby, 13th–20th centuries; Saltmarshe family of Saltmarshe, 16th–20th centuries; Scholfield family of Sand Hall, 16th–20th century; Sotheran Estcourt family, 15th–20th centuries.
Solicitors records of Clark & Co., Snaith, 14th–20th centuries; MacTurk & Co., South Cave, 16th–20th centuries; Powell and Young, Pocklington, 15th–20th centuries; Taylor Bromer & Co., Howden, 17th–20th centuries.

Ecclesiastical records: Anglican, Methodist, Baptist, non-conformist and Society of Friends records.
Public records, including shipping registers, Bridlington, 1786–1847, Goole, 1828–94.
Coroners' records, Hull, 1853–.
East Riding and Scunthorpe AHAs, including Goole and Rawcliffe hospitals, 19th–20th centuries.

Non-manuscript material: Microfilms of non-parochial and Friends registers for the area.

Finding aids: Catalogues, indexes and lists. Lists sent to NRA.

Facilities: Photocopying. Photography. Microfilming. Microfilm/fiche readers.

Conservation: Full conservation facilities within the County Archive Service; the conservation unit for both offices is in the area office at Grimsby. Outside work not generally undertaken.

Publications: Guide to South Humberside Area Archives Office (1993).
Other handlists and guides for sale: list of publications available.

87 Bexley Libraries and Museums Department
Local Studies Centre

Address: Hall Place, Bourne Road, Bexley, Kent DA5 1PQ

Telephone: (01322) 526574

Fax: (01322) 522921

Enquiries: The Local Studies Officer/Archivist, Mr M.D. Barr-Hamilton

Open: Mon–Sat: 9.00–5.00 Winter: 9.00–dusk

Access: Generally open to the public

Historical background: The centre was established in 1972 to preserve the records of former local and semi-official authorities in the area and to collect documentary material relevant to local studies. It combines a local studies library and archive repository, and acts as a Diocesan Record Office for Rochester (Deaneries of Erith and Sidcup).

Acquisitions policy: To increase holdings of material of local relevance.

Major collections: Usual local authority record holdings and deposited collections, including archives of Belvedere, Danson, Footscray Place and Hall Place estates.

Non-manuscript material: OS maps. Large collection of local photographs and prints.

Finding aids: Catalogues and indexes; lists sent to NRA.

Facilities: Photocopying. Microfilm/fiche reader/printers.

Conservation: Contracted out.

Publications: Guide to family history resources and large range of local history publications.

88 Allan Ramsay Library
Leadhills Miners' Library

Address: Main Street, Leadhills, Biggar, Strathclyde ML12 6XP

Telephone: (01659) 74216

Fax: (01659) 74459

Enquiries: The Secretary, the Library Committee

Open: Easter–Oct: Sat, Sun: 2.30–4.00
Other times by appointment.

Access: Generally open to the public. The library is run by a committee of voluntary workers; there is a yearly subscription and donations are welcomed.

Historical background: The Leadhills Miners' Reading Society was founded in 1741 and is the oldest subscription library in the British Isles. Allan Ramsay, poet, was born in Leadhills in 1686, and the library commemorates his name. Members included a number of celebrated men, notably William Symington (1763–1831), mining engineer; Dr John Brown (1786–1854), Edinburgh author; and Dr James Braid (?1795–1860), surgeon. The lead mines in the village closed in the 1930s and the membership of the Reading Society declined. In 1940 the Lanarkshire County Council took over the building, but by 1965 the local authority withdrew financial support. In 1969, with the help of grants, the restoration of the building was started and the library reopened in 1972. The library also has a small exhibition of relics.

Acquisitions policy: The library does not pur-

chase, but from time to time receives gifts of books, photographs etc.

Archives of organisation: Library records, including MS 'Members' Roll', 1741–1903; minute books, 1821–; ledgers of book loans, 1903–.

Major collections: Mining records, 1738– (Leadhills).
Minute books of the local Curling Club, early 19th century.

Non-manuscript material: Photographs. Maps of mining grounds.

Finding aids: NRA 16021.

Facilities: Photography permitted on written application to the committee.

Publications: Information leaflets on the library are available.

89 Moat Park Heritage Centre

Parent Organisation: Biggar Museum Trust

Address: Moat Park, Biggar, Strathclyde ML12 6DT

Telephone: (01899) 21050

Enquiries: The Director, Brian Lambie

Open: Easter–Oct: Mon–Sat: 10.00–5.00 Sun: 2.00–5.00 Nov–Easter: Mon–Fri: 9.30–5.00; Sat and Sun by appointment

Access: Generally open to the public. A charge is made for genealogical research.

Historical background: Previously known as the Albion Archive after one of its main holdings, the records of Albion Motors Ltd. The trust's holdings have expanded in recent years.

Acquisitions policy: Local history material from the Upper Clyde and Tweed valleys; maintaining the Albion material.

Major collections: Albion Motor Car Co., subsequently Albion Motors Ltd (later part of British Leyland Motor Corporation): minute books, documents, photographs, job sheets (164,000) and other memorabilia, 1899–1972.
Miscellaneous day books and ledgers of local businesses, 1797–.
School exercise books, 1807–47, and later.
Young family papers (farming), c1800–60.
Biggar Gaslight Co., miscellaneous papers.
Biggar Horticultural Society, 1861–.
Curling Club minutes, 1887–1901.

Architects' plans of local farms and houses, 1838– (mostly 1898–1910).

Rental books/farm accounts books, 18th and 19th centuries.

Non-manuscript material: Photographs and slide collection covering Scotland and Europe, including that of Rev. G. Allan (23,000 negatives and 8000 transparencies), *c*1935–*c*1970. Transcripts of local MSS in museum.

Finding aids: NRA 13035; NRA(S) 0419.

Facilities: Microfilm/fiche readers.

Conservation: Contracted out.

90 Wanlockhead Miners' Library

Parent organisation: Wanlockhead Museum Trust

Address: Goldscaur Row, Wanlockhead, By Biggar, Strathclyde ML12 6UJ

Telephone: (01659) 74387

Enquiries: The Curator, Ms J. Orr

Open: By arrangement.

Access: Bona fide researchers, by appointment only.

Historical background: A library founded in 1756 by the Miners' Reading Society was taken over by Wanlockhead Museum Trust in 1974 with the intention of preserving the collection and developing an archive of Scottish lead-mining.

Acquisitions policy: The archive is being enlarged, mainly by copies of historical documents and results of mine surveying and industrial archaeology.

Archives of organisation: Records of the library and museum trust.

Major collections: Records of economic and social aspects of the lead-mining industry in Wanlockhead, Leadhills and Strontian.
Records of village institutions, including Curling Society, village band and village council.

Non-manuscript material: Maps and photographs.

Finding aids: Catalogue and list.

Facilities: Photocopying.

91 Wirral Archives

Address: Information Services, Birkenhead Central Library, Borough Road, Birkenhead, Merseyside L41 2XB

Telephone: (0151) 652 6106/7/8

Fax: (0151) 653 7320

Enquiries: The Archivist, Mr D.N. Thompson

Open: Mon, Tues, Thurs: 10.00–8.00 Fri: 10.00–5.00 Sat: 10.00–1.00; 2.00–5.00

Access: Generally open to the public; appointment advisable.

Historical background: The archives department was established at the time of local government reorganisation in 1974 to administer the records inherited by the Wirral Metropolitan Borough Council. The service is, however, based at a reference library which has been collecting material of local interest (including manuscripts, 1856–), and which had gradually been given custody of the former Birkenhead Borough Council's archives in the 1960s. The library is recognised as a place of deposit for public records. A new record office and local history museum is being developed at Birkenhead Town Hall.

Acquisitions policy: To collect, by means of deposit, gift or purchase, records of all kinds relating to the locality.

Archives of organisation: Usual local authority record holdings, late 18th century–, including material relating to Birkenhead Park (designed in 1843–7 by Sir Joseph Paxton and the first municipal park to be laid out at public expense) and to the Birkenhead Street Railway (the first street tramway in Britain, 1860).

Major collections: Many deposited business and private records, including the following which have wider significance: archives of Unichema Chemicals Ltd, formerly the Bromborough (Wirral) branch of the Price's Patent Candle Co. Ltd; this includes material relating to Price's Village, a model village built for the company's workforce at Bromborough Pool in 1853.
Archives, including plans, of Cammell Laird Shipbuilders Ltd of Birkenhead, a major contractor to the Royal Navy, *c*1810–1993.
Archives of local hospitals, including administrative and clinical records, mid-19th century–.
Some antiquarian collections, including that of

John Stafford, a mid-18th century Macclesfield attorney, which relates to Macclesfield Borough and School and to villages throughout Cheshire, 15th–18th centuries.

Finding aids: Handlists and catalogues; sent to NRA.

Facilities: Photocopying. Photography. Microfilm reader/printer.

Publications: Copies of lists available on request.

92 Birmingham and Midland Institute

Address: 9 Margaret Street, Birmingham B3 3BS

Telephone: (0121) 236 3591

Enquiries: The Administrator, Joe Hunt

Open: Mon–Fri: 9.30–6.30

Access: Bona fide students; an appointment is necessary.

The Priestley Library was founded in 1779 and amalgamated in 1965 with the Birmingham and Midland Institute, which had been established in 1854. Records of the institute including minutes, are maintained from its foundation. See J. Hunt's *History of Birmingham and Midland Institute* (1954). Library holdings relate to the Midland Counties (literary, topographical and biographical).

93 Birmingham Central Library

Address: Chamberlain Square, Birmingham B3 3HQ

Telephone: (0121) 235 3586

Fax: (0121) 233 4458

Enquiries: The Head of Service (Social Sciences), Mr. S. Wood or The Head of Music Services, Mr M. Jones or The Head of Service (Local Studies and History), Mr P. Drake

Open: Mon–Fri: 9.00–8.00 Sat: 9.00–5.00

Access: Generally open to the public. Unrestricted, except where controlled by specific agreement with the record owner.

Historical background: The library first opened in 1866 but was completely destroyed by fire in 1879. Reopening later that year, it moved into new premises which it occupied until 1973, when it moved into its present building. It is particularly noted for its unique Shakespeare Library (perhaps second only in the world to the Folger Library) and for a number of special collections of printed books.

Acquisitions policy: Generally, archive materials are collected by the Birmingham City Archives (entry **94**), but the Social Sciences Service Area continues to acquire significant archives relating to political, labour and trade-union movements in Birmingham and, where appropriate, wider afield. It is also the official repository for records from the Co-operative Union.

Major collections: Social Sciences: trade and statistical returns from Co-operative Union member societies; Co-operative Wholesale Society Wage Negotiations Archive; archives of the Birmingham Labour Party, the Birmingham Conservative Party and various local branch records of trade unions; records of the Birmingham Co-operative Movement and the Workers Educational Association; minutes and records of the General Strike in Birmingham; archives of individual Labour activists.
Music: British Organ Archive: accounts, drawings and correspondence of British organ-building firms, 19th–20th centuries, collected by the British Institute of Organ Studies, and formerly deposited at Keele University Library (entry **419**)

Non-manuscript material: Local Studies and History Area: photographic archives, including Francis Frith archive, 1860s-1960s; Sir Benjamin Stone Collection; Warwickshire Photographic Survey; Dyche Collection, 20th century.
Collection of newspapers, pamphlets, seals and maps.

Finding aids: Handlists, copies sent to NRA; index to Local Studies Collection; partial index to photographic collection.

Facilities: Photocopying. Photography. Microfilm/fiche readers.

Conservation: Conservation workshop with two staff on site. Some additional routine work contracted out to commercial binders.

Publications: Birmingham Public Libraries: *Catalogue of the Birmingham Collection* (1918; suppl. 1931).

M. Large: 'Sources of Labour History: Primary Material in the Social Sciences Department of Birmingham Library', in A. Wright and R. Shackleton: *Worlds of Labour: Essays in Birmingham Labour History* (Birmingham, 1983).

94 Birmingham City Archives

Address: Central Library, Chamberlain Square, Birmingham B3 3HQ

Telephone: (0121) 235 4217

Fax: (0121) 233 4458

Enquiries: The City Archivist, Mr N.W. Kingsley

Open: Mon, Tues, Thurs, Fri, Sat: 9.00–5.00

Access: Generally open to the public. Records are closed for 50 years, except where legislation or agreements with owners provide otherwise.

Historical background: The City Archives originated as the manuscript collections of Birmingham Central Library (entry 93). They were separately administered from 1932 to 1968 and then reintegrated with the library collections until 1984, since when they have again been independent. The title 'Birmingham City Archives' was adopted in 1994. It acts as the Diocesan Record Office for Birmingham (parish records) and is recognised as a place of deposit for public records.

Acquisitions policy: To collect and preserve archival material relating to the City of Birmingham, its people, businesses and institutions. Records of some regional and national organisations based in the city are also held. The collections include deeds, estate and family papers relating to the surrounding area acquired before the present network of county record offices was established. Among the places within the present collecting area are the ancient parishes of Birmingham: Aston, Edgbaston, Frankley, Handsworth, Harborne, Kings Norton, Northfield, Sheldon, Sutton Coldfield and Yardley.

Archives of organisation: Official records, including West Midlands County Council, 1974–86; Birmingham City Council archives, 1736–; quarter sessions records, 1839–; Magistrates' Court records, 1860–; coroners' records, 1875–; school records, 1722–; and hospital records, 1756–.

Major collections: Anglican diocesan and parish records for the diocese of Birmingham and parish records for the part of the diocese within the city boundary, 16th–20th centuries; nonconformist church records, 18th–20th centuries.

Business archives include the records of Boulton & Watt, steam engine manufacturers, with the personal, scientific and business correspondence of James Watt and Matthew Boulton; John Hardman & Co., stained glass and metalwork manufacturers, 1839–1970; Boulton & Fothergill, metalwork and silver manufacturers; Soho Mint Ltd, 18th–19th centuries; Metropolitan Cammell Ltd, railway/rolling stock manufacturers, 1860–1940; BSA Ltd, motorbike and gun manufacturers, 1880–1960; IMI plc, ammunition and metalwork manufacturers, 1860–1940; Albright & Wilson, phosphorus manufacturers, 1840–1940; Birmingham Battery & Metal Co., 1836–1991.

Records of authorities and associations include those of West Midlands Regional Health Authority, 1948–; National Association of Health Authorities; British Jewellery & Giftware Federation and its predecessors, 1850–; Birmingham Botanical Gardens, 1820–; Birmingham Royal Institution for the Blind, 1848–; Middlemore Homes, 1870–; Birmingham Triennial Music Festival, c1806–1912.

Family and estate papers include those of Quakers such as the Albright, Cadbury, Hutton and Russell families, as well as records of the Calthorpe, Colmore, Gooch, Holte, Ryland and Taylor estates, which substantially controlled the development of the city, and records of the Hagley Hall, Hams Hall, Westwood Park, Coleshill Park and Elford Hall estates outside the city.

Finding aids: Catalogues are available for about 60% of the collections. Indexes by personal name, place, name and subject. Special indexes for apprenticeships and maps.

Publications: Birmingham Public Libraries: *Catalogue of the Birmingham Collection* (1918; suppl., 1931).

A. Andrews: 'The Birmingham Reference Library', *Archives*, v (1951).

U. Rayska: 'The Archives Section of Birmingham Reference Library', *Archives*, liv (1978).

N.W. Kingsley: *Guide to the Birmingham City Archives* (in preparation).

95 Birmingham Oratory

Address: 141 Hagley Road, Edgbaston, Birmingham B16 8UE

Telephone: (0121) 454 0496

Enquiries: The Librarian and Archivist, Mr Gerard Tracey

Open: Mon–Fri, by arrangement only.

Access: Bona fide researchers or enquirers who have previously contacted the archivist. Records relating to domestic affairs of the oratory may be closed.

Historical background: The oratory was founded in 1847 by John Henry Newman (1801–90), who subsequently founded the Brompton Oratory (entry 505). He left his extensive collection of papers to the oratory, and soon after his death it began to collect together the letters that he had sent out. In the past there has not been a clear distinction made between archives of the oratory and collections of papers given by those connected with it.

Acquisitions policy: Letters by Newman and complementary material is acquired.

Archives of organisation: Records of projects and foundations connected with the oratory, e.g. Catholic University of Ireland, Oratory Public School and other minor educational foundations. Records relating to domestic affairs of the oratory.

Major collections: Documents relating to Newman (*c*120,000): personal papers, theological memoranda, administrative notes, correspondence, 1808–90 (420 files divided into four main subject divisions), also authenticated copies of his letters. These include correspondence of his companions, e.g. Edward Caswall (1814–78), hymn-writer, Ignatius Ryder and Ambrose St John, and those connected with him, e.g. Thomas Mosley and William Palmer (1811–79). A large collection of papers about Newman, assembled since his death.
Papers of members of the oratory, including literary MSS.

Finding aids: Newman letters, indexed by date and correspondents. Description of collection and catalogue of other materials (by type): NRA 27809.

Facilities: Photocopying. Photography.

96 Birmingham RC Diocesan Archives

Address: Cathedral House, St Chad's Queensway, Birmingham B4 6EU

Telephone: (0121) 236 2251

Enquiries: The Archivist, Rev. P. Howell, St Patrick's, 106 Dudley Road, Birmingham B18 7QN

Access: Bona fide scholars, on written application.

Historical background: The records of the Vicars Apostolic of the Midland district are one of the best sources for the history of the Roman Catholic body in England in the 18th century. In 1685, at the request of James II, episcopal government was re-established by the Vicars Apostolic, whose aim throughout the 18th century was to ensure the subordination of the regular clergy to episcopal authority. With the exception of the Bishop of the Western Vicariate they were chosen from the secular clergy and were delegates of the Pope, depending on Rome for facilities to govern their districts. There are some gaps in the archive, notably documents lost in the early 19th century when Bishop Milner, 1806–26, moved to Wolverhampton, and when Dr Kirk abstracted papers for his Church History. Many of the records were received from Oscott College (entry 1044).

Archives of organisation: Records of the Vicars Apostolic of the Midland district, 1700–1850, and of the Bishops of Birmingham, 1850–1900, including correspondence with agents of the Vicars Apostolic in Rome, late 18th–early 19th centuries.
Records of the daily administration of the diocese and parish, 1830–99.
Deeds of the Manor of Erdington, and of the Coyney family properties in north Staffordshire, 13th–17th centuries.
Archives, including annals, ledgers, correspondence and memoirs, of Sedgley Park School, 1763–, and St Wilfrid's College, Cotton, 1873–.

Finding aids: See NRA 8129, 9287, 9289–9.

97 British Association of Social Workers

Address: 16 Kent Street, Birmingham B5 6RD

Telephone: (0121) 622 3911

Fax: (0121) 622 4860

Enquiries: The Hon. Archivist, Prof. Arthur Collis

Open: Mon–Fri: 9.30–4.45
Closed for August, and the last two weeks of December.

Access: Approved research workers and other readers, on written application and by prior appointment only. Restrictions on student training records.

Historical background: The British Association of Social Workers was founded in 1970 when seven former specialist associations came together to form a unified body of professional social workers. The records of the predecessor organisations were lodged with BASW. It has has been agreed that the archive will be transferred to the Modern Records Centre, University of Warwick (entry 229).

Acquisitions policy: To maintain BASW archives and acquire material on activities of professional organisations of social workers.

Archives of organisation: Documents, including membership registers, relating to the formation and activities of the Institute of Medical Social Workers (formerly Almoners), 1890–1970; Association of Psychiatric Social Workers, 1929–70; Association of Child Care Officers, 1950–70; Moral Welfare Workers Association, 1938–70; Association of Family Caseworkers, 1940–70; Society of Mental Welfare Officers, 1963–70; Association of Social Workers (formerly British Federation of Social Workers), 1934–70.
Records of the Standing Conference of Organisations of Social Workers, predecessor of BASW, 1953–70.
Records of the Association of Children's Officers, 1949–71.

Non-manuscript material: Journals and other publications of the organisations.

Finding aids: Detailed list and index for each organisation.

Facilities: Photocopying.

Publications: R.W. Stacey and A.T. Collis: *Catalogue and Guide to the Archives of the Predecessor Organisations, 1890–1970* (BASW, 1988).
Supplementary catalogues are in progress.

98 King Edward VI Schools in Birmingham

Address: Foundation Office, School of King Edward VI in Birmingham, Edgbaston Park Road, Birmingham B15 2UD

Telephone: (0121) 472 1147 ext. 220

Fax: (0121) 472 0221

Enquiries: The Resources Archivist, Kerry York

Open: Mon–Wed: 9.15–5.00 Thurs: 9.00–5.00 Fri: 9.00–4.30

Access: Generally open to the public; an appointment is advisable.

Historical background: King Edward's School was founded in 1552. More schools were established in the 18th and 19th centuries. Today seven schools exist under one administrative umbrella. The Foundation Archive was established in 1980. See also King Edward VI College (entry 1038).

Acquisitions policy: No formal acquisition policy; records accepted from former pupils, teachers and governors if relevant to schools.

Archives of organisation: Records of governing body and individual schools, 1552–.

Major collections: Few surviving records of the Guild of the Holy Cross in Birmingham, 14th century.

Non-manuscript material: School lists and magazines.
Collection of architectural plans by Sir Charles Barry.
Maps and photographs.

Finding aids: MS list at Foundation Office; no external copy.

Facilities: Photocopying at the discretion of the librarian.

Publications: *Dugdale Society*, iv (ed. W.F. Carter); vii (ed. W.F. Carter and E.A.B. Barnard); xx (ed. P.B. Chatwin); xxv (ed. P.B. Chatwin); xxx (ed. J. Izon).

99 St Paul's Convent Archive

Parent organisation: Sisters of St Paul Apostle

Address: St Paul's Convent, Selly Park, Birmingham B29 7LL

Telephone: (0121) 472 0045

Fax: (0121) 414 1063

Enquiries: The Archivist, Sr Phyllis Brady

Open: By prior arrangement.

Access: Bona fide researchers, with a suitable recommendation.

Historical background: The congregation was established in 1847. It now runs St Paul's College of Education and other schools.

Acquisitions policy: To maintain and consolidate the archives.

Archives of organisation: Correspondence relating to the foundation and life of the congregation, 1847–.
Data concerning apostolates' property, 1847–.
Administrative records of the congregation, including constitutions, acts of chapters, council meetings, registers of members, legal documents, baptismal, birth and death certificates, wills, contracts, journals, diaries, annals, circular letters.
Correspondence with Rome, Bishops and other ecclesiastics.
St Paul's College of Education archive and administrative records of other second-level schools owned by the congregation.

Non-manuscript material: Photographs, slides, tapes, videos and artefacts relating to the history and work of the convent. Theses.

Finding aids: Listing in progress.

Facilities: Photocopying.

100 Selly Oak Colleges
Central Library

Address: Bristol Road, Selly Oak, Birmingham B29 6LQ

Telephone: (0121) 472 4231 ext. 153

Fax: (0121) 472 8852

Enquiries: The Librarian, Meline E. Nielsen

Open: Term: Mon–Fri: 9.00–5.30 Vacation:
Mon–Fri: 9.00–5.00
Closed between Christmas and the New Year.

Access: Generally open to the public; appointment necessary.

Historical background: Selly Oak Colleges are a loose confederation of 20th–century interdenominational training and mission colleges, the earliest of which was Woodbrooke College (entry 102).

Acquisitions policy: Archives of missionary and mission history relevance, appropriate to the main research interests of the library.

Major collections: Archives of the Student Christian Movement (including the Church Education Movement), 1890–; also records of the Indian Church Aid Association; Churches of Christ; Korea Mission; Institute of Rural Life, all 20th century.
Papers of individual missionaries, e.g. James Edward Lesslie Newbigin, David Paton, William Paton (1886–1943) and W.C. Willoughby.

Finding aids: Card index to SCM archives.

Facilities: Photocopying. Microfiche reader.

101 University of Birmingham Library

Address: Edgbaston, Birmingham B15 2TT

Telephone: (0121) 414 5838

Fax: (0121) 471 4691

Enquiries: The University Archivist, Miss Christine Penney

Open: Mon–Fri: 9.00–5.00 (5.15 in term)

Access: Bona fide researchers. All new users of MSS and archives should apply first by letter and must supply a formal letter of introduction from an appropriate person. Special collections are made available in the Heslop Room. For enquiries about the Church Missionary Society archive see entry 517.

Historical background: The library began as the library of Mason College in 1880; it is now in various buildings around the university site in Edgbaston. It is recognised as a place of deposit for public records.

Acquisitions policy: To build and strengthen existing collections and to collect in the fields where active academic research is taking place in the university, by purchase, deposit or donation.

Archives of organisation: Mason College and university archives, 1880–.

Major collections: Political archives (*c*200,000 items): papers of the Chamberlain family; Sir Anthony Eden (1897–1977), 1st Earl of Avon; William Harbutt Dawson; Nikolai Shishkin.
Literary papers of Harriet Martineau (1802–76); Francis Brett Young (1884–1954); Edward Arber (1836–1912); David Lodge (*b* 1935).
Papers of Count Vasilii Alexandrovich Pashkov.
Local archives: papers of Bishop E.W. Barnes; Eyton papers of Shropshire local history.
Large collection of music MSS and letters of Sir Granville Bantock (1868–1946); several smaller collections of local companies and personalities, including non-psychic papers of Sir Oliver Lodge (1851–1940).
Papers of Leonard Jay (1905–63), printer.
Other archives: Church Missionary Society records, 1799–; Church Pastoral Aid Society archives.
Letters of the Jerningham and Bedingfeld families in Norfolk, 1780–1843.
Papers of the Cadbury family relating to the cocoa trade in West Africa, 19th and 20th centuries.
British Cotton Growing Association Archive, 19th and 20th centuries.
Archives of St John's College, Nottingham, formerly London College of Divinity.
Archives of the Royal Institute of Public Administration (f. 1922).
Archives of the Association of Metropolitan Authorities.
Leslie Leatherhead Collection.

Non-manuscript material: Birmingham University theses (*c*15,000).
Alma Tadema collection of sketches and photographs (*c*30,000).

Finding aids: Typed handlists to the individual collections (sent to NRA).

Facilities: Very limited photocopying (at the discretion of the University Librarian). Microfilm reader.

Publications: D.W. Evans: *Catalogue of the Cadbury Papers* (1973).
B.S. Benedikz: *The Chamberlain Collection Introduction and Guide* (1978).
National Inventory of Documentary Sources, Chadwyck-Healey microfiche (1984–).
C.L. Penney: 'The Manuscript Collections of the University of Birmingham', *Archives*, XVII (1986).
B.S. Benedikz: 'The Political Archives of Birmingham University', *Diplomacy and Statecraft*, 2 (1991), 321–8.
R. Keen: 'The Church Missionary Society Archives', *Catholic Archives*, 12 (1992), 21–31.
C.L. Penney and E.W. Ives: 'The University of Birmingham and its Archives: Higher Education and Society, 1880–1980', *Archives*, xx (1992).
University of Birmingham: *Research Libraries Bulletin*, 1 (Winter 1994).

102 Woodbrooke College

Address: 1046 Bristol Road, Birmingham B29 6LJ

Telephone: (0121) 472 5171/2

Fax: (0121) 472 5173

Enquiries: The Librarian, Christina M. Lawson

Open: Mon–Fri: 10.00–4.00

Access: Generally open to the public; an appointment is advisable.

Historical background: The college, one of the Selly Oak Colleges (entry 100), was founded in 1903. It is a Quaker centre for religious, social, peace and international studies.

Acquisitions policy: Archives accepted of college connections only.

Archives of organisation: Archives of the college, including minutes of committees, students' lists, timetables and publicity, 1903–.

Major collections: Papers of James Rendel Harris (1852–1941), biblical scholar and director of Woodbrooke, 1903–18.

Non-manuscript material: Photograph collection.
Bevan-Naish collection of 17th-century pamphlets.
Mingana Collection of Syriac MSS (*c*60 boxes of microfilm; originals in Central Library, Selly Oak Colleges).

Finding aids: Lists.

Facilities: Photocopying. Microfilm/fiche reader.

Publications: R. Davis (ed.): *Woodbrooke, 1923–1953* (London, 1953).

R. Ralph Barlow: *Woodbrooke, 1953–1978: a Documentary Account*, ed. D.B. Gray (York, 1982).

103 Blackburn Central Library
Local Studies Department

Parent organisation: Lancashire County Council

Address: Town Hall Street, Blackburn, Lancs BB2 1AG

Telephone: (01254) 661221

Fax: (01254) 690539

Enquiries: The District Librarian, Mrs N.L. Monks

Open: Mon–Wed: 9.30–8.00 Thurs, Fri: 9.30–5.00 Sat: 9.30–4.00

Access: Generally open to the public; prior appointment desirable for some of the material, e.g. rate books.

Historical background: Blackburn Public Library was formed in 1860 and became part of the Lancashire Library in 1974. Some of the records of Blackburn County Borough were deposited after 1965.

Acquisitions policy: Donations of all types of material which relate to the area covered by the Borough of Blackburn are accepted.

Major collections: Usual local history collection for Blackburn District, including Weavers minute books, baptism registers and Lees Hall Collection of temperance material (c2000 items).

Non-manuscript material: Photograph collection (c6000 items).

Finding aids: Newspaper index, 1793–1829, 1837–85, 1887–8, 1891–6. Guide to map collection.

Facilities: Photocopying. Photography by arrangement. Microfilm reader/printer.

Conservation: Contracted out.

Publications: Guide to the Local Studies Collection (1968).
Section in *Local Studies in Lancashire*.

104 Blackburn College Library

Address: Feilden Street, Blackburn, Lancs BB2 1LH

Telephone: (01254) 292120

Fax: (01254) 682700

Enquiries: The Learning Resources Manager, Mr Jeff Cooper

Open: Term: Mon–Thurs: 8.45–8.00 Fri: 8.45–3.00

Access: Generally open to the public. A charge may be made.

The foundation stone of the College (of Technology and Design) was laid in 1888, although teaching did not begin until 1891. The library holds prospectuses, 1891–, student handbooks, plans and photographs, and Blackburn Central Library (entry 103) has some additional material. There are no deposited collections. For further details, see *Blackburn College: 100 years* (1988).

105 Blackburn Museum

Parent organisation: Borough of Blackburn

Address: Museum Street, Blackburn, Lancs BB1 7AJ

Telephone: (01254) 667130

Fax: (01254) 680870

Enquiries: The Curator

Open: Tues–Sat: 9.45–4.45

Access: Bona fide scholars.

Historical background: The Blackburn Museum was founded in 1862 and has been in its present premises since 1874. The museum maintains the collections of the East Lancashire Regimental Museum, founded in 1934, and Lewis Textile Museum, founded in 1938.

Acquisitions policy: Interests restricted to local history, regimental history and the textile trade.

Major collections: The Feilden Papers: documents relating to the Feilden properties in Blackburn, 16th–20th centuries.
The Regimental Museum collection includes records of the East Lancashire Regiment.

Non-manuscript material: Local history collection includes some films and cassette recordings

Textile history collection includes a number of 19th–century pattern books.

Finding aids: Handlists.

Facilities: Photocopying. Photography and microfilming by arrangement.

Publications: J. Horrocks: *My Dear Parents: an Englishman's Letters Home from the American Civil War* (London, 1982).
J. Aytoun: *Redcoats in the Caribbean* (Blackburn, 1984).

106 Blackpool District Central Reference Library

Address: Queen Street, Blackpool, Lancs FY1 1PX

Telephone: (01253) 23977

Fax: (01253) 751670

Enquiries: The District Librarian, Mr J.K. Burkitt or The Reference and Local Studies Librarian, Miss G.H. Marsland

Open: Mon, Tues, Thurs, Fri: 10.00–7.00 Wed: 10.00–5.00 Sat: 10.00–5.00

Access: Generally open to the public. Advisable to book in advance to use the microfilm and microfiche readers; advance arrangements sometimes necessary to use bound volumes of newspapers.

Historical background: The collection concentrates mostly on the town of Blackpool and its history. Material about neighbouring areas has been purchased only in recent years.

Acquisitions policy: Documents relating to Blackpool and it history are purchased. Relevant donations are willingly accepted.

Major collections: Local history collection principally of non-MS material.

Non-manuscript material: Local newspaper, 1873– (on microfilm).
Photographs and postcards relating to local subjects (c5000).

Finding aids: Computer printout of local collections for use in the library.

Facilities: Photocopying. Photography with permission only. Microfilm/fiche readers.

107 Royal Signals Museum

Parent organisation: Royal Signals Institution

Address: Blandford Camp, Blandford Forum, Dorset DT11 8RH

Telephone: (01285) 482413

Fax: (01258) 482603

Enquiries: The Deputy Director, Dr P.J. Thwaites

Open: Mon–Fri: 10.00–5.00

Access: Bona fide researchers; as space is limited an appointment is necessary.

Historical background: The library and archives were formed in 1967, when the Royal Signals Museum was opened at Blandford Camp. The collection covers the history of army communications from the Crimean War to the present time. It also covers the history of the Royal Engineer Telegraph Battalions, the Royal Engineer Signal Service and the Royal Corps of Signals, which was formed in 1920. Records of the Uxbridge and Middlesex Yeomanry Cavalry, previously held by the Middlesex Yeomanry and Signals Historical Trust, Harrow-on-the-Hill, have been transferred to the museum for safekeeping.

Acquisitions policy: To collect and preserve all relevant material relating to the history of military communications by all means, i.e. radio, line, despatch rider service, pigeons. Purchases of relevant material are made.

Major collections: Diaries, journals and letters of officers and soldiers who have served in the RE Telegraph Battalions, the Signal Service and the Royal Signals, 19th and 20th centuries.
Details of Royal Signals units, which include a number of historical records.
Uxbridge and Middlesex Yeomanry Cavalry (f. 1797 and 1830 respectively): archives, plus those of subsequent units and other yeomanry companies and signals regiments.

Non-manuscript material: Personal photographic collections donated by ex-members of the corps.
Technical manuals dealing with military radio and line equipment.

Finding aids: General index to all collections. Index to photographic collection.

Facilities: Photocopying and photography by prior appointment.

108 David Livingstone Centre

Parent organisation: The Scottish National Memorial to David Livingstone Trust

Address: 165 Station Road, Blantyre, Glasgow G72 9BT

Telephone: (01698) 823140

Enquiries: The Director, David O'Neill, The Education Officer, Sheila Watt

Open: April–Sept: Mon–Sat: 10.00–6.00 Sun: 1.00–6.00 Oct–March:Mon–Sat:10.00–5.00 Sun: 1.00–5.00

Access: Generally open to the public, by museum entry ticket. An appointment is necessary.

Historical background: The National Memorial to the David Livingstone Trust was established in 1926, with the building opening to the public in 1929. Its main function is the preservation of his birthplace but it is regarded as the main repository for Livingstonia.

Acquisitions policy: Livingstonia; social history relating to Blantyre Mills, where Livingstone worked as a boy; ethnography and natural history relating to areas in which he explored – southern and East Africa.

Archives of organisation: Records relating to the museum.

Major collections: Letters and journals belonging to David Livingstone (1813–73). Original letters, 1846–76, including notebooks, 1871–4.

Non-manuscript material: Photographs, original hand-drawn maps, books on Livingstone. Blantyre Mill Works Library. Paintings and prints by Haswell Millar (30).

Finding aids: Catalogue is available on request.

Facilities: Photocopying. Photography by arrangement.

109 Bolton Archive and Local Studies Service

Address: Central Library, Civic Centre, Le Mans Crescent, Bolton, Lancs BL1 1SE

Telephone: (01204) 22311 ext. 2179

Fax: (01204) 363224

Enquiries: The Archivist, Mr T.K. Campbell or The Local Studies Librarian, Mr B.D. Mills

Open: Tues, Thurs: 9.30–7.30 Wed: 9.30–1.00 Fri, Sat: 9.30–5.00

Access: Generally open to the public; prior notice appreciated, but not essential.

Historical background: The service was established in 1990 by the amalgamation of the Archive Service (f. 1974) and the Local Studies Section of the Central Reference Library (f. 1853). It is recognised as a place of deposit for public records.

Acquisitions policy: To collect and preserve archives, printed, audio-visual and other material relating to the area administered by Bolton Metropolitan Borough Council.

Archives of organisation: Records of Bolton MBC and eight predecessor local authorities, with inherited archives, including those of townships and civil parishes, 1640–; Improvement Trustees of Great Bolton and Little Bolton, 1792–1850; Turton and Entwistle Reservoir Commissioners, 1832–66; Irwell Valley Water Board, 1853–1963; and Bolton Poor Law Union, 1837–1929.

Major collections: Archives of non-conformist and Methodist Churches, 18th–20th centuries. Records of local estates, families and individuals, including Ainsworth of Smithills, Crompton of Hall i'th'Wood and Heywood of Bolton, 16th–20th centuries. Business records, including textiles; bleaching and finishing; coal-mining; papermaking; brewing and tanning, 17th–20th centuries. Records of societies, trade unions and employers' organisations, 19th–20th centuries. MSS maps and plans of estates, enclosure, turnpike roads, coal-mines and industrial premises, railways, canals, 1620–1950.

Non-manuscript material: Microfilm copies of local newspapers, 1823–; census returns, 1841–91; many local parish registers, 16th–20th centuries; local large scale OS maps, 1845–; photographs and illustrations; collection of oral history tapes and transcripts; biographical and topographical newspaper cuttings; handbills, playbills and ephemera.
Walt Whitman (1819–92) Collection of books, manuscripts and memorabilia.
Books, articles, pamphlets, dissertations relating to the Bolton area (c35,000).

Finding aids: Lists. Indexes of photographs, audio tapes, local newspapers, topographical

and biographical cuttings. Census street and name indexes, 1851.
Local studies catalogue of books, pamphlets and articles.

Facilities: Photocopying. Photography allowed, but no in-house facilities. Microfilm/fiche reader/printer.

Conservation: Work undertaken by Greater Manchester County Record Office (entry **794**).

Publications: Guide to Archive Service (1988). *Handlist of Registers* (1994).

110 Boston Borough Council

Address: Municipal Buildings, West Street, Boston, Lincs PE21 8QR

Telephone: (01205) 357400

Fax: (01205) 364604

Enquiries: The Director of Administration and Legal Services

Open: Mon–Fri: 9.30–12.30; 2.30–4.30

Access: By prior appointment.

The council buildings are recognised as a place of deposit for public records. Records are acquired relating to Boston Corporation as and when they become available; they comprise council and committee minutes, 1545–; and contracts, conveyances and deeds. Donations of other records are welcomed. There are catalogues and a printed index. NRA 11483.

111 The Tank Museum

Address: Bovington Camp, Dorset BH20 6JG

Telephone: (01929) 463953

Enquiries: The Curator, Mr John Woodward or The Librarian, Mr David Fletcher

Open: Mon–Fri: 10.00–1.00; 2.00–4.45

Access: Generally open to the public, by appointment.

Historical background: Founded after World War I as the Royal Tank Corps Museum, the current museum embraces all regiments of the Royal Armoured Corps. The museum exists as an independent registered charity as a corps and

a regimental museum. Exhibits and archives are the property of the trustees.

Acquisitions policy: To collect and preserve material connected with the history and development of mechanised armoured warfare on land, covering all nationalities but with particular emphasis on the UK.

Major collections: A comprehensive collection of handbooks and other documents associated with the development of armoured fighting vehicles, 1914–.
War diaries and histories of many British armoured regiments and the papers of numerous individuals associated with the development of tank warfare.

Non-manuscript material: Photographs, films, technical drawings and maps relating to armoured fighting vehicles and their use, 1914–.

Finding aids: Detailed card index system.

Facilities: Photocopying. Photography.

112 National Meteorological Library and Archive

Parent organisation: The Meteorological Office

Address: Library: London Road, Bracknell, Berks RG12 2SZ
Archive: The Scott Building, Sterling Centre, Eastern Road, Bracknell, Berks RG12 2PW

Telephone: (01344) 854843 (Library) 855960 (Archive)

Fax: (01344) 854849 (Library) 855961 (Archive)

Enquiries: The Library and Archive Services Manager

Open: Mon–Fri: 9.00–4.30; Archive closed for lunch 1.00–2.00

Access: Open to the public, preferably by appointment.

Historical background: The Meteorological Office originated as a department of the Board of Trade in 1855. It is now an agency within the Ministry of Defence. Under Public Records Acts the office is authorised to select technical meteorological records for retention and maintain recognised places of deposit for public records at Bracknell, Edinburgh (entry **292**) and Belfast (entry **72**). The office also holds archives of the Royal Meteorological Society, which was founded in 1850 as the British

Meteorological Society and succeeded the Meteorological Society of London (1823–41). In 1921 the RMS amalgamated with the Scottish Meteorological Society.

Acquisitions policy: Responsible for original meteorological and climatological records and reports from sources in England, Wales and various overseas stations. Donations are welcomed.

Archives of organisation: Published and unpublished reports and scientific papers of the Meteorological Office.
Released administrative records of the Meteorological Office are transferred to the Public Record Office (entry 960).

Major collections: Systematic collections since the formation of the Meteorological Office include: meteorological observation registers for England, Wales and overseas stations; weather charts from the Central Forecast Office; ships' weather logs; climatological returns; private weather diaries, mid-18th century–.
Royal Meteorological Society archives, c1791–, mainly 1850–, including papers of George Symons, founder of the British Rainfall Association, 1851.

Non-manuscript material: The National Meteorological Library includes rare books and a photographic collection.
Royal Meteorological Society: rare books and pamphlets.

Finding aids: Index cards and computer-based lists. NRA 9962/37105.

Facilities: Photocopying. Microfilming.

113 Bradford Cathedral
Archives and Library

Address: 1 Stott Hill, Bradford, West Yorks BD1 4EH

Telephone: (01274) 728955 (enquiries)

Enquiries: The Hon. Librarian,
Miss Connie Priestley, Church Bank, Bradford, West Yorks BD3 9AF or The Hon. Archivist, The Canon Precentor

Open: Mon–Fri: by arrangement.

Access: Bona fide researchers; prior appointment is in every case necessary.

Historical background: The Cathedral Church

of St Peter, Bradford, founded in 1919, is based on the Parish Church of St Peter, which had a muniments room from the 16th century. There are some more recent archival resources in the Cathedral Library, which was begun in 1979.

Acquisitions policy: Continued deposit of registers and records.

Archives of organisations: Baptisms, marriages and burial registers of the Parish Church of St Peter, Bradford, 1599–; vestry minutes, 1686–; churchwardens' accounts, 1667–. The registers and their indexes prior to 1837 are held on microfilm by the West Yorkshire Archive Service, Bradford district (entry 116) and the Library of the University of Bradford (entry 115).

Major collections: Records of Bradford charities and day and Sunday schools, 19th century.

Non-manuscript material: Parish church and cathedral magazines, 1897–; *The Bradford Antiquary*, 1888–.
Architects' plans for extension, 20th century.

Finding aids: NRA 17769. The baptisms and marriages registers are well indexed.

114 National Museum of Photography, Film & Television

Parent organisation: Science Museum, London

Address: Pictureville, Bradford, West Yorks BD1 1NQ

Telephone: (01274) 727488

Fax: (01274) 723155

Enquiries: The Duty Enquiry Officer

Open: Tues–Sun: 10.30–6.00, by arrangement.

Access: Generally open to the public, by appointment. Restrictions according to condition of material.

Historical background: The National Museum of Photography, Film and Television is a unique collaboration between the Bradford Metropolitan Council and the Science Museum. It was opened in 1983.

Acquisitions policy: The museum collects equipment, images and printed ephemera connected with photography, film and television.

Non-manuscript material: Permanent collection of photographs and equipment, 1840–.
Daily Herald newspaper photograph archive, 1914–1960s, but strongest section covers 1929–44.
The Kodak Museum Collection of equipment and images.
Other collections: Talbot, Focal Press, Kraszna Krausz, Frank, Zoltan Glass, Buckingham Movie Museum, Thames Television, Sony.
Photographs, equipment, posters, technical literature, TV Heaven (television programmes), commercials.

Finding aids: Subject index to *Daily Herald* archive. Other items are listed on the museum computer.

Facilities: Photocopying. Photography. Microfilm reader.
Conservation Contracted out.

115 University of Bradford

Address: J.B. Priestley Library, Bradford, West Yorks BD7 1DP

Telephone: (01274) 383400

Fax: (01274) 383398

Enquiries: The Librarian, Dr M.B. Stevenson

The university was founded in 1966 as a successor to Bradford Technical College and Bradford Institute of Technology. The library is responsible for all archives of the university itself and of its predecessors. There are also several significant deposited holdings of archival material relating to peace movements. Further details are not available.

116 West Yorkshire Archive Service
Bradford District Archives

Address: 15 Canal Road, Bradford, West Yorks BD1 4AT

Telephone: (01274) 731931

Fax: (01274) 734013

Enquiries: The District Archivist, Mr D. James or The Archivist to the Joint Committee, Mr R. Frost

Open: Mon–Wed: 9.30–1.00; 2.00–5.00 Thurs:

9.30–1.00; 2.00–8.00 Fri: 9.30–1.00
Closed one week in February for stock-taking.

Access: By appointment.

Historical background: An archive department was established in Bradford Central Library in 1974 by the Metropolitan District Council; in 1982 it joined the West Yorkshire Archive Service and in 1985 it moved from the library to separate premises. Bradford Library's manuscript collection initially formed the core of the department's holdings, now considerably increased from official and other sources. It also acts as the Diocesan Record Office for Bradford and is recognised as a place of deposit for public records.

Acquisitions policy: To acquire archive material relating to the history of the area covered by Bradford Metropolitan District.

Archives of organisation: Records of Bradford Metropolitan District Council and superseded authorities: Bradford County Borough, Keighley Municipal Borough; Urban District Councils of Baildon, Bingley, Denholme, Ilkley, Queensbury, Shipley and Silsden; townships and school boards.

Major collections: Deposited local collections include significant textile, iron and engineering archives, also those of textile trade unions, Independent Labour Party and Yorkshire Co-operatives Ltd.
Family and estate collections include those of Sir Francis Sharp Powell, MP, of Horton Hall (late 19th century), Ferrand of Bingley, Tempest of Tong and Spencer-Stanhope of Horsforth and Cawthorne.
Leeds and Liverpool Canal Company records.

Non-manuscript material: Yorkshire Television Video History Archive.

Finding aids: The majority of collections are catalogued and also accessible through item-level indexes. Links to West Yorkshire Archive Service computerised database and to NRA computer. Catalogues are sent to NRA.

Facilities: Photocopying. Microfiche reader/printer.

Publications: See entries for West Yorkshire Archive Service (**370, 448, 449, 1072**).

117 Brecknock Museum

Parent organisation: Powys County Council

Address: Captain's Walk, Brecon, Powys
LD3 7DW

Telephone: (01874) 624121

Enquiries: The Curator, David Moore

Open: Mon–Fri: 10.00–5.00 Sat: 10.00–1.00;
2.00–5.00 Sun (April–Sept): 10.00–1.00; 2.00–
5.00

Access: Bona fide researchers, by appointment.

Historical background: The museum was
founded in 1928 by the local historical society,
the Brecknock Society. The society handed the
museum and its collections to Breconshire
County Council in 1950, and since 1974 it has
been administered by the new county of Powys.
The archive was begun in 1928 and contains
research papers and other documents collected
by members of the Brecknock Society. Brecon
Assizes Quarter and Petty Sessions records are
now with Powys County Archives (entry **475**).

Acquisitions policy: All archives are now collected and acquired by Powys County
Archives.

Archives of organisation: Minute books and
other documents of the museum and Brecknock
Society, 1928–.

Major collections: Papers of Sir John Conway
Lloyd (1878–1954) and the Dinas Estate.
Papers relating to the enclosure of Breconshire
commons, c1800; railways, canals, turnpikes,
etc, 18th and 19th centuries.

Non-manuscript material: Photographs of Breconshire interest.

Finding aids: General index to all of the
collection. Schedules of major collections.

Facilities: Photocopying. Photography by
arrangement.

118 South Wales Borderers and Monmouthshire Regimental Museum of the Royal Regiment of Wales

Address: The Barracks, Brecon, Powys
LD3 7EB

Telephone: (01874) 623111

Fax: (01874) 613275

Enquiries: Lt.-Col. R.J. Ashwood

Open: 1 Oct–31 March: Mon–Fri: 9.00–1.00;
2.00–5.00 1 April–30 Sept: Mon–Sat: 9.00–1.00;
2.00–5.00

Access: Bona fide scholars, by prior permission
of the Curator.

Historical background: The regiment was
raised in 1689 and in 1969 amalgamated with the
Welch Regiment to become the Royal Regiment
of Wales. See also the Welch Regiment Museum
of the Royal Regiment of Wales (entry **197**). In
1934 the first display was opened in a room in
the Brecknock County Museum; later it moved
to the Keep in the Barracks, and in 1959 it
opened in its present location. The museum is
registered with the Museums and Galleries
Commission and is recognised as a place of
deposit for public records.

Acquisitions policy: Any items which in any
way relate to the history of any unit connected
to the South Wales Borderers, the Monmouthshire Regiments and the Royal Regiment of
Wales.

Archives of organisation: Records of South
Wales Borderers, 24th Foot, Monmouthshire
Regiment and the Royal Regiment of Wales,
1689–, including letters, pay books, citations,
battle reports and officers' records.

Major collections: Usual military museum collection, including war diaries and personal
papers.
MS diaries, letters, journals, scrapbooks.

Non-manuscript material: Photographs, medal
collection (2000), arms, uniforms and artefacts.

Finding aids: Computerised catalogue. Indexes.
NRA 20951.

Facilities: Photocopying. Photography.

119 The Leprosy Mission

Address: 80 Windmill Road, Brentford, Middx TW8 0QH

Telephone: (0181) 569 7292

Fax: (0181) 569 7808

Enquiries: The International General Director, Trevor Durston

Open: Mon–Fri: 9.30–4.00

Access: By written request, giving background for consultation; an appointment is necessary.

Historical background: The Leprosy Mission is a medical missionary society founded in 1874. The principal object of the organisation is 'to minister in the name of Jesus Christ to the physical, mental and spiritual needs of sufferers from leprosy, to assist in their rehabilitation and to work towards the eradication of leprosy'. The mission is currently negotiating a transfer of the archive to SOAS (entry 729).

Acquisitions policy: To maintain the archive of the society.

Archives of organisation: Minutes of council and various committees, 1878–1987.
Reports, 1894–.
Correspondence file series and papers received from more than 50 countries, c1905–c1988.
Personnel files.

Non-manuscript material: Large photographic and film collection; tape-recordings.
Library has various histories, pamphlets, journals and publications of the Mission.
Property plans.

Finding aids: Various interim lists and card index.

Facilities: Photocopying.

120 Brighton College

Address: Eastern Road, Brighton, East Sussex BN2 2AL

Telephone: (01273) 697131

Enquiries: The Archivist, Mr M.D.W. Jones

Open: Term only: Mon–Fri: 9.30–5.00

Access: Generally open to the public, on written application and by appointment only.

Historical background: Brighton College was founded in 1845 by William Aldwin Soames. It obtained charitable tax status for schools in the 1927 Finance Act. The college archives were established in 1950 by the late G.P. Burstow.

Acquisitions policy: Anything to do with the history of the school and its former pupils.

Archives of organisation: Corporate and financial records; pupil records; correspondence and papers of various headmasters, bursars and other officers of the college; magazines, 19th and 20th centuries.

Non-manuscript material: Photographs; uniforms past and present; ephemera; architectural drawings of college buildings; books by or about former pupils.

Finding aids: Card index and typescript catalogue.

Facilities: Photocopying by arrangement.

Publications: G.P. Burstow and M. Whittaker: *A History of Brighton College*, ed. Sir Sydney Roberts (Brighton, 1957).
M.D.W. Jones: 'Brighton College v Marriott: Schools, Charity Law & Taxation', *History of Education*, xii/2 (1983), 121–32.
——: *A Short History of Brighton College* (Brighton, 1986).
——: *Brighton College 1845–1995: Essays in Honour of the Sesquicentenary* (Chichester, 1995).

121 Brighton Reference Library

Parent organisation: East Sussex County Libraries

Address: Central Library, Church Street, Brighton, East Sussex BN1 1UE

Telephone: (01273) 601197/691197

Fax: (01273) 695882

Enquiries: The Reference Library Manager, Mrs E. Jewell

Open: Mon, Tues, Thurs, Fri: 10.00–7.00 Sat: 10.00–4.00

Access: Generally open to the public.

Historical background: The Local Studies Collection contains material on both East and West Sussex. However, in recent years a good deal has been transferred to East and West Sussex Record Offices (entries 455 and 211).

Acquisitions policy: Donations and deposits are accepted in close cooperation with East Sussex County Record Office.

Archives of organisation: Minutes and other records relating to East Sussex County Library.

Major collections: Brighton rate books, 1791–1894.
Minutes and accounts of trade union groups, Brighton and Sussex, 19th–20th centuries.
Minutes of Brighton Labour Party and Friendly Societies.
Working notes and correspondence of Brighton Community Publishing Group, Queenspark.

Non-manuscript material: Sussex newspapers and journals, 18th–20th centuries.
Drawings, prints, photographs, magic-lantern slides, glass negatives, postcards, slides of Brighton and Sussex.
Census returns, East and West Sussex, 1841–81, and Brighton Manor court rolls (on microfilm).

Finding aids: Booklet listing trade union, Friendly Society and Labour Party material. Local history catalogue.

Facilities: Photocopying. Photography by arrangement. Microfilm/fiche reader/printer.

Publications: *A–Z of Special Collections.*
T. Carder: *The Encyclopaedia of Brighton.*

122 Preston Manor

Parent organisation: Royal Pavilion Art Gallery and Museums

Address: Preston Park, Brighton, East Sussex BN1 6SD

Telephone: (01273) 603005 ext. 3239

Enquiries: The Keeper, David Beevers

Open: Mon–Fri, by arrangement.

Access: Generally open to the public, but no children under 16 unless accompanied by an adult. Appointment always necessary.

Historical background: Collection of documents relating to Sussex, the property of Sir Charles Thomas Stanford (1858–1932), who bequeathed Preston Manor and its estate to Brighton Corporation (now Brighton Borough Council).

Acquisitions policy: To maintain the archives relating to the families who owned Preston Manor.

Archives of organisation: Family papers of the Stanfords, who held Preston Manor from 1795, including manorial court rolls, indentures and agreements relating to land holdings and building conveyances.

Major collections: Large collection of deeds and documents relating to East and West Sussex, arranged by parish.
Letters by Sussex authors.

Non-manuscript material: Photographs of Preston Manor.
Collection of Sussex family bookplates; books by Rudyard Kipling and Sussex authors.

Finding aids: Card index. East and West Sussex collections: NRA 1296.

Facilities: Photocopying by arrangement.

123 University of Sussex

Address: Falmer, Brighton, East Sussex BN1 9QL

A Library

Telephone: (01273) 678158

Fax: (01273) 678441

Enquiries: The Librarian, A.N. Peasgood

Open: Mon–Thurs: 9.00–1.00; 2.00–5.00

Access: Academic researchers, on written application.

Historical background: The university library was opened to readers in 1964. In 1970 a section was created within the library to handle the special materials acquired to support research projects which had arisen from the curriculum. In 1973 these special collections were divided into two groups, official published papers and manuscripts, and thereafter the Manuscripts Section has maintained and serviced the manuscript collections, together with small supporting collections of printed books.

Acquisitions policy: To collect papers which support research and teaching in the university, especially literary, political, sociological, and scientific papers of the late 19th and 20th centuries.

Major collections: Collections include the following: Benn Levy, MP, c1930–70; Charles W. Gibson, MP, c1910–70; James Gerald Crowther, papers on scientific journalism and politics; Sir Richard Gregory, c1880–1952; John Hilton Bureau papers: *News of the World* readers' problems, 1945–68; Kenneth Allsop, 1940–68; Kingsley Martin, 1910–69; Rudyard Kipling and family, c1860–1940; Leonard and

Virginia Woolf, 1890–1969; Rosey Pool: American Negro Literature, 1945–70; Sir Lawrence Dudley Stamp, 1910–65.

Common Wealth Party papers, 1940–.

Matusow papers on 20th–century US politics and culture, 1940–74.

Wartime Social Survey papers, 1940–41.

Maurice Reckitt papers on religion, politics and society, 1915–50.

Geoffrey Gorer papers, c1920–1981.

New Statesman archive, 1944–1988.

Nicolson Papers, 1970s: correspondence of Nigel Nicolson while editing the letters of Virginia Woolf.

Non-manuscript material: Printed books associated with individual collections, e.g. works and studies of Virginia Woolf, Leonard Woolf, Rudyard Kipling.

Finding aids: Descriptive handlists to each collection. Indexes of letter writers for main collections in progress. Handlists are lodged with the NRA.

Facilities: Usual reprographic facilities.

Conservation: Contracted out.

B Tom Harrisson Mass-Observation Archive

Telephone: (01273) 678157

Fax: (01273) 678441

Enquiries: The Archivist, Ms Dorothy E. Sheridan

Open: Mon–Thurs: 9.15–5.00, by appointment.

Access: Bona fide researchers, on written application; reference/sponsorship required.

Historical background: Mass-Observation was a social science research organisation set up in 1937 by Tom Harrison and Charles Madge. They aimed to create what they called an 'anthropology of ourselves', using two main approaches: (a) the recruiting of a panel of volunteer 'observers' to record their everyday lives in diaries and to respond to detailed monthly questionnaires; and (b) the establishment of a core of full-time investigators based in London. During World War II Mass-Observation was used by the Ministry of Information for a short period to monitor civilian morale. The papers generated by this work (which continued into the 1950s) were brought to the University of Sussex in 1970. The archive was officially opened in 1975, when it became a charitable trust.

Acquisitions policy: The original Mass-Observation collection is virtually complete, but a small amount of complementary material (private papers, letters, diaries, scrapbooks and personal material donated by individuals), dating from 1937 to the present day, continues to be accepted. In addition, the archive itself is the centre for a nationwide contemporary writing project, 'Mass-Observation in the 1980s and 1990s', begun in 1981 and still in operation, and regularly receives contributions from volunteer writers willing to record their lives in response to thematic open-ended questionnaires sent to them by the archivist.

Major collections: Mass-Observation records: personal diaries, 1937–63; detailed questionnaire replies, 1937–53; papers resulting from a wide range of investigations into British social life before, during and immediately after World War II.

Mary Adams collection: personal papers donated by Mary Adams relating to her work at BBC Television, 1936–9, 1942–58; as Director of Home Intelligence, Ministry of Information, 1939–41; and as Deputy Chairman of the Consumers' Association, 1958–70.

Papers resulting from the contemporary Mass-Observation project (2500 writers since 1981), arranged thematically and chronologically on aspects on everyday life in Britain.

Non-manuscript material: Photographs taken by Humphrey Spender of Bolton and Blackpool, 1937–8, for Mass-Observation's 'Worktown Project' (c400).

The library includes *Mass-Observation* and related publications; these may not be borrowed.

Newspaper cuttings relating to Mass-Observation's history.

Ephemera, including posters, pamphlets, leaflets etc, which are related to topics investigated by Mass-Observation.

Finding aids: Lists and indexes. Sections of the collection are still being catalogued.

Facilities: Photocopying. Microfilm reader. Educational materials for schools.

Conservation: Contracted out.

Publications: D. Sheridan: *Mass-Observation Archive: Guide for Researchers* [pamphlet available for sale from the archive].

A. Calder and D. Sheridan (eds): *Speak for Yourself: a Mass-Observation Anthology* (1984)
——: 'Ordinary Hardworking Folk: Volunteer Writers in Mass-Observation 1939–50 and 1981–91', *Feminist Praxis*, nos. 36/7, (1993) [special issue on Mass-Observation].
——: 'Reading Mass-Observation Writing: Theoretical and Methodological Issues in Researching the Mass-Observation Archive', *Auto/Biography*, the Bulletin of the BSA Auto/Biography Group, 2/2; also pubd as Mass-Observation Archive Occasional Paper No. 1, University of Sussex Library (1993).
'Writing to the Archive: Mass-Observation as Autobiography', *Sociology*, 27/1 (1993), 101–13.
'Using the Mass-Observation Archive as a Source for Women's Studies', *Women's History Review*, 3/1 (1994), 101–13.

124 Bristol Central Library
Reference Department

Parent organisation: Avon County Community Resources Department

Address: County Central Library, College Green, Bristol BS1 5TL

Telephone: (0117) 929 9147 (Reference Enquiry Desk)

Enquiries: The Local Studies Librarian

Open: Mon–Thurs: 10.00–7.00 Fri: 9.30–7.30 Sat: 9.30–5.00

Access: Generally open to the public, but advance notice is required for the use of MSS, early printed material and some other valuable items.

Historical background: The City Library of Bristol has been in existence since 1613. In 1974 Bristol Public Libraries became part of Avon County Library, and much of the early stock survives in the County Reference Library, which also contains the books of the Bristol Library Society, founded in 1772. Most MS material relevant to the history of Bristol is housed in the Bristol Record Office (entry **125**).

Acquisitions policy: To strengthen the existing collections, especially those relating to local history and local literary figures, by purchase and donation.

Major collections: MS and printed material

relating to Thomas Chatterton (1752–70) and Samuel Taylor Coleridge (1772–1834).
Richard Smith Collection: MS and printed material relating to the history of the theatre in Bristol, 1672–1843.
Letters and papers relating to the Southwell family, 1655–1777.
Small collection of documents relating to slavery in the West Indies and the slave trade generally, 1723–36.
The Ellacombe Collection: MSS and other material relating to the history and topography of south-east Gloucestershire (now part of Avon).

Non-manuscript material: Extensive collections on the history of Bristol and its environs, including books, pamphlets, pictorial material, colour and monochrome transparencies, sound archives.
Braikenridge Collection: c9000 items on the history of the city, including engravings, ephemera and other pre-1850 material.
Emanuel Green Collection of books on the history of Somerset.

Finding aids: Catalogues, lists and indexes.

Facilities: Photocopying. Microfilm/fiche readers.

Conservation: Contracted out.

125 Bristol Record Office

Parent organisation: Bristol City Council

Address: 'B' Bond Warehouse, Smeaton Road, Bristol BS1 6XN

Telephone: (0117) 922 5692

Fax: (0117) 922 4236

Enquiries: The City Archivist, John S. Williams

Open: Mon–Thurs: 9.30–4.45
Closed last two weeks of January.

Access: Generally open to the public. Appointments welcomed but not essential.

Historical background: The Record Office was established in 1924. Newly converted premises were opened in 1992. The office also acts as the Diocesan Record Office for Bristol (parish records for the Archdeaconry of Bristol) and is recognised as a place of deposit for public, manorial and tithe records.

Acquisitions policy: The office is interested in all

records relating to the present city and former city and former city and county of Bristol. Acquisitions are mainly by donation or deposit, occasionally by purchase.

Archives of organisation: Usual local authority record holdings, 12th century–.

Major collections: Deposited collections including the following which have a wider significance:
Records of J.S. Fry and Sons Ltd, chocolate manufacturers, 1693–1966.
Records of Imperial Tobacco Ltd, formerly W.D. and H.O. Wills, tobacco manufacturers, late 18th–20th centuries.
Papers of Sir George White, transport pioneer, c1874–1935.
Records of P. and A. Campbell Ltd, paddle-steamer company, 1893–1971.

Non-manuscript material: Large number of plans, drawings and photographs relating to the area.
Over 200 films, 1902– (VHS viewing copies available of some).

Finding aids: Place, subject and personal names indexes compiled from lists of holdings. Various specialist indexes available. Lists sent to NRA.

Facilities: Photocopying. Microfilm/fiche readers/printer. Photography and microfilming by arrangement.

Conservation: Occasional work undertaken by another repository.

Publications: I. Kirby: *Diocese of Bristol: A Catalogue of the Records* (1970).
E. Ralph: *Guide to the Bristol Archives Office* (1971).
Various guides to records, posters, maps and postcards; full list available.

126 Feminist Archive

Address: Trinity Road Library, St Phillips, Bristol BS2 0NW

Telephone: (0117) 935 0025

Open: : Wed: 2.00–5.00

Access: Women; men restricted to published matter. General enquiries will be answered if SAE enclosed, but no prolonged research can be undertaken. Access to some collections may be restricted by the donors.

Historical background: The archive is a charity which was started in 1978 and expanded and outgrew various premises, including a room in Bath University; it moved to its present premises in 1988. It is run by a collective of volunteers. The northern branch of the Feminist Archive is at the Department of Applied Social Studies, Bradford University (entry 115), 21 Ashgrove, Bradford BD7 1BP, tel. (01274) 383502.

Acquisitions policy: To collect and preserve donated material, including audio cassettes, from the 1960s to the present pertaining to the women's movement and feminist issues.

Major collections: Dora Russell Collection: records of the journey through Europe of the Women's Peace Caravan, 1958. Also some of Dora Russell's own papers.

Non-manuscript material: Photographs, drawings, posters, records, stickers, calendars, conference papers, periodicals and various ephemera. Audio cassettes of interviews.

Finding aids: Cataloguing is underway.

Conservation: Contracted out.

Publications: Newsletters and various leaflets available.

127 John Wesley's Chapel
The New Room in the Horsefair

Parent organisation: The Methodist Church

Address: 36 The Horsefair, Bristol BS1 3JE

Telephone: (0117) 926 4740

Enquiries: The Hon. Archivist

Open: By arrangement.

Access: Bona fide researchers, on written application.

The manuscript collection at the New Room (which is the oldest Methodist building in the world, 1739) is built around three collections of letters made by the Rev. Dr William L. Watkinson, president of the Wesleyan Conference in 1897. These were brought together in the early years of this century. Added to these collections are a number of gifts of letters and journals, making a total of some 1200 items, of which most are 19th century. The collections contain letters of John Wesley (1703–91) and all the major figures of 19th-century Wesleyan Methodism. There is a catalogue available.

128 Society of Merchant Venturers of Bristol

Address: Merchants' Hall, The Promenade, Clifton, Bristol BS8 3NH

Telephone: (0117) 973 8058/3104

Fax: (0117) 973 5884

Enquiries: The Hon. Archivist, Miss Elizabeth Ralph

Open: Mon–Fri: 9.00–12.30; 2.00–5.00

Access: Bona fide scholars, with the consent of the society and strictly by appointment only.

Historical background: The society was incorporated by Royal Charter in 1552. Microfilm of books of proceedings, 1605–1900, are at Bristol University (entry **129**).

Acquisitions policy: Acquisitions are mainly by donation or deposit.

Archives of organisation: Archives, cover records of trade, shipping and docks, 17th century–, as well as records relating to the society's administration of almshouses, independent schools and other charities.

Finding aids: Lists sent to NRA.

Facilities: Photocopying. Photography allowed.

Conservation: Contracted out.

Publications: E. Ralph: *A Guide to the Archives of the Society of Merchant Venturers of Bristol* (1988).

129 University of Bristol Library

Address: Tyndall Avenue, Bristol BS8 1TJ

Telephone: (0117) 928 8014

Enquiries: The Archivist

Open: Mon–Fri: 8.45–4.45

Access: Members of the University of Bristol; others on application.

Historical background: University College Bristol was founded in 1876 and became a university on grant of Charter in 1909. The Gladstone Library of the National Liberal Club was purchased by the library in 1976. The University Library is a repository of West Indies archives.

Acquisitions policy: Acquisitions are by donation, deposit and purchase.

Archives of organisation: University College and University of Bristol: archives of the institution, 1876– (incomplete); papers relating to individuals connected with it, including Arthur Roderick Collar (1935–82), Sir Frederick Charles Frank (1935–88), Dr Heinz London (1886–1972), Professor Conwy Lloyd Morgan (1875–1938), Sir Philip Robert Morris (1942–80), Professor Cecil Frank Powell (1916–69), Arthur Mannering Tyndall (1921–84). Also papers of John Beddoe (1854–1907), Cecil Reginald Burch (1901–83), Charles Hubert Sisson, Philip John Worsley.

Major collections: Bristol Moravian Church: diaries, minute books, memoirs and other items of church history, 1760–1893.

Letter-books, sketch books, calculation books, accounts, correspondence etc, of Isambard Kingdom Brunel (1806–59), 1824–59, plus letter-books and journals of Sir Marc Isambard Brunel (1769–1849).

Clifton Suspension Bridge Trust minute books, accounts, plans, 1829–1939.

Letter-books, sketch books, diaries, accounts etc of Henry Marc Brunel, 1860–1903.

General Election addresses, 1892–, European Parliament, 1979–.

Penguin Books Ltd, historical and editorial files, 1935–70. Includes papers of Betty Radice.

Correspondence, notes, papers and publications of Edward Conze in the field of oriental theology.

Autograph scores and correspondence of Philip Napier Miles, 1884–1951.

Paget family: accounts, correspondence, family and estate papers, relating mainly to Somerset and Staffordshire, 1270–1920.

Pinney family: accounts, letter-books, family and estate papers, relating mainly to Dorset and the West Indies, 1650–1986.

Somerset Miners Association: minutes, accounts, correspondence etc, 1868–1964.

John Addington Symonds: correspondence and family papers, 1884–1980.

West Indies Papers: miscellaneous personal and estates records, 1663–1929.

Women's Liberal Federation: minutes, accounts, correspondence, 1888–1988.

Bateman Collection: resources for the history of the Labour movement, 20th century.

Jane Cobden Unwin: letters to Jane Cobden Unwin on Irish independence and anti-slavery, 1880–1939.

Victor and Joan Eyles: papers on the history of geology, including Sowerby family correspondence, 1679–1869, Buckland family wills, 1837–56.

Dame Katharine Furze: correspondence, 1887–1952.

Goldney family: papers, 1681–1891.

Hamish Hamilton Ltd: editorial and historical archive to 1970.

Adey Horton: reproductions of medieval Christian iconography, arranged by subject.

David James Cathcart King: correspondence and papers, 1939–89.

National Liberal Club: small collections of papers (formerly in the Gladstone Library).

Robin Tanner: letters, 1920–88.

Non-manuscript material: Recordings, cassettes, photographs, films, plans and drawings referring to the history of University College Bristol and Bristol University, 1876–.

Fry Collection of Portraits (prints).

Finding aids: Indexes. Lists. Catalogues. Calendars.

Facilities: Photocopying. Photography. Microfilm/fiche reader/printer.

Publications: Guide to Special Collections and *The Brunel Collection* (1993).

130 University of Bristol Theatre Collection

Parent organisation: University of Bristol

Address: Department of Drama, Cantocks Close, Woodland Road, Bristol BS8 1UP

Telephone: (0117) 930 3218 (Keeper) 930 3030 ext. 8074 (Assistant Keeper)

Fax: (0117) 928 8251

Enquiries: The Keeper, Mr Christopher Robinson, The Assistant Keeper, Sarah Morris

Open: Mon–Fri: 9.30–5.30

Access: Bona fide researchers, preferably by appointment.

Historical background: The Theatre Collection was founded in 1951, funded by the Rockefeller Foundation, five years after the founding of the university's department of drama. It was originally conceived as a working collection of graphic material illustrating the development of theatre, based on the earliest acquisitions (the Robinson Collection and the Landstone Bequest). It has grown significantly since the 1970s, with a number of large bequests and purchases as well as the development of the Women's Theatre Collection within the main collection. The holdings now cover the period from the 18th century onwards.

Acquisitions policy: Archive material, original artwork and models, books, and visual material covering all aspects of drama and theatre history. Costumes, props or printed plays are not actively collected unless they are contained within a collection. The main emphasis is on British Victorian and 20th-century theatre, and theatre design.

Major collections: Old Vic Archive: administrative papers and production records, 1816–1963, including photographs, prompt books, playbills, personal papers, etc.

Bristol Old Vic Archive: administrative papers and production records, 1946–1993.

Beerbohm Tree Collection: personal papers of Herbert Beerbohm Tree (1853–1917), actor manager and builder of Her Majesty's Theatre, London, and material covering all aspects of productions, including press cuttings and photographs, 1880–1917; also personal papers of his wife Maud, 1880–1937.

Eric Jones Evans (1899–1989), theatre historian: scripts, photographs, prompt books and personal papers, 19th and 20th centuries.

Kathleen Barker, theatre historian: personal research papers.

Leon Quartermaine (1876–1958), actor: personal papers.

Women's Theatre Collection: scripts, books, personal papers of women playwrights and actors, 1890s-1994.

Non-manuscript material: Robinson Collection: playbills for West Country theatres, 18th and 19th centuries.

Landstone Bequest: London theatre programmes, 1944–69.

Richard Southern (theatre historian) Collection: prints of theatre architecture, costume and scene design; engravings, playbills, designs, paintings, books, 18th–20th centuries.

Miriam Luck Collection: film books.

Extensive collections (mainly British) of programmes and periodicals; slides and photographs; set models; costumes and props; prints and original artwork of costume; set designs and portraits.

Finding aids: Card index system arranged by form/person/subject. Computerised list in preparation.

Facilities: Photocopying. Photography. Microfiche reader.

Conservation: Contracted out.

Publications: C. Robins: 'British Theatre Collection', *Theatrephile*, 1 (Dec 1983).

131 Wesley College

Address: College Park Drive, Henbury Road, Bristol BS10 7QD

Telephone: (0117) 959 1200

Fax: (0117) 950 1277

Enquiries: The Librarian, Mr John Farrell

Open: By arrangement.

Access: Bona fide researchers, on written application.

Historical background: Three colleges have amalgamated to create the Bristol College: Didsbury College, Manchester (f. 1842), Wesley College, Headingley (f. 1868) and Richmond College, London (1843–1972).

Acquisitions policy: To maintain and consolidate the archives and collections relating to Methodism.

Archives of organisation: Archives of the three constituent colleges, Wesley, Disbury and Richmond, 19th and 20th centuries.

Major collections: Antiquarian collections, including papers of Rev. George Morley (*d* 1843) and his son, George Morley, surgeon of Leeds; Dr Adam Clarke (?1762–1832), theologian, and his family.
Correspondence of Methodist worthies, c1790–c1840; letters and papers relevant to the Wesleys, c1700–c1850, (3 vols); letters and newspaper cuttings *re* troubles in Tonga, 1883–7.

Non-manuscript material: Pamphlet collections on church controversy, particularly Methodism, c1680–1850 (153 vols).
Hymnals, 1640–1900.

Finding aids: TS catalogue: NRA 27644.

Facilities: Photocopying. Microfilm/fiche readers.

Publications: D. MacCulloch: 'Manuscript Collections at Wesley College, Bristol: a Handlist', *Proceedings of the Wesley Historical Society*, xliii, 95.

132 Isle of Arran Heritage Museum

Address: Rosaburn, Brodick, Isle of Arran KA27 8DP

Telephone: (01770) 302636

Enquiries: The Archivist, Mrs F. Gorman

Open: Easter–Oct: Mon–Sat: by appointment.

Access: Generally open to the public. An appointment is necessary and a donation is welcomed.

The museum was established in 1979 and it acquires items with an Arran connection. It holds material relating to land tenure, genealogy, emigration, archaeology, music, poetry, geology, shipping, the fishing industry, horticulture, local industries, and most aspects of life on the island. There are also photographic collections, especially those of MacFee and Anderson, c1900–1912. Museum documentation record cards are available as well as photocopying and microfiche reader facilities. The museum has issued two publications by A. Fairhurst, *Arran Heritage Museum Guide* and *Exploring Arran's Past*.

133 Bromley Public Library
Archive Section

Address: Central Library, High Street, Bromley, Kent BR1 1EX

Telephone: (0181) 460 9955

Fax: (0181) 313 9975

Enquiries: The Archivist, Miss E. Silverthorne

Open: Mon, Wed, Fri: 9.30–6.00 Tues, Thurs: 9.30–8.00 Sat: 9.30–5.00

Access: Generally open to the public.

Historical background: The Greater London borough of Bromley was formed in 1965 by the amalgamation of Bromley, Beckenham, Penge, Orpington and Chislehurst, all of which had previously been part of Kent; Penge had been in Surrey until 1889, then in London until 1900. The first archivist was appointed in 1970. Previously there had been haphazard collection of material at all libraries, with the largest at Bromley, the result of the activities of a committee of local historians in the 1920s. There is close liaison with the Centre for Kentish Studies (entry **789**), which has transferred some local material, including Anglican parish records (diocese of Rochester: Beckenham, Bromley and Orpington deaneries). The library is recognised as a place of deposit for public records.

Major collections: Usual local authority record holdings and deposited collections.

Facilities: Photocopying. Photography by arrangement. Microfilm/fiche reader/printer.

Conservation: Contracted out.

134 Lord's Day Observance Society

Address: 6 Sherman Road, Bromley, Kent BR1 3JH

Telephone: (081) 313 0456

Fax: (081) 466 0059

Enquiries: The General Secretary, Mr John Roberts

Open: By arrangement only.

Access: Students and those involved in research regarding the Lord's Day, by appointment with the General Secretary.

Historical background: The society was founded in 1831 by Joseph Wilson and Rev. Daniel Wilson (subsequently Bishop of Calcutta), and it seeks to promote the observance of the Lord's Day for worship. It united with the Working Men's Lord's Day Rest Association in 1920, with the Lord's Day Observance Association of Scotland in 1953 and with the Imperial Alliance for the Defence of Scotland in 1965. Some of the archives were destroyed during World War II.

Acquistions policy: To maintain the archives.

Archives of organisation: Some records of predecessor society. Minutes, reports and journals, 1830–.
Annual accounts, 1978–.

Correspondence with government and local authorities.

Non-manuscript material: Magazines *Joy and Light*, 1948–, *Day and Night*, 1948–.

Facilities: Photocopying.

135 Bromsgrove Library

Parent organisation: Hereford and Worcester County Libraries

Address: Stratford Road, Bromsgrove, Hereford and Worcester B60 1AP

Telephone: (01527) 575855 ext. 5024, 575856 on Sat or after 5.00 pm

Fax: (01527) 575855

Enquiries: The Bromsgrove Librarian

Open: Mon, Fri: 9.30–7.00 Tues, Wed: 9.30–5.00 Sat: 9.30–4.00
Closed on bank holidays and usually on the following day.

Access: Generally open to the public. Some notice is necessary if manuscripts are to be consulted.

Historical background: The library first acquired the Housman collection because of the family's connection with the town.

Acquisitions policy: Donations of relevant material on the Housman family are accepted.

Major collections: Letters of Laurence Housman (1865–1959), pacifist and brother of A.E. Housman, 1927–58 (approx 1200 sheets); and of his sister, Clemence Housman (approx 20 sheets).

Non-manuscript material: Small collection of background material on the Housman family. *Bromsgrove Messenger*, 1860–.

Facilities: Photocopying. Microfilm/fiche readers.

136 St Mary's Convent, Buckfast

Parent organisation: St Scholastica's Abbey, Teignmouth

Address: St Mary's Convent, 7 Buckfast Road, Buckfast, Devon TQ11 0EA

Telephone: (01364) 643280

Enquiries: The Archivist, Dame Mildred Murray Sinclair

Open: By arrangement.

Access: Researchers, and those genuinely interested in monastic history. An appointment is necessary.

The community was founded in 1662 at Dunkirk for English Benedictine nuns on the continent. It also represented a similar monastery founded at Pontoise. During the French Revolution the nuns were imprisoned, and on release they settled at Hammersmith until 1863, when the community removed to Teignmouth. When St Scholastica's Abbey closed in 1987, the recusant library, primarily pre-18th century books, was transferred to Downside Abbey (entry 55). Four of St Scholastica's community (including the archivist) have started a small community at Buckfast and hold the archives there. The archives of St Scholastica's date back to its foundation, although little remains for the early years in Dunkirk. No lists of catalogues are yet available.

137 Buckfast Abbey

Address: Buckfastleigh, Devon TQ11 0EE

Telephone: (01364) 643301

Fax: (01364) 643891

Enquiries: The Archivist

Open: Not open to the public, but the archivist is willing to deal with enquiries about the history of the abbey and aspects of the monastic life which is followed here.

Access: By appointment.

Historical background: The abbey was originally founded in 1018 but, like other abbeys, was suppressed in 1539. In the following centuries the church and monastery became a ruin. The abbey was refounded in 1882 by a group of exiled monks from France. Subsequently the monastery was rebuilt on the medieval foundations.

Acquisitions policy: To maintain the archive of the abbey.

Archives of organisation: Records of the abbey, 1882–. The only notable documentary record of the medieval abbey is a part of the medieval cartulary which the abbey was able to acquire in later years.

Non-manuscript material: A collection of architects' drawings for the rebuilding of the abbey and more recent restorations.

Facilities: Photocopying at the discretion of the Archivist.

Publications: *A Short History of Buckfast Abbey* (in press).

138 Burton Library

Parent organisation: Staffordshire County Council

Address: Riverside, High Street, Burton on Trent, Staffs DE14 1AH

Telephone: (01283) 543271

Fax: (01283) 510938

Enquiries: The Group Librarian

Open: Mon, Tues, Thurs, Fri: 9.30–6.00 Wed: 9.30–1.00 Sat: 9.15–1.00

Access: Generally open to the public; previous notification of visit to Archive Collection essential.

Historical background: The present building was opened in 1976 to house archives from the Burton area, principally Burton borough records.

Acquisitions policy: Local archives are accepted on deposit or as gifts.

Major collections: Burton borough records. Board of Guardians records, 1830s–. Burton Methodist archives, 19th century–. Education records from the former County Borough of Burton, 1870s–.

Facilities: Microfilm/fiche reader.

139 Bury Archives Service

Parent organisation: Bury Metropolitan Borough Council

Address: 1st Floor, Derby Hall Annexe, Edwin Street (off Crompton Street), Bury, Lancs BL9 0AS

Telephone: (0161) 797 6697

Enquiries: The Archivist, Kevin Mulley

Open: Mon–Fri: 10.00–1.00; 2.00–5.00 Sat (1st of each month): 10.00–1.00 Appointments are essential, except on Tuesdays.

Access: Generally open to the public. The

service operates the CARN reader's ticket system.

Historical background: Bury Metropolitan Borough Council was formed in 1974 by the amalgamation of Bury County Borough with Prestwich and Radcliffe boroughs, and Ramsbottom, Tottington and Whitefield urban districts. The archive service was established in 1986 to administer large backlogs of council records created by the local government reorganisation, and scattered private records previously deposited with the borough museum and libraries. In 1992 it moved to new premises in Edwin Street, and certain local authority records previously deposited with Lancashire Record Office were transferred back to Bury. Other records for the locality are held by Lancashire Record Office (entry **944**), (including Bury and Prestwick manorial), Manchester City Record Office (entry **761**), (parish records) and Greater Manchester Record Office (entry **764**) (Wilton estate and some public records).

Acquisitions policy: Archives of organisations and individuals based in, or primarily relating to, the area of the borough, including local branches of national or regional bodies. Records on certain media (film, sound recordings) have been transferred to the North West Film and Sound Archive (entry **771**).

Major collections: Usual deposited local records, including non-conformist churches from 1782; tithe maps, Bury and Prestwich parishes, 1838–42; businesses, 1782–, including Richard Bealey & Co., bleachers and chemical manufacturers, 1750–1935; Bury Savings Bank, 1822–1972; Woodcock & Sons, solicitors, 1780–1980; trade unions and co-op societies, 1858–; local social, recreational and political groups, 1839–; miscellaneous and family papers, including Hutchinson family, 1727–1950.

Non-manuscript material: Plans, drawings, photographs and maps are included in many of the archives listed above; building regulation plans for Bury, 1866–1948, Whitefield, 1866–1927, and Ramsbottom, 1877–1948; tithe maps, Bury and Prestwich parishes (schedules Prestwich only).

Finding aids: Lists (organised by provenance); name and place indexes to deeds and plans. Lists sent to NRA.

Facilities: Photocopying. Microfilm/fiche reader.

Conservation: Provided by agreement with Greater Manchester Record Office.

Publications: 'Routes' guide to family history; quarterly *Newsletter*; interim guide in preparation (1994).

140 Suffolk Record Office
Bury St Edmunds Branch

Parent organisation: Suffolk County Council

Address: 77 Raingate Street, Bury St Edmunds, Suffolk IP33 2AR

Telephone: (01284) 722522

Enquiries: The Archives Service Manager, Miss R.A. Rogers (service) or The Branch Archivist, Mr R.G. Thomas (branch)

Open: Mon–Sat: 9.00–5.00
Material required on Saturdays must be ordered before 1.00 on Friday.

Access: Generally open to the public. The office operates the CARN reader's ticket system.

Historical background: The office was established as Bury St Edmunds Borough Record Office in 1938 and was known as Bury St Edmunds and West Suffolk Record Office from 1950 to 1974. It became the Bury St Edmunds Branch of the Suffolk Record Office in 1974. It is the Diocesan Record Office for St Edmundsbury and Ipwich (Archdeaconry of Sudbury) and a recognised place of deposit for public records. The Local Studies Library is an integral part of the office.

Acquisitions policy: Archival and printed material relating to the former administrative county of West Suffolk.

Archives of organisation: Usual local authority record holdings.

Major collections: Deposited local collections, including estate and family papers of the Dukes of Grafton (the 3rd Duke was Prime Minister, 1768–70); papers of Hervey family, Marquisses of Bristol, in Lincolnshire, Essex and Sussex, 14th–20th centuries; records of Robert Boby, engineers, 1866–1909.

Finding aids: Catalogues and indexes; catalogues sent to NRA; annual summary of accessions published in *Archive News*.

Facilities: Photocopying. Photography. Microfilm/fiche readers/printers (some self-service). Microfilming by arrangement.

Conservation: Available in-house.

Publications: Guide to Genealogical Sources (4/1993); *Archive News* (half-yearly); various history titles.

141 Royal Caledonian Schools

Address: Aldenham Road, Bushey, Herts WD2 3TS

Telephone: (01923) 226642

Fax: (01923) 230148

Enquiries: The Master, Captain D.F. Watts

Open: Mon–Fri: 9.00–5.00
Closed during all state school holidays.

Access: Authorised readers, by appointment only.

The Royal Caledonian Schools were founded in 1815 by the Highland Society of London under the presidency of Queen Victoria's father, the Duke of Kent and Strathearn. The aim was to care for children of Scotsmen lost in the Napoleonic wars. At the turn of the century the schools moved to Bushey, where they have continued to care for children of Scottish parentage. Today most of the children are the sons and daughters of men serving in the Scottish regiments. The schools maintain their own archives, consisting of minutes books, registers, ledgers and other records of the day-to-day running of the schools. There is also a small collection of photographs of schools' events, 19th–20th century.

142 Gwynedd Archives and Museums Service
Caernarfon Area Record Office

Address: Victoria Dock, Caernarfon, Gwynedd LL55 1SH

Telephone: (01286) 679095

Fax: (01286) 679637

Enquiries: The Deputy Director of Culture and Leisure, Mr Bryn R. Parry or The Principal Archivist and Museums Officer, Mr G. Haulfryn Williams, County Offices, Shirehall Street, Caenarfon, Gwynedd LL55 1SH

Open: Mon, Tues, Thurs, Fri: 9.30–12.30; 1.30–5.00 Wed: 9.30–12.30; 1.30–7.00

Historical background: The County Record Office was founded in 1947 and Gwynedd Archive Service was established in 1974, incorporating Anglesey and Merioneth Record Offices. It became the Gwynedd Archives and Museums Service in 1985. The office also acts as the Diocesan Record Office for Bangor and St Asaph (parish records). There are Gwynedd Archives Service Record Offices also at Dolgellau (entry **245**) and Llangefni (entry **477**). The office is recognised as a place of deposit for public records.

Archives of organisation: Usual local authority record holdings.

Major collections: Deposited local collections including the following which have a wider significance: records of the slate quarrying industry; shipping and other maritime history collections; Ffestiniog Railway archives; estate records, notably those of Boduan, Cefnamwlch, Glynllifen, Rug (Clwyd) and Vaynel.

Non-manuscript material: Major collections of topographical prints, photographs, local newspapers and Welsh-language periodicals. Oral history recordings (*c*600).

Facilities: Photocopying. Photography. Microfilm/fiche readers.

Publications: W.O. Williams: *Guide to the Caernarvonshire Record Office* (1952).

143 The Royal Logistic Corps Museum

Address: The Princess Royal Barracks, Deepcut, Camberley, Surrey GU16 6RW

Telephone: (01252) 340984

Enquiries: The Curator, Mr F.G. O'Connell, The Archives Assistant, Mr S. Gill

Open: Mon–Fri: 9.30–4.00, by arrangement.

Access: Bona fide researchers. Some personal collections are restricted. Appointments are necessary.

Historical background: The museum opened in

1993 and has combined the collections of the corps detailed below. Most material dates from 1850 onwards; the collections complement but do not include personnel records and unit war diaries.

Acquisitions policy: To acquire material relating to the history, personnel and equipment of the corps listed below and their predecessors.

Archives of organisation: Archives of the Royal Corps of Transport, the Royal Army Ordnance Corps, the Royal Pioneer Corps, the Army Catering Corps and the Royal Engineers Postal and Courier Service.

Major collections: Documents, publications, personal recollections and photographs donated by individuals who have served with corps supporting the army.
Examples of official documentation.

Non-manuscript material: Photographic collections, corps journals, training manuals.

Finding aids: Individual collection listings.

Facilities: Photocopying.

Conservation: Contracted out.

144 Royal Military Academy Sandhurst
Sandhurst Collection

Address: Camberley, Surrey GU15 4PQ

Telephone: (01276) 412503

Enquiries: The Archivist

Open: Mon–Fri: 9.00–5.00

Access: Approved readers, on written application (normally 48 hours' notice is required) and by prior appointment only.

Historical background: The Royal Military Academy Sandhurst, established in 1947, is an amalgamation of the Royal Military Academy (Woolwich) (f. 1741) and the Royal Military College (Sandhurst) (f. 1800). The archive section was set up in 1986, and is recognised as a place of deposit for public records.

Acquisitions policy: To collect material relating to the history of the RMAS and its predecessors.

Archives of organisation: Archives of the three constituent organisations, including correspon-

dence, letter-books, files and publications, 18th century–.

Major collections: Papers of Gen. Sir J.G. Le Marchant (1766–1812), first Lieutenant-Governor of the Royal Military College.

Non-manuscript material: Large quantity of ephemera.

Finding aids: Some holdings are listed in the Public Record Office and the rest are in the process of being listed. Le Marchant: NRA 0184.

145 Addenbrooke's Hospital
Archives Office

Parent organisation: Addenbrooke's NHS Trust

Address: c/o Administration, Board Room Suite, Addenbrooke's Hospital, Hills Road, Cambridge CB2 2QQ

Telephone: (01223) 245151 ext. 3516

Enquiries: The Hon. Archivist, Mr P. Rundle

Open: Mon–Fri: am

Access: Bona fide researchers. Appointment necessary.

Historical background: The hospital is named after Dr John Addenbrooke (1620– 1719), who left a sum of money to build 'a small physical hospital for poor people of any Parish or any County'. This bequest gave John Addenbrooke the distinction of being the first Englishman to bequeath his private wealth to found a voluntary hospital. The original hospital was in Trumpington Street, Cambridge, but the new hospital was completed in 1984. Addenbrooke's is the district general and teaching hospital for Cambridge. It is recognised as a place of deposit for public records.

Archives of organisation: Records of the hospital, including: minute books, 1766– 1939; rules and orders, 1778–1908; annual reports, 1863–; accounts, 1740–67; 1923–41; clinical records, 1878–1947.

Non-manuscript material: Portraits and photographs of medical staff and governors, 1800–.
Small collection of surgical instruments and ward equipment.

Finding aids: Lists

Facilities: Photocopying.

146 British Antarctic Survey

Address: High Cross, Madingley Road, Cambridge CB3 0ET

Telephone: (01223) 251531

Fax: (01223) 62616

Enquiries: The Archivist and Registrar, Mr M.J. Vine

Open: Mon–Fri: 9.30–1.00; 2.00–5.00

Access: By appointment only. Means of identification may be required.

Historical background: The survey originated as Operation Tabarin, an expedition organised during World War II primarily to maintain a British presence in Antarctica, but scientific work was also undertaken. At the end of the war the operation was transferred to the Colonial Office and renamed the Falkland Islands Dependencies Survey, and scientific research became its main purpose. A scientific bureau was established in London in 1950 and specialist units at various universities from 1956. The organisation was renamed the British Antarctic Survey in 1962 and became a constituent institute of the Natural Environment Research Council in 1967. Its headquarters were moved to Cambridge in 1976 where most of the Survey's activities in the UK were centralised. The five Antarctic stations are involved in a wide spectrum of research in the atmospheric, earth and life sciences. The Archive Service was established in 1979. It is recognised as a place of deposit for public records.

Acquisitions policy: Internal transfers of scientific, logistical and administrative records. Loans and gifts accepted from closely related organisations and from individuals connected in some way with the survey.

Archives of organisation: Field notes, specimen registers, maps, air photographs, processed data and draft papers of scientific staff in the fields of earth, atmospheric and life sciences.
Internal reports on building and maintaining stations in Antarctica and on South Georgia, and on the scientific work carried out from them, 1943–.
Administrative and logistical records from the London and Port Stanley Offices (both now closed) and of the present headquarters in Cambridge.

Non-manuscript material: Large photographic and cine film/video archive relating to British Antarctic Survey activities.
Limited selection of historical books and an extensive collection of relevant scientific publications in the library.

Finding aids: Archival lists produced from computer database, supplemented by indexes, principally to persons, places and subjects.

Facilities: Photocopying. Photography.

Conservation: Contracted out.

Publications: J. Rae and G.J. Smith: *BAS Archives: Guide to Holdings* (Cambridge, 1987).

147 Cambridge University Library

Parent organisation: University of Cambridge

Address: West Road, Cambridge CB3 9DR

A Manuscripts Department

Telephone: (01223) 333000/333143

Fax: (01223) 333160

Enquiries: The Keeper of Manuscripts and University Archives, Dr P.N.R. Zutshi

Open: Manuscripts Room: Mon–Fri: 9.00–6.45
Sat: 9.00–12.30
Closed one week in September and certain other days around public holidays.

Access: Bona fide researchers, on production of satisfactory references in accordance with the Library Syndicate's regulations. A charge may be made and intending readers are advised to write in advance.

Historical background: Cambridge University is known to have possessed a library since the second decade of the 14th century. It retains few MSS from its pre-Reformation holdings, but since 1574 the MS collections have been continuously enlarged. The present library building was opened in 1934. An extension was added in 1972, when the University Archives, until then separately housed, were brought into the library. It is a recognised place of deposit for public records.

Acquisitions policy: MSS of all types are

acquired, with the emphasis on strengthening existing collections.

Major collections: The older collections, both Western and oriental, are mainly of a literary character.

The Taylor-Schechter Genizah Collection of Hebraica.

Western MSS acquired over the past 100 years include: records of the Diocese and Dean and Chapter of Ely; several East Anglian family and estate archives; private papers of Cambridge men, e.g. Adam Sedgwick (1785–1873) and Charles Darwin (1809–82); records of the Bible Society (formerly the British and Foreign Bible Society), 19th–20th centuries, and other national and university societies.

Commerical records, including Phoenix Assurance, 1782–20th century; Jardine Matheson & Co, 19th century; Vickers plc, 19th–20th centuries.

Queens' College Archives.

Medieval MSS of Pembroke College and Peterhouse.

Non-manuscript material: Microfilms of MSS in other locations, e.g. the papers of Field Marshal J.C. Smuts (1870–1950).

Finding aids: Lists and indexes.

Facilities: Photocopying. Photography. Microfilming. Microfilm readers. Ultra-violet light.

Conservation: Full in-house facilities.

Publications: Catalogue of the (Western) Manuscripts Preserved in the Library of the University of Cambridge (Cambridge, 1856–67/R1980) [the preface to the reprint contains details of the principal catalogues of both Western and oriental MS collections published to 1979].

F.H. Burkhardt and others: *Calendar of the Correspondence of Charles Darwin, 1821–1882* (New York and London, 1985).

P. de Brun and M. Herbert: *Catalogue of Irish Manuscripts in Cambridge Libraries* (Cambridge, 1986).

Various published handlists and indexes.

B University Archives

Telephone: (01223) 333147/333148

Fax: (01223) 333160

Enquiries: The Keeper of Manuscripts and University Archives, Dr P.N.R. Zutshi

Open/Access: As Manuscripts Department above.

Historical background: From at least the 14th century the university kept its muniments in a chest in the tower of the University Church. It was from here that they were allegedly removed and destroyed in the 1381 rising. In fact more than 50 items, the earliest dated 1266, survive from before this date. By 1420, when Rysley compiled the first catalogue, the chest had been transferred to the New Chapel above the newly built Divinity Schools. During the Civil War the archives may have been hidden in private houses before being returned, in 1662, to a custom-built muniment room next to the Registrar's office in the Old Schools, the Registrar being recognised henceforth as their keeper. In 1836 the Registrar's office and the archives were moved into the new Pitt Press building and remained there until 1934, when the building of the new University Library (entry **147A**) enabled their return to the Old Schools. In 1972 the archives were transferred physically into the university library and in 1977 came under the librarian's authority. Some of the university's departments and libraries hold papers.

Acquisitions policy: Acquisitions are restricted to records of the administration of the university and its departments.

Archives of organisation: Charters, grants of privilege, title deeds; university statutes; records of the university's legislative and executive bodies and of the Chancellor's and Commissary's jurisdiction; financial records; Syndicate minutes; departmental records; matriculation and degree records; records of charitable foundations and other endowments.

Records of University Press; Board of Extra-Mural Studies; Course on Overseas Development; Botanic Garden; Appointments Board; Department of Geology.

Non-manuscript material: Estate maps and plans. Architectural plans and drawings. Photographs. Items of academic dress (few).

Finding aids: Card index. Typescript lists of many collections, some sent to NRA.

Facilities/Conservation: As Manuscripts Department entry above.

Publications: Statutes, 1785–.

H.R. Luard: 'A List of Documents in the University Registry from the Year 1266 to the

year 1544,' *Proceedings of the Cambridge Antiquarian Society* (o.s.), iii (1864–76), 385–403.
A Chronological List of the Graces, Documents and other Papers in the University Registry which Concern the University Library (Cambridge, 1870).
Grace Books Alpha to Delta (Cambridge 1897–1910) [*Beta* in two parts].
E.S. Leedham-Green: 'University Press Records in the University Archives: an Account and a Checklist', *Transactions of the Cambridge Bibliographical Society*, viii (1984), 398–418.
H.E. Peek and C.P. Hall: *The Archives of the University of Cambridge; a Historical Introduction.*
D.M. Owen: *Cambridge University Archives: a Classified List* (Cambridge, 1989).

C Royal Commonwealth Society Collections

Telephone: (01223) 333000/333198

Fax: (01223) 333160

Enquiries: Miss T.A. Barringer

Open/Access: As Manuscripts Department above.

Historical background: The organisation, founded as the Colonial Society in 1868 and known successively as the Royal Colonial Institute, the Royal Empire Society and the Royal Commonwealth Society, built up a library from its earliest days. The society had its headquarters in Northumberland Avenue, London WC2, from 1885. In the early 1990s the library was threatened with piecemeal sale and dispersal as a result of the society's financial difficulties, but a successful international appeal succeeded in buying the entire collection for the University of Cambridge and it was transferred to the University Library in the summer of 1993.

Acquisitions policy: Newly published material is no longer added to the collection but donations of relevant manuscripts and photographs are welcome.

Archives of organisation: Archives of the Royal Commonwealth Society: substantial collection of minute books of the council of the society and varied committees; correspondence; memoranda; miscellaneous items.

Major collections: Papers of Sir George Arthur (1784–1854) as Superintendent of British Honduras, 1814–24.

Some official correspondence and private papers of Hugh Childers (1827–96), cabinet minister.
Diaries and notebooks of Cuthbert Christy (1863–1932), doctor and traveller.
Correspondence and diaries of Sir John Glover (1829–85), administrator in West Africa.
Papers of Colonel Henry Burney (1792–1845), diplomat in Siam and Burma.
British Association of Malaya: diaries, letters, reminiscences (20 boxes).
Charts and documents relating to the North West Company, the fur trade and Canadian exploration.

Non-manuscript material: Photographs (70,000), including c3000 photographs of members of the society, 1880–1925.
Smaller collection of negatives and some slides.
Several collections of paintings and prints, notably paintings by A.H. Fisher, Gen. Edward Frome, A.A. Anderson, and the Gifford Collection of prints and drawings of St Helena.

Finding aids: Updated typescript catalogue to Manuscript Collection available on request. Detailed handlist to major collections.

Facilities/Conservation: As Manuscripts Department above.

Publications: D.H. Simpson: *Manuscript Catalogue of the Royal Commonwealth Society* (1975).
National Inventory of Documentary Sources, (Chadwyck-Healey microfiche 1984–).
Library Notes, nos. 1–306 (1957–91)

D Royal Greenwich Observatory

Telephone: (01223) 333000, 333056 (direct line)

Fax: (01223) 333160

Enquiries: The Royal Greenwich Observatory Archivist, Mr A.J. Perkins

Open/Access: As Manuscripts Department above. The 30–year rule applies to much of this collection.

Historical background: The Royal Observatory, Greenwich, was founded in 1675 by Charles II for the improvement of navigation. It became the Royal Greenwich Observatory in 1948. In 1988 the collection was moved from Herstmonceux Castle, East Sussex, to Cambridge University Library. The archives were developed largely under George Biddel Airy (1801–92), 7th Astronomer Royal, who also acquired the records of the Board of Longitude. The archives of the RGO are public records. The records reflect the role of the RGO in navigational astronomy, astrometry and astrophysical research.

Acquisitions policy: Modern records of the RGO accrue to the collection in accordance with the Public Records Act 1958. The personal papers of the Astronomers Royal, members of staff, and associated astronomers and scientists are accepted on deposit, as are collections of papers related to the RGO and astronomy.

Archives of organisation: Papers of the Astronomers Royal, 1675–1971, and directors of the RGO, 1972–93.
Papers and records of HM Nautical Almanac Office, 1937–93.
Administrative papers, 1911–90.
Departmental and project papers, 20th century, including records of the Anglo-Australian Telescope Project, 1963–72, and the Northern Hemisphere Observatory (La Palma), 1970–93.

Major collections: Records of the Board of Longitude, 1737–1828; Royal Observatory, Cape of Good Hope, 1820–1978, and Radcliffe Observatory, 1929–67.
Kew Observatory papers, solar observations and records, 1858–93.
Stonyhurst College Observatory sunspot drawings, 1880–1947.
Papers of John Guy Porter (1900–81); Roderick Oliver Redman (1905–75); and Donald Harry Sadler (1908–87).

Non-manuscript material: Plans of the observatory buildings and grounds at Greenwich and Herstmonceux, and of observing sites.
Astronomical drawings and drawings of places with astronomical associations.
Photographs of astronomical subjects, and people and places with astronomical associations.
Maps concerned with the move of the Royal Observatory, c1944.
Some films and videos concerned with telescopes and astronomy.
Sound recordings by working astronomers (oral history of the Royal Observatory).
Microfilms of the earlier papers.

Finding aids: Handlists to the major classes. Catalogue and index to the papers of John

Flamsteed (also in machine readable form). Index to photographs and records of Royal Observatory, Cape of Good Hope. Index to Biddell Airy papers. Lists of papers of the earlier Astronomers Royal sent to NRA.

Facilities/Conservation: As manuscripts department above. Photocopying permitted only from some 20th–century collections.

148 Cambridgeshire Archives Service
Cambridge County Record Office

Address: Shire Hall, Castle Hill, Cambridge CB3 0AP

Telephone: (01223) 317281

Fax: (01223) 317201

Enquiries: The County Archivist, Mrs E.A. Stazicker

Open: Mon–Thurs: 9.00–12.45; 1.45–5.15 (Tues evening to 9.00, by appointment) Fri: 9.00–12.45; 1.45–4.15

Access: Generally open to the public. The office operates the CARN reader's ticket system.

Historical background: The office was established for receipt of records in 1930, but had no staff until 1948. Before 1930 Cambridge University Library (entry 147) acted as a local repository. The office also acts as Diocesan Record office for Ely (parish records) and the Archdeaconry of Ely, and of the deaneries of Ely and March in Wisbech Archdeaconry, and probate records for the Diocesan Archdeaconry. Other diocesan and archdeaconry records are at Cambridge University Library; parish records for other deaneries are at Wisbech Museum (entry 1091) and Norfolk and Norwich Record Office (entry 855). There is a Branch Office at Huntingdon (entry 404).

Acquisitions policy: The service seeks to acquire records of all sorts relating to the area of the present administrative county. This comprises the historic counties of Cambridgeshire, the Isle of Ely, Huntingdonshire and the Soke of Peterborough (but note that parish records and records of pre-1888 private bodies for the area of the Soke are held at Northamptonshire Record Office (entry 848). Records for the

Cambridgeshire and Isle of Ely area are held mainly at Cambridge Record Office.

Archives of organisation: Usual local authority record holdings.

Major collections: Deposited local collections, including records of Bedford Level Corporation, 1663–1920 (with some earlier records); nearly complete series relating to land drainage of fens and adjoining counties; records of various women's groups, of which Cambridge was particularly prolific, 1884–1984.

Non-manuscript material: Aerial photographs, 1949–69; Cambridge Antiquarian Society glass lantern slides, 1920s and 1930s.

Facilities: Photocopying. Photography by arrangement. Microfilming. Microfilm/fiche readers.

Conservation: Paper, parchment and bookbinding in-house; advice relating to record care always available; outside work undertaken occasionally.

Publications: Annual Reports (1965–) [include lists of accessions].
A. Black: *Guide to Education Records* (1972).
M. Farrar: *Genealogical Sources in Cambridgeshire* (2/1994).

149 Cambridgeshire Collection

Parent organisation: Cambridgeshire Libraries and Heritage Service

Address: Central Library, 7 Lion Yard, Cambridge CB2 3QD

Telephone: (01223) 65252 ext. 209

Fax: (01223) 62786

Enquiries: The Local Studies Librarian, Mr M.J. Petty

Open: Mon–Fri: 9.30–5.30 Sat: 9.00–5.00

Access: Generally open to the public.

Historical background: Cambridge Free Library opened in 1855 and from that date collected material relating to Cambridge and Cambridgeshire, both current and retrospective. In 1974 material from the local collection of Cambridgeshire and Isle of Ely County Library was incorporated with the city library collection to form the current collection.

Acquisitions policy: To collect material, principally published, relating to the City of Cambridge and the former county of Cambridgeshire and Isle of Ely, past, present and future.

Non-manuscript material: Photographic record of the Cambridge Antiquarian Society.
Industrial archaeological record of the Cambridge Society for Industrial Archaeology.
Various photographic collections.
Books, articles, annual reports, periodicals and associated monograph material.
Handbills and posters, 1734–; illustrations, 1688– (*c*400,000).
Maps, principally printed, 1574–.
Newspapers, 1764–; printed ephemera.
Tape-recordings and gramophone records relating to Cambridgeshire.

Finding aids: Catalogues. Indexes. Computer link to County Record Office. Listed Buildings and County Council minutes.

Facilities: Photocopying. Photography. Microfilm reader/printer. Tape play-back facilities.

Publications: Guide for Users.
Guide to Catalogues and Indexes.
Cambridgeshire Newspapers and the Local Researcher.
Village Projects: a Guide for Users.
An annotated Catalogue of Books and Articles, Pamphlets and Periodicals Acquired, 1855–1983 [on microfiche].
M.J. Petty: "'The Albatross Inheritance": Local Studies Libraries', *Library Management*, vi/1 (1985).

150 Centre of South Asian Studies

Parent organisation: University of Cambridge

Address: Laundress Lane, Cambridge CB2 1SD

Telephone: (01223) 338094

Fax: (01223) 316913

Enquiries: The Secretary/Librarian, Dr L.J. Carter

Open: Term: Mon–Fri: 9.30–5.30 Vacation: Mon–Fri: 9.30–5.00
Closed August.

Access: By appointment; written application two weeks in advance, with references and statement of study.

Historical background: The archive was begun in 1966 to collect papers relating to economic, social and political conditions during the period of British rule in India, Burma and Ceylon. Contact was made with persons whose papers would not otherwise have found their way into a collection. This was done through the Indian Civil Service Pensioners' Association, and later all recipients of a pension from the former Indian Empire were contacted. Funding has come from various sources.

Acquisitions policy: Contacts made by word of mouth are the main source of material, which is personally collected by the librarian.

Major collections: Papers of Sir Edward Benthall (1893–1961); Sir Malcolm Darling (1880–1969); J.T. Gwynn (1881–1956) and J.P.L. Gwynn, Indian Civil Service, Madras; P.T. Mansfield (1892–1975), ICS Bihar and Orissa; Sir Reginald (1882–1927) and Lady Maxwell, ICS Madras etc.
Collection of writings (memoirs, letters, etc) by British women who lived and worked in India, and a series of answers to questionnaires.

Non-manuscript material: Tape-recordings made in India of people who knew Gandhi and were connected with the early days of the Independence movement; the conditions in Delhi and Punjab in 1947; Anglo-Indians; Roman Catholic missionaries and those who remained in India after 1947.
Tape-recordings made in England of wives and widows of Indian Civil Servants, and other government officers (Forestry etc), missionaries and educationalists.
More than 80,000 photographs, including negatives and glass slides.
Cine films: home movies (16mm, 9.5mm and 8mm) covering aspects of domestic and social life, ceremonial, engineering, indigenous village life, people, crafts, tribals.
Maps on South and South-East Asia (300); an Indian Newspaper Collection (3000 reels of microfilm).

Finding aids: Typescript lists of unpublished material. Handlists of photographic collections. Shotlists for cine films.

Facilities: Microfilm/fiche readers. Editing table for films.

Publications: M. Thatcher and L. Carter (eds): *Cambridge South Asian Archive* (1973, 1980, 1983, 1986) [4 vols], reproduced in: Chadwyck-Healey: *National Inventory of Documentary Sources in the United Kingdom* .
D. Boyes: *Principal Collections of Photographic*

Material in the Cambridge South Asian Archive (1984).
L. Carter and D. Bateson: *Principal Collections of Papers in the Cambridge South Asian Archive* (2/1987).
L. Carter: *Brief Guide to Original Memoirs held in the Cambridge South Asian Archive* (1989).
Annual Reports of the Centre of South Asian Studies, University of Cambridge.

151 Cheshunt Foundation Archives

Address: Westminster College, Madingley Road, Cambridge CB3 0AA

Telephone: (01223) 353997 ext. 5

Fax: (01223) 300765

Enquiries: The Director, The Cheshunt Foundation, Rev. Dr D.G. Cornick, The Hon. Archivist, Dr Edwin Welch

Open: By special arrangement only.

Access: Any person with reasonable grounds; appointment necessary.

Historical background: The Cheshunt Foundation is the legal continuation of the former Cheshunt College, originally founded at Trevecca in 1767 by Selina, Countess of Huntingdon (1707–91), an aristocratic patron of the Wesleys. Cheshunt effectively ceased to operate as a theological college after the early 1970s.

Acquisitions policy: No acquisitions are sought; there is a small inflow of items of new relevant material given by individuals.

Archives of organisation: Records of Cheshunt College, 1767–1970s.
Correspondence of Selina, Countess of Huntingdon (several thousand items).

Finding aids: Catalogue, well indexed. Cheshunt Collection: NRA 12352.

Facilities: Photocopying.

Publications: E. Welch: *Calendar and Index of Cheshunt College Archives*, List and Index Society Special Series 14 (1981).
——(ed.): *Cheshunt College: the Early Years*, (Herts Records Society, 1991).

152 Christ's College

Parent organisation: University of Cambridge

Address: Cambridge CB2 3BU

Telephone: (01223) 334900

Enquiries: The College Archivist

Open: Mon–Fri: 9.00–1.00, by arrangement.

Access: Subject to approval of the governing body of Christ's College.

Historical background: The college was founded in 1439 as God's House, licensed by Henry VI, and refounded in 1505 by the Lady Margaret Beaufort, by whom the college was richly endowed.

Acquisitions policy: To receive gifts and bequests of MSS and photographic material from Fellows.

Archives of organisation: Archives include deeds, grants, manorial rolls, confirmations, conveyances, terriers, grants of advowsons, college account books, student admission books and numerous other records relating to the administration of the college, 12th century–.

Major collections: Western MSS collections.

Non-manuscript material: Some photographic material from the mid-19th century.
A few tape-recordings.
Maps and plans of present and former college estates.
Architectural plans and drawings of college buildings.

Finding aids: Lists and catalogue in preparation.

Facilities: Photocopying.

Publications: M.R. Jones: *A Descriptive Catalogue of the Western Manuscripts in the Library of Christ's College Cambridge* (Cambridge, 1905).
J. Peile: *Christ's College Bibliographical Register* (Cambridge, 1910) [2 vols].
H. Rackham: *Early Statutes of Christ's College* (Cambridge, 1927).
See also HMC First Report, App. 63(1).

153 Churchill Archives Centre

Parent organisation: Churchill College, University of Cambridge

Address: Churchill College, Cambridge CB3 0DS

Telephone: (01223) 336087

Fax: (01223) 336135

Enquiries: The Archivist, Alan Kucia

Open: Mon–Fri: 9.00–12.30; 1.30–5.00

Access: Bona fide researchers, by appointment only. Special conditions apply to a number of collections. In all cases the Archivist should be consulted in writing.

Historical background: Churchill College was founded in 1960 as the UK and Commonwealth memorial to Sir Winston Churchill (1874–1965). The Archives Centre, opened in 1973, constitutes an American tribute to Sir Winston, since the cost of construction and endowment was met by a group of prominent US citizens. The archives of the College are administered separately. Contact the College Archivist, Ms Joan Bullock-Anderson, tel. (01223) 336168, for further details.

Acquisitions policy: The centre was built to house Sir Winston's own papers, and to establish and make available a wide-ranging archive of the 'Churchill Era' and after, covering all those fields in which Churchill played a personal role or took a personal interest.

Major collections: Papers of Sir Winston Churchill and of more than 400 other political, military, naval, diplomatic and scientific figures, including Lord Alexander of Hillsborough, Lord Attlee, Ernest Bevin, Sir Alexander Cadogan, Sir James Chadwick, Sir John Cockcroft, Lord Duncan-Sandys, Admiral of the Fleet Lord Fisher of Kilverstone, Lord Hailsham, Lord Hankey, Lt.-Gen. Sir Ian Jacob, Neil Kinnock, Reginald McKenna, Lise Meitner, Lord Noel-Baker, Sir Eric Phipps, FM Lord Slim, Sir Edward Spears, and Lord Vansittart.

Non-manuscript material: Numerous photographs, mainly on the life and career of Churchill; microfilms; video and audio tapes.

Finding aids: TS catalogues of all major collections. Computerised catalogue and index of Churchill papers in preparation. Catalogues sent to NRA.

Facilities: Photocopying. Photography and

microfilming by arrangement. Accommodation in college usually available during university vacation.

Conservation: In-house paper conservation workshop.

Publications: A Guide to the Holdings of Churchill Archives Centre (1994) [a complete list of collections, reprinted annually].

154 Clare College Archives

Parent organisation: University of Cambridge

Address: Clare College Memorial Courts, Queens Road, Cambridge CB3 9AJ

Telephone: (01223) 333228

Fax: (01223) 333219

Enquiries: The College Archivist, Mrs S.C. Johnston

Open: Mon–Fri: 9.15–12.45, strictly by arrangement; afternoon opening can sometimes be arranged.

Access: Bona fide enquirers, by prior appointment. Restrictions are applied to personal records and all documents under 30 years old.

Historical background: Clare College was founded as University Hall by Richard de Badew in 1326, and refounded and endowed by Elizabeth de Clare between 1338 and 1359. Subsequent benefactions include the college properties. In 1521 a fire destroyed almost all records. The archives were formerly administered by the bursar; an archivist was appointed in 1985 and new accommodation was converted in 1986.

Acquisitions policy: Records relating to the college's administration, properties and affairs, and to related bodies. Papers of alumni and student organisations.

Archives of organisation: Statutes, 1359–1989; minutes of governing body and subsidiaries, 1644–; accounts, including main college accounts, 1549–1977; registers of property transactions, 1354–1950; letter-books and files, 1628–.
Student records, including admission registers, 1631–1979, and tutorial accounts, 1658–1948.
Estate records for college properties in Cambridgeshire and many parts of England, 1298–.
Records of college benefices, 1539–1990.
Records of benefactions and trusts, 1525–1971.

Major collections: Papers of alumni, including

Samuel Blithe (1636–1713), Edward Atkinson (1819–1915), Cecil Sharp (1859–1924), John Reynolds Wardale (1859–1931), W. C. Denis Browne (1888–1915), Mansfield Forbes (1889–1936) and Sir Harry Godwin (1901–85).
Records of student association, 1940–.
Minutes and accounts etc of various student clubs, notably Boat Club, 19th–20th centuries.

Non-manuscript material: Maps and plans, 1634–20th century.
Photographs and engravings of benefactors, alumni and buildings.
Series of student and alumni magazines, 1889–.

Finding aids: Preliminary lists. Computerised catalogue in progress. Classification scheme and handlists. Brief lists sent to NRA.

Facilities: Photocopying.

Conservation: Contracted out to two private organisations.

Publications: J.R. Wardale: *Clare College* (London, 1899).
——: *Clare College Letters and Documents* (Cambridge, 1903).
M.D. Forbes: *Clare College, 1326–1926* (Cambridge, 1927, 1930) [2 vols].
W.J. Harrison: *Notes on the Masters, Fellows, Scholars and Exhibitioners of Clare College, Cambridge* (Cambridge, 1953).
——: *Life in Clare Hall* (Cambridge, 1958).
H. Godwin: *Cambridge and Clare* (Cambridge, 1985).

155 Corpus Christi College Archives

Parent organisation: University of Cambridge

Address: Trumpington Street, Cambridge CB2 1HS

Telephone: (01223) 338049

Enquiries: The Archivists, Mrs N. Levy (modern archives) or Mrs C. Hall (early archives)

Open: College records: by arrangement (may be closed during vacation periods).
Older administrative records kept in the college's Parker Library available for readers in that library only (see below).

Access: College records: open to those having sent a letter of request/reference, subject to the discretion of the keeper of the records. Recent personal and administrative records not yet on open access. For material in the Parker Library apply to the assistant librarian *re* admissions procedure to become a reader.

Historical background: The College of Corpus Christi and the Blessed Virgin Mary was founded in 1352, uniting two town guilds of those names, under the patronage of Henry, Duke of Lancaster. The small medieval college was enlarged, reorganised and generously endowed by Matthew Parker, Queen Elizabeth's first Archbishop of Canterbury, who had been Master of the College under King Edward VI. The MS collection he bequeathed to the college is enshrined in the college's Parker Library, a separate entity within the college with its own librarian.

Acquisitions policy: Acquisitions are restricted to material relevant to the history of the college and the corporate activities of its members. Donations of MSS or papers by old members are housed in the Parker Library.

Archives of organisation: The college muniments proper comprise predominantly bursarial material; there is an incomplete series of college accounts, 1376–. Also medieval charters, especially relating to property in Cambridge, and registers covering the careers of Fellows. There are incomplete series of more recent administrative records with their supplementary ephemera.

Major collections: College library: papers of Arthur Boutwood (1864–1924), philosopher and theologian; correspondence of the Postlethwayt, Rogerson and Kerrich families, 1633–1828.
Parker Collection: bequest of Archbishop Matthew Parker (*d* 1575) of medieval and Reformation MSS, also material relating to Parker and his associates.

Non-manuscript material: Photographs and ephemera relating to the collegiate activities of old members.
Old prints and drawings of the college.

Finding aids: Typescript catalogue. Card catalogue of estate deeds. Handlists of maps.

Facilities: Photocopying. Photography by arrangement.

Publications: M.R. James: *A Descriptive Catalogue of the MSS in the Library of Corpus Christi College Cambridge* (Cambridge, 1912) [2 vols].

R. Vaughan and J. Fines: 'A Handlist of MSS in the Library of Corpus Christi College Cambridge not Described by M.R. James', *Transactions of the Cambridge Bibliographical Society*, iii (1960).

156 Department of Plant Sciences Library

Parent organisation: University of Cambridge

Address: Downing Street, Cambridge CB2 3EA

Telephone: (01223) 333930

Fax: (01223) 33953

Enquiries: The Assistant Librarian, Mr R. Savage

Open: Term: Mon–Fri: 8.30–5.15 Vacation: Mon–Fri: 8.30–5.15

Access: Members of the university; others with an interest in plant sciences.

Historical background: The Department of Plant Sciences was formerly the Botany School. The library was established in 1762 in association with the Botanic Garden; it has been in its present building since 1903.

Acquisitions policy: The library accepts donations of relevant botanical papers.

Major collections: Notes and some correspondence of eminent botanists, including Charles Cardale Babington (1808–95), founder of the Entomological Society; John Stevens Henslow (1796–1861); William Border (1781–1862); A.G. Tansley (1871–1955); and G.C. Evans.

Finding aids: NRA 9541.

Facilities: Photocopying. Microfiche reader.

Conservation: Undertaken by Cambridge University Library (entry **147**).

157 Downing College

Parent organisation: University of Cambridge

Address: Cambridge CB2 1DQ

Telephone: (01223) 334800 College (Porter's Lodge; Archivist) 334829 (Library)

Enquiries: The Fellow Archivist

Open: By arrangement only.

Access: Application must be made to the

librarian to consult the Bowtell Collection. Consultation of archives is by appointment only; application to be made to the Fellow Archivist or Assistant (if available).

Historical background: The college was founded in 1800 following years of litigation over the will of the founder, Sir George Downing (?1684–1749). Acquisition of land for the college site, development of the domus, and the development of the college within the university are reflected in the collection.

Acquisitions policy: Maintenance of archives and addition of modern college records (administrative and academic), where relevant.

Archives of organisation: Records of the college, including: Downing family and estate papers; opinions and petitions *re* legal contest over foundation; college statutes; minute and account books; residence books.

Major collections: Library: Collection of John Bowtell (1753–1813), Cambridge antiquarian: includes Borough of Cambridge records; deeds, 16th–18th centuries; medieval fragments; MSS on bell ringing.

Non-manuscript material: Wilkins Plans: architectural plans for the college; the farm plans of Downing estates in Cambridgeshire, mid-19th century.

Finding aids: Bowtell Collection: NRA 22707. Full lists and indexes to be compiled for archives.

Facilities: Photocopying.

Publications: C.M. Sicca: *Committed to Classicism: the Building of Downing College Cambridge.*
S. French: *The History of Downing College Cambridge.*
——(ed.): *Aspects of Downing History.*

158 East Asian History of Science Library

Parent organisation: Needham Research Institute

Address: 8 Sylvester Road, Cambridge CB3 9AF

Telephone: (01223) 311545/69252

Enquiries: The Librarian, Mr J.P.C. Moffett

Open: Mon–Fri: 9.30–5.00

Access: Bona fide scholars and research workers, by appointment only.

Historical background: The personal collection of Dr Joseph Needham (1900–95) forms the nucleus round which the library is developing. Dr Needham worked, with a number of collaborators, for more than 40 years on the history of Chinese science, technology and medicine. The library, as part of the Science and Civilization in China Project, became a recognised educational charity in 1963. It belongs to, and is governed by, the East Asian History of Science Trust.

Acquisitions policy: Chinese material of all periods connected with the history of science, technology and medicine is constantly being added, with Japanese and Western material on the same subjects.

Major collections: Archival and photographic material, 1940–, including a quantity of MSS in European and Asian languages, especially Chinese and Japanese, comprising principally notes and maps.

Non-manuscript material: Printed books (including many rare Chinese editions), periodicals and offprints.
Microfilm/fiche collections of Chinese material not widely available in the West.

Finding aids: Card catalogues.

Facilities: Photocopying. Microfilm/fiche reader.

Publications: J. Needham and others: *Science and Civilization in China* (Cambridge, 1954–) [15 vols to date].

159 Emmanuel College

Parent organisation: University of Cambridge

Address: Cambridge CB2 3AP

Telephone: (01223) 334292/334200

Fax: (01223) 334426

Enquiries: The Archivist

Open: Mon–Fri: 9.00–5.30, by arrangement.

Access: Bona fide researchers, by appointment.

Historical background: Emmanuel College was founded in 1584 by Sir Walter Mildmay. The archives were first assembled in 1955 by H.S. Bennett.

Acquisitions policy: Consolidation of the college archives by receipt of non-current records from the various college offices.

Archives of organisation: Foundation deeds and statutes; estate deeds and records, 1584–, including a few medieval deeds and manorial court rolls; administrative records, including order books, 1588–, and minute books, 1895–; financial records, 1584–; admission registers, 1584–; records of undergraduate societies, 19th and 20th centuries; chapel records, including accounts and inventories, 1599–.

Major collections: Letters, papers and photographs of past members of the college, including Henry Melville Gwatkin (1844–1916), historian and theologian; Edward Woodall Naylor (1867–1934), composer and musical historian; and Cyril Northcote Parkinson (1910–93), author and historian. Also a collection of letters of F.R. Leavis (1895–1978), English scholar and critic.

Non-manuscript material: Plans of college buildings, maps of college estates, photographs of college and people connected with it.

Finding aids: Handlists and indexes in the College Archives. Not generally sent to NRA. Gwatkin: NRA 27206.

Facilities: Photocopying and photography by arrangement.

Conservation: Contracted out.

Publications: M.R. James: *The Western MSS in the Library of Emmanuel College* (Cambridge, 1904).
P. Hunter Blair: 'The College Archive', *Emmanuel College Magazine*, lxi (1978–9), 14–18.

160 Fitzwilliam College

Parent organisation: University of Cambridge

Address: Huntingdon Road, Cambridge CB3 0DG

Telephone: (01223) 332000

Fax: (01223) 464162

Enquiries: The Archivist

Open: By arrangement.

Access: Bona fide researchers only.

Historical background: The college was founded in 1869 as a non-collegiate organ-

isation catering for students unable to afford college fees and college life. It developed into an identifiable foundation known firstly as Fitzwilliam Hall and then as Fitzwilliam House until 1966, when it received collegiate status. Board meeting minutes are housed in Cambridge University Library (entry **147**), but copies are in the collection at the college.

Acquisitions policy: To maintain the archives of the college.

Archives of organisation: Records of the non-collegiate foundation from its inception, growth and final achievement of collegiate status, 1869–.

Non-manuscript material: Photographs.

Finding aids: Catalogue.

Publications: W.W. Grave: *Fitzwilliam College Cambridge, 1869–1969* (Fitzwilliam Society, 1983).

161 Fitzwilliam Museum
Department of Manuscripts and Printed Books

Parent organisation: University of Cambridge

Address: Trumpington Street, Cambridge CB2 1RB

Telephone: (01223) 332900

Fax: (01223) 332923

Enquiries: The Keeper

Open: Tues–Thurs: 10.00–12.30; 1.30–4.30 Fri: 10.00–12.30; 1.30–4.15

Access: Museum staff, members of the University of Cambridge; others with special research enquiries on written application. The archives of the museum are not open to the public.

Historical background: The museum was founded in 1816 by Richard, seventh Viscount Fitzwilliam of Merrion, when he bequeathed to the University of Cambridge, in which he took his MA in 1764, his fine art collections, his library, and the sum of £100,000 to build a museum. The museum now has five curatorial departments: Antiquities, Applied Arts, Coins and Medals, Manuscripts and Printed Books, and Paintings, Drawings and Prints.

Acquisitions policy: To strengthen the collection by purchase, gifts, bequests and loans.

Major collections: Illuminated MSS (Western and oriental).
MS and printed music.
Literary and historical MSS.
Autograph letters.
McClean Collection of illuminated MSS and incunabula.

Non-manuscript material: Lord Fitzwilliam's Library. Exhibition catalogues. Dealers' catalogues. Sale catalogues. Incunabula. Private press books.

Finding aids: Card and slip catalogues.

Facilities: Photocopying. Photography. Microfilm/fiche reader/printer.

Publications: J.A. Fuller-Maitland and A.H. Mann: *Catalogue of the Music in the Fitzwilliam Museum* (London, 1893).
M.R. James: *A Descriptive Catalogue of the Manuscripts in the Fitzwilliam Museum* (Cambridge, 1895).
——: *A Descriptive Catalogue of the McClean Collection of Manuscripts in the Fitzwilliam Museum* (Cambridge, 1912).
F. Wormald and P.M. Giles: *A Descriptive Catalogue of the Additional Illuminated Manuscripts in the Fitzwilliam Museum Acquired between 1895 and 1979* (Cambridge, 1982).

162 French Resistance Archive

Parent organisation: Anglia Polytechnic University

Address: East Road, Cambridge CB1 1PT

Telephone: (01223) 63271 ext. 2312

Fax: (01223) 352973

Enquiries: The Archive Curator, Jeremy Holford-Miettinen

Open: Term: Mon–Thurs: 9.00–8.30 Fri: 9.00–4.30 Vacation: Mon–Fri 10.00–4.30

Access: Access by non-members of the university is by appointment only; in the case of students up to undergraduate level, a supporting letter from a tutor is required. Users are advised to apply as far in advance as possible.

Historical background: The collection was started in the 1970s when the university was the Cambridgeshire College of Arts and Technology. Dr Hilary Footitt and Dr J.C. Simmonds gathered the material. The collection was used to develop teaching materials as well as providing users with a selection of important primary and secondary sources. The material represents as many different social, economic and political groups as possible. Originally a print collection, the archive now holds audiotapes, videotapes, photographs and slides as well.

Non-manuscript material: Copies of unpublished material concerned with the Resistance in World War II; Resistance journals; photographs and postcards; slides; audio and videotape interviews with former members of different movements and Allied services, e.g. Special Operations Executive (SOE). Microfilms of Resistance journals.

Finding aids: A computer-generated catalogue has been created: copies may be purchased. The development of an indexed CD-ROM of the archive is under consideration.

Facilities: Photocopying. Photography. Slide viewing. Audio and videotape facilities. Microfilm reader/printer.

Publications: H. Footitt and J.C. Simmonds: *The Resistance Experience: Teaching & Resources.*
J. Holford-Miettinen: *The French Resistance Archive: a Brief Introduction*
——: *Two Sticks and TNT: The French Resistance Archive.*

163 Girton College

Parent organisation: University of Cambridge

Address: Cambridge CB3 0JG

Telephone: (01223) 338897

Fax: (01223) 338896

Enquiries: The Archivist, Ms Kate Perry

Open: Mon–Fri: 9.00–5.00, by appointment.

Access: Bona fide scholars and research workers.

Historical background: The college, originally for women, was founded in 1869.

Acquisitions policy: To strengthen the collection by purchase, gifts and bequests.

Archives of organisation: Documents and photographs relating to the college's internal administration, 1869–.

Major collections: Papers relating to the higher education of women and the inception of an organised women's movement, 19th century, including those of Barbara Bodichon (1827–91); Emily Davies (1830–1921), founder; Bessie Rayner Parkes (1828–1925), writer, publisher and editor.

Papers of alumni, including Dorothy Moyle Needham (1896–1987) and Barbara Wooton (1897–1988).

Non-manuscript material: Blackburn Collection: pamphlets and books collected by Helen Blackburn (1842–1903), suffragist.

Finding aids: Catalogues and lists.

Facilities: Photocopying.

164 Gonville and Caius College

Parent organisation: University of Cambridge

Address: Cambridge CB2 1TA

A College Archives

Telephone: (01223) 332446

Fax: (01223) 332456

Enquiries: The College Archivist, Ms A. Neary

Open: Mon–Fri, by appointment.

Access: Members of the college and other bona fide researchers.

Historical background: The archive consists of the undifferentiated muniments of the ancient Treasury, which held all the older records dating from the foundation of Gonville Hall in 1348 to the building of the New Treasury in 1879, apart from certain items in volumes removed to the library MSS.

Acquisitions policy: Acquisitions have in the past been restricted to the normal deposit of formal records produced in or by the college officiary with any related material. There is currently a project for extending the archive to include more personal or social items illustrating the corporate life of the college and of its members.

Archives of organisation: Admission Register, 1560–; reports of college meetings, 1651–; records of scholarships and fellowships, 1581–; bursars' books, 1422–1523, 1608–; bursars' indentures, 1490–*c*1640; archives of the Senior

Bursar and the Registrar, *c*1860–. Estate records, including deeds; lease books, 1559–; maps and architectural plans.

Non-manuscript material: Substantial photographic collection, consisting of college photographs taken by W. Swann and G.W. Wilson, also club photographs.

Finding aids: Historical registers of oldest muniments running from 1657 to 1970. Computerised catalogue of estate deeds, maps and architectural drawings in progress.

Facilities: Photocopying restricted to smaller and less fragile items. Photography by arrangement.

Conservation: Contracted out.

Publications: J. Venn (comp): *Biographical History of Gonville and Caius College*, iii (1901) [contains a summary of some of the more important older muniments]; iv, part 2 (1912) [contains an Estates Chronicle to 1901].
C. Brooke: *A History of Gonville and Caius College* (Boydell, 1985).
A. Neary: 'Bare Bones and Living History: the College Archives', *The Caian* (Nov 1990).

B The Library

Telephone: (01223) 332419

Fax: (01223) 332430

Enquiries: The Librarian, Mr J.H. Prynne

Open: Mon–Fri: 9.00–5.00

Access: Approved readers, on written application and by prior appointment only.

Historical background: The college has possessed a collection of books since 1349 and has housed them in a library since 1441; some 350 volumes survive from this medieval library. The collection has been augmented by the acquisition of printed books and some MSS, while continuing as a working collection for undergraduates.

Acquisitions policy: The library normally acquires MSS only by donation or bequest.

Major collections: Papers of certain members or former members of the college, principally those of: C.M. Doughty (1843–1926), poet and traveller; John Venn (1834–1923), logician and historian of the college; Charles Clayton (1821–83); and Charles Wood (1866–1926), composer.

Non-manuscript material: Collections relating to the Old Catholic movement, including newspaper cuttings, with some correspondence.

Finding aids: Holdings are partially listed in TS. Annotated copy of M.R. James' *Catalogue* (see 'Publications').

Facilities: Photocopying, photography and microfilm (university library facilities). Microfilm/fiche reader by arrangement.

Publications: M.R. James: *A Descriptive Catalogue of the Manuscripts in the Library of Gonville and Caius College* (Cambridge, 1907–11) [2 vols].
Supplement to the Catalogue (Cambridge, 1914).

165 Institute of Astronomy Library

Parent organisation: University of Cambridge

Address: The Observatories, Madingley Road, Cambridge CB3 0HA

Telephone: (01223) 337537

Enquiries: The Librarian

Open: Term: Mon–Fri: 9.00–1.00; 2.00–5.00 Vacation: enquiry necessary.

Access: Members of the university. Accredited readers by prior written request.

Historical background: Founded in 1823 as the library of the University Observatory, it then acquired many earlier books; later the libraries of the former Solar Physics Observatory and Institute of Theoretical Astronomy were incorporated. A move to the University Library is under consideration.

Acquisitions policy: Now mostly books, conference proceedings, periodicals and serials on modern astronomy; also material relating to the history of astronomy.

Major collections: MSS archives and observational records of Cambridge Observatories, 1823–.
Correspondence and some scientific papers of former directors and staff members, especially G.B. Airy (1801–92), R.S. Ball (1840–1913), J. Challis (1803–82) and A. Hinks (1873–1945).

Non-manuscript material: 800 periodical and serial titles relating to astronomy (9300 vols).

5700 monographs. Sky surveys, star maps and catalogues. Offprint and pamphlet collection.

Finding aids: Finding list to 19th–century MS letters etc.

Facilities: Photocopying. Microfilm readers.

Publications: *Notes on the Use of the Library.*

166 Jesus College
The Old Library and Archives

Parent organisation: University of Cambridge

Address: Cambridge CB5 8BL

Telephone: (01223) 339414 (Keeper) 339439 (Archivist)

Fax: (01223) 324910

Enquiries: The Keeper

Open: By arrangement.

Access: Approved readers, on written application.

Historical background: The college succeeded to the buildings and property of St Radegund's Priory, Cambridge, in 1496. The contents of the library reflect the scholarly interests of the Fellows of the college since its foundation.

Acquisitions policy: Materials relating to the college and its old members.

Archives of organisation: Royal and episcopal charters, deeds, etc relating to the priory of St Radegund and the college, 12th and 13th centuries; records relating mainly to property and accounts, 1496–.

Major collections: Archives: biographical material relating to college members.
Library: medieval MSS, including a large group from Durham priory and other northern monasteries (*c*80 items).

Non-manuscript material: Political tracts of the Civil War period.
Malthus family library including books of Thomas Robert Malthus (1766–1834), political economist (*c*2300 vols).

Finding aids: Catalogue of archives. Catalogues and card indexes in library.

Facilities: Photocopying and photography by arrangement.

Publications: M.R. James: *A Descriptive Cata-*

logue of the Manuscripts in the Library of Jesus College, Cambridge (Cambridge, 1895).
A. Gray: *The Priory of St Radegund, Cambridge* (Cambridge Antiquarian Society, 1898).
J. Harrison et al: *The Malthus Library Catalogue* (New York, 1983).

167 Kettle's Yard

Parent organisation: University of Cambridge

Address: Castle Street, Cambridge CB3 0AQ

Telephone: (01223) 352124

Fax: (01223) 324377

Enquiries: The Director, Mr Michael Harrison

Open: Mon–Fri: 2.00–4.00

Access: Generally open to the public, but a letter for an appointment, stating interest, is essential.

Historical background: Kettle's Yard was the home of Jim and Helen Ede from 1957 until 1973, during which time their collection of 20th–century art, and furniture, textiles and ceramics from a wide historical period, was formed; it was given to the university in 1966.

Acquisitions policy: To maintain the Ede Collection.

Major collections: Correspondence of Jim Ede (1895–1990) with Alfred Wallis (1885–1942), Ben Nicholson (1894–1982), David Jones (1895–1974), T.E. Lawrence (1888–1935) and Helen Sutherland.
Material and sketch books of Henri Gaudier-Brzeska (1891–1915) and Christopher Wood (1901–30).

Non-manuscript material: Microfilm of Sophie Brzeska's diaries held by Cambridge University Library (entry **147**).
Personal library (art, literature, religion) of Jim Ede; Jan and Zoe Ellison bequest of literature on pottery and crafts.
Art periodicals, catalogues and publications from major art galleries.

Finding aids: Card index and written lists of archive material in progress.

Facilities: Photocopying.

Publications: J. Lewison: *Kettle's Yard: An Illustrated Guide.*
J. Ede: *Kettle's Yard: A Way of Life* [out of print].

168 King's College

Parent organisation: University of Cambridge

Address: Cambridge CB2 1ST

Fax: (01223) 331315

A College Archives

Enquiries: The Hon. Archivist, Mr A.E.B. Owen, c/o Manuscripts Department, Cambridge University Library (entry **147**)

Open: By arrangement.

Access: Bona fide researchers, on written application to the Hon. Archivist, giving at least two weeks' notice of any proposed visit.

Historical background: The college was founded in 1441. The contents of the Muniment Room are not the responsibility of the college library, but are usually made available for study in its Modern Archive Centre.

Acquisitions policy: Administrative records of the college.

Archives of organisation: Records of internal administration of the college since its foundation, and of its estates from c1200; some monastic records.

Finding aids: Handlists and card index. NRA 3643 and 16444 list a small part of the archives.

Facilities: The Hon. Archivist can arrange most forms of reprography at the University Library.

Publications: J. Saltmarsh: 'The Muniments of King's College', *Proceedings of the Cambridge Antiquarian Society*, xxxiii (1931–2), 83–97.
'Handlist of the Estates of King's College, Cambridge', *Bulletin of the Institute of Historical Research*, xii (1934), 32–8.
Allan Doig: *The Architectural Drawings Collection of King's College* (Cambridge, 1979).

B Library and Modern Archive Centre

Telephone: (01223) 331337 (Librarian) 331444 (Modern Archives)

Enquiries: The Librarian, Mr Peter Jones (for medieval MSS) or The Modern Archivist, Ms Jacqueline Cox (for post-medieval MSS)

Open: Mon–Fri: 9.30–5.15
Closed for six weeks every summer.

Access: Bona fide researchers with letter of introduction, and by appointment with the librarian or modern archivist.

Historical background: The Modern Archive Centre was established in 1983 and contains the papers of former members of the college and other people of historical importance.

Acquisitions policy: Papers of members of the college by gift or deposit.

Major collections: MSS of Isaac Newton (1642–1727) [in Keynes Library]; Rupert Brooke (1887–1915); T.S. Eliot (1888–1964); Richard Kahn (1905–89); John Nicholas Kaldor (1909–86); John Maynard Keynes (1883–1946); Joan Robinson (1902–82); Oscar Browning (1837–1923), Le Fanu family; E.M. Forster (1879–1970); C.R. Ashbee (1863–1942); Roger Fry (1866–1934); Alan Turing (1912–54).

Finding aids: Lists sent to NRA. Integrated name index to all collections.

Publications: M.R. James: *A Descriptive Catalogue of the Manuscripts in the Library of King's College, Cambridge* (Cambridge, 1895).

169 Lucy Cavendish College

Parent organisation: University of Cambridge

Address: Lady Margaret Road, Cambridge CB3 0BU

Telephone: (01223) 332183

Fax: (01223) 332178

Enquiries: The Librarian, Dr J.M. Sheppard

Open: By arrangement only.

Access: Bona fide researchers, by appointment.

The Lucy Cavendish College (f. 1965) is an approved foundation in the university for women, both research students and mature undergraduates. The college holds some papers relating to the life of Lucy, Lady Frederick Cavendish (1841–1925).

170 Magdalene College

Parent organisation: University of Cambridge

Address: Cambridge CB3 0AG

Telephone: (01223) 332100

A Old Library and Archives

Enquiries: The Keeper of the Old Library

Open: Term: Thurs: 12.00–1.00

Access: Qualified scholars; an appointment is necessary. Some modern collections are accessible only with the permission of the governing body or are closed under a time restriction.

Historical background: The college was originally a Benedictine hostel founded in 1428. In c1480 it became known as Buckingham College, which was refounded in 1542 as the College of St Mary Magdalene. The archives commence with the foundation of Buckingham College and continue to the present, but they are comparatively sparse before 1660.

Acquisitions policy: Material relating to former members of the college.

Archives of organisation: College records: a varied collection of administrative and estate records, 12th–20th centuries.

Major collections: Personal and literary papers of those connected with the college, including Charles Kingsley (1819–75), author; A. C. Benson (1862–1925), master; George Mallory (1886–1924), mountaineer; William R. Inge (1860–1954), Dean of St Paul's; I.A. Richards (1892–1979), philosopher and literary critic. Papers of the Ferrar family, of London, Little Gidding and Huntingdon, c1590–1790.

Finding aids: Comprehensive handlists.

Facilities: Photocopying. Photography.

Publications: M.R. James: *A Descriptive Catalogue of the Manuscripts in the College Library of Magdalene College, Cambridge* (Cambridge, 1909).

B Pepys Library

Enquiries: The Pepys Librarian

Open: Michaelmas and Lent terms: Mon–Sat: 2.30–3.30 Easter term and summer extension: Mon–Sat: 11.30–12.30; 2.30–3.30

Access: Qualified scholars; a letter of reference is always required and an appointment is necessary.

Historical background: Samuel Pepys's private library, comprising his entire personal collection made between 1649 and 1703, was conveyed to the college by the terms of his will in 1724. These terms forbid either subtraction from or addition to the collection. The books stand in the original presses as he ordained them to be left at his death.

Major collections: Medieval, music and naval MSS.
Pepys's private and state papers, including his diary and original library catalogues.

Facilities: Photography.

Publications: HMC: *Report on the Pepys Manuscripts* (1911).
R.C. Latham (ed.): *Catalogue of the Pepys Library* (Woodbridge, 1978–94) [11 vols].

171 Marshall Library of Economics

Parent organisation: University of Cambridge

Address: Sidgwick Avenue, Cambridge
CB3 9DB

Telephone: (01223) 335217

Fax: (01223) 335475

Enquiries: The Librarian, H.R. Thomas

Open: Term: Mon–Fri: 8.30–9.00 Sat: 9.00–1.00
Vacation: Mon–Fri: 9.00–5.00
Closed for two weeks in September.

Access: Members of the university; approved readers on written application.

Historical background: The library was established in 1925. The nucleus of the original departmental library was collected by Alfred Marshall for the use of students and placed by him in 1909 at the disposal of the Special Board for Economics. After Marshall's death in 1924, the greater part of his private library was merged with the departmental library. Originally housed in premises known as the Balfour Laboratory, in Downing Place, in 1935 the library moved to the former Squire Law Library in Downing Street. The present building was occupied in 1961. The Pryme Library, part of the Marshall Library since 1935, is now on permanent loan to Cambridge University Library (entry **147**).

Major collections: Notes, lectures, and other papers of Alfred Marshall (1842–1924), 1877–1923.
Correspondence of Herbert Somerton Foxwell (1849–1936), 1894–1926; John Neville Keynes (1852–1949), 1891–1942; and John Maynard Keynes (1883–1946), 1911–28.

Finding aids: Card index of letters. TS

list of papers. Computer catalogue of Marshall papers in progress.

Facilities: Photocopying. Microfiche reader. Photography by arrangement in main University Library.

172 Newnham College Archives

Parent organisation: University of Cambridge

Address: Sidgwick Avenue, Cambridge
CB3 9DF

Telephone: (01223) 335700/335789/335789

Fax: (01223) 357898

Enquiries: The Archivist, Dr C. Hicks

Open: By arrangement .

Access: Bona fide scholars, by appointment.

Historical background: The college was founded in 1871 for the higher education of women. It remains a college for women only.

Acquisitions policy: To maintain college records and receive relevant material by gift or bequest.

Archives of organisation: College records, 1870s-, mainly official papers, including minutes of council, governing body, committees; records of students, estate and finance records; Balfour Laboratory minutes and correspondence.
Papers of Eleanor Mildred Sidgwick (1845–1936), principal, 1892–1910, and sister of A.J. Balfour, including correspondence, addresses and photographs.

Major collections: Papers of Jane Ellen Harrison (1850–1928), classical scholar.
Some papers of Graham Wallas (1858–1932), political psychologist.
A small collection of material relating to Lord John Russell's family.

Non-manuscript material: Women's degrees: press cuttings, 1896 and 1919.
Photographs of members and buildings, 19th and 20th centuries.

Finding aids: Lists and card index.

Facilities: Photocopying. Photography by arrangement.

173 Pembroke College
Archives and Library

Parent organisation: University of Cambridge

Address: Cambridge CB2 1RF

Telephone: (01223) 338121

Fax: (01223) 338163

Enquiries: The Librarian, Mr T.R.S. Allan

Open: By arrangement.

Access: Bona fide scholars, by appointment.

The college was founded in 1347. The library was designed by Waterhouse and built in 1875. It houses the college archives, which comprise a large collection of medieval property deeds and various registers containing lists of Fellows etc, but no medieval accounts pre-1557. A list of the archives is available. The library also holds papers of those associated with the college, including musical MSS of John Dunstable (*d* 1543), mathematician and composer; commonplace books, note-books and correspondence of Thomas Gray (1716–71), poet; and a MS of Sir George Stokes (1819–1903), mathematician and physicist. The medieval MSS are deposited in Cambridge University Library (entry **147**). See M.R. James: *A Descriptive Catalogue of the Manuscripts in the Library of Pembroke College, Cambridge* (Cambridge, 1905).

174 Peterhouse

Parent organisation: University of Cambridge

Address: Cambridge CB2 1RD

Telephone: (01223) 338200

Fax: (01223) 337578

Enquiries: The College Archivist, Dr R.W. Lovatt

Open: By arrangement, preferably during term time.

Access: Approved scholars (references may be required), by appointment in writing.

Historical background: In *c*1200 a hospital was founded on the present site of St John's College, and a community of scholars was also established there, first references being in 1280. Differences between the two communities led to a deed of separation of 1284 (taken to be the foundation date of the college). The college's collection of medieval MSS has been placed on deposit in Cambridge University Library (entry **147**).

Archives of organisation: The medieval holdings are substantial, including charters and deeds *re* property of the college, 12th century–(*c*2000); statutes, 1344–; bursar's account rolls, 1374– [incomplete series]; old registers, 1401–1660s; records of gifts and inventories; accounts and resignations of Fellows, 1420–; bakehouse books, 1542–; governing body minutes, 1650–.

Major collections: The library holds some papers of Matthew Wren (1585–1667), theologian; Joseph Beaumont (1616–99), theologian and poet; James Clerk Maxwell (1831–79), physicist; Peter Guthrie Tait (1831–1901), mathematician and physicist; Edward John Routh (1831–1907), mathematician; Adolphus Ward (1837–1924), historian; and Harold Temperley (1879–1939), historian.

Finding aids: Lists are available in the college. Maxwell: NRA 9500.

Facilities: Photocopying by permission.

Publications: HMC First Report, App. 77–82 (1)

M.R. James: *Descriptive Catalogue of Manuscripts in the Library of Peterhouse, Cambridge* (Cambridge, 1899).

T.A. Walker: *Bibliographical Registers of Peterhouse Men, 1284–1616* (Cambridge, 1927, 1930) [2 parts].

Dom Anselm Hughes (comp.): *Catalogue of the Musical Manuscripts at Peterhouse, Cambridge* (Cambridge, 1953).

R. Lovatt: 'The Early Archives of Peterhouse', *Peterhouse Record* (1975–6), 26–38.

175 Queens' College

Parent organisation: University of Cambridge

Address: Queens' Lane, Cambridge CB3 9ET

Telephone: (01223) 335549 (direct line to College Library) 335511 (enquiries)

Fax: (01223) 335522

Enquiries: The Archivist

Open: Mon–Fri: 10.00–5.00, by prior arrangement only.

Access: Bona fide scholars, by written appointment.

The college was founded in 1448. Administrative and estate archives pre-1800 are housed and administered by Cambridge University Library (entry **147**). Post-1800 archives are held in college and include restricted access materials. The college is a member of Cambridge Colleges Conservation Consortium. See J.F. Williams: 'The Muniments of Queens' College', *Proceedings of the Cambridge Antiquarian Society*, xxvii (1924–5), 43–8; and J. Twigg: *The History of Queens' College, Cambridge, 1448–1986* (1987).

176 Ridley Hall Library

Address: Cambridge CB3 9HG

Telephone: (01223) 353040 (Secretary's office)

Fax: (01223) 301287

Enquiries: The Librarian, Rev. Dr M.C. Sansom

Open: College hours. Closed during vacations.

Access: Bona fide researchers, by permission of the librarian only.

The hall was founded in 1877 and is a member of the Cambridge Federation of Theological Colleges. Apart from theological pamphlets and the library, it houses the papers of Charles Simeon (1759–1836), founder of the Church Missionary Society. There are lists available in the library. See F.W.B. Budlock: *History of Ridley Hall (1941–53)* [2 vols].

177 St Catharine's College

Parent organisation: University of Cambridge

Address: Cambridge CB2 1RL

Telephone: (01223) 338317

Fax: (01223) 338340

Enquiries: The Keeper of Muniments, Professor J.H. Baker

Open: Mon–Fri am, by prior arrangement only.

Access: Approved researchers, on written application; appointment necessary. Some classes of records restricted.

Historical background: The college was founded as St Catharine's Hall in 1473 and incorporated by charter in 1475. The founder made provision for a record tower, but this has long since disappeared and there are no administrative records prior to the 17th century. The college was very small until the present century,

and there are few personal records other than admissions.

Acquisitions policy: Documents of college interest only (mostly transfers from the college office).

Archives of organisation: College archives, including muniments of title, 13th century–; a few court rolls; correspondence, 17th century–, including tutorial correspondence of G.E. Corrie, 1819–43; lease books, 1598–; audit books, 1623–; stewards' accounts, 1622–; admission books, 1642–; order books, 1640–; pupils' accounts, 1670–83, 1748–75, 1849–1940; estate accounts, 18th century–; papers of college societies, 1871–; minutes of governing body, 1873–.

Non-manuscript material: Photographs, mainly sporting; ephemera.

Finding aids: Typescript shelf-lists. Partial card index. See also E.A.B. Barnard: *Catalogue of Documents in the Muniment Room, the Master's Lodge and the College Library* [TS, 1930; addenda, 1934–5; copy in Cambridge University Library].

Facilities: Photocopying (flat documents only).

Publications: H. Philpott: *Documents Relating to St Catharine's College in the University of Cambridge* (Cambridge, 1861).
Some of the older records are summarised in W.H.S. Jones: *A History of St Catharine's College, Cambridge* (1936), 279–89.

178 St Edmund's College

Parent organisation: University of Cambridge

Address: Mount Pleasant, Cambridge CB3 0BN

Telephone: (01223) 336250

Fax: (01223) 336111

Enquiries: The Archivist, Rev. Dr C. Moss

Open: By arrangement.

Access: Bona fide researchers only.

Historical background: The college was founded in 1896 by the 15th Duke of Norfolk as a house of residence for Roman Catholic priests who were taking degrees at the university. It is now a college and an approved foundation of the University of Cambridge, maintaining its Roman Catholic tradition. Its MS collections are held by Cambridge University Library (entry **147**).

Acquisitions policy: To maintain the archives of the college.

Archives of organisation: Records of the college, including correspondence relating to the foundation and recognition by the university, 1895–.

Major collections: Papers of founders and other ecclesiastics, including the 15th Duke of Norfolk (1847–1917) and Baron Anatole von Hügel (1854–1928), president of St Edmund's House.

Non-manuscript material: Photographs.

Finding aids: Catalogue in preparation.

Publications: G. Sweeney: *St Edmund's House: the First Eighty Years.*

179 St John's College

Parent organisation: University of Cambridge

Address: Cambridge CB2 1TP

Telephone: (01223) 338631

Enquiries: The Archivist, Mr M. Underwood

Open: Mon–Fri: 10.00–1.00; 2.15–5.30, by appointment.

Access: Open to those having a letter of reference, subject to the discretion of the archivist. There is a 50–year closure on personal and administrative records unless otherwise approved by the college.

Historical background: The college was founded in 1511 by the executors of Lady Margaret Beaufort, mother of Henry VII, as successor to, and on the site of, the hospital of St John the Evangelist. Statutes made for its government by Bishop Fisher from 1516 to 1530 were all superseded by new ones given by the crown in 1545, and these in turn by others in 1580, until the 19th–century commissions ushered in a period of frequent reform and reorganization. The college is now governed by statutes made in 1926–7 (under powers given to the Universities Commission in 1923), as subsequently amended by the governing body of the college.

Acquisitions policy: Acquisitions are restricted to records relating directly to the college and to members of it.

Archives of organisation: Administrative and financial records of the college from its foundation, including accounts and correspondence of college officers and records of admissions of members (regularly from 1545). Title deeds of college estates and those of the hospital of St John, the hospital of Ospringe, Kent, the priory of Higham, Kent, and the priory of Broomhall, Berkshire. Some household accounts of Lady Margaret Beaufort (1443–1509), 1498–1509.

Major collections: The library's holdings include the papers of John Couch Adams (1819–92) astronomer; C.W. Previté-Orton (1877–1947), historian; Sir Joseph Larmor (1857–1942), physicist; Arthur Caley (1821–95), mathematician; and Sir John Herschel (1792–1871), astronomer.

Non-manuscript material: Printed bills and Acts of Parliament relating to college properties.
Printed matter relating to the university's affairs in the late 18th and the 19th century.
Numerous maps, plans and surveys; architectural drawings relating to the college site.
A few photographs of the college buildings and certain properties.
OS 6 inch and 25 inch maps of Cambridge city and areas in which the college holds property; a few other printed maps.

Finding aids: Calendar with supplementary card index. Computer-based lists and keyword indexes. Previté-Orton papers: NRA 10633. Larmor: NRA 22852. Scientific MSS: NRA 9502.

Facilities: Photocopying, subject to the discretion of the archivist.

Publications: T. Baker: *History of St John's College Cambridge*, ed. J.E.B. Mayor, i (Cambridge, 1869) [calendars of college registers, c1545–1671].
J.E.B. Mayor and R.F. Scott: *Admissions to the College of St John the Evangelist, Cambridge*, i–iv (Cambridge, 1882–1931).
Records printed by R.F. Scott in *Notes from the College Records* [extracts from *The Eagle*, 1889–1915, college magazine].
M.R. James: *St John's College Cambridge, Catalogue of Manuscripts* (Cambridge, 1913).

180 Scientific Periodicals Library

Parent organisation: Cambridge University Library

Address: Bene't Street, Cambridge CB2 3PY

Telephone: (01223) 334744

Fax: (01223) 334748

Enquiries: The Librarian

Open: Mon–Fri: 9.00–6.00 Sat: 9.00–1.00

Access: Bona fide researchers, by appointment.

Historical background: The library was founded in 1820 by the Cambridge Philosophical Society. It was jointly administered by society and university between 1881 and 1976, since when it has been administered by Cambridge University Library (entry **147**) where papers and notes of Charles Babbage (1792–1871), mathematician, 1808–c1866, have been transferred.

Archives of organisation: Records of the Cambridge Philosophical Society, 1819–.

Major collections: Miscellaneous note-books of Vernon Harcourt (1789–1871), chemist; T.R. Robinson (1792–1882), astronomer; J.T. Desaguliers (1683–1744), natural philosopher.
Small collections of records of Natural Science Club; Cambridge Graduate Science Club; Cambridge University Wireless Society.

Facilities: Photocopying. Photography by arrangement with University Library. Microform reader/printer.

181 Scott Polar Research Institute

Parent organisation: University of Cambridge

Address: Lensfield Road, Cambridge CB2 1ER

Telephone: (01223) 336555

Enquiries: The Archivist, R.K. Headland

Open: Mon–Fri: 10.00–12.30; 2.30–5.00

Access: Bona fide students, by appointment.

Historical background: The Scott Polar Research Institute was founded in 1920 as a memorial to Captain Robert Falcon Scott and his four companions, who died returning from the South Pole in 1912. The MS collection was started in the same year with a deposit of papers relating to Scott's two Antarctic expeditions, and has continued to expand ever since with the acquisition of documents relating to all aspects of Arctic and Antarctic exploration and research, particularly expedition diaries and correspondence. The institute is recognised as a place of deposit for public records.

Acquisitions policy: To continue to extend the collection by donations, deposits, and occasional purchases.

Major collections: Records of Captain Scott's Antarctic expeditions, 1901–4 and 1910–13, and of numerous other expeditions in the heroic era of Antarctic exploration, 1900–20.
Records of the search for the North-West Passage in the 19th century, notably the personal papers of Sir John Franklin (1786–1847), Lady Jane Franklin (1792–1875), Sir George Back (1796–1878), Sir William Parry (1790–1855), Sir John (Clark) Ross (1777–1856) and Sir James Clark Ross (1800–62).
Antarctic Treaty papers.
South Georgia whaling and administrative papers, 1904–66.

Non-manuscript material: Extensive collections of watercolours, drawings and prints, photographs, films, sound recordings, press cuttings.

Finding aids: Author/biographical catalogue. Index of expeditions and voyages.

Facilities: Photocopying. Photography and microfilming by arrangement. Microfilm/fiche reader.

Publications: C. Holland: *Manuscripts in the Scott Polar Research Institute, Cambridge, England: a Catalogue* (London and New York, 1982).

182 Seeley Historical Library

Parent organisation: University of Cambridge

Address: Faculty of History, West Road, Cambridge CB3 9EF

Telephone: (01223) 335337

Enquiries: The Seeley Librarian, Miss A.C. Cunninghame

Open: Term: Mon–Fri: 9.00–7.15 Sat: 9.00–6.00 Vacation: Mon–Fri: 9.00–1.00; 2.15–5.00 Closed for three weeks in September.

Access: Bona fide students, by appointment.

Non-manuscript material: Microfilms of Kenya National Archives; British cabinet papers, 20th century; US national archives, mainly consular reports; and papers of Sir John Colborne (1778–1863).

Finding aids: Participating member of the university's union catalogue. Colborne: NRA 5288.

Facilities: Photocopying. Microfilm readers.

183 Selwyn College

Parent organisation: University of Cambridge

Address: Grange Road, Cambridge CB3 9DQ

Telephone: (01223) 335880

Fax: (01223) 335837

Enquiries: The Librarian

Open: By arrangement.

Access: Bona fide researchers, by appointment.

Historical background: The college was founded in 1882. The papers of Brooke Foss Westcott are now held by the library of Westcott House Theological College, Jesus Lane, Cambridge CB5 8BP; tel. (01223) 350074. Contact the librarian for an appointment.

Acquisitions policy: College archives and any material relating to Bishop Selwyn.

Archives of organisation: College archives, 1882–.

Major collections: Papers of George Augustus Selwyn (1809–78), Primate of New Zealand.

Non-manuscript material: Microfilms of the Selwyn sermons, of some of the papers, and of 11 volumes of Bishop Cotton's journals.

Finding aids: Selwyn: NRA 24352.

Facilities: Photocopying (permission of governing body may be required). Microfilm reader only at the University Library.

Conservation: Member of the Cambridge Colleges Conservation Consortium.

Publications: A short history of the college was published in 1973.

184 Sidney Sussex College

Parent organisation: University of Cambridge

Address: Sidney Street, Cambridge CB2 3HU

Telephone: (01223) 338800/338824 (Muniment Room)

Fax: (01223) 338884

Enquiries: The Archivist, Mr N.J. Rogers

Open: Mon–Thurs: 9.00–12.55; 2.00–5.15 Fri: 9.00–12.55; 2.00–4.15

Access: Bona fide researchers; an appointment is necessary; restricted access to some college papers.

Historical background: The college was founded in 1596 by the executors of Lady Frances Sidney, Countess of Sussex. The Muniment Room, established in 1938, houses MSS and early printed books, formerly kept in the Old Library, and the archives, previously housed in the Master's Lodge.

Acquisitions policy: Any material relating to the history of the college and its members.

Archives of organisation: Masters' records, records of college administration, tutorial and bursarial records. Also material relating to college estates.

Major collections: Manuscript collection, mainly Western medieval (119 MSS).
Papers of Richard Allin (?1675-1747), John Hey (1734–1815), George Ralph Mines (1886–1914), David Thomson (1912–70) and Samuel Ward (1572–1643).

Non-manuscript material: Estate maps, architectural drawings.

Finding aids: Various typescript calendars.

Facilities: Photocopying and photography by arrangement.

Conservation: Member of the Cambridge Colleges Conservation Consortium.

Publications: Some of the muniments are described in HMC Third Report, xx and App. 327–29 (2) (1872).
For MSS 1–106, see M.R. James: *A Descriptive Catalogue of the Manuscripts in the Library of Sidney Sussex College, Cambridge* (Cambridge, 1895).
The Ward papers are listed by M. Todd in *Transactions of the Cambridge Bibliographical Society*, 8 (1985), 582–92.

185 Trinity College Library

Parent organisation: University of Cambridge

Address: Cambridge CB2 1TQ

Telephone: (01223) 338488

Fax: (01223) 338532

Enquiries: The Librarian, Dr D.J. McKitterick

Open: Mon–Fri 9.00–5.00

Access: Members of the college; others by appointment.

Historical background: The college was founded by King Henry VIII in 1546. He amalgamated two existing colleges, the King's Hall (f. 1317) and Michaelhouse (f. 1324), with various small hostels, and added to their revenues substantial endowments from the dissolved monasteries.

Acquisitions policy: Records relating directly to the college, and personal and professional papers of past and present members of the college.

Archives of organisation: A few property deeds and 'Black Book' of Michaelhouse, and a large number of records from King's Hall, including Seneschal's accounts, 1337–.
Administrative and financial records of the college, 1546–.
Title deeds and other records relating to the acquisition and administration of college estates, 12th–20th centuries.
Records of college clubs and societies, 19th–20th centuries.

Major collections: Medieval MSS (1500) and a substantial collection of oriental MSS.
Modern MSS include papers of Sir Isaac Newton (1642–1727); William Whewell (1794–1866); Lord Houghton (1809–85); Alfred, Lord Tennyson (1809–92); Thomas, Lord Macaulay (1800–59); A.J. Munby (1828–1910); A.E. Housman (1859–1936); A.A. Milne (1882–1956); Ludwig Wittgenstein (1889–1951); Lord (R.A.) Butler (1902–82); Sir George Pine Thomson (1887–1965), rear-admiral and chief press censor; G.H. Hardy (1877–1947), mathematician; and many other distinguished members of the college.

Non-manuscript material: Printed books (*c*200,000), including 750 incunabula; Sir Isaac Newton's Library; the Capell Collection of Shakespeariana and the Rothschild Collection of 18th-century literature.
Photographs and portraits, maps and plans.

Finding aids: Typescript catalogues and card index of college archives and modern manuscripts. Catalogues sent to NRA.

Facilities: Photocopying, photography and microfilming by arrangement. Microfilm/fiche readers.

Publications: E.H. Palmer: *Catalogue of the Arabic, Persian and Turkish MSS in the Library of Trinity College, Cambridge* (Cambridge, 1870).
M.R. James: *Catalogue of the Western Manuscripts in the Library of Trinity College, Cambridge* (Cambridge, 1900–04) [4 vols].
H.M.J. Loewe: *Catalogue of the Hebrew MSS in the Library of Trinity College, Cambridge* (Cambridge, 1926).

186 Trinity Hall

Parent organisation: University of Cambridge

Address: Trinity Lane, Cambridge CB2 1TJ

Telephone: (01223) 332500

Fax: (01223) 332537

Enquiries: The Librarian or Archivist

The college was founded in 1350. Virtually none of its medieval records survive, although there is a small collection of charters. Apart from M.R. James: *A Descriptive Catalogue of Manuscripts ... (1907)*, there is A.W.W. Dale (ed.): *Warren's Book: Documents etc relating to Trinity Hall, Cambridge* (1911), and a typescript list, by A.L. Pink, of Trinity Hall documents to 1600.

187 Canterbury Cathedral Archives

Address: The Precincts, Canterbury, Kent CT1 2EH

Telephone: (01227) 463510

Fax: (01227) 762897

Enquiries: The Archivist

Open: Mon–Thurs: 9.00–5.00 1st and 3rd Sat of each month: 9.00–1.00
Annual stock-taking closure last week of January and first week of February.

Access: Generally open to the public, by appointment.

Historical background: Cathedral records have been kept here since the foundation of the cathedral in 597. From 1884 to 1915 and from 1956 to 1970 the office acted as the City Record Office, and from 1970 it was run as the joint City and Chapter Record Office. It became the Diocesan Record Office in 1959, and the Archive Filing Unit for Canterbury City Council was opened in 1981. The service has been administered by Kent County Council since 1989. It is recognised as a place of deposit for public records.

Acquisitions policy: Normal statutory acquisitions from all three authorities; deposits or gifts are accepted.

Archives of organisation: Records of Dean and Chapter of Canterbury, 742–; City of Canterbury 1200–; Diocese of Canterbury 1364–.

Major collections: Parish records for the Archdeaconry of Canterbury; private deposits.

Finding aids: Catalogues. On-line computer index to most of the catalogues of the Dean and Chapter records and private deposits can be consulted by staff.

Facilities: Photocopying. Photography. Microfilming. Microfilm/fiche reader/printer.

Conservation: Full range of paper and parchment conservation and binding. Facilities for map repair are limited. Limited outside work undertaken.

188 Canterbury College of Art

Parent organisation: Kent Institute of Art and Design

Address: New Dover Road, Canterbury, Kent CT1 3AN

Telephone: (01227) 769371 ext. 27

Fax: (01227) 451320

Enquiries: The Librarian, Kathleen Godfrey

Open: Term: Mon–Fri: 9.00–8.30 Vacation: Mon–Thurs: 9.00–5.00 Fri: 9.00–4.30

Access: Generally open to scholars; appointment advisable.

The Canterbury College of Art was founded by the Victorian artist Sidney Caper. It was administered by Canterbury City Council until 1974, and thereafter by Kent County Council. Apart from the internal archives, the college holds the Herbert Read archive, consisting of letters, postcards and magazines, pamphlets and

books (*c*300), written by or contributed to by Sir Herbert Read (1893–1963), writer on art, critic and poet.

189 Institute of Heraldic and Genealogical Studies

Address: Northgate, Canterbury, Kent CT1 1BA

Telephone: (01227) 768664

Fax: (01227) 765617

Enquiries: The Registrar, Jeremy Palmer

Open: Mon, Wed, Fri: 10.00–4.30

Access: By appointment with the librarian.

Historical background: A school for the study of the history and structure of the family was founded by Cecil Humphery-Smith on the suggestion of the late Canon K.J.F. Bickersteth in 1957. The institute opened in Canterbury in 1961 and was established as an educational trust. Subsequently it moved into its present premises (which date from 1283 with 16th–century and later additions). Full-time and other courses of instruction are held to train and qualify members of the genealogical profession and provide researchers into the applications of family history studies.

Acquisitions policy: To build a corpus of original material for the study of social, economic and environmental changes and historical structures of family life.

Major collections: Family History: unpublished MSS collections relating to some 15,000 family groups.
Case histories and genealogical tracings.
Estate maps, collections of deeds and related documentation, manorial incidences and papers, 13th–20th centuries.
Tyler Collection: extracts from Kentish parish records, wills, marriage settlements, local history material; several hundred MS note-books by eminent antiquary and family historian, and related documents.
Hackman Collection: similar material for Hampshire.
Humphery-Smith Collection: extensive MS notes on Sussex families, records of coats of arms in all churches of Sussex county, in Canterbury Cathedral and elsewhere, with related research notes; very large British and European armorial indexes; transcripts of rolls

of arms and heraldic treatises with related notes; several original heralds' note-books; painted and blazoned armorials (16th and 17th centuries).

Culleton Papers: four large bound MS books of working papers of 19th–century genealogical and heraldic practice.

MS indexes: the Augmented Pallot Index to several million London marriages; Andrew's Index to British overseas.

Non-manuscript material: Pamphlets relating to parish and local histories (c5000).

A collection of European heraldic works unique in the UK.

An extensive library of secondary source material for genealogical research.

Finding aids: Lists, indexes and guides. A comprehensive classified catalogue is in preparation.

Facilities: Photocopying. Microfilm/fiche reader. Palaeographic aids.

Publications: Family History (1962–) [journal of the institute].
Guide to Pallot Index (1986).
Maps of the parishes and probate jurisdictions of the UK and other research aids.

190 The King's School
Archives and Walpole Library

Address: Canterbury, Kent CT1 2ES

Telephone: (01227) 595501

Enquiries: The School Archivist, Mr P. Pollak

Open: By arrangement.

Access: Bona fide students, by appointment.

Historical background: A school has been attached to the cathedral since 600 AD; however, pre-1750 material is kept in the Canterbury Cathedral Archives (entry 187). The Walpole Library is based on the collection accumulated by Sir Hugh Walpole between the wars.

Acquisitions policy: Material relating to the school is acquired as limited resources permit. Additions to the Walpole Library collection of literary MSS are by gift.

Archives of organisation: Records of pupils, 1750–; lists of King's Scholars, 1541– (incomplete); usual school material: academic, sporting, administrative, 1750–. School magazine *The Cantuarian*, 1882–.

Major collections: Sir Hugh Seymour Walpole (1884–1941), novelist, collection of literary MSS.

Non-manuscript material: Collection of topographical prints and drawings relating to Canterbury premises and the King's School, mainly 18th and 19th centuries. The Walpole and Somerset Maugham libraries.

Finding aids: MS indexes.

Facilities: Photocopying by arrangement.

Publications: Printed catalogues of Walpole and Maugham libraries.

191 University of Kent at Canterbury

Address: Canterbury, Kent CT2 7NU

Telephone: (01227) 764000 ext. 3124

Fax: (01227) 459025

A Library

Enquiries: The Librarian, Ms M. M. Coutts

Open: Mon–Fri: 9.00–5.00

Access: Approved readers, on written application.

Historical background: The university was founded in 1963.

Acquisitions policy: Selected acquisitions of material related to existing collections.

Major collections: Frank Pettingell (1891–1966): collection of 19th–century drama: includes 1000 plays and 350 pantomimes in MS or TS, only 36 of which are known to have been published; several hundred MSS related to productions at the Britannia Theatre, Hoxton; playbills and programmes.

Melville family (late 19th to mid-20th century): records relating to provincial and London theatres run by the Melvilles; plays in MS and TS; playbills.

C.P. Davies Wind- and Water-Mill Collection: press cuttings, MS notes, photographs; archives of millers and mill construction firms.

John Crow (1904–69): papers and correspondence.

Catherine Crowe (1790–1872): material gathered by a researcher for an intended biography.

Hewlett Johnson (Dean of Canterbury, 1931–63): papers and correspondence.

R.E.W. Maddison (1901–93): papers and correspondence.

Alan Reeve-Jones: screenplays in TS and MS.

E.M. Tenison (1880–1962): papers and correspondence.

Lord Bernard Weatherill (Speaker of the House of Commons, 1983–92): papers and correspondence.

Non-manuscript material: Frank Pettingell Collection: printed play texts, separately bound (with many prompt books and actors' copies) (c3000); printed texts in composite volumes (1800); pantomime libretti (331); playbills (c300).

Collection of popular literature, chiefly ballads and popular poetry, with some chapbooks.

Grace Pettman Collection, including her writings in 20th–century popular magazines and religious tracts.

Kingsley Wood Press Cuttings: 25 large press cutting books covering the career of the politician and cabinet minister, 1903–40.

Muggeridge Collection: photographs of English windmills, 1905–.

Finding aids: Catalogue to the Frank Pettingell Collection. Other materials are in the process of being catalogued.

Facilities: Photocopying. Photography. Microfilm/fiche printer.

Publications: G.S. Darlow: 'A Brief Description of the Frank Pettingell Collection of Plays in the University Library, Canterbury, Kent', *Theatre Notebook*, xxxi/3 (1977) 2.

B British Institute for Cartoon Research

Enquiries: The Director, Mr Robert Edwards, The Deputy Director, Mrs Jane Newton

Historical background: The institute was established as the Cartoon Study Centre in 1973 with initial funding from the Nuffield Foundation, and cataloguing and research work has been funded by an additional grant from the Leverhulme Trust.

Acquisitions policy: No purchasing budget; long-term loans and donations/bequests relating to the field of study and existing collections of original cartoon drawings.

Major collections: Original cartoon drawings from British newspapers and journals, 1900–,

including political-humorous, wartime and social comment cartoons (c85,000). Artists represented include Low, Strube, Vicky, Cummings, Lee, Zec, Haselden, Smythe, Jensen, Garland, Dyson, Trog, Horner, Hewison, Mac and Illingworth.

Non-manuscript material: Linfield Library of Humour, comprising volumes on cartoons and caricature and associated graphic and illustrative books (c800). Cartoon Study Centre's small reference library (3000 vols), mainly anthologies of published work and limited amounts of related newspaper cuttings.

Finding aids: On-line computerised database (search by artist, date, persons and keywords) exists for half the collection and is constantly being added to.

192 Central Register of Air Photography for Wales

Parent organisation: Welsh Office

Address: Planning Division, Room G-003, Crown Offices, Cathays Park, Cardiff CF1 3NQ

Telephone: (01222) 823819

Fax: (01222) 825466

Enquiries: The Air Photographs Officer

Open: Mon–Fri, by appointment.

Access: Generally open to the public by arrangement: for a cover search, a map or Ordnance Survey National Grid Reference of the area of interest will be required.

Historical background: The National Air Survey, flown 1945–52 by the RAF, was used to plan post-war development and forms the basis of the collection. Subsequent surveys have been added. The Central Register of Air Photography for Wales was formed in 1975 and is operated by the Air Photography Unit: it is the only comprehensive source of information about air photos of Wales.

Acquisitions policy: Continued updating of the collection.

Major collections: Extensive collection (over 200,000) of air photographs of different scales covering Wales at various dates, including the National Air Survey (1:10,000) flown 1945–52 by the RAF.

Other RAF photographs, including small-scale

national surveys, 1969, 1981; pre-1971 Ordnance Survey air photographs; extensive colour photographs, 1983–92; oblique and infra-red photos of Welsh coastline.

Facilities: Photography from original RAF and pre-1971 Ordnance Survey air film. Photostats (map information superimposed). Reference and loan of library prints.

193 Glamorgan Record Office

Parent organisation: Glamorgan Archives Joint Committee

Address: Mid Glamorgan County Hall, King Edward VII Avenue, Cathays Park, Cardiff CF1 3NE

Telephone: (01222) 780282

Fax: (01222) 780027

Enquiries: The Glamorgan Archivist, Mrs Annette M. Burton

Open: Tues, Thurs: 9.30–1.00; 2.00–5.00 Wed: 9.30–1.00; 2.00–7.00 (for the evening, it is necessary to make an appintment before 4.00) Fri: 9.30–1.00; 2.00–4.30
Appointments necessary to consult microforms.

Access: Generally open to the public.

Historical background: The office was established in 1939 to serve the county of Glamorgan, which was divided into the counties of Mid-, South and West Glamorgan on local government reorganization in 1974. Initially, these three counties combined to provide a joint archives service, but in 1992 West Glamorgan withdrew from this arrangement. Since then, the Glamorgan Record Office has been jointly funded by the counties of Mid- and South Glamorgan. After local government reorganization in 1974, most of the archive collection of the former Cardiff City Library was transferred to the Glamorgan Record Office. It also holds ecclesiastical parish records from the whole of the Diocese of Llandaff. It is recognised as a place of deposit for public and manorial records. Modern records of the county of South Glamorgan are administered by the Records Centre, South Glamorgan County Hall, Atlantic Wharf, Cardiff CF1 5UW.

Acquisitions policy: The office accepts archival material for the geographical area which it serves in the counties of Mid- and South Glamorgan and the Diocese of Llandaff.

Archives of organisation: Glamorgan County Council, 1889–1974, and other local authority record holdings.

Major collections: Deposited collections, including the following which have a wider significance: South Wales Coalfield, pre-1947 records received from the National Coal Board. Dowlais Iron Company Collection, containing extensive correspondence, 1792–.
Society of Friends records relating to the whole of Wales, 1650–.
Bruce Collection, containing correspondence received by the first Lord Aberdare (1815–95).
Papers of John Singleton Copley, Baron Lyndhurst (1772–1863), Lord Chancellor.

Finding aids: Lists and indexes.

Facilities: Photocopying. Photography and microfilming by arrangement. Genealogical Centre microfilm/fiche readers/printer centralising sources for family history.

Conservation: In-house facilities.

Publications: Dowlais Iron Company: Calendar of the London House Letter-book Series, 1837–1867 [42 schedules; reproduced TS].
On the Parish: an Illustrated Source Book on the Care of the Poor under the Old Poor Law (1988).
A Catalogue of Glamorgan Estate Maps (1992).
Hughesovka: a Welsh Enterprise in Imperial Russia (1992).
Poor Relief in Merthyr Tydfil Union in Victorian Times (1992).
The Bridges of Merthyr Tydfil (1992).

194 National Museum of Wales

A Library

Address: Cathays Park, Cardiff CF1 3NP

Telephone: (01222) 397951 ext. 234

Fax: (01222) 373219

Enquiries: The Librarian, Mr John R. Kenyon

Open: Tues–Fri: 10.00–5.00

Access: Bona fide researchers, preferably by prior arrangement.

Historical background: The National Museum of Wales received its Charter of Incorporation in 1907. Besides various outstations (see **B** and

C below), there are five departments in Cathays Park: Archaeology and Numismatics, Art, Botany, Geology and Zoology. There is no archivist in Cathays Park; archives are handled by curatorial staff within the relevant departments and central records are held by the Resource Management Division.

Acquisitions policy: No formal policy; the majority of archives are acquired by donation.

Major collections: John Ward papers (archaeology, local history), in main library.
Files on artists in Department of Art.
Natural history MSS.

Non-manuscript material: Early photographs of Welsh buildings etc in main library.
Collection of maps in Department of Geology.

Finding aids: No formal overall catalogue or list.

Facilities: Photocopying. Photography. Microfilm/fiche readers.

Conservation: Generally contracted out.

Publications: Natural History MSS listed in G.D.R. Bridson et al.: *Natural History Manuscript Resources in the British Isles* (1980), 53–6.
A. Lloyd Hughes: 'G.B. Sowerby Letters in Cardiff', *Archives of Natural History*, x/1 (1981), 172.
J.R. Kemson: 'Some Glamorgan Documents in the National Museum of Wales Library', *Morgannwg*, 37 (1993), 100–2.

B Welsh Folk Museum

Address: St Fagans, Cardiff CF5 6XB

Telephone: (01222) 569441 ext. 237

Fax: (01222) 578413

Enquiries: The Archivist, Mr A. Lloyd Hughes

Open: Mon–Fri: 9.30–1.00; 1.45–4.30

Access: Bona fide researchers, preferably by prior arrangement.

Historical background: In 1946 the Earl of Plymouth offered St Fagans Castle, with its gardens and grounds, to the National Museum of Wales as a centre for a folk museum. It was opened to the public in 1948.

Acquisitions policy: To complement existing collections in the fields of Welsh ethnology by donations or deposits, in cooperation with other archival institutions in Wales.

Major collections: Ty'n-y-pant MSS: c800 MSS in the Welsh language relating to the history and folklore of Cantref Buallt, Breconshire (now Powys).
T.C. Evans and T.H. Thomas MSS, relating to Glamorgan folklore and dialect, the National Eisteddfod, Gorsedd of Bards, heraldry etc.
W. Meredith Morris MSS, relating to the folklore and dialect of Pembrokeshire (now Dyfed), musicology etc.
Farmers' and craftsmen's account books, diaries, eisteddfodic essays etc.
Questionnaires on aspects of Welsh folk culture, dialects, farming etc.

Non-manuscript material: Pamphlets and broadsides.
Photographs (c125,000); cine-films (c200); sound archives (c8000 tapes).
The library houses a unique collection of books (c35,000) and periodicals of historical and ethnological interest with special emphasis on Wales.

Facilities: Photocopying. Photography. Microfilm/fiche reader. Tape-recorders.

Publications: A. Lloyd Hughes: 'The Welsh Folk Museum Manuscripts', *Folk Life*, xvii (1979), 68–70.
Catalogue of Welsh Folk Museum MSS 1–3000 (1979, 1981) [3 vols to date].

C Welsh Industrial and Maritime Museum

Address: Bute Street, Cardiff CF1 6AN

Telephone: (01222) 481919

Fax: (01222) 487252

Enquiries: The Keeper, Dr E.S. Owen-Jones

Open: Tues–Fri: 10.00–5.00

Access: Generally open to the public, by appointment.

Historical background: The museum was established in 1977 within the framework of the National Museum of Wales and deals with the industrial and maritime history of Wales. Archival material, although belonging to the museum, is deposited with the Glamorgan Record Office (entry 193).

Acquisitions policy: To collect relevant MSS, artefacts and photographs relating to industrial and maritime Wales.

Non-manuscript material: An extensive collection of photographs, prints and drawings relating to Wales.

Finding aids: Card index.

195 South Glamorgan Central Library

Parent organisation: South Glamorgan Library Service

Address: St David's Link, Frederick Street, Cardiff CF1 4DT

Telephone: (01222) 382116

Fax: (01222) 238642

Enquiries: The County Librarian, Mr R. Ieuan Edwards

Open: Mon, Tues, Fri: 9.00–6.00 Wed, Thurs: 9.00–8.00 Sat: 9.00–5.30 (MS material not available after 4.30)

Access: Generally open to the public; advance notice of visit preferred.

Historical background: The library was founded in 1862 as the Cardiff Free Library with the following foundation collections: (a) MSS acquired with the Tonn Library, purchased from the Rees family of Llandovery in 1891; (b) literary and historical MSS and deeds of Welsh interest, purchased from the collection of Sir Thomas Phillipps in 1896. Subsequent additions by purchase (especially in the 1920s-1950s) and gift from a variety of sources. The majority of deeds and manorial documents (which relate to Wales and the bordering counties of England) have been transferred to the Glamorgan Record Office, Cardiff (entry **193**). The Mackworth Collection of early music has been placed in the University of Wales College of Cardiff (entry **196**).

Acquisitions policy: Material is no longer acquired.

Major collections: Welsh literary MSS, mostly poetry, medieval–18th century (*c*100 vols).
Non-Welsh medieval MSS, mostly religious (*c*50 vols).
Historical MSS, relating mostly to Wales and including 19th– and 20th–century literary MSS (*c*4300 groups).
Papers of the Marquesses of Bute, mainly 19th century.

Non-manuscript material: Large collection of maps, photographs, prints, original drawings

etc, relating mainly to South Glamorgan and adjacent counties.

Finding aids: Card index and shelf list. TS catalogue of Mackworth Collection: NRA 1142.

Facilities: Photocopying. Microfilm/fiche readers.

Publications: MSS are described in various library reprints, and brief details of recent acquisitions are in *Morgannwg*, ii-xv (1958–71). N.R. Ker: 'Cardiff Public Library', *Medieval Manuscripts in British Libraries*, ii (1977), xx, 331–77.

196 University of Wales College of Cardiff

A The Library

Address: PO Box 430, Cardiff CF1 3XT

Telephone: (01222) 874000

Fax: (01222) 371921

Enquiries: The Librarian

Open: Mon–Fri: 9.00–5.00, appointment preferred.
At other times when the library is open a prior appointment is essential.

Access: Members of the college; others on written application.

Historical background: UWCC came into existence in 1988 as a result of the merger of University College, Cardiff (f. 1883) and the University of Wales Institute of Science and Technology (UWIST). During the century of its existence the library of University College, Cardiff, accumulated a substantial collection of MSS and archives. The Youth Movement Archive has been transferred to the British Library of Political and Economic Science (entry **498**).

Acquisitions policy: There is no acquisitions policy, but collections offered are accepted where appropriate.

Major collections: Edward Thomas (1878–1917), poet: MSS, papers, letters, scrapbooks, photographs, first editions.
E.G.R. Salisbury (1819–90): papers and printed ephemera.
Lower Swansea Valley Project: papers of K.J. Hilton, director, 1960–65.

Educational Settlements: papers of Sir J.F. Rees, 1929–42, especially the Merthyr Settlement. Cardiff Trades Council: records, 1941–82.
Papers of deceased members of the college, including Cyril Brett, professor of English (d 1936); B.J. Morse, lecturer in Italian (d 1977); C.M. Thompson, professor of chemistry (d 1932); S.B. Chrimes, professor of history (d 1984); D.E. Evans, tutor in charge of extra-mural studies (d 1951); E.J. Jones, lecturer in education and professor at University College Swansea (d 1977); H.J.W. Tillyard, professor of Greek (d 1968); T.H. Robinson, professor of Semitic languages (d 1964).

Finding aids: TSS handlists of Salisbury MSS, miscellaneous MSS, Cardiff Trades Council records, Edward Thomas Collection.

Facilities: Photocopying. Microfilm/fiche readers.

B Welsh Music Information Centre

Address: c/o A.S.S. Library, University of Wales College of Cardiff, Cardiff CF1 1XL

Telephone: (01222) 874000 ext. 5126

Fax: (01222) 371221

Enquiries: The Director, A.J. Heward Rees

Open: Mon–Fri: 9.30–12.30; 2.00–5.00, by appointment only.

Access: Any bona fide person seeking relevant information; advance notice is helpful.

Historical background: The Welsh Music Archive was founded in 1976 and re-established in 1983 as the Welsh Music Information Centre. The centre is funded principally by the Welsh Arts Council and has an Advisory Working Committee.

Acquisitions policy: Welsh music, historical and contemporary: also music and music-making relevant to Wales other than folk or popular.

Major collections: Large and comprehensive collection of scores by contemporary Welsh composers (MS, photocopied and printed), including complete MSS of Grace Williams (1906–77), J.R. Heath, Morfydd Owen, and J. Morgan Nicholas.
Mackworth Collection of MS and printed music, mostly 18th century.

Non-manuscript material: Collection of taped broadcast concerts, talks etc; some photographic material; concert programmes etc.

Printed scores and other material on Welsh composers, present and past.

Finding aids: Card index. Catalogues of contemporary Welsh music.

Facilities: Photocopying.

197 The Welch Regiment Museum of the Royal Regiment of Wales

Address: The Black and Barbican Towers, Cardiff Castle, Cardiff CF1 2RB

Telephone: (01222) 229367

Enquiries: The Curator, Lt. (retd) Bryn Owen

Open: Fridays only, by appointment.

Access: Bona fide researchers.

Historical background: The museum developed from a collection displayed in the late 1920s in the old Regimental Depot, Cardiff, for the benefit of recruits under training. During the 1950s that collection formed the basis for a small regimental museum on the same site. In 1964 the museum became a charitable trust by a Declaration of Trust drawn up under the guidance of the Army Museums Ogilby Trust and in 1978 opened in its present location. The museum was one of the first in Wales to be registered under the Museums and Galleries Commission Registration and is recognised as an approved place of deposit for public records. See also the South Wales Borderers and Monmouthshire Regimental Museum of the Royal Regiment of Wales (entry 118).

Acquisitions policy: Archival material and artefacts relating to the history and services of the 41st and 69th Regiments of Foot (later 1st and 2nd Battalions) and of the Welch Regiment, which includes also its Territorial Force and Territorial Army Battalions and wartime Service and Reserve Battalions. Also material relating to the Militia Volunteers, local militia and other affiliated auxiliary units raised within the old 41st Regimental District of South Wales, and the services of all battalions of the Royal Regiment of Wales (24th/41st Foot) from 1969.

Archives of organisation: War diaries, 1914–18, 1941–5, court martial books, letter-books.

Various order books, 1806–; Digests of Service, 1719.
The archives do not include the personal service records of ex-members of the regiment.

Non-manuscript material: Prints, drawings, and a large collection of photographs and albums.

Finding aids: Photo albums and MS books (NRA 20951).

Conservation: Contracted out.

198 The British Deaf Association

Address: 38 Victoria Place, Carlisle, Cumbria CA1 1HU

Telephone: (01228) 48844 (voice) 28719 (vistel)

Fax: (01228) 41420

Enquiries: The Information Department

Open: Normal office hours throughout the year.

Access: Generally open to the public, by appointment only.

The association is the oldest national charity in the United Kingdom for deaf people. It was founded as the British Deaf and Dumb Association in 1890 and the present name was adopted in 1971. Its aim is 'to advance and protect the interests of all deaf people'. The association maintains its own archives and acquires any material relevant to the history of the deaf and to the association.

199 Cumbria Archive Service
Cumbria Record Office (Carlisle)

Address: The Castle, Carlisle, Cumbria CA3 8UR

Telephone: (01228) 812416 or 812391

Enquiries: The County Archivist, Mr Jim Grisenthwaite (service-wide enquiries) or The Assistant County Archivist, Mr David Bowcock (office enquiries)

Open: Mon–Fri: 9.00–5.00
Closed between Christmas and the New Year.

Access: Generally open to the public. The office operates the CARN reader's ticket system.

Historical background: The office was officially opened in 1962, although archives had been collected before then and staff were appointed from c1944. It also acts as the Diocesan Record Office for Carlisle, and is recognised as a place of deposit for public records. Administrative assistance is given to the Egremont Estate Office, Cockermouth Castle. Cumbria Archive Service has other offices at Kendal (entry **423**) and Barrow-in-Furness (entry **49**).

Acquisitions policy: Official and unofficial records for the former county of Cumberland and City of Carlisle.

Archives of organisation: Usual local authority record holdings.

Major collections: Deposited local collections, of which the following have a wider significance: Political and other personal and family papers of Sir Esme Howard (Lord Howard of Penrith), diplomat, 1780–1961.
Papers of Catherine Marshall, suffragist and pacifist, of Hawse End, Keswick, c1880–1956.
Estate and family records of Earl of Lonsdale, 12th–20th centuries, including West Cumberland shipping and coal-mining, 17th–20th centuries.

Finding aids: Catalogues and indexes. Some collections are unlisted. Selected catalogues sent to NRA.

Facilities: Photocopying. Photography. Microfilming. Microfilm/fiche readers/printer.

Conservation: In-house facilities. Outside work is considered, but only on written application to the County Archivist.

Publications: R.C. Jarvis: *The Jacobite Rising of 1715 and 1745*, Cumberland County Council Record Series, i (Carlisle, 1954).
E. Hughes (ed.): *The Fleming Senhouse Papers*, Cumberland County Council Record Series, ii (Carlisle, 1961).
B.C. Jones: 'Cumberland, Westmorland and Carlisle Record Office, 1960–65', *Archives*, vii/34 (1965), 80.
——: 'Cumberland and Westmorland Record Offices, 1968', *Northern History*, iii (1968), 162.
H.W. Hodgson: *A Bibliography of the History and Topography of Cumberland and Westmorland* (Carlisle, 1968).

Cumbrian Ancestors. Notes for Genealogical Searchers (2/1994).

200 Dyfed Archives Service
Carmarthen Office

Address: County Hall, Carmarthen, Dyfed SA31 1JP

Telephone: (01267) 233333 ext. 4182

Enquiries: The County Archivist, Mr J. Owen or The Senior Archivist, Mr J. Davies

Open: Mon: 9.00–7.00 Tues–Thurs: 9.00–4.45 Fri: 9.00–4.15

Access: Generally open to the public.

Historical background: The office was established as Carmarthenshire Record Office in 1959. It also acts as a Diocesan Record Office for St David's (parish registers), and is recognised as a place of deposit for public records. There are branch offices at Aberystwyth and Haverfordwest (entries 9 and 380 respectively).

Archives of organisation: Usual local authority record holdings.

Major collections: Deposited local collections, including the following which has a wider significance: Cawdor Collection, containing the *Golden Grove Book*, an 18th–century collection of pedigrees relating to the whole of Wales.

Facilities: Photocopying. Photography. Microfilming. Microfilm reader.

Publications: S.G. Beckley: *Carmarthen Record Office Survey of Archive Holdings* (1980). *Tracing Your Family History in the Carmarthenshire Record Office* (1992).

201 Castle Ashby Archives

Parent organisation: Compton Estates

Address: Estate Office, Castle Ashby, Northants NN7 1LJ

Enquiries: The Agent

Open: By arrangement.

Access: Bona fide researchers, by appointment only.

The archives of the Comptons, Earls and Marquesses of Northampton, since 1618, include principally estate records for Northamptonshire and Warwickshire as well as some family documents, mostly 19th century. There is a catalogue available, which is also held at Northamptonshire Record Office (entry 848) and at the NRA.

202 Royal Engineers Library

Parent organisation: Institution of Royal Engineers

Address: Brompton Barracks, Chatham, Kent ME4 4UG

Telephone: (01634) 822416

Fax: (01634) 822419

Enquiries: The Librarian

Open: Mon, Wed, Fri: 9.00–12.30; 1.30–5.00

Access: Members of the institution and serving members of the armed forces. Open to the public, by appointment.

Historical background: A Royal Engineers Library was formed at Chatham in 1813. A Corps Library was established in London in 1847 and branch libraries were set up at selected stations as funds permitted; by 1862 there were 16 home station and 19 overseas libraries, excluding India. Between 1924 and 1928 all home station libraries except those at Chatham and Aldershot were abolished and only nine remained abroad. The Corps Library was moved from London to Chatham in 1939. The present library is now the only RE library, inheriting the best of the items of all the other libraries as they closed down. The Institution of Royal Engineers was founded in 1875. The original libraries were set up to hold technical books relevant to the work of the corps in all its varied aspects.

Acquisitions policy: Items on military engineering worldwide, with particular emphasis on the work and history of the Corps of Royal Engineers.

Archives of organisation: RE reports, documents, letters, construction plans etc.

Major collections: Connolly papers: biographical notes on RE officers to 1860.

Non-manuscript material: Photograph albums of Royal Engineers and of their life, work and play, c1855–.

Finding aids: Computer database/card index system. NRA 36689.

Facilities: Photocopying. Photography. Microfilm/fiche readers.

203 Essex Record Office

Address: County Hall, Chelmsford, Essex CM1 1LX

Telephone: (01245) 430067

Fax: (01245) 430085

Enquiries: The County and Hon. Diocesan Archivist, Mr Ken Hall

Open: Mon: 10.00–8.45 Tues–Thurs: 9.15–5.15 Fri: 9.15–4.15

Access: Generally open to the public; appointment advisable. The office operates the CARN reader's ticket system.

Historical background: The Record Office opened formally in 1938, although parish and other records had been collected from 1936. Before the reorganisation of London in 1964 the office covered old Essex, which included the boroughs of Havering, Barking and Dagenham, Waltham Forest, Newham and Redbridge. The office also acts as the Diocesan Record Office for Chelmsford, and is responsible for the cathedral archives. It is recognised as a place of deposit for public records. There are branch offices at Southend and Colchester (entries **1022** and **220** respectively).

Archives of organisation: Usual local authority record holdings.

Major collections: Deposited local collections, including the following which have a wider significance:
Papers of Sir Thomas Smith relating to the colonisation of the Ards in Ulster, 1572–7.
Correspondence of the Cornwallis and Bacon families, 1622–80.
Record book and papers of William Holcroft as JP, verderer and captain of militia, 1661–8.
Journals and correspondence of James Paroissien, relating to South America, 1806–27.

Non-manuscript material: The Essex Sound Archive.
Extensive photographic and pictorial collections.
Collection of local history printed material in the Essex Record Office Library.

Finding aids: Catalogues. Lists. Indexes. Lists sent to NRA.

Facilities: Photocopying. Photography. Microfilming. Microfilm/fiche readers.

Conservation: In-house facilities for paper conservation. Outside work undertaken for institutions and private individuals.

Publications: F.G. Emmison: *Guide to the Essex Record Office* (1969).
Essex Family History: a Genealogist's Guide to the Essex Record Office.
Publications catalogue available.

204 Cheltenham and Gloucester College of Higher Education

Address: The Learning Centre, PO Box 220, Cheltenham, Glos GL50 2QF

Telephone: (01242) 532721

Fax: (01242) 532810

Enquiries: The Learning Centre Manager, Clare Hetherington

Open: Mon–Thurs: 9.00–9.00 Fri: 9.00–5.00 Sat: 9.00–12.00

Access: Any serious student or researcher, strictly by appointment with the librarian, since the college archive is held at the France Close Hall site.

The college was founded in 1847 as the Church of England Training School. It adopted the names St Paul and St Mary some time in the late 19th century but first used them officially in 1906. It was renamed in 1990. From 1921 to 1979 separate principals were appointed to the constituent male and female departments, but they remained under the control of one college council. The colleges merged in 1979 to form a college of higher education. The records of the colleges are, therefore, integrated and are being catalogued accordingly. The development of this important teacher-training establishment is well documented and its archive holdings are of particular value to the educational historian. In addition there are deposited papers of former students and staff, and a large collection of photographs, 1860s–. A catalogue is in progress.

205 Cheltenham College

Address: Bath Road, Cheltenham, Glos
GL53 7LD

Telephone: (01242) 513540

Fax: (01242) 577746

Enquiries: The Librarian, C.E. Cawley

Open: Term: normal school hours. Vacation:
by arrangement only.

Access: Generally open to the public, by
appointment.

Cheltenham College was founded as an educational establishment for boys in 1841. The
archives are in process of collection and arrangement and old Cheltonians are actively
encouraged to deposit material. There are scrapbooks and school magazines, 1841–, as well as
school registers and photographs. A computer
catalogue is in progress.

206 Planned Environment Therapy Trust Archive and Study Centre

Address: Church Lane, Toddington,
Cheltenham, Glos GL54 5DQ

Telephone/Fax: (01242) 620125

Enquiries: The Archivist

Open: Mon–Fri: 9.00–4.00, by prior arrangement.

Access: Open to any bona fide researcher, by
written application to the archivist and by
appointment; much of the material is restricted.

Historical background: The PETT was founded
in 1966 by Dr Marjorie Franklin, a pioneering
psychiatrist/psychoanalyst, using private
monies and funds from Q-Camps Committee
(1935–c1966), and Children's Social Adjust-
ment Ltd (1948–1969), which had earlier
founded and run Alresford Place School.
Founding Trustees with Dr Franklin were W.
David Wills and Arthur T. Barron, both of
whom had extensive experience in therapeutic
community work with children and young
people. The Archive and Study Centre was
established in 1989 to fulfil one of the trust's
founding aspirations. It aims to encourage and
promote research and discussion in the fields
covered by the archive through an active oral
history recording project, seminars and publication, and the projected compilation of a
comprehensive research directory and guide to
published and archival sources.

Acquisitions policy: Papers of individuals, institutions and organisations involved in pioneer
work in environment therapy, milieu therapy
and therapeutic community.

Archives of organisation: Archives of PETT,
1966–.

Major collections: Marjorie Franklin (1877–
1975) Collection and Arthur T. Barron (1919–
93) Collection.
Personal and professional papers of W. David
Wills (1903–81).
Materials related to Otto Shaw, and the archives
of the Red Hill School, 1934–92.
Dr David Clark's papers *re* the founding and
early years of the Association of Therapeutic
Communities, 1970–82.
Archives of the Sussex Youth Trust, Chalving-
ton Trust and School, 1980–92; Westhope
Manor/Shotton Hall School, 1949–94;
Q-Camps Committee, 1935–c1966, including
Hawkspur Camp for Men, one of the earliest
therapeutic communities in England, 1936–40;
Barns School in Scotland, 1940–45; Home Lane
Society, 1964–; New Barns School, 1965–.
Signifiant collections concerning the Associa-
tion of Workers for Maladjusted Children,
1951–, and the Cotswold Community, 1967–.

Non-manuscript material: Growing oral history collection. Expanding collection of films,
photographs, videotapes and sound recordings.

Finding aids: Catalogues and lists, to be sent to
NRA.

Facilities: Limited photocopying. Photography. Audio and video playback and copying
facilities.

Conservation: Contracted out.

207 Cheshire Military Museum

Address: The Castle, Chester CH1 2DN

Telephone: (01244) 327617

Fax: (01244) 327617

Enquiries: Maj. (retd) J.E. Ellis

Open: Tues, Thurs: 9.00–5.00, by appointment.

Access: Bona fide researchers. A small charge is made.

A The 22nd (Cheshire) Regiment

The museum opened in its present location in 1972. The regiment was raised in 1689, although the records date mostly from the late 18th century and include regimental journals, 19th century–. Collections of documents, letters and photographs, 20th century, are held and any material relating to the regiment is acquired. In addition there is a small collection of correspondence of General Sir Charles Napier (1782–1853). There is an index to the collections and photocopying is available.

B Cheshire (Earl of Chester's) Yeomanry

The regiment was raised in 1797. The records are incomplete but include orders and correspondence, mainly late 19th century–.

208 Cheshire Record Office

Address: Duke Street, Chester CH1 1RL

Telephone: (01244) 602574 (enquiries)

Fax: (01244) 603812

Enquiries: The Principal Archivist, Mr J.R.H. Pepler

Open: Mon–Fri: 9.15–4.45, by appointment. Also every 2nd Wednesday evening and 4th Saturday morning of each month.

Access: Generally open to the public.

Historical background: The first professional county archivist was appointed in 1949, though the listing of the county muniments had commenced in 1933. The office was nominated by the Bishop of Chester as the official depository for ecclesiastical parish records in 1954 and became Chester Diocesan Record Office in 1961. The office also acts for the Dean and Chapter of Chester (cathedral and estate records) and for all the districts of Cheshire with the exception of Chester. The office is recognised as a place of deposit for public records.

Acquisition policy: To acquire records of administrative or historical significance for the county of Cheshire and the diocese of Chester.

Archives of organisation: Usual local authority and diocesan holdings.

Major collections: Deposited local collections, including a large range of family and estate collections, e.g. Arderne, Cholmondeley, Crewe, Egerton, Leicester of Tabley, Shakerly, Stanley of Alderley, Tollemache, Vernon/Venables and Wilbraham.
Business collections, including Fodens and ICI, Mond Division.

Non-manuscript material: Maps, including excellent OS coverage of the county at all scales. Newspapers, including *Chester Courant*, 1747–1982; *Chester Chronicle*, 1775–; *Cheshire Observer*, 1856–.

Facilities: Photocopying. Photography and microfilming by arrangement.

Conservation: Full in-house facilities.

Publications: F.I. Dunn: *The Ancient Parishes, Townships and Chapelries of Cheshire* (1987) [with large folding map].
Cheshire Record Office Guide (1991).
Various source sheets; leaflets available singly.

209 Chester City Record Office

Address: Town Hall, Chester CH1 2HJ

Telephone: (01244) 324324 ext. 2110

Fax: (01244) 324338

Enquiries: The City Archivist, Mrs M. Lewis

Open: Mon–Fri: 10.00–4.00
Otherwise by appointment only.

Access: Generally open to the public.

Historical background: Chester City Record Office was established by Chester County Borough Council in 1948. Since 1974 it has served the new City of Chester, one of eight districts of Cheshire. The City Archivist is Honorary Archivist to the Freemen and Guilds of the City of Chester. The office houses Chester Archaeological Society Library and MSS, of which the City Archivist is Honorary Archivist. Access can be arranged to the Duke of Westminster's MSS, Eaton Estate Office, Eccleston, Chester. The office is recognised as a place of deposit for public records.

Acquisitions policy: Records of Chester District Council, covering current district; collection of other records restricted to geographical boundaries of pre-1974 Chester Borough.

Archives of organisation: Usual local authority

record holdings, plus charters, mayors' and sheriffs' records, 12th century–.

Major collections: Deposited collections including: archives of 21 of the city guilds, 15th–20th centuries; Chester Bluecoat Hospital, 1700–1948; Chester College, 1839–1987; Chester Royal Infirmary, 1755–1956.
MSS of J.P. Earwaker, antiquarian, c1200–1897. Extensive collections of non-conformist church records, 17th–20th centuries, and business records, 18th–20th centuries.

Non-manuscript material: Oral history collection (300 recordings).
Collections of lantern slides and photographs transferred from Grosvenor Museum in 1993.

Finding Aids: Source guides. Catalogues and indexes. Computerised system under development. Lists sent to NRA.

Facilities: Photocopying. Photography. Microfiche reader/printers.

Conservation: Subject to contractual arrangement with Cheshire Record Office (entry **208**).

Publications: A.M Kennett: *Chester Schools: A Guide to the School Archives* (1973).
——: *Archives and Records of the City of Chester* (1985).
Family History Sources (1992).

210 Derbyshire Library Service
Local Studies Department

Address: Chesterfield Library, New Beetwell Street, Chesterfield, Derbys S40 1QN

Telephone: (01246) 209292 ext. 38

Fax: (01246) 209304

Enquiries: The Central Librarian, Mr L. Greaves

Open: Mon–Fri: 9.30–7.00 Sat: 9.30–1.00

Access: Generally open to the public, but since some archives are housed in a basement store it is advisable to write in advance.

Historical background: The library was established in 1879 with a strong engineering background due to George Stephenson's influence. It has gradually accumulated archival material over the years. The library came under Derbyshire County Council with reorganisation in 1974 and moved into a new central library in 1985.

Acquisitions policy: While the library retains the existing archive collections, all offers of archival material are now referred to Derbyshire Record Office (entry **813**).

Major collections: Collections of family papers, including: Barnes family, landowners and owners of Grassmoor colliery, including bills and accounts, 18th–19th centuries (c1000 items); Twigg family from Ashover area, some material relating to local mining, mostly 18th century (c500 items).
Records of local businesses, including Plowrights Brothers Ltd, engineering firm; Greaves, chemist shop, mid-19th century–.
Unitarian church records, 1692–1968.
Methodist records for Chesterfield area: church records, 1828–1974; circuit records, 1912–57.
Education records, 1863–1970.
Handford local history collection.
Oakley Collection: deeds (c300) and other documents on north-east and west Derbyshire, c1571–1875, collected by R.H. Oakley, local historian.
Arkwright Cotton Mill, Bakewell: wage books, 1786–1811

Non-manuscript material: Substantial collection of photographs and slides of the Chesterfield area, c1880–.
Stephenson Collection of books, pamphlets etc, showing contribution of George Stephenson to railway history.
Census returns, 1841–91.
Derbyshire Times, 1854–; *Derbyshire Courier,* 1828–1922; *Derby and Chesterfield Reporter,* 1823–1930; *Derby Mercury,* 1732–1800.
Maps, historical and current, of various scales covering Chesterfield area.

Finding aids: Various lists and indexes. Card catalogue.

Facilities: Photocopying. Microfilm/fiche readers/printer.

Publications: Derbyshire Local Studies Collections: a Guide to Resources [new edition in preparation].

211 West Sussex Record Office

Address: County Hall, Chichester, West Sussex PO19 1RN

Telephone: (01243) 533911

Fax: (01243) 777952

Enquiries: The County and Diocesan Archivist, Mr Richard Childs

Open: Mon–Fri: 9.15–4.45 Sat: 9.15–1.00; 2.00–4.30

Access: Generally open to the public.

Historical background: The Records Committee was set up in 1939 and took in records from that date, although an archivist was not appointed until 1946. Since reorganisation in 1974 the office has covered the old West Sussex area and part of what was East Sussex. The office also acts as the Diocesan Record Office for Chichester and is recognised as a place of deposit for public records.

Archives of organisation: Usual local authority record holdings.

Major collections: Deposited local collections, including the following which have a wider significance: Wilfred Scawen Blunt MSS: Irish and Middle Eastern politics, and literary, 19th and 20th centuries.
Cobden MSS: political, 19th century.
Eric Gill Collection: works of art, 20th century.
Goodwood MSS: political and cultural, 18th and 19th centuries.
Maxse MSS: political, 20th century.
Petworth House Archives: Thomas Harriott astronomical papers, 17th century.
Royal Sussex Regiment MSS: military, 18th–20th centuries.

Facilities: Photocopying. Photography. Microfilming. Microfilm reader/printers.

Conservation: In-house facilities.

Publications: Official Guide and Report on the East and West Sussex Record Offices (1954).
F.W. Steer and I.M. Kirby: *Catalogue of the Records of the Bishop, Archdeacons and Former Exempt Jurisdictions* (1966).
P.M. Wilkinson: *Genealogists' Guide to the West Sussex Record Office* (1979).
Over 50 publications [list available].
See also 'Publications' under East Sussex Record Office (entry **455**)

212 The Guild of Handicraft Trust

Address: The Silk Mill, Chipping Camden, Glos GL55 6DS

Telephone: (01386) 841417 (archive)

Enquiries: The Secretary, Frank Johnson

Open: Wed–Fri: 9.30–5.00

Access: Generally open to the public, by appointment only.

Historical background: Established following an inaugural meeting in 1990 and acquired charitable status in 1992.

Acquisitions policy: Working and dimensional drawings, sketches, presentation design prototypes, samples, correspondence, photographic records relating to art, craft and design production in the North Cotswolds since 1900.

Non-manuscript material: Design drawings of jewellery and other silverware by George Hart and Sidney Reeve, Guildsman with the Guild of Handicraft, 1900–39.
Design drawings, sketch pads, samples, prototypes, correspondence of Robert Welch, industrial designer and silversmith (*b* 1929), 1953–94.
Architectural drawings by C.R. Ashbee (1863–1937), 1900–30.
Photographs of the North Cotswolds by Jesse Taylor, 1890s-1910.
Design drawings, samples of APT (Appropriate Technology) Ltd: low-tech engineering solutions for the developing world, 1982–92.
Archive of typographer and graphic artist Douglas Coyne (*b* 1930), 1950s-90s.
Photographs of Chipping Camden by Roland Dyer (*b* 1923), 1950s.
Design drawings, architectural plans, slide collection, small oral history unit, photographs.

Finding aids: Catalogues in preparation.

Conservation: Contracted out.

213 Royal Agricultural College

Address: Stroud Road, Cirencester, Glos GL7 6JS

Telephone: (01285) 652531 ext. 2274

Enquiries: The Librarian

The college was founded in 1845. Its archives are available by appointment only, normally in the college vacations. They include examination papers, course photographs, and RAC *Journals*. A computerised catalogue is in preparation. Appropriate donations of records are accepted.

214 North West Sound Archive

Address: Clitheroe Castle, Clitheroe, Lancs BB7 1AZ

Telephone/Fax: (01200) 27897

Enquiries: The Sound Archivist, Ken Howarth

Open: Mon–Fri: 9.30–5.30

Access: Generally open to the public; an appointment is essential. Charges for loan service.

Historical background: The archive was founded in 1979 in Manchester and transferred in 1981 under the auspices of Lancashire Record Office, although it is still independent with a separate committee.

Acquisitions policy: To record and preserve the recordings of the life, language, traditions and culture of north-west England, i.e. Lancashire, Greater Manchester and the Peak District.

Non-manuscript material: Solidarity recordings (Granada TV).
Jodrell Bank Radio Astronomy collections.
BBC Radio Manchester and Lancashire collections.
Surveys of English Dialects (Leeds University) and children's playsongs.
Oral history collections: Bolton, Manchester Jewish Museum, Manchester Ship Canal, Salford Quays, Strangeways.

Finding aids: Computer catalogue.

Facilities: Photocopying.

215 Stonyhurst College

Address: Clitheroe, Lancs BB7 9PZ

Telephone: (01254) 826345

Fax: (01254) 826732

Enquiries: The Librarian, The Rev. F.J. Turner

Access: On personal application, normally with a letter of introduction, to the librarian.

Historical background: Stonyhurst College dates from the reign of Queen Elizabeth I, when English Catholics wishing to educate their children in their own religion had to send them abroad. A number of institutions were established on the continent, one of the earliest being the English College of St Omers in 1593. Subsequent colleges were set up in Bruges and Liège and, in 1794, in Stonyhurst.

Major collections: A large number of MSS relating to English Catholicism, 1570–1850 (the period known as recusancy), consisting of deeds, returns of recusants, transcripts of various letters, account books, manorial documents and estate papers, including letters *re* English College at Liège, 1780–1814 (3 vols).
Collection of annual letters on the Scottish Mission, 1562–1752.

Finding aids: MS Collection: NRA 22957.

Facilities: Photocopying.

Publications: HMC Second Report, xiii and App. 143–46 (1); Third Report, xxi, and App. 334–41 (2); Tenth Report, xxv and App. IV 176–99 (13).

216 Clogher Diocesan Archives

Address: St MacCartan's Cathedral, Clogher, Co. Tyrone BT76 0AD

Telephone: (016625) 48235

Enquiries: The Rector

Open: By appointment.

Access: Generally open to the public. No charge for reasonable requests.

Historical background: The Diocesan Archives room was set up in 1972 as a memorial to Rt Rev. S.J. Heaslett, the first Anglican bishop of Tokyo (who was later Primate of the Japanese Church). Bishop Heaslett was born in Tedarnet parish in Clogher Diocese. A former diocesan library had existed in Clones.

Acquisitions policy: Archives relating to Clogher Diocese (Church of Ireland).

Archives of organisation: Diocesan visitation books, 1661– (100 vols).
Chapter lease book, 18th–19th century.
Chapter minutes.
Rural deans' reports and cathedral preachers' books, c1800–.

Major collections: Clogher Corporation Book,

1783–1800.
Seal and Letters Patent of Bishop John Porter, 1798.

Non-manuscript material: Some maps, including a set of the first OS series for the Clogher Valley.

Publications: Clogher Cathedral Graveyard (1972) [list of tombstone inscriptions].

217 Clydebank District Libraries and Museum

Address: Central Library, Dumbarton Road, Clydebank, Strathclyde G81 1XH

Telephone: (0141) 952 8765/1416

Fax: (0141) 951 8275

Enquiries: The District Librarian

Open: Mon–Fri: 9.30–8.00 Sat: 9.30–5.00

Access: Generally open to the public, but prior notification appreciated.

Acquisitions policy: Generally to acquire all local studies material relating to Clydebank District, but specific interests are local shipbuilding, Singer Sewing Machine production and the Clydebank Blitz. This archive is supplemented by the museum collection, which has shipbuilding memorabilia and a large collection of Singer and non-Singer sewing machines.

Archives of organisation: Minute books and related records of Clydebank Town Council, 1886–1975, and Clydebank District Council, 1975–.

Major collections: Usual local history material, including local shipbuilding companies: J. & G. Thomson Ltd, John Brown & Co. Ltd, Wm Beardmore & Co. Ltd, Napier Miller; Singer Manufacturing Co.; and the Clydebank Blitz, 1941.

Non-manuscript material: Clydebank & Renfew Post, 1891–1921, *Clydebank Press,* 1921–83 and *Clydebank Post,* 1983–.
Photographs of Clydebank district (including Old Kilpatrick, Hardgate, Duntocher), late 19th century–.
Near complete set of OS maps of Clydebank District from 1st edition, 6 inch (1:10000) and 25 inch (1:2500)

Facilities: Photocopying. Microfiche reader/printer.

Publications: J. Hood (ed): *History of Clyde-*

bank (1988).
List of other local history publications available.

218 Order of the Company of Mary Our Lady

Address: Convent of Notre Dame, Cobham, Surrey KT11 1HA

Telephone: (01932) 868331

Fax: (01932) 867454

Enquiries: The Sr Archivist

Open: Mon–Fri: 9.00–12.00
Closed during school holidays.

Access: Open to members of the Company of Mary. All others by appointment.

The Company of Mary is a Roman Catholic religious order of apostolic religious women founded in 1607 by Saint Jeanne de Lestonnac in Bordeaux with the approval of Pope Paul V. It was the first order dedicated to the education of youth, with Ignatian spirituality, and spread over Europe, North and South America, Asia and Africa. The union of all the Houses and the establishment of central government took place in 1921 with the Generalate in Rome. The General Archivist, resident in Rome, oversees the collections and issues guidelines to ensure the safe-keeping of archival material in the designated repositories. The archives at Cobham form a small collection concerned mainly with the internal affairs of the convent. A catalogue and classification list for the collections worldwide, 1607–1921, can be found in Pilar Foz y Foz ODN, *Primary Sources for the History of the Education of Women in Europe and America: Historical Archives Company of Mary our Lady, 1607–1921* (Rome, 1985).

219 ESRC Data Archive

Parent organisation: Economic and Social Research Council

Address: University of Essex, Wivenhoe Park, Colchester, Essex CO4 3SQ

Telephone: (01206) 872001

Fax: (01206) 872003

Enquiries: The Assistant Director (Information), Bridget Winstanley

Open: Mon–Fri: 9.00–5.15

Access: Data are available at cost to the academic (HEFC-funded) community. Administrative charges and royalties apply for non-academic use. Appointments are necessary.

Historical background: The Data Archive was founded in 1967. It is a national, multi-disciplinary research facility with a brief to acquire, store and disseminate computer-readable copies of social science and humanities datasets for further analyses by the research community. The archive also provides information on the location and availability of social science data and sponsors various activities, including workshops, user groups and regular newsletters, designed to improve the quality of data and their secondary analysis.

Acquisitions policy: To obtain computer-readable files from all areas of the social sciences from academic, governmental and commercial sources, to store them and to disseminate copies for further analyses.

Non-manuscript material: Historical and contemporary research data on a variety of magnetic media (c5,000 datasets). Major holdings include General Household Surveys, Family Expenditure Surveys, CSO Macro-Economic Data, British Crime Surveys, British Household Panel Study, Election Studies, computerised historical records including 19th century censuses.

Finding aids: BIRON, the archive's on-line catalogue and index, is available on JANET and Internet: address: biron essex.ac.uk; login name: biron; password: norib.

Publications: *ESRC Data Archive Bulletin* [published three times a year].
A list of other publications is available on request.

220 Essex Record Office
Colchester and North-East Essex Branch

Address: Stanwell House, Stanwell Street, Colchester, Essex CO2 7DL

Telephone: (01206) 572099

Fax: (01206) 574541

Enquiries: The Branch Archivist, Mr P.R.J. Coverley

Open: Mon: 10.00–5.15 Tues–Thurs: 9.15–5.15

Fri: 9.15–4.15 Mon (2nd of the month): 10.00–8.45

Access: Generally open to the public; an appointment is advisable. The office operates the CARN reader's ticket system.

Historical background: This branch office of Essex Record Office was established in 1985. It is recognised as a place of deposit for manorial and tithe documents as well as public records.

Acquisitions policy: Collections of interest for the county of Essex. The main catchment area consists of the current Colchester and Tendring local authority areas.

Archives of organisation: Usual local authority record holdings.

Major collections: Deposited local collections, including antiquarian and literary correspondence of Charles Grey, 1728–76.

Finding aids: Indexes (place, subject, name), catalogues. Lists sent to NRA.

Facilities: Photocopying. Photography. Microfilming. Microfilm/fiche reader.

Conservation: In-house facility at Essex Record Office, Chelmsford (entry 203).

221 Society of Engineers

Address: Guinea Wiggs, Nayland, Colchester, Essex CO6 4NF

Telephone: (01206) 263332

Fax: (01206) 262624

Enquiries: Mrs L.C.A. Wright

Open: Mon–Fri: 9.00–5.30

Access: By appointment only.

The Society of Engineers was established in 1854 and in 1910 incorporated the Civil and Mechanical Engineers Society (f. 1859). It is the third oldest engineering society in the UK, and uniquely represents the interests of civil, electrical, mechanical, chemical and aeronautical engineers. The library maintains the society's archives as well as collections of memorabilia and photographs relating to members.

222 University of Essex

Address: The Albert Sloman Library, Wivenhoe Park, Colchester, Essex CO4 3SQ

Telephone: (01206) 873333

Fax: (01206) 872289

Enquiries: The Librarian

Open: Term: Mon–Fri: 9.00–10.00 Sat: 9.00–6.00 Sun: 2.00–7.00 Vacation: Mon–Fri: 9.00–5.30

Access: On written application to the librarian.

Historical background: The University of Essex was founded in 1963.

Acquisitions policy: Donation or deposit of records either relevant to the teaching and research at the university or of local interest.

Major collections: Archives of the Colchester and Coggeshall meetings of the Society of Friends, including correspondence of Steven Crisp.
Papers of the Rowhedge Iron Works.
Archives of the Social Democratic Party (SDP) and the Tawney Society, 1981-8.
Papers and reports of the Scientific Committee on Problems of the Environment (SCOPE), International Council of Scientific Unions, 1982-8.
Papers of the National Viewers' and Listeners' Association.
Paul Sieghart (1927–89): Human Rights Archive.
Sir Vincent Evans Collection: papers of the European Court of Human Rights.
Letters and papers of Henri and Sophie Gaudier-Brzeska.
Diaries, papers and work-ledger of John Hassall, poster artist and book illustrator.
Diaries of Samuel Levi Bensusan (1872–1958), author.
Papers of Professor Donald Davie (*b* 1922), author.
Papers of K.F. Bowden *re* computerisation of medical records.

Finding aids: Handlists to SDP, Tawney Society, SCOPE, Sieghart and Evans collections. Bowden: NRA 27778.

Facilities: Photocopying.

Conservation: Contracted out.

Publications: S.H.G. Fich: *Colchester Quakers* (Colchester, 1962).

223 University of Ulster at Coleraine Library

Address: Coleraine, Co. Londonderry BT52 1SA

Telephone: (01265) 44141

Fax: (01265) 40903

Enquiries: The Sub-Librarian, Ms C.P. Ballantine

Open: Term: Mon–Fri: 9.00–10.00 Sat: 9.30–1.00 Vacation: Mon–Fri: 9.30–5.00
Special collections available only up to 5.00, or by arrangement.

Access: Anyone establishing a serious interest.

Historical background: The University of Ulster was established in October 1984 by merging the former New University of Ulster with Ulster Polytechnic. There are four campuses, at Belfast, Coleraine, Jordanstown and Magee College, Londonderry.

Acquisitions policy: To strengthen relevant research areas.

Major collections: Papers of: George Shiels (1881–1949), playwright; Denis Johnston (*b* 1901), playwright and author; George Stelfox (1884–1972), naturalist; E. Norman Carrothers (1898–1977), botanist and railway engineer.
Headlam–Morley correspondence.
Paul Ricard Collection of World War II material.
MSS of John Hewitt (1907–87), poet.

Non-manuscript material: Henry Davis Gift of early books and incunabula.
Henry Morris Collection of Irish material.
E.N. Carrothers bookplates.
Study of Conflict archive.
Considerable runs of newspapers and other material in microtext form.
European Documentation Centre.
Co-operative Documentation Centre.
Library of John Hewitt, including rural Ulster poets of the 19th century.

Facilities: Photocopying. Photography by arrangement. Microtext readers.

Publications: Guide to the libraries [annual].

224 Barnoldswick Library

Parent organisation: Lancashire County Council

Address: Fern Lea Avenue, Barnoldswick, Colne, Lancs BB8 5DW

Telephone: (01282) 812147

Enquiries: The Local Studies Assistant, Miss Karen Green

Open: Mon, Wed: 9.30–7.00 Thurs, Fri: 9.30–5.00 Sat: 9.30–4.00

Access: Generally open to the public; an appointment is advisable as facilities are limited.

Historical background: Barnoldswick New Library was opened in 1989, and the Craven and Yorkshire collections of local history material previously housed at Colne Library (entry **225**) were added to Barnoldswick Library stock. The Barnoldswick Local History Society Collection was added in 1991.

Major collections: Barnoldswick UDC minutes, 1938–71, and abstract of accounts, 1919– 70; Earby UDC minutes, 1915–42, and yearbook, 1955–74.
Earby Co-operative Society Book, 1911–32.
Salterforth Water Company correspondence.
Barnoldswick Local History Society Collection.

Non-manuscript material: OS maps and photographic collections for West Craven area (Barnoldswick, Salterforth, Kelbrook, Earby, Thornton, Bracewell and Brogden).
Plans for Barnoldswick and West Craven area.
Craven Herald, 1929–66.

Finding aids: Catalogue of Barnoldswick Local History Collection. Index to newspapers, maps and censuses.

Facilities: Photocopying. Microfilm/fiche reader.

Publications: K.A. Green: *Barnoldswick & District Maps.*
S. Byrne: *Barnoldswick Jottings.* E. Gregson: *Barnoldswick New Library Brief History.*

225 Colne Library

Parent organisation: Lancashire County Council Library and Museum Service

Address: Market Street, Colne, Lancs BB8 0HS

Telephone: (01282) 871155

Enquiries: The Reference Librarian, Mrs Christine Bradley

Open: Mon, Wed: 9.30–7.00 Tues: 9.30–12.00 Thurs, Fri: 9.30–5.00 Sat: 9.30–4.00

Access: Generally open to the public.

Historical background: The collection relates specifically to the present area of Pendle District, with emphasis on Colne, Trawden and Foulridge. Records relating to the area which was in the West Riding of Yorkshire before local government reorganisation in 1974 are now housed at Barnoldswick Library (entry **224**). See also Nelson Library (entry **830**).

Major collections: Parish registers, 1599– (on microfilm); overseers of poor accounts, 1767–87; surveyors' accounts and minute books, 1767–1876; rate books and tax returns, 1523–.
Council minutes, 1893–; census enumerators' returns, 1841–81.
Methodist church minutes, 1815–; Co-operative Society minute books, 1882–1964.
Friends of Wycoller Collection; Colne Literary and Scientific Society minute books, 1898–1957; records of Colne, Earby and Barnoldswick Amalgamated Association of Beamers and Twisters and Weavers, 1905–71.

Non-manuscript material: Usual local history collection, including: Ernest Spivey photographic negatives (2108 items).
Directories, 1814–.
Local newspapers, 1854–.

Finding aids: Lancashire Record Office: guide to material relating to Pendle District (photocopies of relevant pages of full catalogue).

Facilities: Photocopying. Microfilm reader. Audio and film-viewing equipment.

Publications: The Wills of Colne & District, 1545–1830.
Colne and its Times: an Index to the Local Newspaper, 1874–1974.
Maps of Colne & District: a Catalogue.
Photographic Source Material for Pendle District: a Catalogue.

The Ernest Spivey Collection of Photographic Negatives.
The Local Wotwegot: a Catalogue of Colne Local History Collection.

226 Coventry Central Library

Parent organisation: Coventry City Council

Address: Smithford Way, Coventry, West Midlands CV1 1FY

Telephone: (01203) 832336 (Library) 832329 (Tom Mann Centre)

Fax: (01203) 832440

Enquiries: The Local Studies Librarian

Open: Mon, Tues, Thurs, Fri: 9.00–8.00 Wed: 9.30–8.00 Sat: 9.00–4.30

Access: Generally open to the public. An appointment is preferred for manuscript material.

Historical background: The George Eliot Collection was founded in 1919 to mark the centenary of the author's birth, and the Angela Brazil Collection was presented by her sister in 1947. MS material of the Tom Mann Centre, previously held in the library, is now at the Modern Records Centre at the University of Warwick (entry **229**) but trade union books, pamphlets and periodicals remain.

Acquisitions policy: To acquire further material relating to the collections already held.

Archives of organisation: Minute books and other records of the Coventry Library Society, the predecessor of Coventry City Libraries, and of the Coventry Book Club, the former subscription department of the Central Library.

Major collections: Letters and other MS records relating to George Eliot (1819–80), her friends and relatives, especially those with Coventry connections.
Scrapbooks, photographs and other personal possessions of Angela Brazil (1868–1947), writer of children's stories.

Non-manuscript material: Usual local studies collection covering Coventry and Warwickshire, including newspapers, maps, photographs and recordings.

Facilities: Photocopying. Photography. Microfilm/fiche readers.

Conservation: Access to facilities at Coventry City Record Office (entry **227**).

227 Coventry City Record Office

Address: Mandela House, Bayley Lane, Coventry, West Midlands CV1 5RG

Telephone: (01203) 832418/832421

Enquiries: The City Archivist, Mr Roger Vaughan

Open: Mon–Thurs: 8.45–4.45 Fri: 8.45–4.15

Access: Generally open to the public. Advance notice is needed for some series of records held outside the repository.

Historical background: The St Mary's Hall Muniment Room was constructed in 1892. The City Record Office was established when the first city archivist was appointed in 1938. In 1974 the Record Office was transferred from the Associate Town Clerk's Department to the Department of Libraries, Arts and Museums. After having been housed in temporary accommodation in Hay Lane and Broadgate House, the Record Office moved to a modern purpose-adapted repository in 1986. It is recognised as a place of deposit for public records.

Acquisitions policy: Acquires by gift or deposit records produced by organisations and individuals presently or formerly active in Coventry.

Archives of organisation: Usual local authority record holdings, including borough archives, 12th century–1835.
Records of Coventry City Council, 1836–.
Records of the Mayor's Court concerning apprenticeship and admission to the Freedom of the City, 1722–.
Archives of superseded authorities, including parish councils, boards of guardians and school boards.

Major collections: Local public records: Quarter Sessions, magistrates court, coroner's court and the Coventry and Warwickshire Hospital.
Deposited local collections, including business records, archives of Coventry's trading companies, non-conformist church records and archives of clubs, societies, schools and other organisations and private citizens.

Non-manuscript material: Collection of oral history tapes and transcripts covering most aspects of Coventry's recent history. Microfilm copies of parish registers for Coventry and environs and local cemetery registers.

Finding aids: Guide to the borough archive. Catalogues and indexes of some private accessions and departmental archives. Lists of the records of superseded authorities and of some classes of local public records. Handlist and titular index of all unofficial accessions. Card index of surnames of persons admitted to the Freedom of the City.

Facilities: Photocopying. Photography. Microform readers. Ultra-violet lamp.

Conservation: Conservation unit undertaking full range of paper and parchment conservation. Limited outside work undertaken by arrangement.

Publications: J.C. Jeaffreson: *A Calendar of the Books, Charters in the New Muniment Room of St Mary's Hall* (1896).
F. Smith: *Supplementary Catalogue* (1931).
A.A. Dibben: *Coventry City Charters* (1969).

228 Coventry University
Lanchester Library

Address: Much Park Street, Coventry, West Midlands CV1 2HF

Telephone: (01203) 838435

Fax: (01203) 838686

Enquiries: The University Librarian, Mr P. Noon

Open: Term: Mon–Thurs: 9.00–8.45 Fri: 9.00–5.15 Sat: 10.00–12.45 Vacation: Mon–Fri: 9.00–5.15

Access: Approved readers, on application to the University Librarian.

Historical background: The family of F.W. Lanchester, aeronautical and automotive engineer, presented books and papers to the college (subsequently Coventry Polytechnic now Coventry University) in 1960. Since then, the archive has been added to considerably by purchase of his sketchbooks and other materials. The Lanchester Library is named in his honour. The original papers were microfilmed with the aid of a British Library grant.

Acquisitions policy: To receive, by gift or purchase, any relevant material offered.

Major collections: Papers, publications and sketchbooks of F.W. Lanchester.

Non-manuscript material: Archive of photographs of Lanchester cars.

Finding aids: Catalogue of F.W. Lanchester papers (1966). Indexing in progress.

Facilities: Photocopying. Microfilm/fiche readers/printers.

229 Modern Records Centre

Parent organisation: University of Warwick

Address: University of Warwick Library, Coventry, West Midlands CV4 7AL

Telephone: (01203) 524219

Enquiries: The Archivist

Open: Mon–Thurs: 9.00–1.00; 1.30–5.00 Fri: 9.00–1.00; 1.30–4.00
Other times by arrangement.

Access: All serious researchers; a few days' notice of a visit is advisable. Some accessions subject to restricted access.

Historical background: The centre was established in October 1973 on the initiative of a group of academics at the University of Warwick and with the aid of a grant from the Leverhulme Trust Fund. Its objects are to ensure the preservation (where necessary by collecting) of original sources for British political, social and economic history, with particular reference to labour history, industrial relations and industrial politics, and to make such sources available for research.
Archives of BP International are now housed in the same building as the centre, but administered separately. Records of the former Coventry College of Education, established as an emergency training college in 1946 and merged with the University of Warwick in 1978, are held in Westwood Library.

Acquisitions policy: To build on existing strengths, especially in industrial relations and industrial politics.

Major collections: Confederation of British Industry Predecessor Archive; also some other trade and employers' association records, including Engineering Employers' Federation. Trades Union Congress records, pre-1960.
Trade union archives, including constituents of Manufacturing, Science, Finance Union, Rail, Maritime and Transport Workers Union, Transport and General Workers' Union, Union of Construction, Allied Trades and Technicians;

also unions in the fields of education, the printing industry, public service (UNISON constituents) and the Post Office and telecommunications, as well as in a variety of other occupations.

Political records, including a significant concentration of records of British Trotskyism.

Pressure groups, including Campaign for Nuclear Disarmament; Howard League and NACRO; also comprehensive holdings of public documents of Amnesty International and Anti-Concorde Project.

Charities: Young Women's Christian Association records, mainly pre-1960, including minutes, serials and other publications, ephemera, some files.

Individuals' papers, including those of Lady Allen of Hurtwood (1897–1976); Sir Ernest Benn (1875–1954), publisher and individualist (personal papers); Frank Cousins (1904–86); R.H.S. Crossman (1907–74), full transcripts of published diaries; R.A. Etheridge, convenor at Austin Motor Company, Longbridge; Sir Victor Gollancz (1893–1967), publisher and humanitarian (personal papers); Reg Groves, socialist activist and historian.

Some business records, mostly motor industry under an agreement with British Motor Industry Heritage Trust (entry 338).

Rubery Owen Holdings archives.

Some publishing records of Victor Gollancz Ltd.

Some Cable and Wireless archives are housed in the Centre.

Non-manuscript material: Numerous accessions include printed reports, journals and pamphlets, individual items and small groups of ephemera over a wide range of political, social and economic activity.

The University Library has an extensive collection of journals, reports and pamphlets of trade unions and employers' and trade associations which may be consulted in the centre. This collection includes part of the former Board of Trade Library.

Historical Library of the Howard League (owned by the University Library).

Finding aids: Typescript catalogues or interim finding aids exist for many accessions; search-room card indexes are based on these. Lists sent to NRA.

Facilities: Photocopying (limited). Microfilm/fiche reader. Listening facilities for tapes (limited). Provision for use of lap-top computer.

Publications: R.A. Storey and J. Druker: *Guide to the Modern Records Centre* (1977)

C. Woodland and R.A. Storey: *The Taff Vale Case: a Guide to the ASRS Records* (1978) .

——: *The Osborne Case Papers and other Records of the Amalgamated Society of Railway Servants* (1979).

R.A. Storey and S. Edwards: *Supplement to the Guide to the Modern Records Centre* (1981).

J. Bennett and R.A. Storey: *The First Labour Correspondent and the Board of Trade Library* (1983).

M. Wilcox and R.A. Storey: *The Confederation of British Industry Predecessor Archive* (1984).

N. Baldwin and R.A. Storey: *The International Transport Workers' Federation Archive* (1985).

R.A. Storey and A. Tough: *Consolidated Guide to the Modern Records Centre* (1986).

J. Bennett and R.A. Storey: *Trade Union and Related Records* (6/1991).

C. Wightman and R.A. Storey: *Women at Work and in Society* (2/1991).

L. Smallbone and R.A. Storey: *Employers' & Trade Associations' History* (1992).

S. Duffield and R.A. Storey: *The Trades Union Congress Archive 1920–60* (1992).

R.A. Storey, A. Tough and C. Woodland: *Supplement to the Consolidated Guide* (1992).

Also Information Bulletin, Annual Report and Information Leaflet series, and lists reproduced in the *National Inventory of Documentary Sources*, (Chadwyck-Healey microfiche 1984–).

230 University of Warwick
Centre for Research in Ethnic Relations

Address: Social Studies Building, University of Warwick, Coventry, West Midlands CV4 7AL

Telephone: (01203) 523523 ext. 3607/2364 (Enquiries) ext. 3605 (Librarian)

Fax: (01203) 524324

Enquiries: The Director, Dr Z. Layton-Henry

Open: Mon–Fri: 9.00–4.00

Access: Bona fide researchers, by prior appointment.

The CRER was set up with a grant from ESRC in 1984 to continue the work of the Research

Unit on Ethnic Relations at the University of Aston. It maintains a Documentation Centre and Black Media Archive which holds a variety of documents, newscuttings and audio-visual material in the field of race and ethnic relations. There is a card catalogue and index to the newscuttings. It also houses the National Ethnic Minority Data Archive.

231 Innerpeffray Library

Address: by Crieff, Tayside PH7 3RS

Telephone: (01764) 652819

Enquiries: Mr E.W. Powell

Open: Mon–Wed, Fri, Sat: 10.00–1.00; 2.00–5.00 Sun: 2.00–5.00

Access: Generally open to the public. It is advisable to ring in winter, when opening times may change.

The library dates from 1680 and is probably the oldest public library in Scotland. Its own archives include MS borrowing ledgers, 1747–1968, and visitors books, early 19th century–. There are a few family MSS, e.g. commonplace books, held among the library collections. See NRA(S) 824; NRA 17568.

232 Cromarty Courthouse

Address: Church Street, Cromarty, Highland IV11 8KA

Telephone: (01381) 600418

Fax: (01381) 600408

Enquiries: The Curator, David Alston

Open: April–Oct: Mon–Sun: 10.00–6.00 Oct–March: Mon–Sun: 12.00–4.00

Access: Generally open to the public; an appointment is necessary.

The courthouse holds miscellaneous papers relating to the burgh of Cromarty and court case papers, mostly 19th century, (*c*1500). The latter are held with permission of the Scottish Record Office (entry 313) pending completion of cataloguing. There is also a small archive of oral history recordings and some photographs of the area, early 20th century.

233 Wellington College

Address: Crowthorne, Berks RG11 7PU

Telephone: (01344) 772262

Fax: (01344) 771725

Enquiries: The Archivist, R.C. Sopwith or The Bursar

Open: Most Weds, Thurs: 9.00–12.30; 1.30–5.30

Access: Generally at the archivist's discretion and by appointment giving a week's notice. Some material is restricted. Unsuitable for school or group search.

Historical background: The college, which opened in 1859, is a 'royal and religious foundation'. Foundationers of either sex are children of serving officers killed on active service, but the school is very largely a fee-paying, independent boarding school.

Acquisitions policy: To maintain the college archive.

Archives of organisation: Administrative, domestic, academic and estate records (incomplete).

Major collections: Deposits from old boys and governors, including letters of the Duke of Wellington and some E.F. Benson (1867–1940) material.
Correspondence relating to education of the Princes Adolphus and Francis of Teck, 1883–1910.

Non-manuscript material: Plans and drawings showing the architectural development of the college.

Finding aids: Partial card index. NRA 21772.

Facilities: Photocopying. Photography.

Conservation: Contracted out.

Publications: D.H. Newsome and J. Murray: *A History of Wellington College.*
Register of Wellington College 1859–1984 (1984).

234 London Borough of Croydon Archives Service

Address: Central Library, Katharine Street, Croydon, Surrey CR9 1ET

Telephone: (0181) 760 5400

Fax: (0181) 253 1004

Enquiries: The Archivist, Mr Oliver Harris

Open: Mon: 9.00–7.00 Tues, Wed, Fri: 9.00–6.00 Thurs: 9.30–6.00 Sat: 9.00–5.00

Access: Generally open to the public. Notification of visits is advised.

Historical background: The present London Borough of Croydon was created in 1965 from the former County Borough of Croydon (originally incorporated as a municipal borough in 1883), and the Urban District of Coulsdon and Purley. Croydon Public Library opened in 1890, and began a local collection, including manuscript material, soon afterwards. A distinct local history library was formed in 1973. An archivist was appointed in 1990 and the Archives Service was formally constituted in 1993. The library is recognised as a place of deposit for public records.

Acquisitions policy: To acquire non-current records of Croydon Council and its predecessor authorities, and other archival material relating to the area of the present borough and its inhabitants.

Archives of organisation: Records of Croydon Vestry, 1741–1899; Croydon Local Board of Health, 1849–83; Borough and County Borough of Croydon, 1883–1965; London Borough of Croydon, 1965– ; Croydon Rural District, 1896–1915; Coulsdon and Purley UDC, 1915–65; Croydon Board of Guardians, 1842–1930, Croydon Quarter Sessions, 1889–1965.

Major collections: Records of Croydon Literary and Scientific Institution, *c*1839–1930.
Estate records of Delmé-Radcliffe family *re* Addiscombe etc, 1329–1799; Eldon family *re* Shirley, 1698–1867.
Archives of Gillett and Johnston, bellfounders, 1877–1985; Mission of Hope maternity home/adoption agency/children's home, *c*1900–*c*1970; South Suburban Co-operative Society, 1887–1961; Women's International League (Croydon and District Branch), 1918–76. Items *re* the East India Company's Military Seminary/Addiscombe College, *c*1740–*c*1909.
Personal and family papers of F.G. Creed (1871–1957), inventor, *c*1890–*c*1980; antiquarian papers of C.W. Johnson (1799–1878), C.G. Paget (*d* 1952) and W.H. Mills (1870–1951).

Non-manuscript material: The Archives Service is housed with the Local Studies Library, which holds a large collection of books, pamphlets, periodicals, sale particulars, published maps, photographs, audio-visual material etc.

Finding aids: Various lists and indexes. Lists sent to NRA.

Facilities: Photocopying. Microfilm/fiche reader/printers.

Conservation: Contracted out.

235 Whitgift Foundation Archives

Address: Whitgift School, Haling Park, South Croydon, Surrey CR2 6YT

Telephone: (0181) 688 9222/3/4

Fax: (0181) 760 0682

Enquiries: The Archivist, Mr F.H.G. Percy

Open: Mon, Wed, Thurs: 10.00–4.30; other times by arrangement.

Access: Approved readers, on application by letter or telephone; an appointment is always advisable. Certain information about living persons is restricted at the discretion of the archivist.

Historical background: The Whitgift Foundation of a hospital for aged poor and a grammar school in Croydon was established by John Whitgift, Archbishop of Canterbury, in 1596.

Acquisitions policy: To continue to receive material relevant to the history and development of the foundation, the school and the Old Whitgiftian Association, as well as biographical details relating to old boys, staff and governors.

Archives of organisation: Ancient muniments, foundation deeds and account books, 15th century– ; leases of property, 17th century– .
Administrative records of the hospital and school, including minutes Court of Governors, 1871– (incomplete records prior to this); school rolls, 1871– ; school magazines, 1879– ; research papers relating to the history of Whitgift School.

Non-manuscript material: Maps, plans, architectural drawings, photographs and engravings of buildings and antiquities. Press-cuttings.

Finding aids: Lists and catalogues. Card indexes in progress.

Facilities: Photocopying. Photography by arrangement. Microfilm reader.

Publications: *History of Whitgift Grammar School* (Croydon, 1892).
Abstracts of the Ancient Muniments of the Whitgift Foundation (Croydon, 1934).
F.H.G. Percy: *History of Whitgift School* (Batsford, 1976).
——: *Whitgift School: a History* (Whitgift Foundation, 1991).

236 District History Centre and Baird Institute Museum

Parent organisation: Cumnock and Doon Valley District Council

Address: 3 Lugar Street, Cumnock, Strathclyde KA18 1AD

Telephone: (01290) 421701

Enquiries: The District Librarian, Mr S.C. Brownlee

Open: Mon, Tues, Thurs, Fri: 10.00–1.00; 1.30–4.30 Sat: 11.00–1.00

Access: Generally open to the public.

Historical background: Formerly part of Ayr County, the Cumnock and Doon Valley District was formed in 1975 on local government reorganisation and assumed responsibility for the Baird Institute, founded in 1891 under the will of John Baird (1812–88).

Acquisitions policy: To build up the archival collection for all parishes within the district.

Major collections: Usual local history collection, including local authority department records, 1887–.
Parochial records for Mauchline, New Cumnock and Sorn, 19th and 20th centuries.
Dalmellington District Council minutes, 1932–.

Non-manuscript material: Pamphlets.
Photographs, prints, glass negatives.
Microfilms of parish records and census returns.

Finding aids: Catalogue of archival material.

Facilities: Photocopying. Microfilm/fiche readers. CD-ROM facilities.

Publications: Leaflets and details of microfilm holdings.

237 North East Fife District Museum Service

Address: County Buildings, Cupar, Fife KY15 4TA

Telephone: (01334) 53722 ext. 141

Fax: (01334) 54016

Enquiries: The Assistant Museum Curator, Ms Marion Wood

Open: Mon–Fri: 9.00–5.00

Access: Bona fide researchers, by appointment.

Historical background: The District Museum Service was founded in 1983.

Acquisitions policy: Archaeology and social history of north-east Fife.

Archives of organisation: Records relating to museum collections and collectors.

Major collections: Records of Tayside Floorcloth Co., Newburgh, and Newburgh Friendly Society.
Personal papers of Alexander Laing (1808–92), local antiquarian and collector; Rev. John Anderson (1796–1864), geologist; and Martin Anderson ['Cynicus'] (1854–1932), artist.

Non-manuscript material: Local maps, photographs, postcards.

Finding aids: Card indexes.

Facilities: Photocopying. Photography.

238 Gwent County Record Office

Address: County Hall, Cwmbran, Gwent NP44 2XH

Telephone: (01633) 832214

Fax: (01633) 838225

Enquiries: The County Archivist, Mr David Rimmer

Open: Tues–Thurs: 9.30–5.00 Fri: 9.30–4.00

Access: Generally open to the public. The making of appointments is encouraged.

Historical background: Monmouthshire Record Office was founded in 1938 and Gwent Record Office was established following local government reorganisation in 1974. It also acts as the Diocesan Record Office for Monmouth,

Swansea and Brecon (parish records), and is recognised as a place of deposit for public records.

Acquisitions policy: Accepts collections of archives, by gift or deposit, relating to the county of Gwent and the historic county of Monmouthshire.

Archives of organisation: Usual local authority record holdings, including Quarter Sessions of the County of Monmouth, 18th–20th centuries; Monmouthshire County Council, 1889–1974; Gwent County Council, 1974–.

Major collections: Cwmbran Development Corporation records, 20th century.
1st Baron Raglan and descendants: papers, including those relating to the Napoleonic and Crimean War, 18th–19th centuries.
Lewis of St Pierre: estate papers and deeds, 14th–20th centuries.
Lord Llangattock of the Hendre (Rolls): family and estate papers and deeds, 15th–20th centuries.
Marquis of Abergavenny: estate papers and deeds, 16th–20th centuries.
Hanbury of Pontypool Park: business records and deeds, 16th–20th centuries.

Non-manuscript material: OS maps of Monmouthshire, 1878–1920.

Finding aids: Catalogue and indexes. Lists sent to NRA.

Facilities: Photocopying. Microfilm/fiche reader.

Conservation: Full conservation facilities.

Publications: W.H. Baker: *Guide to the Monmouthshire Record Office* (1959).

239 London Borough of Barking and Dagenham Public Libraries

Address: Valence House Museum, Becontree Avenue, Dagenham, Essex RM8 3HT

Telephone: (0181) 592 8404

Fax: (0181) 595 8307

Enquiries: The Curator/Archivist, Ms Susan Curtis

Open: Tues–Fri: 9.30–1.00; 2.00–4.30 Sat: 10.00–4.00

Access: Bona fide researchers, by appointment only.

Historical background: Dagenham Public Libraries acquired certain parish and urban district records and in 1963 were given the family papers of the late Captain A.B. Fanshawe, RN. In 1974, a curator/archivist, who administers the borough archives from the local history museum, was appointed.

Acquisitions policy: Non-current records of the London Borough of Barking and Dagenham and its predecessors, and of local firms and organizations etc, by donation or deposit.

Major collections: Local government records: Barking, 1666–; Dagenham, 1838–.
Local property title deeds, 15th–19th centuries.
Business archives of Lawes Chemical Co. Ltd, 1872–1969.
Fanshawe family MSS, including genealogical papers and pedigree, and correspondence and papers of Sir Richard Fanshawe (1600–66), mainly as ambassador to Portugal, 1662–3, and Spain, 1664–6.

Non-manuscript material: Photographs, drawings, paintings and prints. Maps and plans.

Finding aids: Local history collection: NRA 1293.

Facilities: Photocopying. Microfilm reader/printer.

Conservation: Contracted out.

Publications: *Guide to Local History Resources.*

240 Bergman Österberg Archives

Parent organisation: University of Greenwich

Address: The Library, Dartford Campus, Oakfield Lane, Dartford, Kent DA1 2SZ

Telephone: (0181) 316 9271/8585

Fax: (0181) 316 9275

Enquiries: The Campus Librarian, Ms E. Johnston

Open: Term: Mon–Fri: 9.00–9.00 Sat: 9.00–5.00 Vacation: telephone for opening hours.

Access: Generally open to the public, by appointment.

Historical background: The Bergman Öster-berg Physical Training College was founded in 1885 by Madame Österberg, who pioneered physical education as a new profession for women. Training continued on the Dartford Heath site until June 1986 and, although courses had become more general and male students were eventually accepted for certain of them, physical education was still the major specialism when training ceased. Latterly the courses were run by the Dartford Faculty of Education and Movement Studies of Greenwich University.

Acquisitions policy: Donations from old students and their relatives of all types of memorabilia, including uniforms, games equipment and badges.

Archives of organisation: Documents and photographs covering the history of the college, 1885–.

Non-manuscript material: One of the early gymslips, a garment invented at Madame Österberg's Physical Training College in about 1893.

Finding aids: Lists and a card index.

Facilities: Photocopying.

241 Dartford Central Library

Parent organisation: Kent County Council Arts and Libraries Department

Address: Central Park, Dartford, Kent DA1 1EU

Telephone: (01322) 221133

Fax: (01322) 278271

Enquiries: The Arts and Libraries Officer, Heritage, Miss P. Stevens or The Information Officer, Mr C. Bull

Open: Mon, Thurs, Fri: 9.00–6.00 Tues: 9.00–7.00 Wed: 9.00–1.00 Sat: 9.00–5.00
Appointment necessary for use of microfilm.

Access: Generally open to the public.

Historical background: The library has collected material on the local area since it was established in 1916.

Acquisitions policy: Local history material is acquired, but archival material is at the Centre for Kentish Studies (entry **789**).

Archives of organisation: Library reports, minutes, cuttings, photographs, statistics and ledgers, 1916–.

Non-manuscript material: Usual local history collection, including glass negatives of Ernest Youens, and drawings of Clement Youens, late 19th–early 20th centuries.
Large collections of maps and photographs.

Facilities: Photocopying. Photography. Microfilm/fiche readers.

Publications: Guide to the Local Studies Collection [pamphlet].

242 Derby Local Studies Library

Parent organisation: Derbyshire Library Service

Address: 25B Irongate, Derby DE1 3HF

Telephone: (01332) 255393

Enquiries: The Local Studies Librarian, Mrs L.G. Owen

Open: Mon, Tues: 9.00–7.00 Wed–Fri: 9.00–5.00 Sat: 9.30–1.00

Access: Generally open to the public. Readers should make prior arrangements to book use of microfilm/fiche readers.

Historical background: The collection is based on two family libraries, the Devonshire and Bemrose libraries, acquired in 1878 and 1914 respectively. The Devonshire Collection consisted of books, pamphlets, prints, election addresses and MSS; the Bemrose Library included some MS items and early editions of the works of Derbyshire authors. There were subsequently a number of deposits, some quite large, before the establishment of the local record office.

Acquisitions policy: To strengthen and enlarge existing primary and secondary collections on the history of Derbyshire and environmental studies within the county.

Major collections: Derby Corporation deeds, 17th–19th centuries (10,000).
Borough court records.
Derby Union Board of Guardians records, 1837–1915.
Various collections of family papers, notably of the Pares family.
Duesbury Collection of records of Derby China Factory, 1780–1800.

Wyatt Collection relating to lead-mining, 1810–50.
Derby Canal Company records, 1793–1974.

Non-manuscript material: Large collections of illustrative material, including photographs (*c*8000), broadsides, tapes and maps.
Newspapers: *Derby Mercury,* 1732–1933; *Derby and Chesterfield Reporter,* 1828–1930; *Derbyshire Advertiser,* 1876–1976; *Derby Evening Telegraph,* 1879–.
Census returns, 1841–91, for Derbyshire and some small portion of surrounding counties.

Finding aids: Various lists and indexes.

Facilities: Photocopying. Microfilm/fiche readers/printer.

Publications: Local Studies Collections Guide [in press].

243 Wiltshire Archaeological and Natural History Society Library

Address: 41 Long Street, Devizes, Wilts SN10 1NS

Telephone: (01380) 727369

Enquiries: The Librarian, Mrs Pamela Colman

Open: Tues–Sat: 10.00–5.00
Closed January.

Access: Generally open to the public and members.

Historical background: The society was formed in 1853 to collect information illustrating the history of Wiltshire, and the library was started immediately.

Acquisitions policy: Collections illustrating the local history of Wiltshire and Wessex. Archives are directed to Wiltshire Record Office (entry 1060).

Major collections: Notes, working papers and correspondence of many local historians, including William Stukeley's Commonplace Book; Sir Richard Colt Hoare's correspondence with William Cunnington and other contemporary antiquaries; Edward Kite's collection of pedigrees; and T.H. Baker's collection of transcripts of monumental inscriptions (23 vols).

Non-manuscript material: John Buckler watercolours of churches and major buildings, 1805–10 (10 vols)
Plans, drawings, photographs and maps.
An extensive pamphlet collection.
Press cutting collection, 1850–.

Finding aids: Catalogues, lists and indexes.

Facilities: Photocopying. Photography. Microfilm reader.

Conservation: Contracted out.

Publications: Wiltshire Archaeological and Natural History Magazine, 1854–.

244 Nazarene Theological College

Parent organisation: Church of the Nazarene

Address: Dene Road, Didsbury, Greater Manchester M20 8GU

Telephone: (0161) 445 3063 ext. 15

Fax: (0161) 448 0275

Enquiries: The Librarian, Mrs Heather Bell

Open: Mon–Fri: 9.00–5.00, by appointment only.

Access: To any person with a relevant enquiry, by arrangement only.

The Church of the Nazarene was founded in 1906 and the Theological College in 1944. Any material relating to the Church in the British Isles is acquired, and personal papers of the Rev. Dr Jack Ford, 1908–80, are held. A card catalogue and subject lists are available. There are photocopying facilities and microfilm/fiche readers are available.

245 Gwynedd Archives and Museums Service
Merioneth Record Office

Parent organisation: Gwynedd County Council

Address: Cae Penarlag, Dolgellau, Gwynedd LL40 2YB

Telephone: (01341) 422341 ext. 3300/3302

Enquiries: The Area Archivist and Museums Officer, Mr E.W. Thomas

Open: Mon–Fri: 9.00–1.00; 2.00–5.00 Closed for first full week in November.

Access: Generally open to the public. An appointment is desirable for microfilm/fiche readers.

Historical background: The office was set up in 1952 as the record office for the County of Merioneth. It is recognised as a place of deposit for public records.

Acquisitions policy: Documentary evidence relating to the old County of Merioneth.

Archives of organisation: Usual local authority record holdings.

Major collections: Deposited local collections.

Non-manuscript material: Slate quarry plans.

Finding aids: Catalogues, indexes. Catalogues sent to NRA.

Facilities: Photocopying. Photography. Microfilm/fiche readers.

Conservation: In-house.

Publications: K. Williams Jones: *Calendars of the Merioneth Quarter Session Rolls* (1965).

246 Dollar Museum

Parent organisation: Dollar Museum Trust

Address: Castle Campbell Hall, High Street, Dollar, Central FK14 7AY

Enquiries: The Hon. Curator, Mrs Janet Carolan, tel./fax: (01259) 742895

Open: Easter to Christmas, by arrangement with the Curator.

Access: An appointment is recommended.

Historical background: The museum was founded in 1987 and inherited material from the defunct Dollar Town Council.

Acquisitions policy: Material relevant to Dollar and the immediate vicinity is collected.

Major collections: Minute books of societies and clubs, 19th century.
Miscellaneous papers relating to the locality.

Non-manuscript material: Large photographic collection, including Devon Valley Railway.
Dollar Magazine, 1902–.
Early guide books; published reminiscences, 19th century; local cemetery inscriptions; scrapbooks.

Finding aids: Catalogue.

247 Doncaster Archives

Parent organisation: Doncaster Metropolitan Borough Council

Address: King Edward Road, Balby, Doncaster, South Yorks DN4 0NA

Telephone: (01302) 859811

Enquiries: The Principal Archivist, Dr B.J. Barber

Open: Mon–Fri: 9.00–12.30; 2.00–5.00

Access: Open to the public, with the customary 30–year restriction on access and, in addition, any restrictions imposed in respect of public records. Appointment advisable for use of the microfilm/fiche readers.

Historical background: The Borough of Doncaster had a series of honorary archivists (including P.G. Bales, later first county archivist of Cambridgeshire) before the appointment of a professional archivist in 1973. In the following year the department took responsibility for the new metropolitan district. In 1979 it became the Diocesan Record Office for the Archdeaconry of Doncaster (Diocese of Sheffield); it is also a recognised place of deposit for public records. The office has received archival holdings transferred from Doncaster Central Library.

Acquisitions policy: To locate, collect and preserve records of all kinds relating to the Doncaster Metropolitan District and make them available to the public in accordance with a policy notified to the Historical Manuscripts Commission.

Archives of organisation: Records of superseded rural and urban district councils; and the borough of Doncaster, 1194–; Quarter Sessions and manorial records.

Major collections: Family and estate archives include Cooke-Yarborough of Campsmount (microfilm); Copley of Sprotbrough; Davies Cooke of Owston, 15th century–; and Warde Aldam of Frickley, notably papers of William Aldam, MP, 1840–90.
Records of the manor of Conisbrough, 1265–1935.
Records of 81 parishes in the Archdeanconry of Doncaster.

Records of Bridon plc (formerly British Ropes), 1751–1974.
Records of Great Northern Railway Locomotive Friendly Society, 1867–1981.

Non-manuscript material: Building control plans for the superseded county borough and rural and urban district councils, 1860–1974.

Finding aids: Lists of holdings of this department and other South Yorkshire archive departments. Lists sent to the NRA. Place and subject card indexes. Names card index to a large proportion of the parish records and some other classes of records.

Facilities: Photocopying. Microfilm/fiche readers.

Conservation: Undertaken by the Conservation Department of Sheffield Archives (entry 1006) under the South Yorkshire Joint Agreement on Archives.

Publications: *Guide to the Archives Department* (2/1981).

248 Dorchester Reference Library
Local Studies Collection

Address: Colliton Park, Dorchester, Dorset DT1 1XJ

Telephone: (01305) 224442/224448/224501

Fax: (01305) 266120

Enquiries: The Reference Librarian, Mr N.G. Lawrence

Open: Mon: 10.00–7.00 Tues, Wed, Fri: 9.30–7.00 Thurs: 9.30–5.00 Sat: 9.00–1.00

Access: Generally open to the public.

Historical background: Much material was acquired in the 1960s on the building of the new library. The Thomas Hardy Society Library is housed here.

Acquisitions policy: Any material relating to Dorset and the existing collections, in particular to Thomas Hardy (1840–1928).

Major collections: Lock Collection (deposited by Henry Lock of the solicitors who dealt with the Hardy family): includes correspondence of the Hardy and Hand families; letters from literary figures, 1868–1940; press cuttings; photographs; play programmes.
Ralph Wightman Collection: scripts with MS

annotations of BBC Radio programme 'Country Magazine', 1942–53.

Non-manuscript material: Maps; illustrations; audio and video cassettes; records; films.
PhD theses relating to the collection (microtext).
Microfilms of census returns and of local newspapers, 1737–.
Printed material and cuttings relating to Rev. William Barnes and T.E. Lawrence.
Typescripts, taken mainly from MSS, connected with the Powys family, primarily T.F. Powys (1875–1953), but also John Cowper Powys (1872–1963).

Facilities: Photocopying. Microfilm/fiche reader/printer.

Conservation: Contracted out.

Publications: C.P.C. Pettit: *A Catalogue of the Works of Thomas Hardy in Dorchester Reference Library* (1984).
J.C. Ward: *A Catalogue of Works by and about William Barnes (1801–1886) in Dorchester Reference Library* (1986).
L.A. Mudway: *A Catalogue of Work by and about T.E. Lawrence ('Lawrence of Arabia') (1888–1935) in Dorchester Reference Library* (1989).

249 Dorset County Museum

Parent organisation: Dorset Natural History and Archaeological Society

Address: High West Street, Dorchester, Dorset DT1 1XA

Telephone: (01305) 262735

Enquiries: Mr Richard de Peyer

Open: Mon–Sat: 10.00–5.00 Sun (July and Aug): 10.00–5.00

Access: Generally open to the public, by appointment. Daily admission fee for research.

Historical background: The Dorset County Museum was founded in 1846 as a private institution, which it still is. The Dorset Natural History and Antiquarian Field Club was founded in 1875. The two bodies joined in 1928 as the Dorset Natural History and Archaeological Society.

Acquisitions policy: The archive collections centre on the geology, archaeology, natural history, local history, literature and fine arts of the county of Dorset.

Archives of organisation: Archives of the museum and predecessor bodies, 1846–.

Major collections: Thomas Hardy (1840–1928) Memorial Collection: MSS, notebooks, diaries, letters, books from Hardy's library, watercolours, photographs and personalia.
Rev. William Barnes (1801–86), poet and grammarian: a large collection of MSS, diaries, letters, scrapbooks, notebooks and personalia.
Sylvia Townsend Warner (1893–1978) and Valentine Ackland: a large collection of MSS, diaries, notebooks, letters, personal items and books.
Natural History MS collections of notebooks, diaries, etc.
Archaeological archives relating to all principal Dorset excavations.
John Cowper, Llewellyn and Theodore Powys letters, short story, novel, and poetry MSS.

Non-manuscript material: Printed material relating to each of the authors noted above.
Photographic archive (46,000 images). Archive of ephemera relating to Dorset places, people and subjects.

Finding aids: Card indexes

Facilities: Photocopying. Photography.

Conservation: Contracted out to Dorset Record Office (entry 250) or Area Museums Council.

Publications: *Proceedings* of the society [annual].
Archaeological Society [monograph series].
County Record Society series.

250 Dorset County Record Office

Parent organisation: Dorset County Council

Address: 9 Bridport Road, Dorchester, Dorset DT1 1RP

Telephone: (01305) 250550

Fax: (01305) 224839 (County Council Offices)

Enquiries: The County Archivist, Mr H. Jaques

Open: Mon–Fri: 9.00–5.00 Sat: 9.30–12.30

Access: Generally open to the public; an appointment is advised to be assured of a place, particularly in the microfilm search room.

Usual closure periods on archives; persons using documents for legal purposes must have the owner's permission.

Historical background: Dorset Record Office was founded in 1955 and in 1957 it received the collections of the Dorset Natural History and Archaeological Society from the Dorset County Museum. The office serves as the Diocesan Record Office for parish records within the diocese of Salisbury (Archdeaconries of Dorset and Sherborne) in the County of Dorset, and is recognised as a place of deposit for public records. In 1974 Bournemouth and Christchurch came into Dorset from Hampshire.

Acquisitions policy: All archives relating to the county of Dorset concerning all aspects of the history and life of the county.

Archives of organisation: Usual local authority holdings, including: Dorset County Council minutes, 1889–; older departmental records and modern legal documents (the latter are not available for research).

Major collections: deposited local collections, including the following which have a wider significance:
State papers of Sir John Trenchard, Chief Secretary of State, 1693–5.
Accounts etc of Sir Stephen Fox and others as Paymasters of the Forces and in other public offices, 1638–1712.
War Office letter-books of Sir W. Yonge, 1741–5, and Henry Fox, Lord Holland, 1746–55; Army Agent's accounts, 1755–64; court of enquiry relating to Gibraltar, 1749–50.
Correspondence and papers of William Bankes, 1803–55.

Non-manuscript material: Photographic, film and sound archive.
Plans and drawings of Ernest Wamsley-Lewis of Weymouth (1889–1978), architect, 1928–71.

Finding aids: Catalogues. Lists. General indexes. Most catalogues sent to NRA.

Facilities: Photocopying. Photography by arrangement. Microfilm/fiche readers/printer. Record-searching service.

Conservation: In-house service and outside work undertaken.

Publications: A.C. Cox: *Index to the Dorset County Records* (1938).

M.E. Holmes: 'The Dorset Record Office', *Archives*, vii (1966), 207.

H. Jaques (ed.): *Guide to the Location of the Parish Registers of Dorset* (1985).

——: *The Archives of Dorset: a Catalogue of an Exhibition to Mark the First 30 Years of the Dorset Record Office.*

Guide to the Transcripts held in the County Record Office (1994).

List of diaries and memoirs in the Dorset Record Office.

Dorset Motor Taxation Records: a Short Guide (1994).

A Guide to the Non-Conformist Registers of Dorset.

251 General Registry, Isle of Man

Parent organisation: Isle of Man Government

Address: The Registries, Deemsters Walk, Bucks Road, Douglas, Isle of Man IM1 3AR

Telephone: (01624) 685233 (Companies Registry) 685250 (Deeds Registry) 685242 (Office of the High Court)

Fax: (01624) 685236

Enquiries: The Chief Registrar, Mr P. Curtis

Open: Mon–Fri: 9.00–1.00; 2.15–4.30

Access: Generally open to the public; a search fee is charged.

Historical background: By the General Registry Act 1965 the General Registry was constituted to carry out the functions of the Rolls Office, the Registry of Deeds and the Registrar General's Department, and the statutory posts of Chief Clerk Rolls Office, the Registrar of Deeds and Registrar General were amalgamated into the one post of Chief Registrar. The General Registry is the Office of the High Court and incorporates the Companies Registry, the Probate Registry, the Business Names Registry and the Industrial and Building Societies Registry. Its functions include the issue of summonses and processes for all divisions of the High Court; the making of Grants of Probate, Administration and other Grants of Representation; and the registration of all deeds and documents leading to title to real estate in the island.

Archives of organisation: Wills, 1911–. Statutory records of registered births, 1878–.

Church of England baptisms, 1611–1878. Marriage records: Church of England, 1629–1849; Church of England and dissenters, 1849–83; statutory records, 1884–. Statutory records of death, 1878–. Church of England burial records, 1610–1878. Records of legal adoptions registered in the Isle of Man, 1928–. Deeds of property, 1911–. Company registration records, 1865–. High Court Records, original Acts and Resolutions of Tynwald; Grants of Representation to the estates of descendants; original plans and valuations of Manx estates; many other documents relating to the history and development of the Isle of Man.

Facilities: Photocopying. Microfilming. Microfilm reader.

252 Isle of Man Public Record Office

Parent organisation: Isle of Man Government

Address: Unit 3, Spring Valley Industrial Estate, Braddan, Douglas, Isle of Man IM2 2QR

Telephone: (01624) 613383

Fax: (01624) 613384

Enquiries: The Public Records Officer, Miss M.J. Critchlow

This service, for Manx government records, is in the process of being established. It will hold the Isle of Man public administration departmental records, including health service records. Many of the older records are presently held in the Manx Museum Library (entry **253**), which should be consulted in the first instance for pre-20th–century records.

253 Manx Museum Library

Parent organisation: Manx National Heritage

Address: Manx Museum and National Trust, Kingswood Grove, Douglas, Isle of Man IM1 3LY

Telephone: (01624) 675522

Fax: (01624) 661899

Enquiries: The Librarian-Archivist, Mr R.M.C. Sims

Open: Mon–Sat: 10.00–5.00 Closed for the last week of January.

Access: Generally open to the public. No appointment is necessary, but notification of an intended visit is appreciated.

Historical background: The Manx Museum Trustees have pursued a policy of collecting Manx books and MS material since their institution in the 1880s. The library, open to the public since 1922, holds certain classes of Manx public records by Act of Tynwald as well as literary papers and the records of Manx families, societies and businesses.

Acquisitions policy: Public and private records relating to the Isle of Man.

Major collections: Isle of Man Government: court records; registered deeds, 1600–1910. Wills: ecclesiastical and civil, 1629–1910. Papers of the Derby family, 17th–18th centuries.
Papers of the Atholl family, 18th–19th centuries.

Non-manuscript material: Printed ephemera and a large collection of Manx books, pamphlets and newspapers.
Microfilms of census returns, 1841–91, parish registers to 1883 and other genealogical sources. Microfilm of majority of Manx newspaper collection, 1793–.

Finding aids: Various lists and indexes. New lists will be sent to NRA.

Facilities: Photocopying. Photography. Microfilm/fiche readers.

Conservation: The library has its own archives conservator and workshop.

Publications: Early Maps of the Isle of Man (1974).
100 Years of Heritage: the Work of the Manx Museum and National Trust (1986) [describes history and scope of library].

254 Down County Museum

Address: The Mall, Downpatrick, Co. Down BT30 6AH

Telephone: (01396) 615218

Enquiries: The Keeper of Collections

Open: Tues–Fri: 11.00–5.00 Sat: 2.00–5.00 Additional opening July–mid Sept: Mon: 11.00–5.00 Sun: 2.00–5.00

Access: Generally open to the public.

The museum maintains collections illustrative of the history of County Down from the earliest times, with documentation relating to the collections, including minute books, certificates, maps and plans. There is also a photograph collection. Photocopying and photography are available.

255 Dudley Archives and Local History Service

Parent organisation: Dudley Metropolitan Borough Council

Address: Mount Pleasant Street, Coseley, Dudley, West Midlands WV14 9JR

Telephone/Fax: (01902) 880011

Enquiries: The Archivist, Mrs K.H. Atkins

Open: Tues, Wed, Fri: 9.00–5.00 Thurs: 9.00–7.00 Sat (1st and 3rd of each month): 9.30–12.30, by appointment. Limited service between 1.00–2.00

Access: Generally open to the public.

Historical background: Archives have been collected since 1947 and the first qualified archivist was appointed in 1972. The service also acts as the Diocesan Record Office for Worcester (Deaneries of Dudley, Himley and Stourbridge parish records). It is recognised as a place of deposit for public records.

Acquisitions policy: Records relating to the area of the present Metropolitan Borough.

Archives of organisation: Usual local authority record holdings.

Major collections: Deposited local collections, of which the following is of wider significance: archive of the Earls of Dudley, 12th–20th centuries.

Non-manuscript material: The Local History Library includes newspapers, cuttings, and local photographs (c14,000).
Local history collections can also be found at the following area libraries: Brierley Hill, Halesowen and Stourbridge.

Finding aids: Lists and handlists. Some lists sent to NRA.

Facilities: Photocopying. Photography. Microfilm/fiche readers/printer.

Publications: Handlist of Parish Registers. Handlist of Non-Conformist Registers.

Checklist of Sources for Genealogical Enquirers.
List of Principal Accessions of Records.

256 Dumbarton District Libraries

Parent organisation: Dumbarton District Council

Address: Dumbarton Library, Strathleven Place, Dumbarton, Strathclyde G82 1BD

Telephone: (01389) 33273/63129

Fax: (01389) 33018

Enquiries: The Local Studies Librarians, Mr A.F. Jones and Mr G.M. Hopner

Open: Mon, Tues, Thurs: 10.00–8.00 Wed, Fri, Sat: 10.00–5.00

Access: Generally open to the public; pre-booking advisable for genealogical research.

Historical background: After the reorganisation of local government in 1975 Dumbarton Library became a recognised repository for archives, and it has acquired the records of the various local authorities which were in existence up to that time. Since 1981 the library has collected any records of societies, institutes, individuals and business organisations which were present in the area.

Acquisitions policy: To collect records relating to the area covered by the district libraries.

Archives of organisation: Dumbarton District Council records, 1974–.

Major collections: Dumbarton Burgh records, 1599–1975.
Collection of charters, documents and letters pertaining to the town of Dumbarton, 15th century-.
Helensburgh Burgh records, 1807–1975.
Records of the Dennystown Forge Company, 1854–1979.
Census returns for Dumbartonshire and West Stirlingshire, 19th century.
Dumbartonshire, West Stirlingshire and some Argyll parish registers.

Non-manuscript material: Maps and plans of the district (c1000).
Drawings, paintings and prints (258).
Photographic prints (c14,300), negatives (c5200) and slides (c4900).
Local newspapers, 1851–.

Finding aids: Various lists and indexes.

Facilities: Photocopying. Photography. Microfilm/fiche readers/printers.

Conservation: Library bindery; other work contracted out.

257 Dumfries and Galloway Health Board Archives

Parent organisation: Dumfries and Galloway Health Board

Address: Crichton Royal Hospital, Easterbrook Hall, Bankend Road, Dumfries DG1 4TG

Telephone: (01387) 55301 ext. 2360

Fax: (01387) 41141 (not direct)

Enquiries: The Archivist, Mrs Morag Williams

Open: Tues–Fri: 9.00–5.00

Access: Bona fide researchers, by appointment only. Searches undertaken by the archivist for a charge.

Historical background: The parent body, the Dumfries and Galloway Health Board, has been fully operational since 1974. Archive work has been pursued since 1983.

Acquisitions policy: All material relating to health care in south-west Scotland in Wigtownshire, Kirkcudbrightshire, Dumfriesshire, now known as Dumfries and Galloway Region.

Archives of organisation: Dumfries and Galloway Royal Infirmary: minutes books and annual reports, 1777–; cash books, ledgers, letter-books and staff registers.
Crichton Royal Hospital: trust documents, 1820s-, minute books, annual reports, case notes, registers of admission, obligants books, staff registers, 1839–; house magazine, 1844–; registers of restraint and seclusion, accident, death, sheriff's warrants, 1858–.
Cottage hospital material relating to Stranraer (Garrick), Kirkcudbright, Castle Douglas, Moffat, Langholm (Thomas Hope), including minutes, annual reports (incomplete), some letter-books, patients' registers, 1892–.
Infectious diseases hospitals, including patients' registers for Newton Stewart, Castle Douglas and Thornhill, 1898–.
Cresswell Maternity Hospital material, 1939–.
Area Health Board minutes, 1973.

Non-manuscript material: Architectural plans, art therapy material, 1839–; extensive collection of (psychiatric) artefacts for Crichton Royal; photographs for all hospitals; limited oral archive.

Facilities: Photocopying. Photography.

Publications: M. Williams and A. C. Morrell: *The History of Kirkcudbright Hospital* (1984).
M. Williams: *The History of Thomas Hope Hospital* (1989).
Geals, Gordon, Paterson, Train and Wiliams, *Cresswell Maternity Hospital, 1939–1989* (1989).
M. Williams: *History of Crichton Royal Hospital 1839–1989.*
——:*The History of Garrick Hospital, 1892–1992* (1992).

258 Dumfries and Galloway Regional Council Library Service Archives

Address: Ewart Library, Catherine Street, Dumfries DG1 1JB

Telephone: (01387) 53820/52070

Fax: (01387) 60294

Enquiries: The Reference and Local Studies Librarian, Ruth Airley

Open: Mon–Wed, Fri: 10.00–7.30 Thurs, Sat: 10.00–5.00

Access: Generally open to the public; prior notice appreciated.

Historical background: The Archives Department was established in 1975 following local government reorganisation; before that local authorities held their own records and there was no formal collecting policy. The records for Wigtownshire (partial) and the Stewartry of Kirkcudbright were joined with those of Dumfriesshire in 1975.

Acquisitions policy: Active collecting policy for all material pertaining to Dumfries and Galloway.

Archives of organisation: Records of Dumfriesshire, 1667–, Stewartry of Kirkcudbright, 1728–, and Wigtownshire, 1736–; includes council and committee minutes, highway authorities records, valuation rolls, education, parish (not Wigtownshire) and militia records.

Major collections: Deposited collections, mostly of family papers, including Grierson of Lag, 1518–1761, and Culvennan charters and MSS (Gordon family), 15th–19th centuries.
Other material includes marriage registers for Gretna Hall, 1829–55, and Sark Toll Bar, 1832–45; and minutes of the Seven Incorporated Trades of Dumfries, 1612–1890.

Non-manuscript material: Local photographic collection (8500 images); *Galloway News* photographic archive, 1947–80 (*c*100,000 negatives). Large collection of OS maps, 1846–; also microfiche collection of 'Historical Maps', including some estate plans and county maps. Memorial inscriptions for Dumfries and Galloway (excluding part of Wigtownshire) (*c*200 vols).
Microfiche of local newspapers, 1977–.
Large local collection of printed books and pamphlets.

Finding aids: Lists. Computer and card catalogues. Indexes to local newspapers.

Facilities: Photocopying. Photography. Microfilm/fiche readers/printers.

259 Dumfries Archives Centre

Parent organisation: Dumfries Museums Service

Address: 33 Burns Street, Dumfries DG1 2PS

Telephone: (01387) 69254

Enquiries: The Archivist, Miss M.M. Stewart

Open: Tues, Wed, Fri: 11.00–1.00; 2.00–5.00 Thurs: 6.00–9.00

Access: Generally open to the public; prior appointment requested. Application to use vehicle licensing records must be supported by the signatures of two referees. Certain records are not available as being too recent or fragile.

Historical background: The records have been the responsibility of the museums service for many years, but have not had one permanent home or any staff to sort and list them or make them readily available to researchers until the establishment of the archive centre in 1987. Hitherto the records were dispersed among numerous stores, and the process of collecting, identifying, repairing and making them accessible is still going on.

Acquisitions policy: Any archival material bearing on the history of Nithsdale or the immediately surrounding areas.

Archives of organisation: Records of Dumfries Burgh and Court, 1506–; Dumfries Treasurer and Chamberlain, 1640–; rentals, rating, taxation and voting, 1674–; Parochial Board and Police Commissioners, 19th century.

Major collections: Dumfries Kirk Session records; Sanquhar Burgh records.
Deposited records of local firms, clubs, businesses, lawyers and architects.
Family papers include Stewart of Shambellie, 1640s-1950s; McCartney of Halketleaths, 1560s-1830s, and Clerk Maxwell of Middlebie, 1640s-1850s.

Non-manuscript material: Microfilm of much local-interest material that is held elsewhere, including census returns and newspapers.
Inscriptions of all the gravestones in Dumfries and Galloway (except Wigtownshire).
Reference library, mainly of topographical and genealogical material.
Sasine Abridgements and Indexes for Dumfriesshire, Kirkcudbrightshire and Wigtownshire.

Finding aids: A shelf list (with index) is available for all the material located so far.
Source lists, pamphlets, various guides and indexes, including council minutes and some Kirk Session minutes and some 1851 census returns.

Facilities: Photocopying. Microfilm/fiche reader. Typewriters or tape recorders may only be used if no other researchers are present. Search room space is limited.

Publications: Ancestor Hunting in Dumfries Archive Centre.
Publications list available.

260 Dumfries Museum

Parent organisation: Nithsdale District Council

Address: The Observatory, Dumfries
DG2 7SW

Telephone: (01387) 53374

Fax: (01387) 65081

Enquiries: The Museums Officer, Siobhan Ratchford

Open: Mon–Sat: 10.00–1.00; 2.00–5.00 Sun:

2.00–5.00 Oct-March: Closed Sun and Mon

Access: Generally open to the public; an appointment is essential.

Historical background: The museum was established by Dumfries Astronomical Society and began collecting in the 1860s, but the Dumfries Archives Centre (entry **259**), opened in 1987, is now the repository for all archival material.

Acquisitions policy: Archival material is now not collected.

Archives of organisation: Dumfries Astronomical Society minute books, 19th century.

Major collections: William Grierson (1773–1852), diaries, 1794–1809.
School scrapbook, produced partly by J.M. Barrie.
Documents relating to witchcraft in Dumfries.

Non-manuscript material: Local photographs, estate maps and plans, OS maps.
Small local history library.

Finding aids: Subject catalogues.

Facilities: Photocopying. Photography. Microfiche reader.

Conservation: Paper conservation is contracted out.

261 Dunblane Cathedral Museum

Parent organisation: The Trustees of the Dunblane Cathedral Museum

Address: The Square, Dunblane, Central FK15 1DD

Telephone: (01786) 824254

Enquiries: The Hon. Curator, Mr J. G. Lindsay, 21 Argile Way, Dunblane, Central FK15 9DX

Open: Late May–early Oct: Mon–Fri: 10.30–12.30; 2.30–4.30

Access: Access by arrangement; a donation is requested.

There is a collection of archives, MSS, books and artefacts concerned with the cathedral. The archives include plans for the restoration of the cathedral, 1889–93, and photographs. Cataloguing is in progress. A *Journal of the Friends of Dunblane Cathedral* is produced annually.

262 The Leighton Library, Dunblane

Enquiries: The Hon. Custodian, Bill Moore, 'Cranford', Smithy Loan, Dunblane, Central FK15 0QH

Telephone: (01786) 822850

Open: May–Oct: Mon–Fri: 10.30–12.30; 2.30–4.30
At other times by arrangement with the Hon. Custodian.
Items required for prolonged study may be consulted at Stirling University (entry **1032**).

Access: Generally open to all, preferably with advanced notice.

Historical background: The library, which is the oldest private library in Scotland, was built between 1684 and 1687 to hold the books of Robert Leighton, Bishop of Dunblane, 1660–71, and Archbishop of Glasgow, 1671–4. It operated as a subscription library from the early 1700s–1840. The contents lay undisturbed until *c*1980, when money was raised for restoration of the building and treatment of the books. The library opened to the general public in 1990. It is run by the Leighton Library Trustees, members of whom are descendants of the original trustees. Papers of the trustees are retained by Tho. & J.W. Batty, Solicitors, 61 High Street, Dunblane, Central FK15 0EH.

Archives of organisation: Minutes and papers relating to the library.

Major collections: Various MSS relating to Scottish history, especially religious history; also literary MSS.
Some MSS may also be seen at Dunblane Cathedral Museum (entry **261**).

Non-manuscript material: Books, 1500–1840 (*c*4500).

Facilities: None at the Leighton Library. Photocopying and photography by arrangement. Microfilm/fiche readers at Stirling University Library.

Publications: G.W. Willis: *The Leighton Library, Dunblane: Catalogue of Manuscripts* (Stirling, 1981).
——: 'The Leighton Library, Dunblane: its History and Contents', *The Bibliothek*, x/6 (1981), 139–57.

263 Dundee Art Galleries & Museums
McManus Galleries

Parent organisation: City of Dundee District Council

Address: Albert Square, Dundee, Tayside DD1 1DA

Telephone: (01382) 432020

Fax: (01382) 432052

Enquiries: The Keeper of Human History, Janice Murray

Open: Mon: 11.00–5.00 Tues–Sat: 10.00–5.00

Access: Bona fide researchers, by appointment.

Historical background: Formerly the Albert Institute, the McManus Galleries opened as a free library in 1867. The Art Galleries and Museum were formed in 1873. Some collections formerly held by Broughty Castle Museum have been transferred.

Acquisitions policy: Ephemera only; other archival collections will be directed to the appropriate archive centre, either Dundee District Libraries (entry **265**) or Dundee District Archive and Record Centre (entry **264**).

Archives of organisation: Acquisition registers and some supporting documentation, 1911–. Annual museum reports, 1958–73 (incomplete).

Major collections: Whaling journals, log-books, certificates, seamen's papers, note-books etc, early 19th–20th centuries.
Correspondence and photographs of Mary Slessor, Church of Scotland missionary in West Africa, *c*1877–1913.
Chalmers Publishing House Collection: including ink recipes and correspondence between James Chalmers (1782–1853) and Rowland Hill (1795–1879) concerning the postal service, early 19th–mid-20th century.

Non-manuscript material: Textile industry: ephemera, machine plans, specifications and technical films, late 19th–20th centuries.
Rail transport: ephemera and plans, especially relating to North British line and the Tay rail bridges, mainly late 19th century.
Shipbuilding: ephemera and plans, particularly of the Caledon and Gourlay shipping yards, 19th–20th centuries.

Friendly societies and trade unions: collection of certificates and rule books etc, late 19th–20th centuries.
Supporting photographic archives, particularly strong for textiles; local topography; whaling; education (including the Tay training ship *Mars*); retail trades.

Finding aids: Card index. Lists sent to NRA.

Facilities: Photocopying. Photography, by arrangement only.

264 Dundee District Archive and Record Centre

Address: 21 City Square (callers use 1 Shore Terrace), Dundee, Tayside DD1 3BY

Telephone: (01382) 434494/434825

Fax: (01382) 434666

Enquiries: The Archivist, Mr Iain Flett

Open: Mon–Fri: 9.15–1.00; 2.00–4.45

Access: Generally open to the public, by appointment.

Historical background: Formerly Dundee City Record Office, the archive was renamed a district office following reorganisation in 1975, but acts on an agency basis for Tayside Regional Council.

Archives of organisation: Usual local authority record holdings; retransmitted records from the Scottish Record Office include Dundee Presbytery, Custom and Excise and Fishery series.

Major collections: Deposited collections, including the following which have a wider significance:
Dundee Chamber of Commerce (formerly Forfarshire Chamber of Commerce, and Baltic Coffee House and Chamber of Commerce) records, 1819–1960.
Dundee Harbour Trustees and various shipping company records, 19th–20th centuries.
Dundee Jute and Flax Union records, 1906–71 (including references to jute industry in India).
Loyal Order of Friendly Shepherds Friendly Society records, 1871–1989.
First Scottish American Trust Co. Ltd, records and those of subsequent investment companies, 1873–1970.
Geekie family, Keillor Co. Angus: correspondence etc, 1646–1850 (includes letters from

Alexander Geekie, surgeon in London, c1678–1724).
Papers of David Greig, FRCSEd (*fl* 1850s): copies of his letters written while serving as assistant surgeon in the Crimea.
Papers of Dr Thomas Dick, LLD, FRAS (1774–1857), 1814–1908.
Account books covering voyages of the brigantines *Flora* and *Tagus*, Dundee, 18th century.
Jas. Scott & Sons, merchants, spinners and jute manufacturers, records (including India and South America), 1861–1969.
Williamson Memorial Unitarian Church records, 1832–1979.
Wedderburn of Pearsie family papers (including service in East India Company), 1483–1918.
Earl of Northesk papers, 13th–20th centuries.

Facilities: Photocopying.

Publications: W. Hay (ed.): *Charters, Writs and Public Documents of the Royal Burgh of Dundee, 1292–1880* (Dundee, 1880).
Archives Argus [newsletter of the Friends of Dundee City Archives].

265 Dundee District Libraries

Address: Central Library, The Wellgate, Dundee, Tayside DD1 1DB

Telephone: (01382) 434377

Fax: (01382) 434643

Enquiries: The Chief Librarian, Mr J.B. Ramage

Open: Mon, Tues, Thurs, Fri: 9.30–9.00 Wed: 10.00–9.00 Sat: 9.30–5.00
Access to some materials may be severely restricted during major refurbishment in 1995.

Access: Generally open to the public. Readers requiring items from special collections are advised to make prior arrangement.

Historical background: The library was established in 1869 after the adoption of the Public Libraries Act 1867, since when the library service in Dundee has been developed steadily. Various special collections, including archival material, have been donated over the years.

Acquisitions policy: The special and archival collections are strengthened by donations or, in special cases, by purchase.

Major collections: The Compt Book of David Wedderburn, 1587–1630.
Letters and other MS material of local persons,

including Edwin Scrymgeour (1866–1947), Prohibitionist and MP; William McGonagall (*d* 1902); Mary Slessor, 1905–14.

Dundee Trades Council Collection, MS and printed material, to *c*1960.

Miscellaneous MS material relating to local authors and organisations.

Some personal whaling log-books.

Non-manuscript material: Dundee Photographic Surveys, 1915 and 1992.

Wilson Collection of photographs, *c*1888–*c*1910.

Local History Library (Dundee and District) includes the Lamb Collection of ephemeral material; books; pamphlets; posters; newspapers; prints; maps; plans.

Wighton Collection of early national music.

Finding aids: Library catalogues and indexes.

Facilities: Photocopying. Photography. Microfilm/fiche readers/printer.

Publications: J. MacLauchlan: *A Brief Guide to the old Dundee Historical Collection* (Dundee, 1901).

266 University of Dundee Library
Archive Department

Address: Dundee, Tayside DD1 4HN

Telephone: (01382) 23181 ext. 4095, 344095 (direct line)

Fax: (01382) 29190

Enquiries: The Archivist, Mrs Joan Auld

Open: Mon–Wed, Fri: 9.30–12.30; 1.30–4.30 Thurs: 9.30–1.30

Access: Generally open to the public. Appointments advisable

Historical background: The university has its origins in University College, Dundee, founded in 1881. The college became part of St Andrews University in 1897, was renamed Queens College, after incorporating Dundee School of Economics, in 1954, and was granted its charter as a university in 1967. In 1994 Duncan of Jordanstone College of Art, formerly an independent institution, became a faculty of the university. The Archive Department is also responsible for the Kinnear Local Collection

(printed books and pamphlets), which complements the MSS holdings.

Acquisitions policy: To strengthen the library's MSS collection, particularly as it relates to the textile industry, local connections with India, and medical history. To accumulate records of the university and its predecessors, University and Queens College, and of prominent staff and students.

Archives of organisation: University archives: records of the university, 1967–, of its predecessors, University College and Queens College, *c*1875–1966, including Dundee School of Economics, and of the Dundee Medical School (University of St Andrews).

Major collections: Records of the textile industry and its links with India and Pakistan, particularly relating to jute and linen and including engineering, 1795–*c*1985.

Shiell and Small, solicitors, Dundee: records of the firm and of principal clients, particularly railway companies and prominent Dundee businessmen, 1826–*c*1935.

Records of local medical associations, 1864–1927, and Dundee Medical Library, 1880–1903; papers relating to the history of medicine in Angus, 16th century–1936; papers of R.C. Alexander (1884–1968), surgeon, *c*1899–1950, including RAMC field service notebooks, 1917–18; R.P. Cook (1906–89), biochemist, papers, including correspondence with Alexander Fleming, Ernst Chain and Howard Florey.

Glassite church sermons and correspondence, 1728–1885; papers relating to the College and Collegiate Church of the Holy Spirit, Isle of Cumbrae, *c*1850–1929.

MSS and correspondence of Thomas Campbell (1777–1844), poet, 1797–1854; Joseph Lee (1876–1949), journalist and poet, papers, 1898–1948, including illustrated journals while prisoner of war in Germany, 1916–18, and correspondence with Robert Bridges (1844–1930), poet, 1914.

Correspondence of Alexander Scott (1853–1947), chemist, 1851–1935, including letters to William J. Russell; papers of Alexander Mackenzie (1869–1951), chemist, *c*1896–1936; Sir Robert Robertson (1869–1948), chemist, 1894–1949; A.D. Walsh (1916–71), chemist, *c*1930–1970; James Ballantyne Hannay (1855–1931), chemist and innovator, papers, including *re* diamond research, 1842–1987, and Prince of Wales Theatre, Glasgow, 1871–87; John Berry (*b* 1907), biologist and ornithologist, papers relating to the North of Scotland Hydro-Electric Board, and to nature conservancy, 1932–89, including correspondence with Sir Peter Scott (1909–89).

Records of Dundee Stock Exchange Association, 1876–1964; papers relating to east of Scotland shipping, including whaling, 1767–1980; papers of Wilson family of Alva, mainly woollen manufacturers, 1771–1976, including letters from America, 1815–29, letters and photographs relating to service in the French and British Red Cross, 1916–18 and letters *re Anschluss* and the German occupation, 1938–45; James Dalyell (1798–1870), naval officer and coastguard, papers, *c*1817–73, including service in West Indies, *c*1817–27, and the Pacific, 1841–5, and journals of walking tours in France, 1828–34; Michael Peto (1908–70), photographer, correspondence, including letters from A.S. Neil, 1943–5; Catherine Kinnear (1912–88), bibliophile and antiquary, papers, 1845–1955; Peter Carmichael of Arthurstone, engineer, biographical writings and papers, 1837–90.

Tayside Health Board: records of Dundee hospitals and boards of management, including the Dental Hospital, 1820–1974.

Brechin Diocesan Library MSS: correspondence of Bishop Alexander Penrose Forbes, 1844–74; transcripts of episcopal registers, *c*1681–1890; records of the Diocese of Brechin and some congregations, *c*1744–1970; William Drummond of Hawthornden (1585–1649), diary and commonplace book; Psalter, Book of Hours, sermons, 15th century.

Non-manuscript material: Maps and plans, particularly Tayside and Fife and including railway plans, 1746–*c*1970 (*c*3500); technical drawings, particularly textile machinery, *c*1850–1960.

Ruggles Bequest: contemporary drawings of American Civil War, 1863–4; David Waterson (*c*1870–1954), artist, watercolour studies; Neil Stewart (*c*1820–*c*1890), medical illustrations; miscellaneous pathological lithographs, *c*1815–*c*1890.

Photographs, particularly the university and its predecessors, including staff and students, *c*1882–, industry in Tayside, jute industry in India, and medical conditions (13,500).

Torrance Collection of photographs of Middle East, *c*1880–1970.

George H. Bell (1905–86), physiologist, collection of photographs of the medical profession and of Scotland, Italy and Africa.

Hugh S. Stannus (1877–1957), specialist in tropical medicine, glass negatives of Central Africa, *c*1905–1918.

Alexander Burn Murdoch (*c*1880–1954), stereoscopic negatives of trans-Canada rail journey, 1912, and stereoscopic glass slides, including Scotland, French and Swiss Alps, 1924–53.

Michael Peto (1909–70) photographs of international figures in politics (especially Hungary) and arts (especially ballet) plus people and social conditions in London, South Wales, Dundee, Europe, India, and Far and Middle East, *c*1946 (*c*120,000).

Finding aids: Summaries of collections in University Library on-line catalogue (access through Telnet, Gopher or World Wide Web); descriptive lists, card indexes, databases of photographs, maps and plans, source lists on various subjects. Lists sent to NRA(S).

Facilities: Photocopying. Photography.

Conservation: The University Library Conservation Unit provides an in-house paper conservation service and also carries out contract work.

267 Andrew Carnegie Birthplace Museum

Address: Moodie Street, Dunfermline, Fife KY12 7PL

Telephone: (01383) 724302

Enquiries: The Custodian, Mr D. Barclay

Open: April–Oct: Mon–Sat: 11.00–5.00 Sun: 2.00–5.00 Nov–March: Mon–Sun 2.00–4.00

Access: Accredited scholars or reseachers, by appointment only. A standard search fee is charged for access to the archives.

Historical background: The main collection of personalia and memorabilia of Andrew Carnegie (1835–1919), manufacturer and philanthropist, was presented by his widow between 1926 and 1928, with occasional subsequent additions. See also Carnegie Dunfermline and Hero Fund Trusts (entry 268).

Acquisitions policy: Items connected with Andrew Carnegie.

Archives of organisation: Annual reports and publications of the Carnegie trusts and institutions.

Major collections: Carnegie Collection includes MSS and typescripts of his publications.

Non-manuscript material: Extensive collection of photographs of Andrew Carnegie, Carnegie Steel Company, Carnegie's family, friends and others, taken at ceremonies throughout the UK. Newspaper cuttings *re* Carnegie's death and centenary (13 vols).
Full set of first editions.

Finding aids: Catalogue; some indexes available.

Facilities: Photocopying and photography can be arranged.

Conservation: Contracted out.

Publications: Collection is fully catalogued and available in bound form or on computer disk.

268 Carnegie Dunfermline and Hero Fund Trusts

Address: Abbey Park House, Abbey Park Place, Dunfermline, Fife KY12 7PB

Telephone: (01383) 723638

Enquiries: The Secretary and Treasurer, Mr W.C. Runciman

Open: Mon–Fri: 9.00–5.00

Access: Access is normally given to accredited scholars or researchers; appointments should generally be made.

Historical background: The Carnegie Dunfermline Trust was established in 1903 to improve social, recreational and cultural amenities of the native town of Andrew Carnegie (1835–1919). The Carnegie Hero Fund Trust was established in 1908 to provide financial assistance if necessary to people who have been injured or sustained financial loss, or to the families of people who have been killed in heroic endeavour to save human life in peaceful pursuits throughout the British Isles. See also Andrew Carnegie's Birthplace Museum (entry **267**).

Acquisitions policy: Consolidation of the trusts' archives.

Archives of organisation: Records of the Carnegie Dunfermline Trust and the Carnegie Hero Fund Trust, including reports, minutes, correspondence files, title deeds, newspaper cuttings, photographs, tape and video recordings and plans.

Finding aids: List of archives, 1977.

Facilities: Photocopying.

269 Dunfermline Central Library

Parent organisation: Dunfermline District Council

Address: Abbot Street, Dunfermline, Fife KY12 7NW

Telephone: (01383) 723661

Fax: (01383) 620761

Enquiries: The Chief Librarian and Museums Officer, John Jamieson

Open: Mon, Tues, Thurs, Fri: 10.00–7.00 Wed, Sat: 10.00–5.00

Access: Generally open to the public; no appointment is necessary, but a preliminary letter or telephone call is welcome.

Historical background: The library, the first Carnegie Free Library in the world, was established in 1883 and the local history collection is based on a collection gifted in 1920.

Acquisitions policy: Local records covering the area of the present local authority boundary.

Archives of organisation: Records of Tradesmen and Mechanics Library, 1826–30; Dunfermline Subscription Library, 1789–1828; and Dunfermline Public Library, 1880–.

Major collections: Usual local history collection, including records of Dunfermline Abbey and non-conformist churches, 19th–20th centuries; turnpike records and papers, 1809–79; Dunfermline Co-operative Society minutes and papers, 1861–1967; Dunfermline Naturalists Society records, 1861–1967; Incorporation of Weavers entry and minute books, 1596–1863.
Erskine Beveridge (1851–1920) Collection: notes on local churchyards.

Finding aids: Card catalogues incorporating subject index. NRA(S) 1834.

Facilities: Photocopying. Microfilm/fiche reader.

270 Dunfermline District Council

Address: City Chambers, Dunfermline, Fife KT12 7ND

Telephone: (01383) 722711

Fax: (01383) 620761

Enquiries: The Director of Central Services, Findlay M. Coutts

Open: Mon–Fri: 9.00–4.00

Access: Generally open to the public; an appointment is not necessary but can be advantageous.

Certain records for Dunfermline and Inverkeithing have been transferred to the Scottish Record Office (entry **313**); however, the City Chambers holds records of the Town Clerk's and Burgh Chamberlain's Departments for all constituent burghs, as well as Social Work Department records for Dunfermline, 1850–. An outline list is available.

271 Scottish Horse Regimental Museum

Parent organisation: Scottish Horse Trust

Address: The Cross, Dunkeld, Tayside PH8 0AN

Enquiries: Miss M. McInnes, Villa Park, Woodside, Coupar Angus, Tayside PH13 9NQ

Open: Easter–end of Sept: Mon, Thurs, Fri: 10.00–12.00; 2.00–5.00

Access: Generally open to the public, by arrangement. Research is undertaken and a donation is required.

Historical background: Raised by the Marquis of Tullibardine (the 8th Duke of Atholl) in South Africa in 1900, the regiment served in the South African Campaign and World Wars I and II.

Archives of organisation: Correspondence and telegrams, diaries and courts martial.
Registers of animals and reports on operations, 1899–1902.
Registers of Scottish Horses, 1901–.
Scottish Horse casualties in Gallipoli, 1915–17.

Major collections: Correspondence and papers, 1902–18, including letters from Viscount Haldane, Secretary of State for War, 1905–12. Miscellaneous files and narratives *re* World War II.

272 Durham County Record Office

Address: County Hall, Durham DH1 5UL

Telephone: (0191) 383 3474/388 3253

Enquiries: The County Archivist, Miss J. Gill

Open: Mon, Tues, Thurs: 8.45–4.45 Wed: 8.45–8.30 Fri: 8.45–4.15 Sat: 9.00–12.00

Access: By appointment. Documents required for Wednesday evening and Saturday morning must be ordered by the previous day.

Historical background: The office was established in 1961 to cover the whole county; no archive service had existed previously. The department moved to its new building in 1964. It also acts as the Diocesan Record Office for Durham (parish records), and is recognised as a place of deposit for public records. The Darlington branch office was closed in 1991.

Archives of organisation: Usual local authority record holdings.

Major collections: Deposited local collections, including the following which have a wider significance:
Londonderry records: estate and business papers, including those relating to Seaham Harbour and coal interests in east Durham; family and personal papers.
Strathmore records: estate records and records relating to 'Grand Allies' and the development of the Durham coalfield in the 18th century.
National Coal Board records: pre-nationalisation records.

Facilities: Photocopying. Photography and microfilming by arrangement. Microfilm reader.

Publications: W.A.L. Seaman: *Durham County Record Office* (1969).

273 Durham Dean and Chapter Library

Address: The College, Durham DH1 3EH

Telephone: (0191) 386 2489

Enquiries: The Deputy Librarian, Mr Roger Norris

Open: Mon–Fri: 9.00–1.00; 2.15–5.00
Closed for the whole of August.

Access: Bona fide students; references are required, with means of identification.

Historical background: The library of the Dean and Chapter of Durham descends in direct historic continuity from the library of the Benedictine house (f. 10th century in Durham), which was dissolved in 1540 and then changed into a capitular foundation of a dean and 12 residentiaries.

Acquisitions policy: Archives are not actively acquired.

Major collections: Extensive collection of medieval MSS (see 'Publications' below).
Papers include those of the following: I.T. Ramsey, Bishop of Durham, 1966–72; General Synod, i.e. Liturgical Commission, 1960s-1970s; J.B. Lightfoot, Bishop of Durham, 1879–89; H.H. Henson, Bishop of Durham, 1920–39.
Parochial clergy correspondence, c1895–1910.
Antiquarian collections of the following: Christopher Hunter (1675–1757); Thomas Randall, headmaster, Durham School, 1761–8; George Allan (1736–1800); Robert Surtees (1779–1834); Sir Cuthbert Sharp (1781–1849); James Raine (1791–1858).
Music MSS, early 17th–19th centuries.

Non-manuscript material: Extensive iconographic material, including photographs, negatives and engravings.

Finding aids: Card indexes. Henson: NRA 28047.

Facilities: Photography by arrangement.

Conservation: Contracted out.

Publications: Sir Roger Mynors: *Durham Cathedral Manuscripts* (1939).
N.R. Ker: *Monastic Libraries in Great Britain* (1964; supplement, 1987).

274 St John's College
College Archives

Address: 3 South Bailey, Durham DH1 3RJ

Telephone: (0191) 374 3579

Fax: (0191) 374 3573

Enquiries: The Librarian, Dr B.W. Longenecker

Open: By prior arrangement.

Access: Approved readers, on written application; an appointment is necessary.

St John's College was founded in 1909 as an independent but constituent college of the University of Durham. The college archives have grown, almost accidentally, with the collection of various documents, including MSS and photographs, associated with the college and with members of staff. These include a collection of sermons by Canon Gouldsmith and dissertations of the Bernard Gilpin Society. There is a TS list available.

275 University of Durham

A Library: Archives and Special Collections, Palace Green Section

Address: Palace Green, Durham DH1 3RN

Telephone: (0191) 374 3003

Fax: (0191) 374 7481

Enquiries: The Sub-Librarian (Special Collections), Miss E.M. Rainey

Open: Term: Mon–Fri: 9.00–6.00 Sat: 9.00–12.30 Vacation: Mon–Fri: 9.00–5.00

Access: Generally open to the public. Advance notice is advisable and proof of identity essential.

Historical background: The University Library, founded in 1833, incorporates Bishop Cosin's Library, founded in 1668. Until 1963 it was the only official archive repository in County Durham apart from Gateshead Borough Library. Its department of Archives and Special Collections was founded in 1990 by a merger of its Special Collections with the university's Department of Palaeography and Diplomatic, which had been established in 1948 under a joint scheme of Durham University and the Dean and Chapter of Durham for the care of archives, mainly from the northern counties, and for the promotion of the study of MS material. It is recognised as a place of deposit for public records.

Acquisitions policy: Material relating to the library's existing collections or relevant to the university's research interests and teaching, particularly, so far as MSS and archives are concerned, material connected with the Palatinate, Diocese, Cathedral, County, City and University of Durham (coordinating policy in this area with Durham Cathedral Library and Durham County Record Office); political papers of national and international significance but with a local connection; the Sudan during the Condominium period, 1899–1955; modern literary MSS; hymnology.

Archives of organisation: Some central administrative records of the university, and some records of its colleges and student societies, 19th–20th centuries. Records and correspondence of the University Observatory (astronomical, meteorological and seismological), 1838–*c*1957.

Major collections: Cosin MSS, largely medieval book MSS, and letter-books of Bishop John Cosin (1595–1672), 11th–19th centuries.
Mickleton and Spearman MSS antiquarian collections relating to the north-east, especially Durham Palatinate, 13th–early 18th centuries.
Greenslade Deeds, mainly Co. Durham, 15th–19th centuries.
Clavering family of Greencroft, letters and papers, 15th–19th centuries.
Wharton family of Old Park, papers, letters and diaries, including Grand Tour correspondence, 18th–19th centuries.
Wright MSS: astronomical papers of Thomas Wright (1711–80) of Byers Green, Co. Durham.
Thorp correspondence, 1831–62: letters and papers of Charles Thorp (1783–1862), first warden of the university.
Earl Grey Papers: political, private and estate papers of the Greys of Howick, 18th–20th centuries, including papers of John, Viscount Ponsonby (*c*1770–1855), and Evelyn Baring, 1st Earl of Cromer (1841–1917).
Abbas Hilmi II Papers: official, personal and estate papers of Abbas Hilmi II (1874–1944), Khedive of Egypt, covering the period of the Khedivate, 1892–1914, and extending after his deposition until his death. Also includes letters of Ibrahim Pasha (1789–1848), eldest son of Muhammad Ali Pasha, Viceroy of Egypt, relating to his military campaigns in Syria in the 1830s and 1840s.
Sudan Archive: official, semi-official and private papers of officials, soldiers, businessmen, missionaries, and many others who served or lived in the Sudan, 1899–1956. Also includes some material of the Mahdist period and substantial quantities of papers relating to countries bordering on the Sudan. Includes papers of Sir Reginald Wingate (1861–1953), Sir Rudolf Baron Slatin (1875–1932), Sir Gilbert Clayton (1875–1929), Sir Harold MacMichael (1882–1969), Sir James Robertson, and the papers of the Gordon Memorial College Trust Fund, and more than 200 smaller collections, mainly of former Sudan Political Service officials.
Papers of John James Lawson, Baron Lawson (1881–1965), miners' leader, MP and cabinet minister, and papers of Malcolm John MacDonald (1901–81), cabinet minster, colonial governor and diplomat.
Abott Literary MSS, 18th–20th centuries: including MSS of John Wolcot (Peter Pindar), George Darley, the Rossetti family, letters of G.M. Hopkins to Coventry Patmore, and MSS and correspondence of Edward Thomas.
Personal papers of Professor Claude Colleer Abbott (1889–1971), including papers of Gordon Bottomley, J.R. Ackerley, Llewelyn Powys.
Papers of William Plomer (1903–71), novelist, poet, and librettist for Benjamin Britten, including literary correspondence.
Pratt Green MSS, 18th–20th centuries: hymns, tunes, papers of hymnologists and hymn writers, including John Wilson (1905–92) and H.C.A. Gaunt (1902–83).
Basil Bunting (1900–85), poet: multi-media archive.

Non-manuscript material: Sudan Archive: photographs (over 36,000), maps, portraits, cine films, museum objects, and a large quantity of related printed material.
Plans, photographs and slides of the restoration of Durham Castle, 1920–39.
Edis and Gibby collections of negatives, lantern slides and photographic prints, principally of buildings, places and people in Co. Durham, 19th–20th centuries.
Durham County parliamentary election poll-books and contest literature in pamphlet and broadside form, with some MS material, 1675–1874.
Playbills for City of Durham theatres, 1769–1859.

Maps of Co. Durham and towns and areas within it, 16th–20th centuries.

Coins of the Durham mint, Henry II–Bishop Tunstall (Bishop of Durham, 1530–59).

Finding aids: Various lists, indexes, catalogues and calendars. Lists sent to NRA.

Facilities: Photocopying. Photography. Microfilming. Beta-radiography. Microform readers. Video-spectral comparator and video and audio playback machines.

Conservation: In-house conservation workshop.

Publications: Durham University Library Archives and Special Collections Introductory Guide.
Sudanese Studies at Durham: a Guide to Resources [free].
Summary Guide to the Sudan Archive [updated annually].
Numerous lists of individual collections. A list of publications is available.

B Library: Archives and Special Collections, The College

Address: 5 The College, Durham DH1 3EQ

Telephone: (0191) 374 3610

Fax: (0191) 374 7481

Enquiries: The Archivist

Open: Mon–Fri: 9.00–1.00; 2.00–5.00 Extended to 8.00 on Tuesday in term by prior booking.

Access: Generally open to the public. Advance notice advisable and proof of identity essential.

For historical background and acquisitions policy see Palace Green section.

Major collections: Durham Dean and Chapter Muniments and associated collections, including Church Commission deposits: archives of Durham Cathedral and its estate, 11th–20th centuries (monastic to 1539).
Durham diocesan records and associated collections; central administrative archives, 15th–20th centuries.
Durham diocesan probate records, 1540–1857, and registered copies of wills for Co. Durham only, 1858–1940.
Church Commission deposits of Durham Bishopric financial and estate records, 15th–20th centuries.
Durham Bishopric Halmote Court (copyhold) records, 16th–20th centuries.
Durham Palatinate Records: some records of the Durham Chancery court, chiefly c1880–1920; and Durham Prothonotary records, chiefly writs and other legal and financial papers, 17th–19th centuries. (Most Durham Palatinate Records are in the Public Record Office, entry **960**).
Durham City Guild records, 16th–20th centuries.
Land tax records: Co. Durham townships, 1780s-20th century.
Manorial records: Chester Deanery, 16th–20th centuries; Frosterly, chiefly 20th–century; and (Weardale Chest Papers) Forest of Weardale and Stanhope Park, Co. Durham, 16th–17th centuries.
Solicitors' papers, and deed groups, including Booth and Lazenby papers, chiefly 19th–early 20th centuries; Clayton and Gibson papers, including Marquess of Bute and Clavering deeds, 16th–19th centuries; and Eden papers, 13th–20th centuries.
Backhouse papers: personal and business papers of a Quaker banking family, and of related families, including the Gurneys of Norwich, chiefly 18th–20th centuries.
Baker Baker papers: family, estate and business papers.
Howard of Naworth papers: family and estate papers of the Earls of Carlisle relating mainly to Cumberland and Northumberland, 12th–20th centuries.
Shafto (Beamish) papers: deeds, estate papers and colliery accounts, estates successively owned by the Davison, Eden and Shafton families, 15th–20th centuries.
Shipperdenson papers: Shipperdenson and Hopper family estate papers, 16th–20th centuries.
Antiquarian collections, including papers of C.R. Hudleston, 1905–92.

Finding aids: Various lists, indexes, catalogues and calendars. Lists sent to NRA.

Facilities: Microfilm reader.

Conservation: In-house conservation workshop.

Publications: List of Deans and Major Canons of Durham, 1541–1900 (1974).

C University of Durham: Russian Research Collection

Address: Department of Russian, Elvet Riverside, New Elvet, Durham DH1 3JT

Telephone: (0191) 374 2687

Fax: (0191) 374 2691

Enquiries: The Secretary, Russian Department

Open: Open by appointment only.

Access: Generally open to the public, by arrangement.

The collection, reflecting Russian history and society of the late 19th and early 20th century, was brought together in the early 1980s through the acquisition by purchase and gift of material belonging to Feliks Volkhorskii, Barry Hollingsworth and Jaakoff Prelooker.

276 Ushaw College Library

Address: Durham DH7 9RH

Enquiries: The Librarian, Dr J.T. Rhodes

Open: By arrangement.

Access: Bona fide scholars, by prior written appointment only.

Historical background: Ushaw College is a direct descendant of the English College, Douai, France (1568–1793), and its archives cover the Roman Catholic history of Northern England from c1700. In 1971, when the English College in Lisbon closed, its archives and MSS were moved to Ushaw College.

Acquisitions policy: Acquires, by gift or loan, documents relevant to English Roman Catholic history.

Archives of organisation: College archives, including MSS from Douai, 1794–.

Major collections: Lisbon Collection: extensive archives of the English College in Lisbon, 1628–1973, and its MSS collections, including correspondence of Bishop Richard Russell (1630–93) and papers of the Jorge and Donovan families relating to Anglo-Portuguese trade, 19th century.

Letters of John Lingard (1781–1851), historian, 1840s; and Cardinal Nicholas Wiseman (1802–65).

Smaller collections of 19th-century letters, including those of Cardinal John Newman (1801–90).

40 medieval MSS.

Non-manuscript material: Books and pamphlets, particularly strong on Roman

Catholic theology, church history and English recusancy (50,000).

Finding aids: Card catalogues. Lisbon College archives: NRA 29239. Ushaw College, archives and MSS: NRA 13674. Other lists in preparation.

Publications: M. Sharratt: 'The Lisbon Collection at Ushaw', *Northern Catholic History*, 8 (1973), 30–34.

——: 'Lisbon College Register 1628–1813', *Catholic Record Society*, 72 (1991).

Articles, principally in the *Ushaw Magazine*, 1891–.

277 North London Collegiate School

Address: Canons Park, Edgware, Middx HA8 7RJ

Enquiries: The School Archivist, Mrs Helen Turner

Open: Term: by arrangement only.

Access: Members of the school under supervision and serious researchers, by appointment only.

Historical background: The school was founded in 1850 by Frances Mary Buss (1827–94), with the assistance of her parents and brothers, in the family house in Camden Town. From the beginning it aimed to give girls an education that would fit them for professional life, with a strong academic bias. The school was later divided into an upper and lower school, the latter eventually becoming the Camden School for Girls, now separately run by the local authority. NLCS moved to Canons Park, Edgware, in 1938, when it became a direct grant school. It is now an independent school and its archive is consulted by students of education for girls and of women's studies.

Acquisitions policy: To maintain the school's archives.

Archives of organisation: Admissions register; governors' minutes; headmistresses' reports; school magazine, 1876–.

Major collections: Paintings and sketch books of R.W. Buss, artist and illustrator.

Non-manuscript material: Works by Old North Londoners and past headmistresses.

Finding aids: Card catalogue.

Publications: The North London Collegiate School 1850–1950: Essays in Honour of the Centenary of the Mary Buss Foundation (Oxford, 1950).

278 Bank of Scotland Archives

Address: The Mound, Edinburgh EH1 1YZ

Telephone: (0131) 243 5830

Fax: (0131) 243 7070

Enquiries: The Archivist and Records Manager, Alan Cameron

Open: By appointment only.

Access: No access to customer records less than 100 years old or to others less than 50 years old without special permission. The bank reserves the right to refuse access.

Historical background: The Bank of Scotland was founded by Act of Parliament of Scotland in 1695. It absorbed the Caledonian Bank in 1907, the Union Bank of Scotland in 1955 and the British Linen Bank in 1971. The Bank has an extensive branch network in Scotland and the right to issue its own bank notes.

Acquisitions policy: Main acquisitions arise as part of the records management programme: only identified strays or items which are directly relevant to the bank's history. Material outside these areas will be acquired only after consultation with NRA(S) and the National Library of Scotland (entry **294**).

Archives of organisation: Archives of the Bank of Scotland, 1695–, and of all banks that are part of the group and its predecessors, including Union Bank of Scotland, 1830–1954; British Linen Bank, 1764–1971.

Non-manuscript material: Pictures, silver coins, bank-notes, firearms and banking memorabilia housed in the bank museum.

Finding aids: NRA(S) 945 and 1110 (in process of recataloguing).

Facilities: Photocopying. Photography. Microfilm reader by arrangement.

Conservation: Contracted out.

Publications: R.S. Rait: *The History of the Union Bank of Scotland* (Glasgow, 1930).
C.A. Malcolm: *The Bank of Scotland, 1695–1945* (1946).
——:*The British Linen Bank* (1950).

C.S. Checkland: *Scottish Banking: a History, 1695–1975* (Glasgow, 1975).
C.W. Munn: *The Scottish Provincial Banking Companies* (Edinburgh, 1981).
N. Tamaki: *The Life Cycle of the Union Bank of Scotland, 1830–1954* (1983).
R.S. Saville: *The Bank of Scotland, 1695–1996* (Edinburgh, 1995).
A. Cameron: *Scotland's First Bank: an Illustrated History* (Mainstream, 1995).

279 British Geological Survey

Address: Murchison House, West Mains Road, Edinburgh EH9 3LA

Telephone: (0131) 650 0307

Fax: (0131) 667 2785

Enquiries: The Records Officer, Mr Richard Gillanders

Open: Mon–Thurs: 9.00–5.00 Fri: 9.00–4.30

Access: Generally open to the public, by appointment only.

Historical background: The Geological Survey Office in Scotland was set up in 1867, although mapping had started in 1854. It holds MS, graphic and photographic material of the British Geological Survey and its predecessors, the Geological Survey of Great Britain and the Institute of Geological Sciences, relating to the geological land survey of Scotland. The archival material, comprising some 25,000 items, is included as part of the wider national geoscience record collection available for reference at BGS Edinburgh. See also British Geological Survey, Nottingham (entry **857**), for central administrative archives.

Acquisitions policy: To add to the existing collection in pursuance of the survey's role as a repository for national geological archives.

Archives of organisation: The survey's own archives, which include correspondence, registered files, papers, photographs and field observations notably official notebooks of Geological Survey staff.

Major collections: Plans of abandoned mines (other than coal and oil shale), c1872–, held on behalf of the Health and Safety Executive, and non-coal mine plans and company borehole journal books, c1800–c1950, deposited by NCB/British Coal.

Non-manuscript material: Photographs (*c*10,000) and mine plans (*c*2000).

Finding aids: Lists of holdings and on-line database index.

Facilities: Photocopying. Photography.

Conservation: Contracted out.

280 Chartered Institute of Bankers in Scotland

Address: 19 Rutland Square, Edinburgh EH1 2DE

Telephone: (0131) 229 9869

Fax: (0131) 229 1852

Enquiries: The Chief Executive, Dr C.W. Munn

Open: Mon–Fri: 9.00–1.00; 2,00–5.00

Access: Bona fide researchers, by appointment.

The institute was founded in 1875 and maintains a collection of Scottish banking documents. The library has a special collection of banking histories.

281 Edinburgh City Archives

Address: Department of Administration, City Chambers, High Street, Edinburgh EH1 1YJ

Telephone: (0131) 529 4614

Fax: (0131) 529 7477

Enquiries: The City Archivist

Open: Mon–Fri: 9.00–4.30

Access: Generally open to the public. A prior consultation is advisable. There is a production fee for the commercial use of Dean of Guild building control plans.

Historical background: The City Archives, as the official local records repository for the City of Edinburgh, house the administrative records of the Burgh and present District Council.

Acquisitions policy: Primary official and non-official records relating to the area covered by the present City of Edinburgh District Council and predecessor authorities of Leith, Edinburgh and their environs.

Archives of organisation: Usual local authority record holdings, 14th century–, with the major part of the holdings relating to the period after 1700.

Edinburgh Town Council minutes, 1551–1975; City of Edinburgh District Council minutes, 1975–; Edinburgh Dean of Guild plans, 1762–1975; building control plans, 1975–; register of Burgesses and Guildbrethren, 1487–1955; Edinburgh Valuation Roll survey books, *c*1850–1975; Burgh Court records, 1900–74; Edinburgh Police Commissioners minutes, 1805–60; Edinburgh Parochial Board, 1845–1900; Edinburgh Parish Council, 1893–1930; Leith Dean of Guild Court, 1870–1920; Edinburgh and Leith Police, *c*1840–1970; Incorporation of Hammermen of Edinburgh, 1494–1963; Edinburgh Extent and Annuity Rolls, 1580–1833; Canongate Jail records, 1750–1840; Incorporation of Bakers of Edinburgh, 1522–1947; Incorporation of United and Incorporated Trades of St Mary's Chapel, 1669–1910; Edinburgh Chamber of Commerce, 1785–1971.

Major collections: Substantial records relating to other bodies, principally those closely associated with the city authorities, such as the Burgh of the Canongate, Trinity Hospital and the Edinburgh Water Company, but also including the Scottish Modern Art Association and Queensferry Town Council.

Finding aids: Lists, reports and historical databases. Lists sent to NRA(S).

Facilities: Photocopying.

Conservation: Contracted out.

282 Edinburgh City Libraries
Edinburgh Room and Scottish Library

Address: Central Library, George IV Bridge, Edinburgh EH1 1EG

Telephone: (0131) 225 5584

Fax: (0131) 225 8783

Enquiries: The Reference Librarian, Morag Kyle

Open: Mon–Fri: 9.00–9.00 Sat: 9.00–1.00

Access: Generally open to the public. Restrictions on certain categories of material.

Historical background: Edinburgh Public Library opened in 1890 with a reference library, newsroom and home reading library serving the City of Edinburgh. The Edinburgh Room opened in 1932 (the fine art and music libraries also opened in the 1930s), and the Scottish Library in 1961. At local government reorganisation they became Edinburgh City Libraries, serving the Edinburgh District.

Acquisitions policy: Edinburgh Room: collects some MSS illustrating the life of the city but does not compete with the City Archives (entry **280**) and the National Library of Scotland (entry **294**). Scottish Library: comprehensive coverage of printed sources and non-book materials illustrating the life of Scotland.

Major collections: Edinburgh Room: 1000 MSS, including school log-books, school board minutes, letters, account books, minutes of local societies and trade unions.
Scottish Library: principally non-MS material (see below); 50 MSS, including Smith's poems *Old Scottish Clockmakers* and *Surfaceman*.

Fine Art Library: Italian architectural folios, sketch books by Scottish artists and art collectors, late 18th and 19th centuries.

Music Library: Edinburgh Music Society minutes, 1728–95, and index to music.

Non-manuscript material: Edinburgh Room: broadsides, including playbills, political broadsides, acts and proclamations, ballads (*c*2200).
Large collection of press cuttings.
Maps and plans, 16th century– (*c*2800).
Prints and drawings, excellent for costume and architecture (*c*10,000).
Photographs, including large callotype collection from the 1840s of the work of D.O. Hill and Robert Adamson, and Dr Thomas Keith (*c*12,000).
Films and tapes.

Scottish Library: large collection of press cuttings.
Extensive map and print collections, 17th century–.
Parish registers and census returns for the Lothians, Borders, Dumfries and Galloway, Ayrshire, Stirlingshire, Clackmannanshire, Kinrosshire, Shetland, Orkney, Caithness and Sutherland.
Photographs (*c*1000), negatives (*c* 950), and lantern slides (*c*1700), including Dr I.F. Grant's Highland Folklife Collection, and the Dr Thomas Keith Collection, 1855–6.

Fine Art Library: Dyer Collection of Japanese prints and books.
Press cuttings on Scottish art, architecture and design.

Music Library: extensive collection of programmes relating to local musical events, early 19th century–.
Scottish music, late 18th century–.

Finding aids: Indexes to much of non-MS material.

Facilities: Photocopying. Photography by arrangement. Microfilm/fiche reader/printer.

283 Edinburgh College of Art

Address: Lauriston Place, Edinburgh EH3 9DF

Telephone: (0131) 221 6034

Fax: (0131) 221 6001

Enquiries: The Librarian, Glenn Craig

Open: Term: Mon–Thurs: 9.00–8.30 Fri: 9.00–5.00 Vacation: Mon–Fri: 9.00–4.00

Access: Advance notice required.

Historical background: The college was founded in 1907 from predecessor institutions dating from the early 19th century. These were: the Board of Trustees for Manufacturers in Scotland (the Trustees Academy), whose records up to and including the creation of the college are housed in the Scottish Register Office (entry **313**); and the Royal Scottish Academy and Heriot-Watt College (now Heriot-Watt University), both of which house their own records (entries **305** and **288**). Copies of those records dealing with the creation of the college are housed in the college library.

Archives of organisation: The present college archive comprises minute books, letter-books, annual reports, and prospectuses, 1907–.

Non-manuscript material: Small collection of early photographs and a very inconsistent collection of subsequent photographs, with varied ephemera of people, events and college work.

Finding aids: A computerised name record is available.

Facilities: Photocopying. Microfilm readers.

284 Fettes College

Address: Carrington Road, Edinburgh
EH4 1QX

Telephone: (0131) 332 2281

Fax: (0131) 332 3081

Enquiries: The Hon. Archivist

Open: By arrangement only.

Access: Bona fide researchers, by appointment.

Historical background: The college was founded in 1870 under the terms of the will of Sir William Fettes Bart. of Comely Bank and Redcastle (1750–1836): 'It is my intention that the residue of my whole Estate should form an Endowment for the maintenance, education and outfit of young people whose parents have either died without leaving sufficient funds for that purpose, or who from innocent misfortune during their lives, are unable to give suitable education to their children.' He very wisely gave his trustees ample and unlimited powers for the making of regulations and general management of the funds. The college is a co-educational boarding school.

Acquisitions policy: Records relating directly to the history of the college and to prominent Old Fettesians.

Archives of organisation: School records. Minutes of meetings of Governors of the Fettes Trust.

Non-manuscript material: Photographs, plans, maps.
Portraits.
Selwyn-Lloyd Memorial Library.

Publications: A Hundred Years of Fettes (1970).

285 Free Church College

Address: The Mound, Edinburgh EH1 2LS

Telephone: (0131) 226 4978

Fax: (0131) 220 0597

Enquiries: The Hon. Librarian

Open: Mon–Fri: 9.00–4.30

Access: Approved readers, on written application.

Historical background: The college became the Free Church College in continuity from New College, subsequent to the reorganisation of the Free Church College and Offices by the Execu-

tive Commission after the emergence of the United Free Church in 1900. The building originally comprised luxury flats occupied by leading notables of Edinburgh society. Kirk Session and Presbytery records are deposited in the Scottish Record Office (entry **313**); finance papers, 1848–1910, are deposited in the National Library of Scotland (entry **294**).

Major collections: Many documents of historical and antiquarian significance, relating mainly to the Scottish Church.

Non-manuscript material: Portraits of leading Scottish churchmen; D.O. Hill's famous painting 'The First Free Church General Assembly', 1843.
Celtic library, housed in Senate Hall.

Finding aids: Lists of archives. NRA 23336.

Facilities: Photocopying by arrangement.

286 General Register Office for Scotland

Address: New Register House, Edinburgh EH1 3YT

Telephone: (0131) 334 0380

Enquiries: The Registrar General

Open: Mon–Thurs: 9.00–4.30 Fri: 9.30–4.00

Access: Records available in microform to the public on payment of a fee (list of charges available). Advance booking recommended.

Historical background: The office was established in 1855 on the introduction of compulsory registration of births, deaths and marriages in Scotland. New Register House was designed by Robert Mathieson, an assistant surveyor of HM Office of Works. The office provides a facility for record searching thought to be unique in the UK, housing under one roof the old parochial registers, the statutory registers and open census records.

Acquisitions policy: Intake of statutory or closely allied material only.

Archives of organisation: Statutory registers of births, deaths and marriages, 1855–.
Open census records, 1841–91.
Minor records of births, deaths and marriages registered abroad, 1855– (Scottish nationals only).

Major collections: Old parish records of Church of Scotland, 1553–1854 (incomplete).

Non-manuscript material: Microfilm/fiche of records.
Registrar General's published weekly, monthly, quarterly and annual reports, 1855–. Published census reports, 1841–1991.

Finding aids: Statutory registers: computer indexes. Old parochial registers: computer indexes to birth and marriages; a few death indexes. Open census records: street indexes for larger towns. Minor records: index.

Publications: Information leaflet (including guidance for family historians).
List of Registration District.
Family tree chart of Scotland, 1855–.

287 Grand Lodge of Scotland

Address: Freemasons' Hall, 96 George Street, Edinburgh EH2 3DH

Telephone: (0131) 225 5304

Fax: (0131) 225 3953

Enquiries: The Grand Secretary

Open: Mon–Fri: 9.00–5.00, by arrangement.

Access: Bona fide scholars and anyone genuinely interested in freemasonry, by appointment

Historical background: The Grand Lodge of Scotland of Ancient, Free and Accepted Masons was established in 1736.

Acquisitions policy: To maintain its own archives and those of other Scottish lodges, as appropriate.

Archives of organisation: Minutes, 1736–1893; cartulary and lists of lodges and members, 1736–; registration books, 1799–; statutes and ordnances of the masons of Scotland, 1598–9; records of Aitcheson's Haven Lodge, 1598, 1738–1851.

Major collections: Miscellaneous lodge minutes, including Lodge of Scotland.
Freemasons in Rome, 1735–7.

Non-manuscript material: Collection of masonic certificates.

Finding aids: NRA(S) 2612 (NRA 27749).

288 Heriot-Watt University Archive

Address: Riccarton, Edinburgh EH14 4AS

Telephone: (0131) 451 3218

Fax: (0131) 451 3164

Enquiries: The University Archivist, Dr Norman Reid

Open: Mon–Fri: 9.30–4.45 Other times by arrangement.

Access: By appointment. Certain classes of records are accessible at the discretion of the archivist.

Historical background: The institution was founded in 1821 as an evening school for mechanics under the title of the School of Arts of Edinburgh. In 1852 it incorporated the Edinburgh memorial to James Watt and thus became the Watt Institution and School of Arts. In 1885, merged with the charitable trust founded by George Heriot in 1623, it became Heriot-Watt College. From 1928 to 1966 it was an autonomous Scottish Central Institution, and in 1966 it became the Heriot-Watt University. The university archive was established as an administrative department in 1984, and was incorporated within the university's Institutional Development Division in 1993. The Scottish Brewing Archive has been transferred to Glasgow University (entry **351E**)

Acquisitions policy: To strengthen existing collections on the history of the institution and its background, including relevant biographical material; the history of technical education; and the history of Riccarton and its locality.

Archives of organisation: University records: administrative, financial and academic records of the institution from its foundation to the present day, including private papers of individuals concerned with it, records of student bodies etc.

Major collections: Watt Collection: biographical works, with some artefacts and ephemera, relating to James Watt, and records of the Watt Club (f.1854, now the university's Graduates Association).
Gibson-Craig Papers: records of the Riccarton estate and its owners, 15th–19th centuries.
Papers of Sir Robert Blair (1859–1935), first Chief Education Officer of London County Council, 1904–24.
Leith Nautical College records, 1855–1987.

Non-manuscript material: University records: many printed calendars and publications; also photographs, films, tapes and medals.

The archive also administers the university's collections of works of art and historical artefacts.

Finding aids: Lists and indexes of all collections, at various stages of preparation, to be available in hard-copy and database form. Partial computer index of past students and staff.

Facilities: Photocopying. Photography by arrangement.

Conservation: Contracted out.

Publications: Heriot-Watt University: from Mechanics Institute to Technological University, 1821–1973 (1973).

Heriot-Watt University Archive Catalogue, vol. 1: *Collections Relating to the Edinburgh School of Arts, the Watt Institution and School of Arts, and Heriot-Watt College, 1821–1966* (1983); vol. 2: *Collections relating to the Watt Club and James Watt* (1984).

L.A. Wallace: *1821–1992: Physics at Heriot-Watt University, Edinburgh,* (1993).

Various pamphlets.

289 Huntly House Museum

Parent organisation: Edinburgh City Museums and Galleries

Address: 142 Canongate, Edinburgh EH8 8DD

Telephone: (0131) 225 2424 ext. 6678

Fax: (0131) 557 3346

Enquiries: The Assistant City Curator, Derek Janes

Open: June–Sept: Mon–Sat: 10.00–6.00 Oct–May: Mon–Sat: 10.00–5.00

Access: Generally open to the public, by appointment.

Acquisitions policy: It is not general policy to acquire archives, but the holdings of taped interviews, personalia and political/trade union material will be developed.

Major collections: Business records, including: Forde Ranking Glass Works; Norton Park Glass Works (Edinburgh and Leith Flint Glass Works), *c*1791–*c*1917; A.W. Buchan & Co., Thistle Potteries, 1867–1972.

Collections of local history material relating to Edinburgh.

Non-manuscript material: Memorabilia of FM Earl Haig (1861–1928); Sir Walter Scott (1771–1832); Robert Burns (1759–96); R.L. Stevenson (1850–94).

Taped interviews.

Photographs of Edwardian interiors at Laurieston Castle.

Photographic collections of life and work of Edinburgh's people.

NB Photographs and associated documentary material relating to South Queensferry and Dalmeny and the Forth road and rail bridges is also held at the Queensferry Museum, 53 High Street, South Queensferry EH30 9HN; tel. (031) 331 5545.

Finding aids: NRA(S) 17572 (NRA 19065).

Facilities: Photocopying. Photography by arrangement.

Conservation: Contracted out.

290 Institute of Chartered Accountants of Scotland

Address: 27 Queen Street, Edinburgh EH2 1LA

Telephone: (0131) 225 5673

Enquiries: The Librarian, Mrs D. F. Hogg

Open: Mon–Fri: 9.00–5.00

Access: Bona fide researchers, by appointment.

The institute has the distinction of being the oldest professional body of accountants in the world. The Society of Accountants in Edinburgh was formed in 1854, the Institute of Accountants and Actuaries in Glasgow in 1855 and the Society of Accountants in Aberdeen in 1867. In 1951 the three bodies amalgamated to become the Institute of Chartered Accounts of Scotland. The archives comprise the records of the three societies, those of Edinburgh and Aberdeen being held in Edinburgh and the Glasgow records being held at Glasgow. The archives have been listed.

291 Jewel and Esk Valley College

Address: 24 Milton Road East, Edinburgh EH15 2PP

Telephone: (0131) 669 8461 ext. 209

Fax: (0131) 657 2276

Enquiries: The Chief Librarian, Mrs Suzette Bell

Open: Term: Mon–Thurs: 8.45–8.00 Fri: 8.45–4.30 Vacation: Mon–Fri: 9.00–4.30

Access: On application to the chief librarian.

Historical background: The college was founded in 1855, following the Merchant Shipping Act 1850. It became a Central Institution in 1903 and moved to new purpose-built premises in 1978, with three academic departments for marine electronics, marine engineering and navigation. A specialised unit for hazardous cargo handling was created in 1978 but was closed in 1987. A Centre for Advanced Maritime Studies was subsequently opened in Leith.

Acquisitions policy: The main emphasis is on the acquisition of current textbooks. However, it is also policy to retain or acquire examples of texts and teaching materials for the education and training of merchant seamen, 1850–.

Major collections: Historical collection of texts and teaching materials, including former students' log-books, examination primers and notebooks.

Non-manuscript material: Selected examples of navigation instruments.

Finding aids: Card catalogue to historical collection. List of navigation instruments.

Facilities: Photocopying. Microfiche readers.

292 Meteorological Office Edinburgh

Parent organisation: Meteorological Office

Address: Saughton House, Broomhouse Drive, Edinburgh EH11 3XG

Telephone: (0131) 244 8358/244 8368

Fax: (0131) 244 8389

Enquiries: The Superintendent, Mr M.R. Porter

Open: Mon–Fri: 9.00–4.00

Access: Generally open to the public, preferably by appointment.

Historical background: The Meteorological Office originated as a department of the Board of Trade in 1854. Under the Public Records Acts the office is authorised to select technical meteorological records for retention and main-tain approved places of deposit in Edinburgh, Bracknell (entry **112**) and Belfast (entry **72**). In 1920 the Meteorological Office took over responsibility for climatological observations in Scotland from the Scottish Meteorological Society and agreed to maintain an office in Edinburgh for the records.

Acquisitions policy: Responsible for original meteorological and climatological records from any source in Scotland. Donations are welcomed.

Archives of organisation: Minute books of the Scottish Meteorological Society, 1859–81.
Daily and some hourly climatological data for locations in Scotland; extensive coverage since 1857 plus some earlier data.
Complete hourly data and log-books from meterological observatories on Ben Nevis, 1883–1904, and at Fort William, 1890–1904.

Non-manuscript material: Library collection of the Scottish Meteorological Society, including some rare books.

Finding aids: Index of contents of archives. Work has started on a computer-based catalogue of the climatological records.

Conservation: Contracted out.

Facilities: Photocopying by arrangement.

293 National Gallery of Scotland Library

Parent organisation: National Galleries of Scotland

Address: The Mound, Edinburgh EH2 2EL Administrative Dept: 13 Heriot Row, Edinburgh EH3 6HB

Telephone: (0131) 556 8921 ext. 501

Fax: (0131) 220 0917

Enquiries: The Librarian, Mrs Julia Rolfe

Open: Mon–Fri: 10.00–12.30, 2.00–4.30, by prior arrangement only.

Access: Bona fide researchers, by appointment.

The National Gallery of Scotland was founded in 1850 and opened in 1859. It maintains research files on all items in its paintings, drawings and sculpture collections, with related catalogues. There is also a collection of photographs and slides with miscellaneous notes on artists. Archives, 1856–1906, are deposited at the Scottish Record Office (entry **313**) where there are indexes. See also the Scottish National Portrait Gallery (entry **312**) and Scottish National Gallery of Modern Art (entry **311**). The gallery produces the following publications: annual reports of the National Gallery of Scotland, catalogues of gallery collections, and exhibition catalogues.

294 National Library of Scotland
Department of Manuscripts

Address: George IV Bridge, Edinburgh EH1 1EW

Telephone: (0131) 226 4531

Enquiries: The Keeper of Manuscripts

Open: Mon, Tues, Thurs, Fri: 9.30–8.30 Wed: 10.00–8.00 Sat: 9.30–1.00
Closed completely on some public holidays, restricted service on others. Annual closure for stock-taking: 1st week of October.

Access: The great majority of holdings are available for consultation by serious researchers; a library reader's ticket, temporary or long term, which is issued on completion of the register and production of identification, is necessary. A few items or collections are restricted by date or require the permission of the owner. An appointment is not essential, but note that material for use in the evening must be ordered (in person or in advance) by 4.00.

Historical background: The National Library of Scotland was created by Act of Parliament in 1925, on the basis of the gift to the nation of the non-legal collections of the Advocates' Library. The Faculty of Advocates had collected a wide range of MS material since the 1680s, and the National Library has continued and expanded this activity.

Acquisitions policy: All MS material relating to Scotland and the activities of Scots worldwide. All subject areas are covered and there are few geographical restrictions. Medieval MSS, literary MSS and papers of all periods, historical documents, family papers and archives of organisations (cultural, political, commercial) are all represented. A detailed acquisitions policy statement is available.

Non-manuscript material: Some architectural and engineering plans. Important MS maps and estate plans (mostly stored and consulted in the Map Library, Salisbury Place, Edinburgh). Oral history tapes.

Finding aids: Inventories of large uncatalogued accessions available in typescript (sent to NRA and included in the *National Inventory of Documentary Sources*); various subject lists also available.

Facilities: Photocopying. Photography. Microfilm/fiche readers. Only battery-operated portable computers are presently allowed.

Conservation: Paper and vellum repair and all aspects of binding in-house.

Publications: National Library of Scotland: *Catalogue of Manuscripts acquired since 1925*, vols 1–8 (HMSO, 1938–92); later vols available in typescript.
Summary Catalogue of the Advocates' MSS (HMSO, 1971).
A variety of leaflets on library services.

295 National Monuments Record of Scotland

Parent organisation: Royal Commission on the Ancient and Historical Monuments of Scotland

Address: John Sinclair House, 16 Bernard Terrace, Edinburgh EH8 9NX

Telephone: (0131) 662 1456

Fax: (0131) 662 1477/1499

Enquiries: The Curator

Open: Mon–Thurs: 9.30–4.30 Fri: 9.30–4.00

Access: Generally open to the public. An appointment is preferable for complex enquiries.

Historical background: The RCAHMS is an independent non-departmental government body financed by Parliament through the Scottish Office under the sponsorship of Historic Scotland. The amalgamation in 1966 of the Royal Commission on the Ancient and Historical Monuments of Scotland, founded in 1908 to make an inventory of all ancient and historical monuments in Scotland, and the Scottish National Buildings Record, set up in 1941 to make and preserve records of buildings in anticipation of their possible destruction by enemy action, enabled the two largest collections of photographs and drawings of ancient monuments and historic buildings in Scotland to be combined in a single archive known as the National Monuments Record of Scotland (NMRS). In 1976 an aerial survey component was added to its recording programme, and in 1993 it became responsible for running the Air Photographic Unit, formerly part of the Scottish Office.

Acquisitions policy: Records of archaeological sites, built environment and design for all of Scotland and Scotland's architects. The NMRS adds to the existing collection of drawings, prints, photographs, slides and MSS by purchase, donation and deposit, and by making photographic copies of relevant material in other public and private muniments.

Major collections: Principally non-MS material (see below).
Society of Antiquaries of Scotland collection, MSS and drawings, 19th century.
Ordnance Survey record cards of archaeological sites.

Non-manuscript material: Extensive collection of plans, drawings, photographs and maps, including the following:
Burn Collection: office collection of architectural drawings from the London office of William Burn (1789–1870).
Lorimer Collection: office drawings of the architectural practice of Sir Robert Lorimer (1864–1929), and engineering drawings of the Northern Lighthouse Board.
Erskine Beveridge collection of photographs of archaeological sites and buildings in the West Highlands and Fife.
Royal Commission on the Ancient and Historical Monuments of Scotland: aerial photographs of archaeological and architectural sites.
Library of more than 11,000 books and pamphlets.

Finding aids: Topographical and subject indexes to the NMRS collection. Alphabetical slip index to architects and their works. Summary guide slip index containing references to material in the NMRS, outside collections and published sources.

Facilities: Photocopying. Photography. Microfilm/fiche reader/printer.

Conservation: In-house and contracted out.

Publications: Inventories of ancient and histori-

cal monuments, lists of archaeological sites and monuments, catalogues of aerial photographs, monographs etc. A detailed list of publications is available.
RCAHM (Scotland): *National Monuments Record of Scotland Jubilee: a Guide to the Collections* (HMSO, 1991).

296 National Museums of Scotland Library

Address: Chambers Street, Edinburgh EH1 1JF
Queen Street, Edinburgh EH2 1JD

Telephone: (0131) 225 7534
Chambers Street Library ext. 153
Queen Street Library ext. 369

Fax: (0131) 226 5682

Enquiries: Chambers Street Library, Elize Rowan
Queen Street Library, Dorothy Laing

Open: Mon–Thurs: 10.00–12.30; 2.00–5.00 Fri: 10.00–12.30; 2.00–4.30

Access: Generally open to the public; Chambers Street Library is by prior appointment only.

Historical background: The National Museums of Scotland came into being with the passing of the National Heritage (Scotland) Act 1985. The present National Museums of Scotland Library was formed from the libraries of the three national museums in the group which were formerly the Royal Scottish Museum, the National Museum of Antiquities of Scotland and the Scottish United Services Museum. It functions now as a unified service on three sites. The Chambers Street Library, originally founded with the Royal Scottish Museum in 1854, covers the decorative arts, the history of science and technology and natural history. The curatorial departments have their own archives relating to objects in the collections. The library archives cover the history of the museum and its building, material relating to the Edinburgh University Natural History Museum and the papers of natural historians. Some listing of the collection has been made but the latter is not actively curated or developed.
The Queen Street Library, originally the Society of Antiquaries of Scotland's Library, is concerned with Scottish history and culture and the archaeology of Europe. It has an extensive archive of papers, formerly the property of the society, which passed into the library's care in the 19th century. As at Chambers Street, there

has been some listing of the collection and, currently, a conservation project is under review, but there is no active collecting policy in place.
See also the Scottish United Services Museum (entry **314**) and Scottish Ethnological Archive (entry **310**).

Acquisitions policy: No active collecting policy. New acquisitions are normally by donation or acquired with an object/specimen.

Archives of organisation: Directors' correspondence 1861– (very incomplete, outgoing correspondence only, 1861–1937). Edinburgh University Natural History Museum report books: daily 1822–30, 1845–54; weekly 1822–31; annual 1834–6.
Society of Antiquaries of Scotland archives.

Major collections: Natural historians' correspondence, field notes, journals etc, particularly those of J.A. Harvie-Brown (1844–1916), William Jardine (1800–74), William S. Bruce (1867–1921), diary of A. Forbes Mackay. Other, uncatalogued, natural historians' material is in the Natural History Department.
Society of Antiquaries of Scotland: letters of William Smellie (1697–1763), surgeon; papers of Robert Riddell and miscellaneous antiquarian MSS, 18th and 19th centuries.

Non-manuscript material: Science, Technology and Working Life Department: photography collection, including examples of early photographic techniques and photographs (e.g. Hill and Adamson); technical drawings (*c*300).

Finding aids: Lists of NMS archives for internal use.

Facilities: Photocopying. Photography. Microfilm/fiche readers.

Conservation: Limited in-house paper conservation, otherwise contracted out.

Publications: J. Pitman: *Manuscripts in the Royal Scottish Museum*, part 1: *William Jardine Papers*, Royal Scottish Museum Information Series: Natural History, 7 (1981).
——:*Manuscripts in the Royal Scottish Museum*, part 2: *William S. Bruce Papers and Diary of A. Forbes Mackay*, Royal Scottish Museum Information Series: Natural History 8 (1982).
——:*Manuscripts in the Royal Scottish Museum*, part 3: *J.A. Harvie-Brown Papers*, Royal Scottish Museum Information Series: Natural History, 9 (1983).

297 National Trust for Scotland

Address: 5 Charlotte Square, Edinburgh EH2 4DU

Telephone: (0131) 226 5922

Fax: (0131) 243 9501

Enquiries: The Director of Administration, Mr E.D. Cameron

The trust, which was founded in 1931, holds only its own archives dealing with internal matters (see NRA(S) 1562). Any archives acquired with properties are usually deposited with the appropriate local record office.

298 Royal Botanic Garden Library

Address: 20A Inverleith Row, Edinburgh EH3 5LR

Telephone: (0131) 552 7171

Fax: (0131) 552 0382

Enquiries: The Chief Librarian, Dr C.D. Will

Open: Mon–Thurs: 9.00–5.00 Fri: 9.00–4.30

Access: Generally open to the public.

Historical background: The garden was founded in 1670. Its large archival collection is the result of its long history and activities, particularly in the field of botany and horticulture.

Acquisitions policy: Attempts to acquire comprehensively material relevant to the research interests of the scientific staff.

Archives of organisation: Archives of the garden and its predecessors: administrative records and scientific papers, including papers of Regius Keepers and staff.

Major collections: Records of botanical clubs and societies, including the Botanical Society of Edinburgh minute books, 1836–, and the Royal Caledonian Horticultural Society.
Transcribed material and notes made by historians of the garden.
Papers, including J.F. Rock's diaries and photographs; James MacNab's journals and scrapbooks; several files of papers and letters related to expeditions to different parts of the world.
Collection of *c*30,000 letters including John Hutton Balfour's worldwide correspondence

(*c*4000) and George Forrest's letters from China (*c*4000).

Non-manuscript material: Extensive collection of plant drawings, paintings and prints.

Finding aids: MSS indexes.

Facilities: Photocopying. Photography. Microfilm/fiche reader.

Publications: H.R. Fletcher and W.H. Brown: *The Royal Botanic Garden, Edinburgh, 1670–1970* (1970).
I.C. Hedge and J.M. Lamond (eds): *Index of Collectors in the Edinburgh Herbarium* (1970).
M.V. Matthew: *The History of the Royal Botanic Garden Library, Edinburgh* (1987).

299 Royal College of Nursing Archives

Address: 42 South Oswald Road, Edinburgh EH9 2HH

Telephone: (0131) 662 1010

Fax: (0131) 662 1032

Enquiries: The Archivist, Ms Susan McGann

Open: Mon–Thurs: 10.00–4.45 Fri: 10.00–4.15

Access: Bona fide researchers. Some administrative records are confidential.

Historical background: The RCN Archives record the growth of the college from its foundation in 1916 to its present position as the largest professional union of nurses, with more than 300,000 members. The records document its role as a professional organisation with international links, as an education body providing the first post-registration courses for nurses, and as a trade union negotiating and campaigning on behalf of nurses. The headquarters are at 20 Cavendish Square, London, a site occupied by the college since 1919. The Scottish Board of the College was also founded in 1916, and in 1991 the RCN Archives were transferred to Edinburgh. An archivist was first appointed in 1986.

Acquisitions policy: Papers relating to the history of nursing, including those of nursing-related organisations and nurses.

Archives of organisation: Council and committee minutes; reports of working parties and surveys on nursing policy and practice; records of the professional nursing department, the education department, the labour relations department and the international department; records of fund-raising and public relations; membership records; records of the Scottish Board, the Irish Board, 1917–25, and of various branches.

Major collections: Records of the following nursing organisations: the National Council of Nurses, 1908–62; the Association of Hospital Matrons, 1919–72; the Society of Registered Male Nurses, 1937–67; the National Association of State Enrolled Nurses (NASEN), 1948–70; the Students' Nurses' Association, 1925–68.
Papers and certificates of hundreds of individual nurses.

Non-manuscript material: Photographs and glass slides (*c*2000).
Oral history collection (80).
Badges (*c*700).

Finding aids: Catalogues and lists.

Facilities: Photocopying. Photography. Microfiche reader.

Publications: G. Bowman: *The Lamp and the Book: the story of the RCN* (London, 1967).
S. McGann: *The Battle of the Nurses* (London, 1992).
Archives and Oral History Collection leaflet [free].

300 Royal College of Physicians of Edinburgh Library

Address: 9 Queen Street, Edinburgh EH2 1JQ

Telephone: (0131) 225 7324

Fax: (0131) 220 3939

Enquiries: The Librarian

Open: Mon–Fri: 9.00–5.00

Access: Fellows, members of the college and bona fide researchers.

Historical background: The library was founded in 1681 by Sir Robert Sibbald, the principal founder of the college, and has had a continuous existence as a working medical library since then. It also contains good collections of works on botany and natural history down to the mid-19th century.

Acquisitions policy: To fill gaps in historical collections and augment the history of medicine section.

Archives of organisation: College archives relating to the institution, with lists of members, minutes, accounts and records, general correspondence, college buildings, Fellows' petitions etc, 1681–.

Major collections: Reports and correspondence concerning lunatic asylums in Scotland, 1814–85.
Records and papers of the Medical Provident Institution of Scotland, 1826–34.
MSS Collection: c1000 vols, including 18th–century lecture notes of lectures in Edinburgh medical school; MSS of William Cullen (1710–90), including consultation letters; MSS of Sir James Young Simpson (1811–70); MSS of the three Alexander Monros (1697–1767, 1733–1817, 1773–1859).
MSS of Thomas Laycock (1812–76); diaries of Sir Alexander Morison (1779–1866); MSS of Sir R.W. Philip (1857–1939); MSS of Sir Sydney A. Smith (1883–1969).

Non-manuscript material: College portraits.
Albums of engravings of medical men, 18th and 19th centuries.
Other prints, engravings and photographs, including those from the collection of J.D. Comrie.

Finding aids: Inventory of muniments (1914; typescript; copy in Scottish Record Office). Various other indexes. W.J. Robertson: *A Checklist of Manuscripts in the RCPEd* (TS). Detailed and summary listings of larger MSS collections.

Facilities: Photocopying. Photography. Microfilm/fiche reader.

301 Royal College of Surgeons of Edinburgh

Address: Nicolson Street, Edinburgh EH8 9DW

Telephone: (0131) 556 6206 ext. 211

Fax: (0131) 557 6406

Enquiries: The Hon. Secretary, I.B. Macleod or The Archivist, Miss A.M. Stevenson

Open: Mon–Fri: 9.00–5.00, by prior arrangement.

Access: Enquirers should first write to the Hon. Secretary for written permission to use the college's archives and, with that, then contact the college's archivist to arrange a suitable time.

Historical background: From the beginning the college has been concerned with the training, examination and licensing of prospective surgeons. In 1505, after petitioning the Town Council, the barbers and surgeons of Edinburgh were granted a Seal of Cause, which enabled them to be enrolled among the Incorporated Crafts of the Burgh. The crafts of Barbers and Surgeons were separated by a decree of the Court of Session in 1722, after which records were kept separately for the two crafts. Both the Barbers and Surgeons continued to use the same premises for meetings until 1893, when the Society of Barbers met for the last time. In 1778 a Royal Charter was granted to the Incorporation of Surgeons, which conferred the present title, and in 1979 a new charter was granted.

Acquisitions policy: The college collects all papers relating to itself and papers belonging to its fellows and licentiates or concerning them.

Archives of organisation: Bound records of the college, 1581–; College Council minutes, 1822–; charters, 1504–1979; examination records, 1581–; apprentices' indentures, 1709–1872; building of Old Surgeons' Hall, 1696–1710; records of the Surgeons Widows' Fund, 1820–90; plans for the present college building, 1829–32; list of fellows, 1581–; lists of licentiates, 1770–1873; triple qualification examination schedules, 1886–; annual reports of the college, 1937–; laws of the college, 1793–1977.

Major collections: Papers of the extra mural medical school of the royal colleges.
Papers of the Society of Barbers.
Papers of the Royal Odonto-Chirurgical Society of Scotland.
Papers of Sir James Young Simpson (1811–70), physician; John Robert Hume (?1781–1857), physician; John Smith (1792–1833), professor of medical jurisprudence; Sir John Struthers (1823–99), anatomist; Joseph Lister (1827–1901) and Sir Henry Wade (1877–1955).

Finding aids: Summary of the college's archival holdings freely available on the computer. Sent to the NRA(S) and the Medical Archives and Manuscripts Survey at the Wellcome Institute for the History of Medicine (entry **768**).

Facilities: Photocopying. Photography.

Publications: Detailed guide to the college's archives in preparation.

302 Royal Highland and Agricultural Society of Scotland

Address: The Library, Royal Highland Centre, Ingliston, Edinburgh EH28 8NF

Telephone: (0131) 333 2444 ext. 237

Enquiries: The Librarian, Mrs M.N. Ramsay

Open: Mon–Fri: 9.30–5.00

Access: Generally open to the public, by appointment.

Historical background: The society was founded in 1784 to promote agricultural interests and education, as well as the study of the Gaelic language and Scottish poetry and music.

Acquisitions policy: To maintain the archives and collections.

Archives of organisation: Minutes, 1784–1967; abstracts of premiums offered, 1874– 1925; reports and premium certificates, 1785–1890; accountancy records, 1834–1967; plans of show yards, 1837–47.
Sederunt books, 1842–1945, and journals.
Correspondence, papers and photographs *re* St Kilda Fund, 1851–1931; also J.M. Macleod of St Kilda, letters to J.M. Maxwell *re* conditions on St Kilda, 1859–66.

Major collections: Gaelic MSS: Ingliston papers: MSS relating to Gaelic matters, including essays on Highland music, fisheries and other subjects, 1793–1809; papers *re* publication of Gaelic dictionary, 1809–38; and much other correspondence, mainly 19th century.

Non-manuscript material: Transactions of the Highland Society, 1799–. Large collection of bound volumes of pamphlets.

Finding aids: NRA 12271.

Facilities: Photocopying.

303 Royal Observatory

Parent organisation: Particle Physics and Astronomy Research Council

Address: Blackford Hill, Edinburgh EH9 3HJ

Telephone: (0131) 668 8397

Fax: (0131) 668 8264

Enquiries: The Librarian, Mr A.R. Macdonald

Open: Mon–Fri: 9.00–5.30

Access: Serious researchers in the history of science, by appointment.

Historical background: The observatory was founded in 1818 as the Observatory of the Astronomical Institution of Edinburgh and was designated 'Royal' in 1822. It moved to its present site in the 1890s.

Acquisitions policy: To maintain and consolidate the archives.

Archives of organisation: Correspondence, administrative and scientific papers and notebooks of the Astronomical Institution of Edinburgh and the Observatory, 1764–.
Papers and correspondence of Astronomers Royal for Scotland and their staffs, 1834–, including those of Charles Piazzi Smyth (1819–1900).
Considerable collection of material from the (26th) Earl of Crawford's private observatory at Dunecht, Aberdeenshire, 17th–19th centuries.

Major collections: Royal Society of Edinburgh's collections on Charles Piazzi Smith.
Notes of A.P. Norton, Astronomical Society of Edinburgh.

Non-manuscript material: Photographic collection of glass negatives and prints.

Finding aids: NRA(S) 2657.

Facilities: Photocopying. Photography.

Publications: H.A. Brück: *The Royal Observatory, Edinburgh, 1822–1972* (Edinburgh, [1972]).
Catalogue of the Archives of the Royal Observatory Edinburgh, 1764–1937 (Edinburgh, 1981).

304 The Royal Scots Regimental Museum

Parent organisation: The Royal Scots Regimental Headquarters

Address: The Castle, Edinburgh EH1 2YT

Telephone: (0131) 310 5014

Fax: (0131) 310 5019

Enquiries: The Curator, Major R.P. Mason

Open: April–Oct: Mon–Sun: 9.30–5.30 Oct–March: Mon–Fri: 9.30–4.00

Access: Bona fide researchers, on written application.

Acquisitions policy: Collection of documents relevant to the regimental history.

Archives of organisation: Regimental war diary, 1914–, and register of services, 1877–.
Regimental record books; minutes of officers' mess.
Account book of distribution of pay and subsistence *re* 1st Battalion, 1776–9.
Official correspondence of officers of the Royals, Ireland, 1786.

Major collections: Diaries, autobiographies and memoirs, mainly World War I.
Miscellaneous documents and letters, some concerning the early history of the regiment, 1650s.

Non-manuscript material: Photographs and albums, drawings and scrapbooks.
Copies of *The Thistle* and regimental magazines; rolls of honours and materials (mainly printed) on casualties and war graves.

Finding aids: Card index. NRS(S) 2273.

305 Royal Scottish Academy

Address: The Mound, Edinburgh EH2 2EL

Telephone: (0131) 225 6671

Fax: (0131) 225 2349

Enquiries: The Assistant Librarian/Keeper, Mrs Joanna Soden

Open: Mon–Fri: 10.00–1.00; 2.00–4.00

Access: Generally open to the public, by appointment only. Enquiries may be answered by letter; a donation is requested for this service, except from schoolchildren and matriculated students.

Historical background: The Royal Scottish Academy was founded in 1826 to promote the visual arts in Scotland and to improve conditions of living artists. It is therefore the oldest surviving art organisation in Scotland. One of the founding aims was to establish a library devoted to the visual arts, and this has been maintained since that time. The archives of the RSA date back to its foundation and they form part of the Library collections.

Acquisitions Policy: The library of the Royal Scottish Academy aims to collect material relevant to past and present members of the academy and to the visual arts generally in Scotland. Archival material is acquired mainly by gift or bequest.

Archives of organisation: Annual reports, minute books and other records, 1826–.
Annual exhibition catalogues, and sales records, 1861–.
Life class registers and associated material, 1843–53; 1866–1901.
Letter collection, 1825–94.

Major collections: William George Gillies RSA (1898–1973) Bequest: letters, cuttings, photographs, notes, catalogues, personal memorabilia and an extensive collection of paintings and drawings.
Files on most 20th-century members and associate members of the RSA, including correspondence, news cuttings and catalogues.

Non-manuscript material: Paintings, drawings, sculptures, photographs, books, catalogues, news cuttings, memorabilia and objects.

Finding aids: Main letter collection listed chronologically with partial name index. Some minute books indexed. Photographs indexed by sitter. NRA(S) 1464.

Facilities: Photocopying.

Conservation: Limited contracting out.

Publications: E. Gordon: *The Royal Scottish Academy, 1826–1976* (1976).
——: *The Making of the Royal Scottish Academy* (RSA, 1988).

306 The Royal Society for the Relief of Indigent Gentlewomen of Scotland

Address: 14 Rutland Square, Edinburgh EH1 2BD

Telephone: (0131) 229 2308

Enquiries: The Secretary, George F. Goddard, MBE

Open: Mon–Fri: 8.45–5.00

Access: Bona fide researchers; an appointment is necessary.

The society was founded in 1847 to assist spinsters and widows with professional or business backgrounds who exist on low incomes and have limited capital resources. It has enjoyed royal patronage since 1930. Among archives held are loose application books of ladies seeking admission to the roll, records of donations and legacies and annual reports, 1850–.

307 The Royal Zoological Society of Scotland

Address: Scottish National Zoological Collection, Murrayfield, Edinburgh EH12 6TS

Telephone: (0131) 334 9171/2/3

Fax: (0131) 316 4050

Enquiries: The Director, Prof. R. J. Wheater

Open: Mon–Fri: 9.00–5.00

Access: Bona fide researchers, by appointment only.

The Royal Zoological Society was constituted in 1910 and opened its zoological gardens in Edinburgh in 1913. It received its royal charter in 1947. The society has been involved in recent years in the provision of a major zoological collection, for conservation of species, environment education, research and recreation. Although there is no formal archive, correspondence documenting the society's history and animal collection is maintained. There are also collections of plans, drawings and photographs. Films have been deposited with the Scottish Film Archive (entry 348).

308 School of Scottish Studies

Parent organisation: University of Edinburgh

Address: 27–29 George Square, Edinburgh EH8 9LD

Telephone: (0131) 650 4160 (Archivist); (0131) 650 4159 (Archive Assistant)

Fax: (0131) 650 6553 (Faculty of Arts)

Enquiries: The Archivist, Dr Alan Bruford or The Archive Assistant, Ms Rhona Talbot

Open: Mon–Fri: 9.30–5.00 (may be closed 12.30–2.00)

Access: Bona fide researchers, with advance notice; charges for extensive use of tape-recordings.

Historical background: The school was founded as an independent research institute of the University of Edinburgh, and the first fieldworker started accumulating transcripts and sound recordings in January 1951. The Sound Archive, backed by photographic, film and videotape archives and a manuscript collection, is the basis for the school's research and its undergraduate teaching, which started in 1971 after the school had become part of the Faculty of Arts in 1965.

Acquisitions policy: Ethnology, including material culture information; folklore, including custom and belief, traditional tales, songs, riddles, rhymes, proverbs etc; ethnomusicology/folk and national music; oral history, including local and social history, life stories and reminiscences, place names, Scots and Gaelic dialects. Principally sound recordings made by own staff and students in Scotland and Scots communities elsewhere, augmented by donations.

Major collections: Written material in this archive supports sound material which constitutes the main archive.
Manuscript Archive: fieldwork notes, tape transcripts and other relevant typescripts, cuttings, microfilms etc, student projects and dissertations, 1951–.
Lucy Broadwood folksong MSS, mainly Gaelic.
Lady Evelyn Stewart-Murray Gaelic folktales MSS from Atholl.
Royal Celtic Society MSS from storytelling competitions at various Gaelic Mòds, 1920s-40s.
Maclagan MSS: information on Gaelic folklore (mostly in English) collected by helpers of Dr R.C. Maclagan (9200 sheets; deposited by the Folklore Society; entry 540).

Non-manuscript material: Sound Archive: field recordings, with place-name survey, linguistic survey, lecture tapes, cassettes, direct-recorded discs and commercial discs, 1951– (c8000).
John Levy archive: ethnomusicological recordings, mainly Asian, and ancillary material, including photographs and films.
Will Forret Bequest: large collection of sound

recordings of Scottish popular and folk music, 1930s-.

Tapes and transcripts from MSC oral history projects in Scotland, e.g. Working People's Oral History in SE Scotland, 1983-5.

There is also a separate photographic archive, including the Atkinson Collection on Scottish islands, for which the archivist is not responsible.

Finding aids: Card index for all media. Sound recordings catalogued in detail, since the early 1980s are now accessible only on a database held in the CASTLE system and tape-by-tape register printouts. NRA(S) informed of oral history recordings.

Facilities: Photocopying. Photography. Sound recording technician available to approved researchers (price-lists available). Printouts from computerised catalogue.

Publications: Material from the archives is published regularly in the school's magazine *Tocher* and the Scottish Tradition series of recordings (now published by Greentax). Information on oral history holdings has been published in the Newsletter of the Scottish Oral History Group, *By Word of Mouth*, 15.

309 Scottish Catholic Archives

Address: Columba House, 16 Drummond Place, Edinburgh EH3 6PL

Telephone: (0131) 556 3661

Enquiries: The Keeper, Dr Christine Johnson

Open: Mon–Fri: 9.30–1.00; 2.00–4.30

Access: Bona fide researchers, by appointment only.

Historical background: Material was collected by Bishop Kyle from various sources at the seminary of Aquhorties College (Deeside), 1799–1829; Preshome (near Buckie), 1829–69; and Blairs College (near Aberdeen), 1829–. The Blairs material was brought to Edinburgh in 1958, the Preshome material in the 1970s and other collections have been added. NB There is no genealogical material.

Acquisitions policy: Each diocese or other body preserves its own modern records but they are encouraged to deposit their older records cen-

trally. Material is acquired throughout Scotland, with priority given to older records.

Major collections: Archives of Archdiocese of St Andrews and Edinburgh and of dioceses of Argyll, Dunkeld, Galloway and Motherwell, 1878–1980.

Archives of Blairs College, 1829–1986.

Records of Friendly Societies, 1812–1970s.

Papers relating to the post-Reformation Roman Catholic Church in Scotland: Archbishop James Beaton (*d* 1603); Scottish mission, 16th–19th centuries, including the Blairs and Preshome letters (*c*50,000 items).

College of the Continent, 16th–19th centuries; in Scotland, 18th–20th centuries; Scots Abbey in Germany, 1177–19th century; Eastern District of Scotland, 19th–20th centuries; Northern and Western Districts of Scotland, 19th century.

Non-manuscript material: Printed books and pamphlets relevant to post-Reformation Scottish Catholicism.

Finding aids: Catalogues. All material prior to 1878 also calendared or (for large collections of letters) at least indexed. A computerised printout of *Summary Handlist of Holdings up to 1878* is available.

Facilities: Photocopying.

Publications: D. McRoberts: 'The Scottish Catholic Archives, 1560–1978', *Innes Review*, xxviii (1977), 59–128.

M. Dilworth: 'The Scottish Catholic Archives', *Catholic Archives*, 1 (1981), 10–19.

See also articles on ongoing work in *Catholic Archives* 4–6, 9–10.

National Inventory of Documentary Sources, Chadwyck-Healey microfiche (1984–).

310 Scottish Ethnological Archive

Parent organisation: National Museums of Scotland

Address: York Buildings, Queen Street, Edinburgh EH2 1JD

Telephone: (0131) 225 7543 ext. 303/347

Fax: (0131) 557 9498

Enquiries: The Curator, Ms D.I. Kidd

Open: Mon–Fri: 9.00–5.00

Access: Bona fide researchers; prior appointment advised and preferred. A charge may be made for any research which is undertaken.

Historical background: The National Museums of Scotland were formed in 1985 from the amalgamation of the Royal Scottish Museum and the National Museum of Antiquities of Scotland (NMAS). The archive, established in 1959 as the Country Life Archive of the NMAS, has since extended its remit to include maritime, urban and industrial collections.

Acquisitions policy: To acquire, through research, donation or purchase, material illustrating Scotland's social and economic history from the early 18th century onwards.

Major collections: Memoirs, diaries, letters, scrapbooks and recorded MS evidence.

Non-manuscript material: Printed ephemera, cuttings, maps, plans and bibliographical references.
Photographs (c100,000) and slides (c10,000).
Small collection of tape-recorded interviews, film and videotape.

Finding aids: Subject catalogue.

Facilities: Photocopying. Photography.

Conservation: In-house paper conservators.

Publications: Guide and Subject Index to the Scottish Ethnological Archive (NMS, 1988).
D.I. Kidd: *To See Ourselves: Rural Scotland in Old Photographs* (NMS/Harper Collins, 1992).
L. Leneman: *Into the Foreground: a Century of Scottish Women in Photographs* (NMS/Alan Sutton, 1993).

311 Scottish National Gallery of Modern Art

Parent organisation: National Galleries of Scotland

Address: Belford Road, Edinburgh EH4 3DR

Telephone: (0131) 556 8921 ext. 312

Fax: (0131) 343 2802

Enquiries: The Librarian/Archivist, Mrs Ann Simpson

Open: Mon–Fri, by arrangement.

Access: Bona fide scholars, strictly by appointment.

Historical background: The Scottish National Gallery of Modern Art opened in 1960 and is part of three sister institutions which make up the National Galleries of Scotland (see also Scottish National Portrait Gallery (entry **312**) and National Gallery of Scotland (entry **293**)). The collection numbers some 4500 items of paintings, sculpture, drawings and prints from about 1900 to the present day. The archive has grown alongside the collection.

Acquisitions policy: Letters, sketchbooks, photographs, videos and tapes concerning 20th-century art, especially material relating to the main collection, as well as 20th-century Scottish art and artists.

Archives of organisation: Material relating to exhibitions organised by the gallery.

Major collections: Artists' papers, including those of Joan Eardly (1921–63), Ian Hamilton Finlay (*b* 1925), W.O. Hutchison (1889–1970), William MacTaggart (1903–81), James Pryde (1866–1941) and Scottie Wilson (1889–1972).

Finding aids: Card catalogue.

312 Scottish National Portrait Gallery

Parent organisation: National Galleries of Scotland

Address: Reference Archive, 1 Queen Street, Edinburgh EH2 1JD

Telephone: (0131) 556 8921

Fax: (0131) 558 3691

Enquiries: The Assistant Keeper, Dr Rosalind K. Marshall

Open: Mon–Fri: 10.00–12.30; 2.00–4.30

Access: Generally open to the public. For lengthy enquiries it is advisable to write in advance.

Historical background: Since the establishment of the gallery in the late 19th century, comprehensive records have been kept of Scottish portraits and portrait painters (see also National Gallery of Scotland (entry **293**) and Scottish National Gallery of Modern Art (entry **311**)).

Acquisitions policy: Engravings, drawings, early photographs and photographs of portraits are acquired on a historical basis for the importance of the sitter in Scottish history, rather than for aesthetic merit. The gallery does not collect MS material.

Non-manuscript material: Portrait engravings (14,000).
Portrait drawings (750).
Hill and Adamson calotypes (5000).
Photographs of portraits in other collections (30,000).
Biographical details of Scottish artists.
Analyses of information about costume, furniture and other aspects of social history.

Finding aids: All materials are indexed by sitter, by artist and for all social history features.

Publications: R.K.Marshall: 'The Scottish National Portrait Gallery as a Source for the Local Historian', *Local Historian*, ii (1975), 382.
R.K. Marshall: 'Scottish Portraits as a Source for the Costume Historian', *Costume*, xv (1981), 67.
S. Stevenson: *David Octavius Hill and Robert Adamson* (National Galleries of Scotland, 1981) [catalogue of holdings].
H. Smailes: *Concise Catalogue* (Edinburgh, 1990) [illustrated; lists portrait drawings as well as paintings in the collection].

313 Scottish Record Office

Address: HM General Register House, Princes Street, Edinburgh EH1 3YY

Telephone: (0131) 556 6585

Fax: (0131) 557 9569

Enquiries: The Keeper of the Records of Scotland

Open: Historical and West Search Rooms: Mon–Fri: 9.00–4.45 Legal Search Room: Mon–Fri: 9.30–4.30

Access: Legal Search Room, HM General Register House: searches of a legal or commercial nature; a fee is charged.
Historical Search Room, HM General Register House, and West Search Room, West Register House: readers' tickets are issued on personal application (not by post). Tickets valid for three years; personal identification necessary before issue. Advance notification strongly advised as 50% of records out-housed.

Historical background: The department originated in the office of the Clerk of the Rolls (13th century), who was responsible for the custody of the non-current records of government and whose successors, the Lord Clerk Register and Deputy-Clerk Register, were also responsible for supervising the framing of the public legal registers and their safe-keeping. The General Register House (f.1774) was designed by Robert Adam as the earliest purpose-built record repository in the British Isles, in order to centralise most of the public and legal records and facilitate access to them. In 1847 the Antiquarian Room, now the Historical Search Room, was opened to the public for the purposes of historical and literary research free of charge. The office of Keeper of the Records of Scotland and the modern development of the Scottish Record Office date from the Public Registers and Records (Scotland) Act, 1948. In 1971 the West Register House, an internal conversion of the former St George's Church, Charlotte Square (f. 1811), was opened as a branch repository, mainly for modern records. In 1994 Thomas Thompson House was opened to store c50% of the records of the SRO.

Acquisitions policy: The SRO is the repository for the public (government and legal) records of Scotland and also assists in preserving Scotland's archival heritage by accepting custody of records for which it is the most suitable repository.

Major collections: The surviving legislative and administrative records of the kingdom of Scotland prior to the parliamentary union with England in 1707, thereafter the records of the various government agencies and departments in Scotland until the present, with regular transmissions of records from the departments of the Secretary of State for Scotland and nationalised industries.
Records of the Scottish central courts (Court of Session and High Court of Justiciary) and many local courts.
Public registers of sasines and deeds relating to property and private rights.
Records of local authorities and churches.
Over 450 separate collections of private archives, family papers, records of institutions, businesses and industrial firms.
Much of the material in private archives, and even in certain public record groups, relates to overseas.
Details of records not in official custody are contained in surveys carried out by the NRA (S), which is a branch of the SRO.

Non-manuscript material: Large collection of maps and plans, many of them hand-drawn, 18th century-.
Photographs in certain record groups; micro-

film holdings of records held both within and outside the SRO; modern records in microfiche (e.g. valuation rolls).

Early printed material, including books, in private archive deposits.

Printed books reference library (limited access), mainly legal, topographical, biographical and general Scottish history, as well as many standard reference works and historical clubs' publications.

Finding aids: Catalogue or reference rooms in both repositories (readers are advised on how to use the repertories, inventories and handlists); indexes in the reference rooms for some record groups. Computerised database of Scottish Office department files now being compiled in West Search Room (interrogated by staff on request). Source lists, prepared and distributed to certain interested bodies and institutions, on major themes, e.g. overseas countries, communications, industry, education, medicine, maritime history etc.

Facilities: Electrostatic copies. Photography and microfilming. The West Search Room is also equipped for map and plan consultation and the use of tape-recorders and portable computers. Computer and Microfilm Search Room with facilities for on-line searches of Gift and Deposit (GD) on CLIO text base (General Register House).

Publications: Full information on accessions and surveys in *Annual Report of the Keeper of the Records of Scotland* [available from SRO and on microfiche from Chadwyck-Healey, *Catalogue of British Official Publications not published by HMSO*].

SRO record publications in print are listed in *British National Archives: Sectional List 24*; SRO Leaflet 15 (free on request) gives details of publications for sale.

Descriptive Lists of Plans and Gifts and Deposits (i.e. private archives) and *A List of American Documents* [obtainable from HMSO and government bookshops].

Guide to the Scottish Record Office [in preparation].

A series of free information leaflets on the history, holdings and facilities of the office, including facilities for research and services for schools, is available free on request.

314 Scottish United Services Museum Library

Parent organisation: National Museums of Scotland

Address: The Castle, Edinburgh EH1 2NG

Telephone: (0131) 225 7534 ext. 404

Fax: (0131) 225 3848

Enquiries: The Library Assistant-in-Charge, Edith Philip

Open: Mon, Wed: 10.00–12.30; 2.00–5.00 Tues, Thurs: 10.00–12.30, by arrangement.

Access: Bona fide researchers, by appointment only.

Historical background: The Scottish United Services Museum was established in 1930.

Acquisitions policy: To acquire by purchase and donation material on the history of the Scottish soldier, sailor and airman. There is limited purchase of MSS material. Most new items are acquired with museum objects.

Archives of organisation: Complete MSS accessions register.

Correspondence of former keepers of the Museum.

General records of buildings and administration.

Major collections: 603 (City of Edinburgh) Squadron correspondence, combat reports, benevolent fund etc, 1927–52.

Ronald Ball's notes on the Scots Army.

Dalrymple-White papers, 1720–1954.

Henry McCance: notes for regimental history of the Royal Scots, 1913.

Regimental order books, 1745–.

Wilson of Bannockburn (clothing contractors): correspondence with regiments, 18th and 19th centuries.

Scots Greys MSS.

Papers relating to Maj. John McBlain, Scots Guards, c1830–c1884.

Correspondence of Gen. Sir David Baird (1759–1829), 1799–1828, with other related papers, 1772–c1855.

Non-manuscript material: Set of World War I trench maps and aerial photographs.

Print and photographs collection (c10,000 items).

World War I service medal roll (microfiche, slightly imperfect).

Cumberland Papers (microfilm; originals in Royal Archives, Windsor, entry 1088).

Finding aids: Catalogues of all material. Baird: NRA 27982.

Facilities: Photocopying. Photography. Microfilm/fiche readers.

Conservation: Limited paper conservation through National Museums of Scotland Library (entry **296**).

315 University of Edinburgh Library

Address: George Square, Edinburgh EH8 9LJ

A Special Collections

Telephone: (0131) 650 3412 (Special Collections) 650 6865 (Edinburgh University Archives)

Fax: (0131) 650 6863

Enquiries: The Librarian, Special Collections or the University Archivist, Mr A.T. Wilson

Open: Term: Mon–Thurs: 9.00–9.00 Vacation: Mon–Fri: 9.00–5.00
Closed 2nd week of August, Scottish spring and autumn holidays.

Access: By written application to the University Librarian.

Historical background: The library was founded by the bequest of books from the library of Clement Little in 1580 to the Town and Kirk of Edinburgh; it was transferred to the town's college (later university) in 1584. The Librarian, Special Collections, is also responsible for the small collections in the Reid Music Library and Royal Dick Veterinary College.

Acquisitions policy: To strengthen existing collections in certain fields by purchase and donation.

Archives of organisation: University archives: historical collections relating to students and teaching in the university, including Medical School, 18th and 19th century; papers of Robert Jameson, Sir A. Geikie, Sir C. Lyell and Sir R.I. Murchison *re* natural history and geology.

Major collections: Laing Collection: rich in material relating to Scottish letters and history. Oriental MSS (*c*650): include MSS transferred from New College (entry **315C**), and a small collection of palm-leaf MSS. Western MSS: medieval items (*c*330), MSS in Scottish Enlightenment medicine, Africa, Scot-

tish Gaelic; modern Scottish literary collections include Hugh MacDiarmid (1892–1978), George Mackay Brown (*b* 1921); archives of other 20th-century writers: Arthur Koestler, Thomas Allinson, John Middleton Murry, Colin Legum and John Wain; papers of many scientists, geologists and doctors; Edinburgh University staff and student correspondence and papers.
Business archives, including Thomas Nelson & Son Ltd, publishers (includes John Buchan correspondence); Christian Salvesen Ltd, Leith (whaling in Antarctica).
Records of Scottish Liberal Association.

Non-manuscript material: Architectural drawings and plans of W.H. Playfair, Sir Rowand Anderson, Sir Robert Lorimer.
Thomson-Walker collection of engraved portraits of medical men.
University medals.
Sir Patrick Geddes (1854–1932) archive: urban planning.
Kennedy-Fraser wax cylindrical recordings.
Rare book collections in all fields, 15th–20th centuries.

Finding aids: Guide to MSS collections in the main library. Index to MSS, with separate files relating to individual collections. Shelf-lists of business and university archives.

Facilities: Photocopying. Photography. Microfilm/fiche reader.

Conservation: In-house conservators.

Publications: Rev. J. Anderson (ed.): *Calendar of the Laing Charters, AD 854–1837, Belonging to the University of Edinburgh* (Edinburgh, 1899).
Report on the Laing Manuscripts Preserved in the University of Edinburgh, Historical Manuscripts Commission (London, 1914–25) [2 vols].
C.R. Borland: *A Descriptive Catalogue of the Western Medieval Manuscripts in Edinburgh University Library* (Edinburgh, 1916).
M.A. Hukk, H. Ethé and E. Robertson: *A Descriptive Catalogue of the Arabic and Persian Manuscripts in Edinburgh University Library* (Hereford, 1925).
R.B. Serjeant: *A Handlist of the Arabic, Persian and Hindustani MSS of New College* (London, 1942).
J.R. Walsh: 'The Turkish Manuscripts in New College, Edinburgh', *Oriens*, xii (1959), 171.
Index to Manuscripts (Boston, 1964) [2 vols]; *First Supplement* (Boston, 1981).

N.R. Ker: *Medieval Manuscripts in British Libraries*, ii (Oxford, 1977), 589.

M.C.T. Simpson: 'The Special Collections', in J.R. Guild and A. Law (eds), *Edinburgh University Library, 1580–1980* (1982).

The Koestler Archive in Edinburgh University Library: a Checklist (Edinburgh, 1987).

B Lothian Health Services Archive

Telephone: (0131) 650 3392

Enquiries: Dr Mike Barfoot

Open: Mon–Fri: 9.00–5.00

Access: Generally open to the public, by appointment. Patient records have a 100–year closure period. Administrative records are closed for 30 years.

Historical background: The Royal Infirmary of Edinburgh was founded in 1729. It appointed an archivist in 1967. In 1974 the remit of the archivist was widened to include all the hospitals of Lothian Health Board. The collections are managed by the University Library by agreement with the various hospital trusts.

Acquisitions policy: To acquire or catalogue *in situ* records of the Lothian Health Services hospitals.

Archives of organisation: Records of Royal Infirmary, Chalmers Hospital, Royal Hospital for Sick Children, Leith Hospital, City Hospital, Simpson Maternity Hospital.

Major collections: Papers of: Alexander Murray Drennan (1884–1984), pathologist; Sir Derrick Melville Dunlop (1902–80), Christison Professor of Therapeutics and Clinical Medicine, Edinburgh University; Ernst Julius Levin (1887–1975), neurologist; Elsie Stephenson (1916–67), Director of Nursing Studies Unit. Medical-Chirurgical Society of Edinburgh; transactions, laws, lists of members, minutes, letter-book, agendas, 1821–1959.

Non-manuscript material: Photograph collection.

Finding aids: There are typescript lists, which are sent to NRA(S), for most collections. Card index to photographs.

Facilities: Photocopying. Photography. Microfilming.

C New College Library

Address: Mound Place, Edinburgh EH1 2LU

Telephone: (0131) 650 9856

Fax: (0131) 650 6579

Enquiries: The Librarian, Special Collections, (see **A** above), or direct

Open: Term: Mon–Thurs: 9.00–9.30 Fri: 9.00–5.00 Sat: 9.00–12.30 Vacation: Mon–Fri: 9.00–5.00

Access: By written application to the Librarian of New College, Dr M.C.T. Simpson.

Historical background: The college was founded in 1843 when training for the Free Church ministry began. The library has become one of the chief British research collections in theological, religious, historical and other subjects. After the Church Union of 1900, a large proportion of the library of the United Presbyterian Church College (Synod Hall) was acquired, and in more recent years the General Assembly (Tolbooth) Library of the Church of Scotland was incorporated. In 1935, as a result of the 1929 Reunion, New College formally became also the university's Faculty of Divinity, and in 1963 the library was placed on permanent deposit with the university. It is now administered as a detached section of the university library.

Acquisitions policy: To add to the Thomas Chalmers archive by purchase or gift. To add to existing collections of papers of Scottish church leaders, and, selectively, other material relevant to the religious life of Scotland, and to the ecumenical and hymnology collections.

Archives of organisation: New College archives and historical papers. Papers of principals and professors of New College, 19th and 20th centuries, including John Baillie (1886–1960) and James Stuart Stewart (1896–1990).

Major collections: Archive of Thomas Chalmers (1780–1847), leader of Free Church of Scotland, social reformer, c1760–1890.

MSS relating to individuals and events in Scottish church history, including Alexander Thomson (1798–1868) of Banchory; papers of John White (1867–1951) relating to reunion of Church of Scotland and United Free Church of Scotland, 1929; James King Hewison papers on the Covenanters, 17th century; letters, journals and sermons of Robert Baillie, 1637–62; James Kirkwood, provision of the Irish Bible in Scotland, and establishment of Highland Libraries, 1676–1709; Thomas Brown, archive for Annals of the Disruption, 1843; James

Denney (1856–1917) of Glasgow United Free College; Scottish Ecclesiological Society papers. Westminster Assembly of Divines minutes, 1643–52.

Sermons of Covenanters, 17th century; and Secession ministers, 18th century.

Ecumenical Collection, including: Church of Scotland Special Committee on Anglican–Presbyterian relations, 1961–6; Christian Unity Association, 1904–56;

Balfour of Burleigh papers on church reunion, to 1913.

Archibald Campbell Craig (1888–1985), British Council of Churches.

J.H. Oldham (1874–1969), papers.

Non-manuscript material: Ecumenical collection of printed books, pamphlets and microfilm of the World Council of Churches, British Council of Churches and Scottish Council of Churches.

James Thin hymnology collection (7000 printed items).

Finding aids: Inventories and indexes.

Facilities: Photocopying. Microfilm/fiche readers. Microfilming and photography in main university library building.

Publications: H. Watt: *New College, Edinburgh: a Centenary History* (Edinburgh, 1946).

316 Royal Holloway and Bedford New College
College Archives

Parent organisation: University of London

Address: Egham Hill, Egham, Surrey TW20 0EX

Telephone: (01784) 434455

Fax: (01784) 473662

Enquiries: The Archivist

Open: By appointment.

Access: Approved researchers, on written application to the secretary/registrar.

Historical background: The Royal Holloway College, built in French Renaissance style to the design of the architect William Henry Crossland, was founded and endowed in 1883 by Thomas Holloway, the Victorian philanthropist who made a fortune from patent medicines. It was officially opened by Queen Victoria in 1886. Originally instituted as a women's college, it began admitting men in 1965. In 1985 the new college was formed by a merger with Bedford College (f. in 1849 as a women's college), which moved to Egham from Regent's Park. It has faculties of arts, music and science.

Acquisitions policy: To collect official records of the college in all its aspects and to acquire miscellaneous material relating to the history of the Royal Holloway College, including its picture gallery, and of Bedford College. Collections are being sought in support of the archive's developing role as a focus for a centre for the history of women.

Archives of organisation: Board of Governors' records, 1886–1949, and Council records, 1949–; records of the academic board, academic departments, library, administrative and residence departments, associations, committees, clubs and societies.

Major collections: Some deposited papers of those associated with the colleges.

Non-manuscript material: A variety of miscellaneous material relating to the college and the parent colleges, including photographs of the buildings and of members of the college and their activities; items relating to Thomas Holloway and his family; historical notes, newspaper articles and cuttings; reminiscences and memoirs of members of the college; verses and fiction; prints, drawings and watercolours.

Finding aids: TS catalogue of the archives of Bedford College, 1849–1985, 143pp.

Facilities: Photocopying.

Publications: D. Paul: *Royal Holloway College Archives: a Guide* (1973).
J. Chapel: *Victorian Taste: the Complete Catalogue of Paintings in the Royal Holloway College* [of relevance to letters in the archives about the picture gallery and its paintings].

317 Gordonstoun

Address: Elgin, Grampian IV30 2RF

Telephone: (01343) 830 445

Fax: (01343) 830 074

Enquiries: The Hon. Archivist, D.A. Byatt

Open: By arrangement only.

Access: By appointment to researchers.

Historical background: An ancient Scottish estate since the 13th century, Gordonstoun has been a public school since 1934. Gordon Cumming private family papers (owners of Gordonstoun from 17th century to 1934) are deposited in the National Library of Scotland (entry **294**).

Acquisitions policy: Any papers on the estate, past and present staff, former pupils or past governors are most welcome.

Archives of organisation: Minutes of boys', staff and governors' meetings; material relating to the school's varied activities; letters to/from past headmasters, governors and old boys; general administrative papers.

Non-manuscript material: Pamphlets and photographs.
Plans, maps and drawings.

Finding aids: Various lists and indexes.

Facilities: Photocopying.

Publications: H.L. Brereton: *Gordonstoun* (Aberdeen, 1968/R1981).
D.A. Byatt: *Kurt Hahn: an Appreciation of his Life and Work* (Gordonstoun).

318 David Owen Archive

Parent organisation: Boat Museum Trust

Address: The Boat Museum, Dockyard Road, Ellesmere Port, South Wirral L65 4EP

Telephone: (0151) 355 5017

Fax: (0151) 355 4079

Enquiries: The Archive Office, Mr Lynn Doylerush

Open: Mon–Thurs: 11.00–4.00

Access: Generally open to the public with canal-related enquiries.

Historical background: The Boat Museum opened in 1976 with a modest collection of four craft of the inland navigations and then began gathering documents, photographs, artefacts, books and information relating to canals worldwide. The David Owen Archive was officially opened in 1990 and is now an important repository of canal records. The museum is situated in the old transhipment dock of Ellesmere Port which connects the Shropshire Union Canal to the Manchester Ship Canal. The museum represents an embodiment of the canal age based very largely on the evidence of the archive.

Acquisitions policy: To collect material and informative evidence relating to the history of inland navigations. This includes craft, artefacts, boatbuilding drawings, maps, working records, documents, parliamentary material, photographs, books, audio-visual evidence and other relevant items. The collecting policy extends beyond British canals to world canals where appropriate.

Archives of organisation: Archives of the Boat Museum Trust.

Major collections: David Owen Collection of documents, photographs, slides and artefacts. Denys Hutchings Collection of papers, books and slides.
Weaver Navigation Files (on loan from British Waterways, NW Division).

Non-manuscript material: Michel Ware Collection of photographs and postcards.
John Heap Collection: Library of the Inland Waterways Association (on long-term loan).
Daphne Roswell Collection of artefacts, books and slides.
Hadfield Collection of books, articles and slides relating to World Canals.

Finding aids: Card indexes and collection lists. Computerisation in progress.

Facilities: Photocopying.

Conservation: Paper conservation is carried out by the North West Museums Service.

Publications: The Boat Museum Brochure.
Development of a Dock Area (Archive Pack no. 1).
Canals in Cheshire (Archive Pack no. 2).

319 Fermanagh District Museum

Parent organisation: Fermanagh District Council

Address: Enniskillen Castle, Castle Barracks, Enniskillen, Co. Fermanagh BT74 7HL

Telephone: (01365) 325000

Fax: (01365) 327342

Enquiries: Ms H. Lanigan Wood

Open: By appointment only.

Access: Bona fide researchers, by prior arrangement.

Historical background: The County Museum is situated within the precincts of the 15th-century Enniskillen Castle, which houses a separate regimental museum for the Royal Enniskillen Fusiliers.

Acquisitions policy: To maintain and build on the collection relating to Co. Fermanagh only.

Major collections: Co. Fermanagh criminal books, 1861–1969, and proclamations.
Parish of Derrymacausey primary school register, 1844–1954.
Lady Dorothy Lowry-Corry correspondence, 1931–5.
Canon W.H. Dundas (*d* 1941), family papers.

Non-manuscript material: Photographs, maps, posters, sound archives and ephemera.

Facilities: Photocopying.

Conservation: Contracted out.

320 Epsom College Archive

Address: Epsom College, Epsom, Surrey KT17 4JQ

Telephone: (01372) 721973 (Epsom College Common Room)

Enquiries: The Archivist, Mr A.G. Scadding

Open: During school term, by arrangement.

Access: Bona fide researchers, by appointment.

Historical background: Epsom College was founded in 1851 as the Royal Medical Benevolent College in direct response to the inadequacies perceived in the medical profession during the epidemics of the 1830s and 1840s. It opened as a school and asylum for the medical profession in 1855. Development by 1900 resulted in an independent school of international reputation. Strong links with medical colleges were formed in the 1890s, by which time the college was one of the pioneers of science education. The archive was begun in 1980, but inherited an important run of scrapbooks and minute books, beginning with the foundation in 1851. Material relates to the money-raising activities of the profession, the public elections to pensioners and scholarships, the growth of the school, royal connections and the development of buildings.

Archives of organisation: Bound minutes, accounts, photograph albums, headmasters' book, scrapbooks etc.
Headmasters' archive: collection of interesting correspondence.
Bursars' archive: documents relating to diet; trenches and evacuation in event of invasion in 1940s; rationing; employment and plans of development.
Trivia boxes: general collections of school-related items for every ten years.
Special collections of sports club and departmental material.

Non-manuscript material: Photograph boxes, 19th century–.
Maps and plans.
Drainage and works records, including plans by Sir Joseph Bazalgette (1819–91).

Finding aids: Handlists with keys to main sources.

Facilities: Photocopying and some photographic facilities on request.

Publications: M.A. Salmon, *Epsom College: the First 125 Years.*

321 Evesham Public Library

Parent organisation: Hereford and Worcester County Council

Address: Oat Street, Evesham, Worcester WR11 4PJ

Telephone: (01386) 442291

Fax: (01386) 765855

Enquiries: The Librarian, Mrs C. Evans

Open: Mon, Tues, Fri: 9.30–5.30 Thurs: 9.30–8.00 Sat: 9.30–4.00

Access: Generally open to the public. No appointment necessary. Restriction on use of photograph collection.

Major collections: Principally non-MS material, including collection of E.A.B. Barnard (*d* 1953), local historian.
Complete holding of *Evesham Journal* and its photograph collection.

Facilities: Photocopying. Microfilm/fiche reader/printer.

322 The Courtenay Archives

Address: Powderham Castle, Kenton, Exeter, Devon EX6 8JQ

Telephone: (01626) 891367

Fax: (01626) 890729 or 890187 (Archivist)

Enquiries: The Archivist, Lt.-Col. C.G. Delforce

Open: By arrangement.

Access: Approved researchers and genealogists, by appointment only. Charge depends on staff involvement.

Powderham Castle has been owned and occupied by the Courtenay family, Earls of Devon, since 1393. The archives consist of family and estate records, plans and maps, mainly for the 19th and 20th centuries, earlier material being deposited in Devon Record Office, Exeter (entry **323**). Genealogical records of the Courtenay family worldwide are maintained. There is an index to the MSS and pictures, and photocopying and photography are available.

323 Devon Record Office

Address: Castle Street, Exeter, Devon EX4 3PU

Telephone: (01392) 384253

Fax: (01392) 384250

Enquiries: The County Archivist, Mrs M.M. Rowe

Open: Mon–Thurs: 9.30–5.00 Fri: 9.30–4.30 Sat (1st and 3rd of each month): 9.30–12.00
There is a daily or annual charge, but some exceptions.

Historical background: The old County Record Office was established in 1952 and the former Exeter City Record Office (originally Exeter MSS Department of the library) was established in 1947. In 1974 the latter became the East Devon Office, and it amalgamated with the old County Office in 1977. The office also acts as the Diocesan Record Office for Exeter and is recognised as a place of deposit for public records. There are branch offices at Plymouth (entry **939**), Barnstaple (entry **48**), and Exeter Cathedral (entry **324**).

Acquisitions policy: Archival material relevant to the historic county of Devon.

Archives of organisation: Usual local authority record holdings.

Major collections: Deposited collections, including the following which have a wider significance:
Papers of Henry Addington, first Viscount Sidmouth (1757–1844); Gen. John Graves Simcoe, relating to Canada and the campaign in the West Indies, 1776–97.

Non-manuscript material: Microfilms of papers of William Buckland (1784–1856), geologist, and his son Frank Buckland (1809–91), naturalist.

Facilities: Photocopying. Photography and microfilming by arrangement. Microfilm reader/printer.

Finding aids: Catalogues and indexes; sent to NRA.

Conservation: In-house department.

Publications: List available on request.

324 Exeter Cathedral

A Archives

Address: Diocesan House, Palace Gate, Exeter, Devon EX1 1HX

Telephone: (01392) 495954

Enquiries: Mrs A.A. Doughty

Open: Mon–Fri: 2.00–5.00, by arrangement.

Access: Serious researchers, by appointment only.

Historical background: A monastery existed here as early as 670 AD. A cathedral church was established in 1050 and consecrated in 1113. The archives are now administered by the Devon Record Office (entry **323**) on behalf of the Dean and Chapter of Exeter Cathedral.

Acquisitions policy: Restricted to records directly relating to the cathedral, its personnel and its present and former properties.

Archives of organisation: Capitular archives: royal diplomas, 10th–11th centuries; charters, deeds, leases; lawsuits etc; chapter acts, late 14th century–; registers, cartularies etc; rentals, surveys, manorial records, maps, plans etc; accounts, 12th century–; deeds, agreements and manorial records, 18th–19th century, redeposited by the Church Commissioners.
Archives of Vicars Choral, 13th–20th centuries, of a similar nature to the capitular archives.

Archives of Archdeaconry of Exeter: court records, visitations etc, 17th century–.
Paper of Henry Phillpotts, Bishop of Exeter (1778–1869).

Non-manuscript material: Accumulating collection of photographs and coloured photographic slides, mainly of architectural and sculptural details of the cathedral, primarily to record the continuing conservation programme.

Finding aids: MS catalogue of part of the capitular archives (compiled by A. Stuart Moore, 1873); gradually being superseded by numerous lists, card catalogues and indexes in progress. Complete summary class lists in typescript of records of the College of Vicars Choral and of the Archdeaconry of Exeter. Phillpotts: NRA 25909.

Facilities: Photocopying. Photography by arrangement. Microfiche reader.

Conservation: Work undertaken by Devon Record Office, with grants from the Friends of the Cathedral.

Publications: L.J. Lloyd and A.M. Erskine: *The Library of Exeter Cathedral, with a Short Description of the Archives* (Exeter, 1967/ R1974).
A.M. Erskine (ed. & trans.): *The Accounts of the Fabric of Exeter Cathedral, 1279–1353*, Devon & Cornwall Record Society, new series, vols 24, 26 (Exeter, 1981–3).

B Library

Address: Diocesan House, Palace Gate, Exeter, Devon EX1 1HX

Telephone: (01392) 72894

Enquiries: Mr P.W. Thomas

Open: Mon–Fri: 2.00–5.00

Access: Generally open to the public; appointment appreciated if medieval MSS required for study.

Historical background: The library was founded by a gift of 66 MSS by Leofric, Bishop of Exeter (*d* 1072), and has had a continuous history since that date. The medieval MSS, including the Exeter Book of Poetry (10th century) and the Exon Domesday (11th century), remain in the library under the administration of the University of Exeter (entry

326). Books, pamphlets and a few MSS have accumulated since the post-medieval period.

Acquisitions policy: The collection is virtually static, though gifts would be considered, and an attempt might be made to acquire any MSS of direct relevance to the existing stock.

Facilities: Photocopying. Photography. Microfilming (by Exeter University reprographic department).

Publications: HMC *Report on Manuscripts in Various Collections*, IV, 23–95 (1907).
M.P. Crichton: *A Catalogue of the Medical Books and Manuscripts, including a Selection of Scientific Works, in Exeter Cathedral Library* (Exeter, 1934).
N.R. Ker: *Medieval Manuscripts in British Libraries*, ii (Oxford, 1977), 800–46.

325 Exeter Central Library

Parent organisation: Devon County Council Libraries

Address: Castle Street, Exeter, Devon EX4 3PQ

Telephone: (01392) 384216 (direct line)

Fax: (01392) 385905

Enquiries: The Westcountry Studies Librarian

Open: Tues, Thurs: 9.30–8.00 Wed, Fri: 9.30–6.00 Sat: 9.30–4.00

Access: Generally open to the public; prior enquiry advisable.

Historical background: Devon Library Services was formed out of a number of separate library authorities on local government reorganisation in 1974. Two of these authorities, Exeter and Plymouth, were established in the 19th century and had considerable MS collections. They both suffered in World War II and their archives are now administered by Devon Record Office (entry 323). Most MSS in Devon Library Services are now non-archival in nature and relatively few in number. They are to be found mainly in the Westcountry Studies Library in Exeter, with some local history collections at Barnstaple, Plymouth, Torquay and central libraries (entries 48, 937 and 1056).

Acquisitions policy: To acquire non-archival MSS which reflect the development of Devon and South-West England.

Major collections: Several hundred MSS and

TSS, mainly on local antiquarian or genealogical topics, including the writings of historians such as Tristram Risdon (?1580–1640) and James Davidson (1793–1864), and several surveys of Devon churches.

A few literary MSS by R.D. Blackmore (1825–1900), John Galsworthy (1867–1933), Eden Phillpotts (1862–1960), Sabine Baring-Gould (1834–1924) and Neil Bell.

Devon and Cornwall Record Society collection of transcripts of parish records (1200 vols; available to members only).

J. Brooking Rowe Collection of rubbings of monumental brasses.

Non-manuscript material: Extensive collections of illustrations, newspaper-cutting files, ephemera, maps relating to South West England.

Rare book collection, including 2500 pre-1800 imprints.

Small collections of sound and film recordings.

Finding aids: Card indexes and computerised files giving access by author, place and subject.

Facilities: Photocopying. Microfilm/fiche reader/printers.

Conservation: Some work undertaken by Devon Record Office; other work contracted out.

Publications: Some material listed in A. Brockett (comp.): *The Devon Union List* (Exeter, 1977).

Some MSS items in *Abbots Bickington to Zeal Monachorum: a Handlist of Devon Parish Histories* (Exeter, 1994).

Publications list available.

326 University of Exeter Library

Address: Stocker Road, Exeter, Devon EX4 4PT

Telephone: (01392) 263870

Fax: (01392) 263871

Enquiries: The Librarian

Open: Mon–Fri: 9.00–5.30

Access: By written application to the librarian.

Historical background: The university library dates from 1955, when the university received its charter, but some of its stock dates back to the early years of the 20th century.

Acquisitions policy: Archives and MSS are occasionally purchased but the majority of items are gifts.

Archives of organisation: University archives, 1955–.

Major collections: Literary: papers and MSS of R.D. Blackmore (1825–1900), Henry Williamson (1895–1977), Jack Clemo, Charles Causley (*b* 1917) and Ted Hughes (*b* 1930).

Local history: local newspapers, prints and MSS.

Theatre: large collection of playbills of the Theatre Royal, Exeter, *c*1890 to early 1950s.

Autographs: small collection of 19th–century autographs and letters.

Astronomy: archives of Sir Norman Lockyer (1836–1920).

West Indies: collection of papers relating to estates and slavery in Jamaica.

Non-manuscript material: Early maps, mainly of Devon and Cornwall.

Photographs relating to former British colonies.

Very large collection of tapes, records and CDs of American music, especially jazz and blues (*c*7500; see *Archives*, xx/87 (1992), 121).

Finding aids: Lists.

Facilities: Photocopying. Photography. Microfiche.

Publications: *Manuscript Collections* (1984).

327 Eyam Hall

Address: Eyam, Sheffield S30 1QW

Telephone: (01433) 631976

Fax: (01433) 631976

Enquiries: The Administrator, Miss Carolyn Fooks

Open: By appointment.

Access: Generally open to scholars by prior arrangement.

Eyam Hall was built in 1671–2 by a junior branch of the Derbyshire family of Wright of Great Longstone. It has been the home of the Wrights of Eyam ever since and is today the home of R. H. V. Wright Esq. Archives consist of family papers, deeds (mainly for Derbyshire), late 17th century–, papers relating to lead-mining, and photographs. A list of the collection is in preparation. Photocopying, with some restrictions, is available.

328 Falkirk Library

Parent organisation: Falkirk District Council

Address: Hope Street, Falkirk, Central
FK1 5AU

Telephone: (01324) 624911 ext. 2316/2259

Fax: (01324) 614027

Enquiries: The Reference Librarian

Open: Mon–Tues, Thurs: 9.30–8.00 Wed, Fri–
Sat: 9.30–5.00

Access: Generally open to the public, by
appointment.

Major collections: Scottish Metalworkers'
Union minutes; Town Council minutes.

Non-manuscript material: Local newspapers,
1845–.
Census returns.
Press cutting collection.
Small collection of photographs, films and
videos of Falkirk district social events.

Finding aids: Index to press cuttings; partial
index to newspapers.

Facilities: Photocopying. Microfilm reader/
printer.

329 Falkirk Museums, History Research Centre

Parent organisation: Falkirk District Council

Address: Callendar House, Callendar Park,
Falkirk, Central FK1 1YR

Telephone: (01324) 612134

Fax: (01324) 614026

Enquiries: The Museum Archivist, History
Research Centre

Open: Mon–Fri: 10.00–12.30; 1.30–5.00

Access: Generally open to the public.

Historical background: The museum was
founded in 1926 as a bequest by Mungo Buchanan, architect and antiquarian, and was based on
his collection of MSS and photographic material. The collections were extended to form a
local history archive primarily for the town of
Falkirk, and, with local government reorganisation in 1975, for the whole of Falkirk District.

Acquisitions policy: To strengthen existing
primary and secondary collections in the local
history and industrial history fields by purchase

and donation of material related to Falkirk
District.

Archives of organisation: Museum records,
1926–.

Major collections: Burns Collection: diaries,
MSS and ephemera, 1796–1860.
Kirklands diary, transcript and notes, 1722–6.
Love Collection: note-books and MSS, 1877–
1928.
Buchanan Collection: site plans, sketches.
Grangemouth Dockyard trial books and ship
plans, 1860–1970.
Grangemouth Cooperative Society: adminis-
trative records, minutes.
Bo'ness Seabox Society (beneficent society),
papers, 1634–20th century.
Bo'ness Town Council: administrative records,
and ephemera, 1663–1975.

Non-manuscript material: Maps and plans,
Falkirk District, 18th and 19th centuries.
Foundry catalogues, 1860–1960.
Photographic collection: townscapes, people,
industries, archaeological excavations, 1860–
(21,000 items).
Small oral history series on cassettes.
Offprint collection of secondary reference
material.

Finding aids: Card and computerised lists and
indexes. NRA(S) 1003. Bibliographical and
trades indexes.

Facilities: Photocopying. Photography.
Microfiche reader/printer. Slide hire.

330 St Michael's Abbey

Address: 280 Farnborough Road,
Farnborough, Hants GU14 7NQ

Telephone: (01252) 546105

Fax: (01252) 372822

Enquiries: The Archivist/Librarian

Open: Strictly by appointment only.

Access: By previous private arrangement.

The church and monastery were built between
1883 and 1888 and stand opposite the former
residence of the Empress Eugénie (1826–1920).
In 1895 they were occupied by Benedictine
monks from the Abbey of Solesmes, France,
and 50 years later were handed over to English
monks. Monastic archives exist, 1895–, plus
plans, drawings etc of the grade I abbey church.

There is also an abbey library with special reference to the French Second Empire (1848–70).

331 Kent Archives Office
South East Kent Branch

Address: Folkestone Central Library, Grace Hill, Folkestone, Kent CT20 1HD

Telephone: (01303) 850123

Fax: (01303) 242907

Enquiries: The Heritage Officer, Mrs Janet Adamson

Open: Heritage Room: Mon–Sat: 9.30–5.00

Access: Generally open to the public, by appointment.

Historical background: The office was established in 1976 following local government reorganisation. The library had already accumulated a considerable collection of archives, the bulk pertaining to the Borough of Folkestone.

Acquisitions policy: Archival material relating to the Shepway District.

Archives of organisation: Usual local authority record holdings, including records and MSS for Folkstone Town Council and Boards of Guardians for Eltham and Romney Marsh.

Major collections: Deposited collections, primarily of local interest, including company papers, school log-books, Methodist Circuit records.

Non-manuscript material: Photograph albums, glass negatives, maps and plans.

Facilities: Photocopying. Microfilm/fiche reader/printer.

Publications: Second Supplement to the Guide to the Kent Archives Office.
Guide to Folkestone Heritage Services.

332 German Occupation Museum

Address: Forest, Guernsey, Channel Islands GV8 0BG

Telephone: (01481) 38205

Enquiries: The Director

Open: Summer: Mon–Sun: 10.30–5.00 Winter: Sun: 2.00–5.00
Closed December and January.

Access: By appointment only.

Historical background: The museum was founded by the present director, R.L. Heaume, in 1966 to document and depict the German occupation in the Channel Islands, 1940–45.

Acquisitions policy: German occupation material, including archives and photographs relating solely to the Channel Islands, 1940–45.

Major collections: Diaries of Frank Barton, 1940–44, and Rev. Ord, 1940–45.

Non-manuscript material: Complete set of newspapers of Guernsey, 1940– 45 (censored by the German Press Censor).
Video and sound archives.

Finding aids: List of video and sound archives.

Publications: Numerous publications on the German occupation (list on request).

333 Falconer Museum

Parent organisation: Moray District Council, Museums Division

Address: Tolbooth Street, Forres, Grampian IV36 0PH

Telephone: (01309) 673701

Enquiries: The Museums Development Officer, R.B. Inglis

Open: April–May, Oct: Mon–Sat: 10.00–5.30
June, Sept: Mon–Sat: 9.30–6.00 Sun: 2.00–5.00
July–Aug: Mon–Sat: 9.30–6.00 Sun: 12.00–5.30
Nov–April: Mon–Fri: 10.00–12.30; 1.30–4.30

Access: Bona fide researchers, preferably with a reference and by written appointment.

The Falconer Museum is the headquarters of the Museums Division. It was established following a bequest by Alexander Falconer in the 1860s and was transferred to the custody of the local authority in 1975. The holdings include the archive of Hugh Falconer (1808–65), palaeontologist and botanist, 1836–65; and diaries and correspondence of Peter Anson (1889–1975), marine painter and recorder of maritime topics, 1919–75. Photography is available. See P.J. Boylan: *The Falconer Papers, Forres* (Leicestershire Museums, Art Galleries and Records Services, 1977).

334 Moray District Record Office

Address: The Tolbooth, Forres, Grampian IV36 0AB

Telephone: (01309) 673617

Fax: (01309) 674166

Enquiries: The District Archivist, Dr David Iredale

Open: Mon–Fri: 9.00–4.30

Access: Generally open to the public.

Historical background: The department was established by Moray District Council in 1975.

Acquisitions policy: To collect and preserve official archives and private muniments referring to the Moray District.

Archives of organisation: Usual local authority record holdings: archives of pre-1975 authorities in Moray, including three royal and nine police burghs, county councils and commissioners of supply, district councils, water authorities, schools, parishes, 1268–1975.

Major collections: Records of Anderson's Institution (free school), Forres, 1823–88; Forres guildry, 1767–1888; county turnpike and commutation roads, 1805–64; customs and excise (Moray), 1870–1915; Justice of the Peace courts (Moray), 1712–1975; Kirk sessions (Moray parishes), 1584–1994; Presbytery (Moray), 1635–1972.
Papers of Isaac Forsyth, bookseller, Elgin: correspondence with his brother Joseph, 1800–15; Duff (solicitor; town, county, JP and sheriff clerk), correspondence, 1752–1861; Grant of Tannach family, 1783–1857.

Non-manuscript material: Architectural plans of J.W. Wittet, 1826–1990, and Doig & Morrison, including distillery, 1850–1980.

Finding aids: Lists, calendars and card index of persons, places and subjects.

Facilities: Photocopying.

335 West Highland Museum

Address: Cameron Square, Fort William, Highland PH33 6AJ

Telephone: (01397) 702169

Enquiries: The Curator, Fiona C. Marwick

Open: Mon–Fri: 10.00–1.00; 2.00–5.00

Access: Anyone may consult the records but preference will always be given to members; an appointment is essential.

The museum was founded in 1922. It is independent and self-financing and was set up to collect and preserve everything of relevance to the West Highlands. The principal collection is of Jacobite papers, including Cluny family correspondence, 1578–1825 (NRA 13685).

336 Gateshead Libraries and Arts Service
Local Studies Department

Address: Central Library, Prince Consort Road, Gateshead, Tyne and Wear NE8 4LN

Telephone: (0191) 477 3478

Fax: (0191) 477 7454

Enquiries: The Local Studies Librarian, Miss E. Carnaffin

Open: Mon, Tues, Thurs, Fri: 9.00–7.00 Wed: 9.00–5.00 Sat: 9.00–1.00

Access: Generally open to the public.

Historical background: The local history collection has existed since the opening of the library in 1884. It became a separate local studies and archives department in 1974.

Acquisitions policy: Documents relating to the area covered by Gateshead Metropolitan Borough Council.

Major collections: The collections include the Cotesworth MSS: estate papers for the 17th and 18th centuries; important for the early history of coal-mining in the Gateshead/North Durham area.

Non-manuscript material: Thomas Bell estate plans, c1780–1840 (c1000).

Finding aids: Calendars. MSS accessions book. Indexes.

Facilities: Photocopying. Photography. Micro-film/fiche reader/printer.

Publications: F.W.D. Manders: *Gateshead Archives: a Guide* (1968).
Local and Family History in the Gateshead Area (1992).

337 The Northern Film and Television Archive

Parent organisation: Trade Films Ltd

Address: 36 Bottle Bank, Gateshead, Tyne and Wear NE8 2AR

Telephone: (0191) 477 3601

Fax: (0191) 478 3681

Enquiries: Bob Davis

Access: Generally open to the public, by appointment only.

Historical background: The Northern Film and Television Archive was established in 1983 as a wing of Trade Films, an independent film company. Financial support is received from Northern Arts.

Acquisitions policy: Film and videotape material produced in, or relating to, the social, economic, industrial and political history of the North-East, both amateur and professional productions. Any MS material offered would be referred to the relevant local record office and any film material from outside the North-East would be offered to other film archives.

Non-manuscript material: National Coal Board films, 1947–83, with photocopies of material from the NCB production files.
North-East Development Council films, 1966–74.
Trade Film productions, 1981–; home movies.
A collection of film material produced during the Miners' Strike, 1984–5.

Finding aids: A provenance-based catalogue and a computerised index of persons, places, subjects, production companies and titles.

Facilities: Film and videotape viewing facilities.

338 British Motor Industry Heritage Trust

Address: Banbury Road, Gaydon, Warks CV35 0BJ

Telephone: (01926) 641188

Fax: (01926) 641555

Enquiries: The Archivist, Anders Ditlev Clausager

The trust, formerly Leyland Historic Vehicles and BL Heritage Ltd, was established in 1983. It holds technical and production records, including engineering drawings, photographs, and technical and sales literature, for Austin, Morris and other Nuffield group makes, Rover and Standard-Triumph. At the same address the trust operates the Heritage Motor Centre (Motor Museum). Material relating to British commercial vehicles may be found in the British Commercial Vehicle Museum, at King Street, Leyland, Lancashire. Some business records of the Rover Group and associated companies are in the trust's deposit at the Modern Records Centre, University of Warwick Library (entry **229**).

339 Eastwood District Libraries
Local History Department

Address: Giffnock Library, Station Road, Giffnock, Glasgow G46 6JF

Telephone: (0141) 638 6349

Fax: (0141) 620 0884

Enquiries: The District Reference and Local History Librarian, Mrs M. Devine

Open: Mon, Wed, Fri: 2.00–8.00 Tues, Thurs, Sat: 10.00–5.00

The library holds local authority records, 1975–, including minutes, annual reports and financial statements, and valuation and voters' rolls. There is also a local history collection of letters, local newspapers, photographs (*c*1100) postcards, ephemera, publications and extensive community information files. Photocopying and microfilm/fiche readers are available.

340 Gillingham Central Library

Address: High Street, Gillingham, Kent ME7 1BG

Telephone: (01634) 281066

Fax: (01634) 855814

Enquiries: The Information Officer

Open: Mon, Tues: 9.30–7.00 Wed: 9.30–1.00; 2.00–5.00 Thurs, Fri: 9.30–6.00 Sat: 9.30–5.00

Access: Generally open to the public.

Historical background: The present library was built and opened in 1937, but local collections predate this. Methodist Church archives have been transferred to Rochester-upon-Medway Studies Centre (entry **966**).

Acquisitions policy: To strengthen the existing collection of Gillingham material by purchase and donation.

Major collections: Special collections relating to Louis Brennan (1852–1932); J.B. McCudden, VC (1895–1918); and Will Adams (1564–1620), the first Englishman to settle in Japan (the Adams collection contains little original archival material).

Non-manuscript material: Photographs and prints (*c*800); slides (250).
Oil paintings, mostly by Henry Hill.
Gramophone records of Kent folk music.
Microfilms of census returns for Gillingham, Rainham and parts of north-east Kent, 1841–91, and of parish records, *c*1558–1927.

Finding aids: Indexes and lists.

Facilities: Photocopying. Microfilm reader/printer.

Publications: Local History Series nos 1–13 and leaflets 1–6.

341 Angus Folk Museum

Parent organisation: National Trust for Scotland

Address: Kirkwynd Cottages, Glamis by Forfar, Tayside DD8 1RT

Telephone: (01307) 840288

Enquiries: The Property Manager, Mrs Valerie McAlister

Open: May–Sept: Mon–Sun: 11.00–5.30

Access: Only serious students; appointment preferred.

The museum was founded in 1957. It acquires items relating to rural Angus, domestic and agricultural, until *c*1920. The museum holds a small quantity of items, including school exercise books, 19th century, farm account books, 1834–1961, and town plans, *c*1832, plus miscellaneous accounts and correspondence relating to the Shaw family, 1759–1916. There are also photographs of the Angus area.

Non-manuscript material: Photographs of Angus, 19th century–.

Finding aids: NRA 19893 (NRS(S) 1262).

Publications: H. Cheape and G. Sprott: *Angus Country Life*, National Trust Scotland (1980). *Angus Folk Museum Guide* (1994).

342 Archdiocese of Glasgow Archive

Address: 196 Clyde Street, Glasgow G1 4JY

Telephone: (0141) 226 5898 ext. 154

Fax: (0141) 221 1962

Enquiries: Rt Rev. Mgr Hugh N. Canon Boyle or Dr Mary McHugh

Open: By appointment.

Access: Approved readers, usually on written application. Restrictions on certain categories of records containing personal details of individuals.

Historical background: The modern Archdiocese of Glasgow was established in 1878, although some papers date from the arrival of Archbishop Charles Eyre (1817–1902) in 1869.

Acquisitions policy: To collect material relating to the Archdiocese of Glasgow and its parishes. Deposits from related diocesan organisations and parishes are encouraged.

Archives of organisation: Archives of the Episcopal Chancery and Diocesan Curia, 1878–.
Archdiocesan parish registers, including the cathedral parish, 1795–.
Education papers prior and subsequent to Education (Scotland) Act 1918.

Major collections: Catholic Union records, 1885–1940s.

Non-manuscript material: Plans of some ecclesiastical buildings.
Archbishop J.D. Scanlon, photographs, 20th century.
Canon Michael Condon, photograph albums, 19th century.

Finding aids: Catalogue, which is being computerised.

Facilities: Photocopying.

Publications: M. McHugh: 'Glasgow Archdiocesan Archive', *Catholic Archives*, 5 (1985), 19–33.

343 Glasgow School of Art

Address: 167 Renfrew Street, Glasgow G3 6RQ

Telephone: (0141) 353 4551

Fax: (0141) 353 4746

Enquiries: The Principal Librarian, Mr I. Monie

Open: Mon–Fri: 9.30–5.00 by arrangement.

Access: Bona fide scholars, strictly by appointment. Access to many of the records is restricted because of their fragile condition.

Historical background: Glasgow School of Art was founded c1845 in Ingram Street, then moved to the McLellan Buildings, and eventually to its present site in 1899, where it occupies a building designed by Charles Rennie Mackintosh (1868–1928), a former pupil.

Archives of organisation: Governors' minute books, 1854–; letter-books, 1854–1913 (incomplete); student registers, 1878–; academic records of students, 1920s–; prospectuses, 1893–; annual reports, c1845– (incomplete).

Non-manuscript material: Press cuttings, 1864–.

Facilities: Photocopying.

Conservation: Some work contracted out.

344 The Mitchell Library, Arts Department

Parent organisation: Glasgow City Libraries

Address: North Street, Glasgow G3 7DN

Telephone: (0141) 305 2933/4

Fax: (0141) 305 2815

Enquiries: The Departmental Librarian, Ms K. Cunningham

Open: Mon–Fri: 9.00–9.00 Sat: 9.00–5.00

Access: Generally open to the public; prior notice of particular requirements is helpful.

Historical background: The library was opened in 1877 as Glasgow's first free public reference library, following a bequest by Stephen Mitchell, a tobacco manufacturer in Glasgow, of £70,000 to the town council for that purpose. Baillie's library stock was incorporated in 1982. The Rare Books and Manuscripts Department was incorporated in the Arts Department in 1994. The library's own archives are deposited with Strathclyde Regional Archives (entry 350).

Acquisitions policy: Archives are sought relating to Glasgow, and to the library's major special collections in Scottish poetry, drama, family history and regimental history, and trade unions. Other archives are normally now directed to Strathclyde Regional Archives (entry 350) or the Glasgow University Business Record Centre (entry 351C) as appropriate.

Major collections: Extensive MSS and archival holdings, including estate and family papers, records of business, societies, schools, and trade unions (c100). Examples include Glasgow and West of Scotland Association for Women's Suffrage, 1902–19; Alfred Morton diaries, 1887–1941; Scottish Council for Community Service during Unemployment, 1935–51; Guy Aldred papers, 1905–67; Scottish Women's Hospitals, 1914–22.

Non-manuscript material: North British Locomotive Company Collection includes plate glass negatives (10,000) in addition to order books and weight diagram books.
History and Glasgow Room: material relating to Glasgow, including MSS, maps and illustrations; Scottish local history, topography and genealogy, with extensive map collection.

Finding aids: Interim catalogue of MSS (cards xeroxed in sheets and bound), gradually being superseded by detailed looseleaf catalogue with card index. Aldred: NRA(S) 1410; John L. Kinloch: NRA(S) 0465.

Facilities: Photocopying. Photography. Microfilm/fiche reader/printers.

Conservation: Minor repairs done in-house; other work contracted out.

Publications: The North British Locomotive Company Collection (1974).
The Mitchell Library, Glasgow, 1877–1977 (Glasgow, 1977).

345 Royal College of Physicians and Surgeons of Glasgow

Address: 234–242 St Vincent Street, Glasgow G2 5RJ

Telephone: (0141) 221 6072

Enquiries: The Librarian, Mr A.M. Rodger

Open: Mon–Fri: 9.30–5.30

Access: Fellows and members of the college; registered medical practitioners; college examination candidates and postgraduate students. Other approved readers, on written application to the librarian.

Historical background: The college was established in 1599 by the grant of a Royal Charter from King James VI to Maister Peter Lowe and Professor Robert Hamilton, to regulate the practice of medicine in the west of Scotland. The original title of the college was the Faculty of Physicians and Surgeons of Glasgow. The faculty's privileges were confirmed by Act of Parliament in 1672. It had the exclusive right to examine and license practitioners of surgery in the west of Scotland, and no individual could practise medicine within its boundaries without its express permission. In 1909 the corporation became the Royal Faculty of Physicians and Surgeons of Glasgow, until the change to its present designation as a Royal College in 1962. Many outstanding individuals, such as Lister, Macewen, Livingstone and many names famous in the context of the Glasgow Medical School, have been associated with the college.

Acquisitions policy: The college aims to supplement and improve in any way it can its archives and rare-book holdings. The completion of the setting up of an archives section attached to the library has expanded that area of interest in the college library's remit.

Major collections: Sir William Macewen (1848–1924) Collection: correspondence, lecture notes, private ward journals, photographs and memorabilia.
Sir Ronald Ross (1857–1932) Collection: correspondence, private writings, pamphlets and memoirs.

Lord Lister (1827–1912) Collection: correspondence and memorabilia.
Large collection of student lecture notes, 19th-century; records of seven major Glasgow medical societies.

Non-manuscript material: Extensive collection of medical tracts, 15th–19th centuries, and works by authors such as Boerhaave, Cullen etc. The collection of early Latin and English medical books is very strong.

Finding aids: List of archives and MSS (typescript, 1987).

Facilities: Photocopying.

Publications: A. Duncan: *Memorials of the Faculty of Physicians and Surgeons of Glasgow* (1894).

346 Royal Faculty of Procurators Library

Address: 12 Nelson Mandela Place, Glasgow G2 1BT

Telephone: (0141) 332 3593

Fax: (0141) 333 9104

Enquiries: The Librarian, Mr Edward M. Pierce

Open: Mon–Fri: 9.00–5.00

Access: Members of the Royal Faculty of Procurators of Glasgow; authorised members of the legal profession (sheriffs, advocates); bona fide research workers, on application to the librarian.

Historical background: Although its existence dates from the latter part of the 18th century, the library was officially founded by the Faculty of Procurators in 1817 and has been housed in the present building since 1857. Its purpose was, and is, to provide practising members of the legal profession in Glasgow with a specialised law library where they can find all the legal information necessary for their daily work and research.

Acquisitions policy: No active policy for acquiring archives.

Archives of organisation: Archives of the Royal Faculty of Procurators, 1668–.

Major collections: Archives of the Hutcheson-Hill family, 16th century–, including some genealogical MSS.
Hill Collection: a record of Glasgow

in the 19th century, of sociological interest.

Non-manuscript material: Maps of Glasgow, 18th century–.
Prints.

Finding aids: Catalogue. Card index to Hill Collection, also NRA(S) 0534.

Facilities: Photocopying.

Publications: Printed catalogue of Hill Collection (1905).

347 Royal Scottish Geographical Society

Address: Graham Hills Building, 40 George Street, Glasgow G1 1QE

Telephone: (0141) 552 3330

Fax: (0141) 552 3331

Enquiries: The Director, A.B. Cruickshank

Open: By prior arrangement.

Access: Bona fide researchers, providing a written reference, by appointment.

Historical background: The society was founded in 1884.

Acquisitions policy: To maintain its own archive.

Archives of organisation: Council and committee minutes and papers; correspondence.

Non-manuscript material: Photographic slides; a substantial collection of maps of Scotland.

Finding aids: Indexes to maps.

Publications: Early maps of Scotland [published by the society; 2 vols].

348 Scottish Film Archive

Address: Dowanhill, 74 Victoria Crescent Road, Glasgow G12 9JN

Telephone: (0141) 334 4445

Fax: (0141) 334 8132

Enquiries: The Archivist, Ms Janet McBain

Open: Mon–Fri: 9.00–12.30; 2.00–5.00

Access: Initial enquiries free; researchers are advised to give prior notice of their intention to visit. Viewings of film by appointment only, free to academic and bona fide students; a fee is charged for commercial and television users. Consultation on premises preferred, although arrangements can be made to despatch available viewing copies to an enquirer.

Historical background: The Scottish Film Archive, a division of the Scottish Film Council, was established in 1976 as a Job Creation Project, and permanent status followed in 1978. Active research into the sources of film and cinema history in Scotland has been undertaken since 1977, with a steadily growing collection of material.

Acquisitions policy: Actuality and non-fiction film relating to Scottish culture and history in the 20th century. Emphasis on local material.

Archives of organisation: Archives of the Scottish Film Council and its constituents, 1934–, including minute books 1934–74, publications, reports of conferences, papers of the Scottish Educational Film Association, Scottish Central Film Library, Edinburgh Film Festival and Cosmo Cinema (now Glasgow Film Theatre).

Major collections: Principally non-MS material (see below); also Scottish film and cinema industry records.

Non-manuscript material: Locally produced cinema newsreels, comprising calendar customs, visits of celebrities, freedom of city ceremonies etc.
Upper Clyde Shipbuilders Ltd: official films of launches and trials of vessels constructed by component companies, 1926–71.
Educational and documentary films on Scotland, 1935–.
Television news and documentaries, c1965–.
Oral recordings: former cinema staff, film renters, exhibitors in Scotland.
Photographs of cinemas. Cinema memorabilia and publicity.

Finding aids: Subject and personality index system. Alphabetical and chronological lists of titles. Cataloguing in progress.

Facilities: 35mm and 16mm film viewing facilities. U-matic and VHS video.

349 Scottish Jewish Archives Centre

Parent organisation: Scottish Jewish Archives Committee

Address: Garnethill Synagogue, 127 Hill Street, Glasgow G3 6UB

Telephone: (0141) 332 4151, 649 4526 (Director)

Enquiries: Director, Mr Harvey Kaplan

Open: Monthly open day; otherwise by arrangement.

Access: Generally open to the public, by appointment only.

The collection was begun in 1984 and the Archives Centre opened in 1987. The centre collects a wide range of material relating to the history of Jews in Scotland from the late 18th century. The holdings include synagogue and communal organisations' minutes and registers; financial records, accounts and annual reports; newspapers and cuttings books; brochures and other publications; and photographs. There is a computerised catalogue and a biannual *Newsletter* issued to Friends of Scottish Jewish Archives. See also K. Collins: *Second City Jewry* (1950).

350 Strathclyde Regional Archives

Parent organisation: Strathclyde Regional Council

Address: Mitchell Library, North Street, Glasgow G3 7DN

Telephone: (0141) 227 2401/5

Fax: (0141) 226 8452

Enquiries: The Principal Archivist, Mr A.M. Jackson

Open: Mon–Thurs: 9.30–4.45 Fri: 9.30–4.00 At other times by arrangement.

Access: Generally open to the public.

Historical background: The Glasgow City Archives Department was established in 1964, and following reorganisation in 1975 became the Strathclyde Regional Archives. The sub-office in Ayr (entry **39**) is a dependent repository.

Acquisitions policy: The geographical area of the Strathclyde Region, but Ayrshire material is held in the Ayr sub-office and Argyll and Bute material is normally directed to Argyll and Bute Archives (entry **479**).

Archives of organisation: Usual local authority record holdings.

Major collections: Deposited collections, including the following which have a wider significance:
Extensive shipbuilding and engineering records, including the Fairfield Shipbuilding and Engineering Co. Ltd and its predecessors, 1860–c1970; G.L. Watson & Co., marine architects; and Sir William Arrol & Co. Ltd, bridge builders.
Records of Clyde Port Authority (formerly Clyde Navigation Trust) and the Scottish Co-operative Wholesale Society.
Family collections, including Maxwell of Pollok, Stirling of Keir, Colquhoun of Luss and Cochrane-Baillie of Lamington.

Non-manuscript material: Large collection of architectural and estate plans; photographs, including commercial collections; some audio material.

Finding aids: Lists, indexes and computer files. Lists are sent to NRA(S).

Facilities: Photocopying and plan printing. Photography and microfilming by arrangement. Microfilm/fiche readers.

Conservation: In-house conservation. Outside work is undertaken occasionally.

351 University of Glasgow

A University Archives

Address: The University, Glasgow G12 8QQ

Telephone: (0141) 330 5516 (direct line) 339 8855 ext. 6494

Fax: (0141) 330 4158

Enquiries: The University Archivist, Mr Michael Moss

Open: Mon–Fri: 9.15–4.45 Evenings and Saturdays by arrangement

Access: Generally open to the public, by appointment, subject to normal confidentiality.

Historical background: The archives department holds the records of the university since its foundation in 1451. The earliest volumes include the *Annales Universitatis Glasguensis, 1451–1558*. The records become fuller after the *Nova Erectio* of 1577 and the construction in the following century of the Old College building in the High Street. For the 17th and 18th centuries the archive is the fullest of the four ancient Scottish universities. By the 1780s Glasgow had about 1800 students, making it of equivalent size to Oxford or Cambridge.

The university had authority to teach in all the faculties, but arts and theology were exclusively taught until the early 17th century, when medicine and law were included. In the last 50 years it has built up large collections of records relating to business and health care in the west of Scotland. See below for the Business Record Centre, Greater Glasgow Health Board and Scottish Brewing Archive.

Acquisitions policy: To collect records relating to the university and to business and health care in the west of Scotland.

Archives of organisation: University records: relating to the administration, finance, students, staff and teaching of the university, 1451–, with papers from institutions affiliated to the university, including Anderson's College of Medicine (1841–1965), Queen Margaret College (1835–1935), Glasgow Veterinary School (1866–1990) and the Royal Scottish Academy of Music and Drama (1870–1985), student clubs and societies, and individual professors and other staff.

Major collections: Beith and other Ayrshire parish papers, 1610–1924; Garscube Estate (Sir Archibald Campbell), 1837–1960; Hamilton of Rozelle, Ayrshire, and Rozelle and Pemberton, Jamaica, 1682–1939; Lumsden of Arden, stationers, Glasgow, 1661–1984; MacFie family, sugar refiners, Greenock, Edinburgh and Liverpool, 1709–1960; Napier family, shipbuilders, engineers and textile manufacturers, 1764–1963. Personal papers, including Duncan Black (1908–91), economist; Frederick O. Bower (1885–1928), botanist; Archibald A. Bowman (1883–1936), philosopher; Sir Alec Cairncross (*b* 1911), economist; Archibald C. Corbett, MP (1856–1933), 1st Baron Rowallan; Sir Maurice Denny (1886–1955), shipbuilder; John 'Soda' Ferguson (*d* 1915), chemist; Sir Hector Hetherington (1888–1956), university administrator; Sir Robert Horne, MP (1871–1940), Chancellor of the Exchequer, 1921; Sir John Graham Kerr (1869–1957), zoologist; Sir James Lithgow (1883–1952), shipbuilder; John Scott Maclay, 1st Viscount Muirshiel, MP (1905–90), Secretary of State for Scotland; Very Rev. Robert Herbert Storey (1835–1907), Principal, Glasgow University; Viscount William Weir (1877–1959), industrialist and public servant.

Non-manuscript material: Jackson collection: photographs relating to the university and Scottish topography, 1902–1930s (50,000). Plans relating to the university (3000).

Finding aids: Computerised catalogues, handlists and indexes. Lists sent to NRA(S).

Facilities: Photography. Photography. Microfilming. Microfilm/fiche reader.

Conservation: Contracted out.

Publications: Summary guide to University Archives and Business Records Centre collections.
Munimenta Alme Universitatis Glasguensis: Records of the University of Glasgow from its Foundation till 1727 (Glasgow 1854) [3 vols].
W.I. Addison: *A Roll of the Graduates of the University of Glasgow, 1727–1897* (Glasgow, 1898).
James Coutts: *A History of the University of Glasgow From its Foundation in 1451 to 1909* (Glasgow, 1909).
W.I. Addison: *The Matriculation Albums of the University of Glasgow from 1728–1858* (Glasgow, 1913)
J.D. Mackie: *The University of Glasgow, 1451–1951* (Glasgow, 1954).

B Library Department of Special Collections

Address: University of Glasgow, Hillhead Street, Glasgow G12 8QE

Telephone: (0141) 339 8855 ext. 6767

Fax: (0141) 330 4952

Enquiries: The Keeper of Special Collections, Dr Timothy Hobbs

Open: Term: Mon–Thurs: 9.00–8.30 Fri: 9.00–5.00 Sat: 9.00–12.30 Vacation: Mon–Fri: 9.00–5.00 Sat: 9.00–12.30 (not Christmas) Closed Glasgow Fair Monday (July); Glasgow Autumn Holiday Monday (September).

Access: Members of Glasgow University and all other bona fide researchers. Prior written application is desirable.

Historical background: Glasgow University was founded in 1451. A MS catalogue of 1691

shows the library with a stock of 3300 volumes. From 1709 to 1836 the library enjoyed the copyright privilege and by 1790 (the year of its first published catalogue) its holdings had risen to 20,000 volumes. Vast collections were acquired by gift and bequest in the 19th and 20th centuries, and in 1994 the library's stock approached 1,700,000 volumes.

Acquisitions policy: To augment the following archival collections by purchase, gift and deposit: 18th–century medicine, with special emphasis on William Hunter and his work in anatomy and obstetrics.
Scottish theatre history in the 19th and 20th centuries.
History of art in the 19th and 20th centuries, with special emphasis on James McNeill Whistler and the painter-etchers of his period, and Scottish artists.
Papers of the physicist William Thomson, Lord Kelvin.
Alchemy and the early history of chemistry.

Major collections: 316 medieval MSS; *c*250 oriental MSS.
Post-medieval MSS, particularly covering the following subjects: 18th–century medicine and anatomy; alchemy and early chemistry; 19th– and 20th–century art history; Gaelic literature (over 30,000 separate items).
Music: scores of several late 19th– and early 20th–century Scottish composers.
Papers of individuals, including: James Douglas (1675–1742); William Hunter (1718–83); William Cullen (1710–90); Theophilus Siegfried Bayer, early 18th century; William Thomson, Lord Kelvin (1824–1907); Adam Smith (1723–90); James McNeill Whistler (1834–1903); Dugald Sutherland Macoll (1859–1948); Harold James Lean Wright; Henry George Farmer (1882–1965); Edwin Morgan (*b* 1920).
Scottish Theatre Archive, mainly 19th and 20th century.

Non-manuscript material: D.O. Hill Collection: early photographs, *c*1843–60.
Caricatures of the Franco-Prussian War and the Paris Commune (*c*3000).

Finding aids: Main sheaf index (TS) to the MS collections; access points include names of persons, institutions and subjects. Special TS lists and abstracts of certain collections. It is hoped to bring the MS catalogue on-line in the near future.

Facilities: Photocopying. Photography. Microfilming. Microfilm/fiche readers.

Publications: J. Young and P. Henderson Aitken: *A Catalogue of the Manuscripts in the Library of the Hunterian Museum in the University of Glasgow* (Glasgow, 1908).
J. Mackechnie: *Catalogue of Gaelic Manuscripts in selected Libraries in Great Britain and Ireland*, i (Boston, MA, 1973), 365–454.
N.R. Ker: *Medieval Manuscripts in British Libraries*, ii (Oxford, 1977), 871–933 [details of the non-Hunterian medieval MSS in Glasgow University Library].
J. Baldwin: 'Glasgow University Library's Manuscripts: the non-Hunterian Collections', *The Bibliotheck*, viii (1977), 127.
Kelvin Papers: Index (Glasgow, 1977).
Whistler, MacColl, Wright: Art History Papers, 1850–1950, in Glasgow University Library (Glasgow, 1979).
N. Thorp: *The Glory of the Page: Medieval & Renaissance Illuminated Manuscripts from Glasgow University Library* (London, 1987).

C Business Records Centre

Address: 13 Thurso Street, Glasgow G11 6PE

Telephone: (0141) 330 5515 (direct line) 339 8855 ext. 6079

Fax: (0141) 330 4158

Enquiries: The Manager, Miss Vanora Skelley

Open: Mon, Tues, Thurs, Fri: 9.30–12.30; 1.30–4.00

Access: Generally open to the public, by appointment only.

Historical background: The Business Records Centre contains the largest dedicated collection of business records in Europe. It was inaugurated by Sydney Checkland, the first Professor of Economic History, in 1959. The centre holds records of almost every type of commercial and industrial activity that has been pursued in the west of Scotland in the last two hundred years.

Acquisitions policy: To collect records relating to business in the west of Scotland.

Major collections: Allied Distillers Ltd, Dumbarton, 1668–1980; Anchor Line, shipowners, Edinburgh and Glasgow, 1790–1980; Babcock & Wilcox Ltd, boilermakers, Renfrew, 1891–1985; Andrew Barclay Sons & Co. Ltd, locomotive builders, Kilmarnock, 1876–1970; Barr & Stroud Ltd, optical instrument makers, Glasgow, 1880s-1980s; William Beardmore & Co., engineers, Glasgow, 1864–1976; Blackie & Son, publishers, Glasgow, 1794–1980s; British Alcan plc (including British Aluminium Corporation Ltd), London and Fort William, 1880s-1980s; John Brown & Co. (Clydebank) Ltd, shipbuilders, 1847–1971; City of Glasgow Bank, 1840–82; Clyde Shipping Co. Ltd, Glasgow, 1875–1980s; Coats Patons plc, cotton thread manufacturers, Glasgow and Paisley, 1830–1980s; William Collins, Son & Co. Ltd, publishers, Glasgow, 1822–1986; William Denny & Bros, shipbuilders, Dumbarton, 1844–1952; John Elder & Co., shipbuilders, Glasgow, 1869–1916; Ellerman Lines Ltd (including City Line), shipowners, London, 1839–1970s; James Finlay & Co. plc, textile manufacturers and merchants, Glasgow, 1789–1972; Gartshore Estate (Viscount Whitelaw), Glasgow, 1849–1953; Gourock Ropework Co., Port Glasgow (including New Lanark Mills), 1774–1972; Highland Distilleries Co. plc, whisky distillers, Glasgow, 1882–1984; House of Fraser Group (Army & Navy Stores, Dickens & Jones, Binns, D.H. Evans etc), Glasgow, London and elsewhere, 1820s-1980s; Ivory & Sime plc, investment trust managers, Edinburgh, 1880–1986; John Lean & Sons, muslin manufacturers, Glasgow, 1850–1925; Lithgows Ltd, shipbuilders, Port Glasgow, 1875–1977; Long John International, whisky distillers, Dumbarton, 1840–1991; Sir Robert McAlpine & Sons Ltd, Glasgow, 1882–1971; North British Locomotive Co. Ltd, locomotive builders, Glasgow, 1903–48; Robertson & Baxter Ltd, whisky merchants, Glasgow, 1903–82; Scott & Sons, shipbuilders, Bowling, 1857–1979; Scotts Shipbuilding & Engineering Co., Greenock, 1780–1984; A.W. Smith & Co. Ltd, sugar machine manufacturers, Glasgow, 1841–1966; Alexander Stephen & Sons, shipbuilders, Glasgow, 1848–1968; William Teacher & Sons Ltd, whisky distillers, Glasgow, 1856–1900.

Non-manuscript material: Photographs relating to Scottish topography and industry, ships, building, boilers, locomotives, shipbuilding, engineering, optical instruments, machine-tool making and department stores (100,000).
Technical drawings of buildings, locomotives, cranes, optical instruments and ships (200,000). Technical and business history library (6000).

Finding aids: Computerised databases, catalogues, handlists and indexes. Lists sent to NRA(S).

Facilities: Photography. Photocopying. Plan copying. Microfilming. Microfilm/fiche reader.

Conservation: Contracted out.

Publications: Summary guide to collections.

D Greater Glasgow Health Board Archive

Address: University of Glasgow, Glasgow G12 8QQ

Telephone: (0141) 330 5516 (direct line) 339 8855 ext. 5516

Fax: (0141) 330 4158

Enquiries: The Archivist, Alistair Tough

Open: Mon–Fri: 9.00–1.00; 2.00–5.00

Access: Generally open to the public, subject to normal confidentiality; an appointment is advisable.

Historical background: The Greater Glasgow Health Board was created in 1974 to assume the functions of the former Western Regional Hospital Board and its boards of management in the Greater Glasgow area. The GGHB Archive was established in 1975 to collect and administer the records of the GGHB and its predecessor bodies.

Acquisitions policy: Records relating to the hospital service and health care in Glasgow and the west of Scotland.

Archives of organisation: Administrative, financial and clinical records of Glasgow and Paisley hospitals, 1787–; administrative records of Western Regional Hospital Board and constituent Boards of Management and GGHB, 1948–1990.

Non-manuscript material: Small collection of medical and surgical instruments and equipment.
Videotaped interviews.

Finding aids: Catalogues and handlists. Summary guide to collections.

Facilities: Photocopying. Photography.

Publications: D.A. Dow: 'The Archives of the Greater Glasgow Health Board', in O. Checkland and M. Lamb: *Health Care as Social History: the Glasgow Case* (Aberdeen, 1982), 158–69.
A.G. Tough: *Medical Records of Glasgow and*

Paisley: a Guide to the Greater Glasgow Health Board Archive (Glasgow, 1993).

E Scottish Brewing Archive

Address: Business Records Centre, 13 Thurso Street, Glasgow G11 6PE

Telephone: (0141) 330 5515 (direct line) 339 8855 ext. 6079

Fax: (0141) 330 4158

Enquiries: The Archivist, Mrs Alma Topen

Open: Tues–Thurs: 9.30–12.30; 1.30–4.30

Access: Open to the public, by appointment only.

Historical background: The Scottish Brewing Archive was established in 1981 at Heriot-Watt University, an institution with a long connection with the industry through its degree course in brewing. The archive moved to Glasgow University in 1991.

Acquisitions policy: To collect records of brewing, malting and other related industries (excluding distilling), and the licensed trade in Scotland.

Major collections: Records of more than 50 companies, including James Aitken & Co. (Falkirk) Ltd, 1900–65; T. & J. Bernard Ltd, Edinburgh, 1895–1960; Drybrough & Co. Ltd, Edinburgh, 1778–1970; Belhaven Brewery, Dunbar, 1871–1973; John Fowler & Co. Ltd, Prestonpans, 1926–69; John Jeffrey & Co. Ltd, Edinburgh, 1850–1970; Lorimer & Clark Ltd, Edinburgh, 1871–1973; Wm McEwan & Co. Ltd, Edinburgh, 1856–; J. & R. Tennent Ltd and Tennent Caledonian Breweries Ltd, 1776–1985; Thomas Usher & Son Ltd, Edinburgh, 1834–1980; George Younger & Son Ltd, Alloa, 1875–69; Wm Younger & Co. Ltd, Edinburgh, 1805–.

Non-manuscript material: Photographs of brewing processes, buildings and workers, 1860s-1980s; plans of buildings, c1900–1970s; anti-prohibition leaflets, 1920s; library of technical and historical books, 1726–, periodicals; beer labels, 1850–, and beer mats, 1950s-; advertising ephemera, 1880s-; artefacts, including bottles, cans, glasses, trays, coopering and malting tools, hydrometers, c1850s-.

Finding aids: Catalogue of archive collections (new version in progress). Lists sent to NRA(S). Computerised database for library and artefacts.

Facilities: Photocopying. Photography. Plan copying. Microfilming. Microfilm/fiche reader.

Conservation: Contracted out.

Publications: Scottish Brewing Archive *Newsletter* (1982–).

352 University of Strathclyde

A John Anderson Campus

Address: Strathclyde University Archives, McCance Building, 16 Richmond Street, Glasgow G1 1XQ

Telephone: (0141) 552 4400 ext. 2318

Fax: (0141) 552 0775

Enquiries: The Archivist, Dr James S. McGrath

Open: Mon–Fri: 9.15–4.45

Access: Bona fide researchers, by appointment. Recent official records by arrangement with the Secretary to the University.

Historical background: Anderson's Institution was established in 1796 according to the instructions contained in the will of John Anderson, Professor of Natural Philosophy at the University of Glasgow, as a 'place of useful learning' for those excluded from the university system. During the 19th century, the institution spawned the Glasgow Mechanics' Institution, developed a medical school and changed its name (Anderson's University, then Anderson's College). In 1887 it became the Glasgow and West of Scotland Technical College, at which point the Medical School became independent and was finally absorbed into Glasgow University in 1947. The Technical College was renamed the Royal Technical College in 1912 and then the Royal College of Science and Technology in 1956. In 1964 it merged with the Scottish College of Commerce (which started in 1847 as the Glasgow Athenaeum). Later in 1964 the merged institution became the University of Strathclyde. In 1993 the university merged with the Jordanhill College of Education. Strathclyde University Archives (John Anderson Campus) was established in 1977. Most of the archives previously held by the Department of History have been transferred to Glasgow University Business Records Centre (entry **351C**.

Acquisitions policy: The University Archives

collect the records of the university and its antecedents, and the papers of former staff and students. There is no policy of seeking other records, although some non-university collections were inherited.

Archives of organisations: Anderson's Institution and University, including Anderson's Medical School, Allan Glen's Institution, the Atkinson Institution etc, 1796–1887.
Glasgow Mechanics' Institution, 1823–87.
Glasgow and West of Scotland Technical College, later the Royal Technological College, then the Royal College of Science and Technology, 1887–1964.
Glasgow Athenaeum, later the Glasgow and West of Scotland Commercial College, then the Scottish College of Commerce, 1847–1964.
University of Strathclyde, 1964–.

Major collections: Leith-Buchanan family and estate papers (Dunbartonshire and Invernessshire), c1600–1900.
Glasgow Typographical Society, 1817–1960.
Glasgow Dilettante Society, 1825–43.
Wm Baird & Co. (steelworks), c1840–1968.
Society of Chemical Industry (Glasgow and West of Scotland branch), 1884–1962.
Scottish Association for the Promotion of Technical and Secondary Education, 1891–1925.
Gem Line (steamship company), c1945–1960.
International Union of Food Science & Technology, c1970–.
Papers of James 'Paraffin' Young, c1811–1883; Sir Patrick Geddes, c1854–1932; Sir George Pepler, c1882–1959.

Non-manuscript material: Photographs and films of campus, staff and students; some sound material; some supporting printed material.

Finding aids: Most collections are catalogued and indexed.

Facilities: Photocopying. Photography. Microfilm reader.

Publications: S.E.G. Lythe and J.S. McGrath: *Catalogue of the Papers of Sir Patrick Geddes* (Glasgow, 1983–) [3 vols].

B Jordanhill Campus

Address: Jordanhill Library, University of Strathclyde, 76 Southbrae Drive, Glasgow G13 1PP

Telephone: (0141) 950 3300 ext. 3308

Fax: (0141) 950 3268

Enquiries: The Librarian, Mrs Margaret Harrison

Open: Term: Mon–Thurs: 9.00–9.00 Fri: 9.00–5.00 Sat: 9.00–12.00 Vacation: Mon–Fri: 9.00–5.00

Access: Bona fide researchers. Readers are advised to contact the librarian before visiting the collection.

Historical background: Jordanhill College of Education originated in the pioneering teacher-training work of David Stow (1793–1864) and had become, on the eve of its merger with Strathclyde University, the largest teacher training institution in the UK. The Jordanhill archive was set up as a special collection within the college library in 1983, and the archives are now managed by the Jordanhill Campus Library on behalf of Strathclyde University Archives.

Acquisitions policy: Records of the college and its antecedents, and the papers of former staff and students. Also material relating to the development of teacher training and education in Scotland.

Archives of organisation: Glasgow Infant School, 1828–34.
Glasgow Normal Seminary, 1835–45.
Glasgow Church of Scotland Training (or Normal) College, 1845–1907.
Glasgow Free Church Training (or Normal) College, 1845–1907.
University of Glasgow Local Committee for the Training of Teachers (King's students), 1903–06.
Glasgow Provincial Training College, later Jordanhill College of Education, 1907–93.
Hamilton College of Education, 1966–81.

Non-manuscript material: Photographs etc of the former college and its staff.
Materials relating to the educational pioneer David Stow, 1793–1864 (chiefly secondary sources).
Similar collections relating to the development of teacher training education, including Robert Rusk and Marjorie Cruickshank collections, to the Jordanhill estate and district of Glasgow, and to Jordanhill College School.

Finding aids: Most collections are catalogued.

Facilities: Photocopying. Photography. Microfilm reader.

353 Glossop Library

Parent organisation: Derbyshire County Council

Address: Victoria Hall, Talbot Street, Glossop, Derbyshire SK13 9DG

Telephone: (01457) 852616

Enquiries: The Librarian, Mrs J. Powell

Open: Mon, Wed–Fri: 10.00–7.00 Tues, Thurs: 10.00–5.00 Sat: 9.30–1.00

Access: Generally open to the public.

Acquisitions policy: To acquire, by donation, deposit or purchase, material relevant to the history and study of Glossop and its immediate surroundings in liaison with Derbyshire Record Office (entry **813**).

Major collections: Usual local history collection, including papers and estate records of the Howard family, Dukes of Norfolk; material on local cotton production; parish registers; records of Littlemoor Congregational Church.

Non-manuscript material: Local newspapers, 1859– (on microfilm) and newspaper cuttings. Census returns.

Finding aids: Non-conformist records: NRA 19179. Card index of newspaper cuttings.

Facilities: Photocopying. Microfilm/fiche readers.

354 British Waterways Archive

Parent organisation: British Waterways

Address: Llanthony Warehouse, Gloucester Docks, Gloucester GL1 2EJ

Telephone: (01452) 318041

Fax: (01452) 318075

Enquiries: The Archivist, R.A. Jamieson

Open: Mon–Fri: 10.00–5.00

Access: Generally open to the public; an appointment is appreciated.

Historical background: Nationalisation of the canals and inland waterways in 1947 was followed by the setting up of the British Transport Commission, which was succeeded by the British Waterways Board. The collection was started in 1963, when the museum was established at Stoke Bruerne. It moved to Gloucester in 1989 and is the main repository of canal records of British Waterways, receiving much canal material from the British Transport Historic Collection (formerly at Clapham) in the 1960s and 1970s.

Acquisitions policy: Principally internal records of British Waterways, but other material relating to canals is also acquired.

Archives of organisation: Records of canal companies pre-nationalisation, 1750–1947. Records of British Waterways, 1947–.

Major collections: MS plans by William Jessop (1745–1841), Thomas Telford (1757–1834), John Rennie (1761–1821) and Sir Joseph Whitworth (1803–87).

Non-manuscript material: Photograph collection, 1890–, including work of J.W. Millner, Cyril Arapoff and Arthur Watts (10,000 negatives).

Finding aids: Computer database of archives and photographs.

Facilities: Photocopying. Microfilm/fiche reader/printer.

355 Gloucester Cathedral Library

Address: 17 College Green, Gloucester GL1 2LR

Telephone: (01452) 528095

Enquiries: The Cathedral Librarian, Mr L. Maddison

Open: By arrangement only.

Access: Bona fide researchers, by appointment only.

Historical background: The long room which contains the present cathedral library dates from the end of the 14th century during the time of Abbot Froucester, who built it to house the monastic library of St Peter's Abbey. When Henry VIII dissolved the abbey early in 1540, he dispersed the books. The present cathedral library dates from the end of the Commonwealth period, when the cathedral received 200 books from the library of John Selden; thanks to the interests of the Dean and Chapter, there were many fine acquisitions during the 18th century.

Acquisitions policy: To maintain the archives.

Archives of organisation: Archives of the Dean and Chapter, 1617–1990.

Major collections: Medieval MSS and registers, including 400 charters, 1072–1539.
Post-medieval MSS, including tithes and offerings of Trinity Parish, Gloucester, 1618–45.
Three Choirs Festival collection of programme books, and documents, 19th century–.

Non-manuscript material: Architectural plans and photographs of the cathedral.
Selden and Wheeler Collection of 17th- and 18th-century books.

Facilities: Photocopying.

Publications: S.M. Eward and others: *Catalogue of Gloucester Cathedral Library* (1972). A. Boden: *Three Choirs: a History of the Festival* (1992).

356 Gloucester Library
Gloucestershire Collection

Parent organisation: Gloucestershire County Library, Arts and Museums Service

Address: Brunswick Road, Gloucester GL1 1HT

Telephone: (01452) 426979

Fax: (01452) 521468

Enquiries: The Senior Librarian, Local Studies, Graham Baker

Open: Mon, Tues, Thurs: 10.00–7.30 Wed, Fri: 10.00–5.00 Sat: 9.00–1.00

Access: Generally open to the public; restricted access on some collections. An appointment for film/fiche readers is advisable.

Historical background: The nucleus of the Gloucestershire Collection was a bequest by J.J. Powell, QC, who left to the City of Gloucester several volumes of cuttings from Gloucestershire newspapers, with the understanding that should a public library be established they be kept there. On the death of Judge Powell in 1891 the bequest was added to by others, and since the library opened in 1900 other gifts and bequests, coupled with a policy outlined below, has seen the collection become a major one.

Acquisitions policy: All forms of material relating to the county, city, towns and villages of Gloucestershire, and items written by persons connected by birth or residence with the city or county.

Major collections: Hockaday MSS Collection: abstracts of ecclesiastical records relating to the diocese of Worcester and Gloucester, 1187– (compiled from diocesan records and other sources).
Ivor Gurney MSS Collection: material, comprising music, poems, correspondence.
Smyth of Nibley Papers: papers, documents and letters concerning the business and personal affairs of John Smyth the elder, who was steward of the Hundred of Berkeley (*c*2000 items).
The Dancey Gift: MSS, books, pamphlets and prints relating to the city and county of Gloucester (225 vols, 321 pamphlets, 282 prints and portraits), includes a series of MSS illustrating the histories of the Saxon churches of Gloucestershire which have been compiled from city records, parish registers and records and other sources; and Dancey's handbooks, which are full of matters relating to local history.

Non-manuscript material: *Gloucester Journal*, 1722–1992; *Citizen*, 1876–; *Gloucester Chronicle*, 1833–1928.
Hitchings Collection of Bibles and New Testaments, 1540–1906.
Hannam-Clark Collection of books pertaining to the topography and history of Palestine.

Finding aids: Card catalogue.

Facilities: Photocopying. Photography. Microfilm/fiche readers.

Conservation: Contracted out.

Publications: *Catalogue of the Gloucester Collection* (1928).
Your Local History and *Your House Has History* [leaflets].

357 Gloucestershire Record Office

Address: Clarence Row, Alvin Street, Gloucester GL1 3DW

Telephone: (01452) 428295

Fax: (01452) 426478

Enquiries: The County and Diocesan Archivist, Mr D.J.H. Smith

Open: Mon: 10.00–5.00 Tues, Wed, Fri: 9.00–5.00 Thurs: 9.00–8.00

Access: By reader's ticket, on application. Proof of identity is required and a fee is charged.

Historical background: The County Record Office was founded in 1936 and was appointed Diocesan Record Office for Gloucester in 1954. Some archives of the diocese and of the city previously held in the City Library were transferred to the Record Office at local government reorganisation in 1974. The office is recognised as a place of deposit for public records. The county archivist acts as honorary archivist to Berkeley Castle, where muniments are kept, and enquiries for access to these should be sent to the county archivist in the first instance.

Acquisitions policy: Public and private archives relating to Gloucestershire.

Archives of organisation: Records of Gloucestershire County Council, 1889-, and predecessor authorities, including records of Gloucestershire Quarter Sessions with indictment books, 1660-, order books, 1672-, order rolls, depositions and gaol calendars, 1728-; records relating to the administration of bridges, highways, prisons, police stations and asylums, mainly 19th century; land tax assessments, 1775-1832, and registers of electors, 1832-; police records, 1839-1980s.

Major collections: Other public and local authority records, including borough, district and parish councils and their predecessor bodies; hospital and health authority records including Gloucestershire Royal Hospital, 1754-1972, and Barnwood House Private Mental Hospital, 1794-1970s; poor law unions records, 1835-1930s; records of individual schools, school boards and managers, mainly 19th-20th centuries; water authorities' records including waterworks companies, drainage boards and Severn River Board, mainly 19th-20th centuries; coroners' records, 17th-20th centuries; records of the Lord Lieutenant and militia, 19th-20th centuries.
Registers and records of Anglican parishes, 16th-20th centuries; of the Diocese of Gloucester, 1541-, which includes probate records, 1541-1858, and tithe maps, mid-19th century; of the estates of the Dean and Chapter of Gloucester, 16th-20th centuries; and of many non-conformist churches, 17th-20th centuries.
Records of local societies and voluntary associations, mainly 19th-20th centuries; and of local charities, 16th-20th centuries.
Estate and family archives, often including records relating to property and family elsewhere in Britain and overseas, including:
Bathurst of Cirencester, 14th-20th centuries.
Bathurst of Lydney: correspondence of C.B. Bathurst, MP, 1767-1828.
Beaufort of Badminton, 13th-20th centuries.
Berkeley of Berkeley: correspondence of Capt. H. Berkeley, RN, in Zanzibar, 1843-98, and of F.H.F.Berkeley, MP, 1854-64.
Berkeley of Stoke Gifford, 13th-20th centuries.
Blathwayt of Dyrham: estates in Somerset, 16th-20th centuries; drawings for the building of Dyrham Park by James Wyatt, 1692-1706; political papers of William Blathwayt, Secretary at War, Commissioner of Trade etc, 1662-1716.
Bowly of Cirencester: diplomatic papers of Melchior Guydickens in Russia, 1749-53, and Gustavus Guydickens in Germany, 1760-68.
Codrington of Dodington: Bethell family estates in East Yorkshire, 1795-1846.
Colchester-Wemyss of Westbury-on-Severn: correspondence of M.W. Colchester-Wemyss with the King of Siam, 1903-25
Commeline of Gloucester: correspondence from a soldier in South Africa, 1879-84.
Ducie of Tortworth: architectural drawings by A.W.N. Pugin and B. Bucknall, c1848-55.
Dutton of Sherborne: Stawell family, c1200-18th century; papers of the Rt Hon. H.B. Legge, Chancellor of the Exchequer, 1742-64.
Freeman-Mitford of Batsford: 16th-20th centuries; political papers of John Freeman-Mitford, 1st Baron Redesdale, 1748-1830; John Thomas Freeman-Mitford, 2nd Baron and 1st Earl of Redesdale, 1805-86 and Algernon B. Freeman-Mitford, 1st Lord Redesdale of the 2nd creation, 1837-1916.
Hanbury-Tracy of Toddington: estate records, c1300-19th century.
Hicks Beach of Coln St Aldwyn: political papers of Sir Michael Hicks Beach, 1st Earl St Aldwyn, *re* South Africa and Ireland, 1865-1915.
Hyett and Dickinson of Painswick: political papers of Sebastian Dickinson, MP, 1820-78, and W.H. Dickinson, MP, 1878-1943; correspondence of Gen. Sir Richard Meade in India, 1857-93.
Jenner-Fust of Hill: Indian and Afghanistan records, 1803-82.
Kingscote of Kingscote: Colonel R.N.F. Kingscote's Crimean War journal, 1854-6.
Lloyd-Baker of Hardwicke Court: papers relating to Hardwicke Reformatory, 1882-1910; correspondence and other records of Bishop William Lloyd of Worcester, 1627-1717, Arch-

bishop John Sharp of York, 1645–1714, and Granville Sharp, philanthropist, particularly relating to the anti-slavery movement and parliamentary reform, 1735–1813.

Maclaine of the Isle of Mull: estate records, 18th–19th centuries; Gaelic songs, 1689–c1810.

Provost of Stinchcombe: correspondence from John and Thomas Keble, 1824–93.

Price of Tibberton: papers of Morgan Philips Price, MP (1855–1973).

Ridley of Naunton: constituency correspondence files of Nicholas Ridley, MP, 1970–78.

Rooke of St Briavels: naval orders and letters of Admiral Sir George Rooke, 1694–1702.

Sotheron-Estcourt of Shipton Moyne: political papers of Thomas Estcourt, MP (1748–1818), T.G.B. Estcourt, MP (1775–1853) and T.H.S. Sotheron Estcourt, MP (1801–76); also military records of Admiral F. Sotheron (d 1859) and Gen. J.B. Estcourt (1802–55) while serving in Canada, the Middle East and the Crimea.

Whitmore of Lower Slaughten: diaries and other papers re military service of Maj.-Gen. F.L. Whitmore, Gen. Sir A. Whitmore and Maj.-Gen. G.S. Whitmore in France, the Mediterranean and the Crimea, 1789–1882.

Records of the local businesses and firms, including many solicitors' practices, comprising family and estate papers, and details of local societies, public undertakings and commercial activities, mainly 17th–20th centuries; canal companies' records, including the Thames and Severn Canal, 1792–20th century.

Businesses, including Winterbotham, Strachan and Playne of Minchinhampton, cloth manufacturers, 1829–1980; Gloucester Railway Carriage and Wagon Company, 1860–1880s; Lister & Co. of Dursley, cycle manufacturers etc, 1867–1971; Sisson & Co. of Gloucester, marine engineers, 1850s-1960s; H.H. Martyn & Co. of Cheltenham, sculptors, woodcarvers and architectural decorators, 1900–65; Bruton Knowles and Co. of Gloucester, estate agents, 19th–20th centuries.

Antiquarian collections, including Sir Thomas Phillipps' relating to Gloucestershire, 13th–19th centuries (mainly title deeds but also including an account roll for Gloucester Castle, 1263–66); Rev. D. Royce's notes and transcripts of the histories of many Cotswold churches and parishes, 19th–20th centuries.

Non-manuscript material: Substantial photographic collection relating to Gloucestershire and elsewhere, 19th–20th centuries.

Large collection of microfilm/fiche copies of material held elsewhere, including Gloucester Cathedral act books, 1617–19th century; the 1851 census enumerators' returns; medieval accounts and title deeds for the Berkeley family's estates in Gloucestershire and elsewhere; part of the West Indian correspondence of the Codrington family of Dodington, 17th–20th centuries.

The Library of Sir Francis Hyett, containing a collection of contemporary tracts on the Civil War in Gloucestershire; full series of the *Transactions* of the Bristol and Gloucestershire Archaeological Society and of the Cotteswold Naturalists Field Club.

Printed county maps and sets of the 1st, 2nd and 3rd edition OS maps of Gloucestershire.

Finding aids: Catalogues, lists and indexes. All catalogues sent to NRA.

Facilities: Photocopying. Photography. Microfilming. Microfilm reader.

Conservation: Paper, parchment, seal and map conservation facilities in-house.

Publications: I.M. Kirby: *Catalogue of the Records of the Dean and Chapter* (1967) [Diocese of Gloucester].

——: *Catalogues of the Records of the Bishop and Archdeacons* (1968) [Diocese of Gloucester].

Handlist of the Contents of the Gloucestershire Record Office (1988).

Handlist of Genealogical Records (1992).

Archive teaching books: *Gloucestershire Turnpike Roads* and *Gloucestershire Towns*.

358 Charterhouse

Address: Godalming, Surrey GU7 2DX

Telephone: (01483) 291508/291516 291671 (to leave a message)

Enquiries: The Librarian, Mrs A.C. Wheeler

Open: By arrangement, preferably during term.

Access: Approved researchers, on written application and by appointment.

Historical background: Sutton's Hospital in the Charterhouse was founded in 1611 by Thomas Sutton to provide a home for 40 deserving men pensioners and to offer board and education to 40 boys, nominated in turn by the governors. They were housed in London until 1872, when the school was moved to newly built premises in Godalming. In London the school also educated day boys, who lodged in private boarding houses, though for many years these were not recorded as part of the establishment.

Acquisitions policy: To add, by purchase or donation, books, photographs, documents etc, by or about Old Carthusians. To house anything of interest to the school, its history and pupils.

Archives of organisation: School admission, discipline and minute books.

Major collections: Personal scrapbooks relating to the school, kept by Mrs Haig Brown, wife of the headmaster who moved the school from London, and Mr Girdlestone, an assistant master who, having founded the house which bears his name, was housemaster of it for many years, 1872–c1902.

Non-manuscript material: School photographs, 1870–.
Cartoons of John Leech and Max Beerbohm. School magazines, 1872–.
Carthusian Collection: works by and about Old Carthusians, notably John Wesley, Thackeray and Baden-Powell.

Facilities: Some photocopying and photography may be possible.

359 Gracehill Moravian Church

Parent organisation: Moravian Church, London (entry 635)

Address: Moravian Manse, 25 Church Road, Gracehill, Co. Antrim BT42 2NL

Telephone: (01266) 653141

Enquiries: The Minister, Rev. Victor D. Launder

Open: By appointment.

Access: Generally open to the public by appointment; a donation towards the church is appreciated.

The Moravian Church in Gracehill was started in 1759. Records consist of church diaries (kept by the Moravian ministers), accounts, deeds, registers of members, baptisms, marriages and burials. There are also diaries and records of the former Dublin congregation, 1748–1980, and registers and records of the former congrega-

tions. Microfilm and lists are at Public Record Office of Northern Ireland (entry78).

360 Belvoir Castle

Address: Grantham, Lincs HG32 1PD

Telephone: (01476) 870262

Enquiries: The Secretary to the Duke of Rutland, Mrs D.A. Staveley

Open: Mon–Fri: 9.00–5.00

The Belvoir Archive contains MSS, estate records, accounts and maps 14th century–; and personal papers of the Marrens family, 15th century–. The muniment room is not open, but applications from bona fide researchers may be given consideration. There is a very brief catalogue.

361 The Wordsworth Library

Parent organisation: The Wordsworth Trust

Address: Dove Cottage, Townend, Grasmere, Cumbria LA22 9SH

Telephone: (015394) 35003/35544

Fax: (015394) 35748

Enquiries: The Registrar, Jeff Cowton

Open: Mon–Fri: 9.30–1.00; 2.00–5.30; weekends by arrangement.

Access: Bona fide researchers, by prior arrangement with the trustees (please allow 3–4 weeks).

Historical background: This charitable trust was founded in 1890 with the purchase of Dove Cottage and a mission to preserve Dove Cottage and its collections 'for lovers of poetry all over the world'. A museum opened in 1935, with provision for a library in 1950. The current specially designed museum opened in 1981 and houses special exhibitions, an education programme, a 'writer-in-residence' scheme, and special events and conferences.

Acquisitions policy: The trust collects manuscripts, books, artefacts and fine art related to Wordsworth and the development and influence of Romanticism; and to the development of the Lake District, art and culture.

Major collections: Verse, prose and correspondence of William Wordsworth (1770–1850), his family and circle, including Dorothy Wordsworth (1771–1855), Samuel Taylor Coleridge (1772–1834) and Thomas De Quincey (1785–1859).

Integral collections of papers associated with Wordsworth and the Lake District and associated family estate papers including the Shepherd papers, the 'G' papers, the Spedding papers (c1700–1940), and the Moorsom papers of the Calvert and Stanger families of Keswick, 18th century–.

Non-manuscript material: Paintings, drawings, prints, photographic archive.
Lifetime editions, collected works, biographical and critical works of William Wordsworth and his contemporaries.
Books owned by, and associated with, Wordsworth and his circle.
Collection of Lake District books.

Finding aids: Indexes, lists, catalogues, computer records available, to varying degrees of detail; Calvert and Stanger papers: NRA 26173.

Facilities: Photocopying by arrangement. Photography.

Conservation: Preventative conservation in-house. Remedial conservation contracted out.

Publications: Catalogues relating to special exhibitions. Publication list available.

362 Great Yarmouth Central Library

Parent organisation: Norfolk County Council

Address: Tolhouse Street, Great Yarmouth, Norfolk NR30 2SH

Telephone: (01493) 844551

Fax: (01493) 857628

Enquiries: The Senior Librarian, Peter Ransome

Open: Mon–Fri: 9.30–6.00 Sat: 9.00–5.00

The library houses local studies material on Great Yarmouth and East Norfolk consisting mainly of books, pamphlets, newspaper cuttings and illustrations. Most archival material relating to Great Yarmouth is held by Norfolk Record Office (entry **855**). There is a local studies catalogue with indexes to newspaper cuttings and local illustrations. Facilities include photocopying and microfilm/fiche readers, and a guide to the local history collections is available.

363 Inverclyde District Libraries

Address: Watt Library, 9 Union Street, Greenock, Strathclyde PA16 8JH

Telephone: (01475) 720186

Enquiries: Mrs I. Couperwhite

Open: Mon, Thurs: 2.00–5.00; 6.00–8.00 Tues, Fri: 10.00–12.30; 2.00–5.00 Wed, Sat: 10.00–1.00

Access: Generally open to the public.

Historical background: Opened in 1837 as a memorial to James Watt, the Watt Library was originally a subscription library; it was taken over in 1974 by Inverclyde District Council and is used as a centre for the local archive material for the area.

Acquisitions policy: To collect material relating to the Inverclyde area, by purchase, donation or deposit.

Major collections: Corporation minutes of Greenock, Gourock and Port Glasgow.
Local cemetery, hospital and institutions records.

Non-manuscript material: Pamphlets; photographs; tapes; newspapers; rare books.
Scott's photographs and ship details.

Finding aids: Indexes to newspapers, including ship-launches, and births, marriages and deaths. Catalogue of main collections.

Facilities: Photocopying. Microfilm reader/printer.

364 South Humberside Area Archive Office

Parent organisation: Humberside County Archive Service (Beverley)

Address: Town Hall Square, Grimsby, South Humberside DN31 1HX

Telephone: (01472) 353481

Enquiries: The Area Archivist, Mr J.F. Wilson

Open: Mon, Wed, Thurs: 9.30–12.00; 1.00–5.00 Tues: 9.30–12.00; 1.00–5.00; 5.00–9.00, by appointment only Fri: 9.30–12.00; 1.00–4.15

Access: Generally open to the public. An appointment is advisable.

Historical background: The office was established in 1976 following reorganisation to cover the administrative areas of Grimsby, Scunthorpe, Glanford and Cleethorpes, and it is a recognised place of deposit for public records. The office is a branch of Humberside County Archive Service (entry **86**). It is not a diocesan record office, and enquiries about parish registers, wills and bishops' transcripts should be directed to the Lincolnshire Archives Office (entry **460**). Archives formerly in the custody of the Scunthorpe Borough Museum and Art Gallery, Oswald Road, Scunthorpe, DN15 7BD, are now deposited and available in this office, but can also be returned to the museum for study by arrangement with the Keeper of Local History there.

Acquisitions policy: Humberside County Council and predecessor local authorities; geographical county of Humberside.

Archives of organisation: Usual local authority record holding of archives, created by Great Grimsby Borough, 1227–; and by rural district councils and urban district councils in South Humberside, including records of lighting inspectors, local boards of health, sanitary authorities, burial boards, school boards, parish councils (15), schools (100), Grimsby Borough Police and Grimsby Education Committee.

Major collections: Deposited local collections, including Board of Trade records for Grimsby, notably merchant vessel crew lists, 1863–1913, fishing vessel crew lists, 1884–1914, registers of sea-going apprentices, 1880–1937.
Parkinson family of East Ravendale: family and estate papers, 1699–1937.
Sheffield family of Normanby Hall: family and estate papers, 1720–1927.
Winn family of Nostell Priory (Yorks) and Appleby Hall: ironstone leases and related papers for North Lincolnshire, 1839–1942, principally of Rowland Winn (1820–93), 1st Lord St Oswald.

Non-manuscript material: Oral history recordings of domestic servants, farm and fishing workers, in Grimsby and North Lincolnshire, 1900–85.

Finding aids: Lists sent to NRA.

Facilities: Photocopying. Microfilm readers.

Conservation: Comprehensive in-house facilities. The conservation unit for Humberside County Archive Service is in this office. Outside work is not generally undertaken.

Publications: Guide to the South Humberside Area Archive Service (1993).

365 British Red Cross Museum and Archives

Address: Barnett Hill, Wonersh, Guildford, Surrey GU5 0RF

Telephone: (01483) 898595

Fax: (01483) 892836

Enquiries: The Archivist, Miss Alison Kearns

Open: By appointment only.

Access: Generally open to the public.

Historical background: The Red Cross movement was started in 1863 to help the sick and wounded of both sides in war. The British society was founded in 1870, when it was known as the British National Society for Aid to the Sick and Wounded in War. In 1905 it became the British Red Cross Society.

Acquisitions policy: To acquire all documents and museum items relating to Red Cross history.

Archives of organisation:: Minute books, 1905–; other records of the society, including official reports on British Red Cross activities in a number of wars, *c*1870–; Voluntary Aid Detachment record cards, World Wars I and II. Records of a number of British Red Cross county branches, 1909–.

Major collections: Records of Royal Star and Garter Home for Disabled Sailors, Soldiers and Airmen, Richmond, Surrey, 1915–87.
Voluntary Blood Donor's Association, minute books, 1932–64.
Records of the Joint Committee of the British Red Cross Society and Order of St John, including records of its predecessor bodies the Joint War Committee, Joint Council and Joint War Organisation, 1914–. These bodies coordinated voluntary aid to the armed services during both World Wars, and their records include information about services to prisoners of war, medical work, fund-raising and personnel.
Papers of Col. Robert Lloyd-Lindsay, later Lord Wantage (1832–1901), founder and first

chairman of BRCS. These contain important material on the Franco-Prussian War, 1870–71, and the South African War, 1899–1902.

Non-manuscript material: Large amount of printed and published posters, leaflets, first aid handbooks, reports, etc, c1870–.
Large photograph collection.
Small collection of oral history tapes.
Old training films and films showing International Red Cross work.

Finding aids: Lists. Accessions register with subject and personal names indexes. Some indexes for items acquired before May 1985. General survey list for whole collection.

Facilities: Photocopying. Photography by arrangement.

Conservation: Contracted out.

Publications: M. Poulter: 'The Archives of the British Red Cross', *Social History of Medicine* vi/1(1993), 143–7.

366 Guildford Institute

Parent organisation: University of Surrey

Address: Ward Street, Guildford, Surrey GU1 4LH

Telephone: (01483) 62142

Enquiries: The Librarian, Patricia Chapman

Open: Mon–Fri: 10.00–3.00

Access: Bona fide research students, who must normally become members of the institute on payment of an annual subscription.

The institute was founded in 1834 (not in the present building) as part of the Mechanical Institutes movement. In 1980 the building passed into the trusteeship of the University of Surrey and was completely repaired and refurbished. The aims and objectives and property rights are fully protected by Charity Commissioners. Archives of the institute, 1834–, are now held at Surrey Record Office, Guildford Muniment Room (entry **368**). Playbills of Guildford Theatre, the Theatre Royal and Borough Halls, 1822–; scrapbooks and newspaper cuttings, 1870–1922; and photographs of local worthies, events and topography are maintained at the institute.

367 Surrey Local Studies Library

Parent organisation: Surrey County Libraries and Leisure Department

Address: Branch Library, 77 North Street, Guildford, Surrey GU1 4AL

Telephone: (01483) 34054

Enquiries: The Local Studies Librarian

Open: Mon, Fri: 10.00–8.00 Tues, Thurs: 10.00–5.00 Wed: 10.00–1.00 Sat: 9.30–4.00

Access: Generally open to the public; appointment necessary to use microform material.

Historical background: The Local Studies Library was established in 1981 and since then has brought together various collections of local history material. These now form a comprehensive collection relating to the whole of the present administrative county of Surrey.

Acquisitions policy: To collect any items, including ephemera, of history, geology and related subjects relevant to the present administrative county of Surrey, having regard to the acquisitions policy of Surrey Record Office, Guildford Muniment Room (entry **368**).

Archives of organisation: Many items relating to the Surrey County Library founded in 1924.

Major collections: MS note-books and scrapbooks of various deceased local historians, including the Gladwin note-books, Green note-books, Williamson note-books and scrapbooks.
MS diaries of Henry Peak (1832–1914), architect and mayor of Guildford.
MS of Gertrude Jekyll's *Old West Surrey*, published in 1904.
MS note-book of Sgt Alexander Alexander, who served in the Scots Guards, 1844–66.

Non-manuscript material: Maps of Surrey (c4000).
Illustrations collection, including photographs, postcards, engravings, lithographs and glass plates (c15,000 items).
Microfilms, including local newspapers, 1837–, Surrey parish registers and census returns, 1841–91.
Large collection of property sales catalogues, 19th century–.

Finding aids: Card and microfiche catalogue, indexes to illustrations, parish records (on microfilm and hard copy), sales catalogues, censuses (population and places), Surrey Information Index, Surrey Biography Index.

Facilities: Photocopying. Microfilm/fiche readers/printer.

Conservation: Contracted out.

368 Surrey Record Office
Guildford Muniment Room

Parent organisation: Surrey County Council

Address: Castle Arch, Guildford, Surrey GU1 3SX

Telephone: (01483) 573942

Enquiries: The Archivist-in-charge, Miss M. Mackey

Open: Tues–Thurs: 9.30–4.45 Sat (1st and 3rd of each month): 9.30–12.30

Access: Generally open to the public; an appointment is necessary.

Historical background: The office was established in 1928 by the Surrey Archaeological Society and originally collected material from all over Surrey; it is now concerned mainly with south-west Surrey. It also acts as the Diocesan Record Office for Guildford (parish records, excluding Emly and Epsom deaneries) and is recognised as a place of deposit for public records. See also Surrey Record Office, Kingston-upon-Thames (entry **429**).

Acquisitions policy: Archival material relating to the area of south-west Surrey and the Diocese of Guildford (excepting deaneries of Emly and Epsom).

Archives of organisation: Local authority archives of Guildford Borough.

Major collections: Deposited collections, of which the following have a wider significance: Papers of More of Loseley, including records of the office of the King's Tents, 1542–58, and of the Lieutenancy of the Tower of London, 1615–17.
Wey Navigation, 17th–20th centuries.
Godalming Navigation, 18th–20th centuries.
Billings & Sons of Guildford, printers, 19th–20th centuries.
Dennis Bros. of Guildford, motor manufacturers (including plans), 20th century.
Papers of Lewis Carroll, 1832–98.
Onslow estate and family papers, c1232–1968.

Non-manuscript material: Dennis Bros. photographic collection.

Finding aids: Lists sent to NRA. Personal name, place and subject indexes.

Facilities: Photocopying. Photography. Microfilm reader.

Conservation: In-house facilities at Surrey Record Office, Kingston-upon-Thames.

Publications: Surrey Record Office Guide to Parish Registers [updated regularly].
Lewis Carroll in Guildford Muniment Room (1989).

369 University of Surrey

Address: Guildford, Surrey GU2 5XH

A Library

Telephone: (01483) 259287

Fax: (01483) 259500

Enquiries: The Librarian, Mr T.J.A. Crawshaw

Open: Term: Mon: 10.00–10.00 Tues–Fri: 9.00–10.00 Sat: 1.00–6.00 (autumn and spring); 9.00–6.00 (summer) Sun: 2.00–6.00 Vacation: Mon–Fri 9.00–5.00
Details of weekend opening on application.

Access: Bona fide researchers.

Historical background: Battersea College of Technology, founded in 1894 as the Battersea Polytechnic, was awarded a charter as the University of Surrey in 1966. The library supports the teaching and research of the university. The archives are housed in the library and are under the control of the librarian, supported by part-time archives staff.

Acquisitions policy: The library collects administrative and other documents from departments. There is no other policy, except to preserve items of historical interest about the institution and its courses.

Archives of organisation: Administrative and other records of the university and its predecessors. Calendars, staff and student magazines and newsletters.

Non-manuscript material: Some tape-recordings of older staff and others on the institution's history. Some photographs and insignia.

Finding aids: Collection partly indexed, with work still in progess.

Facilities: Photocopying. Photography. Microfilm/fiche reader/printer.

B National Resource Centre for Dance

Telephone: (01483) 259316

Enquiries: The Manager, Judith A. Chapman

Open: Tues–Fri: 9.30–5.00

Access: Researchers, students and teachers, by appointment. A visit facility fee is charged.

Historical background: The NRCD was established at the University of Surrey in 1982 as a result of the Calouste Gulbenkian Foundation report on dance education and training in the UK (1980) and operates as a self-financing fee-based service. There are several collections built up by companies, solo artists, dance organisations and individuals involved in dance.

Acquisitions policy: The focus of the collection is on dance, especially dance heritage of the UK. Materials acquired include manuscripts, visual materials and sound recordings, mainly 20th century.

Major collections: Arts Council Dance Panel records, c1950–c1990.
Records of many dance associations and societies, e.g. Dance and the Child International, International Council for Kinetography Laban.
Archives of dance companies and artists, e.g. EMMA/Midlands Dance Company; Extemporary Dance Theatre; Kickstart.
Joan Russell Archive: dance education.
Warren Lamb Archive: early movement analysis and profiling work.
Laban Archive: original drawings and papers of R. Laban (see also entry **590**).

Non-manuscript material: Collection of UK and foreign dance journals.

Finding aids: Lists of some major archives; others in preparation.

Facilities: Photocopying and photography (central university facilities).

Conservation: Conservation facilities are available in-house.

Publications: J.A. Chapman (comp.): *Dance Film and Video Catalogue* (1992).
A List of the Dance Periodical and Newsletters Holdings at the University of Surrey (NRCD, 1993).

370 West Yorkshire Archive Service
Calderdale District Archives

Address: Calderdale Central Library, Northgate House, Northgate, Halifax, West Yorks HX1 1UN

Telephone: (01422) 357257 ext. 2636

Fax: (01422) 349458

Enquiries: The District Archivist or The Archivist to the Joint Committee, Mr R. Frost

Open: Original documents, by appointment: Mon, Tues, Thurs, Fri: 10.00–5.30 Wed: 10.00–4.00
Documents on microfilm: Mon, Tues, Thurs, Fri: 10.00–8.00 Wed, Sat: 10.00–5.00

Access: Generally open to the public.

Historical background: The Calderdale Archives Service is very much a development of the Halifax Borough Archives Service, which was established in 1964 and which acquired the accumulations of the Halifax Museums Service and the Halifax Antiquarian Society. In 1974 the Archives Service took control of the archival records of the nine amalgamating local authorities within Calderdale, and in 1983 it joined the West Yorkshire Archive Service. It moved to its present purpose-built accommodation in 1983. It acts as the Diocesan Record Office for Bradford (Shelf parish records) and is recognised as a place of deposit for public records.

Acquisitions policy: Archives relating to the Calderdale MBC geographical area.

Archives of organisation: Records of Calderdale MBC and nine predecessor authorities, with inherited archives, including records of civil townships, 1665–, and Halifax Town Trustees, 1762–1849.

Major collections: Family and estate archives, including Lister of Shibden Hall, 1329–1937, Armytage of Kirklees Hall, 1200–1800, and Stansfeld of Fieldhouse Sowerby, 1701–1920.
Political and labour holdings, including records of local Co-operative Societies, 1832–1972, friendly societies, 1769–1981, political parties, 1874–1981, and trade unions, 1834–1983.
Business archives, especially textile records, 1562–1983, including John Crossley and Sons, carpet manufacturers, 17th–20th centuries.

Finding aids: Lists and detailed indexes available. Link to West Yorkshire Archive Service computerised database. Catalogues sent to NRA.

Facilities: Photocopying. Photography by arrangement. Microfilm/fiche readers/printers.

Conservation: Undertaken by West Yorkshire Archive Service Headquarters, Wakefield (entry 1072).

Publications: Archives in Calderdale (1976; annual supplements, 1977–84).
A. Betteridge and P. Sewell (comp.): *Calderdale Archives, 1964–1989: an Illustrated Guide to Calderdale District Archives* (1990); supplement covering 1990–92 accessions (1993).

371 Hamilton District Libraries

Address: 98 Cadzow Street, Hamilton, Strathclyde ML3 6HQ

Telephone: (01698) 894044 ext. 2403

Fax: (01698) 286334

Enquiries: The Libraries Manager, Mr W.K. McCoubrey

Open: Mon, Tues, Thurs: 9.30–7.30 Wed: 9.30–1.00 Fri, Sat: 9.30–5.00

Access: Generally open to the public.

Historical background: Hamilton District Libraries was formed in 1975. Hamilton Burgh Library joined with part of Lanark County Libraries to form the new authority.

Acquisitions policy: To collect material relating to Hamilton District and the surrounding area. Photographs of the area have been transferred to the Museum Service.

Major collections: Burgh of Hamilton: Council minute books, 1701–1975; abstract of accounts, 1879–1975; Register of Electors, 1851– (incomplete); Hamilton Police Commissioners minute books, 1857–1901; Hamilton Road Trustees minute books, 1808–65; Hamilton Combination Poor House (later Hamilton Home) minute books, 1864–1975.
Lanark County Council minute books, 1890–1975.
Small collection of 18th– and 19th–century estate papers relating to the Duke of Hamilton's estates in Lanarkshire.

Non-manuscript material: Maps of Hamilton and the surrounding area (*c*1000).

Microfilm of census returns for the Hamilton area 1841–1891.
Local newspapers, 1856–.

Finding aids: List of Hamilton estates papers; sent to NRA and NRA(S).

Facilities: Photocopying. Microfilm/fiche reader/printer.

372 Rothamsted Experimental Station Library

Parent organisation: AFRC Institute of Arable Crops Research

Address: Rothamsted Experimental Station, Harpenden, Herts AL5 2JQ

Telephone: (01582) 763133

Fax: (01582) 760981

Enquiries: The Librarian

Open: Mon–Thurs: 9.00–5.30 Fri: 9.00–5.00

Access: Bona fide enquirers, by prior arrangement only.

Historical background: Rothamsted Experimental Station was founded in 1843 by Sir John Bennett Lawes and his partner Sir Henry Gilbert to study crop nutrition. A number of the experiments they began continue today, and Rothamsted's remit is still to study the processes involved in plant growth.

Acquisitions policy: No active policy for collecting archives; other departments retain their own records.

Major collections: Sir John Lawes and Sir Henry Gilbert: a few personal papers and much correspondence and other documents relating to scientific work, preparation of lectures and printed papers and Rothamsted administration, 1840s–early 20th century.
Sir A.D. Hall and Sir E.J. Russell, 20th–century directors of Rothamsted: personal and working papers.
Lawes Agriculture Trust: correspondence and minutes, 1880s–early 20th century.
Rothamsted Farm, Woburn Experimental Station and Fruit Farm: diaries and working note-books, mid-19th–mid-20th centuries.
Rothamsted staff: working note-books of Robert Warrington (1838–1907), and of a few 20th–century staff members.

Non-manuscript material: British livestock

prints and paintings (*c*200).
Early agricultural books, 1480–1840 (*c*3500).

Finding aids: Various catalogues and lists; some sent to NRA.

Facilities: Photocopying. Microfilm/fiche reader.

Conservation: Contracted out.

Publications: M. Harcourt Williams: *Rothamsted Experimental Station: Catalogue of the Records in the Station Library* (1987).
Catalogue of the Correspondence of Lawes and Gilbert (1989).
G.V. Dyke: *John Bennett Lawes: the Record of his Genius* (Research Studies Press, 1991).
——: *John Lawes of Rothamsted* (Hoos Press, 1993).

373 Harrow School

Address: 5 High Street, Harrow-on-the-Hill, Middx HA1 3HP

Telephone: (0181) 422 2196 ext. 305

Fax: (0181) 423 311

Enquiries: The Archivist, A.D.K. Hawkyard

Open: By arrangement.

Access: Bona fide students or researchers.

Historical background: The school was founded *de novo* in 1572 in the parish of Harrow by John Lyon of Preston, who, in the absence of children of his own, endowed it with a series of properties. The income from the Lyon estates was also used towards the maintenance of local roads, the provision of apprenticeship money and of dowries and other approved purposes until the Public Schools Act of 1868, when a second school, the John Lyon School, was partially funded from the surplus of the original endowment. Although the school was originally established as a free grammar school for boys from the locality, as early as 1592 the headmaster was permitted to take in fee-paying pupils, who shortly outnumbered the parishioners. It is now an independent fee-paying school controlled by a board of governors.

Acquisitions policy: To consolidate the existing collection of material relating to the school, its governors, staff and pupils, and to John Lyon's other charities.

Archives of organisation: Estate documents, 14th century–.
Governors' minutes and account books, 1615–.
Headmasters' papers, *c*1805–; masters' papers, *c*1800–.
School lists, 1770–.

Major collections: Literary and other autographs; material relating to Richard Brinsley Sheridan (1751–1816) and Lord Byron (1788–1824).

Non-manuscript material: Photographs of individuals, groups, teams and buildings, late 1850s–.
Architectural drawings, particularly by William Burges (1827–81).

Finding aids: Card index in progress.

Facilities: Photocopying.

Publications: E.J.L. Scott: *Records of the Grammar School Founded by John Lyon* (Harrow, 1886).
J.S. Golland: *The Harrow Apprentices* (Harrow, 1981).

374 The Society of the Divine Saviour (SDS)

Address: Salvatorian Provincial Office, 129 Spencer Road, Harrow Weald, Middx HA3 7BJ

Telephone: (0181) 427 4673

Fax: (0181) 427 6924

Enquiries: Fr Edmund Lanning

Open: By appointment.

Access: Bona fide scholars, by appointment only.

The Salvatorians were founded in Rome in 1882 and came to England in 1901. Their archives relate to the administration of the Province, its houses and members, and links with various dioceses and international houses. The society is a registered charity. There is a catalogue and further listing is in progress.

375 Hartlepool Central Library

Parent organisation: Cleveland County Libraries

Address: 124 York Road, Hartlepool, Cleveland TS26 9DE

Telephone: (01429) 263778/272905

Enquiries: The Reference Librarian, Miss M.E. Hoban

Open: Mon–Thurs: 9.30–7.00 Fri, Sat: 9.30–5.00

Access: Generally open to the public. Prior notice is needed for access to older and more fragile material; a booking system operates for microfilm readers.

Acquisitions policy: The primary area of interest is the geographical area within the Hartlepool District boundaries; material for neighbouring areas is included in the collection, which is based on a stock covering the old counties of Northumberland, Durham and North Yorkshire. All subjects are included and all formats – books, pamphlets, ephemera, photographs, postcards, maps, periodicals, videos, manuscripts.

Major collections: Usual local history collection, including William Grey & Co., shipbuilder: yardbooks, 1878–1942 (incomplete). Blumer's, shipbuilder & ship repairer: account books, 1853–68 (4 vols).
J. Proctor, printer, binder and stationer: invoices and accounts, 1865–7.
Sir Cuthbert Sharp, author and antiquary, MSS. NB Hartlepool Port and Harbour Commission records are now at Cleveland County Archives (entry 819).

Non-manuscript material: Local studies collection covering the North-East, with special emphasis on Hartlepool.
Photographs (c4000), including the Ferriday Collection.
Substantial collection of 19th-century maps.

Finding aids: Selective index to newspapers, 1865–89; index to photograph collection; card catalogue of maps.

Facilities: Photocopying. Photography by arrangement. Microfilm/fiche readers/printers.

Conservation: By arrangement with Cleveland County Archives.

Publications: List of Directories in the Local Studies Collection.
Selective List of Genealogical Sources in the Local Studies Collection.

376 Haslemere Educational Museum

Address: High Street, Haslemere, Surrey GU27 2LA

Telephone: (01428) 642112

Enquiries: The Curator, Diana M. Hawkes

Open: April-Oct: Tues–Sat: 10.00–5.00 Sun: 2.00–5.00 Nov-March: Tues–Sat: 10.00–4.00

Access: Generally open to the public; appointment essential.

Historical background: The museum, which is a charitable trust, was founded in 1888 by Jonathan Hutchinson (1828–1913), surgeon and local landowner.

Acquisitions policy: Suitable documents relating to local history and personalities connected with the district and museum.

Major collections: Field note-books, sketches and MSS belonging to Sir Archibald Geikie (1834–1924), geologist.
Flora and fauna records of the district, c1870–.

Non-manuscript material: Press cuttings, early photographs etc relating to Haslemere district and celebrated personalities, c1870–.

Facilities: Photocopying strictly by arrangement.

377 Haslingden Library

Address: Higher Deardengate, Haslingden, Rossendale, Lancs BB4 5QL

Telephone: (01706) 215690

Enquiries: The Librarian

Open: Mon, Thurs: 9.30–5.00 Tues, Fri: 9.30–7.30 Sat: 9.30–4.00

Access: Generally open to the public.

Historical background: The local history collection was started before World War II, but more recently some items have been copied and originals placed in Lancashire Record Office (entry 944).

Acquisitions policy: Acquires local history material relevant to Haslingden and neighbouring towns in Rossendale.

Major collections: Usual local history collec-

tion, including: minutes of Haslingden Borough, 1927–74, Rossendale, 1974–.
Halstead Collection: a few transcripts of local church and other records, including Haslingden Parish Church registers, 1650–96, and Haslingden vestry books, 1780–1911, with diaries and scrapbooks.
Collection *re* local cricket club and Lancashire League, 1875–.

Non-manuscript material: Cassette recordings of local dramatic society productions and of the Rossendale Male Voice Choir.

Finding aids: NRA 1296 and more recent typed list.

Facilities: Photocopying. Microfilm reader. Film projectors.

378 Hastings Museum and Art Gallery

Address: Cambridge Road, Hastings, East Sussex TN34 1ET

Telephone: (01424) 721202

Enquiries: The Curator, Miss V.A.G. Williams

Open: Museum: Mon–Fri: 10.00–5.00 Sat: 10.00–1.00; 2.00–5.00 Sun: 3.00–5.00
Access to records is by appointment, Monday to Friday only.

Access: Generally open to the public.

Historical background: The museum was founded in 1890 and moved to its present site in 1928. Originally only a museum and art gallery, it gradually attracted records. In 1973 parish and other ecclesiastical records were transferred to the East Sussex Record Office (entry **455**).

Acquisitions policy: Donations of local MSS are accepted from time to time.

Major collections: Archives of Hastings and the Cinque Ports, 12th century-.
Archives of local families, including the Milwards.

Non-manuscript material: Large collections of photographs, prints and ephemera with the gallery collections.

Finding aids: Various registers and indexes.

Facilities: Normal archive office facilities cannot be provided. However, help will always be given to genuine researchers. Not suitable for student projects.

Publications: Various historical publications relating to Hastings.

379 Hatfield House Library

Address: Hatfield House, Hatfield, Herts AL9 5NF

Enquiries: The Librarian and Archivist to the Marquess of Salisbury, Mr R.H. Harcourt Williams

Open: By arrangement with the librarian.

Access: Approved academic (normally postgraduate) researchers, on written application.

Historical background: Hatfield House was built in 1612 by Robert Cecil, 1st Earl of Salisbury. It has remained in the possession of his direct descendants and is now the home of the 6th Marquess of Salisbury.

Archives of organisation: Papers of William Cecil, 1st Baron Burghley (1520–98), Secretary of State and afterwards Lord Treasurer to Queen Elizabeth I.
Papers of Robert Cecil, 1st Earl of Salisbury (1563–1612), Secretary of State and Lord Treasurer to King James I (a microfilm copy of these papers may be consulted in the British Library, Special Collections (entry **495**)).
Papers of Robert Gascoyne-Cecil, 3rd Marquess of Salisbury (1830–1903), Foreign Secretary and Prime Minister to Queen Victoria.

Non-manuscript material: Maps and architectural drawings.

Finding aids: Calendar of the Salisbury (Cecil) Manuscripts, vols i–xxiv (1883–1976), covers all papers up to 1668 (i.e. those of Lord Burghley and the 1st and 2nd Earls of Salisbury).
J.F.A. Mason: *Calendar of the Private Foreign Office Correspondence of Robert, 3rd Marquess of Salisbury*, 2 vols (NRA typescript, 1963; available at the NRA).
Card index at Hatfield House for remaining correspondence of the third Marquess.

Facilities: Photocopying (certain collections only).

Publications: Robert, 5th Marquess of Salisbury: 'The library at Hatfield House, Hertfordshire', *The Library*, 5th ser., xviii/2 (1963), 83.
R.A. Skelton and Sir J. Summerson: *A Description of Maps and Architectural Drawings in the Collection made by William Cecil, First Baron*

Burghley, now at Hatfield House (Oxford, 1971).
Royal Commission on Historical Manuscripts: 'Estate papers of the Cecil family, Marquesses of Salisbury', HMC *Annual Review 1989–1990* (HMSO, 1990), 29–31.

380 Dyfed Archives Service
Pembrokeshire Record Office

Parent organisation: Dyfed County Council

Address: The Castle, Haverfordwest, Dyfed SA61 2EF

Telephone: (01437) 763703

Enquiries: The Archivist, Mrs Marie Steele-Morgan

Open: Mon–Thurs: 9.00–4.45 Fri: 9.00–4.15 Sat (1st and 3rd of each month, except bank holiday weekends): 9.30–12.30

Access: Generally open to the public. Some restrictions on deposited material.

Historical background: The first county archivist was appointed in 1963 and the office was established as Pembrokeshire Record Office in 1967. It also acts as the Diocesan Record Office for St David's (parish records only) and is recognised as a place of deposit for public records. There are associated offices at Aberystwyth and Carmarthen (entries 9 and 200).

Acquisitions policy: The area covers the old county of Pembrokeshire.

Archives of organisation: Usual local authority record holdings.

Major collections: Deposited local collections, including solicitors', estate agents' and family records relating to Angle (John Mirehouse); Bush (Meyricks); Carew Court (Carew); Cresselly (Allen); Lawrenny (Lort-Phillips); Pentre (Saunders-Davies); Scotlon (Higgon) and Henlan (Lewis).
Deeds and documents of the Starbuck family of Sherborn, Nantucket Island, Massachusetts, 1660–1780.

Finding aids: Catalogues and indexes. Lists sent to NRA.

Facilities: Photocopying. Microfilm/fiche reader.

Conservation: Conservator employed for the three Dyfed Archives Service offices; minimum outside work undertaken.

381 Haverfordwest Public Library
Local Studies Department

Parent organisation: Dyfed Cultural Services Department

Address: Dew Street, Haverfordwest, Dyfed SA61 1SU

Telephone: (01437) 764591 ext. 5248

Fax: (01437) 769218

Enquiries: The Assistant Librarian, Reference and Local Studies, Mrs A. Thomas

Open: Mon, Wed, Thurs: 9.30–5.00 Tues, Fri: 9.30–7.00 Sat: 9.30–1.00

Access: Generally open to the public; advance notice preferred but not essential.

Historical background: The Local Studies Collection contains material relating to Pembrokeshire which has been collected over a period of more than 50 years. Much of the archival material was gathered in the absence of a record office before local government reorganisation in 1974.

Acquisitions policy: To collect material directly related to Pembrokeshire. Donations of relevant material are accepted.

Major collections: Francis Green Collection of genealogical material, comprising copies of documents dating from 13th to early 20th centuries (33 vols). There is also a supplementary collection of sheet pedigrees relating to West Wales families.

Non-manuscript material: Photographs and slides, mainly topographical, 19th and 20th centuries (c5500).
Maps, 17th–20th centuries (c1000).
Local newspapers, 1844–1924 (on microfilm), 1960– (bound, incomplete); newspaper cuttings, 1976–.

Finding aids: Card indexes. Bibliographies prepared for certain localities (copies sent to National Library of Wales, Aberystwyth; entry 10).

Facilities: Photocopying. Microfilm/fiche readers.

Publications: *Genealogical Sources in Haver-*

fordwest Library.
Newspapers and Periodicals in Haverfordwest Library.

382 Clwyd Record Office
Hawarden Branch

Address: The Old Rectory, Hawarden, Deeside, Clwyd CH5 3NR

Telephone: (01244) 532364

Fax: (01244) 538344

Enquiries: The County Archivist, Mr C.J. Williams

Open: Mon–Thurs: 9.00–4.45 Fri: 9.00–4.15 Two days' notice required for access to Glynne-Gladstone MSS

Historical background: Flintshire Record Office was established in 1951 and was incorporated in Clwyd Record Office, which was formed after local government reorganisation in 1974, also taking in what was formerly Denbighshire and part of Merioneth. The office also acts as the Diocesan Record Office for St Asaph (parish records) and is recognised as a place of deposit for public records. There is a branch office at Ruthin (entry **972**). The county archivist is honorary archivist to the St Deiniol's Library, Hawarden, whose archive collections (Glynne-Gladstone MSS) are made available for research at the Record Office.

Archives of organisation: Usual local authority record holdings.

Major collections: Deposited collections, of which the following has a wider significance: Glynne-Gladstone MSS, deposited in St Deiniol's Library by Sir William Gladstone in 1968, comprising family correspondence and papers of the Glynne and Gladstone families of Hawarden Castle, mostly c1800–1930; includes correspondence of W.E. Gladstone (1809–98), Herbert, Viscount Gladstone (1854–1930) and the 5th Duke of Newcastle (1811–64).

Finding aids: Lists (including detailed list of Glynne-Gladstone MSS).

Facilities: Photocopying. Photography. Microfilming by arrangement. Microfilm/fiche reader/printer.

Publications: A.G. Veysey: *Guide to the Flintshire Record Office* (1974) [includes St Deiniol's Library collections].

D. Pratt and A.G. Veysey: *Handlist of Topographical Prints of Clwyd* (1977).
D. Pratt: *Calendar of the Flintshire Quarter Sessions Rolls, 1747–52* (1983).
A.G. Veysey: *Guide to the Parish Records of Clwyd* (1984).
C.J. Williams: *Handlist of the Grosvenor (Halkyn) MSS* (1988).
——: *Handlist of the Glynne-Gladstone MSS in St Deniol's Library, Harwarden* (List and Index Society, Special Series Vol. 24, 1990).

383 Hawick Museum

Parent organisation: Roxburgh District Council

Address: Wilton Lodge Park, Hawick, Roxburghshire TD9 7JL

Telephone: (01450) 73457

Fax: (01450) 78526

Enquiries: The Assistant Curator, Elizabeth Hume

Open: April-Sept: Mon–Sat: 10.00–12.00; 1.00–5.00 Sun: 2.00–5.00 Oct-March: Mon–Fri, Sun: 1.00–4.00

Access: Generally open to the public, preferably by appointment.

Historical background: Hawick Museum's collection was founded in 1857 as a result of the collecting activities of the Hawick Archaeological Society. The current museum has been on the site since 1910 and now houses that collection and the library and archive of the society.

Acquisitions policy: Actively seeks to augment existing MS material and contemporary photographs relating to all aspects of Roxburgh District.

Major collections: Hawick Archaeological Society archive and strong local collections, including:
Roxburgh copy of the *National Covenant*, 1638.
Ancrum Papers (Buccleuch), 18th century.
Heritors papers from the original parish church.
Comprehensive monumental inscriptions of Roxburghshire graveyards.
Local estate, church and farming papers, 18th century–.
Local knitwear records, mid-19th century–.

Local archaeological excavations records.
Motor vehicle licensing records (Roxburgh), 1904–27.

Non-manuscript material: Photographic archive (*c*4500 originals) and glass negatives and early slides, late 19th century–.
Extensive maps and plans of Hawick area, 1658–.
Local newspapers, 1877–.

Finding aids: Lists available. Computerised indexes underway. Estate plans and photographs: NRA 17662.

Facilities: Photocopying and photography by arrangement.

Conservation: Contracted out to Scottish Museums Council or Gateshead College.

Publications: Z. Oddy: *A History of Wilton Lodge* (Jedburgh, 1990).

384 Brontë Parsonage Museum Library

Parent organisation: The Brontë Society

Address: Church Street, Haworth, Keighley, West Yorks BD22 8DR

Telephone: (01535) 642323

Fax: (01535) 647131

Enquiries: The Assistant Curator/Librarian, Kathryn White

Open: Mon–Fri: 10.00–4.30 Annual closed period in January/February. The Brontë Parsonage Museum itself is also open at weekends.

Access: Bona fide researchers, with written academic references and strictly by prior appointment.

Historical background: The Brontë Society was founded in 1893 and a museum opened in Haworth in 1895. Early Brontë Society representatives obtained material from important sales of MSS. The Brontë's former home was purchased for the society by a local benefactor and it became a museum in 1928. Since then items have been donated, purchased, bequeathed or loaned, thus adding to the collection. The research library is housed within the museum itself.

Acquisitions policy: The acquisition of material related to, or connected with, the Brontë family, their friends and relatives, and the work of the Brontës.

Archives of organisation: Early Brontë Society correspondence.

Major collections: Brontë Society Collection: work of the Brontë family, including MSS, juvenilia, letters, poetry, French exercises, drawings, administration papers and books. Letters and miscellaneous items of the Brontës' friends and relatives.
Indentures, letters, certificates concerning Haworth and district.
Bonnell Collection: MSS, letters, books and drawings, bequeathed by Henry Houston Bonnell.
Seton Gordon Collection: mainly letters from Charlotte Brontë to her publishers, Smith Elder & Co.
Grolier Collection: mainly letters.

Non-manuscript material: Library collections, including transcripts of Brontë MSS; complete set of Brontë Society *Transactions*; editions of the works, biography, literary criticism and drama archive related to the Brontës.
Collection of published material and facsimiles.

Finding aids: Several catalogues. Computer database of books, MSS and museum objects for staff use only, to prepare selective listings for researchers. Facsimiles of primary source material available for study.

Facilities: Photocopying.

Conservation: Contracted out to Museums Council recommended conservators.

Publications: Brontë Society *Transactions* [published biannually].
C. Alexander: *A Bibliography of the Manuscripts of Charlotte Brontë* (1982).
C. Lemon: *A Centenary History of the Brontë Society, 1893–1993.*

385 The Boys' Brigade

Address: National Training Centre, Felden Lodge, Hemel Hempstead, Herts HP3 0BL

Telephone: (01442) 231681

Fax: (01442) 235391

Enquiries: The Brigade Secretary

Open: Mon–Fri: 9.00–5.00

Access: Members and bona fide researchers, usually by appointment.

Historical background: The Boys' Brigade was founded by William A. Smith in Glasgow in 1883 as part of the Free Church College Mission. It was the first uniformed youth organisation and now has a membership of about 400,000 in more than 60 countries. The celebration of the centenary in 1983 prompted the development of brigade archives.

Acquisitions policy: To acquire records, publications and other relevant material relating to the brigade and its close links with other similar organisations.

Archives of organisation: Archives of the brigade both at central and local level, 1883–.
The *BB Gazette* (in which the original *Scouting for Boys* by Baden-Powell was published), 1889– (monthly).

Major collections: Records and papers of William A. Smith (1854–1914).

Non-manuscript material: Photographs, programmes, certificates, publicity material, handbooks, badges, medals, uniform regalia and other artefacts; film library.

Finding aids: Cataloguing not complete or comprehensive; personal assistance provided if necessary.

Facilities: Photocopying. Photography by arrangement.

Publications: *The Boys' Brigade Gazette* [published bi-monthly].
Archives Press [booklet series dealing with a variety of aspects of Boys' Brigade history].

386 Hereford Cathedral

Address: Hereford HR1 2NG

Telephone: (01432) 359880

Fax: (01432) 355929

Enquiries: The Cathedral Librarian, Miss J. Williams

Open: Tues–Thurs, 1st Sat of month: 10.00–12.30 Other times by arrangement.

Access: Approved readers, by appointment.

Historical background: The archives are formed by the natural accretion of records relating to the history and administration of the Cathedral of Hereford and of the affairs of the Dean and Chapter. They are closely associated with the cathedral library, which acts as a repository for the cathedral music and material relating to the cathedral's function as a place of learning. A new building for archives and rare books is due to open in 1996.

Acquisitions policy: The archives continue to take in material from the administrative and legal offices of the Dean and Chapter. Gifts and deposits are accepted of material relating to or associated with any aspect of the cathedral's history.

Archives of organisation: Acts of the Dean and Chapter; records of the Dean's Consistory court; manorial records; muniments of title and administrative papers of the Dean and Chapter and of the prebendaries. A subsidiary group is formed by the records of the now defunct Vicars Choral. The earliest deed is *c*840.

Major collections: Library: 227 MS works, 8th–15th centuries.

Non-manuscript material: Library: photographic negatives of the Cathedral and contents (*c*1000).
Early books, still chained, 1611– (*c*1500).

Finding aids: Typescript calendars and lists. Card indexes.

Facilities: Photocopying and photography by arrangement. Microfilm reader. Reference library equipped for students.

Publications: F.C. and P.E. Morgan: *Hereford Cathedral Libraries and Muniments* (2/1975) [illustrated].

387 Hereford Record Office

Parent organisation: Hereford and Worcester County Council

Address: The Old Barracks, Harold Street, Hereford HR1 2QX

Telephone: (01432) 265441

Enquiries: The Assistant County Archivist, Miss D.S. Hubbard

Open: Mon: 10.00–4.45 Tues–Thurs: 9.15–4.45 Fri: 9.15–4.00
Prior booking for microfilm/fiche readers essential.

Access: Generally open to the public. The CARN reader's ticket system is operated.

Historical background: Hereford County Record Office was established in 1959 and since 1974 has been a dependent repository of Hereford and Worcester Record Office (entry

1094). It also acts as the Diocesan Record Office for Hereford and is recognised as a place of deposit for public records.

Acquisitions policy: Records of the County and predecessor authorities. Hereford diocesan records: parish records within the old county of Hereford area. Private records within the old Hereford county area are accepted as gifts (preferred) or on deposit.

Archives of organisation: Records of Hereford County Council, 1888–1974. Most HWCC records, 1974–, are held at the Worcester branch.

Major collections: Deposited local collections, some of national standing, including Edward Elgar correspondence with Percy Hull, 1903–33.

Non-manuscript material: Bustin of Hereford, photographers: plate glass negatives, c1890–1920 (c6000).

Finding aids: Parish, subject and biographical indexes; most lists are indexed. Lists sent to NRA.

Facilities: Photocopying. Photography. Microfilming. Microfilm/fiche readers.

Conservation: Joint conservation unit for both Hereford and Worcester Record Office is based here. Outside work is undertaken to a limited degree.

Publications: General leaflets: *Sources for Genealogy*; *Sources for House History*.

388 Haileybury and Imperial Service College

Address: Haileybury, Hertford, SG13 7NU

Telephone: (01732) 352703 (Archivist) (01992) 443050 (College)

Fax: (01732) 352703 (Archivist) (01992) 467603 (College)

Enquiries: The Archivist, Mr Alistair Macpherson

Open: Weekdays, by arrangement.

Access: Bona fide scholars, by appointment with the archivist.

Historical background: Haileybury was founded in 1862 on the site of the East India College, which between 1802 and 1858 trained administrators for the Honourable East India

Company. The library and records of the East India College were transferred to the India Office (entry **497B**) on its closure, although a small proportion has since been returned to Haileybury.

Acquisitions policy: The acquisition of archive material by purchase is minimal, but gifts of material of interest are welcomed by the archivist.

Archives of organisation: A wide range of historical material originating from the following institutions: The East India College, Haileybury College, United Services College, Imperial Service College, Haileybury & ISC, and the Haileybury Junior School Windsor; and some items from Haileybury College, Melbourne, and the Haileybury School of Mining, Ontario.

Non-manuscript material: Complete run of *The Haileybury Observer* and *The Haileyburian* magazines.

Finding aids: Comprehensive indexing in progress.

Publications: I. Thomas: *Haileybury 1807–1987*.
W. Blunt: *The Buildings of Haileybury*.
R.L. Ashcroft: *Random Recollections of Haileybury*.
The Haileybury Register [published by the Haileybury Society about every tenth year].

389 Hertford Museum

Parent organisation: Trustees of Hertford Museum

Address: 18 Bull Plain, Hertford, SG14 1DT

Telephone: (01992) 582686

Enquiries: The Senior Curator, Andrea George

Open: Tues–Sat: 10.00–5.00

Access: Generally open to the public; appointment preferred.

Historical background: The museum was founded by Robert and William Andrews during the 19th century and is owned by the trust they set up in 1914.

Acquisitions policy: Material relating to the East Hertfordshire area.

Major collections: Usual local history collections, including: amateur dramatic handbills, property deeds, auction details, and a large collection of election posters, mainly 19th century.

Andrews family collections of topographical and antiquarian notes.

Wigginton Collection: papers of Wigginton family of Hertford.

East Hertfordshire Archaeological Society collection of MSS.

Non-manuscript material: James Wilcox (1778–1861): collection of his topographical sketches and watercolours.

Other prints and postcards.

Facilities: Photocopying.

390 Hertfordshire Record Office

Address: County Hall, Hertford SG13 8DE

Telephone: (01992) 555105

Fax: (01992) 556622

Enquiries: The County Archivist, Dr Kate Thompson

Open: Mon; Wed–Thurs: 9.15–5.15 Tues (2nd and 4th in month): 10.15–7.45 Fri: 9.15–4.30

Historical background: A records committee was established in 1895 and the present premises opened in 1939. The office also acts as the Diocesan Record Office for St Albans and is recognised as a place of deposit for public records.

Archives of organisation: Usual local authority record holdings.

Major collections: Deposited local collections, of which the following have a wider significance:

Family and estate papers of Cowper (Panshanger), 13th–19th centuries; Desborough, 19th and 20th centuries; Lytton (Knebworth), 14th–19th centuries; Delme-Radcliffe, 13th–20th centuries; Martin Leake, including explorers in the Near and Middle East, 15th–20th centuries; Verulam (Gorhambury), 14th–19th centuries.

Facilities: Photocopying. Photography. Microfilming. Microfilm/fiche readers.

Conservation: In-house; some outside work undertaken.

Publications: W. Le Hardy: *Guide to the Hertfordshire Record Office*, Part 1: *Quarter Sessions and other Records in the Custody of the Officials of the County* (1961).
Catalogue of Manuscript Maps (1969).
Genealogical Sources (rev. 1982).

391 Rochdale Libraries
Local Studies Collection

Address: Heywood Library, Church Street, Heywood, Lancs OL10 1LL

Telephone: (01706) 60947

Enquiries: The Town Librarian or The Local Studies Librarian at Rochdale Library

Open: Mon: 9.00–5.30 Tues, Fri: 10.00–5.30 Wed: 10.00–12.30 Thurs: 10.00–7.30 Sat: 9.30–1.00; 2.00–4.00

Access: Generally open to the public.

Historical background: The dynamic growth of Rochdale, Middleton and Heywood during the 19th century produced a wealth of material relating to the area. In 1974 it was decided that the local collection pertaining to Heywood only should be retained at Heywood Library, under the general supervision of the Local Studies Librarian at Rochdale Area Central Library (entry 963).

Acquisitions policy: The collection of documentary material relating to all aspects of life in the former Borough of Heywood.

Major collections: Administrative material from the former Heywood Borough, mainly 20th century, including council minutes and accounts; the Medical Officer of Health's reports; records of the Heywood and Middleton Water Board; electoral registers.

Non-manuscript material: Complete runs of local newspapers (original and microfilm copies).
Books, pamphlets, audio-visual material, photographs, maps, plans, 19th–20th centuries.

Facilities: Photocopying. Microfilm/fiche readers.

Publications: *Introduction to Local Studies Collections* (1981).
J. Cole: *Tracing your Ancestors through Local Libraries: a Guide to Genealogical Sources* (1983).

392 Ulster Folk and Transport Museum

Address: Cultra, Holywood, Co. Down BT18 0EU

Telephone: (01232) 428428

Fax: (01232) 428728

Enquiries: The Librarian

Open: Mon–Fri: 9.00–5.00

Access: Researchers seriously pursuing a specific enquiry, preferably by appointment.

Historical background: The museum represents a merger of two institutions – the Ulster Folk Museum, established by Act of Parliament in 1958, and the Belfast Transport Museum, established by Belfast City Council and opened to the public in 1962. The merger occurred in 1967 to provide for the eventual transfer of the Transport Museum from Belfast. The museum is administered by a statutory board of trustees representing central government, local government and Northern Ireland's two universities. It is funded by statutory grants from the Department of Education, Northern Ireland.

Acquisitions policy: The collection of information and material for purposes defined by Act of Parliament as 'illustrating the way of life, past and present, and the traditions of the people of Northern Ireland'. Essentially small country-based industries and crafts.

Major collections: Professor K.H. Connell Collection: material covering Irish economic and social history, 18th–20th centuries.
Miscellaneous collections include old account books of farms or mills, recipe books, transports etc.
Material generated by researchers, especially surveys.

Non-manuscript material: Ephemera; ballads; pamphlets.
Photographic collections, especially W.A. Green Collection of several thousand photographs and glass plates; Harland & Wolff Collection (25,000 items).
Sound archive of folklore, oral history, folk music and song (c3000 items).

Finding aids: Various lists and indexes.

Facilities: Photocopying. Photography.

393 Christ's Hospital Archives

Address: Horsham, West Sussex RH13 7LE

Telephone: (01403) 252547

Fax: (01403) 211580

Enquiries: The Curator, N.M. Plumley

Open: By arrangement only, and usually during school term.

Access: Any responsible person with a serious interest in the history of the school, by appointment only.

Historical background: Christ's Hospital was founded in 1552 for the children of those in need in the City of London. The boys' school moved to Horsham in 1902, and the girls' school moved from Hertford in 1985, thus re-establishing a co-educational school. Most of the administrative records and registers of children prior to the 20th century are deposited at Guildhall Library, London (entry 553).

Acquisitions policy: By donation, deposit and occasionally by purchase, anything relevant to the history of the school.

Archives of organisation: MS material of administrative and educational interest, primarily 20th century.

Major collections: MSS of Edmund Blunden (1896–1974).

Non-manuscript material: Ephemera of educational and antiquarian interest.
Portraits of benefactors and a fine photographic archive collected within the new Christ's Hospital Museum.

Finding aids: Catalogue and inventory in progress.

Facilities: Photocopying. Photography.

Publications: G.A.T. Allan: *Christ's Hospital.*

394 Horsham Museum

Parent organisation: Horsham District Council

Address: 9 The Causeway, Horsham, West Sussex RH12 1HE

Telephone: (01403) 254959

Enquiries: The Curator, J. Knight

Open: Tues–Sat: 10.00–5.00, by arrangement only.

Access: Generally open to the public. An appointment needs to be made to consult documents, with the minimum of notice of three (preferably five) days.

Historical background: Horsham Museum was founded by Horsham Museum Society in 1893. From its beginnings the society collected documents, and in 1950 William Albery, saddler, local historian and author, gave his collection to the town and Horsham Museum Society looked after them. In 1989 the collection of documents was handed over to the museum staff to manage. Since 1966 the Museum Society has ceased to collect documents but Horsham Museum continues to collect as a function of the council.

Acquisitions policy: Documents relating to the town, surrounding area and people/businesses connected with Horsham. A close liaison is maintained with West Sussex Records Office (entry **211**) over acquisitions.

Archives of organisation: Archives of Horsham Museum Society, 1893–.
Archives of Horsham Museum collections, 1893–.

Major collections:: William Albery Collection, consisting of:
Medwin papers: records of elections, Horsham, New Shoreham, Steyning, 1736–1832; Horsham Borough records; Norfolk papers; private and business papers of T. Medwin, P. Medwin (1770–1870).
Albery papers: business and personal records of a saddler, c1830–1950s, local history research records, c1910–50.
MSS relating to Clough and Butler, Fletcher, Padwick, Rawlinson, Lord and Lady Irwin.
Miscellaneous documents, title deeds, inventories, wills, plus a number of documents relating to the Shelley family, including Percy Bysshe Shelley (1792–1822), poet, and Thomas Medwin (biographer of Byron, Shelley).

Non-manuscript material: Extensive holdings of ephemera, notably political squibs and sale posters, 1790–1990; civic functions and miscellaneous items.
Maps, postcards and photographs of the town, plus Felici Beato/Samuel Bourne photographs of India, Japan, Borneo, China and USA (320).

Finding aids: Catalogue produced by West Sussex Records Office in preparation.

Facilities: Photocopying. Photography.

Conservation: Contracted out.

Publications: Sussex Archaeological Collections, 69, p.117, describes many of the Albery manuscripts.

395 Royal Society for the Prevention of Cruelty to Animals

Address: The Causeway, Horsham, West Sussex RH12 1HG

Telephone: (01403) 264181

Fax: (01403) 241048

Enquiries: The Information Officer, Olive Martyn or The Archivist, Rita Mayer

Open: Mon–Fri: 9.00–5.00

The society was founded in 1824 as the Society for the Prevention of Cruelty to Animals and royal patronage was granted in 1840. The archives are maintained and include minutes and journals, which are indexed, as well as annual reports. Access is available, by appointment only, to bona fide research students, with a letter from their university or supervisor, but the minutes from 1944 onwards are not available for research.

396 London Borough of Hounslow
Local History Collection

Parent organisation: Leisure Services Department, Libraries Division

Address: Local Studies Department, Hounslow Library, 24 Treaty Centre, Hounslow, Middx TW3 1ES

Telephone: (0181) 570 0622 ext. 7892

Fax: (0181) 569 4330

Enquiries: The Senior Librarian, Local Studies, Miss Andrea Cameron

Open: Mon, Wed, Fri, Sat: 9.30–5.30 Tues, Thurs: 9.30–8.00

Access: Generally open to the public.

Historical background: Material is collected pertaining to all aspects of the history of the London Borough of Hounslow and its predecessors. The collections at Chiswick Library, Dukes Avenue, London W4 2AB, and Hounslow Library have been built up since the beginning of this century and contain material on all the original parishes within those two areas. The collection at Feltham Library, 210 The Centre, Feltham, London TW13 6AW, has been in existence only since 1965 and is much smaller in extent, although containing material relating to the original parishes within the area.

Acquisitions policy: All material pertaining to the history of the London Borough of Hounslow or any of its constituent parts, by purchase, donation or deposit.

Archives of organisation: Local authority archives, minutes, ratebooks, electoral registers etc, *c*1870–.
Parish records: All Saints Church, Isleworth, 1564–*c*1900; St Lawrence's Church, Brentford, 18th century only; St Mary the Virgin, transcript copies only.

Non-manuscript material: Layton Collection: 12,000 books, maps and prints of British topography, 16th–19th centuries.
Several hundred large-scale maps covering most parts of the borough, 1635–.
Prints, paintings and photographs covering all parts of the borough, *c*1750–.
Local newspapers, *c*1870–.

Finding aids: Chiswick and Hounslow libraries: subject catalogue and indexes to local newspapers and deeds. Hounslow Borough Records: NRA 13857.

Facilities: Photocopying. Photography. Microfilm/fiche reader/printer.

Publications: A wide range of local publications are available from Chiswick and Hounslow libraries.

397 Hove Reference Library
Wolseley Collection

Parent organisation: East Sussex County Library

Address: 182–186 Church Road, Hove, East Sussex BN3 2EG

Telephone: (01273) 324274

Fax: (01273) 822932

Enquiries: The Reference Librarian

Open: Tues: 9.30–7.30 Wed–Fri: 9.30–5.30 Sat: 9.30–5.00

Access: Bona fide scholars, preferably by appointment.

Historical background: The Wolseley Collection was offered to the library in 1924, and an additional accession via the Royal United Services Institute came in 1965. The collection was officially opened in 1970.

Acquisitions policy: Anything relating to Lord Wolseley and his family, by gift, purchase or deposit.

Major collections: Collection of Field Marshal Lord Wolseley (1833–1913): covers his career and campaigns and includes scrapbooks and autograph letters from leading figures in his day; also correspondence of his wife and with his family, who lived in East Sussex (*c*8000 items).
Papers of Lord Wolseley's daughter, Lady Frances Garnet Wolseley, who was a pupil of Gertrude Jekyll and had a school of gardening in Glynde.
Scrapbooks, pedigree notebooks and privately printed catalogue (biography) of Sir Walter Miéville (1855–1929) and his family.

Non-manuscript material: Small collection of early children's books and private press books.

Finding aids: Name index, rough lists, catalogue of Wolseley Collection.

Facilities: Photocopying. Photography by arrangement. Microfilm reader.

Publications: J. Dale: *All Sir Garnet* [catalogue of exhibition on Lord Wolseley, 1981].

398 University of Huddersfield Library

Address: Queensgate, Huddersfield, West Yorks HD1 3DH

Telephone: (01484) 422288 ext. 2119, 472119 (direct line)

Fax: (01484) 517987

Enquiries: The Archivist, Mrs E.A. Hilary Haigh

Open: Term: Mon–Fri: 8.45–9.00 Sat: 9.30–5.00 Sun: 1.00–5.00 Vacation: Mon–Fri: 8.45–5.00, by appointment only.

Access: Researchers from within and beyond the University. Appointments should be made with the archivist.

Historical background: The university has its origins in the Huddersfield Mechanics' Institute, founded in 1841 as the Young Men's Mental Improvement Society. In 1884 the Mechanics' Institute amalgamated with the Female Educational Institute and became the Technical School and Mechanics' Institution. This, successively, became the Huddersfield Technical College (1896–1958), Huddersfield College of Technology (1958–70), the Polytechnic of Huddersfield (1970–92) and the University of Huddersfield (1992–). The archive was established in the 1960s by the Principal of the College of Technology, Dr W.E. Scott. Much of the institution's historical archive was transferred to the library during the 1970s and 1980s. A profession archivist was first employed in 1991.

Acquisitions policy: Official archives of the university and its predecessors, and collections of archives and other materials deposited by reason of their direct connection with the work of the University and its predecessors. Major collections reflect research interests in educational and political history.

Archives of organisation: Huddersfield Mechanics' Institute, 1843–84; Huddersfield Female Educational Institute, 1846–83; Huddersfield Technical School and Mechanics' Institution, 1884–96; Huddersfield Technical College, 1896–1958; Huddersfield College of Technology, 1958–70.
Huddersfield Foreign Library Society, 1851–70; Huddersfield Literary and Scientific Society, 1857–82; Huddersfield Fine Art and Industrial Exhibition, 1882–84.

Major collections: Records of Colne Valley Labour Party, 1891–1970 (including bound volumes of the *Colne Valley Guardian*, 1896–1976), and Huddersfield Labour Party, 1918–63.

Non-manuscript material: G.H. Wood Collection: Journals, pamphlets and books, c1850–1910 (5000), on economics, politics, and social and industrial history. Wood was a professional statistician and social reformer ultimately employed as the Secretary of the Huddersfield Woollen Manufacturers' Association. The collection includes 300 pamphlets on the Labour Problem; other areas of special significance include trade unions, wage histories, bimetallism, free trade, early socialism, Fabianism, the textile and mining industries, and industrial health, safety and welfare; MS wage

notes covering all industries, 1850–1910 (20 vols).
Microfilm copies of manuscripts and indexes held in the PRO and other repositories; significant holdings of newspapers, both local and national; some census material.

Finding aids: Lists of all the archive collections; some sent to NRA. Detailed catalogue of the G.H. Wood Collection.

Facilities: Photocopying. Photography. Microfilm/fiche readers/printer.

Conservation: contracted out.

Publications: Annual report.
Catalogue of the G.H. Wood Collection and *A Guide to the Archives and Special Collections* [in preparation].
A note on the G.H. Wood Collection appeared in *Bulletin of the Society for the Study of Labour History*, 4 (spring 1980), 47.

399 West Yorkshire Archive Service: Kirklees

Address: Central Library, Princess Alexandra Walk, Huddersfield, West Yorks HD1 2SU

Telephone: (01484) 513808 ext. 207

Enquiries: The District Archivist, Miss J. Burhouse or The Archivist to the Joint Committee, Mr. R. Frost

Open: Mon–Fri: by arrangement.

Access: Generally open to the public, by appointment.

Historical background: The post of archivist was established in 1959. In 1982 Kirklees joined the West Yorkshire Archive Service; close links with the local studies department are still maintained.

Archives of organisation: Local authority records of all predecessor authorities.

Major collection: Estate and family records of the Beaumonts of Whitley, 12th–19th centuries; Ramsdens of Longley and Huddersfield, 16th–20th centuries; Thornhills of Fixby, 18th–20th centuries; Saviles of Thornhill, 17th–18th centuries (held at Dewsbury Library).
Parish and non-conformist church records, 17th–20th centuries.

Education records: school boards' records, education departments' log-books, minutes, 19th–20th centuries.

Societies' records: Co-operative, Chamber of Commerce, Thespians, Glee and Madrigal, Oddfellows, 19th–20th centuries.

Business records of firms of architects, joiners, accountants, engineers, woollen manufacturers.

Poor Law records, 18th–20th centuries.

Finding aids: Lists sent to NRA. Link to West Yorkshire Archive Service computerised database.

Facilities: Photocopying. Photography. Microfilm/fiche readers.

Publications: See West Yorkshire Archive Service, Wakefield (entry **1072**).

400 Hull Local Studies Library

Parent organisation: Humberside Libraries

Address: Central Library, Albion Street, Kingston upon Hull, Humberside HU1 3TF

Telephone: (01482) 210077

Enquiries: The Local Studies Librarian, Miss J. Crowther

Open: Mon–Thurs: 9.30–8.00 Fri: 9.30–5.30 Sat: 9.00–4.30

Access: Generally open to the public.

Historical background: The local history collections were originally part of the Central Reference Library, which opened in 1901 and became a separate department in 1962, with collections covering the city of Kingston upon Hull and the old East Riding of Yorkshire. The service became part of Humberside Libraries on local government reorganisation in 1974, and the coverage was extended to include printed material on the new county of Humberside.

Acquisitions policy: To maintain and strengthen the collections of printed, manuscript and ephemeral material on the areas covered. Archive material is collected by purchase, donation and deposit, in conjunction with the statutory acquisition requirements of the Hull City Record Office (entry **401**) and the Humberside County Record Office (entry **86**).

Major collections: Non-conformity: Congregational records, 1768–1942; Primitive Methodist, district, circuit and church records, 1833–1920.

Society of Friends: collection on East Yorkshire meetings, c1700–1910.

Winifred Holtby (1898–1935), writer: letters, cuttings, literary MSS etc (c25,000 items); includes material on the writer's social and political activities, reflecting her work for the League of Nations Union in the cause of world peace, for feminism, and for the cause of South African trade unionism.

Log-books of Hull whaling vessels, 19th century.

Non-manuscript material: Illustrations, 18th century– (c7000).

Theatre bills for Hull and district, late 18th century– (c7000).

Hull and district newspapers, 1787– (most on microfilm).

Extensive collection of maps (c1500).

Small collection of audio tapes, slides, records, videotapes.

Finding aids: Classified card catalogues. Various lists and indexes.

Facilities: Photocopying. Photography by arrangement. Microfilm/fiche reader/printer.

Publications: Select Bibliography of the County of Humberside (1980).

Winifred Holtby (1898–1935): a Catalogue (1985).

Local history study sheets: series of annotated student guides.

401 Kingston upon Hull City Record Office

Parent organisation: Kingston upon Hull City Council: Museums, Art Galleries and Archives

Address: 79 Lowgate, Kingston upon Hull, Humberside HU1 2AA

Telephone: (01482) 595102/595110

Fax: (01482) 593710

Enquiries: The Archivist, Mr Geoffrey W. Oxley

Open: Mon–Thurs: 9.00–12.15; 1.30–4.45 Fri: 9.00–12.15; 1.30–4.15

Access: Generally open to the public, subject to relevant closure periods; appointments highly desirable.

Historical background: The office was established in 1968 and moved to specially converted premises in 1979. It is recognised as a place of deposit for public and manorial records.

Acquisitions policy: Records relating to all subject areas within the City of Hull.

Archives of organisation: Usual local authority record holdings.

Major collections: Deposited local collections.

Finding aids: Guide (in progress); lists; indexes of names, places and ships. Lists sent to NRA.

Facilities: Photocopying. Photography. Microfilm/fiche reader.

Conservation: Provided by Humberside Record Office (entry **86**) conservation unit.

Publications: L.M. Stanewell: *City and County of Kingston upon Hull: Calendar of the Ancient Deeds, Letters, Miscellaneous Old Documents* (1951).
Guide Part I.
World War II.
Transport by Sea, Rail and Inland Navigation.

402 Town Docks Museum

Parent organisation: Kingston upon Hull City Council: Museums, Art Galleries and Archives

Address: Queen Victoria Square, Kingston upon Hull, Humberside HU1 3DX

Telephone: (01482) 593902

Enquiries: The Keeper, A.G. Credland

Open: Mon–Fri: 10.00–5.00

Access: Generally open to the public; an appointment, preferably in writing, is essential.

Historical background: The museum was established in 1912 as the Hull Maritime Museum, and the collections derive from those of the Hull Literary and Philosophical Society, which was founded in 1823.

Acquisitions policy: To acquire material relating to whaling, especially arctic, fishing, merchant shipping and Hull docks.

Major collections: Hull whaling: ship log-books and minute books of shipowners, 1754–1869; records of fishing and trawler companies, 19th and 20th centuries.
Merchant shipping: logs, journals and miscellaneous material, 18th–20th centuries.
Wilberforce Collection: personal and family papers of William Wilberforce (1759–1833) and

slavery archive collected since 1906. Maintained at Wilberforce House; contact Keeper of Social History, tel. (01482) 593902.

Non-manuscript material: Small collection of rare pamphlets on whaling, 1826–35.

Finding aids: Handlists, card indexes.

Facilities: Photocopying. Photography.

403 University of Hull
Brynmor Jones Library

Address: Cottingham Road, Kingston upon Hull, Humberside HU6 7RX

Telephone: (01482) 465265

Fax: (01482) 466205

Enquiries: The University Archivist, Mr B. Dyson

Open: Mon–Fri: 9.00–1.00; 2.00–5.00
Other times by arrangement.

Access: Bona fide researchers, with initial contact in writing and by appointment.

Historical background: Hull University College was opened in 1928 and received its charter as a university in 1954. Archives and manuscripts have been collected since 1928.

Acquisitions policy: To extend and strengthen existing collections, by gift, purchase or deposit, particularly in the fields of labour and political history.

Archives of organisation: Records of principal officers and administrative departments, 1928–.

Major collections: Pressure groups: records of Justice, 1959–; Liberty (formerly the National Council for Civil Liberties), 1934–; Women's Co-operative Guild, 1886–; Union of Democratic Control, 1914–66; Socialist Health (formerly Medical) Association, 1930–; Joint Council for the Welfare of Immigrants, 1967–.
Business records: Ellerman's Wilson Line, 1825–1972; Earle's Shipbuilding and Engineering Company, 1858–1909; Hull Printers, 1897–1978; Hull & East Riding Co-operative Society, 1858–1980; Horsley Smith Ltd, 1864–1968; Kay and Backhouse Ltd, 1891–1970; Needlers Ltd, 1901–86.
Landed families and estates: Barnard of South Cave, 1400–1945; Beaumont (Stapleton) of Carlton, late 11th century–1979; Forbes-Adam (Beilby, Lawley, Thompson, Wenlock) of

Escrick, 1387–1988; Gee (Hall, Watt) of Bishop Burton, 1194–1931; Hotham of South Dalton, 1311–1982; Lloyd-Graeme of Sewerby, 12th century-1950; Maxwell-Constable of Everingham, 1125–1959; Pennington of Warte, 1538–1877; St Quintin of Harpham, 1220–1960; Sykes of Sledmere, 1300–1980; Wickham-Boynton of Burton Agnes, 1172–1944.

Trade union and labour: local (Hull and East Yorkshire) trade union and friendly society records, 19th–20th centuries; Frederick W. Dalley (1885–1960); W.E. Jones (1895–1973); Charles George Ammon, 1st Baron Ammon (1873–1960); Julia Varley (1871–1952); Vicky (Victor Weisz) (1913–66).

Political archives: records and papers of Hull Labour Party, 1955–; Beverley and Haltemprice Social Democratic Party, 1981–8; Campaign for Labour Party Democracy, 1973–91; Revolutionary Communist Party, 1944–9; Bernard Floud, MP (1915–67); Anne Kerr, MP (1925–73); Kevin McNamara, MP (b 1934); John Prescott, MP (b 1936); Austin Mitchell, MP (b 1934); Christopher Price, MP (b 1932); David Winnick, MP (b 1933); Eric Lubbock (Lord Avebury) (b 1928); Thomas Perronet Thompson, MP (1783–1869); Sir Mark Sykes, MP (1879–1919); Sir Patrick Wall, MP (b 1916); Henry Grattan (1746–1820); Howard Hill (1913–80); Robin Page Arnot (1890–1980); Jock Haston (1913–86); Harold Laski (1893–1950).

Religious archives: records and papers of Society of Friends, Hull & Pickering Monthly Meeting, 1636–1990; some records of Selby Abbey, 1349–1538, and Marrick Priory, 1154–1539; papers of the Anglican Evangelical Group movement 1907–72; papers of the Christian Socialists Rev. Conrad Noel (1869–1942) and Canon Stanley Evans (1912–65).

Modern English literary MSS and archives: papers of Douglas Dunn (b 1942), Gavin Ewart (b 1916), Philip Larkin (1922–1985), Andrew Motion (b 1952), Alan Plater (b 1935), Stevie Smith (1902–71), Henry Treece (1911–66) and Anthony Thwaite (b 1930); records of the magazines *Wave*, 1970–74, *Phoenix*, 1967–75 and *Reality Studio*, 1978–88; and the archives of Hull Literary Club, 1879–1979, and Hull Subscription Library, 1775–1970.

South-East Asian texts and research collections, 19th century–.

Non-manuscript material: Pamphlets, maps, local playbills and broadsides in general collection in main library.

Finding aids: 'HUMAD' on-line guide. Calendars or initial lists of collections; copies sent to NRA. Indexes of places, personal names and subjects. Subject and other guides issued regularly. Lists of maps, manorial records, enclosure records, wills, etc.

Conservation: Minor repairs in-house; otherwise contracted out.

Publications: Paragon Review (1992–) [annual].
P. Larkin: *A Lifted Study-Storehouse: the Brynmor Jones Library, 1929–1979* (Hull, 1979; rev. 1987).
S.K. Mitra, D.A. Reid and G.D. Weston (eds): *Catalogue of Primary and Secondary Material on Indian Studies in the Brynmor Jones Library, University of Hull* (Hull, 1989).
J. Saville: *The Labour Archive at the University of Hull* (Hull, 1989).
B. Dyson: 'Business Records in the Archives of the University of Hull', *Business Archives* (Nov 1990), 14–23.
——: 'Records and Research for Co-operation: Records in Britain', *Journal of Co-operative Studies*, 69 (Sept 1990), 52–6.
——: 'Archives at the University of Hull: a Research Resource', *History of Education Society Bulletin*, 47 (spring 1991), 62–4.
——: 'HUMAD: Hull University's On-Line Guide to Archives and Manuscripts', *Local Studies Librarian*, 10 2 (autumn 1991), 13–15.
B. Dyson and H. Roberts: 'The University of Hull Brynmor Jones Library', *Archives* (forthcoming).

404 County Record Office, Huntingdon

Parent organisation: Cambridgeshire County Council

Address: Grammar School Walk, Huntingdon, Cambridgeshire PE18 6LF

Telephone: (01480) 425842

Fax: (01480) 459563 (Huntingdon Library)

Enquiries: The Deputy County Archivist, Dr P.C. Saunders

Open: Mon–Thurs: 9.00–12.45; 1.45–5.15 Fri: 9.00–12.45; 1.45–4.15 Sat (2nd of every month): 9.00–12.00, by appointment.

Historical background: The office was established in 1947. Between 1969 and 1974 it was administered with the Northamptonshire

Record Office. Since 1974 it has been one of two offices serving the enlarged county of Cambridgeshire responsible for official and unofficial deposited records within the area of the former county of Huntingdonshire, and local government records of the former Soke of Peterborough, which was amalgamated with Huntingdonshire in 1965. Some official and most deposited collections relating to Peterborough remain the responsibility of the Northamptonshire Record Office (entry 848). The office contains the records of the Archdeanconry of Huntingdon (until 1837 in Lincoln Diocese, since then in Ely), is a Diocesan Record Office for parish records in the archdeanconry and is recognised as a place of deposit for public records.

Acquisitions policy: Records relating to the area of the present county (see also Cambridge Record Office, entry 148).

Archives of organisation: Usual local authority record holdings.

Major collections: Deposited local collections, including the following which have a wider significance:
Records of the Earls and Dukes of Manchester of Kimbolton, 13th–20th centuries.
Bush Collection of Cromwell family records, 1579–1832 (some exhibited in adjacent Cromwell Museum).
Estate records of the Fellowes family, Baron De Ramsey, of Ramsay and Abbots Ripton.

Non-manuscript material: OS papers and plans for Huntingdon.
Photographs of Maddison and Hinde of Huntingdon, 1867–1925.

Facilities: Photocopying. Photography. Microfilming. Microfilm reader/printer.

Conservation: Undertaken in-house at the Cambridge Office.

Publications: G.H. Findlay: *Guide to the Huntingdonshire Record Office* (1958).
P.G.M. Dickinson: *Maps in the County Record Office, Huntingdon* (1968).
Annual Reports: Northants and Hunts Archives Committee, 1969–74, Cambridgeshire County Archivist 1974–.

405 Knowsley Archives

Parent organisation: Knowsley MBC

Address: Knowsley Central Library, Derby Road, Huyton, Merseyside L36 9UJ

Telephone: (0151) 443 3740

Fax: (0151) 489 9405

Enquiries: The Archivist, Ms H. Ford

Open: Mon–Wed, Fri: 10.00–7.00 Sat: 10.00–1.00; 2.00–4.00

Access: Bona fide researchers.

Historical background: Knowsley Library Service came into being in 1974 following local government reorganisation. The area covers Cronton, Huyton, Kirkby, Knowsley, Prescot, Roby, Simonswood, Tarbock and Whiston. The Local Studies and Archives Collection was assembled during the first years of the library service, before the new Central Library was opened in Huyton in 1978.

Acquisitions policy: To strengthen existing collections regarding the history of areas presently incorporated in the Metropolitan Borough of Knowsley, by purchase, donation or deposit.

Major collections: Council minutes for Huyton-with-Roby, Kirkby and Prescot UDCs; Council minutes and Clerks' working papers for Whiston RDC, c1890–1974.
Prescot Grammar School archives, 15th–19th centuries.
National Union of Mineworkers (Cronton Branch) minute books, 1952–71.
Huyton Cricket Club records, 1860–c1970.
Preston and Whiston Co-operative Society records, c19th–20th centuries.

Non-manuscript material: Photographic collection (c6000).
Large map collection.
Prescot Report, 1858–1975.
Parish registers, census returns, directories, copies of tithe maps and awards, newspaper cuttings and electoral registers.

Finding aids: Most archive collections listed and partly indexed. Indexes to photographic collection. Some census returns indexed by street and name.

Facilities: Photocopying. Photography by arrangement. Microfilm/fiche readers/printer.

Publications: W.L. French (ed.): *Registers of Kirkby St Chad's Chapelry, i: Baptism, 1610–*

1839 (1977); ii: *Marriages and Burials, 1610–1839* (1979).

J. Knowles (ed.): *Prescot Records: the Court Rolls, 1602–1648* (1980–81).

B. Burgess: *Tracing your Family History in the Knowsley Area at Huyton Library* (1989).

406 Hythe Town Archives

Parent organisation: Hythe Town Council

Address: Town Council Offices, Stade Street, Hythe, Kent CT21 6BG

Telephone: (01303) 266152/3

Enquiries: The Hythe Town Archivist, Mrs M.P. Shaw

Open: Wed: 9.45–1.00; 2.00–4.45
Other days may be possible by prior arrangement.

Access: Generally open to the public, by appointment.

Archives of organisation: The Town Council holds the records of the former Borough of Hythe, *c*1278–1974; some records, not registers, of the parish of St Leonard, Hythe, *c*1412–1850; and various private deposits.

Finding aids: Catalogue in house style of Kent Archives Office, in preparation. NRA 19570.

Facilities: Limited photocopying.

Publications: H.D. Dale and C. Chidell: *Catalogue of Documents Belonging to the Corporation of Hythe, 11th to 20th century.*
M.P. Shaw: *A Revised Catalogue of Documents* (1985).

407 Barnardo's Photographic and Film Archive

Address: Tanners Lane, Barkingside, Ilford, Essex IG6 1QG

Telephone: (0181) 550 8822 ext. 345

Fax: (0181) 551 6870

Enquiries: The Photographic Resources Officer/Archivist, John Kirkham

Open: Mon–Fri: 9.30–4.30

Access: Bona fide researchers, by appointment only.

The photograph and film archive complements the Barnardo Archive held by the University of Liverpool (entry *472*). It consists of prints, negatives and plates, 1864– (500,000), and of films, 1905– (200), illustrating the history of childcare and residential education. A database of the collection is maintained and there is in-house conservation. Photocopying and photography are available.

408 London Borough of Redbridge
Libraries Department

Address: Redbridge Central Library, Local History Room, Clements Road, Ilford, Essex IG1 1EA

Telephone: (0181) 478 7145 ext. 225

Fax: (0181) 553 4185

Enquiries: The Local History Librarian, Mr Ian Dowling

Open: Tues–Fri: 9.30–8.00 Sat: 9.30–4.00

Access: Generally open to the public; appointment preferred.

Historical background: Archival material was acquired haphazardly over a number of years from 1909, mainly by donations from local residents. Since 1965 a more definite policy has been pursued. The Local History Library has been designated as the repository for all council archives, and to this end departments are transferring material to the library.

Acquisitions policy: To acquire, by donation or purchase, when practicable, all documentary material relating to the borough. The accession of archives from council departments.

Archives of organisation: Material relating to the activities and functions of the various departments of the council of the London Borough of Redbridge.

Major collections: Admission registers, reports, papers etc, relating to the former Infant Orphans Asylum (later the Royal Infant Orphanage, later the Royal Wanstead School), Snaresbrook, Wanstead.
Sales reports, staff and workforce details, reports, maps, minutes of board meetings etc, relating to the former chemical manufacturers Howards of Ilford, Ltd.

Non-manuscript material: Local History Collection: local maps and plans of Ilford, Wanstead and Woodford, mainly 19th and 20th centuries; pamphlets and news cuttings (*c*45,000); photographs (8000) and slides (1600). Local newspapers, 1900– (earlier issues on microfilm).

Finding aids: The majority of archive material is as yet uncatalogued. Classified index for all illustrative material and pamphlet file material (not complete). Ilford Local History Collection: NRA 3007. 4th Earl of Mornington correspondence: NRA 24051.

Facilities: Photocopying. Photograph copying service. Microfilm reader/printer.

Publications: A Catalogue of Local History Documents (1977) [lists the majority of the archives held at that time, together with the holdings of various societies and organisations in the borough].
Redbridge in World War II: a Perspective (Ilford, 1986).
Domesday Redbridge (Ilford, 1987).
G. Tasker: *Ilford Past and Present* (1992).

409 Highland Health Board Archives

Address: Highland Health Sciences Library, Raigmore Hospital, Inverness, Highland IV2 3UJ

Telephone: (01463) 705269

Fax: (01463) 713454

Enquiries: The Area Librarian, Rebecca Higgins

Open: By appointment only.

Access: Bona fide researchers. Administrative records are closed for 30 years, medical records for 75 years.

Acquisitions policy: Pre- and post-NHS material from the Highlands and inner Islands of Scotland.

Archives of organisation: Records relating to hospitals and health authorities in the area including minutes, financial records, patient and staff registers, case notes, nurse training records and annual reports, *c*1850–.
Administrative records of the Northern Regional Hospital Board and local authority health departments, including MOH annual reports.
Minutes and financial records of the Royal Northern Infirmary, 1798–1950.

Finding aids: Lists.

Facilities: Photocopying. Photography.

410 Highland Regional Archive

Address: The Library, Farraline Park, Inverness, Highland IV1 1NH

Telephone: (01463) 220330

Fax: (01463) 711128

Enquiries: The Regional Archivist, Mr R. Steward

Open: Mon–Fri: 9.30–1.00; 2.00–5.00

Access: Generally open to the public; appointment preferred.

Historical background: The archive was formed in 1975 on the reorganisation of local government and the creation of the Highland Region. A full-time archive service was established in 1990.

Acquisitions policy: To acquire and manage the records of the Regional Council and the former county authorities within the region (Caithness, Sutherland, Ross and Cromarty, Invernessshire, Moray and Nairn). In addition, to acquire, by donation, loan or copying, documentary material relating to the Highlands from whatever source.

Archives of organisation: Material relating to activities and functions of the Highland Regional Council, including those records for which the council has a statutory responsibility.

Major collections: Records of the parochial boards, parish councils and school boards within the region.
Papers of MacDonald and Fraser, solicitors, Skye, 1850–1910; John and Alexander Fraser, merchants, Inverness, 1790–1840.
Records of Northern Meeting, 1780–1960, and various clan societies.

Finding aids: Catalogues and lists, though many collections are not properly listed.

Facilities: Photocopying. Microfilm/microfiche reader/printer. Genealogical research service employing full-time genealogist.

411 Inverness Museum and Art Gallery

Parent organisation: Inverness District Council

Address: Castle Wynd, Inverness, Highland IV2 3ED

Telephone: (01463) 237114

Fax: (01463) 712850

Enquiries: The Museum Curator

Open: Mon–Sat: 9.00–5.00
Closed some local public holidays.

Access: Generally open to the public, by appointment.

Historical background: The museum dates from 1825, when the Northern Institution for the Promotion of Science and Literature in Inverness was founded. The collection, badly neglected, was taken over by the Inverness Field Club in 1876 and a permanent building was opened in 1882. In 1907 a new policy of making the museum chiefly a Highland and Jacobite collection was adopted and in the following year management was transferred to the library committee. A new building was erected on the same site in 1966, and in the 1975 local government reorganisation the museum assumed an independent role under the district council's Leisure and Recreation Committee.

Acquisitions policy: Items relating to Inverness and the surrounding area.

Archives of organisation: Inverness Museum guide books, 1909–.

Major collections: Inverness Town Council and District Council committee minutes, 1894–. Small collections of estate papers, accounts and letters of local families, 18th–20th centuries.

Non-manuscript material: M.E.M. Donaldson collection of glass plates of the Highlands, c1900–1920.
Photograph collection: Inverness and district, topography, industry, agriculture, society, architecture, transport, communications etc.
Inverness Courier, 1915–; *Northern Chronicle*, 1915–49.
Local prints and drawings.

Finding aids: Donaldson catalogue.

Facilities: Photocopying. Photography with difficulty.

412 Queen's Own Highlanders Regimental Archives

Address: Cameron Barracks, Inverness, Highland IV2 3XD

Telephone: (01463) 224380

Fax: (01463) 224380

Enquiries: The Regimental Secretary

Open: Mon–Fri: 9.00–5.00

Access: Anyone with a genuine interest in the history of the regiment, by appointment.

There is a museum at Fort George, Ardersier, Highland IV1 2TD. The regiment maintains photograph albums, war diaries, documents, some enlistment books, and published records, and actively acquires material relating to its own history and the military history of the North Highlands.

413 Suffolk Record Office
Ipswich Branch

Parent organisation: Suffolk County Council

Address: Gatacre Road, Ipswich, Suffolk IP1 2LQ

Telephone: (01473) 264541

Enquiries: The Archives Service Manager, Miss R.A. Rogers or The Branch Archivist, Mr D.R. Jones

Open: Mon–Thurs: 9.00–5.00 Fri: 9.00–4.00 Sat: 9.00–1.00; 2.00–5.00 Material required on Saturday must be ordered before 1.00 on Friday.

Access: Generally open to the public. The office operates the CARN reader's ticket system.

Historical background: The Ipswich and East Suffolk Record Office was established in 1950 and became the Ipswich Branch of the Suffolk Record Office in 1974. It also acts as the Diocesan Record Office for St Edmundsbury and Ipswich (Archdeanconries of Ipswich and Suffolk) and is recognised as a place of deposit for public records. The Local Studies Library is an integral part of the Record Office.

Acquisitions policy: Archival and printed material relating to the former administrative county of East Suffolk, excepting the area served by the Lowestoft Branch (entry **786**).

Archives of organisation: Usual local authority record holdings of East and West Suffolk County Councils, 1889–1974; Ipswich Borough, 13th century-1974; Suffolk County Council, 1974–.

Major collections: Deposited local collections, including the following which have a wider significance:
Sir Thomas Phillipps Collection of medieval manuscripts and Suffolk antiquaries' notes; Cornwallis papers, including letter-book of 1st Marquis Cornwallis, Governor-General of Bengal; diaries and political papers of Gathorne Hardy, 1st Earl of Cranbrook; correspondence of William Lowther MP and James William Lowther, 1st Viscount Ullswater; military, naval and political papers of 1st–7th Earls of Albemarle, Admiral Viscount Keppel, General Sir William Keppel and Baron Egerton; naval papers of Admiral Sir James Saumarez and Sir Philip Bowes Vere Broke; papers of George Pretyman (Tomline), Bishop of Lincoln and Winchester, including material *re* William Pitt the Younger; papers of Mary C. Greenup (wife of Gen. J.T. English) *re* South America; diaries of Canon J.H. Turner *re* the Canadian Arctic; papers of William Leathes, ambassador, and of Carteret Leathes and Hill Mussenden, MPs.
Collections relating to Jamaican estates of the Long family; Bristol and Gloucestershire estates of the Gonning family; London and Lincolnshire estates of the Boucherett family; Kent estate of the Barne family; various lands of the Hanbury-Bateman families; London estate of the Kerrison family; South Carolina estate of the Middleton family; Lincolnshire estate of the Pretyman-Tomline families; Nevis (West Indies) estate of the Maynard family; Lancashire, Northamptonshire and Irish estates of the Purcell-Fitzgerald family; Hertfordshire and other estates of Lord Rendlesham.
Business archives of Richard Garrett and Sons of Leiston; British Xylonite Co. of Homerton, Hale End and Brantham; Ransomes and Rapier of Ipswich, and the Norsk Hydro Fertilisers Group.

Non-manuscript material: Local Studies Library: extensive photographic and illustrative collections, oral history collection.

Finding aids: Catalogues and indexes; catalogues sent to NRA; annual summary of accessions published in *Archive News*.

Facilities: Photocopying. Photography. Micro-filming. Microfilm reader/printers. Micro-filming.

Conservation: Available in-house.

Publications: *Guide to Genealogical Sources* (4:1993).
Archive News [half-yearly].
Various local history titles.

414 Salford City Archives

Parent organisation: City of Salford Arts and Leisure Department

Address: Archives Centre, 658–662 Liverpool Road, Irlam, Greater Manchester M44 5AD

Telephone: (0161) 775 5643

Enquiries: The Archivist, Mr A.N. Cross

Open: Mon–Fri: 9.00–4.30

Access: Open to the public by appointment. Usual embargoes on local authority and personal records.

Historical background: The Archives Centre was established in 1974 with the reorganisation of local government. Before then archives were kept by various libraries, which have subsequently transferred some material. Salford Town Hall, Bexley Square, Salford, is recognised as a place of deposit for public records and keeps Quarter Sessions, Coroner's and local Health Authority records.

Archives of organisation: Records of the City of Salford and its local authority predecessors, 1687–.

Major collections: Bridgewater Estates plc Collection, 1771–1980 (chiefly 19th century). Nasmyth, Wilson and Co., records, 1836–1922. James Nasmyth correspondence, 1849–88.

Non-manuscript material: F. Mullineux's photograph collection of glass plates and prints, including photos by Samuel L. Coulthurst, covering local district, Manchester Ship Canal and Holland and Wales, 1880s-1910.

Finding aids: Catalogues, indexes. Copies of catalogues sent to NRA. Duplicated handlist, 1978.

Facilities: Photocopying.

Publications: Information leaflets on genealogical sources and the history of houses [available on request].

415 Ironbridge Gorge Museum Trust

Address: The Wharfage, Ironbridge, Telford, Shropshire TF8 7AW

Telephone: (01952) 432751 ext. 27

Fax: (01952) 432204

Enquiries: The Museum Archivist, Miss Dianna Stiff

Open: Mon–Fri: 9.00–5.30

Access: By prior appointment only, with the Archivist or the Librarian, Mr John Powell.

Historical background: The Ironbridge Gorge Museum Trust was established in 1968 to conserve for posterity the unique industrial remains of the area's former period of greatness. It consists of the world's first iron bridge (1779), the furnace where coke smelting was first introduced in 1709, the Coalbrookdale Museum of Iron, the Severn Warehouse, Blists Hill Open Air Museum, Coalport China Works Museum and other sites within an area of six square miles. The library and archive collections have been built up since 1968. Telford Development Corporation archives and the Omnibus Society library, including an archive of the bus and coach industry, are now held at the museum.

Acquisitions policy: Material relating to social, industrial and economic history of the East Shropshire coalfield. Technological history in general and industrial archaeology. Special interest in Thomas Telford, oral history and notable industrial historians. The majority of items are received as donations.

Archives of organisation: Internal administrative records of IGMT and Friends of IGMT, 1969–.

Major collections: Archives relating to the following companies: Coalbrookdale Company; Horsehay Company; Lilleshall Company; Maw & Co.; Hathernware Company (of Loughborough, Leics).
Material *re* Dunhill decorative tiles.
Collection pertaining to the life and works of Thomas Telford (1757–1834): official correspondence, reports and accounts of the Gloucester and Berkeley Canal and his involvement in the Exchequer Loans Commission Board; draft versions of Telford's autobiography, with correspondence relating to its publication.
Darby family archives.

Non-manuscript material: Illustrative material in the Telford Collection and Xerox and microfilm copies of all known Telford MS material and printed parliamentary reports containing Telford references.
Elton Collection: material relating to the Industrial Revolution.
Maps and plans (*c*200); postcards and photographs (*c*15,000).
Film collection on local industries and Ironbridge; oral history recordings (*c*100).

Finding aids: Lists and indexes. Major lists sent to NRA.

Facilities: Photocopying. Photography. Microfilming.

416 Scottish Maritime Museum

A Museum Collection

Address: Laird Forge, Gottries Road, Irvine, Strathclyde KA12 8QE

Telephone: (01294) 278283

Fax: (01294) 313211

Enquiries: The Curator, Veronica Hartwich

Open: Mon–Fri: 9.00–4.30
NB Study times are not identical with those of the museum.

Access: Bona fide researchers, by appointment.

Historical background: The Scottish Maritime Museum Trust was founded in 1983. The museum itself offers harbour quayside exhibits and vessels with visitor access and an exhibition hall. It is housed in a Grade A-listed engine shop rebuilt in 1991 from the Linthouse Shipyard, Govan. The collections are broad and include vessels, machinery, archives and a special library.

Acquisitions policy: All aspects of Scottish maritime history and activity, including inland water, with particular interest in shipbuilding. Archival collections are being developed in cooperation with other major Scottish depositories and include ship/boatbuilding business records.

Archives of organisation: Records relating to the museum and the Scottish Maritime Museum Trust, 1981–.

Major collections: Business records of Wm Fife & Sons of Fairlie and their successors, the Fairlie Yacht Slip Co., 1915–85.

(The main block of technical material is at Fairlie Restoration Ltd, c/o Hamble Yacht Services, Port Hamble, Batchell Lane, Hants, tel. (0703) 456336.)

Non-manuscript material: Samples, manufacturers' catalogues, photographs, postcards, ephemera and cuttings albums.

Finding aids: Business archives cataloguing in progress. Details to be sent to Scottish Record Office (entry 313).

Facilities: Photocopying. Photography.

Conservation: Contracted out.

B Denny Ship Model Experiment Tank

Address: Castle Street, Dumbarton, Strathclyde G82 1QS

Telephone: (01389) 63444

Fax: (01389) 43093

Enquiries: The Research Officer, Niall McNeill

Open: Mon–Sat: 10.00–4.00

Access: Bona fide researchers, by appointment.

Historical background: The Experiment Tank was founded in 1883 by Messrs Wm Denny & Bros and was operated by them until 1963, when ownership passed to Vickers Shipbuilding & Engineering Ltd. The establishment was closed down in 1983. The building and its contents were salvaged by a consortium of museums, including the Scottish Maritime Museum, which owns the building and ground and most of the collections.

Acquisitions policy: Existing collections (object and archival) are defined by their direct association with the tank itself. The general objective is to improve and fill gaps in the archive. Expansion to include records of hydrodynamics not ongoing in Dumbarton is under consideration.

Archives of organisation: Hydrodynamic test records of Messrs Wm Denny & Bros, tank business records, 1883–1963.
Vickers records, mainly lists of models and dates of tests, 1963–83.

Non-manuscript material: Large number of hull lines, plans and drawings for models tested.

Photographic archive of Vickers tests at Dumbarton, 1960s.
Tank original library of books and periodicals appropriate to work.

Finding aids: Master list summarising the content of the collections; detailed catalogue of test records.

Conservation: Contracted out.

417 British and Foreign School Society
Archives Centre

Address: Brunel University College, Lancaster House, Borough Road, Isleworth, Middx TW7 5DU

Telephone: (0181) 568 8741 ext. 2615

Fax: (0181) 569 9198

Enquiries: The Archivist, Bryan E. Seagrove

Open: Tues, Thurs: 10.00–4.00

Access: Generally open to the public; no prior appointment necessary. Access to some recent records is at the discretion of the archivist.

Historical background: BFSS was founded in 1808 by supporters of Joseph Lancaster (1788–1838) and his system of non-conformist popular education. Its headquarters were at Borough Road, Southwark, where the society's original training institution for elementary teachers was established by 1814. When Borough Road College was moved to Isleworth in 1890, many of the society's records were moved there and so escaped the destruction of the society's London offices in 1940–41. The society's recent records were moved to West London Institute (now Brunel University College) in 1980.

Acquisitions policy: To add to the society's collection documents, photographs and printed books relevant to the history of its colleges, schools and overseas work, as well as its central administration.

Archives of organisation: Records of the BFSS, including minute books, secretaries' letters and papers, overseas correspondence, annual reports 1808–.
Records of the society's schools and colleges: Borough Road College, Saffron Walden College, Stockwell College and Darlington College,

including minute and log-books, registers, students' journals and prospectuses, *c*1814–.

Major collections: Correspondence of Joseph Lancaster and his contemporaries, 1810–12.

Non-manuscript material: The Salmon Collection of books and pamphlets on elementary education, early 19th century.
Photographs and prints of the society's colleges and schools.
Educational Record, 1848–1929.

Finding aids: Typescript bibliography of books, articles, unpublished typescripts, relevant to the history of BFSS and produced since 1965. Lists sent to NRA.

Facilities: Photocopying. Photography by arrangement.

Publications: BFSS Archives Centre General Prospectus [available on request].
Detailed reports of the Archives Centre are given in the following: *Journal of Educational Administration and History* (July 1980); *History of Education* (Oct 1981); *The Local Historian*, xiv/4 (1984).

418 University of Keele
Air Photo Library

Address: Department of Geography, Keele University, Keele, Staffs ST5 5BG

Telephone: (01782) 583395

Enquiries: The Archivist, Mrs S. Walton

Open: Mon–Wed: 9.30–4.30

Access: Access is strictly by appointment. Requests for access to photographs covering specific areas should state the name of the site and position to nearest latitude and longitude. There is an administrative search fee.

Historical background: The library is composed of a significant part of the air photo print library of the Allied Central Interpretation Unit from RAF Medmenham, and it holds allied forces reconnaissance air photographs. It is recognised as a place of deposit for public records.

Major collections: Exclusively non-MS material (see below).

Non-manuscript material: Vertical air photographs from World War II (5½ million).

There is no cover of any country which was neutral during World War II nor of the UK.

Finding aids: The collection is catalogued by latitude and longitude.

Facilities: Copy-print service.

419 University of Keele Library

Address: Keele, Staffs ST5 5BG

Telephone: (01782) 621111 ext. 3741

Fax: (01782) 711553

Enquiries: Special Collections and Archives, Mr M. Phillips

Open: Mon–Fri: 9.00–5.00

Access: Bona fide researchers, by appointment. A reader's ticket is essential for access to the Wedgwood MSS; application forms are available from the Curator, Wedgwood Museum, Darlaston, Stoke-on-Trent ST12 9ES.

Historical background: In 1957 the University College of North Staffordshire (later the University of Keele) purchased the papers of the Sneyds of Keele, which had by then become part of the collection of the late Raymond Richards MA, FSA, FRHistS, of Gawsworth, Cheshire. Most of the rest of this collection was purchased at the same time and became the nucleus of the MS holdings. Subsequent deposits and gifts and some further purchases, mainly of archive material, have been added.

Acquisitions policy: To consolidate relevant holdings having regard to the interests of neighbouring repositories.

Archives of organisation: Keele University Senate minutes, 1951–.

Major collections: Wedgwood MSS: reflecting the history of the family and of the firm; rich in material relating to the fine arts, the history of science and the development of humanitarian movements, as well as the history of the manufacture of ceramic products (*c*75,000 separate items, plus vols).
Spode MSS: business records, correspondence etc, 19th–20th centuries (*c*1000 items).
Raymond Richards Collection: Sneyd family papers and older collections such as the Hatton Wood MSS, a large proportion of which consists of medieval evidence of title, 12th century–.
Tamworth court rolls, items, 1284– (*c*250).

Arnold Bennett (1867–1931): literary MSS, letters, pictorial material.

Non-manuscript material: Photographs, including Warrillow Collection of Potteries material; cartoons; drawings and paintings; music; printed ephemera.

Finding aids: Calendars, lists, indexes.

Facilities: Photocopying. Photography. Microcard/fiche/film readers.

Conservation: Contracted out.

Publications: M.K. Dale: *Abstracts of Tamworth Court Rolls* (1959).
I.H.C. Fraser: 'Sneyd MSS, University of Keele', *Bulletin of the National Register of Archives*, 14 (1967).
——: 'Manuscripts in the Library of the University of Keele', *North Staffordshire Journal of Field Studies*, vii (1967).
C. Fyfe: 'Manuscripts in Keele University Library', *Staffordshire Studies*, i (1988).

420 Cliffe Castle Museum

Address: Spring Gardens Lane, Keighley, West Yorks BD20 6LH

Telephone: (01535) 618230

Fax: (01535) 610536

Enquiries: The Curator

Open: Tues–Sun: winter: 10.00–5.00 summer: 10.00–6.00

Access: Bona fide students and researchers, by appointment only.

The collection of local documentary material was formed by Keighley Museum. It includes papers relating to the Butterfield family of Keighley, builders of Cliffe Castle, and printed ephemera, mainly of local interest. Most MS material, including the Eshton Hall Collection of estate papers of the Currer and Wilson families, is now deposited with Bradford Archives (entry 116).

421 Keighley Reference Library

Parent organisation: Bradford Metropolitan Libraries

Address: Public Library, North Street, Keighley, West Yorks BD21 3SX

Telephone: (01274) 758215

Fax: (01274) 758214

Enquiries: The Reference Librarian, Mr J.S. Cardwell

Open: Mon, Wed: 9.00–7.00 Tues: 9.00–1.00 Thurs: 9.30–7.00 Fri, Sat: 9.00–5.00

Access: Generally open to the public, but 24 hours' notice is necessary for archives.

Historical background: Although now part of Bradford Metropolitan Libraries, the Reference Library remains largely a relic of the former Keighley Borough (1882–1974), within which its local collection has been steadily accumulating from 1904 onwards. The main emphasis of the archives relates to Keighley and outer communities which were formerly included in Keighley Borough, such as Haworth and Oxenhope, although there is a smaller amount of wider West Yorkshire material.

Acquisitions policy: To collect materials relating primarily to the area of the former Keighley Borough. A major subject area tends to be local government, owing to the demise of the borough in 1974, with consequent movement of its records.

Major collections: Minutes of Keighley Improvement Commissioners, 1824–57; Select Vestry, 1798–1854; Local Board of Health, 1855–82; Borough Council, 1882–1974; Poor Law Union, 1837–1930; North Bierley Poor Law Union, 1848–1930.
Miscellaneous letter files.
Keighley and Worth Valley Methodist archives, 18th–20th centuries; Keighley Independent and Congregationalist archives and Baptist archives (excluding registers), 19th and 20th centuries.
Brigg Collection: mainly documents relating to Yorkshire/Lancashire border properties, 15th–19th centuries.
Records of Keighley Independent Labour Party c1890s-1920s, and Keighley Co-operative Society, c1860–1950.
Gordon Bottomley (1874–1948), poet and playwright: letters, photographs, inscribed first editions.

Non-manuscript material: Philip Snowden Library: personal book collection of former Chancellor of the Exchequer, particularly strong in early socialist pamphlets.
Brontë Collection: scrapbooks and ephemera, 19th century.

Finding aids: Catalogue (but only of broad headings); local index (in permanent process of compilation). Lists of Brigg Collection and Methodist Archives.

Facilities: Photocopying. Microfilm reader.

422 Abbot Hall Art Gallery and Museums

Address: Kendal, Cumbria LA9 5AL

Telephone: (01539) 722464

Fax: (01539) 722494

Enquiries: The Director, Mr Edward King

Open: Mon–Fri: 10.30–5.00 Sat, Sun: 2.00–5.00

Access: Bona fide researchers, by appointment only.

Most archival records relating to Abbot Hall are housed in the Cumbria Record Office (entry 423). Collections held relate to museum items. There are also typescripts etc relating to Arthur Ransome (1884–1967); and material relating to John Harden of Brathay Hall (?1772–1847), including transcripts of Harden Diaries.

423 Cumbria Archive Service
Cumbria Record Office (Kendal)

Address: County Offices, Kendal, Cumbria LA9 4RQ

Telephone: (01539) 814330

Enquiries: The County Archivist, Mr Jim Grisenthwaite (service-wide enquiries) or The Assistant County Archivist, Ms Anne Rowe (office enquiries)

Open: Mon–Fri: 9.00–5.00

Access: Generally open to the public. The office operates the CARN reader's ticket system.

Historical background: The office was established in 1962 under a joint archives committee for the former counties of Cumberland and Westmorland and the City of Carlisle. Few archives other than local authority records had been acquired before that date. The office is recognised as a place of deposit for public records and acts as the Diocesan Record Office for Carlisle (former Westmorland parishes), and holds records of Cumbrian parishes in the Diocese of Bradford. It provides administrative assistance to Levens Hall near Kendal (see also the offices at Carlisle (entry 199) and Barrow-in-Furness (entry 49)).

Acquisitions policy: Official and unofficial archives for the former county of Westmorland and the Sedbergh, Garsdale and Dent areas (formerly West Riding of Yorkshire).

Archives of organisation: Usual local authority record holdings.

Major collections: Deposited local collections, of which the following have a wider significance:
Lady Anne Clifford (1590–1676): Appleby Castle estate and personal records.
T.H. Mawson, landscape architect, plans and photographs of gardens and parks, late 19th–20th centuries.

Finding aids: Catalogues and indexes. Some collections are unlisted. Selected catalogues sent to NRA.

Facilities: Photocopying. Photography. Microfilming. Microfilm/fiche readers/printer.

Publications: B.C. Jones: 'Cumberland, Westmorland and Carlisle Record Office, 1960–65', *Archives,* vii/34 (1965), 80.
——: 'Cumberland and Westmorland Record Offices, 1968', *Northern History,* iii (1968), 162.
E.M. Wilson: *Much Cry of Kendal Wool: an Anthology (1420–1720),* Curwen Archives Trust, Occasional Publications No. 1 (1980).
E.L. Ashcroft: *Vital Statistics: the Westmorland 'Census' of 1787,* Curwen Archives Texts No. 1 (1992).
Cumbrian Ancestors (2/1993).
Curwen Archives Trust: *Plans of Kendal in 1787, 1833 and 1853 by John Todd, John Wood and Henry Hoggarth* [reproductions].

424 Keswick Museum and Art Gallery

Parent organisation: Allerdale Borough Council

Address: Fitz Park, Station Road, Keswick, Cumbria CA12 4NF

Telephone: (017687) 73263

Enquiries: The Curator, Hazel Davison

Open: Apr–Oct: Mon–Sat: 10.00–4.00

Access: Generally open to the public, by appointment only.

Historical background: The museum was founded in 1873 and has been administered by the Fitz Park Trust for much of its history. In 1994 it was taken over by Allerdale Borough Council. Literary collections of the Romantic poets made during the latter part of the nineteenth century were donated to the museum during the 1930s.

Acquisitions policy: MSS of the Romantic poets.

Major collections: MSS of Robert Southey (1774–1843), Poet Laureate, 1813–43; William Wordsworth (1770–1850) and Sir Hugh Walpole (1884–1941), novelist (all microfilmed).
Records of Keswick Gas Company and Crosthwaite Boys School.
Miscellaneous material relating to Keswick.

Non-manuscript material: Maps of Keswick and district.
Photographic collection. Newspapers: *English Lakes Visitor* and *Keswick Guardian*, 1882–1910.

Facilities: Photocopying by arrangement.

Conservation: North West Museums Service.

Publications: MSS listed in *The Wordsworth Circle* (winter 1980).

425 Drayton House

Address: Lowick, Kettering, Northants NN14 3BG

Telephone: (01832) 732405

Enquiries: The Librarian

Open: Strictly by appointment only.

Access: Approved academic researchers, on written application.

Historical background: Drayton House dates from medieval times. It was owned by the Mordaunt family during the 16th and 17th centuries, passed to the Sackvilles in 1769 and is still with their descendants. Medieval and 16th–century estate records are held at Northamptonshire Record Office (entry **848**).

Archives of organisation: Background material to estate and house, mainly c1700–1800.

Major collections: Material on Lord George Germain (Sackville) (1716–85), who inherited Drayton in 1769 (mostly published in *HMC Report*).

Finding aids: Historical Manuscripts Commission: *Report on the manuscripts of Mrs Stopford-Sackville*, 1904, 1910 [2 vols]. Northamptonshire Record Office *Calendar* lists some material. Other material is still being sorted and catalogued.

Facilities: Limited photocopying.

426 Kilmarnock and Loudoun District Museums
The Dick Institute

Address: 14 Elmbank Avenue, Kilmarnock, Strathclyde KA1 3BU

Telephone: (01563) 26401

Fax: (01563) 29661

Enquiries: The Curator, Mr James Hunter

Open: Mon, Tues, Thurs, Fri: 9.00–8.00 Wed, Sat: 9.00–5.00

Access: Generally open to the public; access to MSS by appointment.

Historical background: The foundation stone of the Dick Institute was laid in 1898 by Mrs Dick, wife of the donor, and the building was formally opened in 1901. The museum owes its origin chiefly to James Thomson, who gifted a rare and valuable collection of corals, fossils and minerals, to which extensive additions were made by Dr Hunter-Selkirk of Braidwood and others.

Acquisitions policy: MSS of local interest or relating to museum subject areas.

Major collections: Various collections, 14th–20th centuries, including poems and letters of Robert Burns (1759–96); papers of Boyds of Kilmarnock, and Rawden-Hastings and Campbell families; records of local town councils, trade guilds and trade unions.

Non-manuscript material: Local maps.
Engineering and architectural plans and drawings.
Paintings and prints (*c*1500).
Photographs and slides (*c*10,000).
Local newspapers.

Finding aids: Catalogues and indexes to most collections. Rawden-Hastings and Campbell: NRA 18854.

Facilities: Photocopying. Photography. Microfilming. Microfilm reader.

427 The Lynn Museum

Parent organisation: Norfolk Museums Service

Address: Old Market Street, King's Lynn, Norfolk PE30 1NL

Telephone/Fax: (01553) 775001

Enquiries: The Curator, Miss L. Brewster

Open: Mon–Sat: 10.00–5.00

Access: There is a small admission charge to the museum, subject to seasonal alterations.

Historical background: The museum was founded as a society museum in 1844 with a collection of natural history specimens and curiosities. It was taken over by King's Lynn Borough Council and the present building was opened in 1904. In 1973 a branch museum of social history was opened, now located at 46 Queen Street, King's Lynn, and in 1974 both museums were included in the newly formed Norfolk Museums Service.

Acquisitions policy: To collect material and information relating to King's Lynn and West Norfolk.

Archives of organisation: Museum records, 1844–. Natural history: a few records relating to the museum's collections.

Major collections: Archaeological: records of excavations in King's Lynn etc.
Engineering: a vast collection of works' drawings and accompanying ledgers and papers from Dodman's of Lynn (founded *c*1850) relating to boilers, agricultural machinery, traction engines, marine equipment etc; works' drawings, ledgers etc relating to Savages of Lynn,

important manufacturers of fairground machinery, traction engines etc.
Topographical: papers, MS letters etc, relating to the history of Lynn, including some deeds and business records.
Miscellaneous MSS relating to Thomas Baines (1822–75) and Captain G.W. Manby (1765–1854).

Non-manuscript material: Pamphlets and broadsheets relating to Lynn.
Poster Collection: local theatres, politics, religion, sales and auctions etc, 18th century–(*c*6000).
Photographic collections relating to the museum collections and to West Norfolk.
Local paintings, prints, sketches etc, including maritime subjects.

Finding aids: Various lists and indexes. A few select catalogues.

Facilities: Photocopying of small documents at the discretion of the curator.

428 Kingston Museum and Heritage Service

Parent organisation: Royal Borough of Kingston upon Thames

Address: North Kingston Centre, Richmond Road, Kingston upon Thames, Surrey KT2 5PE

Telephone: (0181) 547 6753

Fax: (0181) 547 6747

Enquiries: The Assistant Archivist, Mrs Jill Lamb

Open: Mon, Wed, Thurs, Fri: 10.00–5.00 Tues: 10.00–7.00

Access: Generally open to the public, by appointment (two days' notice required). Council material is restricted for at least 30 years. Records are made available at Surrey Record Office (entry **429**).

Historical background: Archives are held under the various provisions of the Municipal Corporations Act 1882, the Local Government (Records) Act 1962, as modified by the London Government Act 1963, and the Public Records Acts 1958 and 1967. In 1965 the County Archivist of Surrey became the Honorary Borough Archivist and Kingston Corporation employed an assistant archivist.

Acquisitions policy: Records of the Royal Borough of Kingston upon Thames, its predecessors, other bodies, businesses and individuals living in, or connected with, places within the royal borough.

Archives of organisation: Records of the Royal Borough of Kingston, including substantial deed groups for corporation property, 1238–.

Major collections: A small number of private papers.

Non-manuscript material: Plans (all other material is held by the local history library at the same address).

Finding aids: Lists and name and place index to deeds. Lists sent to NRA.

Facilities: Photocopying and microfilm readers available in the Local History Room.

Conservation: Undertaken by Surrey County Record Office.

Publications: Guide to the Borough Archives (1971).
Guide to the Post-1965 Archives (1994).
Archive Teaching Units: *Kingston Children; Kingston Market Place; Kingston in Maps.*

429 Surrey Record Office

Address: County Hall, Penrhyn Road, Kingston upon Thames, Surrey KT1 2DN

Telephone: (0181) 541 9065

Enquiries: The County Archivist, Dr D.B. Robinson

Open: Mon–Thurs: 9.30–4.45 Sat (2nd and 4th of each month): 9.30–12.30, by appointment only. Weekday appointments also advisable.

Access: Generally open to the public. The office operates the CARN reader's ticket system.

Historical background: Records have been received since 1926. The first county archivist was appointed in 1951. Archives of the Royal Borough of Kingston (entry **428**) are consulted in Surrey Record Office search room. The office also acts as the Diocesan Record Office for Southwark (parts) and Guildford (deaneries of Emly and Epsom) and is recognised as a place of deposit for public records (see also Surrey Record Office, Guildford (entry **368**)).

Archives of organisation: Usual local authority record holdings.

Major collections: Deposited local collections, of which the following have a wider significance:
Papers of the Goulburn family of Betchworth relating to sugar estates in Jamaica, 1795–1858, and correspondence with Sir Robert Peel (1788–1850).
Records of the Royal Philanthropic Society's School, Redhill (founded in London for the reform of juveniles), 1788–, and of several other educational and welfare institutions which relocated from London.
Records of the Broadwood family of Lyne, including those of John Broadwood & Sons, piano manufacturers, 1800–.

Finding aids: Lists sent to NRA and some published in *National Inventory of Documentary Sources*, Chadwyck-Healey microfiche (1984–).

Facilities: Photocopying. Photography. Microfilming. Microfilm reader. Limited reader–printer service.

Conservation: Paper conservation in-house. Insect eradication service (leaflet available).

430 Kirkcaldy Central Library

Parent organisation: Kirkcaldy District Libraries

Address: War Memorial Grounds, Kirkcaldy, Fife KY1 1YG

Telephone: (01592) 260707

Enquiries: The Reference Librarian, Miss Sheila Campbell

Open: Mon–Thurs: 10.00–7.00 Fri, Sat: 10.00–5.00

Access: Generally open to the public, preferably by prior appointment. A booking system is in operation for the use of microform readers.

Historical background: Kirkcaldy Central Library opened in 1928, and was part of Kirkcaldy Public Libraries until local government reorganisation in 1975, when Kirkcaldy District Libraries was set up.

Acquisitions policy: To collect material for Kircaldy District in particular and the Fife region in general.

Major collections: Box of deeds and letters.

MSS of Jessie Patrick Findlay, local author, 20th century.

Non-manuscript material: Local history collection: books, maps, press cuttings, slides and photographs.
Kirkcaldy District census records, 1841–81, and old parochial registers.
Newspapers.

Finding aids: Press cuttings index. List of deeds, NRA(S).

Facilities: Photocopying by arrangement. Microfilm/fiche reader/printer.

Publications: List of local history publications available.

431 Kirkcaldy Museum and Art Gallery

Parent organisation: Kirkcaldy District Council

Address: War Memorial Gardens, Kirkcaldy, Fife KY1 1YG

Telephone: (01592) 260732

Enquiries: The Curator

Open: Mon–Fri: 9.00–5.00

Access: Generally open to the public, by appointment only.

Historical background: The museum and art gallery was founded in 1925 as a general museum for Kirkcaldy. In 1975 it became responsible for Kirkcaldy District. The archive is only part of the large general museum and art collections. Much earlier local material is deposited with the Scottish Record Office (entry 313). The bulk of the 19th– and 20th–century government material is held by Kirkcaldy District Council, Town House, Kirkcaldy.

Acquisitions policy: By donation and deposit, material relevant to the museum collections and to the history of Kirkcaldy District.

Major collections: Records of the linoleum industry, including plans, buildings and machinery, 1840–1990s; trade guilds, 1700–1850; trade unions, local branches, 20th century; local government, 19th–20th centuries; friendly societies, 19th century.

Non-manuscript material: Photographic collections of the district. Most non-MS material is held by Kirkcaldy Central Library (entry **430**).

Finding aids: Some indexing. NRA(S) lists, including Kirkcaldy Burgh Museum and Art Gallery: NRA(S) 744.

Facilities: Photocopying by arrangement.

432 Hornel Art Gallery and Library

Parent organisation: National Trust for Scotland

Address: Broughton House, 12 High Street, Kirkcudbright, Dumfries and Galloway DG6 4JX

Telephone: (01557) 330437

Enquiries: The Property Manager

Open: Apr-Oct: Mon–Sun: 1.00–5.30 At other times by arrangement only.

Access: Generally open to the public; an appointment is necessary.

Historical background: The property and its contents, including the library, were left to the community by the artist E.A. Hornel, under a trust deed which became operative in 1950. In 1994 the property was transferred to the National Trust for Scotland by the E.A. Hornel Trust.

Acquisitions policy: Acquisition by donation, deposit or purchase within the fields covered by the collection.

Major collections: The Dumfries and Galloway Collection, covering the old counties of Dumfries, Kirkcudbright and Wigtown: diaries, accounts, military documents, genealogies, ecclesiastical papers, writs, covenanting papers, 17th–19th centuries.
Literary MSS, including correspondence of Sir Walter Scott, 1802–31, and Thomas Carlyle, 1819–78.
Large collection of MSS of local authors and correspondence *re* ballads and local traditions, including the William McMath Collection, relating mainly to English and Scottish popular ballads.

Non-manuscript material: Robert Burns Collection, including many early editions, and information about Burns clubs throughout the world.

Finding aids: Catalogues. NRA(S) 0118 (NRA 10178).

Facilities: Photocopying and photography by arrangement.

433 The Stewartry Museum

Parent organisation: Stewartry District Council

Address: Department of Environmental Health and Leisure Services, Cannonwalls, High Street, Kirkcudbright, Dumfries and Galloway DG6 4JG

Telephone: (01557) 331643

Fax: (01557) 330005

Enquiries: The Curator, Dr D. Devereux

Open: Mon–Fri: 9.00–5.00, subject to the availability of the curator
NB These opening times are not identical with those of the museum.

Access: Open to all responsible researchers; an appointment with the Curator is necessary. A postal enquiry service is offered on a fee-paying basis.

Historical background: The archive collection was begun in 1881 with the foundation of the Stewartry Museum. The operation of the museum was taken over by Stewartry District Council in 1990, and at this time responsibility for the district council's collection was transferred to the Museum Service.

Acquisitions policy: Material of all types relating to the human and natural history of the collecting area, which is the area currently under the local government administration of Stewartry District Council, together with those areas formerly administered by the County Council of the Stewartry of Kirkcudbright and now outwith the bounds of Stewartry District.

Archives of organisation: Records relating to the foundation and subsequent management of the Stewartry Museum, 1881–1990; these include minute books, financial accounts, correspondence and the collections register of the Stewartry Museum Association.

Major collections: Kirkcudbright Town Council records, later 16th century-1975, including minute books, 1576–1975.
Burgh court records and annual accounts, c1700–.

Stewartry Burgh records for New Galloway, Castle Douglas and Gatehouse of Fleet (various dates).
Kirkcudbrightshire Yeomanry Cavalry records, 1804–36.
Local estate records: Auchendolly, Redcastle, Queenshill, Gelston, Orchardton, Livingstone.

Non-manuscript material: Small collections of plans and drawings of local bridges.
Maps, especially Kirkcudbright, late 18th century–.
Photographic collection for the Stewartry area.
Small collection of films.
Supporting printed material includes graveyard surveys and newspaper indexes.

Finding aids: A computer-based inventory is in preparation. Survey of Stewartry Museum Collection: NRA 9002.

Facilities: Photocopying. Photography by arrangement.

Conservation: Active conservation programme, contracted out.

434 William Patrick Library

Parent organisation: Strathkelvin District Libraries

Address: 2 West High Street, Kirkintilloch, Glasgow G66 1AD

Telephone: (0141) 775 1613

Fax: (0141) 776 0408

Enquiries: The Principal Assistant (Reference), Mr Don Martin

Open: Mon, Tues, Thurs, Fri: 9.30–8.00 Wed: 9.30–1.00; 2.00–5.00 Sat: 9.30–1.00

Access: Generally open to the public.

Historical background: The department was set up in 1975 as a result of the reorganisation of local government in Scotland.

Acquisitions policy: To provide accommodation for local authority records which vest in Strathkelvin District Council; also material belonging to local individuals, firms and organisations who wish to deposit locally.

Archives of organisation: Records of the former burghs of Kirkintilloch and Bishopbriggs; also a small quantity of records of former county district councils which now vest in Strathkelvin District Council.

Major collections: Archives of local organisations, families and individuals, including minute books, accounts books, scrapbooks etc, of Kirkintilloch YMCA, Kirkintilloch Funeral & Mortcloth Society, Lenzie Public Hall Trustees and Kirkintilloch Town Mission.
J.F. McEwan Collection of Scottish railway history.
Documents of local interest collected by individuals and families.

Non-manuscript material: Catalogues, drawings and photographs of the former Lion Foundry Co.
Extensive holdings of local material, including books, pamphlets, maps, photographs, photographic slides, local newspapers, news cuttings, leaflets and posters.

Finding aids: Catalogue of the archive (3 vols).

Facilities: Photocopying. Photography. Microfilm/fiche reader/printer.

Publications: Leaflets available on 'Archives', 'Local History' and 'Family History'.

435 Orkney Archives

Parent organisation: Orkney Islands Council

Address: The Orkney Library, Laing Street, Kirkwall, Orkney KW15 1NW

Telephone: (01856) 873166

Fax: (01856) 875260

Enquiries: The Archivist, Miss Alison Fraser

Open: Mon–Fri: 9.00–1.00; 2.00–5.00
Closed for annual stock-taking last two weeks of February and 1st week of March.

Access: Generally open to the public, by appointment.

Historical background: The office was formally established in 1973 by Orkney Education Authority; it is now administered by the Department of Education and Recreation Services of Orkney Islands Council.

Acquisitions policy: MS and printed material; film, video, photographs, sound recordings, maps, plans etc relating to Orkney.

Archives of organisation: Usual local authority holdings, 1669–.

Major collections: Balfour of Balfour and Trenabie, c1570–1886; Watt of Breckness & Skaill, c1720–1850; Sutherland Graeme of Graemeshall, c1600–1938; Ernest W. Marwick, c1770–1977; Earldom of Orkney, 1536–1880. Business records of Highland Park Distillery and Orkney Islands Shipping Company.

Non-manuscript material: Plans and maps. Photographs (20,000).
Sound archive (1600 tapes).
Microfilm copies of local newspapers, census and old parish registers.

Finding aids: Descriptive lists available for main series of records and many of the deposited collections; lists sent to NRA(S).

Facilities: Photocopying. Photography. Microfilm/fiche readers/printer.

436 Saint David's University College

Parent organisation: University of Wales

Address: Lampeter, Dyfed SA48 7ED

Telephone: (01570) 422351 ext. 234

Enquiries: The Hon. Archivist, Rev. Canon D.T.W. Price

Open: By appointment.

Access: Generally open to the public.

Historical background: The college opened in 1827 and for many years most of the graduates entered the ministry of the Anglican Church, although the college was never simply a theological college. In 1971 the college became a constituent institution of the University of Wales.

Acquisitions policy: To retrieve and preserve all material concerned with the history of the college.

Archives of organisation: Archives of the college, including tutors' registers, which provide biographical material on all students of the college.

Non-manuscript material: College magazines; many photographs.

Finding aids: Various lists and indexes.

Facilities: Photocopying.

437 Lindsay Institute

Parent organisation: Clydesdale District Council, Libraries, Information and Museums Service

Address: Hope Street, Lanark, Strathclyde ML11 7LZ

Telephone: (01555) 661331 ext. 269

Fax: (01555) 665884

Enquiries: The Support and Information Librarian, Mr J. McGarrity

Open: Mon, Tues, Wed, Fri: 9.30–7.30 Thurs, Sat: 9.30–5.00

Access: Generally open to the public. An appointment is advisable if a microfilm reader is required.

Historical background: The collection was founded for Clydesdale District in 1975, parts having formerly been held by the Royal Burgh of Lanark, the Burgh of Biggar and Lanark County Council. The institute also holds the libraries of Dr William Smellie (1697–1763) and the Robert Owen Collection of books and pamphlets.

Acquisitions policy: Since 1975 collecting has concentrated on archival materials relevant to the Clydesdale District.

Archives of organisation: Local government records covering Clydesdale District, 1150–.
Records of the Royal Burgh of Lanark, 1150–1975.
Records of Biggar Town Council, 1863–1963 (incomplete).

Non-manuscript material: Microfilms of old parish registers, 1645–1854, census returns, 1841–91.
Maps and plans (c1750).
Photographs and illustrations (c2300).

Finding aids: Lists sent to NRA(S). Royal Burgh of Lanark: NRA 26114.

Facilities: Photocopying. Photography. Microfilm/fiche readers.

Conservation: Minor work and protective measures carried out in-house; otherwise contracted out.

438 Lancaster District Library
Local Studies Department

Address: Market Square, Lancaster LA1 1HY

Telephone: (01524) 63266

Fax: (01524) 842629

Enquiries: The District Librarian, Mr S.J. Eccles

Open: Mon, Thurs, Fri: 9.30–7.00 Tues, Wed: 9.30–5.00 Sat: 9.30–4.00

Access: Generally open to the public; a prior appointment will save time.

Historical background: Formerly Lancaster City Library, the library became part of the Lancashire Library in 1974. The City Library was formed in 1893, inheriting volumes from the Mechanics' Institute, Amicable Society etc, which date from the late 18th century. Between World Wars I and II the library was designated an official repository of archives by the Master of the Rolls before the creation of Lancashire Record Office (entry **944**). Most archive material has been acquired since 1900. The Yorkshire Collection is now housed at Morecambe Library.

Acquisitions policy: Material is acquired only by donation. All types of maps and unmounted illustrations etc are accepted. Ephemera is collected. MSS would now normally be donated to Lancashire Record Office.

Major collections: Local history collection (c 9000 MSS), for the area within 15 miles radius of Lancaster, including: apprentice registers; Port Commissioners archives.
Cumbria and Lancashire Collection: general interest material.

Non-manuscript material: Cumbria, Lancashire and Yorkshire map collections.
Local newspapers, 1801–.

Finding aids: Indexes to all local collections are sheaf catalogues with general subject lists as guides to their use. Newspapers are partly indexed, but the quality of the indexing varies.

Facilities: Photocopying (excluding bound newspapers). Photography (subject to conditions). Microfilm reader/printer.

439 Lancaster University Library

Address: Bailrigg, Lancaster LA1 4YH

Telephone: (01524) 65201

Fax: (01524) 63806

Enquiries: The Assistant Librarians, Mr J.L. Illingworth and Dr L.M. Newman or The Centre for NW Regional Studies, Dr Elizabeth Roberts

Open: Term: Mon, Tues, Thurs, Fri: 8.45–9.45 Wed: 9.30–9.45 Sat: 9.00–4.45 Sun: 2.00–6.45 (no service after 7.00 or at the weekend) Vacation: Mon, Tues, Thurs, Fri: 9.00–4.45 Wed: 9.30–4.45

Access: Members of the university library and other accredited research workers; prior written application is desirable.

Major collections: MSS from the library of Burnley Grammar School, 13th–17th centuries (9 items).
Miscellaneous correspondence of John Ruskin.
Wordsworth MSS, including a variant of a late sonnet.
Wolfenden Report: papers and oral evidence submitted to the Wolfenden Committee on the future of voluntary organisations, 1974–6.
Barclay Report: papers and oral evidence submitted to the Barclay Committee on the role and task of social workers, 1981.
Robert Fitzgibbon Young (*d*1960): some papers and press cuttings.

Non-manuscript material: Map collection, census, slides, extensive microfilm archives.
Centre for North West Regional Studies: tapes, with transcripts, of interviews on social and family life in Barrow, Lancaster and Preston, 1890–1970 (500).

Finding aids: Some indexes, including full index to CNWRS transcripts.

Facilities: Photocopying. Photography. Microfilm/fiche reader/printers.

Conservation: In-house bindery; otherwise contracted out.

440 Lancing College Archives

Address: Lancing College, Lancing, West Sussex BN15 0RW

Telephone: (01273) 452213 ext. 267

Fax: (01273) 464720

Enquiries: The Assistant Archivist, Mrs J. Pennington

Open: By arrangement.

Access: Approved readers, on written application. An appointment is necessary and a small search fee is made for lengthy postal requests.

Historical background: The college was founded by Nathaniel Woodard (1811–91), canon of Manchester, in 1848. A basic collection of Woodard schools papers, made by Henry M. Gibbs during the 19th century, has been gradually added to since. See also Woodard Corporation (entry **779**).

Acquisitions policy: To acquire further material relating to the past of Lancing College and the other 22 Woodard schools, and to preserve present material, including tape-recordings and video recordings.

Archives of organisation: Correspondence and papers of Nathaniel Woodard, 1846–90 (*c*10,000).

Major collections: Papers of Edmund Field, chaplain of Lancing College, 1854–92.
Memoirs and other papers.

Non-manuscript material: Photographs and architectural drawings, in particular the construction of the chapel, 1868–1979.

Finding aids: Catalogue. Report on the records compiled by the Royal Commission on Historical Manuscripts.

Facilities: Photocopying. Photography.

Conservation: Conservation of Woodard's correspondence and papers with a grant by the National Manuscripts Conservation Trust. The Hampshire Archives Trust is undertaking the repair work.

Publications: K.E. Kirk: *The Story of the Woodard Schools* (Abbey Press, *R*1952).
B. Heeney: *Mission to the Middle Classes: the Woodard Schools, 1848–1891* (SPCK, 1969).
B. Handford: *Lancing College: History and Memoirs* (Phillimore, 1986).

441 Henry Moore Centre for the Study of Sculpture

Parent organisation: The Henry Moore Sculpture Trust

Address: The Henry Moore Institute, 74 The Headrow, Leeds LS1 3AA

Telephone: (0113) 246 9469

Fax: (0113) 246 1481

Enquiries: The Research Assistant, Ben Dhaliwal

Open: Mon–Sat: 10.00–5.30 Wed: 10.00–9.00

Access: Open to everyone with a serious interest. An appointment is necessary and at least two days' notice is normally required.

Historical background: The centre was established by the Henry Moore Foundation and Leeds City Council in 1982. In 1993 it moved from Leeds City Art Gallery to the new Henry Moore Institute next door, where it shares premises with the Henry Moore Sculpture Trust. The centre works with the trust to develop a programme to promote the study of sculpture. Most material relating to Henry Moore (1898–1986) is kept at the foundation's premises in Much Hadham, Hertfordshire.

Acquisitions policy: To maintain and develop a library and archive devoted to the history and practice of sculpture. The centre aims to preserve documents relating to the preparation, production and reception of sculpture, and holds a significant collection of sculptors' drawings in addition to other kinds of documentation.

Major collections: Thornycroft family papers from three generations of sculptors, including Thomas Thornycroft (1816–85) and his wife Mary (1809–95), and Sir Hamo Thornycroft RA (1850–1925).
James Sherwood Westmacott (1823–88), drawing books.
Thomas Woolner (1825–98), photographs and diaries.
Alfred Gilbert (1854–1934), letters (*c*50).
Jacob Epstein (1880–1959), complete studio photographs and sketchbooks.
Henry Moore, early note-book and juvenilia from his time at Leeds; archive of photographs of his works.
Gilbert Ledward (1888–1960), preparation drawings for 'Westminster Guards Memorial'

(1922); typescript of his unpublished autobiography; all studio photographs.
Eric Gill (1882–1940), correspondence with the sculptor Joseph Cribb.
Stephen Cox (*b*1946), two sketchbooks.
Wood's Monumental Masonry Album of 222 designs for church monuments by various artists working in Britain, used by the workshop of the Wood family of Bath and Bristol, late 18th and early 19th century.
John Galizia Foundry, London, casting ledgers, 1930–65 (4 vols), and photographic archive (500).

Non-manuscript material: Erroll Jackson Photographic Archive.
Henry Hugh Armstead, Count Gleichen, albums of photographs of sculpture.
Studio photographs and portraits of Eric Gill and his family (145).
Slide library, especially of exhibitions, outdoor sculpture and ecclesiastical sculpture (6000 images).

Finding aids: Thornycroft papers indexed and catalogued. Cataloguing in progress on other material. Detailed catalogues of slide sets.

Facilities: Photocopying, except for drawings. Slide sets for loan.

442 Leeds Central Library
Local History Department

Parent organisation: Leeds City Libraries

Address: Municipal Buildings, Calverley Street, Leeds LS1 3AB

Telephone: (0113) 247 8290

Fax: (0113) 247 8268

Enquiries: The Senior Librarian, Local and Family History, Mrs Sandra L. Smith

Open: Mon, Wed: 9.00–8.00 Tues, Fri: 9.00–5.30 Thurs: 9.30–5.30 Sat: 9.00–4.00

Access: Generally open to the public.

Historical background: The reference library has always maintained a collection of material relating to Leeds and the rest of Yorkshire. In 1991 the Local History Department was expanded to include material and research facilities for the study of family history and became the Local and Family History Library. The Leeds Archives Department (now West Yorkshire Archive Service: Leeds, entry **448**), originally housed in the library building, moved to separate premises in the 1960s and is administered independently.

Acquisitions policy: Maps, periodicals, newspapers etc relating to Leeds or by Leeds authors, and some relating to the rest of Yorkshire, are purchased.

Major collections: Usual local history collection, including a minor collection of such items as minutes of local societies and original MSS of works by local authors.

Non-manuscript material: Maps of Leeds and Yorkshire.
Illustrations of Yorkshire, mostly of the Leeds area (*c*32,000).
Leeds playbills (6000).
Wide range of printed transcripts and microfilm copies of parish registers.
Microfilm of Yorkshire census returns and Leeds newspapers.
Books and pamphlets on Leeds and Yorkshire or by local authors (*c*90,000).

Finding aids: Index to Leeds and Yorkshire items in newspapers and periodicals (incomplete). Index to illustrations. Index to census returns: Yorkshire by town and village, Leeds Metropolitan District by street names.

Facilities: Photocopying. Photography. Microfilm/fiche readers/printer.

Publications: Leeds City Libraries: Guides to *Local and Family History* and *Census Enumerator's Returns, Yorkshire.*

443 Leeds Diocesan Archives

Address: Diocesan Curia, 7 St Marks Avenue, Leeds LS2 9BN

Telephone: (0113) 244 4788

Fax: (0113) 244 9084

Enquiries: The Diocesan Archivist, Very Rev. Mgr G.T. Bradley or The Assistant Archivist, Mr Robert Finnigan

Open: Mon–Fri: 10.00–4.00, by appointment

Access: Bona fide students, by written application to the Archivist.

Historical background: The collection is part of the archives of the Vicars Apostolic of the Northern District (1688–1840) and the papers of the Vicar Apostolic of the Yorkshire District

(1840–50), the Bishop of Beverley (1850–78) and the Bishops of Leeds (1878–).

Acquisitions policy: The records of the Diocese of Leeds are all eventually passed to the Diocesan Archives; also deposited are any records of importance from parishes in the diocese. The registers of certain parishes established before 1900 have been microfilmed.

Major collections: Papers of the Roman Catholic Church in Yorkshire, 1688–; some papers for other parts of the North of England before 1840.
Hogarth MSS: 19th–century transcripts of the papers of the secular clergy in Yorkshire, 1660–.

Non-manuscript material: Printed pastorals of bishops.
Small collection of theological pamphlets for the period of the archives.

Finding aids: Some lists and indexes (1821–61); other parts are in the process of being catalogued.

Facilities: Photocopying by arrangement. Microfiche reader.

Publications: G.T. Bradley: 'Leeds Diocesan Archives: a Provisional Summary', *Newsletter for Students of Recusant History*, 4 (Nijmegen, 1962), 26.
——: 'The Leeds Diocesan Archives', *Catholic Archives*, 2 (1982), 46–51.

444 Museum of the History of Education

Parent organisation: University of Leeds

Address: Parkinson Court, University of Leeds, Leeds LS2 9JT

Telephone: (0113) 233 4665

Enquiries: The Curator, Dr E.J. Foster

Open: Mon–Fri: 9.30–12.30; 1.30–3.30

Access: Generally open to the public, by arrangement.

Historical background: The University of Leeds was founded as the Yorkshire College in 1874. The museum was established in the 1950s, aimed at the documentation of the history of education and the promotion of research and publication.

Acquisitions policy: Acquires children's work, equipment, artefacts and books to illustrate the history of education.

Major collections: Children's exercise books, 17th century–.

Trainee teachers' work and records of their progress.

Records of education societies and material concerning education in the former West Riding of Yorkshire, 1902–74.

Non-manuscript material: Children's practical work, including needlework.

School textbooks, 17th century–.

Examples of science teaching apparatus and school furniture.

Finding aids: Computerised catalogue in progress.

445 Thoresby Society

Address: Claremont, 23 Clarendon Road, Leeds LS2 9NZ

Enquiries: The Hon. Librarian

Open: Tues, Thurs: 10.00–2.00 (except Tues following a bank holiday).

Access: Members of the society; others on written application.

The Thoresby Society was founded in 1889 to foster interest in the history of Leeds and district; it collects relevant MSS, pictures, maps and plans and printed material. A catalogue, lists and indexes are available.

446 University of Leeds
Brotherton Library

Address: Leeds LS2 9JT

A Special Collections

Telephone: (0113) 233 5518 (direct line)

Fax: (0113) 233 5561

Enquiries: The University Librarian and Keeper of the Brotherton Collection, Mr R.P. Carr or The Head of Special Collections, Mr C.D.W. Sheppard

Open: Mon–Thurs: 9.00–1.00; 2.15–5.00 Fri: 9.30–1.00; 2.15–5.00

Access: Open to all at the discretion of the Librarian. Non-members of the university should apply in advance to the Librarian and should provide a letter of introduction from a person of recognised status if so required.

Historical background: The university library, of which the Brotherton Library forms part, began as the library of the Yorkshire College in 1874.

Acquisitions policy: General, with a bias towards the research interests of the university.

Major collections: Archives of West Riding wool textile manufacturers, mainly 18th century–; Dean and Chapter of Ripon, medieval; various Yorkshire Quaker meetings, 17th century–; Leeds Chamber of Commerce, 19th century–; Leeds Philosophical and Literary Society, 19th and 20th centuries; Association of Education Committees, 20th century.

Woolley Hall estate papers, medieval.

Roth MSS on Jewish history and culture, medieval.

Papers and diaries of Herbert Thompson, music critic, 19th and 20th centuries.

Correspondence of Jethro Bithell, mainly with mid-20th–century German writers.

Papers of John Wilson of Broomhead, near Sheffield, antiquarian, 18th century.

Leeds Russian Archive, 20th century.

Miscellaneous cookery and recipe books, 16th century–; medical treatises and papers, 18th century–.

Diaries, letters and papers of various professors and other members of the university staff, 19th and 20th centuries.

Papers of Lord Boyle, and other political papers, 20th century.

Leeds Queen's Square and Park Square art gallery archives, 20th century.

Finding aids: Various handlists.

Facilities: Photocopying. Photography. Microfilming. Microfilm/fiche reader.

Conservation: Contracted out.

Publications: C. Roth: 'Catalogue of Manuscripts in the Roth Collection', *Alexander Marx Jubilee Volume: English Section* (1950), 503–35.
P. Hudson: *The West Riding Wool Textile Industry: a Catalogue of Business Records* (1975).

B The Brotherton Collection

Historical background: The basis of the collection is the private library of Lord Brotherton of Wakefield (1856–1930), presented to the university 'for the Nation' shortly after his death. It is now greatly increased in size through subsequent purchases from endowed funds and through further gifts. Since 1993 the Brotherton Collection has been amalgamated with the other Special Collections of the University Library, but for historical and funding reasons it retains a degree of autonomy.

Acquisitions policy: Major current collecting fields are: English drama and poetry, 1600–1750, and material from this period relating to travel, science, language, translation, and political and economic thought; 19th– and 20th-century literary MSS and printed books; Romany subjects.

Major collections: Literary MSS, especially verse miscellanies, 17th and 18th centuries.
MSS of 19th–century writers, including the Arnolds, the Brontës, A.C. Swinburne (1837–1909) and George Borrow (1803–81).
Marrick Priory deeds and charters, 12th century–.
Archives of the Loder-Symonds family and Henry Marten (1602–80), regicide.
Papers of Thomas Townshend, 1st Viscount Sydney (1733–1800); the Novello and Cowdon-Clarke families, 19th century.
MSS and correspondence of: Sir Edmund Gosse (1849–1928), P.H. Gosse (1810–88) and Dr Philip Gosse, 1867–1928; Edward Clodd (1840–1930); W.W. Gibson; Lascelles Abercrombie (1881–1938); John Drinkwater (1882–1937); W.R.M. Childe; Bonamy Dobrée; Francis Berry and G. Wilson Knight.
Correspondence of: Bram Stoker (1847–1912) and Sir Henry Irving (1838–1905); Henry Arthur Jones (1851–1929); G.A. Sala (1828–96); Clement Shorter (1857–1926).
Papers of Arthur Ransome (1884–1967).
Letters and MSS of Mendelssohn.
Correspondence files of the *New Statesman*, 1914–19.
Archives of *The London Magazine*, 1972–.
Documents relating to the Chevalier D'Eon.
Papers of Alf Mattison relating to the development of socialism in Great Britain, late 19th and early 20th centuries.
Papers of T.W. Thompson, gypsy scholar.

Non-manuscript material: Some paintings and other artefacts, particularly in Romany and Novello and Cowden-Clarke collections.

Finding aids: Many lists and indexes.

Facilities: Photocopying. Photography. Microfilming. Microfilm/fiche reader.

Conservation: Contracted out.

Publications: J.S. Symington: *The Brotherton Library: a Catalogue of Ancient Manuscripts and Early Printed Works Collected by Edward Allen, Baron Brotherton of Wakefield* (Leeds, 1931).
Annual Report of the Brotherton Collection Committee (1936–).
A Catalogue of the Gosse Correspondence in the Brotherton Collection 1867 to 1928 (Leeds, 1950).
The Novello Cowden-Clarke Collection (Leeds, 1955).
Catalogue of the Romany Collection formed by D.U. McGrigor Phillips LL.D and Presented to the University of Leeds (Edinburgh, 1962).
D.I. Masson: 'The Brotherton Collection of Rare Books and Manuscripts', *University of Leeds Review*, xxi (1978), 135.
The Brotherton Collection, University of Leeds: its Collections Described with Illustrations of Fifty Books and Manuscripts (Leeds, 1986).
The Brotherton Collection Review (1989–) [triennial account of selected new acquisitions].

C The Liddle Collection

Telephone: (0113) 233 5566 (direct line)

Fax: (0113) 233 5561

Enquiries: The University Librarian, Mr R.P. Carr or The Keeper, Mr P.H. Liddle

Open: Generally open to the public, by appointment.

Access: Open to all at the discretion of the Librarian. Non-members of the university should apply in advance to the Librarian and should provide a letter of introduction from a person of recognised status if so required.

Historical background: The collection dates from 1964, conceived by Mr Peter Liddle as a source of original material for research on World War I, with a particular emphasis on the personal experience of individuals involved in the conflict. In 1988 the collection was acquired by the university library, with Mr Liddle retaining responsibility for its administration.

Acquisitions policy: Any original documentary material in the form of letters, diaries, artwork, scrapbooks and official papers, and also maps, books, artefacts, souvenirs, weapons and uniforms relating to 1914–18 and the period immediately before and after World War I. Also MS, typescript and tape-recorded recollections of personal experience in any aspect of the war. The domestic front and conscientious objection are areas considered as significant as the fighting fronts.

Major collections: The 1914–18 papers and/or recollections of over 5000 veterans (many men and women of outstanding eminence). A special feature of the archives is that there is first-hand evidence of the early active service careers of about 150 men who later rose to the highest army, navy and air force ranks. The same can be claimed for outstanding politicians, scientists, businessmen and men of the arts and sport. The war in the air, at sea, Gallipoli and conscientious objection are among the areas most comprehensively covered, but of special interest is the material relating to less well-documented aspects of the war, such as German East Africa, Dunsterforce, the Caspian Naval Force and British intervention in Russia.

Non-manuscript material: Large newspaper collection of national, local, army and navy, and foreign issues, with many unusual specialist items, including trench news sheets.
Map collection for all the fighting fronts.
Museum collection of uniforms, weapons, souvenirs and various artefacts.
Tape-recorded recollections of all areas of personal experience in the war, with the social background and pre-1914 working experience of the interviewees, who include Harold Macmillan, Henry Moore, Lord Shinwell and Fenner Brockway as well as a number of marshals of the Royal Air Force, field marshals and an Admiral of the Fleet.

Finding aids: Leaflets fully listing individuals represented in the archive. Everything except the British Occupation of Germany material is fully listed. Special aspects catalogues for army service, RFC, RNAS and RAF and the Royal Navy and Mercantile Marine. Card index to tape-recordings; transcripts in progress. Lists for the newspapers, maps and museum collections.

Facilities: Photocopying. Photography.

Conservation: Contracted out.

Publications: P.H. Liddle: 'The First World War: Teaching and Research', *Teaching History* (May 1974).
——: *Men of Gallipoli* (1976).

——: 'The Distinctive Nature of the Gallipoli Experience', *RUSI* (June 1977).
——: *World War One Archive* (1977).
——: 'Recollections of the Great War', *Journal of Oral History* (1979).
——: 'The Tragedies of Loos', *Army Quarterly* (April 1983).
——: *The Sailor's War* (1985).
——: 'Aspects of the Employment of the British Air Arm, 1914–18', *RUSI* (Dec 1986).
——: *The Airman's War* (1987).
——: *The Soldier's War* (1988).

447 University of Leeds Archive

Parent organisation: The University of Leeds

Address: Baines Wing, University of Leeds, Leeds LS2 9JT

Telephone: (0113) 233 5061 (direct line) 243 1751 ext. 5061

Enquiries: The University Archivist

Open: Mon, Wed, Thurs: 9.30–5.00

Access: Personal enquiries, preferably by appointment.

Historical background: The Yorkshire College of Science, precursor of the University of Leeds, was founded in 1874 and merged with the Leeds School of Medicine (itself founded in 1831) in 1884 to become one of the constituent colleges of the Victoria University in 1887. The University of Leeds was created an independent institution in 1904 and the university archives were established in 1977.

Acquisitions policy: Administrative and teaching records and papers of the University of Leeds and such personal papers as may be appropriate.

Archives of organisation: Administrative records of Leeds School of Medicine, 1831–84; Yorkshire College (of Science), 1874–1903; University of Leeds, 1904–.
Some early teaching and student material and personal papers.

Non-manuscript material: Photographs; building plans.

Finding aids: Various lists and indexes in process of compilation.

Facilities: Photocopying. Photography.

448 West Yorkshire Archive Service: Leeds

Address: Chapeltown Road, Sheepscar, Leeds, LS7 3AP

Telephone: (0113) 262 8839

Fax: (0113) 262 4707

Enquiries: The District Archivist, Mr W.J. Connor

Open: Tues–Fri: 9.30–5.00 (limited service 12.00–2.00)
Annual stock-taking closure usually early February; generally closed on the day following public holidays.

Access: Bona fide researchers, subject to any restrictions laid down by depositors; an appointment is essential.

Historical background: The office was established in 1938 in Leeds City Reference Library, where manuscripts had been collected since the late 19th century. It moved to its present premises in 1965 and became part of the West Yorkshire Archive Service in 1982. It does not incorporate a printed local history collection. As one of the few offices established in the West Riding before 1974, its collections derive from a much wider geographical area than might be expected, including Craven, Ripon and Harrogate as well as the heartland of the present West Yorkshire. It is a Diocesan Record Office for the dioceses of Bradford and Ripon and is recognised as a place of deposit for public records.

Acquisitions policy: Archives of all kinds arising within the local authority area or associated with existing holdings.

Archives of organisation: Leeds City Council and absorbed authorities, 1662–, including the boroughs and districts of Aireborough, Garforth, Horsforth, Morley, Otley, Pudsey, Rothwell, Wetherby and Wharfedale.

Major collections: Family and estate archives, including Baines family of Leeds, 1784– 1890, notably Edward Baines (1774–1848), Matthew Talbot Baines (1799–1860) and Sir Edward Baines (1800–90); Gascoigne family of Parlington; Earls of Harewood, notably papers of George Canning, 1780–1827, Earl Canning, 1833–62, and Marquises of Clanricarde, 1816–1910; Ingilby family of Ripley Castle; Lane Fox family of Bramham Park; Earls of Mexborough, notably correspondence of Sir John Reresby, 1639–88; Newby Hall Estate, notably London

Port Books, 1717–20, and correspondence of 1st and 2nd Lords Grantham, 1736–1801; Nostell Priory; Ramsden family of Byram, notably Rockingham and Fitzwilliam correspondence, 1765–1801, and Sir J.W. Ramsden (1831–1914); Samuel Smiles (1812–1904), papers; Studley Royal Estate, notably Fountains Abbey monastic records, 12th century-1540, and correspondence of 1st and 2nd Lords Grantham, 1725–71; Temple Newsam (Ingram family and estate), notably English and Irish customs accounts, 1604–45, the Commissary of Minorca, 1735–55, and records of the Council of the North, 1585–1636.

Antiquarian collections include Bacon Frank, J.E.F. Chambers (including Plumpton family) and papers of William Farrer.

Business records include T. and M. Bairstow of Sutton in Craven, worsted manufacturers, 1801–1964; British Coal, pre-vesting date records for North Yorkshire Area; Burton group of Leeds, clothing manufacturers, notably papers of Sir Montague Burton, 1896–1952; Fairbairn Lawson of Leeds, engineers, 1843–1980; Ford Ayrton of Bentham, silk spinners, 1871–1971; Grand Theatre and Opera House, Leeds, 1876–; Greenwood and Batley of Leeds, engineers, 1856–1969; Hathorn Davey of Leeds, pump manufacturers, 1852–1939; Kirkstall Forge of Leeds, engineers, 1752–; Leeds Industrial Co-operative Society, 1847–; Middleton Colliery of Leeds, 1760–1907; Joshua Tetley of Leeds, brewers, 1786–; John Waddington of Leeds, printers and games manufacturers, 1907–; John Wilson of Leeds, linen manufacturers, 1754–1836; Yorkshire Patent Steam Waggon Co. of Leeds, 1903–53; and solicitors' and estate agents' papers.

Ecclesiastical records of Anglican and nonconformist churches, including Diocese of Ripon and Archdeaconry of Richmond, 1474–, deposited parish records and Yorkshire Congregational Union, 1812–.

Records of charities and societies include Arthington Trust, Conchological Society of Great Britain and Northern Ireland, Leeds Institute, Yorkshire Ladies' Council of Education, Yorkshire Naturalists' Union.

Non-manuscript material: Some photographs, usually associated with archives, such as surveys of slum clearance areas.

Finding aids: Card indexes of names, places and probate records. Links to West Yorkshire Archive Service and NRA computerised databases. Catalogues sent to NRA.

Facilities: Photocopying. Photography. Microfilm/fiche readers. Ultra-violet lamp.

Conservation: In-house department which undertakes outside work.

Publications: A Brief Guide to Yorkshire Record Offices (1968)
P. Hudson: *The West Riding Wool Textile Industry: a Catalogue of Business Records* (1975).
J.M. Collinson: *Sources of Business and Industrial History in the Leeds Archives Department* (Leeds, 1977).
——: 'The Leeds Archives Department', *Northern History*, xv (1979), 210.
Leeds Archives, 1938–1988: an Illustrated Guide to Leeds District Archives (Wakefield, 1988).
West Yorkshire Archive Service: *Guide for Family Historians* (1992).

449 West Yorkshire Archive Service: Yorkshire Archaeological Society

Address: Claremont, 23 Clarendon Road, Leeds LS2 9NZ

Telephone: (0113) 245 6362

Enquiries: The Archivist-in-charge, Mrs S. Thomas or The Archivist to the Joint Committee, Mr R. Frost

Open: Tues, Wed: 2.00–8.30 Thurs, Fri: 9.30–5.00 Sat: 9.30–5.00, by appointment.

Access: Generally open to the public; an appointment is required for Saturdays, and appreciated for other days.

Historical background: The society was formed in 1863 and has built up extensive collections of books and documents relating to the whole of Yorkshire. From 1976 to 1982 the society's archives were administered by West Yorkshire County Council, and since 1982 they have formed part of the West Yorkshire Archive Service, which seconds staff from its headquarters in Wakefield (entry 1072). The Thoresby Society (entry 445) operates from the same address.

Acquisitions policy: To acquire items additional to collections already held, material relating to Yorkshire as a whole, antiquarian MSS and the results of research and fieldwork carried out by society members.

Archives of organisation: The society's own records, 1863–.

Major collections: Estate and family archives, including Osborne, Duke of Leeds; Clifford of Skipton; Slingsby of Scriven; Fawkes of Farnley; Lister, Lord Ribblesdale of Gisburn; Middleton of Stockeld; Beaumont, Viscount Allendale of Bretton; Clarke-Thornhill of Fixby.
Manorial, most notably Wakefield court rolls, 1274–1940s.
Leeds Freemasons' records, 18th–20th centuries.
Antiquarian collections, including those of the Horsley family, herald painters, 16th–17th centuries; Roger Dodsworth, 17th century; Ralph Thoresby (1658–1725), historian of Leeds, and Joseph Hunter, historian of South Yorkshire.

Non-manuscript material: The society maintains an extensive library of Yorkshire books, prints, maps and photographs.

Finding aids: Lists and indexes. Link to West Yorkshire Archive Service computer database. Lists sent to NRA.

Facilities: Photocopying. Microfilm/fiche readers.

Conservation: Undertaken at West Yorkshire Archive Service HQ.

Publications: E.W. Crossley: *Catalogue of Manuscripts and Deeds in the Library of the Yorkshire Archaeological Society, 1867–1931* (2/1931/R1986).
S. Thomas: 'The Archives of the Yorkshire Archaeological Society', *Yorkshire Archaeological Journal*, lvi (1984).
——: *Guide to the Archive Collections of the Yorkshire Archaeological Society, 1931–1983, and to Collections Deposited with the Society* (Wakefield, 1985).

450 John Doran Gas Museum

Parent organisation: British Gas plc

Address: PO Box 28, Aylestone Road, Leicester LE2 7QH

Telephone: (0116) 253 5506

Fax: (0116) 253 5942

Enquiries: The Curator, Lesley Davis

Open: Tues–Fri: 12.30–4.30 Closed Tuesdays after Bank Holidays.

Access: Generally open to the public, by appointment only.

The museum opened in 1977 to preserve the history of the East Midlands gas industry. It actively acquires archives and artefacts of all East Midlands pre- and post-nationalisation gas undertakings, both independent and local authority, 1820–. There is also a small collection of photographs, plans and ephemera. The material is catalogued, including NRA 23245, and several publications are available.

451 Leicestershire Record Office

Address: Long Street, Wigton Magna, Leicester LE8 2AH

Telephone: (0116) 257 1080

Fax: (0116) 257 1120

Enquiries: The County Archivist, Mr C.W. Harrison

Open: Mon, Tues, Thurs: 9.15–5.00 Wed: 9.15–7.30 Fri: 9.15–4.45 Sat: 9.15–12.15

Historical background: Archives were collected by the city from 1849 and the City Museums Archives Department was set up in 1930. The County Record Office was established in 1947. With reorganisation in 1974 the Museum Archives Department came under the county and was amalgamated with the County Record Office. In 1992 the Leicestershire Collection, the county's local studies library, was amalgamated with the Record Office. The office also acts as the Diocesan Record Office for Leicester (parish records) and Peterborough (Rutland parish records) and is recognised as a place of deposit for public records.

Archives of organisation: Usual local authority record holdings.

Major collections: Deposited local archive collections. Local studies library.

Facilities: Photocopying. Photography. Microfilming. Microfilm/fiche readers/printers.

Publications: M. Bateson, H. Stocks and G.A. Chinnery: *Records of the Borough of Leicester, 1103–1835*, vols. I-VII (1899–1974).

Brief Guide to the Muniment Room, City of Leicester Museum and Art Gallery (1949).
Handlist of the Records of the Leicester Archdeaconry (1954).
A.M. Woodcock: *Records of the Corporation of Leicester* (1956).
H. Broughton: *Village History in Records* (1982).
G. Jones: *Quarter Sessions Records in the Leicestershire Record Office* (1985).
J. Farrel: *A Guide to Tracing your Family Tree in the Leicestershire Record Office* (1987).
G. Jones: *The Descent to Dissent: a Guide to the Nonconformist Records at the Leicestershire Record Office* (1989).
H.E. Broughton: *Family and Estate Records in the Leicestershire Record Office* (2/1991).

452 University of Leicester Library

Address: PO Box 248, University Road, Leicester LE1 9QD

Telephone: (0116) 252 2046

Fax: (0116) 252 2066

Enquiries: The Stack Librarian

Open: Mon–Fri: 9.00–5.00

Access: Any registered readers. External readers should give prior notification of their visit.

Acquisitions policy: By donation only.

Archives of organisation: Archives of Leicester University Library. The university archives are kept separately; contact Miss E.M. Davies.

Major collections: Papers of Sir B.C. Brodie (1817–80), Waynflete Professor of Chemistry at Oxford.
Capital Guarantee Society: minutes, correspondence, registers of borrowers, share certificates, 1874–1914.
Robert Benson Dockray, resident engineer of the London & Birmingham Railway and L&NWR: journal, 1850–60 (3 vols) and commonplace book, 1852–69.

Finding aids: Brief catalogue; sent to NRA. Brodie papers: NRA 9991.

Facilities: Photocopying. Photography by arrangement. Microfilm/fiche/card readers.

453 Wigan Archives Service

Address: Town Hall, Leigh, Lancs WN7 2DY

Telephone: (01942) 672421 ext. 266

Enquiries: The Archivist, Mr N.P. Webb

Open: Mon, Tues, Thurs, Fri: 10.00–1.00; 2.00–4.30, by appointment.

Access: Generally open to the public, subject to the usual closure rules. NB Church registers are normally shown on microfilm only, and these are now accessible at the History Shop, Rodney Street, Wigan WN1 1DG, not at the Archives Service.

Historical background: Wigan Record Office was established in 1968 to serve the former Wigan County Borough. In 1974, when the present Wigan Metropolitan Borough was created, the office moved to larger premises in Leigh. In 1989 the office became part of the new Wigan Heritage Service, which also includes local history libraries and museums, and the title Archives Service was adopted. The service acts as Diocesan Record Office for Liverpool (parish records), and is approved as a place of deposit for public, manorial and tithe records.

Acquisitions policy: Records relating to the locality, by deposit or gift.

Archives of organisation: Records of the old borough, including charters, court leet, borough sessions, burgess lists, accounts.
Records of Wigan Municipal and County Borough, 1974–, and of the other pre-1974 constituent authorities, including Leigh Municipal Borough.

Major collections: Family and estate archives, including: Anderton, Earls of Crawford, Holt Leigh, Scarisbrick, Standish.
Edward Hall Collection of diaries.
Wigan Grammar School.
Wigan and Leigh Boards of Guardians.
Records of solicitors, businesses and societies.

Non-manuscript material: Local photographic collection of regional significance.
Comprehensive OS map collection for the locality.
Census microforms, 1841–91, for the present Metropolitan Borough area.

Finding aids: Most collections have been listed and indexed.

Facilities: Photocopying. Photography. Microfilming. Microform readers.

Conservation: Mostly contracted out.

Publications: Guide to Wigan Record Office. Guide to Genealogical Sources in Wigan Record Office (1994).
Past Forward [Heritage Service magazine].
Information leaflets (free); local history publications programme (list available).

454 Shetland Archives

Parent organisation: Shetland Islands Council

Address: 44 King Harald Street, Lerwick, Shetland ZE1 0EQ

Telephone: (01595) 3535 ext. 402

Fax: (01595) 6533

Enquiries: The Archivist, Mr Brian Smith

Open: Mon–Thurs: 9.00–5.00 Fri: 9.00–4.00 Closed on local public holidays.

Access: Generally open to the public. An Appointment is preferable but not essential.

Historical background: The archives department was founded in 1976 and is now part of the leisure and recreation department of Shetlands Islands Council.

Acquisitions policy: Records and oral material relating to Shetland.

Archives of organisation: Usual local authority record holdings, 1750–.

Major collections: Deposited collections, 16th century–; Crown records, including sheriff court, customs and exise and procurator fiscal, 15th century–.

Non-manuscript material: Oral history collections, with transcripts.

Finding aids: Lists, some available on computer with text-search facilities.

Facilities: Photocopying. Photography. Microfilm reader/printer.

455 East Sussex Record Office

Address: The Maltings, Castle Precincts, Lewes, East Sussex BN7 1YT

Telephone: (01273) 482347

Fax: (01273) 482341

Enquiries: The County Archivist, Mr C.R. Davey

Open: Mon, Tues, Thurs: 8.45–4.45 Wed: 9.30–4.45 Fri: 8.45–4.15 Sat (2nd of each month): 9.00–1.00; 2.00–4.45

Historical background: The office was established in 1949. It also acts as a Diocesan Record Office for Chichester (East Sussex parish records), houses Sussex Archaeological Society records, and is recognised as a place of deposit for public records.

Archives of organisation: Usual local authority record holdings.

Major collections: Deposited collections, including the following which have a wider significance:
Sheffield Park archives concerning John Baker Holroyd, 1st Earl of Sheffield, politician and authority on commercial and agricultural topics, late 18th century.
Sussex Archaeological Society records, including papers of the Gage family (American material) and the Fuller family of Rosehill (West Indian material).

Facilities: Photocopying. Microfiching by arrangement. Microform reader/printer.

Publications: Descriptive Report on the Quarter Sessions, other Official, and Ecclesiastical Records in the Custody of the County Councils of West and East Sussex (1954).
F.W. Steer: *The Records of the Corporation of Seaford* (1959).
——: *Catalogue of the Shiffner Archives* (1959).
R.F. Dell: *Winchelsea Corporation Records* (1963).
——: *The Glynde Place Archives* (1964)
H.M. Warne: *Catalogue of the Frewen Archives* (1972).
J.A. Brett: *Catalogue of the Battle Abbey Estate Archives* (1973).
——: *The Hickstead Place Archives* (1975).
——: *East Sussex Record Office: a Short Guide* (1988).
F.W. Steer: *The Ashburnham Archives* [out of print].
R.F. Dell: *The Records of Rye Corporation: a Catalogue* [out of print].

456 Glyndebourne Festival Opera Archive

Address: Glyndebourne, Lewes, East Sussex BN8 5UU

Telephone: (01273) 812321 ext. 2214

Fax: (01273) 812783

Enquiries: The Archivist, Rosy Runciman

Open: Mon–Fri: 9.30–5.30

Access: Researchers by prior appointment. A research fee is charged.

Historical background: Glyndebourne Festival Opera was founded in 1934 by John Christie (1882–1962) and his wife Audrey, and has become renowned for its annual festival. Glyndebourne Touring Opera was established in 1968, with Arts Council support, to encourage young singers and to take the festival's productions to a wider audience. The archive was set up in 1987.

Acquisitions policy: To acquire, by gift or purchase, all material relevant to the history of Glyndebourne and the personnel connected with it.

Archives of organisation: Large collection of correspondence relating to the Festival and Touring Opera companies, 1930s-.

Major collections: Material relating to James Atkins, singer (1912–91).

Non-manuscript material: Plans, posters, programmes, leaflets, press cuttings, recordings, videos, costume and set designs.
Oral history interviews, in association with the National Sound Archive (entry **496B**), with singers, conductors, former members of the administrative staff etc (c40).
Black and white contact sheets (c170) and colour slides (2000) recording the demolition of the old theatre and building of the new Opera House, 1991–4.

Finding aids: Computer database for all Glyndebourne Festival productions and performers, 1934-. Many lists detailing archive holdings.

Facilities: Photocopying.

Publications: W. Blunt: *John Christie of Glyndebourne* (London, 1968).
S. Hughes: *Glyndebourne: a History of the Festival Opera* (London, 1981).
J. Julius Norwich: *Fifty Years of Glyndebourne: an Illustrated History* (London, 1985).

M. Binney and R. Runciman: *Glyndebourne: Building a Vision* (London, 1994).
P. Campion and R. Runciman: *Glyndebourne Recorded* (London,1994).

457 Lichfield Joint Record Office

Address: Lichfield Library, The Friary, Lichfield, Staffs WS13 6QG

Telephone: (01543) 256787

Fax: (01543) 411138

Enquiries: The Archivist-in-charge, Mark Donington

Open: Mon–Fri: 9.30–5.00, by arrangement.

Access: Generally open to the public, by appointment only.

Historical background: The office was established in 1959 as a branch of the Staffordshire Record Office to house the Lichfield probate and, on completion of purpose-built accommodation in 1968, diocesan records, since when it has been jointly financed by the Lichfield City (now District) and Staffordshire County councils. It is now run as part of the Staffordshire Archive Service (entry 1028). It also acts as the Diocesan Record Office for Lichfield, and is recognised as a place of deposit for public records. Assistance is given to Burton on Trent Archives (entry 138).

Acquisitions policy: Archives from the City of Lichfield and Lichfield diocesan records.

Archives of organisation: Usual local authority record holdings.

Major collections: Lichfied diocesan archives. Deposited local collections relating to Lichfield and including Lichfield Cathedral archives.

Facilities: Photocopying. Microfilming by arrangement. Microfilm/fiche readers.

Finding aids: Lists sent to NRA.

Publications: *Staffordshire Record Office Cumulative Hand List*, part 1: *Lichfield Joint Record Office, Diocesan, Probate and Church Commissioners Records* (2/1978).
Other Staffordshire Archive Services publications.

458 Museum of the Staffordshire Regiment

Address: RHQ Staffords, Whittington Barracks, Lichfield, Staffs WS14 9PY

Telephone: (0121) 311 3229/3263/3240

Fax: (0121) 311 3205

Enquiries: The Curator

Open: Mon–Fri: 9.00–4.00, by arrangement.

Access: Generally open to the public, by appointment only.

The Staffordshire Regiment (The Prince of Wales's) incorporates the former South and North Staffordshire Regiments, which were amalgamated in 1959. Its origins go back to 1705, when the 38th Foot, later the 1st Battalion of the South Staffordshire Regiment, was raised at Lichfield. The 64th Foot, later the 1st Battalion of the North Staffordshire Regiment, was formed in 1758. During the 18th century the regiments served in the Caribbean and were also involved in the American War of Independence. The Muniment Room contains diaries and other documents, photographs and newspaper cuttings. Catalogues are produced and photocopying facilities are available.

459 Samuel Johnson Birthplace Museum

Parent organisation: Lichfield City Council

Address: Breadmarket Street, Lichfield, Staffs WS13 6LG

Telephone: (01543) 264972

Fax: (0543) 258441

Enquiries: The Curator, Dr G. Nicholls

Open: Mon–Fri: 10.00–5.00

Access: Generally open to the public, by appointment.

Historical background: The museum was opened in 1901. A large number of papers relating to Samuel Johnson (1709–84) was acquired in the first decade of this century; these have subsequently been added to by donation and purchase.

Acquisitions policy: MS material relating to Samuel Johnson, especially his family, and other eminent Lichfeldions, including Anna Seward

(1747–1809) and David Garrick (1717–79), actor.

Major collections: A.C. Reade Collection: documents and papers relating to Johnson's family.
Lichfield and Johnson papers collected by Thomas George Lomax.
Papers relating to Johnson and Jacob Tonson.
Anna Seward papers.
Gregory King (1648–1712), statistical papers.

Non-manuscript material: Large library relating to Johnson and the 18th century, including association copies.

Conservation: Contracted out.

Publications: K.K. Yung: *Handlist of Manuscripts and Documents in the Johnson Birthplace Museum* (1972).

460 Lincolnshire Archives

Parent organisation: Lincolnshire County Council

Address: St Rumbold Street, Lincoln, LN2 5AB

Telephone: (01522) 525158/526204

Fax: (01522) 530047

Enquiries: The County Archivist, Dr G.A. Knight

Open: Mon: 1.30–7.15 Tues–Fri: 9.00–5.00 Sat: 9.00–4.00

Access: By reader's ticket only. There is an admission charge (some exemptions apply).

Historical background: A Diocesan Record Office was established in 1936 and Lincolnshire Archives Office was formally established in 1948. It also acts as the Diocesan Record Office for Lincoln, and is recognised as a place of deposit for public records. It gives administrative assistance to Lincoln Record Society.

Acquisitions policy: Documents, in any category, which are of lasting historical significance and relate to the county of Lincolnshire, are accepted either by gift or on indefinite loan.

Archives of organisation: Usual local authority record holdings.

Major collections: Deposited local and family collections, 11th century-.

Finding aids: Lists and indexes. Longer lists sent to NRA.

Facilities: Photocopying. Photography. Microfilming. Microfilm/fiche reader.

Conservation: Full conservation service available; outside contracts accepted.

Publications: *Archivist's Reports* (1948–77; with indexes, 1948–68) [available from the office].
K. Major: *Handlist of the Records of the Bishop of Lincoln and of the Archdeacons of Lincoln and Stow* (1953).
D.M. Williamson: *Muniments of the Dean and Chapter of Lincoln* (1956).
Lists and indexes series (1987–).
Genealogical sources series.

461 Lincolnshire County Library

Address: Local Studies Library, The Castle, Lincoln LN1 3AA

Telephone: (01522) 523019

Enquiries: The Local Studies Librarian

Open: Mon–Fri: 10.00–12.30; 1.30–5.00 Sat: 10.00–12.30
Tennyson Research Centre: by appointment only.

Access: Generally open to the public, on application. A letter of authority is usually required for the Tennyson Research Centre.

Historical background: The Tennyson Research Centre was founded in 1964 following the deposit by the Tennyson Trustees. Since 1983 the collection has been owned by Lincolnshire County Council.

Acquisitions policy: Any material relating to Sir Joseph Banks (1743–1820), botanist, or Alfred, Lord Tennyson (1809–92).

Major collections: Joseph Banks Collection: MS material covering a range of subjects relating to Lincolnshire, the militia etc, including many letters to and from Banks (c700 items).
Tennyson Centre: correspondence between Tennyson and members of his family, and letters from Browning, Gladstone, Lear, Sullivan, FitzGerald etc (c8000 items); most complete MS of *In Memoriam*, plus MSS of Tennyson's plays, poems, extracts from poems etc; miscellaneous material, including daybooks, diaries, journals, household account books, 19th century (mainly 1850–92).

Non-manuscript material: Joseph Banks Collection: topographical drawings of Lincolnshire by C. Nattes and others, late 18th century, commissioned by Banks (4 folio vols, c770 sketches); biographies of Banks together with copies of his works.

Tennyson Centre: proofs and trial-books of Tennyson's poems (c220 items); illustrations, including photographs by Julia Margaret Cameron (c100); sound recordings and tapes of Tennyson's works; music based on Tennyson's poetry; biographical and critical material, mainly monographs and pamphlets (c1200 items); Tennyson family library and collection of his works.

Finding aids: Banks: NRA 5342.

Facilities: Photocopying. Photography. Microfilm/fiche reader/printer.

Publications: The letters in the Banks Collection are included in W.R. Dawson (ed.): *The Banks Letters* (1958).
N. Campbell (comp.): *Tennyson in Lincoln: a Catalogue of the Collections in the Research Centre*, vol. 1: *The Family Libraries*; vol. 2: *Tennyson's Works, Biographies and Criticism, Parodies, Music, Illustrations* (Tennyson Society, 1971, 1973).
C.Y. Langand and E.F. Shannon (eds): *The Letters of Alfred, Lord Tennyson, 1821–1870* (1981, 1987).

462 National Primary Education Archive

Address: Bishop Grosseteste College, Newport, Lincoln LN1 3DY

Telephone: (01522) 527347 ext. 227

Fax: (01522) 530243

Enquiries: The Archivist, Miss E. T. Wagstaffe

Open: Tues: 9.30–12.30 Wed: 9.30–12.15; 1.30–4.30 Seven days' notice by telephone is required.

Access: Bona fide students and researchers. No access to unlisted material; restricted access to some other material. Charges may be made for some services.

Historical background: Bishop Grosseteste College, a college of higher education specialising in primary education, was founded in 1862 as the Lincoln Diocesan Training College. The archive is a registered charity, founded in 1990, when the papers of several influential

figures in the field of primary education were received. Other gifts, both personal and corporate, have been made since. Pending cataloguing only one collection is available. The archive collection is the responsibility of six trustees and an archivist was appointed in 1990.

Acquisitions policy: The archive concentrates on material relating to the development of primary education in England and Wales, especially since the publication of the Hadow Report (1931), though earlier material is not necessarily excluded. Types of material collected include private papers, talks, lectures, articles, examples of the work of children and student teachers and evidence offered to national and local committees.

Major collections: Papers of Robin Tanner, teacher and Her Majesty's Inspector, including significant photograph collection, 1904–88.

Finding aids: Internal indexes. Lists will be sent to NRA.

Facilities: Photocopying.

Conservation: Contracted out.

Publications: *Papers of Robin Tanner, HMI, 1904–1989: a Summary List* (Bishop Grosseteste College, 1993).

463 Littlehampton Museum

Parent organisation: Littlehampton Town Council

Address: Manor House, Church Street, Littlehampton, West Sussex BN17 5EP

Telephone: (01903) 715149

Enquiries: The Curator, Dr I. Friel

Open: Tues–Sat: 10.30–4.30

Access: Generally open to the public, on application one week in advance.

Historical background: The museum was founded in 1926 by the local Natural History and Archaeology Society and the Town Council. It was taken over in 1974 by Arun District Council and is now administered by Littlehampton Town Council. The museum's own archive was established in 1928 and a town photo archive in the 1930s.

Acquisitions policy: To add to collections on the town's and the district's history, with emphasis on seafaring and shipbuilding.

Archives of organisation: Documentation, including photographic prints and negatives, supporting the museum's collections, 1928–.

Major collections: Local history collection, including:
Records of the Romano-British villa excavation in Gosden Road and Angmering.
Transcripts of Capt. Robinson's history of the Robinson shipping family.

Non-manuscript material: Maps of the harbour development, mid- 18th century–.
Extensive ephemera collection.
Prints of railway charts and maps, mid-19th century–.
Photographs, prints and paintings concerning the history of the town.

Finding aids: Card index. Computerisation started in 1994.

Facilities: Photocopying. Photography by arrangement.

464 Athenaeum

Address: Church Alley, Liverpool L1 3DD

Telephone: (0151) 709 7770

Enquiries: The Librarian

Open: Mon–Fri: 10.00–5.00

Access: This is a private library for use by the proprietors. Facilities are made available to researchers on application in writing.

Historical background: Founded in 1797 as a literary and scientific institution, the Athenaeum contains a historic general library strong in local history.

Acquisitions policy: Acquisitions are now limited to works of local interest.

Major collections: Roscoe Collection: Renaissance Italian and English MSS collected by William Roscoe (1753–1831), historian.
Gladstone Collection: papers, documents and MSS relating to local history collected by Robert Gladstone (1866–1940).

Non-manuscript material: Liverpool playbills, 1773–1830 (22 vols).
Comprehensive collection of maps of Liverpool and district included in local collection.
Extensive pamphlet collection: J. Hampden Jackson economic pamphlets (60).
Bound single plays, mainly 18th century (100 vols).

Finding aids: Card and shelf catalogues; indexes to pamphlets and plays; handlist of maps.

Facilities: Limited photocopying. Microfiche reader.

Publications: *Catalogue* (1864; supplements, 1892, 1905).
R.W. MacKenna: *The Athenaeum* (Liverpool, 1928).

465 British Psychological Society Archives

Address: c/o Dept of Psychology, The University, PO 147, Liverpool L69 3BX

Telephone: (0151) 794 2962 (Hon. Archivist) 794 2957 (Department Secretary)

Enquiries: The Hon. Archivist, Dr A. D. Lovie

Open: By written appointment only.

Access: Scholars with an interest in the history of psychology.

Historical background: The archive was founded in the 1950s, originally to house the records of the British Psychological Society and associated bodies, but has now expanded its remit.

Acquisitions policy: Welcomes both complete collections of material and single items of significance. No predetermined policy as to the type or extent of the material providing that it falls within the purview of the historian of psychology.

Archives of organisation: Minute books of the Council of the British Psychological Society and some of its subsidiary branches, 1904–.
Material from the Child Study Society, 1891–1939.
Publications of the British Psychological Society.

Major collections: C.E. Spearman (1863–1945): letters, lecture notes and research papers.
H. Tajfel: letters, minutes of meetings, book drafts and research material.
Note-books from C.W. Valentine (1879–1964).
Collection of test results for the Ravens Matrix Test.

Non-manuscript material: Collection of photographs of prominent British, European and American psychologists.
Small collection of tapes and records of remi-

niscences, interviews and lectures by various psychologists.

Finding aids: Short catalogue (1982).

Facilities: Photocopying.

466 Liverpool Medical Institution

Address: 114 Mount Pleasant, Liverpool L3 5SR

Telephone: (0151) 709 9125

Fax: (0151) 707 2810

Enquiries: The Resident Librarian, Mr D.M. Crook

Open: Mon–Fri: 9.30–6.00 Sat: 9.30–12.30

Access: Approved readers, by appointment.

Founded in 1779 as the Liverpool Medical Library, the institution adopted its present name in 1840 and was granted a Royal Charter of Incorporation in 1964. The archives comprise minutes of council meetings, 1779–, ordinary meetings (scientific), 1839–, and the Library Committee, 1840–. There are also deposited MSS, which are included in W.A. Lee: *Catalogue of the Books in the Liverpool Medical Institution Library* (Liverpool, 1968). See also J.A. Shepherd: *A History of the Liverpool Medical Institution* (1979).

467 Liverpool Record Office and Local History Library

Parent organisation: Liverpool Libraries and Information Services

Address: William Brown Street, Liverpool L3 8EW

Telephone: (0151) 225 5409 (Local Studies and Archives Officer) 225 5417 (General Enquiries) 225 5433 (Microfilm/fiche bookings)

Fax: (0151) 207 1342

Enquiries: The Local Studies and Archives Officer

Open: Mon–Wed: 9.00–7.30 Thurs: 1.00–7.30 Fri, Sat: 9.00–5.00

Access: Generally open to the public, on application. 30–year closure on some collections; permission of depositor needed for others. Authorised reader's ticket required for archives, rare books, maps, photographs, watercolours. Appointments are necessary to use microfilm/fiche.

Historical background: The 'Local Collection' was begun in the Liverpool Public Library in 1852 and local material has been acquired continuously since then. The Liverpool Record Office was formally opened in 1953 as a repository for Liverpool archives. It is recognised as a place of deposit for public records and since 1977 has acted as the Diocesan Record Office for Liverpool.

Acquisitions policy: Archives of and relating to Liverpool. Books and other non- manuscript material covering Liverpool, Merseyside and the surrounding areas of Lancashire and Cheshire.

Archives of organisation: Usual local authority records of Liverpool City Council and Corporation, including city charters, 1207–, minutes of the council and committees, 1550–, freeman's registers, 1692–. Department records, including cemeteries: interment registers; education: school managers' minutes, log-books, registers; housing: photographs of corporation estate and clearance areas.

Major collections: Liverpool Diocesan Registry, parish records: Church of England, 1586–, and Roman Catholic, 1741–; non-conformist and Jewish records.

Liverpool Borough Sessions, 1836–.

Statutory Authorities, 19th–20th centuries: Liverpool School Board, Board of Guardians, including workhouse registers; records of out-townships subsequently incorporated.

Business organisations, including Liverpool Chamber of Commerce, 1860–, Liverpool Cotton Association, 1842–, Liverpool Stock Exchange, 1836–.

Local general and specialist hospitals, 18th–20th centuries.

Records relating to public health, including MOH letter and report books, 1849–89, and extensive correspondence of Florence Nightingale (1820–1910) and William Rathbone VI (1819–1902).

Papers of prominent Liverpool figures and local families, including letters of Dr James Currie (1756–1805), physician and slave-trade abolitionist; non-estate papers of the Earls of Derby, statesmen, 19th–20th centuries; Holt and Durning-Holt families, 19th–20th centuries; papers of Joseph Mayer (1803–86), antiquarian and collector; correspondence of George Melly (1830–94), merchant and MP; Moore deeds and papers, 13th–18th centuries; papers of James Muspratt (1798–1886), founder of alkali industry in Lancashire; Nicholson family, merchants and Unitarians, 17th–20th centuries; deeds and papers of the Norris family of Speke, 15th–18th centuries; papers of the Parker family, with interests in America and the West Indies, 18th–19th centuries; Plumbe Tempest, deeds of property in and around Liverpool, 16th–19th centuries; letters of William Roscoe (1753–1831), banker, MP, poet and philanthropist who corresponded with many eminent figures, early 19th century; the Liverpool estate and manorial records of the Marquess of Salisbury, 15th–20th centuries; Molyneux, Earls of Sefton, diaries and papers, 1815–1953; papers of the Tarleton family of Liverpool, landowners and West India merchants, 17th–19th centuries.

Records of many Liverpool societies, charities and trade unions, including Literary and Philosophical Society, 1812–1937, Liverpool Society for the Prevention of Cruelty to Children, 1883–1957, Sheltering Homes for Destitute Children, 1873–1933, Liverpool Trades Council, 1852–.

Records of the Liverpool Playhouse (Repertory) Theatre, 1911–.

Non-manuscript material: Maps (7200).
Newspapers, 1756–.
Photographs and prints (70,000), topographical watercolours (6000), films, tape and video recordings.
Microfilm of Liverpool directories, 1766–1904, Liverpool newspapers, Town Books, 1550–1835, obituary notices, 1879–1920s, census returns.

Finding aids: Archive lists; copies sent to NRA. Calendars of older collections and index to unlisted archives accessions. Handlist of maps. Indexes to photographs and watercolours.

Facilities: Photocopying. Photography by arrangement. Microfilm/fiche readers.

Conservation: Paper and bookbinding Conservation Department on premises; outside binding work occasionally undertaken.

Publications: Guides in preparation. Brief information sheets available.

468 Liverpool School of Tropical Medicine

Address: Pembroke Place, Liverpool L3 5QA

Telephone: (0151) 708 9393

Fax: (0151) 708 8733

Enquiries: The Archivist, Miss Patricia J. Miller

Open: Mon–Wed: 9.00–4.00

Access: Archive materials may be consulted by bona fide scholars, by permission of the Director and by arrangement with the Archivist. Some material is deposited in the strongroom of the University of Liverpool (entry 473).

Historical background: The school was founded in 1898.

Archives of organisation: Administrative records, 1898–.
Biographical materials on eminent school staff.
Records of research and teaching at home and overseas.

Major collections: Publications, letters and photographs relating to Sir Ronald Ross (1857–1932).

Finding aids: Lists sent to NRA.

469 Merseyside Record Office

Parent organisation: Liverpool City Council

Address: 4th Floor, Cunard Building, Water Street, Liverpool L3 1EG

Telephone: (0151) 236 8038

Fax: (0151) 236 5827

Enquiries: The Archivist-in-Charge

Open: By appointment only.

Access: Generally open to the public, by prior appointment.

Historical background: The Merseyside County Archives were established in 1974 as part of the new county's museum service. At the abolition of the County Council (MCC) in 1986 the records passed to the Merseyside Residuary Body (MRB), with the exception of maritime archives, records relating to the museums' artefact collections and archives acquired by the museums before 1974, which were transferred to the National Museums and Galleries on Merseyside (successor to the County Museums). In 1989 the records, now including the records of the MCC (and later of the MRB), passed to Liverpool City Council, which administers the service on behalf of the five Merseyside District Councils by means of an endowment from the funds of the MRB. The office is recognised as a place of deposit for public records.

Acquisitions policy: Seeks to acquire records and documents relating to the whole of the county of Merseyside or to more than one of the Metropolitan Districts.

Archives of organisation: Usual local authority record holdings of Merseyside County Council and Merseyside Residuary Body.

Major collections: Deposited local collections of coroners, hospitals, Methodist and United Reformed Chuches, social welfare organisations, businesses, societies and some family and estate papers, including records of Merseyside Passenger Transport Executive and Merseyside Fire Service and their predecessor bodies, 1845–1970s; Rainhall Hospital, 1851–1981; Peter Walker, brewers, 1850s-1970s; Crawfords Biscuits, family and business papers, 20th century; Woodall, architects, 1864–1980; Child Welfare Association, 1870–1970; League of Welldoers, 1856–1986; Personal Service Society, 1858–1983; Weld-Blundell family, c1667–1974; Merseyside Communist Party, 1940s-1992.

Finding aids: Lists and indexes. Handlists of holdings and of genealogical sources.

Facilities: Photocopying. Photography by arrangement.

Publications: Public Health on Merseyside: a Guide to Local Sources (1991).
Archives on Merseyside (1992).
Education on Merseyside: a Guide to the Sources (1992).
The Irish Community in North-West England: a Guide to Local Archive Sources (1993).
Transport on Merseyside: a Guide to Local Sources (1994).
Annual union accession lists for Merseyside repositories (1990–).

470 National Museums and Galleries on Merseyside
Archives Department

Address: c/o Maritime Archives and Library, Merseyside Maritime Museum, Albert Dock, Liverpool L3 4AA

Telephone: (0151) 207 0001 (Switchboard) 478 4418 (Enquiries)

Fax: (0151) 478 4590

Enquiries: The Curator of Archives, Mr J. Gordon Read

Open: Generally open to the public, preferably by prior appointment. A small charge is made for a reader's ticket.

Access: Bona fide researchers. Several collections require at least two weeks' notice. Modern business and charity records may include confidential material.

Historical background: An archivist was appointed after the County of Merseyside came into existence in 1974, and the museum archives collections (which had themselves developed from Liverpool City functions) were incorporated; the latter included valuable maritime archives, particularly in connection with the Maritime Museum, finally established in 1980. The abolition of the County Council led to the transfer of charity, hospital and non-conformist archives to the Merseyside Residuary Body and subsequently to Merseyside Record Office (entry **469**). The department is recognised as a place of deposit for public records. A small collection of business and other modern records, plus the military records of the King's (Liverpool) Regiment, are housed separately as part of the Regional History Department of the National Museums and Galleries on Merseyside; access can be arranged via the Archives Department. For horological material previously held, contact Prescot Museum, 34 Church Street, Prescot, tel. (0151) 430 7787.

Acquisitions policy: To extend the holdings of the following categories of archives: archives of the National Museums and Galleries on Merseyside; maritime and business archives; archives associated with museum specialisms, especially shipping and trade, natural history, the King's Regimental Museum and the Museum of Labour History.

Archives of organisation: Records of the Museums and Art Galleries, 1849–.

Major collections: Maritime archives: Mersey Docks and Harbour Company and its antecedents; Dockland Survey Archive (South Docks); register of ships, 1739–1860.
Business records: including extensive ship records and correspondence about American Civil War, trade abroad, slave trade, marine insurance, associations for shipping, and corn, sugar and provision trade; BICC plc (cables); Meccano Ltd; engineering records, including Vulcan Locomotive Works.
Natural history records, including 13th Earl of Derby's correspondence, 1799–1850.
Business and family papers: Danson family of Barnston and Birkenhead in Wirral (shipping insurance), 19th–20th centuries; Bryson Collection, 17th–20th centuries.
Emigration records research collection, UK, USA, Canada, Australia and New Zealand.

Non-manuscript material: Stewart Bale photographic archive: glass negatives covering all aspects of business activity in the North-West and elsewhere, c1910–1975.
Maritime history research library, photographic and sound archives.
Reference library of printed books, pamphlets and periodicals, including Lloyd's Registers, 1764–, Lloyd's Lists, 1741–, Customs Bills of Entry, c1820–1939 (incomplete), and museum catalogues.

Finding aids: Some 100 lists and indexes.

Facilities: Photocopying. Photography. Microfilm/fiche reader.

Publications: Reproductions of posters and documents.
Archive Teaching Unit: *The Leaving of Liverpool* and *Ships and Seafarers of 19th-century Liverpool.*
G. Read: 'The Bryson Collection of Business Archives and Ephemera', *Business Archives*, 47 (Nov 1981), 18–30.
N. Ritchie-Noakes: *Liverpool's Historic Waterfront* (1984).
Guide [in press].

471 Science Fiction Foundation Collection

Parent organisation: SF Foundation/University of Liverpool

Address: Sydney Jones Library, PO Box 123, Liverpool L69 3DA

Telephone: (0151) 794 2733/2696

Fax: (0151) 794 2681

Enquiries: The Librarian/Administrator, Mr Andy Sawyer

Open: Mon–Fri: 10.00–1.00; 2.00–5.00

Access: Generally open to the public, by appointment.

Historical background: The SFF was established in 1970 as a central office of information for the genre and was offered a home in the North-East London Polytechnic. In 1993 the SFF Collection was deposited with the University of Liverpool, and is a major resource for an MA in Science Fiction Studies. It is an independent organisation (membership is by invitation only). The educational role of the SFF is important; it provides a discriminating understanding of the nature of science fiction, and the library provides research facilities. The nucleus of the library is that of the British Science Fiction Association Library, deposited in 1972.

Acquisitions policy: To maintain the collections.

Major collections: MSS, correspondence and legal papers of a number of prominent science fiction writers, including Christopher Priest, Ian Watson and Ramsay Campbell.
Archive of Eric Frank Russell
Myers Collection of Russian SF.
Correspondence of John W Campbell (Xeroxes).
Papers relating to the Flat Earth Society.

Non-manuscript material: Small selection of recorded readings, broadcasts and lectures.
Collection of fanzines, ephemera and newspapers.

Finding aids: Card catalogue in process of computerisation.

Facilities: Photocopying. Microfilm/fiche readers.

472 University of Liverpool Archives Unit

Address: PO Box 147, Liverpool L69 3BX

Telephone: (0151) 794 5424

Fax: (051) 708 6502

Enquiries: The University Archivist

Open: Mon–Fri: 9.30–5.00, by prior appointment only.

Access: Generally open to the public. Archives relating to children are subject to restrictions: for these prior application is necessary.

Historical background: The University of Liverpool was founded (as University College initially) in 1881, but its medical school goes back to 1834 and there are certain other earlier constituent bodies. The university archives were set up in 1968.

Acquisitions policy: In association with the Merseyside Archives Liaison Group: archives of the university administration, research and teaching; archives of members and former members of the university. Externally, to strengthen existing research resources, particularly in the field of social work with children, architecture and town planning. There is is also a concern for medical and sport archives, but no intention to acquire material where there are more natural repositories.

Archives of organisation: Archives of the university, its constituents and affiliated bodies.

Major collections: Papers of former members of staff: principally Sir Cyril Burt: psychology; Lord Holford, Sir Charles Reilly, Sir Patrick Abercrombie, Professor George Stephenson: town planning and architecture.
Cunard Steamship Company, 1840–c1950; Dr Barnardo's, 1867–c1980; National Children's Home, 1867–c1980; Family Service Units, 1940–c1990; Fairbridge Society, 1912–c1990; Simon Community and Trust, 1964–88; Universities Athletic Union (and its Western Division), 1919–c1987; English Table Tennis Association 1919–83; Ling Physical Education Association, later the Physical Education Association of Great Britain and Northern Ireland, 1910–86.

Non-manuscript material: Publications and prints emanating from the university, including student journals and publications of certain societies and clubs.
Recorded interviews with certain individuals.

Finding aids: Typescript lists with access point on computer catalogue. Printed catalogue of the Cunard archive available, but with restricted circulation. Lists sent to NRA.

Facilities: Photocopying. Photography (by central university service). Microfilming.

Publications: Annual reports in the annual reports of the university (to 1990), and in annual *Research Reports* of the university.
A.R. Allan and J.A. Carpenter (comps): *Redbrick University: a Portrait of University College Liverpool and the University of Liverpool, 1881–1981* (Liverpool, 1981).
M. Proctor (ed.): *Education on Merseyside: a Guide to the Sources* (Merseyside Archives Liaison Group, 1992).
S. Harrap: *Decade of Change: the University of Liverpool, 1981–1991* (Liverpool, 1994).
T. Kelly: *For Advancement of Learning: the University of Liverpool, 1881–1981* (Liverpool, 1994).

473 University of Liverpool Sydney Jones Library

Address: PO Box 123, Liverpool L9 3DA

Telephone: (0151) 794 2696

Fax: (0151) 794 2681

Enquiries: Special Collections Department, Ms K.J.C. Hooper

Open: Mon–Fri: 9.00–1.00; 2.00–5.00 Evenings and Saturday mornings by arrangement.

Access: Approved readers, on written application. Restrictions on certain deposited archives.

Historical background: Collections were deposited in the library, or given to it. The first important collection was that of Thomas Rylands (acquired in 1900), which reflects a wide range of interests, in particular the history of Lancashire and Cheshire.

Acquisitions policy: To strengthen existing holdings, especially in the following areas: Liverpool shipping, trade and slave trade records, MS facsimiles (especially illuminated), selected local poets.

Major collections: MSS include: Oxyrhynchus papyri; collection of medieval and Renaissance

MSS (56); some oriental MSS, mostly of late date and of no textual or artistic importance.

Mayer MSS, 114 items, of which more than half are oriental, the rest mainly medieval Western with a small group of Irish 18th–century items (on loan from National Museums and Galleries on Merseyside).

Radcliffe Library, Liverpool Cathedral (Anglican), chiefly Western medieval liturgical MSS (63).

Modern papers, autograph letters and deeds, including those of José Blanco White (1775–1841); Sir John Tomlinson Brunner (1842–1919); Josephine Butler (1828–1906); John Bruce Glasier (1859–1920) and Katherine Glasier (1867–1950); Rathbone family of Greenbank, Liverpool, 18th–20th centuries; Sir Oliver Lodge (1851–1940); D.H. Lawrence (1885–1930); Cecil Day Lewis (1904–72).

Personal archive of Olaf Stapledon (1886–1950), philosopher and science fiction writer.

Merseyside Poets Collection.

Records of Gypsy Lore Society, c1896–1974, and other gypsy and Romany material in Scott Macfie Collection, including photographs of gypsies, taken chiefly by Fred Shaw, late 19th–early 20th centuries; Liverpool Psychological Society, 1923–30; Liverpool Literary and Philosophical Society, 1812–27; Liverpool Royal Institution, 1813–1942 (incomplete).

A few items relating to the history of the university.

The School of Education Library includes MS examples of school work.

Non-manuscript material: Maps, pamphlets and early printed books.

Microforms and slides; seals; prints and drawings; news cuttings; photographs; records and tapes.

Finding aids: Lists (sent to NRA) and indexes, including author index to MS collections. Detailed subject handlist. Detailed catalogues for most of the larger collections. Guide to Special Collections (1978).

Facilities: Photocopying. Photography. Microfilming. Microfilm/fiche readers.

Conservation: Contracted out.

Publications: J. Sampson (comp.): *A Catalogue of the Books, Printed and in Manuscript, Bequeathed by the Late Thomas Glazebrook Rylands to the Library* (Liverpool, 1900).
Guide to the Manuscript Collections in Liverpool University Library (Liverpool, 1962).

474 Llandaff Cathedral Library

Parent organisation: The Dean and Chapter, Llandaff Cathedral

Address: The Ollivant Room, Saint Michael's College, Llandaff, Cardiff CF5 2YJ

Telephone: (01222) 563379

Enquiries: The Rev. Librarian

Open: By arrangement with the librarian.

Access: Generally open to the public, by appointment.

The Cathedral Library at Llandaff was established during the episcopate of Bishop Alfred Ollivant (1798–1882) DD, Lord Bishop of Llandaff, 1849–82. Owing to re-organisation in the cathedral, the whole library was moved to the Ollivant Room at St Michael's College in 1986. The library holds sermon notes and letters and diaries of Ollivant and Bishop Edward Copleston (1776–1849). See M. Tallone: *Cathedral Libraries of Wales* (Athlone Press, 1962).

475 Powys County Archives Offices

Parent organisation: Powys County Council

Address: County Hall, Llandrindod Wells, Powys LD1 5LG

Telephone: (01597) 826087

Fax: (01597) 826230 (County Hall)

Enquiries: The County Archivist, Gordon Reid

Open: Mon–Thurs: 9.00–12.30; 1.30–5.00 Fri: 9.00–12.30; 1.30–4.00

Access: Generally open to the public. An appointment is recommended to avoid disappointment.

Historical background: An archivist was first appointed in Powys in 1985, based in the County Library Headquarters in Llandrindod. In 1991 the new County Archives Office was established on the County Hall site and the collections were relocated here. In addition, virtually all collections of official and public records relating to the old counties of Brecon, Montgomery and Radnor have been transferred from the National Library of Wales (entry 10). Many private deposits relating to these counties and all ecclesiastical parish records remain at the National Library. However, the County Archives Office has purchased copies of all tithe maps and registers of baptisms, marriages and burials for Powys.

Acquisitions policy: To collect archival material relating to the old counties of Brecon, Montgomery and Radnor and the modern county of Powys, as laid down in a policy document agreed with the county's libraries and museums.

Archives of organisation: Virtually all records of local government for the three counties, including quarter sessions, county councils, urban and rural district councils, and parish and community councils. Also some Brecon Beacons National Park records.

Major collections: Deposited local collections, of which the following have a wider significance:
The Abercamlais Estate: deeds, correspondence and related papers, 16th–19th centuries, including correspondence and other papers of Archdeacon Richard Davies of Brecon, late 18th–early 19th centuries.
Brecknock Museum Transfer: large collection of assorted material relating to Breconshire, including papers of the Brecon and Abergavenny Canal and miscellaneous Great and Quarter Sessions records.
Bonner-Maurice of Llanfechain, 17th–early 20th centuries.
Sandbach Family of Bryngwyn: diaries, correspondence and papers, 1813–1929.
Lewis of Y Neuadd: Lewis Lloyd and Lewis families of Nantgwyllt, 1548–1973.
Welsh Water Authority: records and plans of Elan Valley waterworks, 1890s-1930s.

Non-manuscript material: OS and other maps; topographical prints and engravings. Some photographs and postcards.

Finding aids: TS catalogues; sent to NRA and National Library of Wales. Detailed card index to places only. Accessions catalogued since 1992 on computer with free text-search facility.

Facilities: Photocopying. Photography. Microfilm/fiche readers/printer.

Conservation: Contracted out.

Publications: Guide to the Powys County Archives Office (1993).
G. Reid: 'The County Archives', *Transactions of the Radnorshire Society*, LXIII (1993).

Regular reports, including new accessions relating to Breconshire, are published in *Brycheiniog*, the journal of the Brecknock Society.

476 Llanelli Public Library

Address: Vaughan Street, Llanelli, Dyfed SA15 3AS

Telephone: (01554) 773538

Fax: (01554) 750125

Enquiries: The Borough Librarian

Open: Mon, Thurs, Fri: 9.30–7.00 Tues: 9.30–6.00 Wed: 9.30–1.00 Sat: 9.30–5.00

Access: Generally open to the public.

Historical background: The Public Library was established in 1892; it incorporated the Mechanics' Institute, which was established in 1847.

Acquisitions policy: The library is a general library which also has collections on all aspects of local matters, with special emphasis on the coal industry, tinplate making, ships and shipbuilding and local government. Material in any form in these specialised areas is collected.

Major collections: Llanelli Harbour Trust records.
Local Government records for Llanelli area.

Non-manuscript material: Coal-mining plans for Carmarthenshire.
Photographic prints (c15,000), transparencies (c2000) and 16 mm cine-films, all devoted to local subjects (e.g. industry, town development, special events).
Tape interviews of local people.

Finding aids: Indexes, including local newspapers, 1863–.

Facilities: Photocopying. Microfilm/fiche readers. Cine-film and slide projectors.

Publications: Llanelli Public Library Local History Research Group Series [details on application].

477 Gwynedd Archives and Museums Service
Llangefni Area Record Office

Address: Shire Hall, Llangnefni, Gwynedd LL77 7TW

Telephone: (01248) 750262 ext. 271/269

Enquiries: The Senior Archivist, Anne Venables

Open: Mon–Fri: 9.00–1.00; 2.00–5.00 Annual closure 1st week of November.

Access: Generally open to the public. The office operates the CARN reader's ticket system.

Historical background: The office was set up in 1974 following local government reorganisation, and before that Anglesey County Library did some collecting. It is recognised as place of deposit for public records.

Acquisitions policy: Material relating to Anglesey.

Archives of organisation: Usual local authority record holdings.

Major collections: Deposited local collections.

Non-manuscript material: Plans, photographs, tape interviews.

Finding aids: Indexes, catalogues. Lists sent to NRA.

Facilities: Photocopying. Photography. Microfilm/fiche readers.

Conservation: Undertaken at Caernarfon Area Record Office (entry **142**).

478 Midlothian District Library

Address: Library Headquarters, 2 Clerk Street, Loanhead, Midlothian EH20 9DR

Telephone: (0131) 440 2210

Fax: (0131) 440 4635

Enquiries: The Archivist, Ms Ruth Calvert

Open: Mon: 9.00–8.00 Tues, Thurs: 9.00–5.00 Fri: 9.00–3.45

Access: Generally open to the public.

Historical background: The library was established as Midlothian County Library in 1921 under the Education (Scotland) Act of 1919. Following local government reoganisation parts of the area were transferred to East Lothian, West Lothian and Edinburgh district and to the Borders region. Material previously deposited with Edinburgh District Archives has now been returned to the library.

Acquisitions policy: The library attempts to acquire, by purchase, gift or otherwise, items relating to the area.

Major collections: Local collection covering Midlothian district.
Records of the former burghs of Dalkeith, 1760–1975; Bonnyrigg and Lasswade, 1865–1975; Loanhead, 1909–75; and Penicuik, 1867–1975.
School Board letter-books and cash books; school log-books, c1870–1970.
County council and district council minutes.
Family papers.

Non-manuscript material: Maps and plans, prints and photographs.

Finding aids: Bibliographies, catalogues and shelf-lists. Local newspaper index in preparation.

Facilities: Photocopying. Microfilm/fiche reader/printers.

Publications: *New Statistical Account of Midlothian*, pt 1 (1987); pts 2 & 3 (1988) [reprint of the 1845 2nd Statistical Account with additional notes and illustrations].
J. Wilson: *The Annals of Penicuik, being a History of the Parish and of the Village* (1985) [reprint of the 1891 history of Penicuik].

479 Argyll and Bute District Council

Address: Kilmory, Lochgilphead, Strathclyde PA31 8RT

Telephone: (01546) 604120

Fax: (01546) 604138

Enquiries: The Archivist, Mr Murdo Mac-Donald

Open: Mon–Thurs: 9.00–1.00; 2.00–5.15 Fri: 9.00–1.00; 2.00–4.00

Access: Generally open to the public. An appointment is advised.

Historical background: The archives department was established in 1975 following the setting up of the district council under local government reorganisation. The district archives also act on a local agency basis for Strathclyde Regional Archives (entry **350**).

Acquisitions policy: To encourage the deposit and donation of records relating to the district in general.

Archives of organisation: Usual local authority record holdings.

Major collections: Deposited local collections, including records of the Episcopal Diocese of Argyll and the Isles, 19th–20th centuries.
Malcolm of Poltalloch papers, 18th–20th centuries.
Campbell of Kilberry papers, 18th–20th centuries.

Finding aids: Lists sent to NRA(S).

Facilities: Photocopying.

Conservation: Contracted out.

480 Alpine Club

Address: 55 Charlotte Road, London EC2A 3QT

Telephone: (0171) 613 0755

Enquiries: The Hon. Archivist, via Assistant Secretary

Open: Mon–Fri: 10.00–5.00, by appointment.

Access: Members of the Alpine Club and bona fide researchers. It is necessary to make an appointment with the Hon. Archivist through the Assistant Secretary of the club.

Historical background: The Alpine Club was founded in 1857 and its archives include mountaineering records dating back to the 18th century. The material comprises a unique collection of MSS, letters and photographs of mountain exploration, in which the Alpine Club has always played a leading role, from the earliest days up to the present time.

Acquisitions policy: To encourage the deposit and donation of records relating to the Alpine Club and its members and mountaineering in general.

Archives of organisation: Alpine Club records: minutes and correspondence, 1857–.
Ladies' Alpine Club records, 1907–75.

Major collections: Collections of personal papers, including the following: diaries of J.P. Farrar (1857–1929); W.N. Ling (1873–1953); C. Schuster (1869–1956) and T.G. Longstaff (1875–1964).
Papers of S. Spencer (1862–1950); E. Strutt (1874–1948) and H. Montagnier (1877–1933).
Correspondence of E. Whymper (1840–1911); G. Winthrop Young (1876–1958); D. Freshfield (1854–1934); W. Coolidge (1850–1926) and M. Bourrit (1739–1819).

Non-manuscript material: Newspaper cuttings, 1891– (36 vols).
Photographs held in the Alpine Club Library.

Finding aids: Indexes.

Facilities: Photocopying.

481 Architectural Association Library

Address: 36 Bedford Square, London WC1B 3ES

Telephone: (0171) 636 0974 ext. 233

Fax: (0171) 414 0782

Enquiries: The Deputy Librarian, Miss E.A. Underwood

Open: Term: Mon, Wed: 10.00–6.00 Tues, Thurs: 10.00–6.30 Fri: 10.00–7.00 Vacation: Mon–Fri: 10.00–5.00
Closed July to September.

Access: Bona fide scholars and members of the Architectural Association. An appointment is necessary and a research fee is charged to non-members.

Historical background: The Architectural Association was founded as an evening school for architectural students in 1847. A day school was started in 1901. The library began in 1862 and is principally a resource for staff, students and members.

Acquisitions policy: Material relating to subject areas of teaching units in general: architecture, art, landscape planning, town planning, philosophy.

Archives of organisation: Archives of the AA, including membership index, 1847–.

Major collections: Small MS collection, including a Repton 'Red Book'.

Non-manuscript material: Slide library and print studio.
Theses and essays.

Facilities: Photocopying. Microfiche reader.

Publications: *Guide to the Library.*
Annual Reports.

482 Art Workers' Guild

Address: 6 Queen Square, London WC1N 3AR

Telephone: (0171) 837 3474

Enquiries: The Hon. Librarian

The guild is an association of architects and

artists founded in 1884 by members of the arts and crafts movement. It maintains its own archives, including minute books, and accepts deposits relating to members. There is a card catalogue and the archive is open to bona fide researchers by appointment with the Honorary Librarian. See H.J.L.J. Masse: *The Art Workers' Guild, 1884–1934* (London 1935).

483 Arts Council of England

Address: 14 Great Peter Street, London SW1P 3NQ

Telephone: (0171) 973 6574 (direct line) 333 0100

Fax: (0171) 973 6584

Enquiries: The Head of Secretariat, Lawrence Mackintosh

Open: Mon–Fri: 9.30–5.30

Access: Bona fide researchers, strictly by appointment.

The Council for the Encouragement of Music and the Arts (CEMA) was set up in 1940 with grants from the Treasury and the Pilgrim Trust. The Arts Council of Great Britain was founded in 1945 to continue this work in peacetime and operated under its second Royal Charter, granted in 1967. On 1 April 1994 the functions and responsibilities of ACGB were transferred to three successor bodies, each with its own Royal Charter: The Arts Council of England, The Scottish Arts Council (SAC), 12 Manor Place, Edinburgh EH3 7DD, and The Arts Council of Wales (ACW), Museum Place, Cardiff CF1 3NX. The Arts Council of England is currently (1995) in negotiation with the Victoria and Albert Museum (entry **641c**) for the transfer to its Theatre Museum of the English Archive of ACGB covering the period from inception to March 1994. The wartime records of the CEMA are at present deposited with the PRO, and these too are to be transferred to the Theatre Museum. Lists and catalogues exist for the material deposited with the PRO.

484 The Athenaeum

Address: 107 Pall Mall, London SW1Y 5ER

Telephone: (0171) 930 4843

Fax: (0171) 839 4114

Enquiries: The Librarian, Miss S.J. Dodgson

Open: Private club. Visiting by arrangement only.

Access: Bona fide researchers, on written application to the Librarian.

The Athenaeum was founded in 1824 by John Wilson Croker (1780–1857) and others, and is one of the most celebrated London clubs. Its archives consist solely of internal administrative records. The librarian will answer reasonable requests about them submitted in writing. The club has no papers of past members; the letters of Herbert Spencer (1820–1903) have been transferred to the University of London (entry **762**). An automated catalogue of former members is in progress, and a handlist of archives has been compiled which may be consulted only in the club. The Victorian periodical *The Athenaeum* is not connected with the club or library in any way.

485 Bank of England

Address: Threadneedle Street, London EC2R 8AH

Telephone: (0171) 601 4889/5096

Fax: (0171) 601 3240

Enquiries: The Archivist, Henry Gillett

Open: By appointment only.

Access: Records over 30 years old are normally available for inspection, although records relating to customers may need to be withheld.

Historical background: The Bank of England was incorporated by Act of Parliament and Charter in 1694, and in return its proprietors subscribed funds to help finance the war being fought by William III against Louis XIV of France. The subscribers were granted a Royal Charter on 27 July 1694, under the title 'The Governor and Company of the Bank of England'. Of the original Charter, the only clauses now remaining unrevoked are those relating to the incorporation of the bank, the Common Seal, legal suit and the holding of property. The Bank of England Act of 1946 brought the bank into public ownership, but provided for the continued existence of 'the Governor and Company of the Bank of England' under Royal Charter.

Acquisitions policy: No external acquisitions.

Archives of organisation: Records covering the principal activities of the bank: advice to government; market operations; management of government, bank and private accounts; management of government and other stock issues; economic intelligence; relations with financial institutions abroad; industrial liaison; banknote printing; supervision of UK financial institutions; exchange control.

Finding aids: Descriptive lists and computer database. Lists sent to NRA.

Facilities: Limited photocopying.

Conservation: In-house.

486 The Barbers' Company

Address: Barber-Surgeons' Hall, Monkwell Square, Wood Street, London EC2Y 5BL

Telephone: (0171) 606 0741

Enquiries: The Archivist, Mr I.G. Murray

Open: Strictly by prior arrangement.

Access: To approved researchers, on written application. Users are referred in the first instance to the microfilmed copies of company records at Guildhall (entry **553**).

Historical background: The company, which practised both barbery and surgery, is first mentioned in 1308, when Richard le Barbour was presented as Master before the Court of Aldermen. It had a hall in Monkwell Street by 1443 and received its Charter of Incorporation in 1462. In 1540 by Act of Parliament it was united with the Fellowship of Surgeons to form the Worshipful Company of Barbers and Surgeons of London, with a monopoly of the two trades throughout London and the suburbs, and later the right to examine surgeons for the Navy and East India Company. In 1745 the surgeons left to form what was to become the Royal College of Surgeons (entry **689**), leaving the hall and its contents to the Barbers. The present hall dates from 1969, the previous ones having been destroyed in 1666 and 1940.

Acquisitions policy: Modern records are added to the archives from time to time in the usual

way. The company also maintains a library, to which material is added by gift or purchase.

Archives of organisation: Charters, ordinances, Grant of Arms etc, 1462–1685; court minutes, 1551–; court and livery lists, 1711–; freedom admission registers, 1522–1801; apprentice bindings and turnover books, 1657–1829; quarterage books, 1717–1860; company accounts, 1603–1881; dinner accounts, 1676–1790; tradesmens' receipt books, 1722–1818; records of examination of naval surgeons, 1709–45; charity fund accounts, 1764–1917; pension accounts, 1716–1894; property inventory, 1711–45; title deeds to company property, 1555–.

Non-manuscript material: Biographical material on members.
Photographs, portraits and illustrative material.

Finding aids: List of archive holdings; sent to NRA. Indexes to court minutes.

Publications: S. Young: *Annals of the Barber-Surgeons* (London, 1890).
J. Dobson and R. Milnes-Walker: *Barbers and Barber-Surgeons of London* (London, 1979).

487 Birkbeck College

Parent organisation: University of London

Address: Malet Street, London WC1E 7HX

Telephone: (0171) 631 6239

Fax: (0171) 631 6270

Enquiries: The Librarian

Open: By prior arrangement only.

Access: Bona fide researchers.

Historical background: The college was founded in 1823 as the London Mechanics' Institution and was modelled on the Glasgow Mechanics' Institution. Dr George Birkbeck (1776–1841) became its first president. Its original building was in Chancery Lane. In 1891 it was called the Birkbeck Institute and combined with two other bodies to form the City Polytechnic; however, in 1907 it reverted to being a separate institution called Birkbeck College. Although it had teachers recognised by the University of London from the 1890s, it became part of the university only in 1920. The college maintains a commitment to provide education to working people and mature students.

Acquisitions policy: To maintain the archive.

Archives of organisation: Early registers and papers, 1823–1910 (incomplete); governor's minutes and records, 1910–50; financial records, including appeals, 1897–1925; staff records; building records, 1914–45; departmental papers.

Papers *re* London County Council, 1906–35; University of London, including records of first application, 1908–50; and University Grants Committee, 1921–48.

War papers, 1938–46.

Major collections: Letters of George Birkbeck. Papers of Sir John Lockwood (1903–65), principally concerning development of university education in East Africa, and Dr R. Fürth, physicist.

Papers of J.D.Bernal (1901–71) are at Cambridge University Library (entry **147**).

Non-manuscript material: Photographs and college calendars.

Finding aids: Outline list.

Publications: C. Delisle Burns: *A Short History of Birkbeck College* (London, 1924).

E.H. Warmington: *A History of Birkbeck College, University of London, during the Second World War, 1939–1945* (London, 1955).

488 Bishopsgate Institute Reference Library

Address: 230 Bishopsgate, London EC2M 4QH

Telephone: (0171) 247 6844

Fax: (0171) 375 1794

Enquiries: The Reference Librarian, Dr David Webb

Open: Mon–Fri: 9.30–5.30

Access: Generally open to the public.

Historical background: The institute began as a cultural centre in 1894, funded by the Bishopsgate Foundation, a federation of St Botolph parish charities. The reference library opened in 1895 and is still supported entirely by the foundation.

Acquisitions policy: The library acquires the archives of associations and individuals connected with radical politics, especially the co-operative movement, and secularism.

Major collections: Howell Collection: Papers and library of George Howell (1833– 1910), chartist and MP, including the archives of the Reform League; the diaries of Ernest Jones (1819–69), chartist; and the minutes of the First International, 1864–76.

Holyoake Collection: Diaries and MSS of George Jacob Holyoake (1817–1906), socialist and founder of the co-operative movement.

New Secular Society Archives (f. 1866), including correspondence and papers of its founder, Charles Bradlaugh (1833–91), and archives of the Rationalist Peace Association, 1910–21.

London Co-operative Society Archives, including those of constituent societies, and their predecessors, *c*1850–.

Women's Co-operative Guild.

Finding aids: Typescript lists. NRA 10203, 10204.

Publications: George Howell Collection: Index to the Correspondence (rev. edn, 1975).

E. Royle: *The Bradlaugh Papers: a Descriptive Index* (East Ardsley, 1975).

D.R. Webb: *Bishopsgate Foundation Centenary History* (1991).

489 The Black Cultural Archives

Parent organisation: The African People's Historical Monument Foundation

Address: 378 Coldharbour Lane, Brixton, London SW9 8RP

Telephone: (0171) 738 4591

Fax: (0171) 738 7168

Enquiries: The Director, Mr S.H. Walker

Open: Mon–Fri: 10.00–4.00

Access: Researchers and interested members of the public; an appointment is essential.

Historical background: The African People's Historical Monument Foundation (UK) exists to promote the collection, documentation and dissemination of the culture and history of African peoples in the diaspora. The Black Cultural Archives project was begun in 1982 as a centre for collection and preservation of all primary source materials relating to black experience and community events, both past and present. Display and exhibition of materials are top priorities.

Acquisitions policy: To acquire, by donation or

purchase, historical and contemporary material by, or pertinent to, people of African origin.

Archives of organisation: Official records, working papers and photographic evidence of the growth of the archives project, 1982–.

Major collections: Jamaican slave papers, 18th century–.
Documentation of the lives and achievements of eminent black persons in Britain, 18th–20th centuries.

Non-manuscript material: Rare books documenting European imperialism in Africa.
Handbills, posters and photographs of community events, both current and historical.
Rare maps.
Paintings by local and international artists; African sculpture and carvings.
Oral evidence of black experience.

Finding aids: General index to all collections.

Facilities: Photocopying. Photography by arrangement. Computers.

Publications: Mary Seacole Teacher Resource Pack.

490 Brewers and Licensed Retailers Association

Address: 42 Portman Square, London W1H 0BB

Telephone: (0171) 486 4831

Fax: (0171) 935 3991

Enquiries: The Archivist, Dr Fiona Wood

Open: Mon–Fri: 9.00–5.30, by arrangement only.

Access: Bona fide researchers, strictly by appointment.

Historical background: The County Brewers' Society was formed in 1822, and in 1904 it amalgamated with the London Brewers' Association and the Burton Brewers' Association to form the Brewers' Society, subsequently the Brewers and Licensed Retailers Association.

Acquisitions policy: To maintain the archive. The library includes works on brewing history, prohibition and temperance.

Archives of organisation: Archives of the association and its predecessors, 1894–.
Daily precis of information about brewing appearing in the press, 1937–71.

Non-manuscript material: Photographs of brewers, production and retailing.
Biographies of brewers.
Brewing journals, 1876–.

Finding aids: Photographs catalogued in part. Index to press cuttings.

Facilities: Photocopying.

Publications: *Brewers' Guardian* (centenary edn, 1971) [includes history of the Brewers' Society].
T. Gourvish and R.G. Wilson: *British Brewing Industry* (Cambridge, 1994).

491 The British Academy

Address: 20–21 Cornwall Terrace, London NW1 4QP

Telephone: (0171) 487 5966

Fax: (0171) 224 3807

Enquiries: The Secretary

Open: Mon–Fri: 9.30–5.30

The British Academy is the premier national learned society for the humanities and the social sciences. It was founded in 1902 by Royal Charter, and the official records and working papers from that time are maintained and made available to bona fide researchers by appointment. No other material is acquired but there is a collecion of photographs of Fellows.

492 British Dental Association Library

Address: 64 Wimpole Street, London W1M 8AL

Telephone: (0171) 935 0875 ext. 205

Fax: (0171) 487 5232

Enquiries: The Librarian

Open: Mon–Fri: 9.00–5.30

Access: Bona fide researchers. An appointment is essential.

Historical background: The BDA was founded in 1880, and in 1923 it was linked with the Incorporated Dental Society through the Public Dental Service Association, which provided a forum for both professional negotiating bodies. Following the establishment of the NHS in 1948, all three associations amalgamated as the BDA.

Acquisitions policy: To maintain BDA records, and other collections or material of historical dental interest.

Archives of organisation: Records of BDA, including minutes of central committees, e.g. Council and Representation Board, and of branches and sections, 1880–.
Records of Incorporated Dental Society, 1934–49, and Public Dental Service Association, 1923–49.

Non-manuscript material: Dental manufacturers' catalogues, 1839–.
Scrapbooks of press cuttings relating to 1876 and 1921 Dentists Acts.

Finding aids: Holdings list.

Facilities: Photocopying.

493 British Film Institute

Address: 21 Stephen Street, London W1P 1PL

Telephone: (0171) 255 1444

Fax: (0171) 436 7950

A Special Materials Unit

Enquiries: The Special Materials Librarian, Ms Janet Moat

Open: Mon, Tues, Thurs, Fri: 10.30–5.30 Wed: 1.30–5.30

Access: Bona fide researchers, by appointment only. Preference given to BFI library members and postgraduates.

Historical background: The BFI was founded in 1933 'to encourage the development of the art of the film, to promote its use as a record of contemporary life and manners, and to foster public appreciation and study of it'. In 1961 the BFI's Memorandum of Association was amended to include television. The Special Materials Unit is located within the Library and Information Service, and was established in 1992 to incorporate the holdings of unpublished scripts, press-books and special collections which have been acquired gradually since 1933.

Acquisitions policy: All types of material relating to film and television, including ephemera, are acquired by purchase, donation and exchange, but priority is given to British cinema and TV.

Major collections: These currently number more than 100, and include papers of: Carol Reed, director/producer (1906–76); Michael

Balcon, producer (1896–1977); Joseph Losey, director (1909–84); Derek Jarman, director/ scriptwriter/designer (1942–94); David Putnam, producer (*b* 1941); Ivor Montagu, director/producer /scriptwriter (1904–84).
Unpublished scripts (*c*16,000) and press-books (25,000).

Non-manuscript material: Audio cassettes (*c*100), plus listening copies of the BECTV Oral History Project cassettes; see also section B.

Finding aids: Script card catalogue. Lists of special collections; sent to NRA. Computerisation in progress.

Facilities: Photocopying. Photography. Microfilm/fiche readers.

Conservation: Contracted out.

B National Film and Television Archive

Enquiries: The Curator, Mr Clyde Jeavons

Open: Mon–Fri: 10.00–5.30

Access: The catalogue of the film and TV collection is generally open to the public for consultation. Research viewings can also be arranged by appointment. Details of charges are available on request. The film and TV collection is not available for loan or hire.

Historical background: The NFTVA, a division of the British Film Institute, was founded in 1935 'to maintain a national repository of films of permanent value'. Its brief was extended to include television in the 1950s. A large complementary collection of stills, posters and designs is also held by the Stills, Posters and Designs Department. The NFTVA is a founder-member of the International Federation of Film Archives.

Acquisitions policy: To select, acquire, preserve, document and make permanently available for research and study a national collection of films and television programmes of all kinds exhibited or transmitted in the UK, from any source and of any nationality, which have lasting value as works of art, or are examples of cinema and television history, historical or scientific records, portraiture, or records of contemporary life and behaviour.

Major collections: Film and television collection: more than 200,000 titles comprising feature and short films, documentaries, newsreels, animation and amateur films, 1895–.

Finding aids: Computerised database to holdings with search criteria such as title, country or director. Comprehensive subject and personality indexes, plus shot-lists for *c*10% of the collection.

Facilities: Microfilm reader. 35mm and 16mm table viewers for film study. Video players and monitors for video-cassette viewings. Stills copying service.

Publications: British Films, 1927–39, 1971–81. Catalogue of Stills, Posters and Designs. Film and Television Periodical Holdings (1982). *Film/Video Production and Funding* (1984). *TV Documentation: a Guide to BFI Library Services Resources* (1985). *British Cinema Resource Book* (1994).
Some special subject bibliographies.
BFI annual listing of publications: full list of publications available.

494 British Institute of Radiology
Bernard Sunley Library

Address: 36 Portland Place, London W1N 4AT

Telephone: (0171) 580 4085, 436 2644 (answerphone)

Fax: (0171) 255 3209

Enquiries: The Library and Information Services Manager, Mrs Maryam Molana-Stone

Open: Mon, Wed, Fri: 9.00–5.00 Tues, Thurs: 10.00–6.00 By prior arrangement only.

Access: Bona fide scholars may apply for research tickets. Special permission is required to consult the archives and historic books. Charges are made for certain services.

Historical background: The present British Institute of Radiology, incorporated by Royal Charter in 1958, has its origin in the Röntgen Society, founded in March 1897, 16 months after the discovery of X-rays. The basic constitution of the institute dates from 1927. Application for membership may be made by any person, medically qualified or not, with interests in radiology. The archives derive from the initial collection of minutes and associated correspondence; artefacts derive from the initial gifts of X-ray tubes (currently on loan to the

Science Museum) and historic books. Journals commence with the *Archives of Clinical Skiagraphy* (1896–), gaining considerably from the Mackenzie Davidson Collection donated in 1923.

Acquisitions policy: To maintain and extend records of the evolution of the institute and of activities stimulated by its members.

Archives of organisation: Minute books of the Röntgen Society and successive bodies, including records of property transactions, membership lists and handbooks, 1897–.

Major collections: Minutes of the British X-Ray and Radium Protection Committee, 1921–48. Proceedings of the Radium Commission, 1929–48.
Book of Radiation Martyrs, with source material collected by F.G. Spear, 1895–1980.
Notebooks of J. Read, 1908–93, pioneer in radiation biology and the effects of oxygen on radiosensitivity.

Non-manuscript material: Group photographs of institute and international meetings and individual portraits.
Recordings of lectures.
Manufacturers' catalogues.
Newspaper cuttings on radiology, 1921–3.
Collections of X-ray prints in albums.
K.C. Clark Slide Library on Positioning in Radiography, based on lectures, 1935–80.

Finding aids: Outline list of archives (full details in preparation). Full catalogue of historic books.

Facilities: Photocopying.

Publications: P.J. Bishop: 'The Evolution of the British Journal of Radiology', *British Journal of Radiology*, x/6 (1973), 833–6.
——: 'The Library's Historical Collection', *British Institute of Radiology Bulletin*, i/3 (1975), 5.
Annual Reports of the British Institute of Radiology include summaries of work on archives and books.

495 British Library
Special Collections

Address: Great Russell Street, London WC1B 3DG

Telephone: (0171) 412 7501

Fax: (0171) 412 7745

Enquiries: The Director of Special Collections, Dr A. Prochaska
NB The Special Collections of the British Library will move in about 1997 to the new British Library at St Pancras (96 Euston Road, London NW1 2DB). There are at the time of going to press no plans for the Newspaper Library to move there.

A Manuscripts Collections

Telephone: (0171) 412 7513/7514

Fax: (0171) 412 7745

Enquiries: The Manuscripts Librarian

Open: Mon–Sat: 10.00–4.45 (last admission/enquiry 4.30) Closed one week in November as announced.

Access: Reader's pass plus supplementary pass. Applicants must be aged 21 or over.

B Map Library

Telephone: (0171) 412 7700/7747

Fax: (0171) 412 7780

Enquiries: The Map Librarian

Open: Mon–Sat: 10.00–4.30 (or from 9.30 with a reader's pass)
Closed the week following the last complete week of October.

Access: On application (no pass needed).

C Music Library

Telephone: (0171) 412 7527/7752

Fax: (0171) 412 7751

Enquiries: The Music Librarian

Open: Mon–Fri: 9.30–4.45
On Saturdays apply to the Manuscripts Students' Room.
Closed the week following the last complete week of October.

Access: Reader's pass.

D Philatelic Collections

Telephone: (0171) 412 7635/7636

Fax: (0171) 412 7745

Enquiries: The Head of Philatelic Collections

Open: Mon–Fri: 10.00–4.00, by appointment.

Access: Reader's pass and appointment necessary.

Historical background: The foundation collections (Sloane, Cotton, Harley) date back to the establishment of the British Museum in 1753. MSS of all kinds, including music, maps and oriental material, were represented in these early collections and have been added to constantly ever since. The Philatelic Collections were founded in 1891 with the Tapling Collection bequest. The British Library was founded from the library departments of the British Museum in 1973. In 1982 the administration of the India Office Library and Records was transferred from the Foreign and Commonwealth Office to the British Library Board and has since been amalgamated with the Oriental Collections (entry 497). The separate departments listed above, all of which contain material of potential interest to archive and manuscript researchers, were united in the Directorate of Special Collections in 1985. The British Library is recognised as a place of deposit for public records.

Acquisitions policy: There is an active policy of acquisition by purchase and gift in the field of historical papers and in many others, literary, artistic, cartographic, musical etc, of national interest.

Archives of organisation: The British Library has held its own archives since its foundation in 1973.

Major collections: See finding aids for named collections.

Non-manuscript material: Large collection of seals (MS Collections).
Original photographs (MS Collections).
Good collection of facsimiles and microfilms of MSS not in the British Library (all departments).
Printed maps and music (Map and Music departments, which also hold some MS materials).
Stamps and related materials (Philatelic).
Lord Chamberlain's plays, MS, typewritten and printed (MS Collections).

Portraits, paintings, prints, drawings, plans (Maps and MS Collections).
(For newspapers and sound archive materials, entry **496**).

Finding aids: Published catalogues of additions and catalogues of named collections; Catalogue of Manuscript Maps, Charts and Plans; Catalogue of Manuscript Music (see M.A.E. Nickson: *Guide to the Catalogues and Indexes of the Department of Manuscripts*).
Amalgamated *Index of Manuscripts*.
NRA holds published catalogues and annual printouts.
Some manuscripts catalogues expected to be mounted on OPAC in 1995.
Supplementary unpublished finding aids available in Manuscripts Students' Room.
Card catalogues, lists and indexes, and many contemporary finding aids are available. See NRA 13548 [*Guide to MSS*].

Facilities: Photocopying. Photography. Microfilm/fiche readers. On-line Public Access Catalogue for Printed Books. See Initiatives for Access announcements for availability of digitalised text and images. Light sources, watermark readers, microscopes etc in reading rooms, Video-spectral comparator and other specialist equipment on application to Conservation. 'Visualtek' miniviewer.

Conservation: Full range of conservation and binding processes from in-house specialist department. Services available to the public: see leaflet; also consultancy and advice: tel. (0171) 412 7740. Advice also from National Preservation Office: tel. (0171) 412 7612 or fax (0171) 412 7768.

Publications: Catalogues of collections, monographs and illustrated books; exhibition catalogues; *British Library Journal*; multi-media publications, etc. Annual list of publications from BL Marketing and Publishing Office, 41 Russell Square, London WC1B 3DG, tel. (0171) 412 7704, fax (0171) 412 7768.

496 British Library
Humanities and Social Sciences

A Information Sciences Service

Address: 7 Ridgmount Street, London WC1E 7AE

Telephone: (0171) 412 7688

Fax: (0171) 412 7691

Enquiries: The Reader Services Librarian

Open: Mon, Wed, Fri: 9.00–6.00 Tues, Thurs: 9.00–8.00

Access: Generally open to the public.

Historical background: The library was founded by the Library Association *c*1900 and was maintained as a service to the association's members until 1974. In that year it was transferred to the British Library, which wholly finances it as a service to the UK library community.

Acquisitions policy: Maintains the existing collections and acquires publications on library and information science throughout the world.

Major collections: Archives of the following organisations: Association of Assistant Librarians; Library Association Cataloguing and Indexing Group; Library Association, London and Home Counties Branch; Art Libraries Society; Association of Metropolitan Chief Librarians.
H. Evelyn Bliss papers relating to the Bliss Classification.

Non-manuscript material: Collection of books and periodicals, including much that is relevant to the history of libraries and librarianship.
Extensive collection of library annual reports, notably of UK public libraries.

Finding aids: Catalogues of the books and pamphlets. Other aids are planned.

Facilities: Photocopying. Microfiche readers.

B National Sound Archive

Address: 29 Exhibition Road, London SW7 2AS

Telephone: (0171) 412 7440/7430

Enquiries: The Information Service

Open: Mon–Wed, Fri: 10.00–5.00 Thurs: 10.00–9.00

Access: Open to the public; listening service by appointment only.

Historical background: The NSA was founded as the British Institute of Recorded Sound and acquired its first premises in 1955. It became a department of the British Library in 1983. It will move to the new St Pancras British Library in the late 1990s.

Acquisition policy: The following main subject areas are represented by curatorial sections: Western art and music; drama, poetry and documentary recordings; folk, traditional and non-Western classical music; jazz; popular music; wildlife sounds; languages and dialect; industro-mechanical sound; oral history. British and Anglophone material are given priority where appropriate.

Major collections: UK commercially published recordings (through a system equivalent to legal deposit of books at the British Library).
Overseas commercially published recordings.
Recordings of BBC, ITV and Channel 4 broadcasts off transmission.
Duplicate pressings of tapes of BBC Sound Archive recordings.
NSA's own recordings.
Deposited collections of commercial and non-commerical recordings.

Non-manuscript material: Relevant museum artefacts and obsolescent recording equipment are also collected for display and study and as an adjunct to older recording media.
Published discographies and record company catalogues.

Finding aids: NSA on-line catalogue. National Discography on-line database. BBC Sound Library catalogue. NSA Library Card catalogue.

Facilities: Photocopying. Microfilm/fiche reader/printer. Listening service (including group listening and remote listening at BL Document Supply Centre, Boston Spa, Yorkshire, and at North Devon Library, Barnstaple). Commercial transcription service. Conference and event recording service.

Publications: Various discographies, leaflets, books and sound recordings; full list available. *Playback* [tri-annual bulletin].

C Newspaper Library

Address: British Library Newspaper Library, Colindale Avenue, London NW9 5HE

Telephone: (0171) 412 7353
Fax (071) 412 7379

Enquiries: The Information Officer, Jill Allbrooke

Open: Mon–Sat: 10.00–5.00
Closed for a week at the end of October.

Access: Holders of a Newspaper Library pass or British Library pass (for the purposes of research and reference not readily available in other libraries). No access for those under 18.

Historical background: The library was opened in 1905 as the British Museum Newspaper Repository to house English provincial, Welsh, Scottish and Irish newspapers. In 1932 it became the Newspaper Library and all the British Museum's newspapers were transferred to Colindale, with the exception of the pre-1801 London newspapers and newspapers in oriental languages. In 1973 it became part of the British Library.

Acquisitions policy: All UK and Irish newspapers received through legal deposit, also weekly and fortnightly popular magazines, comics and specialist titles (trade, etc). Foreign newspapers are acquired in Western and Slavonic languages.

Major collections: Newspapers and magazines (600,000 vols; 270,000 reels of microfilm).
Includes full sets of the main London editions of all national daily and Sunday papers from start of publication to the present day. Local newspapers are held from all over England, Wales, Scotland and Ireland. Foreign newspapers in Western and Slavonic languages are acquired from almost every country in the world.

Finding aids: Catalogues available at Colindale and Bloomsbury.

Facilities: Full range of copying services, including self-service microfilm reader/printers.

Conservation: In-house conservation workshop and bindery.

Publications: *Catalogue of the Newspaper Library, Colindale* (1975).
J. Westmancoat: *Newspapers* (1985).
Newsplan reports (in progress).
Bibliography of British Newspapers (vols in progress).

497 British Library
Oriental and India Office Collections

Address: 197 Blackfriars Road, London
SE1 8NG

Telephone: (0171) 412 7873

Fax: (0171) 412 7858

Enquiries: The Archivist and Deputy Director

Open: Mon–Fri: 9.30–5.45 Sat: 9.30–12.45

Access: Approved readers.

A Oriental Collections

Historical background: The foundation collections of MSS and printed books of the British Museum (1753) contained some material in the languages of Asia. A rapid increase in the quantity of this material during the 19th century led to the creation of an oriental sub-department in the Department of Manuscripts in 1867. This was enlarged by taking over the collections of printed books in Asian languages from the Department of Printed Books to form a new Department of Oriental Printed Books and Manuscripts in 1892. On the inauguration of the British Library in 1973, incorporating the former library departments of the British Museum, it was renamed the Department of Oriental Manuscripts and Printed Books and subsequently the Oriental Collections. In 1991 it merged with the India Office.

Acquisitions policy: All significant material in the fields of the humanities and social sciences in the languages of Asia and of North-East Africa.

Major collections: More than 45,000 oriental MSS: the largest collections are in Hebrew, Arabic, Persian, Turkish, Chinese, and the languages of South and South-East Asia; especially rich in illuminated and illustrated Islamic MSS and Hebrew and Arabic religious and literary texts.
Stein Collection of Chinese fragments (*c*20,000 items).

Non-manuscript material: Early blockprinted books from the Far East. Over 630,000 printed books, serials and newspapers, representing all the literary languages and cultures of Asia and of North and North-East Africa.
Growing collections of microforms.

Large intake of official publications from Asian countries.

Finding aids: Current catalogues in card form and in a computer-generated file supplement the printed catalogues.

Facilities: Photocopying. Photography. Microfilm/fiche readers. Information is given to enquiries in person, by telephone and by post.

Publications: Guide to the Department of Oriental Manuscripts and Printed Books (1977) [published catalogues (covering more than 100 languages) are listed and described].
Educational and popular booklets on various aspects of the collections.

B India Office Collections

Historical background: The office holds the archives of the East India Company from its formation in 1600 to 1858; the Board of Control, 1784–1858; the India Office, 1858–1947; and the Burma Office, 1937–48; as well as MSS collected by the Library (f. 1801) of the East India Company and the India Office. The administration of the India Office Library and Records was transferred from the Foreign and Commonwealth Office of the British Library Board in 1982. Merger with the Oriental Collections took place in 1991. It is recognised as a place of deposit for public records.

Acquisitions policy: Following the independence of India, Pakistan and Burma in 1947–8, the official India Office archive closed, although certain related official series continue for a few years after. Papers of individuals, ranging from Viceroys to private soldiers, are still being acquired with selected maps and microfilms of archives held in South Asia.

Archives of organisation: India Office Records: the official archive (*c*200,000 vols, files and boxes); while concentrating upon South Asia, the archive also covers the general history of the British penetration of Asia, ranging at different periods from St Helena, via South and East Africa, the Middle East, Malaysia, Indonesia and China, to Japan; includes maps (*c*20,000 items).

Major collections: Oriental MSS: (*c*27,800); major collections in Persian and Arabic, many illuminated and illustrated.
European MSS: private papers of such individuals as Robert, 1st Baron Clive, and his son,

1733–1832; Robert Orme (1728–1801); Sir Stamford Raffles and family, 1799–1957. Vice-regal collections include 1st Viscount Chelmsford, 1916–21; 1st Marquess of Curzon, 1899–1905; 1st Marquess of Dufferin and Ava, 1884–8; 1st Earl of Halifax, 1926–31; 5th Marquess of Lansdowne, 1888–94; 1st Baron Lawrence, 1841–79; 1st Earl of Northbrook, 1872–90; 1st Marquess of Reading, 1898–1935 (*c*13,600).

Non-manuscript material: India Office Records: official publications (*c*70,000 vols). India Office Library: European printed books (*c*158,000).
Oriental printed books (*c*270,000).
Prints, drawings and paintings (*c*30,000).
Photographs (*c*250,000).

Finding aids: A large number of lists and indexes is available, including many contemporary finding aids. Some data on OPAC. NRA 13548 [*Guide to MSS*].

Facilities: Photocopying. Photography. Microfilm/fiche reader.

Conservation: Full in-house department.

Publications: A list of publications, giving details of earlier catalogues of the official archive (many of which are gradually being superseded), together with catalogues of the European MSS, oriental MSS, European and oriental printed books, and prints and drawings, is available upon request. The *Annual Report* lists MSS accessions and contains articles on all aspects of the collections.
W. Foster: *A Guide to the India Office Records, 1600–1858* (London, 1919).
S.C. Hill: *Catalogue of the Home Miscellaneous Series of the India Office Records* (London, 1927).
J.C. Lancaster: 'The India Office Records', *Archives*, ix (1970), 130.
A. Farrington: *The Records of the East India College, Haileybury, and other Institutions* (London, 1976).
I.A. Baxter: *A Brief Guide to Biographical Sources* (London, 1979).
A. Griffin: *A Brief Guide to Sources for the Study of Burma in the India Office Records* (London, 1979).
P. Tuson: *The Records of the British Residency and Agencies in the Persian Gulf* (London, 1979).
A.K. Jasbir Singh: *Gandhi and Civil Dis-* *obedience: Documents in the India Office Records, 1922–1946* (London, 1980).
L.A. Hall: *A Brief Guide to Sources for the Study of Afghanistan in the India Office Records* (London, 1981).
J. Sims: *A List and Index of Parliamentary Papers relating to India, 1908–1947* (London, 1981).
A. Farrington: *A Guide to the Records of the India Office Military Department* (London, 1982).
A Select List of Private Collections in the European Manuscripts (London, 1985).
R. Seton: *The Indian 'Mutiny', 1857–58. A Guide to Source Material in the India Office Library and Records* (London, 1986).
S. Ashton and P. Tuson: *India Office Library and Records: A Brief Guide for Teachers* (London, 1987).
M.I. Moir: *A General Guide to the India Office Records* (London, 1988).

498 British Library of Political and Economic Science
London School of Economics

Parent organisation: University of London

Address: 10 Portugal Street, London WC2A 2HD

Telephone: (0171) 955 7223

Fax: (0171) 955 7454

Enquiries: The Archivist, Dr G.E.A. Raspin

Open: Term: Mon–Fri: 10.00–5.30 Vacation: Mon–Fri: 10.00–5.00

Access: Approved readers undertaking original research; students must produce evidence of their status and degree course. Some categories of reader will be charged a fee. An appointment is not necessary but readers are strongly advised to contact the archivist before their first visit.

Historical background: The library of the London School of Economics was founded in 1896.

Acquisitions policy: Modern British political, economic and social history, social anthropology (mainly post-1890); history of the London School of Economics.

Archives of organisation: LSE archives, 1894–1968.

Major collections: Papers of Beatrice Webb (1858–1943) and Sidney Webb (1859–1947); John Stuart Mill (1806–73); Hugh Dalton (1887–1962); Bronislaw Malinowski (1884–1942); George Lansbury (1859–1940); Walter Citrine (1887–1983).

Archives of National Institute of Industrial Psychology, 1919–74; Political and Economic Planning, c1931–73; Independent Labour Party National Administrative Council, minutes and other papers, c1893–1950; Liberal Party, c1924–1982; Nationalised Industries Chairmen's Group, 1973–89.

Charles Booth Survey of London, 1885–1905 (426 vols).

New Survey of London Life and Labour, 1928–33.

Hall-Carpenter Archives of Lesbian and Gay History, c1957–1994.

Non-manuscript material: Webb Collection on Trade Unions.

Extensive collections of rare books on political, economic and social questions, and on socialism, 1485–1951.

UK election leaflets and other ephemera for most general and some other elections, 1945–.

Finding aids: Catalogues/handlists for most collections. Card index of letters. Cataloguing data in machine readable form are available for the school archives, for most election ephemera and for about one-third of deposited collections. There is also a database containing descriptions of all major collections. Searches are carried out by arrangement with the archivist.

Facilities: Photocopying, microforms and photography by arrangement. Readers may use personal computers (but not scanners) and power points are provided. Microfilm/fiche readers/printers.

Publications: A Guide to Archives and Manuscripts in the University of London, 1 (1984), 1–35.

499 British Medical Association

Address: BMA House, Tavistock Square, London WC1H 9JP

Telephone: (0171) 383 6588

Fax: (0171) 383 6717

Enquiries: The Archivist, Emily Naish

Open: Mon–Fri: 9.30–4.30

Access: BMA members and other bona fide researchers, by appointment only. Official records of the association are subject to a 30-year closure period.

Historical background: The BMA was founded in 1832 by Sir Charles Hastings to promote the medical and allied sciences and to maintain the honour and interests of the medical profession. Originally called the Provincial Medical and Surgical Association, it adopted its present name in 1856. The BMA is also a registered company and trade union. The archive was set up in 1993.

Acquisitions policy: The records of the association at both central and local level and other material relating to the history of the BMA, including personal papers of BMA members and officers.

Archives of organisation: Minutes of committees and annual meetings, 1834–.
Correspondence, c 1950s–.
Deposited collections of minutes and other records of BMA divisions and branches, mid-1830s–.

Major collections: Various small collections, including correspondence of Joseph Lister, 1884–1908; and of Sir Charles Hastings, 1837–53.

Records of Hackney Medical Society, including minutes and some correspondence, 1913–38.

Other historical MSS.

Non-manuscript material: Photographs of members, 19th and 20th centuries.

Finding aids: Lists and indexes (not sent to NRA).

Facilities: Photocopying and photography by arrangement.

Conservation: Contracted out.

500 British Museum
Central Archives

Address: Great Russell Street, London WC1B 3DG

Telephone: (0171) 323 8768/8243/8224

Fax: (0171) 323 8480

Enquiries: The Museum Archivist, Miss K.J. Wallace

Open: Tues, Thurs: 10.00–1.00; 2.00–4.30

Acess: Generally open to the public by appointment. Records less than 30 years old are closed under the terms of the Public Records Act 1958, and a small number of other records are closed for a longer period by order of the Lord Chancellor.

Historical background: The British Museum was founded in 1753 and has been governed throughout its history by a board of trustees. Its ten present-day departments have evolved from one original department of antiquities. It also included, until the 1880s, the departments which now form the Natural History Museum and, until 1973, the departments which now form part of the British Library. The museum's archives became public records in 1958 and an archivist was first appointed in 1974.

Acquisitions policy: Material relating to the administrative history of the museum is accepted by gift and may be acquired by purchase when appropriate.

Archives of organisation: Archives of the British Museum Trustees, Director and Museum Secretary, 1753–; records of buildings and staff; purchases and donations of museum objects; finance; reading room of the former British Museum Library; excavations; deeds of title; administrative correspondence and papers, 1753–.
Printed staff lists, 1847–1967.

Major collections: Papers of Charles Townley (1737–1805).
Detailed documentation of the museum's collections of antiquities is held by the various departments.

Non-manuscript material: Printed copies of statutes and proceedings of parliamentary commissions relating to the museum, 18th and 19th centuries.
Microfilm of the main classes of archives.

Finding aids: Class lists and indexes to main classes.

Facilities: Photocopying (unbound MSS only). Photography. Copies from microfilm.

Publications: J Wallace: 'The Central Archives of the British Museum', *Archives*, xix/84 (1990), 213–23.

501 British Orthodox Church

Parent organisation: Coptic Orthodox Patriarchate of Alexandria

Address: Church Secretariat, 10 Heathwood Gardens, Charlton, London SE7 8EP

Telephone: (0181) 854 3090

Fax: (0181) 244 7888

Enquiries: The Librarian, Dr Judith E. Pinnington or The Archivist, Dr Gregory Tillet

Open: By appointment only.

Access: Bona fide enquirers, on written application.

Acquisitions policy: To maintain all records of the church.

Archives of organisation: Church records, registers and correspondence, 1866–.

Major collections: Private papers of Metropolitan Mar Georgius (1905–79), Bishop W.B. Crow (1895–1976) and Bishop U.V. Herford (1866–1938).
Papers of the now defunct Archdiocese of Antwerp, 1947–85, and Apostolic Vicariate for France, 1952–70.
Collection relating to the history of the Orthodox Church in Great Britain; Old Catholicism and various small autocephalous churches.

Non-manuscript material: The Newman Collection of books, pamphlets and photographs relating to the Catholic Apostolic Church (commonly known as Irvingites).
Photographic collection, press cuttings and pamphlets.
Library specialises in books on liturgy and Eastern Christendom, especially the Coptic and other oriental Orthodox Churches.

Finding aids: Card index. Catalogues of books and MSS (still in process of being compiled).

Facilities: Very limited photocopying and photography.

502 British Province of the Society of Jesus Archives

Address: 114 Mount Street, London W1Y 6AH

Telephone: (0171) 493 7811

Fax: (0171) 495 6685/499 0549

Enquiries: The Archivist, Rev. Thomas M. McCoog or The Archivist Emeritus, Rev. T.G. Holt

Open: Mon–Fri: 10.00–1.00, by appointment only. (Arrangements may be made for longer daily periods where researchers come from a distance.)

Access: Bona fide students, on written application. Official policy forbids access to any Jesuit's papers until forty years after his death.

Historical background: The province archives supplement and continue the collection of MSS held at Stonyhurst, which virtually began with the Jesuit mission to England, Scotland and Wales from 1580. Original papers at Farm Street begin *c*1623 and cover England and Wales, and Scotland from *c*1857.

Acquisitions policy: All kinds of archival material concerning the history of the Society of Jesus, especially in England, Scotland and Wales, is received. The main accessions come from Jesuit houses, especially those which close, and from the papers of deceased Jesuits.

Archives of organisation: Official and private correspondence, registers and accounts of missions, *c*1623–.

Major collections: Correspondence of John Morris (1826–93); John Hungerford Pollen (1820–1902); Joseph Stevenson (1806–95); Herbert Thurston (1856–1939) and other members of the British Province.
Large collections of transcripts, photocopies and microfilms of material from many British and continental archives concerning the British Jesuits in particular and British Catholics in general.

Non-manuscript material: Extensive collection of printed books and pamphlets on Jesuit and British Catholic topics, 1525–, with special emphasis on the 16th and 17th centuries and the Victorian period.
Complete set of the English Recusant Literature reprint series. The archives holds copies of most of the works written by members of the British Province and is currently seeking to fill in the gaps.

Finding aids: Card index (not in general available, but cards of subjects of interest to researchers are shown them by an archivist or assistant).

Facilities: Limited photocopying. Microfilm reader.

Publications: F. Edwards: 'The Archives of the English Province of the Society of Jesus', *Journal of the Society of Archivists*, iii (1966), 107.

503 British Psycho-Analytical Society

Address: Institute of Psycho-Analysis, 63 New Cavendish Street, London W1M 7RD

Telephone: (0171) 580 4952

Fax: (0171) 323 5312

Enquiries: The Hon. Assistant, Miss Pearl King

Open: Mon–Fri: 10.00–6.00
Closed August.

Access: Researchers are allowed access by previous permission of the honorary archivist.

Historical background: The BPAS was founded in 1919 and the institute's library started in 1926. Ernest Jones (1879–1958) was president of the society and his correspondence forms the basis of the collections. A working party now exists to deal with the archives and MS collections.

Acquisitions policy: Donations of papers of people associated with the society.

Archives of organisation: British Psycho-Analytical Society archives, including minutes, correspondence and memoranda, 1919–.

Major collections: Personal and professional papers of Ernest Jones, *c*1900–1958.
Papers of James Strachey (1887–1967), translator of Freud; John Rickman (*c*1890–1951); Sylvia Payne (1880–1971); and Susan Isaacs (1885–1948), colleague of Melanie Klein.

Non-manuscript material: Newspaper cuttings.

Finding aids: The archives are currently being reorganised and indexed on a computer database.

Facilities: Photocopying.

504 British Veterinary Association

Address: 7 Mansfield Street, London W1M 0AT

Telephone: (0171) 636 6541

Fax: (0171) 436 2970

Enquiries: The Head of Veterinary Services, Ms Chrissie Nicholls

Open: Mon–Fri: 9.30–5.00

Access: Members and bona fide researchers only. An information service is provided for the media, parliamentarians and occasional researchers.

The association was founded in 1881 and retains its own archives. Collections of veterinary interest are normally referred to the Royal College of Veterinary Surgeons (entry **690**).

505 Brompton Oratory

Address: Brompton Road, London SW7 2RP

Telephone: (0171) 589 4811

Fax: (0171) 584 1095

Enquiries: The Fr Librarian

Open: By arrangement only.

Access: Bona fide researchers, by appointment.

Historical background: The oratory was opened in 1854, although a library had existed from 1847.

Acquisitions policy: The oratory maintains its own archives and collections.

Archives of organisation: Internal records, 1854–.
Recorded notes of general congregations.

Major collections: Letters of or about F.W. Faber (1814–63), superior of the oratory; Ralph Francis Kerr (1874–1932); and John Henry Newman (1801–90); as well as other London oratorians.
MSS of works by Faber.
MSS of Thomas Francis Knox (1822–82).

Finding aids: NRA 16631.

Publications: The London Oratory, 1884–1984 (London, 1984).

506 BT Archives

Parent organisation: British Telecommunications plc

Address: G09, Telephone House, 2–4 Temple Avenue, London EC4Y 0HL

Telephone: (0171) 822 1002

Fax: (0171) 822 1010

Enquiries: The Group Archivist, David Hay

Open: Mon–Fri: 9.30–4.30

Access: All records over 30 years old are available to all members of the public, and many records of more recent date. Prior appointments are necessary.

Historical background: The telegraph service, begun by private companies from the 1830s, was taken over by the Post Office (PO) in 1870. The telephone service, also initiated by private companies from 1878, was taken over in 1912. As a central government department (the Postmaster General sat in Cabinet) the PO was the virtual monopoly supplier of telecommunications services in the UK from this date. In 1969 the PO was established as a public corporation under the Post Office Act of that year and was split into two divisions, Posts and Telecommunications. The British Telecommunications Act 1981 established British Telecom as a distinct corporation, although the telecommunications division of the PO had been known as British Telecom since the previous year. British Telecom was incorporated as a public limited company in 1984 as British Telecommunications plc under the Telecommunications Act of that year. The 1984 Act also abolished British Telcom's exclusive privilege of running telecommunications services. It now requires a licence to operate such services and is subject to scrutiny and review by the Office of Telecommunications. BT, the company's trading name since 1991, remains legally obliged under the Public Records Acts to safeguard its historical records created up to the date of privatisation, including those of its predecessors. BT Archives, created in embryonic form during 1984, rapidly expanded from 1986 to consolidate in one repository the various telecommunications collections held throughout BT and elsewhere. It is recognised as a place of deposit for public records.

Acquisitions policy: To collect all multi-media

material on the development of services provided in the UK and overseas by BT and its predecessors.

Archives of organisation: Private telegraph companies, 1846–70; private telephone companies, 1878–1912; PO telegraph service, 1866–1969; PO telephone service, 1878–1969; PO telecommunications, 1969–80; British Telecommunications (public corporation), 1980–84; British Telecommunications plc, 1984–.

Major collections: Records of telegraph companies taken over by the PO, including: English Telegraph Co., 1852–69; Electric (and International) Telegraph Co., 1846–70; London and Provincial Telegraph Co., 1859–68; United Kingdom Telegraph Co., 1851–70; Universal Private Telegraph Co., 1861–70.
Records of telephone companies taken over by PO including: The Telephone Co. Ltd, 1878–80; Edison Telephone Co., 1879–80; United Telephone Co., 1880–88; National Telephone Co., 1892–1913.

Non-manuscript material: Historical phone book collection, 1880–.
Historical telecommunications photograph and film library, 19th century–.
Phonecard collection, 1985–.
Publicity artwork, 1930s-1960s.
Telecommunications library, 1769–.

Finding aids: Catalogues. Card index (currently being computerised).

Facilities: Photocopying. Photography. Microfilm/fiche readers.

Conservation: Contracted out.

Publications: F.G.C. Baldwin: *History of the Telephone in the United Kingdom* (1938).
H. Robinson: *Britain's Post Office* (1953).
D.C. Pitt: *The Telecommunications Function in the British Post Office* (1980).
BT Archives: *Guide to Events in Telecommunications* (1993).

507 Carlton Club

Address: 69 St James's Street, London SW1A 1PJ

Telephone: (0171) 493 1164

Fax: (0171) 495 4090

Enquiries: The Secretary, Mr R.N. Linsley

Open: Mon–Fri: by arrangement. Closed August.

Access: Bona fide researchers, by appointment.

The Carlton Club, a club for Conservative Party supporters, was founded in 1832. Most of the records and the library were destroyed by enemy action in 1940, but some archives of the club survive, including members' records from 1832. The club owns a number of portraits of 19th- and 20th-century Conservative leaders. Photocopying facilities are available. See Sir Charles Petrie: *The Carlton Club*; Barry Phelps: *Power and the Party* [includes 1st and 2nd Carlton Lectures].

508 Central Saint Martins College of Art and Design

Parent organisation: The London Institute

Address: Southampton Row, London WC1B 4AP

Telephone: (0171) 753 9090

Fax: (0171) 831 0735

Enquiries: The Director of Learning Resources, Sylvia Backemeyer

Open: By arrangement only.

Access: Staff and students of London Institute and bona fide researchers, by appointment.

The college was founded in 1896 by W.R. Lethaby (1857–1931) as the Central School of Arts and Crafts, under the auspices of the Technical Education Board, which later became the London County Council. The college maintains its own archives, a collection of material related to design history, and the Central Lettering Record, a collection of letter forms. The collections are not yet fully catalogued or generally accessible.

509 Central School of Speech and Drama Library

Address: Embassy Theatre, 64 Eton Avenue, London NW3 3HY

Telephone: (0171) 722 8183

Fax: (0171) 586 1665

Enquiries: The Librarian, Linda Dolben

Open: Term: Mon: 10.00–7.00 Tues–Thurs: 9.00–7.00 Fri: 9.00–5.00

Access: Generally open to the public; an appointment is necessary and fees are charged on a daily basis.

The Central School of Speech and Drama was founded in 1906 by Elsie Fogerty, offering an entirely new form of training in speech and drama for young actors and other students. In 1956 the school moved to its current location at the Embassy Theatre in Swiss Cottage. There is a very small archive concerned with the history and development of the school. Donations of material concerned with the history of CSSD are accepted, although current space constraints mean that it is not current policy to expand the archive significantly.

510 Charing Cross and Westminster Medical School

Parent organisation: University of London

Address: Library, The Reynolds Building, St Dunstan's Road, London W6 8RP

Telephone: (0181) 846 7152

Fax: (0181) 846 7565

Enquiries: The Librarian and Information Services Manager, Mrs Susan V. Howard

Open: Mon–Thurs: 9.00–9.00 Fri: 9.00–8.00 Sat: 9.00–12.00

Access: Bona fide readers, preferably by appointment.

Historical background: Charing Cross Medical School was founded in 1822 and Westminster in 1834. The Charing Cross and Westminster schools were merged in 1984. Westminster Hospital records are at the Greater London Record Office (entry 550).

Acquisitions policy: Material of relevance to the history of Charing Cross Hospital and Westminster Medical School and related hospitals is accepted.

Archives of organisation: Charing Cross Hospital and Medical School records, including management minutes, 1823–, and registers of students, 1882–. Westminster School records, including registers

of students, 1893–, are with the Assistant Secretary (Chelsea and Wesminster).

Non-manuscript material: Photographs, albums, newspaper cuttings. The library includes a collection of articles and books relating to the hospital.

Finding aids: Interim lists.

Facilities: Photocopying. Photography.

511 Charity Commission for England and Wales

Address: St Alban's House, 57/60 Haymarket, London SW1Y 4QX

Telephone: (0171) 210 4533/4405 (Central Register of Charities) 210 4438 (access to records)

Enquiries: The Central Register

Open: Mon–Fri: 10.00–4.00, by appointment.

Access: The Central Register of Charities is open to the public; charity records over 30 years old are open to inspection on application.

Historical background: The Charity Commission was established on a permanent basis by the Charitable Trusts Act 1853, following the report of a Royal Commission set up in 1849. The commissioners were given full powers of investigation and inquiry, including that of scrutiny of annual accounts, powers of advice, control over the institution of legal proceedings on behalf of charitable trusts and control over dealings with the real estate of charitable trusts in England and Wales. In 1860 the commissioners were given important additional powers concurrent with those of the High Court to remove and appoint trustees; to vest property and to establish or to vary the purposes of a trust by means of a scheme, subject to appeal to the High Court. Their powers were confined to charity property which was permanent endowment or which the trustees wished to become subject to the commissioners' jurisdiction. The Charities Act 1960, which followed upon the Nathan Committee's Report of 1952, consolidated the existing law of charity and to some extent extended its scope. It set out the position and functions of the commissioners, extended their powers to all charities, established machinery to enable the needs of charities to be considered in relation to each other and to the statutory welfare services, provided for the registration of charities and widened the range of circumstances in which trust purposes could be revised. The London office covers national and overseas charities and those in England south of the River Severn to the Wash. (Contact the Liverpool Office, Graeme House, Derby Square, Liverpool L2 7SB, tel. (0151) 227 2191 ext. 22801 for Wales and the rest of England.) It is recognised as a place of deposit for public records.

Major collections: Records relating to 170,000 charities.

Finding aids: The central register has four main indexes: by name (nominal index); by object (classified index); by place (geographical index); and by diocese in respect of Church of England charities.

Facilities: Photocopying. Microfilm reader.

512 Chartered Institute of Bankers

Address: 10 Lombard Street, London EC3V 9AS

Telephone: (0171) 623 3531

Enquiries: The Librarian, Mr Jim Basker

Open: Mon–Fri: 9.00–5.00

Access: Anyone wishing to consult the institute's archives should apply to the librarian in writing.

The Institute of Bankers was founded in 1879 to provide the educational background for bankers at all stages of their careers. The organisation maintains a library, formed in 1879, and has a historical collection of paper money which is now housed in the British Museum. The archives include council minutes and there is a small collection of documents relating to the work of the institute in the field of banking education. See E. Green: *Debtors to their Profession: a History of the Institute of Bankers, 1879–1979* (Institute of Bankers, 1979).

513 Chartered Institute of Public Finance and Accountancy

Address: The Library, 3 Robert Street, London WC2N 6BH

Telephone: (0171) 895 8823 ext. 314

Enquiries: The Librarian/Information Officer, Chris Wilson

Open: Mon–Fri: 9.00–5.00

Access: Members and bona fide researchers, by prior appointment only. A daily research fee is charged.

The institute was founded in 1885 as the Corporate Treasurers' and Accountants' Institute. It was incorporated under the Companies Acts in 1901 as the Institute of Municipal Treasurers and Accountants (IMTA), and was granted a Royal Charter under that name in 1959. In 1973 the present name was adopted. A library was formally established in 1985 and this includes the institute's archives, including the institute journal, annual report and publications, 1885–; archives of associated bodies are also held, including Association of Health Service Treasurers and IMTA students' societies.

514 Chartered Insurance Institute

Address: The Library, 20 Aldermanbury, London EC2V 7HY

Telephone: (0171) 606 3835 ext. 3218

Open: Mon, Tues, Thurs: 9.00–5.00 Wed: 10.00–5.00 Fri: 9.00–4.45

Access: Members and bona fide researchers; a charge is usually made to use the library.

The Federation of Insurance Institutes of Great Britain and Ireland was established in 1897. Ten years later it was replaced by the Chartered Insurance Institute of Great Britain and Ireland, which in 1912 became the Chartered Insurance Institute. The institute holds its own archives, which are primarily for internal use only, and it does not actively acquire records. There are also substantial catalogued collections of insurance policies and other insurance ephemera, 17th–20th centuries, as well as a rare book collection. See *Sources of Insurance History: a*

Guide to Historical Material in the CII Library (London, 1990). The institute's Insurance History Committee actively promotes interest in insurance archives.

515 Chelsea Physic Garden

Parent organisation: Chelsea Physic Garden Company

Address: 66 Royal Hospital Road, London SW3 4HS

Telephone: (0171) 352 5646

Enquiries: The Curator

Open: Mon–Fri: 9.30–4.30
NB The garden is open on Wednesday and Sunday afternoons only, from mid-April to mid-October.

Access: Bona fide scholars, by appointment only.

Historical background: The Chelsea Physic Garden Company is a registered charity set up in 1983 to continue to administer the Chelsea Physic Garden, founded in 1673 by the Society of Apothecaries. In 1899 control of the Society of Apothecaries passed to the City Parochial Fund. Most of Chelsea Physic Garden's archives are housed at the Guildhall Library (entry **553**).

Acquisitions policy: To maintain its archives.

Archives of organisation: A few fragmentary records, including catalogues of seeds sown and accounts, 1785–1842.
Committee of management minutes, 1899–; attendance records, 1912–76.

Major collections: Alicia Amherst, Lady Rockley (1865–1941): MSS, including material on gardening history.

Non-manuscript material: Photographs of the garden, including collection of William Hales, curator, 1899–1937.
Publications, including guide books, seed lists etc, 1900–.
Herbarium collection.

Facilities: Photography by prior arrangement.

Publications: *Catalogue of the Library of the Chelsea Physic Garden* (1956) [includes MSS].

516 The Children's Society Archive

Address: Edward Rudolf House, Margery Street, London WC1X 0JL

Telephone: (0171) 837 4299

Fax: (0171) 837 0211

Enquiries: The Archivist, Mr Ian Wakeling

Open: Mon–Fri: 9.30–5.00

Access: Generally open to the public, by appointment. Restricted access to case records.

Historical background: The society was founded in 1881 by Prebendary Edward de Mountjoie Rudolf (1852–1933) as the child-care organisation of the Church of England. Known originally as the Church of England Society for Providing Homes for Waifs and Strays, it was renamed the Church of England Children's Society in 1946. The society adopted its present title in 1987. Until the 1970s it ran a large number of residential children's homes and specialised in the field of adoption, fostering and boarding-out. The 1970s saw a shift in practice that led to the development of community-based social work projects and preventative work with children, young people and their families. The earlier records are incomplete, some having been lost through bombing during the war.

Acquisitions policy: Records relating to the development of the society's child-care and fundraising practices and policies.

Archives of organisation: Annual reports, branch minute books, diet books, admission and discharge registers, correspondence *re* the administration of children's homes and projects, and general promotional material, including leaflets and posters.
Society journals: *Our Waifs and Strays* (1882–1953), *Gateway* (1953–93) and *Brothers and Sisters* (1891–1971).

Major collections: Children's case files, 1882–1925 (30,000).
Papers of the Churches Association for Family Welfare, 1924–90.

Non-manuscript material: Photograph collection of prints and negatives, 19th century– (10,000).

Finding aids: A provisional catalogue for the records of the society's homes is available. The majority of the earlier photographs have catalogue lists and an index. Index entries to homes and projects in the publications *Our Waifs and Strays* and *Gateway*.

517 Church Missionary Society

Address: 157 Waterloo Road, London SE1 8UU

Telephone: (0171) 928 8681

Fax: (0171) 401 3215

Enquiries: The Archivist, Ken Osborne

Open: Mon–Fri: 9.30–4.00

Access: 40–year closure period for official archives; closure for unofficial deposited material varies according to the request of the depositor. Material available for research is being transferred gradually, on deposit, to the University of Birmingham Library (entry 101), but enquiries about the CMS are answered by the archivist in London.

Historical background: The Church Missionary Society was founded in 1799. Its missionary activity is worldwide. The society amalgamated with the Church of England Zenana Missionary Society (CEZMS) in 1957.

Acquisitions policy: Confined to records of former missionaries and staff and material relating specifically to CMS and CEZMS institutions.

Archives of organisation: CMS archives, 1799–. Church of England Zenana Missionary Society archives, 1880–1957.

Major collections: Female Education Society archives, 1834–99.
Loochoo Naval Mission archives, 1842–57.
Eclectic Society of London notes, 1798–1814.
Venn MSS, 1679–1955.

Non-manuscript material: Photographs of missionaries and CMS institutions.

Finding aids: Catalogues and/or detailed lists of records of all CMS departments. Calendars of pre-1820 CMS mission series. Brief catalogues for Loochoo Mission and Female Education Society. Catalogues of *c*200 of the accessions of deposited unofficial material. Card indexes of names, places and subjects. Card index to some photographs.

Publications: Catalogues of East Asia (Group 1) Missions, 1821–1934, i: *Canada*; ii: *China*: iii: *Japan*.
Catalogues of West Asia (Group 2) Missions,
1811–1934, i: *Ceylon*; ii: *North India*; iii: *South India*; iv: *Western India*; v: *Mauritius and Madagascar*; vi: *Persia and Turkish Arabia*.
Catalogues of Africa (Group 3) Missions, 1804–1934, i: *West Africa (Sierra Leone)*; ii: *Nigeria*; iii: *South and East Africa (South Africa, Kenya and Tanzania)*; iv: *East Africa (Nyanza, Uganda and Ruanda/Burundi)*; v: *Egypt and Sudanese Missions*; vi: *Mediterranean and Palestine*; vii: *New Zealand*; viii: *West Indies* .
Summary of archive holding in R. Keen: *Survey of Archives of Selected Missionary Societies*, NRA Report (1968).

518 The Church of England Record Centre

Address: 15 Galleywall Road, Bermondsey, London SE16 3PB

Telephone: (0171) 222 7010 ext. 4155 (general enquiries)

Fax: (0171) 231 5243

Enquiries: The Archivist, Dr B.L. Hough, The National Society Archivist, Ms S. Duffield

Open: Mon–Fri: 10.00–5.00

Access: Bona fide researchers, by appointment. Records are open to the public, except for 100–year closure on personal files and 30–year closure on certain administrative files. Access to the archives of the ecumenical bodies is at the discretion of the organisation concerned.

Historical background: The record centre came into operation in 1989, and incorporates the former archives of the Church Commissioners, the General Synod, and the National Society for Promoting Religious Education, with a few smaller collections, including the records of the former British Council of Churches. The centre also assists the voluntary organisations of the Church of England on request, and acts as a clearing-house for information on all Anglican records.

Acquisitions policy: Generally restricted to the records of the parent organisations, but the papers of voluntary bodies are occasionally housed as an emergency measure, and there are papers of leading churchmen (normally having connections with one or more of the parent bodies). Only central Anglican records are accepted; parish and diocesan records are cared for by the Diocesan Record Office (normally the County Record Office).

Major collections: Church Commissioners: archives, including those of predecessor bodies, Queen Anne's Bounty, 1704–1948, the Church Building Commissioners, 1818–56, and the Ecclesiastical Commissioners, 1836–1948; the bulk relates to the estates which were inherited from the bishops and deans and chapters in the 19th century, and the involvement of the Church Commissioners and their predecessors in a great variety of specific church matters as a result of various Acts and Measures.
General Synod: departmental material, mainly 20th century, but inherited papers include those of the Church of England Purity Society, 1887–; the Church Defence Institution, 1859–; the Church Reform League, 1895–, and the Colonial/Overseas Bishoprics Fund (f. 1841).
Personal papers include those of Dr Francis Eeles (1876–1954), former secretary of the Central Council for the Care of Churches, a leading liturgical scholar and an authority on women's ministry; and certain correspondence of Lord Hugh Cecil, Lord Quickswood (1869–1956), primarily on church affairs of the 1920s and 1930s.
National Society: minute books and annual reports, 1811–; School and Teaching Training College, correspondence, c1816–.
Records of Church of England Sunday School Institute, 1843–1936, and St Christopher's College, Blackheath, 1908–1960s.
Records of Church of England schools in the diocese of London and Southwark.

Non-manuscript material: The reference library includes sets of published Church Assembly/General Synod debates and papers; *Church of England Yearbook*, 1883–; *Crockford/Clergy List; and Chronicles of the Convocation of Canterbury.*
Small photographic archive.
The National Society has an important library relating to the history of education.

Finding aids: Listing and indexing in progress. Lists sent to NRA.

Facilities: Photocopying. Limited photography. Microfilm/fiche reader/printer.

Conservation: Very limited in-house facilities.

Publications: A. Savidge: *The Foundation and Early Days of Queen Anne's Bounty* (1955).
M.H. Port: *Six Hundred New Churches* (1961) [history of the Church Building Commissioners].
G.F.A. Best: *Temporal Pillars* (1964) [history of

Queen Anne's Bounty and the Ecclesiastical Commissioners].
A. Savidge: *The Parsonages in England* (1964).
C.J. Kitching: *The Central Records of the Church of England: a Report and Survey presented to the Pilgrim and Radcliffe Trustees* (London, 1976).
Series of leaflets on main classes of records.

519 City of London Club

Address: 19 Old Broad Street, London EC2N 1DS

Telephone: (0171) 588 7991

Fax: (0171) 374 2020

Enquiries: The Club Secretary, Mr Glenn Jones

Open: Mon–Fri: 8.00–5.00

Access: Non-members of the club must write to the general committee via the Club Secretary for access.

Historical background: The City of London Club was founded in 1832 by a group of prominent bankers, merchants and shipowners, who formed a committee under the chairmanship of Mr John Masterman MP.

Archives of organisation: Minutes of committee meetings (c30 vols); membership lists; menus; album of photographs of original members of the club; miscellaneous documents, 1832–.
Original plans drawn by Philip Hardwick, the architect of the club (52).

Facilities: Photocopying.

520 City University Library

Address: Northampton Square, London EC1V 0HB

Telephone: (0171) 477 8000

Fax: (0171) 490 4419

Enquiries: The Sub-Librarian

Open: Term: Mon–Thurs: 9.00–9.00 Fri: 9.00–8.00 Vacation: Mon–Fri: 9.00–5.00

Access: Bona fide researchers.

Founded in 1894 as the Northampton Institute and renamed the City University in 1966, the university does not have an active policy relating to its archives. Surviving material, including some council minutes, is held with special collections in the library. In addition the library has marked files with contributors' names of *The Athenaeum*, a forerunner of the *New Statesman*, late 19th–early 20th centuries, and papers of Sir Robert Birley (1903–82), educationist and Professor of Social Sciences and Education in the university. There is a published history by J. Teague: *The City University History* (London, 1980).

521 The Clothworkers' Company

Address: Clothworkers' Hall, Dunster Court, Mincing Lane, London EC3R 7AH

Telephone: (0171) 623 7041

Fax: (0171) 283 1289

Enquiries: The Archivist, Mr D.E. Wickham

Open: Mon–Fri: 9.30–4.30

Access: After acceptance of details of purpose and requirements of study, and by appointment only. Suitable written reference required in advance. Problems of supervision and accommodation mean that random enquiries are not encouraged.

Historical background: The company was incorporated by Royal Charter in 1528 and its records are practically complete to date. The company's involvement with clothworking (i.e. cloth finishing) was always limited to London, and the records are not normally of use for any aspect of the cloth trade of Kent, East Anglia or the Cotswolds.

Acquisitions policy: Restricted to records relating directly to the company, its prominent members, its history, and its post-industrial revolution status as a charitable organisation. To a large extent these items are self-generating.

Archives of organisation: All aspects of the history and modern work of this City of London livery company and its associated charitable foundation, 1528–.

Finding aids: Some lists and indexes.

Publications: T. Girtin: *The Golden Ram: a Narrative History of the Clothworkers' Company, 1528–1958* (1958).

D.E. Wickham: *Clothworker's Hall in the City of London* (1989).

522 The College of Arms

Address: Queen Victoria Street, London EC4V 4BT

Telephone: (0171) 248 2762

Fax: (0171) 248 6448

Enquiries: The Officer in Waiting (heraldic and genealogical matters) or The Archivist, Mr R.C. Yorke (academic matters)

Open: Mon–Fri: 10.00–4.00

Access: Through an officer of arms or the archivist; prior contact by academic enquirers recommended. A fee may be charged.

Historical background: The English heralds were made a body corporate in 1484. The College of Arms has been on its present site since 1555, being rebuilt after the Great Fire of 1666. The archives comprise both the official records of the college and the collections of many individual heralds, who have included well-known antiquaries. There is medieval material dating from well before 1484.

Acquisitions policy: The archives are augmented by the generation of records within the college, and by the acquisition of collections from heralds. Relevant material may be purchased from, or given by, outside sources.

Archives of organisation: Official records: these include visitations; grants of arms; enrolments of royal warrants, pedigrees etc; royal and other ceremonials; records of Garter King of Arms; records of the Court of Chivalry; and the administrative records of the college. Semi-official and unofficial records include rolls of arms, armorials, pedigrees, painters' work-books, and papers relating to orders of chivalry.

Major collections: Arundel MSS; Combwell Priory and other charters; miscellaneous family and estate papers. Some 50 collections of individual heralds and others.

Non-manuscript material: Bookplate and seal collections.

Finding aids: Various lists and indexes. L.M. Midgley: *Report on Miscellaneous Deeds, including Charters relating to Combwell*

Priory in the Collections of the College Arms (1980) [typescript].

Facilities: Photocopying. Photography and microfilming by arrangement. All reproduction is subject to permission; official records may not be copied.

Publications: W.H. Black: *Catalogue of the Arundel Manuscripts in the College of Arms* (1829).
A.R. Wagner: *The Records and Collections of the College of Arms* (1952).
F. Jones: *Catalogue of Welsh Manuscripts in the College of Arms.*
L. Campbell and F. Steer (comps): *A Catalogue of Manuscripts in the College of Arms: Collections*, i (1988).

523 Commonwealth Institute
Commonwealth Resource Centre

Address: Kensington High Street, London W8 6NQ

Telephone: (0171) 603 4535 ext. 210

Fax: (0171) 602 7374

Enquiries: The Librarian, Head of Information

Open: Tues–Fri: 11.00–4.30 Sat: 1.00–5.00, by appointment only
Closed August.

Access: Serious users over the age of 18.

Historical background: The present library and resource centre dates from 1962, when the new institute building was opened in Kensington High Street. Before that, as the Imperial Institute at a site in South Kensington, there had existed a library, most of which was dispersed at the time of removal. It is believed that some archival materials, dealing with life in the colonial possessions, and particularly a large collection of photographic slides, were destroyed before removal to the new premises. The library in the new building was originally intended for use by teachers and collected materials mainly concerning contemporary life in Commonwealth countries. The library was opened to the general public from c1972, and has gradually broadened its acquisitions policy to include historical and archival materials, though the holdings of these are still extremely modest. In 1977 most of the archives of the Imperial Institute, up to 1958, were deposited at the

Public Record Office (entry **960**), though there is still a small collection which has accumulated from donations or office turnouts since that date.

Acquisitions policy: There is no positive acquisitions policy, and no funding is available to acquire archival material relating to the Commonwealth from external sources. Donations of materials which seem likely to explain and put into historical context the present state of Commonwealth countries excluding Britain are accepted.

Major collections: Garfield Todd (Zimbabwe) Archive: letters from Mrs G. Todd and her husband, ex-Prime Minister of Rhodesia, explaining conditions under detention, confinement and imprisonment during the period of Unilateral Declaration of Independence, c1965–.
Harold Ingrams Archive: miscellaneous papers, articles and MS books covering his career as colonial administrator, journalist and writer, c1900–1970s.

Non-manuscript material: Small collection of exploration literature, 19th century.
Some exhibition catalogues, 19th–early 20th centuries.
Recordings of music on disc, cassette and reel-to-reel tape; much is traditional and ethnic, though modern music, popular and composed, is also collected. Because of the wide spread of Commonwealth countries, music from most of the main cultural and ethnic areas of the world is represented.
Special collection of Commonwealth literature (in English), consisting of published creative writing and critical responses from most Commonwealth countries.
Newscuttings and articles on writers; recordings of readings, dramatic productions and interviews.

Finding aids: Lists of some collections, including literature, recordings and audio-visual materials [list available on application].

Facilities: Photocopying. Photography. Microfilm/fiche reader. Range of audio-visual hardware.

524 Corporation of London Records Office

Address: PO Box 270, Guildhall, London EC2P 2EJ

Telephone: (0171) 606 3030 ext. 1251, 332 1251 (direct line)

Fax: (0171) 332 1119

Enquiries: The City Archivist, Mr J.R. Sewell

Open: Mon–Fri: 9.30–4.45
Appointment necessary to see rate books.

Historical background: The office is the official record office for the archives of the Corporation of the City of London. It is recognised as a place of deposit for public records.

Archives of organisation: Official archives of the Corporation, 11th–20th centuries, including records of admissions to the freedom of the City, 1681–1940; at many periods the principal classes include much of national interest.
Other classes of records reflect special responsibilities or associations of the corporation and jurisdiction and property interests outside the city boundaries; these records include:
Bridge House Estates, deeds, rentals, accounts, minute books etc, relating to maintenance of London Bridge and, later, other bridges within the city, 11th century–.
Royal Contract Estates, records of estates in many counties granted by the Crown in 1628 for sale to settle crown debts, 17th century.
Brokers' admission records, 1691–1886.
Southwark: coroners' records, 1788–1932; sessions of the peace records, 1667–1870; manorial records, 1539–1959.
Finsbury: manorial records, 1550–1867; property records, 1567–1867.
City of London Lunatic Asylum (later known as City of London Mental Hospital and Stone House Hospital) records, 1859–1948.
Guildhall School of Music and Drama records, 1878–1989.
Emanuel Hospital, Westminster, and Brandesburton Estate, Yorkshire, records, early 17th–20th centuries.
Thames Conservancy records, 17th–19th centuries.
Lieutenancy of the City of London, commissions, lists and minutes, 17th–19th centuries.
Irish Society records of the plantation of Ulster and management of estates there, 17th–20th centuries.

Facilities: Photocopying. Photography by arrangement. Microfilm/fiche readers.

Conservation: In-house.

Publications: P.E. Jones and R. Smith: *Guide to the Records at Guildhall London*, pt I: *The Corporation of London Records Office* (1951).
H. Deadman and E. Scudder: *An Introductory Guide to the Corporation of London Records Office* (1994).
Many calendars of medieval and later records [list available].

525 Council for the Care of Churches

Parent organisation: General Synod of the Church of England

Address: 83 London Wall, London EC2M 5NA

Telephone: (0171) 638 0971

Fax: (0171) 638 0184

Enquiries: The Librarian, Miss Janet Seeley

Open: Mon–Fri: 9.30–5.00

Access: Generally open to the public, by appointment only.

Historical background: The council was established in 1921 as the central co-ordinating body for the Diocesan Advisory Committees for the Care of Churches. The library and National Survey of Churches were developed from the outset. The council supplies photographic and documentary information on the work of contemporary artists and craftsmen who are interested in ecclesiastical commissions.

Acquisitions policy: To strengthen the National Survey of Churches, by donation and purchase; to acquire special collections through bequests and gifts; to augment records of contemporary craftsmanship and conservation, by donation from practitioners.

Archives of organisation: National Survey of Churches files, many including photographs and guide books, on most of the 17,000 churches and chapels of the Church of England; the collection is particularly rich in postcards and photographs, c1900–50.

Major collections: Canon B.F.L. Clarke Collection of MS notes, covering c11,000 Anglican

churches, with details of 18th– and 19th–century restorations; also photographs.
Canon P.B.G. Binnall's card index and MS notes on 19th–century stained glass.
Gordon Barnes Collection of MS notes and photographs, with emphasis on Victorian church architecture, especially in London and Worcestershire.

Non-manuscript material: Canon B.F.L. Clarke Collection of postcards (*c*20,000).
Printed items on ecclesiastical art and architecture, with special reference to Anglican churches and their furnishings (*c*12,000).

Finding aids: Card catalogue.

Facilities: Photocopying.

Publications: Information sheet [available from the librarian].

526 Courtauld Institute of Art

Parent organisation: University of London

Address: Somerset House, The Strand, London WC2R 0RN

Telephone: (0171) 873 2701

Fax: (0171) 873 2772

Enquiries: The Librarian, Mr P.M. Doran

Open: Term: Mon–Fri: 9.30–7.00

Access: Normally restricted to university staff and students, on the basis of satisfactory identification. Enquiries about archive material should be made well in advance of a visit.

Historical background: The institute was founded in 1931; it moved to Somerset House in 1989. The library (called the Book Library) was started in 1933.

Acquisitions policy: No proactive acquisitions policy, but material offered is accepted if considered appropriate.

Major collections: Papers of Lord Lee of Fareham (1868–1947).
Correspondence of Philip Webb (1831–1915), architect.

Finding aids: Individual check-lists.

Facilities: Photocopying. Photography.

527 The Dickens' House Museum

Address: 48 Doughty Street, London WC1N 2LF

Telephone: (0171) 405 2127

Fax: (0171) 831 5175

Enquiries: The Curator, Dr David Parker

Open: Mon–Fri: 9.00–5.00
NB Opening times are not identical to those of the museum.

Access: The museum is required to make its collections available for study to any Dickens lover who may be deemed responsible; appointments are necessary.

Historical background: The Dickens' House Museum was founded by the Dickens' Fellowship in 1925. The fellowship acquired the house, where Dickens had lived, put together the basis of a collection, and set up an independent trust to run the museum. Working in close co-operation with the fellowship since that date, the house has gradually built up a major collection of memorabilia, pictures, books, ephemera and MSS (not Dickens' papers as such, since in 1858 Dickens himself burnt all the letters he had received).

Acquisitions policy: Dickensiana: MSS and objects which concern the life, works, circle and times of Charles Dickens (1812–70), especially during the period he lived at Doughty Street.

Archives of organisation: Records relating to the museum and the Dickens Fellowship.

Major collections: Collections assembled by Dickens scholars and admirers, including the following: B.W. Matz (1865–1925); F.G. Kitton (1856–1903); Thomas Wright (1859–1936); Comte Alain de Suzannet (1882–1950), these include letters and scrapbooks; Sir Felix Aylmer (1889–1979), concerning his acting studies of Dickens; W.J. Carlton (1886–1973); Leslie Staples (1896–1980); Gladys Storey (1892–1978); Noel O. Peyrouten (1924–68); and the National Dickens Library. In addition there are various collections built up piecemeal by the museum.

Non-manuscript material: Memorabilia, pictures, photographs, books (including Dickens first editions in volume form and parts), scrapbooks.
Copies of *The Dickensian*, 1902– [journal published by the Dickens' Fellowship].

Finding aids: A new catalogue currently in preparation; details will be sent to the NRA.

Facilities: Photocopying. Photography by arrangement.

Conservation: Contracted out.

Publications: Useful articles in *The Dickensian. Museum Guide.*

528 Dr Williams's Library

Address: 14 Gordon Square, London WC1H 0AG

Telephone: (0171) 387 3727

Fax: (0171) 388 1142

Enquiries: The Librarian, Mr John Creasey

Open: Mon, Wed, Fri: 10.00–5.00 Tues, Thurs: 10.00–6.30
Closed 24 December–2 January; Thursday before to Tuesday after Easter Day; first fortnight of August (exact dates printed in *Annual Bulletin*).

Access: Open to persons duly introduced and guaranteed in accordance with the regulations made by the trustees. Regulations, membership forms etc may be had on personal application or by post from the Librarian.

Historical background: The library forms part of the charitable trust established under the will of Daniel Williams DD (*d* 1716), a Presbyterian minister; its nucleus was the founder's personal library, principally of divinity. To this collection of printed books, MSS, for the most part relating to English non-conformity, began to be added by purchase, gift or deposit very soon after the library opened in 1729/30. The library also administers the Congregational Library (f. 1831).

Acquisitions policy: Very little is added by purchase. Such MSS as are acquired are given or, in some cases, deposited. Very little is added that is not related to English non-conformity or to material already held.

Major collections: Minutes of the Westminster Assembly, 1643–52, and the Fourth London Classis, 1646–59; John Evans List of Dissenting Congregations, 1715–29, and similar lists of *c*1770 by Josiah Thompson; correspondence of Joseph Priestley, Theophilus Lindsey and oth-

ers associated with them; correspondence and other papers of Richard Baxter (1615–91); collections made by Roger Morrice, including the late 16th–century *Second Parte of a Register* and Morrice's political diary covering the years 1677–91; the collections for the history of dissenting churches made by Walter Wilson (1781–1847); the miscellaneous and largely personal collections of John Jones (1700–70), which includes a MS of George Herbert's poems, English and Latin; the diary, reminiscences and letters of Henry Crabb Robinson (1775–1867); items by William Law and others in the collection of books and MSS deposited by Christopher Walton (1809–77); the MSS from New College, London, including much correspondence and papers of Philip Doddridge (1702–51).
The Congregational Library collection includes correspondence of Isaac Watts (1674–1748), as well as letters and sermons of prominent nonconformists.

Non-manuscript material: The MSS are really an adjunct to the printed books (133,000 vols), which are pre-eminent for the study of English Protestant non-conformity.

Finding aids: Handlists of MSS and partial name index.

Facilities: Microfilm reader. Some items suitable for photocopying on premises.

Publications: The Baxter Treatises: a Catalogue of the Richard Baxter Papers (other than the Letters) in Dr Williams's Library (1959).
I. Elliott: *Supplement* to index in Edith Morley: *Henry Crabb Robinson on Books and their Writers* (1960).
J. Creasey: *Index to the John Evans List of Dissenting Congregations and Ministers, 1715–1729, in Dr Williams's Library* (1964).
K. Twinn: *Guide to the Manuscripts in Dr Williams's Library* (1969).
Nonconformist Congregations in Great Britain: a List of Histories and other Material in Dr Williams's Library (1974).
Thomas Jollie's papers: a List of the Papers in Dr Williams's Library, Manuscript no. 12.78.

529 Drapers' Company

Address: Drapers' Hall, Throgmorton Avenue, London EC2N 2DQ

Telephone: (0171) 588 5001

Fax: (0171) 628 1988

Enquiries: The Archivist, Miss P.A. Fussell

Open: Mon–Fri: 10.00–4.30

Access: Generally open to the public, by prior appointment only.

Historical background: The company evolved from a religious fraternity and trading association of cloth merchants in the city of London, and was granted a Royal Charter in 1364. The hall has occupied its present site since 1543, although it has since been damaged by fire; the facade and interior of the present hall date mainly from 1860. The company is principally concerned with supporting charities, especially in education, medicine and the arts, and the relief of need.

Acquisitions policy: To maintain its archives.

Archives of organisation: Land and other documents, 1180–; accounts, 1415–; meetings, 1515–; grants of arms, including earliest surviving English grant, 1439–; charters, 1364–; charity trust deeds and documents, 1408–.

Finding aids: Catalogues and lists; sent to the NRA.

Facilities: Photocopying and photography only by express permission of the Master and Wardens.

Publications: A.H. Johnson: *History of the Worshipful Company of Drapers of London* (1914) [5 vols].
T. Girtin: *The Triple Crowns: a Narrative History of the Drapers' Company, 1364–1964* (1964).
P. Hunting: *A History of the Drapers' Company* (1989).

530 Duchy of Cornwall Office

Address: 10 Buckingham Gate, London SW1E 6LA

Telephone: (0171) 834 7346

Fax: (0171) 931 9541

Enquiries: The Archivist and Records Manager, Miss E.A. Stuart

Open: Wed: 2.00–5.00

Access: On written application. In order to protect the privacy of lessees, material less than 100 years old is available for inspection only with the specific permission of the Secretary.

Historical background: The Duchy of Cornwall was created by Edward III in 1337 to provide an income for his eldest son, Edward (often called the Black Prince). As such, it is a major landed estate whose holdings are concentrated largely, though not exclusively, in the West Country. Apart from the Interregnum, the Duchy has existed continuously since the fourteenth century and continues to maintain the heir to the throne.

Acquisitions policy: Material relating to the Duchy, mainly from within the organisation.

Archives of organisation: Mainly records of a landed estate with some significant additions:
Extensive series of medieval account rolls of the receivers, ministers and court officials of the Duchy.
Household receipts and vouchers for Frederick and subsequently Augusta, Prince and Princess of Wales respectively, 1728–72.
Estate correspondence, 19th–early 20th centuries.

Non-manuscript material: Duchy photograph collection. Prints and engravings, including 18th-century Vauxhall Gardens prints.

Finding aids: Cataloguing is in progress.

Facilities: Photocopying. Photography by arrangement. Record Agency service available.

Publications: R.L. Clowes: 'On the Historical Documents in the Duchy of Cornwall Office', *Royal Cornwall Polytechnic Society Annual Report* (1930).

531 Dulwich College
The Wodehouse Library

Parent organisation: Alleyn's College of God's Gift

Address: College Road, London SE21 7LD

Telephone: (0181) 693 3601

Fax: (0181) 693 6319

Enquiries: Dr J.R. Piggott or Mr A.C.L. Hall

Open: Term only, by prior arrangement.

Access: Bona fide researchers, by appointment.

Historical background: Founded in 1619 by Edward Alleyn (1566–1626), the college is administered by a board of governors. In the mid-19th century it was refounded as a public school. The archives of the original library were rehoused in air-conditioned units in 1981.

Archives of organisation: Alleyn's personal papers and those of Philip Henslowe (c1555–1616), his wife's step-father.
Records of the college, 1619–.
Deeds of the Manor of Dulwich, 14th century–.

Major collections: P.G Wodehouse (1881–1975) collections, including assorted MSS and his voluminous correspondence with William Townend.
Music MSS collection, early 18th century.

Non-manuscript material: Architectural drawings for college buildings by Charles Barry (1823–1900).
Sir Ernest Shackleton: original photographs of *The Endurance* expedition.
Alleyn's library and subsequent gifts.

Finding aids: Computerised catalogues in preparation.

Facilities: Photocopying. Photography and microfiche by arrangement.

Publications: G. Warner: *Catalogues of the Manuscripts and Muniments* (1881; 2nd series, 1903).

532 Egypt Exploration Society

Address: 3 Doughty Mews, London WC1N 2PG

Telephone: (0171) 242 1880

Fax: (0171) 404 6118

Enquiries: The Secretary, Dr Patricia Spencer

Open: Mon–Fri: 10.30–4.30, by appointment only .

Access: Bona fide researchers approved by the society's committee.

Historical background: The Egypt Exploration Society was founded (as the Egypt Exploration Fund) in 1882 by Amelia Edwards, Sir Erasmus Wilson and scholars from the British Museum to study the culture of ancient Egypt and promote excavation and survey work in the Nile Valley. The society's excavation costs are mostly covered by an annual grant from the British Academy, with donations from museums and individuals; it also maintains an Egyptological library for the use of members. The Graeco-Roman branch of the society was established in 1897 for the discovery and publication of Greek or Latin documents from Egypt.

Archives of organisation: The society's archive consists mainly of the records of excavations, as well as note-books, correspondence, photographs and negatives, 1882–.

Finding aids: Handlist of early correspondence. Lists for most of the photographic record.

Facilities: Photocopying. Photography by arrangement.

Publications: Journal of Egyptian Archaeology. Results of fieldwork are incorporated in more than 170 publications.

533 Electoral Reform Society of Great Britain and Ireland

Address: 6 Chancel Street, London SE1 0UU

Telephone: (0171) 928 1622

Fax: (0171) 928 4366

Enquiries: The Secretary or Information Officer

Open: Mon–Fri: 9.30–5.30, by arrangement.

Access: Bona fide researchers, by appointment.

Historical background: Founded in 1884 as the Proportional Representation Society, it changed its name in 1959 but holds the same aims. The library, the Arthur McDougall Library for Electoral Studies, is administered by trustees of the Arthur McDougall Fund, which is a registered charity.

Acquisitions policy: Maintains own archives and accepts material relating to elections and electoral methods. An active policy of acquiring papers, books and journals on all aspects relating to democracy and elections in the newly emerging democracies in Eastern Europe.

Archives of organisation: Records of the society, including minute books and early publications.

Major collections: Papers of individuals associated with reform and parliamentary change, including Lord Courtenay of Penwith, Sir John Lubbock (Lord Avebury), A.R. Droop and Dr J.F.S. Ross.

Non-manuscript material: Publications from various electoral reform groups in the UK, Ireland and abroad *c*1880s.

Large collection of dated and sourced newspaper cuttings about electoral politics, 1905– (also on microfilm).

Parliamentary papers about reform from Commonwealth and European countries.

Finding aids: Database catalogue.

Facilities: Photocopying.

Publications: The Best System (London, 1984) [centenary history].

E. Lakeman: *Twelve Democracies: Electoral Systems in the European Community* (1991).

Representation: Journal of Electoral Record and Comment [published quarterly by the Arthur McDougall Fund].

534 English Heritage

Address: 23 Savile Row, London W1X 1AB

Telephone: (0171) 973 3000 (Record Office) 973 3533 (Historic Properties Group) 973 3731 (London Sites and Monuments Record)

Fax: (0171) 973 3001

Enquiries: Record Office: Bronwen Knox Historic Properties Group: Kathy McCracken London Sites and Monuments Record: Ian Morrisson

Open: By arrangement.

Access: Generally open to the public, by prior appointment only.

Historical background: The Historic Buildings and Monuments Commission, the predecessor of English Heritage, was set up in 1984 to be responsible for securing the preservation of England's architectural and archaeological heritage and for the management of more than 350 monuments and buildings formerly under the Secretary of State for the Environment (DoE). In 1986 it took over the conservation work carried out by the GLC Historical Buildings Division. The public repository for records of historic monuments is the National Monuments Record (entry 645) and enquiries should normally be directed to them in the first instance. English Heritage's record holdings relate to its own statutory and management responsibilities and are working papers rather than archives.

Acquisitions policy: To maintain the archives of the commission.

Archives of organisation: Record Office: records related to scheduled ancient monuments, listed historic buildings and gardens.

Historic Properties Group: the Historic Plans Room is the official repository for English Heritage and the DoE/Property Services Agency permanent record drawings, survey notes, photographs of work in progress, glass negatives, deeds and deed plans.

London Division: London Sites and Monuments Record, London blue plaques files, survey drawings associated with the Survey of London volumes, some research reports prepared in connection with public enquiries and proposals to change the character of listed buildings. (Survey drawings were sent to the archives division of the Royal Commission of Historical Monuments of England in April 1995, but English Heritage has kept copies.) Files on buildings recommended for listings.

The Photographic Unit, Fortress House, provides new photography for internal use for works and presentation purposes.

Publications: Annual reports; Conservation Bulletin; list of publications available.

535 English National Ballet Archives

Address: Markova House, 39 Jay Mews, London SW7 2ES

Telephone: (0171) 581 1245

Fax: (0171) 225 0827

Enquiries: The Archivist, Ms Jane Pritchard

Open: By appointment only.

Access: Bona fide research students, on written application.

Historical background: The archive was established in 1975 to maintain the records of English National Ballet (formerly known as London Festival Ballet), which was founded by Julian Braunsweg, Anton Dolin and Alicia Markova in 1950.

Acquisitions policy: Primary and secondary material relating to the history of London Festival Ballet. Also material relating to the history of ballets in the company's repertoire and to the careers of artists who have worked with the company. The emphasis is on 20th–

century ballet. Material is acquired by donation, purchase and deposit.

Archives of organisation: Principally records of the English National Ballet Company.

Non-manuscript material: Photographic collection.
Video library, including tapes of productions and classes; some films.
Audio recordings.
Designs for Festival Ballet productions.

536 English National Opera Archive

Address: 185 Broadhurst Gardens, London NW6 3AX

Telephone: (0171) 624 7711

Enquiries: The Archivist, Ms C. Colvin

Open: By arrangement.

Access: Bona fide researchers, by appointment only.

Historical background: Sadler's Wells Opera moved to the London Coliseum in 1968 and changed its name to English National Opera (ENO) in 1974. ENO purchased the London Coliseum in 1992.

Acquisitions policy: To acquire material relevant to ENO, Sadler's Wells Opera and the Coliseum.

Archives of organisation: Administrative records of Sadler's Wells Opera and ENO, 1931–.

Major collections: Material on the Coliseum, 1904–.

Non-manuscript material: Photographs of productions; press cuttings; posters, audio and video tapes.

Finding aids: Lists and indexes.

Facilities: Photocopying. Photography. Tape copying.

537 The Evangelical Library

Address: 78A Chiltern Street, London W1M 2HB

Telephone: (0171) 935 6997

Enquiries: The Librarian

Open: Mon–Sat: 10.00–5.00

Access: Bona fide scholars may use the archives by arrangement. They are also open to members who pay an annual donation.

Historical background: The library was begun in about 1924 as the personal collection of Geoffrey Williams (1886–1975), whose aim was to build up a worldwide evangelical library. Towards the end of World War II the library was moved from Surrey into central London, largely due to the influence of the preacher Dr D. Martyn Lloyd-Jones (1899–1981). In addition to the stock at headquarters there are holdings in over 100 branches throughout the world.

Major collections: MSS and letters of eminent non-conformists, including sermon notes of Matthew Henry (1662–1714), commentator and non-conformist minister; letters received by George Whitefield (1714–70), leader of Calvinistic Methodists.

Non-manuscript material: Large collection of small portraits of evangelicals. Wilberforce and McGhee collections of, pamphlets of the National Club, 19th century.
Puritan and Robinson collections of works by Evangelicals of the 17th and 18th centuries.

Facilities: Photocopying.

Publications: Bulletin [biannual].
Numerous printed catalogues for sale.

538 The Fawcett Library

Parent organisation: London Guildhall University

Address: Calcutta House, Old Castle Street, London E1 7NT

Telephone: (0171) 247 5826 (direct line) 320 1189

Fax: (0171) 320 1177

Enquiries: The Fawcett Development Librarian

Open: Term: Mon: 11.00–8.30 Wed–Fri: 10.00–5.00 Vacation: Mon–Fri: 10.00–5.00, preferably by appointment

Access: By subscription. Charges payable for a day visit, or at different rates per annum for individuals, full-time students and the unwaged.

Historical background: The library began as the Women's Service Library, which was the library of the London and National Society for Women's Service (now the Fawcett Society), the direct descendant of the London Society for Women's Suffrage, founded in 1867. The society was at the centre of the non-militant campaign for women's suffrage under the leadership of Millicent Garrett Fawcett, and accumulated a certain amount of material from the campaign and related issues. In the 1920s the society decided to organise this material for the use of members and in 1926 the first librarian was appointed. Over the years the library acquired a number of other smaller collections, including the Cavendish-Bentinck and Edward Wright libraries (originally suffrage collections with a high proportion of old and rare books), the Crosby Hall Collection, the Sadd Brown Library (on women in the Commonwealth) and the library of the Josephine Butler Society (formerly the Association for Moral and Social Hygiene). Gradually the Fawcett Library became a major national research resource. In 1977, as the society could no longer support the library, it was transferred to the City of London Polytechnic, which became the London Guildhall University in 1993.

Acquisitions policy: Papers relating to women's organisations and prominent women are actively collected, mainly by gift.

Major collections: Archive material, mainly 19th and 20th centuries, including records of societies concerned with suffrage, especially the archive of the Fawcett Society; equal status; emigration; business and professional bodies, including trade unions; repeal of the Contagious Diseases Acts and other moral issues, including papers of feminists involved in the controversy of 1863–6; and records of the Association for Moral and Social Hygiene and the National Vigilance Association.
Papers of individuals, including Millicent Garrett Fawcett (1847–1929) and Dr Elizabeth Garrett Anderson (1836–1917).
40 folders of correspondence of Josephine Butler (1828–1906).
80 folders of miscellaneous letters and autograph letters.
c200ft of archives awaiting listing.

Non-manuscript material: Photographs, many of individual women involved in suffrage movements; posters relating to suffrage campaign; newspaper cuttings on all aspects of women.
Special collections include: Josephine Butler Library (previously library of the Association for Moral and Social Hygiene); Cavendish-Bentinck Collection (mainly rare and antiquarian works); Sadd Brown Collection, devoted to the role of women in the Commonwealth.

Finding aids: Typed list to major collections. NRA 8556, 10648, 20625, 21465.

Facilities: Photocopying. Microfiche reader.

Publications: M. Barrow: *Women, 1870–1918: a Select Guide to Printed and Archival Sources in the United Kingdom* (1981), 192–215.
J. Uglow: 'The Fawcett Library', *Times Literary Supplement* (7 Sept 1984), 994–5.
Women's Studies International Forum, x/3 (1987) [special issue on the Fawcett Library].
H.L. Smith: 'Archival Report: British Women's History: the Fawcett Library Archival Collections', *Twentieth century British History,* 2/2 (1991), 215–23.

539 Federation of British Artists

Address: 17 Carlton House Terrace, London SW1Y 5AH

Telephone: (0171) 930 6844

Fax: (0171) 839 7830

The federation was established in 1962 and links the following organisations: the Hesketh Hubbard Society; the New English Art Club; the Pastel Society; the Royal Institute of Painters in Water Colours (f. 1831); the Royal Society of British Artists (f. 1823); the Royal Society of Marine Artists; the Royal Society of Portrait Painters (f. 1891) and the Society of Wildlife Artists. In spite of the age of some of these bodies, it appears that archives have not been systematically preserved and details are not available. A fire in 1985 destroyed some material, although this was mainly catalogues. Some records are held by presidents of the societies and, although access is not encouraged, enquiries can be addressed to the federation.

540 The Folklore Society

Address: University College London, Gower Street, London WC1E 6BT

Telephone: (0171) 387 5894

Enquiries: The Hon. Archivist

Open: Strictly by arrangement only.

Access: Members of the society and bona fide researchers, by appointment.

Historical background: The Folklore Society was formed in 1878 and was the first organisation in the world to be devoted to the study of traditional culture. Today the society continues to stimulate folklore studies throughout the world, and it provides a valuable point of contact for isolated collectors and scholars.

Acquisitions policy: Most acquisitions are by donation from society members, mainly in the form of TS and MS materials, but also a limited number of photographic materials.

Major collections: Collections, large and small, deposited by past society members, including Sir George and Lady Alice Gomme, T.F. Ordish and Andrew Lang, 1890s-.
Daily Mirror 'Live Letters' collection.

Finding aids: Cataloguing and indexing in progress.

Facilities: Photocopying and photography by arrangement.

Publications: Folklore and *FLS News*, in which reports of past donations to the archive and a current annual report are included.

541 The Football Association

Address: 16 Lancaster Gate, London W2 3LW

Telephone: (0171) 262 4542

Enquiries: Mr David Barber

The association was founded in 1863 and retains its minutes from that time, as well as a collection of historical books and programmes. The library holds *c*2000 volumes, including early *Annuals*, 1870-. A short article by D. Barber, 'FA Records', appeared in the *FA Year Book, 1980-81*.

542 Franciscan Archives English Province

Address: Franciscan Friary, 56 St Antony's Road, Forest Gate, London E7 9QB

Telephone: (0181) 472 6012

Fax: (0181) 503 5797

Enquiries: The Archivist

Open: By arrangement.

Access: Bona fide scholars, by appointment only.

Historical background: The archive collection was begun in 1629.

Acquisitions policy: To acquire any material dealing with the English Franciscan Province.

Archives of organisation: Chapter Registers, 1629–1838.
Correspondence dealing with the business of the province.
Deeds and wills connected with benefactors and relatives of Franciscans.
Provincial registers; procurators' account books; note-books of Franciscan provincials; notifications from Major Superiors in Rome and the Low Countries.

Facilities: Photocopying.

543 French Protestant Church

Address: 8 & 9 Soho Square, London W1V 5DD

Telephone: (0171) 437 5311

Enquiries: The Archivist

Open: By arrangement.

Access: Bona fide researchers, by appointment.

Historical background: The French Protestant Church was founded in 1550, when Edward VI gave a charter to Protestant refugees. French Huguenots occupied a church in Threadneedle Street from 1550 to 1841, then in St Martins le Grand until 1887. Links were maintained with other Huguenot churches in England, notably at Canterbury, Norwich and Southampton. The church moved to its present site in 1893.

Acquisitions policy: To complement the archives of the past and document the church's ongoing activities.

Archives of organisation: Records, including *actes du consistoire* (vestry minutes), 1560-; account books; lists of members' pews and poor relief; indentures of apprentices; *livres des témoignages*; royal approbations.

Non-manuscript material: Library of specialist literature, including incunabula, particularly 18th century- (*c*1400 vols).

Facilities: Photocopying by arrangement.

Publications: R. Smith (comp.): *The Archives of*

the French Protestant Church of London (London, 1972).
Y. Jaufres: *The French Protestant Church of London and the Huguenots* (London, 1993).

544 Froebel Institute College
Early Childhood Collection

Parent organisation: Roehampton Institute

Address: Grove House, Roehampton Lane, London SW15 5PJ

Telephone: (0181) 392 3000 (switchboard) 392 3323 (answerphone for out of hours enquiries)

Fax: (0181) 392 3331

Enquiries: The Archivist, Mrs Jane Read

Open: Term: Mon, Tues, Thurs: 9.30–2.00 Fri: 9.30–1.30 Vacation: by arrangement.

Access: Bona fide researchers and other interested persons; a prior appointment is required, especially as some archives are stored elsewhere.

Historical background: The Froebel Society was founded in 1874 to promote the Kindergarten system, and the Educational Institute was founded in 1892. The institute moved to its current site in Roehampton in the early 1920s, and since 1978 has been a constituent college of the Roehampton Institute of Higher Education. The Early Childhood Collection was established to preserve a unique set of source material tracing the development of the Froebel movement in this country, and to provide information and research facilities for the college community and researchers from this country and abroad.

Acquisitions policy: To acquire any further relevant material to strengthen the existing collection.

Archives of organisation: Archives of the institute, 1892–.
Minute books of the Froebel Society and the National Froebel Foundation, 1874–.

Non-manuscript material: Examples of students' work.
Photographs of college, staff, students, Kindergartens, demonstration schools and nursery schools.
Publications relating to the work of Friedrich Froebel (1782–1852) and his followers, with examples of his educational apparatus.

Finding aids: Card catalogue of holdings. 'Who's Who' of Froebelian pioneers in course of preparation.

Facilities: Photocopying and photography through Roehampton Institute Media Resources Service.

Publications: An Introductory Guide to the Early Childhood Collection [pamphlet outlining holdings etc].
The Froebel Educational Institute: a Centenary Review (London, 1992).
Froebel: Drawings and Photographs of the Froebel Institute College (London, 1992).

545 Garrick Club

Address: 15 Garrick Street, London WC2E 9AY

Telephone: (0171) 836 1737

Enquiries: The Librarian

Open: Wed: 10.00–5.00, by arrangement. Closed last two weeks of August and first week of September.

Access: Bona fide researchers, who should write stating the subject of their research. An appointment is necessary and a fee may be charged.

Historical background: The Garrick Club was founded in 1831 by the art collector Francis Mills. The formation of a library was in the first constitution. It now contains *c*7500 volumes connected with the theatre.

Acquisitions policy: Material relating to British drama and the theatre, especially 18th and 19th centuries.

Major collections: Garrick Collection: correspondence, cuttings and illustrations relating to David Garrick (1717–79).
Northcote Collection: archives of Drury Lane Theatre.

Non-manuscript material: Irving Collection: 20 scrapbooks relating to Henry Irving (1838–1905).
Playbills and programmes, 18th century–.
Press cuttings.

Finding aids: Card index.

Facilities: Photography by arrangement only.

Publications: G. Boas: *The Garrick Club, 1831–1947* (1948).

546 The Geological Society

Address: Burlington House, London W1V 0JU

Telephone: (0171) 434 9944

Enquiries: The Hon. Archivist, J.C. Thackray

Open: Mon–Fri: 10.00–5.00

Access: Bona fide researchers, by appointment.

Historical background: The Geological Society of London was founded in 1807.

Acquisitions policy: Any donations of MSS relating to the society and its Fellows are gratefully received.

Archives of organisation: Administrative records: a full series of official records, including minutes, 1807–; fellowship and financial records; MSS relating to society publications, including the *Journal.*

Major collections: Collections from Fellows and others, in particular Roderick I. Murchison (1792–1871).
Collection of note-books, diaries and letters.

Non-manuscript material: Maps. Illustrations.

Finding aids: MSS catalogue in preparation.

Facilities: Photocopying.

Publications: Various 19th–century catalogues of the library.

547 Girls' Public Day School Trust

Address: GPDST Head Office, 26 Queen Anne's Gate, London SW1H 9AN

Telephone: (0171) 222 9595 ext. 151

Fax: (0171) 222 8771

Enquiries: Research and Statistics Officer (Archivist), Mr P.F.V. Waters

Open: Mon–Fri: 9.00–5.30

Access: Any bona fide researcher may consult the archives by appointment. A few confidential files may not be consulted without the permission of the Council of the Trust.

Historical background: The Girls' Public Day School Trust was founded in 1872 as the Girls' Public Day School Company to provide junior day schools. The first school was established the following year in Chelsea, and the trust cur-

rently runs 25 schools in England plus one (in association) in Wales. Teacher-training departments were often attached to the schools, and the trust also had responsibility for Clapham Teacher Training College from 1900 to 1949. Charitable status was acquired in 1950.

Acquisitions policy: To maintain the archives of the trust and its schools.

Archives of organisation: Records of the trust, including minutes of council and committees, 1874–; financial and legal papers, 1872–; correspondence, 1879–; estate and building records, including architects' plans, 18th–20th centuries; pupil admission registers, 1873–; inspectors' and headmistresses' reports, 1880s–; prospectuses and press cuttings, 1860s–.

Facilities: Photocopying. Microfilm/fiche reader.

Publications: J. Sondheimer and P. Bodington (eds): *A Centenary Review* (1972).
L. Richmond and B. Stockford: *Company Archives* (1986), 118–23 [gives a detailed survey of the trust's records].

548 Grand Lodge Library and Museum

Parent organisation: United Grand Lodge of Free and Accepted Masons of England

Address: Freemasons' Hall, Great Queen Street, London WC2B 5AZ

Telephone: (0171) 831 9811 ext. 260

Fax: (0171) 404 7418

Enquiries: The Librarian and Curator, J.M. Hamill

Open: Mon–Fri: 10.00–5.00 Sat: mornings, by arrangement
Closed Saturdays preceeding public holidays.

Access: The library and museum are open to the public. Access to the records is free to members and, after discussion with the Librarian and Curator, to non-members by appointment. There is a charge for genealogical enquiries.

Historical background: The Grand Lodge of England was formed in 1717. The library and museum were established in 1837 to manage the archives of the Grand Lodge and its sister organisation the Grand Chapter of the Royal Arch, and to develop a comprehensive library on freemasonry, together with a reference collection of regalia, medals and orders, and artefacts with either a masonic use or incorporating masonic decoration in their design. While concentrating on the development of English freemasonry, the collections include material on freemasonry wherever it is or has been practised throughout the world.

Acquisitions policy: Active policy of collecting printed, MS, documentary and ephemeral material on English freemasonry.

Archives of organisation: MS and printed minutes of Grand Lodge, 1723–, and Grand Chapter, 1766–.
Membership registers of Grand Lodge, 1751–, and Grand Chapter, 1766–.
Letter-books, c1770.

Major collections: Historical correspondence: correspondence from lodges and individual freemasons (worldwide), c1770–c1890 (c150,000 items).
Masonic warrants, charters, patents of appointment, certificates etc (c200,000 items).

Non-manuscript material: Large collection of printed ephemera concerning lodges, personalities and masonic events.
Portraits, prints, drawings, photographs, engravings of persons, masonic scenes, artefacts (c100,000 items).
Printed books and pamphlets (c44,000).

Finding aids: Documents indexed by recipient and issuing body. Correspondence indexed by writer, recipient and subjects.

Facilities: Photocopying and photography by arrangement.

Publications: J. Stubbs and T.O. Haunch: *Freemasons' Hall: Home and Heritage of the Craft* (London, 1983).
J.M. Hamill: *The History of Freemasonry: Souvenir of an Exhibition* (London, 1986).

549 Gray's Inn Library

Parent organisation: Honourable Society of Gray's Inn

Address: South Square, Gray's Inn, London WC1R 5EU

Telephone: (0171) 242 8592, 405 8164 exts 143/4/5

Enquiries: The Librarian, Mrs T.L. Thom

Open: Legal term: Mon–Fri: 9.00–8.00
Shorter hours during vacations: please enquire.

Access: Members only, though others may be admitted by arrangement at the Librarian's discretion and after written application.

Historical background: The library has been in existence since the mid-16th century, although bombing destroyed a large part of the collections in 1941.

Archives of organisation: Records of Gray's Inn, mainly 18th and 19th centuries, but including orders in pension, 1569–, MS books, 12th–16th centuries.
Records of Barnard's Inn, 17th–19th centuries.

Major collections: Papers of James Richard Atkin, Baron Atkin (1867–1944), judge.

Non-manuscript material: Portraits, prints and photographs.
Roman law books collected by Robert Warden Lee (1868–1958), lawyer.

Finding aids: Typescript guide, 1971; NRA 17004.

Facilities: Photocopying. Microfilm reader.

Publications: A.J. Horwood: *Catalogue* (1869).
N.R. Ker: *Medieval Manuscripts in British Libraries*.

550 Greater London Record Office

Parent organisation: Corporation of London

Address: 40 Northampton Road, London EC1R 0HB

Telephone: (0171) 332 3824 (not Mondays)

Fax: (0171) 833 9136

Enquiries: The Head Archivist

Open: Tues: 9.30–7.30; from 4.45 by prior appointment only. Wed–Fri: 9.30–4.45
Closed 3rd and 4th weeks of October.

Access: Generally open to the public.

Historical background: The Greater London Record Office was formed in 1965 by the amalgamation of the London and Middlesex county record offices. The offices were physically amalgamated at County Hall in 1980 and moved to Clerkenwell in 1982. Both these offices had their origins in the records inherited by their respective county councils in 1889. The office also acts as the Diocesan Record Office for London, Southwark and Guildford and is recognised as a place of deposit for public records.

Acquisitions policy: Official records of the Greater London Council, the London County Council, the Middlesex County Council and their predecessors. Deposited and non-official archives relating to the area of the former counties of London and Middlesex.

Archives of organisation: Records of London Residuary Body, Greater London Council and their predecessors, including: records of the Middlesex Sessions, 1549–1971, with the Gaol Delivery of Newgate for Middlesex, 1549–1834, and the Westminster Sessions records, 1620–1844; records of various commissions of sewers, 16th century–1855, and of the School Board for London, 1870–1904.

Major collections: Records of St Thomas Hospital Group (including Nightingale School), Guy's Hospital, Westminster Hospital Group, 1556–1974.
Records of the Foundling Hospital (Thomas Coram Foundation for Children from 1954), 1739–1968.
Records of businesses, including brewing companies: Truman Hanbury and Buxton; Barclay Perkins; Fuller Smith and Turner; Meux; Reid; Sich; Courage; 17th–20th centuries.
Records of the charities, societies and schools, including the Charity Organisation Society (Family Welfare Organisation from 1946), excluding local area material outside London, 1869–1966.
Records of predecessors of Thames Water Authority, late 18th century-1974.
Records of Anglo-Jewish institutions and organisations, 19th–20th centuries.
Manorial, family and estate records.

Non-manuscript material: Associated collections of primary sources in Record Office Library (*c*100,000 books); map and print collections (*c*15,000 maps and plans; *c*40,000 prints). photograph collection (*c*500,000 images).

Facilities: Photocopying. Prints from microfilms. Photography by arrangement. Microfilm readers.

Conservation: Archive conservation section provides full service.

Publications: *Guide to the Records in the London County Record Office*, pt 1: *Records of the Predecessors of the London County Council, except the Boards of Guardians* (1962).

Guide to the Middlesex Sessions Records, 1549–1889 (1965)
Guide to Parish Registers Deposited in the Greater London Record Office (rev. 2/1991).
Greater London Record Office: a General Guide to Holdings (1994) [2 vols].
Free information leaflets about holdings.

551 Grenadier Guards Regimental Archives

Address: Regimental Headquarters, Wellington Barracks, Birdcage Walk, London SW1E 6HQ

Telephone: (0171) 414 3221

Fax: (0171) 414 3443

Enquiries: Maj. P.A. Lewis

Open: Tues, Thurs: 7.00–4.00, by appointment.

Access: Open to ex-Grenadiers and their relations, and also to bona fide researchers on application.

Historical background: The regiment was founded in 1656 by Charles II.

Acquisitions policy: Maintains the regimental archive and accepts personal papers.

Archives of organisation: Records of the regiment, including activities of each Battalion, 1656–.
Records of promotions, awards, births, deaths and marriages.
Attestation papers of all members of the regiment (3000 box files).

Major collections: Diaries, letters and biographical material.

Non-manuscript material: Photographs, 1850–1.
Grave locations.

Finding aids: Catalogue in preparation. Personal files of all officers in alphabetical order and other ranks by regimental number.

Facilities: Photocopying.

552 The Guide Association

Address: 17–19 Buckingham Palace Road, London SW1W 0PT

Telephone: (0171) 834 6242 ext. 255

Fax: (0171) 828 8317

Enquiries: The Archivist, Mrs M.S. Courtney

Open: Mon–Fri: 10.00–4.00

Access: Bona fide scholars, who should supply references and make an appointment. There are restrictions on certain records.

Historical background: The Guide Association was founded as the Girl Guides Association in 1910 by Lord Baden-Powell (1857–1941) as a counterpart to the Boy Scouts (see National Scout Archive entry **649**).

Acquisitions policy: Accepts donations of guiding material and papers relating to guiding personnel. Local records are held by regional and county offices.

Archives of organisation: Records and publications of the association, 1910–, including minutes of council and committees; annual and conference reports and correspondence; training material.

Major collections: Small collection of Baden-Powell family letters.

Non-manuscript material: Photographic collection, 1908–.
Film collection (transferred to video).
Badges, awards and souvenirs.

Finding aids: Catalogues. Indexes. Photographic catalogue in preparation.

Facilities: Photocopying. Microfiche reader.

553 Guildhall Library Manuscripts Section

Parent organisation: Corporation of London

Address: Guildhall Library, Aldermanbury, London EC2P 2EJ

Telephone: (0171) 332 1863

Fax: (0171) 600 3384

Enquiries: The Keeper of Manuscripts

Open: Mon–Fri: 9.30–4.45 Sat: 9.30–4.45 (but no delivery from strongrooms, 12.00–2.00)

Access: Generally open to the public; appointment not normally necessary. Access to some modern (mostly business) records dependent on depositor's permission and requires 24 hours' notice of visit.

Historical background: Guildhall Library was founded in 1824 and is primarily a library of London history, holding not only printed books but also prints, maps, drawings and paintings and MSS. The Manuscripts Section is, in effect, the local record office for the City of London (excepting the archives of the Corporation of London, entry **524**). The office also acts as Diocesan Record Office for London and is recognised as a place of deposit for public records.

Acquisitions policy: Records relating to or emanating from the City of London (excepting the archives of the Corporation of London).

Major collections: Records of Diocese of London, 14th–20th centuries; Archdeanconry of London, 14th–20th centuries; parish records for the City of London, 15th–20th centuries.
Dean and Chapter of St Paul's Cathedral, 11th–20th centuries.
79 of the City of London's ancient livery companies and related organisations, 12th–20th centuries.
Businesses and business organisations, 16th–20th centuries, including merchant banks: Brown Shipley, Hambros, Kleinwort Benson, Morgan Grenfell; insurance companies: Commercial Union, Hand in Hand, Royal Exchange, Sun Insurance Office; London Chamber of Commerce; Association of British Commerce; London Stock Exchange; Lloyd's Marine Collection; Institute of Chartered Accountants.
Christ's Hospital School, 16th–20th centuries.
Corporation of Trinity House, 16th–20th centuries.

Finding aids: General catalogue. General subject, name and place indexes. Several specialised indexes, lists and guides.

Facilities: Photocopying. Microfilm/fiche readers.

Conservation: Parchment, paper and photograph conservation and binding are undertaken in house. Some work is contracted out, e.g. binding.

Publications: Vestry Minutes of Parishes within the City of London (2/1964).
London Rate Assessments and Inhabitants Lists in Guildhall Library and the Corporation of London Records Office (2/1968).
Churchwardens' Accounts of Parishes within the City of London (2/1969).
Guide to the Archives of City Livery Companies and Related Organisations in Guildhall Library (3/1989).

A Guide to Archives and Manuscripts at Guildhall Library (2/1990).
Handlist of Parish Registers, pt 1: *Parishes within the City of London* (6/1990); pt 2: *Parishes in Greater London outside the City* (7/1994).
A Handlist of Business Archives at Guildhall Library (2/1991).
Handlist of the Non-Conformist, Roman Catholic, Jewish and Burial Ground Registers (2/1993).
D.T. Barriskill: *A Guide to the Lloyd's Marine Collection at Guildhall Library* (2/1994).
G. Yeo: *The British Overseas: a Guide to Records of their Births, Baptisms, Marriages, Deaths and Burials available in the United Kingdom* (3/1994).
R. Harvey: *A Guide to Genealogical Sources in Guildhall Library* (4/1995).

554 Hall-Carpenter Archives

Address: c/o BM Archives, London WC1N 3XX

Enquiries: The Hon. Secretary, Oliver Merrington

Open: By arrangement.

Access: By appointment on written application to the address above.

Historical background: The Hall-Carpenter Archives were founded in 1982 as the national UK Lesbian and Gay Archive from the Campaign for Homosexual Equality's media monitoring service. From 1984 to 1986 it received funding from the Greater London Council and was housed in the London Lesbian and Gay Centre (now closed). Its collections have now been dispersed as follows:
British Library of Political and Economic Science (entry **498**): organisational archives, including Albany Trust; Campaign for Homosexual Equality; Gay Liberation Front; Gay News Ltd; and Scottish Homosexual Rights Group; papers of gay rights campaigners; and periodicals (*c*250 titles).
National Sound Archive (entry **496B**): major oral history project investigating the lives of lesbians and gay men in the London area over the last 60 years, with transcripts.
Greenwich Lesbian and Gay Centre (contact address above): see non-manuscript material below.

Acquisitions policy: Material in any format that relates to the history, social and personal experiences of lesbians and gay men. Priority is given to material from the UK and Eire, and relating to women and people from ethnic minorities.

Non-manuscript material: Press cuttings, *c*1960–87, including a large collection on AIDS (many thousands). Gay ephemera, including banners, badges, leaflets and posters.

Finding aids: List of press cuttings in preparation. Computer catalogue at BLPES and handlist at NSA.

Publications: *Inventing Ourselves: Lesbian Life Stories* (Routledge, 1989).
Walking After Midnight: Gay Men's Life Stories (Routledge, 1989).

555 Highgate Literary and Scientific Institution

Address: 11 South Grove, London N6 6BS

Telephone: (0181) 340 3343

Enquiries: The Secretary, Archives Committee

Open: Tues–Fri, by arrangement.

Access: Members and bona fide scholars, by appointment only.

Historical background: The institution was founded in 1839 by Harry Chester (1806– 68), educationalist, and others. It has been at the present address since 1840. The scientific book collection was completely dispersed after World War II and the institution now concentrates on literature and local history.

Acquisitions policy: Material of local interest accepted by donation.

Archives of organisation: Records of the institution, including minute books, annual reports, printed programmes, lectures, correspondence, scrapbooks and newspaper cuttings, 1838–.

Major collections: Deeds of Pauncefort Almshouses, *c*1700–*c*1900.
Book Society minute books, 1822–1922.
Highgate Dispensary books, 1787–1840.
Mothercraft Training Society archives, 1918–1950s.
Highgate Horticultural Society minute books, 1903–.
Robert Whipple Trust minute books.
Papers of Samuel Taylor Coleridge (1772–1834) and Sir John Betjeman (1906–84).

Non-manuscript material: Local history collection, including photographs and prints. Glass plate slides and negatives.

Finding aids: Outline lists and card indexes for some collections.

Publications: `A.E. Barker: 'Improving the Records of Highgate: the Story of the Literary and Scientific Institution', *Camden History Review*, no. 8 (1980), 13–16.
Heart of a London Village (Archives Committee, 1989).

556 Highgate School

Address: North Road, London N6 6AY

Telephone: (0181) 340 1524

Fax: (0181) 340 7674

Enquiries: The Record Keeper, Mr T.G. Mallinson

Open: By prior arrangement only.

Access: Bona fide researchers, by appointment.

Historical background: Highgate School is an independent institution, founded in 1565 by Sir Richard Cholmeley. The archives have been developed systematically only since the 1980s following the return of the governors' records, formerly housed separately, into school curatorship.

Acquisitions policy: All items in any way connected with Highgate School and its present and former staff and pupils.

Archives of Organisation: Documents relating to the foundation, history, administration, finance, staff and pupils of the school, mid-16th century-.

Major collections: Some documentary material relevant to the history of Highgate village.

Non-manuscript material: Plans, drawings, photographs and uniforms, as integral part of the archive.
Tape-recorded interviews of former staff and pupils, mainly covering early 20th century (with transcripts).

Finding aids: Manual card index catalogue and users' guide.

Publications: T. Hinde: *Highgate School: a History* (London, 1992).

557 HM Customs and Excise

Address: New King's Beam House, 22 Upper Ground, London SE1 9PJ

Telephone: (0171) 620 1313 (switchboard) 865 5729 (direct line)

Fax: (0171) 865 5670

Enquiries: The Archivist, Mr I.F. Wright

Open: Mon–Fri: 8.30–5.00, by appointment only.

Access: 30–year closure on most departmental records. Some items are housed in remote storage.

Historical background: The library dates from 1671, when the Board of Customs was established. Certain excise records were deposited after amalgamation of HM Customs and Excise in 1909. There is also a small display showing the historical and modern work of the department.

Acquisitions policy: Directly relating to present functions of the department and to support historical collections.

Archives of organisation: Trade and shipping statistics (imports and exports).
Background material on taxation of goods, smuggling etc.
Books of rates, 16th century–.
Parliamentary papers, 1820–.
Annual register, 1756–.
Current records of the department.

Non-manuscript material: Small collection of prints and photographs on subjects relating to the work of the department.
Some 18th–century maps and charts of the British coast.

Finding aids: Index.

Facilities: Limited photocopying.

Publications: E. Carson: 'Customs Records as a Source for Historical Research', *Archives*, xviii (1977), 74.
Handouts on various historical subjects.

558 HM Land Registry

Address: 32 Lincoln's Inn Fields, London WC2A 3PH

Telephone: (0171) 917 8888

The Land Registry does not, as a rule, retain the deeds of title which are submitted for registration. The records kept by the registry are retained only for the periods required by the Public Records Act 1958, except in the case of permanently retained documents still under the provisions of the Land Registration Acts 1925–1988, and Rules. Under the Land Registration (Open Register) Rules 1991, anyone may inspect and obtain copies of the register and filed plan and any documents (other than a charge or a lease) referred to in the register that the Land Registry holds. A fee is payable for this service.

559 Honourable Artillery Company

Address: Armoury House, City Road, London EC1Y 2BQ

The company was founded in 1537, making it the oldest volunteer regiment in the world. The archives are of particular interest for 17th- and 18th-century militia and city matters. They are open to bona fide researchers, strictly by written appointment with the Honorary Archivist, Jean Tsushima. Queries are answered by post and a donation is requested. In 1989 the HAC Biographical Dictionary was launched. It aims to create a database with details of those in the HAC and the London Trained Bands, 1537–1914. Publication is planned.

560 House of Lords Record Office

Address: House of Lords, London SW1A 0PW

Telephone: (0171) 219 3074

Fax: (0171) 219 2570

Enquiries: The Clerk of the Records, Mr D.J. Johnson

Open: Mon–Fri: 9.30–5.00
Closed last two weeks of November.

Access: Open to the public, preferably by appointment. There is a 30–year closure period on administrative records and longer closure periods on a few classes, e.g. certain committee records.

Historical background: The records of the House of Lords have been kept at Westminster since 1497 (earlier records are to be found among the Chancery and Exchequer records in the Public Record Office). The House of Lords records escaped the fire of 1834 which gutted most of the medieval Palace of Westminster, but the House of Commons records were destroyed, with the exception of the original Journals dating from 1547. In 1864 the Lords records were moved into the Victoria Tower of the new Palace of Westminster, where they are still housed. The record office was established in 1946 and now has custody of both the House of Lords records and of the House of Commons Journals and post-1834 records, and of some deposited private papers.

Acquisitions policy: To acquire records relating to proceedings in either House of Parliament; the history, architecture and decoration of the Palace of Westminster; peers, MPs and officials particularly concerned with the running of Parliament.

Archives of organisation: Acts of Parliament, 1497– (c 60,000).
Papers laid before the House of Lords, 1531–.
House of Lords Journals, 1510–.
House of Commons Journals, 1547–.
Committee proceedings, 1610–.
Plans of canals, railways, roads and other works, 1794–.
Peerage claims, 1604–.
Historical collections: parliamentary diaries, clerks' papers etc, 1545–.

Major collections: Private political papers, 1712–, including those of Lord Beaverbrook (1879–1964), David Lloyd George (1863–1945) and Andrew Bonar Law (1858–1923).

Non-manuscript material: Plans and drawings of the Palace of Westminster, including drawings by Barry and Pugin, c1840–60.
Photographs of the Palace of Westminster and of peers and MPs, 1852–.
Audio-visual material relating to Parliament.
NB Recordings of proceedings in both Houses are now available from the Parliamentary Recording Unit, 7 Millbank, London SW1P 3JA.

Finding aids: Various typescript and MS lists and indexes.

Facilities: Photocopying. Photography. Microfilm/fiche reader.

Conservation: In-house bindery; outside work undertaken.

Publications: M.F. Bond: *Guide to the Records of Parliament* (1971).

A Guide to Historical Collections of the Nineteenth and Twentieth Centuries Preserved in the House of Lords Record Office, House of Lords Record Office *Memorandum,* no. 60 (1978).

M.F. Bond: *A Short Guide to the Records of Parliament* (3/1980).

Historical Manuscripts Commission Reports 1–14 [include lists of House of Lords MSS, 1498–1693].

The Manuscripts of the House of Lords, 1693–1718 [12 vols].

561 The Huguenot Library

Parent organisation: The Huguenot Society of Great Britain and Ireland

Address: University College London, Gower Street, London WC1E 6BT

Telephone: (0171) 380 7094

Enquiries: The Librarian

Open: Tues–Thurs: 10.00–4.00, strictly by appointment with the librarian.

Access: Fellows of the society and bona fide researchers. Genealogical enquiries from non-members are dealt with by the society's research assistant (details on application).

Historical background: The Huguenot Library is the joint library of the French Protestant Hospital, founded by Royal Charter in 1718 (now at Rochester), and of the Huguenot Society of London, founded in 1885. It was housed at the hospital until its transfer on deposit to University College in 1957, but it is not administered by the college archivists.

Acquisitions policy: The collection of books and archives relating to the Huguenots, in particular those who came to Britain, and their descendants.

Major collections: 'Royal Bounty' MSS.
French Hospital archives, with some associated Huguenot philanthropic bodies.
Collection of Huguenot pedigrees and other genealogical material made by the late Henry Wagner.

Finding aids: OPAC catalogue available through JANET.

Conservation: Contracted out.

Publications: Huguenot Society: *Quarto Series* (1885–) [57 vols], including all surviving registers of the Huguenot churches in England and Ireland; lists of denizations and naturalisations, the 'Royal Bounty' papers by Raymond Smith (vol. 51); and all remaining archives by Irvine Gray (vol. 56). Vols 1–18 available in microfiche.

Annual *Proceedings* (1885–).
General Index to the Proceedings and Quarto Series 1885–1985 (1986).
Huguenot Society New Series (monographs) No. 1–.

562 Hulton Deutsch Collection

Address: Unique House, 21–31 Woodfield Road, London W9 2BA

Telephone: (0171) 266 2662

Fax: (0171) 289 6392

Enquiries: The Picture Research Manager

Open: Mon–Fri: 9.00–6.00

Access: Bona fide researchers, by appointment; a charge is made. Researchers can also telephone with a description and then fax the information.

Historical background: The Hulton Deutsch Collection is the direct descendant of the Library originally created by Edward Hulton, the publisher of *Picture Post.* The collection was part of the BBC until 1988, when it was acquired by Brian Deutsch. Since then the collection has expanded to over 15 million images, with the addition of the Keystone, Fox and Central Press archives.

Acquisitions policy: Hulton Deutsch represents Reuter News Pictures and manages Mirror Syndication International, ensuring contemporary images are being added to the collection.

Non-manuscript material: Many photographic collections, including:
Picture Post Collection, 1938–58.
Topical Press Agency, 1902–57.
Sasha, 1920s and 1930s (theatre portraits and literary figures).
Baron, 1935–56 (personalities, society and performing arts).
Studio Lisa, 1936–54 (royal family).
Charles Downey, 1860–1920 (portraits).
London Stereoscopic Company, 1854–1914 (topographical).
Keystone, Fox, Central Press and Three Lions, 20th century.
Large collection of historical engravings.

Finding aids: Subject lists. Promotional catalogue. The Hulton has an on-going programme of digitising the collection and creating keyword access to images.

Facilities: Photocopying. CD-ROM research facilities.

Conservation: In-house conservation department for photographs. Outside work undertaken (e.g. nitrate copying).

Publications: Quarterly newsletter *HDC*, 1994–.
CD guides: *The Decades*, 1920s-1950/60s, with 2,500 images each.

563 Imperial College Archives

Parent organisation: University of London

Address: Room 455, Sherfield Building, Imperial College, London SW7 2AZ

Telephone: (0171) 594 8850

Fax: (0171) 584 3763

Enquiries: The College Archivist, Mrs Anne Barrett

Open: Mon–Fri: 10.00–12.30; 2.00–5.00, by appointment.

Access: Open to bona fide scholars who produce evidence of their identity. There is a 25–year closure on administrative records. There is a longer period for some records and some material is not available for consultation.

Historical background: Imperial College was established by Royal Charter in 1907 and was a federation of the Royal School of Mines, the Royal College of Science and the City and Guilds College. In 1988 St Mary's Hospital Medical School was merged with the college. See entry 691 for the archives of the Royal Commission for the Exhibition of 1851.

Acquisitions policy: Material collected is directly related to the college or any of its past or present staff and students.

Archives of organisation: Records of the Royal College of Chemistry, 1845–53; the Royal School of Mines, 1851–; the Royal College of Science, 1881–; the City and Guilds College, 1884–; Imperial College, 1907–.

Major collections: Collections of papers of scientists associated with the college include

those of: Sir Andrew Ramsay (1814–91), geologist; Lyon Playfair (1818–98), chemist and politician; T.H. Huxley (1825–95), member of staff, 1854–95; William Cawthorne Unwin (1838–1933), civil engineer; Henry Edward Armstrong (1848–1937), chemist; Silvanus P. Thompson (1851–1916), electrical engineer; H.A. Humphrey (1868–1951), engineer; Edward Frankland Armstrong (1878–1945), chemist; James Watson Munro (1888–1968), entomologist; Herbert Dingle (1890–1978), historian of science; Dennis Gabor (1900–79), electrical engineer, inventor of holography and television engineering pioneer; Willis Jackson (1904–70), electrical engineer; Sir Patrick Linstead (1902–66), chemist and rector of the college; Colin Cherry (1914–79), electrical and telecommunications engineer.

Non-manuscript material: Photographs, maps, plans and models of college buildings; photographs of staff and students; records and videotape interviews; microfilms of financial records; scientific drawings and teaching apparatus; medals etc.

Finding aids: Handlists for most collections. Lists sent to NRA.

Facilities: Photocopying. Photography at archivist's discretion. Microfilm/fiche readers in college library.

Conservation: Contracted out.

Publications: J. Pingree: *A Guide to Imperial College Archives* (London, 1982).
J. Percival (ed): *A Guide to Archives and Manuscripts in the University of London*, vol. 1 (London, 1984), 36–42.
R.G. Williams and A. Barrett: *Imperial College: a Pictorial History* (London, 1988).
A. Barrett and K. Brown: *St Mary's Hospital Medical School: a Pictorial Anthology* (London, 1990).

564 Imperial War Museum
Department of Documents

Address: Lambeth Road, London SE1 6HZ

Telephone: (0171) 416 5000 ext. 5220/1/2/3

Fax: (071) 416 5374

Enquiries: The Department of Documents

Open: Mon–Sat: 10.00–5.00, preferably by appointment (essential for Sats)
Closed last two full weeks of November.

NB Other reference departments in the museum have different opening hours.

Access: Bona fide researchers over the age of 15. Some collections are governed by special access conditions.

Historical background: Although the museum has been collecting MSS relating to 20th–century warfare since its formation in 1917, the Department of Documents has its origins in the Foreign Documents Centre, which was set up in the museum and supported by a grant from the Leverhulme Trust from 1964 to 1969. On the expiry of the grant the centre was incorporated into the museum as the Department of Documents and assumed responsibility for the acquisition and administration of collections of British private papers, while continuing in its role of custodian of major series of foreign records for the period 1933 to 1945. The department is recognised as a place of deposit for public records.

Acquisitions policy: To expand the museum's holdings of unpublished records written by officers and other ranks of all three services and by civilians where they relate to their experiences in twentieth century conflict, particularly World Wars I and II.

Major collections: Foreign documents: copies of papers relating to the following areas: the German military high command and the conduct of land campaigns of World War II; Luftwaffe planning and supply, 1939–45; German aerial, armaments, industrial and technical research during the period of the Third Reich; the Nuremberg and Tokyo War Crimes Trials. British private papers: notable collections include the papers of Field Marshals Sir John French (1852–1925), Sir Henry Wilson (1864–1922) and Viscount Montgomery of Alamein (1887–1976); Sir Henry Tizard (1885–1959), scientist; Isaac Rosenberg (1890–1918), war poet.
Several thousand collections of unpublished diaries, letters and memoirs written by officers and other ranks, many of them civilians in uniform (i.e. not regulars), during, between and since World Wars I and II.
Series of biographical files on persons who have been decorated with the Victoria or George Crosses.
Department of Art: unique collection of correspondence with artists who were commissioned under the war-artist schemes in World Wars I and II.

Non-manuscript material: Department of Films: including record footage from service film units, officially sponsored information and propaganda films and newsreels, equivalent material from Allied and enemy sources, television 'histories' and amateur records (c45 million feet).
Department of Photographs: including those taken by official war photographers and others acquired from private sources (c5 million).
Department of Printed Books: reference library comprising books (c100,000) as well as extensive collections of pamphlets, propaganda leaflets, periodicals, maps and technical drawings.
Department of Sound Records: recorded material, including interviews conducted by museum staff covering the period from the Boer War to Bosnia; also broadcast recordings and sound effects (c20,000 hours/45 million feet).

Finding aids: In-house lists and indexes.

Facilities: Photocopying and microfilm services. Special area for readers wishing to use typewriters or dictaphones. Copy prints can be made to order from the Department of Photographs' collections.

Conservation: Contracted out.

Publications: Leaflet outlining the holdings of the department.
A Catalogue of the Records of the Reichsministerium für Rüstung und Kriegsproduktion, pt 1 (1969).
For further information about individual collections of British private papers in the museum, readers should consult C. Cook: *Sources in British Political History, 1900–1951* (especially vols ii and vi), and S.L. Mayer and W.J. Koenig: *The Two World Wars: a Guide to Manuscript Collections in the United Kingdom*.

565 Inner Temple

Address: c/o Treasurer's Office, Inner Temple, London EC4Y 7HL

Telephone: (0171) 797 8251 (Archivist) 797 8219 (Librarian)

Fax: (0171) 797 8178 (Archives) 797 8224 (Library)

Enquiries: The Archivist, I.G. Murray or The Librarian

Open: By arrangement.

Access: Approved researchers, strictly by appointment.

Historical background: The Temple acquired its name from the Knights Templars, who held the site from about 1150 until 1320 when the order was dissolved. It was then granted to the Order of St John of Jerusalem, but after 1339, when the courts were permanently established at Westminster, it became increasingly the home of lawyers, who very soon formed themselves into two legal societies, the Inner and Middle Temples. These were two of the four Inns of Court with powers to train barristers and call them to the Bar, and their authority was confirmed by Letters Patent of 1608 when the Temple was conveyed to the two societies for this purpose 'for all time to come'. The division of the site between them was also confirmed by a formal Deed of Partition in 1732. The library is recognised as a place of deposit for public records.

Acquisitions policy: Modern records are added to the archives from time to time in the usual way.

Archives of organisation: Records of the Inn relating to admission and call, domestic administration, and the building and maintenance of chambers, including: admission registers, 1547–; admission papers, 1804–1927; students' address books, 1871–1962; bar bonds, 1642–1873; records of call to the Bar, 1590–; Bench Table orders, 1668–; committee minutes, 1876–; Acts of the Parliament of the Inn, 1505–; admissions to chambers, 1615–67; chamber reference books, 1693–1962; chamber rent accounts, 1821–1962; Commons records, 1672–; Christmas account book, 1614–82; financial records, 1606–1962.

Major collections: Library: MS collections of historical, legal and literary interest, principally the Petyt Collection (386 vols); the Barrington Collection (57 vols); the Mitford Collection of legal MSS (79 vols); miscellaneous MSS (211 vols).
Series of bound volumes of administrative records, 16th–18th centuries, separate from the archives.

Non-manuscript material: Building plans, c1820–; photographs, engravings etc of the Inn. Library: printed books on the Inn and the Inns of Court in general.

Finding aids: Handlist of the archives; sent to NRA. Index to admissions, 1505– 1850 (1851– in progress).

Facilities: Photocopying.

Publications: F.A. Inderwick and R.A. Roberts (eds): *Calendar of Inner Temple Records* (1896–1937) [5 vols, covering the period 1505–1800; 1800–50 in progress].
J.C. Davies (ed.): *Catalogue of Manuscripts in the Library* (1972) [3 vols; sets available for sale on application to the librarian].
J.H. Baker: *The Inner Temple: a Brief Historical Description* (1991).

566 Institute of Actuaries

Address: Staple Inn Hall, High Holborn, London WC1V 7QJ

Telephone: (0171) 242 0106

Fax: (0171) 405 2482

Enquiries: The Assistant Librarian or The Librarian, Miss Sally Grover

Open: Mon–Fri: 9.15–4.30

Access: Actuaries and bona fide researchers, by appointment only. A charge is made for prolonged work by staff.

Historical background: The institute was formed in 1848 and received the Royal Charter of Incorporation in 1884. It has been housed in Staple Inn since 1887, apart from a break of 11 years following the destruction of the Hall in 1944. In 1990 the education service and the main library moved to Oxford, leaving the rest of the secretariat, archives and historical texts in Staple Inn. The formation of a library was one of the original objects of the institute, and many early members were also FRS or FSS.

Acquisitions policy: Maintaining the institute archives and acquiring collections on actuarial and related material, including MSS and associative copies of historical texts.

Archives of organisation: Minutes of council, and miscellaneous committee minutes, formal business of council; lists of members, 1848–.
Year Book and *Members' Handbook*, 1851–.

Major collections: Correspondence and MSS of Frank Mitchaell Redington (1906–84), president, 1958–83.
Records relating to the Students' Society/Staple Inn Actuarial Society.

Non-manuscript material: Photographs of presidents and other prominent members.

Newmarch Collection of 19th-century pamphlets.

Books, journals and papers on actuarial and related matters, including historical texts (mainly British).

A few early 20th-century calculating machines.

Finding aids: Database includes details of major MS collections. Lists available; sent to NRA. Council and committee minutes indexed in each volume.

Facilities: Photocopying. Photography.

Conservation: Only rudimentary in-house facilities. Binding of archival and historical texts contracted out.

Publications: Printed catalogue, 1835; later additions listed in *Journal* or *The Actuary*. Reading lists available covering historical texts. Occasional articles and reviews in *Journal* and *The Actuary* on historical texts and MSS. *Landmarks of actuarial science* (1985) [exhibition catalogue].

567 Institute of Archaeology

Parent organisation: University of London

Address: 31–4 Gordon Square, London WC1H 0PY

Telephone: (0171) 380 7485

Enquiries: The Librarian, Ms Belinda Barrat

Open: Term: Mon–Fri: 10.00–8.00 Sat: 10.00–4.30 Vacation: Mon–Fri: 10.00–5.30 Sat: 10.00–4.30; closed during summer vacation.

Access: Members of London University, and bona fide researchers on application.

Historical background: The Institute of Archaeology was founded in 1937 by Dr (later Sir) Mortimer Wheeler as a 'laboratory of archaeological science' where 'the archaeologist of the future may learn his business'. Originally a postgraduate institute only, in 1968 it began to take undergraduate students, and at present it is by far the largest archaeological teaching and research institute in the country.

Acquisitions policy: The library acquires books by purchase, exchange and donation, but has no deliberate policy in acquiring archival material, all of which has come by unsolicited gift.

Major collections: Excavation records: field note-books, photographs, maps, indexes of finds etc, predominantly of Western Asiatic sites.

Working note-books of Professor Gordon Childe, former director of the institute.

Non-manuscript material: Negatives and prints of air-photographs of the Middle East taken by the RAF after World War I.

Various collections of photographs of general archaeological interest.

Finding aids: Brief lists of the excavation material. Detailed finding lists for the air-photographs.

Facilities: Photocopying. Photography. Microfilm/fiche reader.

568 The Institute of Brewing

Address: 33 Clarges Street, London W1Y 8EE

Telephone: (0171) 499 8144

Fax: (0171) 499 1156

Enquiries: Principal Technical Support, C.J. Marchbanks

Open: Mon–Fri: 9.00–5.00

Access: Members of the Institute of Brewing, and bona fide scholars, by appointment only.

Historical background: The institute's origins date back to 1886, with the foundation of a Laboratory Club by a group of brewing chemists. In 1940 Brewers Hall was bombed and most of the archives were destroyed.

Acquisitions policy: Books and occasionally MSS on historical technical machinery and brewing.

Archives of organisation: Charters and list of members, 1886–1935.
Minutes and records, 1940–.

Non-manuscript material: Institute's publications and journals, 1895–.
Technical brewing journals and brewing trade magazines, 1941–.

Facilities: Photocopying.

Publications: *A History of the Institute of Brewing 1886–1951* (1955)
The Institute of Brewing Centenary, 1886–1986 (1987) [pictorial history].

569 Institute of Chartered Accountants in England and Wales

Address: Chartered Accountants' Hall, Moorgate Place, London EC2P 2BJ

Telephone: (0171) 920 8620

Fax: (0171) 920 8621

Enquiries: The Librarian, Ms S.P. Moore

Open: Mon–Thurs: 9.00–5.30 Fri: 10.00–5.30 Closed for three weeks in August.

Access: On written application.

Historical background: The institute was founded in 1880 by the amalgamation of the Institute of Accountants of London (f. 1870) with five smaller societies of accountants. It absorbed the Society of Incorporated Accountants and Auditors (f. 1886) in 1956. The institute is the major professional body for accountants in England, with 100,000 members. The library was founded on the basis of the small collection made by the Institute of Accountants and is now the major accounting library in Britain. It began collecting early books on book-keeping in 1882, and continues to do so.
Records of the ICAEW and of Incorporated Accountants are now housed at the Guildhall Library (entry **553**).

Acquisitions policy: Occasionally acquires interesting MS account books and other material relevant to the history of accounting.

Major collections: Files of comments by interested persons, companies, firms etc on accounting standards issued by the Accounting Standards Board and on exposure drafts of auditing standards and guidelines issued by the Auditing Practices Board; both are committees of the Consultative Committee of Accountancy Bodies (f. 1971).
Account books illustrating the development of book-keeping practice, including the journal of Francesco Doni, 1534–42; Linzer Marckt-Strazza journal, 1659; and a West Country draper's waste book, 1654–67 (10 vols).
Miscellaneous collection of letters, documents and MSS relating to the history of accounting, including the notebook of R.P.A. Coffy (*d* 1867); the patent granted on his book-keeping system to E.T. Jones (1767–1833); a number of MSS of 19th– and early 20th–century books on accounting; copies of indentures, articles and partnership agreements of some 19th–century accountants; letters and the MS library catalogue of C.P. Kheil (1843–1908).
Leaf of a piyyut for Yom Kippur, 15th century, used as a binding for Pacioli's *Summa de arithmetica*, 1494.

Non-manuscript material: Books on book-keeping and accounts in English, French, German, Dutch, Russian, Spanish, Japanese and ten other languages, 1494–1914 (*c*3000 vols).

Finding aids: Handlist of MSS. Computer database of 20th-century collection. NRA 36719.

Facilities: Photocopying allowed only of comments on ASB and APB exposure drafts.

Publications: G.A. Lee, 'The Melekh Manuscript: a Discovery in the English Institute Library', *The Accountant* (16 Nov 1972), 622–4.
Library of the ICA: *Historical Accounting Literature: a Catalogue of the Collection of Early Works on Book-Keeping and Accounting* (London, 1975).
M.F. Bywater and B.S. Yamey: *Historical Accounting Literature: a Companion Guide* (London, 1982).

570 Institute of Commonwealth Studies

Parent organisation: School of Advanced Study, University of London

Address: 28 Russell Square, London WC1B 5DS

Telephone: (0171) 580 5876

Fax: (0171) 255 2160

Enquiries: The Librarian, David Blake

Open: Term: Mon–Wed: 10.00–7.00 Thurs, Fri: 10.00–6.00 Vacation: Mon–Fri: 10.00–5.30

Access: Postgraduate and other bona fide research students, on production of identification; undergraduate students on the recommendation of a teacher. Charges are made for the use of the library by certain categories of user; details on application.

Historical background: The institute was founded in 1949 to promote advanced study of the Commonwealth and Empire, and to provide facilities for postgraduate students and academic staff engaged in research on the Comnonwealth in the fields of politics, recent history and economic development.

Acquisitions policy: Advanced level monographs, research papers, official and other primary documents on and from countries of the Commonwealth are collected. Archival collections are normally built up by donation rather than purchase.

Archives of organisation: A complete set of unpublished papers presented to seminars and conferences held at the institute, 1949–.

Major collections: The collection is particulary strong in material relating to the history and politics of southern Africa. Important collections on other areas include the papers of Richard Jebb (1874–1953), Sir Ivor Jennings (1903–65), Sir Keith Hancock (Buganda crisis, 1954), Simon Taylor (1740–1813) (Jamaica), Richard Hart (Caribbean papers, 1937–63), C.L.R. James (West Indian politics) and the minutes of the West India Committee, 1769–1924.
The papers of Ruth First (1925–82) are held on behalf of the Ruth First Memorial Trust.

Non-manuscript material: Collection of materials issued by political parties in the Commonwealth, including manifestos, conference proceedings, posters, car stickers, constitutions, and campaign literature (*c*12,000 items).

Finding aids: Catalogues: card (material received to end of 1984); microfiche (1985–1990); on-line public access catalogue (1990 onwards). Lists sent to NRA.

Facilities: Photocopying. Microfilm/fiche readers.

Publications: New Titles Added to the Library (quarterly).
Regional lists also produced on Africa, Asia, Australia, the Commonwealth Caribbean, New Zealand and the Pacific, the Mediterranean and the Middle East.
Series of short leaflets on materials on the regions of the Commonwealth.
V.J. Bloomfield: 'African Ephemera', *Proceedings of the International Conference on African Bibliography, Nairobi, 1967*, ed. J.D. Pearson (London, 1969) [on political party collection].
B. Willan: *The Southern African Materials Project, University of London, 1973–76* (London, 1980).

D. Blake: 'Indian political ephemera at the Institute of Commonwealth Studies', *South Asia Library Group Newsletter*, no. 29 (Jan 1987), 1–7.

571 Institute of Contemporary Arts

Address: The Mall London SW1Y 5AH

Telephone: (0171) 930 0493

Fax: (0171) 873 0051

Enquiries: The Director

Open: Fri: 10.00–6.00

Access: Bona fide researchers, by appointment only. Access likely to be curtailed pending move of the archive.

Historical background: The ICA was founded in 1947 by the late Herbert Read and Sir Roland Penrose as a centre for all forms of contemporary arts. Its first permanent premises were in Dover Street, and since 1968 it has been housed in Nash House, Carlton House Terrace. The first exhibition was mounted in 1948, and activities include theatre, film, poetry, seminars, conferences and, more recently video, television and radio, as well as visual arts exhibitions. The institute is currently seeking a permanent home for the archive with a major institution.

Acquisitions policy: To maintain the archives and find a suitable home for it where public access can be given.

Archives of organisation: Papers of council, departments and individuals working at the ICA.
Large collection of official papers of Sir Roland Penrose.

Non-manuscript material: Catalogues of exhibitions; photographs; press cuttings; ICA monthly Bulletins.

Finding aids: Preliminary lists for 1947–68 material. Class lists and subject/personal name indexes for 1968–78 material. Post-1978 material in process of accessioning and listing.

Facilities: Photocopying. Photography by arrangement (post-1985 material only).

572 Institute of Contemporary History and Wiener Library

Address: 4 Devonshire Street, London
W1N 2BH

Telephone: (0171) 636 7247

Fax: (0171) 436 6428

Enquiries: The Librarian, Mrs C.S. Wichmann

Open: Mon–Fri: 10.00–5.30

Access: Accredited researchers, who may become members on payment of a moderate fee.

Historical background: The Wiener Library collection was founded by Dr Alfred Wiener in Amsterdam in 1933 and brought to London in 1939. It covers totalitarianism, the history of Germany since 1914 and Jewish history. Most of the books were transferred to Tel Aviv University in 1980, but much of its unique material is available on microfilm. The Institute of Contemporary History and Wiener Library is recognised as an educational charity.

Acquisitions policy: To build on existing collections covering the rise of the Nazis and the subsequent history of Europe.
NB Most material is on microfilm.

Major collections: Eye-witness and fate of survivors reports.
Collection on the Nazi Party in Spain.
Gestapo files and Himmler papers.
International War Crimes Tribunal prosecution documents (*c*40,000).

Non-manuscript material: Press archives: over a million cuttings drawn from an international range of newspapers and covering a wide range of subjects relating to events in Europe and other countries before, during and after World War II; also includes a special collection of files covering biographical information on several thousand individuals considered relevant to the library's holdings. Ephemeral pamphlets, leaflets and brochures.

Finding aids: Guides and indexes.

Facilities: Photocopying. Microfilm reader/printer.

Conservation: Contracted out.

Publications: Various reference works, including:

I. Wolff and H. Kehr (eds): *Wiener Library Catalogue Series* (1949–78) [7 vols].
The Wiener Library Bulletin.

573 Institute of Education Library

Parent organisation: University of London

Address: 20 Bedford Way, London
WC1H 0AL

Telephone: (0171) 612 6080

Fax: (0171) 612 6126

Enquiries: The Head of Reader Services, S. Pickles

Open: Term: Mon–Thurs: 9.30–8.00 Fri: 9.30–7.00 Sat: 9.30–5.00 Vacation (Christmas and Easter): Mon–Fri: 9.30–7.00 Sat: 9.30–5.00 (summer): Mon–Fri: 9.30–6.00

Access: Generally open to the public, but written application should be made.

Historical background: The University of London Institute of Education came into existence in 1902 as the London Day Training College, financed and controlled by the London County Council with the academic support of the University of London. In 1932 it was agreed that the college should be transferred wholly to the control of the University of London with the title Institute of Education. In 1987, though retaining its title, it became a school of the university.

Acquisitions policy: Archives of organisations concerned with education are accepted, if sufficient storage space is available.

Archives of organisation: The library is responsible for administering the institute's own archives.

Major collections: German archive: papers relating to German educational reconstruction after World War II (mainly microfiche).
Incorporated Association of Assistant Masters in Secondary Schools papers, *c*1899–*c*1960.
National Union of Women Teachers minute books and other administrative papers.
World Education Fellowship (formerly the

New Education Fellowship) papers, c1936–c1972 (further papers may be deposited).

College of Preceptors minutes and committee papers, including examination papers and results, 1848–1945.

Society of Teachers opposed to Physical Punishment: policy papers and confidential case material, 1968–89.

Schools Council correspondence and memoranda on curriculum projects, 1964–84.

Non-manuscript material: World Education Fellowship: tape-recordings of conference speeches and Mrs Ensor's reminiscences.

Finding aids: NRA 18109–11, 18116, 18866, 20822.

Facilities: Photocopying. Microfilm/fiche readers.

Publications: *World Education Fellowship,* Royal Commission on Historical Manuscripts Report no. 74/1 (1974).
Incorporated Association of Assistant Masters in Secondary Schools, Royal Commission on Historical Manuscripts Report no. 75/12 (1975).

574 Institute of Germanic Studies

Parent organisation: University of London

Address: 29 Russell Square, London WC1B 5DP

Telephone: (0171) 580 3480

Fax: (0171) 436 3497

Enquiries: The Librarian, Mr W. Abbey (general archive queries) Professor J.L. Flood (History of German studies in Great Britain) The Honorary Secretary (English Goethe Society papers) Professor C.V. Bock (Gundolf Archive)

Open: Mon–Fri: 9.45–6.00

Access: Staff and postgraduates of departments of Germanic Languages and Literature in the University of London; all others on written application.

Historical background: The institute was founded in 1950 as an independent institute of the University of London. It is sponsored by the Senate of the university. The objects of the institute are to promote the advancement of the study of Germanic languages and literature and

to provide facilities for research and opportunities for contacts between scholars, the former through its library, which concentrates its resources mainly on primary texts and journals, the latter through regular seminars and lectures. The initiator of the institute and its first honorary director (1950–53) was Professor L.A. Willoughby.

Acquisitions policy: To strengthen existing archive collections by encouraging donations or deposits, and, if necessary, by purchase.

Major collections: Majut Correspondence: letters to Dr R. Majut from German scholars in Berlin, 1920s-1930s; letters from Jethro Bithell, 1940s-1950s.
Bithell Correspondence: letters to Jethro Bithell from various correspondents.
Breul Correspondence: letters to Karl Breul, first Schröder Professor of German at Cambridge, from various correspondents, c1900–1932.
Correspondence of German writers and scholars with Professor E.M. Butler, Professor W. Rose, Professor L.W. Forster and others.
Papers of Berthold Auerbach, Germany's leading theatre agent before World War II, and of Dr Mary Beare.
Papers of Professor August Closs (1898–1990) and of Professor Gilbert Waterhouse (1888–1977).
Gundolf Archive: letters to and from Professor Friedrich Gundolf of Heidelberg, with TSS and MSS of lectures, poems and publications, c1900–1931 (c1000 items).
History of German studies in Great Britain: records collected on behalf of the Conference of University Teachers of German in Great Britain and Ireland.
English Goethe Society: records and papers.

Non-manuscript material: Photographs; printed material such as offprints, newspaper articles, theatre programmes, invitation cards etc.
Large collection of pamphlets and cuttings.
Books on German languages and literature, many of which complement the MSS collection.

Finding aids: Handlists to all collections.

Facilities: Photocopying. Microfilm/fiche reader.

Publications: C.V. Bock: 'First Report on the Gundolf Papers at the Institute of Germanic Languages and Literature in the University of London', *German Life and Letters* (new series) 15 (1961–2), 16–20.

C. Neutjens: *Friedrich Gundolf: ein bibliographischer Apparat* (Bonn, 1969) [includes almost complete list of the Gundolf Archive].

J.L. Flood: 'Die Mittelalterlichen Handschriften der Bibliothek des Institute of Germanic Studies, London', *Zeitschrift für deutsches Altertum und deutsche Literatur*, 129 (1991), 325–30.

575 Institute of Historical Research

Parent organisation: University of London

Address: Senate House, London WClE 7HU

Telephone: (0171) 636 0272

Fax: (0171) 436 2183

Enquiries: The Academic Secretary, Dr Steven Smith

Open: Mon–Fri: 9.00–9.00 Sat and most public holidays: 9.00–5.00

Access: Open to graduates engaged in historical research. Details of membership scheme available on request.

Historical background: Founded in 1921 as the University of London's centre for postgraduate study in history, the institute functions as a national and international focus and meeting place for historians. It runs research programmes, including the Victoria County History, and the projects of its Centre for Metropolitan History, as well as seminars, courses and conferences; it also produces publications. Its library of about 140,000 volumes, all on open access, plus a growing collection of microforms, concentrates on research tools and primary tools. In 1994 the institute became part of the School of Advanced Study of the University of London. With the exception of the institute's own records, all archival material is deposited in the University of London Library (entry 762).

Non-manuscript material: Microforms include the collections held at the Huntingdon Library and some other foreign collections and finding aids.
Guides to archives, bibliographies, printed primary sources, official publications, University of London history theses, runs of journals, e.g. *Gentleman's Magazine, Edinburgh Review*, reports of the NRA. A collection of current leaflets from archive repositories and libraries is also maintained.

Facilities: Photocopying. Microfilm/fiche reader/printer.

576 Institute of Ophthalmology

Parent organisation: University of London

Address: Bath Street, London EC1V 9EL

Telephone: (0171) 608 6815

Fax: (0171) 608 6859

Enquiries: The Librarian, Mrs C.S. Lawrence

Open: Mon–Fri: 9.00–5.00

Access: Bona fide researchers, by appointment.

The institute, previously located in Judd Street, holds archival material, notably personal papers, medical illustrations, photographs and letters concerning patients, of Edward Nettleship (1845–1913) *re* heredity and eye disorders, 1870–1913. There is a card index to historical work in the library. Photocopying and a microfiche reader are available.

577 Institute of Physics

Address: 47 Belgrave Square, London SW1X 8QX

Telephone: (0171) 235 6111

Fax: (0171) 259 6002

Enquiries: The Chief Executive, Dr Alun Jones

Open: Mon–Fri: 9.30–5.00

Access: Bona fide researchers, by appointment.

The present institute is the result of the amalgamation of the Physical Society (f. 1874), the Optical Society (f. 1907) and the Institute of Physics (f. 1918). It was granted a Royal Charter in 1970. It holds its own archives, which include minute books of council and some committees, and all publications of constituent bodies, 1874–.

578 Institution of Civil Engineers

Address: 1–7 Great George Street, Westminster, London SW1P 3AA

Telephone: (0171) 222 7722

Fax: (0171) 222 7500

Enquiries: The Archivist, Mrs M.K. Murphy or The Librarian, Mr M.M. Chrimes

Open: Mon–Fri: 9.15–5.30

Access: Items may be consulted in the library by members of the institution, and by approved readers by prior arrangement.

Historical background: The institution was founded in 1818. The first royal charter was received in 1828. The institution is the learned society and qualifying body for the civil engineering profession. The library has as its nucleus the gifts of Thomas Telford (1757–1834), who became the institution's first president in 1820. The archive collections consist of records relating to the institution and to the civil engineering profession.

Acquisitions policy: All important ICE records. Select civil engineering archives, usually acquired by gift, very occasionally by purchase.

Archives of organisation: ICE archives: records of meetings, membership, accounts; council and committees' minutes; MSS of early papers; minute books of the Society of Civil Engineers, 1771–92, and the Society of Smeatonian Civil Engineers, 1793–.
Archives of the Institution of Municipal Engineers (absorbed in 1984); Society of Civil Engineering Technicians; Société des Ingénieurs Civils de France (British section); Council of Engineering Institutions.

Major collections: MS records relating to the work of Thomas Telford; the Rennie family: John Rennie (1761–1821), George Rennie (1791–1866) and Sir John Rennie (1794–1874); John Smeaton (1724–92); William Mackenzie (1794–1851), contractor, and his family (non-engineering material in Buckinghamshire CRO, entry **34**); Joseph Bazalgette (1819–91); Robert Stephenson (1803–59); Sir Marc Isambard Brunel (1769–1849); the Thames Tunnel.
J.G. James Collection relating to the history of iron bridges.

Non-manuscript material: Engineering draw-

ings and plans; prints; paintings; portraits; slides; photographs.
J.G. James Collection of architectural and civil engineering slides.
Medals; various artefacts, e.g. drawings and instruments belonging to Telford.

Finding aids: Various indexes and lists, including Archives of the ICE provisional list (1979) and Collections of Prints and Drawings (1978) [duplicated TS].
All recent additions notified to NRA.
On-line computer catalogue.

Facilities: Photocopying. Microform reader/printer.

Conservation: Contracted out.

Publications: Save Engineering Records (1979) [pamphlet].
M.M. Chrimes: 'The Institution of Civil Engineers Library and Archives: a Brief Introduction', *Construction History*, 5 (1989), 59–65.

579 Institution of Electrical Engineers
Archives Department

Address: Savoy Place, London WC2R 0BL

Telephone: (0171) 240 1871 ext. 2228, 344 5462

Fax: (0171) 240 7735

Enquiries: The Archivist, Mrs E.D.P. Symons

Open: Mon–Fri: 10.00–5.00

Access: Bona fide researchers, by appointment.

Historical background: The institution was founded in 1871 as the Society of Telegraph Engineers, taking its present name in 1888. A Royal Charter granted in 1921 recognised it as the representative body of electrical engineers in the United Kingdom. The institution houses a library (formed in 1880) and an archives department (formed in 1975), which holds MS material relating to the history and development of magnetism and electricity from medieval times to the present, and modern papers relating to the development of telegraphy, the submarine cable, electrical engineering and physics.

Acquisition policy: To acquire, by donation, deposit or purchase, material relevant to the history and development of electrical engineering and electronics, and allied fields, including modern industrial records.

Archives of organisation: Archives of the institution: official records and working papers, 1871–.
Archives of the Institution of Electronic and Radio Engineers (amalgamated 1988) and the Institution of Protection/Manufacturing Engineers (merged 1991).

Major collections: Special Collection MSS: including medieval MSS; the scientific papers of Michael Faraday (1791–1867); Sir Francis Ronalds (1788–1873); Oliver Heaviside (1850–1925); Sir William Fothergill Cooke (1806–79), including letters from Sir Charles Wheatstone (1802–75); several 19th– and 20th–century engineers and academics.
National Archive for Electrical Science and Technology: modern technical and manufacturing records and engineering drawings.
Archives of the Women's Engineering Society, 1919–85, and of the Electrical Association for Women, 1924–86.

Non-manuscript material: Portraits (mainly photographs and engravings) of eminent scientists and electrical engineers, presidents of the institution, 18th–20th centuries.
Photographs of electrical equipment and institution events.
Silvanus Phillips Thompson Collection of rare books relating to magnetism and electricity, 15th–19th centuries (1000).
Sir Francis Ronalds Collection of rare books (2000) and pamphlets (3000) relating to magnetism and electricity and the development of the telegraph, 17th–19th centuries.

Finding aids: General index to all collections. Handlists for most collections. Index to photograph collections. Lists sent to NRA.

Facilities: Photocopying. Photography by arrangement.

Conservation: Contracted out.

Publications: F. Ronalds: *Catalogue of Books and Papers relating to Electricity, Magnetism, the Electric Telegraph* (1880).
S.P. Thompson: *Handlist of Magnetic and Electrical Books* (1914).

580 Institution of Gas Engineers

Address: 21 Portland Place, London W1N 3AF

Telephone: (0171) 636 6603

Fax: (0171) 636 6602

The institution was founded in 1863 and retains some archives, including printed bound transactions, as well as a small number of MS items donated by individuals. Access is limited and requests to consult material should be made by appointment with the librarian.

581 Institution of Mechanical Engineers

Address: 1 Birdcage Walk, Westminster, London SW1H 9JJ

Telephone: (0171) 222 7899

Fax: (0171) 222 8762

Enquiries: The Information Services Manager, Ms. J. Ollerton or The Senior Librarian/Archivist, Mr Keith Moore

Open: Mon–Fri: 9.15–5.30

Access: Bona fide researchers, by appointment only.

Historical background: The institution was founded in Birmingham in 1847, moving into its current premises in 1899. The library contains some 150,000 publications covering all aspects of engineering and associated subjects.

Acquisitions policy: To maintain the collection on mechanical engineering, by purchase, donation or presentation.

Archives of organisation: Council and committee minutes; biographical records of members (proposal forms) and signature books, 1847–.
Archives of organisations later merged with IMechE, including the Institute of Automobile Engineers (f. 1905) and the Institution of Locomotive Engineers (f. 1911).

Major collections: Correspondence and papers of George Stephenson (1781–1848), first president of the institution, and Robert Stephenson (1803–59).
Note-books and engineering drawings of James Nasmyth (1808–90); Charles Algernon Parsons (1854–1931); Frederick William Lanchester

(1868–1946); David Joy (1825–1903); Joseph Whitworth (1803–87).

Personal papers of Christopher Hinton (1901–83), Baron Hinton of Bankside, nuclear engineer.

Non-manuscript material: Portraits of eminent engineers, 19th century.

Photographs of engineering works, notably Robert Howlett's series on Isambard Kingdom Brunel and the construction of the 'Great Eastern'.

Engineering medals and artefacts.

Finding aids: Catalogue on a CAIRS-IMS database.

Facilities: Photocopying. Microfilm reader/printer.

Conservation: Contracted out.

Publications: R.H. Parsons: *A History of the Institution of Mechanical Engineers, 1847–1947* (1947)

582 The Institution of Mechanical Incorporated Engineers

Address: 3 Birdcage Walk, Westminster, London SW1H 9JN

Telephone: (0171) 799 1808

Fax: (0171) 799 2243

Enquiries: The Assistant Secretary, Diane Davy

Open: Mon–Fri: 9.00–5.00

Access: Generally open to the public, by appointment.

Historical background: The institution was incorporated in 1988 on the amalgamation of two organisations, the Institution of Technical Engineers in Mechanical Engineering (ITEME, f. 1988) and the Institution of Mechanical and General Technician Engineers (IMGTechE, f. 1864). IMGTechE was started as the Vulcanic Society by apprentices at Maudsley Sons at Field Ltd of Lambeth. Its name was changed several times before the present one was adopted in 1976.

Acquisitions policy: To maintain membership records and associated memorabilia.

Archives of organisation: Institution of Junior Engineers council minute books, 1894–98.

Junior Institution of Engineers council minute books, 1903–.

Minutes of committees, including finance and general purposes/publications, 1898–1912; benevolent fund, 1947–88.

Minutes of members' ordinary meetings 1912–61.

Membership registers, 1914–38.

Subscription book, 1919–68, and other financial records.

Papers on awards of medals, 1953–78.

Non-manuscript material: Architectural plans relating to former HQ at 33 Ovington Square, London.

Small collections of photographs and memorabilia.

Finding aids: Brief listing in preparation.

Facilities: Photocopying. Photography.

Publications: Institution of Mechanical and General Technical Engineers Centenary 1884–1984 (IMGTechE, 1984).

583 Institution of Mining and Metallurgy

Address: 44 Portland Place, London W1N 4BR

Telephone: (0171) 580 3802

Fax: (0171) 436 5388

Enquiries: The Head of Library and Information Service, Mr M. McGarr

A library was started in 1894 soon after the founding of the institution; it holds a historic collection of early books on mining. Internal administrative archives are held; there is also an extensive map collection and a small group of unpublished articles dating from the 1900s and 1940s.

584 Irish Studies Resource Centre Archive

Parent organisation: University of North London

Address: Faculty of Humanities and Teacher Education, 1 Prince of Wales Road, London NW5 3LB

Telephone: (0171) 753 5018 ext. 4092

Fax: (071) 753 7069

Enquiries: The Director

Open: By arrangement.

Access: Generally open to the public, by appointment.

Historical background: The Irish Studies Resource Centre was established by the University of North London in 1986 and the archive is housed in the university library. Much material is on permanent loan from the Irish in Britain History Group and the video collection was recently donated by the Activision Irish Project. It focuses on a wide range of topics, including the Irish in London, migration, racism, homelessness and Irish culture, and is particularly rich in materials covering the experience of the 1940s/50s migrants.

Acquisitions policy: Actively welcomes donations of material covering Irish culture of contemporary or historical interest.

Major collections: Subject files of personal reminiscences, memorabilia, photographs and pamphlets, including also British media and Ireland.

Non-manuscript material: Activision Irish Project: large video collection.
Irish Post, 1970–.
Books and articles of Irish literary and historical interest (*c*400).
Cassette recordings.

Publications: Guide to Resource Centre (1994). Information packs.

585 Japan Society Library

Address: Suite 6/9, Morley House, 314–22 Regent Street, London W1R 5AH

Telephone: (0171) 636 3029

Fax: (0171) 636 3089

Enquiries: The Hon. Librarian, Mr Kenneth B. Gardner via Secretariat of the Japan Society at above address

Open: Thurs: 2.30–5.30
Closed only when national holidays (British and Japanese) fall on a Thursday.

Access: Members of the Japan Society. Others by appointment,

Historical background: The society and library were founded in 1891, and the archives, where they survive, are retained from that time. The name changed to the Japan Society in 1986.

Acquisitions policy: To maintain the archives and MSS.

Archives of organisation: Some archive material, including minutes of the council, are held by the secretariat and the library. Records of the society are incorporated in *Transactions and Proceedings of the Japan Society of London* (1891–World War II), continued by *Bulletin of the Japan Society of London* (1950–85) and *Proceedings* (of the Japan Society, 1986–).

Non-manuscript material: Some early printed books, 17th–18th century.

Finding aids: Card catalogues under author, subject and title.

586 The Jewish Museum

Address: 129/131 Albert Street, London NW1 7NB

Telephone: (0171) 284 1997

Fax: (0171) 267 9008

Enquiries: The Curator

Open: Sun-Thurs: 10.00–4.00
Closed Jewish and public holidays.

Access: The museum has no search room, therefore MSS can only be inspected by prior appointment, by qualified researchers.

The museum has a small MSS collection, which includes a limited quantity of archival material. Most of this is listed in an appendix to an article by Edgar Samuel in vol. iii of the *National Index of Parish Registers.* However, since that was published the museum's collections of secondary genealogical material have been transferred to the Anglo-Jewish Archives, now at University of Southampton (entry **1021**) and the Mocatta Library, now incorporated into University College London (entry **761A**). See also NRA 10098.

587 Jews' College Library

Address: 44a Albert Road, London NW4 2SJ

Telephone: (0181) 203 6427/8/9

Enquiries: The Librarian, Mr Ezra Kahn or The Catalogue Librarian, Mr Aron Prys

Open: Term: Mon–Wed: 9.00–6.00 Fri: 9.00–1.00 Vacation: Mon–Thurs: 9.00–5.00 Fri: 9.00–1.00
Closed all Jewish holy days and public holidays.

Access: Open to those who are interested in

Hebrew and Jewish studies. Students, scholars and other enquirers who need guidance should telephone prior to a visit and produce a letter of introduction.

Historical background: The library was founded in 1860. It is part of Jews' College, which trains students to become rabbis, cantors and teachers; it is also used for general Jewish studies.

Acquisitions policy: Acquisition is dependent on the amount of donations received. Financial assistance is welcomed as well as donations, from individual books to entire collections.

Major collections: Jews' College Collection of MSS (*c*150 vols).
Montefiore Collection of MSS (*c*600 vols).

Non-manuscript material: Collection of printed books and pamphlets (*c*70,000 vols).
Montefiore Collection of printed books (*c*3000 vols).
Hebrew and Jewish periodicals collection.

Finding aids: Lists and indexes. NRA 22093.

Facilities: Photocopying. Microfilm reader.

Conservation: Contracted out.

Publications: H. Hirschfield: *Descriptive Catalogue of the Hebrew MSS of the Montefiore Library* (London, 1904, 1969).

588 Keats House

Parent organisation: London Borough of Camden

Address: Wentworth Place, Keats Grove, Hampstead, London NW3 2RR

Telephone: (0171) 435 2062

Fax: (0171) 431 9293

Enquiries: The Curator, Mrs C.M. Gee

Open: April-Oct: Mon–Fri: 10.00–1.00; 2.00–6.00 Sat: 10.00–1.00; 2.00–5.00 Sun: 2.00–5.00
Nov-March: Mon–Fri: 1.00–5.00 Sat: 10.00–1.00; 2.00–5.00 Sun: 2.00–5.00

Access: Approved readers, on written request.

Historical background: The Keats Collection was begun in 1897 by Hampstead Public Library and transferred in 1921 to Keats House, where John Keats lived 1818–20. It was opened to the public in 1925. The London Borough of Camden continues to maintain the collection and the house as part of the Libraries and Arts Department.

Acquisitions policy: To add to the collections on Keats, Shelley, Byron, Leigh Hunt and their circles and to maintain the collection on general Romantic literature. To add, where possible, to the relics of the poets.

Major collections: Dilke Collection: MSS, books, paintings, relics of Keats.
Leigh-Browne Lockyer Collection: commonplace books relating to friends of Keats (20).

Non-manuscript material: Kate Greenaway Collection: original drawings, proofs, Christmas cards and books.
Charles Lamb Collection: books on Lamb (*c*1000).
Maurice Buxton Forman Collection: books on Keats and his circle (*c*2500).
Smaller collections from the families of Fanny Brawne, Charles Brown, Joseph Severn and Fanny Keats.

Finding aids: Catalogue of MSS and relics (1966). Card catalogue of pamphlets and ephemera. Recataloguing in progress.

Facilities: Photocopying. Microfilm reader.

Conservation: Contracted out.

589 King's College London

Parent organisation: University of London

Address: Strand, London WC2R 2LS

Telephone: (0171) 873 2187/2015 (direct lines)

Fax: (0171) 873 2760

Enquiries: The College Archivist, Miss Patricia Methven

Open: Term: Mon–Fri: 9.30–5.30 Vacation: Mon–Fri: 9.30–4.30
Closed last fortnight of August.

Access: Open to bona fide scholars and members of the public able to demonstrate a serious interest in the records, by appointment. Records relating to college business are closed for 30 years. Student and personnel files are closed for 80 years. A limited number of the collections in the Liddell Hart Centre for Military Archives are closed. Readers seeking to use the Centre for Military Archives and the

Modern Greek Archives are required to agree to submit texts for publication to the trustees and/or another designated authority.

A College Archives and Library Manuscripts

Historical background: KCL was founded in 1828. Both King's College (the senior department) and King's College School (the junior department) opened to students in 1831. In 1839 the first King's College Hospital was established in Portugal Street, moving to Denmark Hill in 1913, where the Medical School followed in 1915. From 1849 the college provided evening and occasional education for Londoners. Academic education coexisted with training for would-be entrants to the Civil Service, telegraphists and surveyors of taxes, and workshop classes were set up with, among others, the Clothworkers' Company (entry 521). An offshoot of the Civil Services classes was a commercial school, the Strand School, which moved into the basement of the college when the boy's school moved to Wimbledon in 1897. With reconstitution of the University of London in 1900, the college shed its non-academic commitments. In 1909 responsibility was transferred to independent governing bodies for the hospital and KCS and to the LCC for the Strand School. The abolition of the Test Act in 1903 led to the partial separation of the college into University of London King's College for the majority of subjects and KCL for the Theological Department. In 1915 King's College for Women (f. 1871) transferred from Kensington, except for the Household and Social Science Department, which became recognised as a school in its own right. In 1953 it was renamed Queen Elizabeth College. In the 1980s the divisions of the college went into partial reverse. The Theological College was reunited with the rest of the college in 1980, the whole to be known again as KCL. In 1983 King's College Hospital Medical and Dental School was also reunited, followed in 1985 by Queen Elizabeth College. In 1985 the college was merged with Chelsea College, founded in 1891 as the South Western Polytechnic, later Chelsea Polytechnic, a college of advanced technology, and eventually a school of the university in 1966. The records of the College School of Medicine and Dentistry have recently been transferred to the college.

Acquisition policy: Internal records, private papers of members of the college, and papers supporting research in the specialist fields of literature in translation and modern Greece.

Archives of organisation: All major records relating to KCL, 1828–, including its constituent colleges.

Records relating to KCS, and the Strand School, mainly during the periods when they formed part of the college, but 19th-century pupil admission forms are held by KCS.

King's College Hospital records, 1839–1976, including minutes, policy files and title deeds; case files, 1840–1939; Belgrave Hospital for Children case papers, 1904–39.

Major collections: Papers of former members of the college, including Prof. T.J. Brown (1923–87); Dr R.M. Burrows (1867–1920); Prof. J.F. Daniell (1790–1845); Maureen Duffy (*b* 1933); Prof. R.R. Gates (1882–1962); Prof. E.J. Hanson (1919–73); Prof. F.J.C. Hearnshaw (1869–1946); Prof. Donald Hey (1904–87); Dr C.W.F McClare (1937–77); Rev. W.R. Matthews (1881–1974); Rev. F.D. Maurice (1805–72); Prof. J.C. Maxwell (1831–79); Evelyn Underhill (1875–1941); Prof. Sir Charles Wheatstone (1802–75).

Other collections: P.H. Leathes (*d* 1838), especially 18th–century antiquarian and topographical literature, *c*1650–1844; William Marsden (1754–1836), especially oriental MSS and records *re* Portuguese missionaries, 1580–1780; Frida Mond Collection, including Goethe and Schiller papers, 1794–1831; King George III Museum Collection, especially Richmond Observatory records, 1769–83.

Archives of *Modern Poetry in Translation*, 1965–83; *Adam International Review*, 1920–86; the Greek Relief Fund, 1948–84; League for Democratic Freedom in Greece, 1940–83.

Non-manuscript material: Photographs and engravings of college life and history. Sir Charles Wheatstone Collection of photographs *re* his work on stereoscopes.

Finding aids: Handlists; some sent to NRA.

Facilities: Restricted photocopying and photography.

Publications: F.J.C. Hearnshaw: *The Centenary History of King's College London* (London, 1929).

H. Willoughby Lyle: *King's and Some King's Men: being a Record of the Medical Department of King's College London from 1830–1909 and of King's College Hospital Medical School from*

1909–1934 (London, 1935; addendum to 1948, 1950).

H. Silver and S.J. Teague (eds): *Chelsea College: a History* (London, 1977).

G. Huelin: *King's College London, 1828–1978* (London, 1978).

F. Miles and G. Cranch: *King's College School: the First 150 Years* (London, 1979).

W.O. Skeat: *King's College London Engineering Society, 1847–1947* (London, 1979).

N. Marsh: *The History of Queen Elizabeth College* (London, 1986).

D.J. Britten (ed.): *The Story of King's College Hospital and its Medical School* (London, 1991).

B Liddell Hart Centre for Military Archives

Historical background: The centre was opened in 1964 to provide a repository for documents bearing on the military affairs of the 20th century which would respect their confidential nature. It was named after Captain Sir Basil Liddell Hart (1895–1970) to mark the acquisition of his papers and library in 1973.

Acquisitions policy: Private papers of higher commanders of the armed services and defence personnel holding senior office during the 20th century.

Major collections: Collections of private papers (*c*500), including those of FM Viscount Alanbrooke (1883–1963); FM Viscount Allenby (1861–1936); ACM Sir Robert Brooke-Popham (1878–1953); Sir Arthur Bryant (1899–1985); Brig. John Charteris (1877–1946); Sir Frank Cooper (*b* 1922); Sir Maurice Dean (1906–78), Maj.-Gen. C.H. Foulkes (1875–1969); Maj.-Gen. J.F.C. Fuller (1878–1966); Gen. Sir Ian Hamilton (1853–1947); Gen. Lord Ismay (1887–1965); Sir Charles Johnson (1912–86); Gen. Sir Richard O'Connor (1889–1981); ACM S.W.B. Menaul (1915–87); FM Sir Archibald Montgomery-Massingberd (1871–1947); FM Sir William Robertson (1860–1933); Gen. Sir Hugh Stockwell (1903–86).

Non-manuscript material: Numerous photographs illustrating the life and work of the armed services from the Boer War onwards; especially important are those relating to the development of photographic reconnaissance at the turn of the century.

Microfilm (800 reels) and microfiche (5000) copies of original material, mainly American, relating to defence studies.

Finding aids: Handlists; some sent to NRA.

Facilities: Restricted photocopying and photography.

Publications: *Consolidated List of Accessions* (London, 1986); *Supplement, 1985–1990* (1991).

590 Laban Centre for Movement and Dance

Address: Laurie Grove, New Cross, London SE14 6NW

Telephone: (0181) 692 4070 ext. 32

Fax: (0181) 694 8749

Enquiries: The Librarian, Peter Bassett

Open: Term: Mon, Wed, Fri: 8.45–5.30 Tues, Thurs: 8.45–7.30 Vacation: Mon–Fri: 9.00–5.00

Access: Generally available to the public. An appointment is necessary and a charge is made.

Historical background: The Laban Centre for Movement and Dance is an institution for higher education in dance offering graduate, postgraduate and research degree courses. The centre developed from the Art of Movement Studio opened by Lisa Ullmann, an associate of Rudolph Laban, in Manchester in 1946. The library and archives developed considerably during the early 1980s into a major dance resource, although the archives of the Art of Movement Studio and the Laban Centre are not at present available for public use.

Acquisitions policy: All forms of dance and movement are covered, including dance therapy and dance in the community. Equally all forms of printed and audio visual materials on dance are acquired.

Major collections: Peter Williams Collection: the working collection of Peter Williams, editor of the journal *Dance and Dancers*, 1950–77, consisting principally of photographs, theatre programmes, publicity material.
Laban Collection: documents, books and photographs of the work of Rudolph Laban (*d* 1958) in pre-war Europe.

Finding aids: Computer catalogues for both collections, and general collections of the library, are in preparation.

Facilities: Photocopying. Microfilm/fiche reader. Video viewing facilities.

591 Lambeth Palace Library

Address: London SE1 7JU

Telephone: (0171) 928 6222

Enquiries: The Librarian and Archivist,
Dr Richard Palmer

Open: Mon–Fri: 10.00–5.00

Access: Bona fide students, at the discretion of the Librarian; new readers are required to provide a letter of introduction from a person or institution of recognised standing. Special permission is needed for access to some categories of MSS (e.g. illuminated MSS).

Historical background: Lambeth Palace Library is the historic library of the archbishops of Canterbury. It was founded as a public library by Archbishop Bancroft in 1610. Its original endowment included a celebrated collection of medieval MSS and a large quantity of English and foreign printed books, to which considerable additions have been made over the past 350 years. The Church Commissioners are now responsible for the maintenance of the library, and it is recognised as a place of deposit for public records.

Acquisitions policy: Records of the archbishops of Canterbury. Historical records of the central institutions of the Church of England, with the exception of records of the Church Commissioners and the General Synod and its associated bodies (see Church of England Record Centre, entry **518**). Papers of ecclesiastics of national distinction and of statesmen where these fall within the library's general area of interest.

Archives of organisation: Registers of the archbishops of Canterbury, 13th–20th centuries.
Correspondence and papers of the archbishops of Canterbury, 16th century–.
Records of the estates of the See of Canterbury, 13th–19th centuries.
Archives of the Province of Canterbury, including those of the Court of Arches, the Faculty Office, the Vicar General's Office, and Convocation, mainly 17th century–.
Records of the Archbishop's Peculiars of Arches, Croydon and Shoreham, particularly testamentary, 17th century–.
Records of the Lambeth Conferences, 1867–.

Major collections: Medieval MSS.
Collections of 16th-century MSS, including Bacon, Carew, Shrewsbury and Talbot papers.

Records of societies within the Church of England, including the Church of England Men's Society, Church of England Temperance Society, Church Society, Church Union, Clergy Orphan Corporation, Confraternity of the Blessed Sacrament, Incorporated Church Building Society.
Papers of the bishops of London, including extensive collections concerning colonial America and the West Indies, 17th century–.
Papers of distinguished bishops, churchmen and statesmen, such as G.K.A. Bell, Bishop of Chichester; A.C. Headlam, Bishop of Gloucester; E.J. Palmer, Bishop of Bombay; Christopher Wordsworth, Bishop of Lincoln; Baroness Burdett-Coutts; John Keble; Athelstan Riley; Isaac Williams; 1st Earl of Selborne; William Gladstone.
Ecclesiastical records of the Commonwealth, 1643–60.
Records of the Commission for Building Fifty New Churches in London and Westminster, 18th century.
Records of Doctors Commons.
Registers of foreign churches, e.g. Basra, Khartoum, Shanghai and Shangtung.

Non-manuscript material: Books (c150,000), particularly strong in English and foreign books published from the invention of printing to 1800.
Large collection of pamphlets.

Finding aids: Catalogues and indexes.

Facilities: Photocopying. Photography and microfilming by arrangement. Colour transparencies available for loan.

Publications: Apart from catalogues noted in Robert Collison: *Published Library Catalogues* (1973), 137–8, see:
C.R. Batho: *A Calendar of the Shrewsbury and Talbot Papers in Lambeth Palace Library and the College of Arms, ii: Talbot Papers in the College of Arms* (1971) [collection purchased by Lambeth Palace in 1983].
E.G.W. Bill: *A Catalogue of Manuscripts in Lambeth Palace Library, MSS 1222–1860* (1972).
J. Houston: *Index of Cases in the Records of the Court and Arches at Lambeth Palace Library, 1660–1913* (1972).
J.E. Sayers and E.G.W. Bill: *Calendar of the Papers of Charles Thomas Longley, Archbishop of Canterbury, 1862–1868, in Lambeth Palace Library* (1972).

Index to the Papers of Anthony Bacon (1558–1601) in Lambeth Palace Library (MSS 647–662) (1974).

W.W. Manross: *S.P.G. Papers in the Lambeth Palace Library: Calendar and Indexes* (1974).

M. Barber: *Index to the Letters and Papers of Frederick Temple, Archbishop of Canterbury, 1896–1902, in Lambeth Palace Library* (1975).

E.G.W. Bill: *The Queen Anne Churches: a Catalogue of the Papers in Lambeth Palace Library of the Commission for Building Fifty New Churches in London and Westminster, 1711–1759* (1979).

Index to the Letters and Papers of Edward White Benson, Archbishop of Canterbury, 1883–1896, in Lambeth Palace Library (1980).

E.G.W. Bill: *A Catalogue of Manuscripts in Lambeth Palace Library, MSS 2341–3119* (1983).

For recent accessions, see Library's *Annual Review*.

592 The Law Society Library

Address: 113 Chancery Lane, London WC2A 1PL

Telephone: (0171) 320 5946

Fax: (0171) 831 1687

Enquiries: The Librarian

Open: Mon–Fri: 9.00–5.00

Access: Members and academic researchers, by written appointment. Charges for enquiries passed to records department on individual solicitors and firms.

Historical background: The Law Society was formerly known as the Society of Attorneys, Solicitors and Proctors and others not being Barristers, practising in the Courts of Law and Equity of the United Kingdom; the Law Institution and the Incorporated Law Society. It was founded in 1832 and remains on the same site. The archives are limited and do not include the papers of individual solicitors, their firms or their clients.

Acquisitions policy: To maintain the society's archives. Private papers and MSS are not acquired.

Archives of organisation: Incomplete archives, including minutes of council and committees; annual reports; committee reports; charters and bye laws.

Major collections: Records of the Society of Gentlemen Practicers. Certain records of Staple Inn.

Non-manuscript material: Architectural plans of 113 Chancery Lane by Vulliamy, Hardwick and others.

Some photographs of solicitors, mainly presidents of the society.

Publications of the Metropolitan Provincial Law Association.

Finding aids: Computer catalogue (limited detail); also on microfiche.

Facilities: Archival material is not normally copied, but photocopying and microform reader/printers are available.

Conservation: Contracted out.

Publications: *Handbook of the Law Society* (London, 1938) [gives brief description].

D. Sugarman: *History of the Law Society* (1995).

593 The Leathersellers' Company

Address: 15 St Helen's Place, London EC3A 6DQ

Telephone: (0171) 588 4615

Enquiries: The Clerk

Open: Strictly by appointment only.

Access: On a restricted basis following discussion with the clerk.

Historical background: The Leathersellers' Company appears to have been the successor of two earlier and minor fraternities that existed in the early 13th century. Reference to a Fraternity of Leathersellers appears in 1372. Articles for the regulation of the craft were applied for in 1398, and in 1444 the Leathersellers obtained a Charter of Incorporation. The company has possessed six halls and has provided technical education since 1909, with the establishment of the Leathersellers' Technical College, re-established as the National Leathersellers' College in 1951, and now known as the British School of Leather Technology, Nene College, Northampton.

Acquisitions policy: To maintain the company's archives; the company also relies on the goodwill of members of the profession and families who present items of historical interest.

Archives of organisation: Minutes, 1608–; warden's accounts, 1471–; books of wills, 1470–1799; apprenticeship books, 1629–; registers for freedom, 1630–; livery books, 1706–; charters and ordinances.

Publications: W.H. Black: *History of the Antiquities of the Worshipful Company of Leathersellers of the City of London* (London, 1871) [includes facsimiles and lists archives].
P. Hunting: *The Leathersellers' Company: a History* (London, 1994).

594 Leighton House Museum and Art Gallery

Parent organisation: Royal Borough of Kensington and Chelsea

Address: 12 Holland Park Road, London W14 8LZ

Telephone: (0171) 602 3316

Fax: (0171) 371 2467

Enquiries: The Curator, Julia Findlater

Open: Mon–Sat: 11.00–5.30

Access: Bona fide researchers, by appointment.

Leighton House acquired the papers of Frederic, Lord Leighton (1830–96), which consist of c600 items of juvenilia and correspondence with family and friends, 1840–96. Some of the letters have been transferred from the G.F. Watts Gallery, Compton, and those are listed in B. Curle: *Catalogue of Leighton Letters* (Royal Borough of Kensington and Chelsea, 1983). A computerised catalogue is in progress.

595 Lesbian Archive and Information Centre

Address: London Women's Centre, 4 Wild Court, Holborn, London WC2B 4AU

Telephone: (0171) 405 6475

Enquiries: The Lesbian Archive

Open: Sat: 2.00–6.00 Other times by arrangement.

Access: Access is for women only; there are restrictions on some materials according to donors' wishes.

The archive was established in 1984 to collect material past and present of specific interest to lesbians and to house it safely and confidentially. It is unfunded and relies on membership and donations. The archive currently holds a wide variety of records, including MSS, diaries and letters as well as oral histories, press cuttings, artwork, reference fiction books, magazines, newspapers and newsletters and audio-visual material, which dates mostly from 1950 onwards although it relates to earlier decades. Catalogues, indexes and lists are available. There is a computerised information database and photocopying is available. See NRA 36162.

596 Liberal Jewish Synagogue

Address: 28 St John's Wood Road, London NW8 7HA

Telephone: (0171) 286 5181

Fax: (0171) 266 3591

Enquiries: The Archivist, Mr Bryan Diamond (home tel. (0171) 433 1876)

Open: By arrangement with the archivist (not Saturdays or Jewish holy days).

Access: Generally open to the public, by appointment.

Historical background: The LJS was founded in 1911, as an offshoot of the Jewish Religious Union formed in 1902 by the Hon. Lily Montagu and Claude Goldsmid Montefiore. Archives were transferred to the present building in 1925.

Acquisitions policy: Acquisitions are normally restricted to records directly related to the LJS and its ministers.

Archives of organisation: Administrative records and minutes of Jewish Religious Union, 1902–, and of Liberal Jewish Synagogue, 1911–.

Major collections: Correspondence, sermons, articles and press cuttings *re* Rabbis Israel Mattuck (1883–1954) and Leslie Edgar (1905–84); smaller amounts of correspondence, sermons etc of Hon. Lily Montagu (1873–1963) and Claude Montefiore (1858–1938).

Non-manuscript material: Plans and photographs of the previous and present synagogue buildings.
Portraits of council presidents and senior ministers.

Finding aids: TS box list.

Facilities: Limited photocopying.

597 Library of the Hellenic and Roman Societies
Institute of Classical Studies

Address: 31–4 Gordon Square, London WC1H 0PP

Telephone: (0171) 387 7697

Fax: (0171) 383 4807

Enquiries: The Librarian

Open: Mon–Fri: 10.00–6.00 Sat: 10.00–4.00
Term: Tues, Thurs: 10.00–8.00
Closed for two weeks to include the late summer bank holiday.

Access: Open to members of the Hellenic Society and the Roman Society (subscription and sponsor required) and the Institute of Classical Studies (university teachers, museum staff and registered postgraduate students are eligible for membership if working on subjects within the scope of the institute). Postal and telephone enquiries accepted from the general public. Appointment preferable for consultation of MSS.

Historical background: The Hellenic Society was founded in 1879 and the library was begun in 1880; the Roman Society was formed in 1910 and the library became a joint library. The Institute of Classical Studies (University of London) was founded in 1953. The societies then handed over primary published material to the institute, which took responsibility for the primary (reference) library; they kept responsibility for the secondary (lending) library and slides collection. The two libraries are housed and run as one unit, but separate ownership is maintained. Black and white slides are now housed at King's College London (entry **589A**).

Acquisitions policy: MSS: to accept donations where appropriate. Printed material and slides: to maintain and improve the coverage of all aspects of classical antiquity, in close co-operation with other libraries whose interests overlap.

Major collections: Wood donation (property of the Hellenic Society): 27 items, including diaries and sketchbooks relating to Robert 'Palmyra' Wood (?1717–71) and his travels.
Bent diaries and notebooks (property of Hellenic Society): 25 items, mainly diaries of Mabel Bent (*d* 1929) with note-books of Theodore Bent, covering travels, 1883–98.

Non-manuscript material: Unpublished University of London theses on classical subjects, mainly 1954– (337 vols).
Library covering all aspects of classical antiquity: *c*83,000 books, pamphlets and bound periodicals; *c*1100 sheets of maps (*c*60 items on microfilm or microfiche); 2″ coloured slides (6,500).
Photographic collections on microfiche: the index of ancient art and architecture of the German Archaeological Institute in Rome; Ancient Roman architecture.

Finding aids: Handlist to Wood Collection. List of the Bent papers. Card catalogue of unpublished theses, which are listed in University of London and Aslib lists. Catalogues, including catalogue of colour slides (1977; addenda 1978).

Facilities: Photocopying and photography by courtesy of neighbouring libraries. Microfilm/fiche reader.

Publications: *Annual Report of the Hellenic Society*, xxii (1926) [on the Wood donation].
C.A. Hutton: 'The travels of "Palmyra" Wood in 1750–51', *Journal of Hellenic Studies*, xlvii (1927), 102.
University of London Bulletin, xiv (1974), 5.
P.T. Stevens: *The Society for the Promotion of Hellenic Studies, 1879–1979: a Historical Sketch* (London, 1979).
Guide to Classic Libraries and Collections (LRCC Classics Sub-Committee) (London, 1993).
Hellenic and Roman Societies Slides Collections: Greek Catalogue (1993); *Roman Catalogue* (1994).
Guide to the Library of the Institute of Classical Studies and the Library of the Hellenic and Roman Societies (London, 2/1994).
J.A. Butterworth: 'Robert Wood and Troy', *Bulletin of the Institute of Classical Studies*, xxxii (1985), 147.
——: 'The Wood Collection', *Journal of Hellenic Studies*, cvi (1986), 197.

598 Lincoln's Inn Library

Address: Holborn, London WC2A 3TN

Telephone: (0171) 242 4371

Fax: (0171) 831 1839

Enquiries: The Librarian

Open: Mon–Fri: 9.30–7.00 August: Mon–Fri: 9.30–5.30

Access: Members of Lincoln's Inn, and bona fide enquirers bringing a letter of recommendation.

Historical background: The library was established c1475.

Archives of organisation: Black Books: minutes of the governing body, 1422–; Red Books: finance and building, 1614–1877 [7 vols]; Account Books Vacation Commons, 1629–35, 1649–58, 1660–80; Treasurers' accounts, 1672–81, 1713–22; Works Department accounts, 1779–84; Cook's accounts, 1806–32; Admission registers, 1573–; Bar Books, 1757–.

Finding aids: Catalogue. NRA 17005.

599 Linnean Society of London

Address: The Library, Burlington House, Piccadilly, London W1V 0LQ

Telephone: (0171) 434 4479

Fax: (0171) 287 9364

Enquiries: The Librarian and Archivist, Miss Gina Douglas

Open: Mon–Fri: 10.00–5.00

Access: Bona fide scholars; non-fellows by written appointment only.

Historical background: The society was founded in 1788. Linnaeus's MSS were acquired in 1828 from the founder, J.E. Smith, who purchased them in 1784. Other MSS have been acquired by bequest or gift.

Archives of organisation: Including charters, minute books, accounts, records relating to collections of specimens, correspondence, ephemera etc, 1788–.
Papers read at society meetings, most published in society *Transactions*.
Zoological Club of the Linnean Society, minutes and papers, 1822–9.

Major collections: Carolus Linnaeus (1707–78), MSS, including correspondence, MS copies of his work and other MSS from contemporary naturalists.
James Edward Smith (1759–1828), MSS, including correspondence (c3000 letters)
William Swainson (1789–1855) correspondence.

MSS, including correspondence of Alexander and William Sharpe MacLeay; Richard Pulteney (1730–1801) and John Ellis (?1705–1776). Archives of the Society for Promoting Natural History, 1783–1801; Selborne Society, including minute books and Gilbert White MSS; and the Council for Nature.

Non-manuscript material: Prints, watercolours and sketches included in collections.
Collection of portraits of naturalists.

Finding aids: Card catalogue; slip index of correspondents; individual handlists. Swainson papers: NRA 22111.

Facilities: Photocopying. Photography by arrangement. Microfiche reader.

Conservation: Limited in-house facilities. Specific projects contracted out.

Publications: Linnean Society of London: *Catalogue of the Manuscripts in the Library of the Linnean Society of London*, pt I: *The Smith Papers* (by Warren Dawson, 1934); pt II: *Caroli Linnaei Determinationes in Hortum Siccum Joachimi Burseri* (by Spencer Savage, 1937); pt III: *Synopsis of the Annotations by Linnaeus and Contemporaries in his Library of Printed Books* (by Spencer Savage, 1940); pt IV: *Calendar of the Ellis Manuscripts* (by Spencer Savage, 1948).
W.T. Stearn and G. Bridson: *Commemorative Catalogue* (1978).
G. Bridson, W. Phillips and A.R. Harvey: *Natural History Manuscript Resources in the British Isles* (Mansell, 1981) [lists collections and holdings].
National Inventory of Documentary Sources, Chadwyck-Healey microfiche (1984–).
W.T. Stearn: *History of the Linnean Society London* (1988).

600 Little Sisters of the Assumption
Anglo-Scottish Province Archives

Address: Provincial House, 52 Kenneth Crescent, Willesden Green, London NW2 4PN

Telephone: (0181) 452 1687

Fax: (0181) 452 1687

Enquiries: The Provincial Archivist, Sr Margaret Lonergan

Open: By arrangement.

Access: The archives are private, and access is

normally limited to members. However, bona fide researchers who can in writing authenticate their request by a letter of referral are assured that enquiries are welcome. 50-year closure on personal records.

Historical background: The religious order known as the Little Sisters of the Assumption was founded in 1865 in Paris for the care of needy families by means of nursing and social work. The first convent in England opened in Bow, London, in 1880 and the first Scottish community opened in 1946. It is now present in 30 countries. The Welsh communities are linked to the Irish Province.

Acquisitions policy: To maintain, preserve and acquire archival material relating to the order and its associate works and organisations.

Archives of organisation: Archives relating to the early history of the province, 1865–83, as well as sisters, communities and convents in England, 1880–, and in Scotland, 1946–.
Administrative records of the history of each convent, nursing and social work.
Medical registers detailing patients nursed, 1880– (closed).

Major collections: Pernet MSS: correspondence and transcripts relating to the Founder, Venerable Stephen Pernet, 1824–99.
Fage papers: correspondence of Antoinette Fage, foundress with Fr Pernet, and first sister, 1824–83.

Non-manuscript material: Albums and photographs depicting the sisters, convents and associates.
Films and transparencies.

Finding aids: Some lists and indexes.

Facilities: Photocopying.

Publications: Sr M. Lonergan: 'The Archives of the Anglo-Scottish Province of the Little Sisters of the Assumption', *Catholic Archives*, 11 (1991), 17–24.

601 Lloyd's Register of Shipping
Records Centre

Address: 71 Fenchurch Street, London EC3M 4BS

Telephone: (0171) 423 2475 (Information Officer and Archivist) 423 2348 (Records Centre Manager)

Fax: (0171) 488 4796

Enquiries: The Information Officer and Archivist, Mrs Barbara Jones, The Records Centre Manager, Mr Iain Mayoh

Open: Information Office: Mon–Fri: 9.30–12.00; 1.00–4.30
Records Centre: by appointment only.

Access: Information Office: generally open to the public. Records Centre: bona fide researchers, by appointment; prior application is necessary to view records of ships (existing or wreck); owner's permission must be obtained by enquirer.

Historical background: Lloyd's Register was founded in 1760 and is now the oldest and largest ship classification society. It has diversified into many other technical areas, notably offshore gas and oil and land-based industrial work of all kinds. The Information Office holds a complete collection of all the published works of Lloyd's Register, including the Register of Ships, 1764–. The Records Centre holds plans and survey reports of classed ships and an index to those of Lloyd's Registers plans and reports retained by the National Maritime Museum (entry **645**).

Acquisitions policy: Lloyds's Registers own publications and additions to reference library.

Archives of organisation: Register of ships, 1764–.
Merchant shipbuilding returns, 1888–.
Statistical returns, 1878–.
Casualty Returns, 1890–.
Liverpool Underwriters Register for Iron Ships, 1862–84.
British Corporation Registers, 1893–1947.
Plans and reports of ships classed by Lloyd's Register, 1834– (incomplete).
Register of yachts, 1878–1980.

Non-manuscript material: Reference library concerning marine history (*c*3000).

Facilities: Photocopying.

602 London Borough of Barnet
Archives and Local Studies Department

Address: Hendon Catholic Social Centre, Egerton Gardens, Hendon, London NW4 4BE

Telephone: (0181) 202 5625 exts 55, 27

Enquiries: The Archivists, Mrs J.M. Corden, Mrs P.J. Taylor, c/o Hendon Library, The Burroughs, Hendon, London NW4 4BQ

Open: Mon–Wed, Fri: 9.30–5.00 Thurs: 9.30–7.30 Sat: 9.30–1.00; 2.00–5.00

Access: Generally open to the public, preferably by appointment.

Historical background: Archives have been collected by the library since 1932. Administrative assistance is given to Barnet Local History Society.

Acquisitions policy: Material of relevance relating to the London Borough of Barnet (former boroughs of Finchley and Hendon, and urban districts of Barnet, East Barnet and Friern Barnet). There is no modern records management programme.

Archives of organisation: Usual local authority record holdings.

Major collections: Deposited local records.

Non-manuscript material: Maps, photographs, prints, local newspapers, iconographic material.

Publications: J. Hopkins: *A History of Hendon* (Barnet, 1964).
P. Taylor (ed.): *A Place in Time* (Barnet, 1991) [a history of the borough to c1500].
A. Godfrey edition reprinted large-scale OS maps with historical notes.
Full list of publications available.

603 London Borough of Brent
Community History Library and Archive

Address: Cricklewood Library, 152 Olive Road, London NW2 6UY

Telephone: (0181) 908 7430/450 5211

Fax: (0181) 081 450 0744

Enquiries: The Community History Librarian/Archivist, Adam F. Spencer

Open: Mon: 11.00–5.00 Tues, Sat: 10.00–5.00 Thurs: 10.00–8.00

Access: Generally open to the public, by appointment.

Historical background: A local history library was opened in 1977 in the Grange Museum. The collections were moved to Cricklewood Library (f. 1929) in 1993.

Aquisitions policy: Material illustrating the life of the people of the Borough of Brent and its predecessors, Wembley, Willesden and Kingsbury.

Archives of organisation: Minutes of the present borough and its predecessors, with Medical Officer of Health reports.
Vestry minutes, overseers' and churchwardens' records for Willesden, 17th century–.

Non-manuscript material: British Empire Exhibition, Wembley, 1924–5; including guides, maps, photographs, music and souvenirs.
Wembley History Society Collection, including hundreds of mounted photographs.
Photographs and postcards, prints and drawings of the area.
Large map collection, especially strong on Willesden, including tithe and enclosure maps.
Collections of work by local authors, including Harrison Ainsworth, W.H.G. Kingston, Louis Wain, Gunby Hadath.

Finding aids: Index to the collection and partial index to the local newspapers *Willesden Chronicle*, 1880–1985, and *Wembley Observer*, 1965–85. Some lists sent to NRA.

Facilities: Photocopying. Photographic reprint service. Microfilm/fiche reader/printer.

Conservation: Contracted out.

Publications: Brent Streetnames (1975).
Brent Placenames (1977).
A History of Wembley (1980).
Roots in Britain (1981).
Aviation in and around Brent (1984).
The Metropolitan Railway and the Making of Neasden (1986).

604 London Borough of Camden
Local Studies and Archives Centre

Address: 32–38 Theobalds Road, London WC1X 8PA

Telephone: (0171) 413 6342

Enquiries: The Local Studies Manager, Mr R.G. Knight

Open: Mon–Wed, Fri: 9.30–5.00 Tues: 9.30–7.30 Sat: 9.00–4.00
Opening hours may vary with the move of the Swiss Cottage Library collections to Holborn.

Access: Generally open to the public, preferably by appointment.

Historical background: In 1965 the London Borough of Camden was formed by the amalgamation of the former metropolitan boroughs of Hampstead, Holborn and St Pancras. Each library system had a collection of archive and local history material which had been gathered continuously since the first of the library services was established in 1896. The Local Studies Centre acts as a repository for many archives of the London Borough of Camden and its predecessors, and many local organisations have deposited their records. The Swiss Cottage Library collections are due to move to Holborn Library during 1995.

Acquisitions policy: The aim of the Local Studies Centre is to record life in Camden: its people, buildings and institutions. Any material which helps to record this is acquired: museum objects, printed matter, illustrations, ephemera, tape-recordings, maps and a wide variety of archives.

Archives of organisation: London Borough of Camden: archives of Camden and the various vestries, boards and boroughs forming the present borough; earliest minutes, 1617–; rate books, 1726–1966 (c13,000 vols).

Major collections: Highgate Cemetery: registers of burials and other records, 1839– 1984.
Hampstead Manor: minute books, 1742–1843, plus many papers concerning disputes and court cases, particularly concerning Hampstead Heath.
Original census returns for Hampstead, 1801, 1811.
Transcriptions of tombstone inscriptions covering most burial grounds, 1860s-1880s, by F.T. Cansick for St Pancras and Holborn and R. Milward for Hampstead.
Deeds (c15,000; c3000 are catalogued and indexed).

Non-manuscript material: Slides (5000).
Paintings, drawings, prints, photographs (c31,000).
Maps (c3000, plus many uncatalogued).
Bellmoor Collection: material collected by Thomas J. Barratt, mainly printed or illustrated items (21 vols).
Heal Collection: rich collection of MSS, maps, drawings, paintings, playbills, ephemera etc.
G.B. Shaw Collection: biographies, his works (many first editions), pamphlets by him and on him, news cuttings, playbills, ephemera, records, photographs, original letters.
Dalziel Collection: c250 proof copies of engravings, the work of the Dalziel brothers who lived and worked in Hampstead and Camden Town.
Parish registers, 1560–1840s (microfilm).
Census returns for Camden area, 1841–91 (microfilm).

Finding aids: Card catalogues. Various lists and indexes. Lists sent to NRA.

Facilities: Photocopying. Photography by arrangement. Microfilm/fiche readers/printers.

Conservation: In-house conservation unit.

Publications: Camden Past and Present: a Comprehensive Guide to the Collections (1989).
Camden Now and Then: a Student's Guide to the Local Studies Library (1989).
Camden Local Studies and Archives Centre: a Brief Guide to the Collections (1994).
Various other publications; list available.

605 London Borough of Ealing
Local History Library

Address: Central Library, 103 Ealing Broadway Centre, London W5 5JY

Telephone: (0181) 567 3656 ext. 37

Enquiries: The Local History Librarian, Miss M. Gooding

Open: Tues, Thurs, Fri: 9.00–7.45 Wed, Sat: 9.00–5.00

Access: Generally open to the public.

Historical background: The Local History Library is formed from the collections of the former boroughs of Acton, Ealing and Southall and contains material on the area of the London Borough of Ealing. There is no archivist for the borough and therefore archives for the area are scattered.

Acquisitions policy: Donations and deposits of material covering the London Borough of Ealing are accepted.

Major collections: Minutes of the Acton School Board, 1875–1903; Acton Education Committee, 1903–44; Ealing Works Committee, 1886–1926; Ealing Education Committee, 1903–65; Southall Council School Managers, 1903–31; Ealing Sanitary Inspectors' Journal, 1899–1940. Large collection of school log-books. Hanwell Wesleyan Methodist Church minutes and miscellaneous documents, 1882–1960. Ealing Swimming Club, 1882–1934. League of Nations Union (Ealing Branch), including minute books, 1928–45. Martin Brothers & Martinware: papers of Sydney K. Greenslade.

Non-manuscript material: Photographic survey of Borough of Ealing, c1902, and other photographs and postcards (c18,500).

Finding aids: Accession lists: copies sent to Greater London Record Office (entry 550). Much of the material is not yet listed. Index to local newspaper, 1866–.

Facilities: Photocopying strictly at the discretion of the local history librarian: in general no archival material may be copied. Microfilm reader/printer.

Publications: Full list of reproduction maps, postcards and monographs available.

606 London Borough of Enfield Libraries
Local History Unit

Address: Southgate Town Hall, Green Lanes, Palmers Green, London N13 4XD

Telephone: (0181) 982 7453

Fax: (0181) 982 5450

Enquiries: The Local History Officer, Mr G.C. Dalling

Open: Mon–Sat: 9.00–5.00

Access: Generally open to the public, by appointment.

Historical background: The former boroughs of Enfield and Edmonton each had a local collection, and there was also a collection of books, pamphlets, photographs and drawings at Broomfield Museum in Southgate. All archive material was removed from the museum to Southgate Town Hall in 1975 and escaped the fire in 1984.

Acquisitions policy: To obtain, by donation, purchase or photocopy, material on the area of the London Borough of Enfield. To acquire non-current documents by transfer from other local authority departments.

Archives of organisation: Usual local authority record holdings.

Major collections: Local history and topography collections relating to Edmonton, Enfield and Southgate, including Edmonton Friendly Benefit Society records, 1820–1912; Stamford Hill and Green Lanes Turnpike Trust records, 1764–1805. Edmonton rate books, 1764–1850, and valuation lists, 1878, 1884, 1892 and 1905; Edmonton and Enfield Enclosure Awards.

Non-manuscript material: Paintings, drawings and prints (500). Photographs (15,000) and transparencies (1500). Newspaper cuttings (14,000). Local newspapers and microfilms of census returns. All non-current maps of the area.

Finding aids: General index on cards. Detailed classified catalogue: books, pamphlets and printed ephemera. Name indexes to census records, World War II civilian casualties etc. NRA 25942, 25947.

Facilities: Photocopying. Microfilm reader/printer.

Publications: Brief guide.

607 London Borough of Greenwich
Local History and Archives Library

Address: 'Woodlands', 90 Mycenae Road, Blackheath, London SE3 7SE

Telephone: (0181) 858 4631

Fax: (0181) 293 4721

Enquiries: Mr Julian Watson

Open: Mon, Tues: 9.00–5.30 Thurs: 9.00–8.00 Sat: 9.00–5.00

Access: Generally open to the public. Appointments desirable for use of microfilm and fiche readers.

Historical background: The department opened as a local library and art gallery in 1970, enabling the separate collections of the former metropolitan boroughs to be amalgamated. There is as yet no systematic records programme. The department also acts as the Diocesan Record Office for Southwark (Greenwich parish records), and is recognised as a place of deposit for public records.

Acquisitions policy: Printed documents, MSS, illustrations, and other visual media for the London Borough of Greenwich (Greenwich, Deptford, Charlton, Woolwich, Plumstead, Shooters Hill, Eltham, Kidbrook and Blackheath). Relevant archives of local organisations except those within the collections policy of the Greater London Record Office, i.e. parish, schools, hospitals, magistrates courts etc.

Archives of organisation: Usual local authority record holdings. Archives of London Borough of Greenwich, 1965–, and its predecessors: metropolitan boroughs of Woolwich and Greenwich and former civil parishes of Greenwich, St Nicholas Deptford, Charlton, Plumstead, Kidbrooke, and Woolwich Board of Health, 1848–99.

Major collections: Deeds, 16th–20th centuries. Family and estate papers relating to Martin, Newton and Fuller families.
Records of Christchurch School, East Greenwich, 1870–1950.
Business records, including Woolwich Ferry Company, 1811–15; Furlongs Estate Agency and Sykes Pumps.
Records of Greenwich and Lewisham Antiquarian Society, 1905–; Greenwich Historical Society and West Kent Natural History Society, 1871–.
The collection of Alan Roger Martin (1901–74).

Non-manuscript material: MS plans and surveys.
Extensive picture and photographic collections.
Spurgeon Collections of photographs of street life in Greenwich, 1884.
Watercolours and drawings, early 18th century– (c900).

Finding aids: Catalogues, lists and indexes.

Some lists sent to NRA, including NRA 7826, 26583.

Facilities: Photocopying. Photography. Microfilm/fiche reader.

Conservation: Contracted out.

Publications: Greenwich Local History Library: *A Guide to Sources.*
L. Reilly: *Family History in Greenwich, a Guide to Sources* (1992).

608 London Borough of Hackney
Archives Department

Address: 43 De Beauvoir Road, London N1 5SQ

Telephone: (0171) 241 2886

Fax: (0171) 241 6688

Enquiries: The Archivist, Mr D.L. Mander

Open: Mon, Tues, Thurs: 9.30–1.00; 2.00–5.00 Sat (1st and 3rd of each month): 9.30–1.00; 2.00–5.00

Access: Generally open to the public; an appointment is necessary. Certain classes of records are closed for specified periods (details from the department).

Historical background: The department was established in 1965 and administers the official and inherited records of the former metropolitan boroughs of Hackney, Shoreditch and Stoke Newington and their predecessors, as well as the local history collections of the former authorities. Deposited records are also held.

Acquisitions policy: Formal policy approved by Hackney Council. Collects records about or associated with the area of the London Borough of Hackney and its immediate environs. In certain cases records relating to areas outside the geographical boundaries may be acquired, either because they form part of a record group with a Hackney association or for other reasons.

Archives of organisation: Usual local authority record holdings, including those transferred from the former Greater London Council.

Major collections: Deposited records with substantial business collections, including records of Abney Park Cemetery Company, 1840–1980; Berger, Jenson & Nicholson, paint manufacturers, 1773–1980; Bryant & May Ltd, match manufacturers, and subsidiaries, c1850–c1965, J. & W. Nicholson of Clerkenwell and Bow, gin distillers, 1763–1969; British Xylonite Co. Ltd, plastic manufacturers, corporate and some manufacturing records, 1877–1969.

Non-manuscript material: Local history library, which includes local directories; local newspapers (available on microfilm); theatre material, including posters and programmes for four Shoreditch Theatres, c1831–1910, and for the Hackney Empire, c1910–; and OS and other printed and copy maps of the Hackney area. Visual collection of photographs; oil, watercolour and other paintings; film (mostly available on VHS video).
John Dawson Collection: books printed before 1767 (600), believed to be the only surviving parochial library in London, with MS notebooks and Dawson's dairy.

Finding aids: Lists of archive collections sent to NRA. Lists of deposited records have been microfilmed by Chadwick-Healey. Indexes. General information available on local Viewdata (via Prestel).

Facilities: Photocopying. Photographc service. CAPPS copying service (via another council dept). Microprinter reader and microfilm/fiche readers. Video monitor. Casette listening facility. Paid search service.

Conservation: In-house service; available to external institutions.

Publications: Hackney section of *Guide to London Local History Resources.*
Leaflets on using sources.
Various publications on the history of Hackney stocked for sale; publications list available (send SAE).

609 London Borough of Hammersmith and Fulham
Archives and Local History Collection

Address: The Lilla Huset, 191 Talgarth Road, London W6 8BJ

Telephone: (0181) 741 5159, 748 3020 ext. 3850

Fax: (0181) 741 4882

Enquiries: The Borough Archivist and Local History/Records Manager

Open: Mon: 9.30–8.00 Tues, Thurs: 9.30–1.00 Sat (1st of each month): 9.30–1.00

Access: Generally open to the public, by appointment only

Historical background: Hammersmith and Fulham libraries accumulated material from the late 19th century. In 1955 the Metropolitan Borough of Hammersmith appointed an archivist, and on the amalgamation of the borough with Fulham in 1965 appropriate material was also transferred to the archives, then based at Shepherds Bush. In 1992 the entire archives plus the two separate local history collections moved into a new purpose-built Archives and Local History Centre next to the London Ark building in Hammersmith. The centre is recognised as a place of deposit for public, manorial and tithe records. A computerised modern records management system is run from the centre.

Acquisitions policy: In addition to preserving and making available the records of the London Borough of Hammersmith and Fulham and its predecessors, deposits are accepted, and in some cases purchases are made, of material relevant to the history of the area.

Archives of organisation: Usual local authority record holdings, including vestry minutes, rate books etc, 1620s–.

Major collections: Deposited local collections, including records of some local churches, businesses and schools, plus the following of particular note: Hammersmith Bridge Company records, 1824–80; Fulham Bridge Company records, 1729–1865; Dorville and Scott families, estate papers, 1607–1853; Bult family of Brook Green, correspondence, 1796–1846; Fulham manorial records, 1810–1929; West London Hospital records, 1866–1979; Fulham Pottery records, 1865–1968; Sir William Bull's collection of antiquarian papers, 1882–1930; Hammersmith Convent's records (IBVM, later Benedictine, now Sacred Heart), 1672–1866; William Morris (1834–96) and Burne-Jones (1833–98), miscellaneous papers.

Non-manuscript material: Extensive collection of photographs, drawings and prints (c60,000); maps, printed ephemera, theatre programmes; local newspapers, including *West London Observer*, 1855–1984, and *Fulham Chronicle*, 1888–; newspaper cuttings; electoral registers. Collections of local pottery and paintings, such as the Cecil French Bequest, which includes 25 works by Burne-Jones.

Census returns, 1841–81 (microform).

Finding aids: Name and place index. Lists of deposited collections: copies sent to NRA.

Facilities: Photocopying and photography by arrangement. Microfilm/fiche reader.

Conservation: Conservation section with one in-house full-time conservator. Outside work is not undertaken.

Publications: See contribution to *Guide to London History Resources.*

610 London Borough of Haringey
Bruce Castle Museum

Address: Lordship Lane, London N17 8NU

Telephone: (0181) 808 8772

Fax: (0181) 808 4118

Enquiries: The Archivist

Open: Wed–Sun: 1.00–5.00

Access: Generally open to the public, by appointment.

Historical background: Bruce Castle was opened as a world history museum in 1926 and subsequently acquired an important collection of material on the history of the British Post Office. It is now a museum of local and postal history. The collection of archival material relating to Tottenham commenced early; since the formation of the London Borough of Haringey in 1964, Hornsey and Wood Green material has been added. The material comprising the museum of the Middlesex Regimental Association has been transferred to the National Army Museum (entry **640**).

Acquisitions policy: Limited to public and private records relating to the Haringey area.

Archives of organisation: Usual local authority record holdings, 1850–.

Major collections: Court rolls of the Manor of Tottenham, 1318–1732.
Records of the parishes of Tottenham and Hornsey, 15th century–.
Administrative records of the Alexandra Park and Palace, 1866–1966.

Non-manuscript material: Collection of local history material, consisting of printed books and pamphlets, maps and plans (*c*1000); news-papers; photographs (*c*10,000); prints and paintings; census returns.

Finding aids: Lists of parochial and manorial holdings and indexes by person and place to the archive collections in general. Translations of manorial court rolls fully indexed. Census material and newspapers in process of indexing.

Facilities: Photocopying. Photography by arrangement. Microfilm reader.

Publications: *Guide to London Local Studies Resources* [includes details of archive holdings and local history material in the Haringey return].
Handlist no. 1: Deposited Parish Records [Tottenham and Hornsey].
Court Rolls of the Manor of Tottenham [translations appearing so far (6 vols): 1318–99 and 1510–82].
Illustrated exhibition catalogues covering education, leisure activities, housing and transport.

611 London Borough of Islington

A Islington Central Library

Address: 2 Fieldway Crescent, London N5 1PF

Telephone: (0171) 609 3051 ext. 216/217

Fax: (0171) 607 6409

Enquiries: The Local History Librarian, Ms Vada Hart

Open: Mon, Wed, Thurs: 9.00–8.00 Tues, Sat: 9.00–5.00

Access: Generally open to the public; an appointment is necessary. Appointment times are more restricted than general library opening hours.

Historical background: The London Borough of Islington was formed in 1965 by the amalgamation of the metropolitan boroughs of Finsbury and Islington. Both library services had collections of local history material and held records of the borough councils and their predecessors. The two local history collections are housed separately and their scope reflects the pre-1965 borough boundaries. Some post-1965 records have been transferred to the Islington collection. The metropolitan borough of Islington (1900–65) was formed from only one civil parish, St Mary's, Islington.

Acquisitions policy: To acquire all possible material relating to the local area by purchase, donation or deposit.

Archives of organisation: Local government records: some post-1965 council records; records of the metropolitan borough of Islington, including council minutes and rate books; records of the civil parish of St Mary's, Islington, including vestry minutes, rate books, churchwardens' and overseers' accounts.
Records of Islington Turnpike Trust (later Hampstead and Highgate Turnpike Trust), 1717–1826.

Major collections: Records of Islington Literary and Scientific Society, 1832–76.
Records of the Royal Agricultural Hall, Islington, 1862–1981.
Records of Dove Brothers, builders, 1855–1970.

Non-manuscript material: Very large collections of graphic material and news cuttings.
Registers of electors for Islington, 1860– (incomplete).
Many local newspapers, 1865– (mainly on microfilm).
Islington local directories, 1852–1916.
Census returns, 1841–81 (microfilm).
Special collections relating to Walter Sickert (1860–1942) and Joe Orton (1933–67).

Finding aids: Various catalogues, card indexes and lists. Where possible lists sent to NRA.

Facilities: Photocopying. Photography by arrangement. Microfilm/fiche reader/printer.

Conservation: Contracted out.

B Finsbury Library

Address: 245 St John Street, London EC1V 4NB

Telephone: (0171) 278 7343 ext. 25

Fax: (0171) 278 8821

Enquiries: The Finsbury Reference Librarian, Mr D. Withey

Open: Mon, Thurs: 9.30–8.00 Tues, Sat: 9.30–5.00 Fri: 9.30–1.00

Access: Generally open to the public; an appointment is necessary. Appointment times are more restricted than general library opening hours.

Historical background: The metropolitan borough of Finsbury (1900–65) was formed from the civil parishes of St James and St John,

Clerkenwell, St Luke, the Liberty of Glasshouse Yard, St Sepulchre (part) and Charterhouse (part). In 1965 it became part of the London Borough of Islington. The collection covers the area within the former borough boundaries, i.e. the Pentonville district, north of the Angel and Islington south of the Angel.

Acquisitions policy: To acquire all possible material relating to Finsbury, by purchase, donation or deposit.

Archives of organisation: Inherited Finsbury records include the following:
Records of the constituent parishes of Finsbury, including vestry minutes and rate books; Clerkenwell and St Luke's Guardians' records.
Records of the metropolitan borough of Finsbury, including council minutes and rate books.
Records of Old Street Turnpike, 1752–1826, and City Road Turnpike Trust, 1786–1827.
Records of the Clerkenwell Explosion Relief Fund (set up after the Fenian bomb incident), 1867–81.

Major collections: Sadler's Wells Theatre Archives (includes much printed material), 18th century–.
Penton estate records, 1695–1938. Records of Finsbury Dispensary, 1795–1920.

Non-manuscript material: Very large collections of graphic material and news cuttings.
Islington Gazette, 1856–1904, 1955–60 (on microfilm).
Registers of electors: Clerkenwell, 1842; combined parishes of Islington and Finsbury etc, 1873–85 (arranged in alphabetical order of electors).
Census returns, 1841–81 (microfilm).

Finding aids: Various catalogues and card indexes. Where possible lists sent to NRA.

Facilities: Photocopying. Photography by arrangement. Microfilm/fiche readers.

Conservation: Contracted out.

612 London Borough of Kensington and Chelsea Libraries

Address: Kensington Central Library, Hornton Street, London W8 7RX
Chelsea Reference Library, Old Town Hall, King's Road, London SW3 5EZ

Telephone: Kensington: (0171) 937 2542 ext. 3038

Chelsea: (0171) 352 6056, 361 4158

Enquiries: The Local Studies Librarian, Ms Carrie Starren

Open: Kensington: Tues, Thurs: 10.00–1.00; 2.00–8.00 Wed: 10.00–1.00 Fri, Sat: 10.00–1.00; 2.00–5.00
Chelsea: Mon, Tues, Thurs: 10.00–8.00 Wed: 10.00–1.00 Fri, Sat: 10.00–5.00

Access: It is necessary to telephone to make an appointment. Restrictions on certain deposits and council records.

Historical background: The Royal Borough of Kensington and Chelsea was formed in 1965 by the amalgamation of the boroughs of Kensington and Chelsea. Both library services had collections, founded in 1887, of local history materials and held records of the councils and their predecessors. The two collections reflect the pre-1965 borough boundaries. Post-1965 civic records are held at Kensington with current materials at Chelsea. A borough records management scheme is in operation at Kensington.

Acquisitions policy: To acquire by donation, deposit or purchase material of relevance to the history of the boroughs.

Archives of organisation: Usual local authority record holdings.

Major collections: Kensington: Correspondence of Frederic, Lord Leighton (1830–96). Local deeds (50,000 items).
Chelsea: Records of Chelsea Arts Club, 1890–.

Non-manuscript material: Original sketches, design material relating to work of Walter Crane (1845–1915).
Extensive collections of illustrations, topographical prints, photographs, newspaper cuttings and maps.

Finding aids: Some card catalogues and indexes. Transcript of Leighton collection. Lists sent to NRA.

Publications: A number of publications, including *Historic Kensington in Maps, 1741–1894* and *Historical Chelsea in Maps, 1700–1894* [list of publications available at the Central Library].

613 London Borough of Lambeth
Lambeth Archives Department

Address: Minet Library, 52 Knatchbull Road, London SE5 9QY

Telephone: (0171) 926 6076

Fax: (0171) 926 6080

Enquiries: The Archivist, Mr Jon Newman

Open: Mon: 10.30–7.30 Tues, Thurs: 9.30–5.30 Alternate Sats: 9.30–1.00; 2.00–4.30

Access: Generally open to the public; it is necessary to telephone to make an appointment. Restrictions on certain deposited and council records.

Historical background: William Minet donated the library to the vestries of Lambeth and Camberwell in 1890, together with his local history collection, which related to the whole of Surrey before 1888. The collection of MSS, illustrations, maps and printed material was built up, and in 1956 the library became part of the Borough of Lambeth public library service and took on its archive function. It is recognised as a place of deposit for public records.

Acquisitions policy: The records of the London Borough of Lambeth and predecessor authorities and of business organisations and individuals situated within or connected with the borough.

Archives of organisation: Usual local authority record holdings of Lambeth, Clapham and Streatham civil parish records up to 1855; Vestry of St Mary Lambeth, 1855–1900; Metropolitan Borough of Lambeth, 1900–65; London Borough of Lambeth, 1965–.

Major collections: Manorial, parochial, charity, Poor Law and non-conformist records.
Deeds (*c*13,000).
Special collections, including: Magdalen Hospital Trust, 1757–1975.
Theobald Papers, papers of an 18th–century steward of the Dukes of Bedford at Streatham.
Minet Estate records, Camberwell, 1767–1975.
Papers of the Graham and Polhill families of Clapham, including letters and diaries, 1803–55; and of the Thorntons of Clapham, mainly 19th century.
Correspondence of Henry Beaufoy, relating

mostly to the setting up of Ragged Schools, 1847–51.
Artagen records (Artisans, Labourers and General Dwellings Company), 1867–1975.

Non-manuscript material: 10,000 illustrations, including 'extra-illustrated' vols (e.g.Manning and Bray's Surrey); 4 vols of Phillips watercolours; Petrie watercolours.
Playbills and theatre programmes.
Vauxhall Gardens song books, playbills, news cuttings etc.
Printed books, guides, pamphlets and news cuttings relating to the Crystal Palace.
Cuttings collection (includes ephemera), mainly post-1956.
Maps and plans (printed and MS), 17th century–.
Periodicals, newspapers, directories, pamphlets, including all standard printed material as well as rarer items.

Finding aids: Person, place and subject indexes to deeds and special collections. Catalogue of deeds and special collections. Street index to census returns (on microfilm) and trade index to 1841 census. Vauxhall Gardens songs index. Rate books name index, 1729–73. Lambeth Vestry minutes subject index, 1652–1858. Norwood Cemetery index to tomb inscriptions. South London Press index, 1909–14. Lists sent to NRA.

Facilities: Photocopying. Photography. Microfilm/fiche reader/printer. Map copying service.

Conservation: Contracted out.

Publications: Catalogue of Works Relating to the County of Surrey (1900; suppl. 1923).
M.Y. Williams: *A Short Guide to the Surrey Collection* (1965).
Series of *Information Guides* including *Records for Family Historians*; *Maps*; *Record Agents*; *Business Records*; *Entertainment Records*.

614 London Borough of Lewisham
Lewisham Local Studies Centre

Address: Lewisham Library, 199–201 Lewisham High Street, London SE13 6LG

Telephone: (0181) 297 0682

Fax: (0181) 297 1169

Enquiries: The Archivist, Ms Jean Wait

Open: Mon: 10.00–5.00 Tues: 9.00–8.00 Wed, Fri, Sat: 9.00–5.00

Access: Generally open to the public. Appointments are advisable. Restrictions on a few official and deposited collections.

Historical background: An archives and local history department (later called the Local History Centre) was established by the Metropolitan Borough of Lewisham in 1960 at the Manor House, Lee. Since 1965 it has acted as the archive repository and local history library for the London Borough of Lewisham, including the former Metropolitan Borough of Deptford. In October 1994 it changed its name to Lewisham Local Studies Centre and moved to the new Lewisham Library. The centre is recognised as a place of deposit for local public, manorial and tithe and parish records (parishes in East and West Lewisham).

Acquisitions policy: To collect, preserve and make available all types of archive and local history materials relating to the London Borough of Lewisham, within the terms of the relevant Local Government Acts and the centre's formal appointments.

Archives of organisation: Local government records: metropolitan boroughs of Lewisham and Deptford, Lewisham Board of Works, Lee and Plumstead Board of Works, Greenwich Board of Works, St Paul's Deptford Committee, parishes of Lewisham, Lee and St Paul's Deptford, 18th–20th centuries.

Major collections: Anglican parish records: parishes within the deaneries of East and West Lewisham, 16th–20th centuries.
Non-conformist records: Lewisham and Peckham Methodist Circuit and constituent churches, 19th–20th centuries; Deptford Wesleyan Mission, 19th–20th centuries; Deptford and Brockley Congregational churches, 18th–20th centuries.
Family and estate records: Baring Estate, Lee, including manorial records, 16th–19th centuries; Mayow Estate, Sydenham, 17th–20th centuries; Evelyn Estate, Deptford, 19th–20th centuries; other lesser estates and miscellaneous deeds, 16th–20th centuries; Forster estate, southern Lewisham, 18th–20th centuries.
Charity records: Deptford Fund (Albany Institute), 19th–20th centuries; parochial and other charities and voluntary bodies, 17th–20th centuries.

Business records: Chiltonian Ltd, biscuit manufacturers, 20th century; Cobbs of Sydenham, department store, 19th–20th centuries; Stone's foundry, Deptford, 19th–20th centuries (restricted access).

Education records: Blackheath Proprietary School, 19th–20th centuries; St Dunstan's College, Catford, 19th–20th centuries.

Clubs and societies records: Bellingham Bowling Club, 20th century; Catford Cycling Club, 19th–20th centuries.

Non-manuscript material: Prints of Lewisham, London and Kent, 18th–20th centuries (1400 items).

Art collection: mainly Lewisham topography and local artists, 19th–20th centuries (500 items).

Photographic prints, postcards, negatives and transparencies, *c*1857– (*c*30,000 items).

Printed maps and plans: Lewisham, London, Kent, OS etc, 16th–20th centuries.

Local newspapers, 1834– (originals and microfilm).

Local census returns, 1841–91 (microfilm).

Audio-visual materials: miscellaneous local films (mainly home movies); tape-recordings of local events and oral history reminiscences.

Printed books and pamphlets: Lewisham, London and Kent, local history topics, works by local authors (e.g. John Evelyn, Edgar Wallace, Henry Williamson), 16th–20th centuries.

Finding aids: Various card indexes. Lists of archive collections.

Facilities: Photocopying. Photography. Microfilm/fiche readers/printer.

Publications: Lewisham Section of the *Guide to London Local History Resources.*
Various local history publications.

615 London Borough of Newham
Local Studies Library

Address: Stratford Library, Water Lane, London E15 4NJ

Telephone: (0181) 557 8856

Fax: (0181) 503 1525

Enquiries: The Local Studies Librarians, Mr H. Bloch and Ms D. Sanders

Open: Mon, Thurs: 9.30–8.00 Tues: 9.30–6.30 Wed, Fri, Sat: 9.30–5.30

Access: Generally open to the public. Intending readers should telephone first to ensure that a local studies librarian will be on duty; an appointment is preferred.

Historical background: The Local Studies Library was opened in 1978 and forms part of the Stratford Library, but is housed in a separate room. The collection contains material on Essex, London and the former county boroughs of East and West Ham. A large amount of pre-20th century material, especially official records, is in Essex Record Office (entry 203). The library is recognised as a place of deposit for public records.

Acquisitions policy: To collect materials directly related to the London Borough of Newham, the former county boroughs of East and West Ham, and Essex and London materials where relevant.

Archives of organisation: Archives of Newham Borough and its former constituent authorities. West Ham Quarter Sessions rolls, 1894–1965; manorial rolls and books, 1603–24, 1736–1922.

Major collections: Parochial and religious records: East Ham, 1809–1965; Little Ilford, 1887–1900; West Ham, 1646–1965; Newham, 1964–.

Minute and rate books of Stratford Abbey Landowners, 1715–1874.

Records of local charities, 17th–19th centuries.

Deeds and family papers: Rawstorne of Plaistow, 17th–19th centuries; Henniker of Stratford and East Ham, 17th–19th centuries.

Non-conformist records, 19th and 20th centuries.

Air Raid Precaution files relating to East and West Ham, 1939–45.

Records relating to HMS *Albion* disaster, 1898, and Silvertown Explosion, 1917, relief funds.

Jack Cornwell VC (1900–16) papers.

James Keir Hardie, first Labour MP (South West Ham, 1892–5), letters, photographs etc.

Non-manuscript material: Newspapers and journals; newspaper cuttings, 18th–20th centuries. Maps and surveys of East and West Ham, 1741–.

Photographs (*c*25,000), paintings, drawings, films, videos, sound recordings.

Microfilms of directories, electoral registers, newspapers and parish registers.

Theatre Royal, Stratford, posters, programmes.

Wanstead House scrapbooks, 19th and 20th centuries.

Finding aids: Catalogue. Various indexes.

Facilities: Photocopying. Microfilm reader/printer.

Publications: Family History Notes; Local Studies Notes.

616 London Borough of Southwark
Local Studies Library

Address: 211 Borough High Street, London SE1 1JA

Telephone: (0171) 403 3507

Enquiries: The Local Studies Librarian, Janice Brooker

Open: Mon, Thurs: 9.30–12.30; 1.30–8.00 Tues, Fri: 9.30–12.30; 1.30–5.00 Sat: 9.30–1.00, by appointment.

Access: Generally open to the public, except in the case of some categories of modern council records, to which restrictions of varying duration apply.

Historical background: The London Borough of Southwark was formed in 1965 by the merger of the metropolitan boroughs of Southwark, Bermondsey and Camberwell. These metropolitan boroughs in their turn were formed in 1900 from ten vestries which had governed their parishes from Tudor times.

Acquisitions policy: Acquisitions comprise records which are transferred from the custody of departments of the London Borough of Southwark, and various private deposits which relate to institutions and individuals within the borough or its predecessors.

Archives of organisation: Records of the civil parishes up to 1900: vestry minutes, rate books, Poor Law records, churchwardens' accounts, highway records and other series of the parishes of St Saviour, St Olave, St Mary Magdalen (Bermondsey), St Mary (Rotherhithe), St Mary (Newington), St Giles (Camberwell), St John Horseleydown, St Thomas, St George and Christ Church, 1347–; notably Poor Law records, late 18th and early 19th centuries, and vestry records, 1856–1900.
Records of the boroughs, 1900–.

Major collections: Deposited private collec-

tions, including local deeds (20,000) and a large collection of local Methodist records.

Non-manuscript material: Printed books, pamphlets, press cuttings and other ephemera; microfilms of local newspapers, census returns and directories; photographs and prints; maps; gramophone records and tape-recordings of older residents' memories; videos and films.

Finding aids: Calendar of the deeds, with indexes by name and place; more detailed aids in progress. Author and subject card catalogue of the non-MS items.

Facilities: Photocopying. Microfilm/fiche reader/printer.

Publications: A Guide to the Archives in Southwark Local Studies Library (1992).

617 London Borough of Tower Hamlets
Local History Library and Archives

Address: Bancroft Library, 277 Bancroft Road, London E1 4DQ

Telephone: (0181) 980 4366 ext. 134

Fax: (0181) 981 9965

Enquiries: The Archivist, Jane Kimber or The Local History Librarian, Mr C.J. Lloyd

Open: Mon, Thurs: 9.00–8.00 Tues, Fri: 9.00–6.00 Wed, Sat: 9.00–5.00

Access: Generally open to the public; an appointment is preferred. Intending users of archive material are asked to telephone in advance to ensure the archivist will be on duty. An appointment is advisable for microform use.

Historical background: Following the creation of the London Borough of Tower Hamlets in 1965, the local collections of archives and local history material from the former Metropolitan Boroughs of Bethnal Green, Poplar and Stepney were amalgamated to form Tower Hamlets Local History Library. Some local records are held by the Greater London Record Office (entry 550) and Guildhall Library (entry 553), and others were destroyed during World War II. In 1986 an archivist was appointed, and in 1988 an air-conditioned strongroom was opened to house the archives.

Acquisitions policy: To collect, preserve and make available material in all formats relevant to the history of the London Borough of Tower Hamlets and its people.

Archives of organisation: Committee minutes and other records of the London Borough of Tower Hamlets, 1965–, and the metropolitan boroughs of Bethnal Green, Poplar and Stepney, 1900–65.
Records of their predecessor authorities, including rate books, land tax assessments, vestry records, Poor Law records etc, 16th century–.
No original ecclesiastical parish records; some parish registers on microfilm.

Major collections: Deposited records of some local organisations, including non-conformist churches and schools, 18th–20th centuries; some East India Company records, 1709–1871.
Census returns for Poplar and Blackwall, 1821, 1831, and (on microfilm) for the whole borough, 1841–91.
Title deeds, 16th century– (c15,000)
Daniel Bolt Shipping Collection: books, pamphlets, illustrations, MS ship indexes, mostly 1850–1920, and MS ships' log-books, 1797–1914 (c10).

Non-manuscript material: Photographs and prints (c20,000), transparencies (c5000); books, pamphlets and theses (c18,000); newspaper cuttings (c500 boxes); maps (c2000). Small collections of sound recordings, films and videos. Microfilms of local newspapers, 1857–, and some parish registers.

Finding aids: Several catalogues and indexes to the local history collections. Handlists; sent to NRA.

Facilities: Photocopying. Photography by arrangement. Microfilm/fiche readers/printer.

Conservation: Contracted out.

Publications: C. Kerrigan: *History of Tower Hamlets.*
Leaflets on family history and other resources in the collection are available.

618 London Borough of Waltham Forest
Archives and Local History Library

Parent organisation: Arts and Leisure Department

Address: Vestry House Museum, Vestry Road, Walthamstow, London E17 9NH

Telephone: (0181) 509 1917, 527 5544 ext. 4391

Enquiries: The Archivist, Josephine Parker

Open: Tues, Wed, Fri: 10.00–1.00; 2.00–5.15
Sat: 10.00–1.00; 2.00–4.45

Access: Generally open to the public, strictly by appointment.

Historical background: Vestry House Museum was opened as the Walthamstow Borough Museum in 1931, with recognition as an approved repository for local manorial records. Following the formation of the London Borough of Waltham Forest in 1965, the manuscript and printed local history collections of the former boroughs of Chingford, Leyton and Walthamstow were amalgamated at the museum, forming the basis of Waltham Forest Archives and Local History Library. Records of parishes in Waltham Forest Deanery have been held since 1982, when diocesan approval was granted.

Acquisitions policy: To hold the records of the former boroughs of Chingford, Leyton and Walthamstow; to hold and continue to receive official and private records relevant to the Waltham Forest area.

Archives of organisation: Usual local authority records.

Major collections: Deposited local collections, including research notes and transcripts of state papers relating to the Leyton area, by John Brant, c1919–1929.
MS works of John Drinkwater (1882–1937), poet and dramatist, c1912–1934.
Records of Chingford Mount Cemetery, 1884–1970.

Non-manuscript material: Prints, drawings and some ephemera.
Waltham Forest Photographic Archive (c 60,000 images).
Tape-recordings, with transcripts, generated by

the Waltham Forest Oral History Workshop (enquiries to Nigel Sadler, Museum Keeper).
The Local History Library holds books, directories, pamphlets, ephemera, printed maps and plans (enquiries to Brian Mardall, Local History Librarian).

Finding aids: Archive catalogues: lists sent to NRA. Name index to Chingford, Leyton and Walthamstow parish registers and rate books, pre-1880, and to local census returns up to 1881. Indexed calendars of certain deeds series for Leyton and Walthamstow.

Facilities: Photocopying. Microfilm/fiche reader/printer.

619 London Borough of Wandsworth
Local History Collection

Address: Battersea Library, 265 Lavender Hill, London SW11 1JB

Telephone: (0181) 871 7467

Enquiries: The Local History Librarian, Mr Richard A. Shaw

Open: Tues, Wed: 10.00–1.00; 2.00–8.00 Fri: 10.00–1.00; 2.00–5.00 Sat: 9.00–1.00
Other times by appointment.

Access: Generally open to the public; an appointment is advised. The Thomas Collection is currently not available.

Historical background: The London Borough of Wandsworth is an amalgamation of the two old metropolitan boroughs of Battersea and Wandsworth and, the collection covers the old parishes of Battersea, Putney, Streatham, Tooting Graveney, Wandsworth and, to a small extent, Clapham. Original paintings and drawings previously in the library are now held at the Wandsworth Museum.

Acquisitions policy: Any material relating to the above, by purchase, donation and deposit.

Major collections: Records of parishes listed above, including rate books; vestry minutes; Poor Law records; minutes of Metropolitan and Local Boards of Works; metropolitan boroughs of Battersea and Wandsworth and London Borough of Wandsworth.
Correspondence of Edward P. Thomas (1878–1917) of Battersea, poet and critic.

Non-manuscript material: Illustrations, mainly photographs, *c*1870– (14,000).

Finding aids: Card and loose-leaf indexes only. Very few MSS catalogued.

Facilities: Limited photocopying. Photography by arrangement. Microfilm/fiche readers.

620 London College of Furniture

Parent organisation: London Guildhall University

Address: 41 Commercial Road, London E1 1LA

Telephone: (0171) 320 1867

Fax: (0171) 320 1865

Enquiries: The Subject Librarian, Richard Farr

Open: Term: Mon, Fri: 9.30–5.00 Tues–Thurs: 9.30–7.00

Access: Bona fide enquirers, by appointment.

In 1992 the London Guildhall University (previously the City of London Polytechnic) incorporated the London College of Furniture. The library of the Commercial Road site houses the Atcraft Archive Collection, which was deposited after the closure of Atcraft of Wembley, manufacturers of furniture, formerly active in East London. The collection consists primarily of ledgers, accounts books and product catalogues.

621 London College of Printing and Distributive Trades
Department of Learning Resources

Parent organisation: The London Institute

Address: Elephant and Castle, London SE1 6SB

Telephone: (0171) 514 6500 ext. 6527

Fax: (0171) 514 6597

Enquiries: The Head of Learning Resources, Pat Batley

Open: Term: Mon–Thurs: 9.00–7.15 Fri: 9.00–5.45 Vacation: Mon–Fri: 9.00–4.30
Closed in August.

Access: External researchers should apply in writing to the Head of Learning Resources.

Historical background: The London College of Printing was an ILEA specialist college until the formation of its new parent body, when it became a federated member of the London Institute. It has since merged with the College for the Distributive Trades and now operates on three sites across London, the Elephant and Castle being its main site.

Acquisitions policy: To maintain the college archives and acquire materials to support the teaching, learning and research needs of the staff and students of the college. Principal areas of work include printing, graphic design, media, business and management, retail studies and professional studies.

Archives of organisation: College archives, including those of its predecessor, the London School of Printing, 1894–1922.

Non-manuscript material: Printing Historical Collection: specimens of printing, 1485–; private press and artists books; substantial ephemera collection, including posters and calendars. Collection of film scripts (located at Back Hill site); Distribution Industrial Training Board Collection (located at Davies Street site).

Finding aids: Catalogue on BLCMP library system. Manual index to special collections' catalogues are held at each site.

Facilities: Photocopying. Photography. Microfilming.

Conservation: In-house facilities.

Publications: Series of guides to collections.

622 The London Library

Address: 14 St James's Square, London SW1Y 4LG

Telephone: (0171) 930 7705

Fax: (0171) 930 0436

Enquiries: The Librarian, Mr Alan Bell

Open: Mon–Wed, Fri, Sat: 9.30–5.30 Thurs: 9.30–7.30

Access: Members and accredited students. A prior appointment is essential.

Historical background: The London Library was established in 1841 as a subscription library with an extensive collection of printed books (now c1 million vols) for reference and loan to members.

Acquisitions policy: Collecting is now concentrated on the library's own history, from the founder Thomas Carlyle (1795–1881) onwards.

Archives of organisation: Minute books, 1845–; some early issue registers; membership lists, annual reports etc.

Major collections: Thomas Carlyle, various letters.
J.F. Baddeley Collection on Caucasian studies, 1882–1914.
C.W. Shirley Brooks (1816–74), editor of *Punch*, diaries.
Sir Samuel Egerton Brydges (1762–1857), miscellaneous papers.
James Mill (1773–1836), commonplace books (5 vols).
John Addington Symonds (1840–93), MS memoirs.
James Maurice Wilson (1836–1931), canon of Worcester, memoirs, books and family papers.

Non-manuscript material: Charles Reade (1814–84), scrapbooks.

Finding aids: NRA 20043 (summary only).

Facilities: Photocopying. Microfilm/fiche readers.

Conservation: Contracted out.

Publications: J. Wells: *Rude Words: a Discursive History of the London Library* (London, 1991).

623 London Museum of Jewish Life

Address: The Sternberg Centre, 80 East End Road, London N3 2SY

Telephone: (0181) 349 1143

Enquiries: The Curator

Open: Mon–Thurs: 10.30–5.00

Access: Generally open to the public, by appointment.

Historical background: The museum was initially established as the Museum of the Jewish East End in 1984.

Acquisitions policy: Documents, photographs, artefacts and memorabilia relating to the social and cultural history of London's Jewish community.

Major collections: Personal papers and records of organisations relating to the Jewish East End, including immigrant trades, Yiddish theatre, East End synagogues and refugees from Nazism.

Records of Jewish Friendly Society, late 19th and 20th centuries.

Collection of unpublished memoirs and research papers.

Personal papers of Israel Zangwill.

Non-manuscript material: Boris the Studio Photographer Collection: photographs of Jewish weddings, 1920s and 1930s.

Photograph archive and oral history library.

Collection of gramophone records.

Facilities: Photocopying. Photography by arrangement.

Publications: Exhibition catalogues: *The East End Synagogues; Boris the Studio Photographer; The Jewish West End.*

Research Paper series.

624 London School of Hygiene and Tropical Medicine

Parent organisation: University of London

Address: Keppel Street, London WC1E 7HT

Telephone: (0171) 927 9276

Enquiries: The Librarian, Mr R. Brian Furner

Open: Term: Mon–Fri: 8.30–8.25 Sat: 9.00–12.30 Vacation: Mon–Fri: 9.30–7.30 Sat: 9.00–12.30

Access: Bona fide researchers. Records containing personal information are generally closed for 100 years.

Historical background: The school was opened in 1899 and the library has existed since that date. It is the largest medical library in the University of London. There is a broad coverage of all aspects of exotic diseases and public health as well as the history of both subjects. The school's administrative archives are kept by the secretary's office and are not available. The Centre for Human Nutrition maintains its own archive collections, including papers of Prof. B.S. Platt (*d* 1969).

Acquisitions policy: To maintain the existing archival collections.

Archives of organisation: Papers, architects' drawings and correspondence *re* competition for the design of LSHTM, 1924, and its construction in Keppel Street, 1926–9.

Papers of Sir Andrew Balfour (1873–1930), first director of LSHTM.

Student registers, 1899–.

Examination records of candidates for service in the 'Colonies and Protectorates', 1898–1919.

Major collections: Sir Ronald Ross (1857–1932) Archives: MSS, correspondence and reprints relating to his life and work (*c*20,000 items).

Sir Patrick Manson (1844–1922) Collection: diaries covering his work in China and including many case histories, also artefacts.

Robert Thomson Leiper (1881–1969), Professor of Helminthology: material relating to his work and family.

Sir (William) Allen Daley (1887–1969): papers relevant to his life and work.

Sir Leonard Rogers: MSS and original medical illustrations concerning leprosy.

Timothy Lewis note-books, including case histories, 1870s.

Records of the Mott Malaria Clinic, Horton Hospital, Epsom: clinical records of patients treated for neurosyphilis by induced malaria, 1925–60.

Non-manuscript material: Photographs of personalities connected with the history of the school and Ross Institute.

Finding aids: Catalogue of the Ross Archives. Some MSS in library card catalogue.

Facilities: Photocopying. Microfilm/fiche reader.

Publications: G.K Hall: *Dictionary Catalogue of the London School of Hygiene and Tropical Medicine* (Boston, 1965; suppl. 1970) [7 vols].

M.E. Gibson: *Catalogue of the Ross Archives* (London, 1983) [microfiche].

625 Madame Tussaud's Archives

Address: Marylebone Road, London NW1 5LR

Telephone: (0171) 935 6861

Fax: (0171) 465 0862

Enquiries: The Archivist, Ms Undine Concannon

Open: By prior arrangement only.

Access: Bona fide researchers, by appointment only. Restrictions on certain material.

Historical background: Madame Marie Tussaud (1760–1850) inherited a small wax exhibition from her uncle in Paris. She brought it to England in 1802 and travelled with it for many years, settling in London permanently in 1835. Other members of the Tussaud's group include Rock Circus, London; the London Planetarium; Warwick Castle; Chessington World of Adventures; Alton Towers, and Scenerama, Amsterdam.

Acquisitions policy: To enlarge the collection of material relating to or produced by Madame Tussaud's; and, to a much lesser extent, to collect material relating to 19th–century wax exhibitions.

Archives of organisation: Archives of Madame Tussaud's group; Tussaud family documents.

Non-manuscript material: Collection of embossed scrap reliefs and scrap albums, 18th and 19th centuries.
Exhibition catalogues, posters, publications written by members of staff.

Finding aids: List in course of preparation.

Facilities: Photocopying. Photography of certain items.

626 Marx Memorial Library

Address: Marx House, 37a Clerkenwell Green, London EC1R 0DU

Telephone: (0171) 253 1485

Enquiries: The Librarian

Open: Mon: 1.00–6.00 Tues–Thurs: 1.00–8.00 Sat: 10.00–1.00

Access: Library members. An annual subscription is charged. Enquiries are welcomed.

Historical background: The library was started in 1933 as a response to Hitler's Fascism and the burning of Marxist and progressive books, and to commemorate the fiftieth anniversary of Karl Marx's death.

Acquisitions policy: To build and maintain a library relating to all aspects of Marxism, the history of Socialism and the working-class movement.

Major collections: Spanish International Brigade Archives, including letters, cuttings, pamphlets and books.

Non-manuscript material: Books, pamphlets and periodicals on all aspects of Marxism and the Labour movements, with particular reference to Great Britain, including: John Williamson Collection of the American Communist and Labour Movement; James Klugmann Collection of Chartist and early radical literature, 1649–; J.D. Bernal Peace Collection.

Finding aids: Author, subject and title catalogues. NRA 11083.

Publications: A. Rothstein: *The House on Clerkenwell Green.*
Marx Memorial Library Bulletin.

627 Marylebone Cricket Club Library

Address: Lord's Cricket Ground, St John's Wood, London NW8 8QN

Telephone: (0171) 289 1611

Fax: (0171) 289 9100

Enquiries: The Curator, Mr Stephen E.A. Green

Open: Mon–Fri: 9.30–5.30, by appointment. Most Saturdays and some Sundays in the cricket season.

Access: Approved readers, on written application.

Historical background: Lord's was founded in 1787 and has had a historical collection of paintings since 1864. All the early records of the club were destroyed by a fire in 1825. The MCC library dates from 1893.

Acquisitions policy: To build up a representative body of material on the history of cricket.

Archives of organisation: Domestic archives of the MCC, 1787–.

Major collections: Middlesex County Cricket Club archives.
MS collections concerning other cricket clubs and famous players.

Non-manuscript material: Books, photographs, films and oral history collections concerning cricket.

Finding aids: Catalogues to much of the collection. NRA informed of accessions.

Facilities: Photocopying. Photography.

Conservation: Contracted out.

Publications: S. Green: 'Some Cricket Records', *Archives*, 80 (Oct 1988), 187–98.
Many publications relating to Lord's.

628 Medical Mission Sisters Central Archives

Address: 41 Chatsworth Gardens, Acton, London W3 9LP

Telephone: (0181) 992 6444

Enquiries: The Archivist

Access: Not open to the public but the Archivist will deal with enquiries.

Historical background: The Society of Catholic Medical Missionaries, also known as Medical Mission Sisters, is an international religious congregation founded in 1925 in Washington, DC. In 1939 the motherhouse moved to Philadelphia, and in 1958 the Society's Generale was established in Rome. It moved to its present location in 1983. District archives are held at individual houses but are mainly duplicated in the central archives.

Acquisitions policy: Society archives.

Archives of organisation: The history of the society.
Papers of the foundress, Dr Anna Dengel.
Papers of the society.

Non-manuscript material: Collection of photographs and slides of the foundress, the sisters and the work of the society in various countries.
Books and other printed works relating to medical missions.

Finding aids: Some preliminary inventories are available.

Facilities: Photocopying.

Conservation: Facilities for paper conservation.

629 Medical Research Council Archives

Address: MRC Archives (Information Group), 20 Park Crescent, London W1N 4AL

Telephone: (0171) 636 5422 ext. 6428/9

Fax: (0171) 436 6179

Enquiries: The Archivist, Alexandra McAdam Clark

Open: Tues–Fri: 9.00–5.00

Access: Bona fide researchers, who will need to provide referee(s) and sign an undertaking. Researchers normally write in with details of their research and are sent or told what information is available. Archives less than 30 years old are closed.

Historical background: The Medical Research Council was preceded by the Medical Research Committee (1913–20), which originated in the National Insurance Act, 1911. Sub-sections of the Act created a national fund for medical research. In 1913 the Medical Research Committee was set up to administer this fund. The Medical Research Council was formed in 1920 and has continued to promote the development of medical and related biological research in the UK. The Public Record Office (entry 960) has recently received early records of the MRC. Some additional files may be transferred at a later date.

Archives of organisation: Council minutes and related papers, 1920–.
Council documents and committee papers, 1950–1960s.
Personal files of early administrators and early history of the MRC, 1913–1960s.

Finding aids: Index of files (1913–c1954).

Facilities: Photocopying.

Publications: A. Landsborough Thomson, *Half a Century of Medical Research* (HMSO, 1978) [the official history of the MRC].

630 The Mercers' Company

Address: Mercers' Hall, Ironmonger Lane, London EC2V 8HE

Telephone: (0171) 726 4991

Fax: (0171) 600 1158

Enquiries: The Archivist, Miss Anne F. Sutton

Open: Mon–Fri: 9.30–5.00

Access: Approved readers, by appointment only.

Historical background: The Worshipful Company of Mercers is the premier city livery company and one of the ancient merchant guilds of London. The word 'mercer' derives originally from the French word for merchant, but later became associated particularly with the trade in luxury goods, especially cloth. The records start in 1347 but the company is certainly older. From an early date the mercers administered estates in land and money left to them by wealthy members and non-members, such as Richard Whittington; Dean Colet, the founder of St Paul's School; Sir Thomas Gresham, the founder of the Royal Exchange and Gresham College; and the Earl of Northampton. These charities were and are for the poor and for educational purposes.

Acquisitions policy: To acquire material closely related to the history of the company and its members, by purchase, permanent loan or donation.

Archives of organisation: Records of the Mercers' Company and of the charitable estates in its care.

Non-manuscript material: A small collection of books printed 'at' the Mercers' Chapel, London.

Finding aids: Extensive lists and catalogues.

Facilities: Limited photocopying.

Publications: J. Watney: *Some Account of the Hospital of St Thomas of Acon and of the Plate of the Mercers' Company* (London, 1892; 2/1906).

——: *An Account of the Mistery of Mercers of the City of London* (London, 1914).

L. Lyell and F. Watney (eds): *The Acts of Court of the Mercers' Company, 1453–1527* (Cambridge, 1936).

J. Imray: *The Charity of Richard Whittington, 1424–1966* (London, 1968).

——: *The Mercers' Hall,* London Topographical Society Publication No. 143 (1991).

A.F. Sutton: *The Mercers' Company's First Charter, 1394* (Mercers' Company, 1994).

I. Doolittle, *The Mercers' Company 1579–1959* (Mercers' Company, 1994).

G. Huelin: *Think and Thank God: the Mercers' Company and its Contribution to the Church and Religious Life since the Reformation* (Mercers' Company, 1994).

631 Merchant Taylors' Company

Address: Merchant Taylors' Hall, 30 Threadneedle Street, London EC2R 8AY

Telephone: (0171) 588 7606

Fax: (0171) 528 8332

Enquiries: The Clerk of the Company

Microfilm copies of all records are available at Guildhall Library (entry **553**). Any request for research at the hall will be dealt with only by letter, and a charitable contribution may be requested. Records are also held by the Merchant Taylors' School (entry **852**).

632 Middle Temple Archive

Parent organisation: The Honourable Society of the Middle Temple

Address: Middle Temple Library, Middle Temple Lane, London EC4Y 9BT

Telephone: (0171) 353 4303

Fax: (0171) 583 6674

Enquiries: The Librarian and Keeper of the Records, Mrs J.E. Edgell

Open: Mon–Fri: 10.00–5.00 Closed for the first fortnight in August.

Access: Access to non-members is strictly by appointment and at the Librarian's discretion.

Historical background: The Middle Temple is one of the four Inns of Court, which alone have the right of calling members to the Bar, i.e. of admitting them as barristers with exclusive right of audience in the superior courts of England and Wales. Apprentices in law first settled in the Temple in the mid-14th century. The earliest records of the Middle Temple date from 1501, by which time it was already providing education for students, accommodation for practitioners and a professional and social framework for barristers, functions which it continues to discharge. The governing body of Parliament is composed of Masters of the Bench and the Under Treasurer is responsible to Parliament for the running of the Inn.

Acquisitions policy: There is no active acquisitions policy. The Inn maintains its own archive and this involves the transmission of non-current administrative and financial records to the archive. Occasional gifts and deposits of papers of members or societies associated with the Inn are accepted.

Archives of organisation: Records relating to: administration, 1501–1988; finance, 1608–1991; membership, 1501–1987; deeds and legal papers, 1608–1994; rents, chambers and property, 1621–1969; building works, 1670–1976; commons, kitchens, entertainment, 1612–1971; staff, 1601–1991; library, 1641–1992; scholarships, prizes, charities, 1877–1985; pictures and plate, 1717–1967; New Inn, 1605–1904; legal education, 1846–1993; liaison with legal institutions, 1894–1992; Temple Church, 1591–1990; House of Commons Bills affecting Middle Temple, 1855–1958; Inns of Court Regiment, 1896–1959.

Major collections: A small number of deposited records, mainly letters patent, matriculations of arms and collections of papers pertaining to prominent lawyers, including Sir Alexander Cockburn, QC, mid-19th century; A.M. Sullivan, KC, 1919; John Dunning, Lord Ashburton, 1768; Lord Diplock, 1948–56; Helena Normanton, KC, 1948.
Records of societies, including the Pegasus Club, 1895–1939.
Correspondence of Samuel Annesley, East India Company, Surat, 1695–7.
The library holds MSS (mostly law case notes and judgements) by Sir George Treby (?1644–1700), Charles Butler (1750–1832), Sir Soulden Laurence (1751–1814), Sir Vicary Gibbs (1751–1820), John Scott, Earl of Eldon (1751–1838) and Sir Henry Dampier (1758–1816).

Non-manuscript material: Plans and architectural drawings include those by Sir Christopher Wren, 1680; H.J. Wadling, 1903; Sir Aston Webb, 1924; Clyde Young, 1946–7; Sir Edward Maufe RA, 1950–58.
Large illustration collection relating to the Inn and its members and to Temple Church.
Video (taken from nitrate film), with sound track, of the Inns of Court during the blitz.

Finding aids: Most of the archive is catalogued; catalogues will be sent to NRA when listing is completed.

Facilities: Photocopying by approval of the archivist. Photography on payment of a disturbance fee.

Conservation: Conservation programme being undertaken by Camberwell College of Art paper conservation students. Specific repairs also contracted out.

633 The Middlesex Hospital
Archives Department

Parent organisation: University College London Hospitals

Address: The Middlesex Hospital, Mortimer Street, London W1N 8AA

Telephone: (0171) 636 8333 ext. 4498

Enquiries: Mr Marvin Sturridge

Open: Thurs: 10.30–3.00

Access: By written application only; an appointment is essential. Closure on some records depending on the date.

Historical background: The Middlesex Hospital was founded in 1745. The Hospital for Women, Soho Square, was founded in 1842. St Luke's Woodside, Psychiatric Hospital, was founded in 1751 and houses its own records. The other collections were brought together in 1971.

Acquisitions policy: To strengthen the existing collection of written, printed and photographic records relating to the Middlesex Hospital and illustrating its work and organisation since its foundation in 1745.

Archives of organisation: Middlesex Hospital: Board of Governors' minutes, 1748–1975; Medical Committee minutes, 1851–; admissions registers, 1747–; lying-in registers, 1747–1829; case notes 1855–; register of surgeons' pupils and house surgeons, 1763–; physicians' pupils, 1766–; register of refugee French clergy, 1789–1814; hospital reports, 1820–1940 (incomplete); register of nurses, 1867–.
The Hospital for Women: reports, 1843–1940; Committee of Management minutes, 1843–1939.

Non-manuscript material: Numerous photographs, etchings, portraits, maps and some film. Pamphlets.

Finding aids: List and indexes in course of revision.

Facilities: Limited facilities by arrangement only.

634 Ministry of Defence

Address: Whitehall Library, 3–5 Great Scotland Yard, London SW1A 2HW

Telephone: (0171) 218 9006 218 4445 (enquiries) 218 5456 (Air Historical Branch) 218 5251 (Army Historical Branch) 218 5450/5451 (Naval Historical Branch)

Fax: (0171) 218 5413

Enquiries: The Chief Librarian, MOD, Mr Richard Searle or The Marketing Librarian, MOD, Mrs C.C. Basinger or direct to the relevant branch

The MOD Whitehall Library opened in its newly refurbished building in 1989. The emphasis on the historical work of the library has declined in recent years and it is now essentially a working collection geared to current information needs. Nevertheless a small amount of archival material is still held and the separate branches will give advice and information. A charge is made for genealogical and general interest enquiries.

The Air Historical Branch has transferred a number of unit diaries and miscellaneous material to the RAF Museum (entry **673**), while other unit diaries and the papers of Sir John Slessor (1897–1979) have been placed at the Public Record Office (entry **960**), which receives regular transfers of the former.

Papers of John Arbuthnot, Lord Fisher (1841–1910), Admiral of the Fleet, 1900–10, as well as pamphlets, monographs, charts and atlases, previously noted as being in the Naval Historical Branch Library, remain with the MOD Library and are made available to bona fide researchers.

635 Moravian Church Archive and Library

Address: Moravian Church House, 5–7 Muswell Hill, London N10 3TH

Telephone: (0181) 883 3409

Enquiries: Ms Janet Halton

Open: By arrangement only.

Access: On written application, and by appointment only.

Historical background: The Moravian Church is a Protestant sect, and the London congrega-tion settled in 1742. It included James Hutton (1715–95) and has been active in the missionary field since 1735. Archives and MSS are expected to be transferred to John Rylands University of Manchester Library (entry **806**) in late spring or early summer 1995.

Acquisitions policy: To maintain the archives of the church.

Archives of organisation: Records of the Moravian Church (British Province), including *Periodical Accounts* of missions and despatches from missionaries, 1790–.

Major collections: Collection of diaries and MSS, including correspondence of John Wesley (1703–91) and Charles Wesley (1707–88) with James Hutton.

Non-manuscript material: Portraits of early Moravians.
Prints and sketches of Moravian locations.

Finding aids: Comprehensive index and catalogue.

636 Morden College Archives

Address: 19 St Germans Place, London SE3 0PW

Telephone: (0181) 858 3365 ext. 228

Fax: (0181) 293 4887

Enquiries: The Archivist and Librarian, Mrs Elizabeth Wiggans

Open: By arrangement only.

Access: Researchers, by appointment arranged on application to the Clerk to the Trustees.

Acquisitions policy: To maintain the archives.

Historical background: The archives department holds administrative records from the foundation of the charity in 1695 and other documents relating to its endowment, the Manor of Old Court.

Archives of organisation: Minute books, 1708–.
Early account books, 1705–.
Maps, plans and expired leases relating to the college estates.
Deeds relating to the appointment of visitors.
Documents relating to the admission of members.

Major collections: Charles Kelsall (1782–1857): sketch books, architectural drawings, literary works.

Non-manuscript material: Plans, drawings, photographs, maps.

Finding aids: Database in course of compilation.

Conservation: Contracted out.

Publications: H. Lansdell: *Princess Aelfrida's Charity* (1911–15) [7 vols; history of the college; index in course of compilation].
P. Joyce: *Patronage and Poverty in Merchant Society: the History of Morden College, Blackheath* (1982).
Morden College: a Brief Guide and Handbook (5/1984).

637 Museum in Docklands

Parent organisation: Museum of London

Address: Unit C14, Poplar Business Park, 10 Prestons Road, London E14 9RL

Telephone: (0171) 515 1162

Fax: (0171) 538 0209

Enquiries: The Librarian, Mr R. Aspinall

Open: Tues, Wed, Fri: 10.00–5.00

Access: Generally open to the public, students and researchers, strictly by appointment with the librarian.

Historical background: The Museum of London began collecting material relating to London's docklands, with the assistance of the Port of London Authority, in the 1970s. In 1985 discussions between the two institutions resulted in the PLA's library and archives being deposited with the museum for curatorial purposes. Until then, this was the largest collection of business records in the UK outside a museum or record office.

Acquisitions policy: To maintain and consolidate the collections relating to the Port of London and London's docklands.

Major collections: Port of London Authority archives, including minute books of London dock companies and Thames navigation authorities, 1770–, and departmental records of PLA administration, 1909–.
British Ports Association archives, 1911–70.
Registers of vessels licensed to operate on the tidal River Thames, 1890–1950.

Non-manuscript material: Newspaper cuttings, a unique collection *re* all events in the docks, including dock strikes, 1889–1960s.
Photographs, including dock activities, riverside and aerial views, 1865–1970 (c20,000).
Films and videos, 1924–70.
Engineering and architectural drawings of docks, 1805–1970s (20,000).
Expanding collection on the regeneration of Docklands, 1981–, drawn from a wide variety of sources.

Finding aids: Catalogues and indexes for PLA and BPA archives and newspaper cuttings collection. Computer list of dock company employees, 1800–1909. See also NRA 25615.

Facilities: Photocopying. Photography by arrangement.

Publications: M. Chrimes: 'Drawing on the Past', *New Civil Engineer* (19 May 1988), 26 [gives details of engineering drawings].

638 Museum of London
Library

Address: 150 London Wall, London EC2Y 5HN

Telephone: (0171) 600 3699 ext. 221

Fax: (0171) 600 1058

Enquiries: The Librarian, Ms Joanna Clark

Open: Mon–Fri: 9.30–5.30

Access: Generally open to the public, by appointment only.

Historical background: The Museum of London was opened in 1976, created by the amalgamation of two major collections, the Guildhall Museum of the City of London (1826–1975) and the London Museum (1911–75).

Acquisitions policy: The museum collects, conserves and records evidence relating to the development of London and to life in London from earliest times. Documentary evidence is excluded unless it falls within one of the following categories: records created by the museum or by others (individuals or societies) in the course of research on London; material relating to or illuminating aspects of the existing object-collections. Archives which form an integral part of an object-collection are acquired.

Archives of organisation: Archives of the Guildhall and London museums, c1908–75.

Major collections: Site records of archaeological excavations in the City, 1930s-; miscellaneous other site records from other parts of Greater London.

The Young MSS: commonplace books, household accounts and letters of the Young family of Limehouse (family of G.F. Young, shipbuilder), 1736–1862.

Whitefriars Glass Company archives, 1680–1980.

Suffragette Collection, 1800–: includes Women's Social and Political Union Archive and the research papers of David Mitchell, author of *The Fighting Pankhursts*.

Miscellaneous deeds, letters etc, 15th century–.

Non-manuscript material: Library: Tangye Collection, contemporary printed works and some MSS of Civil War/Commonwealth period.

W.G. Bell Collection, similar collection of material concerning the Plague and Fire of London.

London guide books, 18th century–.

Maps and plans of London, 1553–1994.

Historic Collections: printed ephemera collection, includes trade cards, 16th century–; valentines, 19th century; material from London pleasure gardens and theatres, 18th–20th centuries.

Historic photograph collection, 1840s–.

Prints, drawings and paintings of London.

Finding aids: Indexes and catalogues to the collections.

Facilities: Photocopying. Photography. Microfilm/fiche reader/printer.

Conservation: Limited in-house facilities; some work contracted out.

639 Musicians' Union

Address: Union Headquarters, 60–62 Clapham Road, London SW9 0JJ

Telephone: (0171) 582 5566

Fax: (0171) 582 9805

Enquiries: The General Secretary, Dennis Scard

Open: By arrangement.

Access: Bona fide scholars, by appointment.

Historical background: The Manchester Musical Artistes' Protective Association, 1874–6 (a branch of a similar organisation in London), and the Birmingham Orchestral Association, 1874–8, were forerunners of the Amalgamated Musicians' Union established in Manchester in 1893. In 1921 this merged with the National Union of Professional Orchestral Musicians and adopted its present name.

Acquisitions policy: To maintain its archives.

Archives of organisation: Manchester Musical Artistes' Protection Association minutes, 1874–6. Musicians' Union Executive Committee minutes, 1894–, and Glasgow Branch minutes, 1902–.

Rules, 1894– (incomplete), and membership records, c1930–.

Reports and Journals, 1895–.

Finding aids: NRA 9877.

Publications: E.S. Teale: 'The Story of the Amalgamated Musicians' Union', *Musicians' Journal* (1929–30) [4 articles].

640 National Army Museum

Address: Royal Hospital Road, London SW3 4HT

Telephone: (0171) 730 0717 ext. 2222

Fax: (0171) 823 6573

Enquiries: The Head of Archives, Photographs, Film and Sound, Dr P.B. Boyden

Open: Tues–Sat: 10.00–4.30

Access: By reader's ticket, which must be obtained in advance.

Historical background: The museum developed from the collections of the Royal Military Academy Sandhurst (entry **144**), which provided museum facilities for relics of the pre-partition Indian Army and the Irish regiments disbanded in 1922. In 1960 the National Army Museum was established by Royal Charter. The museum moved to purpose-built premises in Chelsea in 1971, an extension to which was opened in 1980.

Acquisitions policy: The acquisition by gift and purchase of collections of private, regimental and business archives relating to the history of the British Army, the Indian Army to 1947, and British colonial land forces to relevant independence dates.

Major collections: Papers of Gen. Lord Rawlinson of Trent (1864–1925); Gen. Sir James Outram (1803–63); Gen. Sir Aylmer Hunter-

Weston (1864–1940); Lt.-Gen. Sir William Inglis (1763–1837); Maj.-Gen. Sir Clement Milward (1877–1951); FM Lord Birdwood (1865–1951); FM Sir George Nugent (1757–1849); Lt.-Gen. Robert Ballard Long (1771–1825); Gen. Lord Chelmsford (1827–1905); Gen. Lord Raglan (1788–1855) and Gen. Sir William Codrington (1804–84) *re* Crimean war; 1st Marquis of Anglesey (1768–1854), as Colonel of 7th Hussars; FM Lord Roberts (1832–1914); FM Viscount Gough (1779–1869); Gen. Sir Frederick Haines (1812–1909); Gen. Sir Henry Warre (1819–98); Lt.-Gen. Reginald Savory (1894–1980); Gen. Sir Roy Bucher (1895–1980); FM Lord Harding of Petherton (1896–1989); Maj.-Gen. Sir Edmund Hakewill Smith (1896–1986); Brig. Peter Young (1915–88); Sir A.F. Andrew N. Thorne (1885–1970); Lt.-Gen. Sir Gerald Ellison (1861–1947); Professor H. Spenser Wilkinson (1853–1937); Brig. Gen. J.E. Gough (1871–1915); and others.

Regimental records of 9th/12th Royal Lancers, Middlesex Regiment, Womens Royal Army Corps (and predecessors), Westminster Dragoons, Surrey Yeomancy, 4th Battalion London Regiment, and various Indian Army units. Business archives of Gaunt and other military tailors.
Tidworth Tattoo records, 1920–39; United Service Club records, 1815–1970.

Non-manuscript material: Prints and drawings, including the Crookshank Collection of British military campaigns and the Cambridge Collection of British military costumes (*c*25,000).
Albums (*c*1000) and photographs (*c*400,000).
Printed books (*c*40,000).
Oral history interviews (*c*300) and sound discs of military music (*c*300).
Small collection of privately shot cine film.

Finding aids: Card catalogue for pre-1984 accessions; more recent additions on microfiche catalogue and computer database. Lists and calendars of large collections. Lists regulary sent to NRA.

Facilities: Photography. Photocopying. Microfilming. Microfiche/film reader.

Conservation: Facilities available in-house.

Publications: Articles on the collections in the archives appear in the *Annual Report* and *Yearbook*.
P.B. Boyden: 'The National Army Museum Archive Collection, 1960–1985', *Journal of the Society of Archivists*, viii/1 (1986), 23–9.

641 National Art Library

Parent organisation: Victoria and Albert Museum

A Manuscript Collection

Address: South Kensington, London SW7 2RL

Telephone: (0171) 938 8500

Fax: (0171) 938 8461

Enquiries: The Head of Special Collections

Open: Tues–Sat: 10.00–5.00 Closed for three weeks after late August bank holiday for stocktaking.

Access: Researchers with reader's ticket (for special collections application forms obtainable from library); bona fide researchers.

Historical background: MSS have entered the library from the inception of the School of Design after 1836. Documentary and illuminated MSS were collected from the 19th century and consolidated into a collection in the 1950s.

Acquisitions policy: To collect MSS that document the history and practice of all branches of art and design; to collect illuminated and calligraphic MSS that document the development of book production and book design from the Middle Ages, with special emphasis on the post-medieval survival of medieval book-making crafts, the 19th–century revival and subsequent development in the 20th century of calligraphy, lettering and illumination. The MSS Collection usually acquires material that lacks an archival context; archive groups are now passed to the Archive of Art and Design.

Archives of organisation: The MSS Collection holds material relating to the history of the V & A, most notably the papers of Henry Cole (1808–82), but has no responsibilities for the V & A's archives.

Major collections: Edwin Landseer (1802–73), correspondence.
Records of Carrington & Co., silversmiths and jewellers, 1870–1930.
Records of J. Smith & successors, picture dealers, 1812–1908.
Pugin family records, 19th century.
The Library of John Forster (*d* 1876) includes MSS of Charles Dickens's novels; the correspondence of David Garrick (1717–79); papers

of James Butler, Duke of Ormonde, and his successor, relating to Ireland, *c*1642–*c*1700; miscellaneous papers of Jonathan Swift (1667–1745).

Finding aids: Card catalogue available in library; acquisitions from 1987 being entered onto the library computer catalogue. Annual returns made to NRA.

Facilities: Photocopying and photography of some material; microfilming.

Conservation: In-house museum department; some work contracted out.

Publications: J.I. Whalley: *Catalogue of English Non-Illuminated Manuscripts in the National Art Library up to December 1973* (1975) [reproduced typescript; with annual supplements up to 1978].
For the Forster Collection, see Science and Art Department of the Committee on Council on Education, South Kensington Museum: *Forster Collection: a Catalogue of the Paintings, Manuscripts, Autograph Letters, Pamphlets, etc with Indexes* (HMSO, 1893).

B Archive of Art and Design

Address: 23 Blythe Road, London W14 0QF

Telephone: (0171) 602 5349

Fax: (0171) 602 6907

Enquiries: The Curator, Ms Serena Kelly

Open: Tues–Thurs: 10.00–4.30
Closed for three weeks after late August bank holiday for stock-taking.

Access: An appointment, by telephone or in writing, is required. References may be necessary for access to certain materials.

Historical Background: The Archive of Art and Design was set up in 1978 to conserve, catalogue and make available archive groups formerly held by and offered to the curatorial departments of the Victoria and Albert Museum, with particular emphasis on the 20th century.

Acquisitions policy: To collect archive groups that complement existing primary collections in the National Art Library and Archive of Art and Design, with special reference to the fields covered by the collections of the Victoria and Albert Museum. Major strengths are in the fields of textiles, fashion, graphic design and book illustrations, stained glass, exhibition design, interior design, metalwork and ceramics.

Major collections: Archives of Heal & Son Ltd, bedding and furniture manufacturers, 1840–1956; John French, fashion photographer, *c*1948–65; Misha Black, industrial and exhibition designer and architect (1928–77); The Rt Hon. Baron Reilly of Brompton, former director of the Design Council (1920–90); Gaby Schreiber, consultant designer for industry (1938–89); Francis Marshall, fashion and social illustrator (1928–80); Japan Festival 1991 Ltd, *c*1989–91; the Crafts Council, *c*1968–94; Department of Design Research, Royal College of Art, *c*1960–86; Bernhard Baer-Ganymed Press and Ganymed Original Editions Ltd, 1947–85; *The Ambassador*, the British export magazine for textiles and fashion, 1933–70.
Records of James Powell & Sons (Whitefriars) Ltd, stained-glass making company, 1845–1973; William Comyns & Sons Ltd, manufacturing silversmiths, *c*1900–86; Arts and Crafts Exhibition Society (later Society of Designer Craftsmen), papers, 1886–1984.
E.W. Godwin, architect, furniture and theatre designer: papers, 1855–86.
Eileen Gray, interior and furniture designer and architect: papers, designs and photographs, 1917–37.

Non-manuscript material: A large number of the archive groups contain a wide variety of media from glass negatives to film and other audio-visual material.
The Krazy Kat Arkive of 20th-century popular culture includes toys, robots, games, books, journals and tear sheets.
Ephemera collection.

Finding aids: Each archive group is described on the computer catalogue of the National Art Library; list of titles of all archive-groups and lists for larger collections also available.

Facilities: Photocopying. Photography. Microfiche readers. Video and tape recorders. Slide projector. Light table.

Conservation: As for Manuscript Collection above.

Publications: Guide forthcoming.

C Museum Archive

Address: 23 Blythe Road, London W14 0QF

Telephone: (0171) 602 5349

Fax: (0171) 602 0980

Enquiries: The Archivist, Victoria and Albert Museum

Open: By arrangement.

Access: Strictly by appointment. Records less than 30 years old are closed under the terms of the Public Records Act 1958; some confidential material is closed for longer.

Historical background: The museum was established on its present site in South Kensington in 1857. Papers in the archive go back to the 1840s but are not rich for the 19th century. The Museum Archive was formally set up when an archivist was appointed in 1992 to take charge of records management procedures and to look after the museum's historical archives. It is recognised as a place of deposit for public records.

Major collections: Victoria and Albert Museum Registry. Material formerly held in the PRO. National Art Library archives.

Finding aids: Some lists available.

Facilities: Photocopying at the discretion of the Archivist.

Conservation: As for Manuscript Collection above.

Publications: Guide forthcoming.

642 National Council for Voluntary Organisations

Address: Regent's Wharf, 8 All Saints Street, London N1 9RL

Telephone: (0171) 713 6161

Fax: (0171) 713 6300

Enquiries: The Information and Technology Team

Open: Mon–Fri: 2.00–5.00, by prior arrangement.

Access: Bona fide researchers. Not all material is available.

Historical background: The National Council of Social Service (NCSS) was founded in 1919 to promote the systematic organisation of voluntary social work, both nationally and locally. In 1980 it became the NCVO, with aims of encouraging and supporting voluntary organisations.

Acquisitions policy: Retains own working papers only. In certain circumstances these have been handed over to repositories (see below).

Archives of organisation: Correspondence, minutes and other papers, 1919–; documents covering the development of the welfare state, the NHS, amateur drama and music societies, unemployment in the 1930s, the formation of councils for voluntary service and rural community councils, and specific projects such as International Year of the Disabled.
Some records have been deposited elsewhere: Standing Conference of Women's Organisations and Women's Group (Fawcett Library; entry **519**); Goodman Committee (House of Lords; entry **560**); material relating to village halls, including architects' drawings (largely transferred to local rural community councils).

Non-manuscript material: Some maps and photographs (mostly uncatalogued).
Newspaper cuttings kept by Information Team.

Finding aids: Still in process of being catalogued. TS lists available.

Facilities: Photocopying.

Publications: M. Brasnett: *Voluntary Social Action* (1969) [history of the NCSS].
K. Cole: *NCVO from 1919 to 1993: a Selective Summary of NCVO's Work and Origins*, Information Briefing No. 8 (NCVO, 1993).

643 National Gallery Archive

Address: Trafalgar Square, London WC2N 5DN

Telephone: (0171) 389 1731

Fax: (0171) 753 8179

Enquiries: The Archivist

Open: Mon–Fri: 10.00–5.30, by appointment

Access: Bona fide researchers.

Historical background: The National Gallery, founded in 1824, houses the national collection of European painting from the mid-13th to the early 20th century. The archive is recognised as a place of deposit for public records.

Acquisitions policy: To collect, by purchase, gift or deposit, material related to the National Gallery and the people associated with it.

Archives of organisation: Records of the activities of the National Gallery, 1824–, including minutes, correspondence, photographs, plans, publications and press cuttings.

Major collections: Correspondence of Sir Abraham Hume and Giovanni Maria Sasso, 1787–1805.
Note-books of Sir Charles Eastlake (1793–1865), 1852–64, and his correspondence with Jeremiah Harman, 1821–5.
Diaries of Otto Mündler, 1855–8.
Correspondence of Sir William Boxall, 1848–78; and of Ellis Waterhouse, 1925–56.

Finding aids: Basic lists of most of the collection; some detailed lists and indexes.

Facilities: Photocopying. Photography of some material permitted. Microfilm reader/printer.

644 National Institute for Social Work
Dame Eileen Younghusband Collection

Address: 5–7 Tavistock Place, London WC1H 9SN

Telephone: (0171) 387 9681

Fax: (0171) 387 7968

Enquiries: The Librarian

Open: Mon–Fri: 9.30–5.30

Access: Bona fide research students; a letter of application and an appointment are essential; certain materials are restricted.

The institute was started in 1961 by Eileen Louise Younghusband (1902–81), a pioneer in social work, and on her death it accepted her extensive collection of papers (NRA 24768). Information about the institute's own archives is not available.

645 National Maritime Museum

Address: Romney Road, Greenwich, London SE10 9NF

Telephone: (0181) 858 4422 ext. 6722/6691, 312 6722/6691 (direct line)

Fax: (0181) 312 6632

Enquiries: The Head of Manuscripts or The Enquiry Service

Open: Mon–Fri: 10.00–5.00 Sat: 10.00–1.00; 2.00–5.00; prior arrangement necessary. Closed for the third week of February.

Access: By reader's ticket, issued to prospective readers who can prove their identity. Access to certain items, including the museum's archives, is restricted. A large amount of material is housed away from the museum; prior arrangement may therefore be necessary.

Historical background: The museum was formally established by Act of Parliament in 1934 for the instruction and study of the maritime history of Great Britain; it opened in 1937. The MS collections began to be assembled before this date. The museum is recognised as a place of deposit for public records. The Information Access Section of the museum's Maritime Information Centre is responsible for MSS.

Acquisitions policy: To collect, by purchase, gift or deposit, MSS relating to British maritime affairs.

Archives of organisation: Records of acquisitions, policy and management, early 1930s-, including papers of first director, Sir Geoffrey Callender.

Major collections: Public records, including Admiralty, Navy Board and dockyard records, 17th–19th centuries.
Business records, including P&O and subsidiary companies; Lloyd's Register Surveys, c1833–c1964; Shipbuilders and Repairers National Association, c1889–1977; Marine Society, 1756–1977.
Personal papers: c300 collections, including papers of Edward Hawke (1705–81); Lord Hood (1724–1816); Viscount Nelson (1758–1805); Matthew Flinders (1774–1814); Lord Beatty (d 1936); Baron Chatfield (1873–1967); John Montagu, 4th Earl of Sandwich (1718–92).
Artificial collections, including the maritime papers collected by Sir Thomas Phillipps.
Items acquired singly by the museum, e.g. atlases, logs, signal books, letter- and order-books; tapes relating to seamen and shipboard life.

Non-manuscript material: Maritime Information Centre: books and pamphlets (c50,000).
Ships' Draught Collection, including the Admiralty Draught Collection.
Chart collection.
Photographic collection.

Finding aids: Lists are available for most of the collections. Index of people, places, ships and subjects. Lists sent to NRA.

Facilities: Photocopying. Photography. Microfilming. Microfilm/fiche reader.

Conservation: In-house service; outside work undertaken occasionally. Some binding contracted out.

Publications: R.J.B. Knight (ed.): *Guide to the Manuscripts in the National Maritime Museum*, i: *The Personal Collections* (1977); ii: *Public Records, Business Records and Artificial Collections* (1980).
Guide to British Naval Papers in North America.

646 National Monuments Record

Parent organisation: Royal Commission on the Historical Monuments of England

Address: National Monuments Record Centre, Kemble Drive, Swindon SN2 2GZ
NMR London public search room: 55 Blandford Street, London W1H 3AS

Enquiries: Customer Services

Open: Mon–Thurs: 9.30–5.30; Fri: 9.00–5.00
Please phone for details of Saturday opening.

Access: Generally open to the public.

Historical background: Founded in 1941 as the National Buildings Record, it was formed to be a systematic photographic record of English architecture. In 1963 the record became part of the Royal Commission on Historic Monuments (f. 1908); the name was changed to the National Monuments Record when its work was extended into the fields of archaeology and air photography. It is recognised as a place of deposit for public records and is England's public archive of the historical environment.

Archives of organisation: Records of RCHME architectural and archaeological survey work, 1908–.

Non-manuscript material: The architectural record consists of major collections of architectural drawings and photographs, including those of the National Buildings Record, the Property Services Agency, and a range of notable architectural photographers.
Air photographs include total coverage of

England in vertical photography and a large collection of oblique photographs, 1908–.
Archaeology includes OS record cards of archaeological slides and the national index of excavations, as well as a large and historic collection of drawings and photographs.
Major library of architecture and archaeology (32,000 vols).

Finding aids: Databases of heritage information and air photographs. Various indexes and catalogues.

Facilities: Photocopying. Photography. Microfilm/fiche readers/printers. Laser copying.

Publications: *Annual Report.*
Newsletter.
RCHME books catalogue available on request.

647 National Portrait Gallery
Heinz Archive and Library

Address: St Martin's Place, London WC2H 0HE (entrance in Orange Street)

Telephone: (0171) 306 0055

Fax: (0171) 306 0056

Enquiries: The Research Assistant (Archive), Jonathan Franklin

Open: Tues–Sat: 10.00–5.00

Access: Researchers in the field of portraiture who cannot find their material elsewhere, by appointment.

Historical background: The National Portrait Gallery was founded in 1856. The archive and library were originally built up to aid staff in the acquisition of portraits, in the compiling of catalogues of the collection, and to help answer general enquiries. The gallery is recognised as a place of deposit for public records.

Acquisitions policy: Photographs, engravings, drawings and MSS that extend the collection of information on British portraiture are acquired by purchase and donation.

Major collections: Sketchbooks and diaries of Sir George Scharf (1820–95), first director.
Artists' sitters' books, notably Joseph Wright of Derby (1734–97), account books, and letters, including many by George Frederic Watts (1817–1904).
Collection of MSS on the history of the National Portrait Gallery and the building.

Non-manuscript material: Extensive collection of reference photographs and other reference material on portraits in collections other than the gallery's.
Portrait engravings.
Original portrait photographs and negatives (*c*150,000 items), including large collections of the work of Camille Silvy, Madame Yevonde, Howard Coster, the Bassano Studio and Cecil Beaton (1904–80).

Finding aids: Card catalogue to library and MSS. Card index of portraits. Listing of special collections.

Facilities: Limited photocopying. Photography.

Publications: A. Davies and E. Kilmurray: *Dictionary of British Portraiture* (1979–81) [4 vols; based on information in the archive].
K.K. Yung (comp.): *Complete Illustrated Catalogue* (1981).

648 National Postal Museum

Address: King Edward Building, King Edward Street, London EC1A 1LP

Telephone: (0171) 239 5420

Fax: (0171) 600 3021

Enquiries: The Manager, Mr Stan Goron

Open: Mon–Thurs: 9.30–4.30 Fri: 9.30–4.00

Access: Generally open to the public, by arrangement only, to view material not on display.

Historical background: The National Postal Museum was established on the initiative of R. M. Phillips, who donated his stamp collection to the Post Office in 1965.

Acquisitions policy: The museum makes purchases of philatelic and other postal material from time to time to develop its collections. It also receives much internal material from the Post Office.

Archives of organisation: The Post Office's collection of artists' designs for postage stamps, essays, die proofs and registration sheets mid-19th century–.
Stamps of the world collection.

Major collections: The R.M. Phillips Collection of British stamps and related material, 1837–1901 (available on microfilm).
Correspondence of the De La Rue Company,

stamp printers, 1855–1955 (available on microfilm).
The Frank Staff postal history collection.

Non-manuscript material: Artefacts relating to Post Office operations.

Finding aids: Catalogues of philatelic records held.

Facilities: Photocopying (NB photocopying of philatelic material is limited for reasons of conservation). Photography.

Conservation: In-house paper conservation studio.

Publications: Research articles and notes on material in the R.M. Phillips and other philatelic collections are published in the monthly *British Philatelic Bulletin* and the biannual *Crosspost* (published by the Association of Friends of the NPM); these and a list of museum publications are available from the museum.

649 National Scout Archive

Parent organisation: The Scout Association

Address: Baden-Powell House, Queen's Gate, London SW7 5JS

Telephone: (0171) 584 7030

Fax: (0171) 581 9953

Enquiries: The Archivist, Mr Paul Moynihan

Open: Mon–Fri: 10.00–4.00, by appointment.

Access: Members of the scout movement, and other approved readers by application in writing to the Archivist.

Historical background: The Scout Association's national archive was established in 1976 to provide the movement with a reference facility covering the history of scouting and the life of its founder, Lord Baden-Powell (1857–1941).

Acquisitions policy: To receive, by gift or purchase, any relevant material.

Archives of organisation: Minute books, letters, documents and official documents of the movement, 1907–.
Some material relating to the Boer War and the Siege of Mafeking.

Major collections: Diaries, papers and original MSS of Lord Baden-Powell.
Papers and letters of Sir Percy W. Everett

(1870–1952), Deputy Chief Scout, and Percy B. Nevill (1887–1975).

Non-manuscript material: Large collection of photographic items, including prints, negatives and slides relating to world scout jamborees, rover moots and scouting activities generally. Also cine and video films and sound recordings. Large collection of uniforms, badges, postcards, cigarette cards, artefacts and memorabilia. Collection of pamphlets, secondary works and general reference works on the history of scouting.

Finding aids: General card index.

Facilities: Photocopying. Photography. Microfilm/fiche reader.

Conservation: Contracted out.

Publications: Subject fact sheets.

650 National Society for the Prevention of Cruelty to Children (NSPCC)

Address: The Library, NSPCC National Centre, 42 Curtain Road, London EC2A 3NH

Telephone: (0171) 825 2767

Fax: (0171) 825 2525

Enquiries: The Archivist, Nicholas Malton

Open: Strictly by prior appointment only.

Access: Bona fide readers. 100–year closure period for any records from which children can be identified, and 30–year closure for most unpublished administrative records. Children's legal case files are not included in the archive.

Historical background: The NSPCC was founded by Rev. Benjamin Waugh (1839–1908) in 1884, following the example of local societies in New York and Liverpool.

Acquisitions policy: Records of or directly relating to the NSPCC and of local societies that have merged into it.

Archives of organisation: National and local administrative records and annual reports. The Society's official journals and other NSPCC publications.

Major collections: Collection of material relating to Rev. Benjamin Waugh, founder and first director.

Non-manuscript material: Photographs and films.
Collecting boxes, badges, uniforms, portraits, plaques and posters.

Finding aids: Catalogues: due to confidentiality, these are not open to public use, but it may be possible to supply researchers with lists tailored to their specific enquiry.

Facilities: Limited photocopying by permission.

651 National Trust
Archive and Library

Address: 36 Queen Anne's Gate, London SW1H 9AS

Telephone: (0171) 227 4957

Fax: (0171) 222 7691

Enquiries: The Archivist/Records Manager, Miss Janette Harley

The trust was established in 1895 and holds its own internal archives. Papers acquired with properties are generally family and estate papers, and are normally deposited in an appropriate local repository. The trust also owns: papers of Rudyard Kipling (1865–1936), housed at University of Sussex library (entry **123A**); family and political papers of Benjamin Disraeli (1804–81), at the Bodleian Library (entry **871**); and papers of Thomas Carlyle (1795–1881), at the National Library of Scotland (entry **294**).

652 Natural History Museum

Address: Cromwell Road, London SW7 5BD

Telephone: (0171) 938 9238

Fax: (0171) 938 9290

Enquiries: The Museum Archivist, Mr J. Thackray

Open: Mon–Fri: 10.00–4.30

Access: Tickets are issued (no museum admission charge applies); prior notice is required.

Historical background: The British Museum (Natural History) was established at South Kensington in 1881, having separated from the British Museum, Bloomsbury, in that year. The natural history collections date from the time of Sir Hans Sloane (1660–1753), who bequeathed his vast private collection to the nation. This formed the nucleus of the British Museum. A few important MS collections were transferred to South Kensington in 1881, but the bulk of the museum's holdings have been acquired since that date. It is recognised as a place of deposit for public records. The museum changed its name to the Natural History Museum in 1989.

Acquisitions policy: To obtain, by purchase, gift or exchange, all published and unpublished materials relevant to the work of the museum.

Archives of organisation: The museum archives comprise mostly post-1881 documents, although some departmental records go back to 1800 and a few are pre-1800. They contain reports, correspondence etc relating to the collections and the development of the museum.

Major collections: Large collections of MSS associated with the following scientists: Sir Joseph Banks (1743–1820) and his associates; Robert Brown (1773–1858); Albert C.L.G. Günther (1830–1914); Sir John Murray (1841–1914); Sir Richard Owen (1804–92); Lionel Walter, 2nd Baron Rothschild (1868–1937); Daniel Solander (1736–82); James Sowerby (1757–1822) and subsequent generations of the Sowerby family; Richard Meinertzhagen (1878–1967); Miles J. Berkeley (1803–89); William Jardine (1800–74); David A. Bannermann (1886–1979); John Gould (1804–81); Philipp C. Zeller (1808–83); Arthur Russell (1878–1964); William Roxburgh (1759–1815); Henry T. Stainton (1822–92); Alfred Russel Wallace (1823–1913); Edward A. Wilson (1872–1912). Documents relating to Captain James Cook's three expeditions, 1768–71, 1772–5, 1776–80.

Non-manuscript material: Large collections of watercolour paintings, pencil sketches etc, of natural history subjects, including works by, or commissioned by, the following: Ferdinand Bauer (1760–1826); Franz Bauer (1758–1840); Thomas Baines (1822–75); Georg D. Ehret (1708–70); Thomas Hardwicke (1755–1835); Bryan H. Hodgson (1800–94); Sydney Parkinson (1745–71); John Reeves (1774–1856); John Latham (1740–1837); Alfred Waterhouse (1830–1905); Richard Owen (1804–92); George E. Lodge (1860–1954); John Abbot (1751–c1842); Eugel Terzi (*d* c1944); Arthur Smith (1916–91); Thomas Watling (1762–?). Challenger voyage photographs; Indian botanical drawings; portraits of naturalists collection.

Finding aids: The automated catalogue of the museum libraries contains catalogue entries for MSS and drawings; various more detailed lists are available. Lists and indexes of the museum archives are available. An index of letters is in the course of compilation. Lists sent to NRA.

Facilities: Photocopying. Photography. Microform viewing.

Publications: Catalogue of the Books, Manuscripts, Maps and Drawings in the British Museum (Natural History) (London, 1903–40) [8 vols].
The History of the Collections Contained in the Natural History Departments of the British Museum (London, 1904–06) [2 vols].
Bulletin of the British Museum (Natural History), Historical Series (1953–).
W.R. Dawson: *The Banks Letters: a Calendar of the Manuscript Correspondence of Sir Joseph Banks Preserved in the British Museum (Natural History) and other Collections in Great Britain* (London, 1958).
F.C. Sawyer: 'A Short History of the Libraries and List of Manuscripts and Original Drawings in the British Museum (Natural History)', *Bulletin of the British Museum (Natural History)*, Historical Series, (1971), 77–204.
J.B. Marshall: 'The Handwriting of Sir Joseph Banks, his Scientific Staff and Amanuenses', *Bulletin of the British Museum (Natural History)*, Botanical Series, 6 (1978), 1–85.
W.T. Stearn: *The Natural History Museum at South Kensington* (London, 1981).
R.E.R. Banks: 'Resources for the History of Science in the Libraries of the British Museum (Natural History)', *British Journal for the History of Science*, xxi (1988), 91–7.

653 New Church Conference Library

Parent organisation: The General Conference of the New Church

Address: 20 Bloomsbury Way, London WC1A 2TH

Telephone: (01206) 302932 (Secretary) or (0171) 229 9340

Enquiries: Mr G.S. Kuphal, Secretary of Conference, 20 Red Barn Road, Brightlingsea, Colchester, Essex CO7 0SH

Open: Mon–Fri: 9.30–5.00

Access: The collections may be consulted by anyone, but an appointment is necessary.

Historical background: The General Conference of the New Church is an organisation of followers of the Christian theological teaching of Emanuel Swedenborg (1688–1772), the Swedish scientist, philosopher and theologian. They first met for separate worship in 1787 and a national organisation began in 1789. The General Conference was incorporated in 1872. It is a registered charity under the Companies Act. The library was established in 1913 and is under the supervision of a library and documents committee.

Acquisitions policy: To collect as fully as possible records of New Church organisations in this country.

Archives of organisation: Minute books and similar records, with some correspondence, of the General Conference, its various committees and some related bodies, early 19th century–.
Baptismal, marriage and funeral registers and minute books of individual New Church societies (congregations) in the UK.

Non-manuscript material: Photographs of New Church buildings, meetings and individuals.
Early Latin editions and English translations of the works of Emanuel Swedenborg.
Many miscellaneous New Church printed pamphlets.

Finding aids: Loose-leaf catalogue of principal archives.

654 Newham Museum Service

Parent organisation: London Borough of Newham

Address: c/o Leisure Service Department, 292 Barking Road, London E6 3BA

Telephone: (0181) 472 4785

Fax: (0181) 503 5698

Enquiries: The Museum Services Manager

Access: By appointment only.

Historical background: The Newham Museum Service, formerly the Passmore Edwards Museum, was reviewed in 1994 and the collections rationalised to retain principally material relating to the London Borough of Newham:

non-Newham archives are being transferred to the Essex Record Office (entry 203).

Acquisitions policy: Acquisition, by donation or purchase, of material relating to the London Borough of Newham and any material relating to the Great Eastern Railway.

Archives of organisation: Some East and West Ham and London Borough of Newham archives.

Major collections: Great Eastern Railway records, 19th and 20th centuries.
Local manorial and industrial records, 16th century–.
Correspondence and papers of Raphael Meldola (1849–1915), chemist, 1864–1908.

Non-manuscript material: Essex Pictorial Survey (photographs and engravings).

Finding aids: Lists. Meldola: NRA 12102.

Facilities: Photocopying. Photography by arrangement.

655 North London University

Address: Holloway Road, London N7 8DB

Telephone: (0171) 607 2789

Enquiries: The Archivist

Open: By appointment.

Access: Open to students studying the history of education.

Historical background: North London University was formerly the Polytechnic of North London which was the amalgamation of the Northern Polytechnic (f. 1896) and North Western Polytechnic (f. 1929).

Acquisitions policy: Active collection of relevant material. Everything welcome.

Archives of organisation: Archives date from the 1890s and include internal and external correspondence.
Receipts and invoices relating to the supplies bought by the polytechnics.
Student record cards.

Non-manuscript material: Departmental and committee papers and reports.
Polytechnic anniversary documents.
Prospectuses, annual reports, governors' minutes, student union publications, arts societies programmes, annual accounts, course leaflets, house journals.

Files of press cuttings relating to the polytechnic.

Large collection of photographs of buildings and classrooms.

Oral history collection (in progress).

Finding aids: Card index in preparation.

Facilities: Photocopying. Photography.

656 Office of Population Censuses and Surveys

Address: General Register Office, St Catherine's House, 10 Kingsway, London WC2B 6JP

Telephone: (0171) 242 0262

Fax: (0171) 439 1779

Enquiries: The Registrar General (postal enquiries) or The Information Branch

Open: Mon–Fri: 8.30–4.30

Access: The search rooms are open to the public. 100–year closure on census returns; some other papers have an extended closure beyond the normal 30–year period.

Historical background: The General Register Office was founded in 1837, when a service was created for the state registration of births and deaths and the solemnisation and registration of marriages in England and Wales; registration commenced from 1 July 1837. In 1970 the General Register Office merged with the Government Social Survey to form the Office of Population Censuses and Surveys. The General Register Office still exists as a statutory body under the direction of the Registrar General, who is also Director of OPCS. The decennial census returns and departmental papers worthy of preservation are transferred to the Public Record Office under the provisions of the Public Records Acts 1958 and 1967.

Acquisitions policy: The records accumulate as registration proceeds.

Archives of organisation: Birth, death and marriage registers, 1 July 1837–.
Records kept by British consuls and high commissioners in respect of British subjects abroad, 1849–.
Army records (personnel and families), some of which date back to 1761.
Royal Air Force returns, 1920–.

Births and deaths on board British registered vessels, 1894–.

Finding aids: Indexes to birth, death and marriage registers.

Publications: Information leaflets (available on request).

657 Order of St John
Library and Museum

Address: St John's Gate, Clerkenwell, London EC1M 4DA

Telephone: (0171) 253 6644 exts 13, 27, 28

Fax: (0171) 490 8835

Enquiries: The Curator, Ms Pamela Willis

Open: Mon–Fri: 10.00–5.00, by arrangement.

Access: Generally open to the public, by appointment.

Historical background: The collection was started after the establishment of the Venerable Order of St John in 1831 and more particularly after the acquisition of St John's Gate in 1874, where the collection is housed. St John's Gate and Priory Church are the remains of the priory of the Medieval Order of St John, dissolved in 1540. The museum was opened to the public on a regular basis in 1978. The British Royal Order of Chivalry runs two major charitable foundations, St John Ambulance and St John Ophthalmic Hospital.

Acquisitions policy: Material relevant to the history of the Knights of St John, the Most Venerable Order and the charitable foundations, by purchase and donation.

Archives of organisation: MS records of the Order of St John, including documents relating to British properties, and estates in France, Malta and Rhodes, 1140– (c5000).
Records relating to the foundation of St John Ambulance and its activities in various wars, including Zulu, Boer and World Wars I and II, 1860s–.
Records of the St John Ophthalmic Hospital, Jerusalem.

Non-manuscript material: Prints and drawings collection. Photographs and glass negatives.
Pamphlets and books relating to the Order of St John, 15th–20th centuries.
Coins: Crusader and Order of St John (includ-

ing the King, Wilkinson and Sprawson collections).

St John Ambulance Collections.

Finding aids:. Catalogue and handlists. Indexes. Lists sent to NRA.

Facilities: Photocopying. Photography.

Publications: The Early Statutes of the Knights Hospitallers (1932).
The Thirteenth-Century Statutes of the Knights Hospitallers (1933).
Six Documents relating to Queen Mary's Restoration of the Grand Priories of England and Ireland (1935).
Notes on the History of the Library and Museum (1945).
J. Toffoto: *Image of a Knight* (1988)
P. Willis: *Brief History of the Order of St John.*
Mason and Willis: *Maps of Malta* (1989).
Knights of St John in Essex (1992).
St John Ambulance in Victorian Britain (1992).

658 Palestine Exploration Fund

Address: 2 Hinde Mews, Marylebone Lane, London W1M 5RR

Telephone: (0171) 935 5379

Enquiries: The Executive Secretary, Mr R. Chapman

Open: By arrangement.

Access: Bona fide researchers, by appointment.

Historical background: The fund was established in 1865 and supports archaeology in the Holy Land.

Acquisitions policy: To maintain the archives and acquire the papers of individuals associated with the fund.

Archives of organisation: Records of the fund, including reports of Jewish excavations, 1865–6, 1867–70; and other excavations, 1860s-1930s; Western survey 1871–7; and Eastern survey.

Major collections: Papers, including those of Edward Henry Palmer (1840–82); Sir Walter Besant, secretary of PEF, 1868–86; Prof. T. Hayter Lewis, 1870s-1890s; William Flinders Petrie (1853–1942); and documents by and relating to Gen. Sir Charles Warren (1840–1928), Maj.-Gen. Sir Charles Wilson (1836–1905), FM Lord Kitchener of Khartoum (1850–1916) and T.E. Lawrence (1891–1936).

Records of excavations of Prof. J. Garstang (1876–1956).

Non-manuscript material: Photographs, mainly of Palestine, 19th century (*c*10,000).
MSS maps of Palestine, including the fund's Survey of Western Palestine MSS and the surviving MSS of the map of Lt. C.W.M. Van de Velde, RE.

Finding aids: Detailed list: NRA 16370. The material is being systematically catalogued.

659 Peabody Trust

Address: 45 Westminster Bridge Road, London SE1 7JB

Telephone: (0171) 928 7811 ext. 228

Fax: (0171) 620 1269

Enquiries: The Assistant Secretary, Mr D. Delmar

Open: By prior arrangement only.

Access: Generally open to the public, strictly by appointment with at least four weeks' notice required.

Historical background: The Peabody Trust was founded in 1862 by George Peabody (1795–1869), an American philanthropist whose gift, which became known as the Peabody Donation Fund, was administered by trustees to 'ameliorate the condition of the poor' of London. It was agreed that the trust would concentrate on the provision of cheap clean housing, and the first estate was opened in Spitalfields in 1864. The trust took over the Labour's Friend Society (f. 1830), later renamed the 1830 Housing Society, in 1965 and the Westminster Housing Trust Ltd in 1972. The archives were catalogued and established within the trust by the Business Archive Council in 1985.

Acquisitions policy: To maintain the historical records of the trust, its founder and any inherited records, principally relating to its estates.

Archives of organisation: Peabody Trust: agenda books, annual reports, accounts, letterbooks, estate records, including births, deaths and population books, and registers of tenants, *c*1862–1984.
Affiliated bodies: the Labourer's Friend Society/1830 Housing Society, minutes, 1832–, and annual reports, 1850–; miscellaneous

property records, and correspondence; publications.

The Westminster Housing Trust Ltd: records, including minutes, ledgers and annual reports, 1929–.

Non-manuscript material: Scrapbooks, plans, drawings, paintings, photographs and glass slides, ephemera.
Journals and official reports *re* housing and related subjects.
Unpublished histories and dissertations.

Finding aids: Business Archives Council list: NRA 27933.

Publications: J.N. Tarn: 'The Peabody Donation Fund', *Victorian Studies*, 10 (1966).
George Peabody: a Biography (Nashville, 1971).

660 The Polish Institute and Sikorski Museum
Archives Department

Address: 20 Princes Gate, London SW7 1PT

Telephone: (0171) 589 9249

Enquiries: The Keeper of Archives, Andrzej Suchcitz

Open: Tues–Fri: 9.30–4.00

Access: All bona fide researchers; there are restrictions on certain deposited collections.

Historical background: The institute was founded in 1945 as the General Sikorski Historical Institute, taking its present name in 1966 after amalgamating with the Polish Research Centre. The institute's archives contain the largest collection outside Poland of primary sources concerning that country, with special emphasis on World War II. The documents in the institute's archives do not concern only Polish history and related subjects, nor are they exclusively in Polish. Researchers will also find sources relating to international politics in general, and to Central and East European affairs in particular.

Acquisitions policy: To acquire, by donation or deposit, material relevant to the history of Poland and her citizens.

Major collections: Records of Polish Civil Service, including the Chancellery of the President of Poland, the Polish National Council, the Council of Ministers, ministries, embassies,

legations and consulates, 1939–49; Polish armed forces, including army, navy and air force, 1939–47.
Papers of the Polish government in exile, 1945–90.
Private and subject collections, including those of Gen. Władysław Sikorski (1881–1943), soldier and statesman; Gen. Władysław Anders (1892–1970); Count Edward Raczyński (*b* 1891), diplomat; Tadeusz Romer (1894–1978), diplomat; Josef Retinger (1888–1960), political adviser; Adam Ciołkosz (1901–78), politician and writer; Jan Ciechanowski (1887–1973), diplomat; Count Jan Szembek (1881–1945), diplomat; Stanisław Kot (1888–1975), professor of literature and politician (*c*350 collections).

Non-manuscript material: Maps, paintings and engravings, 15th–19th centuries. Military memorabilia, 20th century.

Finding aids: General index to all collections. Register of subject files to most collections.

Facilities: Photocopying. Microfilm reader.

Publications: Guide to the Archives of the Polish and Sikorski Museum, i (London, 1985).

661 The Polish Library

Parent organisation: Polish Social and Cultural Association

Address: 238–46 King Street, London W6 0RF

Telephone: (0181) 741 0474

Enquiries: The Librarian, Dr Z. Jagodziński

Open: Mon, Wed: 10.00–8.00 Fri: 10.00–5.00 Sat: 10.00–1.00

Access: Scholars and researchers, subject to library rules and the reservations of depositors, which in some cases means closure until the end of the 20th century.

Historical background: The Polish Library was established in 1942 by the Ministry of Education of the Polish government in exile. Between 1948 and 1953 it became part of the Polish University College in London; later it was taken over by the Committee for the Education of Poles in the United Kingdom. Since 1967 the Polish Social and Cultural Association has accepted full responsibility for the library as its legal owner on behalf of the Polish community in Great Britain.

Acquisitions policy: To collect and preserve

records of cultural, social, political, literary etc activities and life of Poles abroad, especially in the UK, since 1939.

Major collections: Private archive of Jozef Retinger (1888–1960).
Archives of Polish wartime or post-war periodicals in the UK and some Polish émigré organisations.
MSS, private papers, diaries, memoirs, biographical materials, literary works etc of Polish writers, scholars, politicians, artists and other members of Polish communities abroad.

Non-manuscript material: Large collections of periodicals (c3300 titles), bookplates, photographs, maps and engravings.
Books, pamphlets etc, including special collections of Conradiana (in co-operation with the Joseph Conrad Society).
Polish underground and Solidarity publications (1976–90) and works on Anglo-Polish relations.

Finding aids: Inventory books. Card catalogues. Conrad: NRA 15220.

Facilities: Photocopying.

662 Post Office Archives and Records Centre

Parent organisation: The Post Office

Address: Freeling House, Mount Pleasant Complex, London EC1A 1BB (entrance in Phoenix Place)

Telephone: (0171) 239 2570

Fax: (0171) 239 2576

Enquiries: The Chief Archivist, Mrs Jean Farrugia

Open: Mon–Fri: 9.00–4.15
Closed Maunday Thursday afternoon.

Access: Generally open to the public, but with proof of identity required.

Historical background: The General Post Office was founded by royal proclamation in 1635, and at first operated on a farming basis. Its public records date from 1677, and these were being administered as a public archive by 1890. The archives unit holds all the archives of the GPO, including those on broadcasting, the Post Office Savings Bank, and some on telecommunications, up to 1969. The Post Office was established as a public corporation in 1969, when its archives unit continued to be recog-

nised as a place of deposit for the organisation's public records; but its stamp collections are deposited separately in the National Postal Museum (entry **648**). Girobank (Nigel Hardman, Archivist/Librarian, 5 North, The Triad, Stanley Road, Bootle, Merseyside L20 3LT, tel. 0151 928 8181 ext. 3413) and British Telecom (entry **506**) are now separate organisations, with their own archives units.

Acquisitions policy: Through the operations of its records centre, to maintain the archive and ensure its completeness from 1969. All aspects of the development of Post Office operations and services are covered, wherever these occur.

Archives of organisation: Administrative records reflecting all aspects of Post Office operations and services, at home and overseas, and employee records, late 17th century–.

Major collections: Papers of Sir Roger Whitley, Deputy Postmaster-General, 1672–77; John Palmer (1742–1818), Surveyor and Comptroller of Mails, 1788–1813; Sir Rowland Hill (1795–1879), Secretary to the Post Office, 1836–79; and Sir William Preece (1834–1913), Engineer-in-Chief, 1854–1913.

Non-manuscript material: Portraits and other pictures, c1800–.
Maps showing the circulation of mail in local areas as well as over major routes, 1807–.
Photographs reflecting the work of the Post Office, late 19th century–.
Library covering the history of the Post Office, c1850–.

Finding aids: Catalogues for records held. Copies held at Public Record Office (entry **960**).

Facilities: Photocopying. Photography. Microfilm/fiche readers. Use of laptop computers.

Conservation: Contracted out.

Publications: J. Farrugia: *A Guide to the Post Office Archives* (1986).
Information leaflet.
A list of other publications, and products, is available from the archives unit.

663 Principal Registry of the Family Division

Address: Somerset House, Strand, London WC2R 1LP

Telephone: (0171) 936 7000 (Probate) 936 6940 (Divorce)

Enquiries: Probate Enquiries Room G25
Divorce Enquiries Room 37

Open: Mon–Fri: 10.00–4.30

Access: Generally open to the public, to view
and purchase copies of grants of representation
and wills of deceased persons' estate issues in
England and Wales since 1858. There is a
restriction on most divorce records, but copies
of some documents are available to the public.
The office is recognised as a place of deposit for
public records.

Major collections: Probate: copies of all grants
of representation and all wills proved in
England and Wales, 1858–.
Divorce: petitions issued in PRFD, 1858–; index
of all decree absolutes issued throughout
England and Wales, 1858–.

Finding aids: Probate: index available for public
inspection.
Divorce: index for staff inspection only.

Facilities: Photocopying. Microfiche readers.

664 Queen Mary and Westfield College

Parent organisation: University of London

Address: Mile End Road, London E1 4NS

Telephone: (0171) 775 3305

Fax: (0171) 975 5500

Enquiries: The Archivist, Mr Anselm Nye

Open: Mon–Fri: 9.00–5.00 by arrangement.

Access: Approved readers, on written application.

Historical background: Westfield College,
Hampstead, was founded in 1882 as a residential
college for women preparing for University of
London degrees. The MS collection was built
up from donations and occasional purchases.
Queen Mary College traces its foundation from
the opening of the People's Palace in the East
End in 1884 and the start of its Technical
Schools in 1887. The latter expanded from
part-time evening classes to the status of a full
school of the University of London, shown in
its changes of name first to the East London
Technical College, in 1892, then to East London
College and finally to Queen Mary College, in
1934. The two colleges merged in 1990. The

Geology Department holds records of the
Geologists' Association.

Acquisitions policy: To maintain archives of
relevance to both colleges.

Archives of organisation: Westfield College
archives, 1882–.
Archives of the People's Palace, minutes, correspondence and press cuttings, 1884–1920.

Major collections: Letters of the Lyttelton
family, with relevance to British and South
African history, late 19th and early 20th centuries (*c*10,000).
Small collections on 19th–century British art,
especially Benjamin Robert Haydon, John
Martin and James Smetham.

Finding aids: Draft catalogue for Westfield
College archives. Lyttelton Collection catalogue almost complete.

Facilities: Photocopying. Photography. Microfilm reader.

Publications: J. Sondheimer: *A Castle Adamant
in Hampstead* (London, 1983) .
G.P. Moss and N.V. Saville: *From Palace to
College* (London, 1985).
C.M. Maynard: *The Diaries of Constance Maynard* (Brighton, 1987) [14 reels of microfilm,
including the diaries, Effie note-books and
unpublished autobiography].

665 Queen's College

Address: 43–49 Harley Street, London
W1N 2BT

Telephone: (0171) 580 1533

Fax: (0171) 436 7606

Enquiries: The Principal, the Hon. Lady Good-
hart

Open: Term: Mon–Fri: 10.30–2.30

Access: Bona fide researchers, at the discretion
of the Principal and by appointment only.
Restrictions on certain MSS.

Historical background: Queen's College, the
first institution to provide a sound academic
education and proper qualifications for women,
was founded in 1848 by F.D. Maurice. The
college had strong links with King's College in
the University of London (entry **589**), many of
whose professors also lectured at Queen's, and
with the Governesses' Benevolent Association.
In 1853 Queen Victoria, the first patron,

granted a Royal Charter to the college and a school for younger girls was started. The college continues to flourish in its present site (now considerably expanded) in Harley Street.

Acquisitions policy: Anything of major interest concerning former students or members of staff.

Archives of organisation: Records and registers of students, 1848–. Minutes of the Committee of Education and college council.

Major collections: Early correspondence of founders and original professors, including F.D. Maurice, David Laing, W. Sterndale Bennett (1816–75), R. Chenevix Trench (1807–86). Articles and note-books of early students, including Katherine Mansfield (1888–1923), writer, and Louisa Twining (1820–1911), social reformer.

Non-manuscript material: Early photographs of the college and former students.
Queen's College Calendar, 1879–1931; *Queen's College Magazine*, 1881–.

Facilities: Photocopying.

Publications: *The First College for Women: Memories and Records of Work Done, 1848–1898.*
R.G. Grylls: *Queen's College, 1848–1948* (1948).
E. Kaye: *A History of Queen's College, London* (1972).

666 Rambert Dance Company Archives

Address: 94 Chiswick High Road, London W4 1SH

Telephone: (0181) 995 4246

Fax: (0181) 747 8323

Enquiries: Jane Pritchard

Open: By appointment only.

Access: Company members and bona fide researchers.

Historical background: The archive was established in 1982 to document the history of Ballet Rambert/Rambert Dance Company and related organisations. The archive documents the life and career of the company's founder, Marie Rambert (1888–1982), choreographers, composers, designers and dancers who worked with the company and the productions they created.

Acquisitions policy: The collection and preservation of a wide range of documentation on the history and activities of the company. This is primarily British, but includes records of overseas tours.

Archives of organisation: Administrative and artistic records, 1926–.

Major collections: Marie Rambert Collection, 1888–1982.
Papers from numerous former company members.

Non-manuscript material: Production designs, set models, video and sound tapes.

Finding aids: Cataloguing in progress.

Facilities: Photocopying.

Conservation: Occasionally contracted out.

Publications: J. Adshead Lansdale and J. Layson, 'Rambert Dance Company Archive', *Dance History* (Routledge, 1994).

667 Ramblers' Association

Address: 1/5 Wandsworth Road, London SW8 2XX

Telephone: (0171) 582 6878

Fax: (0171) 587 3799

Enquiries: The Director

Open: By appointment only.

The Ramblers' Association is a voluntary organisation which was established in 1935. The association promotes the recreation of rambling and works to protect rights of way, to promote access to open country and to defend the natural beauty of the countryside. It maintains its own archives, which comprise minute books, 1930–, committee papers, 1949–, and correspondence with local areas of the RA, as well as publicity material, 1967–. See NRA 24474. Photocopying is available.

668 Reform Club

Address: 104–5 Pall Mall, London SW1Y 5EW

Telephone: (0171) 930 9374

Fax: (0171) 930 1857

Enquiries: The Librarian

Open: Strictly by arrangement only.

Access: Members only; other bona fide researchers by member's introduction or special arrangement with the librarian.

Historical background: The Reform Club was founded in 1836 by Edward Ellice (1781–1863), MP and promoter of the 1832 Reform Bill, for the benefit of Liberal politicians.

Acquisitions policy: To maintain its own archives.

Archives of organisation: Extensive archives of the club, including committee and AGM minutes, annual reports and membership records, 1836–.

Major collections: Papers of W.M. Eager (1884–1966), secretary of the Liberal Land End Industrial Inquiries, 1920s.
Papers of political agents of David Lloyd-George (1863–1945), prime minister.

Finding aids: Catalogue.

Facilities: Photocopying.

Conservation: Contracted out.

Publications: L. Fagan: *The Reform Club: its Founders and Architect, 1836–1886* (1887).
G. Woodbridge: *The Reform Club, 1836–1978* (1978).

669 Royal Academy of Arts
The Library

Address: Burlington House, Piccadilly, London W1V 0DS

Telephone: (0171) 494 5737

Enquiries: The Deputy Librarian, Nicholas Savage or The Librarian, Maryanne Stevens

Open: Mon–Fri: 10.00–1.00; 2.00–5.00 by appointment only.

Access: Bona fide students and scholars.

Historical background: The library was established in 1771, in accordance with the intentions of the founding members of the Royal Academy, to provide a repository of 'things useful to students in the Arts'. Since then the collection has grown to cover books on the history of art, with specific emphasis upon British art. In addition, all archival material

pertaining to the Royal Academy and its members is held. The Royal Academy's collection of works of art is also administered by the library.

Acquisitions policy: To maintain the archives of the academy and to accept donations of members' papers.

Archives of organisation: Archives of the Royal Academy, including Summer and Loan Exhibition catalogues, General Assembly and Council minutes, annual reports and students' register.

Major collections: Summer Exhibition catalogues, 1769–1850, annotated by J.H. Anderdon (26 vols).
Graphic Society: laws, minutes and letters, 1833–90.
Society of Artists records, 1759–1807.
Papers of Sir George Clausen (1852–1944); John Gibson (1790–1866); Ozias Humphry (1742–1890) (8 vols); Sir Thomas Lawrence (1769–1830) (5 vols); Sir Joshua Reynolds (1723–92), including 27 sitters' books.
Thomas Miller archive.

Non-manuscript material: Collection of works of art and photographs, mostly connected with members of the Royal Academy.
Rare books relating to architecture and bound volumes of engravings by artists.

Finding aids: General and separate indexes to most MS material. NRA 14837.

Facilities: Photocopying. Photography by arrangement.

Publications: 'The Royal Academy Schools, 1768–1830', *Walpole Society*, xxxvii [includes transcript of first schools' register].

670 Royal Academy of Dramatic Art

Address: 62–64 Gower Street, London WC1E 6ED

Telephone: (0171) 636 7076

Enquiries: The Librarian, Clare Hope

Open: Term: Mon–Fri: 11.00–1.30; 2.30–7.00

Access: Generally open to the public, by appointment.

Historical background: The academy was founded in 1904 by Sir Herbert Beerbohm-Tree (1852–1917) and has been in its present home since 1905. It received its Royal Charter in 1920.

Members of Council have included Bernard Shaw (a major benefactor of RADA library) and Irene Vanbrugh, and many distinguished members of the theatrical profession have attended RADA.

Acquisitions policy: To maintain the archives. The library expands to support productions.

Archives of organisation: Archives include records of Council meetings, 1906–, student records and cast lists.

Major collections: 40 albums of press cuttings on Bernard Shaw.

Facilities: Photocopying.

671 Royal Academy of Music Library

Parent organisation: Royal Academy of Music

Address: Marylebone Road, London NW1 5HT

Telephone: (0171) 873 7323

Fax: (0171) 873 7374

Enquiries: The Librarian, Ms Katharine Hogg

Open: Term: Mon–Thurs: 9.00–9.00 Fri: 9.00–6.00 Sat: 9.00–12.00 Vacation: enquire before visit.

Access: Generally open to the public, by appointment.

Historical background: The academy was founded in 1822 to provide training facilities for those seeking careers in all branches of music. The library recently obtained a room to house early printed music and MSS.

Acquisitions policy: Material relating to music and performance.

Archives of organisation: Academy archives, including student registers, papers and prospectus (incomplete).

Major collections: Papers and scores of Sir Henry Wood (1869–1944), conductor, a former student and teacher at RAM. Papers of other eminent performers, including Harriet Cohen (1896–1967), pianist.
Savage-Stevens Collection of 18th-century musical scores.

Non-manuscript material: Collection of early sound recordings.

Large collection of printed music, pre-1850, and supporting collection of early literature.

Finding aids: Computerised catalogues, lists and indexes.

Facilities: Photocopying. Photography. Microfilm/fiche reader. Sound recording listening facilities.

Publications: Catalogue of Microfilms of RAM Holdings.

672 Royal Aeronautical Society Library

Address: 4 Hamilton Place, London W1V 0BQ

Telephone: (0171) 499 3515 exts 233, 234

Fax: (0171) 499 6230

Enquiries: The Librarian and Information Officer, A.W.L. Nayler

Open: Mon–Fri: 10.00–5.00

Access: Any member of an Engineering Council institution may have access to the society's library. Non-members are charged a small daily access fee.

Historical background: The society was founded in 1866 and is the oldest aeronautical society in the world; it incorporated the Institute of Aeronautical Engineers in 1927. A Royal Charter, granted in 1949, recognised it as the representative body for those concerned with the general advancement of aeronautical art, science and engineering, and that it facilitated the exchange of information and ideas. The library, formed in 1866, holds an extensive collection of books, technical reports, papers and archival material.

Acquisitions policy: To acquire, by donation, deposit or purchase, material relevant to the history and development of aeronautical engineering, aviation and aerospace, and allied fields.

Archives of organisation: Official records and working papers of the society, 1866–.

Major collections: Collections built up by John Cuthbert (*fl.* 1820s), John Hodgson (1875–1952) and Frederick Poynton (1869–1944), including MSS, prints and ephemera relating to early flight and ballooning, mainly 19th century.
Papers of Sir George Cayley, 1800–50; John

Stringfellow (1799–1883); William Wright (1867–1912); Orville Wright (1891–1948); Katherine Wright (1874–1929); Lawrence Hargrave (1850–1915); Maj. B.F.S. Baden-Powell (1860–1937); and G.G. Grey (1875–1953).

Non-manuscript material: Portraits of eminent aeronautical engineers and aviators, presidents of the society, 1866–.
Photographs of aircraft, equipment, society events and members.

Finding aids: General catalogue to all collections. Index to the photographic collections. Cayley: NRA 1055.

Facilities: Photocopying. Photography by arrangement.

Publications: J.E. Hodgson: *History of Aeronautics in Great Britain* (Oxford, 1924) [includes details of collections].
F. MacCabee: *Publications Index, 1897–1977* [index to the *Aeronautical Journal*, Aerospace Conferences etc].

673 Royal Air Force Museum
Department of Research and Information Services

Address: Grahame Park Way, Hendon, London NW9 5LL

Telephone: (0181) 205 2266 ext. 273 (General enquiries, appointments etc) ext. 250 (Keeper, Mr P.J.V. Elliott) ext. 245 (Curator of Fine Art) ext. 246 (Curator of Photographs) ext. 230 (Curator of Film)

Fax: (0181) 200 1751

Open: Mon–Fri: 10.00–5.00, by appointment.

Access: Bona fide researchers.

Historical background: The museum was founded in 1964 and opened at Hendon in 1972. The Department of Research and Information Services comprises the former departments of Aviation Records (archives and library) and Visual Arts (film, photographs and fine art). The museum is recognised as a place of deposit for public records.

Acquisitions policy: To collect material, by donation and purchase, which relates to the history of the RAF and its antecedents, associated air forces and aviation generally where a link with the RAF is established. The subject

emphasis is on British military aviation, but includes records of British aircraft companies.

Archives of organisation: Museum files, 1964–; minutes of trustees' meetings, 1965–.

Major collections: Papers of a number of senior officers of the period up to 1945, including Marshal of the RAF Lord Trenchard (1873–1956), ACM Sir Arthur Harris (1892–1984), and Lt.-Gen. Sir David Henderson (1862–1921); also leading figures in British aviation, including Lord Brabazon of Tara (1884–1964) and Sir Frederick Handley Page (1885–1962), and aircraft companies, including Supermarine, Fairey and Handley Page.
Material relating to ordinary airmen and women, notably aircrew log-books, World War I casualty records and record cards for RAF aircraft, vehicles and marine craft.

Non-manuscript material: Extensive collections of manufacturers' drawings of aircraft and engines, with site plans for RAF airfields and non-flying stations.
Photographs, films and works of art, including the Air Ministry element of the collection assembled by the War Artists Advisory Committee.

Finding aids: Catalogues and accession lists for most collections. Lists sent to NRA.

Facilities: Photocopying. Microform (fiche, film and aperture card). Photography. Researchers may use their own tape-recorders and other aids in the reading room.

Conservation: Contracted out.

Publications: Series of leaflets explaining how to trace unit and personnel records, the history of RAF stations and the service histories of individual aircraft.

674 Royal Albert Hall

Address: Kensington Gore, London SW7 2AP

Telephone: (0171) 589 3203 ext. 2207

Fax: (0171) 823 7725

Enquiries: The Archivist, Ms Jacky Cowdrey

Open: Tues–Thurs: 10.00–6.00, strictly by appointment only.

Access: Bona fide researchers. Charges are applicable for any commercial use applied for and approved by the hall. Please note seating is very limited.

Historical background: The Royal Albert Hall was opened in March 1871.

Acquisitions policy: The collection, acquisition and preservation of all material relating to events staged at the Royal Albert Hall and to the building itself.

Archives of organisation: Royal Albert Hall Council minutes, 1869–.
Programmes of events, 1913–.

Non-manuscript material: Drawings of the Hall, 1871–.
Original sepia photographs of the building; Heraton's photographs, 1940s-60s.
Transparencies and colour negatives of events, 1982–94.

Finding aids: Various lists. Programmes arranged chronologically.

Facilities: Photocopying. Photography.

Publications: R.W. Clark: *The Royal Albert Hall* (London, 1958).
J.R. Thaderah: *The Royal Albert Hall* (1983).

675 Royal Anthropological Institute of Great Britain and Ireland

Address: 50 Fitzroy Street, London W1P 5HS

A Manuscript and Archive Collection

Enquiries: The RAI Representative, c/o Museum of Mankind, 6 Burlington Gardens, London W1X 2EX, tel. (0171) 437 2224 ext. 8052

Open: Mon–Fri: 10.00–5.00; appointment preferred.

Access: Accredited scholars after written application. Fragile collections are closed.

Historical background: The institute was founded in 1871, incorporating the Ethnological Society and the Anthropological Society of London. It is recognised internationally as the representative body in the UK for the whole field of the study of man. In 1976 the library was donated to the British Museum and merged with the departmental library of the Museum of Mankind, where the Manuscript and Archive Collection is now also stored.

Acquisitions policy: Donations are accepted.

Archives of organisation: Domestic archives of the institute, consisting of minute books, committee reports and other documents relating to its administrative history, mid-19th century–.

Major collections: MSS of fieldwork and papers of the following: E.H. Man, 1875–1920; Sir Everard im Thurn, 1887–1923; H.B.T. Somerville, 1889–1900; M.E. Durham, 1900–36; M.W. Hilton-Simpson, 1906–9; R.S. Rattray, 1919–27; J.D. Unwin, 1919–34; Marian W. Smith, 1945.

Non-manuscript material: See entry **675B**.
Film library of *c*150 films is managed by the Scottish Film Archive, Glasgow (entry **348**).

Finding aids: Typescript catalogues, entry by author with author/subject index (compiled by B.J. Kirkpatrick).

B Photographic Collection

Telephone: (0171) 387 0455

Fax: (0171) 383 4235

Enquiries: The Photo-Librarian

Open: By appointment, preferably on written application because of limited staff.

Access: Consultation of the illustrated catalogue is open to all. Access to the original photographs is restricted and by written application only.

Historical background: The photographic collection predates the institute (f. 1871), some of the photographs having come from one or other of the parent societies – the Ethnological Society and the Anthropological Society of London. Few photographs in the collection can be dated earlier than the 1860s. The taking of photographs was actively encouraged by the institute in *Notes and Queries on Anthropology* (first published in 1874). The photographs taken by these early 'travellers and anthropological observers', as well as those by some of the pioneers of modern anthropological fieldwork, were lodged with the institute. Attempts to classify the photographs began in 1899, at first independently, and then in conjunction with the British Association. This scheme was abandoned by 1911. After a period of inactivity work began again on the collection in 1974 and this has led to more recent acquisitions. A register of photographs in private collections is being compiled. This is seen largely as a communication network for academic researchers.

Anyone who would be willing to give access to their photographic collections should contact the Photo-Librarian at the above address.

Acquisitions policy: To encourage the deposit or donation of photographs relating to the study of anthropology, including early photographs with anthropological content, and recent or present-day fieldwork photographs with associated documentation. The institute has very limited resources for purchase.

Non-manuscript material: Two sets of photographs of 'The Natives of Greater Russia', organised by Professor A. Bogdanov for the Moscow Ethnographic Exhibition in 1867.
Prince Roland Bonaparte's portraits of the Lapps, 1884.
Album of *c*700 photographs selected from the collection of portraits of North American Indians made by the US Geological Survey in the 1870s, and presented by F.V. Hayden, geologist in charge of the survey.
Other collections: E.H. Man (Andaman and Nicobar Islands), Sir Everard im Thurn (Indians of Guyana), P.A. Johnston and T. Hoffman (Sikkim, Nepal and Tibet), Vice-Admiral H.B.T. Somerville (Solomon Islands and New Hebrides), all 19th century; R.W. Williamson (Melanesia), C.G. Seligman (Vedda of Sri Lanka, Sudan, New Guinea), Emil Torday (Congo), Mary Edith Durham (Bosnia, Serbia and Albania), Prof. I. Schapera (Southern Africa), M.W. Hilton-Simpson (Algeria), all early 20th century; E.E. Evans-Pritchard (Africa), Sir Max Gluckman (Southern Africa), 1930s and 1940s; Dr Audrey Richards (East Africa).

Finding aids: Illustrated catalogue cards for three-quarters of the prints and some of the negatives. Various lists.

Facilities: Photocopying. Photography. Copy prints may be supplied on loan to general users (publishers etc), as well as to specialists and students. Loan and reproduction fees charged are available on application.

Publications: R. Poignant: *Observers of Man: a Catalogue of an Exhibition of a Selection of Photographs from the Collection of the Royal Anthropological Institute* (1980).

676 Royal Armouries Library

Parent organisation: Trustees of the Royal Armouries

Address: HM Tower of London, London EC3N 4AB

Telephone: (0171) 480 6358

Enquiries: The Librarian, Mrs S.E. Barter Bailey

Open: Mon–Fri: 10.00–12.30; 2.00–5.00

Access: Serious students, by appointment.

The Royal Armouries is the national collection of arms and armour. Archives of the modern museum, *c*1900–, are maintained with papers of students of armoury, 19th and 20th centuries. There is also a photographic library.

677 Royal Artillery Institution

Address: Old Royal Military Academy, Woolwich Common, London SE18 4DN

Telephone: (0181) 781 5623/4

Enquiries: The Historical Secretary

Open: Mon–Fri: 10.00–12.00; 2.00–4.00

Access: Bona fide historians and researchers who are approved by the Royal Artillery Historical Affairs Committee, by written appointment only.

Historical background: The Royal Artillery Library and Archives were founded in 1778. The library is a private reference library relating to the tactics, technology application and history of both British and foreign artillery and to all aspects of the Royal Regiment of Artillery from 1716.

Acquisitions policy: Only books and papers directly concerned with artillery are sought. The majority of acquisitions are donated to the institution; few are purchased.

Major collections: Military documents covering a variety of artillery topics, 1716– (*c*2000).
Papers of Gen. Gardiner, Gen. Biddulph and Lt.-Gen. Lefroy.
Collections of Lt.-Gen. Samuel Cleaveland and Maj.-Gen. Sir A. Dickson.
Regimental archives.

Non-manuscript material: Photographs.
2 portfolios of 19th–century military sketches and caricatures by Col. L.G. Fawkes RA.

Royal Carriage Dept, Woolwich, 19th–century lithographed general assembly plates of artillery equipment.
Rare books.

Finding aids: Cross-referenced lists.

Facilities: Photocopying. Microfilm/fiche reader.

Publications: M.E.S. Laws: *Battery Records of the Royal Artillery, 1716–1877* (London, 1952) [2 vols].
C.A.L. Graham: *The Story of the Royal Regiment of Artillery* (London, 7/1983).
Proceedings of The Royal Artillery Historical Society.
M. Farndale: *History of the RA*, vol. I: *Western Front, 1914–1918*; vol. II: *Forgotten Fronts and the Home Base.*
B.P. Hughes: *History of the RA*, vol. III: *Between the Wars.*
N.W. Routledge: *History of the RA*, vol. IV: *Anti-Aircraft Artillery, 1914–1955.*

678 Royal Asiatic Society Library

Address: 60 Queen's Gardens, London W2 3AF

Telephone: (0171) 724 4741

Enquiries: The Librarian, M.J. Pollock

Open: Mon, Wed, Thurs: 10.00–5.00 Tues: 10.00–8.30

Access: Fellows, and approved scholars on written or telephone application.

Historical background: The society was founded by Henry Thomas Colebrooke in 1823 and received its first Royal Charter that year for 'the investigation of subjects connected with and for the encouragement of science, literature and the arts in relation to Asia'. Many distinguished scholars have been associated with the society and their work has been presented at its meetings.

Acquisitions policy: Material in the field of oriental studies, mainly by donation, but some limited purchases.

Archives of organisation: Minutes of the Council, 1823–.

Major collections: The collection is devoted to the history, culture and languages of Asia and North Africa.

Large collections of oriental MSS, including Arabic, Persian, Malay, Javanese, Urdu, etc.
Eckstein Collection, includes letters from and about Sir Richard Burton (1821–90).

Non-manuscript material: Drawings, engravings and paintings (*c*3000).
Books (*c*100,000), including Persian and Arabic books given by the late Professor C.A. Storey in 1967.
Periodicals (*c*400), titles of which 165 are current.

Finding aids: Catalogues and handlists for all book, MSS and prints and drawings collections.

Facilities: Photocopying. Photography. Microfilm/fiche readers.

Conservation: Some in-house service for prints and drawings collection.

679 Royal Astronomical Society

Address: The Library, Burlington House, Piccadilly, London W1V 0NL

Telephone: (0171) 734 3307/4582

Fax: (0171) 494 0166

Enquiries: The Librarian, Mr P.H. Hingley

Open: Mon–Fri: 10.00–5.00, by arrangement.

Access: Private library, but access may be granted to bona fide researchers on application in writing to the Librarian or by recommendations of a Fellow.

Historical background: The astronomical library has been accumulated by the Royal Astronomical Society since its foundation in 1820. The founder president was William Herschel, and through the benefactions of his family and others associated with it the society has become the owner and guardian of many MSS and archives of value. The archives were temporarily stored at Churchill College, Cambridge, and the collection was catalogued by a temporary archivist (appointed by the Council of the Society), 1974–6.

Acquisitions policy: Gifts of astronomically significant archives and books are considered on their merits.

Archives of organisation: The society's general correspondence, 1820–.
Papers generated by the society: minutes, register books, papers relating to expeditions etc.

Major collections: MSS, mainly 35 named collections.
Herschel Archive: papers of Sir William Herschel (1738–1822), Sir John Herschel (1792–1871) and Caroline Herschel (1750–1848) (housed at Churchill College, Cambridge (entry **153**) and not available for study, but microfilm copy at Burlington House).

Non-manuscript material: Astronomical drawings.
Astronomical portrait and telescope photographs.
Extensive library of astronomical and some other scientific works (of which *c*2500 are pre-1850).

Finding aids: Guide to library.

Facilities: Photocopying. Microfilm/fiche reader. Microfilming.

Publications: J.A. Bennett: 'Catalogue of the Archives of the Royal Astronomical Society', *Memoirs of the RAS*, lxxxv (1978).

680 Royal Automobile Club

Address: 89–91 Pall Mall, London SW1Y 5HS

Telephone: (0171) 930 2345 ext. 398

Fax: (0171) 976 1086

Enquiries: The Librarian, Joan Williamson

Open: Mon–Fri: 9.00–5.00

Access: Members and bona fide scholars, by appointment only.

Historical background: The club was founded as the Automobile Club of Great Britain in 1897, the society for the protection, encouragement and development of automobilism. It was granted a Royal Charter and renamed the Royal Automobile Club in 1907. Since 1911 it has been housed at its present address, previous locations being in Whitehall Court and Piccadilly. The archives are still in the process of being sorted.

Acquisitions policy: To maintain the club's archive and to acquire documentation and memorabilia relating to the history of motoring, by purchase or donation.

Archives of organisation: Archives of RAC,

including minute books, 1897–, annual reports, letters, journals and programmes.

Major collections: Early correspondence of F.S. Simms (1863–1944), founder of the club.

Non-manuscript material: Photographs (*c*4000).
Small collection of films and videos.
Memorabilia, including badges and models.

Finding aids: Lists and computerised catalogue.

Facilities: Photocopying. Microfilm reader/printer.

Conservation: Contracted out.

Publications: Dudley Noble (ed.): *The Jubilee Book of the Royal Automobile Club, 1897–1947* (London, 1947).
Guide to Library and Archives.

681 Royal British Nurses' Association

Address: 94 Upper Tollington Park, London N4 4NB

Telephone: (0171) 272 6821

Enquiries: The Acting President, Mrs H.M. Campbell

The association maintains its considerable archive, which dates from its foundation in 1887 and includes records of the Bedford Fenwick era. Access to consult this material is, however, normally restricted to members only.

682 Royal College of Art

Address: College Library, Kensington Gore, London SW7 2EU

Telephone: (0171) 584 5020 ext. 318

Fax: (0171) 584 8217

Enquiries: The Archives Assistant, Eugene M. Rae

Open: Mon–Fri: 10.00–5.00

Access: Generally open to all researchers, by appointment only.

The archives contain material relating to the administration of the college, including reports and prospectuses; student magazines; degrees, show and exhibition catalogues; newspaper cuttings, 1890s-; student records, 1898–; staff records, 1930s (housed in the college registry). There are internal lists and photocopying is available.

683 Royal College of Midwives

Address: 15 Mansfield Street, London W1M 0BE

Telephone: (0171) 580 6523/4/5

Fax: (0171) 436 3951

Enquiries: The Librarian, Mrs Jan Ayres

Open: By arrangement only.

Access: Bona fide researchers, by appointment.

Historical background: The RCM was founded in 1881 as the Matrons' Aid or Trained Midwives' Registration Society (later the Midwives' Institute) to campaign for the registration and training of midwives. The former aim was realised with the Midwives Act of 1902. By 1905 there were over 22,000 registered midwives; other midwives' associations were encouraged to affiliate with the institute, which became the leading representative of the profession. Its importance as a training institution was recognised by the change of title to College of Midwives in 1941, and the prefix Royal was granted six years later. The college moved to its present premises in 1957. Building works in the college may inhibit access to the archives for some time.

Acquisitions policy: To maintain and consolidate the college's archives and collections.

Archives of organisation: Records of the college, including incorporation documents; minutes of Council and other committees, including advisory and teachers; financial records, including benevolent funds, 1881–c1960; reports and correspondence *re* maternal mortality, 1934–8, and Rushcliffe Committee on salaries, 1941–7.

Major collections: Individual midwives' case books, 1917–59; lecture notebooks, 1924, 1938.

Non-manuscript material: Memorabilia, including certificates and photographs.

Finding aids: Preliminary inventory, 1981. NRA 19150.

Publications: B. Cowell and D. Wainwright: *Behind the Blue Door: a History of the Royal College of Midwives, 1881–1981* (London, 1981).

684 Royal College of Music

Address: Prince Consort Road, London SW7 2BS

Telephone: (0171) 589 3643

Fax: (0171) 589 7740

Enquiries: The Reference Librarian, Mr Christopher Bornet, The Keeper of Portraits, Mr Oliver Davies, The Museum Curator, Mrs Elizabeth Wells

Open: Library: Mon–Fri: 9.30–6.00 Portraits: Mon–Fri: 10.00–5.30 Museum: Term: Wed: 2.00–4.30 (admission charge)

Access: Generally open to the public, but space is extremely limited during term. Specialised enquiries and parties by appointment only.

Historical background: The Royal College of Music was founded by the Prince of Wales, later King Edward VII, in 1883. The important library of the Sacred Harmonic Society was bought for it by public subscription in that year, and very large collections of MSS and early printed music, musical instruments and portraits have accumulated since, mainly by donation. The Museum of Instruments opened in 1970 and the Department of Portraits opened in 1971.

Acquisitions policy: Library: to extend all classes of material held, by purchase as well as donation.

Major collections: Library: MSS, much of English origin, 16th century–.
MSS of people connected with the college, e.g. Hubert Parry (1848–1918) and Herbert Howells (1892–1983).
Full scores of British choral music, mainly autograph, from Novello's publishing house, 19th century.
Autograph MSS of Walford Davies (1869–1941), Frank Bridge (1879–1941) Trust MSS, Havergal Brian (1876–1972) and Malcolm Arnold (*b* 1921).

Non-manuscript material: Portraits Department: the most comprehensive British collection of likenesses of musicians, comprising 320

original portraits and many thousands of prints and photographs.

Extensive collections of opera illustration, instrumental and concert hall design, title pages. Concert programmes, 1780– (600,000).

Reference library on musical iconography and performance history; documentation on musical portraiture.

Museum: Keyboard, stringed and wind instruments, c1480– (c600), including the Tagore, Donaldson, Hipkins and Ridley and Hartley collections.

Reference library on musical instruments.

Finding aids: Author-title index to MSS and printed books. Handlist of original portraits. Indexes of sitters, opera representation, illustration in music periodicals.

Programme index: (a) artists (b) first performances.

Facilities: Photocopying of approved material. Photography. Microfilm readers/printer.

Publications: Guide to the Collection (1984).
H. Howells: *The Music Manuscripts in the Royal College of Music* (1992).
J. Doane: *A Musical Directory for the Year 1793* (1993).

685 Royal College of Obstetricians and Gynaecology

Address: 27 Sussex Place, London NW1 4RG

Telephone: (0171) 262 5425

Fax: (0171) 723 0575

Enquiries: The College Archivist, Clare Cowling

Open: By arrangement with the College Archivist.

Access: Bona fide researchers may apply for access; letters sent to the archivist will be vetted by the president. A 30–year closure rule is applied. A written undertaking must be given, and an appointment is necessary.

Historical background: The college was founded in 1929 from a group within the Gynaecological Visiting Society in the north of England. It moved from Queen Anne Street to a new building on its present site, that of the former Sussex Lodge, in 1960. A Royal Charter was granted in 1947.

Acquisitions policy: To acquire papers of former presidents and Fellows of the college.

Archives of organisation: Records of the founding of the college, 1926–9; Council and committee minutes and papers with records of honorary officers, 1929–; Fellowship selection records, 1930–76.

Special reports, surveys and projects conducted or supported by RCOG, including abortion, contraception, artificial insemination by donor, childbirth, maternity services in general and rare tumour registry, 1950s-90s.

Major collections: Papers of William Blair-Bell (1871–1936), founder and first president, and of William Fletcher Shaw (1878–1961), first honorary secretary and later president.

NB The library also holds a number of MS collections (unlisted).

Non-manuscript material: Aquarelles (cystoscopic drawings), 1930–45. X-rays, photographs, plans and drawings and press cuttings. Obituary notices (in college library).

Finding aids: Class lists. Indexes. Updated lists will be sent to NRA.

Facilities: Photocopying. Microfilm reader.

Publications: W. Fletcher Shaw: *Twenty Five Years: the Story of the Royal College, 1929–54* (London, 1954).
J. Peel: *The Royal College of Obstetricians and Gynaecologists, 1929–1979* (London, 1979).

686 Royal College of Pathologists

Address: 2 Carlton House Terrace, London SW1Y 5AF

Telephone: (0171) 930 5861

Fax: (0171) 321 0523

Enquiries: The College Secretary

Open: Mon–Fri: 9.30–5.00, by arrangement.

Access: Bona fide researchers, by appointment.

Historical background: The college was founded in 1962 and effectively succeeded the Pathological Society of Great Britain and Ireland, which was established at the beginning of the century when academic pathology became recognised as a distinct subject.

Acquisitions policy: To maintain the college archives and, where relevant, acquire material in all branches of pathology.

Archives of organisation: Minutes of the Pathological Society of Great Britain and Ireland, 1906–62.
Archives of the college, including annual reports, 1962–.

Major collections: Collections of papers of Herbert Maitland Turnball (1875–1955), director, Institute of Pathology, 1906–46, and Professor Sir Roy Cameron (1899– 1966), founder president.
Autobiographical notes by numerous members.

Non-manuscript material: Photographs and memorabilia of members and Fellows.

Facilities: Photocopying.

687 Royal College of Physicians of London

Address: 11 St Andrews Place, Regent's Park, London NW1 4LE

Telephone: (0171) 935 1174

Fax: (0171) 487 5218

Enquiries: The Archivist, Mr G.E. Yeo (archives and manuscripts), The Librarian, Mr G. Davenport (non-manuscript sources and general historical enquiries)

Open: Mon–Fri: 9.30–5.30

Access: Most materials are open to bona fide researchers. There is restricted access to college archives less than 30 years old. Documents containing medical details of patients are not normally available until they are 100 years old.

Historical background: The college was granted its first charter in 1518. It has maintained a library since the 16th century. In 1950 the college decided that its library should concentrate on medical history, and in recent years the library has assumed responsibility for college archives in addition to its MS collections. It is recognised as a place of deposit for public records.

Acquisitions policy: To collect material relating

to medical history and biography, with special reference to the college and its Fellows.

Archives of organisation: Annals, i.e. records of proceedings of the college, 1518–; deeds and charters, 1510–1865; other records, 1607–20th century.

Major collections: Western MSS; 13th–20th centuries (several thousand), including collections of papers of individual physicians, mainly 19th and 20th centuries.
Oriental MSS: mostly Arabic, 12th–20th centuries (*c* 66 vols).

Non-manuscript material: Paintings, prints and photographs (chiefly medical portraits).
Books, pamphlets and journals.
Sound and video tapes from the college's oral history programme.

Finding aids: Card index. Catalogues of legal documents (1924) and oriental MSS (1951).

Facilities: Photocopying. Photography and microfilming by arrangement (advance notice required).

Conservation: Contracted out.

Publications: *National Inventory of Documentary Sources,* Chadwyck-Healey microfiche (1984–).

688 The Royal College of Psychiatrists Library

Parent organisation: The Royal College of Psychiatrists

Address: 17 Belgrave Square, London SW1X 8PG

Telephone: (0171) 235 2351

Fax: (0171) 245 1231

Enquiries: The Archivist (part-time) or The Librarian

Open: Mon–Fri: 9.30–4.30
Closed in August.

Access: Bona fide researchers, strictly by appointment. A letter of introduction is required. There is a day charge.

Historical background: The Association of Medical Officers of Asylums and Hospitals for the Insane was founded in 1841 and changed its name to the Medico-Psychological Association in 1865. It was granted a Royal Charter in 1926 and in 1971 became the Royal College of Psychiatrists.

Acquisitions policy: To maintain the college's archives.

Archives of organisation: Minutes of annual meetings, 1841–; quarterly, council, education and parliamentary committee meetings, mid/late 19th century-1971.
Lists of successful candidates in mental nursing examinations (examinees' names and hospitals only), 1890s-1950s.

Non-manuscript material: Small collection of prints, photographs and newspaper cuttings.

Finding aids: Minutes of annual, quarterly, council, education and parliamentary committee meetings have been abstracted onto an in-house database. Card index to prints, photographs and news cuttings collection.

Facilities: Photocopying.

Conservation: Contracted out.

Publications: The Journal of Mental Science, 1850s– [includes minutes and membership lists].

689 Royal College of Surgeons of England

Address: 35–43 Lincoln's Inn Fields, London WC2A 3PN

Telephone: (0171) 405 3474

Fax: (0171) 831 9438

Enquiries: The Librarian, Mr I.F. Lyle

Open: Mon–Fri: 10.00–6.00
Closed August.

Access: Approved readers, on written application. New readers should enclose with their application a letter of introduction from a Fellow of the college, the dean of a medical school, or a medical librarian.

Historical background: The college was founded in 1800 as successor to the Surgeons' Company, which broke away from the Barber-Surgeons' Company in 1745. The library, opened in 1828, maintains a reference collection of monographs and journals on surgery and its specialities, as well as historical collections. It is recognised as a place of deposit for public records.

Acquisitions policy: To acquire, by gift, deposit or purchase, material relating to the college and its Fellows and the history of surgery and its specialities.

Archives of organisation: Records of the college and of the Surgeons' Company, 1745–.

Major collections: Hunter-Baillie Collection: papers and letters to, or collected by, members of the Hunter, Baillie and Denman families, 18th and 19th centuries.
Papers and letters of Matthew Baillie (1761–1823); William Clift (1775–1849); Thomas Denman (1733–1815); John Hunter (1728–93); William Hunter (1718–83); Edward Jenner (1749–1823); Frederic Wood Jones (1879–1954); Sir Arthur Keith (1866–1955); Lord Lister (1827–1912); Sir Richard Owen (1804–92); Sir James Paget (1814–99).
Records and correspondence of the Hunterian Museum.
Records of the London Lock Hospital, 1746–1948.
Autograph letters, mainly 19th and 20th centuries.
Surgical papers, casebooks and lecture notes, 18th–20th centuries.

Non-manuscript material: Engraved portraits (3000).
Book-plates (2000).

Finding aids: Various lists and indexes.

Facilities: Photocopying. Microfiche reader.

Conservation: Contracted out.

690 Royal College of Veterinary Surgeons
Wellcome Library

Address: 62–64 Horseferry Road, London SW1P 2AS

Enquiries: The Librarian, Miss B. Horder

Open: Mon–Fri: 10.00–5.00

Access: All those on the statutory register of the college. Others on introduction by a member of the college or a librarian.

Historical background: The college was incorporated by Royal Charter in 1844, and members immediately offered to present books to form the nucleus of a library. Several important collections have been acquired by bequest.

Acquisitions policy: To strengthen existing collections, by purchase, exchange and donation.

Archives of organisation: Minute books and other records of the college, 1844–.

Major collections: Papers of Sir Frederick Smith (1857–1929) concerning veterinary history, veterinary physiology and army history, particularly South African Wars.

Non-manuscript material: Portraits of presidents of the college.
A few drawings and prints; small collection of photographs.

Finding aids: Individual MSS indexed in main library catalogue. Contemporary indexes to some minute books.

Facilities: Photocopying.

Conservation: Contracted out.

691 Royal Commission for the Exhibition of 1851 Archive

Address: Room 456A, Sherfield Building, Imperial College, Exhibition Road, London SW7 2AZ

Telephone: (0171) 589 5111 ext. 58850

Fax: (0171) 584 3763

Enquiries: The Archivist, Mrs Valerie Phillips

Open: Mon–Fri: 10.00–12.30; 2.00–5.00

Access: Bona fide scholars, with evidence of identity, by appointment only. 30-year closure on most material; 50 years on personal files.

Historical background: The commissioners were appointed by Royal Charter in 1850 to plan and promote the Exhibition of the Works of Industry of All Nations (held in London in 1851). When the affairs of the exhibition were wound up, the commissioners remained a permanent body to administer the surplus funds to 'increase the means of industrial education and extend the influence of science and art upon productive industry'. On their estate in South Kensington they have established an educational centre as well as schemes of fellowships and scholarships.

Acquisitions policy: Maintaining the records of the 1851 commission and acquiring some material from other organisations relating to the commissioners' activities.

Archives of organisation: 1851 exhibition correspondence.
Correspondence on the South Kensington estate, including institutions, e.g. Royal Albert Hall, Royal College of Music, Royal College of Art, Science Museum, Natural History Museum, Victoria and Albert Museum, Royal College of Organists, Imperial Institute, Imperial College.
Files of science research scholars, industrial bursars and naval architecture scholars.
Windsor archives on the 1851 exhibition (on permanent loan).

Non-manuscript material: Maps, plans, drawings, photographs.
Publications of the commissioners.

Finding aids: Detailed list in preparation.

Facilities: Photocopying. Photography.

Conservation: Contracted out.

692 Royal Entomological Society

Address: 41 Queen's Gate, London SW7 5HR

Telephone: (0171) 584 8361

Fax: (0171) 581 8505

Enquiries: The Registrar, Mr C.G. Bentley

Open: Mon–Fri: 9.30–5.00

Access: Bona fide scholars, by appointment only.

Historical background: The society was founded in 1833 as the Entomological Society of London. In 1885 a Royal Charter was granted to the society, and the privilege of adding the word 'Royal' to its title was bestowed in 1933. Most internationally recognised entomologists have been, and are, numbered among its Fellows.

Acquisitions policy: To maintain its own archives and accept the papers of eminent entomologists.

Archives of organisation: Council, general and other committee meetings, minute books, 1833–.
Signature book of Fellows, illuminated by J.O. Westwood (1805–93), 1833.
Correspondence with Fellows, 19th and 20th centuries.

Major collections: Correspondence of Herbert Druce (1846–1913) and Alexander H. Haliday (1806–70).
Various entomological diaries and note-books, c1850–c1916, including those of Roland Trimen (1840–1916), 1858–1912.

Non-manuscript material: Numerous drawings and photographs.

Finding aids: Catalogue with index of correspondents.

Facilities: Photocopying.

Publications: S.A. Neave: *The History of the Entomological Society of London, 1833–1933* (London, 1933).

693 Royal Free Hospital Archives Centre

Parent Organisation: Royal Free Hampstead NHS Trust

Address: The Hoo, 17 Lyndhurst Gardens, Hampstead, London NW3

Telephone: (0171) 794 0692

Enquiries: The Archivist, Dr Lynne Amidon

Open: Mon–Sat: by arrangement only.

Access: Generally open to the public, strictly by appointment. There is a 30-year closure on administrative records and 100-year closure on clinical records.

Historical background: The Free Hospital was founded in Hatton Garden by William Marsden in 1828, became the Royal Free in 1837 and in 1842 moved to Gray's Inn Road, where it remained until transferring to the new building in Hampstead in 1974. This brought together on one site Hampstead General, the London Fever Hospital and Lawn Road Hospital, which had formed the Royal Free Group following the establishment of the National Health Service in 1948. New End and Coppett's Wood Hospitals joined the group in 1966. In 1974 the group became North Camden District (later Hampstead Health Authority). The Royal Free Hampstead NHS Trust was set up in 1991. From 1878 the Royal Free provided clinical teaching facilities for the London School of Medicine for Women, which was founded in 1874 and became the Royal Free School of Medicine when it became co-educational in 1947. The Archive Centre was opened in 1992 and is recognised as a place of deposit for public records. The archivist can also provide access to the records of the medical school.

Acquisitions policy: Records produced by or directly relating to any of the hospitals or staff associated with the Royal Free Hospital and Hampstead Health Authority and its predecessors.

Archives of organisation: Royal Free Hospital administrative records, 1828–, and case books, 1891–1920; London Fever Hospital administrative records, 1802–1948, and patient records, 1837–1938; Hampstead General Hospital, including North West London Hospital, administrative records, 1882–1948; Children's Hospital, Hampstead, administrative records, 1876–1948; New End Hospital patient records, including birth registers, 1914–86 (pre-1948 administrative records in Greater London Record Office (entry 550)); North Western Fever Hospital nursing and domestic staff records, 1887–1950 (patient registers, 1900–48, in GLRO); Coppett's Wood Isolation Hospital case notes, 1936–1970s.
Records of North Camden and Hampstead health authorities, 1974–89.

Major collections: Royal Free Hospital Medical School records, 1874–, including annual reports, council and committee minutes and application forms.

Non-manuscript material: Medical school press cuttings, 1878–83; photograph collection; various paintings and objects.

Finding aids: All main collections listed and partly indexed; lists sent to NRA.

Facilities: Photocopying. Photography.

Conservation: Contracted out.

694 The Royal Fusiliers (The City of London Regiment) Museum and Archives

Parent organisation: The Royal Regiment of Fusiliers

Address: HM Tower of London, London EC3N 4AB

Telephone: (0171) 488 5611

Fax: (0171) 481 1093

Enquiries: The Chief Clerk and Archivist, Mr J.P. Kelleher

Open: Mon–Fri: 10.00–3.30

Access: Generally open to the public, by appointment and with 48 hours' notice. Postal enquiries welcome; SAE required.

The regiment was raised in the Tower of London in 1685 and amalgamated in 1968 into the Royal Regiment of Fusiliers. There have always been close links with the City of London. The archive includes documents about the raising of the regiment but the bulk of the material dates from World War I. There is a substantial number of deposited collections relating to members of the regiment as well as photographic and sound archives. Indexing is in progress and additions to the collections are actively acquired.

695 Royal Geographical Society

Address: 1 Kensington Gore, London SW7 2AR

Telephone: (0171) 589 5466

Fax: (0171) 584 4447

Enquiries: The Archivist, Ms Paula Lucas or The Keeper, Dr Andrew Tatham

Open: Usually Tues, Thurs: 10.00–5.00

Access: Normally restricted to Fellows of the society. Bona fide scholars may be admitted on application to the Director. An appointment is necessary.

Historical background: The society was founded in 1830 to encourage exploration and geographical research. From the time of its foundation the society collected books, maps, pictures, MSS and museum items relevant to its interests.

Acquisitions policy: To accept gifts of MSS relevant to the history of exploration and travel or relevant to notable Fellows of the society.

Archives of organisation: Minute books, administrative records, correspondence and working papers of the society.

Major collections: Special collections of the papers of Dixon Denham (1786–1828); Ney Elias (1844–97); David Livingstone (1813–73); Sir Clements Markham (1830–1916); F.W.H. Migeod; Sir Henry C. Rawlinson (1810–95); Henry M. Stanley (1841– 1904); Captain R.F. Scott's *Discovery* expedition, 1901–04.
Files of worldwide astronomical observations (to fix positions) and meteorological and topographical observations.

Non-manuscript material: Large collections of maps and pictorial material (Map

Room and Picture Library respectively; enquiries should be directed to the Map Curator or Picture Library Manager as appropriate).
Archives: illustrated MSS diaries, photographs and press cuttings, mostly 19th century.

Finding aids: Author card index. Catalogues available on microfiche.

Facilities: Photocopying. Photography and microfilming and by arrangement.

Publications: C. Kelly (comp.): *The RGS Archives: a Handlist* [reprinted from *Geographical Journal*, 141, 142 and 143, plus supplement, vol. 154, part 2; lists accessions up to December 1987].

696 Royal Historical Society

Address: c/o University College London, Gower Street, London WC1E 6BT

Telephone: (0171) 387 7532

Enquiries: The Hon. Librarian, Mr D.A.L. Morgan

Open: Mon–Fri: 10.00–5.00, by prior arrangement with the executive secretary.

Access: Bona fide researchers, on written application to and at the discretion of the Hon. Librarian.

Historical background: The Historical Society was founded in 1868 and became the Royal Historical Society in 1887. In 1897 the Camden Society was amalgamated with the Royal Historical Society.

Acquisitions policy: No intention of acquiring MSS.

Archives of organisation: Archives of the society and the Camden Society, including minute books, accounts and correspondence, 1867–.

Major collections: Papers of Sir George Prothero (1848–1922), including diaries, letters, notebooks, newspaper cuttings, printed pamphlets and proofs.
Solly Flood MS (a history of the writ of Habeas Corpus by Solly Flood, HM Attorney General in Gibraltar).

Non-manuscript material: The library consists mainly of printed primary sources of British history.

Finding aids: Duplicated list and supplementary handwritten list of the Prothero papers.

Publications: Report on the Archives of the Camden Society and the Royal Historical Society, 1867–97, Royal Commission on Historical Manuscripts (1977).
Transactions; Camden Series; Guides and Handbooks series; Guides and Handbooks supplementary series.

697 Royal Horticultural Society
Lindley Library

Address: Vincent Square, London SW1P 2PE

Telephone: (0171) 821 3050

Fax: (0171) 630 6060

Enquiries: The Librarian, Dr Brent Elliott

Open: Mon–Fri: 9.30–5.30

Access: Members of the RHS; members of the public with bona fide horticultural enquiries, preferably by appointment.

Historical background: The Horticultural Society of London was founded in 1804, becoming the Royal Horticultural Society in 1861. The original library was sold in 1859 and the Lindley Library established in 1868.

Acquisitions policy: Material relating to horticulture worldwide, with subordinate emphasis on botany, garden history, garden design, flower arrangement and botanical art.

Archives of organisation: Archives of Horticultural Society of London, later Royal Horticultural Society: minutes of council and committees.
Architectural drawings for RHS garden at Kensington (1861–88), exhibition halls in Westminster (1904 and 1928), and sundry other buildings.
Flower show records.

Major collections: Personal papers of Edward Augustus Bowles (1865–1954); Ernest Tetley Ellis (1893–1953); Vera Higgins (1892–1968); Lanning Roper (1912–83).

Non-manuscript material: Botanical drawings (*c*18,000).
UK's largest collection of horticultural trade catalogues.
Photographic collections.

Finding aids: Archives in course of cataloguing.

Facilities: Photocopying and photography may be arranged.

Conservation: Contracted out.

Publications: G. Bridson and others: *Natural History Manuscripts Resources in the British Isles* (1981), 273.
W.L. Tjaden: 'The Loss of a Library', *Garden* (Journal of RHS), 112 (1987), 386–8.
——: 'The Lindley Library of the Royal Horticultural Society, 1866–1928', *Archives of Natural History,* 20 (1993), 93–128.
B. Elliott: 'Pictures at an exhibition', *Garden* (Journal of RHS), 118 (1993), 108–112.
——: *Treasures of the Royal Horticultural Society* (Herbert Press, 1994).

698 Royal Humane Society

Address: Brettenham House, Lancaster Place, London WC2E 7EP

Telephone: (0171) 836 8155

Enquiries: The Secretary

Open: Mon–Fri: 10.00–4.00

Access: Generally open to the public, by appointment.

The society was founded in 1774 to save the lives of those rescued from drowning. It is a national charity supported by voluntary contributions, and grants awards to rescuers. It maintains its archives, which consist principally of casebooks, minutes, printed annual reports, transactions and proceedings, 1774–. There are photocopying facilities. See P.J. Bishop: *A Short History of the Royal Humane Society* (London, 1974).

699 Royal Institute of British Architects
British Architectural Library

Address: 66 Portland Place, London W1N 4AD and British Architectural Library Drawings Collection 21 Portman Square London W1H 9HF

Telephone: (0171) 580 5533

Fax: (0171) 631 1802

Enquiries: The Director of Library Services

Open: Mon: 1.30–5.00 Tues: 10.00–8.00 Wed, Fri: 10.00–5.00 Sat: 10.00–1.30 Closed August.

Access: Generally open to the public. A charge may be made. Drawings Collection and Photograph Collection by appointment only.

Historical background: The RIBA was founded in 1834 for the general advancement of civil architecture and for promoting and facilitating knowledge of the various related arts and sciences. From the beginning the British Architectural Library (BAL) has formed an important part of the institute's activities and has always included special collections of drawings, MSS, photographs, pamphlets, and early printed works, in addition to its reference and loan libraries. There is a long tradition of members and well-wishers presenting material to the library, which is funded by members of the RIBA and by a trust fund of donated money.

Acquisitions policy: To strengthen existing collections relating to the work of architecture, and in particular British architecture, by encouraging donations or deposits, and by purchase.

Archives of organisation: RIBA Archives: administrative records of the institute, documenting the affairs of the RIBA and the preoccupations of the architectural profession, and containing biographical information on its members, 1834–; includes the archives of the Society of Architects, 1884–1926, and the Architectural Union Company, 1857–1916.

Major collections: BAL MSS Collection: the largest collection in Britain of the papers of architects, architectural organisations and related groups (including MSS, TSS and printed ephemera), 17th century–, but mainly British 19th- and 20th–century material (400 metres).

Non-manuscript material: BAL Drawings Collection (*c*500,000 drawings): the largest collection in Britain of architectural drawings, mainly British, but including important groups of foreign drawings, 16th century– (particularly rich in 19th-century material).
BAL Photographic Collection (*c*400,000 prints): several collections covering British and foreign architecture and topography of all periods; collection of photographic portraits of architects.

Finding aids: Various lists, card indexes and computer databases for use in the library. The MSS Collection and the Photographs Collection are in the process of being fully catalogued, and catalogues are being prepared for publication. NRA 13990.

Facilities: Photocopies or photographs may sometimes be provided. Microfilm/fiche readers.

Publications: Catalogues of the Drawings Collection of the Royal Institute of British Architects (Amersham, 1969–) [8 alphabetical vols; 11 special vols (on Colen Campbell, Gentilhatre, Inigo Jones and John Webb, Lutyens, J.B. Papworth, the Pugin family, the Scott family, Alfred Stevens, Visentini, Voysey, the Wyatt family)].
National Inventory of Documentary Sources, Chadwyck-Healey microfiche (1984–).
A. Mace: *The RIBA: a Guide to its Archive and History* (London, 1986).

700 Royal Institute of International Affairs

Address: Chatham House, 10 St James's Square, London SW1Y 4LE

Telephone: (0171) 957 5700

Fax: (0171) 957 5710

Enquiries: The Librarian, Miss Susan Boyde (written only)

Open: Mon–Fri: 10.00–6.00
Closed part of August each year and for occasional extra days around some public holidays.

Access: Bona fide researchers, with suitable references and on written application. A fee is charged. 30–year closure on all archives; archives dealing with purely internal Chatham House affairs are closed indefinitely.

Historical background: The institute was established in 1920 as a result of discussions between British and US delegates to the Paris Peace Conference of 1919. Its Royal Charter, granted in 1926, precludes it from expressing opinions of its own, so opinions expressed in its publications or at meetings are the responsibility of the authors and speakers. Its aim is to advance the objective study and understanding of all aspects of international affairs and to encourage informed policy-oriented debate on these issues.

Acquisitions policy: To maintain the institute's archives.

Archives of organisation: Records of Chatham House from its foundation, including correspondence and texts of off-the-record meetings held at the institute (speakers include many of international repute); unpublished material from the research and meetings departments of the institute.

Non-manuscript material: An important press-cuttings collection on most aspects of international affairs, 1924– (1924–39, 1972– on film at Chatham House; 1940–71 in use at the British Library Newspaper Library (entry **496C**)).

Finding aids: Handlists.

Facilities: Photocopying (self-service copying facilities for the press cuttings). Microfilm/fiche readers.

701 Royal Institution of Great Britain

Address: 21 Albemarle Street, London W1X 4BS

Telephone: (0171) 409 2992 ext. 413/416/211

Fax: (0171) 629 3569

Enquiries: The Librarian/Archivist, Mrs I.M. McCabe

Open: Mon–Fri: 10.00–5.00 (closed Fridays during the academic term), by appointment

Access: Approved readers, on written application.

Historical background: Founded in 1799 by Benjamin Thompson, Count Rumford, to promote the study and advancement of science, the institution has since that time occupied the same premises, where many major scientific discoveries have been made. Apart from specific research project grants, the Royal Institution receives no financial support from government and activities are funded by income from property endowments, donations and subscriptions from members.

Acquisitions policy: Donations and deposits.

Archives of organisation: Royal Institution archives.

Major collections: MSS, including correspon-

dence and research notes of eminent scientists of the 19th and 20th centuries associated with the Royal Institution, notably Sir Humphry Davy (1778–1829); Michael Faraday (1791–1867); Sir William Grove (1811–96); John Tyndall (1820–93); Sir William H. Bragg (1862–1942); William Lawrence Bragg (1890–1971); Sir Eric K. Rideal.
Journals of Thomas Archer Hirst (1830–92).

Non-manuscript material: Pictures and busts.
Large photographic archive.
Prospectuses and lecture lists.

Finding aids: Lists and indexes. Rideal: NRA 22229.

Facilities: Photocopying. Photography. Microfilm/fiche reader.

Publications: T. Martin (ed.): *Faraday's Diary, 1820–1862* (London, 1932).
Proceedings of the Royal Institution: Managers' Minutes, 1799–1903 (1971).
J.R. Friday, R.M. MacLeod and P. Shepherd: *John Tyndall: Natural Philosopher, 1820–1893: Catalogue of Correspondence, Journals and Collected Papers* (1974) [microfiche].
W.H. Brock and R.M. MacLeod: *The Journals of Thomas Archer Hirst, FRS* (1980) [microfiche].
I.M. McCabe and F.A.J.L. James: 'History of Science and Technology Resources at the Royal Institution of Great Britain', *British Journal for the History of Science*, xvii (1984).
Publications list available.

702 Royal Institution of Naval Architects

Address: 10 Upper Belgrave Street, London SW1X 8BQ

Telephone: (0171) 235 4622

Fax: (0171) 245 6959

Enquiries: The Assistant Secretary (Technical), Mr Michael S. Porter

Open: Mon–Fri: 9.30–5.00

Access: Bona fide researchers, by appointment.

The institution was founded in 1860 and incorporated by Royal Charters in 1910 and 1960. It has established an international reputation as a qualifying body and learned society in the field of marine technology. It maintains its own archives, which include membership records;

institution transactions and written papers; and shipping registers, 1860–. Photocopying is available.

703 Royal London Hospital Archives

Parent organisation: The Royal Hospitals NHS Trust

Address: The Royal London Hospital Archives and Museum, Royal London Hospital, Whitechapel, London E1 1BB

Telephone: (0171) 377 7000 ext. 3364

Fax: (0171) 377 7677

Enquiries: The Archivist, Mr R.J. Evans

Open: Mon–Fri: 10.00–4.30 (reading room open to 7.30)
Closed hospital statutory holidays.

Access: Generally open to the public, by appointment. Usual restrictions on public (hospital) records: bona fide researchers can be granted access on completion of relevant documentation.

Historical background: The London Hospital (now Royal London) was founded in 1740 and was granted a Royal Charter in 1758. It was controlled by a Court (later Board) of Governors, which continued after the hospital joined the NHS in 1948 until it became part of Tower Hamlets Health District in 1974. After the first archivist was appointed in 1984, the archives assumed responsibility for the records of all hospitals within the district and became a recognised repository for public records. From 1994 the hospital was joined by St Bartholomew's Hospital (entry 720) and the London Chest Hospital as part of the Royal Hospitals NHS Trust.

Acquisitions policy: Records produced by or relating to the Royal London Hospital, its alumni and staff. Records of health care in Tower Hamlets. The archives also collect records of the London Hospital Medical College and training schools, past and present, associated with health care in the district.

Archives of organisation: The London (now Royal London) Hospital, 1740–; The Royal London NHS Trust, 1991–; Albert Dock Hospital, 1890–1979; Bethnal Green Hospital, 1906–90; East London Hospital for Children, 1868–1948; East End Maternity Hospital, 1884–1991; London Jewish Hospital, 1926–80; Mildmay Mission Hospital, 1878–1982; Mile End Hospital, 1898–1988; Poplar Hospital, 1858–1964; Queen Mary's Maternity Home, Hampstead, 1919–72; St Andrew's Hospital, Bromley-by-Bow, 1873–1977; St Clement's Hospital, Bow, 1891–1974.

Pre-1948 records of Mile End Hospital are held at the Greater London Record Office (entry 550).

Major collections: London Hospital Medical College records, including records of students, 1741–; London Hospital Medical Club, 1792–1985; Marie Celeste Samaritan Society, 1837–1983; City & East London Area Health Authority (Teaching) records, 1973–82; Tower Hamlets District Health Authority records, 1982–91; British Society for the Study of Orthodontics records, 1907–90; Henry Hamilton Bailey, medical teacher and author: papers and medical illustrations, 1928–61; Eva Luckes, matron and writer: letters, including correspondence with Florence Nightingale and Edith Cavell, 1880–1919.

Non-manuscript material: A registered museum containing paintings, silverware, instruments and uniforms, trophies etc relating to the Royal London Hospital.
Photographs of wards, medical and nursing staff, 19th and 20th century.
Films of hospital subjects, 1930s–.
Library of books about and by 'Old Londoners', 18th–20th centuries.
Reference library of historical medical texts, 16th–20th centuries (2000 items).

Finding aids: All main archives of organisations and many of the major collections catalogued. Lists sent to NRA.

Facilities: Photocopying. Photography. Microfiche readers.

Conservation: Contracted out.

Publications: J. Pepler: 'The Archives of Tower Hamlets Health Authority', *Society for the Social History of Medicine Bulletin,* xxxix (Dec. 1986), 80–82.

704 Royal National Mission to Deep Sea Fishermen

Address: 43 Nottingham Place, London W1M 4BX

Telephone: (0171) 487 5101

Fax: (0171) 224 5240

Enquiries: The Secretary or The Office Manager, Mr Lawrence V. Taylor

Open: Mon–Fri: 8.30–4.30

Access: Generally open to the public, by appointment.

Historical background: The mission was founded in 1881 by Ebenezer Mather, and granted a Royal Charter in 1896, to offer a spiritual and welfare ministry to fishermen and their families. In early years it visited and ministered to fleets of fishing-boat crews from its own mission ships, known as 'Bethel' ships. Present operations are centred on mission centres located in fishing ports.

Acquisitions policy: To acquire, nearly always by donation, material relevant to early days of fishing and obscure records of the mission's service.

Archives of organisation: Archives of the mission, 1881–, including council and other minutes (mainly on microfiche).

Major collections: Papers of Sir Wilfred Grenfell (1865–1940), medical missionary in Labrador.

Non-manuscript material: Photo album relating to early history, including photographs of mission ships and a few hospital ships. Mission magazines (many on fiche).

Facilities: Photocopying. Microfiche readers.

705 Royal National Theatre

Address: National Theatre Archive, Rear of Salisbury House, 1–3 Brixton Road, London SW9 6DE

Telephone: (0171) 820 3512

Enquiries: The Archivist, Nicola Scadding

Open: Mon–Fri: 10.30–4.30

Access: Accredited researchers, by appointment

only. Restricted access to certain categories of administrative records.

Historical background: The first detailed scheme for a national theatre was drawn up in 1907 by the critic William Archer and the actor/playwright Harley Granville-Barker. In 1908 supporters of the scheme joined forces with a group interested in establishing a national memorial to Shakespeare to campaign for a Shakespeare Memorial National Theatre. The committee of the SMNT purchased a site in Cromwell Road in 1937, but the outbreak of World War II delayed the building of a theatre. In 1949 the National Theatre Bill was passed, authorising the use of public funds to establish a National Theatre on a South Bank site. The first NT performance took place on 22 October 1963 at the Old Vic, which housed the NT for the next 13 years. Building on the present site began in 1969 and in 1976 the first production was staged in the Lyttelton Theatre. The archive was established in 1993 with the assistance of the Foundation for Sport and the Arts.

Acquisitions policy: Records and memorabilia of the Royal National Theatre Company's work since 1963. Material relating to the Shakespeare Memorial National Theatre Committee and the early initiatives for a National Theatre.

Archives of organisation: Company archives of the Royal National Theatre, including programmes, posters, press cuttings, production and administrative files, prompt scripts, board minutes, 1963–.

Non-manuscript material: Production and press photographs; production ground plans and some original costumes.

Finding aids: Index in preparation.

Facilities: Photocopying. Photography.

Conservation: Contracted out.

706 Royal Opera House

Address: The Archives, Royal Opera House, Covent Garden, London WC2E 7QA

Telephone: (0171) 240 1200 ext. 353

Fax: (0171) 836 1762

Enquiries: The Archivist, Miss Francesca Franchi

Open: Mon, Tues, Thurs, Fri: 10.30–1.00; 2.30–5.30

Access: Approved readers, by appointment. Some administrative records are confidential, some available only following written application.

Historical background: The Royal Opera House is the third theatre to have been built on the Covent Garden site and was opened in 1858. The first two theatres opened in 1732 and 1809. On account of the fires that destroyed these two buildings in 1808 and 1856, relatively little material remains relating to their history. There have been various museums and archives at Covent Garden over the years, and when the Royal Opera House reopened after World War II the archives were re-established in the 1950s. The collection concentrates on performances that have been given at Covent Garden and by the Royal Opera House companies, the Birmingham Royal Ballet, the Royal Ballet and the Royal Opera, with biographical information on the people involved and related general information where possible (e.g. prints/photos of world premières of operas/ballets not at Covent Garden). There has been a full-time archivist since 1969, when the present cataloguing system was introduced.

Acquisitions policy: Material mainly from within the Opera House and from donations. Acquisitions are restricted to items necessary to consolidate the collection and provide general reference material.

Archives of organisation: Correspondence and administrative papers.

Non-manuscript material: Playbills, 1750s-1840s (c5000).
Programmes, 1850s- [complete from 1946].
Prints and photographs of singers, dancers, composers, choreographers, designers, producers, productions, Royal Opera House personnel.
Prints, plans and photographs of the three theatres.
Costume designs by Attilio Comelli (c1000); some other costume and set designs, stage plans etc.
Small reference library of books and periodicals.
Press-cutting library.

Finding aids: Various lists and statistics available. Opera and theatre collection almost completely catalogued; ballet catalogue in the process of being fully completed.

Facilities: Photocopying. Photography.

707 Royal Pharmaceutical Society of Great Britain

Address: 1 Lambeth High Street, London SE1 7JN

Telephone: (0171) 735 9141 ext. 354

Fax: (0171) 735 7629

Enquiries: The Museum Curator, Caroline M. Reed

Open: By appointment.

Access: Bona fide researchers.

Historical background: The society was founded in 1841 and material was acquired over the years. The Scottish department is a separate department of the society with its own library and archive collection (see NRA(S) 6743) located in Edinburgh.

Acquisitions policy: Material relating to the profession of pharmacy, by donation or purchase.

Archives of organisation: Archives of the society (some were destroyed during World War II).

Major collections: Small MSS collection, 15th–20th centuries; these include personal correspondence of Jonathan Pereira (1804–53), Jacob Bell (1810–59) and Daniel Hanbury (1825–75); business records, including Allen & Hanburys; La Portes; John Bell & Co.; Savory and Moores; accounts and recipe books; prescription books; named collections of teaching and research material relating to pharmacy and allied sciences.

Non-manuscript material: Early printed works, including herbals, pharmacopeias and prints. Photographs.
Ephemera and artefact collection. Audio taped interviews.

Finding aids: MSS are described in the main catalogue; see also NRA 26284.

Facilities: Photocopying.

708 The Royal Society

Address: 6 Carlton House Terrace, London SW1Y 5AG

Telephone: (0171) 839 5561

Fax: (0171) 930 2170

Enquiries: The Librarian, Mrs Sheila Edwards or Archivist, Mary Sampson

Open: Mon–Fri: 10.00–5.00

Access: Fellows of the Royal Society and those introduced by Fellows. Bona fide scholars of the history of science, on written application to the Librarian.

Historical background: The Royal Society was founded in 1660 and has been in continuous existence since that date. One of its earliest activities was to collect scientific books and MSS to form a library.

Acquisitions policy: To collect administrative records of the Royal Society, as well as original papers and correspondence of past presidents and officers and some Fellows.

Archives of organisation: Royal Society Archives: journal books (of meetings), 1660–; register books, 1661–1738 (21 vols); letter-books, 1661–1740 (31 vols); classified papers, 1660–1740 (39 vols); early letters, 1660–1740 (38 vols); letters and papers, 1741–1806 (70 vols); referees' reports, 1832–.

Major collections: MSS collections, including: Robert Boyle (1627–91), letters and papers (53 vols); Charles Blagden (1748–1820), letters and papers, diary (25 vols); Sir John Herschel (1792–1871), scientific correspondence (35 vols). Sir John William Lubbock (1803–65), correspondence (42 vols), John Smeaton (1724–92), engineering drawings (11 vols). Papers of Sir Frederick Bawden (1908–72); Lord Blackett (1897–1974); Sir George Lindor Brown (1903–71); Sir Henry Dale (1875–1968); Sir Alfred Egerton (1886–1959); Lord Florey (1898–1968); Sir John Henry Gaddum (1900–65); Sir Cyril Hinshelwood (1897–1967); Sir James Jeans (1877–1946); Otto Loewi (1873–1961); Sir Robert Robinson (1886–1975); Sir Francis Simon (1893–1956); Sir Arthur Tansley (1871–1955); Sir Harold Thompson (1908–83); Lawrence Wager (1904–65).

Non-manuscript material: Tape-recordings of some Fellows, also the society's named lectures, 1974–.
Some collections of early photographic material.
A limited number of artefacts from the society's history.

Finding aids: General card catalogue in the library.

Facilities: Microfilming. Microfilm/fiche reader/printer.

Conservation: In-house facilities for paper conservation.

Publications: M. Boas Hall: *The Library and Archives of the Royal Society, 1660–1990* (London, 1992).
K. Moore and M. Sampson: *A Guide to the Archive and Manuscripts of the Royal Society* (in preparation).

709 Royal Society for the Encouragement of Arts, Manufactures and Commerce

Address: 8 John Adam Street, London WC2N 6EZ

Telephone: (0171) 930 5115 ext. 276

Fax: (0171) 839 5805

Enquiries: The Archivist, Susan Bennett

Open: Mon, Tues, Thurs: 10.00–1.00 Wed: 10.0–1.00; 2.00–5.00

Access: Fellows and bona fide researchers.

Historical background: The society was founded in 1754 to encourage arts, manufactures and commerce. Its present headquarters was built for it by the Adam brothers in 1774. It was incorporated by Royal Charter in 1847 and granted the title 'Royal' in 1908.

Acquisitions policy: Fugitive items and other material relevant to the society's history.

Archives of organisation: The society's records: minutes, 1754–; correspondence, c1755–1851 (c10,000 items).

Major collections: John Scott Russell Collection on the Great Exhibition of 1851 (5 vols).
Catalogues of exhibitions held by Free Society of Artists, 1760–90.
Collection of material relating to international exhibitions in UK and overseas, 1848–1951.

Non-manuscript material: Pamphlets and tracts forming part of the society's library, all pre-1830 (*c*400).
Collection of mechanical and architectural drawings and paintings relevant to its early 'premium' offers, 1754–*c*1840.

Finding aids: Card catalogue for MS correspondence.

Facilities: Photocopying of unbound MS items only.

Conservation: Contracted out.

Publications: Series of studies in the society's history and archives, published in *Journal of the Royal Society of Arts* (1958–).

710 Royal Society of Chemistry
Library and Information Centre

Address: Burlington House, Piccadilly, London W1V 0BN

Telephone: (0171) 437 8656

Fax: (0171) 287 9798

Enquiries: The Librarian, Peter Hoey

Open: Mon–Fri: 9.30–5.30

Access: Bona fide researchers; an appointment is necessary.

Historical background: The Royal Society of Chemistry was founded in 1980 as a result of the unification of the Chemical Society (f. 1841) and the Royal Institute of Chemistry (f. 1877).

Acquisitions policy: To maintain the archives and accept donations of other relevant material.

Archives of organisation: Minutes of council meetings, 1841–.

Major collections: Note-books, lecture drafts and correspondence of Sir Henry Enfield Roscoe (1833–1918)(*c*700 items).

Non-manuscript material: Nathan Collection of monographs on explosives and firearms, 1598–1990 (978).
Cribb Collection of portraits and cartoons of chemists, 1538–1890 (433).

Finding aids: Computerised catalogue.

Facilities: Photocopying. Microfilm/fiche readers.

Conservation: Contracted out.

711 Royal Society of Literature

Address: 1 Hyde Park Gardens, London W2 2LT

Telephone: (0171) 723 5104

Fax: (0171) 402 0199

Enquiries: The Secretary, Maggie Parham

Open: By arrangement.

Access: Bona fide researchers, by appointment.

The society was founded in 1823 by George IV, but many moves of premises have resulted in the loss of much of its archival material. What remains is concerned largely with the administration of the society and consists principally of council minutes and correspondence, with reports of its proceedings and lectures. Photocopying is available.

712 Royal Society of Medicine

Address: 1 Wimpole Street, London W1M 8AE

Telephone: (0171) 290 2906/2930

Fax: (0171) 290 2939

Enquiries: The Archivist

Open: Mon–Fri: 10.00–5.00

Access: By arrangement with the Archivist and at the discretion of the Executive Director.

Historical background: The society was formed in 1907 by the amalgamation of a number of specialist societies, but its origins go back to 1805.

Acquisitions policy: Papers and minute books relating to the work of the society and its sections.

Archives of organisation: The papers of 17 predecessor societies, including:
Royal Medical and Chirurgical Society, 1805–1907; Pathological Society of London, 1846–1907; Epidemiological Society of London, 1850–1907; Odontological Society of Great Britain, 1856–1907; Obstetrical Society of London, 1858–1907; Society of Anaesthetists, 1893–1908.

Major collections: Considerable collection of lecture notes and some correspondence of eminent medical and surgical practitioners, 18th–19th centuries.

Finding aids: Preliminary short title list in typescript. NRA 19231.

Facilities: Photocopying. Photography. Microfilm/fiche reader.

Publications: Report on the Records of the Royal Society of Medicine, 1805–1968, Royal Commission on Historical Manuscripts no. 75/42 (London, 1975).

713 The Royal Society of Musicians of Great Britain

Address: 10 Stratford Place, London W1N 9AE

Telephone: (0181) 462 1631

Enquiries: The Secretary

Open: Mon, Wed, Fri: 10.15–3.45

Access: Approved readers, on written application.

Historical background: Founded in 1738 as a benevolent fund for musicians and their families, the society took its present name in 1785 and was granted a Royal Charter five years later. The Royal Society of Female Musicians was subsequently absorbed in 1866. The society is still administered by governors and a court of assistants.

Acquisitions policy: Donations of relevant material are accepted.

Archives of organisation: Minute books of governors, 1785–; minutes of annual general meetings, 1792–; files on members, c1776–; other minute books and cash books; annual lists of subscribers, 1742–.
Many letters from distressed musicians and correspondence relating to public functions.

Major collections: MS scores of Joseph Haydn (1732–1809), Carl Maria von Weber (1786–1826), Philip Cipriani Potter (1792–1871) and Sir Henry Rowley Bishop (1786–1855).

Non-manuscript material: Portraits and photographs of members, 19th and 20th centuries.

714 Royal Society of Painters in Watercolour

Address: c/o Bankside Gallery, 48 Hopton Street, London SE1 9JH

Telephone: (0181) 928 7521

Fax: (0181) 928 2820

Enquiries: The Director, Judy Dixey

The society was founded in 1804; the Royal Society of Painter-Etchers and Engravers is at the same address. A considerable archive survives and there are internal catalogues. Bona fide researchers wishing to consult the records should apply in writing to the Director.

715 Royal Society of Tropical Medicine and Hygiene

Address: Manson House, 25 Portland Place, London W1N 4EY

Telephone: (0171) 580 2127

Enquiries: The Hon. Secretaries

Open: By arrangement.

Access: Fellows only; other bona fide scholars strictly by arrangement with the Hon. Secretaries.

The society was founded in 1906 and retains its council minutes and membership applications from that date. All other material has been transferred to the Wellcome Institute (entry 768).

716 Royal Statistical Society

Address: 25 Enford Street, London W1H 2BH

Telephone: (0171) 723 5882

Fax: (0171) 706 1710

Enquiries: The Secretary, Mr I.J. Goddard

The Statistical Society of London was founded in 1834 and renamed the Royal Statistical Society in 1887. It retains a complete set of minutes, 1834–, and the Yule Library. The main library has been transferred to University College Library (entry 761A). Administrative records and collected MSS, 1850–, including papers of William Stanley Jevons (1835–82) and William Newmarch (1820–82), were listed by R.P. Sturges for *Survey of Archive Sources in the History of Economic Thought* (1971) (NRA 14718).

717 Royal Television Society

Address: Tavistock House East, Tavistock Square, London WC1H 9HR

Telephone: (0171) 430 1000

Fax: (0171) 430 0924

Enquiries: The Consultant Archivist, Ms C. Colvin

Open: By arrangement with the archivist.

Access: Members of the society and bona fide researchers, by appointment only.

Historical background: The Television Society was founded in 1927 and granted the royal title in 1966. The society's activities include the organisation of lectures and a major annual symposium, the publication of *Television* and the Society's *Bulletin*, annual awards to the industry, and, more recently, courses of training for television. In these activities it is supported by 14 regional centres. The library and archives suffered considerable damage during the war and were not maintained until the appointment of an archivist in 1986. The records chart the history and development of television and include material on electrical engineering.

Acquisitions policy: To acquire material relevant to the society about the history and development of television.

Archives of organisation: Archives of the society: official and working papers, 1927–.

Major collections: Lecture notes of Sir Ambrose Fleming (1849–1945).
MSS, photographs and printed ephemera on John Logie Baird (1888–1946), W.C. Fox (*b* 1889) and other pioneers of television.

Non-manuscript material: Photographs of television equipment, personalities and society events.
Small collection of books on the history of television.

Finding aids: A catalogue of the collection is in preparation.

Facilities: Photocopying. Photography and the copying of tapes by arrangement.

718 The Royal Veterinary College
Historical Collections and Veterinary Museum

Parent organisation: University of London

Address: Royal College Street, London NW1 0TU

Telephone: (0171) 387 2898 ext. 331

Fax: (0171) 388 2342

Enquiries: The Archivist

Open: Mon–Fri: 9.00–4.45, by appointment.

Access: Generally open to the public; a donation to assist in the preservation of the collections would be appreciated. A charge is made for research by staff.

Historical background: The Royal Veterinary College was established in 1791. The college was the first of its kind in the English-speaking world, and was granted its Royal Charter in 1875. The RVC became a school of the University of London in 1949. The historical collections have been formally gathered together since 1990 and the Veterinary Museum was created in 1992.

Acquisitions policy: Primarily material relating to the history of the college, but gifts of material relating to the development of veterinary science in general are very welcome.

Archives of organisation: Archives of the college, including minutes, 1790–; examination minutes, 18th–19th centuries; student registers, 19th–20th centuries; patient treatment records, 20th century; general correspondence, 19th–20th centuries.

Major collections: James Beart Simonds (1810–1904) Collection: veterinary matters, especially cattle plague, pleuro-pneumonia, variolar ovina, 19th century (9 scrapbooks and 70 'tract volumes'). Simonds was the first Chief Inspector and Veterinary Advisor to the Privy Council (1865), and RVC Principal (1872–1881).
A.M. Johnston Collection: papers relating to cattle plague in Scotland, 19th century.
Letter-books of Richard Atherton Norman Powys (1843–1913), first college secretary (1876–1913), 1879–1909 (7 vols).

Non-manuscript material: Books, pamphlets and periodicals, pre-1901 (*c*4000)

reputedly one of the finest historical veterinary collections in the world.

Veterinary instruments.

Photographs of college staff, students and buildings, c1860-.

Finding aids: NRA 35652.

Facilities: Photocopying. Photography by arrangement. Microfilm reader/printer.

Publications: Catalogue of the Books, Pamphlets and Periodicals up to 1850 (1965).

'Historical Manuscripts at the Royal Veterinary College, University of London', *Librarians World,* 1/2 (1992), 2–4.

'The Scrapbooks of the Simonds Collection at the Royal Veterinary College', *Veterinary History,* 7/2(1992), 39–45.

Royal Commission on Historical MSS: *Annual Review, 1992–1993* [gives a summary of the archives].

Guide to Historical Collections and *A brief history of the RUC* leaflets [available free].

719 Saddlers' Company

Address: Saddlers' Hall, 40 Gutter Lane, London EC2V 6BR

Telephone: (0171) 726 8661/6

Fax: (0171) 600 0386

Enquiries: The Clerk to the Company, Group Captain W.S. Brereton Martin or The Archivist to the Company, Ms Elizabeth Salmon

Open: Mon–Fri: 9.00–5.00, strictly by appointment.

Access: At discretion of the company, by writing to the Clerk.

Historical background: The Worshipful Company of Saddlers is one of the oldest established livery companies in the City of London; its first recorded charter was granted in 1363. The company maintained close control over the saddlery trade well into the 19th century and even today plays an active role through the Society of Master Saddlers, although its main concerns now are the administration of its charities and estates, which has led to the establishment of several companies in recent years. The company lost nearly all its records when the hall was destroyed in the blitz of 1940.

Acquisitions policy: To acquire material closely related to the history of the company, its members and the saddlery trade.

Archives of organisation: Records of the Worshipful Company of Saddlers, mainly 1946–, but including 'Testament' or record book, 1440–, and 'Freedom Roll', which is signed by all new members, 17th century–.

Non-manuscript material: Audio and visual material recording the history of the company and the saddlers' craft.

Information on the company through research at other archives.

Small collection of books on saddlery.

Finding aids: Handlists and indexes of company members.

Facilities: Photocopying.

Publications: J.W. Sherwell: *The History of the Guild of Saddlers of the City of London* (1889; rev. 1937, 1956).

K.M. Oliver: *The History of the Worshipful Company of Saddlers of the City of London* (1995).

——: *The Treasures and Plate of the Worshipful Company of Saddlers* (1995).

720 St Bartholomew's Hospital

Parent organisation: The Royal Hospitals NHS Trust

Address: West Smithfield, London EC1A 7BE

Telephone: (0171) 601 8152

Fax: (0171) 601 7899

Enquiries: The Archivist, Mr A. Griffin

Open: Mon–Fri: 9.00–5.00

Access: Open to the public, by appointment. There is a 30–year closure on administrative records and a 100–year closure on medical records.

Historical background: St Bartholomew's Hospital was founded, with a monastic priory, in 1123. It was re-established by Henry VIII in 1546 and thereafter controlled by a board of governors, which continued after the hospital joined the National Health Service in 1948 but became defunct following the reorganisation of the NHS in 1974. The archives department at St Bartholomew's was set up after the appointment of the hospital's first achivist in 1934. In 1974 St Bartholomew's became part of the City and Hackney Health District, and the archives department assumed responsibility for the records of all hospitals within the district. In 1994 the hospital joined the Royal London and London Chest Hospitals to form the Royal Hospitals NHS Trust. The archives department is recognised as a place of deposit for public records.

Acquisitions policy: Restricted to records produced by St Bartholomew's and associated hospitals, or directly relating to any of them or to prominent members of staff.

Archives of organisation: Records of St Bartholomew's Hospital, 12th century–; Medical College, 1832–; School of Nursing, 1877–1970s; Alexandra Hospital for Children with Hip Disease, 1866–1958; Eastern Hospital, 1874–1972; German Hospital, Dalston, 1843–1970; Hackney Hospital, 1876–1983; Metropolitan Hospital, 1836–1977; Mothers' Hospital, 1913–84; St Leonard's Hospital, 1885–1969; and St Mark's Hospital, City Road, 1857–1988.
Records of the Central Group Hospital Management Committee, 1948–66; Hackney Group Hospital Management Committee, 1948–74.

Major collections: Parish records of St Bartholomew the Less, 1547–, and St Nicholas Shambles, 1452–1546.
Records of the Royal General Dispensary, Bartholomew Close, 1894–.

Non-manuscript material: Maps and plans of St Bartholomew's Hospital and its estates, 17th–20th centuries (c500 items).
Photographs, mainly of hospital buildings, staff and patients, c1880–.
Portraits and sculptures of eminent physicians, surgeons and benefactors of St Bartholomew's Hospital, and prints and drawings, mainly 17th–20th centuries.
Artefacts and museum objects.
Hospital publications.

Finding aids: Index and calendar of medieval deeds of St Bartholomew's. Card catalogues of all holdings (computerised catalogue in preparation). St Bartholomew the Less: index of baptisms, 1547–1894, marriages, 1547–1847, burials, 1547–1848.

Facilities: Photocopying. Photography. Microfilm reader.

Conservation: Contracted out.

Publications: N.J. Kerling: *Cartulary of St Bartholomew's: a Calendar* (London, 1973).

——: 'Archives', in *The Royal Hospital of St Bartholomew 1123–1973*, ed. V. Medvei and J.H. Thornton (London, 1974), 299.
——: *Descriptive Catalogue of Archives of the Hospitals in the City and Hackney Health District from the beginning of each Hospital to 1974* (Historical Manuscripts Commission, 1977) [includes records held by other repositories].
Minute Books, Accounts and other Records, 1547–1801 (World Microfilms Publications, 1988).
G. Yeo: *Resources in the Archives Department: a Guide for Users* (London, 1990).

721 St Bride Printing Library

Address: St Bride Institute, Bride Lane, London EC4Y 8EE

Telephone: (0171) 353 4660

Fax: (0171) 583 7073

Enquiries: The Librarian, Mr J. Mosley

Open: Mon–Fri: 9.30–5.30

Access: Generally open to the public; an appointment is recommended for special collections.

Historical background: The parish of St Bride has long been a centre of printing and allied trades. In 1894 the St Bride Foundation Printing School opened, its library financed by J. Passmore Edwards. The school moved in 1922 to Southwark, to form the London School of Printing (entry 621), but the library remained and has been administered by the City Corporation since 1966.

Major collections: Records of several firms and printing organisations, including Association Typographique Internationale; Double Crown Club; Electrotypers and Stereotypers Managers' and Overseers' Association; Printing Historical Society; Wynkyn de Worde Society.
London Society of Compositors and other unions, archival material and publications.
Collections of trade documents on labour relations in trade, 1785–1913.
Richard Taylor (1781–1858), personal and family papers re printing and publishing of scientific journals, records of his business and re development of Koenig's printing machine, 1810.
Specimens of printing: a small group of Western and oriental MSS.

Non-manuscript material: Newspapers, broadsides, book jackets, chapbooks etc, with a large collection of ephemera, mostly 18th–19th centuries (c6000 entries).

Finding aids: Lists and indexes.

Facilities: Photocopying.

722 St George's Hospital NHS Trust and Medical School

Address: The Library, Hunter Wing, St George's Hospital Medical School, Cranmer Terrace, London SW17 0RE

Telephone: (0181) 725 5466

Fax: (0181) 767 4696

Enquiries: The History Librarian, Christine Patel or The Hon. Archivist, Dr T.R. Gould

Open: Mon–Fri: 9.00–6.00, by appointment.

Access: Accredited researchers and interested persons.

A Archives

Historical background: St George's Hospital was founded in 1733. It was controlled by a board of governors, which continued after the hospital joined the National Health Service in 1948. The Atkinson Morley Hospital at Wimbledon was built (1867–9) originally for convalescents, but is now the neurological and neurosurgical department; in addition it provides some psychiatric in-patient facilities. The governors were given the management responsibility for the Victoria Hospital for Children and the Royal Dental Hospital, Leicester Square, which closed in 1964 and 1985 respectively. In 1954 St George's began to refurbish derelict wards at the Grove Fever Hospital, Tooting, and in 1968 the building of the new St George's began on the sites of the Grove and Fountain Hospitals. In 1974 the board of governors was replaced by Merton, Sutton and Wandsworth Health Authority, which was itself replaced by the Wandsworth District Health Authority in 1981. In these reorganisations St George's and the Atkinson Morley hospitals were grouped with St James', South London, for Women, St Benedict's, Weir, Springfield and Bolingbroke hospitals. Closures of the Weir, St Benedict's, South London for Women and St James' took place in 1979,

1980, 1984 and 1988 respectively. The Wilkins' St George's at Hyde Park Corner was closed in 1980 and the new hospital at Tooting was formally opened in 1980. St George's NHS Healthcare Trust was formed in 1993 and includes St George's, Atkinson Morley and Bolingbroke hospitals.

Acquisitions policy: Restricted to records relating to St George's, Atkinson Morley and Tite Street hospitals, St James', South London, for Women and Bolingbroke hospitals.

Archives of organisation: Records of weekly boards of St George's Hospital, 1733–1948. Records of Tite Street, Atkinson Morley, Bolingbroke, St James', South London, for Women and Springfield hospitals.

Non-manuscript material: Photographs, pictures, plans.

Finding aids: List of main material. NRA 9767.

Facilities: Photocopying.

B Medical School Library

Historical background: The medical school at St George's was built in 1834, but the hospital has been associated with the teaching of medicine since its foundation in 1733. Physicians and surgeons of the hospital were permitted to have a limited number of pupils and the register of these past students is still preserved in the medical school. A number of celebrated men have been associated with the school, including John Hunter (1728–93), Edward Jenner (1749–1823), Sir Benjamin Brodie (1783–1862) and Henry Gray (1872–1912). In 1901 the school was incorporated as a clinical school within the University of London and in 1976 pre-clinical teaching began at Tooting. All clinical teaching ended at Hyde Park Corner in 1980, when the medical school was transferred to the Tooting site.

Acquisitions policy: Donations of material directly related to the existing collection.

Archives of organisation: Records of the library, 1836–1946 (incomplete).

Major collections: MSS of or relating to Sir Benjamin Collins Brodie.
Student notes of lectures delivered at St George's Hospital, late 18th and 19th centuries.
MSS of Hyde Park Corner Whist Club, 1891–1925.
MSS of St George's Hospital Medical and

Surgical Society (later Hunterian Society), 1833–1956.

Non-manuscript material: Photographs, pictures, plans, late 19th and 20th centuries.

Finding aids: List of principal items of interest.

Facilities: Photocopying.

Publications: *National Inventory of Documentary Sources*, Chadwyck-Healey microfiche (1984–).

723 St Joseph's Missionary Society
Archives of the Mill Hill Missionaries

Address: St Joseph's College, Lawrence Street, Mill Hill, London NW7 4JX

Telephone: (0171) 959 8254

Enquiries: The Archivist, Fr W.J. Mol

Open: Mon–Fri: 9.00–12.30; 2.00–4.00

Access: Bona fide researchers. 50–year closure on all personal correspondence.

Historical background: St Joseph's is a Roman Catholic missionary society, founded in 1866 by Herbert Vaughan (1832–1903), Archbishop of Westminster. It is concerned with the unevangelised peoples outside Europe.

Acquisitions policy: Maintaining the archives: also minor acquisitions of printed material and photographs sent by missionaries.

Archives of organisation: Correspondence between the headquarters at Mill Hill and missionaries in the field. The society's magazines and other publications.

Major collections: Papers and memorabilia of Cardinal Vaughan; diaries of other missionaries.

Non-manuscript material: Large collection of photographs from missionary countries.

Finding aids: Catalogue and computerised index in progress.

Facilities: Photocopying.

Publications: D. Henige: 'The Archives of the Mill Hill Fathers', *African Research and Documentation*, xxii (1980), 18–20.

W. Mol: 'Our Archives', *Millhilliana*, 1 (1981), 31–6.

——: 'The Archives of the Mill Hill Missionaries', *Catholic Archives* (1982), 19–27.

724 St Paul's Girls' School

Address: Brook Green, Hammersmith, London W6 7BS

Telephone: (0171) 603 2288

Fax: (0171) 602 9932

Enquiries: The Librarian and Archivist, Mrs J. Childs

Open: Term: Mon–Fri: 8.40–5.00

Access: Generally open to the public, by appointment.

Historical background: The school was founded in 1904 by the Mercer's Company, and is a sister school of St Paul's School (entry **725**).

Acquisitions policy: The school always purchases anything by an old Paulina.

Archives of organisation: Archives of the school, 1904–, including MSS of Gustav Holst (1874–1934), Director of Music at the School, 1905–34; Imogen Holst (1907–84); and Ralph Vaughan Williams (1872–1958).

Non-manuscript material: The personal library of Sir Siegmund Warburg (*b* 1902).

Facilities: Photocopying. Photography. Microfiche readers.

Conservation: Contracted out.

Publications: *Catalogue of the Warburg Library*.

725 St Paul's School Archives

Address: Lonsdale Road, London SW13 9JT

Telephone: (0181) 748 9162

Enquiries: The Archivist

Open: Mon–Fri: 9.30–4.30 during term, by appointment.

Access: Open for research, on written application.

Historical background: St Paul's School was founded by Dean Colet, probably in 1509. The school and most of its records were destroyed in the Great Fire of London (1666); any surviving early records are held by the Mercers' Company (entry 630). The library and archives both have items connected with the history of the school and its pupils.

Acquisitions policy: The library purchases books and MSS by Old Paulines. The archives have no funds but actively encourage donations and deposits by the school, old boys and masters.

Archives of organisation: School Archives: apposition lists, 1749–; governors' minutes, 1876–1973.
School magazines, 1831–; calendars, 1881–; club lists of masters and boys, 1918–; examination papers; team photographs.

Major collections: Correspondence of Duke of Marlborough (1650–1722); William Camden (1551–1623); Judge Jeffreys (1648–89); Benjamin Jowett (1817–93); Thomas Clarkson (1760–1846); Ernest Raymond (1888–1974); Viscount Montgomery (1887–1976).
Literary MSS of Rev. R.H. Barham (1788–1845); Laurence Binyon (1869–1943); G.K. Chesterton (1874–1936); E.C. Bentley (1875–1956).

Non-manuscript material: Engravings of the school.
Newspaper cuttings collection.
Naimaster Collection of engravings of Old Paulines and High Masters.
Books by and about Edward Thomas (1878–1917).
Books relating to the early history of the school, including grammars, 1575–, preces, 1644–, and sermons, 1674–.
School copy books, 17th and 18th centuries.

Finding aids: Card indexes of authors, subjects, masters and boys.

Facilities: Photocopying.

726 Salters' Company

Address: The Salters' Hall, 4 Fore Street, London EC2Y 5DE

Telephone: (0171) 588 5216

Enquiries: The Clerk of the Salters' Company

Open: By appointment only.

Access: Bona fide researchers, by arrangement. Access is restricted.

Historical background: The company had its origins in a religious fraternity founded in 1394 and received charters of incorporation as a livery company in 1559 and 1607.

Acquisitions policy: Continuous policy of incorporating current material in the company archives and of acquiring relevant material for the company and other (e.g. almshouses) archives as they become available.

Archives of organisation: Charters and other constitutional documents.
Court minutes, 1627–.
Reports of other committees.
Documents on charitable matters (e.g. almshouses and Salters' Institute of Industrial Chemistry).
Documents relating to the company's English and Irish estates.
Records relating to the admission to the Freedom, 1716–; apprenticeship, 1678–; and livery, 1714–.

Non-manuscript material: Photographs, drawings and plans.

Finding aids: Check-list; calendar.

Publications: J. Steven Watson: *History of the Salters' Company* (1963).
H. Barty-King: *The Salters' Company, 1394–1994* (1994).

727 Salvation Army International Heritage Centre
Archives

Address: 117–121 Judd Street, London WC1H 9NN

Telephone: (0171) 387 1656 ext. 244/256

Fax: (0171) 387 3768

Enquiries: The Archivist/Director, Maj. Jenty Fairbank

Open: Mon–Fri: 9.00–3.30

Access: Generally open to the public, by appointment; access may be restricted on some documents.

Historical background: The East London Christian Mission was founded by William Booth in 1865, changing its name to the Salvation Army in 1878. As well as being a denomination of the Christian Church, the army is active in all areas of social welfare. The archives were first officially organised in 1978, although much material was lost in World War II.

Acquisitions policy: To maintain the archives and accept donations of material relevant to the army and Salvationists.

Archives of organisation: Minute books, conference minutes, files and correspondence, 1866–. Some records of army establishments, e.g. Mother's Hospital, Clapton (f. 1884).

Major collections: Papers of William Booth (1829–1912), his daughter Catherine Booth-Clibborn (1858–1955), his grand-daughter Catherine Bramwell-Booth (1883–1987) and James Allister Smith (1866–1960).
Diaries, letters and papers of Salvationists in Britain and abroad, 19th–20th centuries.

Non-manuscript material: Pamphlets, photographs, artefacts.

Finding aids: Computer databases, catalogue, lists and indexes.

Facilities: Photocopying. Photography. Microfilm reader/printers.

728 Save the Children Fund Archives

Address: Mary Datchelor House, 17 Grove Lane, Camberwell, London SE5 8RD

Telephone: (0171) 743 5400 ext. 2067

Fax: (0171) 708 2508

Enquiries: The Archivist, Rodney Breen

Open: Mon–Fri: 10.00–5.30, by arrangement.

Access: Bona fide researchers. There is a general 30–year closure rule, although this may vary in certain cases.

Historical background: The Save the Children Fund was founded in 1919 by Eglantyne Jebb to distribute money for the relief of children and their families in postwar Europe. Since then the fund has given grants or run projects in more than 130 countries. It has also campaigned on behalf of children's rights in the UK and internationally. It was a pioneer of development aid and started the playgroup movement in the UK. The archives have been organised since 1991.

Acquisitions policy: Archives of the fund, through an active records management pro-

gramme. Outside material relating to the fund's work, especially in the early years.

Archives of organisation: Minutes of committees, 1920–85; administrative papers, 1920–27; Director-General's papers, 1965–86; finance papers, 1963–86; Overseas department, 1946–80; UK department, 1926–80.

Major collections: Various papers relating to Eglantyne Jebb (1876–1928); Edward Fuller (1889–1958), editor of *The World's Children*; Mosa Anderson (c1895–1978) and Bridget Stevenson (1909–85), relief workers; and Dorothy Buxton (née Jebb, 1881–1962).
Material relating to the International Save the Children Union, 1926–46.

Non-manuscript material: *The World's Children*, 1920–, and advertising material 1919–85; films and photographs, 1919–90; artefacts relating to Eglantyne Jebb.

Finding aids: General guide to the collections, continuously updated.

Facilities: Photocopying.

Publications: *Brief Guide to the Archives* [free leaflet].

729 School of Oriental and African Studies
SOAS, Centre for Africa and Asia

Parent organisation: University of London

Address: Thornhaugh Street, Russell Square, London WC1H 0XG

Telephone: (0171) 637 2388 (school) 323 6112 (direct line)

Fax: (0171) 436 3844

Enquiries: The Archivist, Mrs R.E. Seton

Open: Term, Christmas and Easter vacations: Mon–Fri: 9.00–8.45 Sat: 9.30–5.00 Summer vacation: Mon–Fri: 9.00–5.00 Sat: 9.30–5.00

Access: An archives ticket permits free access to the archives and manuscripts for up to twenty days in any one year. For a longer period a reference ticket should be requested, for which there is, in certain circumstances, a charge. A letter of recommendation should be submitted with the completed application form. The Archivist is most willing to help with guidance and advice, but it is first advisable to make an appointment.

Historical background: SOAS, founded in 1916, provides courses in the study of the art, archaeology, languages, literature, history, geography, law, religion and social sciences of Africa, Asia and the Pacific area. It also acts as a centre of research in those areas. The library holds some 750,000 volumes, receives 5000 periodicals currently, and has many thousands of microforms, 45,000 sheet maps, 45,000 photographs and sound recordings on disc and tape. The archives and MSS division of the library has grown rapidly since the library moved into its new accommodation in 1973.

Acquisitions policy: Primary source materials of research value relating to Asian and African studies in the following categories: (i) missionaries, missionary organisations and religious groups; (ii) business organisations and individuals involved in business; (iii) humanitarian organisations and political non-governmental groups; (iv) individuals whose life or work has been of special relevance to the study of Asia and Africa.

Major collections: Missionary Archives: archives of missionary and related organisations, including the China Inland Mission (now the Overseas Missionary Fellowship) *c*1872–1951; the Conference of British Missionary Societies, 1910–12; the London Missionary Society (now the Council for World Mission), 1795–1970; the Melanesian Mission, *c*1872–1970; the Presbyterian Church of England's Foreign Missions Committee, *c*1900–, and the Religious Tract Society (now the United Society for Christian Literature), 1799–1976. Individual missionaries represented in the collections include Gladys Aylward, James Legge, David Livingstone, Robert Morrison, Mabel Shaw and James Hudson Taylor.
Overseas Aid Agencies: records of Christian Aid, 1946–70.
Business and Trade: collections include the archives of John Swire & Sons, 1869–1967; the China Association, 1889–1969; the Guthrie Corporation, *c*1900–1960; the Imperial British East Africa Company, *c*1874–1892, and the British India Steam Navigation Company (in the papers of Sir William Mackinnon); papers of members of the Chinese Maritime Customs.
Private Paper Collections: papers of overseas administrators, diplomats, scholars and businessmen, including Sir Charles Addis (1861–1945), Sir John Addis (1914–83), Sir T.W.

Arnold (1864–1930), Dr R.W. Cole (*b* 1907), Professor C. von Führer Haimendorf (*b* 1909), J.S. Furnivall (1878–1960), Andrew Hake (*b* 1925), Sir Robert Hart (1835–1911), Sir Alwyne Ogden (1899–1981), Sir Denison Ross (1871–1940) and A.N. Stencl (1897–1983).

Non-manuscript material: Cassettes (with transcripts) of reminiscences of men and women who experienced the closing years of British rule in India (*c*300).
Photographs, many relating to missionary work (22,000).

Finding aids: Various lists and inventories. Card index to MSS, arranged by language.

Facilities: Photocopying. Photography and microfilming (small orders only). Microfilm/fiche readers.

Publications: Guide to Archive and Manuscript Collections (1994).
Published guides to the archives of the London Missionary Society, the Methodist Missionary Society, John Swire & Sons, the papers of Sir William Mackinnon and Sir Charles Addis, and the collection of Arabic MSS in the school's library.

730 School of Slavonic and East European Studies

Parent organisation: University of London

Address: Senate House, London WC1E 7HU

Telephone: (0171) 637 4934

Fax: (0171) 637 8916

Enquiries: The Librarian, Mr J.E.O. Screen

Open: Term: Mon–Fri: 9.00–7.00 Christmas and Easter vacations: Mon–Fri: 10.00–7.00 Summer vacation: Mon–Fri: 10.00–6.00

Access: Approved readers, following written application.

Historical background: The school was founded at King's College London in 1915 and became an institute of the University of London in 1932.

Acquisitions policy: The library accepts donations and deposits of MS material relating to its areas of interest: Russia, the countries of Eastern and South-Eastern Europe (excluding Greece) and Finland.

Major collections: Papers of Manó Kónyi

(1842–1917) and Count Menyhért Lónyay relating to Hungarian politics and the constitutional settlement of 1867.

Correspondence, notes and papers of Sir Bernard Pares (1867–1949) relating to Russia and Russian history.

Papers of Robert William Seton-Watson (1879–1951), historian, publicist and politician; and Karel Lisicky, Czech diplomat.

Non-manuscript material: Photograph albums depicting the life of Countess Natalia Sergeevna Brasova (1880–1952) with the Grand Duke Mikhail Aleksandrovich, 1909–13.

Finding aids: Lists. NRA 24277.

Facilities: Photocopying. Photography and microfilming by arrangement. Microfilm/fiche readers.

731 Science Museum Library

Parent organisation: National Museum of Science and Industry

Address: Imperial College Road, South Kensington, London SW7 5NH

Telephone: (0171) 938 8218/8234

Fax: (0171) 938 8213

Enquiries: The Archivist, Robert Sharp

Open: Mon–Fri: 9.30–9.00 Sat: 9.30–5.30

Access: For collections housed in the library, most MS material is available without an appointment on production of a reader's ticket; an appointment is, however, advisable on a first visit. Collections housed in other museum departments (see 'Historical background') are accessible at the discretion of the keeper of the department concerned, to whom application should be made in writing. Archive readers must register and an appointment is sometimes necessary. The library can advise on the location of individual collections.

Historical background: The Science Museum evolved from the science-based collections of the South Kensington Museum (f. 1857) and from the Patent Office Museum (merged 1883–7), and became administratively separate from the Victoria and Albert Museum in 1909. Both the museum and its library (which is housed in a separate building) have acquired MS material, including large archival collections, throughout their history. An archives collection was set up within the library in 1979 to co-ordinate future acquisitions and to centralize and catalogue existing MS collections. It is a recognised place of deposit for public records. Notes and correspondence of W.H. Fox Talbot, pioneer of photography, 1837–76, have been transferred to the National Museum of Photography, Film and Television (entry 114).

Acquisitions policy: Records relating principally to the museum's collecting areas in the history of science, technology and medicine; records in the general field of physical science and technology for which there is no suitable local or specialist repository.

Archives of organisation: Administrative records of the Science Museum, 1851–, are the responsibility of the Science Communications Division of the museum. Selected non-current records are deposited with the Public Record Office (entry 960), but some early material remains on deposit with the archives collections in the library.

Major collections: Major MS collections of individuals include: Charles Babbage, mathematician, notes and drawings relating to calculating engines, 1832–71.

Papers of Stanley Gill, computer scientist, 1947–75.

Papers and drawings of Simon Goodrich, engineer to the navy, 1770–1850; George Neumann, railway engineer, 1830s-1850s.

Papers of Barnes Wallis, 1905–1973; Sir Charles A. Parsons, c1895–1915; R.E.B. Crompton, c1870–1940; Joshua Field, c1810–70; Oswald Gilberrad and the Gilberrad Laboratory, c1900–50.

Schneider Trophy papers and drawings of H. Kavelaars.

Research notes of H.E.S. Simmons on British wind- and watermills.

Charles Urban papers, 1905–24, re early motion pictures.

Major collections of industrial records include: Maudslay, Sons & Field, engineers, 1800–92; Alexander Morton & Co. and Morton Sundour Fabrics Ltd (Edinburgh Weavers), textile manufacturers, 1862–1963; North British Locomotive Co. and its predecessors, 1842–1909; S. Pearson & Son Ltd, civil engineering contractors with major subsidiary oil interests, 1876–1960; Robert Stephenson & Co. Ltd, locomotive manufacturers, 1825–1901; Price & Reeves, civil engineering contractors, 1890–1927. Engineering drawings of Bramah & Robinson, c1830–1918; John Taylor/Taylor & Sons, 1846–1957; Hooper (coachbuilders) & Co., c1910–59.

Non-manuscript material: Extensive collections of portraits, photographs, prints, technical drawings and ephemera (within the library's archives collection and the museum's pictorial collection).
Map collection, including early railway maps (in library).
The following types of material are divided between the library and museum curatorial departments: trade literature, chiefly 19th and 20th centuries; newspaper cuttings collections; transport ephemera; ships' plans.

Finding aids: Various lists and indexes to major collections. Lists sent to NRA. A microfiche catalogue of library stock catalogued after 1984 is available. This is updated every two months and contains entries for all recently acquired archive material.

Facilities: Photocopying. Photography. Microfilming. Beta-radiography for the identification and recording of watermarks. Dyelining.

Conservation: Contracted out.

732 Shaftesbury Homes and Arethusa

Address: Shaftesbury House, 3 Rectory Grove, London SW4 0EG

Telephone: (0171) 720 8709

Fax: (0171) 720 2516

Enquiries: Commander Paul Bolas, RN

Open: Mon–Fri, by appointment only.

Access: Bona fide researchers, plus all Friends, old boys and girls. Access to personnel files may be restricted. No charge will be made but donations will be most welcome.

Historical background: The organisation was founded by William Williams in 1843 and staunchly supported by the 7th Earl of Shaftesbury, from whom the society takes its name. The aim of the society is to help, educate and care for children and young people who are suffering from the lack of a stable family upbringing or other social or educational disadvantage, and to enable them to take their place in society as happy and responsible citizens. Throughout its history the society has maintained a number of residential schools, at Bisley, Twickenham, Esher, Sudbury and Ealing, and supported over 250 boys at any one time in the training ship *Arethusa*. The collection has grown considerably since the late 19th century and has only recently been consolidated.

Acquisitions policy: To maintain and accrue archives.

Archives of organisation: The material relates solely to the work and records of the Shaftesbury Homes and *Arethusa*, and includes:
Minutes of the General Committee of the National Refuges, 1904–, and of the Shaftesbury Homes and *Arethusa*, c1850–.
Admission/discharge registers for the Homes c1870–.
Annual reports, 1843–.
Deeds of properties and trust funds.

Non-manuscript material: Photographs, c1900–.
The Fo'c's'le, 1920–1940s; *Our Log Book*, c1900–.

Finding aids: Catalogue of holdings and alphabetical index to admission registers (in preparation).

Facilities: Photocopying, restricted at the discretion of the Director.

Publications: History of the Shaftesbury Homes (in preparation).

733 The Shaftesbury Society

Address: 16 Kingston Road, London SW19 1JZ

Telephone: (0181) 542 5550

Fax: (0181) 545 0605

Enquiries: The Public Relations Manager

Open: By arrangement only.

Access: Bona fide scholars, by appointment.

The society was founded as the Ragged School Union in 1844, added Shaftesbury Society to its name in 1914, and has been known by that title only since 1944. Its early concern with the education and welfare of poor children has led the society to develop a number of socio-medical functions. The society has moved frequently, with resultant loss of records; however, some archives have survived and are maintained. These include minutes, 1841–; and correspondence with reports relating to individual homes, schools and centres, mainly post-1945. Bound copies of the society's magazine exist from 1849. Photocopying is available.

734 Silver Studio Collection

Parent organisation: Middlesex University

Address: Bounds Green Road, London
N11 2NQ

Telephone: (0181) 362 5244

Fax: (0181) 361 1726

Enquiries: The Keeper, Mr Mark Turner

Open: Mon–Fri: 10.00–4.00

Access: Generally open to scholars and the public, by appointment.

Historical background: Middlesex Polytechnic was founded in 1974 on the amalgamation of several institutions. There is no centralised systematic storage of records, but some minutes of constituent bodies survive in the Education Offices etc. The Silver Studio Collection was acquired in 1967. The polytechnic became a university in 1992.

Acquisitions policy: The main effort is concentrated on the conservation, cataloguing and exhibiting of the existing collection, but examples of Silver Studio designs are added as discovered and the library's holdings are being enlarged.

Major collections: Records of Arthur Silver (1852–96) and Rex Silver (1879–1965), wallpaper and textile designers of London, including business and personal correspondence from manufacturers and others, e.g. Walter Crane (1845–1915) (*c*2000 letters), day books, diaries (30 vols), 1880–1960.

Non-manuscript material: Photographic record albums (60); designs for textiles and wallpapers (*c*40,000); textile samples (*c*5000); wallpaper samples (*c*3000); postcards (*c*5000).
Newspaper cuttings, scrapbooks, ephemera.
Large library.
Design objects.

Finding aids: Letters preliminarily sorted but not fully catalogued. Typed catalogue.

Facilities: Photocopying.

Conservation: In-house facilities for paper conservation.

Publications: *Catalogue of Museum of London Exhibition of Silver Studio Work* (1980).

Silver Studio Collection Textile Design, 1850–1950 (1983).
Art Nouveau Designs from the Silver Studio Collection, 1885–1910 (1986).
A Popular Art – British Wallpapers, 1920–1960 (1989).

735 Sion College Library

Address: Victoria Embankment, London
EC4Y 0DN

Telephone: (0171) 353 7983

Enquiries: Sion College: The Librarian,
Mr Stephen Gregory
Industrial Christian Fellowship: The Secretary, c/o St Katharine Cree Church, London EC3A 3DA

Open: Mon–Fri: 10.00–5.00

Access: Sion College: open to members and bona fide researchers, by appointment.
ICF: bona fide researchers at the discretion of The College Librarian and/or the Secretary, ICF

Historical background: The college was founded in 1630 under the will of the Rev. Dr Thomas White (?1550–1624) as a guild for the city clergy with an almshouse for 20 people. The library was established at the same time by the Rev. John Simson and was a copyright deposit collection, 1710–1836. The college originally occupied a site on London Wall and the library moved to its present site in 1886, when the affairs of the almshouse were wound up.

Archives of organisation: Court registers (minutes) and Book of Benefactors.

Major collections: Correspondence of William Scott (1813–72), divine, president of Sion College, 1858.
Industrial Christian Fellowship (f. 1877 as Navvy Mission) archives, including minutes and annual reports, 1877–, missioners' reports, records of 'crusades', policy documents and working papers, 1920–.

Non-manuscript material: Major pamphlet collections, *c*1798–1890.
Photographs of ICF personalities and meetings.

Finding aids: MS handlist. Scott papers: NRA 26478. ICF records: NRA 27076.

Facilities: Photocopying.

Publications: E.H. Pearce: *Sion College and Library* (1913).
G. Huelin: *Sion College and Library, 1912–1990* (1992).

736 Sir John Cass's Foundation

Address: 31 Jewry Street, London EC3 2EY

Telephone: (0171) 480 5884

Fax: (0171) 481 3551

Enquiries: The Clerk to the Governors, Mr Michael Sparks

Open: By arrangement.

Access: Bona fide researchers only, by appointment.

The foundation is named after Sir John Cass (1661–1718), who endowed a charity school under his first will, dated 1709. He died while signing his second will, which was upheld in 1748. Many 19th-century charity schools were supported by the Cass Foundation. In 1961 it amalgamated with the Redcoats Schools, Stepney. The Foundation established a College of Science and Technology in the late 19th century, which in 1970 merged with others to become the City of London Polytechnic (now London Guildhall University). The foundation is a major grant-awarding body, providing help in the education of children and young people throughout the Inner London area. It first appointed an archivist in 1982, and lists of the large archival holdings are now available.

737 Sir John Soane's Museum

Address: 13 Lincolns Inn Fields, London WC2A 3BP

Telephone: (0171) 405 2107

Fax: (0171) 831 3957

Enquiries: The Archivist, Susan Palmer

Open: Tues–Sat: 10.00–5.00 First Tues in month: 6.00–9.00
Research Library and Archives: Tues–Fri: 10.00–1.00; 2.00–5.00 Sat: 10.00–1.00

Access: Generally open to the public; an appointment is necessary for the library and archives.

Historical background: The museum was founded by Sir John Soane RA (1753–1837), architect, who obtained an Act of Parliament in 1833 that vested the property in trustees. On his death in 1837 the trustees were placed under obligation to maintain the house and collections as they then stood (from funds left by Soane). The Act remained in force until 1969, when a scheme was made under the Charities Act, but the character of the museum remains unchanged. No. 12 Lincolns Inn Fields was added to the museum in 1970.

Acquisitions policy: The collection being personal and static, there is no provision for acquisitions. Gifts and objects having a close association with Soane are sometimes accepted.

Archives of organisation: The personal and professional papers of Sir John Soane. Administrative records of the museum, 1837–.

Non-manuscript material: Architectural drawings by Sir John Soane and others, including the Adam brothers (c30,000; microfilmed).
Sir John Soane's library.

Finding aids: Archive catalogue in progress. Catalogues of books and drawings.

Facilities: Photocopying. Photography. Microfilm/fiche readers/printers.

Conservation: Paper conservation in-house.

Publications: *A New Description of Sir John Soane's Museum* (1955; 7/1986).

738 The Skinners' Company

Address: Skinners' Hall, 8 Dowgate Hill, London EC4R 2SP

Telephone: (0171) 236 5629

Fax: (0171) 236 6590

Enquiries: The Clerk

Open: By appointment only.

Access: Bona fide researchers.

Historical background: The Skinners, the guild of furriers, had their first hall during Henry III's reign. The first charter was granted in 1327 and the final charter by James I. The present hall was built in 1668–9 following the destruction of the first, Copped Hall, in the Great Fire. The company funds four schools (Tonbridge School, f. 1553; Judd School, Tonbridge, f. 1888; School for Boys, Tonbridge, f. 1886; School for Girls, North London, f. 1889) and has almshouses at Palmers Green, which were established in 1894, and Hounslow, established in 1986.

Archives of organisation: Records of apprentices and freemen admitted, 1496–.
Court books, 1551–.
Account books, 1491–.
Title deeds, 1249–.

Non-manuscript material: Collection of paintings by Sir Frank Brangwyn RA.
Portraits of past masters.

Finding aids: Lists and indexes.

Publications: J.F. Wadmore: *Some Account of the Skinners' Company* (London, 1902).
J. Lambert: *Records of Skinners of London, Edward I to James I* (London, 1933).

739 Society for Promoting Christian Knowledge

Address: Holy Trinity Church, Marylebone Road, London NW1 4DU

Telephone: (0171) 387 5282

Enquiries: The Archivist/Librarian

Open: By appointment.

Access: By written application, except in cases of genuine urgency.

Historical background: In March 1698/9 Dr Thomas Bray, a priest of the Church of England, together with four distinguished laymen, founded the society, now generally known as SPCK, 'to meet and consult upon the best means of promoting religion and learning in any part of His Majesty's plantations abroad and to propagate Christian knowledge at home', this last by the provision of libraries and schools. For nearly three centuries SPCK has performed its vocation of upholding Christian belief and values through educational work and literature. It ranks as the oldest Anglican missionary society and, while it has never sent out missionaries in the accepted sense, it has been able to support a wide range of missionary enterprises. It is now chiefly known for its publishing and bookselling activities at home and its assistance through grant aid to the local agencies responsible for production and distribution of Christian literature in the Third World, where it has special links with the autonomous Churches of the Anglican Communion.

Acquisitions policy: Acquisitions are confined to material bearing directly on the society's history and activities.

Archives of organisation: Minute books of the society and its committees, 1699–1970.
Letter-books of Henry Newman, secretary, 1708–43.
Abstract letter-books, correspondence received, 1699–1771.
East India Mission records, 1710–1825.
Pitcairn Island, community of *Bounty* mutineers, register, committee minutes, correspondence books, 1790–1854.
Salzburg Emigration and French Protestant Relief records, 18th century.
Many volumes of financial transactions, 1699–.

Non-manuscript material: Printed annual reports of SPCK to date.
Printed monthly reports of SPCK, 1838–1917.
Pamphlets, memorials and pronouncements, illustrating controversies and historical turning-points in the life of the society.
Collection of file copies of books, tracts, prints and pamphlets published by SPCK (*c*20,000), including those destined for overseas readers in 207 foreign languages and dialects, among which translations of the Book of Common Prayer are the most prominent.

Finding aids: Card indexes of classified records, by name and subject. Volume indexes. Catalogues of all past publications. File copy list.

Facilities: Photocopying.

Publications: E. McClure (ed.): *A Chapter in English Church History: being the Minutes of the SPCK for 1698–1704, together with Abstracts of Correspondents' Letters* (London, 1888).
W. Allen and E. McClure: *Two Hundred Years: the History of the SPCK, 1698–1898* (London, 1898).
M. Clement (ed.): *Correspondence and Minutes of the SPCK relating to Wales, 1699–1740* (Cardiff, 1952).
W.E. Tate: 'SPCK Archives, with Special Reference to their Value for the History of Education (mainly 1699–*c*1740)', *Archives,* iii/18 (1957).
W.K. Lowther Clarke: *A History of the SPCK* (London, 1959).
SPCK Early 18th–Century Archives (World Microfilm Publications).
The Charity Sermons, 1699–1732, as a Source of Educational History.
Some Yorkshire Charity School References in the Archives of SPCK, 1700–74.

740 The Society for the Protection of Ancient Buildings

Address: 37 Spital Square, London E1 6DY

Telephone: (0171) 937 1644

Fax: (0171) 247 5296

Enquiries: The Archivist, Miss C.Y. Greenhill

Open: Mon–Fri: 9.30–5.00; possibly closed on days following bank holidays.

The society was founded in 1877 by William Morris (1834–98) and maintains its own archives, which include some thousands of case histories as well as minute books (although these are held elsewhere). There is a list available (NRA 24467) and access is given to members of the society and bona fide researchers, by prior appointment only.

741 Society for Psychical Research

Address: 49 Marloes Road, London W8 6LA

Telephone: (0171) 937 8984

Fax: (0171) 937 8984

Enquiries: The Librarian, D.N. Clark-Lowes

Open: Tues–Thurs: 2.00–5.00
Closed in August.

Access: Members and others with permission from council.

Historical background: The society was founded in 1882 to 'examine without prejudice or prepossession and in a scientific spirit those faculties of Man, real or supposed, which appear to be inexplicable on any generally recognised hypothesis'.

Acquisitions policy: Collections given by members on mediumship, especially experiments, psychical research surveys and parapsychology generally.

Major collections: Correspondence of Sir Oliver Lodge (1851–1940), physicist (c3000 items) and Daniel D. Home (1833–66), medium.

Sittings with and investigation of Eusapia Palladino and R. and W. Schneider.
Diaries of Joseph D. Everett (1831–1904), scientist, 1881–1902.
Whately Carington qualitative study of trance personalities and of paranormal cognition of drawings.
Collection of cases of haunts, poltergeists and apparitions and records of sittings with various mediums.

Non-manuscript material: Journal and Proceedings of SPR, 1882–.

Finding aids: Card indexes. Lodge correspondence: NRA 11857.

Facilities: Photocopying.

Publications: W.H. Salter: *The Society for Psychical Research: an Outline of its History* (1948).

742 Society of Antiquaries of London

Address: Burlington House, Piccadilly, London W1V 0HS

Telephone: (0171) 734 0193/437 9954

Fax: (0171) 287 6967

Enquiries: The Librarian, Mr E.B. Nurse

Open: Mon–Fri: 10.00–5.00
Closed in August.

Access: Fellows and approved readers; others by appointment.

Historical background: The present society was founded in 1707 by Humphrey Wanley and has had a continuous existence from 1717. There was no connection with the Elizabethan Society of Antiquaries. A Royal Charter was granted in 1751, commanding the society to devote itself 'to the study of antiquity and history of former times'. The society moved to the present premises in 1875, having previously occupied premises in Chancery Lane (1753–80) and Somerset House (1780–1875).

Acquisitions policy: To acquire material, by purchase, donation, deposit etc.

Archives of organisation: Minutes, accounts, lists of Fellows, election books and certificates, papers and correspondence 1717–.

Major collections: MSS reflecting the varied

interests of past and present Fellows, 10th–20th centuries (c950).

Many MSS of heraldic interest, especially from the collections of Sir A.W. Franks (1821–97), Oswald Barron (1868–1939) and Charles James Russell (fl. 1860–1907); some are described in A.R. Wagner (see 'Publications').

Rubbings are deposited of almost all brasses listed in Mill Stephenson (see 'Publications').

Important local collections include Habington, Lyttelton and Prattinton collections on Worcestershire; Canon J.E. Jackson (1805–91) on Wiltshire; Edward James Willson (1787–1854) on Lincolnshire; John Thorpe (1682–1750) on Kent (Rochester Diocese); and Thomas Wakeman on Monmouthshire.

Archives of the Roxburghe Club, the Society of Dilettanti and the Royal Archaeological Institute are deposited in the library; permission from the respective secretaries must be given before access is granted.

Non-manuscript material: Prints and drawings of a topographical nature (c20,000).
Broadsides, 1400– (3000).
Lowther Collection: Printed books (200) and tracts (1500) relating largely to the Civil War period.
Casts of seals (10,000).

Finding aids: Topographical and subject catalogue. Catalogues of MSS and of broadsides.

Facilities: Photocopying. Photography. Microfilm reader.

Conservation: Contracted out.

Publications: H. Ellis: *A Catalogue of Manuscripts in the Library of the Society of Antiquaries of London* (London, 1816).
Mill Stephenson: *A List of Monumental Brasses in the British Isles* (London, 1926); *Appendix* (Ashford, 1938).
E.A.B. Barnard: *The Prattinton Collections of Worcestershire History* (Evesham, 1931).
A.R. Wagner: *Catalogue of English Medieval Rolls of Arms* (London, 1950).
N.R. Ker: *Medieval Manuscripts in British Libraries*, i (Oxford, 1969).
I. Gray: *Report on the Manuscript Collections of the Society of Antiquaries of London, 12th–20th Century* (1985).

743 The Society of Chiropodists and Podiatrists

Address: 53 Welbeck Street, London W1M 7HE

Telephone: (0171) 486 3381

Fax: (0171) 935 6359

Enquiries: The Editorial Officer, Dr Georgina Stevens

Open: Mon–Fri: 9.30–4.45

The Society of Chiropodists was formed in 1945 by the amalgamation of the following organisations: the Incorporated Society of Chiropodists (f. 1912), the first in Europe; the Northern Chiropodists' Association (f. 1925); the Chelsea Chiropodists' Association (f. 1926); the British Association of Chiropodists (f. 1931); and the Chiropody Practitioners (f. 1942). The society maintains its own archives which include some records of its constituent bodies, dating from 1912. There is material relating to the formation of the London Foot Hospital (f. 1913) and to the schools of chiropody. Access is available to bona fide researchers, by appointment.

744 Society of Friends

Address: Library of the Religious Society of Friends, Friends House, Euston Road, London NW1 2BJ

Telephone: (0171) 387 3601

Enquiries: The Librarian, Malcolm J. Thomas

Open: Tues–Fri: 10.00–5.00 (and approx. 8 Sats per year) Two annual closed weeks (variable year to year); telephone or write for details.

Access: Open to members of the Society of Friends, and to bona fide researchers, who are asked to provide advance introductions or letters of recommendation on arrival. There is an hourly fee for genealogical research. Documents less than 50 years old are not normally available.

Historical background: The library was founded in 1673 and serves as the main reference library and central archive repository of the Religious Society of Friends in Great Britain. It moved from Devonshire House, Bishopgate, London EC2, in 1926 to the present location. Most Irish Quaker records are held at Friends

Historical Library, Dublin, and the Public Record Office of Northern Ireland (entry **78**).

Acquisitions policy: Society archives; to strengthen MS collections of Quaker private and family papers and archives of bodies with Quaker associations, by donation, deposit and (occasionally) purchase.

Archives of organisation: The central archives of London yearly meetings, including digest registers of births, marriages and burials, c1650–(now on microfilm).
Archives of London and Middlesex area meetings. (Most other local Quaker records are deposited in the appropriate local authority record offices.)

Major collections: Swarthmore MSS: c1400 letters and transcripts relating to the early history of Quakerism, 17th century.
A.R. Barclay MSS: 250 letters of early Friends, 1654–88.
Gurney MSS: c1900 letters, written mainly by or to members of the Gurney family of Norfolk (including Joseph John Gurney and Elizabeth Fry), c1750–1850.
Wilkinson MSS: c500 letters, written mainly to Thomas Wilkinson (1751–1836) of Yanwath, Westmorland.
Lloyd MSS: c800 letters and papers relating to the Lloyd family of Dolobran, Montgomeryshire, and Birmingham, c1680–1850.
Barclay (Bury Hill) MSS: letters and papers relating to the Barclay family of Urie, Aberdeenshire, London and Bury Hill, Surrey, c1650–1850.

Non-manuscript material: Picture collections, including some oil paintings and water colours; engravings, etchings and lithographs; a sizeable collection of photographs of Friends, meeting houses and Quaker work.
Most British printed Quaker works since 1650, listed in J. Smith: *Descriptive Catalogue of Friends' Books* (2 vols, London, 1867; suppl., 1893); a substantial proportion of other Quaker printed works to date.
Printed works relating to peace, slavery, conscientious objection and relief work.
Quaker periodicals, early 19th century–.

Finding aids: Card catalogues, lists and indexes. Lists sent to NRA.

Facilities: Photocopying. Photographs. Microfilm reader.

Publications: *Journal of Friends Historical Society* (1903–) [indexed; includes numerous references to material in the library; now published annually c/o the library].
O. Goodbody: *Guide to Irish Quaker Records, 1654–1860* (1968).
A typescript dictionary of Quaker biography (currently 20,000 entries) in collaboration with Haverford College, Pennsylvania, is in preparation.

745 Society of Genealogists

Address: 14 Charterhouse Buildings, Goswell Road, London EC1M 7BA

Telephone: (0171) 251 8799

Enquiries: The Director, Anthony J. Camp

Open: Tues, Fri, Sat: 10.00–6.00 Wed, Thurs: 10.00–8.00 Closed for one week beginning the first Monday in February.

Access: Collections open to members paying an annual subscription; to non-members on payment of hourly, half-daily or daily fees.

Historical background: The society was founded in 1911; there are about 13,000 members, mostly tracing their own ancestry in the vast indexes and collection of transcripts built up over the years.

Acquisitions policy: To maintain a permanent or temporary safe depository for pedigrees, grants of arms and other MSS; and to acquire transcripts and indexes to original records, printed volumes and other sources of data or reference, particularly on matters of genealogical, historical or related interest.

Archives of organisation: Minutes of the executive and other committees, 1911–; correspondence files, 1911–; card index of former members, 1911–; annual reports.
Periodicals: *Genealogists Magazine*, 1925–, and *Computers in Genealogy*, 1978–.

Major collections: Document collection containing material on 14,000 surnames; other documents arranged by place.
Special MS collections relating to inhabitants of London (60,000 family group sheets), Berkshire, Cornwall, Norfolk and Suffolk, Scotland, the West Indies and Irish wills.
Transcripts of the following: 8500 parish registers, 1538–1837; Boyd's Marriage Index (for England), 1538–1837 (7,000,000 entries), and London Burials, 1538–1852 (250,000 entries).

Genealogical index (for world), 1538–1875 (200,000,000 entries).

Monumental inscriptions in churches and churchyards, mostly in British Isles (c5000).

General card index of 3,000,000 names; other specialised indexes, including Bernau's Index to Chancery and other Proceedings (c4,500,000).

Collection of original apprenticeship indentures, 1641–1888; mortgage bonds (18,000); evidences of birth of civil servants, 1820–1939 (70,000); Trinity House petitions, 1780–1854 (128 vols); Bank of England will copies, 1717–1844 (176 vols).

Non-manuscript material: Topographical material arranged by county, including directories and poll-books; family histories; genealogical periodicals; peerages; school and university registers; professions; heraldry; religions; Commonwealth and Empire: passenger lists, emigrants, early directories; visitations; wills; marriage licences.

Book-plates (60,000).

Finding aids: Card catalogue to bound material; unbound material generally arranged in alphabetical order or by place.

Facilities: Photocopying. Microfilm/fiche readers/printers. Microfilming by arrangement.

Publications: Monumental inscriptions (1984). Poll-books and directories (1984).
List of Parishes in Boyd's Marriage Index (1987).
Marriage licences (1991).
Catalogues of parish register transcripts (1992).
Using the Library of the Society of Genealogists (1994).

746 Society of the Sacred Heart
Provincial Archives

Parent organisation: Generalate of the Society of the Sacred Heart, Rome

Address: Convent of the Sacred Heart, Digby Stuart College, Roehampton Lane, London SW15 5PH

Telephone: (0181) 878 7703

Enquiries: The Archivist, Sr M. Coke

Open: Mon–Fri: 9.30–5.00, by previous arrangement.

Access: Anyone interested in archival matters and bona fide researchers with a recommendation; an appointment is necessary.

Historical background: The Society of the Sacred Heart, a Roman Catholic order of nuns, was founded in 1800 in France. It is an international religious institute and houses in the British Isles were first founded in 1842. The work of the society is chiefly education at all levels. The archives of individual houses were centralised in each province in 1972, those of England and Wales at Roehampton, London.

Acquisitions policy: Material relevant to the work of the order and its members, particularly in England and Wales, including publications by members.

Archives of organisation: Records of the order and its work, including St Mary's College, Newcastle, 1906–85; Digby Stuart College, Roehampton, 1874–; Sacred Heart High School, Hammersmith, 1893–, and other boarding and day schools.

Major collections: Plans and legal documents concerning the Goldsmid and Ellenborough families and others, and their tenure of the site of Digby Stuart College, 1724–1850.

Plans and legal documents relating to the previous occupants of the site of the Sacred Heart High School, Hammersmith: the Institute of the Blessed Virgin Mary, 1672–1792, and the Benedictines, 1799–1865.

Letters and writings of Mabel Digby (1835–1911) and Janet Stuart (1857–1914), who promoted education in the late 19th and 20th centuries.

Non-manuscript material: Photographs of pictures of 17th- and 18th-century mansions of the manors of Wimbledon and Mortlake and of many of the personalities involved, e.g. the Ellenborough family.

Photographs and memorabilia supporting printed and MS records of the work of the order, c1820–.

Finding aids: Checklist of holdings. Card index catalogue in preparation.

Facilities: Photocopying.

747 South Bank University
Perry Library

Address: 250 Southwark Bridge Road, London SE1 6NJ

Telephone: (0171) 815 6608 (direct line)

Fax: (0171) 815 6699

Enquiries: The Faculty Librarian, Mrs Alison Cousins

Open: Mon–Fri: 9.00–5.00

Access: Bona fide researchers; an appointment is essential.

Historical background: The institution was originally the Borough Polytechnic (f. 1892), was renamed the South Bank Polytechnic in 1971 and became the South Bank University in 1992.

Acquisitions policy: Any material relating to the history of the university.

Archives of organisation: Collections held include minutes of Brixton School of Building (part); Battersea College of Education; National College of Heating, Ventilation and Fan Engineering; National Bakery School; Westminster College (part).
Articles of foundation, internal committee papers, student magazines, publications, prospectuses, 1892–.

Non-manuscript material: Photographs and a few working drawings on building extensions.

Facilities: Photocopying.

Conservation: Archive restoration under consideration.

748 Southwark Archdiocesan Archives (Roman Catholic)

Address: 150 St Georges Road, Southwark, London SE1 6HX

Telephone: (0171) 928 5592

Fax: (0171) 928 7833

Enquiries: The Diocesan Archivist

Open: By arrangement.

Access: Approved persons, on written or phone application and by appointment only. Restrictions on certain deposited papers.

Historical background: The Diocese of Southwark (Roman Catholic) was formed in 1850 on the restoration of the Hierarchy in that year.

Acquisitions policy: The archive will acquire any historical papers relevant to the development of the Catholic Church in South-East England.

Archives of organisation: Collection of papers, documents and letters on all matters of church administration relevant to the Diocese of Southwark, 1850–; includes collections of letters from

chaplains in the Crimean War and the Indian Mutiny.

Major collections: Tierney/Rock Collection: MSS collected by Dr Daniel Rock, antiquarian and historian, and Dr Mark Tierney, historian, including naval diaries of Admiral Sir William Monson (1569–1643), Dr Stonor's Roman Agency diaries, and correspondence of Cardinal Barberini and his secretary George Conn (*d* 1640), Papal Agent to Queen Henrietta Maria.
Papers of Dr William Brown (*d* 1950) relevant to the visitation of Scottish dioceses in 1919 and the Scots Education Act of 1917.
Research papers of Dr Percival Styche on Marian priests and martyrs (1535–1688).

Non-manuscript material: Many rare works and first editions of religious books, 16th–19th centuries.

Finding aids: TS list. The Tierney/Rock Archives have a separate MSS catalogue: NRA 27760.

Facilities: Photocopying. Microfiche reader.

Publications: Rev. M. Clifton: 'Southwark Diocesan Archives', *Catholic Archives*, 4 (1984), 15–24.

749 Spanish and Portuguese Jews' Congregation of London
Congregational Archives

Address: 2 Ashworth Road, London W9 1JY

Telephone: (0171) 289 2573

Fax: (0171) 289 2709

Enquiries: The Hon. Archivist, Miss M. Rodriguez-Pereira

Open: Strictly by arrangement.

Access: Private archive, not generally open to the public. Queries and requests submitted in writing by bona fide researchers will be considered.

Historical background: The Congregation of Spanish and Portuguese Jews was formed in 1656 under the protection of Oliver Cromwell by Jews escaping from the persecution of the Spanish and Portuguese Inquisitions. The first synagogue was opened in the City of London in 1657. This was replaced in 1701 by a new building in Bevis Marks, which is still in use.

The archives were formally established in 1915 and since then have been maintained by a small number of volunteers.

Acquisitions policy: To acquire, mainly by deposit and donation, material relating to the history of the congregation and its institutions and to the lives of its members.

Archives of organisation: Archives of the congregation and of its charitable and educational institutions, 1663–.
Registers of marriages and burials, 17th century–; registers of births and circumcisions, 17th–early 20th centuries (incomplete).
NB Records were kept in Portuguese (some in Spanish) until 1819.

Non-manuscript material: Printed orders of service for special occasions, 19th and 20th centuries.

Finding aids: Catalogue of MS books and papers in preparation.

Conservation: Contracted out.

Publications: L.D. Barnett: *El libro de los acuerdos: Translation of the Records and Accounts, 1663–1681* (Oxford, 1931).
L.D Barnett (ed.): *Bevis Marks Records*, pt I: *The Early History of the Congregation, 1656–1800*; pt II: *Abstracts of Marriage Contracts, 1686–1837* (Oxford, 1940, 1949).
R.D. Barnett: *The Burial Register of the Spanish and Portuguese Jews, London, 1657–1735* (Jewish Historical Society of England, 1962).
G.H. Whitehill (ed.): *Bevis Marks Records*, pt III: *Marriage Registers, 1837–1901* (with Jewish Historical Society of England, 1973).
R.D. Barnett and M. Rodriguez-Pereira (eds): *Bevis Marks Records*, pt IV: *The Circumcision Register of Isaac and Abraham de Paiba, 1715–1775; Record of Circumcisions, 1679–99, Marriages, 1679–89, and some Female Births, 1679–99* (with Jewish Historical Society of England, 1991).
M. Rodriguez-Pereira and C. Loewe (eds): *Bevis Marks Records*, pt V: *The Birth Register, 1767–1881, of the Congregation, together with Four Related Circumcision Registers, and the Jewish Births, 1707–63, in the Registers of the College of Arms* (1993).
Burial Register, 1734–1905 (in preparation).

750 Spurgeon's College

Address: 189 South Norwood Hill, London SE25 6DJ

Telephone: (0181) 653 0850

Fax: (0181) 771 0959

Enquiries: The Librarian

Open: Mon–Fri: 9.30–5.00

Access: Approved readers, on written application and by prior appointment only.

Historical background: The college was founded in 1856 by the great Victorian preacher Charles Haddon Spurgeon (1834–92) for the purpose of preparing students for the Christian ministry within the Baptist denomination at home and overseas. In 1923 the college, which was originally sited at the rear of the Metropolitan Tabernacle in Newington Butts, became residential and moved to the house and estate of Falkland Park, South Norwood. The Heritage Room above the college chapel was opened in 1957.

Acquisitions policy: To acquire, by donation or purchase all material relating to the life and writings of Charles Haddon Spurgeon.

Archives of organisation: Archives of the college, including reports as published in the *Sword and Trowel*, 1866–.

Major collections: Extensive collection of material by and about Spurgeon, including his sermon notes, letters, and photocopies of published writings.

Non-manuscript material: Most of the publications of Spurgeon (including translations), biographies, volumes of newspaper cuttings and portraits.

Facilities: Photocopying.

751 Stationers' and Newspaper Makers' Company

Address: Stationers' Hall, London EC4M 7DD

Telephone: (0171) 248 2934

Enquiries: The Hon. Archivist, Robin Myers

Open: Mon, Tues: 10.00–4.00, by appointment. Other days by special arrangement.

Access: Approved researchers, on written

application. Members of the Bibliographical Society of London.

Historical background: A guild or fraternity of the London booktrades (stationers or text-writers, illuminators, parchminers, paper-makers and bookbinders) dating from 1403, it was incorporated by Royal Charter in 1557 and liveried in 1560. Until the end of the 17th century entry was restricted to those in the book or allied trades working within the City (a trade qualification is still required for membership, now open to men and women) and all books had to be licensed and entered in the company's Book of Copies. Licensing, abolished in 1695, was replaced by copyright registration at Stationers' Hall. In 1911 this became an automatic entitlement and in 1924 a voluntary registry was set up which is still used for patenting unpublished material. Between 1603 and 1961 the company ran a semi-charitable joint-stock publishing venture known as the English Stock, whose shareholders were members of the company, and which had a monopoly in English almanacs, primers and other popular books. The company's present hall dates from 1674 (the previous one was burnt down in 1666) and is used for company functions and hired to outside bodies and for private parties.

Acquisitions policy: To maintain the company's archives.

Archives of organisation: The records of the company, 1554–, including: royal charters, letters patent, decrees and ordinances, membership registers, entry books of copies, 1556–1842 (thereafter to 1923 on deposit at the Public Record Office, Kew, entry **960**), court books, wardens' accounts and other financial records, pension lists, wills and other charitable documents, deeds, maps, plans and drawings relating to the company's early property.
Records of the English Stock, 1644–1961, including dividend registers, share transfers, wills and stock holdings.

Major collections: Papers and deeds of the Baskett and Tottel families, 18th–20th centuries.
Papers of the Rivington family.
Correspondence of Sidney Hodgson (1879–1973).
Archive of Kellie and Sons, bookbinders, 1767–1962.

Non-manuscript material: Long runs of almanacs, 1675–1920s.
Reference material relating to the company and other City livery companies.

Finding aids: R. Myers: *The Archive of the Stationers' Company* (1990) (copy in NRA).
Database of membership of the company, 1801–30. Indexes and abstracts of the registers (1556–1708) and court books (1554–1604) are contained in the editions by Edward Arber, W.W. Greg, W.A. Jackson and Eyre and Rivington; W.B. Williams, *Index to Stationers' Register, 1640–1708* (1980); typescript indexes to court book (1640–79).

Publications: There is an extensive published literature.
D.F. McKenzie: *Company Apprentices* [3 vols, for membership records, 1603–1800].
E. Arber: *The Stationers Transcript of the Registers 1554–1640* (5 vols, 1875–94).
G.E.B. Eyre and C.R. Rivington: *Transcript of the Registers 1640–1708* (3 vols, 1913).
W.W. Greg and E. Boswell: *Records of the Court 1576–1602* (1930).
W.A. Jackson: *Records of the Court 1602–40* (1957).
C. Blagden: *The Stationers' Company: a History, 1554–1959* (1960).
R. Myers (ed.): *Microfilm Records of the Worshipful Company of Stationers, 1554–1929* (115 reels, Chadwyck-Healey, 1986).

752 Tate Gallery Archive

Address: Tate Gallery, Millbank, London SW1 3RG

Telephone: (0171) 887 8831

Fax: (0171) 887 8007

Enquiries: The Archivist, Jennifer Booth

Open: Thurs, Fri: 10.00–1.00; 2.00–5.30, by appointment only.

Access: Postgraduates and approved readers, by written application with a letter of reference.

Historical background: The archive was established in 1970. It is the national archive of 20th–century British art and a recognised place of deposit for public records.

Acquisitions policy: Personal papers relating to 20th–century British art.

Major collections: Artists International Association official records and correspondence, 1933–71.

Charleston Trust: correspondence of Vanessa Bell, Clive Bell, Roger Fry, Duncan Grant and others, 1902–60.

George Frederick Watts (1817–1904), correspondence, 1846–1904.

Alan Durst (1883–1970), correspondence, drawings and photographs, 1924–70.

Paul Nash (1889–1946), correspondence and papers, 1908–46.

David Bomberg (1890–1957), correspondence and papers, 1917–57.

Stanley Spencer (1891–1959), correspondence and papers, 1910–59.

John Piper (*b* 1903), photographs, *c*1935–1975.

John Rothenstein (*b* 1901), correspondence and papers, 1913–87.

Ben Nicholson (1894–1982), correspondence and papers, 1909–81.

Kenneth Clark (1903–83), correspondence, papers and photos, 1925–81.

Naum Gabo (1890–1977), papers, correspondence and photos.

National Art Collections Fund papers.

Contemporary Art Society papers.

Non-manuscript material: Sales records of MSS relevant to the archive's own collections.
Interviews with artists and personalities in the art world (*c*500).
Drawings and prints, usually part of the MSS collections.
Microform: more than 80 collections of loan material.
Photographs of British and 20th–century art and artists, including installation photographs of exhibitions, photographs of artists, their work and their studios.
Artist-designed posters (*c*1400).
A large collection of press cuttings covering a wide field relating to British and 20th–century art.
Private view cards of exhibitions, mainly 1970–.

Finding aids: Lists and indexes.

Facilities: Photocopying. Photography. Microfilm/fiche reader.

Conservation: Some in-house facilities; work is also contracted out.

Publications: A. Causey: *Paul Nash's Photographs: Document and Image* (1973).
The Tate Gallery Biennial Report (1976–).
S. Fox Pitt: 'The Tate Gallery Archive of 20th–Century British Art and Artists', *AICARA: Journale pour la documentation de l'art moderne* (March 1983).
——: 'The Tate Gallery Archive of 20th–Century British Art, its Formation and Development', *Archives*, xvii/74 (1985), 94–106.
C. Colvin: 'Forms of Documentation and Storage in the Tate Gallery Archive', *Archives*, xvii (April 1986), 144–52.
Index to the Tate Gallery Archive on Microfiche (1986).
M. Compton, S. Fox Pitt and Beth Houghton: *Brief for the Tate Gallery Study Centre, including the Library and Archive* (1986).
Sir Alan Bowness and S. Fox Pitt: *The Tate Gallery Archive: a Booklet* (London, 1986).

753 Theatre Museum

Address: 1E Tavistock Street, Covent Garden, London WC2E 7PA

Telephone: (0171) 836 7891

Fax: (0171) 836 5148

Enquiries: The Curator

Open: Tues–Fri: 10.30–1.00; 2.00–4.30

Access: Readers should write or telephone in advance with specific enquiries. Access is by appointment only.

Historical background: The Gabrielle Enthoven Theatre Collection, which was given to the Victoria and Albert Museum in 1924, formed the basis of the museum, with later additions from the British Theatre Museum Association and the Friends of the Museum of Performing Arts. The Theatre Museum was finally established in 1974, and opened to the public in its new premises in Covent Garden in 1987.

Acquisitions policy: To collect material on all aspects of the performing arts, while strengthening the existing collections.

Major collections: Gabrielle Enthoven Theatre Collection: comprehensive archive of playbills, programmes, letters and prompt scripts relating to the history of the theatre, opera, ballet, pantomime, circus etc in Britain, *c*1718–.
British Theatre Museum Association Collection: extensive collection on the London theatre, 18th–20th centuries.
London Archives of the Dance and Cyril Beaumont Collections: material relating to the history of dance, 19th and 20th centuries.

William Archer Collection *re* British Theatre Association and English Stage Company Archive.

Non-manuscript material: Harry R. Beard Collection of prints and other material, with particular strength in the history of opera and Italian festival theatre.
Gift of Dame Bridget D'Oyly Carte: designs for Gilbert and Sullivan operas.
Antony Hippisley Coxe Circus Collection.
Friends of the Museum of Performing Arts Collection: costumes, backcloths, designs and other material relating to Diaghilev and the Ballets Russes.
Arts Council Collection: modern theatre designs.
British Council Collection: post-war theatre design.
Guy Little Collection of historic photographs, *c*1857–90.
Houston Rogers Collection of theatre photographs, 1930s-1950s.
Baron Nicholas de Rakoczy circus photographs.
British Theatre Association play library.

Finding aids: Various lists and indexes, but no comprehensive catalogue for the entire collection. Catalogues of finite collections are in the course of preparation.

Publications: Spotlight (1981) [exhibition catalogue].
Victorian Illustrated Music Sheets (1981).
Images of Show Business (1982).
Oliver Messel (1983) [exhibition catalogue].
Theatre Posters (1983).
Stage by Stage (1985).
The Theatre Museum (1987).

754 Theosophical Society in England

Address: The Library, 50 Gloucester Place, London W1H 3HJ

Telephone: (0171) 935 9261

Enquiries: The General Secretary, Miss L. Storey

Open: Mon, Fri: 11.00–5.00 Tues–Thurs: 11.00–6.30

Access: Members of the Theosophical Society, or non-members upon previous appointment with the librarian.

The society was formed in New York in 1875 by Madame Blavatsky (1831–91). The international headquarters are now in Madras, India, with branches in more than 60 countries worldwide. The library specialises in theosophy, comparative religion, mysticism and occultism. It holds a collection of the works and pamphlets of Annie Besant (1847–1933), MSS, photographs and a press cuttings book of other members of the society, plus a growing collection of audio cassettes (*c*400) and videos (24). There is a catalogue.

755 Town and Country Planning Association

Address: 17 Carlton House Terrace, London SW1Y 5AS

Telephone: (0171) 930 8903/4/5

Fax: (0171) 930 3280

Enquiries: The Director

Open: Mon–Fri: 9.30–5.30

Access: Town planners and bona fide academic researchers; an appointment is necessary.

Historical background: The association was founded by 13 men, influenced by Ebenezer Howard, in 1899 as the Garden Cities Association. It was renamed the Town and Country Planning Association in 1941. Subsequently Frederick J. Osborn (honorary secretary of TCPA, 1955–70) campaigned against the construction of tower blocks and deck-access flats. In recent years the TCPA has set up demonstration projects to encourage community initiatives and has urged government to decentralise decision-making on environment issues. It is a voluntary body and a registered educational charity. The archive has been substantially depleted by changes of offices and war-time destruction.

Acquisitions policy: To maintain and consolidate the archive.

Archives of organisation: Council and executive committee minutes, 1913–20, 1938–76.
Minutes of AGMs, 1901–67.
Other administrative records, including papers and proceedings of conferences; evidence submitted by the association; correspondence files of F.J. Osborn; complete set of annual reports, 1941–.

Major collections: Administrative material on

Letchworth and Welwyn Garden Cities (2 box files).

Non-manuscript material: Pamphlets and leaflets commissioned or sponsored by TCPA. Press cuttings and scrap books, 1937–70. Photograph albums, glass slides, posters and ephemera.

Finding aids: NRA 24472.

Facilities: Photocopying.

756 Trades Union Congress

Address: Congress House, Great Russell Street, London WC1B 3LS

Telephone: (0171) 636 4030 ext. 220 (Librarian)

Fax: (0171) 636 0632

Enquiries: The Assistant General Secretary (archives post-September 1970) or The Librarian (library collections)

Open: Mon–Fri: 10.00–5.00, strictly by appointment.

Access: Archives post-1970 are not generally accessible; each application is considered on its merits. Library: bona fide researchers.

Historical background: The TUC was founded in 1868, although few pre-1920 archives survive. The library was formed in 1915 on the establishment of the Labour Party Information Bureau and holds important MSS and archive collections relating to the labour and trade union movement. Archives up to August 1970 have been transferred to the Modern Records Centre, University of Warwick Library (entry 229).

Acquisitions policy: To maintain the archives and collections.

Major collections: Records of London Trades Council, 1860–1953, and London Bookbinders and Paperworkers, 1866–1965. Congress annual reports (complete). Notes and press cuttings of Gertrude Tuckwell (1861–1951), philanthrophic worker and president of the Women's Trade Union League.

Non-manuscript material: John Burns Library, including pamphlets, 18th– 20th centuries. Women's Trade Union League papers (microfilm).

Finding aids: MSS collections: NRA 24409.

Facilities: Photocopying. Microfilm/fiche readers.

Publications: C. Cook: *Sources in British Political History, 1900–1957,* i (London, 1975), 261–3.

757 United Kingdom Temperance Alliance

Address: Alliance House, 12 Caxton Street, London SW1H 0QS

Telephone: (0171) 222 4001/5880

Fax: (0171) 799 2510

Enquiries: The Librarian, Mrs L. Webster

Open: Mon–Fri: 10.00–4.30, preferably by appointment.

Access: Generally open to the public.

Historical background: The United Kingdom Alliance was founded in 1853 'to suppress the drink traffic by legislative means'. The United Kingdom Temperance Alliance Ltd was formed in 1942 as an educational charity, taking over all the work of the UKA except for its political activities. The temperance library and research centre was developed in 1975 by the Christian Economic and Social Research Foundation under the umbrella of the UKTA, which (since the removal of the CESRF to another headquarters) now runs the library.

Archives of organisation: Records of UKA, including minute books, 1871–1923; minute book of UKA Agency Committee, 1902–25; *Alliance Reports,* 1953–; *Year Book,* 1910–52. National Commercial Temperance League: general minute books, 1894–1924; minutes of various committees, 1899–1939. Scottish Temperance League register, 1916, and tracts.

Non-manuscript material: Alliance News; Outlook (NCTL) (incomplete run). Pamphlets, duplicated material and memorabilia of the temperance movement. Original prints by Cruikshank of 'The Bottle' and 'The Drunkard's Daughter'.

Finding aids: Card index. List of temperance movement material by B. Harrison.

Facilities: Photocopying.

758 United Medical and Dental Schools (UMDS)
Guy's and St Thomas's Hospitals

Parent organisation: University of London

Enquiries: The Librarian

Open: Mon–Fri: 9.00–5.00

Access: Bona fide researchers, on application to the Librarian.

A Guy's Hospital Campus

Address: The Wills Library, UMDS, Guy's Hospital, London Bridge, London SE1 9RT

Telephone: (0171) 928 9292 ext. 1459/2367

Fax: (0171) 401 3932

Archives of organisation: Student registers, c1770–1900.
NB Guy's Hospital records are held in the Greater London Record Office (entry **550**).

Major collections: Royal Dental Hospital of London Dental School minutes and annual reports, 1838–1983.
Guy's Hospital Physical Society minutes, 1775–1851 (incomplete).
Some case notes and lecture notes, 18th and 19th centuries.

B St Thomas's Hospital

Address: The Library, UMDS, Block 9, St Thomas's Hospital, Lambeth Palace Road, London SE1 7EH

Telephone: (0171) 928 9292 ext. 1569/2367

Fax: (0171) 401 3932

Historical background: St Thomas's Hospital Medical School as an organisation dates from the early 18th century. The first purpose-built accommodation was provided between 1813 and 1815, and in 1844 a medical school committee was established. By 1860 the school was self-sufficient and it was reconstituted with management vested in the teachers, who were to elect a dean annually. The school was established in new buildings at Lambeth in 1871 and affiliated to the University of London in 1948. In 1982 the school united with Guy's Hospital Medical School under its present title. The records of the hospital have been transferred to Greater London Record Office (entry **550**).

Archives of organisation: Registers of students and records of their fees, 1724–.
Minute books of various school committees, c1880–.

Major collections: A few case notes and lecture notes, 18th and 19th centuries.
A small number of autograph letters.

Non-manuscript material: Prints, 18th and 19th centuries.
Photographs of people and places associated with the medical school, 1859–.

Finding aids: Card catalogues. Name indexes to the registers of students.

Facilities: Photocopying. Photography.

Publications: D.T. Bird (comp.): *Catalogue of Printed Books and Manuscripts (1491–1900) in the Library of St Thomas's Hospital Medical School* (London, 1984).

759 United Reformed Church History Society

Address: 86 Tavistock Place, London WC1H 9RT

Telephone: (0171) 916 2020

Fax: (0171) 916 2021

Enquiries: The Hon. Secretary, Rev. Dr S.C. Orchard

Open: Mon–Fri: by appointment only.

Access: Members of the society or the United Reformed Church; other enquirers by arrangement.

Historical background: The largest part of the collection was assembled by the Presbyterian Historical Society and it is strongest in the history of English Presbyterianism. Since 1972 it has been acquiring some Congregational material.

Acquisitions policy: Although a limited amount of archive material is still accepted from former Presbyterian churches which have already deposited at the library, recent policy has been to encourage former Congregational churches to deposit archives locally. The library concentrates on acquiring books and archive material to add to its Presbyterian collection and establish basic reference material concerning the Congregational Churches of Christ and other denominations.

Archives of organisation: United Reformed Church archives.

Major collections: Records of some closed Presbyterian churches, including baptismal registers.
Biographical information about former Presbyterian, Congregational and United Reformed Church ministers.

Non-manuscript material: Collection of 17th-century pamphlets and books.

Finding aids: Author index for books and pamphlets and some MSS. Lists of other items.

Facilities: Limited photocopying service.

Publications: United Reformed Church History Society Journal.

760 United Society for the Propagation of the Gospel (USPG)

Address: Partnership House, 157 Waterloo Road, London SE1 8XA

Telephone: (0171) 928 8681

Fax: (0171) 928 2371

Enquiries: The Archivist, Mrs C. Wakeling

Open: Mon–Thurs: by appointment only.

Access: Open to bona fide researchers, upon production of a letter of introduction. Some records closed for 30 years and personal records closed for 50 years from the date of death.

Historical background: The USPG was formed in 1965 by the merging of two missionary organisations: the Society for the Propagation of the Gospel in Foreign Parts (SPG), founded in 1701, and the Universities Mission to Central Africa (UMCA), founded in 1857. The majority of the archives of SPG (1701–1965), UMCA (1857–1965) and the Cambridge Mission to Delhi (1857–1968) are at Rhodes House Library (entry 907).

Acquisitions policy: Gifts of appropriate missionary papers are accepted.

Archives of organisation: USPG archives, 1965–.
SPG and UMCA missionaries personal files, 19th century–1965.
Small proportion of SPG and UMCA archives, pre-1965.

Non-manuscript material: Photographs.
The society's films are deposited at the National Film and Television Archive (entry 493B).

Finding aids: Calendars of the earliest correspondence and lists of archives at Rhodes House Library. Card index to missionary files. Card index/catalogue ot USPG archives.

Facilities: Photocopying.

Publications: C.F. Pascoe: *Two Hundred Years of the SPG: an Historical Account of the Society for the Propagation of the Gospel in Foreign Parts, 1701–1900* (London, 1901).
H.P. Thompson: *Into all Lands: the History of the Society for the Propagation of the Gospel in Foreign Parts, 1701–1950* (London, 1951).
M. Dewey: *The Messengers* (Oxford, 1975).

761 University College London

Parent organisation: University of London

Address: Gower Street, London WC1E 6BT

A Library

Telephone: (0171) 380 7796 (direct line) 387 7050 ext. 7793 (general enquiries only)

Fax: (071) 380 7727

Enquiries: The Archivist, Ms Gillian Furlong

Open: Mon, Wed–Fri: 10.00–5.00, preferably by appointment; Tues (except long vacation): 10.00–7.00 (material available after 5 pm by prior appointment only)

Access: Open to bona fide scholars, on application to the Librarian or to the Archivist, preferably giving prior notice.

Historical background: The library was opened in 1829, a year after the University of London first admitted students. The first acquisitions of MS material were donations or bequests, the most notable being the Bentham MSS (1849), the Society for the Diffusion of Useful Knowledge (SDUK) papers (1848), the Chadwick papers (1898) and the Graves Library (1870). Major purchases included the Brougham papers and a collection of very interesting MSS that came with the Ogden Library (1953) and a succession of purchases of early MSS in 1911, 1921 and 1927. The large collection of Latin American business archives was transferred to the library, from firms going into liquidation in the 1960s, as a result of a survey undertaken on behalf of the *Guide to MS Sources for the History of Latin America and the Caribbean in the British Isles* (ed. P. Walne, 1973). Following reorganisation in the late 1980s, MSS and archives of Jewish interest, in particular those formerly part of the Library of the Jewish Historical Society of England (or Mocatta Library), were incorporated in 1993. The Gaster papers were transferred in 1994. Records of the Geological Sciences Department are now held by the Zoology Museum, Biology Department.

Acquisitions policy: To strengthen existing collections, by gift, loan, deposit or purchase, and to encourage the deposit of archival material relating to college history, including professorial papers.

Archives of organisation: College archives: including correspondence, 1825– 1905; professorship applications, 1827–1920; professors' fee books, 1833–80; and committee papers, 1836– 1918.
Other records are held by the college records office (contact Ms Elizabeth Gibson).

Major collections: Correspondence and papers of eminent political, literary and scientific figures, including Lord Brougham (1778–1868) (*c*60,000 MSS); Jeremy Bentham (1748–1832) (*c*75,000 MSS); Sir Edwin Chadwick (1800–90); Dr Moses Gaster (1856–1939); George B. Greenough (1778–1855); Karl Pearson (1857–1936); Sir Francis Galton (1822–1911); Lionel Penrose (1878–1972); George Orwell (1903–50).
Publishing archives of Routledge & Kegan Paul Ltd, 1853–1973, and the Society for the Diffusion of Useful Knowledge, 1824–48.
Papers of former UCL professors, including Sir William Ramsay (1852–1916); A.F Murison (1847–1934); W.P. Ker (1855–1923); Sir J. Ambrose Fleming (1849–1945); R.W. Chambers (1874–1942); J.Z. Young, FRS (*b* 1907).
Latin American business archives: the largest collection outside South America, covering, in particular, banking, trade, railways and shipping, mainly 19th century.
Smaller collections include 99 medieval MSS in 9 different languages; 40 Phillips MSS relating to Swiss towns; 40 Graves MSS relating to the history of mathematics and science; 102 Ogden MSS covering a wide range of subjects.
Diaries and letters of Sir Moses Montefiore (1827–72).

Non-manuscript material: Photograph collection covering UCL history: members of staff, buildings etc. Several MS collections contain photographs which are variously listed.
Plans.
Printed material supporting college collections on history and George Orwell.

Finding aids: Handlists and/or card indexes to most collections. Lists sent to NRA.

Facilities: Photocopying. Photography. Microfilming. Microfilm/fiche reader.

Conservation: Contracted out.

Publications: D.K. Coveney: *Descriptive Catalogue of Manuscripts in the Library of University College* (London, 1935).
A. Taylor Milne: *Catalogue of the Manuscripts of Jeremy Bentham in the Library of UCL* (1937).
N.R. Ker: *Medieval Manuscripts in British Libraries*, i: *London* (1969).
J. Percival: *Manuscript Collections in the Library of University College London*,
Occasional Publications of UCL Library no. 1 (London, 2/1978).
Occasional Publications of UCL Library nos. 3–8 [handlists to the Chadwick, Chambers, Sharpe and SDUK papers and to the archives of Routledge & Kegan Paul and of the Peruvian Corporation].
M. Merrington and J. Golden: *A List of the Papers and Correspondence of Sir Francis Galton (1822–1911)* (London, 2/1978).
M. Merrington et al.: *A List of the Papers and Correspondence of Lionel Sharples Penrose (1898–1972)* (London, 1979).
J. Golden: *A List of the Papers and Correspondence of George Bellas Greenough (1778–1855)* (London, 1981).
M. Merrington, J. Golden et al.: *A List of the Papers and Correspondence of Karl Pearson (1857–1936)* (London, 1983).
J. Percival (ed.): *A Guide to the Archives and Manuscripts in the University of London*, i (London, 1984).
J. Golden: *A List of the Papers and Correspondence of Henry Clark Barlow MD (1806–1976)* (London, 1985).

B Slade School of Art

Telephone: (0171) 387 7050 ext. 2317 (Archive) 2313 (Slade General Office, for appointments)

Fax: (0171) 380 7801 (Slade General Office)

Enquiries: The Slade Archivist, Stephen Chaplin

Open: Tues: 10.30–12.00 ('surgery' for telephone callers)
Enquiries by letter or by telephone during normal office hours throughout the year.

Access: Open to the public, by appointment, for

routine enquiries. Much of the material is restricted, and access is at the discretion of the college authorities.

Historical background: The Slade School opened in 1871. Since then it has made a major contribution to education in drawing, painting, sculpture, fine art, print making, stage design, film studies and particularly (in the 1930s) applied art and mural design. Since its inception the Slade has formed a constituent part of University College London (UCL). The school's collection of prize works, together with other bequests and purchases, has been in the charge of the Curator (Strang Print Room: Department of Art History) since the late 1960s. UCL records department holds the financial material, which includes the Slade's earliest years. These give authoritative information on dates, courses, prizes. UCL Library Archives has other important material, minutes, diaries, correspondence. Some losses occurred in World War II.

Acquisitions policy: All forms of papers, ephemera, diaries, memoirs, photographs, catalogues relating to the activity of Slade students, and to their subsequent lives, whether or not dedicated to art. Art works are held by the Curator of the College Art Collections, UCL.

Archives of organisation: Administrative records, student and staff records, committee minutes, examination scripts, mainly 1949–, but including signing-in books, 1878–, daily record of student attendance.
Records of the Film Studies Department, although the films and library are no longer at UCL.

Major collections: Reports by ex-students.

Non-manuscript material: Small library on Slade history.
Exhibition catalogues of work by ex-students.
Collection of photographs, 1890s–; photographs of student works, 1950s– (incomplete).
Tape-recordings on art theory, 1970–75.

Finding aids: Computerised index in preparation. A–Z resource on students and staff being formed.

Facilities: Photocopying and photography by arrangement.

Publications: *A History of the Slade, 1870–1975* (in preparation).

762 University of London Library

Address: Senate House, Malet Street, London WC1E 7HU

Telephone: (0171) 636 8000 ext. 5030

Fax: (0171) 436 1494

Enquiries: The Archivist, Miss Ruth Vyse

Open: Mon–Fri: 10.00–5.00 Sat: 9.45–1.00; 2.00–5.15

Access: By appointment. Restrictions on certain collections and some of the university archives material.

Historical background: The University of London Library has, historically, been the central library of the university. Its origins go back to 1838, though its real expansion dates from the gift of the De Morgan Collection in 1877. The library was based first in Burlington Gardens and then, from 1906, in South Kensington, before it moved to its present accommodation in Senate House in 1937. The Palaeography Room contains a library of printed material on MS studies and archives, and its staff are responsible for administering the library's holdings of MSS and archives. In 1901 Herbert S. Foxwell (1849–1936) sold his collection of books, pamphlets and MSS relating to economic history to the Worshipful Company of Goldsmiths and in 1903 the company gave this collection to the university. This subject interest influenced the subsequent acquisitions policy for MS material, especially for the period covering the 15th to the 19th centuries. The Institute of Historical Research has transferred its MS holdings to the library.

Acquisitions policy: At present the library only accepts MS material which adds to or complements existing collections or which falls within the collecting policy, defined as follows: material relating to the history of the university, especially personal papers of prominent figures, and to the history of higher education; papers of historians and of literary figures, especially 1850–; material which complements the University of London Library's Special Collections, including Goldsmiths' Library: social and economic history, 15th–19th centuries; Sterling Library: literary MSS and correspondence, mainly 19th century; Harry Price Library: psychical research.

Archives of organisation: The archives of the

central administration of the university, 1836–, comprising records created by statutory bodies, administrative departments, federal activities, student facilities and other functions associated with the Federal University.

Major collections: Individual historical and literary MSS and autograph letters, 12th– 20th centuries; includes the foundation collection of MSS acquired with the Goldsmiths' Library of Economic Literature.
Collections of papers of individuals and institutions, including the following: Charles Booth (1840–1916); Professor Augustus De Morgan (1806–71); (Henry) Austin Dobson (1840–1921); Herbert Spencer (1820–1903); Thomas Sturge Moore (1870–1944); Duckworth Publishers, c1936–56.
Captain A.W. Fuller's collection of documents and seals, 13th–20th centuries.
MSS transferred from the Institute of Historical Research.
Papers of Harry Price (1881–1948), including correspondence of Sir A. Conan Doyle (1859–1930).
Literary MSS collected by Sir Louis Sterling (*d* 1958).

Non-manuscript material: Considerable quantity of microfilm copies of MS material held elsewhere.
Detached seals, proofs and casts.
University of London Collection: relating to the history of the university.

Finding aids: Card index to holdings. TS catalogue to post-1930 MS acquisitions. Handlists to many collections. TSS lists. NRA notified of new acquisitions and lists sent.

Facilities: Photocopying. Photography. Microfilm/fiche reader/printer.

Conservation: Full in-house service.

Publications: R.A. Rye: *Catalogue of Manuscripts and Autograph Letters in the University Library* (London, 1921; suppl. *1921–30*, 1930).
P. Kelly: *Modern Historical Manuscripts in the University of London Library: a Subject Guide* (London, 1972).
J. Gibbs and P. Kelly: 'Manuscripts and Archives in the University of London Library', *Archives*, xi/51 (1974), 161.
H. Young: *Guide to Literary Manuscripts.*
Catalogue of the Goldsmiths' Library of Economic Literature, iii (1982) [including MSS].
J. Percival: *A Guide to Archives and Manuscripts in the University of London*, 1 (London, 1984).

763 University of Westminster Archives

Address: Riding House Street Library, 37–49 Riding House Street, London W1R 7PT

Telephone: (0171) 911 5000 ext. 3891

Enquiries: The Archivist, Brenda Weeden

Open: By appointment.

Access: Generally open to the public; evidence of identity is required and an appointment is necessary. Institutional records are generally closed for 30 years; student and staff files are closed for 80 years.

Historical background: In 1881 Quintin Hogg (1845–1903) purchased 309 Regent Street, which had formerly housed the Royal Polytechnic Institute (f. 1838), to accommodate his expanding educational and religious work among the poorer young men of Central London. After the move his Young Men's Christian Institute became known as the Polytechnic Institute, and its technical education became the model for the polytechnic movement. The variety of education activities was matched by the provision of social, religious and recreational opportunities, in accordance with the founder's philosophy of developing the whole man. The Polytechnic of Central London was formed in 1970 by the merger of Regent Street Polytechnic and Holborn College of Law, Languages and Commerce. In 1990 Harrow College of Further Education also merged with PCL. In 1992 the PCL was renamed the University of Westminster.

Acquisitions policy: To acquire and preserve the records of the university and of its antecedents.

Archives of organisation: Royal Polytechnic Institution: a limited amount of legal and other material regarding the founding of the institution; bound volumes of programmes of institution activities, 1873–8.
Regent Street Polytechnic: minutes of the governing body, 1891–1970; *Polytechnic Magazine*, 1879–1971; prospectuses, 1888–1965; administrative records; records of some clubs and societies; some material related to the Sidney Webb College of Education and polytechnic schools.

Non-manuscript material: Photographs of buildings, educational and recreational activities; events. A few tapes of speeches on particular occasions.

Finding aids: In preparation. Partial descriptive list.

Facilities: Photocopying. Photography by arrangement.

764 Upper Norwood Library

Address: Westow Hill, Upper Norwood, London SE19 1TJ

Telephone: (0181) 670 2551

Fax: (0181) 670 5468

Enquiries: The Reference Librarian and Local Librarian, Mr J.G. Savage

Open: Mon: 10.00–7.00 Tues, Thurs, Fri: 9.00–7.00 Sat: 9.00–5.00

Access: Generally open to the public.

Historical background: The library is situated close to the borough boundary between Lambeth and Croydon. It opened in 1900 and has been run since then as an independent public library financed jointly by Croydon and Lambeth.

Acquisitions policy: To supplement the local history collection with any materials of interest concerning the Upper Norwood area.

Major collections: Principally non-MS material (see below).

Non-manuscript material: Local history collection, including pamphlets, programmes and handbills, newspapers, press cuttings, maps, slides and books, covering the Upper Norwood area and to a lesser extent the surrounding localities of Croydon, Dulwich, Camberwell, Sydenham, Southwark, Anerley and Penge. There is a considerable amount on the Crystal Palace, which stood nearby until 1936, including photographs of interior and exterior views. J.B. Wilson (*d* 1949) Collection: personal collection of a local historian, covering Upper and especially West Norwood.

Finding aids: Card indexes of subjects, individuals and buildings.

Facilities: Photocopying.

Publications: Fact-sheets on early history of Norwood and on the Crystal Palace.

765 Vaughan Williams Memorial Library

Parent organisation: English Folk Dance and Song Society

Address: Cecil Sharp House, 2 Regents' Park Road, London NW1 7AY

Telephone: (0171) 284 0523

Fax: (0171) 284 0523

Enquiries: The Librarian, Malcolm Taylor

Open: Mon–Fri: 9.30–5.30 Sound library closed 12.00–2.00 daily.

Access: Generally open to the public but non-members of the society are charged a daily fee. Access to the sound collection is restricted; contact the Librarian for details.

Historical background: Cecil Sharp (1859–1924) was an assiduous collector of English folk music and dance traditions and founded the English Folk Dance Society (EFDS) in 1911 to encourage and promote these traditions. Cecil Sharp House was opened in 1930 and in 1932 the society amalgamated with the Folk Song Society (f. 1898). The library was renamed in 1958 in honour of Ralph Vaughan Williams (1872–1958), president of EFDSS.

Acquisitions policy: To acquire materials of any media relevant to British folk culture and elements it found in other communities, particularly North America and Ireland.

Archives of organisation: Archives of the Folk Song Society, 1898–1932, the EFDS, 1911–32, and the EFDSS, 1932–.

Major collections: MS collections of most early 20th-century folk song and dance collectors, including: Cecil Sharp, Lucy Broadwood, Janet Blunt, Anne Gilchrist, George Gardiner, George Butterworth, Hammond brothers, Maud Karpeles, James Madison Carpenter and others (microfilm).

Non-manuscript material: Sound collection, 1906–, including field recordings of major collectors, e.g. Percy Grainger, Mike Yates, BBC film/video collections.

Finding aids: Indexes to photographs, Cecil Sharp's informants, films and videos, and BBC archive of folk music and folklore. Sound collection catalogue and various indexes. Blunt: NRA 35006; Broadwood: NRA 35004;

Butterworth: NRA 35007; Gardiner: NRA 35005; Sharp: NRA 34987.

Facilities: Photocopying. Microfilm/fiche reader/printer. Audio-visual playback equipment.

Conservation: Contracted out.

Publications: Catalogue (1973).
Study guides to Momi dancing, sword dancing and May Day in England.

766 The Wallace Collection Library

Address: Hertford House, Manchester Square, London W1M 6BM

Telephone: (0171) 935 0687

Fax: (0171) 224 2155

Enquiries: The Senior Museum Assistant, Robert Wenley

Open: Mon–Fri: 9.00–1.00; 2.00–5.00

Access: Bona fide researchers; an appointment by phone or in writing is required.

Historical background: The collection was acquired during the 19th century by the 3rd and 4th Marquesses of Hertford and the latter's illegitimate son, Sir Richard Wallace. It includes old master paintings, 18th–century French works of art, and arms and armour. The collection was bequeathed to the nation by Lady Wallace in 1897 and opened as a national museum in 1900. The library is recognised as a place of deposit for public records.

Acquisitions policy: Any material relating to the founders, their properties and their collections. Also material relating to the history of the museum since 1900.

Archives of organisation: Extensive archives on the founders, their ancestors and descendants; their property and collections, including receipts, inventories, letters and wills.
Archives relating to the Sèvres procelain factory (mainly microfilm).

Major collections: Hertford–Mawson letters, 1848–61.

Non-manuscript material: Photographs of the founders, their properties and collections, and of the museum, 1900–.
Numerous French and British sale catalogues, 18th and 19th centuries.

Books and sale catalogues from Richard Wallace's Library.

Finding aids: Index

Facilities: Photocopying. Microfilm/fiche reader.

Conservation: Contracted out.

Publications: J. Ingamells (ed.): *The Hertford-Mawson Letters* (London, 1981).
P. Hughes: *The Founders of the Wallace Collection* (London, 1992).
The Wallace Collection: Guide (London, 1992).

767 Warburg Institute

Parent organisation: University of London

Address: Woburn Square, London WC1H 0AB

Telephone: (0171) 580 9663

Fax: (0171) 436 2852

Enquiries: The Librarian, Dr W.F. Ryan

Open: Mon–Fri: 10.00–6.00 Sat: 10.00–1.00 (except Aug and Sept)

Access: By reader's ticket, to suitably qualified persons, on application to the director.

Historical background: The institute is named after its founder, Aby Warburg (1866–1929), historian of Renaissance art and civilisation. In 1913 Warburg was joined by Fritz Saxl (1890–1948), who in 1921 turned the library in Hamburg into a research institute. After the rise of the Nazi regime it was transferred to London, where in 1934 it was housed at Thames House, moving in 1937 to the Imperial Institute, South Kensington. In 1944 it was incorporated into the University of London, and it moved to its permanent home in Woburn Square in 1958. The institute is concerned with the study of the Classical tradition, i.e. those elements of European thought, literature, art and institutions which derive from the ancient world.

Major collections: Working papers inherited from private scholars, including Aby Warburg; Fritz Saxl; Henri Frankfort (1897–1954); Robert Eisler (1882–1949); Roberto Weiss (1906–69); Evelyn Jamison (1877–1972); A.A. Barb (1901–79); F.A. Yates (1899–1991).
Papers of and concerning Aleister Crowley and the Order of the Golden Dawn.

Non-manuscript material: Photographic collection, designed primarily for the study of iconography relating to the areas of scholarship represented in the library.

Finding aids: Photographic collection arranged by subject; card index supplies cross-references.

Facilities: MSS are not photocopied.

Publications: Annual Report.
Summary Guide to the Photographic Collection of the Warburg Institute, University of London (London 1988).

768 Wellcome Institute for the History of Medicine

Parent organisation: The Wellcome Trust

Address: 183 Euston Road, London NW1 2BE

Telephone: (0171) 611 8888/8582

Fax: (0171) 611 8703

Enquiries: The Curator of Oriental Collections: Dr N. Allan The Curator of Western MSS: Dr R. Aspin The Archivist of Contemporary Medical Archives Centre (CMAC): Miss J.G.A. Sheppard The Curator of Iconographic Collections: W.M. Schupbach

Open: Mon, Wed, Fri: 9.45–5.15 Tues, Thurs: 9.45–7.00 Sat: 9.45–1.00
Rare materials and archives are available after 5.15 by prior appointment only.

Access: Generally open to bona fide researchers. Readers in the CMAC will be expected to sign a reader's undertaking. Permission of the owner may be required and some collections are closed.

Historical background: The WIHM is owned and maintained by the Wellcome Trust, a charity set up under the will of Sir Henry Wellcome (1853–1936). He built up a historical medical museum and library, the latter being opened to the public in 1949. The museum was transferred on indefinite loan to the Science Museum (entry 731) in 1976, and the institute (so called since 1968) houses the library and academic research centre. Wellcome amassed a vast amount of material covering the whole history of man, with medicine as a central core. Although a great deal of irrelevant material was dispersed by gift or sale after his death,

the collections have a wide scope. The CMAC has existed since 1979 and inherited the collections of the Wellcome Tropical Institute on its closure in 1989. Apart from housing papers and records of 20th–century medical scientists and practitioners, it maintains a Hospital Records Project with the Public Record Office (entry 960). A Medical Archives and Manuscripts Survey has existed since 1986 to locate information about relevant material elsewhere.

Acquisitions policy: To strengthen existing primary and secondary collections in the history of medicine and allied sciences by purchase, donation or deposit.

Major collections: Oriental MSS: representing 43 languages (c11,000 MSS; one of the major collections in the UK), especially Indian material, including Sanskrit and Hindi; Singhalese palm leaf MSS (c400); Batak MSS (24).
Western MSS: includes correspondence, diaries, accounts, minutes, medical treatises, lecture notes, recipe books, case notes, prescription books, laboratory notes, mainly 11th–19th centuries.
Ticehurst House lunatic asylum, Sussex, archives, 1787–1980.
Hunterian Society of London, records, 1819–1989.
Letters and papers of many eminent figures, including Edward Jenner (1749–1823), Florence Nightingale (1820–1910) and Joseph Lister (1827–1912).
MS collection of the Medical Society of London (c140 items).
Contemporary Medical Archives Centre: Papers of individuals, including Sir Ernst Chain (1906–79), Melanie Klein (1882–1960), Sir Thomas Lewis (1881–1945), Sir Peter Medawar (1915–87), E.A. Sharpey-Schäfer (1850–1935), Dr Marie Stopes (1880–1958) and Dr Cicely Williams (1894–1992).
Records of charities, professional bodies and other organisations, including the Abortion Law Reform Association, 1935–83; British Pharmacological Society, 1921–79; Chartered Society of Physiotherapists (f. 1894); Health Visitors' Association (f. 1896); Eugenics Society, 1908–79; Lister Institute, 1889–1960; Medical Women's Federation, 1916–; Pioneer Health Centre, 1920s-; Queen's Nursing Institute (f. 1887).
Records and papers of general practitioners.
Collections of tropical interest, including administrative records of the Royal Society of Tropical Medicine and Hygiene.

Royal Army Medical Corps Muniment Collection: papers of individuals serving in the RAMC, c1850–, including Sir John Hall (1794–1866) and Sir Thomas Longmore (1816–1895) (c2000 accessions).

Non-manuscript material: Iconographic collections: paintings, portraits, posters and prints, Eastern and Western, 14th–20th centuries.
Photographs: collections and albums, including Roentgen X-rays, John Thomson photographs of China and Vietnam; Morestin collection of plastic surgery photographs.
Films. [The Wellcome Trust also maintains a separate film collection and medical photographic library.]
Tape-recordings (c300).

Finding aids: Various guides, handlists, indexes and sources leaflets; on-line catalogue; video-disc.

Facilities: Photocopying. Photography. Microfilm/fiche reader/printer.

Conservation: In-house conservation department.

Publications: Series of descriptive booklets on oriental, S-E Asian, American, Iconographic Collections, Western Manuscripts and Contemporary Medical Archives Centre (1984–95).
Catalogues include: Warren R. Dawson: *Manuscripta medica: a Descriptive Catalogue of the Manuscripts of the Medical Society of London* (1932).
S.A.J. Moorat: *Catalogue of Western Manuscripts on Medicine and Science* (1962, 1973) [3 vols].
A.Z. Iskandar: *A Catalogue of Arabic Manuscripts on Medicine and Science* (1967).
R.M. Price: *An Annotated Catalogue of Medical Americana* (1983).
R.J. Palmer: *Catalogue of Western Manuscripts in the Library of the Wellcome Institute for the History of Medicine: Western Manuscripts, 5120–6790* (forthcoming).
Contemporary Medical Archives Centre: *Guide* (1991) [in process of revision].
J. Symons: *Wellcome Institute for the History of Medicine: a Short History* (1994).
Articles on collections in the library regularly included in series 'Illustrations from the Wellcome Institute Library', in *Medical History*, [journal produced by WIHM].

769 Westminster Abbey Muniments and Library

Address: London SW1P 3PA

Telephone: (0171) 222 5152 ext. 228

Fax: (0171) 233 2072 ('For Attention of Library')

Enquiries: The Keeper of the Muniments, Dr Richard Mortimer or The Assistant Librarian, Dr Tony Towles

Open: Mon–Fri: 10.00–1.00; 2.00–4.45

Access: Consultation by written appointment; restrictions on certain classes of modern records.

Historical background: The Benedictine monastery founded in the 10th century was replaced in 1540 by a collegiate institution; after a brief restoration of the Benedictines under Queen Mary, the present collegiate chapter was founded in 1560.

Acquisitions policy: Anything relevant to the abbey or its special collections.

Archives of organisation: Estate and administrative archives of the medieval monastery and of the post-medieval collegiate foundation; coronation and funeral records; Jewish starrs (shetaroths); coroners' inquests for the City of Westminster, 1760–1880; various papers from St Margaret's Westminster, including the parish registers.

Major collections: Collections of personal papers include those of Lady Margaret Beaufort (1443–1509) and Sir Reginald Bray (*d* 1503), John Nedham (c1670–1710), and Sir Thomas Modyford (?1620–1679), Governor of Jamaica. NB The Chapter Library holds a substantial collection of MSS; access is by arrangement with the Assistant Librarian.

Non-manuscript material: Plans, engravings and photographs relating to the abbey.

Finding aids: Extensive index and calendar to the muniments available in the Muniment Room. Much later material is awaiting cataloguing.

Facilities: Photocopying. Photography by arrangement. Microfilm reader.

Publications: J. Armitage Robinson and M.R.

James: *The Manuscripts of Westminster Abbey* (Cambridge, 1909).

L.E. Tanner: 'The Nature and Use of the Westminster Abbey Muniments', *Transactions of the Royal Historical Society*, xix (1936).

770 Westminster City Archives

Address: City of Westminster Archives Centre, 10 St Ann's Street, London SW1P 2XR

Telephone: (0171) 798 2180

Fax: (0171) 798 2179

Enquiries: The City Archivist, Jerome Farrell

Open: Mon–Fri: 9.30–7.00 Sat: 9.30–5.00

Access: Generally open to the public; permission is needed to consult the Grosvenor Estate archives.

Historical background: Westminster became a city on the foundation of the episcopal see in 1540. From the 16th century local government was by parishes and by the Court of Burgesses, the court gradually losing most of its powers to the parishes and being abolished in 1900. The ten Westminster parishes were united in 1900 to form the City of Westminster. In 1965 the boroughs of Paddington and St Marylebone, which had each been a single civil parish before 1900, and the City of Westminster formed the present city. Westminster City Archives also act as the Diocesan Record Office for London (South Westminster parish records) and are recognised as a place of deposit for public records. Most Westminster City Council records are held at Westminster City Hall. The two separate libraries at Victoria and Westminster were moved to new purpose-built premises in 1994.

Acquisitions policy: Records relating to Westminster are acquired.

Major collections: Records of the parishes which constitute Westminster.
Grosvenor Estate archives, c1700–1960.
Howard de Walden, formerly Portland, Estate archives, 18th–20th centuries.
Royal Botanic Society archives, 1838–1931.
St Marylebone Charity School for Girls archives, 1750–1932.
Jaeger archives, 1883–1987.
Gillow archives, 1731–1932.
Liberty archives, 1883–1988.
Westminster Fire Office archives, 1717–1943.

Royal Institute of Chartered Surveyors records, 1868–1956.
Grey Coat Hospital archives 1698–1950.

Non-manuscript material: Prints and photographs (50,000); theatre programmes (30,000); cuttings (58,000); microfilms (4500); slides (5500); maps (2000); books (23,700).

Finding aids: Lists and indexes. The Grosvenor Estate archives are in the process of being catalogued. Lists sent to NRA.

Facilities: Photocopying. Photography by arrangement. Microfilm readers.

Conservation: In-house facilities.

Publications: Guide to Local History Resources [duplicated].

771 Westminster Diocesan Archives (Roman Catholic)

Address: 16a Abingdon Road, London W8 6AF

Telephone: (0171) 938 3580

Enquiries: The Archivist, Rev. Ian Dickie

Open: Tues–Thurs: 10.00–5.00 (with lunch break) Closed in August.

Access: Generally open to the public, by appointment only. 30–year closure rule as far as possible.

Historical background: After the Elizabethan Reformation settlement in 1559, Roman Catholic life was organised initially from centres abroad such as the seminary college at Douai. From 1623, however, a rudimentary national network, known as the Old Chapter, was created for secular priests, though it lacked papal recognition and ecclesiastical authority, especially *vis-à-vis* the religious orders. In 1688 England and Wales were divided into four districts under bishops, known as Vicars Apostolic, who enjoyed ecclesiastical jurisdiction of a limited nature (albeit under penal laws and some persecution) until 1850; the number of districts was doubled in 1840. In 1850 a normal diocesan jurisdiction was restored, though with the reservation of certain powers to Rome, since Britain was predominantly a non-Catholic country. These reservations have been gradually abolished only in the 20th century. A small amount of St Edmund's College archives remains with the college at Old Hall Green, Ware, Herts.

Acquisitions policy: At present restricted to central diocesan archives, but no relevant deposits are refused.

Archives of organisation: Records of organisation of Catholics in the London district (Home Counties) and correspondence with other areas, 16th–19th centuries; papers of some agents abroad (especially Roman), recovered *c*1815; administration and correspondence of Westminster diocese, 1850– (except 1865–92); records of bishops' meetings, 1865–1945.

Major collections: Records of St Edmund's College, school and seminary, chiefly 1794– *c*1950.

Non-manuscript material: Small pamphlet collection; a few plans and elevations; photographs and scrapbooks concerning most cardinals of Westminster.

Finding aids: Various lists and indexes. Archives of St Edmund's College: NRA 16303.

Facilities: Photocopying, generally of 19th– and 20th–century material. Microfilming of earlier material may sometimes be arranged.

Publications: P. Hughes: 'The Westminster Archives', *Dublin Review*, cci (1937) [gives an account of papers earlier than mid-19th century, but further material of this period has been discovered].

772 Westminster School Archive and Library

Address: 17 Dean's Yard, London SW1 3PB

Telephone: (0171) 963 1018

Fax: (0171) 963 1006

Enquiries: The Archivist

Open: During school terms, by appointment only.

Access: On application, to researchers with specific enquiries or interests.

Historical background: Westminster School has been established on a site adjacent to Westminster Abbey since at least 1361 and its history is closely bound up with the ecclesiastical and political history of Westminster.

Acquisitions policy: To extend the collection of books, relics and records connected with the history of the school.

Archives of organisation: The school archive: an extensive collection of records and documents concerning the history of the school from its foundation.

Non-manuscript material: Prints and photographs of school history.
The Busby Library: a private 17th–century academic library left to the school by Richard Busby, headmaster, in 1695.
The Greene Library: a collection of first editions of works by Westminster authors.

Finding aids: Computerised catalogue and data retrieval system.

773 Whitechapel Art Gallery

Address: Whitechapel High Street, London E1 7QX

Telephone: (0171) 377 0107

Fax: (0171) 377 1685

Enquiries: The Archivist

Open: By appointment.

Access: Access to publicity materials is unrestricted. Permission is required to consult any administrative records. Charges are made for research done on behalf of enquirers.

Whitechapel Art Gallery, which opened in 1901, is an unendowed charitable trust administered by an independent board of trustees representing national and local interests. It has an internationally recognised tradition of presenting major exhibitions of British and international art. It also aims to encourage young artists, to facilitate the exchange of exhibitions with other galleries and to promote contemporary visual arts. Since 1901 the gallery has held more than 600 exhibitions, which are documented with catalogues, press cuttings, other publicity materials and administrative records. There are also photographs of exhibited works of art and of exhibition installations as well as audio tapes of interviews with artists and others associated with the gallery. Photocopying is available and a catalogue is being planned.

774 Whitelands College

Parent organisation: Roehampton Institute, London

Address: West Hill, Putney, London SW15 3SN

Telephone: (0181) 392 3000

Fax: (0181) 392 3531

Enquiries: The Principal's Office, Mrs J. Iles

Open: By prior appointment.

Access: Generally open to all enquirers; there is a 30–year closure on personal records.

Historical background: The college was founded in 1841 by the National Society (Church of England) to be a training institution for women teachers and soon became important in the professional qualification and academic advancement of women generally. It had connections with Baroness Burdett-Coutts (1814–1906) and especially with John Ruskin (1814–1900), who gave substantial donations of books, illustrations etc and who inspired the institution of the May Queen Festival in 1881. Ruskin also interested Edward Burne-Jones and William Morris in the decoration of its chapel. The college was in Chelsea from 1841 to 1930. In the 1920s and early 1930s its interests were greatly promoted by Winifred Mercier OBE, who moved the college to a building in Putney specially designed by Giles Gilbert Scott. Since 1978 it has been a constituent college of Roehampton Institute, offering degrees awarded by the University of Surrey.

Acquisitions policy: To enlarge the existing collection by donations from former staff and students of examples of work, mementos, letters etc.

Archives of organisation: Student records, 1842– (*c*3000).
College annual reports, 1849–; minute books and account books of governing body.
Chapel files: complete correspondence, 1881–1907, including Burne-Jones and William Morris.
Guild of Old Students: annuals and complete records, 1881–.
Documents covering all aspects of college development, including administrative, financial, curricular and social, especially 1870–.

Non-manuscript material: Extensive photographic collection; films and videos.
May Queen collection: dresses, jewellery, books, photographs, some MSS, 1887–.
Gifts from Ruskin of books, illustrations, pictures etc; and other donations from former staff and students to the college and its chapel.

Some educational equipment of historical interest.
Specimens of students' work, e.g. in needlework.

Finding aids: Computer catalogue in progress. Card index.

Facilities: Photocopying. Photography.

Publications: M. Cole: *The History* (1932).
——: *The Chapel* (1935).
H. Henstridge: *Whitelands College Archive Catalogue* (London, 1979).
M. Cole: *The May Queen Festival* (1981).

775 William Morris Gallery Library

Parent organisation: London Borough of Waltham Forest

Address: Water House, Lloyd Park, Forest Road, Walthamstow, London E17 4PP

Telephone: (0181) 527 3782

Enquiries: The Keeper, Norah C. Gillow

Open: Tues–Sat: 10.00–1.00, 2.00–5.00 Sun (1st of each month): 10.00–1.00; 2.00–5.00

Access: The archive/reserve collection can be viewed by prior appointment only, and access is restricted to bona fide students/academics.

Historical background: Water House was the boyhood home of the designer, craftsman, writer and socialist William Morris (1834–96) from 1848 to 1856. Since 1950 it has housed the gallery, a permanent collection illustrating the achievements and influence of Morris as a designer and writer.

Acquisitions policy: By purchase and gift, within the period relevant to the gallery's collections, i.e. Morris and his associates, the Arts and Crafts Movement, early 20th– century design.

Major collections: Correspondence and MS writings of William Morris and his associates; Arthur H. Mackmurdo (1851–1942) and Frank Brangwyn (1867–1956), artist.

Non-manuscript material: In addition to the

main gallery collections there are the following: photographs, articles and catalogues of relevant exhibitions; contemporary periodicals, e.g. *The Studio, The Yellow Book, The Century Guild Hobby Horse.*
Kelmscott Press books and printed ephemera.

Finding aids: All items catalogued on cards/files. NRA 11835, 11836.

Facilities: Limited photocopying. Photography

Conservation: Contracted out via Area Museum Services for South-East England.

Publications: K.L. Goodwin: *A Preliminary Handlist of Manuscripts and Documents of William Morris* (1983).
N. Kelvin: *The Letters of William Morris* (Princeton, 1984).

776 Wimbledon College Archives

Address: Wimbledon College, Edge Hill, London SW19 4NS

Telephone: (0181) 946 2533

Fax: (0181) 947 6513

Enquiries: The Archivist

Open: Term: Mon–Fri: 9.00–3.30

Access: Bona fide researchers, on written application and by prior appointment. Restrictions on certain collections.

Historical background: Wimbledon College was founded by the Jesuit Fathers in 1892 as the first of two secondary day-schools for boys in the London area. In 1893 the school moved to its present buildings, formerly occupied by Wimbledon School, founded by the Rev. John Matthew Brackenbury, an Anglican clergyman, in 1860. Initially a fee-paying school, Wimbledon College became a voluntary-aided grammar school in 1944 and adopted comprehensive status in 1969. From 1898 to 1919 an independent Army Department, also conducted by the Jesuits, flourished on the same site.

Acquisitions policy: To acquire, by donation or deposit, material relevant to the history and development of Wimbledon School, Wimbledon College and Wimbledon College Army Department and their respective pupils.

Archives of organisation: Archives of Wimbledon College, including admissions registers, financial records etc, 1892–.
Archives of Wimbledon College Army Department, 1898–1919.
A very small number of records relating to Wimbledon School, 1860–92.

Non-manuscript material: Photographic collection: staff and pupils, sports clubs etc, 1892–.
Architect's plans, 1938–.
Wimbledon College Magazine, 1923–.

Finding aids: General index to all collections.

Facilities: Photocopying.

Publications: M. Whitehead: *Archives at Wimbledon College* (1980).
A. Poole: *A History of Wimbledon College* (1992).

777 Wimbledon Lawn Tennis Museum
Kenneth Ritchie Wimbledon Library

Parent organisation: The All England Lawn Tennis Club

Address: Church Road, Wimbledon, London SW19 5AE

Telephone: (0181) 946 6131

Fax: (0181) 944 6497

Enquiries: The Hon. Librarian, Mr J.A. Little or The Museum Curator, Miss V.A. Warren

Open: Tues–Fri: 10.30–5.00
Closed during the championships and the previous Friday, Saturday and Sunday.

Access: Approved researchers, on written application and by appointment. Restrictions on certain AELTC documents.

The Wimbledon Lawn Tennis Museum was opened in 1977 to mark the centenary of the championships. The library forms an integral part of the museum and holds minute books, programmes and other records of the AELTC, as well as collecting photographs, prints, a wide range of ephemera and books and periodicals relating to lawn tennis. Photocopying and photography is by arrangement. See J.A. Little: *The Kenneth Ritchie Wimbledon Library* (1993) [catalogue].

778 Women's Art Library

Address: Fulham Palace, Bishop's Avenue, London SW6 6EA

Telephone: (0171) 731 7618

Fax: (0171) 384 1110

Enquiries: The Managing Director, Ms Pauline Barrie or The Librarian

Open: Tues–Fri: 10.00–5.00

Access: Generally open to the public.

Historical background: The library was established in 1984 in Battersea Arts Centre as the Women Artists' Slide Library and renamed in 1993.

Acquisitions policy: Accepts donations of documentation, photographs, cuttings, film and video, and flat work by or about women artists.

Major collections: Archives of Society of Women Artists (f. *c*1855), including minutes, 1920–, and catalogues of annual exhibitions.
Women's International Art Club records, 20th century.
Historical Documentation Collection, including material *re* Elena Gaputyte (1927–91) and Elisabeth Frink (1930–93).
Archival files, including 'Guerrilla Girls'.
Work of Danish and European artists (*c*5000 files).

Non-manuscript material: Photographs, including large collection on life and works of Dame Laura Knight (1877–1970).
Historical unpublished papers and theses.

Finding aids: Indexed and listed on database.

Facilities: Photocopying.

779 Woodard Corporation Archives

Address: c/o Lee, Bolton and Lee, 1 The Sanctuary, Westminister, London SW1P 3JT

Telephone: (0171) 222 5381

Enquiries: The Registrar, P.F.B. Beesley. The Registrar can direct enquirers to the relevant school or office (see below).

Open: Office hours, by arrangement.

Access: Approved readers, on written application.

Historical background: The Rev. Nathaniel Woodard (1811–91) established the corporation in 1848 to provide schools for the middle classes, in which education should be in accordance with Anglican principles. From his first schools at Lancing and Hurstpierpoint, the corporation has developed five geographical divisions which now control 24 schools, the largest single grouping of independent schools in this country. South, Midland, West, North and East Divisions each have a company office from which their schools are controlled. Records are kept in the offices and the schools and also in the registrar's central office, and the corporation's archive provides a unique source for educational development in the independent sector in all parts of England. A consultant has recently identified records throughout the corporation, listing them and advising schools, officers and the corporation on future archive policy.

Acquisitions policy: Each school and office maintains records.

Archives of organisation: The most important single collection is at Lancing College (entry **440**) in Sussex, where the letters of the founder, Nathaniel Woodard, are stored. These may be transferred to Lambeth Palace Library (entry **591**) but enquiries should still be directed to the Registrar.

Finding aids: Every school and office has its own archive list. Each division holds the lists of all its schools. The office of the registrar holds all archive lists for the Corporation. Copies of all lists at NRA.

Facilities: These vary from school to school.

Publications: There is a number of published works on the history of the corporation and of some of its schools; these are noted in the archive lists.

780 Working Men's College

Address: Crowndale Road, London NW1 1TR

Telephone: (0171) 387 2037

Fax: (0171) 383 5561

Enquiries: The Deputy Warden, Mr J. Parry

Open: By arrangement.

Access: Researchers and students, by appointment.

Historical background: The college was founded in 1854 by F.D. Maurice and a group of the Christian Socialists.

Acquisitions policy: To maintain the archive.

Archives of organisation: College records, including committee papers, accounts, records of early students, attendance registers, 1854–.

Major collections: Papers of the founders, lecturers and students, including correspondence of F.D. Maurice (1805–72), Malcolm Forbes Ludlow (1821–1911), F.J. Furnivall (1825–1920), John Ruskin (1819–1900) and Dante Gabriel Rossetti (1828–62).
General correspondence from individuals such as William Morris (1834–96) and E.M. Forster (1879–1970).

Non-manuscript material: Newspaper cuttings and scrapbooks, 1880–, including collected newpaper articles of A.V. Dicey (1835–1922), English jurist.

Finding aids: NRA 16341. Another catalogue in preparation.

Facilities: Photocopying.

Publications: J. Harrison: *History of the Working Men's College, 1854–1954.*

781 Worshipful Company of Goldsmiths

Address: The Library, Goldsmiths' Hall, Foster Lane, London EC2V 6BN

Telephone: (0171) 606 7010

Fax: (0171) 606 1511

Enquiries: The Librarian

Open: Mon–Fri: 10.00–5.30

Access: Generally open to bona fide researchers, by appointment.

Historical background: The library was established after World War II to provide access to company records.

Acquisitions policy: All relevant material on hallmarking, assaying, and the precious metals as functional or decorative works of art.

Archives of organisation: Company records, including wardens' accounts and court minutes, 1334– (lacking 1579–92), books of ordinances, estate documents.
Trial of Pyx records.

London Assay Office records.

Non-manuscript material: Philip Hardwick (1792–1870), drawings of the Hall.
Edward Spencer metalwork designs.
Omar Ramsden workbooks.
Twining Collection: material on regalia throughout the world.
Trade papers, 1950s-.
Photographs; slides; films.

Finding aids: Card catalogue.

Facilities: Limited photocopying.

Publications: The Early History of the Goldsmiths' Company.
Exhibition catalogues [list available from librarian].

782 Young Men's Christian Association

Parent organisation: National Council of YMCA (Inc.)

Address: 640 Forest Road, Walthamstow, London E17 3DZ

Telephone: (0181) 520 5599

Fax: (0181) 509 3190

Enquiries: The Operations Director, Andy Winter

Open: Mon–Fri: 10.00–4.00

Access: Approved readers, on written application.

The National Council was founded in 1882 but YMCAs were founded from 1844 onwards. Records, including photographs, reports and handbooks, relate mainly to the national body but some local YMCA material is available. Papers on certain founder members and material relating to the movement's activities in World War I are also held.

783 Zoological Society of London

Address: Regent's Park, London NW1 4RY

Telephone: (0171) 722 3333

Fax: (0171) 586 5743

Enquiries: The Librarian, Ms Ann Sylph

Open: Mon–Fri: 9.30–5.30

Access: Members of the Zoological Society of

London; other bona fide researchers by permission of the Secretary and on payment of a fee. An appointment is essential.

Historical background: The society was founded in 1826. Most of the correspondence etc for past years was destroyed during World War II.

Acquisitions policy: Important back files from various departments of the society are added to the archives.

Archives of organisation: Administrative records and documents, 1826–, including minutes; scientific meetings; Zoological Club records, 1866–1927; certificates of election of Fellows, 1829–31, 1870–; account books; daily occurrence books for Regent's Park and Whipsnade.
Letters, mainly concerning administrative matters, 19th century (c3000).

Major collections: Sir Hugh S. Gladstone's collection of autographs of naturalists.
Archives of the Fauna Preservation Society.
(Other individuals' collections are principally non-MS material.)

Non-manuscript material: Paintings, drawings, photographs.
List of Fellows.
Zoo guides.

Facilities: Photocopying. Photography. Microfiche reader.

Publications: Annual report.

784 St Columb's Cathedral
Chapter House Library

Address: c/o the Dean, The Deanery, 30 Bishop Street, Londonderry BT48 6PP

Telephone: (01504) 262746

Enquiries: The Dean, Very Rev. Cecil Orr

Open: Mon–Fri: 10.00–4.00

Access: Bona fide scholars; an appointment is advisable.

Historical background: The collection was begun in 1922 by Dean R.G.S. King (*d* 1958), supported by the Cathedral Select Vestry.

Acquisitions policy: To maintain and consolidate the collections relating to the history of Londonderry and Derry Diocese.

Archives of organisation: Parish records, 1642–.

Major collections: Collections of transcripts

relating to the City and County of Londonderry, by A.M. Munn (*d* 1937) and Tenison Groves (*d* 1938).

Non-manuscript material: Sir Frederick Heygate (*d* 1940) Collection of pamphlets on Irish affairs, 17th century.
Prints relating to the cathedral and its history.

Facilities: Reprography by permission of the Dean.

785 Loughborough University of Technology Archives

Address: Pilkington Library, Loughborough University of Technology, Loughborough, Leics LE11 3TU

Telephone: (01509) 222359/222353

Fax: (01509) 234806

Enquiries: The University Archivist, Mrs J.G. Clark

Open: Thurs, Fri: 9.00–12.30; 2.00–4.30

Access: Bona fide researchers, by appointment. Restrictions on some records.

Historical Background: Loughborough Technical Institute (renamed Loughborough College in 1920) was established by the Leicestershire County Council in 1909 and was an 'Instructional Factory' for the Ministry of Munitions during World War I. In 1952 Loughborough College was divided into four separate institutions: Loughborough College of Technology; Loughborough Training College (later renamed Loughborough College of Education); Loughborough College of Further Education (later renamed Loughborough Technical College); and Loughborough College of Art. Loughborough College of Technology received its charter as a university in 1966 and in 1977 the university and the college of education were amalgamated. The University Archives were established in 1980.

Acquisitions policy: Administrative and other records of the university and its predecessors; papers of former staff and students as appropriate.

Archives of organisation: Administrative and other records relating to Loughborough College, 1909–52; Loughborough College of Technology, 1952–66; Loughborough College of

Education, 1952–77; Loughborough University of Technology, 1966–.
Records of Loughborough Students' Union, 1918–, and the Past Students' Association, 1948–.

Major collections: Some papers deposited by former staff and students, including Norman Swindin, Hon. Reader in Chemical Technology.
Dan Maskell Collection, photographs and memorabilia of the tennis commentator.

Non-manuscript material: Photographs of the 'Instructional Factory', 1914–18.
University publications: calendars, prospectuses, journals, newspapers etc, and student publications; photographs; slides; film and tape-recordings of university events; some technical drawings and plans.

Finding aids: Catalogues, lists and indexes; list sent to NRA.

Facilities: Photocopying.

786 Suffolk Record Office
Lowestoft Branch

Parent organisation: Suffolk County Council

Address: Central Library, Clapham Road, Lowestoft, Suffolk NR32 1DR

Telephone: (01502) 503308

Fax: (01502) 503311

Enquiries: The Archives Service Manager, Miss R.A. Rogers, The Branch Archivist, Miss K.A.L. Chantry

Open: Mon, Wed–Fri: 9.15–5.30 Tues: 9.15–6.00 Sat: 9.15–5.00 Material required for Saturday should preferably be ordered on Friday.

Access: Generally open to the public; the office operates the CARN reader's ticket system. Appointments accepted for microform readers.

Historical background: The branch was established in 1985 to serve the north-eastern part of Suffolk. Its area for the purpose of collecting archives and printed local studies material is that of the Waveney District. It is recognised as a place of deposit for public records and is a Diocesan Record Office for parish records.

Acquisitions policy: Archival and printed material relating to the north-east part of Suffolk.

Archives of organisation: Usual local authority record holdings.

Major collections: Deposited local collections, including: shipping records, c1750–1980s; Adair of Flixton Hall family and estate records, 13th–20th centuries.

Non-manuscript material: Local studies library as integral part of record office.

Finding aids: Catalogues and lists; some sent to NRA. Indexes to persons, subjects, places and particular types of record, e.g. photographs, maps and plans, building plans, architects/surveyors.

Facilities: Photocopying. Photography. Microfilming by arrangement. Microfilm/fiche readers/printers (some self-service).

Conservation: In-house service.

Publications: Guide to Genealogical Sources (4/1993).
Archive News (half-yearly) [includes annual summary of accessions].
Various local history titles.

787 Luton Museum

Parent organisation: Borough of Luton

Address: Wardown Park, Luton, Bed LU2 7HA

Telephone: (01582) 746333

Fax: (01582) 483178

Enquiries: The Keeper of Local History, Dr Elizabeth Adey

Open: Mon–Fri: 10.30–5.00

Access: Generally open to the public; an appointment is necessary, and because of the limited space in the study room the number of researchers must be restricted to a maximum of eight.

Historical background: Luton Museum commenced collecting local history material as soon as it was established in 1927. The collection consists of a library, documents and photographs.

Acquisitions policy: Acquisition is limited to items which have a local relevance or which relate to a specific area of the collection, e.g. lace or rural crafts.

Major collections: Documents relating to all aspects of Luton life: industry (particularly hats), education, social life etc.
Maps, plans and other documents produced by local firm of architects, 1890s–1960s (20,000).
MS vols, including the Guild Book of the Fraternity of the Holy Trinity, a guild based in Luton, 1474–1547; the register of the Fraternity of St John the Baptist based in Dunstable.
Vols of sketches and notes produced by W.G. Smith (1835–1917), a Dunstable antiquarian.

Non-manuscript material: Photographic negatives from *Luton News* (c375,000).
Photographs by Frederick Thurston of Luton, 1870s–1930.

Facilities: Photocopying.

Conservation: Contracted out.

788 Lydd Town Council

Address: The Guild Hall, High Street, Lydd, Romney Marsh, Kent TN29 9AF

Telephone: (01797) 320999

Enquiries: The Town Clerk

Open: Mon, Wed, Thurs: 9.00–12.30; 2.00–4.30, at the town clerk's discretion.

Access: By appointment only, and with a letter of introduction from a professional referee with personal knowledge of the applicant. No access to casual callers is permitted. Uncatalogued archives will be made available only in exceptional circumstances.

Historical background: The Borough of Lydd has been a corporate member of the Cinque Ports since at least 1155. The town was a borough by prescription but did not achieve full borough status until 1885. In 1974 the town lost its borough status but, because of its membership of the Cinque Ports, retains its Mayor and has the title of Town Council.

Acquisitions policy: The council will normally accept gifts of documents relating to the town's history but generally does not purchase material.

Archives of organisation: Borough of Lydd records, including charters, court and plea books with other legal documents, militia lists, oath rolls, burgess rolls and freemen records, also some parish, charity and drainage records, c1400–1974.

Finding aids: Catalogue of Lydd Borough Records, 1412–1941. The majority of the 19th- and 20th–century documents are as yet uncatalogued, although most are briefly listed.

Facilities: Very limited photocopying.

Publications: A. Finn (ed.): *The Records of Lydd, 1911* [transcription of the chamberlains' or jurats' accounts, 1422–84, and the churchwardens' accounts, 1519–59].

789 Centre for Kentish Studies

Parent organisation: Kent County Council Arts and Library

Address: County Hall, Maidstone, Kent ME14 1XQ

Telephone: (01622) 694363

Fax: (01622) 694379

Enquiries: The Manager

Open: Tues–Fri: 9.00–5.00 Sat: (2nd and 4th in month): 9.00–1.00

Access: The office operates the CARN reader's ticket system.

Historical background: The office (previously Kent Archives Office) was established in 1933. It merged with the former County Local Studies Library to form the Centre for Kentish Studies in 1990. It also acts as the Diocesan Record Office for Rochester and Canterbury (Archdeaconry of Maidstone). It is recognised as a place of deposit for public records. For branch offices see entries **331, 948, 966** and **1003**.

Archives of organisation: Usual local authority record holdings.

Major collections: Deposited collections, including the following which have a wider significance:
Correspondence of Frederick North, 5th Earl of Guildford, principally concerning activities as Governor of Ceylon, 1798–1805.
Wykeman Martin MSS, including correspondence relating to American affairs, 18th century.
Cornwallis (Mann) MSS, including correspondence of Charles, Marquis Cornwallis, as Governor General of India, later Lord Lieutenant of Ireland, 1786–1804.
Sackville of Knole MSS, including correspondence about the Young Pretender, 1746;

military papers of Lt.-Col. Sir Francis Whitworth concerning Gibraltar and West Indies, 1777–1807.

Mackeson MSS: correspondence from John Mackeson while in the army in India, 1801–3, and in West Indies, 1807–14.

Papers of Sir Jeffrey, 1st Lord Amherst, covering his military career in Europe, America and, after 1764, England.

Talbot MSS, including diaries of Lady Caroline Stuart Wortley, 1814–18; travel diaries of J.G. Talbot and others, 19th–20th centuries.

Garnett MSS, including military correspondence of General Robert Garnett, 1841–64.

Papers of Charles, Baron Hardinge of Penshurst (1858–1944).

Papers of George Harris, 1st Baron Harris, covering his life in India and the Seringapatam Campaign, 1789–1800.

Romney MSS, including correspondence of Sir John, 1st Baronet, 1656–83.

Papers of Thomas Papillon (1623–1702), London merchant and politician, and his Huguenot family.

Business and personal correspondence of Sir Mark Wilks Collett, Bart, especially about the American cotton market, 1816–1905.

Pratt MSS, including political correspondence of Sir Charles Pratt, 1st Earl Camden (1714–94), Lord Chancellor; and John Jeffreys Pratt, 2nd Earl and 1st Marquess, 1795–1829.

United and Cecil Club records, 1882–1961.

Sir John Rodgers, Bart, MP for Sevenoaks, 1950–79, official and family papers.

Society of Holy Cross records, 1855–1978.

Extensive correspondence with many eminent figures is included in the following collections: Faunce Delaune MSS.

Knatchbull and Banks MSS, including correspondence relating to the families of Jane Austen and Sir Joseph Banks.

Sir William Knollys, treasurer and controller of household of Prince of Wales, 1863–77.

Lady Rose Weigal (d 1921) and family.

Rt Hon. J.H. Thomas, MP (1874–1949).

De l'Isle MSS: Sydney family of Penshurst, 14th century–.

Stanhope of Chevening MSS: official, literary and scientific papers of the seven Earls Stanhope, with family and estate papers, including most of the letters from the 4th Earl of Chesterfield to his son, 1738–68.

Facilities: Photocopying. Photography. Microfilming. Microfilm reader.

Conservation: In-house service. Outside work undertaken, contact Canterbury Cathedral Archives (entry **187**).

Publications: Guide to Kent Archives Office (1958); *First Supplement, 1957–68* (1971); *Second Supplement, 1969–80* (1982).
Handlist of County Council Records, 1889–1945 (1972).

790 Kent Biological Archives and Records Centre

Address: Natural History Section, Maidstone Museums & Art Gallery, St Faith's Street, Maidstone, Kent ME14 1LH

Telephone: (01622) 54497

The archive was started in 1971 to keep records of all natural history in the present administrative county of Kent. Photographs of habitats and species (c1000) are kept and a collection of local naturalists' note-books and other MS material has also been started. Since the retirement of the Keeper of Natural History in 1993 the centre is unable to deal with enquiries. Records before 1971 are treated as historical records and are recorded under species headings. All records for 1971 onwards are treated as recent records and are filed under species and locality headings.

791 Thomas Plume's Library

Address: Market Hill, Maldon, Essex CM9 7PZ

Telephone: (01621) 855912

Enquiries: The Librarian, the Secretary to the Plume Trustees, Mrs G.B. Shacklock

Open: Tues–Thurs: 2.00–4.00 Sat: 10.00–12.00
Open at other times by arrangement.

Access: Generally open to the public, by appointment.

The library was the private collection of Archdeacon Thomas Plume (1630–1704) and was bequeathed to the people of Maldon on his death. Minutes books of the Plume Trustees survive from 1704. There are early MS catalogues of the library, which holds pamphlets, bills and miscellaneous documents (c1500) on a wide range of subjects, including theology, mathematics, science, astronomy and travel, 16th–19th centuries.

792 Chetham's Library

Address: Long Millgate, Manchester M3 1SB

Telephone: (0161) 834 7961

Fax: (0161) 839 5797

Enquiries: The Librarian, Michael Powell

Open: Mon–Fri: 9.30–12.30; 1.30–4.30

Access: Material available on request. Readers are asked to provide references. The building may be visited by the public during opening hours.

Historical background: Founded in 1633 by Humphrey Chetham, a Manchester merchant, as a free public library for 'the use of scholars', it was recognised by Royal Charter in 1665; it was founded with Chetham's School (now the School of Music).

Acquisitions policy: The library concentrates on the history and topography of north-western England.

Archives of organisation: Chetham family papers, hospital and library minute books, 1653–.

Major collections: A varied collection, including *c*40 medieval MSS.
The majority of MSS and archives are concerned with the history of Manchester and its region, including:
Papers of the Manchester Sunday Schools, 19th century.
Bishop Fraser, 2nd Bishop of Manchester, Collection, 1818–85.
Hulme Trust deeds, mainly on Manchester, 13th–17th centuries, including papers of John Huntingdon, 1st warden of the Collegiate Church, 1422–58.
Records of Belle Vue Zoological Gardens, 19th–20th centuries.
Poor House and constable's accounts for Sutton, nr Macclesfield, and Over Knutsford, Cheshire, 17th–19th centuries.
Estate papers of Agecroft, nr Manchester, 15th–18th centuries.

Non-manuscript material: Broadsides and tracts (*c*3100); Chetham Popery tracts.
Shorthand collections of John Byrom (1692–1763) and John Harland (1806–38) (*c*49 MSS and 360 printed books).
Photographic slides and engravings (*c*2000).
Scrapbooks (various) relating to the 18th– and 19th–century history of Manchester.
Local newspapers, 18th–19th centuries.

Incunabula (*c*90).

Finding aids: Catalogues, indexes and lists available; the collection is continuously researched and indexed. Lists sent to NRA.

Facilities: Photocopying. Photography by arrangement.

Conservation: In-house service.

Publications: G.H. Tupling: 'A Selection from the List of Historical Manuscripts in the Chetham Library', *Bulletin of Historical Research*, x (1932–3), 69.
H. Lofthouse: 'Unfamiliar Libraries, 1: Chetham's Library', *Book Collector*, v/4 (1956), 323.

793 Co-operative Union of Great Britain and Ireland

Address: The Library, Co-operative Union Ltd, Holyoake House, Hanover Street, Manchester M60 0AS

Telephone: (0161) 832 4300 exts 286, 287

Fax: (0161) 831 7684

Enquiries: The Information Officer and Librarian, Mr T.R. Garratt

Open: Mon–Fri: 10.00–4.45

Access: Bona fide scholars, students and research workers, by appointment only.

Historical Background: The Co-operative Union was founded in 1869 to link the scattered co-operative societies of that time into a movement, to arrange annual national co-operative congresses for the exchange of information and ideas on co-operation, and to advise in the formation of co-operative societies. Today the union is still the national co-ordinating, advisory and information body of the co-operative consumer movement. The library was properly established in 1911, following the erection of Holyoake House, the union's headquarters, and it is primarily the national historical library of the co-operative movement, although it also provides a service of contemporary books for staff and visitors.

Acquisitions policy: History of all branches of the co-operative movement and all aspects of modern co-operation. History of the Labour movement.

Major collections: Letters and documents of Robert Owen (1771–1858), social reformer, philanthropist and co-operator, 1821–58 (c3,000), and George Jacob Holyoake (1817–1906), co-operative leader, secularist and social reformer, 1835–1903 (3500).

Non-manuscript material: Complete run of the co-operative movement's official newspaper, the *Co-operative News*, 1871–, and *The Co-operator* 1860–71, *New Moral World*, 1840–42, and *Brighton Co-operator*, 1828–30.
Pamphlets on co-operation, 19th century–.
Comprehensive collection of jubilee and centenary histories of individual co-operative retail and productive societies.

Finding aids: Catalogues of Owen and Holyoake MS collections. Checklist on historical periodicals and on workers' co-operatives.

Facilities: Photocopying. Photography by arrangement.

794 Greater Manchester County Record Office

Parent organisation: Association of Greater Manchester Authorities (AGMA)

Address: 56 Marshall Street, New Cross, Manchester M4 5FU

Telephone: (0161) 832 5284

Fax: (0161) 839 3808

Enquiries: The County Archivist

Open: Mon: 1.00–5.0 Tues–Fri: 9.00–5.00 Sat (2nd and 4th of month): 9.00–12.00; 1.00–4.00

Access: Generally open to the public. The office operates the CARN reader's ticket system. An appointment is necessary to use microfilm readers.

Historical background: The office was established in 1976 as the county record office for Greater Manchester, with a collecting policy designed to supplement rather than duplicate those of the district record offices. It is recognised as a place of deposit for public records. The Documentary Photography Archive has existed since the early 1970s with Audrey Linkman as its curator.

Acquisitions policy: Archives of the county with a regional significance, i.e. of two or more districts.

Archives of organisation: Usual local authority record holdings, of Greater Manchester Coun-

cil and some predecessor bodies, plus Greater Manchester Residuary Body records.

Major collections: Deposited local collections, of which the following have a wider significance:
Family papers, including Lord Wilton's family and estate papers relating to Heaton Park, Manchester, and estates in Wrinehill, Cheshire/Staffordshire, and Battesley, West Yorkshire, 1304–1970s; archives of the Assheton family of Middleton, c1300–1830s, Legh of Lyme Hall, Stockport.
Entwisle family of Foxholes, nr Rochdale, 1565–1957.
Canal records, including archives of the Manchester Ship Canal, 1883–1970s; archives of Rochdale Canal Company, 1793–1880s.
Archive of the Paul Geary Memorial Folk Trust.
Architectural records, 19th and 20th centuries.
Business archives, including records of National Vulcan Insurance Company, Manchester, c1860s-1950s; records of Robinsons of Ramsbottom, Bury, bleachers and dyers, 1900–1970s.
Manchester Stock Exchange lists.

Non-manuscript material: Documentary Photography Archive.
Engineering drawings (c100,000).

Finding aids: Catalogues being updated. Lists will be sent to NRA.

Facilities: Photocopying. Microfilm readers.

Conservation: Full in-house service except some specialist bookbinding; outside work undertaken.

Publications: Guide to Greater Manchester County Record Office.
A. Linkman: *The Victorians: Photographic Portraits* (London, 1993).

795 Labour History Archive and Study Centre

Parent organisation: National Museum of Labour History

Address: 103 Princess Street, Manchester M1 6DD

Telephone: (0161) 228 7212

Fax: (0161) 237 5965

Enquiries: The Archivist/Librarian, Stephen Bird or The Archivist/Researcher, Andrew Flinn

Open: Mon–Fri: 10.00–5.00

Access: Generally open to the public; an appointment is preferred.

Historical background: The National Museum of Labour History was founded in 1975. In 1988 it moved to Manchester and was located in the Mechanics Institute Building in Princess Street. It was primarily a museum, although it did obtain some large collections, such as those of the Amalgamated Stevedores and Dockers and the Socialist Sunday Schools. In 1990 the Labour Party Archives were deposited and since then an archive centre has been developed based on collections of the British Labour Movement.

Acquisitions policy: The aim is to collect and make available the records of the political wing of the British Labour Movement.

Archives of organisation: Correspondence, circulars and minutes of the National Museum of Labour History.

Major Collections: Labour Party, archives, 1900–, including minutes of National Executive Committee and correspondence, 1900–.
Miniken/Vincent papers, chartist collection, 1837–41.
Michael Foot (*b* 1913), papers, 1926–90.
Amalgamated Stevedores and Dockers, minutes and correspondence, 1883–1982.
Labour and Socialist International, papers, 1917–57.
Socialist Sunday School Collection, 1904–73.
Communist Party of Great Britain, archives, 1943–92.

Non-manuscript material: Photographs, artefacts and banners.
Large pamphlet collection.
Journals relating to Labour history, including *Tribune, Commonweal* and *New Leader*.
Labour Party candidates, election addresses, 1900–70.

Finding aids: Most material has been sorted and listed; lists sent to NRA.

Facilities: Photocopying. Photographic services by arrangement with Manchester City Art Gallery. Microfilm/fiche reader.

Publications: Manchester Women's History Group Bibliography Project, 1993.

796 Manchester Cathedral

Address: Manchester M3 1SX

Telephone: (0161) 833 2220

Enquiries: The Archivist

Open: By arrangement.

Access: Bona fide scholars, by appointment.

Historical background: The cathedral is the ancient parish church of Manchester, formerly known as the Collegiate Church, founded in 1421. It became a cathedral in 1847.

Acquisitions policy: To maintain the parochial and capitular records.

Archives of organisation: The records of the collegiate foundation, including wardens' and fellows' Act books, 1635–20th century; charters, surveys and valuations relating to lands in the Manchester area, 1422–, and financial archives, 1861–. Records of the parish, including parish registers, 1573– (*c*450 vols).

Finding aids: Typewritten catalogue.

Facilities: Photocopying.

Publications: A.E.J. Hollander: 'The Muniment Room of Manchester Cathedral', *Archives*, i/5 (1951), 3–10.

797 Manchester Jewish Museum

Address: 190 Cheetham Hill Road, Manchester M8 8LW

Telephone: (0161) 834 9879
832 7353

Enquiries: The Director, Adrienne Wallman

Open: Mon–Thurs: 10.30–4.00 Sun: 10.30–5.00 Closed Christmas Day, Boxing Day and Jewish holidays.

Access: Generally open to the public; an appointment is always necessary.

The museum's collection includes archives developed out of a Jewish research project at Manchester Polytechnic in the 1970s. The museum opened in 1984 and actively acquires material relating to Manchester's Jewish community, primarily papers of Jewish families. Archives of Jewish organisations are in Manchester Local Studies Unit (entry **799**).

798 Manchester Literary & Philosophical Society

Address: 14 Kennedy Street, Manchester M2 4BY

Telephone: (0161) 228 3638/9

Enquiries: The Hon. Curator, A.L. Smyth

Open: Mon–Fri: 10.30–4.00

Access: Restricted use by the public; an appointment is necessary.

The society was instituted in 1781. Its archives were largely destroyed in 1940 and the surviving Dalton MSS are now in the possession of the John Rylands University Library (entry **806A**). Some deeds are deposited in the Manchester Local Studies Unit (entry **799**). The society houses the *Manchester Memoirs* (formerly *Memoirs and Proceedings*), 1781–. Material is collected on the history of the society and on selected members, and photocopying is available.

799 Manchester Local Studies Unit

Parent organisation: Manchester City Council

Address: Central Library, St Peter's Square, Manchester M2 5PD

Telephone: (0161) 234 1980 (Archives) 234 1979 (non-manuscript material)

Fax: (0161) 234 1963

Enquiries: The Local Studies Officer, Mr R.J. Bond

Open: Mon–Thurs: 10.00–8.00 Fri: 10.00–5.00

Access: Generally available, unless restricted by the terms of the deposit. Archive material must be booked at least 24 hours in advance. No restrictions on access to non-MS material.

Historical background: Manchester Public Libraries have collected local studies material (MS and printed) since the establishment of the service in 1852. A separate Local History Library was established in 1957, and an Archives Department in 1966. The two services were merged in 1991 to provide a combined archives and local studies service. The unit is recognised as a place of deposit for public

records and as the Diocesan Record Office for Manchester (diocesan and parish records).

Acquisitions policy: Records of the local authority, organisations and individuals within the City of Manchester; note, however, that the unit retains records for a wide area around Manchester which were acquired before the mid-1950s.

Archives of organisation: Manchester Public Library archive.

Major collections: Manchester Branch of the National Union of Women's Suffrage Societies, 1867–1919; papers of Mrs Millicent Garrett Fawcett LLD, on women's suffrage etc, 1871–1919.
Manchester Chamber of Commerce minutes, 1794–1964.
Records of the Strutt Mills at Derby, Milford and Cromford, Derbyshire, 1780–1936, and Samuel Greg's Quarry Bank Mill, Styal, Cheshire, 1788–1937.
Papers of Dr William Farrer, editor of Victoria County History of Lancashire, 16th–20th centuries.
Letters, mostly from politicians, to George Wilson, chairman of the Anti-Corn Law League, 1827–85; letters to John Benjamin Smith, MP, 1832–74.
Records of the Lancashire, later the National, Public School Association, 1848–62.
Parish records for the Diocese of Manchester, 16th–20th centuries; Methodist records of circuit and chapels in the Manchester and Stockport district, 18th–20th centuries; records of the Society of Friends, Hardshaw East, monthly and preparative meetings, 17th–20th centuries.
Records of many Manchester Jewish organisations.

Non-manuscript material: Prints and photographs (c143,000), maps (c13,000), broadsides (c6600), and several hundred press cutting volumes. Microforms (c14,000) include local census returns, newspapers, parish registers (including many for Lancashire and Cheshire), directories, electoral registers; also the International Genealogical Index for the British Isles and the National Probate Index, 1858–1930.

Finding aids: Lists and calendars, sent to NRA. Name, place and subject indexes to the calendars.

Facilities: Photocopying. Photography. Microfilm/fiche readers, with print-out service.

Conservation: Work shared by the library's

own bindery and the Greater Manchester County Record Office (entry **794**).

800 Manchester Metropolitan University

Address: All Saints Building, Oxford Road, Manchester M15 6BH

Telephone: (0161) 247 6100

Fax: (0161) 247 6349

Enquiries: The University Librarian, Professor C. Harris

Open: Term: Mon–Thurs: 9.00–9.00 Fri: 9.00–4.45 Vacation: Mon–Fri: 9.00–4.30

Access: Approved external readers, on written application.

Historical background: Manchester Polytechnic was created in 1970, when the Regional College of Art, the John Dalton College of Technology and the Manchester College of Commerce merged. Didsbury College of Education and Hollings College were also brought into the polytechnic in 1977. Further mergers took place in 1983 with the City of Manchester College of Higher Education and in 1992 with Crewe and Alsager College of Higher Education. University status was granted in 1992. The Jimmy Deane Archive has been transferred to the Modern Records Centre, University of Warwick (entry **229**).

Acquisitions policy: To strengthen existing undergraduate research collections in subject areas taught in the university and to acquire specialised materials where necessary.

Major collections: Barnett Freedman Archive: substantial correspondence, books illustrated and dustwrappers designed by Barnett Freedman (1901–58).
Parry Archive: original illustrations, books illustrated and written by Charles James Parry (1824–94).
John Farleigh Archive: correspondence, illustrations, wood-blocks.
Cotton Collection: documents connected with the Lancashire cotton industry, 20th century.

Non-manuscript material: Seddon Collection: Victorian greetings cards (*c*31,000).
Book Design Collection: books demonstrating physical aspects of book production, 19th century–.

Children's Book Collections: 19th– and 20th–century children's books and periodicals.
Manchester Society of Architects Library: historical books on 18th– and 19th–century architecture.
Sir Harry Page Collection of Victorian Ephemera: albums and commonplace books and individual items collected into scrapbooks.
Home Studies Collections: books on cooking and household management, 17th–mid-20th century.

Facilities: Photocopying. Microfilm reader/printers.

Publications: W.H. Shercliff: *Morality to Adventure: Manchester Polytechnic's Collection of Children's Books, 1840–1939* (1988).
G. Smith: *Sentimental Souvenirs: Victorian Scrap Albums from the Sir Harry Page Collection* (1989).
I. Rogerson: *Barnett Freedman: Painter, Draughtsman, Lithographer* (1990).
G. Smith: *Trade Catalogues: a Hundred Years 1850–1949* (1992).
L. Seddon: *A Gallery of Greetings: a Guide to the Seddon Collection* (1992).
I. Rogerson: *The John Farleigh Collection* (1993).

801 Museum of Science and Industry in Manchester Library and Record Centre

Address: Liverpool Road, Castlefield, Manchester M3 4FP

Telephone: (0161) 832 2244 exts 256/275

Fax: (0161) 833 2184

Enquiries: The Senior Archivist

Open: Tues, Thurs: 1.00–4.30 Mon, Wed, Fri: by appointment.

Access: Generally open to the public. Some records are subject to a 30–year closure period. There is an entrance charge to the museum, but free admission to the Library and Record Centre by appointment. The centre is accessible by lift.

Historical background: The Museum of Science and Industry opened in the world's oldest surviving passenger railway station in 1983. Its collections incorporate those developed by the North Western Museum of Science and Technology (f. 1969). The Library and Record

Centre is the searchroom and study centre for the museum.

Acquisitions policy: To acquire records, photographs and secondary material relating to the scientific, technological, industrial, social and economic development of the Greater Manchester region, with national collections relating to the electricity, gas and paper industries.

Archives of organisation: Corporate, departmental and project records relating to the museum's development.

Major collections: Archives of the Electricity Council, 1957–90, and predecessor bodies, including Central Electricity Board 1927–48, British Electricity Authority, 1947–54, Central Electricity Authority, 1955–57, and British Electrical Development Association, 1919–66.
Business records, including Daniel Adamson & Co., Hyde, steam turbine manufacturers, c1865–1976; Beyer Peacock & Co., Gorton locomotive and machine-tool builders, 1854–1966; Joseph Cockshoot & Co. Ltd, Manchester, coach and motor-car body builders, 1867–1965; Craven Brothers Ltd, Reddish, machine-tool makers, 1860–1967; A.V. Roe & Co., aircraft manufacturers; papers of Roy Chadwick (1893–1947), chief designer, and Jimmy Orrell (1903–88), chief test pilot; Mather and Platt, Manchester, engineers; Crossley Brothers, Manchester engine manufacturers, c1890–c1960; W.T. Glover & Co. Ltd, Trafford Park, electric cable makers, 1868–c1968.
John Alcock and Arthur Whitten-Brown: papers relating to transatlantic flight, 1919.

Non-manuscript material: Calico Printers Association and Birch Vale collections of fabric samples, 1795–1946; Dimoldenberg design samples, c1920–1965.
National Paper Museum collections, including Clayton-Beadle, Clapperton, Schieland watermark collections; J.B. Green and Wakeman collections of paper samples; library of publications relating to papermaking history.
Prints, photographs, engineering drawings, trade literature.

Finding aids: Handlists. Card index. Computer database of images in Beyer Peacock Archive. Lists sent to NRA.

Facilities: Photocopying. Photography. Microfilm/fiche reader.

Publications: P. Webb and E. Sprenger: 'Persuading the Housewife to Use Electricity? An Interpretation of Material in the Electricity Council Archive', *British Journal for the History of Science*, 26 (1993).
Electricity Council Archive Handlist and Guide (1994).
Catalogue of Photographic Images in the Beyer Peacock Archive (1995).

802 National Archive for the History of Computing

Parent organisation: University of Manchester

Address: Centre for the History of Science, Technology and Medicine, Mathematics Tower, The University, Manchester M13 9PL

Telephone: (0161) 275 5850

Fax: (0161) 273 1123

Enquiries: The Director

Open: Mon–Fri: 10.00–5.00, by appointment.

Access: Generally open to the public, by arrangement.

Historical background: The NAHC was founded in 1987 within the Centre for the History of Science, Technology and Medicine at Manchester University in collaboration with the Department of Computer Sciences and the John Rylands Library (entry **806A**).

Acquisitions policy: Materials relating to the development of computing in Britain, including company records, personal papers, advertising literature and ephemera, but excluding technical product literature and manuals.

Major collections: International Computers Ltd (ICL) historical collection, c1900–.
Computer records of the National Research Development Corporation, 1949–65.
Records of the Department of Computer Science, University of Manchester, 1946–.
Open System Interconnection, (OSI), records, British Standards Institution, 1978–.

Non-manuscript material: Photographic collection of 20th–century punched-card and computing machinery. Computer industry film and slide collections.
Oral history collection.

Finding aids: Catalogue.

Facilities: Photocopying.

803 North West Film Archive

Parent organisation: Manchester Metropolitan Univeristy

Address: Minshull House, 47–49 Chorlton Street, Manchester M1 3EU

Telephone: (0161) 247 3097

Fax: (0161) 247 3098

Enquiries: The Librarian, Marion Hewitt

Open: Mon–Fri: 9.30–4.30 Viewings by prior appointment only.

Access: Generally open to the public. All viewings are on the premises, supervised, and on an appointment basis. Discretion is exercised where material is in poor physical condition and a viewing copy does not exist.

Historical background: The North West Film Archive (NWFA) grew out of a research project into the history of the local film industry. It was established in 1977 by Manchester Polytechnic (now Manchester Metropolitan University) and the North West Arts Association (now North West Arts Board). The project concentrated on the location and acquisition of film that was made in or about the North-West of England. The success of this search, together with the demand for a documentary collection within the region and the urgent need for specialist preservation work, led to the establishment of a regional film archive.

Acquisitions policy: Documentary material about life in Lancashire, Cheshire and Greater Manchester, and to a lesser extent Merseyside, 1896–. All film gauges are included and the archive also acquires master video tapes. The collection includes cinema newsreels, documentaries, promotional material, television programmes, home movies and other amateur footage.

Non-manuscript material: Films of local events and traditions such as Whit Walks; life at work, e.g. textile industry; leisure activities such as sport; holidaying throughout the region, particularly Blackpool; street scenes; life on the home front in the two world wars; local personalities, such as Gracie Fields.

Corporate collections include Co-operative Wholesale Society films and the Manchester Ship Canal Company Collection.

Extensive collections of television programmes from BBC North and Channel 4, with restrictions on access.

Copy photographs, taped interviews, posters, advertising material and ephemera on the north-west cinema industry.

Finding aids: Computerised database of more than 1000 titles within the film and video collection, by title, date, subject, place and producer. Also detailed shot lists for many.

Facilities: A range of specialised equipment for film, video and sound. Facility to transfer 16mm film to video tape.

Conservation: All conservation work is undertaken in-house. Film copying is undertaken by external professional laboratories.

Publications: *Moving Memories* video series: compilation videos showcasing the archive's collections.

M. Gomes: *The Picture House* (1988) [a photographic album of north-west film and cinema].

804 Portico Library and Gallery

Address: 57 Mosley Street, Manchester M2 3HY

Telephone: (0161) 236 6785

Enquiries: The Librarian, Mrs Jo Francis

Open: Mon–Fri: 9.30–4.30

The Portico is a private subscription library dating from 1806. The archives are a comprehensive record of the library from its foundation, including minute books, annual reports, library acquisition and issue books, members' subscription books, letter-books and press cuttings. Any interested person may consult the archives and there is a detailed list available.

805 Royal Northern College of Music

Address: The Library, 124 Oxford Road, Manchester M13 9RD

Telephone: (0161) 273 6283

Enquiries: The Librarian, Anthony Hodges

Open: Term: Mon–Wed: 9.00–7.00 Sat: 9.00–1.00 Vacation: Mon–Fri: 9.00–1.00; 2.00–4.30 Closed August.

Access: Generally open to the public, by appointment only.

Historical background: The RNCM was

founded in 1972 from an amalgamation of the Royal Manchester College of Music (f. 1893) and the Northern School of Music (f. 1920).

Acquisitions policy: To maintain and consolidate the collections.

Major collections: MS compositions of Alan Rawsthorne (1905–71).
Dame Eva Turner Collection of songs with MS annotations.
Memorabilia of Philip Newman and Adolph Brodsky (1851–1929).
Correspondence of Sir Charles Hallé (1819–95) (*c*200 items).
John Ogdon Archive.

Non-manuscript material: First editions of Handel, Gluck and other 18th– century music.
Hansen Collection of 20th-century Scandinavian music.
Henry Watson Collection of historical music instruments.
Halifax Collection of scores and piano music; Gordon Green collection of piano music.

Finding aids: Card catalogue. Computer catalogue.

Facilities: Photocopying. Microfilm/fiche readers.

806 University of Manchester
John Rylands University Library

Address: Deansgate, Manchester M3 3EH

A Library

Telephone: (0161) 834 5343/6765

Fax: (0161) 834 5574

Enquiries: The Administrator, Dr Peter McNiven

Open: Mon–Fri: 10.00–5.30 Sat: 10.00–1.00, preferably by appointment.

Access: Manchester University reader's ticket holders; approved researchers, on written application.

Historical background: The library was formed by the merger in 1972 of the library of the University of Manchester (f. 1851) and the John Rylands Library (f. 1900). Most MS collections are housed in the former John Rylands Library in Deansgate, notable exceptions being the university's own archives, the *Manchester Guardian* archive and the Manchester Medical Society archives, which are at the University Library, Oxford Road, Manchester M13 9PP.

Acquisitions policy: To strengthen existing collections, by purchase, donation or deposit.

Archives of organisation: University archive, with papers of a number of academics, including W.S. Jevons (1835–82) and Professor T.F. Tout (1855–1929).

Major collections: Oriental collections: including papyri, Hebrew (400 codices and *c*10,000 fragments); Arabic, Persian and Turkish codices (*c*2000); Indian, South-East Asian and Far Eastern collections in 30 languages.
Western MSS: medieval MSS, many from libraries of famous collectors, particularly rich in Latin MSS of early Germanic and Italian provenance.
Charter Rooms: extensive deeds, genealogical and family papers and other material, relating mainly to Cheshire, Lancashire, Derbyshire, Yorkshire, Warwickshire, Lincolnshire and Suffolk, 12th–20th centuries.
Other collections include the following:
Clinton Papers, with ancillary collections relating to Peninsular War and Napoleonic period.
Melville and Pitt Papers and much other material concerning British rule in India.
Papers of FM Sir Claude Auchinleck (1884–1980).
Thrale-Piozzi MSS relating to Johnson circle (3000 items).
Correspondence of John Ruskin and his circle (2000 letters).
Collections of British artists, especially correspondence of Holman Hunt and Pre-Raphaelites.
Papers of modern writers and actor/producers, including Basil Dean, director.
Papers of John Dalton (1766–1844), scientist.
Archives of businesses, especially textile industry, in particular Samuel Oldknow, early cotton industry records, late 18th century–.
Archival collections from Hartley Victoria Methodist College, the Unitarian and Congregational colleges of Manchester and the Moravian Collection.
Manchester Guardian archive.
Manchester Medical Society archives.
Extensive autograph letter collection.

Non-manuscript material: Maps, plans etc, and all supporting materials of a major university library.

Finding aids: Lists and indexes of some collections. Some lists sent to NRA, including university archives: NRA 16039, 18558.

Facilities: Photocopying. Photography. Microfilming. Microfilm/fiche reader/printer.

Conservation: In-house bindery and conservation unit, based in the main university library, with an outpost at Deansgate.

Publications: Many published handlists and catalogues, several of which have appeared in the library *Bulletin* (thrice yearly). Publications list available.

B Methodist Archives and Research Centre

Telephone: (0161) 834 5343/6765

Fax: (0161) 834 5574

Enquiries: The Methodist Church Archivist, Mr Peter Nockles

Open: Mon–Fri: 9.00–5.00 Sat: am, by appointment.

Access: Approved readers, on written application. There is an embargo placed on certain material, and written permission for access to these items must first be obtained from the secretary of the Methodist Church.

Historical background: Established in 1961 by the Methodist Church, the centre was formerly housed in Epworth House, City Road, London. In 1977 the collection was transferred to Manchester, but Wesley's Chapel, London (tel. 0171 253 2262), retains a small amount of material and is developing a film and sound archive relating to Methodism. The collection remains the property of the Methodist Church and consists of books and MSS devoted to the religious history of the denomination and the doctrinal theological controversies relating thereto. Material relating to circuits and churches, and also more recent district material, is deposited in local authority record offices or agreed repositories.

Acquisitions policy: To strengthen existing primary and secondary collections in the history of Methodism and allied subjects, by purchase and donation.

Archives of organisation: Material of a connexional nature, 1739–, including agendas, conference papers and minutes and district synod minutes. Other material, 1700–.

Major collections: J.J. Colman Collection: surviving diaries and sermon notebooks of John Wesley (1703–91).

E.S. Lamplough Collection: letters of John Wesley and other members of the family.

Preachers' Letters and Portraits Section: letters of Methodist ministers, mainly 18th and 19th centuries (*c*50,000), and their diaries and journals (*c*100).

J.T. Wilkinson Collection: letters of Professor A.S. Peak (1865–1929) (*c*4000) and other documents relating to the history of Hartley Victoria College and to Primitive Methodism (11,500 items).

National and district, but not circuit, records. Much material from the various divisions of the Methodist Church, including home missions, finance, social responsibility, ministries, education and youth and property; also from the forces board and conference office, Humnaby Methodist Girls' School, Filey (now closed), and the diaconal order.

No genealogical, baptismal or burial records.

Non-manuscript material: 18th–century editions of Wesley's works (2000 vols); Charles Wesley's library (500 vols); John Fletcher's library (130 vols).

Pamphlets (6000).

Periodicals (more than 5000); hymn books (3000); circuit plans (4000).

Books by Methodist authors; local histories, engravings, portraits and photographs.

Finding aids: Detailed catalogues and finding aids are available for consultation in the Deansgate building of the library. Lists sent to NRA. Calendar and indexes for several major collections, including Wesley family and Thomas Coke.

Facilities: Photocopying. Photography. Microfilms. Colour slides and all other kinds of work may be supplied.

Conservation: In-house.

Publications: D.W. Riley: 'The Methodist Archives and Research Centre', *Bulletin of the John Rylands University Library of Manchester*, lx, 269; lxii, 3.

——: *Proceedings of the Wesley Historical Society*, xli, 139; xlii, 116; xliii, 18; xlvi, 70.

W.F. Swift: *Proceedings of the Wesley Historical Society*, xxxiii, 79.

J.C. Bowmer: *Methodist Magazine* (1963), 251, 288, 335, 368, 413, 452; (1964), 9, 50, 104, 128, 172, 217, 249, 293, 330, 377, 413, 457.

H.L. Calkin (comp.): *Catalog of Methodist Archival and MSS Collections* [worldwide]. List of catalogues and handlists for sale, available from centre.

807 University of Manchester Institute of Science and Technology

Address: PO Box 88, Manchester M60 1QD

Telephone: (0161) 236 3311

Fax: (0161) 200 4941

Enquiries: Mr P.J. Short, ext. 4933 or Mr J.O. Marsh, ext. 3948

Open: By arrangement.

Access: Generally open to the public.

Historical background: Founded as the Manchester Mechanics' Institution in 1824, it was renamed Manchester Technical School in 1883 and Manchester Municipal School of Technology in 1902. It was incorporated as the Faculty of Technology in the University of Manchester in 1905, renamed Manchester Municipal College of Technology in 1918, and Manchester College of Science and Technology in 1955. It was awarded a Royal Charter as an independent university in 1956 and renamed University of Manchester Institute of Science and Technology in 1966.

Acquisitions policy: Material to support the teaching and research of the institute.

Archives of organisation: Records of UMIST and its predecessors, 1824–; some departments retain their own archives as well.

Major collections: Records of the National Federation of Building Trade Operatives, 1918–76.
Note-books and some correspondence of J.P. Joule (1818–89), scientist.

Non-manuscript material: Joule Collection: library of J.P. Joule.
UMIST theses.

Finding aids: Joule: NRA 9527.

Facilities: Photocopying. Microfilm/fiche reader/printers.

808 Central Coal Benefits Archive Centre

Parent organisation: British Coal Corporation

Address: 200 Lichfield Lane, Mansfield, Notts NG18 4RG

Telephone: (01623) 22681 ext. 234

Fax: (01623) 423468

Enquiries: The Head of the Archive Centre, Mr B. Thornton

Open: Mon–Fri: 9.00–4.00

Access: Access to the general public for certain records held at the centre; appointments are necessary.

The centre maintains post-nationalisation records from all departments of the industry for England and Wales pending their transfer to the Public Record Office (entry **960**). Certain pre-nationalisation records (up to 1947) were distributed to relevant county record offices (lists of these deposits are kept at the archive centre). There is also a major photographic archive of the industry. Lists and indexes and photocopying are available.

809 Mansfield Library

Parent organisation: Nottinghamshire County Council

Address: Four Seasons Centre, Westgate, Mansfield, Notts NG18 1NH

Telephone: (01623) 27591

Fax: (01623) 29276

Enquiries: The Local Studies Librarian, Mr D. Crute

Open: Mon, Thurs, Fri: 9.00–7.00 Tues: 9.30–7.00 Wed: 9.00–5.00 Sat: 9.00–1.00

Access: Generally open to the public.

Acquisitions policy: Donations and deposits are accepted if donors are unwilling to let material out of the town; the Nottinghamshire Archives Office (entry **859**) is the designated repository.

Major collections: Mansfield Borough and successor district diaries, 1892–, and council minutes, 1928–.
Note-books of Albert Sorby Buxton (1867–1932).

Correspondence of Joseph Whitaker (1850–1932).

Non-manuscript material: Photographs, slides, prints and picture postcards of Mansfield and environs, 1870–.

Parish registers up to 1900; census returns of Mansfield and nearby towns and villages in Nottinghamshire; local newspapers, 1846–; wills made within the area of the Peculiar Court of the Manor of Mansfield, 1640–1857 (microform).

Oral history recordings with transcripts.

Finding aids: Archive material is catalogued, classified and indexed by subject. Nottinghamshire Archives have a list of major items. Place and subject index to photographs, slides, prints and picture postcards on cards. Subject and place index to *Mansfield and North Nottinghamshire Advertiser*, 1871–1950. Card index to wills.

Facilities: Photocopying. Microfilm/fiche readers/printer.

Conservation: Work undertaken by Nottinghamshire Archive Office conservation unit.

Publications: The census returns have published surname indexes, compiled by the Nottinghamshire Family History Society.

810 Margate Central Library
Local History Collection

Address: Cecil Square, Margate, Kent CT9 1RE

Telephone: (01843) 223626

Fax: (01843) 293015

Enquiries: The Heritage Office, Penny Ward

Open: Tues, Fri: 2.00–6.00 First Sat in month: 9.30–1.00; 2.00–5.00

Access: Generally open to the public.

Historical background: The basis of the Margate Local History Collection was the bequest of a local antiquary, Dr Arthur Rowe, in 1926. It consisted of every kind of material relevant to the development of Margate, which he was researching in order to write and illustrate a parish history. The collection has continued to be augmented by purchases and donations.

Acquisitions policy: To acquire material relating to Margate, by purchase, donation and loan.

Major collections: Rowe MSS: part of Rowe Collection, documenting streets, buildings, local families, sea bathing, archaeology, 1900–20.

Pridden MSS: a description of the Isle of Thanet in Kent, by Rev. John Pridden, 1780–90, including 100 original drawings; *c*100 letters of John Anderson relating to the founders of the Sea Bathing Hospital; pedigrees of Thanet families (copy on microfilm).

Edward White's MS extracts from Kent newspapers, archives, state and domestic papers, parish registers, gravestones; W.J. Mercer's scrapbooks and indexes, 1850–1900.

Non-manuscript material: Rowe Collection: more than 2000 items relating to Margate, including books, pamphlets, programmes, maps, illustrations, plans, photographs, bills, posters.

Parker Collection: more than 10,000 items relating to Kent, including books, pamphlets, maps, 7000 prints and 1000 illustrations.

Other items include press cuttings, illustrations and ephemera, scrapbooks covering Margate and Kent, photographs, postcards and many guide books and directories.

Finding aids: Catalogue. Some original indexes. The collection is being exhaustively recatalogued, with a computer index to the illustrations.

Facilities: Photocopying. Photography by arrangement. Microfilm readers/printer.

811 Marlborough College Archives

Parent organisation: Marlborough College

Address: Marlborough, Wilts SN8 1PA

Telephone: (01672) 515511 ext. 207

Fax: (01672) 516234

Enquiries: The Archivist, Mr D.R.C. West

Open: Mostly Mon and Thurs in term time, but very flexible, being part- time, retired archivist.

Access: Bona fide researchers on written application. Restricted access to personal files.

The college was founded in 1843 as an independent boarding school with a few day pupils. Girls were admitted to the sixth form in 1968 and the college has been co-educational since 1989. The archival collections were first organised in the 1950s and documents and memorabilia appertaining to the college and its former pupils are actively collected. There is extensive documentation of the foundation and earlier years of the college, including architectural drawings, and a large collection of pupils' reminiscences. A partial computerised index exists and photocopying is available. See T. Hinde: *Paths of Progress: a History of Marlborough College* (James and James, 1992); A.G. Bradley and J. Murray: *History of Marlborough College* (1893, 1923).

812 Derbyshire Library Service
Local Studies Department

Parent organisation: British Coal Corporation

Address: County Offices, Matlock, Derbyshire DE4 3AG

Telephone: (01629) 580000 ext. 6579

Fax: (01629) 585363

Enquiries: The Librarian, Mrs J. Radford

Open: Mon–Fri: 9.00–5.00 Sat: 9.30–1.00, by appointment only.

Access: Generally open to the public.

Historical background: The Local Studies Department was originally housed in the Central Lending Library, St Mary's Gate, Derby. The collections were moved to Matlock in 1966 and housed in the branch library, and transferred to the county offices in 1969.

Acquisitions policy: To strengthen and enlarge existing primary and secondary collections on the county of Derbyshire.

Major collections: Peach Collection: MS and printed play, film and radio scripts of L. du Garde Peach (1890–1975), Derbyshire dramatist.
Barmasters Library: includes, in addition to printed material, MSS, account books and ledgers relating to lead-mining industry in Derbyshire, 1730–1915.

Non-manuscript material: Wolley MSS (British Museum Add MSS 6666–6718), on microfilm, covering Derbyshire; MSS 6676–6686 relate to the Derbyshire lead-mining industry.
Census returns for Derbyshire and some small portion of surrounding counties, 1841–91 (on microfilm).
Derby Mercury, 1735–1800; *Derbyshire Times*, 1854–; *Derbyshire Courier*, 1831–53; *High Peak News*, 1890–1959; *Matlock Mercury*, 1937– (on microfilm).
Illustrations covering all aspects of Derbyshire life (c2500).
Maps, historical and modern, of the county (various scales).
A wide range of genealogical research materials, including St Catherine's House indexes, 1839–1911; International Genealogical Index: Quaker registers, Roman Catholic registers (microfilm).

Finding aids: Various lists and indexes. Card index to Wolley MSS.

Facilities: Photocopying. Microfilm/fiche reader/printer.

Publications: *Catalogue and Indexes of the British Museum Additional MSS 6676–6686* (Derbyshire County Library, 1977).
Derbyshire Local Studies Collections: a Guide to Resources (Derbyshire Library Service, rev. 1988).
Family History in Derbyshire (1994).
List of library publications available on request.

813 Derbyshire Record Office

Parent organisation: Derbyshire County Council

Address: Postal: County Education Department, County Offices, Matlock, Derbyshire DE4 3AG
Record Office: New Street, Matlock, Derbyshire

Telephone: (01629) 580000 ext. 7347 (01629) 35207

Fax: (01629) 57611

Enquiries: The County and Diocesan Archivist, Dr Margaret O'Sullivan

Open: Mon–Fri: 9.30–4.45

Access: User registration is required, with proof of identity and address; an appointment is advisable. There is a charge for research services.

Historical background: Derbyshire Record Office was established in 1962, although archive collections had been acquired earlier. It is the Diocesan Record Office for the Diocese of Derby and is recognised as a place of deposit for public records and for manorial and tithe records.

Acquisitions policy: Archival material of all types, of Derbyshire origin: official, ecclesiastical, industrial, business, family and estate.

Archives of organisation: Archives of Derbyshire County Council and its predecessors; ecclesiastical parishes in the diocese of Derby; superseded local authorities and institutions throughout Derbyshire.

Major collections: National Coal Board, Derbyshire colliery records of pre-vesting date. Lead-mining and related records, 17th–19th centuries.
Engineering company records, late 18th–20th centuries.
Private deposits, including:
Estate papers of Harpur-Crewe of Calke, 12th–20th centuries.
Fitzherbert of Tissington papers, including Treby papers concerning the Titus Oates plot and papers of Lord St Helens (1753–1839), diplomat.
Gell of Hopton and Trustees papers, including civil war papers, 17th century.
Longsdon of Little Longstone papers, including textile manufacturing interest, 18th century.
Catton Hall archive, including political papers of Sir Robert Wilmot *re* Ireland, mid-18th century, and Sir Robert John Wilmot Horton *re* population, emigration and slavery, 1820s-1830s.

Non-manuscript material: Strutt Collection of printed Derbyshire topographical material, late 19th century.

Finding aids: Catalogues, card indexes, handlists. Lists sent to NRA.

Facilities: Photocopying. Photography. Microfilming. Microfilm/fiche readers/printers.

Conservation: In-house.

Publications: Handlist of Tithe Maps (1992).
Handlist of Enclosure Maps (1992).
Derbyshire Record Office Guide (2/1994).
List of Derbyshire Parish Registers (1994).
List of Derbyshire Non-Conformist Registers (1994).
Archives First (1994) [series of introductions to Derbyshire Archives].
Full list of publications available on request.

814 National Tramway Museum

Parent Organisation: Tramway Museum Society

Address: Crich, Matlock, Derbyshire DE4 5DP

Telephone: (01773) 852565

Fax: (01773) 852326

Enquiries: The Librarian, Mrs R. Thacker

Open: Mon–Fri: 9.00–5.00

Access: Generally open to the public, by appointment.

Historical background: The Tramway Museum Society was formed in 1955 to preserve tramcars and associated material. The museum premises were acquired in 1959. The depots accommodate over 50 horse, steam and electric tramcars. The library is housed in its own air-conditioned building.

Acquisitions policy: Material relevant to tramways and LRT systems worldwide is acquired, by donation or bequest.

Archives of organisation: Records of the Tramway Museum Society, 1964–, including annual reports.

Major collections: Production records and official photos of Edgard Allen Ltd, Sheffield, tramway equipment manufacturers.
Minutes of the Municipal Tramways and Transport Association and the Municipal Passenger Transport Association.
Records of transport operators, including those previously lodged with the Bus and Coach Council.

Non-manuscript material: Manufacturers and transport department drawings, including Maley & Taunton, Glasgow.
Large photographic collection, including R.B. Parr, N. Forbes and H.B.Priestley.
Film archive (*c*400).

Finding aids: Computer catalogue (not photographs). List sent to NRA.

Facilities: Photography. Photocopying. Microfilm reader.

815 Society of the Holy Child Jesus Provincial Archives

Parent organisation: Society of the Holy Child Jesus

Address: Convent of the Holy Child, Mayfield, East Sussex TN20 6PH

Telephone: (01435) 873667

Enquiries: The Archivist, Sr Winifred Wickens

Open: By arrangement.

Access: Anyone with a genuine interest or connection.

The Society of the Holy Child was established in 1846 by the Venerable Cornelia Connelly as a teaching order. The archives contain material relevant to convents in England, Ireland and France, documenting the lives of the Sisters and the work of the society. Any material relevant to the society, including schools where the Sisters worked, is collected. Lists and indexes are available.

816 Merthyr Tydfil Central Library

Address: High Street, Merthyr Tydfil, Mid Glamorgan CF47 8AF

Telephone: (01685) 723057

Enquiries: The Assistant Chief Officer (Libraries), Leisure and Amenities Department, Mr G.H. James

Open: Mon–Fri: 9.00–6.30 Sat: 9.00–12.00

Access: Generally open to the public.

Historical background: The Central Library opened in 1935.

Acquisitions policy: Primary and secondary material relating to the Merthyr Tydfil area.

Major collections: Borough Council minutes and County Borough Council and education minutes, 19th–20th centuries.
Rate books and rate account books of the iron masters, 19th century.
Dowlais Iron Company letters (at Dowlais Library, Church Street, Dowlais, Merthyr Tydfil).

Non-manuscript material: Photographic collection.
Maps, including OS maps of the Merthyr Tydfil area, 1832–, and later surveys.
Extensive collection of pamphlets and photocopied material.
Oral history collection; small collection of cine and video material.
Merthyr Express, 1864–; *Merthyr Guardian,* 1833–74; *Western Mail,* 1960– (microfilm).
Census returns, 1841–91.
Bishops transcripts, 1717–, and chapel records, 1786–1837 (microfilm).
Register of electors, 1890– (incomplete).

Finding aids: Material is filed by subject with a separate author/title index.

Facilities: Photocopying. Microfilm/fiche reader.

Publications: Guide to the Local History Collection (1976).
Bibliography (1982); *Supplement* (1984).

817 Methil Public Library

Parent organisation: Kirkcaldy District Council

Address: Wellesley Road, Methil, Fife KY8 3QR

Telephone: (01333) 427229

Fax: via (01592) 643399 (Library HQ, Kirkcaldy)

Enquiries: The Librarian-in-Charge, Mrs Jennifer Taylor

Open: Mon–Thurs: 10.00–7.00 Fri–Sat: 10.00–5.00

Access: Open to legitimate enquirers.

The library does not acquire MSS but holds the Proudfoot-Hutt collections of David Proudfoot, a local miner, and G. Allen Hutt, a journalist, 1920s–1940s, comprising posters, pamphlets, newspapers and correspondence, but especially concerning the 1926 General Strike; see NRA(S) 1878. Photocopying is available.

818 Claydon House

Parent organisation: Claydon House Trust

Address: Claydon House, Middle Claydon, Bucks MK18 2EY

Enquiries: The Archivist, Mrs Susan Ranson

Open: By arrangement.

Access: Bona fide researchers, by written application: a daily charge is made.

Historical background: Claydon House has been the home of the Verney family since the 17th century. It is now administered by the National Trust. A member of the Verney family lives in the house, and the archives are managed by a special trust set up for that purpose.

Acquisitions policy: To maintain the archives.

Archives of organisation: Verney family archives, including deeds, 12th century–, estate papers, and letters.

Correspondence of Sir Ralph Verney (1613–98) (microfilm copies at Buckinghamshire Record Office (entry **35**), the British Library (entry **495A**) and Yale University).

Major collections: Nightingale Papers: letters of the Nightingale family, 1796–1874; correspondence of Florence Nightingale (1820–1910) with Frances Parthenope Nightingale (later Verney) and other members of the Verney family, 1827–1910 (photocopies at the Wellcome Institute (entry **768**)).

Non-manuscript material: Maps and plans.

Finding aids: Catalogue now finished and shortly to be available at Buckinghamshire Record Office and NRA. The Verney letters are arranged chronologically but not listed.

Facilities: Photocopying.

Publications: F.P. Verney and M.M. Verney (eds): *Memoirs of the Verney Family*, 4 vols (1892–9; 1970) [relates to the 17th century].
M.M. Verney and P. Abercrombie: 'Letters of an Eighteenth Century Architect, Sir Thomas Robinson Bart., to Ralph, 2nd Earl of Verney', *Architectural Review*, lix (1926), 258–63; lx (1926), 1–3, 50–3, 92–3.
S. Goldie (comp.): *A Calendar of the Letters of Florence Nightingale* (Oxford, c1977; microfiche) [includes the Claydon House letters].

819 Cleveland County Archives Department

Address: Exchange House, 6 Marton Road, Middlesbrough, Cleveland TS1 1DB

Telephone: (01642) 248321

Enquiries: The County Archivist, Mr D.H. Tyrell

Open: Mon, Wed, Thurs: 9.00–5.00 Tues: 9.00–9.00 Fri: 9.00–4.30

Access: Generally open to the public. The office operates the CARN reader's ticket system.

Historical background: The office was established in 1974 following the creation of Cleveland County, comprising the former county boroughs of Teesside and Hartlepool and parts of the former counties of Durham and the North Riding of Yorkshire. Very few collections had been deposited before this. Collections have also been transferred from the Central Library, Victoria Square. The department acts as the Diocesan Record Office for York (Cleveland parish records), and is recognised as a place of deposit for public records.

Archives of organisation: Usual local authority record holdings.

Major collections: Deposited collections, all of purely local interest.

Non-manuscript material: Sound archives of Radio Cleveland, 1971–.

Facilities: Photocopying. Photography. Microfilm/fiche reader/printers, by arrangement.

Conservation: In-house facilities.

Publications: *Cleveland County Archives: Brief Guide* [continually revised].

820 Rochdale Libraries
Local Studies Collection

Address: Middleton Area Central Library, Long Street, Middleton, Greater Manchester M24 3DU

Telephone: (0161) 643 5228

Enquiries: The Assistant Librarians, Mrs P.M. Elliott and Mrs H.M. Haynes or The Local Studies Librarian at Rochdale Library (entry **963**).

Open: Mon: 10.00–7.30 Tues, Fri: 10.00–5.30 Wed: 10.00–12.30 Sat: 9.30–1.00; 2.00–4.00

Access: Generally open to the public.

Historical background: The dynamic growth of Rochdale, Middleton and Heywood during the 19th century produced a wealth of material relating to the area. Before 1974 the substantial local collections of Heywood, Middleton and Rochdale were located at the central libraries in those areas, and on local government reorganisation it was decided that each should retain a separate collection under the general supervision of a local studies librarian based at Rochdale.

Acquisitions policy: The collection of documentary material relating to all aspects of life in the area of the Metropolitan Borough of

Rochdale and its previously independent constituent authorities.

Major collections: Local administrative records: early administrative records, including highway rates, Poor Law administration and administrative material from the constituent authorities of the metropolitan borough, 19th century; includes Middleton Poor Book, 1838, and Sheffield Rental, 1784.
Church records: church rates, leys, tithe commutation maps, plans, deeds etc.

Non-manuscript material: Complete runs of local newspapers, 1877– (originals and microfilm copies).
Books, pamphlets, audio-visual material, photographs, maps, plans, broadsheets, political handbills, theatre posters.

Finding aids: Calendar of archival material. Newspaper index.

Facilities: Photocopying. Microfilm/fiche readers/printer.

Publications: *Introduction to Local Studies Collections* (1981).

821 Heatherbank Museum of Social Work

Address: Glasgow Caledonian University, 1 Park Drive, Glasgow G3 6LP

Telephone: (0141) 337 4402

Enquiries: The Curator, Alastair Ramage

Open: Mon–Fri, Sun: 2.00–5.00

Access: Reference and Picture Library are generally open to the public. An appointment is preferred.

Historical background: The Heatherbank Press and Museum were founded in 1974 to stimulate public interest in social welfare history by developing the Picture Library, encouraging wider preservation of social welfare archives and publishing occasional papers. It is concerned with buildings, costume, objects, literary evidence and visual evidence.

Acquisitions policy: Actively collects archives *re* social work and welfare history.

Major collections: Association of Poor House

Governors of Scotland, register and minute books, 1880–1939.
Lennox Castle, report books, 1930–48.
Glasgow Discharged Prisoners Aid Society, minute books, 1856–1974 (4 items).
Ross and Cromarty County Council records, including asylum patient rolls, 1920–56.
Other odd items of patients' records.

Non-manuscript material: Large collections of photographs, slides, prints and drawings.
Reference library.

Finding aids: NRA 30643.

Facilities: Photocopying.

Publications: C. Harvey: *Social Welfare Archives in Britain and the USA*, Occasional Paper No. 1 (Milngavie, 1980).

822 Society of the Sacred Mission

Address: Willen Priory, Milton Keynes, Bucks MK15 9AA

Telephone and Fax: (01908) 234546

Enquiries: The Administrative Assistant, Mrs Margaret Moakes

Open: By arrangement.

Access: On written application to the Provincial SSM at Willen Priory.

Historical background: The society, an Anglican religious community, was founded in 1893 by Fr Herbert Kelly (1860–1950). The archives were moved to Willen from Kelham, near Newark, in 1973.

Acquisitions policy: To maintain the archives of the society and the collections of papers of members of the society.

Archives of organisation: Administrative records of the society, 1890–, including student and other records of Kelham Theological College, 1891–1971.

Major collections: Personal and academic papers of Herbert A. Kelly (1879–1950), director, 1893–1910; David Jenks (1866–1935), director, 1910–20; Gabriel Hebert (1884–1963), 1884–1963; and Alfred Kelly, Provincial of South Africa, 1903–06, *c*1908–48.

Finding aids: Major revision in progress. NRA 26270.

823 Clwyd Library and Information Service

Address: County Civic Centre, Mold, Clwyd CH7 6NW

Telephone: (01352) 702495

Fax: (01352) 753662

Enquiries: The Director, Mr W. Gwyn Williams

Open: Mon–Thurs: 8.45–5.00 Fri: 8.45–4.30

Access: Generally open to the public; an appointment is recommended for viewing special collections.

There is a local history collection of books, pamphlets, journals, newspapers, maps, prints, a selection of photographs, oral history tapes, in Welsh and English, and ephemeral material relevant to the former counties of Flintshire, Derbyshire and parts of Merioneth. In addition there is a substantial collection of printed material on the Arthurian legends (*c*2000 vols); a collection of works by and about Daniel Owen (1836–95), local novelist; and a significant collection of Welsh bibles, 1567–1992 (*c*400).

824 Clogher RC Diocesan Archives

Address: Bishops House, Monaghan, Co. Tyrone

Enquiries: The Archivist

Open: Mon–Wed: 11.00–1.00

Access: Bona fide researchers.

The archives house the papers of James Donnelly, Bishop of Clogher, 1864–93, and the parish baptismal and marriage records to 1880. Photocopying is available and microfilm copies and a catalogue are in the Public Record Office of Northern Ireland (entry **78**).

825 Montrose Library Archive

Parent organisation: Angus District Council

Address: 214 High Street, Montrose, Angus, Tayside DD10 8PH

Telephone: (01674) 673256

Enquiries: The Local Studies Librarian/Archivist

Open: Mon–Fri: 9.30–5.00

Access: By prior arrangement.

Historical background: Angus District Council was established following local government reorganisation in 1975, taking over the functions of six former burghs and the former county council. In 1989 all archival material held by these burgh libraries was transferred to the Montrose Library.

Acquisitions policy: Administrative, social and economic records relating to the boundaries of Angus District Council.

Archives of organisation: Angus District Council records, 1975– (held by Administration Department, County Buildings, Forfar). Records of former burghs: Arbroath, 1530–1975; Brechin, 1672–1975; Carnoustie, 1884–1975; Forfar, 1666–1975; Kirriemuir, 1834–1975; Montrose, 1458–1975.

Major collections: Council minutes, burgh correspondence and charters.
Montrose Royal Lunatic Asylum and Dispensary, miscellany, 1810–1948.
Kirk session records.
Local trades, voluntary and friendly societies and charities records, 18th–20th centuries.
Forfarshire Gold Cup (Montrose Races) records, 1820–27.
Subscription library and trades library records, 1810–1904.
Genealogical collection: families of Mudy, Scott, Straton and Walker, 12th–19th centuries.
Records of museums, businesses and local societies, schools and churches.
Personal papers, including Frederick A. Ferguson, Andrew Jervise, Margaret F. Mill, James Clark, William Dorward, Patrick Chalmers, Binny family, Duke family, Inglis family, Robert Stevenson, J.M. Barrie (1860–1937), David Waterson.

Non-manuscript material: Dean of Guild plans for Montrose, Forfar and Kirriemuir.

Finding aids: Archive lists for burgh collections, business records and miscellaneous collections. Name and subject index for miscellaneous collection.

Facilities: Photocopying.

Conservation: Contracted out.

Publications: Angus Ancestors: How Do I Find

Them? Scottish Record Association datasheet No. 6 [leaflet]

826 Montrose Museum

Address: Panmure Place, Montrose, Angus, Tayside DDl0 8HE

Telephone: (01674) 673232

Enquiries: The Curator, Mrs Rachel Benvie

Open: Mon–Sat: 10.00–5.00

Access: Generally open to the public, on written application.

Historical background: The museum was built and opened by Montrose Natural History and Antiquarian Society in 1842. Since 1975 it has been part of Angus District Libraries and Museums.

Acquisitions policy: Any local material for Montrose and Angus.

Major collections: Montrose Natural History and Antiquarian Society minutes, 1836–1951. Payroll of Forfar and Kincardine Militia, 1803. Rifle Volunteer papers.
Miscellaneous local voluntary and friendly society records, 18th and 19th centuries.
Log of whaling ship *Snowdrop*, 1907.
Autograph collection includes Sir Walter Scott (1771–1832); Alfred, Lord Tennyson (1809–92); Richard Chenevix Trench (1807–86); William Harrison Ainsworth (1805–82); Alex Burness ('Bokhara Burness') (1805–41); Joseph Bonaparte; Admiral Sir Charles Napier (1786–1860).

Non-manuscript material: Local maps and plans, 17th–19th centuries.
Local photographs.

Finding aids: Index of Montrose Natural History and Antiquarian Society members, 1836–1931.

Facilities: Photocopying by arrangement.

827 Northumberland Archive Service
Morpeth Records Centre

Address: The Kylins, Loansdean, Morpeth, Northumberland NE61 2EQ

Telephone: (01670) 504084

Enquiries: The Heritage Centre Officer

Open: Mon, Wed, Fri: 10.00–1.00; 2.00–5.00 Tues: 10.00–1.00; 2.00–9.00

Access: Generally open to the public. Records in microform are available only in this form; advance booking of a microfilm reader is essential.

Historical background: Opened in 1989 as a Modern Records Centre, part of the building was converted to an archive strongroom and small public searchroom in 1991 to house certain classes of archives formerly held at Northumberland Record Office, Melton Park (entry **838**) The searchroom was further extended in 1994 to allow sources on microfilm to be transferred from Melton Park. The office is recognised as a place of deposit for public records and as a Diocesan Record Office for Newcastle, which is mostly coterminous with the boundaries of Northumberland before 1974 but includes a small part of Cumbria. Principal classes of archives are now divided between the two offices at Morpeth and Melton Park, while there is a branch office at Berwick upon Tweed (entry **84**) which provides a comprehensive service for North Northumberland.

Archives of organisation: Usual local authority holdings, comprising records of the county council and other past and present local authorities, ecclesiastical records and public records.

Major collections: Deposited local collections.

Facilities: Photocopying. Photography and microfilming by arrangement.

828 Motherwell District Libraries
Museum and Heritage Section, Local Studies Centre

Parent organisation: Motherwell District Council

Address: Hamilton Road, Motherwell, Borders ML1 3BZ

Telephone: (01698) 51311

Enquiries: The Museum and Heritage Manager, Mr Richard Devaney

Open: Mon, Tues, Thurs, Fri: 9.00–7.00 Wed: 9.00–12.00 Sat: 9.00–5.00

Access: Generally open to the public.

Historical background: The local studies collection has been gathered gradually since the early years of the library at the beginning of the century and reflects the changes in the administration of the area, from the Burgh of Motherwell, through amalgamation with the Burgh of Wishaw in 1920, to the formation of Motherwell District Council in 1975.

Acquisitions policy: The Museum and Heritage Section attempts to buy historical material relating to the area within the boundaries of the district council, and support material on surrounding Lanarkshire.

Major collections: Minute books of the commissioners of the burghs of Wishaw, 1855–, and Motherwell, 1865–; letter-books covering the two burghs, 1888–1938; burgh rates assessment registers, 1927–35, and more recent valuation rolls.
County of Lanark clothing and boot registers, 1930–55.
Wishaw (later Wishaw & Newmains) Co-operative Society minutes and accounts, 1890–1966.
Lord Hamilton of Dalzell Collection of books and MSS, including several relating to the Owenite Orbiston community experiment.

Non-manuscript material: Hurst Nelson Collection of photographs of rolling stock.
Old parish records and census returns (on microfilm).
Complete runs of local newspapers (on microfilm and/or hard copy).

Finding aids: Microfiche catalogue; microfiche index to the *Motherwell Times*, 1883–1983; index to the *Wishaw Press*, 1872–1984, in progress; index to Hurst Nelson Collection; survey of the Lord Hamilton of Dalzell Collection. Various other source lists and indexes.

Facilities: Photocopying. Microform reader/printer.

Publications: List available.

829 Much Wenlock Town Council

Address: The Corn Exchange, Much Wenlock, Shropshire TF13 6AE

Telephone: (01952) 727509

Enquiries: The Town Clerk

Open: No regular opening. Any time can be arranged after reasonable notice.

Access: Bona fide researchers.

Historical background: The Borough of Wenlock was founded by charter in 1468. The Corn Exchange is recognised as a place of deposit for public records.

Archives of organisation: Borough records, including minutes, 1468–1966; court records, 1611–1815; voters lists and rate records, c1850–; parish minutes, 17th century, and parish records, 18th–19th centuries.

Major collections: Records of Agricultural Reading Society and Olympian Society, which led to modern Olympic Games, 1840–1900.

Non-manuscript material: Penny Brookes Herbarium

Finding aids: Card index.

Facilities: Photocopying.

830 Nelson Library

Parent organisation: Lancashire County Council Library and Museum Service

Address: Market Square, Nelson, Lancs BB9 7LP

Telephone: (01282) 692511

Fax: (01282) 692511

Enquiries: The Reference Librarian

Open: Mon, Wed, Fri: 9.30–7.00 Tues, Thurs: 9.30–5.00 Sat: 9.30–4.00

Access: Generally open to the public.

Historical background: The collection relates specifically to the present area of Pendle District, with emphasis on the western half of the area. See also Colne Library (entry 225). Some collections have recently been transferred to Lancashire Record Office (entry 944) and Barnoldswick Library (entry 224).

Major collections: Council minutes, 1892–.
Rate books; census enumerators' returns, 1841–91.

Non-manuscript material: Usual local history collection, including: local newspaper files, 1863–; maps, 1848–; directories, 1814–.
Microfilm of parish registers, 1599–.

Facilities: Photocopying. Microfilm/fiche readers.

Publications: Local Studies in Lancashire: a Guide to Resources (1986), 78–82.

831 British Horological Institute

Address: Upton Hall, Upton, Newark, Notts NG23 5TE

Telephone: (01636) 813795/6

Fax: (01636) 812258

Enquiries: The Institute Secretary, Mrs H. Bartlett

Open: Mon–Fri: 9.00–1.00; 2.00–5.00

Access: Members. Others by special concession only.

The British Horological Institute is a founder horological society of the world, established in 1858. It moved to Upton in 1972. It retains the archives of the institute as well as a substantial number of MSS, including the Louis Baume Archives and a collection on the history of clock and watch manufacture.

832 Newark Museum

Parent organisation: Newark and Sherwood District Council

Address: Appletongate, Newark, Notts NG24 1JY

Telephone: (01636) 702358

Enquiries: The Assistant Museum Manager, Mr M.J. Hall

Open: Mon–Wed, Fri, Sat: 10.00–1.00; 2.00–5.00 Sun: 2.00–5.00 (April–Sept only)

Access: Generally open to the public; an appointment is always necessary to consult the archives.

Historical background: Established in 1912 as the museum of the Borough of Newark, the collection passed, under local government reorganisation in 1974, to the Newark and Sherwood District Council.

Acquisitions policy: Acquisitions consist of ephemera circulated in the district, items relating to local government and local material.

Major collections: Newark Borough records, 17th–20th centuries.
Newark Improvement Commissioners minutes, 1851–74.
Newark Rural District Council, clerks' files, 1894–1953.
Newark Urban Sanitary Authority/Borough deposited plans, 1875–1970.
Southwell Rural District Council deposited plans, 1903–74 (on microfilm); deposited plans, 1934–70.

Non-manuscript material: W.N. Nicholson & Sons Ltd, agricultural engineers, Newark: printed catalogues, photographs and negatives, c1860–1967.
Negatives and photographs of the locality.
Negatives of illustrations from the *Newark Advertiser*, 1949–.
Pamphlets of local interest.

Finding aids: Place-name, subject, biographical and author indexes.

Facilities: Photocopying. Photography. Microfilm/fiche reader.

833 National Farmers' Union of Scotland

Address: Rural Centre - West Mains, Ingliston, Newbridge, Midlothian EH28 9LT

Telephone: (0131) 335 3111

Fax: (0131) 335 3800

Enquiries: The Director and General Secretary

Open: By arrangement only.

Access: Requests from bona fide researchers will be considered on their merits.

Historical background: The NFUS was founded in 1913 and amalgamated with the Scottish Chamber of Agriculture, which represented the larger tenants, farmers and landlords, in 1938.

Acquisitions policy: To maintain the records of NFUS.

Archives of organisation: Minute books, AGM records, files of copy letters and annual reports, 1919–.
Scottish Farming Leader, official journal (monthly), 1948–.

Finding aids: NRA 24460.

834 Borough Museum and Art Gallery

Parent organisation: Newcastle-under-Lyme Borough Council

Address: Brampton Park, Newcastle-under-Lyme, Staffs ST5 0QP

Telephone: (01782) 619705

Enquiries: The Senior Museum and Arts Officer, Miranda Goodby

Open: Mon–Sat: 10.00–5.30 Sun: 2.00–5.30, by arrangement.

Access: Bona fide researchers, by appointment.

Historical background: The museum was founded in 1943, and the borough archives were deposited at that time.

Acquisitions policy: Continues to acquire borough records and related material, mostly directly from the council.

Archives of organisation: Borough council records, including minute books of council meetings, lists of burgesses (electors), electoral registers, rate books, reports of medical officers of health, minute books of court cases, 14th century–.
Archives of the borough museum, including accession registers, correspondence, committee resolutions, policies, 1943–.

Non-manuscript material: Staffordshire and Newcastle maps, 18th–19th centuries.
Some plans of buildings erected or acquired by the council.
Large photographic collection (duplicated at Newcastle Library).
Town directories.

Finding aids: Subject and author indexes.

Facilities: Photocopying.

Conservation: Contracted out.

835 Hancock Museum
Natural History Society of Northumbria

Parent organisation: University of Newcastle upon Tyne

Address: Barras Bridge, Newcastle upon Tyne NE2 4PT

Telephone: (0191) 222 7418

Fax: (0191) 222 6753

Enquiries: The Curator, A. Coles

Open: Mon–Fri: 10.00–5.00

Access: Any bona fide enquirer.

Historical background: The Natural History Society of Northumberland, Durham and Newcastle upon Tyne was founded in 1829 as an offshoot of the Literary and Philosophical Society of Newcastle upon Tyne (entry **836**). The society's museum included donations made to the parent society, but was founded on the private collections of Marmaduke Tunstall (1743–90) of Lycliffe and George Allan (1736–1800) of Darlington. The museum was administered solely by the society until the later 1950s, when the University of Newcastle began to provide financial support. The university took overall control in 1974, and since 1992 the Hancock Museum has been administered by Tyne and Wear Museums under an agreement.

Acquisitions policy: Archives relating to natural history and natural history collections in northern England.

Archives of organisation: Archives relate principally to the Natural History Society and the scientific achievements of its members; also letters and documents about the Hancock Museum and the Tyneside Naturalists Field Club.

Major collections: Many collections of papers, including those of Joshua Alder (1792–1867); Thomas Belt (1832–78); Thomas Bewick (1753–1828); R.B. Bowman (1808–82); G.S. Brady (1832–1921); H.B. Brady (1835–91); Abel Chapman (1851–1929); Albany Hancock (1806–73); W.C. Hewitson (1806–78); P.J. Selby (1788–1867); N.J. Winch (1768–1838).

Facilities: Photocopying. Photography.

Finding aids: Partly catalogued: lists available on site.

Publications: Natural history collections listed in P. Davis and C. Brewer: *A Catalogue of Natural Science Collections in North-East England*, North of England Museums Service (Durham, 1986).

836 Literary and Philosophical Society of Newcastle upon Tyne

Address: 23 Westgate Road, Newcastle upon Tyne NE1 1SE

Telephone: (0191) 232 0192

Enquiries: The Librarian, Miss Margaret Norwell

Open: Mon, Wed–Fri: 9.30–7.00 Tues: 9.30–8.00 Sat: 9.30–1.00

Access: Generally open to the public; an appointment is desirable.

Historical background: The society was founded in 1793, since when it has had a major role in all scientific, industrial, literary, antiquarian and literary movements in the North-East.

Archives of organisation: Minutes, reports etc, 1793–.

Major collections: Northern Arts MS Collections: works by most of the region's living writers, especially poets and dramatists, including Thomas Bewick, Edward Bond, Basil Bunting, Tony Harrison, Tony Jackson and Alan Plater.
The Douglas W. Dickenson Collection: material relating to the history of the Northern Architectural Association.

Non-manuscript material: Early scientific and technological material. Local collection, including a large number of pamphlets, local maps and plans.
Mordern Tower Poetry Reading posters.
Newcastle University theatre programmes.

Facilities: Photocopying subject to the librarian's consent.

Publications: R.S. Watson: *The History of the Literary and Philosophical Society of Newcastle upon Tyne, 1793–1896* (1897).
C. Parish: *The History of the Literary and Philosophical Society of Newcastle upon Tyne*, vol. II, *1896–1989* (1990).
J. Phillipson (ed.): *Literary and Philosophical Bicentenary Lectures* (1994).

837 Newcastle upon Tyne City Libraries and Arts
Local Studies Library

Address: Central Library, Princess Square, Newcastle upon Tyne NE99 1DX

Telephone: (0191) 261 0691

Fax: (0191) 261 1435

Enquiries: The Local Studies Librarian

Open: Mon, Thurs: 9.30–8.00 Tues, Wed, Fri: 9.30–5.00 Sat: 9.00–5.00 Closed Saturdays preceding bank holiday Mondays.

Access: Generally open to the public. An appointment is necessary to consult the Pearse (Bewick) Collection in its entirety.

Historical background: The Mechanics' Institute formed the basis of the central library. The collection was founded in 1884 to include all local material (books, photographs, archives etc). In recent years most of the archives have been transferred to the appropriate record offices.

Acquisitions policy: Any printed works, photographs, maps, audio and video recordings on Northumberland, Durham and Tyne and Wear, with special emphasis on Newcastle upon Tyne.

Major collections: Mechanics' Institute minute books, 1834–.
T. and G. Allan Collection: Tyneside song MSS, 1860s.
Seymour Bell Collection, part of a collection compiled by the Bell family of Newcastle and Gateshead during their work as booksellers and land surveyors. It includes plans, inventories of properties, valuations, correspondence, surveys and auctioneers' notices relating to estates in Newcastle and Northumberland, late 18th–early 20th century (25 portfolios).
T. Bell material about the River Tyne, 1844–50; papers relating to printing, 19th century.
Literary and other correspondence of Wilfred Gibson, poet, 1930–44.
Gowland MSS relating to estates and collieries in Durham, early 18th century (4 vols).
MSS of Joe Wilson, songwriter, c1850s.
Letters relating to Durham collieries, 1838–57 (c100).
Early letters and papers relating to the Stockton and Darlington Railway.
Patent library, including UK patent abridgements, 1617–, and specifications 1924–; USA abridgements, 1954–.

The C.P. Taylor Collection: includes scripts etc written by the local playwright C.P. Taylor (1929–1981) (146 folders).

Non-manuscript material: Pearse (Bewick) Collection: books, engravings, wooden blocks, toolbox of Thomas Bewick (1753–1828) and his pupils, 1753–1882.
Illustrations and photographs (c70,000).
Street plans and early maps.
OS maps from 1st edn to current.

Finding aids: Card catalogue.

Facilities: Photocopying. Microfilm/fiche reader/printers.

Conservation: Contracted out.

Publications: Bewick Collection Catalogue. List of Parish Register Transcripts.
Fact sheets and user guides.

838 Northumberland Archive Service

Parent organisation: Northumberland County Council, Amenities Division, Heritage Section

Address: Northumberland Record Office, Melton Park, North Gosforth, Newcastle upon Tyne NE3 5QX

Telephone: (0191) 236 2680

Fax: (0191) 236 2680

Enquiries: The Heritage Centre Officer, Mr Michael J. Hughes

Open: Mon: 9.00–9.00 Tues, Thurs: 9.00–5.00 Fri: 9.00–4.30

Access: Generally open to the public. Records that have been microfilmed are normally available only in this form. A research service is available, for which a charge is made.

Historical background: In 1957 a county records committee was appointed, which established a record office in the Moothall, Newcastle, in 1958. The record office moved to a former anti-aircraft operations centre in North Gosforth in 1962. It is recognised as a place of deposit for certain classes of public records and as a Diocesan Record Office for Newcastle, which is mostly coterminous with the boundaries of Northumberland before 1974. Since the opening of other repositories for Northumberland, the principal classes of archives are split between the offices at Melton Park and Mor-

peth (entry **827**), while there is a branch record office at Berwick upon Tweed (entry **84**) which offers a comprehensive service for North Northumberland. Melton Park remains the administrative centre for Northumberland Archives Service.

Archives of organisation: Usual local authority record holdings.

Major collections: Deposited local collections, principally family, estate and business archives, including the following of special significance:
Records of the North of England Institute of Mechanical and Mining Engineers, including records of the London Lead Company (f. 1692), with interests in the North Pennines and North Wales, 17th–20th centuries.
Butler (Ewart) MSS: includes papers relating to the social reformer Josephine Butler, 17th–20th centuries.
Ridley (Viscount Ridley) MSS, 16th–20th centuries: includes correspondence relating to national policies, late 19th century.
Culley (agricultural improvers) MSS: includes correspondence with leading agriculturalists in the UK, 18th–19th centuries.
Records of the Society of Antiquaries of Newcastle upon Tyne: includes part of the Bell Collection of plans and valuations relating to Northumberland, 18th–20th centuries.

Non-manuscript material: Extensive photographic collections include those of J.P. Gibson of Hexham (1838–1912) and the Blankenburgs Collection: landscape and forestry in the area of Kielder forest and reservoir, c1947–71.

Facilities: Photocopying. Photography. Microfilming.

839 Tyne and Wear Archives Service

Address: Blandford House, West Blandford Square, Newcastle upon Tyne NE1 4JA

Telephone: (0191) 232 6789

Fax: (0191) 230 2614

Enquiries: The Chief Archivist, Ms E.A. Rees

Open: Mon, Wed–Fri: 8.45–5.15 Tues: 8.45–8.30
Documents required for Tuesday evening

must be ordered before lunchtime that day. Booking is required for microfilm readers.

Historical background: The service is jointly run by the five metropolitan districts which formerly made up Tyne and Wear County: Gateshead (lead authority), Newcastle upon Tyne, North Tyneside, South Tyneside and Sunderland. It is recognised as a place of deposit for public records.

Archives of organisation: Usual local authority record holdings.

Major Collections: Deposited collections, some of which have a wider significance, including:
Papers of Sir W.G. Armstrong & Co. (later Armstrong Whitworth, then Vickers), Elswick, Newcastle upon Tyne, relating to engineering and armaments, 1847–1981.
Papers of Sir Joseph Wilson Swan about the invention of incandescent electric light bulbs, the improvement of photographic processes etc, 1863–1959.
Joseph Cowen, politician and newspaper proprietor, correspondence, 1833–1937.
Messrs Merz & McLellan, Newcastle, consulting engineers; reports, minutes, specifications, photographs, 1900–47.
Sir Charles Parsons' plans of the *Turbinia*, 1893–1904.
A.J. Fenwick Collection of circus material, 1773–1974.
Messrs Ralph Beilby and Thomas Bewick, Newcastle engravers, financial records, 1752–1881.
Associated Lead Manufacturers Ltd, papers, 1780–1980.

Facilities: Photocopying. Photography. microfilming. microfilm/fiche reader/printer.

Conservation: In-house service for all types of archive conservation.

840 University of Newcastle upon Tyne Library

Address: Newcastle upon Tyne NE2 4HQ

Telephone: (0191) 222 7671

Fax: (0191) 222 6235

Enquiries: The Special Collections Librarian

Open: Mon–Fri: 9.15–5.00 (Special Collections Reading Room)

Access: By appointment and written application to the Special Collections Librarian.

Historical background: The university has a complicated history, involving the college of Medicine (f. 1834) and the College of Physical Science (f. 1871). At first part of the University of Durham, the Newcastle colleges, after several changes of name, became in 1963 the independent University of Newcastle upon Tyne.

Acquisitions policy: Selective strengthening of MS and printed materials.

Major collections: Papers of four Trevelyans: Sir Walter Calverley (1797–1879), Sir Charles Edward (1807–86), Sir George Otto (1838–1928), Sir Charles Philips (1870–1958).
Papers of Walter Runciman, 1st Viscount Runciman of Doxford (1870–1949); Bernard Bosanquet (1848–1923) and Helen Bosanquet (1860–1925); Gertrude Bell (1868–1926).
Papers of Frederick Whyte (1867–1941), publisher, translator and biographer of W.T. Stead and William Heinemann.
Papers of Jack Common (1903–68), novelist and journalist.
Travel diaries and book MSS of Thomas Hodgkin (1831–1913), historian.
Musical MSS of Charles Villiers Stanford (1852–1924).
Other MSS include medieval items; a 17th-century poetic miscellany; 19th-century letters; 20th-century literary material.

Non-manuscript material: Robert White Collection, notably border history and ballads.
Ephemeral literature, including election ephemera, chapbooks and broadsides, 19th century.
Newcastle Cathedral books.
Burman Collection of Alnwick printed books.
Joseph Cowen tracts on political, social and economic topics.
Hindson-Reid Collection of 19th-century Newcastle woodblocks.
Thomas and John Bell's material on the northeast book trade.
Pybus History of Medicine Collection.
Heslop Collection of dictionaries
The Gertrude Bell photographic archive is also housed in the university. The originals are kept by the library, but copies are available for viewing in the Department of Archaeology (University of Newcastle upon Tyne, Newcastle upon Tyne NE1 7RU), where all enquiries should be addressed.

Finding aids: Handlists or indexes of the Bosanquet, Whyte, Common and Hodgkin material. Lists sent to NRA. Series of catalogues of Trevelyan papers.

Facilities: Photocopying. Photography. Microfilm equipment.

Conservation: In-house service. Outside work undertaken by arrangement with the conservator.

Publications: B.C. Raw: *Lives of the Saints: a Description of MS.1 in the University Library* (Newcastle upon Tyne, 1961).
S. Hill, L. Ritchie and B. Hathaway (comps): *Catalogue of the Gertrude Bell Photographic Archive* (Newcastle upon Tyne, 2/1965).
W. C. Donkin: *The Letters and Papers of Gertrude Bell: a List* (1966).
J.S. Emmerson (comp.): *Catalogue of the Pybus Collection of Medical Books, Letters and Engravings, 15th–20th Centuries, held in the University Library, Newcastle upon Tyne* (Manchester, 1981).
C.J. Hunt: 'Scottish Ballads and Music in the Robert White Collection', *Bibliothek*, v (1983), 138–41.
Special Collections Guide (1994).

841 University of Northumbria

Address: Library Building, Sandyford Road, Newcastle upon Tyne NE1 8ST

Telephone: (0191) 227 4125 (direct line)

Fax: (0191) 227 4563

Open: Term: Mon–Thurs: 9.00–5.00 Sat: 9.30–5.00 Vacation: Mon–Fri: 9.00–5.00

Newcastle Polytechnic was founded in 1969 incorporating three predecessor colleges: the Rutherford College of Technology, the Regional College of Art and Design and the College of Commerce. It became a university in 1992. The library holds the Thompson Newspaper Archive, comprising cuttings, 1900–81, with particular emphasis on the 1970s. Access for outside researchers may be given on request.

842 National Horseracing Museum

Address: 99 High Street, Newmarket, Suffolk, CB8 8JL

Telephone: (01638) 667333

Enquiries: The Curator, Mr Graham Snelling

Open: Tues–Sat: 10.00–5.00 Sun: 12.00–4.00 Closed December to March.

Access: Generally open to the public on written application. An appointment is necessary.

Historical background: The national horseracing museum is an independent museum which was opened in 1983. Its regency building is an integral part of racing history, being adjacent to the Jockey Club. The archives were established at the time of opening.

Acquisitions policy: Material relating to racing, including racing calendars, paintings, memorabilia and books.

Major collections: Archives of the Jockey Club, early 19th century–.
Small collections of memorabilia of famous jockeys, including Sir Gordon Richards (*b* 1904), Stephen Donoghue (1884–1945), Fred Archer (1857–86).

Non-manuscript material: Heber's Turf Calendar, 1763–, and Stud Books (2nd edn) *c*1750–.
Large collection of photographs of jockeys and horses, 1880s–.
Watercolours, prints and films.

Finding aids: Handwritten index and register. Jockey Club archives to be computerised.

Facilities: Photocopying. Photography by arrangement.

843 Newport Libraries

Address: Central Library, John Frost Square, Newport, Gwent NP9 1PA

Telephone: (01633) 211376 (direct line to Reference Library) 65539

Fax: (01633) 222615

Enquiries: The Reference Librarian, Mrs Gillian Holt

Open: Mon–Wed: 9.30–6.00 Thurs: 9.30–5.00 Fri: 9.00–6.00 Sat: 9.30–5.00

Access: Generally open to the public.

Historical background: Newport Public Library opened in 1870. An extensive general reference library and local collection was built up over 100 years. In 1974 much archival material was transferred to Gwent County Record Office (entry **238**).

Acquisitions policy: MSS are occasionally acquired, by donation only.

Major collections: Chartist riots, verbatim reports of trials affecting Newport and district (30 vols).
Mary Delany (1700–88), correspondence with well-known figures of the day, including Fanny Burney (1752–1840).
Correspondence of Sir Charles Hanbury Williams (1708–59), satirist and diplomat, 1750s.

Non-manuscript material: Maps.

Finding aids: Card catalogues.

Facilities: Photocopying. Microfilm reader.

844 Isle of Wight County Record Office

Address: 26 Hillside, Newport, Isle of Wight PO30 2EB

Telephone: (01983) 823821

Enquiries: The County Archivist, Mr C.D. Webster

Open: Mon–Thurs: 9.00–1.00; 2.00–5.30 Fri: 9.00–1.00, 2.00–5.00

Access: Generally open to the public. Booking is required for microform readers.

Historical background: The record office was founded in 1958. It acts as the Diocesan Record Office for Portsmouth (Isle of Wight parish records), and is recognised as a place of deposit for public records.

Archives of organisation: Usual local authority record holdings.

Major collections: Deposited local collections.

Facilities: Photocopying. Microfilm/fiche reader/printer.

Publications: Hampshire Archivists Group: *Poor Law* (1970); *Transport* (1973); *Education* (1977).
P.D.D. Russell (ed.): *The Hearth Tax Returns*

for the Isle of Wight, 1664–1674, Isle of Wight Record Series, vol. 1.
S.F. Hockey (ed.): *The Cartulary of Carisbrooke Priory,* Isle of Wight Record Series, vol. 2.
——: *The Charters of Quarr Abbey,* Isle of Wight Record Series, vol. 3.

845 Scottish Mining Museum Archives

Parent organisation: The Scottish Mining Museum Trust

Address: Lady Victoria Colliery, Newtongrange, Midlothian EH22 4QN

Telephone: (0131) 663 7519

Fax: (0131) 654 1618

Enquiries: The Curator

Open: Mon–Fri: 9.30–4.30

Access: Generally open to the public, by appointment only. Study times are not identical to those of the museum.

Historical background: The Scottish Mining Museum Trust was formed in 1984 to coordinate previous efforts which had started in the early 1970s. The museum is based at a 90–year old colliery which closed in 1981. The main source of the collection has arisen from the relatively rapid decline of the industry in recent years. The library's core holdings are from the now closed Hood School of Mining, Heriot Watt University.

Acquisitions policy: To collect both artefacts and archival material recording the history of Scottish coal-mining, its life and times from the discovery of coal to the present day.

Major collections: National Coal Board/British Coal Corporation, annual reports and accounts, technical specifications, 1947–.
National Union of Mineworkers (Scottish Area) McDonald Memorial Collection, including Miners Federation of GB/NUM annual reports and minutes, 1900–; Scottish executive committee minutes, 1945–, closure consultation minutes, 1950–70.
Royal commissions on the coal industry, 1842–1940.
Annual reports of the Mines Inspectors (national and divisional), 1900–; Inspectors' incident reports, 1920–.

Lothian Coal Company archives, including ledgers, 1889–1947.

Non-manuscript material: Technical drawings, pictures, photographs, maps.
Tape-recordings.
Official government and union publications, including annual reports of NUM and MFGB.
Trade catalogues.

Finding aids: Catalogues are in preparation.

Facilities: Photocopying. Limited photography.

Conservation: Contracted out.

Publications: A Short History of Mining in Scotland.

846 North Yorkshire County Record Office

Address: Postal: County Hall, Northallerton, North Yorks DL7 8AF
Location: Malpas Road, Northallerton North Yorks

Telephone: (01609) 777585

Enquiries: The County Archivist, Mr M.Y. Ashcroft

Open: Mon, Tues, Thurs: 9.00–4.45 Wed: 9.00–8.45 Fri: 9.00–4.15

Access: Generally open to the public, by appointment. The majority of records are made available on microfilm.

Historical background: The present office was established in 1974 with local government reorganisation; previously the office had covered the old North Riding area. The first archivist was appointed in 1949, although records had been collected from 1938. The office acts as a Diocesan Record Office for Bradford, Ripon and York (parish records), and is recognised as a place of deposit for public records.

Archives of organisation: Usual local authority record holdings.

Major collections: Deposited local collections.

Facilities: Photocopying. Photography. Microfilming. Microfilm reader/printer.

Publications: A list of publications is available.

847 Northampton Museum

Parent organisation: Northampton Borough Council

Address: Guildhall Road, Northampton NN1 1DP

Telephone: (01604) 39415

Fax: (01604) 238720

Enquiries: The Keeper of the Boot and Shoe Collection, Ms V. Wood

Open: Mon–Sat: 10.00–5.00 Sun: 2.00–5.00

Access: Generally open to the public, on application and by appointment.

Historical background: The County Museum was established in 1865. Since 1873 it has collected objects related to shoes and shoemaking worldwide, though the greater part of the collection still relates to shoes as worn in the UK and the history of shoemaking in Northamptonshire.

Acquisitions policy: Objects related to the history of Northampton, and in the shoe department to continue to acquire material related to the history of shoes and shoemaking worldwide.

Major collections: Accounts and account books; apprenticeship indentures; documents relating to shoe unions, and education; shoe designs, mostly 19th century.

Non-manuscript material: Pictures, prints and photographs of shoemakers, factory exteriors, shoe shops and transport.
Shoe price lists and catalogues; shoe tool and machinery catalogues, handbooks, c1870–c1930.
Advertisements.

Finding aids: Card indexes of the above. Card indexes of shoemakers, bucklemakers, lastmakers, machinery makers. History of shoemaking by Northamptonshire parishes. NRA 22281.

Facilities: Photocopying. Photography.

Publications: J.M. Swann: *Catalogue of Shoemaker Pictures and Works of Art* (1975).

848 Northamptonshire Record Office

Address: Wootton Hall Park, Northampton NN4 8BQ

Telephone: (01604) 762129

Fax: (01604) 767562

Enquiries: The County Archivist, Miss R. Watson

Open: Mon–Wed: 9.15–4.45 Thurs: 9.00–7.45 Fri: 9.00–4.15 Sat (2nd in month): 9.00–12.15 Office may close 1.00–2.00 without prior notice; documents required Thursday evenings, Saturday mornings and weekdays, 12.00–2.00, should be ordered in advance.

Access: Generally open to the public.

Historical background: The Northamptonshire Record Society founded and ran an office from 1920 to 1951. Since then it has been administered by the county council. The office also acts as the Diocesan Record Office for Peterborough and is recognised as a place of deposit for public records.

Archives of organisation: Usual local authority record holdings.

Major collections: Deposited local collections, of which the following have a wider significance:
Bridgewater estate and canal accounts, 1759–1806.
Exchequer tellers' accounts, 1568–86.
Militia records of various forces, particularly c1790–1815.
Naval records of Admiral P. Rye, c1791–1815.
Correspondence of Rev. C. Hartshorne, antiquary, 1818–47; and Dr Joan Wake (*d* 1974).
Diaries of Lady Louisa Knightley, 1856–1913, and Lord Dover, 1814–33.
Diplomatic papers of Sir Thomas Cartwright (1795–1850) and Sir Fairfax Cartwright (1857–1928).
Political papers of Duke of Shrewsbury, c1694–1700; Edmund Burke, 1764–97; 4th and 5th Earls Fitzwilliam, 1766–1857; W.C. Cartwright, c1860–1910.
Spencer of Althorp Collection, including charters, deeds and court rolls, mainly for Bedfordshire, Northamptonshire, Surrey and Warwickshire, mid-12th–20th centuries.

Facilities: Photocopying. Photography and microfilming (subject to delays). Microfilm/fiche readers/printers.

Conservation: In-house.

849 Northamptonshire Studies Collection

Parent organisation: Northamptonshire Libraries and Information Service

Address: Central Library, Abington Street, Northampton NN1 2BA

Telephone: (01604) 26774

Enquiries: The Subject Specialist: Local History, Miss M.E. Arnold

Open: Mon: 9.30–8.00 Tues–Fri: 9.30–7.00 Sat: 9.30–4.00

Access: Some public access; an appointment is necessary to see the John Clare Collection.

Historical background: The amalgamation of local collections at Northampton and Northamptonshire County Libraries led to the establishment of the collection in its present form in 1974.

Acquisitions policy: To collect and preserve all printed and photographic material on Northamptonshire, its footwear and leather industry, and on John Clare.

Major collections: John Clare (1793–1864): collection of MSS, with his library; books and cuttings.
Beeby Thompson Geological Collection: files and volumes of published papers on geology and water supply of Northamptonshire.
Sir Henry Dryden (1818–99) Collection: drawings and plans of churches and buildings (several thousand).

Non-manuscript material: Charles Bradlaugh (1833–91) Collection: works by and about him, portraits, illustrations, posters and news cuttings.
Northamptonshire Studies Collection: illustrations; photographs, including glass and celluloid negatives; engravings and printed maps (14,000).
Newspaper files, including *Northampton Mercury*, 1720–.
Large collection of books, theses and journals on leather and footwear.

Finding aids: Indexes. Catalogues of Dryden and Clare Collections: NRA 14253 and 10984.

Facilities: Photocopying. Microfilm reader/printer.

Publications: *Catalogue of the John Clare Collection in the Northampton Public Library* (Northampton, 1965); *Supplement* (1971).

850 Northwich Library
Brunner Library

Parent organisation: Cheshire Libraries, Arts and Archives

Address: Witton Street, Northwich, Cheshire CW9 5DR

Telephone: (01606) 44221

Fax: (01606) 48396

Enquiries: The Area Manager, Mrs Sheila Scragg

Open: Mon, Tues: 9.30–5.00 Wed, Sat: 9.30–1.00 Thurs, Fri: 9.30–7.00

Access: Generally open to the public. Booking is necessary for the microform readers.

Historical background: The public library dates from 1885, and there has always been a small local history collection for reference use.

Acquisitions policy: Donation and purchase of material relating to the history of Northwich and district, and selected material more broadly on Cheshire.

Major collections: Usual local history collection comprising MS material (10 metres), microfilm (200 rolls), printed maps, photographs, printed vols (c1200).

Non-manuscript material: *Northwich Guardian*, 1861–; *Northwich Chronicle*, 1885– (incomplete); census returns (Northwich Area), 1841–91, and parish registers, 1558–1903 (microfilm).

Finding aids: Card index. County-wide local studies computer database.

Facilities: Photocopying. Photography by arrangement. Microfilm/fiche readers.

Conservation: Contracted out to Cheshire County Record Office (entry 208).

851 London Bible College
Centre for Undergraduate and Postgraduate Theological Studies

Address: Green Lane, Northwood, Middx HA6 2UW

Telephone: (01923) 826061

Fax: (01923) 836530

Enquiries: The College Librarian, Alan Linfield

Open: Mon–Fri: 9.00–5.00

Access: Bona fide scholars and researchers engaged in academic study. Due to limited space, access is usually restricted to vacations for those outside the college. An appointment is desirable.

The London Bible College is the largest international theological college in Western Europe, founded in 1943. The library has been built up steadily over the years and now boasts a collection of c40,000 books, making it one of the best collections of academic theology in the UK, being particularly strong in biblical theology. It holds mainly publications, but also some tape-recordings and videos relating to academic theology and contemporary Christianity and the personal papers of Dr Donald Guthrie (1916–92).

852 Merchant Taylors' School

Address: Sandy Lodge, Northwood, Middx HA6 2HT

Telephone: (01923) 820644

Fax: (01923) 835110

Enquiries: The Headmaster

Open: By appointment.

Access: On application to the Headmaster.

Historical background: Merchant Taylors' School was founded in 1561. Documents relevant to the early history of the school are at Merchant Taylors' Hall (entry 631).

Archives of organisation: School registers, 1561–; 'Probation Books', 1933–; information about pupils, 1933–.
Headmasters' reports to Company, 1884–.
School magazines.

Finding aids: Index kept in the school library at Sandy Lodge.

Publications: H.B. Wilson: *History of Merchant Taylors' School* (London, 1814).
F.W.M. Draper: *Four Centuries of Merchant Taylors' School* (London, 1962).

853 The History of Advertising Trust

Address: Unit 6, The Raveningham Centre, Raveningham, Norwich, Norfolk NR14 6NU

Telephone: (01508) 548523

Fax: (01508) 548474

Enquiries: The Secretary, Michael Cudlipp

Open: Mon–Fri, by arrangement.

Access: Generally open to the public, by appointment.

Historical background: The trust, a registered charity, was set up in 1977 as an educational foundation to encourage and sponsor the serious study of all aspects of the growth and development of advertising. It is recognised internally as a prime source of historical research on British print advertising and its rapidly growing collection of more than one million unique images and artefacts dates from the 1820s. Its extensive library dates from the 19th century. There are research facilities and an information service, as well as exhibitions and publications. It has a membership scheme which is open to the public.

Acquisitions policy: Records of organisations connected with advertising; advertising material in general, including advertising proofs, research background to campaigns, competitive press and magazine advertising, artwork, television commercials, point of sale material, early commercial television records and rate cards, posters and historic company records.

Major collections: Collections from advertising associations: Association of Independent Radio Contractors, Institute of Public Relations, and other national bodies; also from major advertising agencies, e.g. Charles Barker Group, Ogilvy & Mather and J. Walter Thompson Co.

Non-manuscript material: Selective record of advertisements in various two-dimensional pictorial forms: posters, cards, slides, transparencies, filmstrips, video cassettes etc.

Specialised library on the history of advertising.

Finding aids: Lists and indexes. Select bibliography of the history of advertising (available on request).

Facilities: Photocopying. Photography by arrangement.

Publications: T.R. Nevett: *Advertising in Britain: a History* (Heinemann, 1982).
B. Henry (ed.): *British Television Advertising: the First 30 Years* (Century Benham, 1986).
Journal of Advertising History.

854 John Innes Centre

Parent organisation: John Innes Foundation and Biotechnology and Biological Sciences Research Council

Address: Colney Lane, Norwich, Norfolk NR4 7UH

Telephone: (01603) 56844 ext. 2674/2676

Enquiries: The Archivist, Mrs R.D. Harvey

Open: Mon–Thurs: 8.00–4.30

Access: Any interested person, by appointment.

Historical background: The centre was previously known as the John Innes Institute, which merged with the Cambridge Laboratory and the Nitrogen Fixation Unit to form the present organisation. From 1910 to 1981, when the archives section was established, the archives were in the care of the librarian.

Acquisitions policy: All material pertaining to the history and work of the John Innes Centre. Also material concerning the Innes family, the history of the Plant Breeding Institute, Cambridge, and the history of genetics.

Archives of organisation: Administrative, scientific and historical records of the institute, 1910–.

Major collections: Note-books, original and copy letters of William Bateson (1861–1926), pioneer geneticist and first director, 1910–26.
Letters and papers of the Innes family.
Papers relating to the work of the Plant Breeding Institute, Cambridge.
Haarland and Hutchinson collections on the genetics of cotton.

Non-manuscript material: John Innes Special Collection: early botanical books and herbals, 1536– (Curator, Mrs E.A. Atchison).

History of genetics library (*c*4000 vols).

Finding aids: Card and computer catalogues of John Innes archive collections.
Computer catalogues of Bateson letters (see also NRA 2554) and history of genetics library.
Catalogue of John Innes Special Collection.

Facilities: Photocopying. Photography. Microfilm/fiche readers/printer.

Publications: R.D. Harvey: 'The William Bateson Letters at the John Innes Institute', *Mendel Newsletter*, no. 25 (Nov. 1985).

855 Norfolk Record Office

Address: Gildengate House, Anglia Square, Norwich NR3 1EB

Telephone: (01603) 761349

Fax: (01603) 761885

Enquiries: The County Archivist, Miss Jean M. Kennedy

Open: To be arranged.

Access: Generally open to the public. The office operates the CARN reader's ticket system.

Historical background: The office was founded in 1963, taking over from the archives department of Norwich Public Libraries. It acts as the Diocesan Record Office for Norwich and Ely (deaneries of Feltwell and Fincham) and is recognised as a place of deposit for public records. The Borough of King's Lynn archives are stored at the Regalia Rooms, Saturday Market Place, King's Lynn PE30 5DQ, but arrangements to see them there should be made in advance with the Record Office. The building housing the records was severely damaged by fire in 1994 but no records were lost. The microform searchroom is open at Shirehall Chambers, Market Avenue, Norwich NR1 3JQ; Fri: 9.15–5.00, Sat; 9.15–12.00: telephone for details of current situation and availability of collections.

Acquisitions policy: Records of historical significance relating to the county of Norfolk, excluding mainly photographic and audiovisual material.

Archives of organisation: Usual local authority record holdings, including records of the City of Norwich and Norwich diocesan records.

Major collections: Deposited local collections, including:
Norwich Cathedral archives to 1900.

Estate and family records, including Hobart of Blickling; Meade of Earsham; Ketton-Cremer of Felbrigg; Bulwer of Heydon; le Strange of Hunstanton; Wodehouse of Kimberley; de Grey of Merton; Hare of Stow Bardolph.
Literary MSS of Sir Henry Rider Haggard (1856–1925) and Ralph Hale Mottram (1883–1971).
Music and other MSS of Dr William Crotch (1775–1847) and musicological notes of Dr Arthur Henry Mann (1850–1929).
Antiquarian collections of Harry Bradfer-Lawrence (*d* 1965), Walter Rye (*d* 1929) and the Colman family.

Finding aids: Lists and card indexes of archives received or catalogued since 1963; lists and card catalogue of MSS held by Norwich Public Libraries pre-1963. Lists sent to NRA.

Facilities: Photocopying. Photography. Microfilming. Microfilm/fiche readers/printer.

Conservation: In-house service; limited outside work undertaken.

Publications: P. Rutledge: *Guide to the Great Yarmouth Borough Records* (1973).
Norfolk Record Office Guide to Genealogical Sources (3/1993).

856 University of East Anglia

Address: The Library, University of East Anglia, Norwich, Norfolk NR4 7TJ

Telephone: (01603) 56161 ext. 2102

Enquiries: The Curator, Archive Collections

Open: Term: Mon–Fri: 9.00–9.00 Sat: 9.00–5.00 Sun: 2.00–7.00 Vacation: Mon–Fri: 9.00–6.00

Access: Generally available to scholars. Prior written application is advised and is essential for weekend visits.

Historical background: The archive collections are housed in the university library, which opened to readers in 1963. Collection of MSS and related material began in 1981 with the transfer from the English Faculty Library, Cambridge University, of the Library of Contemporary Cultural Records, subsequently renamed the Holloway Collection of Modern Cultural Records in honour of its founders, John Holloway, Professor of Modern English at Cambridge, and his wife Joan, formerly librarian of the English Faculty. In recent years papers of former UEA staff and alumni have also been accepted. The university also has a Centre of East Anglian Studies, which includes the East Anglian Film Archives (tel. 01603 592664).

Acquisitions policy: Continuing development of the Holloway Collection; collection of material relating to the history and work of the university. Acceptance of other donations or deposits can be considered only where there is a close relationship with existing collections or with the university's teaching and research programmes. Copies of the full policy statement can be supplied.

Archives of organisation: The bulk of the university records are not yet open to researchers.

Major collections: Holloway Collection: ephemera representative of the arts and media in their institutional aspects, 1965–, with emphasis on regional and local activity.
Papers of Lord Zuckerman (*b* 1904), anatomist and government scientific adviser, including material on medical/biological research, civil defence research and air operations planning in World War II, and post-war science policy.
Papers of John Pritchard, engineer and furniture-maker, including records of the Isokon Company and correspondence relating to architecture and design, with special reference to the work of ex-Bauhaus designers in Britain.
Papers of Anne and Jessie Kenney, suffragettes, including correspondence and MSS writings, suffragette newspapers, photographs, cuttings and memorabilia.
Personal papers of former staff and alumni.

Non-manuscript material: Pamphlets, posters, photographs, news cuttings, some maps,plans, microforms, audio and video tapes, microscopic slides.
Local theatre memorabilia collection based on the personal collections of H.T.G. Tinkler, Alick Williams and Geoffrey Hart (in conjunction with Norfolk County Library Service).

Facilities: Photocopying. Microfilm/fiche readers/printer. Video facility. Provision for use of typewriter or tape recorder. Search service (details and scale of fees supplied on request).

Finding aids: Card indexes and catalogues; handlists; descriptive brochures/leaflets of major collections.

Publications: J. Black and J. Holloway: 'Con-

temporary Culture Records Library', *Times Literary Supplement* (3 March 1972).
H. Temperley: 'Memoirs of a Power-broker: the Solly Zuckerman Archive at UEA', *Times Higher Education Supplement* (14 Feb. 1986).

857 British Geological Survey

Address: Kingsley Dunham Centre, Keyworth, Nottingham NG12 5GG

Telephone: (0115) 936 3472 (Chief Librarian and Archivist) 936 3196 (Records Officer) 936 3205 (Library)

Fax: (0115) 936 3200

Enquiries: The Chief Librarian and Archivist, Mr Graham McKenna, The Records Officer, Mr R.C. Bowie

Open: Mon–Thurs: 9.00–5.00 Fri: 9.00–4.30

Access: Generally open to the public; an appointment is preferred. Charges are made for some services.

Historical background: The collection and organisation of the survey's archives began in1967 in order to bring together and preserve MS, graphic, photographic and ephemeral printed material of all kinds relating to the history of British geological sciences, and in particular to the history of the British Geological Survey and its forerunners, the Institute of Geological Sciences, the Geological Survey, the Museum of Practical Geology, and Overseas Geological Surveys. The scope of the collection, more than 30,000 items, has been widened to include material about geology on an international basis, the overall aim being to provide a national geological archive available for public reference on site at Keyworth comprising the BGS Library Archives and the materials housed in the National Geosciences Records Centre. BGS Keyworth is recognised as a place of deposit for public records.

Acquisitions policy: To add to the existing collection in pursuance of the survey's role as a repository for national geological archives.

Archives of organisation: The survey's own archives, which include constituent bodies, the Geological Survey, Museum of Practical Geology, Mining Record Office and Royal School of Mines.
Correspondence and papers, paintings, draw-

ings, photographs; registered files; official field records generated by the survey's staff, 1835–.

Major collections: A wide range of other collections includes the records of the Palaeontographical Society, 1847–1950.
Correspondence and notes of celebrated geologists in many varied collections.

Non-manuscript material: Photographs (survey and geology) (75,000).
British Association for the Advancement of Science geological photographs of Britain, 1861–1940s.
Drawings and ephemera.

Finding aids: TS registers to the whole collection are available in the survey's libraries at Keyworth and Edinburgh (entry **279**), BGS London Information Office, and the Public Record Office (entry **960**). The collection is currently being indexed in detail and a card index is maintained in each library.

Facilities: Photocopying. Photography. Microfilm/fiche reader/printers.

858 Nottingham Diocesan Archives

Parent organisation: Roman Catholic Diocese of Nottingham

Address: Willson House, Derby Street, Nottingham NG1 5AW

Telephone: (0115) 924 1968

Enquiries: The Diocesan Archivist

Open: By arrangement only.

Access: Any bona fide enquirer, at the Archivist's discretion. A charge is made for work done on behalf of enquirers. No records later than 1944 may be consulted at present.

Historical background: The Diocese of Nottingham was created in 1850 when the Catholic hierarchy was restored in England and Wales. The diocese at present covers Nottinghamshire (except Bassetlaw), Derbyshire (except the Chesterfield area), Leicestershire, Lincolnshire and South Humberside. The diocesan archives have been built up over many decades by various individuals. They were moved to their present site in 1990. Pre-1850 records are held by Birmingham RC Diocesan Archives (entry **96**).

Acquisitions policy: To acquire material relevant

to the history of the Catholic Church, with particular reference to the Diocese of Nottingham and the institutions and individuals which form part of it.

Archives of organisation: Correspondence and other papers of the Bishops of Nottingham.
Files for most of the older parishes of the diocese.
Registers (baptisms, confirmations, marriages, deaths) of many parishes (also on microfiche).

Major collections: Croft papers: material on the history of the diocese collected with a view to publication by Monsignor W. Croft (*d* 1926).
History of the diocese and obituary notices for priests by Canon G.D. Sweeney (*d* 1979).

Non-manuscript material: Catholic Directories, c1840– (incomplete).
Diocesan Year Books, 1921–.

Finding aids: Many of the documents are listed on index cards or on typed sheets. Separate list of parish registers.

Facilities: Photocopying by arrangement. Microfiche reader.

Publications: 'A Short Account of Nottingham Diocesan Archives', *Catholic Archives,* iii (1983), 9–19.

859 Nottinghamshire Archives

Address: Castle Meadow Road, Nottingham NG2 1AG

Telephone: (0115) 950 4524 958 1634 (archival enquiries) 924 2749 (Conservation Unit)

Enquiries: The Principal Archivist, Mr A.J.M. Henstock

Open: Mon, Wed–Fri: 9.00–4.45 Tues: 9.00–7.15 Sat: 9.00–12.15

Historical background: The office was formally established in 1949, although some archives were collected from an earlier date. It acts also as the Diocesan Record Office for Southwell and is recognised as a place of deposit for public records.

Archives of organisation: Usual local authority record holdings.

Major collections: Deposited local collections, of which the following have a wider significance:
Portland papers: medieval charters; disintegration of forests, 16th–17th centuries.

Foljambe papers: medieval charters; correspondence of Sir George Savile MP, late 18th century.

Savile papers: medieval charters; correspondence of Sir John Savile (Lumley), European diplomat, late 19th century.

Papers of Dame Laura Knight (1877–1970), artist.

Raleigh Cycle Co. archive.

Finding aids: Nottingham City Archives: NRA 1165, 3440, 9529.

Facilities: Photocopying. Photography. Microfilming. Microfilm reader.

Conservation: Full in-house service; outside work undertaken.

Publications: P.A. Kennedy: *Guide to the Nottinghamshire County Records Office* (1960). *Nottinghamshire Parish Registers on Microfiche, 1538–1900* (1984). *The Victorian School in Nottinghamshire*, Archive Resource Pack no. 1 (1988). *The Great War and Nottinghamshire*, Archive Resource Pack no. 2 (1989). *Women's History in Nottingham Archives Office, c1550–1950* (1989). *Rufford: From Abbey to Country House*, Archive Resource Pack no. 3 (1990). *Nottinghamshire Archives: Users' Guide* (1993). *Watson Fothergill: a Victorian Architect of Nottingham*, Archive Resource Pack no. 4 (1993).

860 The Sisters of St Joseph of Peace Archive

Address: Sacred Heart Convent, 7 Lucknow Avenue, Nottingham NG3 5AZ
NB The archives are deposited at Sacred Heart Provincial House, 61 Station Road, Rearsby, Leicestershire.

Telephone: (01644) 604718

Enquiries: The Archivist, Sr M. Patricia

Open: By arrangement.

Access: Students and genuine interested researchers only. An appointment is necessary.

Founded in 1884 in Nottingham, the Religious Sisters are concerned with social work, education, the care of sick children, work with people with AIDS, and justice and peace issues.The archive consists mainly of personal papers, including correspondence and photographs of the founder, Mother Francis Clare Cusack

(1829–91), and early members of the Order. There are catalogues and indexes.

861 University of Nottingham Library
Department of Manuscripts and Special Collections

Address: University of Nottingham, University Park, Nottingham NG7 2RD

Telephone: (0115) 951 5151 951 4565 (Secretary and general enquiries) 951 4563 (Keeper of Manuscripts)

Fax: (0115) 951 4558

Enquiries: The Keeper of Manuscripts, Dr D.B. Johnston

Open: Mon–Fri: 9.00–5.00, by appointment.

Access: Open to the public on application. Restrictions on modern records varying from between 30 and 100 years, depending on the type of material.

Historical background: Nottingham University College began collecting MSS in the 1930s after the appointment of the first professional librarian in 1931. The first archivist was appointed in 1947, which led to the development of a separate MSS department within the university library. Nottingham gained full university status in 1948. It is recognised as a place of deposit for public records.

Acquisitions policy: To increase the strength of existing collections, by deposit, donation or occasionally purchase, with particular focus upon local archives, material relating to the research and teaching interests of the university and private papers of former members of the university.

Archives of organisation: Historical records of Nottingham University College (1881–1948); some non-current records of the University of Nottingham.

Major collections: Family collections: title deeds and settlements, manorial and estate records, including court rolls, compoti, accounts, rentals, surveys, maps and plans; estate, political and personal correspondence, with papers covering banking business and other interests, including Chamier, Clifton, Denison, Drury-Lowe, Galway, Manvers, Mellish, Middleton,

Newcastle, Portland, Wrench and Kirke families.

Ecclesiastical records: Church of England (Archdeaconry of Nottingham), Unitarian, Baptist, United Reformed Church (Congregational/Presbyterian).

Literary collections: Restoration and 18th–century verse (Cavendish and Harley material in Portland Collection); Henry Kirke White; Coventry Patmore; D.H. Lawrence.

Hospital records of those hospitals in the Nottinghamshire Area Health Authority (Teaching) Nottingham District.

Water authority: records of the former Trent River Authority and its predecessors and other bodies amalgamated with it, including Hatfield Chase Drainage Authority and Brigg Court of Sewers.

Business records, mainly of firms connected with the lace industry.

Trade union records, including those of the Amalgamated Society of Lacemakers.

Specialised collections, including that of Francis Willoughby (1635–72), naturalist and patron of John Ray (1627–1705), a 17th–century natural history collection within the Middleton (Willoughby family), Collection; meteorological records; and Russian and British posters of World War II.

In total there are more than 2,000,000 MSS, 12th–20th centuries.

Non-manuscript material: Included in the MSS collections are photographic material, printed pamphlets, posters, printed sermons, hymn books and related material.

The library's printed book special collections form part of the department's holdings and complement strengths in the MSS in several areas, especially local history.

Finding aids: Handlists, available for purchase; also sent to NRA, copyright libraries and the local record offices (Nottinghamshire, Derbyshire and Lincolnshire). Detailed calendars for a small number of collections, or sections of collections. Some indexes of personal and place names.

Facilities: Photocopying. Photography. Microfilming. Microfilm reader/printer.

Publications: The University of Nottingham, Manuscripts Department of the University Library, Information leaflet no. 13.

The University of Nottingham, Report of the

Keeper of the Manuscripts [occasional publication].

National Inventory of Documentary Sources, Chadwyck-Healey microfiche (1984–).

862 Nuneaton Library

Parent organisation: Warwickshire County Library

Address: Church Street, Nuneaton, Warks CV11 4DR

Telephone: (01203) 384027/347006

Fax: (01203) 350125

Enquiries: The Area Manager, Mr P.J. Monahan

Open: Mon, Thurs: 9.00–7.00 Wed: 9.00–1.00 Tues, Fri: 9.00–6.00 Sat: 9.00–4.00

Access: Open to the public.

Historical background: Ephemeral material relating to Nuneaton and the surrounding area has been collected on a non-systematic basis. Other libraries at Warwick, Stratford upon Avon and Leamington hold local history collections. Most genuinely archival material is held by the Warwickshire Record Office (entry 1077), and the Jodrell MSS and Cross Collection previously held by the library have been transferred there.

Acquisitions policy: Donations of archival material relevant to the Nuneaton area are accepted, but may be passed to the county record office. Archival material is not normally purchased.

Major collections: Beighton MSS, 1698–1733; MSS relating to Attleborough field, Nuneaton Common fields and the Attleborough and Nuneaton Enclosures of 1731.

Non-manuscript material: George Eliot Collection.

Collection of local illustrations.

Finding aids: Index to George Eliot Collection and to illustrations.

Facilities: Photocopying. Microfilm/fiche reader/printer.

863 Oldham Archives Service

Parent organisation: Oldham Metropolitan Borough

Address: Local Studies Library, 84 Union Street, Oldham, Greater Manchester OL1 1DN,

Telephone: (0161) 911 4654

Fax: via (0161) 627 1025

Enquiries: The Archives Officer, Mr Paul Sillitoe

Open: Mon, Thurs: 10.00–7.00 Tues: 10.00–2.00 Wed, Fri, Sat: 10.00–5.00

Access: Open to the public. The office applies the CARN reader's ticket system. Disabled access. Advance booking is recommended for microform readers.

Historical background: Oldham Metropolitan Borough was established in 1974 within Greater Manchester County. Oldham's Local Studies Library then became responsible for the records of the predecessor local authorities, adding to substantial local history MSS collected over 100 years. It moved to the present premises in 1982 and the first Archives Officer was appointed in 1991.

Acquisitions policy: In cooperation with Great Manchester Record Office (entry **794**) and other GM district archives services, to collect, permanently preserve and make available for research, public, official, ecclesiastical and private records relating to the area of Oldham Metropolitan Borough.

Archives of organisation: Records of predecessor authorities: Oldham County Borough and urban districts of Chadderton, Crompton, Failsworth, Lees, Royton, Saddleworth, Springhead and Uppermill.

Major collections: Extensive records of local Co-operative Society and textile trades unions.
Butterworth MSS: including press reports, 1829–43, and research notes for Baines's *History of Lancashire* (1836).
Rowbottom diaries: daily events in Oldham, 1787–1829.
Personal papers of Dame Sarah and Marjory Lees of Werneth Park, including suffrage material.
Higson antiquarian collection.

Non-manuscript material: Local census and parish registers (microfilm).

Local newspapers and oral history resources.
Local studies collections include photographs (20,000), plans (2000), books (16,000) and pamphlets on the history of Oldham.

Finding aids: Lists and indexes (under revision); lists sent to NRA. Local studies classification scheme and indexes.

Facilities: Photocopying. Photography. Microfilm/fiche readers/printer.

Conservation: Contracted out.

Publications: Archive Guide in preparation.

864 Saddleworth Museum
Archives Room

Parent organisation: Saddleworth Museum and Art Gallery

Address: High Street, Uppermill, Oldham, Greater Manchester OL3 6HS

Telephone: (01457) 874093

Enquiries: The Curator

Open: By arrangement.

Access: By appointment.

Historical background: Saddleworth Museum was opened in 1962, with the aim of displaying local life, and expanded in 1979. Partly due to a policy of displaying travelling exhibitions, attendance increased steadily, resulting in a flow of gifts of documents and artefacts from local people. As well as the museum's collections, those of the Saddleworth Historical Society are housed and made available for general use.

Acquisitions policy: To accept anything which will help bring alive an awareness and understanding of the district and its history.

Major collections: Howcroft/Shaw papers, architectural and antiquarian, 19th and 20th centuries.
Saddleworth deeds and wills, including documents and maps *re* Enclosure Act and Award of 1810 and 1834.
Local mill financial, business and processing records, with sample books and correspondence *re* exports of cloth to the Americas, 1800–.
Weavers' Union books and papers, 1820s-1960s.
Papers of Ammon Wrigley (1861–1946), writer,

painter and folklorist, and E.L. Edwards (c1885–1978), local historian.

Non-manuscript material: Photographic archive of local architecture and textile machinery.
Recorded interviews with local people on the history of the area, and the sound of textile looms in operation.
Taped memoirs of Lord Rhodes of Saddleworth.
Microfilms of census returns and parish registers.

Finding aids: Holdings fully listed in typed calendars and card catalogues.

Facilities: Photocopying.

Publications: Saddleworth Archives: Archives for Research and Education (1982) [descriptive booklet].

865 Salford RC Diocesan Archives

Parent organisation: Salford Roman Catholic Diocesan Trustees

Address: Sacred Heart Presbytery, Whetstone Hill Road, Derker, Oldham, Greater Manchester OL1 4NA

Telephone: (0161) 624 8760

Fax: (0161) 628 4967

Enquiries: Fr David Lannon

Open: By arrangement only.

Access: Bona fide scholars, by appointment.

Acquisitions policy: Relevant diocesan and local RC history material acquired, by donation and purchase.

Archives of organisation: Diocese, parishes and related societies records, 1850–.
NB Parish registers are either in individual parishes or the Lancashire Record Office (entry 944).

Major Collections: Bishops' official Acta.
Bishop Casartelli papers, 1852–1925.
Education and Catholic schools material.

Non-manuscript material: Deed plans and photographs.
Directories and diocesan almanacs.
The Harvest, 1887–1969; *Catholic Federationist,* 1910–23.

Finding aids: Lists and subject index.

Facilities: Photocopying.

866 Cowper Memorial Library

Parent organisation: Cowper Memorial Museum

Address: Orchardside, Market Place, Olney, Bucks MK46 4AB

Telephone: (01234) 711516

Enquiries: The Custodian, Mrs Elizabeth Knight

Open: April-Oct: Tues–Sat: 10.00–1.00; 2.00–5.00 Nov-March: Tues–Sat: 1.00–4.00 Closed 15 December to the end of January.

Access: Bona fide students, by appointment.

Historical background: The museum was founded in 1900 and is an independent museum run by a board of trustees. The founder was Thomas Wright, author and local historian, who continued to add to his personal collection. Over the past 15 years the lace collection has been expanded, lacemaking being the local cottage industry in Cowper's day, now enjoying a craft revival. Collections include local archaeology, geology, palaeontology, local history and, more recently, family history.

Acquisitions policy: The main object of the Cowper and Newton Museum is to obtain objects and memorabilia of the poet William Cowper (1731–1800) and the Rev. John Newton (1725–1807), and to preserve and maintain and display such objects for the benefit of students as well as the general public. The museum also acquires items which have a close association with Olney and the immediate surrounding villages.

Major collections: Avenell Collection, the Drinkwater Collection and the Harvey Collection.
Collection of materials towards a life of Cowper.
John Sparrow Collection.
Brian Spiller working papers.

Non-manuscript material: Photographs.

Finding aids: Catalogue of manuscripts. Card index of pamphlets and photographs. NRA 10540.

Conservation: Contracted out.

Publications: 'Handlist', *Cambridge Bibliographical Society Journal*, IV, 2 (1965) [Letters and MSS relating to Cowper and Newton].

867 Edge Hill College

Address: St Helens Road, Ormskirk, Lancs L39 4QP

Telephone: (01695) 575171

Fax: (01695) 584550

Enquiries: The College Librarian

Open: By arrangement.

Access: Bona fide researchers, by appointment.

Historical background: The college was opened as a teachers' training college for women in 1885. It is now co-educational and offers a wide variety of courses in higher education.

Acquisitions policy: To maintain its archives.

Archives of organisation: Minute books, 1882–1925; governors' minutes, 1933–84; staff meeting minutes, 1937–64; register of students, 1885–1925, 1930–51; college roll, 1885–1947; salaries book, letter-books, register of students' work, 1885–95; correspondence with Board of Education, 1884–1907.
College magazine, 1892–.
Photographs.

Finding aids: Rough catalogue.

Publications: F.A. Montgomery: *Edge Hill College: a History, 1885–1985* (1985).

868 Oswestry Town Council

Address: Powis Hall, Oswestry, Shropshire SY11 1PZ

Telephone: (01691) 652776

Fax: (01691) 671080

Enquiries: The Town Clerk, Mr D.J. Preston

Open: Mon, Tues, Thurs, Fri: 9.45–12.45; 2.15–4.30

Access: Bona fide researchers, by application; a registration form must be completed and submitted before a first appointment. Access to records less than 50 years old may be restricted.

Historical background: Oswestry was a chartered borough and, following local government reorganisation, became in 1967 a rural borough functioning as a traditional parish council. In the 1974 reorganisation the rural borough became Oswestry Town Council. In 1986 a strongroom was equipped in the Guildhall, which is a recognised place of deposit for public records. Searchroom accommodation was provided in Powis Hall in 1987.

Acquisitions policy: To maintain the archives.

Archives of organisation: Charters, 1324–1674; minutes and accounts, 1674–; burgess books, 1674–1899; court records of civil actions, 1661–2, 1714–1843; deeds and papers *re* markets, waterworks and buildings, 17th century–; quarter sessions records, 1737–1951; petty sessions records, 1818–97; letter-books and correspondence files, 1890–; charity records, 1836–; housing trust records, 1928–68.

Finding aids: Draft list.

Facilities: Photocopying.

Conservation: Contracted out.

Publications: S. Leighton (ed.): 'The Records of the Corporation of Oswestry', reprinted from *Transactions of the Shropshire Archaeological Society* (1879–83).

869 All Souls College

Parent organisation: University of Oxford

Address: Oxford OX1 4AL

Telephone: (01865) 279379

Enquiries: The Librarian and Archivist

Open: By arrangement.

Access: Bona fide researchers, on written application only and strictly by appointment.

Historical background: All Souls College was founded by Henry Chichele, Archbishop of Canterbury, 1414–43, and is a college for postgraduates only. The library was established in 1438 and takes its name from Christopher Codrington (1668–1710). The archives were transferred to the Bodleian Library (entry **871**) in 1966, the college retaining a few groups of documents.

Acquisitions policy: To maintain collections, by accepting relevant gifts and bequests.

Archives of organisation: Items retained by the college include deeds, charters, college registers, stewards' books, plans, miscellaneous papers.

Major collections: Luttrell Wynne MSS, including volumes of parliamentary, journals and state papers; East India Company documents, 1619–85; papers concerning maritime law; notebooks of Humphrey Dyson (*d* 1632), lawyer and bibliographer.
Correspondence of Sir George Downing (*c*1623–1684) with Sir William Temple, 1664–7.
Notes of lectures given by Sir William Blackstone (1723–80), judge.
Papers of Sir Charles Vaughan, 1774–1849, traveller and diplomat.
Correspondence of Lord Cranley (5th Earl of Onslow) with Sir Dougal Malcolm (1877–1955) on foreign and domestic politics, 1903–13 (2 vols).
Oriental MSS (50).

Non-manuscript material: Drawings and plans by Sir Christopher Wren (1632–1733) (*c*400 items).

Finding aids: Handlist for History of University Project. Calendar of Vaughan Papers: NRA 10564.

Publications: C. Trice Martin: *Catalogue of the Archives in the Muniment Room of All Souls College* (1877) [2 vols + index; annotated copy in Bodleian].
'Catalogue of Sir Christopher Wren's Drawings at All Souls', *Wren Society*, xx (1943), 1–33.
E.F. Jacob: 'All Souls College Archives', *Oxoniensia*, xxxiii (1969), 89–91.
N.R. Ker: *Records of All Souls College Library, 1437–1600* (Oxford, 1971).

870 Balliol College

Parent organisation: University of Oxford

Address: Oxford OX1 3BJ

Telephone: (01865) 277777 (written enquiries preferred)

Fax: (01865) 277803

Enquiries: The Archivist, Dr J.H. Jones, The Librarian, Dr P. Bulloch

Open: Mon–Fri: 9.00–5.00

Access: Archives: Bona fide researchers, on application in writing; there is a 30-year closure rule.
Library: Bona fide researchers, by appointment.

Historical background: The college was founded in 1263 and given its first statute in 1282. Few records survive for college activities in the medieval period, except title deeds. Recording of membership and internal matters began in *c*1520 and was established by 1550. The Archives Room was instituted in 1966 to bring together scattered items. There is little information about the library prior to the 15th century, but there have been continuous gifts since that time.

Acquisitions policy: Archives: material is transferred from college departments, offices and undergraduate societies, and occasionally donated by members.
Library: papers of those connected with the college are accepted.

Archives of organisation: Statutes and foundation deeds, decrees of and correspondence with visitors, correspondence, papers and registers *re* benefactors, 13th–20th centuries; membership records of Masters, Fellows, 16th–20th centuries; estate records, 12th–20th centuries; building records, including architectural drawings and plans, mostly 18th–20th centuries; administration and finance records, including bursars' accounts and buttery books, 1568–20th century; records of Balliol-Trinity Laboratories 1853–1939; records of undergraduates societies, 19th–20th centuries; library records, 17th–20th centuries.

Major collections: Extensive papers of Masters, Fellows and others connected with the college, including: Conroy family papers; Jenkyns family papers, including Richard Jenkyns (Master, 1819–54); substantial material relating to Benjamin Jowett (Master, 1870–93); and papers of David Urquhart (1805–77), Sir Robert Morier (1826–93), T.H. Green (Fellow, 1861–82) and A.L. Smith (Master, 1916–24), including papers relating to the Workers' Educational Association. Also some papers of Nicholas Crouch (Fellow, 1640–68), Frederick Oakley (Fellow, 1827–45), Arthur Hugh Clough (1819–61), Robert Browning (1812–89), Matthew Arnold (1822–88) and his family, A.C. Swinburne (1887–1909), Arnold Toynbee (1852–83), Sir Harold Nicolson (1886–1968) and Adam von Trott zu Solz (1909–44).

Non-manuscript material: Photographs, portraits, coins, seals, college stamps.

Finding aids: All pre-1939 records are identified, listed and selectively indexed. Lists sent to NRA.

Facilities: Microfilm/fiche reader.

Publications: H.E. Salter: *Oxford Balliol Deeds* (1913).
R.A.B. Mynors: *Catalogue of the Manuscripts of Balliol College, Oxford* (1963).
J. Jones: *The Archives of Balliol College, Oxford: a Guide* (Chichester, 1984).
K. Hudson and J. Jones: *The Conroy papers: a Guide* (1987).
J. Jones: *The Jenkyns Papers: a Guide* (1988).
——: *Balliol College: a History, 1263–1939* (1988).
——: *The Portraits of Balliol College: a Catalogue* (1990).
R. Darwall-Smith: *The Jowett Papers* (1993).

871 Bodleian Library
Department of Western Manuscripts

Parent organisation: University of Oxford

Address: Broad Street, Oxford OX1 3BG

Telephone: (01865) 277158

Fax: (01865) 277187

Enquiries: The Keeper of Western Manuscripts, Mrs M. Clapinson

Open: Term: Mon–Fri: 9.00–10.00 Sat: 9.00–1.00 Vacation: Mon–Fri: 9.00–7.00 Sat: 9.00–1.00
Closed: Encaenia Day and the week beginning with the late summer bank holiday.

Access: By reader's ticket. Applicants must present themselves in person, and must have either a letter of introduction from, or an application form filled in by, a responsible person familiar with their work.

Historical background: Founded in 1488, the Bodleian has a continuous history since the refoundation by Sir Thomas Bodley in 1602. Since that date it has collected MSS and printed books and remains a library of legal deposit. The Indian Institute Library and Rhodes House Library (entry **907**) are dependent libraries but still have a separate identity. Access to the Radcliffe Science Library MSS is now arranged via the Keeper of Western Manuscripts.

Acquisitions policy: Building the collections in existing areas of strength. The chief growth area is modern personal papers of public figures.

Archives of organisation: Bodleian Library administrative records, 1600–. (See entry **896** for University Archives.)

Major collections: Large collections of MSS of all periods, including papyri; Byzantine MSS; medieval text and illuminated MSS, especially Italian and English; English historical collections, especially 17th century; local history collections of antiquarian, topographical and estate records; deeds and rolls; music; archives of societies, including the Church's Ministry among the Jews, the Society for the Protection of Science and Learning and the Conservative Party; papers of politicians, writers, scientists, scholars, churchmen and other public figures.

Non-manuscript material: Oxford University theses.
Maps, drawings and photographs.
The John Johnson Collection of printed ephemera (housed separately).

Finding aids: Variety of lists, catalogues and indexes. Lists sent to NRA.

Facilities: Photography. Microfilm/fiche readers. Facilities for blind readers.

Conservation: Full in-house service.

Publications: Quarto catalogues of older named collections (1845–1900): *I, Greek Manuscripts; II, Laud; III* and *XI, Canonici; IV, Tanner; V, Rawlinson; IX, Digby; X, Ashmole.*
F. Madan et al.: *Summary Catalogue of Western MSS in the Bodleian Library at Oxford* (8 vols, 1895–1953; repr., 1980).
M. Clapinson and T.D. Rogers: *Summary Catalogue of Western MSS Acquisitions, 1916–1975* (3 vols, 1991).
Lists of notable accessions in *Annual Report of the Curators* (1888–) and *Bodleian Library Record* (1914–).

872 Brasenose College

Parent organisation: University of Oxford

Address: Oxford OX1 4AJ

Telephone: (01865) 277826/7

Fax: (01865) 277822

Enquiries: The Archivist, Mrs Elizabeth Boardman

Open: Tues, Wed: 9.00–4.45

Access: Bona fide scholars, by appointment only.

Historical background: The college was founded in 1509, and by the 18th century was considered one of the best endowed colleges in the university. Medieval and other MSS are deposited in the Bodleian Library (entry **871**).

Acquisitions policy: Archives of the college; papers of members of the college.

Archives of organisation: Extensive archive collections include college minutes, 1539–; accounts, 1516–; buttery books, 1639–1931; deeds, 12th century–; other estate records, 1509–; site and buildings records, 1509–; benefactions, 1509–; undergraduate clubs, 1782–; room books, 1747–; records of college library, 1550–.

Major collections: Personal papers of Sir Noel Hall (1902–83), principal.
J.H.A. Sparrow Collection of letters, MSS and memorabilia of Walter Horatio Pater (1839–94), writer, critic and Fellow.

Non-manuscript material: Plans and drawings for college buildings by Nicholas Hawkesmoor, Sir John Soane, Philip Hardwick and Sir Thomas Jackson, 18th–20th centuries.
Estate maps, c1500, 1607–1869.
Photographs of college site and members.
Photograph negatives and albums of W.T.S. Stallybrass (1883–1948), principal.

Finding aids: Calendar of deeds and some administrative papers to mid-19th century (NRA). Handlist of major administrative records, 1509–1960 (NRA). Card index of most remaining material. Comprehensive catalogue in progress.

Facilities: Photocopying.

Publications: Brasenose College Register (1909). Articles about the archive collections appear in *The Brazen Nose* (1909–), including R.W. Jeffrey: 'The Brasenose College Muniment Room', *The Brazen Nose*, v (1933), 290–3.

873 Campion Hall

Parent organisation: University of Oxford

Address: Brewer Street, Oxford OX1 1QS

Telephone: (01865) 286104 (Librarian) 286100 (Enquiries)

Fax: (01865) 286148

Enquiries: The Librarian/Archivist, Rev. Norman Tanner

Open: By arrangement only.

Access: Approved readers, by appointment only.

Campion Hall is a private hall of the University of Oxford, founded in 1896 for members of the Society of Jesus. It holds papers of Gerard Manley Hopkins (1844–89), which are catalogued in H. House and G. Storey (eds): *The Journals and Papers of Gerard Manley Hopkins* (1959), Appendix IV. There are also some drawings by Sir Edwin Lutyens (1869–1944), architect. Photocopying is available.

874 Centre for Oxfordshire Studies

Parent organisation: Oxfordshire County Council

Address: Central Library, Westgate, Oxford OX1 1DJ

Telephone: (01865) 810826/815749

Fax: (01865) 810187

Enquiries: The Head of Oxfordshire Studies, Dr M. Graham

Open: Tues, Thurs, Fri: 9.15–7.00 Wed, Sat: 9.15–5.00

Access: Generally open to the public. Access to city archives is via Oxfordshire Archives (entry **898**).

Historical background: The library was started by Oxford City Council in 1854 and transferred to the county council in 1974. The city archives are now made available in the searchroom of Oxfordshire Archives but are housed in the Town Hall, which is recognised as a place of deposit for public records. The Local History Library was merged with other library and museum resources in 1991 to form the Centre for Oxfordshire Studies.

Acquisitions policy: To maintain the local history collections, which cover Oxford and Oxfordshire, including the area formerly in north Berkshire.

Major collections: Oxford city archives, including council and committee minutes, 1559–; hustings and Mayor's Court proceedings, 16th century–; quarter session minutes, 1687–;

deeds of markets, colleges etc, 13th century–; records of Oxford Municipal Charities Trustees and Folly Bridge Trust, 19th century–.
Log-books and other records of Oxford city schools, 1863–.

Non-manuscript material: H.W. Taunt (1842–1922) and others: collections of topographical photographs, *c*1900– (150,000).
Other extensive collections of illustrative material, including prints and posters.
Local newspapers, 1753– (virtually complete).
Oxfordshire census returns (microfilm).
County Sites and Monuments Record.
Oral History Archive (*c*2000 tapes).

Finding aids: Lists and indexes, including NRA 6396 (city archives), and NRA 13756 (schools records).

Facilities: Photocopying. Microfilm reader.

875 Christ Church

Parent organisation: University of Oxford

Address: Oxford OX1 1DP

Telephone: (01865) 276169

Enquiries: The Archivist or The Librarian

Open: By arrangement.

Access: Bona fide researchers, by appointment.

Historical background: The original college was founded by Cardinal Wolsey in 1525 and refounded by Henry VIII in 1546, although a library was not begun until the 1560s. The medieval records of monasteries suppressed by Wolsey to endow his college have been deposited in the Bodleian Library (entry **871**). Custody of the archives is divided between the library and muniment room.

Acquisitions policy: To maintain the college archives and consolidate the MS collections.

Archives of organisation: Statutes and charters, 1525–20th century; admission books, 1660–*c*1900; records of college government, 1547–; financial records, including accounts and battel books, 1545–; estate records, including accounts and correspondence, 15th–19th century.

Major collections: Papers of C.L. Dodgson (Lewis Carroll) (1832–98) and Claude Jenkins (1877–1939), ecclesiastical historian.

Evelyn family papers and deeds.

Finding aids: TS catalogues of manorial records; maps, plans and drawings; treasury books.

Publications: N. Denholm Young: *Cartulary of the Medieval Archives of Christ Church*, Oxford Historical Society, xcii (1931).

876 Corpus Christi College

Parent organisation: University of Oxford

Address: Merton Street, Oxford OX1 4JF

Telephone: (01865) 276700

Fax: (01865) 793121

Enquiries: The Assistant Archivist

Open: Mon–Fri: 9.30–1.00
Closed during staff summer leave.

Access: Bona fide researchers; an appointment is always necessary.

Historical background: The college was founded in 1517 by Richard Foxe (?1448–1528), who made strict regulations for preserving the muniments.

Acquisitions policy: Internal records as they devolve from office holders. Deeds and documents concerning property and estates.

Archives of organisation: Administrative and estate records of the college, including admission registers, 1517–; bursarial accounts 1521–; buttery records, 1648–; correspondence of Richard Foxe and John Claimond, first president; papers of Robert Newlin, steward, *c*1645–1700; records of undergraduate societies, 19th century.

Major collections: Library Collections: Medieval MSS concerning theology, liturgy, science, medicine and mathematics.
Collection of Christopher Wase (?1625–1690) *re* grammar schools.
Papers of Thomas Hornsby (1733–1810), astronomer, 1768–74.
Correspondence, papers and diaries of Sir Robert C.K. Ensor (1877–1958) *re* foreign policy, socialism and ornithology.
Letters and papers of A.F. Hemming (1893–1964) *re* Irish troubles and the treaty, 1920–22, and the International Committee for Non-Intervention in Spain, 1936–9.
Papers of E.D.M. Fraenkel (1888–1970).

Finding aids: Catalogue.

Facilities: Photography. Microfiche reader.

Conservation: In-house service as part of Oxford Colleges Conservation Consortium.

Publications: J.G. Milne: 'The Muniments of Corpus Christi College', *Oxoniensia*, ii (1937).
——: 'Berkshire Muniments of Corpus Christi College', *Berkshire Archaeological Journal* (1942), 35–44.
——: *The Early History of Corpus Christi College*, (Oxford 1946) [Chap. v covers the archives].
C. Woolgar: 'Two Oxford Archives in the Early Seventeenth Century', *Archives*, xvi/71 (1984), 258–72.

877 Edward Grey Institute of Field Ornithology
Alexander Library

Parent organisation: University of Oxford

Address: Zoology Department, South Parks Road, Oxford OX1 3PS

Telephone: (01865) 271143

Fax: (01865) 271168

Enquiries: The Librarian, Dr M. L. Birch

Open: Mon–Fri: 9.00–1.00; 2.00–5.00

Access: Bona fide researchers.

Historical background: In 1930 W.B. Alexander (1885–1965) was appointed director of the Bird Census and, with the support of Edward Grey, 1st Viscount of Falloden (1862–1933), Chancellor of the University, launched an appeal for funds to establish the British Trust for Ornithology. The EGI received its formal university statute in 1938, with Alexander as the director and only member of staff. He built up an extensive collection of books, journals and reprints, and after his retirement in 1945 continued to look after the library until 1955. In 1947, the university assumed full financial responsibility for the institute which, with the Bureau of Animal Populations, was part of the Department of Zoological Field Studies, and was incorporated into the Department of Zoology in 1967. The institute retains its individuality and strong links with other ornithological organisations, which provide members of its advisory council.

Acquisitions policy: To acquire, by donation,

deposit or purchase, material relevant to the study of orthithology and related biological fields.

Major collections: The MSS diaries, field notes and original data of many eminent ornithologists, including W.B. and H.G. Alexander; O.V. Aplin, 1879–1918; Leslie H Brown, 1932–79; T.A. Coward, 1883–1933; E. Dunlop, 1904–15; E. Howard, 1894–1931; Julian Huxley, 1903–49; Rev. F.C.R. Jourdain, 1876–1937; D.L. Lack, 1925–73; C. Oldham, 1883–1939, and P. Condor.
The Department of Zoology also holds lecture material, laboratory notes and observations, correspondence, drawings, sketches and illustrations of a number of zoologists, including notes on T.H. Huxley's lectures on natural history at the School of Mines, 1869–1871.

Finding aids: Author catalogue for theses and archive material. Lack: NRA 18780.

Facilities: Photocopying. Microfilm/fiche readers.

878 English Faculty Library

Parent organisation: University of Oxford

Address: St Cross Building, Manor Road, Oxford OX1 3UQ

Telephone: (01865) 271050

Enquiries: The Librarian

Open: Term: Mon–Fri: 9.30–7.00 Sat: 9.30–12.30 Vacation: Mon–Fri: 9.30–5.00 Closed during August.

Access: Primarily for members of the university. Other people may be admitted at the discretion of the library committee. Application should be to the librarian giving credentials and special reasons for wishing to use the library.

Historical background: Founded in 1914 to serve the English School, it is essentially a working collection and has been enriched by gifts and bequests.

Acquisitions policy: It is not library policy to buy MS material; working papers of scholars are occasionally deposited.

Major collections: E.H.W. Meyerstein (1889–1952): papers, including unpublished works, copies of letters, collections of family photographs, portraits (40 boxes).
Wilfred Owen (1893–1918) Collection:

includes his personal library, some of his MSS (poems etc), family relics, press cuttings, correspondence about his works, and other papers preserved by his brother Harold Owen (1897–1971), an author in his own right; correspondence by or to Wilfred Owen, and later letters from members of his circle or editors, including Siegfried Sassoon (1886–1967) and Edmund Blunden (1896–1974) to Susan and Harold Owen.

Notes and correspondence of Dr Percy Simpson (1865–1962) relevant to the history of the library; Dr K.D. Büllbring (1863–1917); S. Roscoe (1900–77), bibliographer of the Newbery family of booksellers; and Professor H.J. Davis (1893–1967), editor of Swift.

Non-manuscript material: Pamphlet collection of Prof. A.S. Napier (1853–1916), including scarce academic dissertations on Old and Middle English philology, late 19th–early 20th centuries.

Finding aids: Special handlists for MSS collections. NRA 11902.

Facilities: Photocopying. Microfilm readers.

Publications: P. Morgan: *Brief Calendar* (1965) [available in Bodleian Library].
——: *Oxford Libraries outside the Bodleian: a Guide* (Oxford, 2/1980), 169.
J. Harker: *The Historical Development of the English Faculty Library, Oxford* (London, 1980).

879 Exeter College
The Library

Parent organisation: University of Oxford

Address: Oxford OX1 3DP

Telephone: (01865) 279621

Fax: (01865) 279630

Enquiries: The Librarian and Archivist, Dr J.R. Madicott

Open: Mon–Fri: 9.00–5.00
Closed for two to three weeks in August and September.

Access: Bona fide scholars, by appointment with the Librarian and Archivist.

Historical background: The college was founded in 1314.

Acquisitions policy: Gifts and bequests are occasionally received from old members, and

very occasionally items relating to the college are purchased.

Archives of organisation: College registers, 1539–1915; lists of Fellows; statutes; rectors' and bursars' accounts; financial records, 1592–; buttery books, 1592–1762; SCR papers, 1787–1967; library records; records of clubs and societies; deeds and papers *re* properties in Oxfordshire and elsewhere.

Major collections: Shortridge papers, 1693–. Secondary material and collections relating to college history.

Non-manuscript material: A large number of photographs, prints and original drawings; scrapbooks; rolled maps and plans of estates, 18th and 19th centuries.

Finding aids: Full typescript handlist (1977, rev. 1993; copy in the Bodleian Library).

Facilities: Photocopying.

Publications: A.B. How: *Exeter College Register, 1891–1921* (Oxford 1928).
HMC Second Report, XIV App 127–30 (1).

880 Hertford College

Parent organisation: University of Oxford

Address: Catte Street, Oxford OX1 3BW

Telephone: (01865) 279400

Fax: (01865) 279437

Enquiries: The Archivist, Dr T. Barnard, The Librarian, Dr S. West

Open: By arrangement.

Access: Access to the archives is by courtesy of the principal and Fellows, who reserve the right to refuse permission without giving the reasons for their decision. Post-1920 material is not normally available.

Historical background: The origins of the college lie with the foundation of Hart Hall, a medieval establishment connected with Exeter College, which became the first Hertford College in 1740, and Magdalen Hall. The latter was allied to Magdalen College until 1602, moved to the site of the first Hertford College in 1813 and became the second Hertford college in 1874. MSS were deposited in 1890 in the Bodleian Library (entry **871**) in 1890.

Archives of organisation: Few records survive:

they include Magdalen Hall buttery books, 1661, 1663, 1670–1862; Hertford College buttery books, 1879–.
NB A few Magdalen Hall records are among Magdalen College archives (entry **886**).

Non-manuscript material: Broadsides and proclamations, c1660–18th century.

Finding aids: Typescript catalogue of archives (1985): NRA 27928.

Conservation: Contracted out.

Publications: See preface to S.G. Hamilton: *Hertford College* (College Histories, 1903).

881 The House of St Gregory and St Macrina
Library

Address: 1 Canterbury Road, Oxford OX2 6LU

Telephone: (01865) 52991

Enquiries: The Librarian or Webb Collection: Dr S.P. Brock, Oriental Institute, Pusey Lane, Oxford OX1 2LE

Open: By arrangement.

Access: Bona fide researchers, by appointment.

Historical background: The core of the collection comes from the library of the late Rev. Derwas Chitty.

Acquisitions policy: Funds available are minimal: acquisitions are mainly Greek patristic texts of monastic interest.

Major collections: Chitty Collection of papers left by Rev. D. Chitty.
Webb Collection: transcripts of Syriac liturgical MSS made by Rev. Douglas Webb.

Non-manuscript material: Greek patristic texts.

Publications: K. Ware and S.P. Brock: 'The Library of the House of St Gregory and St Macrina, Oxford: the D.J. Chitty Papers', *Sobornost/Eastern Chronicles Review*, iv/1 (1982), 56–8.

882 Jesus College

Parent organisation: University of Oxford

Address: Oxford OX1 3DW

Telephone: (01865) 279700

Fax: (01865) 279687

Enquiries: The Archivist

Open: By arrangement only.

Access: Bona fide researchers, by appointment after written application.

Historical background: The college was founded by Elizabeth I in 1571 and has had strong connections with Wales throughout its history. In 1886 the medieval MSS, including some important Welsh-language ones, were deposited in the Bodleian Library (entry **871**) and buttery books, 1638–, with some other records have also been transferred there.

Acquisitions policy: Papers of former members may be accepted.

Archives of organisation: Registers and papers relating to the college's internal administration, estates and livings, including bursars' accounts, 1631–; benefactors' registers, 1571–1758; college registers, 1660–; minutes of governing body, 1883–; records of undergraduate societies, 1858–.

Major collections: Private papers of principals Francis Mansell (1579–1665) and Thomas Pardo (1688–1763), and of Edmund Meyricke (1636–1713), Fellow and benefactor.
Papers of John Richard Green (1837–83), historian, and T.E. Lawrence (1888–1935).

Non-manuscript material: Plans, maps and photographs.

Finding aids: Handlist for History of the University Project. Some lists sent to NRA.

Facilities: Photocopying where appropriate. Photography via the Bodleian Library.

Conservation: Member of the Oxford Colleges Conservation Consortium.

Publications: J.N.L. Baker: *Jesus College, Oxford, 1571–1971* (Oxford, 1971).

883 Keble College

Parent organisation: University of Oxford

Address: Oxford OX1 3PG

Telephone: (01865) 272727

Enquiries: The Librarian

Open: By arrangement.

Access: Bona fide scholars, by appointment.

Historical background: The college was founded in 1870 as a memorial to John Keble (1792–1866), poet and divine.

Acquisitions policy: To maintain the archives and accept papers relevant to the theological concerns of the college.

Archives of organisation: Papers of the Keble Memorial Fund, 1866–; council minutes, accounts, admissions, 1870–; academic reports on undergraduates, 1873–; records of student societies, 1870–.

Major collections: Correspondence and papers of John Keble and H.P. Liddon (1829– 90) *re* Tractarian Movement.
Collections of medieval and oriental MSS.

Finding aids: TS lists of Keble and Liddon papers, with index of correspondents.

Publications: B. St G. Drennan (ed.): *The Keble College Centenary Register, 1870–1970* (Oxford 1971).
M.B. Parkes: *The Medieval Manuscripts of Keble College, Oxford* (1979).
P. Morgan: *Oxford Libraries outside the Bodleian* (2/1980), 54–5.

884 Lady Margaret Hall

Parent organisation: University of Oxford

Address: Oxford OX2 6QA

Telephone: (01865) 274300

Fax: (01865) 511069

Enquiries: The College Archivist, c/o the College Librarian

Open: Strictly by arrangement.

Access: Bona fide researchers. There is restricted access to personal records of members of college.

Historical background: Lady Margaret Hall was founded in 1878 as one of the first two halls for women in Oxford. It has been co-educational since 1979.

Acquisitions policy: Strictly limited to records relating to the college, its Fellows, other staff and students.

Archives of organisation: Official records of the college 1878–, including minute books of the History Club, a society for Oxford women history dons, 1899–1939.

Major collections: Commonplace books, notebooks and MSS of Louisa Kathleen Haldane (1863–1961), novelist.
MS and TS poems of Ethel Street (LMH, 1918–21), who worked at the Tavistock Clinic and London School of Economics.

Non-manuscript material: Architectural drawings of college buildings and plans of the grounds.
Photographs of buildings and students.

Finding aids: Summary lists. Lists sent to NRA. Haldane: NRA 11605.

Facilities: Photocopying by arrangement.

Conservation: Contracted out.

Publications: J. Agate (ed.): *Lady Margaret Hall Register, 1879–1966* (Cambridge, 1970).
C. Avent and H. Pipe (eds): *Lady Margaret Hall Register, 1879–1990* (Oxford, 1990).

885 Lincoln College

Parent organisation: University of Oxford

Address: Turl Street, Oxford OX1 3DR

Telephone: (01865) 279831

Enquiries: The Librarian

Open: By arrangement only.

Access: Genuine historical researchers; an appointment must be made well in advance.

Historical background: Lincoln College was founded in 1429 by Richard Fleming, Bishop of Lincoln, under whom the earliest college buildings were erected. In 1479 Bishop Thomas Rotherham, who is regarded as the second founder, further endowed the college and had the statutes drawn up. The college was given estates in Oxfordshire and elsewhere which, with various benefactions, provided the income of Fellows and scholars. The college administration has continued unbroken to the present day, although several series of records survive only from the 17th century. In 1892 the MS collections were deposited in the Bodleian Library (entry **871**).

Acquisitions policy: The college is pleased to accept papers of old members relating to the life of the college.

Archives of organisation: College statutes, charters, registers.
Annual accounts, 15th century (complete from 1600–).
Estate deeds, leases and manorial records, correspondence.
Records of college clubs and societies.

Major collections: Some letters of John Wesley (1703–17), Fellow, and Mark Pattison (1813–84), rector.
Papers of William Ward Fowler (1847–1921), Fellow.
Some MSS of Edward Thomas (1878–1917).

Finding aids: MS catalogue of medieval deeds and charters. Catalogue of later material. Handlist and shelf list of archives. Transcripts with subject indexes available in Bodleian Library.

Facilities: Photocopying.

Publications: V.H.H. Green: *The Commonwealth of Lincoln College, 1427–1977* (Oxford, 1979).

886 Magdalen College

Parent organisation: University of Oxford

Address: Oxford OX1 4AU

Telephone: (01865) 276088

Enquiries: The Archivist, Dr J.B. Cottis

Open: Thurs, Fri: 10.00–1.00; 2.00–4.30, by appointment.

Access: On written application. There is a 30–year restriction on many items; no access is available to records of living persons.

Historical background: The college was founded in 1458 by William Waynflete, Bishop of Winchester.

Acquisitions policy: The integration into the college archive of any material relevant to its history, donated or deposited by former members or by the general public.

Archives of organisation: Administrative and financial records of the college, 15th century–.
Deeds and documents relating to the acquisition and control of college estates, distributed over a wide area of southern and eastern England, 12th century–.
Documents relating to schools founded by the college in Oxford, Brackley (Northamptonshire) and Wainfleet (Lincolnshire), mainly 19th century.

Major collections: Literary and personal papers relating to members of the college and their associates.

Non-manuscript material: Maps, plans and architectural drawings of college buildings and estates.
Prints and photographs of college members.
Printed material relating to the college and the university.
A small number of microfilms and tape-recordings.

Finding aids: Calendar of medieval deeds (49 vols). Catalogue: *The Estate Archives of St Mary Magdalen College, Oxford* (10 vols; copy in NRA). Catalogue of estate papers. Handlists of maps and shelf lists of certain series. MS list and card index to MSS 222–1119. Other lists in process of computerisation. Guide in preparation.

Facilities: Photocopying. Photography.

Conservation: Member of the Oxford Colleges Conservation Consortium.

Publications J.R. Bloxam: *Register of the Members of St Mary Magdalen College* (Oxford and London, 1853–81) [7 vols].
W.D. Macray: *Notes from the Muniments of St Mary Magdalen College, Oxford, from the Twelfth to the Seventeenth Century* (Oxford and London, 1882).
——: *Register of Magdalen College*, new series (London, 1894–1915) [8 vols].
C. Woolgar: 'Two Oxford Archives in the Early Seventeenth Century', *Archives*, xvi/71 (1984), 258–72.

887 Manchester College

Address: Mansfield Road, Oxford OX1 3TD

Telephone: (01865) 271015/6

Fax: (01865) 271012

Enquiries: The Librarian, Mrs M.A. Sarosi

Open: Mon–Fri 9.30–1.00; 2.00–5.00, by appointment.
Closed in August.

Access: Approved readers, on written application. Letters of recommendation/identification may be required.

Historical background: Manchester College was established in 1786 in Manchester under the name of Manchester Academy. It was one of the last of a long line of dissenting academies founded to provide non-conformists with higher education, and was the direct successor to Warrington Academy. It moved successively to York (1803–40), back to Manchester (1840–53), to London (1853–99) and finally to Oxford (1899–). From the first the college was closely linked to the Unitarian denomination.

Acquisitions policy: To collect Unitariana and items relating to the history of the college.

Archives of organisation: Minute books of Warrington and Manchester College, 1757–1820, 1885–; library catalogues from Warrington, Exeter and Manchester Academies; lecture notes by students; student magazines.

Major collections: Letters and papers of teachers at Warrington Academy and Manchester College, including John Seddon (1725–70), Joseph Priestley (1733–1804), Charles Wellbeloved (1769–1858), John Kenrick (1788–1877), James Martineau (1805–1900).
Letters and papers of Unitarians, including William Shepherd (1768–1847), Lant Carpenter (1780–1840), Joseph Blanco White (1775–1841), Mary Carpenter (1807–77), Harriet Martineau (1802–76), Robert B. Aspland (1782–1845).

Non-manuscript material: Portraits and prints of teachers and others.
College photographs etc.
Printed material relating to the college and Unitarian history.
Joseph Priestley's globes.

Finding aids: Descriptive catalogue with index in preparation. Typed handlist to Blanco White Collection. Handwritten index to Shepherd Collection. Priestley: NRA 19870

Facilities: Photocopying. Photographs may be arranged.

Conservation: Contracted out when grants obtained.

Publications: Joseph Priestley 1733–1804: Scientist, Teacher and Theologian: a 250th Anniversary Exhibition (Oxford, 1983).
Manchester College, 1786–1986: a Bicentenary Exhibition Organised by Manchester College Oxford at the Bodleian Library (Oxford, 1986).
B. Smith, (ed.): *Truth, Liberty, Religion: Essays Celebrating Two Hundred Years of Manchester College* (Oxford, 1986).

888 Mansfield College Library

Parent organisation: University of Oxford

Address: Mansfield College, Mansfield Road, Oxford OX1 3TF

Telephone: (01865) 270975

Fax: (01865) 270970

Enquiries: The Librarian, Alma Jenner

Open: Mon–Fri: 9.00–4.00
Closed for two weeks at Christmas and Easter and all of August.

Access: Bona fide researchers, by prior appointment only, on written application to the principal with an accompanying letter of reference.

Historical background: Mansfield College had its origins in Spring Hill College, Birmingham, founded in 1838 for the training of Congregational ministers. The college was transferred to Oxford in 1886, and, being the first nonconformist college to come to Oxford after the abolition of the Religious Tests Act, it trained ministers from any dissenting denomination and provided a free church faculty in theology. In 1955 it was recognised by the university and began to receive undergraduates.

Acquisitions policy: General encouragement from librarian to departments and older members of the college to deposit material.

Archives of organisation: Archives of Spring Hill College, Birmingham, and Mansfield College, Oxford: annual reports; minutes of the governing body and Board of Education; cash books; bursary records, 1838–.
College magazine.
Responses from other dissenting colleges to questions sent by Spring Hill College on the anti-slavery movement, 1841.
Minutes of college societies, including Discussion Society, 1847–66; Debating Society, 1860–77; Oxford University Congregational Society, 1950–57; Oxford University Nonconformists Union; Rural Mission Society; Rural Churches Committee.

Major collections: Samuel Birch (1813–85), Book of Prayers.

Records of chapels and missioners associated with former students of Spring Hill.
A.L. Thomas, note-books of lectures by Selbie et al., 1919–22 (47).
E. Wilton Rix, letters to his family, 1914–18.
A.G. Matthews (1881–1962), papers concerning non-conformist history.
Records of the Frilford and Longworth Home Mission, 1854–1939.
MS sermons.

Non-manuscript material: Photograph albums of college buildings, interiors and college members; news cuttings.
Tapes of reminiscences of older members of the college.

Finding aids: Computerised catalogue; hard copy available. Handlist. NRA 10965

Facilities: Photocopying.

889 Merton College Library

Parent organisation: University of Oxford

Address: Oxford OX1 4JD

Telephone: (01865) 276343 ext. 243

Enquiries: The Librarian, S. Bewdall

Open: Mon–Fri: 10.00–1.00; 2.00–4.00
Closed for the month of August and for a week at Christmas and Easter.

Access: Bona fide researchers only; an appointment is necessary.

Historical background: The college was founded in 1264 and the library building, begun in 1373, is one of the oldest to survive in England.

Archives of organisation: Records of the college, administration and estates, including wardens' accounts, bursars' and subwardens' rolls, c1300–1660; minutes of the governing body, 1483–; admission records, 1758–; parish register of St John the Baptist parish.

Major collections: Two diaries of Griffin Higgs (1589–1659), 1637–8.
Papers of James Harris, 1st Earl of Malmesbury (1746–1820); G.C. Brodrick (1831–1903), warden of the college, and F.H. Bradley (1846–1924), philosopher.
Autobiography of Edward Nares (1762–1841), theological and historical writer.
Papers, drawings and first editions of Sir Max Beerbohm (1872–1956).

Non-manuscript material: First editions of T.S. Eliot.

Finding aids: Supplementary catalogue, 1920. Indexes of deeds, surveys and maps, with handlists. Summary handlist, 1970. *Calendar of Oxfordshire Records at Merton* (typescript list). List of correspondence of 1st Earl of Malmesbury: NRA 9473.

Facilities: Limited photocopying facilities. Microfilms may be ordered via the photographic studio of the Bodleian Library.

Conservation: Member of the Oxford Colleges Conservation Consortium.

Publications: F.M. Powicke: *The Medieval Books of Merton College* (Oxford, 1931) [includes MSS].
Merton College Register, 1900–1964; 1964–84 (Oxford, 1964; 1990) [these registers contain summaries of the biographies of members of the college].

890 Middle East Centre
St Antony's College

Parent organisation: University of Oxford

Address: Oxford OX2 6JF

Telephone: (01865) 59651 ext. 264

Fax: (01865) 311475

Enquiries: The Librarian

Open: Tues, Wed: 9.30–12.45; 1.45–5.00
Closed for five to six weeks during summer (dates available on request) and two weeks at Christmas and Easter.

Access: Members of Oxford University; others at the discretion of the Archivist and strictly by appointment. There is a daily charge for non-academics.

Historical background: The collection was begun in 1961 by Elizabeth Monroe and Albert Hourani with the aim of gathering together the papers, both personal and official, of individuals who served in the Middle East–as senior Government representatives, members of the armed forces etc–or whose main area of concern–as bankers, businessmen, missionaries or travellers–was the Middle East. The collection has expanded rapidly and now contains the papers of well over 200 individuals, covering the period from 1800 to the present day.

Acquisitions policy: To acquire, by donation or deposit, further collections of private papers of individuals who were involved in the Middle East.

Major collections: H.R.P. Dickson (1881–1959) papers: reports, diaries and correspondence concerning his career as political agent in Bahrain, 1919–21; political resident in the Gulf, 1928; and political agent in Kuwait, 1929–36.
Papers of C.J. Edmonds concerning his service in Iraq, 1915–45, and his study of Kurdistan (topography, language and people), 1915–1960s.
H. St John Philby: correspondence, memos, travel diaries, published and unpublished MSS, relating to Transjordan, Iraq, Palestine and Arabia, 1915–57.
Maj.-Gen. Sir E.L. Spears: papers relating to the Spears Mission to Syria and the Lebanon, 1941–4.
Jerusalem and East Mission: records covering the mission's work in Palestine, Syria, Iraq, Jordan, Iran, Gulf, Egypt, Sudan, Cyprus and North Africa, 1841–1970s.

Non-manuscript material: Photographic Archive: covering all areas of the Middle East, c1860–1960 (c70,000 items).

Finding aids: Handlists are available for approximately one-third of the collections and there is an extensive author and subject index. Lists sent to NRA.

Facilities: Photocopying. Photography by arrangement. Microfiche reader.

Publications: D. Grimwood Jones (ed.): *Sources for the History of the British in the Middle East, 1800–1978: a Catalogue of the Private Papers Collection in the Middle East Centre, St Antony's College, Oxford* (London, 1979).
G.M. Grant (ed.): *Historical Photographs of the Middle East from the Middle East Centre, St Anthony's College, Oxford* (1984) [17,000 photographs on microfiche with a catalogue].

891 Museum of the History of Science

Parent organisation: University of Oxford

Address: Old Ashmolean Building, Broad Street, Oxford OX1 3AZ

Telephone: (01865) 277280/4

Enquiries: The Librarian, Mr A.V. Simcock

Open: Mon–Fri: 10.30–1.00; 2.30–4.00

Access: Scholarly readers, by arrangement with the Librarian; prior notice of visits is helpful.

Historical background: Accompanying the collection of scientific instruments of Lewis Evans (1853–1930), with which the museum was founded in 1924, were the founder's library of c1000 books and 120 volumes of MSS on the subjects of his collection – early scientific instruments and associated techniques. The first curator of the museum, R.T. Gunther (1869–1940), built up a museum library around this core, and it has continued to develop by purchase, gift and deposit. The MS collections and iconographic collection (prints, photographs and printed ephemera) have developed in the same way.

Acquisitions policy: MSS are occasionally purchased, but more usually deposited or given, on the subject of scientific instruments, history of science, and other themes relating to the displays, activities and interests of the museum.

Archives of organisation: R.T. Gunther (curator, 1924–40) Archive, relating both to Gunther himself and to the early history and activities of the museum.
Museum Archive, 1924–.

Major collections: Buxton MSS containing important material relating to Charles Babbage (1792–1871).
Radcliffe Observatory MSS, 1750s–c1900.
Papers and antiquarian collections of several historians of science, in particular G.H. Gabb (1868–1948), R.T. Gunther, H.E. Stapleton (1878–1962) and F. Sherwood Taylor (1897–1956).
Small groups of papers of many Oxford scientists, and from various university departments, laboratories and societies, especially strong in the fields of astronomy and chemistry.
Lewis Evans's important collection of MS treatises and other papers on sundials, surveying, and other mathematical instruments and techniques, mostly 17th and 18th centuries.
Archives and collected MSS of the Royal Microscopical Society.

Non-manuscript material: Associated with the general collection of books is a large collection of off-prints and pamphlets.
The iconographic and printed ephemera collection includes portraits of scientists, illustrations of scientific instruments and other scientific subjects, lecture notices and syllabuses and trade literature.
Photographic material–not confined to scien-

tific subjects–ranges from an archive of Sir John Herschel's experimental work from the time of the invention (1839) to pioneering colour photographs (1900s), and to lantern slides used in science lectures (often associated with MS collections).

Finding aids: Catalogue and index of the MSS collections. NRA lists.

Facilities: Photocopying. Photography can be arranged. Microfilm/fiche reader.

Publications: A.V. Simcock: 'An Ark for History of Science', *Iatul Quarterly*, i/3 (1987), 196–215.
P. Morgan: *Select Index of Manuscript Collections in Oxford Libraries outside the Bodleian* (Oxford, 1991) [references for the museum's holdings].

892 New College

Parent organisation: University of Oxford

Address: The Library, New College, Oxford OX1 3BN

Telephone: (01865) 279581

Fax: (01865) 279590

Enquiries: The Archivist, Mrs C. Dalton

Open: Mon–Fri: 9.00–1.00; 2.15–5.00 Sat am at Bodleian Library, by prior arrangement only.
Closed last week of August and first week of September.

Access: Bona fide scholars and researchers, by appointment.

Historical background: New College was founded by William of Wykeham in 1379 as the senior part of two linked educational institutions, New College and Winchester College. The archives have taken their present form partly as a result of provisions made in the founder's statutes for the admission and conduct of members, and partly out of the need to keep track of an income derived from manors and benefices scattered over ten different counties in southern England. Of particular interest is the fact that the endowments of the college already had a written history when they were acquired, together with their documents. This means that the oldest material in the collections antedates the foundation of the college by some 250 years.

Acquisitions policy: The archives absorb as a matter of course non-current administrative papers generated within the college. Any informal record of college life offered by old members or their descendants is accepted with gratitude. The college does not actively seek out archives which might have strayed into private hands in the past, or memorabilia, but if anything is offered for purchase, it is considered on its merits.

Archives of organisation: Records of internal discipline and administration, including bursars' rolls, 1379–, hall books, 1386–, acts of warden and Fellows, 17th century–.
Records of dealings with Winchester College, 16th century–.
Records of the administration of the college estates and of presentations to college livings, 12th century–, including manorial accounts rolls, 15th century–.

Major collections: Woodforde family papers, early 17th–late 19th centuries.
Correspondence of Rev. Sydney Smith (1771–1845) (*c*500 letters).
The residue of the papers of Alfred Milner, 1st Viscount Milner (1854–1925) not transferred to the Bodleian Library, especially press cuttings, 1893–1905, visitors' books, 1897–1905, and addresses presented to Lord Milner, 1897–1906. Letters and papers of Warden A.H. Smith (1883–1958).
Cox Archives: letters and papers covering roughly the first half of the life of Sir Christopher Cox (1899–1982).
Cooke Archive: a collection of papers of A. H. Cooke (1912–87), mainly from his period as warden, 1976–85.

Non-manuscript material: A series of photograph albums depicting rowing crews and some other sporting teams, 1883–.
Estate maps.

Finding aids: Databases of supplementary archive and early deeds. Card indexes of photographs and other graphic material, in process of being computerised. Calendar of the White Book (archive 9654). Handlists of the Cox and Cooke archives. Guide to using printed sources and New College archives for biographical research.

Facilities: Photocopying. Photography by arrangement. Microfilm reader. Researchers may bring laptop computers.

Conservation: Contracted out.

Publications: H. Rashdall and R.S. Rait: *New*

College (London 1901) [part of the college histories series].

H.F. Westlake: *Hornchurch Priory: a Kalendar of Documents* (1923).

T.F. Hobson: *Manorial Documents at New College, Oxford*, Manorial Society no. 16 (1929).

A.H. Smith: *New College and its Buildings* (Oxford, 1952).

F. Steer: *The Archives of New College, Oxford* (London, 1974).

J. Buxton and P. Williams (eds): *New College, 1379–1979* (1979).

893 Nuffield College Library

Parent organisation: University of Oxford

Address: Nuffield College, Oxford OX1 1NF

Telephone: (01865) 278550

Enquiries: The Archives Assistant (postal only)

Open: Mon–Fri: 9.30–1.00; 2.00–5.45 Sat: 9.30–1.00
Usually closed in August.

Access: Bona fide researchers.

Historical background: The college was founded in 1937 as a graduate college in the social sciences. The librarian is responsible for custody of archives and deposited collections.

Acquisitions policy: To serve the research needs of members of the college.

Archives of organisation: College records, including papers of the founder, Viscount Nuffield (1877–1963), and of Nuffield College Social Reconstruction Survey.

Major collections: Nuffield Trust for the Special Areas.
Records of the Fabian Society.
Papers on Guild Socialism.
Papers of individuals, including Lord Cherwell (1886–1957), William Cobbett (1762–1835), G.D.H. Cole (1889–1957), Sir Stafford Cripps (1889–1952), Lord Gainford (1860–1943), Sir Hubert Henderson (1890–1952).

Non-manuscript material: Books, pamphlets, journals, government publications *re* social sciences.

Finding aids: Detailed lists of some collections and catalogues of most others.

Facilities: Photocopying. Microfilm/fiche readers.

894 Oriel College

Parent organisation: University of Oxford

Address: Oriel Square, Oxford OX1 4EW

Telephone: (01865) 276558

Fax: (01865) 791823

Enquiries: The Librarian, Mrs M. Kirwan, The Archivist, Mrs E. Boardman (Mondays only)

Open: Please apply for information as this varies.

Access: Bona fide scholars, who must apply in writing.

Historical background: The college was founded in 1326, and until the Elizabethan period it was primarily a body of graduate Fellows; the number of undergraduates remained small until the nineteenth century. The neighbouring St Mary Hall was absorbed in 1902. The library benefited from a large bequest by Baron Leigh in 1786 as well as the college's connections with the Tractarian movement in the 1830s and 1840s; leaders of the movement were Fellows of the college. Medieval MSS (not college archives) are deposited in the Bodleian Library (entry **871**).

Acquisitions policy: Archives of the college (internal deposits). Papers of members of the college. Letters and documents connected with the Tractarian movement.

Archives of organisation: College minutes 1479–; accounts, 1409– (incomplete); buttery books, 1642–1952; caution books, 1657–; estate records, 1326– (deeds from 12th century); site and building records, 1326–; tutorial registers, 1834–1936; records of undergraduate clubs, 1842–.

Major collections: Archives of St Mary Hall, including Journal, 1764–1899; buttery books, 1715–1874; battels account, 1773–1898.
Extensive collections of letters and papers of those in the Tractarian movement, including John Keble (1792–1866) and John Henry Newman (1801–90).
Correspondence and papers of Edward Hawkins (1789–1882), provost.
Correspondence of Lancelot Ridley Phelps (1853/4–1936), provost.
Papers concerning R.D. Hampden (1793–1868) controversy.

Non-manuscript material: James Wyatt's plans for the college library, 1787.

Estate maps, 1683–1905, and plans of college site, 20th century.

Photographs of college members and site, late 19th and 20th centuries.

Finding aids: Calendar of papers relating to the college's foundation and to medieval estates. Card index of college archives (cataloguing in progress). Index of Tractarian and other correspondence.

Facilities: Photocopying.

Publications: C.L. Shadwell: *Catalogue of Muniments*, i-x (1893–1905) [privately printed].
——: *Registrum Orielense*, i-ii (Oxford 1893, 1902).
G.C. Richards and C.L. Shadwell: *The Provosts and Fellows of Oriel College Oxford* (Oxford, 1922).
G.C. Richards and H.E. Salter: *The Dean's Register of Oriel, 1446–1661* (Oxford, 1926).
C.L. Shadwell and H.E. Salter: *Oriel College Records* (Oxford Historical Society, 1926).
Articles about the archive collections appear in *The Oriel Record* (1909–).

895 Oxfam Archives

Address: 274 Banbury Road, Oxford OX2 7DX

Telephone: (01869) 245011 ext. 229

Fax: (01869) 247348

Enquiries: The Archivist, Chrissie Webb

Open: Mon–Fri: by arrangement.

Access: Generally open to the public; by appointment only. Access to certain items may be restricted.

Historical background: The Oxford Committee for Famine Relief was formed in 1942 in response to the Allied blockade of Greece and the suffering of its population. In 1943 the committee was registered as a charity. Today, Oxfam's main concerns as a development agency are long-term sustainable development (although it continues to provide emergency relief in times of crisis) and international advocacy. The organisation of the overseas project files began in 1980 and the central archives were established in 1994.

Acquisitions policy: To maintain the archives.

Archives of organisation: Minutes of Oxford Committee for Famine Relief, 1942–.
Minutes of Council of Management, executive and other committees; annual reports; records of grants, 1943–.
Overseas project files, c1955–.

Non-manuscript material: Publicity and campaign literature, photographs and films. Oxfam publications.

Finding aids: List of overseas project files.

Facilities: Photocopying.

896 Oxford University Archives

Parent organisation: University of Oxford

Address: Bodleian Library, Broad Street, Oxford OX1 3BG

Telephone: (01865) 277145

Fax: (01865) 277182

Enquiries: The Archivist, Mr Simon Bailey

Open: Term: Mon–Fri: 9.00–10.00 Sat: 9.00–1.00 Vacation: Mon–Fri: 9.00–7.00 Sat: 9.00–1.00
Closed week of August bank holiday. Opening hours are those of the Bodleian Library (entry 871); intending visitors should always contact the Archivist in advance.

Access: By prior arrangement with the Archivist. Material from the University Archives is read in the Duke Humfrey reading room in the old Bodleian Library. Access requires a Bodleian reader's ticket, for which a charge is made. All records are closed for 30 years and access to certain classes of material is restricted for up to 80 years.

Historical background: The date of the first extant university charter is 1214. Since then the university has preserved records such as charters, deeds, financial documents and records of students. The first keeper of the archives was elected in 1634, and he and his successor transferred the records from the old Congregation House adjoining St Mary's Church to the lower of the two top rooms in the tower in the old Bodleian Library quadrangle. Expansion led to the acquisition of the upper room in the tower for the archives in 1854 and accommodation in other university buildings more recently. The Bodleian Library and the University Press maintain their own records.

Acquisitions policy: Acquisitions are restricted to the administrative records of the university and its departments.

Archives of organisation: University charters, statutes and title deeds.
Records of the Congregation, Convocation and Hebdomadal Council; (legislative and executive bodies).
University Chest and Registry (finance and central administration); students (chiefly matriculations and degrees); chancellor's jurisdiction; university delegacies and committees.
Departmental and faculty records.

Non-manuscript materials: Plans of the University Museum and the Taylor Institution, 19th and 20th centuries.
Drawings and photographs of the restoration of the Sheldonian Theatre, 1935–7, 1958–63.

Finding aids: Handlist and index to contents of lower archive room; lists of most other records; detailed index to Chancellor's Court records, 1594–1869 (in preparation).

Facilities: (Shared with Bodleian Library) Photocopying. Photography. Microfilm/fiche reader/printer.

Conservation: Contracted out.

Publications: Corpus Statutorum Universitatis Oxoniensis (Oxford, 1768) [with additions].
J. Griffiths: *Index to Wills and other Testamentary Records of the Chancellor's Court* (Oxford, 1862).
——: *Statutes of the University of Oxford codified in 1636* (Oxford, 1888).
R.L. Poole: *Lecture on the History of the University Archives* (Oxford, 1912).
S. Gibson: *Statuta Antiqua Oxoniensis* (Oxford, 1931).
T.H. Aston and D.G. Vaisey: 'University Archives', in P. Morgan: *Oxford Libraries outside the Bodleian* (Oxford, 2/1980).
All the pre-1500 university records and some 16th– and 17th–century material have been published, chiefly by the Oxford Historical Society.

897 Oxford University Museum

Parent organisation: University of Oxford

Address: Parks Road, Oxford OX1 3PW

Telephone: (01865) 272982

Enquiries: The Librarian

Open: Mon–Fri: 9.00–1.00; 2.00–5.00

Access: Senior members and students of the University of Oxford. Bona fide scholars, by appointment and at the discretion of the Librarian and Curator.

Historical background: The library is based upon two major benefactions, that of the Rev. F.W. Hope (1849) and that of W.J. Arkell (1956), which created outstanding resources for the study of entomology and Jurassic geology and palaeontology. But it also reflects the university's historic decision of 1855 to create a central teaching facility for natural science in a new museum where its scattered natural history collections could be brought together. The library concentrates today on providing curatorial and research resources for the four modern collections of entomology, geology, mineralogy and zoology. The archives of the museum are deposited in Oxford University Archives (entry **896**), but there is a small archive on the history of the building and of the musuem.

Acquisitions policy: There is no policy of adding to the archive by purchase.

Major collections: Each collection holds catalogues and correspondence in various degrees of completeness relating to accessioned specimens. In addition there is the following material:
Entomology: W.J. Burchell (1782–1863), MS notes, paintings, correspondence; J.C. and C.W. Dale (1792–1872; 1851–1906), diaries, catalogues, correspondence; F.W. Hope (1797–1862), note-books and correspondence; W. Jones (*d* 1818) note-books and paintings; O. Pickard-Cambridge (1828–1917) and J.O. Westwood (1805–1893), MS notes.
Geology: W.J. Arkell (1904–56) and W. Smith (1769–1839), papers; W. Buckland (1784–1856) and J. Phillips (1800–74), note-books, letters and papers.
Mineralogy: T.V. Barker (1881–1931), research notes, correspondence; A.H. Church (1834–1915), laboratory note-books, correspondence; H. Muller (1833–1915), correspondence; H.L.

Bowman (1874–1942), M.W. Porter (1886–1981), R.S. Spiller (1887–1954) and E.J.W. Whittaker (*b* 1921), research notes.
Zoology: W.J. Burchell, MS notes etc.

Non-manuscript material: Plans, drawings and photographs of the early museum.
Paintings and drawings of geological phenomena used as teaching aids by Buckland, Phillips and others, 19th century.
Teaching slide collections, early 20th century.

Finding aids: Partial catalogues and handlists. Arkell: NRA 24520.

Facilities: Photocopying. Photography.

Publications: K.C. Davies and J. Hull: *The Zoological Collections of the Oxford University Museum* (Oxford, 1976).
A.Z. Smith: *A History of the Hope Entomological Collections in the University Museum, Oxford* (Oxford, 1986).

898 Oxfordshire Archives

Address: County Hall, New Road, Oxford OX1 1ND

Telephone: (01865) 815203/810801

Fax: (01865) 810187

Enquiries: The County Archivist, Carl Boardman

Open: Mon–Thurs: 8.45–5.00 Fri: 10.00–5.00, by appointment only. Late evening Wed to 8.00, by appointment only.
Closed for last week of January and first week of February for stock-taking.

Access: Prior booking is advisable. The office operates the CARN reader's ticket system; tickets issued require two passport-size photos. A charge is made for postal enquiries. A 30–year closure may apply to some county council records.

Historical background: Oxfordshire County Record Office was established in 1935 as a subsection of the legal department of Oxfordshire County Council. In 1987 it was transferred to the newly created Department of Leisure and Arts, and shortly afterwards changed its name to Oxfordshire Archives. In 1984 it took over from the Bodleian Library as Diocesan Record Office for Oxford, and in 1989 began its policy of providing access to major archive collections held by other organ-

isations in the county through its central searchroom. The archives are still housed in the same (though expanded) premises as in 1935, but some 40 per cent of the records are now maintained in an outstore fifteen miles outside Oxford. The archive arranges access to the archives of Oxford City, 1199–, Woodstock Borough, 15th century–, and University College, *c*1190–, though none of these archives is deposited.

Acquisitions policy: Material of local significance, which may have relevance for the study of both local and national history, from within the old county boundaries of Oxfordshire (excluding the Vale of White Horse) before 1974, and the present county of Oxfordshire since that date. The office is a recognised place of deposit for public records, tithe and manorial documents. As Diocesan Record Office, it accepts the diocesan archives for Oxford (i.e. the Archdeaconries of Oxford, Berkshire and Buckingham), but the archdeaconry and parish records for the Archdeaconry of Oxford only.

Archives of organisation: Records of Oxfordshire Quarter Sessions, 1687–1974, and of Oxfordshire County Council (legal and committee service units), 1888–.

Major collections: Local administration: borough records of Banbury, 1554–1974, Chipping Norton, 1600–1966, and Henley-on-Thames, 12th–20th century; urban and rural district council records for pre-1974 Oxfordshire; parish council records; Oxfordshire coroner's records, mainly 20th century; poor law union and highway board records for pre-1974 Oxfordshire.
Ecclesiastical: records of Oxford Diocese, 1516–20th century; Oxford Archdeaconry, 1516–20th century; records of parishes in Oxford Archdeaconry, 1244–.
Private deposits: papers of landed families, including Valentia, early 16th century–20th century; Dillon, 1267–1929; Dashwood, 1316–1954; Fane, 1498–1884; and Saye and Sele, 1339–1932; business records, including the Early Blanket Company of Witney, 1648–1988; Frank Cooper (Oxford Marmalade), 1881–1992, and the breweries of Halls, 1537–1947; Courage, 1709–1967; and Brakspear, 1782–1940; personal papers of individuals, including Hubert Kestell Cornish, 1803–73, containing extensive correspondence from John Keble and Madeau Stewart, 20th century, notably with many individuals, including the Mitford family,

Stevie Smith, Elizabeth Poston and Elizabeth Gouge; records of organisations, including the Oxford Playhouse, 20th century; manorial records; deeds; maps.

Non-manuscript material: Library of John Marriott Davenport, clerk of the peace and antiquary.

Finding aids: Archway computer catalogue. Lists sent to NRA. Calendar of quarter sessions rolls, 1687–1830. Diocesan and parish records catalogued by Bodleian Library prior to transfer; numerous but incomplete indexes to parts of records. Card index of private deposits; comprehensive personal name and place indexes, less comprehensive subject index.

Facilities: Photocopying. Photography can be arranged with a commercial firm. Small number of microforms for use.

Conservation: In-house conservation.

Publications: Oxfordshire County Record Office and its Records (1938).
A Summary Catalogue of the Privately Deposited Records in the Oxfordshire County Record Office (1966).
J. Howard-Drake: *Oxford Church Courts Depositions, 1542–1550* (1991).
——: *Oxford Church Courts Depositions, 1570–1574* (1993).
C. Boardman: *Oxfordshire Sinners and Villains* (1994).

899 Oxfordshire Health Archives

Address: The Warneford Hospital, Warneford Lane, Headington, Oxford OX3 7JX

Telephone: (01865) 226308

Fax: (01865) 226507

Enquiries: The Archivist, Mrs Elizabeth Boardman

Open: Thurs, Fri: 9.00–4.45

Access: By prior appointment only. There is a 30–year closure on administrative records and 100–year closure on medical material.

Historical background: A part-time archivist was employed by the United Oxford Hospitals in 1969, and this was continued by Oxfordshire Health Authority from 1974 to 1994. The archivist is now employed by the Oxfordshire Mental Healthcare NHS Trust, which contracts the service out to the other Oxfordshire NHS trusts and authorities.

Acquisitions policy: Material relating to NHS hospitals in Oxfordshire and their staff, acquired by internal transfer and by gift or deposit from external sources.

Archives of organisation: Significant archives of the following hospitals and administrative bodies:
Radcliffe Infirmary, 1764–1979; Warneford Hospital (formerly Radcliffe Asylum), 1567–1971; Littlemore Hospital (formerly Oxfordshire County Lunatic Asylum), 1846–1985; Horton Hospital, 1869–1989; Nuffield Orthopaedic Centre (formerly Winfield-Morris Hospital), 1872–1974; Brackley Cottage Hospital, 1876–1968; Oxford Eye Hospital, 1885–1947; Victoria Cottage Hospital, Thame, 1891–1969; Chipping Norton War Memorial Hospital, 1919–86; Bicester Cottage Hospital, 1928–68; hospital management committees, 1948–74.
Records of 15 other hospitals and bodies.

Major collections: Radcliffe Guild of Nurses, 1897–1991; Radcliffe Infirmary League of Friends, 1967–90; League of Friends of the Littlemore, Warneford and Park hospitals, 1961–89.
Miscellanea relating to J.M. Charcot (1825–93), French neurologist.

Non-manuscript material: Paintings, prints and photographs of staff and hospitals; site plans.

Finding aids: Handlists of all material and catalogues of most collections.

Facilities: Photocopying.

Publications: A.G. Gibson: *The Radcliffe Infirmary* (1926).
M. Bone: *Relief of the Sick and Lame* (1970).
A.H.T. Robb Smith: *A Short History of the Radcliffe Infirmary* (1970).
M. Cheney: *The Horton General Hospital, Banbury, 1872–1972* (1972).
B. Parry Jones: *The Warneford Hospital, 1826–1976* (1976).
E.J.R. Burrough: *Unity in Diversity: the Short Life of the United Oxford Hospitals* (1978).
B. Parry Jones: 'Peter Hollins at the Warneford Hospital', *Leeds Arts Calendar*, no. 88 (1981).
J. Selby-Green: *History of the Radcliffe Infirmary* (1990).

900 Pembroke College
McGowin Library

Parent organisation: Oxford University

Address: Oxford OX1 1DW

Telephone: (01865) 276409

Enquiries: The Deputy Librarian

Open: Mon–Fri: 10.00–5.00 Closed in August.

Access: Bona fide researchers, by appointment only. Post-1920 material will not normally be available.

Historical background: Pembroke College, founded by Royal Charter in 1624, inherited the site and buildings of its direct predecessor, Broadgates Hall. The McGowin Library was opened in 1974.

Acquisitions policy: To maintain and consolidate the college archives and collections.

Archives of organisation: Archives of the college, including statutes, 1624–; acts of the governing body, 1712–; accounts, 1651–; admission records, 1678–; student societies records, including the Boat Club and Debating Society, 1842–.

Major collections: Samuel Johnson (1709–84), lexicographer: private devotions and papers (14 bundles).
Log-book of T. Atkinson, Master of *The Victory*, 1804–5.
Correspondence of G.W. Hall, Master, 1809–43, and Sir Peter Le Page Renouf (1822–97).

Finding aids: General index to collection; copy held by NRA.

Facilities: Photocopying. Photography by arrangement. Microfilm/fiche readers.

Publications: J.D. Freeman: *A Preliminary Handlist of Documents and Manuscripts of Samuel Johnson*, Oxford Bibliographical Society Occasional Publications, no. 2 (1967).

901 Pitt Rivers Museum

Parent organisation: University of Oxford

Address: South Parks Road, Oxford OX1 3PP

Telephone: (01865) 270927

Fax: (01865) 270943

Enquiries: The Assistant Curator (Archives), Ms E. Edwards

Open: Mon–Fri: 9.00–5.00, by appointment. Restricted services during August.

Access: Bona fide researchers of postgraduate (or equivalent) status. Others at the discretion of the Assistant Curator. There is no access for persons under the age of 18.

Historical background: The museum has been collecting archival material, especially photography, since its foundation in 1884. Its focus has been to collect material which relates to the intellectual frameworks in which the museum functioned rather than the administrative records of the institution itself. Until 1985 the archives were attached to the museum's Balfour Library, but at that date were restructured as a separate curatorial department of the museum.

Acquisitions policy: To strengthen existing collections to meet the teaching and research needs of the museum and department, and to document the development and history of anthropology. Material is added by purchase, exchange, donation and bequest.

Archives of organisation: Very few, mainly from 1884 to 1900.

Major collections: Henry Balfour (1863–1939): diaries and annotated writings.
Miss B. Blackwood (1889–1975): field notes and correspondence.
Sir Baldwin Spencer (1860–1929): correspondence, notes and other papers.
Prof. Sir Edward B. Tylor (1832–1917): correspondence and notes.
Col. R.G. Woodthorpe (1845–98): diaries and sketches.
Various other smaller collections of MSS of anthropological interest.

Non-manuscript material: Photographic collections which are more significant historically than the MS collections.
A collection of about 125,000 items of anthropological interest, 1860s-. The whole world is represented but coverage is especially strong on Oceania, Central Asia, Assam and North America.
Collections include: E. Evans-Pritchard (Southern Sudan), B. Blackwood (Melanesia), J.H. Hutton and J. Mills (Assam), Charles Bell and F. Spencer Chapman (Tibet), R. Rattray (Ghana) and Wilfred Thesiger (Middle East and Africa).

Finding aids: Computer listing, manual handlists and indexes for different parts of the collection. MS list sent to NRA.

Facilities: Photocopying (restricted). Photography. Microfiche reader.

Conservation: Preventative rather than active. Specialist work is contracted out.

Publications: E. Edwards: 'Collecting with a Camera: Pitt Rivers Museum Photographic Collections', *The General's Gift*, ed. B.A.L. Cranstone and S. Seidenburg (Oxford, 1984). E. Edwards (ed.): *Wilfred Thesiger's Photographs: a Most Cherished Possession* (Oxford, 1993) [exhibition publication].

902 Plunkett Co-operative Library

Parent organisation: Plunkett Foundation for Co-operative Studies

Address: 23 Hanborough Business Park, Long Hanborough, Oxford OX8 8LH

Telephone: (01865) 883636

Fax: (01993) 883576

Enquiries: The Librarian, Talat Stonehouse

Open: Mon–Fri: 9.00–5.00

Access: Generally open to the public; an appointment is preferred.

Historical background: Founded in 1919 by Sir Horace Curzon Plunkett to provide greater facilities for the systematic study of the principles and methods of agricultural and industrial co-operation, the library developed from a nucleus of books collected by Sir Horace for Irish farmers. From 1924, the year of the first conference on Agricultural Co-operation, the foundation has been a clearing house of information for the agricultural co-operative movement throughout the English-speaking world.

Acquisitions policy: To collect all material on co-operation and co-operatives in all sectors, but particularly agricultural and worker, in all parts of the world. Also material supportive of the foundation's educational, consultancy and research work in the UK and overseas.

Major collections: Documents of Independent Commission into Consumer Co- operation (Gaitskell Commission), 1958.
Sir Horace Curzon Plunkett (1854–1932), Irish statesman and pioneer of agricultural co-oper-

ation: diaries and letters, 1881–1932.

Finding aids: List of Plunkett correspondence. NRA 16228.

Facilities: Photocopying.

903 Pusey House Library

Address: Pusey House, St Giles, Oxford OX1 3LZ

Telephone: (01865) 278415

Enquiries: The Custodian of the Library, Rev. W.E.P. Davage or The Archivist, Rev. K.E. Macnab

Open: Library: Mon–Fri: 9.00–5.00 Sat: 9.00–1.00
Archives: Mon–Thurs: 9.00–5.00 Fri: 9.00–12.30
Subject to alteration out of university term.

Access: Library: researchers, on written application to the Custodian.
Archives: by appointment with the Archivist.

Historical background: The library was founded as a memorial library after the death of E.B. Pusey (1800–82) by his friends, who bought Pusey's own library for the purpose. The library concentrates on patristics, church history, Victorian church sources and liturgy. Since 1989 the library of the St Augustine's Foundation has been at Pusey House, and is available on the same terms as the Pusey House collection.

Acquisitions policy: To strengthen the areas noted above, as well as to augment the extensive 19th–century pamphlet collection.

Archives of organisation: Records of Pusey House, 1884–.

Major collections: Papers and correspondence of various important figures and organisations involved in the High Church movement: the nucleus is the collection of Pusey papers, formed by H.P. Liddon for his *Life of Pusey*, which includes papers of Edward Churton (1800–74); W.K Hamilton (1808–69); C. Marriott (1811–58); R. Scott (1811–87); H.A. Woodgate; the English Church Union; the Association for the Promotion of the Unity of Christendom.
Collection by and relating to John Henry Newman (1801–90).
Papers of 20th–century Anglican figures,

including C.H. Turner (1860–1930), Darwell Stone (1859–1941), Sidney Lesley Ollard (1875–1949).

Non-manuscript material: Pamphlets centring on the Tractarian movement, 19th century (21,500). H.E. Hall Collection of photographs of 19th–century clergymen.

Finding aids: Catalogues and provisional author list for much of the MS material. Handlist and indexes to pamphlet collection.

Facilities: Photocopying.

Publications: P.M. Meadows: *Pusey House, Oxford: a Guide to the Library and Archives* (1987) [available from Pusey House].

904 Queen's College

Parent organisation: University of Oxford

Address: High Street, Oxford OX1 4AW

Telephone: (01865) 279121

Enquiries: The Keeper of the Archives, J.M. Kaye or The Librarian, Miss H. Powell

Open: By arrangement.

Access: Bona fide scholars, by appointment. Access to the medieval archives and MSS deposited in the Bodleian Library is via the Keeper of the Archives at Queen's only.

Historical background: The college was founded in 1340. Many of the medieval deeds and MSS books have been deposited in the Bodleian Library (entry 871).

Acquisitions policy: To maintain and consolidate the archives and MSS.

A Archives

Archives of organisation: Statutes, letters patent and foundation documents, 1341–19th century; financial records, including annual accounts, 1348–1900; records of college government, 1565–1827; entrance book, 1635–1890; Butler's College diary, 1844– 1900; records of benefactors and schools, 16th–19th centuries; estate records, principally deeds, c1150–1868, especially *re* Sherborne Priory, Dorset, and God's House, Southampton, c1190–16th century.

Finding aids: NRA 1097. Handlist, History of the University Project.

Conservation: Contracted out.

Publications: HMC 2nd report (1871), 137–42, and 4th Report (1874), 451–8.
N. Denholm-Young: *Archives of the Queen's College, Oxford* (1931) [4 vols; calendar of deeds and documents].

B Library

Archives of organisation: Library records, 1663–1805.
Student note-books, 17th and 18th centuries, including Jeremy Bentham's notes on Sir W. Blackstone's lectures, c1760–; records of undergraduate societies, including Halcyon Club, 1869–96, and Addison Society, 1876–1931.
Minutes of meetings and accounts of the proprietors of *Grub Street Journal*, 1730–38.

Major collections: Collections of Thomas Barlow (1607–91), mainly theological MSS, and of Sir Joseph Williamson (1633–1701), including political correspondence and heraldic and genealogical MSS.
MSS and collections of former students and provosts.
Rev. John Barnabas Maude, diary kept during his detention at Verdun, 1802–14.

Finding aids: Manuscript catalogue.

Conservation: Contracted out.

905 Refugee Studies Programme Documentation Centre

Parent organisation: University of Oxford

Address: Postal: Queen Elizabeth House, 21 St Giles, Oxford OX1 3LA
Location: 1st Floor, Dartington House, Little Clarendon Street, Oxford

Telephone: (01865) 270298

Fax: (01865) 270721

Enquiries: The Archivist, Sarah Rhodes

Open: Mon–Fri: 9.00–5.00

Access: Generally open to the public. There may be access restrictions on recent or sensitive archive material.

Historical background: The Refugee Studies Programme was set up in 1982 and is concerned with the causes, consequences and experiences of forced migration. It promotes inter-disciplinary research, teaching and information provision. The Documentation Centre now holds more than 10,000 items, comprising books and unpublished material.

Acquisitions policy: To complement the interests and ongoing projects of the programme.

Major collections: Papers of Paul Weis (1907–92), international refugee lawyer, 1930s-1980s.
Papers of Tristram Betts (1908–83), famine relief and resettlement worker, 1950–1980s.
Refugee Health Collection (transferred from London School of Hygiene and Tropical Medicine), 1960–1990s.

Non-manuscript material: Video collection.
Conference proceedings, project reports and UN documentation.

Finding aids: On-line computer catalogue, including dedicated archive database. Lists of videos and periodicals. Weis list will be sent to NRA.

Facilities: Photocopying. Printouts from catalogue.

Publications: Documentation Centre: a Guide [free].
Refugee Studies Programme Annual Reports.

906 Regent's Park College
Angus Library

Parent organisation: University of Oxford.

Address: Pusey Street, Oxford OX1 2LB

Telephone: (01865) 59887

Fax: (01865) 311449

Enquiries: The Librarian/Archivist,
Mrs Susan J. Mills

Open: Mon–Fri: 9.30–4.00, by appointment only.
Usually closed late August.

Access: Bona fide researchers, by written application accompanied by a reference, to the Librarian/Archivist. The E.A. Payne papers are closed until 2010. There is a daily charge to private genealogical searchers. Extended use by visiting scholars may incur a fee.

Historical background: The college was founded in Stepney in 1810 as a training centre for Baptist ministers, moving to Regent's Park in 1856. It moved gradually to Oxford between 1927 and 1940 and became a permanent private hall of the University in 1957. In 1985 the Baptist Union Library became part of the Angus Library, and in 1989 the archives of the Baptist Missionary Society were deposited with it.

Acquisitions policy: To maintain the archives and build on existing collections of Baptist records, by purchase or gift.

Archives of organisation: College archives, 1810–.

Major collections: Baptist Union of Great Britain (and Ireland) archives, 1812–, including minute books, plus records of the Particular Baptist Fund and other baptist organisations and associations, 18th century–.
Baptist Missionary Society (BMS) archives, 1792–; and missionary correspondence, including William Carey (1761–1834) and George Grenfell (1849–1906).
Records of some local Baptist churches, 1643–.
Papers of prominent Baptists, including Andrew Fuller (1754–1815), William Newman (1773–1835), Joseph Kinghorn (1766–1832), William Steele (1689–1769), Anne Steele (1717–78), J.H. Rusbrooke (1870–1947), M.E. Aubrey (1885–1957), E.A. Payne (1902–80).

Non-manuscript material: BMS archives: maps, photographs, glass slides and negatives.
Major collection of oriental and African translations of the Scriptures and linguistic material.

Finding aids: Card catalogues. Lists sent to NRA. Computer database of BMS missionaries and their records.

Facilities: Photocopying at the librarian's discretion. Microfilm/fiche readers.

Conservation: Contracted out.

Publications: 'Baptist archives', *Religious Archives Group Conference Proceedings* (Sept 1990).
'Angus Library', *Bulletin ABTAPL*, 2/7 (1990), 15.
'Sources for the Study of Baptist History', *Baptist Quarterly*, xxxiv, 6 (1992).

907 Rhodes House Library

Parent organisation: University of Oxford

Address: South Parks Road, Oxford OX1 3RG

Telephone: (01865) 270909

Enquiries: The Librarian, Mr J.R. Pinfold,
The Archivist, Mrs C.E. Brown

Open: Term: Mon–Fri: 9.00–7.00 Sat: 9.00–1.00
Vacation: Mon–Fri: 9.00–5.00 Sat: 9.00–1.00
Follows Bodleian Library timetable for closure
at Christmas and Easter and in early September.
Intending vacation readers are advised to write
for information.

Access: Approved readers holding a Bodleian
reader's ticket or a short-term ticket available at
Rhodes House Library. Suitable credentials are
required and written application in advance is
preferred.

Historical background: A dependent library of
the Bodleian Library (entry **871**), founded by
the Rhodes trustees in 1929, it houses the
post-1760 Bodleian book and MSS collections
relating to the political, economic and social
history of the British colonies and Commonwealth (excluding the Indian subcontinent), the
USA and sub-Saharan Africa.

Acquisitions policy: Development of existing
holdings as a collecting point for administratively affiliated archive surveys; solicitation of
gifts and deposits (and some purchases) in
continuation of established practice.

Major collections: MS collections relating to
areas mentioned above, notably the personal
papers of former British colonial officials and
development administrators, have been gathered through the Oxford Colonial (and Deve-
lopment) Records Projects, and the library
houses the papers of organisations such as the
Anti-Slavery Society, the Fabian Colonial
Bureau and the Africa Bureau.
Archives of the United Society for the Propagation of the Gospel, 1701–.
Substantial holdings relating to Cecil John
Rhodes (1853–1902) and his family; Sir Thomas
Fowell Buxton (1786–1845) and Charles Roden
Buxton (1875–1942); papers of Arthur Creech
Jones (1891–1964), Dame Margery Perham
(1895–1982), Lord Lugood (1858–1945), Sir
Roy Welensky (1907–91) and Elspeth Huxley
(*b* 1907).

Sarawak materials include papers of the Brooke
family and their associates.

Finding aids: Handlists of larger individual
collections sent to NRA. Accessions lists (irreg-
ular).

Facilities: Photocopying in library; other
photographic services at the Bodleian. Micro-
film/fiche readers/printers. Audio-equipment
for oral history collections.

Publications: *Manuscript Collections of Afri-
cana in Rhodes House Library* (1968; suppls,
1971, 1978)
Manuscript Collections (1970, suppl., 1978)
[excluding Africana].
P.M. Hugh: 'The Oxford Colonial Records
Project and Oxford Development Records Project', *Journal of the Society of Archivists*, vi/2
(1978), 76.

908 Ruskin College

Address: Oxford OX1 2HE

Telephone: (01865) 54331

Enquiries: The Librarian, David Horsfield

Open: Term: 9.00–5.00 Vacation: by arrangement.

Access: Approved readers, by prior application
in writing.

Historical background: Ruskin College was
founded as a residential college for adult education in 1899. The archives collection was commenced in 1969.

Acquisitions policy: Working-class and labour
movement history, mainly 20th century.

Archives of organisation: Archives of Ruskin
College, 1899–.

Major collections: Papers of James Smith Mid-
dleton (1878–1962), secretary of the Labour
Party, and Lucy Annie Middleton MP.
Abe Lazarus Memorial Archives: Oxford
labour history, 1930s and 1940s.
Working-class autobiographies.

Non-manuscript material: Books, periodicals,
pamphlets relating to the labour movement.

Finding aids: Items listed in typescript. Middleton: NRA 27385.

Facilities: Photocopying. Microfilm/fiche reader.

Publications: P. Yorke: *Education and the Working Class: Ruskin College, 1899–1909* (Oxford, 1977).
H. Pollins: *The History of Ruskin College* (Oxford, 1984)

909 St Anne's College

Parent organisation: University of Oxford

Address: Oxford OX2 6HS

Telephone: (01865) 274800

Fax: (01865) 274899

Enquiries: The Librarian

Open: By arrangement.

Access: Bona fide scholars, strictly by appointment.

The college was originally founded as the Society of Oxford Home Students in 1879 and was given collegiate status in 1952. The college archives, as yet unsorted, are held by the library, which also houses correspondence concerning the fight for women's rights to take degrees. See R.F. Butler and M.H. Pritchard (eds): *St Anne's College: a History* (1957) [2 vols].

910 St Edmund Hall

Parent organisation: University of Oxford

Address: Oxford OX1 4AR

Telephone: (01865) 279000 (College) 279015 (Archivist)

Enquiries: The Archivist, Dr R.J. Crampton

Open: By arrangement.

Access: Anyone with a specific reason. An appointment is necessary.

Historical background: St Edmund Hall was, from the 13th century, an academic hall of Oxford University; it has been a college since 1957. MSS and papers of principals and vice-principals, 17th–19th centuries, have been deposited in the Bodleian Library (entry 871).

Acquisitions policy: Material relevant to the history of the hall and its members.

Archives of organisation: Archives of the hall,

including buttery books, 1695–1920; principal's ledger, 1684–; library borrowers' registers, 1666–74; 1838–81; minutes and accounts of the Boat Club and Debating Society, 1869–.

Major collections: Extensive transcripts of documents relating to the hall and its members made by Dr A.B. Emden, principal, 1929–51.

Finding aids: Handlist for History of the University Project.

911 St Hilda's College

Parent organisation: University of Oxford

Address: Oxford OX4 1DY

Telephone: (01865) 276884

Enquiries: The College Librarian

Open: By arrangement.

Access: Bona fide researchers only.

Historical background: The college was founded in 1893 by Dorothea Beale (1831–1906) and maintains associations with Cheltenham Ladies College, also established by her. The archives are in the custody of the Librarian.

Acquisitions policy: Material relevant to the history of the college and its members.

Archives of organisation: Records include correspondence and papers *re* women's struggle for education rights.

Major collections: Papers of C.M.E. Burrows (1872–1959), principal, 1910–19.

Finding aids: Card index. NRA 12369.

Facilities: Photocopying.

Publications: G. Hampshire: *Memorabilia* (Oxford, 1977)
St Hilda's College Register, 1893–1993 (Oxford, 1994).
M.E. Rayner: *The Centenary History of St Hilda's College* (Oxford, 1994).

912 St Hugh's College Library

Address: St Margaret's Road, Oxford OX2 6LE

Telephone: (01865) 274938

Enquiries: The Librarian, Miss D.C. Quare

Open: Mon–Fri: 9.00–5.00
Closed mid-August to mid-September.

Access: Bona fide researchers. Written application must be made.

The college was founded in 1886 and maintains its archive from that date as well as acquiring material from past members, including personal papers, letters and reminiscences, especially relating to the education and awarding of degrees to women. A computerised database is in progress and photocopying is available.

913 St John's College

Parent organisation: University of Oxford

Address: Oxford OX1 3JP

Telephone: (01865) 277300

Fax: (01865) 277435

Enquiries: The Keeper of the Archives, Dr M.G.A. Vale or The Librarian

Open: By arrangement.

Access: Approved readers, by appointment.

Historical background: St John's College was formed in 1555 by Sir Thomas White, and has a continuous history since that date as an academic corporation with its own endowments, including estates. The college archives were brought together in a single muniment room in 1957 and a summary guide was prepared.

Acquisitions policy: To maintain the college archives.

Archives of organisation: The college archives are essentially those of the governing body and its committees and of its agents in the management of its property: these include annual accounts, 1568–; bursars' records, 1562–; estate papers; MS maps and plans, minute books of undergraduate societies, 1880–; photographic collection, c1860–.

Major collections: Library: A large number of MSS, many by or concerning those associated with the college, including lectures, essays, miscellaneous documents.
Correspondence received by Thomas Hare (1806–91), political reformer.
Account books of Henry Handley Norris (1771–1850), leader of High Church party.
Lectures of Rev. John Rose (1754–1821), Fellow and rector of St Martin, Outwith London, describing London society and places, 1800–20.

Letters and papers of Josiah Tucker (1717–99), economist, later Dean of Gloucester.
'Ludicra' collection of limericks and nonsense verses made by Herbert Armitage James, president of college, 1909–31.

Finding aids: General guide to the college archives: NRA 9363, revised 1983, and a detailed card index. MS 213–357 described in NRA 7453.

Facilities: Photocopying and photography by arrangement.

Publications: H.M. Colvin: 'Manuscript Maps belonging to St John's College', *Oxoniensia*, xv (1950).
A. and V. Sillery: *St John's College Biographical Register, 1919–1975* (1978).
V. Sillery: *St John's College Biographical Register, 1875–1919; 1775–1875; 1660–1775* (1981; 1987; 1990)
HMC: 4th Report, xvii App 465–8.

914 St Peter's College

Parent organisation: University of Oxford

Address: New Inn Hall Street, Oxford OX1 2DL

Telephone: (01865) 278900

Fax: (01865) 278855

Enquiries: The Master

Open: By arrangement.

Access: Bona fide researchers, at the discretion of the governing body of the college.

St Peter's Hall was founded in 1929 and achieved full college status in 1961. It maintains only its own archives, primarily the records of the governing body, 1929–. Other records are now deposited elsewhere; the parish records of St Peter-Le-Bailey in Oxfordshire Archives (entry **898**) and a small collection of St Helena letters in the Bodleian Library (entry **871**). See Eric H.F. Smith: *St Peter's: the Founding of an Oxford College* (Gerrards Cross, 1978).

915 School of Geography

Parent organisation: University of Oxford

Address: Library, Mansfield Road, Oxford OX1 3TB

Telephone: (01865) 271911/2

Fax: (01865) 271929

Enquiries: The Librarian and Map Curator, Mrs L.S. Atkinson

Open: Term: Mon–Fri: 9.00–1.00; 2.00–6.00 Sat: 9.00–1.00 Vacation: Mon–Fri: 9.00–1.00; 2.30–5.00

Access: Bona fide researchers, by appointment.

Historical background: The present school was established in 1899 and the library is one of the largest and best in the subject in Great Britain. The archives have mainly been deposited in the Bodleian Library (entry 871).

Acquisitions policy: To maintain the collections, by donation.

Major collections: Papers and lectures notes of Sir Halford Mackinder (1861–1947), geographer and politician; Prof. A.J. Herbertson (*d* 1914); and J.N.L. Baker (1893–1971). Radcliffe Meteorological Station Collection of weather reports, mainly 1935–.

Non-manuscript material: Extensive collection of maps covering the whole world (*c*52,000). Collection of air photographs (*c*4000).

Finding aids: Lists. Mackinder Papers: NRA 18709. Card catalogue of map collection.

Facilities: Photocopying. Photography. Microfilm/fiche readers.

916 Sherrington Library for the History of Neuroscience

Parent organisation: University of Oxford

Address: University Laboratory of Physiology, Parks Road, Oxford OX1 3PT

Telephone: (01865) 272524

Fax: (01865) 282161

Enquiries: The Librarian and Archivist, Ms Wendy Saywood

Open: Mon–Fri: 8.30–5.00 Other times by arrangement. Closed during university closures (except by previous arrangement).

Access: Any interested scholar. There are restrictions on some correspondence and rarer books; an appointment is preferable (to avoid disappointment).

The Sherrington Library was opened in 1984 as a memorial to Sir Charles Sherrington (1857–1952), Waynflete Professor in the University Laboratory of Physiology, 1913–35, who won the Nobel Prize for medicine in 1932. The collection comprises correspondence (mostly photocopies) of Sir Charles and is being computerised. The actual records of the Laboratory of Physiology are held by the University Archives (entry 896).

917 Somerville College

Parent organisation: University of Oxford

Address: The Library, Somerville College, Oxford OX2 6HD

Telephone: (01865) 270694

Enquiries: The Archivist, Miss P.A. Adams

Open: By appointment only.

Access: Scholars, by appointment. There are restrictions on certain college archives.

Historical background: The college was first so designated in 1894, although it had been founded as a hall for women students in 1879. The papers of Mary Somerville (1780–1872), after whom the college was named, are now deposited in the Bodleian Library (entry 871), but the college library holds the archives and important collections of 19th- and 20th–century literary MSS.

Acquisitions policy: To maintain the college archives and collections, by donation.

Archives of organisation: Archives of the college, 1879–.

Major collections: Papers and correspondence of Amelia B. Edwards (1831–92), novelist and Egyptologist; Percy Withers (1867–1945), literary figure.
MSS and correspondence of Violet Paget (1856–1936), author.
Working papers of Muriel St Clare Byrne (1895–1983), historian, and of Gladys Scott Thomson (*d* 1966), archivist and author.
Papers of Margaret Kennedy (1896–1967), novelist; Margaret Mann Phillips (1906–87), Erasmus scholar.

Non-manuscript material: Collection of pamphlets, press cuttings and correspondence on women's suffrage.
The libraries of John Stuart Mill (1806–73) and Amelia B. Edwards.

Finding aids: Summary lists at NRA.

Facilities: Microfilm/fiche reader.

Publications: M. St Clare Byrne and C. Hope Mansfield: *Somerville College, 1879–1921* (1922).
Somerville College Register, 1879–1971.

918 Taylor Institution Library

Parent organisation: University of Oxford

Address: St Giles, Oxford OX1 3NA

Telephone: (01865) 278160

Fax: (01865) 278165

Enquiries: The Librarian, Giles Barber

Open: Oct–June: Mon–Fri: 9.00–7.00 Sat: 9.00–1.00 July–Sept: Mon–Fri: 10.00–1.00, 2.00–5.00 Sat: 10.00–1.00
Please enquire for details of closed days in late August and early September.

Access: Graduates and other established researchers.

Historical background: The institution is a centre for the teaching of modern European languages excluding English. It was provided for in the will of Sir Robert Taylor (1714–88), but the establishment was delayed until 1839 and the library was started in 1848. Records of the institution are deposited in Oxford University Archives (entry **896**).

Acquisitions policy: Material relating to continental European language and literature, including Slavonic and modern Latin American.

Major collections: Autograph material: an extensive collection of MSS and letters of continental European political, musical, literary and artistic writers, 1700–.
Archives of the International Association of Hispanists.
Papers of academics associated with the institution, including Dr T.D.N. Besterman (*d* 1976), Voltaire scholar; H.G. Fiedler (1862–1945), professor of German; F. Max Müller (1823–1900); Sir Robert Taylor.

Finding aids: Card index to MSS. Handlist of autograph materials acquired, 1950–70. NRA 11664.

Facilities: Photocopying. Photography by arrangement.

919 Trinity College

Parent organisation: University of Oxford

Address: Broad Street, Oxford OX1 3BH

Telephone: (01865) 279900

Fax: (01865) 279911

Enquiries: The Archivist, Mrs Clare Hopkins

Open: By arrangement only.

Access: Bona fide researchers. An appointment is always necessary. Some access is restricted.

Historical background: Trinity College was founded by Sir Thomas Pope in 1555. It stands on the site of the Benedictine Durham College (of which no records remain in Trinity). The archive was rehoused in 1987–8. All early library MSS and the collections of Warton, Ingram and Collins have been deposited in the Bodleian Library (entry **871**).

Acquisitions policy: The college is pleased to accept material of or relating to its own former and present members, especially reflecting the life of the college.

Archives of organisation: Statutes and charters, financial records and college government, 1556–; property documents, including court rolls, 1556–; admissions registers, 1648–; other records of benefactions, college library and buildings.

Major collections: Literary papers of Sir Arthur Quiller-Couch (1863–1944).

Non-manuscript material: Prints of college buildings, 1675–; photographs of buildings, 1860–; of members, 1889–; building plans; some estate maps.
Major collection of 20th–century undergraduate ephemera.

Finding aids: Detailed catalogue is under preparation (to be sent to NRA). Brief handlist for History of the University Project.

Facilities: Photocopying. Photography may be permitted.

Conservation: Contracted out.

Publications: Herbert E.D. Bakiston: *Trinity College* (London, 1898).

920 University College

Parent organisation: University of Oxford

Address: High Street, Oxford OX1 4BH

Enquiries: The Archivist, Dr Robin Darwall-Smith c/o Oxfordshire Archives, County Hall, New Road, Oxford OX1 1ND; tel. (01865) 815281 or The Fellow Archivist, Mr A.M. Murray at University College, tel. (01865) 276651

Access: Bona fide scholars. Documents from the college archives are delivered to Oxfordshire Archives (entry 898) every Tuesday, so it is necessary to order items and book a seat in advance. A CARN reader's ticket is essential. Most records are generally available, although there is a closure period on some 20th–century items.

Historical background: Money for a college was bequeathed to Oxford University by William of Durham, Archdeacon of Rouen (*d* 1249), but the exact date of the founding of the college is disputed. It has, however, definitely been in continuous existence since 1280. In 1882 its MS collections were deposited with the Bodleian Library (entry 871). Some later private papers have also been deposited there, including the Robert Ross Collection concerning Oscar Wilde, and the papers of Clement Attlee (1883–1967).

Acquisitions policy: To maintain the college archives.

Archives of organisation: Estate papers, including deeds and ledger books of leases relating to properties in Oxford, 12th century–, and elsewhere, including Essex and Yorkshire, 15th century–.
Administrative records, including bursars' rolls, 1381–1597, and journals, 1616–; college register, 1509–; admissions register, c1600–; papers and correspondence of Obadiah Walker, master, 1676–89.
Financial records, including general accounts, 1632–; and benefactors' books, 17th–18th centuries.
Legal papers relating to laws concerning property, 1380s-1904.
Building accounts for the quadrangle, 1634–77, with many plans and card model.

Non-manuscript material: Plans and drawings of college buildings, 17th century–; plans and maps of college property in Oxford and elsewhere, 18th century; photographs of college sports teams, etc (including some albums from old members), 19th century–.

Finding aids: Initial shelf list with indexes (copies at NRA). Work on a full catalogue is currently in progress.

Facilities: Photocopying.

Publications: W. Carr: *University College* (London, 1902).
University College Record (1952–3), 11–12 [summary of the archives].

921 Wadham College

Parent organisation: University of Oxford

Address: Oxford OX1 3PN

Telephone: (01865) 277900

Fax: (01865) 277937

Enquiries: The Keeper of the Archives, C.S.L. Davies (postal only) or The Librarian

Open: By arrangement.

Access: Bona fide researchers, by prior appointment. Enquiries by post only.

Historical background: The college was founded in 1613, and until 1877 the library was housed in its original room dating from that time.

Acquisitions policy: To maintain and consolidate the archives and collections.

Archives of organisation: Records concerned with the foundation and building of the college; admissions registers, 1613–; bursars' accounts, 1649–; estate records and maps (16 counties).
Series of minute books and papers of undergraduate societies, including various literary and theological societies, 1934–.

Major collections: Various Spanish MSS of Sir William Godolphin (?1634–96), ambassador in Madrid, and Benjamin Barron Wiffen (1794–1867) relating to Church reform in Spain.
Individual MSS of former members of the college, including Mediterranean diary of John Swinton (1703–77), naval chaplain, 1730–31, and some papers of Sir Maurice Bowra (1898–1971), warden.

Finding aids: Catalogue of the Muniments of Wadham College: NRA 8127. Deposited collections: NRA 10095. Handlist for History of the University Project.

Facilities: Photocopying.

Publications: R.B. Gardiner: *The Registers of Wadham College, 1613–1871* (London, 1887–90) [effectively presents everything available in the archives on members of the college]. HMC: 5th Report, pp. 479–81.

922 Westminster College

Address: North Hinksey, Oxford OX2 9AT

Telephone: (01865) 247644 ext. 6226 (Learning Centre) ext. 5271 (WHS Library)

Fax: (01865) 251847

Enquiries: The Director of Wesley and Methodist Studies Centre, Rev. Tim MacQuiban

Open: Term: Mon–Fri: 8.30–6.00 Vacation: Mon–Fri: 9.00–5.00

Access: Open to staff and students of the college or members of the Wesley Historical Society (apply to Librarian, Mrs Joyce Banks, tel. (01243) 776531, for a reader's ticket).

Historical background: The college was founded in London in 1851 for the training of teachers in the Methodist Church. It now serves as a college of higher education with courses validated by the University of Oxford. The college houses the library of the Wesley Historical Society (WHS), which was founded in 1893 and maintained a library from 1959. The official archives of the Methodist Church have been deposited in the John Rylands Library, Manchester (entry **806**).

Acquisitions policy: Maintaining the college archives and acquiring other records relating to Methodism and education.

Archives of organisation: Westminster College archives, 1851–.

Major collections: Wesley Historical Society archives, including minutes and correspondence, 1893–.
Methodist connexional minutes and papers, 18th–20th centuries.
Letters and other material relating to presidents of the Methodist conferences, 1790–1932.
Small collection of letters of John Wesley (1703–91).

Non-manuscript material: WHS Library, including extensive collection of periodicals and a cuttings collection, 1791–. Portraits, photographs and prints of British Methodists.

Finding aids: Lists and indexes of college archives and WHS Library.

Facilities: Photocopying. Microfilm reader.

923 Worcester College

Parent organisation: University of Oxford

Address: Oxford OX1 2HB

Telephone: (01865) 278354

Fax: (01865) 278387

Enquiries: The Librarian, Dr J.H. Parker

Open: Mon–Fri: 9.30–1.00; 2.00–4.30 Closed for a fortnight at Christmas, a week at Easter and a fortnight in the summer.

Access: Any bona fide scholar, on written application and by prior appointment.

Historical background: Worcester College is an 18th–century foundation in the University of Oxford. Its chief benefactor was George Clarke (1661–1736), virtuoso and politician, who not only built the library block with the help of Hawskmoor, but also left money for further building plus his own great collection of books.

Acquisitions policy: To add, if possible, to areas where the collection is already strong.

Archives of organisation: In custody of the college archivist: records of the college, including register, bursars' journals, provosts' accounts and annual lists of members, 1714–.
Student note-books on philosophy, theology and the classics, 17th and 18th centuries.
Records of undergraduate societies, 19th and 20th centuries.

Major collections: A large collection of records accumulated by Sir William Clarke (?1623–66), secretary to Cromwell's army, relating to the activities of the army at the height of its political importance.

Non-manuscript material: Architectural drawings of Inigo Jones (1573–1652) and John Webb (1611–72), and some 30 volumes of the working library of Inigo Jones, copiously annotated in his hand.

Finding aids: MS catalogue of all the holdings. NRA 10396.

Facilities: Photocopying and photography by arrangement. Microfilm reader.

Conservation: Paper conservation is contracted out.

Publications: C.H. Firth (ed.): *The Clarke Papers* (Camden Society, 2nd Series, 1891).
C. Henry Daniel and W.R. Barker: *Worcester College* (London, 1906).
J. Harris and A.A. Tait: *Catalogue of the Drawings by Inigo Jones, John Webb and Isaac de Caus at Worcester College, Oxford.*
H.M. Colvin: *A Catalogue of the Architectural Drawings of the 18th and 19th centuries in Worcester College* (1964).
G. Aylmer: *Clarke Papers* [Harvester Press microfilm edition].

924 Paisley Museum

Parent organisation: Renfrew District Council

Address: High Street, Paisley, Strathclyde PA1 2BA

Telephone: (0141) 889 3151

Fax: (0141) 889 9240

The museum holds records of J. and P. Coats Ltd, thread manufacturers, Paisley, 1808–; including employee records, 1833–, minutes 1890–, and plans etc. NRA 20914 (NRA(S) 3151).

925 Renfrew District Archives

Parent organisation: Renfrew District Libraries Service

Address: Local History Department, Central Library, High Street, Paisley, Strathclyde PA1 2BB

Telephone: (0141) 887 3672/889 2360 ext. Local History Department

Enquiries: The Local History Librarian and Archivist

Open: Mon–Fri: 9.00–8.00 Sat: 9.00–5.00

Access: Generally open to the public. No appointment is necessary but several days' notice is normally required; the user will be notified when material is available.

Historical background: The Local History Department of Paisley's central library had amassed over the years a quantity of MS and other archival material. In 1975, as a result of the reorganisation of Scottish local government, the records of several burghs and of the former Renfrew County relevant to Renfrew District were deposited with the department.

Acquisitions policy: To acquire, by deposit, donation or purchase, material relating to places, persons and companies within Renfrew District.

Major collections: Burgh records of Renfrew, 1655–; Paisley, 1594–; Johnstone, 1857–; and Barrhead, 1894–.
Strathclyde Regional Council minutes, annual financial statements, 1975–; Renfrew District Council minutes, statements of reports, annual financial statements, 1975–; community councils, minutes for all councils within the district, 1975–.
Records of the Co-operative Movement in Paisley, late 19th and 20th centuries.
Antiquarian MSS (45 vols).

Non-manuscript material: Plans from Dean of Guild courts in Paisley and Johnstone, late 19th and 20th centuries (c4000).
Newspapers (various titles), 1824–.

Finding aids: List of local authority records to 1975. Indexes to plans.

Facilities: Photocopying. Microfilm/fiche reader/printer.

926 University of Paisley Library

Address: High Street, Paisley, Strathclyde PA1 2BE

Telephone: (0141) 848 3758

Fax: (0141) 887 0812

Enquiries: The Chief Librarian, Mr S. James

Open: Term: Mon–Fri: 8.30–9.00 Sat: 9.00–5.00 Vacation: Mon–Fri: 9.00–5.00

Access: Upon satisfactory identification and approval of need.

Historical background: The university, previously Paisley College of Technology, was founded in 1897 as Paisley Technical College, with the Paisley Government School of Art and Design (f. 1842) as a constituent. It was granted the status of a central institution in 1950, when the art courses were dropped and development concentrated on science and technology. The library was established in 1963.

Archives of organisation: Materials relating to the history of the college/university.

Major collections: Notes of lectures of Lewis Fry Richardson (1881–1953), prinicipal, 1929–40, and his library, with many volumes annotated by him.
A collection of estimates and contracts relating to the construction of *c*25 Scottish railway companies, donated to the college in 1967, at the time of closure of St Enoch's Station, Glasgow.

Non-manuscript material: Maps and plans relating to above material.

Finding aids: Fry Richardson: NRA 26463.

Facilities: Photocopying. Microfilm/fiche readers. Photography by arrangement.

Publications: Calendar of Scottish Railway Documents (1978).
Calendars of the Papers of L.F. Richardson (1983).

927 Black Watch Museum Archive

Parent organisation: Trustees of the Black Watch

Address: Balhousie Castle, Hay Street, Perth, Tayside PH1 5HR

Telephone: (0131) 310 8530

Fax: (0131) 310 8525

Enquiries: Col. R.T.T. Gurdon

Open: Mon–Fri: 10.00–4.00

Access: Generally open to the public, by appointment. There may be a search charge.

Historical background: The Black Watch (Royal Highland Regiment), 42nd and 73rd, traces its origin to six independent companies dating from 1725. These were regimented in 1739, the first muster parade being held in 1740. Since then the regiment has served in many parts of the world. The archive reflects the history of these activities and is part of a registered charitable trust administered by the regimental trustees. Collection of material was begun in a systematic way in 1925.

Acquisitions policy: Material directly relating to the history of the regiment, its militia and territorial battalions and allied regiments.

Archives of organisation: Regimental records of service and diaries; casualty rolls; description book; order books; depot roll books etc, 18th century–.

Major collections: Diaries and memoirs of various regimental personalities, early 19th century–.

Non-manuscript material: Press cuttings/scrapbooks compiled by members of the regiment, illustrating personal and campaign histories.
Large collection of photographs, 1860s–.
Small collection of oral history tapes, and recordings of regimental bands, in particular illustrating pipe music.
Film collection, 1930s– (transferred to video tape).

Finding aids: Regimental documents survey (NRA(S)).

Facilities: Photocopying. Microfiche reader.

Publications: Bernard Fergusson: *The Black Watch: a Short History.*

928 Perth and Kinross District Archive

Parent organisation: Perth and Kinross District Council

Address: A.K. Bell Library, 2–8 York Place, Perth, Tayside PH2 8EP

Telephone: (01738) 444949

Enquiries: The Archivist, Mr Stephen Connelly

Open: Mon–Fri: 9.30–5.00

Access: Generally open to the public; an appointment is preferable.

Historical background: The archive was established as a result of the reorganisation of local government in Scotland in 1975, the first appointment of a permanent archivist being made in 1978. The archive is concerned principally with the preservation of the former local authority records which now vest in Perth and Kinross District Council, or which vest in Tayside Regional Council, but are held on indefinite loan in Perth.

Acquisitions policy: To locate local authority records for preservation in the district archive and to act as a place of deposit for the records of various local businesses, institutions, families and individuals.

Archives of organisation: Records of the City and Royal Burgh of Perth, 1210–1975.
Records of the burghs of Aberfeldy, Abernethy, Alyth, Auchterarder, Blairgowrie and Rattray, Coupar Angus, Crieff, Kinross and Pitlochry, 1708–1975.

Major collections: Records on indefinite loan from Tayside Regional Council: County of Perth, 1650–1975; County of Kinross, 1738–1975; County of Perth and Kinross, 1930–75.
Many deposited collections, including Stewart-Meiklejohn family of Erdradynate, 1484–1892, Fergusson family of Baledmund, 1328–1900, Perth Theatre, 1900–88.
Barons Kinnaird of Inchture, c1872–1930; Richardson family of Pitfour, 1740–1890.

Non-manuscript material: Reports, posters, photographs, maps and plans.

Finding aids: Descriptive lists are available for the main series of records. Lists are in course of preparation for the papers of various local authority bodies and some private deposits. Lists will be sent to NRA(S).

Facilities: Photocopying. Microfilm/fiche readers.

Conservation: Contracted out.

929 Perth Museum and Art Gallery

Parent organisation: Perth and Kinross District Council

Address: George Street, Perth, Tayside PH1 5LB

Telephone: (01738) 632488

Fax: (01738) 635225

Enquiries: The Keeper of Human History, Ms S. Payne

Open: Mon–Sat: 10.00–1.00; 2.00–5.00

Access: Generally open to the public, by appointment only.

Historical background: The nucleus was the Literary and Antiquarian Society Collection, built up from 1784. In 1822 part of the present museum was erected; it opened in 1824. In 1902 a separate collection built up by the Perthshire Society for Natural Sciences was transferred to

local authority ownership, as was the Literary and Antiquarian Society Collection in 1914. All of the collections were amalgamated in the 1824 building, which was extended and reopened in 1935. The museum has three curatorial sections: Human History, Fine and Applied Art, and Natural Sciences.

Acquisitions policy: The archives are no longer being actively added to, but the museum collects ephemera associated with Perth and Kinross District and the history of Perth Museum and its collections.

Archives of organisation: Records of the museum, 19th century–.

Major collections: Literary and Antiquarian Society Collection, mainly antiquarian tracts and papers, 18th and 19th centuries.
Small MSS collections from Kinross Museum and Alyth Folk Museum.
Local history material, including trade archives, 17th century–.
Records of members of the Perthshire Society of Natural Sciences.

Non-manuscript material: A few plans, mostly of Perth and Perthshire. Photographic collection (c200,000 glass negatives). Scottish paintings and prints.

Finding aids: NRA(S) has made lists of the collection. Kinross: NRA 22369. Photographic collection reasonably well indexed.

Facilities: Photocopying. Photography.

930 English Nature

Address: Northminster House, Peterborough, Cambridgeshire PE1 1UA

Telephone: (01733) 318447

Fax: (01733) 68834

Enquiries: The Archivist, Miss H.J. Taylor

Open: By appointment only.

Access: Bona fide researchers; records are designated public records and held pending transfer to the Public Record Office; the 30-year closure period operates.

Historical background: The Nature Conservancy was founded by Royal Charter in 1949 and for the period 1965–73 formed part of the Natural Environment Research Council. In 1973 the Nature Conservancy Council was established by Act of Parliament, to be succeeded in April 1991 by three country conservation agencies: English Nature, Scottish Natural Heritage and the Countryside Council for Wales. English Nature has inherited and administers the Great Britain headquarters records of the former Nature Conservancy Council.

Acquisitions policy: Internal acquisitions only.

Archives of organisation: Council and committee minutes, papers, annual reports, 1949–.
Records of National Nature Reserve and Sites of Special Scientific Interest, 1952–.
Conservation policy files, scientific research policy and data records, 1973–.

Non-manuscript material: Photographs, maps, slides.
Extensive library material.

Facilities: Photocopying. Microfilm/fiche readers.

931 Peterborough Cathedral

Address: Canonry House, The Precincts, Peterborough, Cambridgeshire PE1 1XX

Telephone: (01733) 62125

Fax: (01733) 52465

Enquiries: Canon J. Higham

Virtually all MSS and early printed books are on loan to Cambridge University Library (entry 147A), but the cathedral holds Act books, early registers and a collection of photographs of the cathedral and precincts. Architects' drawings, 1860–1920, have been transferred to Northamptonshire Record Office (entry 848).

932 Peterborough Central Library
Local Studies Collection

Parent organisation: Cambridgeshire Libraries and Heritage

Address: Broadway, Peterborough, Cambridgeshire PE1 1RX

Telephone: (01733) 348343

Fax: (01733) 555277

Enquiries: The Local Studies Librarian

Open: Mon–Fri: 9.30–7.00 Sat: 9.30–5.00

Access: Generally open to the public; an appointment is preferred for certain items, especially those which require supervision.

Historical background: The Local Studies Collection was established by Peterborough City Council in 1892 with a collecting area of 35 miles radius of the city. In 1900 the Peterborough Gentlemen's Society Library was absorbed, though little now remains. With local government reorganisation in 1974 the collecting area was reduced.

Acquisitions policy: To collect local history printed material relating primarily to Peterborough and its former Soke, and secondarily to the area within a 10- to 15-mile radius.

Archives of organisation: Minutes of Peterborough City Library Committee, 1892–1974, with various correspondence files and statistics.

Major collections: Peterborough Gentlemen's Society, minute books, 1730–1900, with the society's surviving library, which includes a copy of the life of Edward the Confessor by Ailred of Rievaulx, 16th century.

Non-manuscript material: Usual local history collection, including Kitchin Photography Collection (1100 items).
Printed maps and plans, 17th century–; engravings; negatives and photographs, 19th century–.

Finding aids: Author/title and classified card catalogues; other rough indexes for staff use.

Facilities: Photocopying. Photography. Microfilm/fiche readers.

Conservation: Conservation done either by our binders or by the Cambridge County Record Office (entry 148).

Publications: Guide in preparation.

933 Peterborough Museum and Art Gallery

Address: Priestgate, Peterborough, Cambridgeshire PE1 1LF

Telephone: (01733) 343329

Enquiries: The Museum Services Curator, Mr M.D. Howe

Open: Mon–Fri: 8.45–5.00, by prior appointment only.

Access: Bona fide researchers. In the case of

Clare MSS, proof of bona fides will be requested.

Historical background: The museum was founded by the Peterborough Museum Society in 1879 and taken over by the city council in 1968.

Acquisitions policy: The museum now collects material of local interest (i.e. within the Greater Peterborough area), although collections held in the museum cover a wider area.

Major collections: Archaeological records of excavations, mostly 20th century.
Natural history material (acquired in connection with Natural History Resources Centre).
Papers and MSS of John Clare (1793–1864).
Norman Cross Collection: Napoleonic prisoner of war work records, including order of day books, accounts of courts martial, land tenure agreements, inventories, 1797–1816.

Non-manuscript material: Photographs; playbills; maps, 1820–; topographical collection.

Facilities: Photocopying and photography by arrangement only.

Finding aids: Card indexes.

Publications: M. Grainger: *Catalogue of Clare MSS in the Peterborough Museum.*

934 Arbuthnot Museum

Parent organisation: North East of Scotland Museums Service

Address: St Peter Street, Peterhead, Grampian AB42 6QD

Telephone: (01779) 477778

Enquiries: The Museum Curator, Ms J.E. Chamberlaine-Mole

Open: Mon, Tues, Thurs, Fri, Sat: 10.30–1.30; 2.30–5.00 Wed: 10.30–1.00

Access: Generally open to the public, by appointment.

Historical background: The present museums service was formed in 1975 incorporating six local museums: Arbuthnot Museum (f. 1850); Banff Museum (f. 1828), Carnegie Museum, Inverurie (f. 1884); Brander Museum, Huntly (f. 1883); Tolbooth Museum, Stonehaven (f. 1963); and Banchory Museum (f. 1975).

Acquisitions policy: The area covers the districts of Banff and Buchan, Gordon, and Kincardine and Deeside; however, most archive material is referred to Grampian Regional Archives (see entry 7).

Archives of organisation: Small collection of museum's archival material, 1828–.

Major collections: Peterhead Harbours: records of arrivals and sailings, 1865–97; day-books, 1857–1935.
Whaling voyage journals, mid-19th century.
J. Scott Skinner (1843–1927), music MSS.
Arbuthnot family records, 18th–19th centuries.

Non-manuscript material: Maps of Peterhead, Stonehaven and Banff.
James Ferguson (1710–76), astronomical charts.
Large photograph collection covering northern Scotland.

Finding aids: Catalogue to photograph collection.

Facilities: Photocopying. Photography. Microfiche reader.

935 Blair Castle

Parent organisation: Atholl Estates

Address: Blair Atholl, Pitlochry, Tayside PH18 5TL

Telephone: (01796) 481207

Enquiries: The Archivist, Mrs Jane Anderson

Open: Mon–Fri: by appointment only.

Access: Bona fide researchers; an appointment is necessary and a charge is made.

Historical background: Blair Castle has been the seat of the Earls, Marquis and Dukes of Atholl from the 13th century to the present day; the present Duke is the 10th.

Acquisitions policy: Acquires material concerning the Atholl family and their estates (located mainly in Perthshire).

Archives of organisation: Land charters and deeds, 13th–18th centuries.
Correspondence, 17th and 20th centuries.
Estate rentals and accounts, 17th and 20th centuries.

Major collections: Political papers of Katharine, Duchess of Atholl MP (1874–1960).

Non-manuscript material: Estate plans and maps.
Architectural drawings.

Finding aids: NRA(S) 234: covers majority of collection (1600–1900). 19th century MS catalogue of earlier material (1290–1600). MS bundle list of 20th-century materials.

Conservation: Limited paper conservation carried out in-house; more complex work contracted to Dundee University (entry **266**). No outside work is undertaken.

Publications: Atholl and Tullibardine Chronicles (private publication, 1908, 1919).

936 College of St Mark and St John

Address: Derriford Road, Plymouth, Devon PL6 8BH

Telephone: (01752) 777188 ext. 4200

Fax: (01752) 761120

Enquiries: The Deputy Head of Learning Resources, Alison Bidgood

Open: Mon–Fri: 9.00–5.00

Access: Generally open to the public, by appointment.

Formerly Battersea College (later St Johns College, Battersea), 1840–1923, and St Mark's College, Chelsea, 1841–1923, the colleges were merged by the National Society in 1923 on the Chelsea site, and moved to Plymouth in 1973. The founding principals were Sir James Kay-Shuttle (1840–79) at Battersea and Derwent Coleridge (1800–83) at St Marks. Until 1977 the college was solely for teacher training. An archive exists for the early colleges and the combined college on both sites. Records include registers, council minutes, photographs, plans, books, journals, papers, artefacts and, more recently, video and audio recordings. There is a card catalogue of the collection and computerisation is being considered.

937 Devon Library Services (West)

Address: Plymouth Central Library, Drake Circus, Plymouth, Devon PL4 8AL

Telephone: (01752) 385909

Fax: (01752) 385905

Enquiries: The Local and Naval History Librarian

Open: Mon–Fri: 9.00–9.00 Sat: 9.00–4.00

Access: Generally open to the public. Prior enquiry is advisable.

Historical background: Devon Library Services were formed from a number of separate library authorities on local government reorganisation in 1974. Two of these authorities, Exeter and Plymouth, were established in the 19th century and had considerable MS collections. They both suffered losses in World War II and West Devon Record Office (entry **939**) now holds records relating to Plymouth and West Devon. Any MSS in Devon Library Services are non-archival in nature and relatively few in number. They are mainly in the local studies collections in Plymouth and Exeter Central Library (entry **325**).

Acquisitions policy: To acquire non-archival MSS that reflect the development of Devon and the South-West of England.

Major collections: A small number of MSS, including antiquarian notes and the collections of Sabine Baring-Gould (1834–1924) on folksongs and parish history.

Non-manuscript material: Extensive collections of illustrations, newspaper cuttings, ephemera, maps, films.
Collection of theses on Plymouth and surrounding area.

Facilities: Photocopying. Photography by arrangement. Microfilm/fiche reader/printers.

Publications: Some material included in A. Brockett: *The Devon Union List* (Exeter, 1977).

938 Marine Biological Association of the United Kingdom

Address: Citadel Hill, Plymouth, Devon PL1 2PB

Telephone: (01752) 222772

Fax: (01752) 226865

Enquiries: The Head of Library and Information Services, David Moulder

Open: Mon–Fri: 9.00–5.15

Access: By appointment only.

Historical background: The Marine Biological Association was founded in 1884 and the Plymouth laboratory opened in 1888. The aims are to promote scientific research into all aspects of life in the sea, and the MBA has gained an international reputation for excellence in research, both by resident staff and the many British and overseas visiting workers. The library is one of the most comprehensive in the world in its coverage of the marine literature and maintains an archive collection.

Acquisitions policy: Material related to the history of the MBA and of British marine science.

Archives of organisation: Material relating to the history of the association, laboratory, research programmes, staff, visiting workers, ships, and governing council. Including personal and scientific papers, letters, note-books and MSS, 1870–.

Non-manuscript material: Photographs and illustrations of people, ships, equipment and buildings.

Finding Aids: Preliminary catalogue (1993). Computer database.

Facilities: Photocopying.

Publications: J. Southward and E.K. Roberts: 'One Hundred Years of Marine Research at Plymouth', *Journal of the Marine Biological Association of the United Kingdom,* 67 (1987), 465–506.

939 West Devon Record Office

Address: Unit 3, Clare Place, Coxside, Plymouth, Devon PL4 0JW

Telephone: (01752) 385940 223939 (searchroom bookings only)

Enquiries: The Senior Assistant Archivist, Mr Paul Brough

Open: Mon–Thurs: 9.30–5.00 Fri: 9.30–4.30 Some late opening (intending visitors are advised to check). There is a daily or annual charge.

Historical background: The office was set up in 1952 as a section of the Plymouth Central Library, which was administered by the city council. Since 1974 it has been a branch of Devon Record Office (entry **323**) under the aegis of Devon County Council. It also acts as the Diocesan Record Office for parishes within the West Devon area and for parts of the South Hams.

Archives of organisation: Usual local authority record holdings.

Major collections: Deposited local collections.

Non-manuscript material: *Western Morning News* photographic collection.

Facilities: Photocopying. Photography by arrangement. Microfilm/fiche readers.

Publications: C.E. Welch: *Guide to the Archives Department of Plymouth City Libraries,* pt 1: *Official Records* (1962).

940 Poole Borough Council

Address: Borough of Poole Museum Service, 4 High Street, Poole, Dorset BH15 1BW

Telephone: (01202) 683138

Fax: (01202) 660896

Enquiries: The Local Studies Officer, Mrs J.A. Norbury

Open: Mon–Fri: by arrangement.

Access: Generally open to the public. The Borough Archive may be viewed by appointment after written application (forms available). The Local Studies Collection is also accessible by appointment.

Historical background: Poole Borough Council houses its own archive, dating back to its first charter in 1248. It was a county incorporate, 1568–1974, and a port of staple; the mayor was also Admiral of the Port. The members of council were trustees of the quays until the late 19th century and the corporation was involved in a wide range of activities linked with its strong Newfoundland and Mediterranean trading interests. The office is recognised as a place of deposit for public records.

Acquisitions policy: Borough Archive: to acquire, by gift, loan or purchase, any material that can be regarded as, or formerly was, part of the borough archive.
Local Studies Collection: to acquire material evidence of Poole, its history and its people, including family records, business and association records, title deeds, photographs and supporting material.

Archives of organisation: Corporate records, minute books and deeds, 16th–20th centuries; courts of record, petty sessions and quarter sessions, mid-17th century–.

Major collections: Records of merchant families.
Research material on the Newfoundland trade.

Non-manuscript material: Local studies collection:, including maps, photographs (*c*12,000), ephemera, biographical material, ship information, trade and commerce data, books and tapes.

Finding aids: Borough Archive: computerised list (copy at PRO) and calendars (4 vols), sent to NRA. Local Studies: name, ship, occupation and information indexes. Photographic collection currently being catalogued.

Facilities: Photocopying (20th-century documents only). Photography.

Conservation: Contracted out.

Publications: Census, 1574.
1803 Levée en Masse [Doc. 1, 1993; another 8 to follow].

941 Portsmouth Central Library
Historical Collections

Parent organisation: Hampshire County Library

Address: Guildhall Square, Portsmouth, Hants PO1 2DX

Telephone: (01705) 819311 ext. 57

Fax: (01705) 839855

Enquiries: The Divisional Librarian, J. Thorn (postal) or The Local and Naval Studies Librarian, A. King (telephone)

Open: Mon–Fri: 10.00–7.00 Sat: 10.00–4.00

Access: Anyone may use the local, naval and genealogical collections on production of proof of name and address. Readers requiring detailed help are encouraged to make an appointment. Dickens researchers should write to the Divisional Librarian with the name of a referee.

Historical background: Portsmouth Public Libraries began in 1883, when a Local Collection was started. The Naval Collection was first brought together in the 1950s and includes the McCarthy Collection of naval history books donated in 1984. The Dickens Collection was transferred from the Charles Dickens Birthplace Museum in Portsmouth in 1967. Portsmouth libraries became part of Hampshire County Library in 1974.

Acquisitions policy: Material, including illustrations, maps, pamphlets, periodicals and ephemera, is acquired by purchase and occasionally by donation. Archives are mostly deposited in Portsmouth City Record Office (entry **942**).

Archives of organisation: Annual reports, catalogues, bye-laws relating to Portsmouth libraries; cuttings and photographs illustrating Portsmouth library history.

Major collections: Dickens Collection: letters, speeches, scrapbooks, first editions etc of Charles Dickens (1812–70).
Minutes and reports of the Portsmouth Literary and Philosophical Society.

Non-manuscript material: Collection of Sir F. Madden's Portsmouth theatre playbills.
Navy lists, 1778–; army lists, 1766–.
Lily Lambert McCarthy Collection of books on naval history, especially Nelson.
Local newspapers, including *Hampshire Telegraph*, 1799–1976.

Finding aids: Items are included in the Hampshire County Library catalogue, with special print-outs for the individual collections.

Facilities: Photocopying. Photography by arrangement. Microfilm/fiche readers (must be booked in advance).

Conservation: Contracted out.

Publications: Booklet and leaflet guides to collections.

942 Portsmouth City Records Office

Address: Museum Road, Portsmouth, Hants PO1 2LJ

Telephone: (01705) 827261

Fax: (01705) 875276

Enquiries: The Collections Manager, Michael Gunton

Open: Mon–Thurs: 9.30–5.00 Fri: 9.30–4.00
Closed the first Monday of every month until 1.15 pm for staff training. Usually closed at the end of December and in early January for stock-taking.

Access: Generally open to the public. Closure periods apply to certain classes of records.

Historical background: The Records Office was established in 1960. It also acts as the Diocesan Record Office for Portsmouth, and is recognised as a place of deposit for public records. Since 1994 it has been part of Portsmouth Museums and Record Service.

Acquisitions policy: Written and printed documents, photographs, maps etc from organisations, families and individuals relating to Portsmouth and south-east Hampshire.

Archives of organisation: Records of Portsmouth City Council and predecessor bodies.

Major collections: Portsmouth Floating Bridge Co., 1838–1961; Portsmouth Water Co., 1741–1967; Portsmouth United Breweries, 1834–1960; Hulbert Jackson, 1650–1985; W. Treadgold & Co. Ltd, iron merchants, 1704–1988; Hoad & Son, wheelwrights, 1777–1984; Portsea Island Gas Co., 1821–1957; Anglican parish records of the Portsmouth, Havant and Alverstoke deaneries of Portsmouth Diocese; records of the Anglican Diocese of Portsmouth; records of Roman Catholic and non-conformist churches on Portsea Island.

Non-manuscript material: Extensive photographic holdings; film and sound archives transferred to the Wessex Film and Sound Archive at Hampshire Record Office (entry **1084**)

Finding aids: Card indexes (name, place, subject); catalogues of collections; ongoing computerisation of indexes and catalogues. Copies of catalogues sent to NRA.

Facilities: Photocopying. Photography by arrangement. Microfilm/fiche readers.

Conservation: Paper and other conservation undertaken in-house. Outside work undertaken by arrangement.

Publications: *Guide to Collections* in preparation; leaflets on various topics are available.

943 The Royal Naval Museum Archive

Address: HM Naval Base, Portsmouth, Hants PO1 3NU

Telephone: (01705) 733060

Fax: (01705) 875806

Enquiries: The Curator of Documents and Manuscripts, Mr Matthew Sheldon

Open: Mon–Fri: 10.00–4.00

Access: To all genuine researchers, by appointment; 24 hours' notice is required.

Historical background: The museum was founded in 1911 as the Dockyard Museum, and the bulk of its collections were transferred to the new Victory Museum in 1938. In 1972 it was renamed the Royal Naval Museum and major expansion began, as a result of which the museum now presents the history of the Royal Navy from Tudor Times until the present day. It is the only museum in the country devoted exclusively to the overall history of the Royal Navy.

Acquisitions policy: The museum aims to collect material for display and research relating to the history of the Royal Navy and its people. Particular emphasis is placed on the navy's social history and the experience of individuals as shown in personal papers and oral history interviews.

Archives of organisation: Correspondence relating to the establishment of the Royal Naval Museum and the formation of the former Victory Museum; correspondence and research notes on museum acquisitions.

Major collections: Personal papers of Admiral Sir Arthur Auckland Cochrane (1840– 1905) and Lt.-Col. Harold Wyllie (1900–70).
Midshipmen's journals, c1800–1940.
Women's Royal Naval Service Historic Collection.

Non-manuscript material: Photographs of ships, men, actions and routines of the Royal Navy, including many private albums, 1870s-1950s (c40,000).
Oral History Collection, 1930–.
The King Alfred Library: reference works, naval journals and biography (18,000 vols).

Finding aids: Computerised catalogues for some of the museum's collection.

Facilities: Photocopying. Photography.

944 Lancashire Record Office

Address: Bow Lane, Preston, Lancs PR1 2RE

Telephone: (01772) 263039

Fax: (01772) 263050

Enquiries: The County Archivist, Mr B. Jackson

Open: Mon, Wed, Thurs: 9.00–5.00 Tues: 9.00–8.30 Fri: 9.00–4.30

Access: Generally open to the public. The office operates the CARN reader's ticket system.

Historical background: The record office was established in 1940. It is also the Diocesan Record Office for Blackburn, part of Liverpool and part of Bradford, and is recognised as a place of deposit for public records.

Archives of organisation: Usual local authority record holdings.

Major collections: Deposited local collections.

Facilities: Photocopying. Photography. Microfilming.

Conservation: In-house. Outside work is not undertaken.

Publications: Handlist of Genealogical Sources (5/1980).
R. Sharpe France: *Guide to Lancashire Record Office* (8/1986).
Janet D. Martin: *Guide to Lancashire Record Office: a Supplement* (1991).

945 Myerscough College Library

Address: Myerscough Hall, Bilsborrow, Preston, Lancs PR3 0RY

Telephone: (01995) 640611 ext. 251

Enquiries: The College Librarian, Mr J. R. Humfrey

Open: Mon–Thurs: 9.00–8.00 Fri: 9.00–5.00

Access: Generally open to the public.

Historical background: The college was founded in 1893, and called Lancashire College of Agriculture and Horticulture until 1993. It is particularly concerned with agriculture, arboriculture, the environment, horticulture, land-based industries, leisure and tourism, equine studies and veterinary nursing.

Acquisitions policy: To maintain the college archives.

Archives of organisation: Archives relating to the college, 1919–, including milking records and farm reports, 1948–; plans and maps of college sites and farms; photographs and glass plates of college and local agriculture, c1900–; slides of conservation/land-based industries/farming (3000) and videos (270).

Finding aids: Lists and indexes.

Facilities: Photocopying. Microfilm/fiche readers.

946 Preston District Library
Local Studies Collection

Parent organisation: Lancashire Library

Address: Market Place, Preston, Lancs PR1 2PP

Telephone: (01772) 253191

Fax: (01772) 555527

Enquiries: The District Librarian, Mrs J.P. Farrell

Open: Mon, Wed, Fri: 10.00–7.30 Tues, Thurs, Sat 10.00–5.00

Access: Open to the general public. A prior appointment will save time.

Historical background: There has been an organised Local Studies Collection since 1967, although material was acquired previously. The library forms part of Preston District Reference Library and collects material relating to Preston and the immediate area around. The bulk of the collection comprises printed material and previously held records of Preston police, schools, trades council and businesses have been transferred to the Lancashire Record Office (entry 944).

Acquisitions policy: MS material is acquired by donation. Printed material is bought as required.

Major collections: Papers of Francis Thompson (1859–1907), poetry and prose.

Non-manuscript material: Local newspapers, 1807–.
Lancashire maps.
Dr Shepherd Library: books on medical and other sciences, plus history, literature, classics, mainly 17th and 18th centuries.
Transactions of the major historical and record societies of the North-West.

Finding aids: Card catalogue of Local Studies Collection.

Facilities: Photocopying (except for bound volumes of newspapers). Microfilm/fiche reader/printer.

Publications: Dr Shepherd's Library Catalogue (Preston, 1870).

Catalogue of the Francis Thompson Collection (Preston, 1959).

947 University of Central Lancashire

Address: Library and Learning Resources Service, Preston, Lancs PR1 2HE

Telephone: (01772) 892284

Fax: (01772) 892937

Enquiries: The University Librarian, Professor Peter Brophy

Open: Term: Mon–Thurs: 9.00–9.00 Fri: 9.00–8.00 Sat: 10.00–6.00 Sun: 10.00–2.00 Vacation: Mon–Thurs: 9.00–5.30 Fri: 9.00–5.00

Access: Written application preferred.

Historical background: Preston Institution for the Diffusion of Knowledge was founded in 1828 by Joseph Livesey (1794–1884), who also founded the British National Temperance League. It was later known as the Avenham Institution until it was re-formed in 1882 as the Harris Institute. This became Harris College in 1956 and Preston Polytechnic in 1973. The Preston Municipal Observatory, (f. 1881) was incorporated into the polytechnic in 1974. In 1984 it was renamed Lancashire Polytechnic and in 1992 it became the University of Central Lancashire.

Acquisitions policy: To collect all material likely to be relevant to the understanding of the history and development of the university and its predecessors.

Archives of organisation: Astronomical and meteorological records for Preston, 1881–1960s.
Index registers of all Harris Institute/College students, 1882–1965.
Committee minutes, 1828–1920s.

Major collections: Archives of BNTL and its two former constituents, including minutes, agents' reports, account books, annual reports, 1845– (incomplete).
Sheffield Temperance Association records, including minutes, correspondence, subscription book, 1856–1919.

Non-manuscript material: All prospectuses and reports, 1928–.
Photographs and ephemera.
Oral history video tapes.

BNTL artefacts, e.g. Joseph Livesey's rattle, memorabilia, lantern slides.

Facilities: Photocopying. Photography. Microfilm readers.

Publications: G. Timmins et al.: *Preston Polytechnic: the Emergence of an Institution, 1828–1978* (Preston, 1979).

948 Thanet Archive Office

Parent organisation: Kent Arts and Libraries

Address: Ramsgate Library, Guildford Lawn, Ramsgate, Kent CT11 9AY

Telephone: (01843) 593532

Fax: (01843) 852692

Enquiries: The Heritage Office, Ms Penny Ward

Open: Thurs: 9.30–1.00; 2.00–6.00 Third Sat of every month: 9.30–1.00; 2.00–6.00

Access: Generally open to the public. An appointment is needed for microfilm/fiche readers.

Historical background: The branch office opened in 1982. The collections comprise material relating to Thanet transferred from Margate, Broadstairs and Ramsgate libraries, from the previous local authorities which were superseded by Thanet District Council following local government reorganisation in 1974, and from the Kent Archives Office at Maidstone (entry **789**).

Archives of organisation: Usual local authority record holdings.

Major collections: Deposited local collections.

Finding aids: Indexes, catalogues, lists.

Facilities: Photocopying and photography by arrangement. Microfilm reader/printer, microfiche reader.

949 Rawtenstall District Central Library
Rossendale Collection

Parent organisation: Lancashire County Library

Address: Haslingden Road, Rawtenstall Rossendale, Lancs BB4 6QU

Telephone: (01706) 227911

Fax: (01706) 217014

Enquiries: The Reference Librarian, Susan A. Halstead

Open: Mon, Tues, Thurs: 9.30–7.30 Wed: 9.30–1.00 Fri: 9.30–5.00 Sat: 9.30–4.00

Access: Generally open to the public.

Historical background: Before 1974 Rawtenstall was administered by a borough council, and the Local Studies Collection was quite extensively developed to cover Rawtenstall and the surrounding areas. After the 1974 local government reorganisation Rawtenstall became the district headquarters of Rossendale, one of the 14 districts of Lancashire County Library. (See also Haslingden Library, entry 377).

Acquisitions policy: To collect materials directly relevant to the Rossendale area, i.e. Bacup, Haslingden, Rawstenstall, Whitworth, as well as Lancashire and the North-West.

Major collections: Rawtenstall and Rossendale Borough Council minutes and electoral registers, 1891–; Rawtenstall Burial Board records, 1874–9; Rawtenstall Corporation Housing Scheme records, 1922–74.
Sunday school records, 1844–1953; co-operative societies' records, 1876–1956.
Loveclough Printerworkers' Library and Club records, 1892–1944.
Haslingden Gospel Mission minute books, 1890–1983.

Non-manuscript material: Copies of music scores written and used by Deighn Layrocks, group of 18th-century musicians. Originals on permanent loan to Lancashire Record Office (entry 944)
News cuttings and photographs.
Rossendale Free Press, 1883 (on microfilm).
Dissertations on the development of industry within Rossendale.

Facilities: Photocopying. Microfilm/fiche readers/printer.

Conservation: Conservation work undertaken by Lancashire Record Office.

Publications: J. Harrison: *Tracing your Ancestors in Rossendale* (1982).
Directory of Local Studies Resources in Lancashire (1986).

950 BBC Written Archives Centre

Address: Caversham Park, Reading, Berks RG4 8TZ

Telephone: (01734) 472742, exts 280/1/2

Fax: (01734) 461145

Enquiries: The Written Archivist, Mrs J.M. Kavanagh

Open: Wed–Fri: 9.45–1.00; 2.00–5.15, by appointment. Telephone calls taken Mon–Fri, 9.30–5.30

Access: By written appointment, giving full details of the nature of the enquiry. Correspondence, 1922–69, is open for research. There is unrestricted access to programme records, programmes-as-broadcast, news bulletins and scripts. Certain charges are made.

Historical background: The centre was established at Caversham in 1970, when it was decided to move the Historical Records Office (set up in London in 1957 mainly to assist Asa Briggs in his work on *The History of Broadcasting in the UK*) to more spacious accommodation and allow greater access for research. BBC sound archives are held in Broadcasting House in London. Requests for access to recorded material should be made to the National Sound Archive (entry 496B) and the National Film and Television Archive (entry 493) respectively.

Acquisitions policy: To maintain the records of the corporation, including BBC publications, and acquire papers of prominent BBC figures.

Archives of organisation: Non-current records of the corporation for permanent preservation, including regional and World Service papers.
Correspondence, minutes and reports covering all areas of the BBC's activities: programmes (including correspondence with contributors), policy, scripts, news bulletins, daily programme logs, audience research, technical developments.

Major collections: Papers of people closely connected with the BBC in some way.

Non-manuscript material: Plans and illustrations; microfilm; BBC publications, including *Radio Times* (with regional volumes), *The Listener, World Radio, London Calling*; BBC schools publications; BBC Symphony and Promenade Concert programmes; the *Summary of World Broadcasts* (produced by the BBC Monitoring Service); broadcasting press cuttings; small collection of books on broadcasting.

Finding aids: Various lists and indexes.

Facilities: Photocopying. Microfilm readers.

Publications: For a general introduction to the range and nature of the material available, see A. Briggs: *The History of Broadcasting in the United Kingdom* (Oxford, 1961–) [4 vols].

951 Berkshire Record Office

Parent organisation: Royal County of Berkshire

Address: Shire Hall, Shinfield Park, Reading, Berks RG2 9XD

Telephone: (01734) 233184

Fax: (01734) 233203

Enquiries: The County Archivist

Open: Tues, Wed: 9.00–5.00 Thurs: 9.00–9.00 Fri: 9.00–4.30
Closure for stock-taking: normally the first two weeks in November.

Access: Generally open to the public. The office operates the CARN reader's ticket system. An appointment is essential as space is limited.

Historical background: The office was established in 1948. It also acts as the Diocesan Record Office for Oxford (Archdeaconry of Berkshire), and is recognised as a place of deposit for public records.

Archives of organisation: Usual local authority record holdings, including Corporation of Reading records.

Major collections: Deposited local collections.

Finding aids: Catalogues and indexes, catalogues sent to NRA.

Facilities: Photocopying. Photography. Microfilming. Microfilm reader/printer.

Conservation: In-house service; outside work occasionally undertaken.

Publications: F. Hull: *Guide to the Berkshire Record Office* (1952).

952 County Local Studies Library

Parent organisation: Royal County Berkshire: Cultural Services

Address: Central Library, Abbey Square, Reading, Berks RG1 3BQ

Telephone: (01734) 509243

Fax: (01734) 589039

Enquiries: The Local Studies Librarian

Open: Mon, Wed: 9.30–5.00 Tues, Thurs, Fri: 9.30–7.00 Sat: 9.30–4.00

Access: Generally open to the public, although an appointment is required to consult some material.

Historical background: Reading is the main local studies library for Berkshire. It has been collecting material on Reading and Berkshire since a public library was first opened in the town in the 1880s. Maidenhead Library also holds a small amount of MS material on Cookham and Maidenhead.

Acquisitions policy: To collect material relating to the whole of Berkshire and neighbouring areas of bordering counties.

Major collections: Literary MSS, diaries, letters and local history note-books and scrapbooks, including: Mary Russell Mitford (1787–1855), correspondence and diary; Thomas Noon Talfourd (1795–1855), judge and author, correspondence and legal note-books; Treacher family note-books of River Thames surveyors and their accounts, c1800–c1860.

Non-manuscript material: Illustrations, photographs, prints, slides, maps and plans, books and directories, newspaper files and cuttings. Printed ephemera.

Finding aids: Catalogues.

Facilities: Photocopying. Photography. Microfilm/fiche readers/printer. Self-service microfiche printer.

Conservation: In-house service.

Publications: *Local Collection Catalogue* (1958; suppl., 1967).
Bibliography of Mary Russell Mitford (1787–1855).

953 Douai Abbey

Address: Upper Woolhampton, Reading, Berks RG7 5TH

Telephone: (01734) 715340

Fax: (01734) 715203

Enquiries: The Archivist, Dom Geoffrey Scott

Open: By arrangement.

Access: Bona fide researchers, by appointment.

Historical background: The English Benedictine community was founded in Paris in 1615, and settled at Douai in northern France after the French Revolution. In 1903 it transferred to Woolhampton. The collections divide into two: material relating to the English Benedictine Congregation, of which the abbey is a member, and archives belonging to Douai Abbey, its parishes, school and other apostolates.

Acquisitions policy: The abbey serves as a repository for archives of the parishes it administers. It specialises in 18th–century Benedictine and Jacobite material. Microfilms are made of dispersed records.

Archives of organisation: English Benedictine Congregation, 1619–.
Records of community, school and missions attached to the community, including apostolates in Mauritius and Australia.

Major collections: Collections of Dom Benet Weldon (1674–1713), Benedictine annalist.

Non-manuscript material: English Benedictine congregation photographs.

Finding aids: Subject and chronological catalogues.

Facilities: Photocopying. Microfilm/fiche reader.

954 Rural History Centre

Parent organisation: University of Reading

Address: Whiteknights, Reading, Berks RG6 2AG

Telephone: (01734) 318666 (Archivist), 318660

Fax: (01734) 751264

Enquiries: The Archivist, J.H. Brown

Open: Mon–Fri: 9.30–1.00; 2.00–5.00, by prior appointment.

Access: Generally open to the public. A user's card may be issued for study of research collections over a long period. One week's notice is required for consultation of Agricultural Co-operative Society and certain deposits of national agricultural organisations' records. There are restrictions on some deposited collections.

Historical background: The Institute of Agricultural History was established in 1968 to co-ordinate and extend teaching and research in agricultural history; to collect, preserve and publish records, documents and other relevant material; and to maintain the Museum of English Rural Life founded within the University of Reading in 1951 and opened to the public in 1955. The institute became the Rural History Centre in 1993.

Acquisitions policy: To collect material concerned with rural and agricultural history, with special reference to national organisations concerned with agriculture, the countryside, rural and agricultural industry, and food. Geographical coverage: Britain, mainly England.

Major collections: Trade Records Collection: business records of over 30 agricultural engineering, servicing and processing firms; technical and advertising literature issued by c3000 UK and foreign firms, 19th century–.
National agricultural organisation records: records of Royal Agricultural Society of England (f. 1838), including archives of the Board of Agriculture and Internal Improvement, 1793–1822; National Union of Agriculture and Allied Workers, 1906–1970s; National Farmers' Union, 1909–43; Country Landowners' Association, 1907–58; Royal Agricultural Benevolent Institution, 1880s–1960s; Council for the Protection of Rural England, 1930s–1970s; Council for National Parks; Agricultural Apprenticeship Council, 1949–74.
Agricultural Co-operative Society records, mostly 20th century.
General collections, including personal papers of agricultural writers and scientists.
Shorthorn Society and Jersey Cattle Society records and publications.
Farm records, 18th–20th centuries, are housed at Reading University Library (entry 955): enquiries should be made in the first instance to the university archivist.

Non-manuscript material: Engineering drawings, trade catalogues and printed ephemera; film and audio tapes.

Photograph library, including reference collections of agricultural organisations and the farming press, mid-19th century– (c500,000 prints and negatives).

Finding aids: Lists and catalogues for all principal deposits. Specialised indexes for certain collections. Lists of principal deposits are sent to NRA.

Facilities: Photocopying. Photography. Microfilming. Microfilm reader. Copying of engineering drawings.

Publications: Historical Farm Records: a Summary Guide (Reading, 1973).
Ransomes: a History of the Firm and Guide to its Records (Reading, 1975).

955 University of Reading
Department of Archives and Manuscripts

Address: Whiteknights, Reading, Berks RG6 2AE

Telephone: (01734) 318776

Fax: (01734) 316636 (library)

Enquiries: The Keeper of Archives and Manuscripts, Mr Michael Bott

Open: Mon–Fri: 9.00–1.00; 2.00–5.00, by appointment.

Access: Generally open to the public. Certain records are restricted.

Historical background: Archives and Manuscripts was established as a department of the library in 1966 on the appointment of Dr J.A. Edwards. Until recently it was the base for work on a location register of 20th–century English literary MSS and letters (published 1988) and its extension to the 18th and 19th centuries (publication forthcoming).

Acquisitions policy: To acquire literary and historical MSS related to teaching and research in the University of Reading. To preserve university archives through the operation of a records management system.

Archives of organisation: University archives: records of university departments and their antecedents and of members of staff, 1860–.

Major collections: Records of British publishing and printing: collections include George Allen & Unwin; George Bell & Sons; The Bodley Head; Jonathan Cape; Chatto & Windus; Heinemann Educational Books; The Hogarth Press; Isotype Institute; Longman Group; Macmillan & Co.; Routledge & Kegan Paul; Secker & Warburg.

Historical farm records: mainly of individual working farmers from every English county, 16th–20th centuries.

Records of contemporary writing: letters and MSS of some 200 authors, 1880–, including the largest collection of Samuel Beckett MSS in Europe.

Modern political papers: six collections of 20th-century papers, of which most important are those of Waldorf, 2nd Viscount Astor, and Nancy, Lady Astor.

Non-manuscript material: Maps. Photographs. Audio-visual material.

Finding aids: Various indexes, catalogues and inventories.

Facilities: Access to all the resources of the university library, including photocopying and photographic services.

Publications: Accessions of General Manuscripts up to June 1970 (1970).
Historical Farm Records: a Summary Guide to Manuscripts and other Material in the University Library Collected by the Institute of Agricultural History (1973).
University of Reading Records Handbook (1977).
M. Bott and J.A. Edwards: *Records Management in British Universities: a Survey with some Suggestions* (1978).
J.A. Edwards: *The Samuel Beckett Collection: a Catalogue* (1978).
——: *A Brief Guide to Archives and Manuscripts in the Library, University of Reading* (1980).
The Kingsley Read Alphabet Collection: a Catalogue (1982).
Location Register of Twentieth-Century English Literary Manuscripts and Letters (1988).
One Hundred Years of University Education in Reading: a Pictorial History, 1892–1992 (1992).

956 Redcar Reference Library

Parent organisation: Cleveland County Libraries

Address: Central Library, Coatham Road, Redcar, Cleveland TS10 1RP

Telphone: (0642) 489292

Enquiries: The Reference Librarian, Miss B. Collett

Open: Mon–Wed, Fri: 9.30–7.00 Thurs, Sat: 9.30–5.00

Access: Generally open to the public.

Redcar was a borough library from 1937 to 1967. From 1967 it was part of Teesside Libraries and later of Cleveland. It maintains the usual local history collection, which includes the Graham Collection of social history photographs, 1890s–1940s (*c*3000). Photocopying and microfilm/fiche readers are available.

957 Cornish Studies Library

Parent organisation: Cornwall County Council Libraries and Arts Department

Address: 2–4 Clinton Road, Redruth, Cornwall TR15 2QE

Telephone: (01209) 216760

Enquiries: The Principal Librarian, Cornish Studies: Mr G.T. Knight

Open: Tues–Thurs: 9.30–12.30; 1.30–5.00 Fri: 9.30–12.30; 1.30–7.00 Sat: 9.30–12.30

Access: Generally open to the public. An appointment is strongly advised for the use of microfilm. Some material is in store so prior enquiry is suggested.

The Cornish Studies Library was established in 1974, based on an earlier large collection at Redruth, but adding collections from Truro and items from elsewhere. A local history collection is maintained, including the A.K. Hamilton Jenkin Collection relating to metal-mining in Cornwall and the Hambly and Ashley Row general Cornish collections. This is actively developed to complement the archival holdings of the Cornwall Record Office (entry **1061**). There are also 30 newspaper files, Cornish census returns, and a large photograph collection. A full computer catalogue is avail-

able and there is the usual range of reprographic services.

958 British Mycological Society Library

Address: c/o The Herbarium, Royal Botanic Gardens, Kew, Richmond-upon-Thames, Surrey TW9 3AE

Telephone: (0181) 948 0556 (Librarian's home)

Enquiries: The Librarian, Dr B.L. Brady

Open: Open by prior arrangement with the Librarian.

Access: Members and associates of BMS.

The BMS was founded *c*1949 and originally housed at the Commonwealth Mycological Institute, moving to the Herbarium in 1990. It holds 1890s drawings by Worthington G. Smith and photographs of early mycologists, but only acquires publications. There is a 1983 catalogue which is currently being revised.

959 London Borough of Richmond-upon-Thames
Libraries Department

Address: Local Studies Library, Old Town Hall, Whittaker Avenue, Richmond-upon-Thames, Surrey TW9 1TP

Telephone: (0181) 940 9125/5529 ext. 32

Fax: (0181) 940 6899

Enquiries: The Local History Librarian, Miss Jane Baxter

Open: Tues: 1.00–5.00 Wed: 1.00–8.00 Thurs, Fri: 1.00–6.00 2nd, 4th and 5th Sat: 10.00–12.30; 1.30–5.00

Access: Generally open to the public. A telephone call in advance is advisable to establish the exact location of any given material.

Historical background: The London Borough of Richmond-upon-Thames was formed in 1965 by the amalgamation of the boroughs of Richmond, Twickenham and Barnes. The local material relating to Richmond and East Sheen, Ham, Kew, Mortlake and Petersham is located at Richmond. There is no borough archivist or archives department and the library is not an official archive depository. Local material relating to Twickenham, The Hamptons, Teddington and Whitton is located at Twickenham District Reference Library. The majority of council records are in the custody of the Chief Executive and Town Clerk's Department, Municipal Offices, Twickenham TW1 3AA, tel. (0181) 891 1411.

Acquisitions policy: Very little money is available each year to spend on local history material that comes on the market, but anything significant is obtained when possible. A number of additions are donations from members of the public or from other council departments that do not wish to keep older materials.

Major collections: Usual local history collections, including:
Local government records, including rate books, Richmond vestry minutes and workhouse records, 19th and 20th centuries.
School records, 19th and 20th centuries.
Records of various local clubs and societies, mostly 20th century.
Vancouver Collection: pamphlets, cuttings and books relating to Captain George Vancouver, especially concerning his connections with Richmond and Petersham.
Sladen Collection: scrapbooks of his correspondence, bills, reviews etc (*c*70), compiled by Douglas Sladen, editor of *Who's Who*, who knew many of the literary and society figures of his day.
Long Collection: local material (books, playbills etc).
Collections of the works of local authors, e.g. James Thomson and Mrs Braddon.

Non-manuscript material: Maps, 1635–; photographs; prints; postcards; slides; news cuttings and microfilms of local newspapers; copies and microfilms of census returns, 1841–81.
Collection of playbills relating mainly to the Theatre Royal, Richmond, 1765–1884 (*c*1000).
Ionides Collection: topographical paintings, drawings and engravings of Richmond, Twickenham and the Lower Thames area (housed at Orleans Gallery, Twickenham).

Facilities: Photocopying. Microfilm/fiche reader/printer.

Finding aids: Index to Sladen letters: NRA 14252. Card catalogues of prints. Index to playbills, artists and local authors.

Publications: The library produces a series of about 60 brief notes on local history which are currently being revised; a complete list of local publications is available.

960 Public Record Office

Address: Ruskin Avenue, Kew, Richmond-upon-Thames, Surrey TW9 4DU
Chancery Lane, London WC2 1LR

Telephone: (0181) 876 3444 ext. 2350 (enquiries)

Fax: Kew: (0181) 878 8905
Chancery Lane: (0181) 404 7248

Enquiries: The Keeper (postal enquiries) or Enquiries (telephone)

Open: Mon–Fri: 9.30–5.00 Census Room: Sat: 9.30–5.00 (except Sat prior to bank holidays) Closed public and privilege holidays and usually the first fortnight of each October (for stock-taking).

Access: Generally open to the public by reader's ticket issued on production of formal documentary proof of identity.

Historical background: The Chancery Lane building was constructed, following the Public Records Act 1838, between 1851 and 1899. By the 1960s overcrowding led to the building of a new repository at Kew, which was opened in 1977. Records of medieval and early modern government, the Prerogative Court of Canterbury and the census of England and Wales (1841–1891), with all legal records, are held at Chancery Lane. Records of modern government departments are housed at Kew. Following extensive new building currently being undertaken at Kew it is planned to move all Chancery Lane records to Kew and reunite the collections from 1 January 1997. Census records will remain in central London.

Acquisitions policy: All government archives selected for permanent preservation are transferred to the PRO for the use of the public 30 years after their creation, unless retained for a longer period by the department concerned under statute or on application to the Lord Chancellor.

Major collections: Many private and semi-official collections of public figures, including the Chatham, Russell, Ramsay MacDonald,

Kitchener and Milner papers, and archives of some national non-governmental organisations, including the Imperial Institute, the Association of Municipal Corporations and the Queen's Institute of District Nursing.

Non-manuscript material: One of the most significant collections of maps and plans in the world.
Extensive photograph holdings (mostly scattered among administrative archives).
Some film, sound and machine-readable material (no facilities for use).
Official printed material.
Large staff library, very strong on English topography, administrative, legal and archival history, and a large collection of periodicals which is due to open to the public in 1997.

Finding aids: Lists (mainly typed), card indexes, indexes, calendars, handbooks etc. Typed lists sent to NRA.

Facilities: Photocopying. Photography. Microfilming. Microfilm/fiche reader/printer.

Conservation: Full in-house facilities.

Publications: Guide to Contents of the Public Record Office (1963–8) [3 vols].
Tracing your Ancestors in the Public Record Office (2/1991).
The Public Record Office Current Guide [regularly updated microfiche edition].
Calendars, handbooks, pamphlets, readers' guides.

961 Royal Botanic Gardens, Kew
Library and Archives

Address: Kew, Richmond-upon-Thames, Surrey TW9 3AE

Telephone: (0181) 332 5417

Fax: (0181) 332 5278

Enquiries: The Chief Librarian and Archivist, Miss S.M.D. Fitzgerald

Open: Mon–Thurs: 9.00–5.30 Fri: 9.00–5.00

Access: On written application.

Historical background: A botanic garden at Kew was begun in 1759 by Princess Augusta. The gardens of the Royal Estates at Kew became a Department of the Crown in 1840. They have been successively managed by the Commissioners of Woods and Forests (1841–51), the Board of Works (1851–1903), the Board of Agriculture (later Ministry of Agriculture, Fisheries and Food) (1903–84), and since 1984 by a board of trustees appointed under the National Heritage Act 1983. The buildings in the Royal Botanic Gardens, including Kew Palace, are maintained by the Department of the Environment. The library was set up in 1852; it is recognised as a place of deposit for public records.

Acquistions policy: Official papers are selected according to Public Record Office rules. Other papers are accepted if relevant to Kew's plant collections and research on tropical botany, plant conservation, anatomy, taxonomy and biochemistry.

Major collections: Archives include over 250,000 letters from all over the world, also modern registered files, field note-books, diaries etc, mostly 1840–.
Notable are the papers of Sir William Jackson Hooker (1785–1865), his son Sir Joseph Dalton Hooker (1817–1911) and George Bentham (1800–84); correspondence with overseas botanic gardens and departments of agriculture and forestry, especially in colonial territories.
Fewer papers relating to the gardens before 1840 survive: most of the papers of the superintendents William Aiton (1731–93) and his son William Townsend Aiton (1766–1849) were burnt in 1849; some were rescued, including inwards and outwards books and records books, 1793–, and correspondence with Kew collectors, e.g. Francis Masson and others; there are some papers of Sir Joseph Banks (1743–1820).

Non-manuscript material: Periodicals (4000); printed books (120,000); pamphlets (140,000); microforms (10,000); illustrations (175,000); maps (11,000); portraits (500).
Kewensia; nurserymen's catalogues.
Sound archive.
Large collection of plant illustrations, including many originals, e.g. the Church, Roxburgh, Tankerville and Curtis's *Botanical Magazine* collections.

Finding aids: General author and subject catalogues. Inventory and Public Record Office lists being computerised. Name index of correspondents. Artists' name index. NRA 25004, 25005.

Facilities: Photocopying. Photography. Microfilm/fiche readers.

Conservation: In-house service.

Publications: G.D.R. Bridson et al.: *Natural History Manuscript Resources in the British Isles* (London, 1980) [RBG, Kew entries, nos 269.1–387].
Royal Botanic Gardens Bibliography, 3: *Kew Gardens: Selected References on the History of the Royal Botanic Gardens, Kew* (1980) [8pp].

962 Yorkshire Film Archive

Address: University College of Ripon and York St John, College Road, Ripon, North Yorks HG4 2QX

Telephone: (01765) 602691

Fax: (01765) 600516

Enquiries: The Director, Ms S. Furness

Open: Mon–Fri: 9.00–5.00

Access: Generally open to the public, by appointment. Search and viewing fees charged for TV and commercial use.

Historical background: The archive was founded in 1986. With renewed funding it is now able to rationalise the collection and procedures. A film survey is in progress which will both considerably increase holdings and lead to the establishment of an electronic database and catalogue. This will detail holdings, other relevant collections in the region and outside sources such as the National Film Archive (entry 493B) and the BBC.

Acquisitions policy: Film that either reflects or illustrates the culture and history of the Yorkshire area (old county boundary).

Non-manuscript material: David Brown tractors, promotional material and films of farming equipment in action worldwide.
Several local film makers' collections covering the area and their travel abroad, 1897–, mostly 1930s and 1950s.
Yorkshire Image, a collection of photographic material of the region; oral history collection.

Finding aids: Nominal list. Catalogue in preparation. Photographic collection card catalogue.

Facilities: Film viewing facilities. Photography.

963 Rochdale Local Studies Library

Parent organisation: Rochdale Metropolitan Borough Council

Address: Arts and Heritage Centre, The Esplanade, Rochdale, Lancs OL16 4TY

Telephone: (01706) 864915

Enquiries: The Local Studies Officer, Mrs P.A. Godman

Open: Mon: 2.00–7.30 Tues, Thurs, Fri: 10.00–1.00; 2.00–5.30 Sat: 9.30–1.00; 2.00–4.00

Access: Generally open to the public. Storage of records on a separate site necessitates prior notice for access.

Historical background: The dynamic growth of Rochdale, Middleton and Heywood during the 19th century produced a wealth of material relating to the area. The town of Rochdale in particular was fortunate in that the early pioneers of the library service were keenly interested in the development of the area and helped to acquire a large amount of material which formed the basis of the Local Collection. Before 1974 the substantial local collections of Heywood, Middleton and Rochdale were located at the central libraries in those areas, and on local government reorganisation it was decided that each should retain a separate collection under the general supervision of a local studies librarian based at Rochdale (see also Middleton Area Central Library, entry 820; Heywood Area Central Library, entry 391).

Acquisitions policy: The collection of documentary material relating to all aspects of life in the area of the Metropolitan Borough of Rochdale and its previously independent constituent authorities.

Major collections: Local administrative records: early administrative records, including highway rates, Poor Law administration and administrative material from the constituent authorities of the metropolitan borough, mid-18th–early 19th centuries.
Church records: church rates, leys, tithe commutation maps, plans, deeds, etc; Methodist archives, 18th century–.
Family records: material relating to local families, including manorial records, deeds, indentures etc, mainly 19th century.
Trade union records: records of the Rochdale Operative Cotton Spinners Association; the

Rochdale Weavers, Winders and Beamers Association, 19th and 20th centuries.

Non-manuscript material: Complete runs of local newspapers (original and microfilm copies).
Books, pamphlets, audio-visual material, photographs, maps, plans, broadsheets, political handbills, theatre posters.

Finding aids: Archive lists.

Facilities: Photocopying. Microfilm/fiche readers.

Conservation: Contracted out.

Publications: Introduction to Local Studies Collections (1981).

964 Rochester Bridge Trust

Address: The Bridge Chamber, 5 Esplanade, Rochester, Kent ME1 1QE

Telephone: (01634) 846706/843457

Fax: (01634) 840125

Enquiries: The Bridge Clerk, Mr Glyn C. Jones, The Archivist, Dr James M. Gibson

Open: By arrangement.

Access: Archives are not normally available to the public, but may be consulted by bona fide scholars, with the approval of the Rochester Bridge Trust.

Historical background: In 1399 Sir Robert Knolles and Sir John de Cobham, prominent local men, gave and collected endowments in money and lands and obtained a Patent of Incorporation to ensure a responsible administration of the Rochester Bridge. A new bridge was built and two wardens appointed, who, with the help of a Court of Assistants added in 1576, administered the bridge. This arrangement still pertains. The bridge was specifically excluded from the provisions of the Trunk Roads Act of 1946. The wardens were appointed ex officio presidents of the New College of Cobham when it was refounded under the will of William Brooke, Lord Cobham, a descendant of the original founder, and college records are therefore lodged with those of the bridge, forming a distinct series.

Acquisitions policy: Working papers of the trust.

Archives of organisation: Rochester Bridge: Administrative records, early 15th century–.
Wardens' accounts, 1391–, including rentals of bridge lands and inventories of tools, boats, furniture etc, 17th–18th centuries.
Records about the maintenance and construction of the bridge, including technical reports, correspondence etc, 1561–, and reports by George Dance, James Rennie, Robert Smirke and Thomas Telford, early 19th century.
Rentals and surveys, 1506–.
Legal records, 1529–1835, and records relating to maintenance of property other than the bridge 1740–.
Estate deeds, including documents for property elsewhere.
Manorial records.
New College of Cobham: administrative records, including payment to pensioners, 1599–; accounts, 1599–; bonds, 1599–1877; nominations, certificates and material concerning elections, 1632–1890; estate deeds and surveys.

Non-manuscript material: Maps.
Plans, 1780–1932.
Photographs and drawings.

Finding aids: Cobham College: NRA 10439, 20714.

Publications: E.S. Scroggs: *Rochester Bridge Trust and the New College of Cobham, Kent: Guide to Classification and Indexing of Records at the Bridge Chamber, Rochester* (1954).
——: 'The Records of Rochester Bridge and the New College of Cobham', *Archives*, ii/12 (1954), 183.
N. Yates and J.M. Gibson (eds): *Traffic and Politics: the Construction and Management of Rochester Bridge, AD43–1993* (Boydell and Brewer, 1994).

965 Rochester Diocesan Registry

Address: The Precinct, Rochester, Kent ME1 1SZ

Telephone: (01634) 843231/2, 847067 (mornings only)

Fax: (01634) 843159

Enquiries: The Diocesan Registrar

Open: During office hours, by appointment.

The diocesan records comprise principally faculties, early 19th century–.

966 Rochester-upon-Medway Studies Centre

Address: Civic Centre, Strood, Rochester, Kent ME2 4AW

Telephone: (01634) 732714

Fax: (01634) 297060

Enquiries: The City Archivist, Mr S.M. Dixon (archives collections), The Heritage Officer, Mrs A. Myers/Miss E. Dixon (local studies collections)

Open: Mon, Thurs, Fri: 9.00–5.00 Tues: 9.00–6.00 Sat (1st and 3rd of each month): 9.00–1.00 Closed for stock-taking first two full weeks of November.

Access: Generally open to the public. Archives are available by appointment only and the centre operates the CARN reader's ticket system. Bookings are required for microfilm and microfiche holdings.

Historical background: Medway Area Archives Office was established on the present site in 1989 as a result of a partnership agreement between Kent County Council and Rochester-upon-Medway City Council. Previously the same agreement had allowed for the employment of an archivist based at the Guildhall Museum Annexe in Rochester (1987–9). By 1990 collections relating to the local government and private organisations of the Medway Towns, formerly located in city council premises in Rochester and Chatham and Kent Archives, Maidstone, were centralised at this site. Following further negotiations between the partner authorities the existing archives office and local studies collections at Rochester, Strood and Chatham libraries were merged in 1993 to form an enhanced and expanded integrated service.

Acquisitions policy: Archives: local government and private records relating mainly to the Medway Towns and Medway area, but including parish records for the wider Rochester Archdeaconry area.
Local studies: printed matter, including newspapers and maps, oral history and census for Kent County Council Medway Library Group area and Wouldham.

Major collections: Records of Rochester City Council, 1227–1974; Chatham Borough Council, 1890–1974; Strood Rural District Council, 1897–1974; Hoo Rural District Council, 1897–1935.
Post-1974 local authority records.
Records of Medway area schools, 19th–20th centuries, and the Poor Law Unions of Medway, Strood and Hoo, 1835–1930.
Parish records for Rochester Archdeaconry area, 14th–20th centuries.
Records of Methodist Church, Medway Towns Circuit, 1768–1988, and Chatham Memorial Synagogue, 1834–1972.
Archives of the Dean and Chapter of Rochester, 1541–1983.
Records of other religious foundations, including King's School, Rochester, 1660–1964; the priories of St Andrew's, Rochester, c1080–1540, and St Mary and St Nicholas, Leeds, 1095–1535; Newark Hospital, Strood, 1150–1540, and the Rochester Chapter and Bishopric estates, 14th–20th centuries.
Family and estate papers of the Earls of Darnley of Cobham Hall, 1537–1940, and the Best family of Boxley and Chatham, 1596–1905.
Business records of Winget of Strood, engineers, 20th century; Blaw Knox of Rochester, engineers, 20th century; Winch & Winch of Chatham, solicitors, 19th and 20th centuries.
Records of charities, including Richard Watts' Charity, Rochester, 1579–1979; Hospital of Sir John Hawkins, Chatham, 1500–1980s; St Bartholomew's Hospital, Rochester, 1627–1948.
Canon S.W. Wheatley: antiquarian notes on Rochester from ancient times, early 20th century.
Rochester Book Society records, 1797–1965.
Port of Rochester, shipping registers and crew lists, 1824–1927.
North Aylesford and Medway Petty Sessions records, 1754–1982.

Non-manuscript material: Local newspapers, 1830– (microfilm), and periodicals.
Census index, 1841–91 (microfilm).
Maps and plans.
Photographs and prints, including: Rochester Castle, Rochester Cathedral and Rochester Bridge.
Dickens Collection: books, journals and ephemera by or on Charles Dickens (formerly housed at Rochester Library).
General printed topographical and historical research on Medway area.

Finding aids: Archives: personal names, place names and subject indexes. Descriptive lists of collections.

Local Studies: topographical, author, and map indexes.

Facilities: Photocopying. Photography by arrangement. Microfilm/fiche reader/printer. Power points for lap-top computers. Limited disabled access.

Publications: Guide to Location of Sources for Armed Forces Genealogy in Medway Area, (1993).
Subject Guide to Records (1994).

967 London Borough of Havering

Address: Central Library, St Edward's Way, Romford, Essex RM1 3AR

Telephone: (01708) 772393/772394

Fax: (01708) 772391

Enquiries: The Reference and Information Librarian

Open: Mon–Wed, Fri: 9.30–8.00 Sat: 9.30–4.00

Historical background: Until 1965 Havering was part of the County of Essex, and much archive material relating to the area is therefore to be found at the Essex Record Office (entry 203). However, a small collection of items is held at Romford.

Acquisitions policy: To obtain further archives relevant to the area where possible and also to acquire copies of those deposited in other collections such as the Essex Record Office (mainly in microfilm form).

Major collections: Usual local history collections, including parish rate books for selected areas (especially Romford), 19th century.
Council minute books for Hornchurch UDC; Romford UDC; Romford Borough; Romford Local Board of Health, 1851–89.
Liberty of Havering treasurer's book, 1835–43.

Non-manuscript material: Microfilm copies of items held at the Essex Record Office, including Romford Workhouse Guardians minutes; and South Divisional Parliamentary Committee for Essex minute book, 1643–56.
Microfilm and transcript of some of the local parish registers, to mid-19th century.
Pamphlets, posters, postcards and other illustrations (*c*2200).
Census, 1841–91, for London Borough of Havering area (1891 census covers parts of London and Essex).
Local newspapers (microfilm, 1866–; bound vols, 1930s-).
Maps and plans.

Finding aids: Some lists and indexes available for census and parish material.

Facilities: Photocopying. Microfilm/fiche reader/printers.

Publications: Romford Record, nos 1–27 (1969–94).
Subject Index to Havering Review, nos 1–10.
Pamphlet about old Upminster and old Collier Row.

968 Rotherham Archives and Local Studies Section

Address: The Brian O'Malley Central Library and Arts Centre Walker Place, Rotherham, South Yorks S65 1JH

Telephone: (01709) 382121 ext. 3616, 823616 (direct line)

Fax: (01709) 823650

Enquiries: The Archivist, A.P. Munford

Open: Mon, Tues, Wed, Fri: 10.00–5.00 Thurs: 1.00–7.00 Sat: 9.00–5.00

Access: Generally open to the public.

Historical background: The library was administered by Rotherham County Borough until 1974 and then, after local government reorganisation, began collecting material relating to the new metropolitan borough. It is recognised as a place of deposit for public records.

Acquisitions policy: To collect material connected with the area of Rotherham Metropolitan Borough.

Major collections: Local government archives of Rotherham Metropolitan Borough Council and the former constituent authorities of Rotherham County Borough, Kiveton Park and Rotherham rural district councils, and the urban district councils of Maltby, Swinton Rawmarsh and Wath-upon-Dearne.
Non-conformist and quarter sessions records.
Hospital, business and workhouse records.

Non-manuscript material: Photographs and other illustrations of the area. Oral history tapes. Pamphlets, press cuttings, newspapers, maps.

Finding aids: Lists sent to NRA.

Facilities: Photocopying. Microfilm/fiche readers.

Conservation: Work undertaken by Sheffield Archives Conservation Unit (entry 1006).

969 Bute Museum Library

Parent organisation: Bute Museum Trustees

Address: The Museum, Stuart Street, Rothesay, Isle of Bute PA20 0BR

Telephone: (01700) 502540

Enquiries: The Hon. Librarian/Archivist, Mrs Anne Buchanan

Open: Wed: 2.30–4.30
Other times by appointment only.

Access: Generally open to the public. No charge is made but donations are welcomed.

Historical background: The Archaeological and Physical Society of Bute was founded in 1872 and started a library and museum. Interest in the society waned at the end of the century but was resuscitated in 1905 when the Buteshire Natural History Society was founded. The library and museum had various locations before the present building was erected in 1926. The society continued the administration until 1992, when a trust was formed and the museum became a registered charity.

Acquisitions policy: Archival material and books which are concerned with the history, natural history, geology and archaeology of the Isle of Bute are actively acquired.

Archives of organisation: Records of Archaeological and Physical Society, 1872–; Buteshire Natural History Society, 1905–; Bute Museum Trust, 1992–.

Major collections: Examination rolls, marriage and baptismal records for Rothesay parish, 1775–1835 (incomplete).
Deeds and papers *re* parish of Kingarth, 1504–1745, and Ascog Estate, 1507–1752.
Rothesay Town Council records, 1653–1766, Parish Session records, 1658–1750, and Kingarth Parish Session records, 1641–1703.
MS sermons, 1765–1824.

Non-manuscript material: Pictures, books,

memorabilia, photographs (*c*1500) and glass negatives (200), including several minor collections of photographs of Clyde steamers, buildings on the island now demolished and general landscapes.

Facilities: Photocopying. Photography by arrangement.

Publications: Transactions of Buteshire Natural History Society [23 vols].
D. N. Marshall, *History of Bute* (rev., 1992).

970 Rugby Library

Parent organisation: Warwickshire County Library

Address: St Matthew's Street, Rugby, Warks CV21 3BZ

Telephone: (01788) 542687/571813/535348

Fax: (01788) 573289

Enquiries: The Regional Information Officer, Mrs J. Grindle

Open: Mon, Thurs: 9.30–8.00 Tues, Fri 9.30–5.00 Wed: 9.30–1.00 Sat: 9.30–4.00

Access: Generally open to the public.

The library was founded in 1890. It maintains the usual local history collection relating to the Borough of Rugby and parts of east Warwickshire, which also includes school registers; a large photographic collection; *Rugby Advertiser*, 1846– (microfilm); and a significant collection of almanacs, 1854–1960. A card catalogue, photocopying and microfilm/fiche reader/printers are available. See *Family History and Local Studies Sources in the County Library.* Conservation work is carried out in-house by staff at Warwick County Record Office (entry 1077).

971 Rugby School

Address: Temple Reading Room, Rugby School, Barby Road, Rugby, Warks CV22 5DW

Telephone: (01788) 573959 (Temple Reading Room) 543465 (main school)

Fax: (01788) 569124

Enquiries: The Librarian, Mr D.S.R. MacLean

Open: Term: Mon–Fri: 9.00–4.00, by appointment.

Access: Approved readers on written application. All research undertaken by the school will be charged for. Applications may also be made to the Sub-Librarian (Special Collections), University of Birmingham Library (entry 101).

Historical background: Rugby School was founded by Lawrence Sheriff in 1567.
Originally a free grammar school for local boys, it began to attract pupils from further afield during the late 17th century, and 100 years later was an established public school. Dr Thomas Arnold (1795–1842) and Dr Frederick Temple (1821–1902), later Archbishop of Canterbury, were among the 19th-century headmasters. The game of rugby football originated at the school. Old Rugbeians include W.S. Landor (1775–1867), Matthew Arnold (1822–88), A.H. Clough (1819–61), Thomas Hughes (1822–96), Rupert Brooke (1887–1915), Lewis Carroll (1832–98), Arthur Ransome (1834–1922) and William Temple (1881–1944).

Acquisitions policy: Items connected with the school.

Archives of organisation: School records: registers, governing body papers, collections of boys' letters etc; the earliest date from the 1670s, most from 1750–.

Major collections: Arnold MSS: letters, diaries and note-books of Dr Thomas Arnold.
Rupert Brooke Collection: MS poems and scrapbook given by Mrs Brooke.
Various items associated with Brooke's schooldays.
Rugby football: MSS and drawings concerning the early history of the game.

Non-manuscript material: Photographs, 1861–. Portraits of headmasters and distinguished Rugbeians.
Natural History Society: published reports, 1867–, and supporting collections.

Finding aids: Various lists available. NRA 5282.

Facilities: Photocopying and photography, by arrangement.

972 Clwyd Record Office, Ruthin Branch

Parent organisation: Clwyd County Council

Address: 46 Clwyd Street, Ruthin, Clwyd LL15 1HP

Telephone: (01824) 703077 (enquiries) 705532 (Senior Archivist)

Fax: (01824) 705180

Enquiries: The Senior Archivist, R.K. Matthias

Open: Mon–Thurs: 9.00–4.45 Fri: 9.00–4.15

Access: Generally open to the public. Prior reservation of microfilm and microfiche readers is necessary.

Historical background: Denbighshire Record Office was set up in 1972 and was incorporated into the Clwyd Record Office upon local government reoganisation in 1974. It is recognised as a place of deposit for public records.

Archives of organisation: Usual local authority holdings.

Major collections: Deposited local collections.

Non-manuscript material: Denbighshire photographic collection; newspapers; index to births, marriages and deaths, 1837–66; index to registers of probate, England and Wales, 1858–1928; database of information on more than 800 non-conformist chapels in the county, with photographic records, 1988.

Finding aids: Lists sent to NRA. Indexed catalogues and handlists. Leaflet aids for searchers. Finding aids to Clwyd Record Office, Hawarden branch (entry 382). Access to computerised index for appropriate enquiries.

Facilities: Photocopying. Photography. Microfilming by arrangement. Microfilm/fiche reader/printer. Refreshment room.

Publications: Handlist of Denbigh Borough Records (1975).
Handlist of Denbighshire Quarter Sessions Records (1991).

973 Saffron Walden Town Council

Address: 18 High Street, Saffron Walden, Essex CB10 1AX

Telephone: (01799) 527661

Enquiries: Mr M.D. White

Open: Mon–Fri: 9.00–5.00, by appointment.

Access: Approved readers, on written application.

Historical background: The Borough of Saffron Walden was granted its first charter in c1300. Saffron Walden Town Council was formed in 1974. It is recognised as a place of deposit for public records.

Acquisitions policy: Anything relating to Saffron Walden Town Council and of general interest concerning Saffron Walden.

Archives of organisation: Borough council and court records, c1300–1974.
Town council records, 1974–.

Major collections: Charity minutes and papers.

Non-manuscript material: Drawings, paintings and prints of Saffron Walden, mainly late 19th and early 20th centuries.

Finding aids: Index available from the Town Clerk.

Facilities: Photocopying available on request.

974 Victorian Studies Centre

Address: Saffron Walden Library, 2 King Street, Saffron Walden, Essex CB10 1ES

Telephone: (01799) 523178

Fax: (01799) 513642

Enquiries: The Librarian and Arts Director, J.M. Crofts

Open: Mon, Tues, Thurs, Fri: 9.00–7.00 Sat: 9.00–5.00

Access: Generally open to the public. An appointment is necessary.

The Victorian Studies Centre houses the archives of the Saffron Walden Literary and Scientific Institute, which flourished between 1832 and 1967. The records include minute books, reports of various committees, and documents relating to the activities and the winding up of the organisation. A full catalogue is available. There is also the Dawson-Turner Collection of correspondence relating to London booksellers and publishers, 18th and 19th centuries.

975 Museum of St Albans

Address: Hatfield Road, St Albans, Herts AL1 3RR

Telephone: (01727) 819340

Fax: (01727) 859919

Enquiries: The Keeper of Local History, H. Purkis or The Keeper of Natural History, D. Curry

Open: Mon–Sat: 10.00–5.00

Access: Generally open to the public, strictly by appointment only.

Historical background: The museum began life as the Hertfordshire County Museum, run by private trust, which collected books, prints, and drawings and watercolours of Hertfordshire, as well as newspapers and cuttings. It was taken over by the district council c1956, and the museum established an environmental records centre as a repository for all forms of information in 1973.

Acquisitions policy: The policy of the original body of trustees was to collect material on Hertfordshire; the museum now collects only items from the area covered by St Albans District Council in the field of local history and South Hertfordshire in natural history.

Major collections: Local History Collection, including local MSS, antiquarian notes and children's writing books.
Natural History Collection, including field note-books of collections of ecological and geological field data for South Hertfordshire.

Non-manuscript material: Prints, drawings and watercolours.
Posters, bills, and other relevant printed ephemera.
Photographs.
Slide collection of ecologically important sites and of geological sections, exposures, etc (7000).

Finding aids: Natural History Collection catalogue is computerised.

Facilities: Photocopying and photography by arrangement.

976 St Albans Abbey
Muniment Room

Parent organisation: Cathedral and Abbey Church of St Alban

Address: c/o The Deanery, Sumpter Yard, St Albans, Herts AL1 1BY

Telephone: (01727) 52120 (The Deanery)

Enquiries: The Archivists, Mrs G. Peyton-Jones and Mr F.I. Kilvington

Open: Monday pm; otherwise by arrangement.

Access: Any bona fide student, by previous appointment.

Historical background: The abbey church has a long and varied history dating back to Norman times. The diocese was founded in 1877 and the collection, which has only recently been organised, dates mainly from 1800. There is, however, some earlier material in the Hertfordshire County Record Office (entry **387**).

Acquisitions policy: To maintain the records of the cathedral and abbey church.

Archives of organisation: Records relating to the building, its precincts and other property, the parish and its administration, including material relating to the establishment of the See of St Albans and the controversial restoration of the abbey church by Lord Grimthorpe and others, 1870–.

Non-manuscript material: A number of drawings, plans etc, especially those by J.S. Neale, 19th century.
A small collection of pictures and a large collection of photographs and slides, 19th and 20th centuries.

Finding aids: Catalogue. Card index.

Publications: R.M. Thomson: *Manuscripts from St Alban's Abbey, 1066–1235* (1902) [2 vols].

977 St Albans Central Library

Parent organisation: Hertfordshire Library and Information Service

Address: The Maltings, Victoria Street, St Albans, Herts AL1 3JQ

Telephone: (01727) 860000 (Library) 866100 (City Council)

Enquiries: Library: The Reference and Information Team Leader or City Council: The Museum Administrator or The Honorary Archivist, Mr John Cox

Open: Mon, Wed, Fri: 9.30–7.30 Tues: 9.30–5.30 Thurs: 9.30–1.00 Sat: 9.00–4.00

Access: Generally open to the public, by appointment. There are rules for use compiled by the council. Notice is necessary for items to be acquired. Research is undertaken by a part-time Honorary Archivist employed by the council.

Historical background: St Albans Corporation opened a library in 1882, five years after it was granted city status. It liaises with Hertfordshire Record Office (entry **387**) about microfilm copies, and is recognised as a place of deposit for public records.

Acquisitions policy: To maintain the council records and local history collections.

Archives of organisation: St Albans Council records, including letters, documents, municipal and manorial records, 1580–.

Major collections: Usual local history collection, including printed maps, 1607–1850.

Facilities: Limited photocopying.

978 Youth Hostels Association

Address: Trevelyan House, 8 Stephen's Hill, St Albans, Herts AL1 2DY

Telephone: (01727) 855215

Fax: (01727) 844126

Enquiries: The National Secretary

Open: By arrangement.

Access: Researchers should apply in writing.

Historical background: A growing interest in the enjoyment of the countryside from the late 19th century led to the setting up of a number of regional bodies and, in 1930, the establishment of a national association to promote youth hostels in Britain. The YHA is governed by a national council and by regional groups, and is now one of the largest youth organisations in the country. Records of Herbert Gatliff, much of which relates to YHA, are at the Bodleian Library (entry **871**).

Acquisitions policy: To maintain the archive.

Archives of organisation: General minute books, 1930– (including minutes of a number of committees).
Complete set of annual reports.
Files of memoranda (which were presented to committees, regional groups and secretaries etc), 1933–.
Hostel files (administrative, legal etc) 1936– (incomplete).
Financial records, 1930s– (incomplete).
Copies of all official magazines and some regional booklets, leaflets etc.
Correspondence and administrative files *re* activities and facilities offered by YHA.

Non-manuscript material: Film strips, 1950s. Slides.
Press cuttings, 1970s-.
Maps and plans.

Finding aids: NRA 24465.

Publications: O. Coburn: *Youth Hostel Story* (1950).

979 British Golf Museum

Address: Bruce Embankment, St Andrews, Fife KY16 9AB

Telephone: (01334) 478880

Fax: (01334) 473306

Enquiries: The Museum Director, Peter N. Lewis, The Assistant Curator, Katie H.M. Page

Open: Mon–Sat, by arrangement.

Access: Bona fide researchers, by appointment only.

Historical background: The British Golf Museum opened in 1990 and took responsibility for the administration of the archives of the Royal and Ancient Golf Club in addition to its own resources. The Royal and Ancient Golf Club was founded in 1754 and became the governing authority for the rules of golf in 1897. Among other events it runs the open and amateur championships each year.

Acquisitions policy: Material relating to the development and history of golf in Britain and to British influences on the game abroad.

Major collections: Royal and Ancient Golf Club archives, including minutes, 1754–; secretary's correspondence, 1890s, and records of the open championship, 1860–.

Non-manuscript material: Photographs, press cuttings, films and artefacts.
Supporting printed material and comprehensive museum collections.

Finding aids: Computerised catalogues.

Facilities: Photocopying.

Publications: Royal and Ancient Championship Records, 1660–1980 (1980; suppl. 1983).

980 The Hay Fleming Reference Library

Address: St Andrews Branch Library, Church Square, St Andrews, Fife KY16 9NN

Telephone: (01334) 473381

Fax: (01334) 653722

Enquiries: The Branch Librarian or The District Librarian, North East Fife District Library, County Buildings, Cupar, Fife KY15 4TA, tel. (01334) 53722

Open: Mon–Wed, Fri: 10.00–7.00 Thurs, Sat: 10.00–5.00

Access: Generally open to the public.

Historical background: David Hay Fleming (1849–1931), a native of St Andrews and an eminent historian and critic, built up a substantial personal library for his own research and studies. On his death the collection was bequeathed to the town of St Andrews to form the nucleus of a public reference library and further the study of Scottish history. The main scope for the collection is Scottish history, literature, theology and the local history of St Andrews. The library is administered on a day-to-day basis by the staff of North East Fife District Library Service and is managed by a management committee of trustees.

Acquisitions policy: The terms of David Hay Fleming's will stipulated that 'the proceeds of the endowment spent in increasing the said library shall be mainly devoted to the purchase of works bearing directly or indirectly on the civil, political, ecclesiastical and social history of Scotland and on the antiquities of Scotland'. A few important works were purchased each year. Archival material is occasionally acquired by donation.

Major collections: David Hay Fleming Collection: research note-books, correspondence, press cuttings, proofs of publications, local historical records and broadsheets.
Collections of Church of Scotland sermons.
Title and legal documents, 1467–1595.
Ecclesiastical documents, 1613–58.
Papers relating to the financial effects of the town of St Andrews, 1614–1702.
Titles to lands in the town, 1622–1724.
Papers of local trades, including wrights, tailors, weavers.
Congregational rolls of churches.

Non-manuscript material: Printed books and pamphlets (*c*13,000), early photographs and postcard views of St Andrews.
Prints, maps and plans of historical buildings.
Press cuttings.
Broadsides and antiquarian material.

Finding aids: NRA(S) 1882. MS index to correspondence.

Facilities: Photocopying.

Publications: H.M. Paton: *David Hay Fleming, Historian and Antiquary* (1934).
A. Rodden: 'The Hay Fleming Reference Library, St Andrews', *SLA News*, cxxii (1974), 109 [precis of a paper given to the Dundee Branch of the Library Association, 3 April 1974].

981 St Andrews University

Address: North Street, St Andrews, Fife KY16 9TR

Telephone: (01334) 462324

Enquiries: The Keeper of Manuscripts, Mr R.N. Smart

Open: Term: Mon–Fri: 9.00–1.00; 2.00–5.00 Sat: 9.00–12.00, by prior arrangement. Vacation: Mon–Fri: 9.00–1.00; 2.00–5.00

Access: Bona fide researchers. Visitors from a distance are advised to give forewarning.

A Library Manuscripts Department

Historical background: A few MSS from the medieval religious house and college libraries of St Andrews survive, but the greater portion has been acquired in the 19th and 20th centuries.

Acquisitions policy: To acquire MSS with a local connection and scholarly material of or relating to members of the university. The library is also interested in material to support teaching and research in the university.

Major collections: Western MSS: a miscellaneous collection of more than 100,000 Codex MSS, letters and documents, early Middle Ages–. It is strong in material of local and university interest, scientific correspondence, 19th and 20th centuries, and papers relating to the Roman Catholic Modernist Movement. Includes papers of Sir James Donaldson (1831–1915), James David Forbes (1809–68), Baron Friedrich von Hügel (1852–1925), Sir D'Arcy Wentworth Thompson (1860–1948), and Wilfrid Ward (1856–1916).
Oriental MSS: small collection (*c*100 vols), mostly in Arabic, Persian or Turkish. Contains some especially fine copies of the Qur'ān.

Non-manuscript material: Photographs: Valentine Ltd (120,000), British Isles, 1878–1967; G.M. Cowie, press photography, Fife, 1930–81 (60,000); R.M. Adam, Scottish landscape and botany, especially Highland scenery and crofting agriculture, 1901–56 (14,000). Miscellaneous collections, zoology, Turkey, Italian architecture, Canada, Fife, continental scenery, farm animals, art photography, Highland scenery, 1839– (70,000).

Finding aids: Unpublished inventories and descriptive lists for particular parts of the collection. Name indexes available for both MSS and photographs. Lists sent to NRA(S). Database available via the Internet.

Facilities: Photocopying. Photography. Microfilm/fiche reader/printer.

Publications: HMC 2nd Report (1871), 206–9.
St Andrews University Library: an Illustrated Guide (St Andrews, 1948).
R.N. Smart: *An Index to the Correspondence and Papers of James David Forbes (1809–1868) and also to some Papers of his son George Forbes* (St Andrews, 1968).
J.D. Pearson: *Oriental Manuscripts in Europe and North America* (Zug, 1971).
R.N. Smart: *Index to the Correspondence and Papers of Sir D'Arcy Wentworth Thompson* (St Andrews, 1987).
C.M. Gascoigne: *Cedric Thorpe Davie, 1913–*

1983: *Catalogue of Works and Index to Correspondence* (St Andrews, 1988).

B Muniments

Historical background: The university was founded in 1411; St Salvators College in 1450; St Leonard's College in 1512; St Mary's College in 1538; United College in 1747; and University College was conjoined in 1897 (erected into the University of Dundee in 1967). Although there has been continuous provision for custody of the records since the foundation, the muniments department dates only from 1892.

Acquisitions policy: Only the official records of the university and its constituent parts are acquired. Certain other archival collections are held on deposit.

Archives of organisation: The university's own records.

Major collections: Records of the following former burghs of North East Fife District are held on deposit from the Keeper of the Records of Scotland: Anstruther, Auchtermuchty, Crail, Cupar, Elie and Earlsferry, Falkland, Kilrenny, Ladybank, Newburgh, Newport, Pittenweem, St Andrews, St Monance, and Tayport, as well as records of the parishes in the former presbyteries of St Andrews and Cupar.
Dundee Royal Infirmary minutes, 1793–1902.

Non-manuscript material: Pictures, medals, and a wide miscellany of objects relative to the university's history.

Finding aids: Typescript guide; separate name indexes to the college papers, Acta Rectorum, Senatus minutes and other series.

Facilities: Photocopying. Photography. Microfilm/fiche reader/printer.

Publications: No general published guide, but see HMC 2nd Report (1871), 206.
R.G. Cant: *The University of St Andrews: a Short History* (Edinburgh, 1970).
See also the introductions to J.M. Anderson: *Matriculation Roll of the University of St Andrews, 1747–1897* (Edinburgh, 1905).
——: *Early Records of the University of St Andrews, 1413–1579* (Edinburgh, 1926).
A.I. Dunlop: *Acta Facultatis Artium Universitatis Sancti Andree, 1513–1588* (Edinburgh, 1964).

982 St Helens Local History and Archives Library

Address: Central Library, Gamble Institute, Victoria Square, St Helens, Merseyside WA10 1DY

Telephone: (01744) 456952

Fax: (01744) 20836

Enquiries: The Local History Librarian and Archivist, Mrs V.L. Hainsworth

Open: Mon, Wed: 9.30–8.00 Tues, Thurs–Sat: 9.30–5.00

Access: Generally open to the public.

Historical background: The borough library service was established in 1872. A separate local history and archives library was established in 1974 to expand existing collections in the reference library and to implement an active archive policy to deal with local government records on reorganisation.

Acquisitions policy: Records of the St Helens Borough Council are stored where appropriate. Donations of other records are accepted. Other records are acquired when known to be at risk.

Major collections: Records of the borough council and historic constituents, 1845–1980. Poor Law papers for the Township of Parr, 1688–1828.
Sherdley estate papers, 1477–1900 (c1500 items).
Records of Grundy's Ironmongers, 1913–70.
Total archive holdings, c1,500,000 items.

Non-manuscript material: Maps, local newspapers, 1859–. Photographs, pamphlets and books (c10,000) relating to St Helens, Lancashire and local history in general.

Finding aids: Index to most archive collections. Newspaper index.

Facilities: Photocopying. Microfilm/fiche readers/printer.

Publications: Frequent leaflet guides to types of material (e.g. *Genealogical Sources*).

983 Jersey Archives Service

Address: Jersey Museum, The Weybridge, St Helier, Jersey, Channel Islands JE2 3NF

Telephone: (01534) 617441

Fax: (01534) 66085

Enquiries: The Head of Archives Service

Open: Mon–Fri: 9.00–1.00; 2.00–5.00

Access: Generally open to the public, by appointment.

Historical background: The Jersey Archives Services was established in 1993. It is administered by the Jersey Heritage Trust and at present is housed in temporary premises at the Jersey Museum.

Acquisitions policy: The archives service will seek to acquire records of Jersey organisations and individuals.

Archives of organisation: Official records, including states departmental records, 17th century- (early records very incomplete).
Occupation records, 1940–45.
War files from the Bailiff's Chambers, 1940s; these include registration cards and photographs of the entire population.

Finding aids: Catalogues.

Facilities: Photocopying.

984 Judicial Greffe

Address: Burrard House, Don Street, St Helier, Jersey, Channel Islands JE2 4TR

Telephone: (01534) 50200

Fax: (01534) 502399

Enquiries: The Judicial Greffier

Open: Mon–Fri: 9.00–1.00; 2.00–5.00

Access: Public Registry: members of the public, 8.30–5.15, as and when working space permits. Facilities are limited and research is not generally possible during office hours, when the records are in use for business purposes.
Royal Court records: members of the public, by prior arrangement with the Judicial Greffier only. Permission is not automatially granted. Some records (e.g. criminal matters) are not available for consultation.
Probate Registry: not open to unsupervised inspection by members of the public.

Historical background: The Judicial Greffe is a civil service department which, among other responsibilities, has custody of records, although this is not a primary function.

Acquisitions policy: The department houses only the documents of the court.

Archives of organisation: Three major categories of documents, as follows:
Public Registry, containing deeds of sale and conveyance, mortgage etc, of real property, 1602–; wills of real estate, 1851–; powers of attorney.
Records of the Royal Court, comprising all acts etc of the Royal Court and other related documents.
Probate Registry, containing wills of personal estate, c1660–; letters of administration, 1848–.

Finding aids: Indexes to relevant court books.

Facilities: Photocopying of some court records and extracts from the Public Registry. The department does not provide a research service by post.

985 Société Jersiaise

Address: 9 Pier Road, St Helier, Jersey, Channel Islands JE2 4UW

Telephone: (01534) 30538

Fax: (01534) 888262

Enquiries: The Librarian, Miss Mary Billot or The Assistant Librarian, Miss Sally Knight

Open: Mon–Fri: 9.30–4.30 Sat: 9.30–12.30; 2.00–4.30

Access: Members of the Société Jersiaise and other bona fide researchers.

Historical background: The Société Jersiaise was founded in 1873, and includes among its aims the promotion and encouragement of the study of the history, archaeology, natural history, language and many other subjects of interest in the Island of Jersey. The société has a very comprehensive local history library with local genealogical research facilities.

Major collections: family papers and correspondence, including La Hague Manor, Pipon and Le Vavasseur dit Durrell families.
Authors' MSS and notes, including Philip Ahier, E.T. Nicolle, Joan Stevens and Marguerite Syvret.
Ancient MSS, including Chevalier's diary, 1643–51, with translation.
Parish church records, 1540–1842.
Jersey Merchant Seamen's Benefit Society registers, c1830s-1880s (some on microfilm).

Non-manuscript material: Mullins' albums of identified photographic portraits, 1848–73.
German Occupation Ephemera Collection,

including ration books, identity cards and *Evening Post*, 1940–45, in English.

Almanacs, 1800– (lists of residents by address and/or trade, officers of the militia, shipping, clubs etc, diaries of local events).

Indices to the parish registers of baptisms, burials and marriages (but not all years or parishes are held).

Index of civil registers (births, deaths and marriages), 1842–1900 on microfiche.

Maps of Jersey and St Helier.

States of Jersey publications, including *Ordres du Conseil*, 1536–1812; *Recueil des Lois*, 1771–, and *States' Minutes*.

Facilities: Photocopying. Microfilm/fiche readers.

986 Norris Library and Museum

Address: The Broadway, St Ives, Huntingdon, Cambridgeshire PE17 4BX

Telephone: (01480) 465101

Enquiries: The Curator, Mr R.I. Burn-Murdoch

Open: May–Sept: Tues–Fri: 10.00–1.00; 2.00–5.00 Sat, Sun: 10.00–12.00 Oct–April: Tues–Fri: 10.00–1.00; 2.00–4.00 Sat: 10.00–12.00

Access: Bona fide researchers.

Historical background: The library and museum opened in 1933, according to the terms of the will of Herbert Ellis Norris (1859–1931). Norris assembled a large collection of antiquities, both historical and archaeological, which he left, together with a substantial trust fund to pay for a building to house them and to allow for future maintenance, to St Ives Borough Council. The present town council continues to administer the library and museum as trustees. Norris collected material from the former county of Huntingdonshire (technically abolished in 1974). Since 1933 other collections of a similar scope have been added to his foundation, notably those of the Huntingdonshire Literary and Scientific Institution (1840–1959). The present Norris Library and Museum houses material from every part of Huntingdonshire and every period of history.

Acquisitions policy: Material relating to all parts of Huntingdonshire and all periods of history and pre-history. There is a small accessions fund

for the library. The museum is dependent on gifts.

Major collections: MS material, including various legal documents, wills etc, 16th–18th centuries.

Field survey of St Ives, 17th century.

MSS by John Clare (1793–1864).

Many minute books etc relating to local government and local charities, 19th century.

Notes by local historians and antiquarians, notably S. Inskip Ladds, Ely Diocesan architect and editor of the Victoria County History of Huntingdonshire.

Non-manuscript material: Pamphlets etc relating to the Civil War period, and to Cromwell, in Huntingdonshire.

Runs of local newspapers, including 19th-century editions.

Maps, including Saxton, Speed, Blaeu, 16th–19th centuries.

Photographs, postcards, prints, paintings and drawings of local scenes, various periods.

General collection of books relating to all aspects of the history of Huntingdonshire.

Finding aids: Comprehensive card index in preparation.

Facilities: Limited photocopying by arrangement. Photography by arrangement. Microfilm reader.

987 Isles of Scilly Museum

Parent organisation: Isles of Scilly Museum Association

Address: Church Street, St Mary's, Isles of Scilly TR21 0JT

Telephone: (01720) 422337

Enquiries: The Librarian, Mrs Peggy Symonds, The Honorary Secretary, Mr Steve Ottery

Open: Summer season: 10.00–12.00; 1.30–4.30

Access: Generally open to the public, by appointment. Only three seats are available at any one time.

The museum commenced in 1967 and collects anything relevant to the history of the Isles of Scilly. Its local history collection includes custom house books, court record books, ships' logs and lifeboat records, wills and scrapbooks, 17th century–. NRA 33099.

988 The Greffe

Address: The Royal Court House, St Peter Port, Guernsey, Channel Islands GY1 2PB

Telephone: (01481) 725277

Fax: (01481) 715097

Enquiries: Her Majesty's Greffier, Mr K.H. Tough
Assistance is by arrangement with the Archiviste de la Cour Royale (Island Archivist; entry **989**).
Genealogical enquiries should first be addressed to the Priaulx Library (entry **990**).

Open: Mon–Fri: 9.00–1.00; 2.00–4.00

Access: Written application should be made to Her Majesty's Greffier. A letter of introduction is recommended.

Historical background: As the record office of the Royal Court of Guernsey, the Greffe has existed in various forms throughout the history of the Royal Court, which is first referred to in a document of 1179. Virtually all records prior to 1948 are in French, and a command of that language is essential for all serious students researching at the Greffe.

Acquisitions policy: All island judicial and legislative records. Deposits of private collections and documents relating to Guernsey are welcomed.

Archives of organisation: Contemporary copies of charters granted to the Bailiwick, 1394–.
Judicial records of the Royal Court of Guernsey, 1526–.
Legislative records, 1553–.
Royal Court letter-books, 1737–.
Documents issued by the Royal Court, c1350–.
Records of land conveyance etc, 1576–.
Records of the Assembly of the States of Guernsey, 1605–.
Registers of births, marriages and deaths, 1840–.
Wills of Real Property from 1841, when it first became possible to make Wills of Realty (Wills of Personalty are held by the Ecclesiastical Court, tel. (01481) 721732).

Major collections: Feudal Court registers, especially Cour St Michel, 1537–.
Private collections deposited by local families, notably the de Sausmarez papers.

Transcripts of documents elsewhere, especially of the Mont St Michel collection (originals destroyed in 1944) and of minute books etc of the Calvinist regime in Guernsey, c1558–1660.
Identity card files, comprising personal forms and photographs, 1940–45 (c20,000).

Finding aids: Typescript calendar of all single documents. Summary of Family History Sources at the Greffe (copies available on request).

Facilities: Photocopying (limited to certain records only). Microfilm reader/printer.

Publications: Lists of records in the Greffe published by the List and Index Society (Special Series, continuing): (i) *Registers and Records in Volume Form* (1969); (ii) *Single Documents under the Bailiwick Seal* (1969); (iii) *Other Documents under Sign Manual, Signature or Seal* (1983).
Recueil d'Ordonnances de la Cour Royale de l'Île de Guernesey 1533– [24 vols to date].
Actes des Etats de l'Île de Guernesey, 1605–1843 [8 vols; thereafter published as *Billets d'Etat*, in annual vols to date].
Recueil d'Ordres en Conseil d'un Intérêt Général enregistrés sur les Records de l'Île de Guernesey, 1800– [30 vols to date].
For a general introduction, see J.C. Davies: 'The Records of the Royal Court', *La Société Guernesiaise, Report and Transactions*, xvi (1956–60), 404.

989 Island Archives Service

Parent organisation: States of Guernsey

Address: 29 Victoria Road, St Peter Port, Guernsey, Channel Islands GY1 1HU

Telephone: (01481) 724512

Fax: (01481) 715814

Enquiries: The Island Archivist, Mr J.H. Lenfestey

Open: Mon–Fri: 9.00–4.30

Access: Written application must be made to the Island Archivist. Some material post-1948 is subject to restriction.

Historical background: The Island Archives Service was established in 1986 by the States of Guernsey for the cataloguing, indexing and retention of committee and departmental records from the 19th century onwards.

Acquisitions policy: All island records of an official or unofficial character, public and private.

Archives of organisation: Records of states committees and departments, 1890–1939; occupation records and files, 1940–45; states' records, 1948–.

Major collections: St Peter Port Hospital records, including day-books, accounts, ledgers, trade and occupation registers, hospital domestic services, lunatic asylum, children's home, stranger poor, outdoor relief, 1742–1950. Stevens Guille Collection of MSS, 1350–1850 (2000 items). Miscellaneous minor collections of family papers, 19th and 20th centuries.

Non-manuscript material: States' architectural drawings, 1800– (none from private practice). Film/sound archive, 1917–.

Finding aids: Office catalogues and indexes.

Facilities: Photocopying (limited to certain records only), by order.

Conservation: Contracted out in the UK.

990 Priaulx Library

Address: Candie Road, St Peter Port, Guernsey, Channel Islands GY1 1UG

Telephone: (01481) 721998

Fax: (01481) 713804

Enquiries: The Chief Librarian, Dr H. Tomlinson

Open: Mon–Sat: 9.30–5.00

Access: Generally open to the public. An appointment is necessary for the use of microfilm readers.

Historical background: The Priaulx Collection, along with Candie House where it is contained, was donated to the people of Guernsey in 1891, for use as a free library, by Osmond De Beauvoir Priaulx (1805–91). The library is designated as a local studies centre.

Acquisitions policy: Purchasing is now restricted to works produced in the islands or relating to them, plus relevant back-up material.

Major collections: Correspondence relating to shipping and privateering from the firm of Carteret Priaulx, 19th century.

Records of the Royal Guernsey Militia, 18th–19th centuries (incomplete). Records of the Onesimus Dorey Shipping Co., 19th and 20th centuries. Genealogical files and pedigree rolls relating to many local families.

Non-manuscript material: Parish registers, cemetery records, civil records of births and deaths and census of Guernsey and Jersey, 1841–91 (microfilm). Photographs and prints of various locations and personalities of local interest. Newspapers published in Guernsey, 1812–50 (mostly in French). Army lists, 1661–1714, 1756–1920. Regimental histories. Works of fiction produced by local or locally resident authors, Guernsey imprints, 19th and 20th centuries.

Finding aids: Card index, currently being transferred to computer.

Facilities: Photocopying. Some photography. Microfilm/fiche readers/printer.

Conservation: Contracted out.

991 La Société Guernesiaise

Address: Candie Gardens, St Peter Port, Guernsey, Channel Islands GY1 1UG

Telephone: (01481) 725093

Fax: (01481) 66217

Enquiries: The Secretary, Mrs L. Sherwill

Open: On demand.

Access: Generally open to the public, by appointment.

Historical background: La Société Guernesiaise is a society of natural science and local research, founded in 1882 to encourage interest in all aspects of Guernsey's natural and local history, geography and geology. It has a small library of local books which members can consult by arrangement. It does not hold historical documents or records: these are kept by the Island Government in its record office, the Greffe (entry 988), and by the Royal Court of Guernsey with the Island Archives Service (entry 989).

Acquisitions policy: Items are acquired by purchase, donation and deposit.

Major collections: Diaries and accounts of island life written in Guernesiais.

Non-manuscript material: Survey maps of the island.
Local books, 1600–.
Transactions, bulletins and periodicals of most French historical and archaeological societies.
Report and Transactions of la Société Guernesiaise, 1882–.
Herbarium, 1790 (island plants); modern herbarium.

Finding aids: Comprehensive index to the *Report and Transactions.*

Facilities: Photocopying.

992 Lancashire Mining Museum, Salford

Address: Buile Hill Park, Eccles Old Road, Salford, Greater Manchester M6 8GL

Telephone: (0161) 736 1832

Enquiries: The Museum Officer, Mr A. Davies

Open: Mon–Fri: 10.00–12.30; 1.30–5.00 Sun: 2.00–5.00

Access: Generally open to the public, by appointment only.

Historical background: The museum opened in 1906 with natural history collections. Mining interest began in the late 1950s and the museum was completely redisplayed and opened as the Mining Museum in 1980. The business archives of John Wood Ltd and Walker Bros Ltd of Wigan, previously held by the museum, have been transferred to Wigan Archives Service (entry 453).

Acquisitions policy: To collect, display or make available anything relating to the Lancashire/Cheshire coalfields, including items relating to social history.

Major collections: Administrative and financial records of closed local collieries, late 18th century–.

Non-manuscript material: Large collections of National Coal Board underground layout plans relating to South Lancashire collieries (*c*400); other plans of Lancashire area (*c*300).
Extensive photographic archive of local collieries; 16mm film collection, 1910–80 (*c*200).
Several thousand books and journals relating to all aspects of coal-mining.

Finding aids: Some lists and indexes. Clifton and Kersley Coal Co.: NRA 22633.

Facilities: Photocopying and photography to order.

993 Salford Art Gallery
L.S. Lowry Archive

Parent organisation: City of Salford

Address: Peel Park, Salford, Greater Manchester M5 4WU

Telephone: (0161) 736 2649

Enquiries: The Museums Officer, Fine Art, Judith Sandling

Open: Mon–Fri: 10.00–4.45 Sun: 2.00–5.00

Access: Bona fide researchers, by appointment only. Some parts of the archive have mandatory restrictions.

Salford Museum and Art Gallery was established in 1850. The gallery's association with L.S. Lowry (1887–1976) began in the 1930s and continued until his death. A special exhibition, on permanent display, records the artist's life and work through his drawings and paintings and is supplemented with documents, photographs and audio-visual material, which is actively augmented by donation, deposit or purchase. See M. Leber and J. Sandling: *L.S. Lowry* (Phaidon Press, 1987).

994 Salford Local History Library

Address: Peel Park, Salford, Greater Manchester M5 4WU

Telephone: (0161) 736 2649

Fax: (0161) 745 9490

Enquiries: The Local History Librarian, Mr Tim Ashworth

Open: Mon, Tues, Thurs, Fri: 10.00–5.00 Wed: 10.00–9.00

Access: Generally open to the public.

The library holds local history collections, including the following: James Nasmyth (1808–90), locomotive engineer and inventor of steam hammer: collection of correspondence, engineering drawings and photographs; and Harold Brighouse, author of *Hobson's Choice*: collection of letters and some MSS of his works.

995 University of Salford Library

Parent organisation: University of Salford, Academic Information Services

Address: The Crescent, Salford, Greater Manchester M5 4WT

Telephone: (0161) 745 5000

Fax: (0161) 745 5888

Enquiries: The Assistant Librarian, Mr A.J. Percy (ext. 3662) or The Director of Academic Information Services

Open: Term: Mon–Fri: 9.00–9.00 Sat: 9.00–12.00 Vacation: Mon–Fri: 9.00–5.00

Access: Bona fide scholars. An appointment is necessary for consultation of archive material.

Historical background: The university is descended from the Salford Royal Technical Institute, founded in 1896. The institute became the Salford Royal College of Advanced Technology before receiving its university charter in 1967. The library was founded in 1957.

Acquisitions policy: To support the teaching and research interests of the university.

Archives of organisation: Documentary and photographic archives of the institution, 1896–. Press cuttings and departmental papers, 1967–. Papers of the Salford Technical and Engineering Association.

Major collections: Walter Greenwood (1903–74): comprehensive collection of MSS and published works, with correspondence, press cuttings and photographs.
Stanley Houghton (1881–1913): MSS of published and unpublished plays, photographs, correspondence.
Bridgewater Collections: archive of Francis Egerton, 3rd Duke of Bridgewater (1736–1803), the pioneer of the great age of canal building in Britain; Bridgewater Estates Company papers, 1895–1950; working papers used by the late Professor F.C. Mather in his study of the Bridgewater Trust, *After the Canal Duke*, covering the period 1825–72.
Lionel Angus-Butterworth papers *re* the history of glassmaking, including a draft of his treatise *The British Glass Industry, 1700–1850*, and company material *re* the family firm, Butterworth Bros, Newton Heath Glass Works, Manchester.

Richard Badnall (*d* 1842): correspondence concerning his proposal for an 'undulating railway'.
William Willink papers: material relating to the Birmingham Canal Company, 1830–1920.

Non-manuscript material: British Election Pamphlet Collection, 1949–74: a substantial collection of election leaflets.
Tape-recordings with transcripts of interviews of Salford residents conducted in 1970 by J.M. Goodger for his film *The Changing Face of Salford*.

Finding aids: Lists for most collections. Special card catalogue of Bridgewater Estates papers, with subject index. Published works recorded on library's on-line catalogue. Collections notified to NRA.

Facilities: Photocopying. Microfilm/fiche readers.

Publications: *Special Collections* (Academic Information Services Leaflet 11). There are separate leaflets describing the Bridgewater Archives and the British Election Pamphlet Collection.

996 Working Class Movement Library

Address: Jubilee House, 51 The Crescent, Salford, Greater Manchester M5 4WX

Telephone: (0161) 736 3601

Enquiries: The Librarian, Alain Kahan

Open: Tues, Thurs, Fri: 10.00–5.00 Wed: 10.00–9.00 Alternate Sun: 2.00–5.00, by arrangement only

Access: Generally open to the public, by appointment.

Historical background: The collections were started by Ruth and Edmund Frow *c*1955. Until 1987 the library was housed in their private home in Stretford. It is now administered by the City of Salford, although the collection is owned by trustees: the Frows still play an active role in acquiring new accessions.

Acquisitions policy: Anything to do with the experience of working people from the 18th century onwards, mostly in Britain, although some international material is acquired.

Major collections: Archives principally of trade unions and political organisations including

local Labour Party archives (not all complete). These include:
General and Municipal Boiler Makers and Allied Trade Unions (NBATU), print unions (NATSOPA and NGA), Amalgamated Engineering Union (AEU and ASE), Gasworkers and General and Municipal Workers Union, and Furniture Timber and Allied Trades (FTAT), plus unions absorbed into these.
Trades and professions covered include: boilermakers, shipwrights, tailor and garment workers, clerks, foundry workers, cabinet makers, organ makers.
A few papers of individuals, including activists and members of the Communist Party.

Non-manuscript material: Large amount of pamphlet material in archive collections.
Rare books and periodicals, 19th century–; radical periodicals on microfilm.
Artefacts and books.

Finding aids: Card catalogue. NRA reports: 1008; 31932 (MS collections); 35557 (Salford Trades Council); 35561 (National Association of Powerloom Overlockers); 35562 (Bolton and District Card and Ring-Room Operators); 35565 (Swinton and Pendlebury).

Facilities: Photocopying. Photography by arrangement. Microfilm/fiche reader.

Conservation: Undertaken by City of Salford, and Museums and Art Galleries Service for the North West.

Publications: *Library Bulletin* (annually, 1989–) [includes information on important recent accessions].

997 Salisbury Cathedral Chapter Archives

Address: 6 The Close, Salisbury, Wilts SP1 2EF

Enquiries: The Librarian and Keeper of the Muniments, Miss S.M. Eward

Open: Mon–Fri: 10.00–12.30; 2.15–4.00, by appointment only.

Access: Bona fide researchers, on written application.

Salisbury Cathedral was begun in 1220 and has had a continuous history since that date. It has Dean and Chapter archives from the medieval period onwards. There is a brief general catalogue.

998 Harrowby Manuscript Trust

Parent organisation: The Earldom of Harrowby

Address: Sandon Hall, Sandon, Stafford ST18 0BZ

Telephone: (01889) 508338, ext. 47

Fax: (01889) 508586

Enquiries: The Archivist, Mr M.J. Bosson

Open: By arrangement only.

Access: Scholars and researchers, with a reference and by appointment.

Historical background: The earldom was created in the late 17th century for Lord Chief Justice Dudley Ryder. Sandon Hall has always been the seat of the earldom; the present house is the third on this site and and dates from the mid-19th century. The collection is principally that of the 5th and 6th Earls and is held in trust for the Bodleian Library (entry **871**).

Acquisitions policy: To maintain and consolidate the records of the Earls of Harrowby and their estates.

Archives of organisation: Estate papers: deeds, correspondence etc relating to administration of estates in Staffordshire, Lincolnshire and Oxfordshire and small subsidiary lands, 12th–20th centuries.
Political correspondence with cabinet ministers, MPs etc, 18th and 19th centuries.
Diary series, including those of Lady Mary Wortley Montagu (1639–1762) 17th–20th centuries, especially World Wars I and II.

Non-manuscript material: Iconographic material, including cartoons and a complete collection of World War I recruiting posters.

Finding aids: Various catalogues, lists, and indexes.

Facilities: Photocopying at nearby office.

999 Royal Society for the Protection of Birds
The Library

Address: The Lodge, Sandy, Beds SG19 2DL

Telephone: (01767) 680551

Fax: (01767) 692365

Enquiries: The Librarian, I.K. Dawson

Open: Mon–Fri: 9.00–5.15, by arrangement.

Access: Bona fide researchers, by appointment.

Historical background: The RSPB was founded in 1889 to fight the trade in bird plumes used in millinery. It was granted its Royal Charter in 1904. The work rapidly expanded to cover all fields of bird protection and the society is now the largest conservation organisation in Europe.

Acquisitions policy: To maintain and consolidate the society's archives.

Archives of organisation: Records of the society, including council and other committee minutes, 1898–; membership and associates registers, 1893–1924; annual reports, 1889–; watchers' reports and diaries, 1911–1950s; files on legislation and individual reserves, 1930s-1950s; *Bird Notes and News*, 1905–.

Major collections: Papers, correspondence and publications of and relating to William H. Hudson (1864–1922), naturalist and writer, 1890s-1960s.

Finding aids: NRA 24476.

Facilities: Photocopying. Microfiche reader.

1000 North Yorkshire County Library
Scarborough Group

Address: Central Library, Vernon Road, Scarborough, North Yorks YO11 2NN

Telephone: (01732) 364285

Fax: (01732) 353893

Enquiries: The Group Librarian (postal enquiries) or The Information Librarian (telephone)

Open: Mon–Thurs: 10.00–5.30 Fri: 10.00–7.00 Sat: 10.00–4.00

Access: Admission to the local history room is on production of a library ticket or other identification. Archive material is generally available to the public on request.

Historical background: The local history collection was founded in 1930. Archives are acquired by deposit, solicited and unsolicited.

Acquisitions policy: To accept deposit of relevant material within accommodation limits and where the donor wishes the material to remain in Scarborough.

Major collections: School log-books, minute books etc, from Scarborough and the immediate area, c1870–c1950 (c120 vols).
Scarborough town rate books, 1837–1900 (c150 vols).
Minutes and accounts of Scarborough Harbour Commissioners, 1752–1904 (20 vols); Scarborough Cliff Bridge Company, 1826–1920; Spa (Scarborough) Ltd, 1920–37.
Minutes and accounts of several local societies, 19th and 20th centuries.
Minor collections of family papers, indentures, property deeds, ships' logs etc.

Non-manuscript material: Prints, topographical, 18th and 19th centuries (c700).
Photographs, topographical and local subjects.

Finding aids: Descriptive typescript catalogues of archive holdings (compiled 1968, not updated).

Facilities: Photocopying. Microfilm/fiche readers/printer.

Publications: *Family History in Scarborough Library.*

1001 The Oates Memorial Library and Museum and the Gilbert White Museum

Address: The Wakes, Selborne, Alton, Hants GU34 3JH

Telephone: (01420) 511275

Enquiries: The Secretary, Mrs N.E. Mees

Open: By arrangement.

Access: Bona fide researchers, by appointment.

Historical background: The museum is housed in The Wakes, the former home of the Rev. Gilbert White. The house was purchased by the Oates Memorial Trust in 1954 and the dual museums opened in 1955. The Wakes passed out of the White family in 1839 and Gilbert White's possessions were auctioned in the following year. The collection of White's personal items and documents is therefore limited, although a substantial collection, including the *Naturalists' Journal*, is held by the British Library (entry **495A**). The bulk of the MS collection is on loan from the Holt-White family. Robert Washington Oates provided the museum with a range of note-books and drawings by members of the Oates family.

Acquisitions policy: To acquire further MSS relevant to Gilbert White and his work and relating to Lawrence Oates, the Antarctic Expedition and Frank Oates in Africa.

Major collections: Gilbert White Collection: original MS of *The Natural History of Selborne*; record of wine and beer brewing, 1771–93; account book, 1758–93, and memoranda; Thomas White's personal copy of the first edition of *The Natural History of Selborne* (reputedly bound in the skin of Gilbert White's dog) and his commonplace book.
Holt-White family documents: including an account book of Gilbert White, 1745–65; sermons; household receipts; various letters to Gilbert White from members of the family. Various White family papers, 1678–1820, including personal letters, legal documents, MS note-books, estate papers, family wills and settlement deeds,
Selborne tithes.
Frank Oates (1840–75) Collection: original note-book from the journey in America and Africa together with a small collection of ethnographic items.
Lawrence Oates (1880–1912): original letters and papers from his childhood and early military career in South Africa, Egypt and India. A comprehensive collection of printed material relating to the Scott Polar Expedition and Lawrence Oates's death.

Non-manuscript material: A few items of Gilbert White personalia. Oates family portraits and paintings by members of the Oates family.
Newspapers relating to the Antarctic Expedition.

Finding aids: Person index and catalogue of the Holt-White collection.

Facilities: Photocopying.

1002 Borders Regional Archive and Local History Centre

Address: St Mary's Mill, Selkirk, Borders TD7 5EW

Telephone: (01750) 720842

Fax: (01750) 722875

Enquiries: The Principal Librarian/Archivist, Ms R. Brown

Open: Mon–Thurs: 9.00–1.00; 2.00–5.00 Fri: 9.00–1.00; 2.00–4.00

Access: Generally open to the public; an appointment is necessary to consult records on microfilm.

Historical background: Established in 1984 and housed within the Regional Library Headquarters, the Borders Regional Archive and Local History Centre developed from a policy to provide essential sources for the study of local history under one roof.

Acquisitions policy: Items of Borders area interest which can strengthen the collection are added as the opportunity offers and where space permits.

Archives of organisation: Pre-1975 records of the county councils of Berwickshire, Roxburghshire, Peeblesshire and Selkirkshire, including valuation rolls, county council minutes, school board minutes, school logbooks and minutes of turnpike trusts.

Major collections: Aimers, McLean & Co. Ltd, machinery manufacturers.
James McCaig & Sons, wool merchants and importers.
Border Union Agricultural Society.

Non-manuscript material: Census returns, 1841–91 and pre-1855 Old Parish records for Roxburghshire, Peeblesshire, Berwickshire and Selkirkshire (microfilm).
Old Parish record index on microfiche.
Usual local history collection of non-manuscript material, including maps, postcards and newspapers (many on microfilm).

Finding aids: Lists of collections. Card catalogues for local books and postcard collection.

Facilities: Photocopying. Microfilm/fiche readers/printer.

1003 Sevenoaks Archives Office

Parent organisation: Kent County Council Arts & Libraries

Address: Sevenoaks Library, Buckhurst Lane, Sevenoaks, Kent TN13 1LQ

Telephone: (01732) 453118/452384

Fax: (01732) 742682

Enquiries: The Arts & Heritage Officer, Ms Amber Baylis

Open: By appointment.

Access: Generally open to the public.

Historical background: In the 1930s a muniment room was built at Sevenoaks Library and a considerable quantity of archives deposited; in 1962 the majority of these were transferred to the Kent Archives Office, Maidstone, now the Centre for Kentish Studies (entry **789**), but on the opening of the new library at Sevenoaks in 1986 these documents were returned and now form the basis of the collection, with other material from Sevenoaks Library as well as the records of local authorities superseded by Sevenoaks District Council in 1974.

Acquisitions policy: All material relating to Sevenoaks District.

Archives of organisation: Usual local authority record holdings.

Major collections: Deposited local collections.

Finding aids: Catalogues. Subject, author and place index.

Facilities: Photocopying. Microfilm/fiche readers.

1004 Centre for English Cultural Tradition and Language

Address: University of Sheffield, Sheffield S10 2TN

Telephone: (0114) 282 6296

Enquiries: The Archivist

Open: Mon–Thurs: 10.00–4.00

Access: Bona fide scholars, by appointment.

Historical background: The centre was established as the Survey of Language and Folklore

in 1964 as part of the English Language Department. It has close links with departments of Folklore, English and Linguistics at the Memorial University of Newfoundland.

Acquisitions policy: The centre relies greatly on voluntary help from local representatives and correspondents in the collection of material: MSS, photographs, tape-recordings, printed books and ephemera relating to folklore, folklife, language and cultural tradition.

Major collections: Richard Blakeborough MSS, late 19th century.
Local business archives.
Russell Wortley Collection of folk dance and song; card index of examples of language and folklore usage; original student monographs.

Non-manuscript material: Tape archive collection, including c700 of Newfoundland folklore (c2300).
Edgar Wagner and AKA film collections.
Examples of a wide range of artefacts relating to folklife and traditional industry.

Finding aids: Handlist of Blakeborough and Wortley MSS.
Catalogue of student monographs in progress.

Facilities: May be arranged through university library and other departments.

Publications: Lore and Language (1969–) [biannual].

1005 Geographical Association

Address: 343 Fulwood Road, Sheffield S10 3BP

Telephone: (0114) 267 0666

Fax: (0114) 267 0688

Enquiries: The Administrator, Miss Julia Legg

Open: By arrangement only.

Access: Academic researchers, subject to prior written application and receipt of written permission.

The association was founded in 1893 'to further the study and teaching of geography', and continues that role today as a forum for teachers of geography at all educational levels. It holds its own archives, although some papers have been deposited with Sheffield Archives (entry **1006**), including minutes of the governing committee and annual meetings, 1893–, and correspondence. There is a complete set of

Geography (previously *The Geography Teacher*), 1901–, and a small collection of lantern slides. NRA 24477.

1006 Sheffield Archives

Address: 52 Shoreham Street, Sheffield S1 4SP

Telephone: (0114) 273 4756

Fax: (0114) 273 5009

Enquiries: The Principal Archivist

Open: Mon–Thurs: 9.30–5.30 Sat: 9.00–1.00; 2.00–4.30

Access: A reader's ticket system is in operation.

Historical background: The library had acquired a small collection of documents of local interest by 1912; the Jackson Collection was received in the same year and the archive collections have continued to accumulate since then. Until the early 1960s the collections were mainly private, of local families, businesses and solicitors, but since then substantial deposits of parish, public and local authority records have been received. From the beginning, MSS relating to an area within a 30–mile radius of the centre of Sheffield, covering the southern half of the West Riding of Yorkshire and North Derbyshire, were collected as there was no county record office for the West Riding, nor, until 1962, for Derbyshire. Since local government reorganisation in 1974 only MSS relating to the area of the Metropolitan District of Sheffield, or additions to existing collections from outside that area, have normally been accepted. Everything held by South Yorkshire County Record Office up to the abolition of the county council in April 1986 has passed to the office, which also acts as the Diocesan Record Office for the Archdeaconry of Sheffield and is recognised as a place of deposit for public records.

Acquisitions policy: The office is now lead district for archives in South Yorkshire and is responsible for records of county-wide significance, i.e. anything which relates to more than one of the districts, as well as collecting for Sheffield Metropolitan District.

Archives of organisation: Usual local authority record holdings, including records of South Yorkshire Police, 1831–1975.

Major collections: Deposited collections, of which the following have a wider significance:

Wentworth Woodhouse Muniments, including correspondence and papers of Thomas Wentworth, 1st Earl of Strafford, the 2nd Marquis of Rockingham (1730–82); the 2nd Earl Fitzwilliam (1748–1833); and Edmund Burke (1729–97).

Muniments of Spencer Stanhope of Cannon Hall; Vernon Wentworth of Wentworth Castle; Crewe of Fryston Hall.

Correspondence and papers of Edward Carpenter (1844–1929); H.J. Wilson, Liberal MP, 1885–1912; and John Mendelson, MP for Penistone, c1940–78.

Arundel Castle MSS: the Duke of Norfolk's Sheffield, Derbyshire and Nottinghamshire estate papers, maps and plans.

Bacon Frank Collection, including papers of the Talbot Earls of Shrewsbury, 1549–1617.

Fairbank Collection: maps and plans of Sheffield and South Yorkshire (1500), with related note-books and surveys, c1736–1848.

Yorkshire Engine Company records, including photographs and plans of arrangement of locomotives, 1865–c1960.

Correspondence relating to Barnsley Canal, 1820–50.

Major holdings of business records, particularly for the steel industry (e.g. Firth Brown); metalware manufacture (e.g. James Dixon & Co.) and coal industry (National Coal Board), 19th–20th centuries.

Non-manuscript material: Early industrial films, late 1920s.

Collection of local architects' plans and drawings, 19th and 20th centuries.

Facilities: Photocopying. Photography. Microfilming. Microfilm/fiche readers/printer.

Conservation: Full in-house department; outside work undertaken.

Publications R. Meredith: *Guide to the Manuscript Collections in the Sheffield City Libraries (1956; suppl., Accessions 1956–76, 1976).*

Catalogue of the Arundel Castle Manuscripts (1965).

Catalogue of Business and Industrial Records (1977).

Handlist of Records of Education in Sheffield, 1862–1944 (1978).

Handlist of Records relating to Politics in Sheffield, 1832–1980 (1982).

1007 Sheffield Hallam University Library

Address: Psalter Lane, Sheffield S11 8UZ

Telephone: (0114) 253 2721

Enquiries: The Campus Librarian, Mr John Kirby

Open: Term: Mon–Thurs: 8.45–9.00 Fri: 8.45–6.00 Sat: 10.00–5.00 Sun: 1.00–800 Vacation: Mon–Fri: 9.00–5.00

Access: Generally open to the public, on application to the Campus Librarian.

Historical background: The Psalter Lane site of the Sheffield Hallam University is the present form of the Sheffield School of Art, which was founded as the Government School of Design (Sheffield) in 1843. The library acts as a repository for the records of the School of Art until its amalgamation to form Sheffield Polytechnic in 1969. This polytechnic became a university in 1994.

Acquisitions policy: To acquire any material relating to the Sheffield School of Art.

Archives of organisation: Subscription lists and documents relating to the Sheffield School of Art.

Non-manuscript material: Drawings, sculpture, slides and photographs relating to the School of Art.
Annual reports, prospectuses etc.
Published material on artists connected with the school.

Finding aids: General index to the collection. Index of names of pupils and staff, 1843–1969.

Facilities: Photocopying. Microfilm/fiche readers. Slide projectors.

1008 University of Sheffield Library

Address: Western Bank, Sheffield S10 2TN

Telephone: (0114) 276 8555 ext. 4343

Fax: (0114) 273 9826

Enquiries: The Curator of Special Collections & Library Archivist

Open: Term: Mon–Thurs: 9.00–9.30 Fri: 9.00–5.00 Sat: 9.00–1.00 Vacation: Mon–Fri: 9.00–5.00 Sat: 9.00–12.30

Access: Bona fide researchers, preferably by written application. University records are subject to a 30–year closure and certain other records are restricted.

Historical background: Sheffield University received its charter in 1905 and the MS collections have been acquired from 1907 onwards. The official university archives, including the records of the institutions which merged to form the university, date from 1833 and have been administered by the library since 1974.

Acquisitions policy: Principally material relating to the university itself and persons and institutions associated with it. Other, mainly local, records are acquired where there is no conflict of interest with the neighbouring local authority repositories. The National Fairground Archive, established in 1994, will collect multimedia material recording the history of fairs and show people.

Archives of organisation: Records of Firth College (f. 1879), the Sheffield Medical School (f. 1829), the Sheffield Technical School (f. 1886) and the University of Sheffield, 1905–.

Major collections: Samuel Hartlib (c1600–70) MSS: an internationally important collection relating to education, intellectual history, religious movements, agricultural improvements and scientific inventions and including a significant collection of Comenius material, 17th century.
A.J. Mundella (1825–97) papers: correspondence of a Gladstonian Liberal cabinet minister, 1860s-1890s.
W.A. Hewins (1865–1931) papers: correspondence and papers of a leading protectionist economist, founder of the London School of Economics, secretary of the Tariff Commission, Conservative MP and junior minister, 1880s-1930s.
Sir Hans Adolf Krebs (1900–81) papers: Nobel prizewinner, lecturer and professor in biochemistry, Sheffield, 1935–54; Whitley Professor of Biochemistry, Oxford, 1954–67.
Peter Redgrove (*b* 1932) papers: working papers and correspondence of a contemporary poet and dramatist, 1970–89.

Non-manuscript material: Official university archives include a collection of photographs and plans.
Innes-Smith Collection of medical engravings, mainly medical men, 17th–20th centuries.

Finding aids: Lists available of Hartlib, Hewins,

Krebs and Mundella collections as well as several of the smaller archives. Partial lists and indexes available for official university archives. Computerised database for all archives in progress.

Conservation: Contracted out.

Facilities: Photocopying. Photography. Microfilm/fiche reader/printers.

1009 Sherborne Castle

Parent organisation: Sherborne Castle Estates

Address: Estate Office, Cheap Street, Sherborne, Dorset DT9 3PY

Enquiries: The Archivist

Open: By prior arrangement.

Access: Bona fide researchers, by appointment and with the permission of the owner, Mr Simon Wingfield Digby.

Historical background: Sherborne Castle was built in 1594 and came to the Digby family in 1617. In 1698 the estates of the Digby family in Warwickshire and Ireland were united with those in Dorset, and Sherborne Castle became the principal seat of the family.

Acquisitions policy: To maintain the archive.

Archives of organisation: Estate papers of the Digby and Wingfield Digby families relating to estates in Dorset, Somerset and Warwickshire and in Ireland, 15th century–.
Correspondence of the Earls of Bristol and other members of the Digby family, 1538–1696 (2 vols); and of Henry Fox, 1st Lord Holland, 1753–57 (1 vol).
Microfilms of the correspondence are available at Dorset County Record Office (entry **250**).

Finding aids: Summary list of the Sherborne Castle Estate Archive available at Dorset County Record office. Lists of the Digby MSS available at Birmingham Central Library (entry **93**). Summary list of the Irish estate correspondence in the Wingfield Digby papers available at the Public Record Office of Northern Ireland (entry **78**).

Facilities: Photocopying.

1010 Sherborne School

Address: Abbey Road, Sherborne, Dorset DT9 3AP

Enquiries: The Librarian

Open: Term: Mon–Fri: 8.30–6.00 Sat: 8.30–1.00
Vacation: Mon–Fri: 8.30–12.00

Access: Bona fide researchers, by prior appointment only.

Historical background: The school was founded as a monastery school in 705 and refounded after the dissolution by Edward VI in 1550.

Acquisitions policy: To acquire school records when they cease to have immediate administrative use and all school publications.

Archives of organisation: Governors' minute books, estate, financial and other records, 1550–.
Some architectural plans.
Shirburnian, 1859–; school lists, 1869–91, 1898–1904; Shirburnian Society annual reports, 1897– (incomplete).

Major collections: Collections of papers of headmasters and relating to old boys.
Alex Waugh (1898–1981): MS of *Loom of Youth* and his collection of reviews and related correspondence.

Finding aids: Brief handlist.

Facilities: Photocopying.

1011 Shrewsbury School

Address: Shrewsbury, Shropshire SY3 7BA

Enquiries: The Librarian and Archivist, J.B. Lawson

Open: Term: by appointment.

Access: Bona fide scholars, on written application.

Historical background: The school was founded by Edward VI in 1552 and the library in 1606. From that time the library has had a continuous policy of acquiring books and MSS.

Acquisitions policy: Current acquisition policy is confined to the history of the school and of old members.

Archives of organisation: Admission registers, accounts, minute books, legal papers, tithe maps, 1552–.

Papers of the clerk to the governing body, 1840–.
Sporting, society and house 'Fasti', c1860–.
Headmasters' and bursars' files, 20th century.

Major collections: Charles Darwin (1809–82), letters.
Samuel Butler (*Erewhon*) (1835–1902), letters and MSS.
Charles Morgan (1894–1958), letters.
Rev. Prof. E. Burton (1794–1836), letters.
Shropshire Local History Collection, including deeds and antiquarian MSS.

Non-manuscript material: Photographic archive, 1860–; plans and architectural drawings.
Shrewsbury poll books, 19th century.
Large quantity of printed ephemera relating to the school.

Finding aids: MS lists and indexes.

Facilities: Photocopying.

Publications: J.B. Oldham: *History of Shrewsbury School* (1952).

1012 Shropshire Records and Research Centre

Address: Castle Gates, Shrewsbury, Shropshire SY1 2AQ

Telephone: (01743) 255350

Fax: (01743) 255355

Enquiries: The Head of Records and Research, Miss R.E. Bagley

Open: Tues: 10.00–9.00 Wed–Fri: 10.00–5.00 Sat: 10.00–4.00.

Historical background: The centre holds the collection of the former Shropshire Record Office (established in 1946) and the Local Studies Library. The latter's MS collection was acquired by Shrewsbury Public Library, 1882–1974. The centre is a diocesan branch record office for Hereford (Archdeaconry of Ludlow) and Lichfield (Archdeaconry of Salop) and is recognised as a place of deposit for public records. The centre includes the staff of the Shropshire Victoria County History.

Acquisitions policy: Archive and local studies material relating to the County of Shropshire.

Archives of organisation: Records of Shropshire County Council, 1889–, are retained at the

Shirehall, Abbey Foregate, Shrewsbury SY2 6ND.

Major collections: Numerous Anglican parish collections and Methodist archives.
Estate collections, including the Attingham, More and Powis archives.
Local authority collections, including medieval borough archives of Ludlow and Shrewsbury.
Lily F. Chitty Collection: Shropshire archaeology and local history.
King's Shropshire Light Infantry Collection.

Non-manuscript material: Watercolours and drawings by J. Holmes Smith and others, including watercolours of Shropshire churches, 1830–50 (c400).
Shropshire Photographic Archive (c18,000 prints; 10,000 negatives).

Finding aids: Various lists and indexes. On-line computer index to former local studies MSS.

Facilities: Photocopying. Photography. Microfilm/fiche readers/printers.

Publications: Family History Guide (1995).
L.F. Chitty Collection Catalogue (1992).

1013 Sidmouth Museum

Parent organisation: Sid Vale Association

Address: Hope Cottage, Church Street, Sidmouth, Devon EX10 8LA

Telephone: (01395) 516139

Enquiries: The Curator, Mrs Erica Connelly

Open: Tues–Sat: 10.00–12.30; 2.00–4.30 Sun, Mon: 2.00–4.30
Closed November to Easter.

Access: Bona fide researchers, by written appointment (with SAE) via the curator. Donations are appreciated.

Historical background: A museum was first established in 1873 and moved to its present site in 1971. The museum is part of the Sid Vale Association, the first civic society (f. 1846). It maintains a local history library, which began as a private collection. The association remains an independent, voluntary institution now housed in a Grade II building.

Acquisitions policy: To maintain and consolidate the collection related to Sidmouthians on Sidmouth.

Archives of organisation: Records of the Sid Vale Association, 1846–.

Major collections: Literary MSS of R.F. Delder-field.

Non-manuscript material: Newspapers and print collections.

1014 Skipton Branch Library

Parent organisation: North Yorkshire County Library

Address: High Street, Skipton, North Yorks BD23 1JX

Telephone: (01756) 792926

Enquiries: The Librarian: Information Services, Ms K.A. Pitt

Open: Mon, Wed–Fri: 9.30–7.00 Sat: 9.30–1.00

Access: Open to all serious researchers; an appointment is advisable.

Historical background: The present collection derives from that formed in Skipton Urban District Council Library before it passed to North Yorkshire in 1974.

Acquisitions policy: Accepts donations principally of local historians' papers.

Major collections: Skipton Board of Guardians records, 1873–1930, including smallpox hospital records, 1912–15.
Rowley MSS: history of Skipton, particularly properties in central Skipton.
Raistrick MSS: Yorkshire deeds, overseers papers, enclosure papers, tithes and terriers, lead-mining etc, c1600–1930s.
Susan Brooks MSS: mainly concerning her work on the history of Grassington and area.
Serjeantson MSS: relating to Hanlith Hall, estates at Carthorpe, Calton and Hanlith, and Camp Hill (Hall) near Bedale, 1331–1868.
Complementary collections from the same depositors are held in the Craven Museum, Town Hall, High Street, Skipton BD23 1AH.

Non-manuscript material: Maps (c400), 1854–.
Photographs covering Craven area, 19th–20th centuries.

Finding aids: Lists. Board of Guardians: NRA 15616; Raistrick MSS: NRA 14065; Skipton Library Collection: NRA 10242; Serjeantson MSS: NRA 5794.

Facilities: Photocopying. Microfilm/fiche readers (booking essential).

1015 Royal Air Force College Archives

Address: The Library, Cranwell, Sleaford, Lincs NG34 8HB

Telephone: (01400) 261201 ext. 6329

Fax: (01400) 261201 ext. 6266

Enquiries: The College Librarian and Archivist, Mrs J. M. Buckberry

Open: Mon, Tues, Thurs: 8.15–5.00 Wed, Fri: 8.15–4.00

Access: Bona fide researchers, by prior written appointment.

Historical background: A Royal Naval Air Service Station was established at Cranwell in 1915, and in 1918 RAF Cranwell was formed with the merging of the Royal Naval Air Service and the Royal Flying Corps. The RAF Cadet College, Cranwell, was opened in 1920.

Acquisitions policy: To collect any material relating to the college's history.

Archives of organisation: Records of administration, course syllabuses, programmes, standing orders, students lists, 1920–.

Major collections: Papers and reminiscences of former members of staff and students.

Non-manuscript material: Photographic collection, including staff and student photographs, 1915–.
Videos of graduation parades.
Maps, drawings and plans of the site, 1915–.
Large scrapbooks of newspaper and periodical articles, 1920–.
Journal of the Royal Air Force College (complete set), 1920–.
Piloteer Magazine, 1916–19.

Facilities: Photocopying.

1016 Solihull Library

Parent organisation: Solihull Libraries & Arts

Address: Homer Road, Solihull, West Midlands B91 3RG

Telephone: (0121) 704 6977

Fax: (0121) 704 6991

Enquiries: The Local History Librarian, Mrs S. Bates

Open: Mon–Wed: 9.30–5.30 Thurs, Fri: 9.30–8.00 Sat: 9.30–5.00

Access: Generally open to the public.

A local history collection has existed since 1974 and is designed to provide a general coverage of those areas within the Solihull Metropolitan Borough. It includes maps, photographs, newspapers, books and a few archives, including records of the BSA motorcycle factory, Small Heath, Birmingham. However, archives are generally deposited at the County Record Office, Warwick (entry 1077). A readers' guide to the collection is available and there is a card index. Facilities include photocopying, photography and microfilm/fiche reader/printers.

1017 Hopetoun House

Parent organisation: Hopetoun House Preservation Trust

Address: South Queensferry, West Lothian EH30 9SL

Telephone: (0131) 331 2451

Fax: (0131) 319 1885

Enquiries: The Archivist, Mrs Patricia Crichton

Open: Papers to be consulted are not available at Hopetoun House. When research has been approved, papers are made available at West Register House, Edinburgh (see entry 313) to be studied there.

Access: Approved academic researchers on written application to the Secretary, NRA (Scotland), PO Box 36, General Register House, Edinburgh EH1 3YY. There is no charge at present, but a copy of all completed research is requested. Genealogy questions should be similarly addressed and will be charged per hour of research. There is also a charge made for any approved commercial reproduction. Access is not normally granted to material post-1908 (the death of the 1st Marquess of Linlithgow).

Historical background: The trust is responsible for the private archives of the family and the estate papers, 17th century–.

Acquisitions policy: To maintain the existing archive.

Archives of organisation: Hope family papers, early 17th century–1703.
Earls of Hopetoun, 1703–1902.
Marquesses of Linlithgow, 1902–.

Non-manuscript material: Maps; estate plans; architectural drawings.

Finding aids: Catalogue available in Register House, Edinburgh, and at NRA. Catalogue and card index at Hopetoun House.

Facilities: Photocopying at West Register House has to be approved by the Archivist at Hopetoun House.

Conservation: Contracted out when funds are available.

1018 South Tyneside Central Library
Local History Department

Parent organisation: South Tyneside Borough Council

Address: Prince Georg Square, South Shields, Tyne and Wear NE33 2PE

Telephone: (0191) 427 1818 ext. 2135

Fax: (0191) 455 8085

Enquiries: The Local History Librarian, Miss D. Johnson

Open: Mon–Thurs: 9.30–7.00 Fri: 9.30–5.00 Sat: 9.30–4.00

Access: Generally open to the public.

Historical background: South Shields Public Library was opened in 1874 and in 1879 a local history collection was started. On local government reorganisation in 1974 South Shields Public Library became South Tyneside Central Library, which meant that the area was expanded from specifically South Shields to cover Jarrow, Hebburn, The Boldons, Cleadon and Whitburn.

Aquisitions policy: Consolidation of existing holdings and strengthening of the collection in areas not covered before 1974.

Archives of organisation: South Shields Library Committee minutes and annual reports, 1874–1974.

Non-manuscript material: Kelly Collection: posters representing business, industry and entertainment in South Shields, 1790–1880 (c2000).

Photographs (c3000) and negatives (10,000), including:

Flagg Collection, amateur photographer and historian, c1925–c1950.

Cleet Collection, professional photographer, slums of South Shields in the 1930s.

Jarrow March Collection, various professional photographers on this event.

Willits Collection, amateur photographer, 1890s and 1900s.

Parry Collection, firm of professional photographers, 1900–50.

Finding aids: Most of the photographs have been catalogued and indexed and work on indexing the posters has begun.

Facilities: Photocopying. Photography. Microfilm/fiche readers/printers.

Conservation: Contracted out.

1019 Ancient Order of Foresters Heritage Trust

Parent organisation: Ancient Order of Foresters

Address: College Place, Southampton, Hants SO9 1FP

Telephone: (01703) 229655

Fax: (01703) 229657

Enquiries: The Heritage Trust Co-ordinator

Open: Mon–Fri: 9.00–5.00, by appointment.

Access: Approved readers, on written application.

The order in its present form dates from 1834 and the Heritage Trust Museum was established in 1992. There is a complete set of executive council reports, journal and annual directories of 'courts' (branches), plus a small but growing collection of 'court' minutes, membership records and accounts. A. Fisk and R. Logan: *'My forebears were members of the Ancient Order of Foresters Friendly Society'* (1993).

1020 Southampton City Record Office

Address: Civic Centre, Southampton, Hants SO14 7LY

Telephone: (01703) 832251/223855 ext.2251

Enquiries: The Archives Services Manager, Mrs S.L. Woolgar

Open: Tues–Fri: 9.30–4.30; one evening each month to 9pm, by appointment only.

Access: Generally open to the public.

Historical background: The office was established in 1953. It also acts as the Diocesan Record Office for Winchester (Southampton parish records) and is recognised as a place of deposit for public records.

Acquisitions policy: Archives relating to the City of Southampton

Archives of organisation: Usual local authority record holdings of present and former authorities for Southampton, including records of the borough, 1199–.

Major collections: Deposited collections, of which the following have a wider significance: Molyneux MSS, including letters on astronomy and scientific experiments, 1681–1713.

Cobb MSS: Smyth and Gee families, including letters from the Duke of Kent, 1808–20, and papers about New Brunswick, Canada, 1820s.

South Coast Engineering and Shipbuilding Employers' Association records, c1902–78.

John I. Thornycroft MSS: financial, publicity and photographic holdings on ship-building and transport-vehicle manufacturing activities of firm in UK and abroad, c1870s-1967.

John H. Isherwood Collection of ships' drawings.

Southampton Chamber of Commerce minutes, 1851–1973.

Southampton Trades Council minutes and notes, 1929–84.

Garrett and Haysom, monumental masons, records, including accounts and ledgers, c1809–1962.

Southampton Test Conservative Association minutes and files, 1912–81.

Finding aids: Catalogues and indexes; lists sent to NRA.

Facilities: Photocopying. Photography. Microfilm/fiche reader.

Conservation: In-house service.

Publications: Southampton Records, i: *A Guide to the Records of Southampton Corporation and Absorbed Authorities* (1964).
Sources for Family History (1993).
Hampshire Archivists' Group guides: *Poor Law* (1970); *Transport* (1973); *Education* (1977).

1021 University of Southampton Library
Special Collections

Address: Highfield, Southampton, Hants SO9 5NH

Telephone: (01703) 592721/593724

Fax: (01703) 593007

Enquiries: The Archivist and Head of Special Collections, Dr C.M. Woolgar

Open: Mon, Tues, Thurs, Fri: 9.00–5.00 Wed: 10.00–5.00

Access: Open to all by appointment.

Historical background: Southampton University received its charter in 1952, having developed from the Hartley Institution (f. 1862), which became a university college of London University in 1902. Most of the holdings of the Anglo-Jewish Archive were moved from UCL to the library in 1990.

Acquisitions policy: Archives of national and international significance having a connection with the university's region or its special collections; papers of individuals associated with the university; archives of Anglo-Jewry.

Archives of organisation: Archives of Hartley Institution, 1862–1902; University College, 1902–52; Southampton University, 1952–.

Major collections: More than 2000 collections, principally of private papers and records of organisations, comprising four groups:
Political, military, diplomatic and official papers, including those of the 1st Marquis Wellesley (1760–1842); 1st Duke of Wellington (1769–1852); 3rd Viscount Palmerston (1784–1865); 7th Earl of Shaftesbury (1801–85); 1st Marquis of Milhaven (1854–1921); and Earl Mountbatten of Burma (1900–79).
Anglo-Jewry archives including papers of Rev. Dr James Parkes (1896–1981); Chief Rabbi J.H. Hertz (1872–1946); Rabbi Dr Solomon Schonfield (1912–84); Anglo-Jewish Association,

1871–1983; Union of Jewish Women, 1902–76; *Jewish Chronicle,* 1841–1990; International and Nuremburg Military Tribunals, 1945–9; Jewish care, including Board of Guardians for the Relief of the Jewish Poor, the Jewish Association for the Protection of Girls, Women and Children and the Jewish Blind Society, 1757–1989; Council of Christians and Jews, 1940–84; World Congress of Faiths, 1934–92.
Papers of members of the university, including Professors N.K. Adams (1891–1973), A.A. Cock (1883–1953), H. Stansfield (1872–1960) and F.W. Wagner (1905–85).
Supporting collections including Spanish archive material relating to the Peninsular War and the Liberal Triennium, 1805–23; records of National Association of Divisional Executives for Education, 1934–71; Joint Four Secondary Teachers' Associations, 1921–78; literary and musical material, including the papers of N.J. Crisp (*b* 1923) and conducting scores of Gustav Mahler (1860–1911).

Non-manuscript material: Photographs, prints and drawings, especially topographical, relating to Hampshire and the Isle of Wight.
Norman del Mar (*b* 1919) Collection of recordings of orchestral music.

Finding aids: Summary and detailed catalogues. On-line computer databases of the same information plus databases of surveys of related sources: Jewish archives and senior UK defence personnel, 1793–70 (jointly with the Liddell Hart Centre, King's College London, entry **589**). These are accessible via JANET and the Internet; enquiries for on-line access via e-mail to Archives@soton.ac.uk.

Facilities: Photocopying. Photography. Microfilming.

Conservation: Full in-house facilities.

Publications: G. Cheffy: *Dr L.F.W. White Memorial Collection of the Records of the National Association of Divisional Executives for Education* (1975) [USL Occasional Paper no. 5].
G. Hampson: *Records of the University of Southampton* (1980) [USL Occasional Paper no. 7].
C.M. Woolgar: *A Summary Catalogue of the Wellington Papers* (1984) [USL Occasional Paper no. 8].
L.M. Mitchell, K.J. Sampson and C. Woolgar: *A Summary Catalogue of the Papers of Earl*

Mountbatten of Burma (1991) [USL Occasional Paper no. 9].

C.M. Woolgar and K. Robson: *A Guide to the Archive and Manuscript Collections of the Hartley Library, University of Southampton* (1992) [USL Occasional Paper no. 11].

K. Robson: *MS 200 Papers of the International Military Tribunal and the Nuremberg Military Tribunals, 1945–9* (1993) [USL Archive Lists, Catalogues and Guides series no. 1].

C.M. Woolgar: *MS 173 Archives of Jewish Care, 1757–1989* (1993) [USL Archive Lists, Catalogues and Guides series no. 2].

K. Robson: *MS 175 Papers of Chief Rabbi J.H. Hertz (1872–1946), 1853–1949* (1993) [USL Archive Lists, Catalogues and Guides series no. 3].

1022 Essex Record Office
Southend Branch

Address: c/o Central Library, Victoria Avenue, Southend-on-Sea, Essex SS2 6EX

Telephone: (01702) 612621 ext. 215

Fax: (01702) 469241

Enquiries: The Branch Archivist, Mr J.R. Smith

Open: Mon, Wed, Thurs: 9.15–5.15 Tues: 9.45–5.15 Fri: 9.15–4.15

Access: Generally open to the public, by appointment. The office operates the CARN reader's ticket system.

Historical background: This branch office of Essex Record Office, Chelmsford (entry **203**) was established in 1974.

Acquisitions policy: Local government and other archives, including parish, family and estate records, relevant to the area of south-east Essex.

Archives of organisation: Usual local authority record holdings.

Major collections: Deposited local collections.

Finding aids: Lists sent to NRA.

Facilities: Photocopying. Photography. Microfilm/fiche readers.

Conservation: Full in-house service at Essex Record Office, Chelmsford.

1023 Sefton Metropolitan Borough
Libraries and Arts Service

Address: Pavilion Buildings, 99–105 Lord Street, Southport, Merseyside PR8 1RH

Telephone: (0151) 934 2119 (Southport Library) 928 6487 (Crosby Library) (01704) 560090 (General enquiries)

Enquiries: The Local History Librarians

Open: Mon, Tues: 10.00–5.00 Wed, Fri: 10.00–8.00 Thurs, Sat: 10.00–1.00, by appointment

Sefton Metropolitan Borough was formed after local government reorganisation in 1974. It combined the areas of Bootle, Crosby, Southport with parts of the West Lancashire district, and some local government records for the authorities pre-1974 are held (see NRA 25531). There is no active collecting policy, but archives are taken in on request and local history collections are held at each library; of particular interest is the Cheetham Collection at Southport. There are photocopying facilities and microfilm/fiche reader/printers at both libraries.

1024 The Royal Marines Museum

Address: Southsea, Hants PO4 9PX

Telephone: (01705) 819385 exts 24/25

Fax: (01705) 838420

Enquiries: The Archivist, Mr Matt Little, The Photo Librarian, Mr Ed Bartholomew

Open: Mon–Fri: 10.00–4.30

Access: Bona fide researchers, by appointment.

Historical background: In 1963 it became necessary to establish a reference library and archive repository for the use of the Royal Marines Historian and Museum, and a certain amount of money was made available for the purchase of items by the Commandant General Royal Marines. This was supplemented by gifts from individuals. In 1965 a number of military and naval reference books were transferred to the museum from the Royal Marines Officers' Mess Library at Plymouth. This was the first of such transfers. Meanwhile the Commandant General's grant continued, which provided the basis for further purchases. In 1988 the museum was designated and is now a registered charity with a board of trustees and a grant-in-aid provided under the terms of the National Heritage Act 1983.

Acquisitions policy: To strengthen the collection by the acquisition of both modern and antiquarian material, by purchase, donation or bequest.

Archives of organisation: Archives of the Royal Marines Corps, comprising derestricted material from official sources; divisional order books concerning marines administration, organisation and deployment, 1644–.

Major collections: An extensive collection of personal diaries and letters; unofficial logbooks; correspondence; and orders.

Non-manuscript material: Extensive photograph library.
Drawings, maps and plans relating to operations, equipment and barracks.
Navy and Marine Lists.
Oral history tapes (52).

Finding aids: Various card indexes, including name, unit, operation and location.

Facilities: Photocopying. Photograph copying. Microfilm/fiche reader.

Publications: From Trench and Turret: Letters and Diaries, 1914–18 (RMM, c1989).
The Royal Marines Victoria Crosses.

1025 Southwell Minster Library

Address: Southwell Minster Office, Trebeck Hall, Bishop's Drive, Southwell, Notts NG25 0JP

Telephone: (01636) 812649

Fax: (01636) 815904

Enquiries: The Hon. Librarian, Mr H. Brooke

Open: By appointment only.

Access: Approved readers, students and researchers.

The cathedral library was re-created at the restoration in 1660. It holds chapter records, 14th century–; Bishops' transcripts of parish registers in the Diocese of Southwell; and some

local photographs. It acquires local history material and publications relevant to Southwell Minster and the diocese.

1026 Lincolnshire and Humberside Film Archive

Address: 16 Cathedral Drive, Spalding, Lincs PE11 1PG

Telephone: (01775) 725631

Enquiries: The Archivist, Peter Ryde

Open: By appointment only.

Access: Bona fide potential users, researchers, students of local history etc. Viewing will normally be on video in the first instance. By arrangement (and subject to copyright/donor's restrictions, if any) material can be made available on video for approved uses. Showings on film can be arranged for societies etc, although films themselves are not available on loan to the public.

Historical background: The archive was established in 1986 and operates in association with the Museum of Lincolnshire Life, Lincoln.

Acquisitions policy: To locate, preserve and make accessible film on all aspects of the life and work in historic Lincolnshire (Lincolnshire and South Humberside), especially pre-1960, though later items are not refused.

Non-manuscript material: Documentary and non-fiction film illustrating the life and work of the region, 1904–early 1970s, but principally 1930s and 1940s (306 titles).
Supplementary documentation is available in some cases, including press cuttings, and commentary scripts for local newsreel items. General background information can be supplied for most items.

Finding aids: Full descriptive catalogue. Computer database for search by date, place, region and broad subject area. A detailed subject index is still in preparation, but information on specific subject content is available on application.

1027 Spalding Gentlemen's Society

Address: The Museum, Broad Street, Spalding, Lincs PE11 1TB

Telephone: (01775) 724658

Enquiries: The Hon. Secretary, Mr D.C. Archer

Open: By appointment.
Closed in August and December.

Access: By arrangement; visitors wishing study facilities will be asked for a reference.

Historical background: One of the oldest learned societies, it was founded by Maurice Johnson, FSA (1688–1755) in 1710, and early members included notable 18th–century figures. Discussion of politics and religion are banned under the founder's ruling. With the exception of the Ashmolean, the museum is the oldest in the UK.

Acquisitions policy: To maintain the collections.

Major collections: Manorial, local government and some monastic records and MSS.
Fens drainage records, 17th–19th centuries.

Non-manuscript material: Portfolios of prints, drawings and plans, early 18th century.
Maps.
Society's library created by purchases and the gift of a volume from every new member.

Finding aids: NRA 4862.

Publications: Annual Report, 1899– .
Various histories, including: *Nichol's Bibliotheca Topographica Britannica* (1790) [history of early days of society with list of members]; and *Literary Anecdotes,* vol. 6 (1812).
W. Moore: *The Gentlemen's Society at Spalding: its Origin and Progress* (London, 1851).
D.M. Owen: *The Minute Books of the Spalding Gentlemen's Society, 1712–1755,* Lincoln Record Society, 73 (1981).

1028 Staffordshire Record Office

Address: Eastgate Street, Stafford ST16 2LZ

Telephone: (01785) 223121 exts 8373/80

Enquiries: The County Archivist, Mr D.V. Fowkes

Open: Mon–Thurs: 9.00–1.00; 1.30–5.00 Fri: 9.00–1.00; 1.30–4.30 Sat: 9.30–1.00, by arrangement

Historical background: The record office was established in 1947; before then records were collected by the William Salt Library. The office also acts as the Diocesan Record Office for Lichfield (Archdeaconry of Stafford parish records), and is recognised as a place of deposit for public records. The William Salt Library, Stafford (entry **1029**) and Lichfield Joint Record Office (entry **1457**) are dependent repositories.

Archives of organisation: Usual local authority record holdings.

Major collections: Deposited collections, including the following which have a wider significance:
Dartmouth Family Collection, including papers of the Legge family who held various government appointments, notably Secretary of State for the Colonies and Admiral of the Fleet, 17th–18th centuries.
Hatherton Collection, including political papers of the 1st Lord Hatherton (1791–1863), Chief Secretary to the Lord Lieutenant of Ireland, 1833–4.
Business records of Birmingham Rail, Carriage and Wagon Works, with worldwide connections, 19th century.

Facilities: Photocopying. Photography and microfilming by arrangement. Microfilm/fiche readers.

Conservation: Full in-house service.

1029 William Salt Library

Address: Eastgate Street, Stafford ST16 2LZ

Telephone: (01785) 52276

Enquiries: The Librarian, Mr D.V. Fowkes

Open: Tues–Thurs: 9.00–1.00; 2.00–5.00 Fri: 9.00–1.00; 2.00–4.30 Sat (2nd and 4th in each month): 9.30–1.00

Access: Generally open to the public.

Historical background: Founded in 1872, the library is based on the collections of William Salt (1808–63), a member of a Stafford banking family. It is administered by trustees, but since 1935 its connection with the Staffordshire County Council has become close, at first by grant, and since the creation of the Staffordshire Record Office in 1947, also by sharing of staff:

the County Archivist acts as William Salt Librarian. Most of the collections deposited with, or loaned to, the library earlier this century are now housed in Staffordshire County Record Office (entry **1028**).

Major collections: William Salt MSS Collection, 9th–20th centuries: reflects his interests and contains a considerable number of autograph letters, only some of which have Staffordshire connections; also many transcripts of Staffordshire material in the Public Record Office, British Library, College of Heralds, much of which is still unpublished (e.g. the Staffordshire entries in the Thomason Tracts and Dr Burney's newspapers).
Subsequent donations and loans still in the library include Anglo-Saxon charters and the Parker-Jervis of Meaford papers.

Non-manuscript material: The original collection of William Salt includes printed books, pamphlets, broadsheets, drawings, engravings and other ephemera relating to Staffordshire. Staffordshire heraldry (2 vols).
Topographical drawings (3000) and prints; also engraved drawings of personalities.

Finding aids: Dictionary index and catalogue of accessions.

Facilities: Photocopying. Photography, by appointment in special circumstances only.

Conservation: Service provided by Staffordshire County Record Office.

1030 Tameside Local Studies Library

Address: Stalybridge Library, Trinity Street, Stalybridge, Cheshire SKl5 2BN

Telephone: (0161) 338 2708/3831

Fax: (0161) 303 8289

Enquiries: The Archivist, Ms Gillian Cooke

Open: Mon–Fri: 9.00–7.30 Sat: 9.00–4.00

Access: Generally open to the public. An appointment is necessary for the use of microfilm.

Historical background: The Tameside Local Studies Library was set up in Stalybridge in 1976. It took over the local history collections of the libraries of the local authorities which preceded Tameside. It is recognised as a place of deposit for public records.

Aquisitions policy: To locate, acquire and preserve all types of printed, illustrative and archive material related to the Tameside area: Ashton, Audenshaw, Denton, Droylsden, Dukinfield, Hyde, Longdendale, Mossley and Stalybridge.

Archives of organisations: Usual local authority record holdings of the authorities which preceded Tameside.

Major collections: Deposited collections of some local organisations, for example churches (including non-conformist); schools; trade unions; mechanics' institutes; also some hospitals; local business, including mills; family, including Lee family of Park Bridge, and individuals' records.
Archives of the Manchester Regiment.

Non-manuscript material: Maps of the Tameside area, Lancashire and Cheshire, 1577– (c1500).
Photographs, 1860s- (14,500); engravings, pamphlets and broadsides, 1790s-.
Oral history interviews, including those by the former Manchester Studies Unit.
Microfilms of local newspapers, census returns and parish registers.

Finding aids: Catalogues, indexes and typescript guide to the archive collection. Card catalogue of photographs, maps and broadsheets. Indexes of the *North Cheshire Herald* (1895–1972) and *Ashton Reporter* (incomplete). Surname index (incomplete) and street index to the census returns.

Facilities: Photocopying. Photography. Microfilm/fiche readers.

Publications: Guide to the Archives (1994).

1031 Central Regional Council Archives Services

Address: Unit 6, Burghmuir Industrial Estate, Stirling FK7 7PY

Telephone: (01786) 450745

Enquiries: The Regional Archivist, Mr G.A. Dixon

Open: Mon–Fri: 10.00–4.30

Access: Generally open to the public.

Historical background: The office was established in 1975 on local government reorganisation. Some material is still retained by appropriate departments in district offices. Stirling Burgh records, 14th century-, and some church, JP and customs and excise records have been transferred from the Scottish Record Office (entry 313).

Archives of organisation: Usual local authority record holdings including burgh records for region, 19th and 20th centuries.

Major collections: Deposited local collections, including MacGregor of MacGregor, Murray of Polmaise and Stirling of Gargunock estate papers, 14th–20th centuries.

Facilities: Photocopying. Photography by arrangement. Microfilm/fiche reader.

1032 University of Stirling Library

Address: Stirling FK9 4LA

Telephone: (01786) 673171

Fax: (01786) 466866

Enquiries: The Librarian Mrs C. Rowlinson (John Grierson Archive) Mr G.W. Willis (all other collections)

Open: Mon–Fri: 9.00–5.00

Access: Available to all on prior application.

Historical background: The university was founded in 1967. The library supervises access to the Leighton Library Dunblane Collection in the Rare Books Department of the university library.

Acquisitions policy: Interested in acquiring material relating to Scottish literature, especially from the 19th century. MSS mostly acquired as gifts or bequests.

Major collections: John Grierson Archive: personal papers, writings on documentary film of John Grierson (1898–1972), with related material.
W. Tait Collection: covering left-wing political matters, 1883–1943.
Howietown Fish Farm records, 1873–1978.
Leighton Library MSS Collection, 16th–20th centuries (c80 MSS).

Finding aids: Grierson Archive: list of contents and card index. Catalogue of Tait Collection. NRA(S) lists of other collections.

Facilities: Photocopying. Photography. Microfilm/fiche reader/printer.

Publications: F. Hardy: *John Grierson Archive List of Contents* (1978).
G. Willis: *The Leighton Library, Dunblane: Catalogue of Manuscripts* (Stirling, 1981).

1033 Stockport Archives Service

Parent organisation: Metropolitan Borough of Stockport

Address: Central Library, Wellington Road South, Stockport, Cheshire SK1 3RS

Telephone: (0161) 474 4530

Fax: (0161) 474 7750

Enquiries: The Archivist, Mrs M.J. Myerscough

Open: Mon–Fri: 9.00–8.00 Sat: 9.00–4.00
An appointment is advisable for evenings (5.00–8.00) and Saturdays.

Access: Generally open to the public. There are restrictions on some records. Contact in advance of a visit is preferable.

Historical background: Active collecting, focused on the county borough area, began in the 1960s to supplement documents already held by the library. In 1974 the Archives Service took over the records of the disbanded urban districts included in the new metropolitan borough: Bredbury and Romiley, Cheadle and Gatley, Hazel Grove and Bramhall, and Marple. It is recognised as a place of deposit for public records.

Aquisitions policy: Acquisition of records relating to any aspect of life in the area of the metropolitan borough.

Archives of organisation: Usual local government records for the area of the metropolitan borough.

Major collections: Deposited local collections, including records of Stockport Sunday School, 1784–1970; Christy & Co. Ltd, hat manufacturers, 1773–1969; Bradshaw-Isherwood estate, 1274–1919; R. Greg & Co., 1850–1980.

Finding aids: 16 calendars and indexes for part of the holdings. Lists sent to NRA.

Facilities: Photocopying. Photography. Microfilm readers.

Publications: M.J. Critchlow: *Guide to Calendars, 1–14* (1983).

1034 Stockton Reference Library

Parent organisation: Cleveland County Libraries

Address: Church Road, Stockton-on-Tees, Cleveland TS18 1TU

Telephone: (01642) 672680

Enquiries: The Reference Librarian, Mrs Joyce E. Chesney

Open: Mon–Wed, Fri: 9.30–7.00 Thurs, Sat: 9.30–5.00

Access: Generally open to the public. An appointment is necessary to use the microfilm/fiche readers.

Historical background: Local historical collection built up over several years.

Acquisitions policy: To add any material relevant to the history of the Stockton District.

Major collections: Usual local history collection, mainly of non-MS material, including council minutes, 1903–; photographs; OS early editions; newspapers, census and parish registers (microfilm).

Finding aids: Card indexes for photographic collection and for weekly newspaper, 1920–60.

Facilities: Photocopying. Microfilm/fiche readers/printer.

Conservation: Contracted out to Cleveland County Archives Department (entry 819).

Publications: *Sources for Family Historians in Stockton Reference Library* [free leaflet].

1035 Hanley Library Information Services

Parent organisation: Staffordshire Libraries, Arts and Archives Department

Address: Hanley Library, Bethesda Street, Hanley, Stoke-on-Trent, Staffs ST1 3RS

Telephone: (01782) 281242/23122/215108

Fax: (01782) 285773

Enquiries: The Assistant County Librarian: North, Ms June Williams

Open: Mon, Wed: 9.00–7.00 Tues, Thurs, Fri: 9.30–5.00 Sat: 9.30–1.00

Access: Generally open to the public. A few items are closed or on restricted access. An initial appointment is advisable; prior booking is essential for use of microfilm.

Historical background: The City of Stoke-on-Trent was formed in 1910 by the Federation of the Independent Local Authorities of Tunstall, Burslem, Hanley, Stoke-upon-Trent, Fenton and Longton. The present collection houses material from these former authorities and relating to Stoke-on-Trent post-1910. From 1974 it became part of Staffordshire County Library, which amalgamated with the Staffordshire Record Office (entry 1028) to become the Libraries, Arts and Archives Department in 1985. It is recognised as a place of deposit for public records.

Acquisitions policy: Collects material relating to Stoke-on-Trent and North Staffordshire in collaboration with the County Record Office.

Archives of organisation: Minute books, and local school board minute books where appropriate, of Burslem Borough Council and predecessors, 1825–1910; Fenton UDC and predecessors, 1842–1910; Hanley County Borough and predecessors, 1847–1910; Longton Borough Council, 1873–1910; Smallthorne UDC, 1875–1922; Stoke-upon-Trent Borough Council and predecessors, 1839–1910; Tunstall UDC and predecessors, 1886–1910. School logbooks.

Major collections: Adam Collection: mainly title deeds relating to North Staffordshire, 12th–19th centuries.
Wilkinson/Newport Collection: documents relating to Clarice Cliff, ceramics designer.
Heathcote Collection.
Local Methodist records.

Non-manuscript material: Large local studies collection relating to Stoke-on-Trent and Staffordshire.
Ceramics collection.
Solon Collection of books on ceramics in many European languages.

Finding aids: Lists for some collections; sent to NRA. Various indexes.

Facilities: Photocopying. Microfilm/fiche readers (printouts can be ordered).

1036 Western Isles Islands Council (Comhairle Nan Eilean)

Address: Sandwick Road, Stornoway, Isle of Lewis PA87 2BW

Telephone: (01851) 703773

Fax: (01851) 705349

Enquiries: The Director of Administration and Legal Services, Mr Robert J.C. Barnett

Open: Mon–Fri: 9.00–5.00

Access: By written application.

Historical background: Comhairle Nan Eilean is a multi-purpose single-tiered local authority (except police and fire) created on local government reorganisation in 1975, combining the Ross and Cromarty and Inverness-shire parts of the Outer Hebrides.

Acquisitions policy: Maintenance of local authority records for the Western Isles.

Archives of organisation: Minute books of the following:
Stornoway Town Council, 1863–1975 (under all forms of name); Western Isles Islands Council (Comhairle Nan Eilean), 1974–; Ross and Cromarty and Inverness-shire District Councils, 1930–70, parochial boards/parish councils, 1890s–1930, and education district sub-committees, 1927–1970s. Also housing registers, 1931–; abstracts of accounts (Stornoway Burgh), 1901–60; and valuation rolls (Stornoway Burgh and Lewis parishes), 1947–67.

Major collections: Records of Stornoway Road Trustees, 1866–1901 (also under later form of name); Stornoway Young Men's Mutual Association, 1871–8; Lewis Coffee House Committee, 1878–1910; D.L. Robertson Trust, 1930–; Dean of Guild Court, 1947–65.

Finding aids: Partial indexes to Stornoway Town Council minutes and Western Isles Islands Council minutes, for internal use.

Facilities: Photocopying.

1037 Western Isles Libraries (Comhairle Nan Eilean)

Address: 2 Keith Street, Stornoway, Isle of Lewis PA87 2QG

Telephone: (01851) 703064

Fax: (01851) 705657

Enquiries: The Chief Librarian, Mr Robert Eaves

Open: Mon–Thurs: 10.00–5.00 Fri: 10.00–7.00 Sat: 10.00–1.00

Access: Generally open to the public, following written or telephone enquiry.

Historical background: The Town Council Library until 1964, then Ross and Cromarty Branch Library until 1975, the Stornoway library is now the headquarters for the whole of the Western Isles.

Aquisitions policy: Building up local history and Gaelic collections, including archive material.

Major collections: Lewis School Board minute books, 1873–1919. Log-books of closed schools.
Aircraft movement log-books for Stornoway and Benbecula, 1972–.
Barvas parish rent ledgers, 1854–1920.

Non-manuscript material: T.B. Macaulay photographic collection; other miscellaneous photographs, postcards, slides.
Newspapers: *Stornoway Gazette*, 1917– (microfilm), 1940– (bound vols); *West Highland Free Press*, 1883–1952 (microfilm), 1972–; *Highland News*, 1883–1952 (microfilm).
Western Isles Islands Council (Comhairle Nan Eilean) agendas and minutes, 1974– (microfilm).

Finding aids: Local history catalogue. Partial subject index being compiled.

Facilities: Photocopying. Microfilm reader.

1038 King Edward VI College

Address: Stourbridge, West Midlands DY8 1TD

Telephone: (01384) 394223

Fax: (01384) 441699

Enquiries: The Keeper of the Archives

Open: Term: Mon–Fri: 9.30–4.00

Access: Bona fide researchers, by prior appointment only. Restrictions on certain deposited archives.

King Edward VI College was established in 1976 as a mixed sixth-form college on the site of the former King Edward VI Grammar School for boys. The grammar school had been established in 1552 by Royal Charter and replaced the school attached to the Chantry Chapel dating from about 1430. The archives department was set up in 1983 and holds material relating to the history and development of the school and college, including records of governors, property, finance, staff and students. There is a general index. Access is granted by the King Edward VI Foundation Trustees, and application to consult the archives should be made in writing to the Chairman of the Foundation Trustees.

1039 Wigtown District Museums Service

Parent organisation: Wigtown District Council

Address: Stranraer Museum, 55 George Street, Stranraer, Dumfries and Galloway DG9 7JP

Telephone: (01776) 705088

Fax: (01776) 704819

Enquiries: The Curator, Miss A. Reid

Open: Mon–Fri: 10.00–1.00; 2.00–5.00

Access: Generally open to the public, by appointment.

Historical background: Stranraer Museum was founded in 1939.

Acquisitions policy: Material from or relating to places, the environment, people and businesses within the Wigtown District.

Archives of organisation: Burgh archives of Stranraer, Wigtown, Newton Stewart and Whithorn, 16th century–. Some Wigtownshire County Council archives; Machars and Rhins councils administrative records; Commissioners of Police records.

Major collections: Business archives, including protocol books, 17th century–.
Collections of personal papers.

Non-manuscript material: Building warrant plans, late 1800s-.
Photograph collection.

Finding aids: Collections listed by NRA(S);

National Farmers' Union of Scotland, Wigtown area: NRA 24706.

Facilities: Photocopying.

1040 Shakespeare Birthplace Trust Records Office

Address: Henley Street, Stratford-upon-Avon, Warks CV37 6QW

Telephone: (01789) 204016

Fax: (01789) 296083

Enquiries: The Senior Archivist, Dr R. Bearman

Open: Mon–Fri: 9.30–1.00; 2.00–5.00 Sat: (except before bank holidays) 9.30–12.30

Access: Bona fide researchers.

Historical background: The records office was founded in the early 1860s, primarily as a repository for Shakespearean and allied material, but this limited objective was eclipsed at an early date on the rapid accumulation of documents relating to Stratford-upon-Avon and the surrounding district. It also acts as the Diocesan Record Office for Stratford and Shottery parishes, and is recognised as a place of deposit for public records.

Acquisitions policy: Until about 1945 the record office acted as a repository for any material from the locality which became available for deposit; as a result, not only Stratford-upon-Avon, but most places in Warwickshire and many in the neighbouring counties of Gloucestershire, Worcestershire and Oxfordshire are represented in the collections. Since c1945, with the expansion of neighbouring county offices, most acquisitions relate only to Stratford-upon-Avon and its immediate hinterland.

Major collections: Stratford-upon-Avon Borough Muniments.
Manorial records.
Warwickshire family collections: Ferrers of Baddesley Clinton; Throckmorton of Coughton Court; Gregory-Hood of Stivichal; Willoughby de Broke of Compton Verney; Leigh of Stoneleigh Abbey; Archer of Umberslade.
Robert Bell Wheler Collection: antiquarian papers, c1800–1820.
Records of Stratford-upon-Avon established and non-conformist churches; businesses and industries; clubs and societies.

Non-manuscript material: Large collection of topographical views (photographs, prints, drawings).

Local history and family history library, with usual reference collection on local history sources, including local newspapers.

Finding aids: Summary list of accessions reproduced by NRA and available in major libraries. Lists and persons, places and subjects indexes.

Facilities: Photocopying. Photography. Microfilm/fiche reader.

Conservation: Contracted out.

Publications: J.O. Halliwell: *A Descriptive Calendar of the Ancient Manuscripts and Records in the Possession of the Corporation of Stratford-upon-Avon* (1863).
L. Fox: 'Shakespeare's Birthplace Library, Stratford-upon-Avon', *Archives*, v/126 (1961), 90.
R. Bearman: *Shakespeare in the Stratford Records* (1994).

1041 Street Library

Parent organisation: Somerset County Library

Address: 1 Leigh Road, Street, Somerset BA16 0HA

Telephone: (01458) 42032

Fax: (01458) 841961

Enquiries: The Area Librarian, Ms Sue Crawley

Open: Mon, Tues, Thurs: 9.30–5.00 Fri: 9.30–7.00 Sat: 9.30–4.00
Closed Saturday preceding Easter Monday.

Access: Generally open to the public.

Historical background: The library was run privately by C. & J. Clark (shoe manufacturers) until 1959, and much archive material for the town is retained at their HQ, 40 High Street, Street.

Acquisitions policy: Occasional purchase of material on Lawrence and Clemence Housman, who lived in the town for 30 years.

Archives of organisation: Stock accession registers, 1900–c1950.

Major collections: Housman Collection: correspondence of Laurence (1865–1959) and Clemence (1861–1955) Housman, brother and sister of A.E. Housman (1859–1936), with Roger and Sarah Clark, 1908–c1930; original

sketches and writings; also correspondence with contemporary literary and artistic figures.

Non-manuscript material: First and other editions of publications of Laurence and Clemence Housman.

Finding aids: Catalogue and amendments.

Facilities: Photocopying. Microfilm/fiche readers.

1042 Gainsborough's House

Parent organisation: Gainsborough's House Society

Address: 46 Gainsborough Street, Sudbury, Suffolk CO10 6EU

Telephone: (01787) 372958

Enquiries: The Curator, H.G. Belsey

Open: Easter–Oct: Tues–Sat: 10.00–5.00 Sun: 2.00–5.00 Nov–Easter: Tues–Sat: 10.00–4.00 Sun: 2.00–4.00

Access: Bona fide researchers, by appointment only.

Historical background: Gainsborough's House Society was founded in 1958 and the house was opened in 1961. It is a small art centre which has collected information about Thomas Gainsborough (1727–88) and his associates over this period.

Acquisitions policy: Material relating to Thomas Gainsborough.

Archives of organisation: Minutes and papers relating to the activities of the society (incomplete).

Major collections: Correspondence and other papers relating to Thomas Gainsborough, including two collections from the Lane Poole family, descendants of Thomas Gainsborough's sister Susan Gardner.

Non-manuscript material: Photographs of paintings by Gainsborough and material relating to Sudbury.

Finding aids: Calendars and accession registers. NRA 33367.

Facilities: Photocopying. Photography. Microfiche reader.

Conservation: Contracted out.

Publications: Annual Review [includes references to new acquisitions].

1043 London Borough of Sutton
Heritage Service Archives Section

Address: Central Library, St Nicholas Way, Sutton, Surrey SM1 1EA

Telephone: (0181) 770 4745

Fax: (0181) 770 4666

Enquiries: The Archivist, Ms Kathleen Shawcross

Open: Tues, Fri: 9.30–12.00 Wed, Thurs: 2.00–7.30 Sat (1st and 3rd): 9.30–1.00; 2.00–4.45 Sun (1st and 3rd): 2.00–5.30

Access: Generally open to the public; an appointment is necessary and there is a booking system for microfiche readers.

Historical background: The present borough includes the ancient parishes of Beddington and Wallington, Sutton and Cheam, and Carshalton, with small areas of Cuddington and Woodmansterne. The library service began in 1935 and a collection of local history material was started in the 1940s. Following local government reorganisation in 1965 the present local history collection was formed by the amalgamation of the collections for the ancient parishes. The archives are kept separately from the local studies collection and comprise primary source material relating only to the borough, with the exception of Wallington (previously Croydon) Magistrates Court records and copies of Surrey parish registers. The archives section is recognised as a place of deposit for public records.

Acquisitions policy: To preserve primary documentation relating to the London Borough of Sutton from the earliest times. Material is accepted from within the council as well as from private individuals, organisations and institutions.

Archives of organisation: Records of the London Borough of Sutton, its predecessors and constituent parishes, including rate books, minute books and poor records, 1730–.

Major collections: Court rolls for the manors of Sutton, 1720–1907; and Carshalton, 1346–1701, 1834–1946; with financial papers, plans and deeds, 19th and 20th centuries.

Carshalton charities records, 1766–1940.
Non-conformist records, including Sutton Congregational Church, 1870–1960.
Phillips Collection relating to the Carew family of Beddington, 15th–17th centuries.
Dr Peatling Collection relating to Carshalton, including notes, pamphlets and cuttings, and transcriptions, 20th century.
River Wandle Collection of deeds relating to fishing rights and milling, 1640–1864.
Royal Female Orphanage, Beddington: minutes, pupil records and records of diphtheria epidemic, 1871–1968.

Non-manuscript material: Croydon Airport Collection, 1915–.
Photographs and glass negatives, 1860–(c20,000); slides (5000); paintings, drawings and prints (500).
Transcripts of Beddington parish registers and microfiche of Surrey parish registers.
Early editions of Surrey maps.
Newspapers, 1863–; newspapers and census returns (microfilm).
Films and tapes, including Sutton weekly talking newspaper, 1976–, oral history interviews and talks.

Finding aids: Catalogue with name, place and subject indexes. Calendar of Phillips papers. Surname indexes to censuses, 1841–81.

Facilities: Photocopying. Photograph copying. Microfilm/fiche readers/printers.

1044 Oscott College Archives

Parent organisation: Archdiocese of Birmingham

Address: St Mary's College, Oscott, Sutton Coldfield, West Midlands B73 5AA

Telephone: (0121) 354 2490

Fax: (0121) 355 3422

Enquiries: The Archivist, Miss Judith Champ

Open: By arrangement.

Access: Bona fide scholars, by written appointment.

Historical background: Founded in 1794 as a joint public school and theological training college, from 1899 the college has been a seminary for the training of Catholic clergy.

Acquisitions policy: Small accrual of rectors' papers and material produced by students.

Archives of organisation: Administrative records from the college's foundation, although more survives, 1830s-; includes account books, lectures notes of rectors, note-books of student societies and correspondence.

Finding aids: Catalogue of early records held at the college. See also NRA 8129.

Publications: J. Champ: *Oscott* (1987) [no. 3 of a series produced by the Archdiocese of Birmingham Historical Commission].

1045 Swansea City Archives

Parent organisation: Swansea City Council

Address: Guildhall, Swansea, West Glamorgan SA1 4PE

Telephone: (01792) 302126

Fax: (01792) 467432

Enquiries: The City Archivist, Dr J.R. Alban

Open: Tues, Wed: 9.30–12.45; 2.15–4.30

Access: Bona fide researchers. An appointment is preferred. Written application is needed for consultation of cine films and sound archives.

Historical background: Before 1835 the care and custody of the records were the responsibility of the Portreeve and thereafter of the Town Clerk. In the 1840s the older records were arranged and repaired by the antiquarian George Grant Francis. During the 1920s an honorary borough archivist was appointed, but from 1932 until 1974 the council's estate agent had a responsibility for historical records. Since 1974 an archivist, attached to the Chief Executive and Town Clerk's Department, has had charge of the records and responsibility for the management of modern departmental records. In 1968 the medieval charters and most of the early minute books were transferred to the Library of the University of Wales Swansea (entry **1046A**).

Aquisitions policy: Care and custody of the records of the city council and its departments.

Archives of organisation: Official records of the city council and its predecessor authorities, 18th–20th centuries.

Non-manuscript material: Photographic col-

lection, including prints, negatives, slides and printing blocks, relating to the Swansea area, mid-19th century– (*c*55,000).
Cine films of important civic events, 1936– (*c*110); videotapes of local events, 1979– (*c*30).
Sound Archive: tape-recordings of work experience in local industries in the Lower Swansea Valley; agricultural life in Gower; war; women in society (*c*130).
Collection of pamphlets and books on the history of the locality.

Finding aids: Lists and descriptive lists of most processed classes. General subject index in progress. Lists sent to NRA.

Facilities: Photocopying. Photography. Microfilm/fiche reader. Facilities for viewing cine films and listening to tapes (strictly by appointment only).

Conservation: Full in-house service for paper and parchment and bookbinding; outside work undertaken for other archives, libraries and museums (leaflet available).

Publications: *Air Raids on Swansea* (1981) [document resources pack].
J.R. Alban: *Calendar of Swansea Freemen's Records* (1982).
List of other publications available.

1046 University of Wales Swansea

A Library

Address: Singleton Park, Swansea, West Glamorgan SA2 8PP

Telephone: (01792) 205678 ext. 4048

Fax: (01792) 295851

Enquiries: The Archivist, Mrs Elizabeth Bennett

Open: Mon–Fri: 9.15–12.45; 2.00–5.00, afternoons strictly by appointment.

Access: Bona fide researchers; a prior arrangment is preferred. Permission is required to use the St David's Priory records.

Historical background: The University College of Swansea was founded in 1920. The library archives department has been built up over the last three decades. In 1969 the South Wales Coalfield Archive was established to preserve the documentary records of the mining community of South Wales.

Acquisitions policy: Documents which relate to existing material in the South Wales Coalfield Archive and local collections, or to University College Swansea, its research interests and prominent figures associated with it.

Major collections: South Wales Coalfield Archive: a large number of separate collections, including records of South Wales Miners' Federation/National Union of Mineworkers (South Wales area) and individual lodges; welfare associations, co-operative societies, political parties and individuals in the community.
Corporation of Swansea medieval charters and administrative records, c1530–c1850.
Family, estate and topographical papers of the Royal Institution of South Wales, including the Mackworth and Dillwyn-Llewelyn families and George Grant Francis (1814–82), antiquarian.
Industrial records of the main metallurgical firms in the area.
Mumbles Railway minutes, financial records and parliamentary and legal papers, 1804–1959.
St David's Priory parochial registers and records, 1808–1982.
Swansea and Gower Methodist circuit records, excluding registers, 1859–1984.

Non-manuscript material: Large collection of local material.
Swansea and Gower census returns, 1841–91 (microfilm).

Finding aids: Lists of collections, sent to NRA.

Facilities: Photocopying. Microfilm/fiche readers.

Publications: D. Bevan: *Guide to the South Wales Coalfield Archive* (1980).
Supplementary Guide to the South Wales Coalfield Archive (1983).

B South Wales Miners' Library

Address: Hendrefoelan House, Sketty, Swansea, West Glamorgan SA2 7NB

Telephone: (01792) 201231 ext. 2003

Enquiries: The Resource Co-ordinator, Ms Nicola Stonelake

The library, opened in 1973, is part of the University of Wales Swansea, which also houses the South Wales Coalfield Archive (entry **1046A**). A full description of the historical origins of the Miners' Library can be found

in H. Francis: 'The Origins of the South Wales Miners' Library', *History Workshop*, no. 2 (autumn 1976). It has a particularly strong socialist and trade union pamphlet collection, with sound, video and photographic collections.

1047 West Glamorgan County Archive Service

Parent organization: West Glamorgan County Council

Address: County Hall, Oystermouth Road, Swansea, West Glamorgan SA1 3SN

Telephone: (01792) 471589

Fax: (01792) 471340

Enquiries: The County Archivist, Miss S.G. Beckley

Open: Mon–Thurs: 9.00–5.00 Mon evening: 5.30–7.30, by appointment.

Access: Generally open to the public. Microfilm readers must be reserved in advance and a charge is made for microfilm use.

Historical background: The office was established in 1983 as a branch office of the Glamorgan Archive Service when West Glamorgan County Council built a new County Hall in Swansea. Documents relating to the West Glamorgan area were transferred from Cardiff to form the nucleus of the collection. In 1992 West Glamorgan County Council withdrew from the Glamorgan Joint Archive Service and established an independent county archive service. Since then the manuscript collections at Swansea, Neath and Port Talbot reference libraries have been transferred. The office holds ecclesiastical parish records from the West Glamorgan area of the Diocese of Swansea and Brecon. It is recognised as a place of deposit for public records.

Acquisitions policy: Archival material relating to the area of the county of West Glamorgan.

Archives of organisation: Usual local authority record holdings.

Major collections: Deposited local collections, including Neath Abbey Ironworks collection, containing plans, 1792–1892.

Finding aids: Major lists sent to NRA.

Facilities: Photocopying. Microfilm/fiche readers/printer.

Conservation: Contracted out to neighbouring record offices.

Publications: List of books, booklets, maps and facsimiles available on request.

1048 Bible Society

Address: Stonehill Green, Westlea, Swindon, Wilts SN5 7DG

Enquiries: The Senior Information Officer/Archivist, Mrs Ingrid A. Roderick (postal only)

Fax: (01793) 512539

Open: By arrangement with the Senior Information Officer/Archivist

Access: Generally open to the public; there is a 75–year closure period.

The British and Foreign Bible Society was formed in 1804 'to encourage a wider circulation of the Holy Scriptures'. It was and remains a non-denominational voluntary society, financed by the donations of its supporters and involved in the translation, publication and distribution of the Bible and related Christian materials throughout the world. It was incorporated by Royal Charter in 1948. In 1985 the majority of materials predating 1960 were transferred to the Cambridge University Library (entry 147A) where the same access conditions apply. The society continues to accept material directly related to the work and staff of the society. See *Historical Catalogue of Manuscripts in Bible House Library* (1982).

1049 Wiltshire Library and Museum Service

Address: Swindon Divisional Library, Regent Circus, Swindon, Wilts SN1 1QG

Telephone: (01793) 616277

Fax: (01793) 541319

Enquiries: The Divisional Librarian

Open: Mon–Thurs: 9.00–8.00 Wed: 9–00-5.00 Sat: 9.00–4.00

Access: Generally open to the public. Visitors who wish to use microfilm/fiche readers should telephone beforehand.

Historical background: The public library service in Wiltshire comprises (since 1974) the former Wiltshire County Library, Swindon Borough Library (successor to the Great Western Railway Mechanics' Institute Library) and Salisbury City Library. The archaeological sites and monuments record for Wiltshire, with more than 2000 archival aerial photographs of archaeological features, is maintained on computer database at Wiltshire Library and Museum Service HQ, Bythesea Road, Trowbridge, Wilts BA14 8BS. Its use is restricted to bona fide researchers. The collection of Alfred Williams (1877–1930), poet and author, has been transferred to Wiltshire Record Office, Trowbridge (entry 1060)

Acquisitions policy: Archival material is not now acquired, such material being directed to the Wiltshire Record Office.

Major collections: Great Western Railway: administrative and miscellaneous papers relating to the locomotive works and GWR generally (58 items).

Non-manuscript material: Local studies material in various media, including illustrations, maps, ephemera, newspapers and a few sound recordings as well as books and periodicals are collected and maintained principally in three collections, at Salisbury, Swindon and Trowbridge Headquarters.
Census enumerators' books, 1841–91; some records, principally minute books, of the Old and New Swindon Local Boards and UDCs; records of the Great Western Railway Medical Board Fund Society (microform).

Finding aids: A computerised union catalogue of local studies holdings.

Facilities: Photocopying. Microfilm/fiche readers/printer.

1050 Hydrographic Office

Parent organisation: Ministry of Defence

Address: Taunton, Somerset TA1 2DN

Telephone: (01823) 337900 ext. 3469

Fax: (01823) 284077

Enquiries: The Curator, Hydrographic Data Centre

Open: Mon–Fri: 9.00–4.30, by appointment

Access: Bona fide researchers, on written application.

Historical background: The department was established in 1795 to supply navigational charts to the navy. It is recognised as a place of deposit for public records.

Aquisitions policy: Continual addition of the results of hydrographic surveys and other worldwide hydrographic documents and information.

Archives of organisation: Reports, correspondence and record copies of sailing directions and other Hydrographic Department publications, 1795–.

Non-manuscript material: Royal Navy hydrographic surveys, 1750–, record copies of superseded Admiralty charts, 1800–, and other published charts, views and photographs.

Finding aids: Graphic indexes. Catalogues. Geographical and numerical listings.

Facilities: Photocopying. Photography. Microfilm/fiche readers.

Conservation: In-house service.

1051 Somerset Archive and Record Service

Parent organisation: Somerset County Council

Address: Somerset Record Office, Obridge Road, Taunton, Somerset TA2 7PU

Telephone: (01823) 337600 (appointments only) 278805 (enquiries and staff)

Fax: (01823) 325402

Enquiries: The County Archivist, Mr Adam Green

Open: Mon: 10.30–4.50 Tues–Thurs: 9.00–4.50 Fri: 9.00–4.20 Sat (usually 1st & 3rd of each month): 9.15–12.15
Closed for two weeks beginning the last Monday of January.

Access: All but a few restricted classes are available for consultation by the public, by appointment.

Historical background: Archives were first housed in a repository in 1929 and a professional archivist was appointed in 1935. The office acts as the Diocesan Record Office for the Diocese of Bath and Wells and is recognised as a place of deposit for public records. It also houses the document collection of the Somerset Archaeological and Natural History Society.

Acquisition policy: Archives illustrative of the history and heritage of Somerset, also covering the pre-1974 county.

Archives of organisation: Usual local authority holdings: the archives and modern records of Somerset County Council.

Major collections: Deposited collections, including the following which have a wider significance:
Dickinson MSS: merchants' accounts etc relating to Jamaica and trade with the Americas and the Baltic, 18th century.
Tudway MSS concerning the family estate on Antigua, late 17th–20th centuries.
Helyar MSS: Jamaican estate papers, c1660–1713.
Phelips MSS: political papers, mainly of Sir Robert Phelips, early–mid-17th century.
Papers of: William Kirkpatrick relating to India, 1787–1811; John Strachey, historian and scientist, early 18th century; Sir William Joliffe, politician, 1845–66; Edward Lear (1812–88), 1847–86; John Braham (1774–1856), singer, early 19th century; Chichester Fortescue, Lord Carlingford, politician, 1854–90; Hon. Aubrey Herbert relating to Albania and the Near East, c1900–23.

Finding aids: Catalogues; those of more significant collections are sent to the NRA. Name, place (including manorial) and subject indexes compiled from catalogues of holdings. Indexes to 1851 census; marriages, 1754–1837; marriage licences, 1765–; and apprenticeship, settlement and bastardy papers (all in progress).

Facilities: Photocopying. Microfilm/fiche readers.

Conservation: Full in-house paper repair service; outside work undertaken.

Publications: Interim Handlist of Somerset Quarter Session Documents and Other Official Records (1947).
Proceedings, Somerset Archaeological and Natural History Society [includes annual lists of main MS accessions].
Primary Genealogical Holdings.

1052 Ancient House Museum

Parent organisation: Norfolk Museums Service

Address: White Hart Street, Thetford, Norfolk
IP24 1AA

Telephone: (01842) 752599

Enquiries: The Curator, Mr Oliver Bone

Open: Mon–Fri: 10.00–5.00

Access: Generally open to the public, by
appointment.

Historical background: The Ancient House
Museum was founded in 1924 by Thetford
Borough Council following the donation to the
town of the building by Prince Frederick
Duleep Singh (1867–1926). Since 1974 it has
been part of the Norfolk Museums Service, a
joint district and county council service.

Acquisitions policy: The museum collects material relating to the local history and archaeology
of Thetford and surrounding parishes.

Archives of organisation: Accessions registers
for the museum and its predecessor Mechanics
Institute, and correspondence with donors,
1924–, minutes of governing body, 1974–, posters relating to events and press cuttings, mainly
1974–.

Major collections: Duleep Singh Collection:
manuscripts, personalia, maps, portraits, prints,
watercolours.

Non-manuscript material: Plans, drawings,
photographs and maps.

Finding aids: Card index. Computerised catalogue in progress.

Facilities: Photocopying. Photography.

Conservation: Paper conservation available
in-house; some outside work is undertaken.

1053 Blundell's School

Address: Muniment Room, Tiverton, Devon
EX16 4DN

Telephone: (01884) 252543

Fax: (01884) 243238

Enquiries: The Head of History, Mr T.H.C.
Noon

Open: School term.

Access: Generally open to the public, by
appointment only.

Historical background: The school was
founded in 1604 and its records have accumulated since then. There has been an organised
muniment room since before World War II.

Acquisitions policy: We accept anything of
local/school importance.

Archives of organisation: Various wills and
deeds relating to Peter Blundell (1520–1601),
merchant and endower of the school, and the
Feoffees of his Good Uses in Tiverton, 1456–.
Order books of Feoffees, 1660–; Great Account
Book of Peter Blundell's Good Uses, 1610–
1847, and three volumes since; register of pupils,
1770–; register/minutes of old boys, 1775–1850,
1870–; *Blundellian* (school magazine), 1861–6;
1877–.
Records relating to the 'Case in Chancery',
1839–46.

Non-manuscript material: Collection of watercolour portraits of Tivertonians by George
Capron, c1840–50. Various etchings/prints of
old school and new school.
Tiverton Gazette, 1890–1939.

Finding aids: The collections are catalogued for
the most part.

Facilities: Photocopying. Photography.

1054 Isle of Mull Museum

Address: Columba Buildings, Tobermory, Isle
of Mull PA75 6NY

Enquiries: The Librarian, B. B. Whittaker

Open: Easter–mid-Oct: Mon–Fri: 10.30–4.30
Sat: 10.30–1.30 Mid-Oct–Easter: by arrangement.

Access: Generally open to the public on payment of Museum Association membership fee.
An appointment is necessary during the
museum closure period.

Acquisitions policy: To collect and keep material
of historic interest to the Isle of Mull, adjacent
islands and the nearby mainland, particularly
Morren and Ardnamurchan.

Major collections: Solicitors' and tradermen's
papers and legal documents relating to Mull,
mid-19th century–.
Records of Alexander Crawford Trust, 1854–
1911; George Willison (1741–97) Trust, and

British Fisheries Society, early–mid-19th century.
Macquarie papers, 1846–86.

Non-manuscript material: Plans and photographic collection, mainly Tobermory and Tobermory Bay, 1880.

Finding aids: Subject index.

Facilities: Photography. Photocopying.

Conservation: By Scottish Museum Council.

1055 Tonbridge Central Library

Parent organisation: Kent County Council

Address: Avebury Avenue, Tonbridge, Kent TN9 1TG

Telephone: (01732) 352754

Fax: (01732) 358300

Enquiries: The Reference Librarian

Open: Mon, Tues, Thurs: 9.30–7.00 Wed, Fri: 9.30–6.00 Sat: 9.30–5.00

Access: Generally open to the public, on prior application.

Historical background: The public library started in Tonbridge in 1882, but most archival material has been collected only since the 1960s.

Acquisitions policy: To strengthen the existing collection relating to the Tonbridge area, although the library does not seek to compete with the local county record office.

Major collections: Local history collections, including minutes of Tonbridge Local Board, 1870–94; Tonbridge UDC, 1895–1970.
Census returns for Tonbridge/Malling Division, 1841–91.
Some items from local families, including wills.

Non-manuscript material: Pamphlets and posters relating to the Tonbridge area.

Finding aids: Indexes.

Facilities: Photocopying. Microfilm reader/printer.

1056 Torquay Central Library

Parent organisation: Devon Library Services

Address: Lymington Road, Torquay, Devon TQ1 3DT

Telephone: (01803) 386505

Fax: (01803) 386507

Enquiries: The Reference Librarian

Open: Mon–Wed, Fri: 9.30–7.00 Thurs,Sat: 9.30–4.00

Access: Generally open to the public; prior enquiry is advisable.

Historical background: Torbay Library Services operated as an independent library authority before local government reorganisation in 1974 and now forms part of Devon Library Services.

Acquisitions policy: To acquire MSS that reflect the development of the Torbay area. Certain categories of records, such as parish registers and school board records have been transferred to the Devon Record Office, Exeter (entry **323**).

Major collections: Archives of the predecessor authorities of Torbay District Council, including Torbay, Paignton, Brixham, Churston Ferrers, St Marychurch, Cockington and Tormohun.

Non-manuscript material: A good local studies collection, including illustrations, maps, newspapers and cutting files.

Facilities: Photocopying. Microform reader/printers.

Publications: J.R Pike: *Torquay, Torbay: a Bibliographical Guide* (Torquay, 1973).
Similiar guides to Brixham (1973) and Paignton (1974).

1057 Torquay Museum

Parent organisation: Torquay Natural History Society

Address: 529 Babbacombe Road, Torquay, Devon TQ1 1HG

Telephone: (01803) 293975

Enquiries: The Curator, Dr M.J. Bishop

Open: Mon–Fri: 10.00–4.45

Access: Strictly by appointment.

Historical background: The Torquay Natural History Society was founded in 1844 for the study of the natural sciences. Its primary aim was the establishment of a natural history library, but in the following year a museum to illustrate Devonian natural history was also set up.

Acquisitions policy: To acquire material illustrative of natural history, archaeology, anthropology, history, folklore and the industrial and fine arts, especially in relation to the Torquay area.

Archives of organisation: Records of the society, including annual reports, 1845–; *Journal* and *Transactions*, 1909–.

Major collections: Papers of William Pengally (1812–94), founder member, honorary secretary and president; and of Father John MacEnery, particularly concerning the study of Kent's Cavern.
Hester Pengelly Collection of autograph letters.

Non-manuscript material: Hambling Collection of photographs (*c*3500).
Torquay Directory, 1846–1948.

Finding aids: Complete index of pictorial records. Catalogue in preparation.

Facilities: Photocopying. Photography by arrangement.

1058 Dartington Hall Records Office

Parent organisation: Dartington Hall Trust

Address: Highcross House, Dartington Hall, Totnes, Devon TQ9 6ED

Telephone: (01803) 864114

Fax: (01803) 867057

Enquiries: The Archivist and Curator, Ms Maggie Giraud

Open: By arrangement.

Access: Bona fide researchers, by appointment.

Historical background: Dartington was founded in 1925 by Leonard and Dorothy Elmhirst, who established a programme of rural regeneration on the estate and funded various pioneering educational and artistic ventures. It received many refugees from Nazi Germany during the 1930s.

Acquisitions policy: To consolidate the archives of the Dartington Hall Trust.

Archives of organisation: Records of the Dartington Hall Trust, including estate documents and plans, 1925–.
Papers of Leonard and Dorothy Elmhirst.
Correspondence files of staff, visitors, students and those connected with the arts, including Imogen Holst (1907–84), Aldous Huxley (1894–1963), Rudolph Laban (*d* 1958), Bernard Leach (1887–1979), Henry Moore (1898–1986), A.S. Neill (1883–1973), Sean O'Casey (1884–1964), Arthur Waley (1889–1966) and H.G. Wells (1866–1946).

Non-manuscript material: Photographs of individuals and of all aspects of the estate; film and video collections; tape-recordings.

Facilities: Photocopying. Photography.

Conservation: In-house bookbinder; conservation work contracted out.

Publications: M. Young: *The Elmhirsts of Dartington: the Creation of a Utopian Community* (London, 1982).

1059 Treorchy Library

Parent organisation: Rhondda Borough Council

Address: Station Road, Treorchy, Mid Glamorgan CF42 6NN

Telephone: (01443) 773204

Fax: (01443) 777047

Enquiries: The Borough Librarian, Miss Susan Scott

Open: Mon–Thurs: 9.30–5.15 Fri: 1.00–8.00 Sat: 9.00–12.00

Access: Generally open to the public.

Historical background: The Library Acts were adopted in 1933 but the service commenced in 1939.

Major collections: Various MSS and archival collections of local history interest, including Welsh Congregational Church records.

Non-manuscript material: Music scores and literature in the Welsh collection.
Rhondda area OS maps, photographs and census, 1841–91 (microfilm).
Burial registers, 1877–, for municipal cemeteries in Rhondda.

Rhondda Leader, 1897–; *Western Mail*, 1947–; and *South Wales Echo*, 1987– (microfilm).

Finding aids: Local history catalogue.

Facilities: Photocopying. Microfilm/fiche readers/printers.

1060 Wiltshire Record Office

Address: County Hall, Trowbridge, Wilts BA14 8JG

Telephone: (01225) 713138

Enquiries: The County Archivist, Mr S.D. Hobbs

Open: Mon, Tues, Thurs, Fri: 9.00–5.00 Wed: 9.00–7.45

Access: Generally open to the public. The office operates the CARN reader's ticket system.

Historical background: The office was established in 1947. Previously, the Wiltshire Archaeological Society collected material and this was incorporated in 1947. When the Salisbury Diocesan Office was closed in 1980 the great majority of records was transferred to Wiltshire Record Office. Salisbury District Council Muniment Room records were transferred in 1982 and collections of papers have also been transferred from Wiltshire Library and Museum Service, Swindon Divisional Library (entry **1049**). The office is the Diocesan Record Office for Salisbury and also Bristol (Wiltshire parish records). It is recognised as a place of deposit for public records.

Archives of organisation: Usual local authority holdings.

Major collections: Deposited local collections, including records from Wilton House, Salisbury Museum Collection and Wiltshire Archaeological Society.

Facilities: Photocopying. Photography and microfilming by arrangement. Microfilm reader/printer.

Conservation: A full in-house service, including advice to owners of archives.

Publications: M.G. Rathbone: *Guide to the Records in the Custody of the Clerk of the Peace for Wiltshire* (1959).
P.M. Stewart: *Guide to the Records of the Bishop, the Archdeacons of Salisbury and Wiltshire* (1973).

1061 Cornwall County Record Office

Address: County Hall, Truro, Cornwall TR1 3AY

Telephone: (01872) 73698/323127

Fax: (01872) 70340

Enquiries: The County Archivist, Mrs C.R. North

Open: Tues–Thurs: 9.30–1.00; 2.00–5.00 Fri: 9.30–4.30 Sat: 9.00–12.00
Closed the Saturday preceding every bank holiday; enquire for December stock-taking closure.

Access: Generally open to the public, by appointment only. The office operates the CARN reader's ticket system. Written enquiries must be made beforehand to the County Archivist concerning the availability of Truro Cathedral and Arundel records.

Historical background: The office was established in 1951 with the appointment of an archivist. A newly built office was opened in 1988. It also acts as the Diocesan Record Office for Truro and is recognised as a place of deposit for public records.

Acquisitions policy: Historical material relating to the county of Cornwall.

Archives of organisation: Usual local authority record holdings.

Major collections: Deposited collections, primarily of local interest, including Truro Cathedral and Arundel family records.

Facilities: Photocopying. Photography and microfilming by arrangement. Microfilm reader/printer.

Conservation: Full in-house service; some outside work is undertaken.

Publications: Series of free information leaflets available (send SAE), including list of publications (no. 3).
A Brief Guide to Sources (revision in progress).
List of Accessions (1981–) [annual].
Sources for Cornish Family History (rev. 1994).

1062 Courtney Library and Cornish History Library

Parent organisation: The Royal Institution of Cornwall

Address: River Street, Truro, Cornwall TR1 1HN

Telephone: (01872) 72205

Fax: (01872) 40514

Enquiries: The Librarian, Ms Angela Broome, The Hon. Archivist, H.L. Douch

Open: Mon–Fri: 10.00–1.00; 2.00–5.00

Access: Generally open to the public; an appointment is recommended.

Historical background: Founded in 1818, the institution sponsored a museum from the beginning. The muniment room was added in 1936 and in 1990 its contents were transferred to a modern archive and book store. Until 1951 the institution was the official repository for historic documents in Cornwall.

Acquisitions policy: Principally non-archival material, including local historians' collections, relating to Cornish life as represented in the museum's collections.

Archives of organisation: Records of the institute, including minutes, 1818–; letter-books, c1905–38; accession lists, accounts and building plans, 19th and 20th centuries.

Major collections: Charles Henderson Collection: Cornish family estate documents, medieval–17th century.
Couch Family of Fowey Collection, 18th and 19th centuries.
Shaw Collection *re* Cornish Methodism.
Hamilton-Jenkin Collection of mine-plans and mine account-books, 18th–19th centuries.
Enys Collection of autographs, many of national importance.
Richard Trevithick and Jonathan Hornblower, correspondence with Davies Gilbert, mainly *re* steam-engines.

Non-manuscript material: Cornish photograph collection, 19th and 20th centuries (c25,000).
Heard of Truro, printers, job-work, including posters,1830s-1840s.
Local newspapers: *Royal Cornwall Gazette*, 1801–1951; *West Briton*, 1810–56.

Microfilms of parish registers, about half the ancient parishes, mainly those in the West.

Finding aids: Catalogues of all collections. Place, name and various subject indexes.

Facilities: Photocopying. Microfilm/fiche readers/printer.

Conservation: Contracted out.

Publications: Annual *Journal* of the institution. Newsletter (bi-annual).
Lists of transcripts and microfilms of Cornish parish registers.

1063 Truro School

Address: Trennick Lane, Truro, Cornwall TR1 1TH

Telephone: (01872) 72763

Enquiries: The Director of Studies, Mr Nigel Baker

Open: Mon–Fri: 9.00–4.30

Access: Bona fide researchers, by appointment. Records may not always be accessible during school holidays.

Historical background: Founded as the Wesleyan Middle Class School for Boys in 1880, its name was changed to Truro College and then in 1931 to Truro School.

Acquisitions policy: To maintain the school's archives.

Archives of organisation: Minutes of governors' and staff meetings; register of pupils; fee books; accounts, 1880–. School magazine and photographs.

Facilities: Photocopying.

Publications: N.J. Baker (ed.): *Truro School Centenary Booklet* (1980).

1064 Rugby Football Union Museum and Library

Address: Twickenham, Middx TW1 1DZ,

Telephone: (0181) 892 8161 ext. 246

Enquiries: The Curator and Librarian

Open: Mon–Fri, by arrangement.

Access: Bona fide researchers, by prior appointment

The English Rugby Football Union is an amateur association founded in 1871 in London. The museum and library were opened in 1984, but memorabilia has been collected throughout the union's existence, and there is the only complete set of *Football Annuals*, 1865–. The archives comprise a fairly complete set of minutes, 1871–, and correspondence. The museum is currently being rebuilt and will be reopened at the same address with improved facilities for research at the end of 1995, when it will be called 'The Twickenham Experience'.

1065 St Mary's University College

Parent organisation: University of Surrey

Address: Waldegrave Road, Strawberry Hill, Twickenham, Middx TW1 4SX

Telephone: (0181) 892 0051 ext. 252 (Library)

Fax: (0181) 744 2080

Enquiries: The College Archives, Mr Ken Breen, Walpole House Library, The Librarian, Miss Sheila F Kent

Open: College Archives by arrangement only. Library: Term: Mon–Fri: 9.00–9.00 Sat: 9.30–12.30 Vacation: Mon–Fri: 9.00–5.00 Closed for one week for stock-taking at the end of June.

Access: Open to members of the public.

Historical background: The college was founded in 1850 to train Catholic teachers for Catholic schools. It removed from Hammersmith to Strawberry Hill in 1925. In 1972 the college diversified and began to provide general degrees in humanities and sciences as well as teaching degrees. Its degrees were originally validated by London University but are now validated by the University of Surrey.

Acquisitions policy: To maintain the collections.

Archives of organisation: Archives of the college.

Major collections: Leigh Bequest: books and MSS on medieval philosophy donated by Dr Yolanthe Leigh, including research papers relating mainly to Duns Scotus.
Anthony West (*d* 1993) Bequest: MSS and research papers, concerned mainly with Irish history and literature.

Finding aids: Typed list of Leigh Bequest, excluding research papers.

Facilities: Photocopying. Microfilm reader/printers.

1066 Laurel and Hardy Museum

Address: 4c Upper Brook Street, Ulverston, Cumbria LA12 7LA

Telephone: (01229) 582292

Enquiries: The Curator, Mr Bill Cubin

Open: Mon–Sat: 10.00–4.00

Access: Generally open to the public.

Since the early 1970s a private collection of material relating to the film comedians Stan Laurel (1890–1965) and Oliver Hardy (1892–1957) has been built up. This includes personal scrapbooks, letters, films, photographs and audio-visual tapes. The collection is being actively augmented by purchase.

1067 Brunel University Library

Address: Kingston Lane, Uxbridge, Middx UB8 3PH

Telephone: (01895) 274000 ext. 2785

Fax: (01895) 232806

Enquiries: The Sub-Librarian, Mr John Worthy

Open: Mon: 10.00–9.00 Tues–Thurs: 9.00–9.00 Fri: 9.00–6.00 Sat: 9.30–1.00 Sun: 2.00–7.00

Access: Bona fide researchers.

Historical background: The university developed from the College of Advanced Technology, Acton, London, and received its Royal Charter in 1966.

Archives of organisation: Minutes and other records of the university, *c*1960–.

Major collections: Transport history collections of the following railway historians: Harold Borley (1895–1989), Charles Clinker (1906–83), David Garnett (1909–84), Stuart Leslie Kear and John Palmer.

Working-class autobiographies, 1800–1945 (*c*400).

Non-manuscript material: Railway photographic collections of Charles Clinker, Charles Mowat and Chris Wookey.

Finding aids: Lists of photographs, maps and Railway Clearing House material.

Facilities: Photocopying. Microfilm/fiche readers.

Publications: Railway Maps and the Railway Clearing House: the David Garnett Collection in Brunel University Library (1986).

1068 Hillingdon Heritage Service

Parent organisation: London Borough of Hillingdon

Address: Central Library, High Street, Uxbridge, Middx UB8 1HD

Telephone: (01895) 250702

Fax: (01895) 239794

Enquiries: The Local Studies Librarian, Mrs C. Cotton

Open: Mon: 9.30–8.00 Tues–Thurs: 1.00–5.30 Fri: 9.30–5.30 Sat: 9.30–12.00; 1.00–4.00

Access: Generally open to the public; an appointment is preferred for detailed enquiries.

Historical background: The Uxbridge Collection began in the 1930s when the library opened under the guidance of H.T. Hanson, editor of the *Uxbridge Gazette*. In 1965, with the formation of the present borough, the archives of the constituent authorities (Uxbridge Borough, Ruislip-Northwood, Hayes and Harlington, and Yiewsley-West Drayton UDCs) were acquired. Following internal reorganisation in 1991, the Heritage Service was formed comprising local studies, museum and archives services.

Acquisitions policy: To collect and make available all material relating to the past, present and future of the borough.

Archives of organisation: Records of Uxbridge Board of Health, UDC and Borough, 1856–1965; Ruislip-Northwood and Hayes and Harlington UDCs, 1904–65, Yiewsley-West Drayton UDC, 1911–65 and the London Borough of Hillingdon, 1965–.

Major collections: Charters and other records of the Lords in Trust for the Manor of Uxbridge, 1188–1802.
Minet Family Collection: deeds, maps and plans *re* property in Hayes, 1699–1960s.
Parish records, excluding registers, of St John the Baptist, Hillingdon, 1695–1897.
Records of Providence Congregational Church, Uxbridge, 1789–1962.
W.F. Eves, architects, plans, 1894–1949.

Non-manuscript material: Maps (*c*800), photographs (*c*10,000), prints and drawings. Cine films (22).
Middlesex Advertiser and Gazette, 1871– (bound vols).

Finding aids: Typescript guide to London Local History Resources: London Borough of Hillingdon (1993). Lists; sent to NRA. Local studies catalogue.

Facilities photocopying: Microfilm/fiche readers/printers.

Conservation: Contracted out.

1069 The John Goodchild Collection
Local Studies Centre

Address: The Basement, Drury Lane Library, Drury Lane, Wakefield, West Yorks WF1 2TE

Telephone: (01924) 891871

Enquiries: John Goodchild

Open: By prior arrangement.

Access: Generally open to the public, by appointment.

Historical background: Previously based with Wakefield Department of Archives and Local Studies, the collection will open in 1995.

Major collections: MSS, books, pamphlets, maps and illustrations relating to industry, transport, government, and social, political and religious life in the central part of the West Riding, 12th century–.

Facilities: Card indexes. Advice service.

1070 National Arts Education Archives
The Lawrence Batley Centre

Parent organisation: National Arts Education Archive Trust

Address: University College, Bretton Hall, West Bretton, Wakefield, West Yorks WF4 4LG

Telephone: (01924) 830261 ext. 211 (Director) ext. 278 (Curator)

Fax: (01924) 830521

Enquiries: The Director, Prof. Ron George or The Centre Administrator, Mr Leonard Bartle

Open: Mon–Fri: 9.30–5.00

Access: Scholars, students and members of the general public; an appointment with the Centre Administrator is preferred.

Historical background: The archive was established in 1985 to provide a trace of the developments in art, craft and design education, primarily in the United Kingdom. It has increasingly developed international links and reflects the development of the arts in education. In 1989 a new purpose-designed, environmentally safe centre was built to house the growing collection. The archive is registered with the Museums and Galleries Commission.

Acquisitions policy: Seeks to acquire, by gift, fixed-term loan or purchase, examples of significant material relevant to the purpose of the archive, and to maintain and develop the archive for the advancement of the education of the public in the arts and the promotion of research into the arts.

Archives of organisation: Papers of early discussions and establishment of the NAEA.

Major collections: These are principally non-MSS (see below), illustrating the developments in the child art and basic design movements in art education, in particular the papers of the Society for Education through Art Conference, 1956.
Barclay Russell Collection: papers and correspondence concerning the art movement, 1930–60.
Papers, speeches and writings of Sir Alec Clegg (1909–86), art educationalist, as Chief Education Officer, West Riding of Yorkshire, 1945–74.

Non-manuscript material: Paintings, drawings, sculptures, ceramics, books, periodicals, films, videos, slides, photographs, audio tapes, games and puzzles are represented throughout the collections, which include:
Basic Design Movement Collections: Victor Pasmore, Harry Thubron, Richard Hamilton, Tom Hudson and others, c1950–60s.
Franz Cizek, Austrian progressive art educationalist, early 20th century.
A.E. Halliwell, graphic and industrial design work, 1920–50.
ILEA collection of child art in London, 20th century.
Don Pavey Collection: art-based games, puzzles and artefacts, 19th and 20th centuries.
William Johnston Collection: selection of paintings and drawings, 1920–80.
Brian Allison International Collection *re* world presidency of INSEA and presidency of NSEAD, 20th century.
National Media Education Archive, 20th century.
Independent Television Commission Collection: educational television broadcasts with supporting material, 20th century.
National Exhibition of Children's Art, 1980–92.

Finding aids: Computerised catalogue, printouts available on request. Search facilities are available to visitors.

Facilities: Photocopying. Photography. Audio and visual playback. Slide projector.

Conservation: Contracted out when funding allows.

Publications: List of collections.
Publicity booklet/leaflet.
Series of occasional papers.

1071 Wakefield Metropolitan District
Department of Archives and Local Studies

Address: Library Headquarters, Balne Lane, Wakefield, West Yorks WF2 0DQ

Telephone: (01924) 371231 ext. 213/214

Fax: (01924) 379287

Enquiries: The Assistant Librarian, Local Studies and Archives HQ

Open: Mon: 9.30–7.00 Tues–Fri: 9.30–5.00 Sat (2nd of each month): 9.30–1.00

Access: Generally open to the public, preferably by appointment.

Historical background: The office was established in 1975 and houses a number of small collections from the former Wakefield City Library, with further collections added by Wakefield Metropolitan District Libraries. The John Goodchild Collection has now been established as an independent collection (entry **1069**).

Major collections: Pilkington family papers, 18th–19th centuries.
R.L. Arundale Antiquarian Collection relating to Horbury.
Wakefield Street Commissioners records, late 18th–early 19th centuries.

Non-manuscript material: Wakefield Corporation minutes.
OS maps and local illustrations in library.

Finding aids: Card indexes.

Facilities: Photocopying. Photography. Microfilm reader/printer.

Publications: *Wakefield District Archives: a Handlist for Students*, Part I: *Manuscripts relating to Local Social Life* (1976).
More than 100 other publications on regional historical themes.

1072 West Yorkshire Record Office: Wakefield Headquarters

Address: Registry of Deeds, Newstead Road, Wakefield, West Yorks WF1 2DE

Telephone: (01924) 295982

Fax: (01924) 201651

Enquiries: The Principal Archivist, Mr P.M. Bottomley or The Archivist to the Joint Committee, Mr R. Frost

Open: Mon: 9.30–8.00 Tues–Thurs: 9.30–5.00
Closed on council holidays and for one week of February for stock-taking.

Access: Free public access to all records not subject to depositors' closure periods.

Historical background: The former West Yorkshire Metropolitan County Council established a county record office in 1974. In 1982–3 the then separate district archive services in Bradford, Calderdale, Kirklees, Leeds and Wakefield were joined with the county's service to form the West Yorkshire Archive Service. When the county council was abolished in 1986 the five districts agreed to continue operating a unified archive service with Wakefield as the lead authority. The joint service accordingly operates record offices in each of the five districts and also administers the archive collections of the Yorkshire Archaeological Society in Leeds (entry **449**). It is recognised as a place of deposit for public records.

Acquisitions policy: Archives relating to Wakefield Metropolitan District, or to existing holdings of county-wide significance.

Archives of organisation: West Riding Quarter Sessions, 1637–1971; West Riding County Council, 1889–1974; West Yorkshire Metropolitan County Council, 1974–86; West Riding Registry of Deeds, 1704–1970; the boroughs, UDCs and RDCs of Altofts, Barnsley, Castleford, Featherstone, Hemsworth, Horbury, Knottingley, Normanton, Ossett, Pontefract, Sandal Magna, Stanley, Wakefield and Whitwood, 1894–1974; Wakefield Metropolitan DC, 1974–.

Major collections: Wakefield Diocese parishes and cathedral, 1538–, and non-conformist circuits and chapels, 1718–.
West Riding wills, 1858–1941; West Yorkshire valuation offices, petty sessions, coroners, motor taxation offices, prisons and hospitals; Wakefield schools.
Political parties, trade unions, trades councils, transport undertakings (notably British Waterways Board, 1652–1976) and businesses.

Non-manuscript material: OS maps of the West Riding, *c*1948–.
West Riding electoral registers, 1840–; national probate calendars, 1858–; general statutes, 1215–; local Acts, 1810–; Journals of the Houses of Lords and Commons.

Finding aids: Catalogues sent to NRA. Listed collections indexed at accession level. An increasing proportion of the holdings is summarised and indexed on a computerised county-wide database.

Facilities: Photocopying. Photography. Microfilm/fiche readers.

Conservation: Full in-house archive conservation and binding service. The office participates in the Society of Archivists' conservator training scheme. Some outside work is undertaken.

Publications: B.J. Barber and M.W. Beresford: *The West Riding County Council, 1889– 1974: Historical Studies* (1978).
R.W. Unwin: *Search Guide to the English Land Tax* (1982).
Guide to the West Yorkshire Archive Service for Family Historians (1984).
B.J. Barber: *Guide to the Quarter Sessions of the West Riding of Yorkshire, 1637–1971, and other Official Records* (1984).
E. Berry: 'The West Yorkshire Archive Service: the Development of a Unified Service, 1974– 1983, and its Work to 1986', *Journal of the Society of Archivists*, viii/4 (1987).
S. Thomas: 'The West Yorkshire Archive Service', *Northern History*, xxiii (1987).
See also West Yorkshire Archive Service, entries **370**, **448** and **449**.

1073 Walsall Local History Centre

Address: Essex Street, Walsall, West Midlands WS2 7AS

Telephone: (01922) 721305, 34954 (conservation)

Enquiries: The Archivist/Local Studies Office, Mr C.S. Latimer

Open: Tues, Thurs: 9.30–5.30 Wed: 9.30–7.00 Fri: 9.30–5.00 Sat: 9.30–1.00

Access: Generally open to the public. Booking is necessary for microfilm/fiche readers.

Historical background: The Local Studies Room of Walsall Central Library was established by a local newspaper, the *Walsall Observer*, to mark its centenary in 1968. It housed the Local Studies Library and a collection of miscellaneous MS material acquired over the years by successive librarians. A full archives service, serving the whole of the Metropolitan Borough of Walsall, has been in operation since 1978. In 1986 the service was relocated at a former school which had been specially converted and in 1990 a conservation workshop and photography darkroom were added. It is recognised as a place of deposit for public records.

Acquisitions policy: To locate, collect and preserve archival and local studies material relating to all aspects of life and work in Walsall.

Archives of organisation: Records of Walsall Quarter Sessions, magistrates' and coroners' courts, 19th–20th centuries.
Local government records: Walsall Metropolitan Borough and the superseded Urban Districts of Aldridge, Brownhills, Darlaston and Willenhall, mainly 19th–20th centuries; Walsall Corporation, 17th–20th centuries.

Major collections: Local non-conformist church records, 18th–20th centuries.
Many important collections of records of local businesses, societies and organisations, mainly 19th–20th centuries.
Walsall Hospital records, 19th–20th centuries.

Non-manuscript material: Photographs (*c*10,000) and videos of all parts of the borough.
Microfilm copies of local newspapers, 1856–; census, 1841–91; and church and cemetery registers, 17th–20th centuries.
Large collection of local posters, pamphlets, sale and trade catalogues
Tape-recordings (*c*700) of reminiscences of local residents.

Finding aids: Most material is listed and indexed.

Facilities: Photocopying. Photography. Microfilm/fiche reader/printers.

Conservation: In-house service; undertakes outside work.

Publications: *Handlist of Accessions* [updated annually].
3–4 publications on local history published annually; free list available.

1074 Sandwell Community History and Archives Service

Address: Smethwick Community Library, High Street, Smethwick, Warley, West Midlands B66 1AB

Telephone: (0121) 558 2561

Fax: (0121) 555 6064

Enquiries: The Local Studies Officer, Mr J.K. Maddison, The Archivist, Miss C.M. Harrington

Open: Mon, Fri: 9.00–7.00 Tues–Thurs: 9.30– 6.00 Sat: 9.00–1.00

Access: Generally open to the public. It is

advisable to book for use of the microfilm/fiche readers.

Historical background: Libraries in Sandwell have collected archival material since the 19th century. In 1988 the archives and local history material from Oldbury, Rowley Regis, Smethwick, Tipton, Wednesbury and West Bromwich, the predecessor authorities of Sandwell Metropolitan Borough, were brought together in a purpose-adapted centre at Smethwick Community Library. The Community History and Archives Service acts as a Diocesan Record Office for Birmingham (Rural Deanery of Warley) and is recognised as a place of deposit for public records.

Acquisitions policy: To acquire any documents that become available from industry, local government, or any other source relating to the Sandwell area.

Major collections: Parish registers, 1539–; Methodist records, 1832–.
Local government records, mid-19th century–.
Records of Patent Shaft Steel Works, Wednesbury.
Records of T.W. Camm stained glass studio, Smethwick, 1866–1960.

Non-manuscript material: Maps; local newspapers; photographs (*c*12,000).

Finding aids: Catalogues and indexes.

Facilities: Photocopying. Photography. Microfilm/fiche readers/printer.

1075 Longleat House

Address: Warminster, Wilts BA12 7NN

Telephone: (01985) 844400

Fax: (01985) 844885

Enquiries: The Librarian and Archivist, Dr K.D. Harris

Open: Mon–Fri: 10.00–1.00; 2.15–4.15

Access: Access is by appointment only and is usually restricted to established scholars and research students. Written application is preferred and a charge is made. Computer catalogue searches are available by post for a fee.

Historical background: The collection is owned by the Marquess of Bath. It has grown up with the house, largely completed in 1580 when the builder, Sir John Thynne, steward to Protector Somerset, died. It reflects the family's land

acquisitions, as well as its marital alliances, and the history of the house, its contents and the surrounding parkland.

Acquisitions policy: Limited acquisition of items connected with the existing holdings.

Archives of organisation: Papers of the following families and individuals: Thynne, Devereux, Dudley, Talbot, Coventry, Whitelocke, Granville-Carteret, Portland, Prior, Seymour.
Monastic records, e.g. Glastonbury Abbey, Cirencester, Amesbury, Maiden Bradley and Longleat.
Estate papers, mainly for Wiltshire, Somerset, Dorset, Shropshire and Herefordshire, and also for Northamptonshire (Norton Hall estate) and lands held in Ireland and North Carolina. The records include manorial court rolls, papers and accounts, 14th–19th centuries, surveys, 14th–19th centuries, and rentals, 17th–20th centuries.
Estate maps and plans, 16th–20th centuries; title deeds, 16th–20th centuries, and enclosure papers, 18th–19th centuries.
Miscellaneous MSS, including household books and accounts, 15th–17th centuries.

Non-manuscript material: A collection of more than 40,000 books is housed in seven libraries. The collection includes medieval codices (*c*100).

Finding aids: Computer catalogues of estate records and the second series of Thynne papers are in preparation. The named collections all have 19th-century calendars and indexes.

Facilities: Photocopying (for certain restricted documents only). Photography. Microfilm reader.

Publications: HMC Reports (1872–1980); see *Guide to the Locations* of Collections.
Microfilm publications: calendars and indexes to the named collections; catalogue (1864) of the MSS collection; catalogue of miscellaneous MSS; named collections; Glastonbury Court and Compotus Rolls.
K. Harris and W. Smith: *Glastonbury Abbey Records at Longleat House*, Somerset Record Society, 81 (1991).

1076 Warrington Library

Address: Museum Street, Warrington, Cheshire
WA1 1JB

Telephone: (01925) 571232/631873

Fax: (01925) 411395

Enquiries: The Area Librarian, D. Rogers

Open: Mon, Tues, Fri: 9.30–7.30 Wed: 9.30–
5.00 Thurs: 9.30–1.00 Sat: 9.00–1.00

Access: Generally open to the public, on
application.

Historical background: Warrington Library
claims to be the first rate-supported library.
Opened in 1848, it has always concentrated on
collecting local material. In 1974 the formerly
independent borough library became part of the
Cheshire County Library Service.

Acquisitions policy: To strengthen existing
primary and secondary collections in Warrington history, by purchase, donation or deposit.

Archives of organisation: Town council
minutes and rate books, 1847–1974.
Early Poor Law rate and account books, c1729–
1834; Police Commissioners' minutes, 1813–47,
and borough police records, 1838–1965.

Major collections: Manorial records, 1580–
1778.
Quaker records, including Penketh Meeting,
1663–1904.
Rev. E. Sibson papers relating to Ashton in
Makerfield, 1588–1847.
Records of some local companies and many
local societies, 18th and 19th centuries.
Papers of W.D. Jeans, solicitor, 19th century.

Non-manuscript material: Handbills, engrav-
ings, photographs, postcards, posters and other
ephemera, mid-18th century– (c19,500).
Warrington Photographic Survey: photographs
of streets and buildings, 1973–9 (c2000).
Books and pamphlets, including Lewis Carroll
Collection and Eyres Press books (c15,500).
Warrington Parish Church records, 1591–1969,
and census returns, 1841–91 (microfilm).
Warrington newspapers, 1853–.
Town maps, 1772–.

Finding aids: Catalogue. Indexes. NRA 9201,
14607.

Facilities: Photocopying. Photography and
microfilming, by arrangement.

Conservation: Some work undertaken by
Cheshire Record Office (entry 208); other work
contracted out.

1077 Warwickshire County Record Office

Address: Priory Park, Cape Road, Warwick
CV34 4JS

Telephone: (01926) 412735

Fax: (01926) 412509

Enquiries: The County Archivist, Mr Christopher Jeens

Open: Mon–Thurs: 9.00–1.00; 2.00–5.30 Fri:
9.00–1.00; 2.00–5.00 Sat: 9.00–12.30

Access: Generally open to the public, by
reader's ticket (available on application).

Historical background: The office was established in 1931 and is recognised as a place of
deposit for public records. It also acts as the
Diocesan Record Office for parish records for
Birmingham (non-city parishes) and Coventry.

Acquisitions policy: Archives relating to the
historic county, excluding, for most purposes,
Birmingham, Coventry and Stratford-upon-
Avon.

Archives of organisation: Usual local authority
record holdings.

Major collections: Deposited local collections.

Non-manuscript material: Large collections of
photographs, maps and prints.
Major local history library, including unpublished material.

Finding aids: Catalogues/lists of archival collections (copies sent to NRA). Indexes to all
collections (principally by place, but also by
person and subject; some specialised indexes).

Facilities: Photocopying. Photography. Microfilming. Microfilm/fiche readers.

Conservation: In-house service.

Publications: Guide to Parish Registers, Non-
conformist Registers and Census Returns in the
Warwickshire CRO.

1078 British Steel
East Midlands Records Centre

Parent organisation: British Steel plc

Address: By-Pass Road, Irthlingborough, Wellingborough, Northants NN9 5QH

Telephone: (01933) 650277

Fax: (01933) 652689

Enquiries: The Records Analyst, Mr Andrew Burns

Open: Mon–Fri: 9.45–4.15 (lunchtime closure), by appointment to be confirmed in writing.

Access: At the discretion of the Records Analyst.

Historical background: The records service was established in 1970 to look after the archives of the constituent companies that made up British Steel on its formation in 1967 and to provide a records management service. The archives and records are now housed in three records centres: East Midlands Region; Northern Region, covering north-east England and Sheffield, at Commerce Way, Skippers Lane Industrial Estate, South Bank, Middlesbrough TS6 6UT; and North Western Region, covering north-west England, South Wales and Scotland, at Shotton Works, Deeside, Clwyd CH5 2NH. Certain non-statutory records have been transferred to local authority record offices.

Acquisitions policy: Restricted to records relating to British Steel plc, its constituent companies and related bodies.

Archives of organisation: Records of the pre-nationalised steel companies, relevant to the archival holdings of the East Midlands Records Centre: Colvilles Ltd, Dorman Long & Co. Ltd, English Steel Corporation Ltd, Richard Thomas & Baldwin Ltd, Stewarts & Lloyds Ltd, and the United Steel Companies Ltd.
Records of the British Iron and Steel Federation and its predecessor the National Federation of Iron & Steel Manufacturers.
Records of the Iron & Steel Trades Employers' Association and related bodies.

Non-manuscript material: Film archive.
Small collections of publications relating to the history of the iron and steel industry.

Finding aids: Records transmittal lists. Computer indexes. Lists sent to NRA.

Facilities: Photocopying. 16mm film projector.

1079 Wells Cathedral Library

Address: Cathedral Offices, West Cloister, Wells, Somerset BA5 2PA

Telephone: (01749) 674483 (messages)

Enquiries: The Hon. Archivist, Mrs F.A. Neale

Open: By arrangement only.

Access: Bona fide researchers, on written application and by appointment only.

Historical background: The library is a working library and muniment depository for the Dean and Chapter and has existed since the 13th century. In the 19th century a number of the deeds of former manorial properties were taken over by the Ecclesiastical Commissioners and were eventually transferred to Somerset Record Office (entry 1051), which also holds all the episcopal and diocesan material formerly housed in the Bishop's Registry.

Acquisitions policy: Material relating to Wells Cathedral administration.

Archives of organisation: Charters, 958–; registers, c1240–.
Administrative records of Wells Cathedral and title deeds of former estates.
Old Wells Almshouse archives.
Archives of College of Vicars Choral.

Finding aids: Copies of calendars of Vicars Choral archives: *The Earliest Extant Register, 1393–1534*; *Act Book, 1541–1593*, and *Documents, 1348–1600*, of the Vicars Choral of Wells (1985, 1986). Calendars of Cathedral and Almshouse archives, plus consolidated index. *Fabric Accounts, 1390–1600, Communars' Accounts, 1327–1600, and Escheators' Accounts, 1372–1600* (in English translation), Friends of Wells Cathedral, Xeroxed typescript (1983, 1984, 1988).

Facilities: Photocopying. Photography.

Conservation: Contracted out.

Publications: *Calendar of MSS of Dean and Chapter of Wells Cathedral*, HMC (1907, 1914) [2 vols].
Wells Cathedral Miscellany, Somerset Record Society, vol. 56 (1941).
Wells Chapter Act Book, 1666–1683, HMC, joint publication no. 20 (with Somerset Record Society), vol. 72 (1973).

1080 Wells City Record Office

Parent organisation: Wells City Council

Address: Town Hall, Wells, Somerset BA5 2RB

Telephone: (01749) 673091

Enquiries: The Archivist

Open: Thurs, Fri: 10.00–4.00

Access: Generally open to the public, by appointment with a week's notice. There are restrictions on some classes of records, e.g. town clerk's files less than 30 years old. Charges may be made for postal enquiries requiring searches.

Historical background: Wells City Council is the lineal descendant of the old corporation, which was formally established by Royal Charter in 1589. Previously, the borough or commonalty (which dates from the second half of the 12th century, when the earliest bishops' charters were issued) was headed by a *magister* or master supported by common councillors. The first Royal Charter was issued by King John in 1201 and the latest by Elizabeth II in 1974. The city record office was established in 1979 after discussions with the Somerset Record Office, and was intended primarily as a repository for the archives of the city council, though other material relating to Wells is also acquired from time to time.

Acquisitions policy: Records of the city council, such as minutes, town clerk's files, title deeds and plans. Other acquisitions include material relating to Wells in general, such as photographs and the records of clubs and societies, and small local businesses.

Archives of organisation: Borough charters, granted by bishops and ruling monarchs, late 12th century–1974; convocation (corporation act) books, 1377–c1835, and council and committee minute books, c1835–; title deeds relating to corporation property, c1240–1696, 18th century–; sessions books, 1600–1719; receivers' books, 1652–1835; rate books, mainly 18th and 19th centuries; surveys, 1604–5, c1820 and 1848; letter-books, late 19th century–c1970; cash books, ledgers and other accounting records, late 19th century–early 20th century; tithe maps with award, 1837–8; building records, late 18th century–c1960; railway papers, including committee minutes, subscription lists, correspondence, Acts of parliament and other material, c1853–c1865; records relating to public health and sanitation, education, highways, education and utilities, 1835–c1920; petty sessions information, c1820–c1900, registers of electors and burgess rolls, 1832–c1900; town clerks' files, c1938–.

Non-manuscript material: Plans relating to the town hall and other corporation property, mainly late 19th and early 20th centuries; maps relating mainly to the borough's sewage system and disposal scheme, 1858–c1910; photographs, mainly pictures of mayors and the corporation, c1870–c1950.

Finding aids: Card index.

Facilities: Limited photocopying. Photography.

Conservation: All conservation work is carried out by the Somerset Record Office (entry **1051**)

1081 Holkham Hall

Parent organisation: The Earls of Leicester and the Coke family

Address: The Archivist, c/o Holkham Estate Office, Holkham Hall, Wells-next-the-Sea, Norfolk NR23 1AB

Enquiries: The Archivist, Mrs Christine Hiskey

Open: By prior arrangement; limited hours only.

Access: Bona fide academic researchers; a copy of any subsequent publication is requested. A charge may be made for other searches. An appointment is necessary. The library and manuscript library is administered separately by the Librarian.

Historical background: Property at Holkham was acquired by Edward Coke (1552–1634), Lord Chief Justice; the hall was built by his descendant Thomas Coke (1697–1759), 1st Earl of Leicester, and passed to Thomas William Coke MP (1754–1842), and hence to the later Earls and the present occupant, son of the 6th Earl.

Acquisitions policy: The archive consists of the records of the family, hall and estate, from 16th century–. The estate covered many other areas of Norfolk and some outside the county. There are very few external acquisitions.

Archives of organisation: Family papers of Edward Coke and his descendants.
Domestic and building accounts for the hall (including domestic accounts for the old manor house).
Farm and estate accounts, audit books, surveys, letter-books, plans, architectural drawings.

Non-manuscript material: Some photographs and plans.

Finding aids: General catalogue in process (1994); HMC Report (1990) available at NRA and Norfolk Record Office (see entry **855**). MS calendars of deeds available at Holkham.

Facilities: Limited photocopying. Photography by arrangement. Some volumes on microfilm.

Conservation: Contracted out.

Publications: I.H. Adams: *The Mapping of a Scottish Estate* (1971).
J. Glendevon: *The Viceroy at Bay*, (1971).
Hopetoun House Newsletters (Jan 1981–).
A. Rowan: 'The Building of Hopetoun', *Architectural History*, vol. 27, (1984).
Research papers: 'The Diaries and Travel of Lord John Hope, 1722–1927'; 'The Hopes at War in the 18th Century'; 'Wives and Children of the 1st and 2nd Earls of Hopetoun' [other titles in course of preparation].

1082 Army Museums Ogilby Trust

Address: No. 2 St Thomas Centre, Southgate Street, Winchester, Hants SO23 9EF

Telephone: (01962) 841416

Fax: (01962) 841426

Enquiries: Col. P.S. Walton

Open: Mon–Fri: 10.00–4.00

Access: On written application.

Historical background: AMOT is a charitable educational private trust, set up by the late Colonel R.J.L. Ogilby in 1954 to support and encourage British Army regimental museums. In this capacity it acts as a central information point on all military and regimental museums. See also NRA 20951: Survey of Regimental Museums. Papers of Henry Spencer Wilkinson have been transferred to the National Army Museum (entry **640**).

Acquisitions policy: Acquires papers and books

allied to its interests, principally military costume.

Major collections: Papers arranged by regiment and dealing mainly with the dress of British and Commonwealth forces (1000 box files).
Letters of Lt. Gen. Robert Hawley.

Non-manuscript material: Photographs (*c*30,000).
The library holds regimental material, histories, journals, army lists (British, Indian and Commonwealth).

Finding aids: Card index on various matters. Hawley: NRA 24611.

Facilities: Photocopying.

Publications: Index to British Military Costume Prints, 1500–1914 (1972).
Military Drawings in the Royal Collections [with Phaidon Press].
The Evolution of the Victoria Cross [with Midas Books].
The Uniforms of the British Yeomanry Force, 1794–1914 [a continuing series of booklets; 15 published to date].

1083 Hampshire County Museums Service

Parent organisation: Hampshire County Council

Address: Chilcomb House, Chilcomb Lane, Winchester, Hants SO23 8RD

Telephone: (01962) 846304/11/12

Fax: (01962) 869836

Enquiries: The Librarian, Ms Gill Arnott

Open: Mon–Fri: 9.00–5.00

Access: Bona fide researchers; an appointment is necessary.

A large proportion of the collection was amassed with the amalgamation of local museums into the county museum service. Archives of branch museums are held as well as accession registers and environmental records. Material is acquired relating to Hampshire history and topography, excluding military history and the cities of Southampton and Portsmouth, as well as documentation relating to the collections already held by the museum service. Photocopying, photography and a microfiche reader are available and there is an in-house paper conservation service which undertakes outside work.

1084 Hampshire Record Office

Parent organisation: Hampshire County Council

Address: Sussex Street, Winchester, Hants SO23 8TH

Telephone: (01962) 846154

Fax: (01962) 878681

Enquiries: The County Archivist, Miss R.C. Dunhill

Open: Mon–Fri: 9.00–7.00 Sat: 9.00–4.00

Access: Generally open to the public. The office operates the CARN reader's ticket system.

Historical background: The office was established in 1947 and is housed in a purpose-built repository opened in 1994. It acts as the Diocesan Record Office for Winchester Diocese and for two deaneries of Portsmouth Diocese, and is recognised as a place of deposit for public records. Hampshire Archives Trust (f. 1986) acts as a support body for archives in the county, carrying out extensive survey and advisory/liaison work and running the Wessex Film and Sound Archive. For details, contact the Secretary at the above address.

Archives of organisation: Usual local authority record holdings.

Major collections: Deposited local collections, including the following which have a wider significance:
Winchester Bishopric Estate records, including pipe rolls, 1208/9–1711.
Political correspondence of 1st Baron Bolton (1764–1807); 3rd Baron Calthorpe (1787–1852); 3rd Earl of Malmesbury (1807–89); 1st Earl of Normanton (1736–1809); George Tierney senior (1761–1830); William Wickham (1761–1840).
Bonham Carter family papers, 18th–20th centuries, including correspondence with Florence Nightingale.
Literary and political papers of James Harris (1709–80), including correspondence with Henry Fielding, and Handel MSS.
Lemprière family papers relating to the Channel Islands, 19th century.
Shelley-Rolls papers, including papers relating to Percy Bysshe Shelley (1792–1822).

Non-manuscript material: Wessex Film and Sound Archive: film, video and sound recordings.

Facilities: Photocopying. Microfilming. Microfilm/fiche readers/printer.

Conservation: Full in-house service; outside work is undertaken.

Publications: Hampshire Record Series.
Hampshire Papers.
Portsmouth Record Series.
Various guides to Hampshire Record Office and its collections.

1085 Winchester Cathedral Library

Address: The Close, Winchester, Hants SO23 9LS

Enquiries: The Curator, John Hardacre, 5a The Close, Winchester, Hants SO23 9LS

Telephone: (01962) 853137

Open: April–Sept: Mon–Sat: 10.30–12.30; 2.30–4.30: Oct–March: Wed, Sat: 10.30–12.30; 2.30–4.30 (days and times subject to alteration.)

Access: Bona fide research students, on written application with references.

The Anglo-Saxon minster was succeeded by a Norman cathedral begun in 1079, and there is a continuous history from that date. Archives, including plans and maps, relate to the priory and the cathedral from the Anglo-Saxon period to the present day. The cathedral has one of the oldest book rooms in Europe, including a fine 17th–century collection; many books were bequeathed by Bishop George Morley (1597–1684).

1086 Winchester College Archives

Address: Winchester College, Winchester, Hants SO23 9NA

Enquiries: The Archivist

Open: By written appointment only, during normal school terms.

Access: Approved researchers.

Historical background: Winchester College was founded by William of Wykeham in 1382. His statutes provided for the careful preservation of documents relating to the college's internal administration and to its estates. The oldest documents are still housed in the 14th–century muniment room with its original chests.

Acquisitions policy: To preserve the administrative and educational records of the college.

Archives of organisation: Extensive records of the college's estates, primarily in Hampshire, Wiltshire and Dorset, late 14th century– (some records predate the foundation).
Internal accounts, 1394– (nearly complete).
Assorted educational records, increasingly full from the 18th century–.

Non-manuscript material: Maps and plans of the college's estates.
Photographs of college buildings and portraits.

Finding aids: Various lists and indexes available, especially for pre-1870 records. Copies of the main descriptive list are available at the main university and London libraries, and at relevant county record offices.

Facilities: Limited photocopying. Photography in special cases only.

Publications: J.H. Harvey: 'Winchester College Muniments', *Archives*, v/28 (1962).
S. Himsworth: *Winchester College Muniments* (1976, 1984) [3 vols; descriptive list with indexes by P. Gwyn and others].

1087 Eton College Collections

Address: College Library, Eton College, Windsor, Berks SL4 6DB

Telephone: (01753) 671221

Fax: (01753) 671244

Enquiries: The College Archivist, Mrs Penny Hatfield

Open: Mon–Fri: 9.30–1.00; 2.00–5.00

Access: Bona fide researchers, by appointment. Records are closed for 40 years (unless special permission is obtained from the Provost); records identifying individual boys may be closed for 75 years.

Historical background: Eton College was founded in 1440 by Henry VI in a collegiate parish church: the college was soon enlarged to include 70 scholars and 20 commensals (sons of benefactors or friends of the college, paying for board and lodging but educated free). Commensals were the forerunners of the oppidans, fee-paying boarders of the school, which has grown up around the college and is administered separately. The provost had peculiar jurisdiction from 1443 over the college and parish. Provosts were rectors of Eton until 1875, when a separate vicarage was created, but are still the ordinaries of college and lower (junior boys') chapels. Provosts also had testamentary jurisdiction, which petered out in the 1660s, and the power to issue marriage licences to parishioners. Parish registers were transferred to Buckinghamshire Record Office (entry 35) after the Parochial Registers and Records Measure 1978, but microfilms and an index to baptisms and marriages are held.

Acquisitions policy: Occasional purchases or gifts of archives some time out of custody.

Archives of the organisation: Administrative and financial records only of the college (the provost and Fellows), 1440–, including estate records, 11th century–.
Records of the school, including house books, society records and sporting annals, c1880–.
Enrolled grants of probate and administrations, 1450s-1660s; a few 18th-century marriage licences.

Major collections: College Library: personal papers of some masters and boys.
School Library (separately administered): Papers of the Moulton Barrett family and Anne Thackeray Ritchie; 20th-century literary MSS.

Finding aids: Manuscripts: handlist in continuation of M.R. James: *Catalogue of MSS* (Cambridge, 1895). *Eton College Records*, vols 1–65 (continuing): mainly calendars of estate records to 1871 (sets available in the Public Record Office (entry 960) and NRA.

Facilities: Photocopying. Photography (own cameras also permitted).

Publications: H.E. Chetwynd-Stapylton: *The Eton School Lists from 1791–1877* (Eton, 1884).
Eton School Registers, 1841–1918, Old Etonian Association (1903–32) [8 parts].
Etonians who Fought in the Great War (1921).
Etonians who Fought in the World War 1939–1945.
W Sterry (ed.): *The Eton College Register*, vol. 1: *1441–1698* (1943).
R.A. Austen-Leigh (ed.): vols 2 & 3: *1698–1790* (1927; 1921).
For literary MSS, see D. Sutton (ed.): *Location Register of English Literary MSS*. (London, 1988).

1088 Royal Archives

Address: Windsor Castle, Windsor, Berks
SL4 1NJ

Telephone: (01753) 868286 exts 2260/2465

Fax: (01753) 854910

Enquiries: The Assistant Keeper or The Registrar or The Curator of the Royal Photograph Collection

Open: By arrangement.

Access: Bona fide researchers, on written application and by appointment. Access for students is restricted to postgraduates.

Historical background: The Royal Archives were established in 1912 with the papers of King George III, King George IV, Queen Victoria and King Edward VII, with those of William Augustus, Duke of Cumberland, and the exiled Stuarts. The papers of King George V and King George VI, as well as those of some other members of the royal family, have been added subsequently.

Acquisitions policy: To maintain and consolidate the archive.

Archives of organisation: Official and private archives of the sovereign from King George III to King George VI.

Major collections: Stuart papers: files of the exiled Stuarts, 17th–19th centuries.
Melbourne papers: official correspondence of 2nd Viscount Melbourne (1779–1848).
Cambridge papers: military papers of the 2nd Duke of Cambridge.
Wardrobe accounts, 1660–1749.

Non-manuscript material: Photograph collection, 1842–1930 (more than 100,000) with some later volumes and loose prints.

Facilities: Photocopying, photography and microfilming by arrangement. Microfilm reader.

Conservation: In-house paper conservation studio; outside work is occasionally undertaken.

Publications: HMC: *Calendar of the Stuart Papers (to 1718)* (1902–39) [6 vols].
A.C. Benson and Lord Esher (eds): *The Letters of Queen Victoria, 1837–61* (1907) [3 vols].
G.E. Buckle (ed.): *The Letters of Queen Victoria, 1862–1901* (1926–32) [6 vols].
Sir John Fortescue (ed.): *The Correspondence of King George III, 1760–83* (1927–8) [6 vols].
A. Aspinall (ed.): *The Letters of King George IV, 1812–30* (1938) [3 vols].
——: *The Later Correspondence of George III, 1783–1810* (1962–70) [5 vols].
——: *The Correspondence of George, Prince of Wales, 1770–1812* (1963–71) [8 vols].
R. Fulford (ed.): *Dearest Child, 1858–61; Dearest Mama, 1861–64; Your Dear Letter, 1865–71; Darling Child, 1871–78; Beloved Mama, 1878–85* (1964–81) [Queen Victoria's correspondence with Victoria, Princess Royal].
F. Dimond and R. Taylor: *Crown and Camera: the Royal Family and Photography* (1987).
A. Ramm: *Beloved and Darling Child, 1886–1901* (1990).
Microfilm publications: The Stuart Papers, Cumberland Papers, Melbourne Papers, Peel Correspondence, Cambridge Papers, Cabinet Reports, 1937–1916, Ministerial Correspondence, 1837–1901, Queen Victoria's files on the Eastern question and European foreign affairs, 1840–1900, and a selection from the Royal Photograph Collection.

1089 Royal Borough Collection

Parent organisation: Royal Borough of Windsor and Maidenhead

Enquiries: The Hon. Curator,
Mrs Judith Hunter, 26 Wood Lane, Slough
SL1 9EA, tel: (01753) 525547

Open: By arrangement.

Access: Generally open to the public, by appointment only.

From 1951 to 1982 there was a small local history museum in the Guildhall, Windsor. When this was closed the exhibits were moved to the museum store and the collection was renamed. It consists of miscellaneous MSS, maps, photographs, prints, paintings, artefacts, books and printed material relevant to the history of Windsor and the other towns and villages in the borough. The collection has been listed and indexed; photocopying and photography are available. Records from Windsor Muniment Rooms have been transferred to Berkshire Record Office (entry **951**).

1090 St George's Chapel, Windsor Castle

Address: The Aerary, Dean's Cloister, Windsor Castle, Windsor, Berks SL4 1NJ

Telephone: (01753) 857942/865538

Enquiries: The Archivist, Dr Eileen Scarff

Open: By appointment only.

Access: Approved readers, on written application; there is a 30–year closure rule.

Historical background: The College of St George was founded in 1348/50.

Acquisitions policy: Personal papers of retired or deceased members of the College of St George are preserved. Otherwise internal acquisitions only.

Archives of organisation: Records of the Dean and Canons of Windsor, 1348/50–; some property deeds predate the foundation, the earliest being of 1140.
Records include chapter acts, accounts, attendance books, estate papers, and some records of the Order of the Garter.

Non-manuscript material: Maps, plans and drawings.
Photographs (*c*1500).

Finding aids: Slip index to post-1957 items. Index to photographs. NRA 18513.

Facilities: Photocopying. Copies of photographs may be obtained.

Conservation: Carried out at the Royal Archives (entry **1088**)

Publications: E.H. Fellows: *The Military Knights of Windsor, 1352–1944* (1945).
——: *The Vicars or Minor Canons* (1945).
M.F. Bond: *The Inventories of St George's Chapel, Windsor Castle, 1384–1667* (1947).
A.K.B. Evans: *St George's Chapel, Windsor, 1348–1416* (1947).
S.L. Ollard: *The Deans and Canons of St George's Chapel* (1950).
J.N. Dalton: *The Manuscripts of St George's Chapel* (1957).
E.H. Fellowes and E.R. Poyser: *The Baptism, Marriage and Burial Registers of St George's Chapel, Windsor* (1957).

S.M. Bond: *The Monuments of St George's Chapel* (1958).
——: *Windsor Chapter Acts, 1430–1672* (1966).
C. Mould: *The Musical Manuscripts of St George's Chapel* (1973).
E.H. Fellows: *Organists and Masters of the Choristers* (2/1979).
G. Holmes: *The Order of the Garter: its Knights and Stall Plates, 1348–1984* (1984).

1091 Wisbech and Fenland Museum

Address: Museum Square, Wisbech, Cambridgeshire PE13 1ES

Telephone: (01945) 58381

Enquiries: The Curator and Librarian, Mr David C. Devenish

Open: April–Sept: Tues–Sat: 10.00–5.00 Oct–March: Tues–Sat: 10.00–4.00

Access: Generally open to the public, strictly by appointment only. An hourly charge is made for consulting parish registers.

Historical background: In 1847 the Wisbech Literary Society (f. 1781) and the Wisbech Museum (f. 1835) moved into the present purpose-built premises. The two societies were merged in 1877 after which the library wing was extended. The museum is now a charitable trust. The town library was founded in 1653 and belongs to the town council, but is now housed in the museum.

Acquisitions policy: To maintain and consolidate the collections.

Major collections: Local archives: records of Wisbech Town Council and its predecessor, the Trinity Gild, 1379–; Wisbech Hundred Commissioners of Sewers, 1660–1921; Elm enclosure awards; manorial records, 1753–1940; parish registers.
Medieval religious works, including Wycliffe's sermons, 14th century.
Asian palm leaf MSS.
Collections of Rev. Chauncey Hare Townshend (1798–1868), poet: sketchbooks, literary and other autographs; and of Thomas Clarkson (1760–1846), philanthropist: letters and other material *re* abolition of slavery.
Peckover family papers.
Original MSS of *Great Expectations* by Charles Dickens and *The Monk* by M.G. Lewis (1775–1818).

Non-manuscript material: Maps of the fens, 17th–19th centuries (*c*800).
Photographs by Samuel Smith (1802–92): local scenes, 1852–64; William Ellis: Madagascar, *c*1860–65; Herbert Coates: East Anglian scenes, *c*1920–1950; L.G. Annis: fenland drainage, *c*1950.
Collection of local ephemera, newspapers, playbills and posters.
Town library of 16th- and 17th-century books (12,000); museum library of 18th- and 19th-century books.

Finding aids: Lists: NRA 3642, 9203, 11114, 11115.

1092 Wolverhampton Borough Archives

Parent organisation: Wolverhampton Metropolitan Borough Council: Library Information Services Division

Address: Central Library, Snow Hill, Wolverhampton, West Midlands WV1 3AX

Telephone: (01902) 312025 ext. 129

Fax: (01902) 714579

Enquiries: The Borough Archivist, Ms Caroline Sampson

Open: Mon–Sat: 10.00–5.00 Sat by appointment only.
Limited production of archive materials 12.00–2.00

Access: Generally open to the public.

Historical background: The archives service was founded within the Public Libraries Department of Wolverhampton Borough Council in 1978, although some acquisitions had been made before this date. It is recognised as a place of deposit for public records.

Acquisitions policy: The archives service accepts and cares for records, from both public and private sources, relating to the Borough of Wolverhampton.

Archives of organisation: Records of Wolverhampton Borough Council, 1777–; records of superseded authorities, i.e. Bilston Borough Council and Tettenhall and Wednesfield Urban District Councils, 19th century–1966.

Major collections: Records of Methodist circuits and churches in Wolverhampton, 18th–20th centuries.

Non-manuscript material: Extensive collection of photographs.
A collection of local printed books, pamphlets and newspapers is maintained by the local studies section.

Finding aids: Lists and indexes: a computer database of archives and local studies holdings is being developed. NRA 10951, 23358.

Facilities: Photocopying. Photography. Microfilm/fiche readers/printer.

Conservation: In-house paper conservation.

1093 The Elgar Birthplace Museum

Parent organisation: The Elgar Birthplace Trust

Address: Crown East Lane, Lower Broadheath, Worcester WR2 6RH

Telephone: (01905) 333224

Enquiries: The Curator, Jim Bennett

Open: By appointment only.

Access: Access to any person with a relevant enquiry.

Historical background: The Elgar Birthplace Museum and archive was set up in 1936 by Carice Elgar-Blake to honour the life, music and achievements of her father, the composer Sir Edward Elgar (1857–1934).

Acquisitions policy: To collect material relating to Elgar, including musical MSS, correspondence, photographs and memorabilia.

Major collections: Correspondence and musical MSS, both autographs and sketches, by or relating to Sir Edward Elgar.

Non-manuscript material: Photographs.
Sound archive of the music of Sir Edward Elgar.
Books from the composer's own Library.

Conservation: Contracted out.

1094 Hereford and Worcester Record Office

Parent organisation: Hereford & Worcester County Council

Address: County Hall, Spetchley Road, Worcester WR5 2NA

Telephone: (01905) 766351

Fax: (01905) 766363

Enquiries: The County Archivist, Mr A.M. Wherry

Open: Mon: 10.00–4.45 Tues–Thurs: 9.15–4.45 Fri: 9.15–4.00
Two-week stock-taking closure in November/December.

Access: Generally open to the public. Prior booking for microfilm/fiche readers essential. The office operates the CARN reader's ticket system.

Historical background: Worcester Record Office was established in 1947. Hereford and Worcester Record Office was created in 1974 following local government reorganisation. Hereford Record Office (entry 387) and St Helen's Record Office (entry 1098) are dependent repositories. The office is recognised as a place of deposit for public records.

Acquisitions policy: Records of the parent body and its predecessors, public records as appropriate, diocesan records (Worcester at St Helen's RO; Hereford at Hereford RO) and private records, within the administrative area of the county and its predecessors.

Archives of organisation: Usual local authority record holdings, including Worcester County Council records, 1888–1974; and quarter sessions (Worcestershire), 1600–1973.

Major collections: Deposited local collections, including several of national standing.

Non-manuscript material: Hereford & Worcester Photographic Survey of the former Worcestershire area (*c*70,000).

Finding aids: Inventory lists, indexes and specialised handlists. Some specialised indexes, e.g. wills. Lists sent to NRA.

Facilities: Photocopying. Photography. Microfilming. Microfilm/fiche reader/printers.

Conservation: Full in-house service at Hereford Record Office.

Publications: General information leaflets, including genealogy and house history.
Genealogy Sources in Worcestershire, 1: 'Parish Registers and Transcripts'; 2: 'Trade Directories and Almanacs'.

1095 King's School, Worcester

Address: 15 College Green, Worcester WR0 2LH

Telephone: (01905) 23016

Fax: (01905) 25511

Enquiries: The Headmaster's Secretary

Open: By written appointment.

Access: Genuine researchers.

The Cathedral College was founded by King Henry VIII in 1541 in place of the cathedral monastery and was governed by the Dean and Chapter. Under the monastery there had been an almonry school and links with Oxford University. Records of the school are integral with those of Worcester Cathedral held by the cathedral library (entry 1097), and include King's Scholar's lists, 1545–1820. The school holds pupils' lists, 1820–, governors' minutes, 1828–, and the *Vigornian* school magazine, 1879–. See M. Craze: *King's School, Worcester, 1541–1972.*

1096 Stanbrook Abbey

Address: Callow End, Worcester WR2 4TD

Telephone: (01905) 830209

Fax: (01905) 831737

Enquiries: The Archivist, Dame Eanswythe Edwards

Access: There is no public access to the archives since the abbey is an enclosed religious community. However, the archivist is willing to answer enquiries by post or, if necessary, in the parlour at Stanbrook by appointment.

Historical background: The community was founded in Cambrai in 1625 by English Benedictine monks and remained there until 1793, when the French Revolution forced the nuns to leave. They eventually returned to England in 1795 and finally settled at Stanbrook in 1838 where, as at Cambrai, they continued to run a small school, which was finally closed in 1918. Although the early records were lost to the community, many copies are now held in the archives, which were first organised by the Abbess Lady Gertrude Dubois in 1875.

Acquisitions policy: To maintain and consolidate the records of the community and the nuns.

Archives of organisation: Account books, 1795–; entry books, 1625–1725, 1838–; annals of the community, 1623–1907; house journal, 1869–; papers and letters *re* building of church and monastery, including Pugin's specification, 1860s and 1870s; school records, including list of pupils, 1795–1917.

Abbesses' papers, including correspondence of Lady Gertrude Dubois with a wide range of clerics, 1860s-1890s, and of Dame Laurentia McLachlan *re* plainchant and monastic history, 1930s.

Correspondence with foundations in Australia, 1842–, and Brazil, 1911–.

Knight family of Lincolnshire, correspondence *re* life at Cambrai, 1790s.

Papers *re* beatification of Carmelite Martyrs of Compiègne, 1906.

Finding aids: Listing in progress.

Publications: D. Eanswythe Edwards: 'The Archives of Stanbrook Abbey', *Catholic Archives*, no. 2 (1982), 3–11.

1097 Worcester Cathedral Library

Address: c/o 10a College Green, Worcester WR1 2LH

Enquiries: The Librarian, Canon Iain MacKenzie

Telephone: (01905) 25238

Open: By arrangement with the librarian.

Access: Approved readers, on written application.

Historical background: Worcester Cathedral has had a continuous history since its foundation as a Benedictine House in 962. The University of Birmingham Library is in the process of recording all MS material on microfiche. Positive copies can be obtained on application to the Keeper of Special Collections there (entry 101).

Acquisitions policy: Apart from the muniments the only additions to the collection are books relating to the Cathedral and Diocese of Worcester. There is no purchasing fund.

Archives of organisation: Cathedral archive and muniments, including letter-books, deeds, accounts and chapter act books.

Major collections: Medieval MSS which mainly comprised the working library of the monks (*c*275); some fragments predate the monastic community (the Diocese dates from 680). The Worcester Fragments, a collection of early 13th-century English polyphony.

Non-manuscript material: Church music, 17th–18th centuries.
Maps and plans.
Bishop John Prideaux (1578–1650) collection of books.
Printed 16th–18th century books (*c*4500).

Finding aids: Catalogues of MSS, collections and books. B.S. Benedikz et al.: Worcester Cathedral Catalogue of Muniments (1977–82) [6 vols; TS], sent to NRA.

1098 Worcester (St Helen's) Record Office

Parent organisation: Hereford & Worcester County Council

Address: Fish Street, Worcester WR1 2HN

Telephone: (01905) 765922

Fax: (01905) 765920

Enquiries: The Assistant County Archivist, Mr R. Whittaker

Open: Mon: 10.00–4.45 Tues–Thurs: 9.15–4.45 Fri: 9.15–4.00 Sometimes closed 1.00–2.00 Two-week stock-taking closure in November/December.

Access: Generally open to the public. Prior booking for microfilm/fiche readers is essential. The office operates the CARN reader's ticket system.

Historical background: This branch was established in 1956 and is a dependent repository of Hereford and Worcester Record Office (entry 1094). It acts as the Diocesan Record Office for Worcester. It is recognised as a place of deposit for public records. The substantial archive collection from Kidderminster Library was transferred to the office in 1990.

Acquisitions policy: Records of the parent body and its predecessors, public records as appropriate, diocesan records and private records, within the administrative area of Worcester.

Archives of organisation: Worcester City Council records, 16th century–.
Diocesan records, 12th century–.

Major collections: Deposited local collections, some of national standing, e.g. correspondence of Sir Edward Elgar (1857–1934).
Local estate and family records, including Vernons of Hanbury, 15th–20th centuries; Russells of Little Malvern, 16th–20th centuries, and Rushouts/Spencer-Churchills of Northwick Park, 14th–20th centuries.

Finding aids: Inventory lists, indexes and specialised handlists. Some specialised indexes, e.g. wills. Lists sent to NRA.

Facilities: Photocopying. Photography. Microfilming. Microfilm/fiche reader/printers.

Conservation: Full in-house service at Hereford Record Office (entry **387**).

Publications: General information leaflets, including genealogy and house history.
Genealogy Sources in Worcestershire: 1. 'Parish Registers and Transcripts'; 2. 'Trade Directories and Almanacs'.

1099 Worcestershire and Sherwood Foresters Regiment

Address: Regimental HQ, RHQ WFR, Norton Barracks, Worcester WR5 2PA

Telephone: (01905) 354359

Fax: (01905) 354359

Enquiries: The Regimental Secretary

Open: Mon–Fri: 10.00–4.00

Access: Generally open to the public, on written application. There is no charge, but a donation would be welcomed.

Historical background: Farrington's Regiment of Foot was formed in 1694 and Charlemont's in 1701. These subsequently became the 29th (Worcestershire) and 36th (Herefordshire) Regiments of Foot and were amalgamated to form the Worcestershire Regiment in 1881. In 1970 the Worcestershire Regiment was amalgamated with the Sherwood Foresters to form the Worcestershire and Sherwood Foresters Regiment.

Acquisitions policy: Acquires material of regimental interest to the Worcestershire Regiment and its antecedent regiments and to the Worcestershire and Sherwood Foresters Regiment.

Archives of organisation: Regimental records, early 18th century–.
Records of service for officers and soldiers, including 29th Regiment, 1702–1925.

Major collections: Personal papers, including diaries, letters, journals, order books.

Non-manuscript material: Watercolour sketches of uniforms of 29th Regiment, 1742–1890.
Regimental magazine, 1922–.
Photographs, 1872– (2000).
Regimental histories covering period 1694–1950.

Finding aids: Card index. NRA 20951.

Facilities: Photocopying. Photography.

1100 The Bar Convent

Parent organisation: The Institute of the Blessed Virgin Mary

Address: Blossom Street, York YO2 2AH

Telephone: (01904) 629359

Enquiries: The Archivist and Librarian, Sr M. Gregory

Open: By appointment only.

Access: Bona fide researchers, by prior arrangement.

Historical background: The Institute of the Blessed Virgin Mary is a religious order for women founded by Mary Ward (*d*? 1645) in 1609. The Bar Convent was founded in 1686, and established a boarding school and day school for girls in 1699. The convent has remained on the same site, outside Micklegate Bar, ever since.

Acquisitions policy: To maintain the existing archive.

Archives of organisation: Administrative records of the Bar Convent, 1686–, including wills of Mother Superiors, vows and account books, 1730–.
Lists of pupils, 1710–.
Pupils' accounts, 1761–.
Lists of nuns.
Archives of the English Province of the Institute of the Blessed Virgin, 1929–.

Major collections: Diaries, journals, memoirs, etc, of and by those in the convent, including one on Mary Ward, written *c*1645.
Recipe book, 1753.

Non-manuscript material: Portraits of nuns and benefactors.

Finding aids: Handlist 'The 17th and 18th Century Archives of the Bar Convent, York' (TS).

Facilities: Photocopying. Photography.

Publications: *History of the Bar Convent* [pamphlet].
H.J. Coleridge (ed.): *St Mary's Convent, Micklegate Bar, York* (1887).

1101 Borthwick Institute of Historical Research

Parent organisation: University of York

Address: St Anthony's Hall, Peasholme Green, York YO1 2PW

Telephone: (01904) 642315

Enquiries: The Director, Dr D.M. Smith

Open: Mon–Fri: 9.30–1.00; 2.00–5.00

Access: Bona fide researchers, by appointment. There are restrictions on some modern records.

A Borthwick Institute

Historical background: The Borthwick Institute is a research institute of the University of York specialising in the study of ecclesiastical history, in particular the administrative and legal history of ecclesiastical institutions within the province of York. It was established in 1953 on the initiative of the York Academic Trust and in 1963 became a department of the newly established university. It acts as the Diocesan Record Office for Yorkshire and is a recognised place of deposit for public records.

Acquisitions policy: Principally records of the Church of England in the York Diocese, including papers of the archbishops, archdeacons, rural deans, and certain parishes, and related church material; records of clerics, families, individuals and religious bodies having a connection with the existing deposited collections or the research and teaching interests of the university.

Archives of organisation: Archives of the university, 1963–, and of the predecessor body the York Academic Trust.

Major collections: York diocesan records: records of the archbishops and their subordinate officials, 13th century–, including probate records, 1389–1858.
Mirfield papers: records of the Community of the Resurrection at Mirfield and of several prominent members, 19th and 20th centuries.
Quaker records: archive of the Retreat, York, mental asylum, 18th century–; archives of the Tuke family, 18th and 19th centuries; social survey papers of Seebohm Rowntree (1871–1954), 20th century; archives of Vickers Instruments and Rowntree plc.
Halifax archives: archives and political papers of the Wood family, Earls of Halifax, 18th–20th centuries.
Many smaller collections of a non-ecclesiastical nature, including family papers and guild records.

Non-manuscript material: Gurney Library, principally concerned with ecclesiastical history and archive studies (20,000), a working library (reference only) for use in conjunction with the deposited archives.
Centre for Local History, a resource centre for the location of Yorkshire archives and a microfilm library of Yorkshire archival sources.

Finding aids: Calendars, lists and indexes of the principal areas of the collection.

Facilities: Photocopying. Photography. Microfilming. Microfilm/fiche readers.

Conservation: In-house paper and parchment conservation. Some limited outside work is undertaken for other repositories.

Publications: D.M. Smith: *Guide to the Archive Collections in the Borthwick Institute* (1973; suppl., 1980).
C.C. Webb: *Guide to Genealogical Sources in the Borthwick Institute* (1981).
The institute also publishes the following series:
Borthwick Papers [studies concerned with the ecclesiastical history of northern England and aspects of the history and historiography of Yorkshire].
Borthwick Texts and Calendars [editions, calendars, handlists of records].
Borthwick Lists and Indexes [shorter catalogues, handlists and indexes].
Borthwick Wallets [palaeography wallets].
Borthwick Studies in History [monographs, essays].

B Southern African Archives

Historical background: The Southern African Archives were collected under the Southern African Documentation Project funded by the Leverhulme Trust between 1974 and 1977; further work on the collection and the addition of extra items was funded by the SSRC in 1980. The documentation project was established to build up a collection of primary source material on southern Africa, following a suggestion by the poet Dennis Brutus. Most of the material has come from private individuals and institutions in the UK; it was not the intention to remove MSS from southern Africa, though some have been given and others photocopied.

Acquisitions policy: Donations or deposits which will extend the collection or strengthen existing coverage are welcomed. The regional focus is on southern Africa: Angola, Botswana, Lesotho, Namibia, Malawi, Mozambique, South Africa and related territories, Swaziland, Zambia and Zimbabwe.

Major collections: Papers of Dennis Brutus, poet and anti-apartheid campaigner.
Records and related material of the Capricorn Africa Society.
Tanganyikan papers of Marion, Lady Chesham, mainly 1955–65.
Papers, diaries, correspondence and sermons of the Rt Rev. Joost De Blank (1908–68); with materials collected by his sister, Miss Bertha De Blank.
Papers of the Rt Hon. Sir Patrick Duncan (1870–1943), noted South African radical.
Political papers of the Rev. William D. Grenfell relating to Angola, and the war of liberation, 1960–77.
Dr Franco Nogueria: papers of Dr Antonio D'Oliveira Salazar (1889–1970), former Prime Minister of Portugal.

Non-manuscript material: South African papers of Lord Loch (Henry Brougham), High Commissioner in South Africa, 1890–95 (microfilm; originals in the Scottish Record Office, entry 313).
Some small photographic collections, including an album of photographs of Basutoland.
A few tape-recordings, mainly of political material.

Finding aids: Lists; many collections fully listed. Indexes.

Facilities: Photocopying. Photography. Microfilming. Microfilm/fiche readers.

Publications: A. Ross: *Guide to the Tanganyikan Papers of Marion, Lady Chesham* (1975).
T. Lodge (comp.), A.V. Akeroyd and C.P. Lunt (eds): *A Guide to the Southern African Archives in the University of York* (1979).

1102 Castle Howard Archives

Address: Castle Howard, York YO6 7BZ

Telephone: (01653) 648444 ext. 43

Fax: (01653) 648462

Enquiries: The Keeper of Archives, Mr E. Hartley

Open: Mon–Wed: 9.30–5.00, with an hour closure for lunch

Access: Castle Howard is a private family archive, and all researchers must apply in writing stating clearly their object of study and any qualifications they hold. Access is dependent on the permission of the Howard family and a research fee is charged.

Historical background: The division of the Carlisle Estates in the 1920s resulted in a split archive, of which Castle Howard Archives and the Howard of Naworth papers at Durham University (entry 275) are the two unequal parts.

Archives of organisation: Documents relating to the building of the house and the Yorkshire estates; and personal papers of the owners of Castle Howard, including the 1st–9th Earls of Carlisle, mainly 18th and 19th centuries.
Some earlier material relating to Howard estates in Cumberland, Northumberland and Yorkshire.

Non-manuscript material: Estate maps and plans, 18th–19th centuries.
Architectural drawings. Small photograph collection.

Finding aids: Catalogue, sent to NRA. Index to personal letters.

Facilities: Photocopying at the discretion of the Keeper of Archives.

1103 Company of Merchant Adventurers of York

Address: Merchant Adventurers' Hall, Fossgate, York YO1 2XD

The Assistant Archivist, 11 New Walk Terrace, York YO1 4BG

Telephone: (01904) 654818 (Hall) 645522 (Assistant Archivist, home)

Enquiries: The Assistant Archivist, Mrs Louise Wheatley

Open: Mon–Fri, by prior arrangement only.

Access: Bona fide researchers; an appointment is essential.

Historical background: The Fraternity of our Lord Jesus Christ and the Blessed Virgin Mary was founded in 1357, and its successor, the Guild of Mercers, was incorporated in 1430. The Elizabethan charter of 1581 formally constituted the organisation as the Company of Merchant Adventurers of York.

Acquisitions policy: To acquire, by donation, deposit or purchase, material relevant to the history of the company, and to trade and trading organisations generally in the northeast of England.

Archives of organisation: Archives pertaining to the Company of Merchant Adventurers of York, 1581–, and its precursors, the Fraternity of our Lord and St Mary, 1357–71, the Hospital of Holy Trinity and St Mary, 1373–1549, and the Guild of Mercers of York, 1430–1580. These consist of: royal charters and grants; minute books, copies of acts and ordinances and meetings; Trinity Hospital administration and advowsons; membership records, elections and apprenticeships; correspondence and papers; letters to and from foreign marts, shipping documents, petitions; Corpus Christi Pageant records, accounts and indentures; account rolls, 1357–67, 1432–1682; account books, 1728–1937, draft and subsidiary accounts, annual accounts and balance sheets, 1901–; receipts and vouchers, 1546–; bonds; cartulary, late 15th century; title deeds, mid-13th century; rental books and rolls, mid-15th century–late 19th century; leases, late 14th century–; estate plans and tenancy papers; records of repairs, benefactions and building works; records of the York Residence of Merchant Adventurers of England (Hamburg Court Books), the York Residence of Eastland merchants, the Company of Porters of York; annual reports, 1944–; and some general miscellanea.

Non-manuscript material: Maps, estate plans, architectural drawings.
Portraits of governors, benefactors and families; oil paintings, watercolours, prints and drawings of York and related subjects.
Photographs, 1870s–.
Guild ceremonial items; weights and measures; seal matrices.

Publications: D.M. Smith (comp.): *A Guide to the Archives of the Company of Merchant Adventurers of York* (York, 1994).
D.M. Palliser's short history is soon to be reprinted.

1104 Film Music Resource Centre

Parent organisation: University of York

Address: Music Department, University of York, Heslington, York YO1 5DD

Telephone: (01904) 430000 ext. 5765

Enquiries: Dr David Kershaw

Open: Mon–Fri: 9.30–5.00, by prior appointment only.

Access: Bona fide researchers.

The resource centre was founded in 1985 as a development of studies undertaken in the department since 1974. It houses a growing collection of silent-film print music as well as some British sound-film scores, 1930–, and acquires material relevant to film music composition and allied fields such as film sound techniques.

1105 National Railway Museum Library

Parent organisation: Science Museum

Address: Leeman Road, York YO2 4XJ

Telephone: (01904) 621261

Fax: (01904) 611112

Enquiries: The Librarian, Mr Philip Atkins or The Archivist, Mr Richard Durack

Open: Mon–Fri: by appointment.

Access: Readers' tickets are available on written application.

Historical background: The museum was opened in 1975 following the closure of the former British Museum of Transport at Clapham, London, in 1973. The records collected at Clapham, mainly technical papers and engineering drawings, were transferred to York. All the Science Museum's railway collections are now concentrated in the city. The records from the former British Railways Historical Record Office in York are deposited at the Public Record Office (entry **960**) and for Scottish Railways at the Scottish Record Office (entry **313**).

Acquisitions policy: Material, including papers of individuals and groups, recording the history and development of railways, railway engineering and related manufacturing industries in the British Isles.

Major collections: Technical records and engineering drawings of locomotives and rolling stock from British Railways and former railway companies.
Records of railway stock builders, including Dübs & Co.; Neilson & Co.; Peckett; Charles Roberts & Co.; Sharp Stewart & Co.; Robert Stephenson & Co., and Vulcan Foundry.
Records of Kennedy Henderson & Co., consulting engineers, concerning railways in Africa and South America.
Rugby Locomotive Testing Station records.
Papers of railway officials, historians and enthusiasts, including R.C. Bond, John Click, E.S. Cox, P.C. Dewhurst, Eric Mason and Selwyn Pearce Higgins.
Papers of Tom Purvis, poster artist.

Non-manuscript material: Official glass negatives from British Rail and former railway companies, 1880–1950.
Private negative collections, including P. Ransome Wallis and M.W. Earley.
Extensive collections of paintings, prints, posters, notices, postcards, tickets, labels and ephemera.
Engineering drawings (35,000) on microfiche.
Sound archive of interviews with former railway employees.

Finding aids: Catalogues, lists and indexes. Lists sent to NRA.

Facilities: Photocopying. Photography. Microfilm/fiche readers.

Conservation: Contracted out.

Publications: C.P. Atkins: 'The National Railway Museum Library and its Collections', *Journal of the Railway and Canal Historical Society* (July 1986).
D. Jenkinson (ed.): *The National Railway Collection* (Collins, 1988).
C.J. Heap: 'The NRM Photograph Collection', *British Railway Journal*, 34 (December, 1990).

1106 North Yorkshire County Library
York Central Library

Address: Library Square, Museum Street, York YO1 2DS

Telephone: (01904) 655631/654144

Fax: (01904) 611025

Enquiries: The Group Librarian (postal)
The Librarian, Local Studies (telephone)

Open: Mon–Wed, Fri: 9.00–8.00 Thurs: 9.00–5.30 Sat: 9.00–1.00

Access: Archive material is generally available to the public on request in the reference library, subject to satisfactory proof of identity.

Historical background: A record office was established in the library in 1957, when civic records and deposited collections were place there. Archives were transferred to York City Archives (entry **1107**) in 1980.

Acquisitions policy: Potential donors are advised to discuss the donation with the Group Librarian.

Major collections: Letters of the Thomas Allis (1788–1875) and William Etty (1787–1849) families, and Waterton papers, 1841–65.
Note-books on York subjects.
Records of the Knowles family, stained-glass manufacturers in York, late 19th century.

Non-manuscript material: Small collection of films of local interest.
Local illustrations (9100) and slides (1000).

Finding aids: Card catalogue and index available in the York Reference Library.

Facilities: Photocopying. Microfilm/fiche readers.

1107 York City Archives

Address: Art Gallery Building, Exhibition Square, York YO1 2EW

Telephone: (01904) 551879

Fax: (01904) 654981 (Art Gallery)

Enquiries: The City Archivist, Mrs R.J. Freedman

Open: Tues, Thurs: 9.30–12.30; 2.00–5.30 Wed: 10.15–12.30; 2.00–5.30 Mon, Fri: by arrangement only.

Access: Generally open to the public, by appointment.

Historical background: Civic records and deposited collections were placed in the York Central Library in 1957, when a record office was opened with a full-time archivist. Following reorganisation in 1974 the archives were retained in the administration of the city and transferred to new premises in the art gallery building.

Acquisitions policy: Non-ecclesiastical records for York and the immediate area.

Archives of organisation: York City council records, 12th century–.

Major collections: Deposited local collections, including the Yorkshire Philosophical Society Collection; York cemetery registers and other records, 1837–1961; and the Goodricke-Piggot Astronomical Collection, 1775–1807.

Non-manuscript material: Photograph and glass-negative collection of properties demolished during slum clearance, 20th century. OS maps, 1852–.

Finding aids: Card catalogue and calendars. Some lists at NRA. Yorkshire Philosophical Society: NRA 16393.

Facilities: Photocopying. Photography and microfilming by arrangment. Microfilm reader.

Conservation: Contracted out.

Publications: York City Archives Brief Guide. Richard III and the City of York [wallet of facsimiles and booklet].
R.J. Green: *York City Archives* (1971).

1108 York Health Archives

Parent organisation: York Health Services NHS Trust

Address: c/o The Wheelchair Centre, Shipton Road, York YO3 6SF

Telephone: (01904) 628183

Enquiries: The Archivist, Dr Katherine Webb

Open: Mon–Fri: 9.30–1.00, by arrangement.

Access: Bona fide researchers, by appointment. The normal closure period for public records is in operation; staff records are closed for 75 years and patients' records for 100 years.

Historical background: York Health Authority established the archives in 1990, with a part-time archivist to catalogue and bring together the archives inherited from its predecessor NHS organisations serving York and district: York 'A' Group and 'B' Group hospital management committees, 1948–74, and York Health District and North Yorkshire Area Health Authority, 1974–82. In 1992 York Health Authority became a single district NHS trust, providing hospital and community-based services for York and district.

Acquisitions policy: Archives of NHS hospitals and their predecessors, and of health services in the district, which at present includes York, Easingwold and Selby but previously also included Thirsk.

Archives of organisation: York County Hospital, 1740–1976.
Bootham Park Hospital (formerly York Lunatic Asylum), 1777–.
Clifton Hospital (formerly North Riding Asylum), 1847–1994.
NHS administration in York and district, 1948–.

Non-manuscript material: Plans, drawings and photographs of hospitals.
City of York Medical Officer of Health and School Medical Officer Annual and Special Reports, 1906–72.

Finding aids: Lists for all collections.

Facilities: Photocopying.

Publications: K.A. Webb: *Guide to York Health Archives* (1995).

1109 York Minster Archives

Address: York Minster Library, Dean's Park, York YO1 2JD

Telephone: (01904) 625308

Fax: (01904) 611119

Enquiries: The Archivist, Ms Sarah Costley

Open: Mon–Thurs: 9.00–5.00 Fri: 9.00–12.00

Access: Open to the public, by appointment; there are some restrictions on modern records.

Historical background: The minster archives were transferred in 1960 from the minster to the minster library. This had been housed in a restored medieval chapel in Dean's Park since 1810. To these archives were then added the Hailstone Collection and a number of smaller accumulations already held by the minster library.

Acquisitions policy: Records relating to the minster or complementary existing holdings, by purchase, donation or deposit.

Archives of organisation: Dean and Chapter records, c1150–.
College of Vicars Choral records, 1252–1936.

Major collections: Edward Hailstone collection, comprising deeds and documents relating to Yorkshire (mainly West Riding), 12th–19th centuries.
Private papers of archbishops, deans and canons of York and other accumulations relating to York and Yorkshire.
Additional MSS, 10th–20th centuries.
Music MSS, 16th–20th centuries.

York Wesleyan Methodist records, mainly 19th century.

Non-manuscript material: Pamphlets (especially Civil War tracts); maps and plans (Yorkshire); architectural drawings (York Minster); prints and drawings (Yorkshire, topographical and biographical); photographs (York Minster); newspapers (mainly Yorkshire), 18th and early 19th centuries.

Finding aids: Various lists and card indexes. Database of Minster architectural plans, 18th–20th centuries, and topographical prints, 17th–20th centuries, in progress.

Facilities: Photocopying. Photography. Microfilm/fiche reader/printer.

Conservation: In-house service.

Publications: K.M. Longley: *A Guide to the Archives and Manuscript Collections in York Minster Library* (1977) [typescript available locally and at NRA].
The history of the archives is described in K.M. Longley: 'Towards a History of Archive-Keeping in the Church of York', *Borthwick Institute Bulletin* (1976, 1977).
Other lists of Dean and Chapter Archives are given in HMC First Report (1870), 97.
J. Burton: *Monasticon eboracense*, ix (York, 1758).
G. Lawton: *Collectio rerum ecclesiasticarum de diocesi Ebor*, ii (1842).
Many individual documents have been published in various vols of the Surtees Society, Yorkshire Archaeological Society and elsewhere.

Appendix I

Since the second edition of *British Archives* the following reported that their archives and/or collections had been placed elsewhere as indicated:

Alyth Folk Museum: Perth Museum and Art Gallery (929)

Anglo-Jewish Archive: University College London (761)

Arbroath Library and Art Gallery: Montrose Library Archive (825)

Baptist Missionary Society: Regents Park College (906)

Bateman Collection (Bristol Polytechnic): Bristol University (129)

Brechin Public Library and Museum: Montrose Library Archive (825)

British Athletics: Birmingham University (101)

British Council: Public Record Office (960)

British Theatre Play Library: Theatre Museum (753)

Burnley District Library: Lancashire Record Office (944)

Carlisle Cathedral Library: Cumbria Record Office (199)

Chartered Society of Physiotherapy: Wellcome Institute for the History of Medicine (768)

Christian Aid: School of Oriental and African Studies (729)

Church Army: Cambridge University Library (147A)

Clackmannan District Library: Central Regional Archives (1031)

Communist Party of Great Britain: Labour History Archive and Study Centre (795)

Down, Connor and Dromore Diocesan Library: Public Record Office of Northern Ireland (78)

Dundee Children's Home: Dundee District Archives (264)

Electricity Council Archives: Greater Manchester Museum of Science and Industry (801)

English National Board for Nursing, Midwifery and Health Visiting: Public Record Office (960)

Felsted School: Essex Record Office (203)

Forfar Public Library: Montrose Library (825)

General, Municipal, Boilermakers and Allied Trades Union: Working Class Movement Library (996)

Goldsmiths' College, Rachel McMillan Collection: Lewisham Study Centre (614)

Health Visitors' Association: Wellcome Institute for the History of Medicine (768)

Jewish Welfare Board: University of Southampton (1021)

Kent County Library: Centre for Kentish Studies (789)

Kidderminster Library: Worcester (St Helen's) Record Office (1098)

King Alfred's College: Hampshire Record Office (1084)

London Borough of Merton: Surrey Record Office (429)

London Fire Brigade: Greater London Record Office (550)

Louth Naturalists' Antiquarian & Literary Society: Lincolnshire Record Office (460)

Marsh-Jackson Postgraduate Medical Centre: Somerset Record Office (1051)

Medical Women's Federation: Wellcome Institute for the History of Medicine (768)

Methodist Missionary Society: School of Oriental and African Studies (729)

National Children's Home Archives: University of Liverpool (472)

National Union of Teachers: Modern Records Centre, Warwick (229)

Neath Reference Library: West Glamorgan County Record Office (1047)

Pendlebury Library of Music: Cambridge University Library (147A)

Plant Sciences Library, Sherard Collection: Bodleian Library (871)

Plas Newydd: Clwyd Record office, Ruthin (972)

Port Talbot Reference Library: West Glamorgan County Record Office (1047)

Presbyterian Church of Wales: National Library of Wales (10)

Queen's Nursing Institute: Wellcome Institute for the History of Medicine (768)

Radcliffe Science Library: Bodleian Library (871)

Redditch Public Library: Hereford and Worcester County Record Office (1094)

Riverside Health Authority: Greater London Record Office (550)

Royal Literary Fund: British Library (495A)

Royal Ulster Agricultural Society: Public Record Office of Northern Ireland (78)

Shropshire Libraries Local Studies Department: Shropshire Records & Research Centre (1012)

Southwark Cathedral Archives: London Borough of Southwark (616)

Southwark Diocese: Greater London Record Office (550)

Sutton Housing Trust: Greater London Record Office (550)

Swansea Central Library: West Glamorgan County Record Office (1047)

Syon Abbey: University of Exeter Library (326)

Telford Development Corporation: Ironbridge Gorge Museum (415)

Trinity House Lighthouse Service: Guildhall Library (553)

United Bible Societies: Cambridge University Library (147A)

Wesley Historical Society Library: Westminster College, Oxford (922)

Appendix II

The following, contacted for this edition, reported having no archives:

British Institute of Jazz Studies, 17 The Chase, Crowthorne, Berks RG11 6HT

Colwyn Bay Library, Woodland Road West, Colwyn Bay, Clwyd LL29 7DH

Daughters of Jesus English Province, Brook House, 95 Uxbridge Road, Rickmansworth, Herts WD3 2BU

Dunfermline District Museums, Viewfield Terrace, Dunfermline, Fife KY12 7HY

Norfolk Museums Service, Castle Museum, Norwich NR1 2JU

Penzance Subscription Library, Morab Gardens, Penzance

Scunthorpe Central Library, Carlton Street, Scunthorpe, South Humberside DN15 6TX

Somerset County Council Library Service, Local History Library, The Castle, Castle Green, Taunton TA1 4AD

South London Botanical Institute, 323 Norwood Road, London SE24 9AQ

Taunton Local History Library, Somerset County Council, The Castle, Castle Green, Taunton TA1 4AD

Winchester School of Art, Park Avenue, Winchester, Hants SO23 8DL

Appendix III

The following, contacted for this edition, either did not respond, or were unable to provide sufficient information for an entry, although those preceded by an asterisk indicated that they held archives:

*Amateur Boxing Association of England, National Sports Centre, Crystal Palace, London SE19 2BB

*Amnesty International British Section, 99-119 Rosebery Avenue, London EC1R 4RE

Army and Navy Club, 36-39 Pall Mall, London SW1Y 5JN

*Bedford Estates, Woburn Abbey, Woburn, Beds MK43 0TP

Bewdley Museum, The Shambles, Load Street, Bewdley, Hereford and Worcester DY12 2AE

*Bowood House, Calne, Wilts

Bradford & Ilkley Community College, Westbrook Building, Great Horton Road, Bradford BD7 1AY

*Britannia Royal Naval College, Dartmouth, Devon TQ6 0HJ

*British Federation of Women Graduates, 4 Mandeville Courtyard, 142 Battersea Road, London SW11 4NB

Brooklands Museum, Brooklands Road, Weybridge, Surrey KT13 0QN

Buddhist Society Library, 58 Eccleston Square, London SW1V 1PH

*Cambridge Institute of Education, Shaftesbury Road, Cambridge CB2 2BX

*Coldstream Guards, Wellington Barracks, Birdcage Walk, London SW1E 6HQ

Crompton Public Library, Farrow Street East, Shaw, Oldham, Lancs OL2 8QY

De Montfort University Library, Leicester LE1 9BH

Design History Research Centre, University of Brighton, 10-11 Pavilion Parade, Brighton BN2 1RA

*Down, Connor and Dromore Diocesan Registry, Belfast

Edinburgh Chamber of Commerce, 3 Randolph Crescent, Edinburgh EH3 7UD

*Faculty of Homoeopathy, Royal London Homoeopathic Hospital, Great Ormond Street, London WC1N 3HA

*Francis Skaryna Byelorussian Library & Museum, Marian House of Studies, 37 Holden Road, Finchley, London N12 8HS

Geological Survey of Northern Ireland, 20 College Gardens, Belfast BT9 6BS

*Glenalmond College Library, Glenalmond, Perth, Tayside PH1 3RY

*Gordon Highlanders Regimental Museum, Viewfield Road, Aberdeen AB1 7XH

*Haberdashers' Aske's School, Butterfly Lane, Elstree, Borehamwood, Herts WD6 3AF

*King's Own Scottish Borderers Archives, Regimental Headquarters, The Barracks, Berwick-upon-Tweed TD15 1DG

*Ladywell Convent, Godalming, Surrey GU7 1ST

*London College of Dance, 10 Linden Road, Bedford MK40 2DA

*Lothian and Borders Fire Brigade, Brigade Headquarters, Lauriston Place, Edinburgh EH3 9DE

Madresfield Court, Pinners Place, Madresfield, Malvern, Worcs WR13 5AB

*Malvern College, Malvern, Worcs WR14 3DF

*Marlborough College, Marlborough, Wilts SN8 1PA

*Morton Lodge of Freemasons, Lerwick, Shetland ZE1 0AB

*Mount Stuart, Rothesay, Isle of Bute PA20 9LR

Museum of East Anglian Life, Stowmarket, Suffolk IP14 1DL

*Normal College, George Site, Holyhead Road, Bangor, Gwynedd LL57 2PX

Nottingham City Museums, The Castle, Nottingham NG1 6EL

Oriental Club, Stratford House, Stratford Place, London W1N 0ES

*Performing Right Society Ltd, 29/33 Berners Street, London W1P 4AA

*Prince of Wales's Own Regiment of Yorkshire, 3 Tower Street, York YO1 1SB

*Roedean School, Brighton, East Sussex BN2 5RQ

Royal Caledonian Curling Club, Cairnie House, Avenue K, Ingliston Showground, Newbridge, Midlothian EH28 2NB

*Royal Dragoon Guards, 3 Tower Street, York YO1 1SB

*Royal Naval Engineering College, Manandan, Plymouth PL5 3AQ

*Royal Scottish Academy of Music and Drama, 100 Renfrew Street, Glasgow G2 3DB

*Royal Welch Fusiliers Regimental Museum, The Queen's Tower, Caernarfon Castle, Caernarfon, Gwynedd LL55 2AY

*Scots Regimental Headquarters, Birdcage Walk, London SW1E 6HQ

*Scottish Society for Prevention of Cruelty to Animals, 19 Melville Street, Edinburgh EH3 7PL

*Scottish Trades Union Congress, 16 Woodlands Terrace, Glasgow G3 6DF

*Sea Cadet Association, 202 Lambeth Road, London SE1 7JF

*South Place Ethical Society, Conway Hall, 25 Red Lion Square, London WC1R 4RL

*Strict Baptist Historical Society, c/o 10 Priory Road, Dunstable, Beds LU5 4HR

Teesside University, Main Site Library, Borough Road, Middlesbrough, Cleveland TS1 3BA

*Tony Benn Archive, c/o House of Commons, London SW1A 0AA

*Traquair House, Innerleithen, Peeblesshire EH44 6PW

*Travellers' Club, 106 Pall Mall, London SW1Y 5EP

Ukrainian Association in Great Britain, 49 Linden Gardens, London W2 4HQ

University of Abertay, Dundee Library, Bell Street, Dundee, Tayside DD1 1HG

University of Glamorgan, Learning Resources Centre, Pontypridd, Mid Glamorgan CF37 1DL

*Ursuline Provincialate, 10 Coventry Road, Ilford, Essex IG1 4QR

*Welsh Guards, RHQ, Wellington Barracks, Birdcage Walk, London SW1E 6HQ

*Wesley Historical Society, Irish Branch, c/o Mrs M.G. Kelly, 13 Glencregagh Drive, Belfast BF6 0NJ

*West Dean College, West Dean, Chichester, West Sussex PO18 0QZ

*Whitby Literary and Philosophical Society, Whitby Museum, Pannett Park, Whitby, North Yorks YO21 1RE

Worshipful Company of Carpenters, Throgmorton Avenue, London EC2N 2JJ

York College of Arts and Technology Library, Dringhouses, York YO2 1UA

Index to Collections

This index is to the descriptive sections of the entries only; for repository titles see the Alphabetical listing in the front of the book. In general, personal names have been given birth and the dates or otherwise identified. Aristocratic titles have been cross-referenced to the family only where both appear in the entry.

Readers are directed also to the indexes maintained by the National Register of Archives (see p. lii).

Guide to Key Subjects

This list is compiled mainly from the checklist of key subject headings sent with the entry questionnaire.
Local authority record offices and national repositories have not been included.
The list is not intended as an index to collections, but rather as a general guide to repositories with holdings of relevance in specific subject areas. Where holdings are particularly strong the reference appears in **bold** type.

ACCOUNTING *see* FINANCE
ADDICTION
  general 591, **757**, 768, **947**
ADVERTISING, 278, 427, 662, 803, **853**, 950, 954, 955
AERONAUTICS *see* AVIATION, technology
AGNOSTICISM 563
AGRICULTURE
  general 13, 27, 33, 36, 194B, **213**, 219, 275B, 302, 348, 392, 403, 530, 564, 709, 806A, 818, 840, 856, 861, 895, 902, 935, **945**, 950, **954**, 955, 961, 981, 1032, 1058, 1087, 1101A
  farming 40, 62, 132, 158, 194B, **372**, 383, 394, 530, 591, 769, **833**, 906, 998, 1081
  machinery 427, 962
AIR FORCE *see* ARMED SERVICES
ALCHEMY *see* CHEMISTRY
ANARCHY *see* POLITICAL MOVEMENTS
ANATOMY 301, 351B, 686, 689, 840
ANGLICANISM *see* RELIGIOUS DENOMINATIONS
ANIMALS
  general 82, 143, 271, **395**, 504, 563, 564, 599, 652, 690, 718, 783, 891, 950
  domestic 954
  farming 45B, 275, 580, 945, 954, 998
  wild 82, 296, **307**, 652, 790, 835
ANTHROPOLOGY 82, 123A, 129, 185, 296, 498, 517, 563, 589B, 652, **675**, 729, **901**, 906, 1004
  see also ETHNOLOGY
ARCHAEOLOGY 18, 33, 45, 52, 67, 82, 132, 139, 194A, 243, 249, 295, 351B, **383**, 449, **532**, **567**, **638**, 646, **658**, 737, 742, 840, 861, 866, 890, 901, 917, 985, 990
ARCHITECTURE
  general 12, **13**, 33, 42, 82, 83, 129, 147B, 194B, 221, 278, **295**, 297, 305, 315A, 351A, 357A, 472, **481**, 519, 526, **534**, 641B, 646, 669, **699**, 737, 740, 806A, 811, 856, 861, 923, 981, 1017, 1058, 1102, 1109
  domestic 13, 40, 44, 120, 194B, 261, 392, **534**, 737, 742, 1081
  ecclesiastical **13**, 55, 68, 83, 113, 261, 309, 324, 518, **525**, **534**, 591, 737, 742, 769, 1087, 1101A
  oriental 158, 890
  see also BUILDING CONSTRUCTION
ARMED SERVICES
  general 22, 82, **143**, **153**, 202, 207, 314, **446C**,

564, **589B**, 591, 660, 890, 962, 1017, **1021**, 1088, 1090
  air force 418, 656, **673**, 801, 962, 1015
  army 20, 21, 22, 28, 40, **80**, 105, 107, 111, **118**, 143, **144**, 150, **197**, 207, 271, 304, 403, 412, **458**, 551, **559**, **560**, 561, 590C, **640**, 656, **677**, 694, 776, 806A, 861, 923, 927, 990, 998, **1082**, **1099**
  navy 21, 170B, 403, 634, **645**, 806A, 861, **943**, **1024**
  see also DEFENCE; WAR
ART
  general 2, 17, 33, 40, 82, 83, 161, 181, 188, 288, **293**, **305**, **312**, 343, **441**, 482, 483, **508**, 519, 526, 535, **539**, 561, **641**, 647, 657, 664, **669**, 682, 709, 734, 737, **752**, 766, **767**, 780, 806A, 856, 861, 1007, 1017, 1058, **1070**, 1102
  applied **54**, 63, **167**, **212**, 296, 621, 625, 662, 742, 761B, 781, 853, 891
  artists 2, 83, 101, **167**, 194A, 278, 305, **311**, 351B, 357A, 361, 446A, 564, 571, 588, 594, 641, 669, **752**, **761B**, 773, 775, 778, 800, 840, 993, 998, 1042, 1058, 1081, 1102
  ecclesiastical 55, 212, 261, 315C, 324, 440, 518, **525**, 591, 646, 746, 769, 1109
  fine 40, 42, 167, 278, 282, **305**, 351B, **311**, 361, 441, 571, **643**, 669, 691, 714, **761B**, 773, 840, 998, 1081
ASTROLOGY 351B, 806A, 891, 1004
ASTRONOMY 29, **147D**, 165, 260, 275A, **303**, 645, **679**, **708**, 731, 891
ASYLUMS *see* LUNACY
ATOMIC ENERGY *see* NUCLEAR POWER
AVIATION
  general 296, 392, 418, 563, 578, 662, 672, **673**, 731, 801, 962
  technology 70, 158, 228, 296, 563, 564, 660, **672**, 731, 801
BANKING *see* FINANCE
BAPTISTS *see* RELIGIOUS DENOMINATIONS
BIOCHEMISTRY 156, 563, 701, 708, 961, 1008
BIOLOGY 82, 146, 181, 296, 357A, 376, 563, 599, 652, 692, 701, 708, 835, 854, 856, 938, 958
BOTANY 28, 82, 83, 129, 146, **156**, 194A, 249, **298**, 333, 357A, 372, 376, 461, 470, **515**, 563, **599**, 652, **697**, 783, 790, 835, 840, 854, 861, **961**, 969, 1001
BREWING **351**, 490, 568